Tim Unwin

From the Estate of Michael J
Eden

February 1999

The
INTERNATIONAL
DIRECTORY
of
GOVERNMENT

The
INTERNATIONAL DIRECTORY
of
GOVERNMENT

EUROPA PUBLICATIONS LIMITED

First Edition 1990

© **Europa Publications Limited 1990**
18 Bedford Square, London, WC1B 3JN, England

Australia and New Zealand
James Bennett (Collaroy) Pty Ltd, 4 Collaroy Street,
Collaroy, NSW 2097, Australia

India
UBS Publishers' Distributors Ltd,
POB 7015, 5 Ansari Road, New Delhi 110002

Japan
Maruzen Co Ltd, POB 5050, Tokyo International 100-31

British Library Cataloguing in Publication Data
The international directory of government.
1. Government. Organization structure
351
ISBN 0-946653-56-9
ISSN 0956-0998

Printed and bound in England by
Staples Printers Rochester Limited
Love Lane, Rochester, Kent.

FOREWORD

The first edition of the INTERNATIONAL DIRECTORY OF GOVERNMENT aims to provide a comprehensive guide to government ministries, departments, agencies and corporations for every country in the world.

Each country chapter provides details on the Head of State and legislative system, and a full list of ministries. Government organizations and affiliated groups are arranged by subject heading, and include sections on agriculture, banking and the economy, defence, media and transport. Every entry contains, where appropriate, names of principal officials, full address, telephone, telex and fax numbers and an outline of activities undertaken.

The Editor is grateful to all those government organizations which have returned questionnaires, ensuring that the directory is both reliable and up-to-date. It is hoped that the authoritative and impartial information contained in the INTERNATIONAL DIRECTORY OF GOVERNMENT will provide its users with an invaluable reference aid.

March 1990

CONTENTS

CONTENTS

EXPLANATORY NOTES

Each chapter covering a country or territory is arranged under the following, or similar, headings, where they apply:

HEAD OF STATE

LEGISLATURE

THE GOVERNMENT
CABINET/COUNCIL OF MINISTERS

GOVERNMENT ORGANIZATIONS AND
AGENCIES:
AGRICULTURE
THE ENVIRONMENT
FISHING
FORESTRY

ART AND CULTURE

BUSINESS AND ECONOMY
BANKING
FINANCIAL AGENCIES
INSURANCE
MARKETING
NATIONALIZED INDUSTRY
TRADE

DEFENCE

DEVELOPMENT AND PLANNING
INVESTMENT
REGIONAL DEVELOPMENT

EDUCATION AND RESEARCH

EMPLOYMENT

HEALTH AND WELFARE

INTERNATIONAL AFFAIRS

LEGAL AND JUDICIARY

MEDIA
BROADCASTING
GOVERNMENT PUBLISHER
NEWS AND INFORMATION

MINING AND ENERGY

SCIENCE AND TECHNOLOGY

TOURISM

TRANSPORT AND COMMUNICATIONS
TELECOMMUNICATIONS
CIVIL AVIATION
RAILWAYS
ROADS
SHIPPING

UTILITIES

ABBREVIATIONS

AB	Aktiebolag (Joint Stock Company)	Eng	Engineer
ACT	Australian Capital Territory	esq	esquina
ADC	aide-de-camp	est	established
Adm	Admiral	etc	etcetera
admin	administration; administrator	eV	eingetragener Verein
AIDS	Acquired Immunodeficiency Syndrome	exec	executive
AK	Alaska	Ext	Extension
AM	Amplitude Modulation		
Apdo	Apartado (Post Box)	f	founded
approx	approximately	Fed	Federal
A/S	Aktieselskab (Joint Stock Company)	FM	Frequency Modulation
asst	assistant	fmrly	formerly
Avda	Avenida (Avenue)	Fr	Father
Ave	Avenue	FRG	Federal Republic of Germany
Bhd	Berhad (Public Limited Company)	GDR	German Democratic Republic
Bldg	Building	Gen	General
Blvd	Boulevard	GmbH	Gesellschaft mit beschränkter Haftung (Limited
BP	Boîte Postale (Post Box)		Liability Company)
br(s)	Branch(es)	Gov	Governor
Brig	Brigadier	Govt	Government
bul	bulvar (boulevard)		
		ha	hectares
CA	California	HE	Her/His Excellency; Her/His Eminence
CACM	Central American Common Market	hf	hlutafelag (Limited Company)
Cad	Caddesi (Street)	HM	Her/His Majesty
Capt	Captain	Hon	Honorary; Honourable
CARICOM	Caribbean Community	HQ	Headquarters
Cdre	Commodore	HRH	Her/His Royal Highness
Chair	Chairman/woman		
Cia	Companhia	ie	id est (that is to say)
Cía	Compañía	IMF	International Monetary Fund
Cie	Compagnie	Inc	Incorporated
CMEA	Council for Mutual Economic Assistance		
cnr	corner	Jr	Junior
Co	Company	Jt	Joint
Col	Colonel; Colonia		
Commdr	Commander	KG	Kommandit Gesellschaft (Limited Partnership)
Commdt	Commandant	KK	Kaien Kaisha (Limited Company)
Commr	Commissioner	km	kilometre
Corpn	Corporation	kv	kvartal (apartment block)
CP	Case Postale; Caixa Postal; Casella Postale (Post Box)		
		LNG	Liquefied Natural Gas
CPSU	Communist Party of the Soviet Union	LPG	Liquefied Petroleum Gas
Cres	Crescent	Lt	Lieutenant
		Ltd	Limited
DC	District of Columbia; Distrito Central		
DDR	Deutsche Demokratische Republik (German	Maj	Major
	Democratic Republic)	Man	Manager; managing
Del	Delegacion; delegate	MB	Manitoba
Dep	Deputy	mbH	mit beschränkter Haftung (with limited liability)
Dept	Department	MD	Maryland
devt	development	mem	member
DF	Distrito Federal	Mgr	Monseigneur; Monsignor
Diag	Diagonal	MW	Medium Wave; megawatt
Dir	Director		
DM	Deutsche Mark	N	North; Northern
DN	Distrito Nacional	nab	naberezhnaya (embankment, quai)
Dr	Doctor; drive	nám	náměští (square)
Dra	Doctora	NF	Newfoundland
		no	número; number
E	East; Eastern	nr	nr
Edif	Edificio	NSW	New South Wales
EEC	European Economic Community	NV	Namloze Vennootschap (Limited Company)
eg	exempli gratia (for example)	NY	New York
Eidg	Eidgenössich (Confederate)		

OAS	Organization of American States	s/n	sin número (without number)
OAU	Organization of African Unity	Soc	Society
Of	Oficina (Office)	Sok	Sokkak
ON	Ontario	SP	Sao Paulo
OPEC	Organization of Petroleum Exporting Countries	SpA	Società per Azioni (Joint Stock Company)
opp	opposite	Sq	Square
		Squad Ldr	Squadron Leader
perm	permanent	Srl	Società a Responsabilità Limitata (Limited Company)
PK	Post Box (Turkish)		
pl	platz; place; ploshchad (square)	St	Saint; street
PLC	Public Limited Company	Sta	Santa
PMB	Private Mail Bag	Ste	Sainte
POB	Post Office Box	Supt	Superintendent
PQ	Québec		
Pres	President	Tas	Tasmania
Prof	Professor	tech	technical
PT	Perseroan Tarbates (Limited Company)	tel	telephone
Pte	Private	TN	Tennessee
Pty	Proprietary	TV	Television
publ	publication		
Pvt	Private	u	utca (street)
		UAE	United Arab Emirates
Qld	Queensland	UDEAC	Union Douanière et Economique de l'Afrique Centrale
Rd	Road	UK	United Kingdom
rep	representative	ul	ulitsa (street)
retd	retired	UN	United Nations
Rev	Reverend	USA	United States of America
RJ	Rio de Janeiro	USSR	Union of Soviet Socialist Republics
Rm	Room		
ro-ro	roll-on roll-off	VA	Virginia
Rt	Right	VEB	Volkseigener Betrieb (Public Company)
		VHF	Very High Frequency
S	South; San	Vic	Victoria
SA	Société Anonyme, Sociedad Anónima (Limited Company); South Australia	Vn	Veien (street)
SARL	Sociedade Anônima de Responsibilidade Limitada (Joint Stock Company of Limited Liability)	W	West; Western
		WA	Western Australia
Sdn Bhd	Sendirian Berhad (Private Limited Company)	yr	Year
Sec	Secretary		
Sen	Senior; Senator	z oo	limited (Polish)

INTERNATIONAL TELEPHONE CODES

To use this table:

Select the International Code for the country from which the call is to be made (column 2), then the Country Code for the country to which the call is going (column 1). To make the call, dial the International Code plus the Country Code plus the number required (adding area codes provided in the entries where necessary). For example, to call the Banque Nationale de Belgique (see page 53) from the USA, the following numbers would have to be dialled: 011 (International Code from the USA) + 32 (Country Code for Belgium) + (2) (area code) + 221-21-11 (Bank's Number).

	Column 1 Country Code To	Column 2 International Code From
Afghanistan	*	*
Albania	*	*
Algeria	213	00
Andorra	33 628	0
Angola	244	*
Antigua and Barbuda	1 809	011
Argentina	54	*
Australia	61	0011
Australian External Territories:		
Christmas Island	672 4	*
Cocos (Keeling) Islands	672 2	*
Norfolk Island	672 3	*
Austria	43	00
The Bahamas	1 809	011
Bahrain	973	*
Bangladesh	880	*
Barbados	1 809	011
Belgium	32	00
Belize	501	*
Benin	229	*
Bhutan	*	*
Bolivia	591	*
Botswana	267	*
Brazil	55	00
Brunei	673	*
Bulgaria	359	00
Burkina Faso	226	*
Burundi	257	*
Cambodia	*	*
Cameroon	237	*
Canada	1	011
Cape Verde	238	*
The Central African Republic	236	*
Chad	235	*
Chile	56	00
China, People's Republic	86	*
China (Taiwan)	886	*
Colombia	57	90
The Comoros	*	*
The Congo	242	*
Costa Rica	506	*
Côte d'Ivoire	225	*
Cuba	53	*
Cyprus	357	00
Czechoslovakia	42	00
Denmark	45	009
Danish External Territories:		
Faeroe Islands	298	*
Greenland	299	*
Djibouti	253	*

	Column 1 Country Code To	Column 2 International Code From
Dominica	1 809 44	0
The Dominican Republic	1 809	*
Ecuador	593	01
Egypt	20	*
El Salvador	503	0
Equatorial Guinea	240	*
Ethiopia	251	*
Fiji	679	*
Finland	358	990
France	33	19
French Overseas Departments:		
French Guiana	594	*
Guadeloupe	590	*
Martinique	596	*
Réunion	262	*
French Overseas Collectivités Territoriales:		
Saint Pierre and Miquelon	508	*
French Overseas Territories:		
French Polynesia	689	*
New Caledonia	687	*
Wallis and Futuna Islands	*	*
Gabon	241	*
The Gambia	220	*
German Democratic Republic	37	06
Federal Republic of Germany	49	00
Ghana	233	*
Greece	30	00
Grenada	1 809	011
Guatemala	502	00
Guinea	224	*
Guinea-Bissau	245	*
Guyana	592	*
Haiti	509	*
Honduras	504	00
Hungary	36	00
Iceland	354	90
India	91	00
Indonesia	62	*
Iran	98	*
Iraq	964	*
Ireland	353	16
Israel	972	00
Italy	39	00
Jamaica	1 809	011
Japan	81	001
Jordan	962	*
Kenya	254	*

	Column 1 Country Code To	Column 2 International Code From
Kiribati	686	*
Korea, Democratic People's Republic (North Korea)	*	*
Korea, Republic (South Korea)	82	001
Kuwait	965	*
Laos	*	*
Lebanon	961	*
Lesotho	266	*
Liberia	231	*
Libya	218	*
Liechtenstein	41 75	*
Luxembourg	352	00
Madagascar	261	*
Malawi	265	*
Malaysia	60	*
Maldives	960	*
Mali	223	*
Malta	356	0
Mauritania	222	*
Mauritius	230	*
Mexico	52	98
Monaco	33 93	19
Mongolia	*	*
Morocco	212	00
Mozambique	258	*
Myanmar	95	*
Namibia	264	*
Nauru	674	*
Nepal	977	*
Netherlands	31	09
Netherlands Dependencies:		
Aruba	297	*
Netherlands Antilles	599	*
New Zealand	64	00
New Zealand's Associated Territories:		
Cook Islands	682	*
Niue	*	*
Nicaragua	505	*
Niger	227	*
Nigeria	234	*
Norway	47	095
Oman	968	*
Pakistan	92	*
Panama	507	*
Papua New Guinea	675	*
Paraguay	595	*
Peru	51	*
The Philippines	63	*
Poland	48	00
Portugal	351	00 (07 Porto)
(Madeira	351 91)	
Portuguese Overseas Territory:		
Macau	853	*
Qatar	974	*
Romania	40	*
Rwanda	250	*
Saint Christopher and Nevis	1 809	011
Saint Lucia	1 809 45	0
Saint Vincent and the Grenadines	1 809 45	0
San Marino	39 549	0
São Tomé and Príncipe	239	*
Saudi Arabia	966	*
Senegal	221	*
Seychelles	248	*
Sierra Leone	232	*
Singapore	65	005
Solomon Islands	677	*

	Column 1 Country Code To	Column 2 International Code From
Somalia	252	*
South Africa	27	*
Spain	34	07
Sri Lanka	94	*
Sudan	249	*
Suriname	597	*
Swaziland	268	*
Sweden	46	009
Switzerland	41	00
Syria	963	*
Tanzania	255	*
Thailand	66	001
Togo	228	*
Tonga	676	*
Trinidad and Tobago	1 809	01
Tunisia	216	00
Turkey	90	9 9
Tuvalu	*	*
Uganda	256	*
Union of Soviet Socialist Republics	7	*
United Arab Emirates	971	*
United Kingdom	44	010
United Kingdom Crown Dependencies	44	010
British Dependent Territories:		
Anguilla	1 809 497	011
Ascension Island	247	*
Bermuda	1 809	011
British Virgin Islands	1 809	011
Cayman Islands	1 809 94	0
Falkland Islands	500	*
Gibraltar	350	*
Hong Kong	852	001
Montserrat	1 809 491	011
Pitcairn Islands	*	*
St Helena	*	*
Turks and Caicos Islands	1 809 946	0
United States of America	1	011
United States External Territories:		
American Samoa	684	*
Guam	671	*
Marshall Islands	692	*
Federated States of Micronesia	691	*
Northern Mariana Islands	670	*
Palau	680	*
Puerto Rico	1 809	135
United States Virgin Islands	1 809	011
Uruguay	598	*
Vanuatu	678	*
Vatican City	39	00
Venezuela	58	00
Vietnam	*	*
Western Samoa	685	*
Yemen Arab Republic (North Yemen)	967	*
Yemen, People's Democratic Republic (South Yemen)	969	*
Yugoslavia	38	99
Zaire	243	*
Zambia	260	*
Zimbabwe	263	*

* No Information/Contact International Operator

The
INTERNATIONAL
DIRECTORY
of
GOVERNMENT

AFGHANISTAN

Head of State

The President is the Head of State, and is elected by a majority vote of the highest executive authority, the Loya Jirgah, to which he remains accountable. No President may serve more than two seven-year terms. The President appoints a Prime Minister, who in turn appoints a Council of Ministers to formulate and implement national policies (except during a state of emergency). In February 1989 a 20-member Supreme Council for the Defence of the Homeland was established, headed by the President, which assumed responsibility for economic, military and political policies (although the Council of Ministers continues to function).

President: Dr Najibullah Ahmadzai (took office 30 November 1987).

Office of the President: Kabul; tel (93) 25889.

Vice-Presidents: Abd ar-Rahim Haif, Lt-Gen Mohamed Rafie, Abd al-Hamid Mohtat, Dr Abd al-Wahed Sarabi.

Legislature

Legislative power is normally vested in the Meli Shura (National Assembly), which comprises the Sena (Senate), with 192 members and the Wolasi Jirgah (House of Representatives), with 234 members. A small number of seats in the Senate and 50 seats in the House of Representatives have been reserved for members of the opposition. The 31 provinces of Afghanistan are each administered by an appointed governor.

Sena (Senate): Kabul; Chair: Dr Mahmud Habibi; Deputy Chairs: Helaludin Badri, Shah Ali Akbar Shah-ritany.

Wolasi Jirgah (House of Representatives): Kabul; Chair: Dr Khalil Ahmad Abawi; Deputy Chairs: Dr Saleh Mohamed Zerai, Zohorullah Zohori.

MINISTRIES AND GOVERNMENT DEPARTMENTS

OFFICE OF THE COUNCIL OF MINISTERS
Shar Rahi Sedarat, Kabul
Tel (93) 26926

OFFICE OF THE PRIME MINISTER
Shar Rahi Sedarat, Kabul
Tel (93) 26926
Prime Minister: Sultan Ali Keshtmand
First Deputy Prime Minister: Mahmud Barialay
Deputy Prime Ministers: Sayed Amanoddin Amin, Mohamed Sarwar Mangal, Mahbubollah Koshani
Ministers without Portfolio: Dr Nur Ahmad Barets, Dr Nematullah Pazhwak, Sar Jang Zazi, Faqir Mohamed Yaqubi, Fazul Haq Khaleqyar, Shar Mohamed Dost

Central Office of Personnel and Administrative Reform: Shar Rahi Sedarat, Kabul; oversees the govt's administrative programme; implements training through the National Institute of Management.

MINISTRY OF AGRICULTURE AND LAND REFORM
Jamal Mina, Kabul
Tel (93) 41151
Minister: Mohamed Ghofran

MINISTRY OF BORDER AFFAIRS
Shah Mahmud Ghazi Ave, Kabul
Tel (93) 21793
Minister: Suleiman La'eq

MINISTRY OF CIVIL AVIATION
POB 165, Ansari Wat, Kabul
Tel (93) 21015
Minister: Sher Jan Mazduryar

MINISTRY OF COMMERCE
Darulaman Wat, Kabul
Tel (93) 41041; telex 34
Minister: Burhanuddin Ghiasi

MINISTRY OF COMMUNICATIONS
Puli Bagh-i-Omomi, Kabul
Tel (93) 21341; telex 297
Minister: Mir Azmuddin

MINISTRY OF CONSTRUCTION AFFAIRS
Micro-Rayon, Kabul
Tel (93) 63701
Minister: (vacant)

MINISTRY OF DEFENCE
Darulaman Wat, Kabul
Tel (93) 41232
Minister: Maj-Gen Mohamed Aslam Watanjar

MINISTRY OF EDUCATION AND TRAINING
Shar Rahi Malek Asghar, Kabul
Tel (93) 25151
Minister: Khodaydad Basharmal

MINISTRY OF ENERGY
Micro-Rayon, Kabul
Tel (93) 25109
Minister: Prof Ras Mohamed Patkin

MINISTRY OF FINANCE
Shar Rahi Pashtunistan, Kabul
Tel (93) 26041
Minister: Hamidollah Tarzi

MINISTRY OF FOREIGN AFFAIRS
Shah Mahmud Ghazi St, Shar-i-Nau, Kabul
Tel (93) 25441
Minister: Abd al-Wakil

**MINISTRY OF HIGHER AND VOCATIONAL
EDUCATION**
Jamal Mina, Kabul
Tel (93) 40041
Minister: Prof Mehr Mohamed Ejazi

MINISTRY OF INFORMATION AND CULTURE
Mohd Jan Khan Wat, Kabul
Tel (93) 24089
Minister: Ahmad Bashir Roygar

MINISTRY OF THE INTERIOR
Shar-i-Nau, Kabul
Tel (93) 32441
Minister: (vacant)

**MINISTRY OF ISLAMIC AFFAIRS AND
ENDOWMENT**
Kabul
Minister: Abdol Ghafur Baher

MINISTRY OF JUSTICE
Shar Rahi Pashtunistan, Kabul

Tel (93) 23404
Minister: Mohamed Bashir Baghlani

**MINISTRY OF LIGHT INDUSTRIES AND
FOODSTUFFS**
Ansari Wat, Kabul
Tel (93) 41551
Minister: Abdollah Bahar

MINISTRY OF MINES AND INDUSTRIES
Shar Rahi Pashtunistan, Kabul
Tel (93) 25841
Minister: Mohamed Eshaq Kawa

MINISTRY OF PLANNING
Shar-i-Nau, Kabul
Tel (93) 21273
Minister: Soltan Hosayn

MINISTRY OF PUBLIC HEALTH
Micro-Rayon, Kabul
Tel (93) 40851
Minister: Sayed Amir Zara

MINISTRY OF RETURNEES' AFFAIRS
Kabul
Minister: Sayed Ekram Paygir

**MINISTRY OF REVIVAL AND RURAL
DEVELOPMENT**
Kabul
Minister: Mohamed Asef Zaher

MINISTRY OF STATE SECURITY
Kabul
Minister: Lt-Gen Ghulam Faruq Yaqubi

MINISTRY OF TRANSPORT
Ansari Wat, Kabul
Tel (93) 25541
Minister: Khalilullah

**MINISTRY OF WATER RESOURCES
DEVELOPMENT AND IRRIGATION**
Darulaman Wat, Kabul
Tel (93) 40743
Minister: Prof Ras Mohamed Paktin

GOVERNMENT AGENCIES AND ORGANIZATIONS

Art and Culture

State Committee of Culture: Kabul; Chair: Abdul Qader Ashna.

Business and Economy

BANKING

Da Afghanistan Bank (Central Bank of Afghanistan): Ibne Sina Wat, Kabul; tel (93) 24075; telex 223; Gov: Dr Mohamed Kabir; Pres: Abd al-Bashir Ranjbar; f 1939; central bank; acts as Govt fiscal agency; responsible for issue of banknotes, regulation of foreign exchange and extension of credit to banks and enterprises; 65 brs.

Agricultural Development Bank of Afghanistan: POB 414, Cineme Pamir Bldg, Jade Maiwand, Kabul; tel (93) 24559; telex 274; Chair: Dr Bassir; Pres: M. Ibrahim Dilzada; f 1959;

provides credits for co-operatives, agro-business and farmers.

Banke Milli Afghan (Afghan National Bank): Ibne Sina Wat, Kabul; tel (93) 25451; telex 231; Chair: Hamidullah Tarzi; Pres: Dr Abul Hadi Ahmadyar; f 1932; 68 brs.

Export Promotion Bank of Afghanistan: Park Temor Shahi, Kabul; tel (93) 24447; telex 202; Pres: Mohamed Yaqub Neda; Vice-Pres: Burhanuddin Shahim; f 1976; provides finance for exports and export-oriented investments.

Industrial Development Bank of Afghanistan: POB 14, Jade Maiwand, Kabul; tel (93) 25641; Pres: H. Azizi; Vice-Pres: A. Yarmand; f 1973; provides financing for industrial devt.

Mortgage and Construction Bank: Bldg No 2, First Part Jade Maiwand, Kabul; tel (93) 23341; Pres: Faiz Mohamed Alokozi; f 1955; provides short- and long-term building loans.

Pashtany Tejaraty Bank (Afghan Commercial Bank): Mohd Jan Khan Wat, Kabul; tel (93) 26551; telex 243; Chair: Dr Basir Ranjar; Pres and Chief Exec: Zir Gul Wardak; f 1954; provides short-term finance and forwarding facilities and deals in foreign exchange; 17 brs in Afghanistan and abroad.

FINANCIAL AGENCY

Department of Enterprise: Shar Rahi Pashtunistan, Kabul; oversees financial policy of public and private business corporations.

INSURANCE

Afghan National Insurance Co: POB 329, Afghan Insurance Bldg, Timore Shahi Park, Kabul; tel (93) 26518; telex 231; Pres: M. Y. Deen; Vice-Pres: Abd ar-Razaq; f 1964; provides marine, aviation, fire, motor and accident cover.

TRADE

Afghan Carpet Exporters' Guild: POB 3159, Darulaman Wat, Kabul; tel (93) 41765; telex 234; Pres: Ziaudin Zia; f 1967; asscn of carpet manufacturers and exporters.

Afghan Cart Co: POB 61, Zarghona-Maidan, Kabul; tel (93) 21952; telex 57; largest import/export co in Afghanistan.

Afghan Chambers of Commerce and Industry: Mohd Jan Khan Wat, Kabul; tel (93) 26796; telex 245; Pres: Mohamed Hakim; Vice-Pres: Yar Mohamed Ayubi; f 1931; promotion of trade.

Afghan Fruits Processing Co: POB 261, Industrial Estate, Puli Charkhi, Kabul; tel (93) 5184; telex 61; exports raisins, other dried fruits and nuts.

Afghan Raisin and Other Dried Fruits Institute: POB 3034, Sharara Wat, Kabul; tel (93) 30463; telex 234; Pres: Najmuddin Musleh; f 1975; exporters of dried fruit and nuts.

Afghan Wool Enterprises: Shar-i-Nau, Kabul; tel (93) 31963.

Afghanistan Karakul Institute: POB 506, Puli Charkhi, Kabul; tel (93) 21952; Pres: Mohamed Ghous Bahir; exporters of furs.

Afghanistan Plants Enterprise: POB 122, Puli Charkhi, Kabul; tel (93) 31962; exports medicines, plants and spices.

Customs Administration Department: Shar Rahi Pashtunistan, Kabul; admin of customs and excise duties both within the country and in relation to other countries.

Federation of Afghan Chambers of Commerce and Industry: Darulaman Wat, Kabul; Pres: Mehar Chand Verma; Vice-Pres: Mohamed Hakim; f 1923; includes 10 regional chambers of commerce.

Handicraft Promotion and Export Centre: POB 3089, Sharara Wat, Kabul; tel (93) 32935; telex 34; Pres: Momena Ranjbar.

Defence

Armed Forces: Ansari Wat, Kabul; tel (93) 25715; Supreme Commdr: President Dr Najibullah Ahmadzai; Chief of Gen Staff: Maj-Gen Mohammed Asef Delawar.

Air Force and Air Defence Forces: Ansari Wat, Kabul; tel (93) 20740; Commdr-in-Chief: Gen Nurollah.

Energy

Atomic Energy Commission: Faculty of Science, Kabul University, Jamal Mina, Kabul; tel (93) 40341; Pres: Dr Mohamed Rasul.

Legal and Judiciary

Office of the Attorney-General: Kabul; Attorney-Gen: Syed Sharafuddin Sharaf; supervises implementation and observance of all laws.

Supreme Court: Kabul; Chief Justice: Nezzamuddin Tahzib; Dep Chief Justice: Abdul Wali Hojat; supervises judicial activities of all courts, ensures uniformity of law enforcement.

Media

BROADCASTING

Radio Afghanistan and TV Afghanistan: POB 544, Ansari Wat, Kabul; tel (93) 25241; Pres (Radio): Sayed Yaqub Wasiq; Pres (TV): Abdullah Shadan; domestic and foreign radio broadcasts; 10 hours of TV transmissions per day.

State Committee for Radio, TV and Cinematography: Ansari Wat, Kabul; tel (93) 25241; Chair: (vacant).

GOVERNMENT PUBLISHER

Government Printing House: Kabul; tel (93) 26851; Dir: Mohamed Ayan Ayan; f 1870; publishes newspapers, magazines, books and textbooks; under the supervision of the Ministry of Information and Culture.

NEWS AND INFORMATION

Bakhtar News Agency: Mohd Jan Khan Wat, Kabul; tel (93) 24089; Pres: Gholam Sarwar Yuresh; Dir: Abd al-Quddus Tander; f 1939; under Ministry of Information and Culture.

Central Statistics Office: Kabul; national statistical agency.

Committee of Bakhtar Information Agency: Kabul; Pres: Mohammad Dauod Kawyaan.

Tourism

Afghan Tourist Organization (ATO): Shar-i-Nau, Ansari Wat, Kabul; tel (93) 30323; Pres: M. Omar Karimzada; f 1958.

Afghan Tour: Shar-i-Nau, Ansari Wat, Kabul; tel (93) 30152; Pres: M. Omar Karimzada; official travel agency under the supervision of ATO.

Transport

Afghan Container Transport Co: POB 3234, Shar-i-Nau, Kabul; tel (93) 23088; telex 17; state-owned container transport co.

Afghan Transit Co: POB 530, Ghousy Market, Mohd Jan Khan Watt, Kabul; tel (93) 22654; telex 276; Pres: M. A. Kargar.

Ariana Afghan Airlines: POB 76, Afghan Air Authority Bldg, Ansari Wat, Kabul; tel (93) 25541; telex 28; Pres: Abdullah Samadi; f 1967; merged with Bakhtar Afghan Airlines Co Ltd in October 1985; internal services between Kabul and 18 regional locations; external services to the USSR, Czechoslovakia, India and the UAE.

Milli Bus Enterprise: Ministry of Transport, Ansari Wat, Kabul; tel (93) 25541; Pres: Aziz Naghaban; state-operated transport co.

ALBANIA

Head of State

The President of the Presidium of the People's Assembly acts as Head of State; in addition the Presidium comprises three Vice-Presidents, a Secretary and 10 other members. The Presidium convenes sessions of the People's Assembly and, between sessions of the legislature, supervises the implementation of the laws and decisions of the People's Assembly and controls all state organs.

President of the Presidium of the People's Assembly: Ramiz Alia (elected 22 November 1982; re-elected 19 February 1987).

Presidium of the People's Assembly: Tirana.

Legislature

The supreme organ of government is the unicameral People's Assembly (Kuvendi Popullor), whose 250 deputies are elected (unopposed) by popular vote for a four-year term. In practice the Assembly meets for only a few days each year to ratify actions taken in its name by the Presidium. The Assembly elects a Council of Ministers, whose Chairman is Head of the Government.

Kuvendi Popullor (People's Assembly): Tirana; Pres: Petro Dode; Vice-Pres: Vitori Curri, Ibrahim Hamza; Sec: Sali Shijaku.

MINISTRIES AND GOVERNMENT DEPARTMENTS

COUNCIL OF MINISTERS
Tirana
Chair: Adil Çarçani
Deputy Chairs: Simon Stefani, Manush Myftiu, Pali Miska
Secretary-Gen: Enver Halili

Presidium of the Council of Ministers: Tirana; Minister: Farudin Hoxha.

MINISTRY OF AGRICULTURE
Shtëpia e Propagandës Bujqësore, Tirana
Tel 61-47
Minister: Pali Miska

MINISTRY OF CONSTRUCTION
Tirana
Minister: Ismail Ahmeti

MINISTRY OF EDUCATION
Tirana
Minister: Skënder Gjinushi

MINISTRY OF ENERGY
Tirana
Minister (acting): Besnik Bekteshi

MINISTRY OF FINANCE
Tirana
Minister: Andrea Nako

MINISTRY OF THE FOODSTUFF INDUSTRY
Tirana
Minister: Jovan Bardhi

MINISTRY OF FOREIGN AFFAIRS
Ministria e Punëvet të Jashtme, Tirana
Telex 2164
Minister: Reis Malile
Deputy Minister: Sokrat Plaka

MINISTRY OF FOREIGN TRADE
Ministria e Tregetisë të Jashtme, Tirana
Telex 2152
Minister: Shane Korbeci

MINISTRY OF THE HEALTH SERVICE
Tirana
Minister: Ahmet Kamberi

MINISTRY OF HOME TRADE
Tirana
Minister: Osman Murati

MINISTRY OF INDUSTRY AND MINING
Tirana
Minister: Besnik Bekteshi

MINISTRY OF INTERNAL AFFAIRS
Tirana
Minister: Simon Stefani

MINISTRY OF LIGHT INDUSTRY
Tirana
Minister: Vito Kapo

MINISTRY OF PEOPLE'S DEFENCE
Tirana
Minister: Prokop Murra

MINISTRY OF PUBLIC SERVICES
Tirana
Minister: Xhemal Tafaj

MINISTRY OF TRANSPORT
Tirana
Minister: Hajredin Çeliku

STATE CONTROL COMMISSION
Tirana
Chair: Manush Myftiu

STATE PLANNING COMMISSION
Tirana
Chair: Niko Gyjzari

GOVERNMENT AGENCIES AND ORGANIZATIONS

Advisory and Supervisory Body

Albkontroll: Bulevardi Enver Hoxha 45, Durrës; tel 23-54; telex 2181; Gen Man: Hito Minga; Dep Gen Man: Bardhyl Kellici; f 1962; central control body for inspection of goods for import and export, means of transport, etc; brs throughout the country.

Business and Economy

BANKING

Banka e Shtëtit Shqiptar (Albanian State Bank): Sheshi Skënderbeu 1, Tirana; tel 24-35; telex 2153; Dir-Gen: Qirjako Mihali; f 1945; bank of issue, sole credit institution; brs in 34 towns.

State Agricultural Bank: Tirana; tel 77-38; Dir: S. Kuci; f 1970; grants short- and long-term credits to agricultural co-operatives and enterprises.

FINANCIAL AGENCY

Drejtoria e Përgjithshme e Kursimeve dhe Sigurimeve (Directorate of Savings and Insurance): Tirana; tel 25-42; Dir: Seit Bushati; f 1949.

TRADE

Agroeksport: Rruga 4 Shkurti 6, Tirana; tel 52-27; telex 2137; Gen Man: Luan Shahu; export of vegetables, fruit, canned fish, wine, tobacco, etc.

Albkoop: Rruga 4 Shkurti 6, Tirana; tel 41-79; telex 2187; Gen Man: Jeton Hajdaraj; f 1986; import and export of consumer goods, including textiles, handicrafts, stationery and jewellery.

Arteksportimport: Rruga 4 Shkurti 6, Tirana; tel 45-50; telex 2140; f 1989; exports handicrafts and products of light industry; imports items required by Albanian industries.

Dhoma e Tregtisë e Republikës Popullore Socialiste të Shqipërisë (Chamber of Commerce of the People's Socialist Republic of Albania): Rruga Konferenca e Pezës 6, Tirana; tel 79-97; telex 2179; Chair: Ligor Dhamo; Vice-Chair: Simon Poreçi; f 1958.

Durrësimpeks: Rruga Skënderbeu 177, Durrës; tel 21-99; telex 2181; Dir: Taqo Kosta; f 1988; trade in industrial and agricultural goods.

Gjirokastërimpeks: Rruga Nacionale 55, Gjirokastër; tel 707; f 1988; industrial and agricultural goods; responsible for trade with Greece.

Industrialimpeks: Rruga 4 Shkurti 6, Tirana; tel 45-40; telex 2140; Gen Man: Hazbi Gjikondi; export of textiles, clothing, paper, timber, cement etc; import of cotton, wool, paper etc.

Makinaimport: Rruga 4 Shkurti 6, Tirana; tel 52-20; telex 2127; Gen Man: Theodhor Duma; import of factory installations and machine parts.

Metalimport: Rruga 4 Shkurti 6, Tirana; tel 38-48; telex 2116; Dir: T. Borodni; import of ferrous and non-ferrous metals, electrodes, oil lubricants, minerals, etc.

Mineralimpeks: Rruga 4 Shkurti 6, Tirana; tel 33-70; telex 2123; Dir-Gen: Niqifor Alikaj; import and export of chromium ore, ferro-nickel ore, electricity, etc.

Shkodërimpeks: Shkodër; responsible for trade with Yugoslavia; industrial and agricultural goods.

Transshqip: Rruga 4 Shkurti 6, Tirana; tel 30-63; telex 2131; fax 30-76; Dir-Gen: Giolekë Zeneli; f 1960; transport of foreign trade goods by sea, rail and road; agents in Durrës, Vlorë and Sarandë.

Legal and Judiciary

Office of Investigation: Tirana; Chair: Qemal Lame; state organ for the investigation of criminal acts.

Supreme Court: Tirana; Pres: Aranit Çela; Attorney-Gen: Rrapi Mino; highest national court; elected for a four-year term by the People's Assembly.

Media

BROADCASTING

Radiotelevisioni Shqiptar: Rruga Ismail Qemali, Tirana; tel 81-34; Dir-Gen: Sefedin Çela; f 1944; provides national radio and TV services.

GOVERNMENT PUBLISHERS

Drejtoria Qëndrore e Përhapjes dhe e Propagandimit të Librit (Central Administration for the Dissemination and Propagation of the Book): Tirana; tel 78-41; under the supervision of the Ministry of Education and Culture.

N I Sh Shtypshkronjave Mihal Duri (Mihal Duri State Printing House): Tirana; Dir: Hajri Hoxha; Govt publications, politics, law, education.

NEWS AND INFORMATION

Albanian Telegraphic Agency (ATA): Bulevardi Marcel Cachin 23, Tirana; tel 44-12; telex 2142; Dir: Taqo Zoto; f 1945; state monopoly for news distribution.

Drejtoria e Statistikës (Directorate of Statistics): Tirana; provision and analysis of national statistics.

Tourism

Albturist: Bulevardi Dëshmorët e Kombit 6, Tirana; tel 79-56; telex 2148; Dir-Gen: Ruhi Sheqi; central tourism agency.

Transport

Albtransport: Rruga Kongresi i Përmetit 202, Tirana; tel 30-26; telex 2124; state air agency, providing links with a number of European cities.

Drejtoria e Agjensisë së Vaporave: Enver Hoxha Port of Durrës; shipping directorate.

Drejtoria e Hekurudhave: Tirana; Dir-Gen: Viktor Caprazi; railway admin.

ALGERIA

Head of State

The President, nominated by the Front de Libération Nationale (FLN), is elected by universal adult suffrage for a five-year term. The President holds supreme executive power and is empowered to legislate by decree when the National People's Assembly is not in session. The President presides over a Council of Ministers and a High Security Council, and appoints the Prime Minister, who in turn appoints the Council of Ministers. The Prime Minister is responsible to the National People's Assembly.

President: Ben Djedid Chadli (elected 7 February 1979; re-elected 12 January 1984 and 22 December 1988).

Office of the President: Présidence de la République, el-Mouradia, Algiers; tel (2) 60-03-60; telex 53761.

Legislature

Legislative power is held jointly by the President and by the unicameral National People's Assembly (Assemblée Nationale Populaire), which has 295 members elected for a five-year term by universal adult suffrage. Parties are subject to approval from the Ministry of the Interior. Local government is the responsibility of regional elected assemblies at department and commune level.

National People's Assembly: 18 blvd Zirout Youcef, Algiers; tel (2) 63-86-00; Pres: Rabah Bitat.

MINISTRIES AND GOVERNMENT DEPARTMENTS

OFFICE OF THE PRIME MINISTER
Palais du Gouvernement, Algiers
Tel (2) 60-23-40; telex 52073.
Prime Minister: Mouloud Hamrouche
Minister Delegate for Employment:
Amar Kara Muhammad
Minister Delegate for Local Authorities: Benali Henni
Minister Delegate for the Organization of Commerce:
Smail Goumeziane
Minister Delegate for Universities:
Abd as-Salem Ali-Rachedi
Secretary of State for Maghreb Affairs:
Abd al Aziz Khellef
Secretary-General of the Government:
Ahmad Medjhouda

MINISTRY OF AGRICULTURE
12 blvd Col Amirouche, Algiers
Tel (2) 63-89-50; telex 52984
Minister: Abd al-Kader Bendaoud

MINISTRY OF DEFENCE
ave des Tagarins, Algiers
Tel (2) 61-15-15; telex 52627
Minister: Ben Djedid Chadli

MINISTRY OF ECONOMY
Algiers
Minister: Ghazi Hidouci

MINISTRY OF EDUCATION AND TRAINING
8 ave de Pékin, el-Mouradia, Algiers
Tel (2) 60-54-41; telex 52443
Minister of Education: Muhammad al-Mili Brahimi
Minister Delegate for Professional Training:
Abd en-Nour Keramane

MINISTRY OF EQUIPMENT
Algiers
Minister: Cherif Rahmani

MINISTRY OF FOREIGN AFFAIRS
6 rue 16n- Batran, el-Mouradia, Algiers
Tel (2) 60-47-44; telex 52794
Minister: Sid-Ahmad Ghozali

MINISTRY OF HEALTH
25 blvd Laala Abd ar-Rahmane, el-Madania, Algiers
Tel (2) 66-33-15; telex 51263
Minister: Akli Kheddis

MINISTRY OF HIGHER EDUCATION
1 rue Bachir Attar, Palais du 1er Mai, Algiers
Tel (2) 66-33-61; telex 52720
Minister: Muhammad al-Mili·Brahimi

MINISTRY OF INDUSTRY
rue Ahmad Bey, Immeuble le Colisée, Algiers
Tel (2) 60-11-14; telex 52707
Minister: Hassen Kalouche

MINISTRY OF THE INTERIOR
Palais du Gouvernement, Algiers
Tel (2) 63-23-40; telex 52073
Minister: Muhammad Salah Muhammadi

MINISTRY OF JUSTICE
8 rue de Khartoum, el-Biar, Algiers
Tel (2) 78-20-90; telex 52761
Minister: Ali ben Flis

MINISTRY OF MINES
80 rue Ahmad Ghermoul, Algiers
Tel (2) 66-33-00; telex 52790
Minister: Sadok Boussena

MINISTRY OF POSTS AND TELECOMMUNICATIONS
4 blvd Salah Bouakouir, Algiers
Tel (2) 61-12-20; telex 52020
Minister: Hamid Sidi Saïd

MINISTRY OF PUBLIC WORKS
135 rue Didouche Mourad, Algiers
Tel (2) 59-00-29; telex 52713
Minister: (vacant)

MINISTRY OF RELIGIOUS AFFAIRS
2 ave Timgad, Hydra, Algiers
Tel (2) 60-85-55; telex 52648
Minister: Saïd Chibane

MINISTRY OF SOCIAL AFFAIRS
rue Farid Zouieoueche, Kouba, Algiers
Tel (2) 77-91-33; telex 53447
Minister: Muhammad Ghrib

MINISTRY OF TRANSPORT
chemin Abd al-Kader Gadouche, Hydra, Algiers
Tel (2) 60-60-33; telex 52775
Minister: Al-Hadi Khediri

MINISTRY OF YOUTH
3 place du 1er Mai, Algiers
Tel (2) 66-33-70; telex 52110
Minister: Abd al-Kader Boudjemaa

GOVERNMENT AGENCIES AND ORGANIZATIONS

Agriculture and the Environment

AGRICULTURE

Office Régional des Produits Oléicoles du Centre (ORPO Centre): rue Bey Muhammad, Domaine Garidi, Kouba, Algiers; tel (2) 58-41-70; telex 77098; Dir-Gen: Mustafa Chabour; production and marketing of olives and olive oil.

Société Nationale des Eaux Minérales Algériennes (SN-EMA): 21 rue Bellouchat Mouloud, Hussein Dey, Algiers; tel (2) 77-17-91; telex 52310; Man Dir: Tahar Khenel; production of mineral water.

Société Nationale des Industries des Peaux et Cuirs (SONIPEC): 100 rue de Tripoli, BP 113, Hussein Dey, Algiers; tel (2) 77-66-00; telex 52832; Chair and Man Dir: Muhammad Cherif Azi; Man Dir: Hassan ben Younes; f 1967; production of hides and skins.

THE ENVIRONMENT

Agence Nationale de Réalisation et de Gestion des Infrastructures Hydrauliques pour l'Irrigation et le Drainage (AGID): El Marsa, BP 31, Bordj, el Bahri (W de Boumerdes); national dept for the creation and management of hydraulic irrigation and drainage systems.

FISHING

Entreprise Nationale des Pêches (ENAPECHES): Quai d'Aigues Mortes, Port d'Alger; tel (2) 62-01-00; telex 61346; Man Dir: Al-Okbi Benouaar; f 1979; production, marketing, import and export of fish.

FORESTRY

Secrétariat d'Etat aux Forêts et au Reboisement: Immeuble des Forêts, Bois du Petit Atlas, el-Mouradia, Algiers; tel (2) 60-43-00; telex 52854; Man Dir: Daniel Belbachir; f 1971; central forestry body; produces timber.

Socété Nationale des Industries des Lièges et du Bois (SNLB): 1 rue Kaddour Rahim, BP 61, Hussein Dey, Algiers; tel (2) 77-99-99; telex 52726; Chair: Malek Bellani; f 1973; manufactures cork and wooden goods.

Business and Economy

BANKING

Banque de l'Agriculture et du Développement Rural (BADR): 17 blvd Col Amirouche, BP 484, Algiers; tel (2) 64-72-64; telex 62240; Man Dir: Mustafa Achour; Dir-Gen: Abdelkader Belgherbi; f 1982; commercial and devt bank.

Banque Algérienne de Développement (BAD): 12 blvd Col Amirouche, 16000 Algiers; tel (2) 63-88-95; telex 67220; fax (2) 63-81-73; Pres and Dir-Gen: Sassi Azziza; f 1963; long-term investment programmes to aid national economic growth.

Banque Centrale d'Algérie: 8 blvd Zirout Youcef, 16000 Algiers; tel (2) 64-75-00; telex 66499; fax (2) 64-87-46; Gov: Abderrahmane Hadj-Nacer; Gen Man: Bachir Saïl; f 1962; central bank and bank of issue; 50 brs.

Banque de Développement Local (BDL): 5 rue Gaci Amar, Staoueli, (W Tipaza); tel (2) 81-58-00; telex 63171; Dir-Gen: Muhammad ben Halima; f 1985; 83 brs.

Banque Extérieure d'Algérie (BEA): 11 blvd Col Amirouche, Algiers; tel (2) 61-12-52; telex 67072; Pres and Gen Man: Mourad Khellaf; f 1967; deals mainly with areas of energy and maritime transport; 60 brs.

Banque Nationale d'Algérie (BNA): 8 blvd Ernesto Ché Guévara, Algiers; tel (2) 62-05-44; telex 52788; Pres: Abd al-Moumene Faouzi Benmalik; Gen Man: Abd al-Madjid Nassou; Head, Int Division: Omar Benderra; f 1966; chiefly concerned with heavy industry and transport; 85 brs.

Caisse Nationale d'Epargne et de Prévoyance (CNEP): 42 rue Khélifa Boukhalfa, Algiers; tel (2) 66-33-53; telex 65286; fax (2) 65-28-64; Man: Jakhdar Benouataf; f 1964; savings and housing bank.

Crédit Populaire d'Algérie (CPA): 2 blvd Col Amirouche, Algiers; tel (2) 61-13-34; telex 67170; Gen Man: Mahfoud Zerouta; f 1966; finances building and public works, light industry, transport and tourism; 90 brs.

FINANCIAL AGENCY

Agence Nationale de l'Aménagement du Territoire (ANAT): 30 ave Muhammad Fellah, BP 237, Kouba, Algiers; tel (2) 58-48-12; telex 62369; Dir-Gen: Dr Hocine ben Djoudi; f 1980; study and production of plans relating to national and regional devt.

INSURANCE

Caisse Algérienne d'Assurance: 48 rue Didouche Mourad, Algiers; tel (2) 64-54-32; telex 66669; Dir-Gen: Mahfoud Battata; f 1963.

Caisse Nationale de Mutualité Agricole: 24 blvd Victor Hugo, Algiers; tel (2) 63-76-82; telex 67333; Dir-Gen: Yahia Cherif Brahim.

Compagnie Centrale de Réassurance: 21 blvd Zirout Youcef, Algiers; tel (2) 63-72-88; telex 67092; Chair: Djamel-Eddine Chouaïb Chouiter; Gen Man: Ahmad al-Azhar Nechachby; f 1973; reinsurance.

Société Algérienne d'Assurances (SAA): 5 blvd Ernesto Ché Guévara, Algiers; tel (2) 62-29-44; telex 61216; Chair: Mahfoud Battata; Dir-Gen: Abd al-Krim Djafri; f 1963; state-sponsored co.

NATIONALIZED INDUSTRY

Entreprise Nationale de Cellulose et de Papier (CELPAP): route de la Salamandre, BP 128, Mostaganem; tel (6) 26-54-99; telex 14058; Man Dir: Enwar Tewfik Berbar.

Entreprise Nationale des Corps Gras (ENCG): 13 ave Mustapha Sayed, El-Ouali, Algiers; tel (2) 59-34-22; telex 66075; Dir-Gen: Rachid Hammouche; Dep Dir-Gen: Saïd Bouras; f 1982; fmrly Société de Gestion et de Développement des Industries Alimentaires (SOGEDIA); production of edible oils, soap, margarines and vegetable oils, glycerine, packaging and bottles.

Entreprise Nationale de Développement et de Coordination des Industries Alimentaires (ENIAL): 2 rue Ahmad Ait Muhammad-el-Harrach, Algiers; tel (2) 76-51-42; telex 54031; Dir-Gen: Mustafa Mokraoui; f 1965; production of semolina, pasta, flour and couscous.

Entreprise Nationale d'Engineering et de Développement des Industries Légères (EDIL): 50 rue Khélifa Boukhalfa, BP 1140, Algiers; tel (2) 66-33-90; telex 52883; Dir-Gen: Missoum Abd al-Hakim; f 1982.

Entreprise Nationale de Fer et de Phosphate (EN FERPHOS): Zhun II, BP 122, 12000 Tebessa; tel (8) 97-49-58; telex 95004; Dir-Gen: Ahmed ben Slimane; f 1983; controlled by Ministry of Heavy Industry; production, devt and marketing of iron and phosphate products.

Entreprise Nationale des Industries Electriques (ENIE): route de Mascara, BP 101, Sidi-Bel-Abbès; tel (7) 24-26-28; telex 16041; Dir-Gen: Muhammad Ghrib.

Entreprise Nationale des Industries de l'Electroménager (ENIEM): BP 71A Poste Chikhi, 15000 Tizi-Ouzou; tel (3) 40-78-90; telex 76031; Dir-Gen: Chabane Hammad; f 1983; research, devt and production of household electrical goods.

Entreprise Nationale de Production de Boulonnerie et Robinetterie (BCR): BP 37, Cité Bizard, Sétif; tel (5) 85-63-78; telex 86079; fax (5) 85-67-24; Gen Man: Muhammad Tayeb Doghbal; Foreign Trade Man: M. E. Louadfel; f 1983; manufactures and distributes bolts, taps and cutlery.

Entreprise Nationale de Production des Matériels Agricoles (ENPMA): route de Tenira, BP 151/08, Sidi-Bel-Abbès; tel (7) 24-91-40; telex 16915; fax (7) 24-91-56; Dir-Gen: Djamel Eddine ben Nini; f 1981; manufactures, imports and exports agricultural machinery and equipment.

Entreprise Nationale de Production de Véhicules Particuliers (ENPVP): 28 rue Quaked Ahmed, Delly Brahim, Algiers; tel (2) 78-23-60; telex 61467; Dir-Gen: Slimane Tahari; manufactures cars, bicycles and motorcycles.

Entreprise Nationale de la Sidérurgie (SIDER): Chaiba, Commune Sidi-Amar, BP 342, 23000 Annaba; tel (8) 83-09-99; telex 81661; fax (8) 83-89-57; Gen Man: Messaoud Chettih; f 1964; restructured 1983; produces, imports and exports iron and steel products.

Pharmacie Centrale Algérienne: 2 rue Bichat, Algiers; tel (2) 65-18-27; telex 52993; Man Dir: M. Morsli; f 1969; manufacture of pharmaceutical products.

Société Nationale de l'Artisanat Traditionnel (SNAT): Algiers; tel (2) 62-68-02; telex 53093; Man Dir: Saïd Amrani; traditional crafts.

Société Nationale de Constructions Mécaniques (SONACOME): Birkhadem, Algiers; tel (2) 65-93-92; telex 52800; Dir: Daoud Akrouf; f 1967; to be reorganized into 11 smaller cos.

Société Nationale de Constructions Métalliques (SN METAL): Algiers; tel (2) 63-29-30; telex 52889; Chair: Hachem Malik; Man Dir: Abd al-Kader Maiza; f 1968; manufactures metal products.

Société Nationale de Fabrication et de Montage du Matériel Electrique (SONELEC): 4 & 6 blvd Muhammad V, Algiers; tel (2) 63-70-82; telex 52867; manufacture of electrical equipment.

Société Nationale des Industries Chimiques (SNIC): 4-6 blvd Muhammad V, BP 641, Algiers; tel (2) 64-07-73; telex 52802; Dir-Gen: Rachid ben Iddir; chemical industries.

Société Nationale des Industries Textiles (SONITEX): 4-6 rue Patrice Lumumba, BP 41, Algiers; tel (2) 63-41-35; telex 52929; Man Dir: Muhammad Arezki Isli; f 1966; group of cos dealing with cotton, wool, industrial textiles, silk, clothing and distribution.

Société Nationale des Matériaux de Construction (SNMC): Algiers; tel (2) 64-35-13; telex 52204; Man Dir: Abd al-Kader Maizi; f 1968; produces and holds imports monopoly of building materials.

Société Nationale des Tabacs et Alumettes (SNTA): 40 rue Hocine-Nourredine, Algiers; tel (2) 66-18-68; telex 52780; Dir-Gen: Muhammad Tahab Bouzeghoub; monopoly of production and sale of tobacco, cigarettes and matches.

TRADE

Chambre Nationale de Commerce: Palais Consulaire, 6 blvd Amílcar Cabral, Algiers; tel (2) 57-44-44; telex 61345; Pres: Omar Ramdane; Dir-Gen: Hamza Mesmoudi; Sec-Gen: Rachid Bettahar; f 1980; under control of Ministry of Commerce; promotes and develops external trade, especially in areas other than oil and gas.

Direction Générale des Douanes: rue Dr Saâdane, Algiers; tel (2) 61-16-16; telex 67153; customs directorate.

Entreprise Nationale d'Approvisionnements en Produits Alimentaires (ENAPAL): 29 rue Larbi ben M'hidi, BP 659, Algiers; tel (2) 64-02-75; telex 52991; Chair: Laid Sabri; Man Dir: Brahim Douaouri; f 1983; holds monopoly of import, export and bulk trade in basic foodstuffs; brs in more than 40 towns.

Entreprise Nationale d'Approvisionnement et de Régulation en Fruits et Légumes (ENAFLA): 12 ave des 3 Frères Bouadou, BP 42, Birmandreis, Algiers; tel (2) 56-90-83; telex 62113; Man Dir: Ali ben Segueni; f 1983; part of Ministry of Commerce; marketing, production and export of fruit and vegetables.

Entreprise Nationale de Commerce: 6-9 rue Belhaffat-Ghazali, Hussein Dey, Algiers; tel (2) 77-43-20; telex 52063; Dir-Gen: Muhammad Laïd Belarbia; monopoly of import and distribution of materials and equipment.

Office Algérien Interprofessionel des Céréales (OAIC): 5 rue Ferhat-Boussaad, Algiers; tel (2) 66-38-14; telex 52121; Man Dir: M. Douaouri; f 1962; holds monopoly of trade in wheat, rice, maize, barley and products derived from these cereals.

Office National de la Commercialisation des Produits Viti-Vinicoles (ONCV): 112 Quai-Sud, Algiers; tel (2) 63-09-40; telex 67074; Man Dir: Douaouri Brahim; f 1968; monopoly of import and export of wine industry products.

Office National des Foires et des Exportations (ONAFEX): Palais des Expositions, BP 252, Pins Maritimes, Alger Gare, Algiers; tel (2) 76-31-00; telex 64212; Dir-Gen: Zahir Abd ar-Rahim; f 1982; promotes commercial exchanges, assists exporters and organizes economic and trade fairs, including the Foire Internationale d'Alger.

Defence

Armed Forces: c/o Ministry of National Defence, ave des Tagarins, Algiers; tel (2) 63-14-76; telex 66420; Commdr-in-Chief of the armed Forces: Ben Djedid Chadli; Inspector-Gen of the Armed Forces: Gen El-Hachemi Hadjeres.

> **Air Force:** c/o Ministry of Defence, ave des Tagarins, Algiers; tel (2) 63-14-76; telex 66420; Commdr: Gen Abd al-Malek Guenaizia.

> **Army:** c/o Ministry of National Defence, ave des Tagarins, Algiers; tel (2) 63-14-76; telex 66420; Chief of Staff of the Army: Col Abdallah Belhouchet; Commdr of the Land Force: Gen Khaled Nezzar.

> **Navy:** c/o Ministry of National Defence, ave des Tagarins, Algiers; tel (2) 63-14-76; telex 67172; Commdr: Gen Kamel Abd ar-Rahim.

National Gendarmerie: c/o Ministry of National Defence, ave des Tagarins, Algiers; tel (2) 63-14-76; telex 66420; Commdr: Gen Line-Labidire Hachichi.

Development and Planning

Conseil National de Planification: Chemin Ibn Badis el-Mouiz, el-Biar, Algiers; tel (2) 78-13-23; planning council.

Société Centrale pour l'Equipement du Territoire (SCET) International: Algiers; Dir: A Gambrelle.

Legal and Judiciary

Supreme Court: Palais de Justice, 10 rue Abone Romolone, Algiers; tel (2) 63-28-24; Pres: A. Medjhouda; Procurator-Gen: Y. Bekkouche; f 1963; highest court of justice.

Media

BROADCASTING

Radiodiffusion Télévision Algérienne (RTA): Immeuble RTA, 21 blvd des Martyrs, Algiers; tel (2) 60-23-00; telex 52042; Dir of RTA: Muhammad Ouzeghdou; Dirs of Radio: M. Abd al-Kader, Hachemi Souami; Dir of TV: Abd al-Kader Brahimi.

GOVERNMENT PUBLISHERS

Entreprise Nationale du Livre (ENAL): 3 blvd Zirout Youcef, BP 49, Algiers; tel (2) 63-97-12; telex 53845; Dir-Gen: Seghir Benamar; f 1966; sole importer, exporter and distributor of all printed material, stationery, school and office supplies; retains state monopoly for commercial advertising.

Office des Publications Universitaires: 1 place Centrale de Ben, Aknoun, Algiers; tel (2) 78-87-18; telex 61396; controlled by Ministry of Higher Education; publication of university textbooks.

NEWS AND INFORMATION

Algérie Presse Service (APS): 7 blvd Ernesto Ché Guévara, Algiers; tel (2) 62-10-00; telex 66380; Dir-Gen: Belkacem Ahcene-Djaballah; f 1962.

Office National des Statistiques (ONS): 10 rue des Moussebiline, Algiers; tel (2) 64-77-90; telex 67190; f 1982; carries out censuses of the population; publishes socio-economic analyses.

Mining and Energy

ENERGY

Haut Commissariat à la Recherche (HCR): BP 100, el-Madania, Algiers; tel (2) 66-33-25; telex 65303; f 1986; fmrly Commissariat aux Energies Nouvelles; research and devt of renewable forms of energy, including atomic, solar, wind and geothermal energy.

Société Nationale de l'Electricité et du Gaz (SONELGAZ): 12 blvd Salah Bouakouir, BP 841, Algiers; tel (2) 64-82-60; telex 66381; Man Dir: Mustafa Harrati; f 1969; holds monopoly of production, transport and distribution of electricity; transport and distribution of natural gas.

Société Nationale pour la Recherche, la Production, le Transport, la Transformation et la Commercialisation des Hydrocarbures (SONATRACH): 10 rue du Sahara, Hydra, Algiers; tel (2) 60-60-28; telex 62103; fax (2) 60-70-37; Dir-Gen: Sadok Boussena; f 1963; exploits, transports, markets and conducts research into natural gas, petroleum and their products; since 1980 the following associated companies have shared SONATRACH's functions:

> **Entreprise Nationale de Canalisation (ENAC):** ave de la Palestine, BP 514, Ouargla; tel (9) 70-32-90; telex 42939; Dir-Gen: Hamid Mazri; piping.

> **Entreprise Nationale de Raffinage et de Distribution des Produits Pétroliers (ENRDP):** route des Dunes, BP 73, Chéraga, Algiers; tel (2) 81-09-69; telex 53079; Dir-Gen: Abd al-Madjid Kazi-Tani; export and internal distribution of petroleum products.

> **Entreprise Nationale d'Engineering Pétrolier (ENEP):** 2 blvd Muhammad V, Algiers; tel (2) 63-08-92; telex 66493; Dir-Gen: Mustapha Mekideche; f 1984; chemical and petrochemical industries; engineering.

> **Entreprise Nationale de Forage (ENAFOR):** BP 211, Hassi Messaoud, Algiers; tel (2) 73-85-40; telex 44077; Dir-Gen: Abd ar-Rachid Rouabah; drilling.

> **Entreprise Nationale de Génie Civil et Bâtiments (ENGCB):** route de Corso, BP 23, Boudouaou, Algiers; tel (2) 41-65-26; telex 53653; Dir-Gen: Muhammad Tahar Zemzoum; civil engineering.

> **Entreprise Nationale de Géophysique (ENAGEO):** BP 213, Hassi Messaoud, Ouargla; tel (9) 78-80-03; telex 44053; Dir-Gen: Ali Ouartsi.

> **Entreprise Nationale des Grands Travaux Pétroliers**

(ENGTP): Zone Industriel, BP 09, Reghaïa, Boumerdes; tel (2) 80-06-80; telex 68150; Dir-Gen: A. Benameur; Asst Dir-Gen: M. ben Ameur; major industrial projects.

Entreprise Nationale de Pétrochimie et d'Engrais (ENPE): route des Dunes, Chéraga, Algiers; tel (2) 81-09-69; telex 53876; petrochemicals and fertilizers.

Entreprise Nationale des Plastiques et de Caoutchouc (ENPC): rue des Frères Meslim, BP 452, Aïn Turk, Sétif; tel (5) 90-33-40; telex 86040; Dir-Gen: Mahieddine Echikh; production and marketing or rubber and plastics.

Entreprise Nationale de Raffinage des Produits Pétroliers (ENRP): f 1987; refines petroleum products.

Entreprise Nationale de Service aux Puits (ENSP): 1 blvd Amílcar Cabral, BP 8, Hassi Messaoud, Ouargla; tel (9) 73-89-84; telex 44018; fax (9) 73-82-01; Dir-Gen: O. Bendahou; oil-well servicing.

Entreprise Nationale des Travaux aux Puits (ENTP): BP 71, In-Amenas, Illizi; telex 44052; Dir-Gen: Abd al-Aziz Krissat; oil-well construction.

MINING

Société Nationale de Recherches et d'Exploitations Minières (SONAREM): 127 blvd Salah Bouakouir, BP 860, Algiers; tel (2) 63-15-55; telex 52910; Dir-Gen: Oubraham Ferhat; f 1967; mining and prospecting.

Telecommunications

Entreprise Nationale des Télécommunications (ENTC): 1 ave du 1er Novembre, Tlemcen; tel (7) 26-76-76; telex 18944; fax (7) 26-39-51; Dir-Gen: Abib Abdelkrim; f 1978; national telecommunications organization; joint venture with Sweden.

Tourism

Office National Algérien de l'Animation de la Promotion et de l'Information Touristique (ONAT): 25-27 rue Khélifa-Boukhalfa, 16000 Algiers; tel (2) 74-33-76; telex 66339; fax (2) 74-32-14; Dir-Gen: Rachid Maarif; national tourist office; acts as tour operator; runs travel agencies.

Transport

CIVIL AVIATION

Air Algérie (Entreprise Nationale d'Exploitation des Services Aériens Internationaux de Transport Public): 1 place Maurice Audin, Immeuble el-Djazair, BP 858, Algiers; tel (2) 63-12-82; telex 52436; Pres and Dir-Gen: Elhadju Haoussine; f 1953; state-owned since 1972; deals with external services to Europe, North, Central and West Africa, the Middle East and Asia.

Inter-Air Services (Entreprise Nationale d'Exploitation des Services Aériens de Transport Intérieur et Travail Aériens): address as above; subsidiary of Air Algérie; serves internal destinations.

RAILWAYS

Société Nationale des Transports Ferroviaires (SNTF): 21-23 blvd Muhammad V, Algiers; tel (2) 61-15-10; telex 52455; Dir-Gen: M. Maherzi; f 1976 to replace Société Nationale des Chemins de Fer Algériens; runs passenger train services from Algiers to major provincial cities and to Tunis.

ROADS

Société Nationale des Transports Routiers (SNTR): 27 rue des 3 Frères Bouadou, Birmandreis, Algiers; tel (2) 56-21-21; telex 52962; Chair: Elhadj Haoussine; Dir-Gen: Ben Aouda ben Elhadj Djelloul; f 1967; monopoly of transport of goods by road.

Société Nationale des Transports des Voyageurs (SNTV): 19 rue Rabah Midat, Algiers; tel (2) 66-00-52; telex 52603; Man Dir: M. Dib; f 1967; monopoly of long-distance transport of passengers by road.

SHIPPING

Compagnie Algéro-Libyenne de Transports Maritimes (CALTRAM): 21 rue des 3 Frères Bouadou, Birmandreis, Algiers; tel (2) 63-58-07; telex 62112; Chair: M. O. Das.

Entreprise Nationale de Consignation et d'Activités Annexes aux Transports Maritimes (ENCATM): Algiers; f 1987; responsible for merchant traffic.

Entreprise Nationale de Réparations Navales (ERENAV): Algiers; f 1987; ship repairs.

Entreprise Nationale de Transport Maritime de Voyageurs—Algérie Ferries (ENTMV): Algiers; f 1987; passenger transport; responsible for car ferry services between Algiers, Annanba and Oran.

Entreprise Portuaire d'Alger: 2 rue d'Angkor, BP 708, Algiers; tel (2) 71-55-80; telex 61275; fax (2) 62-44-98; Pres and Dir-Gen: Hani Lazhar; f 1982; piloting; port management; devt and exploitation of port superstructure; runs port policing and security.

NAFTAL Direction Aviation Maritime: Aéroport Houari Boumedienne, Dar-el Beida, BP 70, Algiers; tel (2) 75-73-75; telex 64315; Dir: Z. ben Merabet.

Office National des Ports (ONP): Quai d'Arcachon, BP 830, Port d'Alger; tel (2) 62-57-48; telex 52738; Man Dir: M. Harrati; f 1971; manages and develops port facilities and sea pilotage.

Société Nationale de Manutention (SONAMA): 6 rue de Béziers, Algiers; tel (2) 64-65-61; telex 52339; Man Dir: Amos Belalem; port-handling monopoly.

Société Nationale de Transports Maritimes et Compagnie Nationale Algérienne de Navigation (SNTM-CNAN): 2 quai d'Ajaccio, Nouvelle Gare Maritime, BP 280, Algiers; tel (2) 63-74-13; telex 52980; Chair: Muhammad Guendouz; Man Dir: Ammar Bousbah; f 1964; monopoly in all Algerian ports of conveyance, freight, chartering and transit facilities; operates a fleet of passenger and freight vessels.

Société Nationale de Transport Maritime des Hydrocarbures et des Produits Chimiques (SNTM-HYPROC): BP 60, 31200 Arzew; tel (6) 37-30-99; telex 12097; Dir-Gen: Mourad Belguedj; f 1982; sea transportation of liquified nitrogen and petroleum gases and chemical products.

ANDORRA

Heads of State

Andorra is a co-principality under the suzerainty of the President of France and the Spanish Bishop of Urgel (represented in Andorra by the Veguer de França and the Veguer Episcopal respectively). A Permanent Delegation, comprising representatives of each co-ruler, forms part of the Government and oversees the Principality's legislature.

Episcopal Co-Prince: Dr Joan Martí Alanis, Bishop of Urgel.

French Co-Prince: François Mitterrand.

Office of the Veguer Episcopal: Prat de la Creu 42, Andorra la Vella; tel 20013; telex 313; fax 60297; Veguer Episcopal: Francesc Badia-Batalla; Permanent Episcopal Delegate: Nemesi Marques.

Office of the Veguer de França: Vigalerie Française, Close de Guillamo, Andorra la Vella; Veguer de França: Lluís Deblé; Permanent French Delegate: Maurice Joubert.

Legislature

The General Council of the Valleys (Consell General de las Valls d'Andorra) comprises 28 members, who are directly elected for a four-year term. The General Council, which is headed by the First Syndic (Syndic Procurador General), assisted by the Second Syndic, submits motions to the Permanent Delegation, and appoints an Executive Council, headed by the President of the Government (Cap del Govern).

General Council of the Valleys: Consell General de las Valls d'Andorra, Andorra la Vella; First Syndic: Josep Bal; Second Syndic: (vacant).

MINISTRIES AND GOVERNMENT DEPARTMENTS

OFFICE OF THE CAP DEL GOVERN
Govern d'Andorra, Edifici Administratiu,
Calle de la Creu s/n,
Andorra la Vella
Tel 21234
Cap del Govern: Óscar Ribas Reig

COUNCIL FOR AGRICULTURE
Govern d'Andorra, Edifici Administratiu,
Calle de la Creu s/n,
Andorra la Vella
Minister: Guillem Benazet

COUNCIL FOR EDUCATION AND CULTURE
Govern d'Andorra, Edifici Administratiu,
Calle de la Creu s/n,
Andorra la Vella
Minister: (vacant)

COUNCIL FOR FINANCE, TRADE AND INDUSTRY
Govern d'Andorra, Edifici Administratiu,
Calle de la Creu s/n,
Andorra la Vella
Minister: Jaume Bartomeu

COUNCIL FOR HEALTH, LABOUR AND WELFARE
Govern d'Andorra, Edifici Administratiu,
Calle de la Creu s/n,
Andorra la Vella
Minister: Antoni Armengol

COUNCIL FOR PUBLIC SERVICES
Govern d'Andorra, Edifici Administratiu,
Calle de la Creu s/n,
Andorra la Vella
Minister: Joan Santamaria

COUNCIL FOR TOURISM AND SPORT
Govern d'Andorra, Edifici Administratiu,
Calle de la Creu s/n,
Andorra la Vella
Tel 21234; telex 469; fax 60184
Minister: Candit Naudi

GOVERNMENT AGENCIES AND ORGANIZATIONS

Business and Economy

BANKING

Banc Agricol i Comercial d'Andorra: Mossén Cinto Verda-guer 6, POB 21, Andorra la Vella; tel 21333; telex 201; fax 60133; Pres: Manuel Cerqueda Donadeu; f 1930; commercial bank.

Crèdit Andorra: Avinguda Princep Benlloch 19, Andorra la Vella; tel 20326; telex 200; Chair: A. Pintat; Man Dir: P. Roquet; f 1955; 9 brs.

Legal and Judiciary

Supreme Court of Andorra: Perpignan, France; civil court of third instance (Tercera Sala).

Tribunal des Corts: Andorra la Vella; administers criminal law; comprises seven members, including the two Veguers and a Judge of Appeal.

Media

Radio Andorra: BPI, Avinguda Meritxell, Andorra la Vella; Dir: Gualberto Ossorio; f 1984; public commercial broadcasting service.

Telecommunications

Servei de Telecomunicacions d'Andorra (STA): Avinguda Meritxell 110, Andorra la Vella; tel 20408; provides national and international telecommunications services.

Tourism

Sindicat d'Initiativa de las Valls d'Andorra: Carrer Dr Vilanova, Andorra la Vella; tel 20214; central tourism organiza-tion.

ANGOLA

Head of State

The President of the Republic is also the President of the Movimento Popular de Libertação de Angola—Partido de Trabalho (MPLA—PT), the sole political organization, Commander-in-Chief of the armed forces, and Chairman of the Political Bureau of the MPLA—PT and of the Council of Ministers. The President appoints the Council of Ministers to exercise executive authority.

President: José Eduardo dos Santos (assumed office 21 September 1979).

Office of the President: Palácio do Povo, Luanda; telex 3072.

Legislature

The People's Assembly is the national legislative body, to which the government is responsible. It has 318 members (including 29 alternate members), chosen for five-year terms by electoral colleges composed of representatives elected by all 'loyal' citizens. Between sessions of the People's Assembly, affairs are conducted by its Permanent Commission.

People's Assembly: Luanda.

MINISTRIES AND GOVERNMENT DEPARTMENTS

OFFICE OF THE CHAIRMAN OF THE COUNCIL OF MINISTERS
Luanda
Chair of the Council of Ministers: José Eduardo dos Santos
Secretary of the Council of Ministers: José Leitão da Costa e Silva

MINISTRY OF AGRICULTURE
Avda Norton de Matos 2, Luanda
Telex 3322
Minister: Fernando Faustino Muteka

MINISTRY OF CONSTRUCTION
Prédio da Mutamba, Luanda
Telex 3067
Minister: João Henriques Garcia (Cabelo Branco)

MINISTRY OF DEFENCE
Rua Silva Carvalho ex Quartel General, Luanda
Telex 3138
Minister: Col Pedro Maria Tonha (Pedalé)

MINISTRY OF EDUCATION AND CULTURE
Avda Comandante Jika, Luanda
Minister: Augusto Lopes Teixeira (Tutu)

MINISTRY OF ENERGY AND PETROLEUM
Avda 4 de Fevereiro 105, CP 1279, Luanda
Tel (2) 372300; telex 3300
Minister of State: Zeferino Cassa Yombo

MINISTRY OF EXTERNAL RELATIONS
Avda Comandante Jika, Luanda
Telex 3127
Minister: Lt-Col Pedro de Castro dos Santos Van-Dúnem (Loy)

MINISTRY OF FINANCE
Avda 4 de Fevereiro, Luanda
Tel (2) 344628; telex 3363
Minister: Augusto Teixeira de Matos

MINISTRY OF FISHERIES
Ilha do Cabo Cais do Carvão, Luanda
Telex 3273
Minister: Francisco José Ramos da Cruz

MINISTRY OF HEALTH
Rua Diogo Cão, Luanda
Minister: Flávio João Fernandes

MINISTRY OF THE INTERIOR
Avda 4 de Fevereiro, Luanda
Minister: Lt-Col Francisco Magalhães Paiva (Nvunda)

MINISTRY OF JUSTICE
Largo do Palácio, Luanda
Minister: Fernando José França Van-Dúnem

MINISTRY OF LABOUR AND SOCIAL SECURITY
Largo do Palácio, Luanda
Minister: Diogo Jorge de Jesus

MINISTRY OF PLANNING
Largo do Palácio, CP 1205, Luanda
Tel (2) 39052; telex 3082
Minister: António Henriques da Silva

National Planning Committee: c/o Ministry of Planning, Largo do Palácio, CP 1205, Luanda; tel (2) 39052; telex 3082; Chair: Minister of Planning; f 1977; drafts and supervises the implementation of the National Plan; co-ordinates economic policies.

MINISTRY OF PROVINCIAL CO-ORDINATION
Luanda

The following Provincial Commissioners are ex-officio members of the government:

Bengo: Col Pedro Benga Lima (Foguetão)
Benguela: Paulo Teixeira Jorge
Bié: Luís Paulino dos Santos
Cabinda: Jorge Barros Tchimpuati
Cunene: Pedro Mutinde
Huambo: Lt-Col Osvaldo de Jesus Serra Van-Dúnem
Huíla: Lopo Fortunato Ferreira do Nascimento
Kuando-Kubango: Manuel Francisco Tuta (Batalha de Angola)
Kwanza Norte: Francisco Vieira Dias
Kwanza Sul: Aurelio Segunda
Luanda: Cristovão Francisco da Cunha
Lunda Norte: Norberto Fernades dos Santos
Lunda Sul: Garciano Mende
Malanje: João Ernesto dos Santos (Liberdade)
Moxico: Jaime Baptista Ndonje
Namibe: Domingos José
Uije: Jeremias Dumbo

Zaire: José Aníbal Lopes Rocha

MINISTRY OF STATE SECURITY
Luanda
Minister: Kundi Paihama

MINISTRY OF TRADE
Largo Kinaxixi 14, Luanda
Tel (2) 344525; telex 3282
Minister: Domingo das Chagas Simões Rangel

MINISTRY OF TRANSPORT AND COMMUNICATIONS
Avda 4 de Fevereiro 42, CP 1250, Luanda
Tel (2) 370061; telex 3108
Minister: Carlos António Fernandes

MINISTRY OF YOUTH AND SPORT
Luanda
Minister: Marcolino José Carlos (Moço)

GOVERNMENT AGENCIES AND ORGANIZATIONS

Agriculture and Fishing

AGRICULTURE

Empresa Nacional de Comercialização e Distribuição de Produtos Agrícolas (ENCODIPA): Luanda; central marketing agency for agricultural produce; numerous brs throughout Angola.

FISHING

Empresa de Pesca de Angola (PESCANGOLA), UEE: Luanda; f 1981; state fishing enterprise; responsible to the Ministry of Fisheries.

Business and Economy

BANKING

Banco de Crédito Comercial e Industrial: CP 1395, Luanda.

Banco Nacional de Angola: Avda 4 de Fevereiro 151, CP 1298, Luanda; tel (2) 339141; telex 3005; Gov: António da Silva Inácio; f 1976 to supersede Banco de Angola; bank of issue; 55 brs and agencies.

Banco Popular de Angola: Avda 4 de Fevereiro, Luanda; tel (2) 336598; telex 3367; Dir-Gen: João Abel das Neves; brs thoughout Angola.

INSURANCE

Empresa Nacional de Seguros e Resseguros de Angola (ENSA), UEE: Avda 4 de Fevereiro 93, CP 5778, Luanda; tel (2) 370169; telex 3087.

NATIONALIZED INDUSTRY

Companhia do Açúcar de Angola: Rua Direita 77, Luanda; sugar production.

Companhia Geral dos Algodões de Angola (COTONANG): Avda da Boavista, Luanda; cotton-textile production.

Empresa Abastacimento Técnico Material (EMATEC), UEE: Largo Rainha Ginga 3, CP 2952, Luanda; tel (2) 338891; telex 3349; technical and material suppliers to the Ministry of Defence.

Empresa Açucareira Centro (OSUKA), UEE: Rua Estrada Principal Lobito, CP 037, Lobito; tel 91459; telex 08268; sugar-production co of central Angola.

Empresa Açucareira Norte (ACUNOR), UEE: Rua Robert Shilds, CP 225, Caxito; tel 71720; sugar-production co of northern Angola.

Empresa Angolana de Embalagens (METANGOL), UEE: Rua Estrada do Cacuaco, CP 151, Luanda; tel (2) 370680; production of metal goods.

Empresa de Cimento de Angola (CIMANGOLA-UEM): Avda 4 de Fevereiro 42, Luanda; tel (2) 371190; telex 3142; f 1954; 69% state-owned; cement production.

Empresa de Construção de Edificações (CONSTROI), UEE: Rua Amilcar Cabral 167, 1, Luanda; tel (2) 332679; telex 3165; f 1978; civil construction co.

Empresa de Rebeneficio e Exportação do Café de Angola (CAFANGOL), UEE: Avda 4 de Fevereiro 107, CP 342, Luanda; tel (2) 337916; telex 3011; f 1983; responsible for processing and trading of coffee.

Empresa de Tecidos de Angola (TEXTANG II), UEE: Km 14, Avda N'gola Kiluanji, CP 5404, Luanda; tel (2) 380723; telex 3046; Dir-Gen: António André Lopes; Tech Dir: Jesus Ernesto; f 1984; textile production.

Empresa Nacional de Cimento (ENCIME), UEE: CP 157, Lobito; tel 2325; cement production.

Empresa Nacional de Ferro de Angola (FERRANGOL): Rua João de Barros 26, CP 2692, Luanda; tel (2) 373800; Dir: Armando de Sousa (Machadinho); iron production.

Empresa Nacional de Manutenção (MANUTECNICA), UEE: Rua 7 Avda do Cazenga 10L, CP 3508, Luanda; tel (2) 383646; assembly of machinery and specialized equipment for industry.

Empresa Texteis de Angola (ENTEX), UEE: Avda Comandante Kima Kienda, CP 5720, Luanda; tel (2) 336182; telex 3086; weaving and tissue finishing.

Siderurgia Nacional, UEE: CP Zona Industrial do Forel das Lagostas, Luanda; tel (2) 373028; telex 3178; f 1963, nationalized 1980; steelworks and rolling mill plant.

Sociedade Unificada de Tabacos de Angola (SUT): Rua Deolinda Rodrigues 537, CP 1263, Luanda; tel (2) 360170; telex 3237; Gen Man: António A. C. Campos; f 1919; tobacco products.

TRADE

Angomédica, UEE: Rua Dr Américo Boavida 85-87, CP 2698, Luanda; tel (2) 332945; telex 4195; fax (2) 392836; Dir-Gen: Dr António Pitra; f 1980; import of medicines and medical equipment.

Direcção dos Serviços de Comércio: Largo Diogo Cão, CP 1337, Luanda; tel (2) 344507; f 1970; Department of Trade; brs throughout Angola.

Epmel, UEE: Rua Karl Marx 35-37, Luanda; tel (2) 330943; co-ordinates trade in industrial agricultural machinery.

Exportang, UEE: Rua dos Enganos 1A, CP 1000, Luanda; tel (2) 332363; telex 3318; co-ordinates exports.

Importang, UEE: Calçada do Município 10, CP 1003, Luanda; tel (2) 337994; telex 3169; Dir-Gen: Lourenço M. Neto; f 1977; co-ordinates the majority of imports.

Maquimport, UEE: Rua Rainha Ginga 152, CP 2975, Luanda; tel (2) 339044; telex 4175; f 1981; import of office equipment.

Mecanang, UEE: Rua dos Enganos, 1-7 andar, CP 1347, Luanda; tel (2) 390644; telex 4021; f 1981; import of agricultural and construction machinery, tools and spare parts.

Defence

Forçãs Armadas Populares de Libertação de Angola (FAPLA): Luanda; Commdr-in-Chief of FAPLA: President José Eduardo dos Santos; Chief of Staff of the Armed Forces: Col António dos Santos França (Ndalu).

Mining and Energy

MINING

Empresa Nacional de Diamantes de Angola (ENDIAMA), UEE: Luanda; f 1986, following dissolution of the Companhia de Diamantes de Angola (DIAMANG); controls diamond mining (last functioning diamond mine, at Cafunfo, closed down in September 1989 due to rebel activities).

Fina Petróleos de Angola, SARL: CP 1320, Luanda; telex 3246; Man Dir: J. G. Rebelo; petroleum production, refining and exploration; operates Petrangol oil refinery in Luanda and Quinfuquena terminal.

Sociedade Nacional de Combustíveis de Angola (SON-ANGOL): Rua I Congresso do MPLA, CP 1318, Luanda; tel (2) 31690; telex 3148; f 1976; exploration, production and refining of crude oil; marketing and distribution of petroleum products; supervises foreign oil companies working onshore and offshore, as sole concessionaire in Angola; majority shareholding in joint ventures with Cabinda Gulf Oil Co, Fina Petróleos de Angola and Texaco Petróleos de Angola.

> **Cabinda Gulf Oil Company:** CP 2950, Luanda; tel (2) 392646; telex 3167; Man Dir: W. M. Lewis; exploration and production of petroleum in Cabinda province; 51% owned by SONANGOL.

ENERGY

Empresa Nacional de Construções Eléctricas (ENCEL), UEE: Avda Comandante Ché Guevara 185, RC 187, Luanda; tel (2) 331411; telex 3261; Gen Man: Daniel M. R. M. Simas; f 1982; construction and assembly of electric-power equipment.

Empresa Nacional de Electricidade (ENE), UEE: Edifício Geominas, 6-7 andar, CP 772, Luanda; tel (2) 321499; telex 3170; distribution of electricity.

Legal and Judiciary

Supreme Court: Luanda.

Media

BROADCASTING

Rádio Nacional, UEE: Rua Comandante Jika, CP 1329, Luanda; tel (2) 321190; telex 3066; Dir-Gen: Guilherme Mogas.

Televisão Popular de Angola (TPA): Rua Ho Chi Minh, CP 2604, Luanda; tel (2) 332005; telex 3238; Dir: Carlos Garcia; f 1975.

GOVERNMENT PUBLISHERS

Empresa Distribuidora Livreira (EDIL), UEE: Rua da Missão 107, CP 1245, Luanda; tel (2) 334034; book distribution company.

Imprensa Nacional, UEE: CP 1306, Luanda; Gen Man: Dr António Duarte de Almeida e Carmo; f 1845; Govt publishing house.

NEWS AND INFORMATION

ANGOP: Rua Rei Katiavala 120, Luanda; tel (2) 334595; telex 4162; Dir-Gen and Editor-in-Chief: Avelino Miguel.

Direcção dos Serviços de Estatística: CP 1215, Luanda; national statistical agency.

Tourism

Centro de Informação e Turismo de Angola: Palácio de Vidro, CP 1240, Luanda; tel (2) 372750; national tourist agency.

Transport and Communications

TELECOMMUNICATIONS

Empresa Publica de Telecomunicações (EPTEL), UEE: Rua I Congresso 26, CP 625, Luanda; tel (2) 392285; telex 3012; telecommunications operating company.

TRANSPORT

Angonave—Linhas Marítimas de Angola: Rua Gov Eduardo Costa 31, CP 5953, Luanda; tel (2) 330144; telex 3313; Dir-Gen: Francisco Venâncio; national shipping line; operates 7 vessels.

Cabotang—Cabotagem Nacional Angolana: Avda 4 de Fevereiro 83A, Luanda; tel (2) 373133; telex 3007; Dir-Gen: João Octavio Van-Dúnem; f 1976; maritime affairs; operates 6 vessels.

Caminhos de Ferro de Angola: CP 1250c, Luanda; tel (2) 370061; telex 3108; Nat Dir: A. de S. E. Silva; Dep Dir (Tech):

Eng R. M. da C. Junior; co-ordinates operations of Amboim, Benguela, Luanda and Namibe railway systems.

Amboim Railway: Porto Amboim; Dir: A. V. Ferreira; f 1945; 123 km of track.

Empresa de Caminho de Ferro de Luanda, UEE (Luanda Railway): CP 1250C, Luanda; tel (2) 370061; telex 3108; Dir: J. M. Ferreira do Nascimento; f 1886; 536 km of track.

Namibe Railway: Namibe; Dir: L. da M. G. Cipriano; f 1905; 899 km of track.

Empresa Portuaria do Lobito: Rua Avda da Independencia, CP 16, Lobito; tel 2711; telex 8233; long-range sea transport.

Empresa Portuaria de Moçâmedes—Namibe, UEE: Rua Pedro Benje 10A and 10C, CP 49, Namibe; tel 60643; Dir: Humberto de Ataide Dias; long-range sea transport.

TAAG—Linhas Aéreas de Angola: Rua da Missão, Luanda; tel (2) 332990; telex 3285; Dir-Gen: José Fernandes; f 1939; national airline operating internal and international flights.

ANTIGUA AND BARBUDA

Head of State

Antigua and Barbuda is a constitutional monarchy. The British sovereign, as Head of State, is represented by a Governor-General of local citizenship. Government is effectively by the Cabinet, appointed by the Governor-General, which is headed by the Prime Minister and is responsible to the House of Representatives.

Sovereign: HM Queen Elizabeth II (succeeded to the throne 6 February 1952).

Governor-General: Sir Wilfred Ebenezer Jacobs (took office 1 November 1981).

Office of the Governor-General: Govt House, St John's; tel 462-0003.

Legislature

Legislative power is vested in Parliament, which consists of the British sovereign, the Senate and the House of Representatives. The 17 Senators are appointed by the Governor-General, while the 17 members of the House of Representatives are elected by universal adult suffrage for up to five years. Local government in Barbuda is provided by The Barbuda Council.

Senate: Queen Elizabeth Highway, St John's; tel 462-0518; Pres: Bradley T. Carrot.

House of Representatives: Queen Elizabeth Highway, St John's; tel 462-0518; Speaker: Casford L. Murray; Clerk: L. Dowe.

MINISTRIES AND GOVERNMENT DEPARTMENTS

OFFICE OF THE PRIME MINISTER
Factory Rd, St John's
Tel 462-0773; telex 2127
Prime Minister: Vere C. Bird, Sr
Minister without Portfolio and Leader of Govt Business in the Senate: Bernard S. Percival

OFFICE OF THE DEPUTY PRIME MINISTER
New Admin Bldg, Queen Elizabeth Highway, St John's
Tel 462-0092
Deputy Prime Minister: Lester Bryant Bird

MINISTRY OF AGRICULTURE, FISHERIES, HOUSING AND LANDS
High St, St John's
Tel 462-1007
Minister: Hillroy Humphries

MINISTRY OF ECONOMIC DEVELOPMENT, EXTERNAL AFFAIRS, TOURISM AND ENERGY
Queen Elizabeth Highway, St John's
Tel 462-0092; telex 2122
Minister: Lester Bryant Bird

MINISTRY OF EDUCATION, CULTURE AND YOUTH AFFAIRS
Church St, St John's
Tel 462-0192
Minister: Reuben H. Harris

MINISTRY OF FINANCE
High and Long Sts, John's
Tel 462-4989; telex 2055; fax 462-1622
Minister: John E. St Luce

MINISTRY OF HOME AFFAIRS
St John's St, St John's
Tel 462-1600; telex 2122; fax 462-3249
Minister: Christopher Manasseh O'Mard

MINISTRY OF LABOUR AND HEALTH
Redcliffe St, St John's
Tel 462-0011
Minister: Adolphus Eleazer Freeland

MINISTRY OF LEGAL AFFAIRS
Hadeed Bldg, Redcliffe St, St John's
Tel 462-0017
Minister and Attorney-Gen: Keith B. Ford

MINISTRY OF PUBLIC UTILITIES AND AVIATION
St John's
Tel 462-1000
Minister: Robin Yearwood

MINISTRY OF PUBLIC WORKS AND COMMUNICATIONS
St John's St, St John's
Tel 462-1414; telex 2153; fax 462-3249
Minister: Vere C. Bird, Jr

MINISTRY OF TRADE, INDUSTRY AND COMMERCE
St John's
Minister: Hugh Marshall

GOVERNMENT AGENCIES AND ORGANIZATIONS

Business and Economy

BANKING

Antigua and Barbuda Development Bank: POB 1279, 27 St Mary's St, St John's; tel 462-0838; fax 462-0839; Chair: S. Roy Mendes; Gen Man: Bernard S. Percival; f 1974; lends money for devt projects in tourism, agriculture, industry, higher eduction and housing.

Antigua Commercial Bank: POB 95, cnr St Mary's and Thames Sts, St John's; tel 462-1217; telex 2175; Man: John Benjamin; f 1955; 2 brs.

Bank of Antigua: POB 315, cnr High and Thames Sts, St John's; tel 462-4282; telex 2180; 1 br.

Eastern Caribbean Central Bank (ECCB): POB 89, Basseterre, St Christopher and Nevis; tel 465-2537; telex 6828; Gov: Cecil A. Jacobs; f 1965 as East Caribbean Currency Authority, expanded responsibilities and changed name in 1983; responsible for issue of currency in Anguilla, Antigua and Barbuda, Dominica, Grenada, Montserrat, Saint Christopher and Nevis, Saint Lucia and Saint Vincent and the Grenadines.

INSURANCE

State Insurance Corpn: POB 290, Redcliffe St, St John's; tel 462-0110; telex 2177; fax 462-2649; Chair: A. E. L. Williams; Gen Man: Rolston L. Barthley; f 1977.

MARKETING

Central Marketing Corpn: POB 1202, Kentish Rd, St John's; tel 462-2569.

TRADE

Antigua Chamber of Commerce Ltd: POB 774, Redcliffe St, St John's; tel 462-0743; telex 2105; Pres: Eustace Francis; Exec Dir: Lionel Boulos; f 1946; collects and disseminates information on trade, commerce, shipping and manufacturing.

Antigua Fisheries Corpn: St John's; aids local fishermen; partly funded by the Antigua and Barbuda Development Bank.

Antigua Sugar Industry Corpn: POB 899, Gunthorpes, St George's; tel 462-0653.

Defence

Antigua and Barbuda Defence Force: Botanical Gardens, St John's; tel 462-3363; Commdr: Maj Clyde Walker.

Antigua Police Force: Police Headquarters, American Rd, St John's; tel 462-0125; Police Commr: George Wright.

Development

Barbuda Development Agency: St John's; Chair: Hakim Akbar; economic devt projects for Barbuda.

Industrial Development Board: Newgate St, St John's; tel 462-1038; f 1984; stimulates investment in local industries.

St John's Development Corpn: POB 1473, Redcliffe St, St John's; tel 462-3925; telex 2087; fax 462-2836; Chair: Lester Bryant Bird; Sec (acting): Makeda Mikael; Exec Dir: Winston James; f 1986; revitalization of St John's.

Legal and Judiciary

Eastern Caribbean Supreme Court: POB 1093, Castries, St Lucia; tel 462-2573; Chief Justice: Sir Lascelles Robotham; f 1967; jurisdiction extends to Anguilla, Antigua and Barbuda, the British Virgin Islands, Dominica, Montserrat, Saint Christopher and Nevis, Saint Lucia and Saint Vincent and the Grenadines; comprises a High Court of Justice and a Court of Appeal; High Court is composed of the Chief Justice and seven Puisne Judges; the Court of Appeal is presided over by the Chief Justice and includes two other Justices of Appeal.

Supreme Court: High St, St John's; tel 462-0039.

Media

Antigua and Barbuda Broadcasting Service (ABBS): Public Information Division, Office of the Prime Minister, Factory Rd, St John's; tel 462-0260; comprises:

ABBS Radio: POB 590, St John's; tel 462-3602; telex 2127; Gen Man: Hollis Henry; f 1956.

ABBS Television: POB 1280, St John's; tel 462-0821; Programme Man: F. Liburd; f 1964.

Mining and Energy

West Indies Oil Co (WIOC): POB 230, St John's; tel 462-0141; telex 2112; Man Dir: W. A. Vickery; jointly owned by the Antiguan Govt and National Petroleum; markets petroleum products.

Tourism

Antigua Department of Tourism: POB 363, High St and Corn Alley, St John's; tel 462-0029; fax 462-0480; Dir-Gen: Yvonne Maginley; Man: Edie Hill-Thibou; promotion of tourism; distribution of hotel and general information on the island.

Antigua Hotels and Tourist Association (AHTA): POB 454, St John's; tel 462-0374; telex 2172; fax 462-3702; Pres: Charles Hawley.

Transport

Antigua Port Authority: POB 1052, Deep Water Harbour, St John's; tel 462-0050; telex 2179; fax 462-1273; Port Dir: Emil Sweeney; Port Man: G. W. Benjamin; f 1968; port admin and harbour operation.

Utilities

Antigua Public Utilities Authority: POB 416, Thames St, St John's; tel 462-4990; telex 2090; fax 462-2516; Gen Man: M. R. Rogers; Electricity Man: P. Benjamin; Telephone Man: M. Edwards; Water Man: P. Martin; generation, transmission and distribution of electricity; internal telecommunications; collection, treatment, storage and distribution of water.

Welfare

Medical Benefits Scheme: Redcliffe St, St John's; tel 462-3346.

Social Security Scheme: Long St, St John's; tel 462-1315.

ARGENTINA

Head of State

Executive power is vested in the President, who is elected for a six-year term by an electoral college. The President handles the general administration of the country, by issuing instructions and rulings, and appoints cabinet ministers, as well as senior members of the judiciary, the civil service and the armed forces (of which he is Commander-in-Chief).

President: Carlos Saúl Menem (took office 8 July 1989)

Vice-President: Eduardo Duhalde.

Office of the President: Casa de Gobierno, Balcarce 50, 1064 Buenos Aires; tel (1) 33-5041; telex 21464.

General Secretariat to the Presidency: Balcarce 50, 1064 Buenos Aires; tel (1) 46-9841; Sec-Gen: Alberto Kohan.

Legislature

Legislative power is vested in the bicameral Congress: the Cámara de Diputados (Chamber of Deputies) has 254 members, elected by universal adult suffrage for a term of four years (with one-half of the seats renewable every two years), while the Senado (Senate) has 46 members, nominated by provincial legislatures for a term of nine years (with one-third of the seats renewable every three years).

Cámara de Diputados (Chamber of Deputies): Rivadavia 1864, 1033 Buenos Aires; tel (1) 40-3441; Pres: César Jaroslavsky.

Senado (Senate): Hipólito Yrigoyen 1849, 1089 Buenos Aires; tel (1) 953-0070; telex 17100; fax (1) 953-35746; Pres: Dr Víctor Martínez.

MINISTRIES AND GOVERNMENT DEPARTMENTS

MINISTRY OF THE ECONOMY
Hipólito Yrigoyen 250, 1310 Buenos Aires
Tel (1) 34-6411; telex 21952
Minister: Antonio Ermán González

Secretariat of Agriculture and Livestock: Avda Pueyrredón 2446, 1119 Buenos Aires; tel (1) 803-3728; telex 21535.

Secretariat of Co-operative Action: Avda Belgrano 172, 1092 Buenos Aires; tel (1) 33-9543.

Secretariat of Domestic Commerce: Avda Julio A. Roca 651, 1322 Buenos Aires; tel (1) 34-2458.

Secretariat of Finance: Avda Julio A. Roca 651, 1322 Buenos Aires; tel (1) 34-2240; Sec: Humberto Bertaina.

Secretariat of Industry and Foreign Commerce: Avda Julio A. Roca 651, 1322 Buenos Aires; tel (1) 30-3242.

Secretariat of Mining: Avda Santa Fe 1548, 14, 1060 Buenos Aires; tel (1) 44-7608.

Secretariat of Programming and Economic Co-ordination: Hipólito Yrigoyen 250, 1310 Buenos Aires; tel (1) 34-6411.

Secretariat of Regional Development: Hipólito Yrigoyen 250, 1310 Buenos Aires; tel (1) 33-5795.

Secretariat of the Treasury: Hipólito Yrigoyen 250, 1310 Buenos Aires; tel (1) 34-1890.

MINISTRY OF EDUCATION AND JUSTICE
Pizzurno 935, 1020 Buenos Aires
Tel (1) 42-4551; telex 22646
Minister: Antonio Francisco Salonia

MINISTRY OF FOREIGN AFFAIRS AND WORSHIP
Reconquista 1088, 1003 Buenos Aires
Tel (1) 311-0071; telex 21194
Minister: Domingo Cavallo
Deputy Minister: Juan Archibald Lanus

MINISTRY OF THE INTERIOR
Balcarce 24, 1064 Buenos Aires
Tel (1) 46-9841
Minister: Julio Mera Figueroa

MINISTRY OF LABOUR AND SOCIAL SECURITY
Avda Julio A. Roca 609, 1067 Buenos Aires
Tel (1) 33-7888; telex 18007
Minister: Alberto Jorge Triaca

MINISTRY OF NATIONAL DEFENCE
Avda Paseo Colón 255, 1063 Buenos Aires
Tel (1) 30-1561; telex 22200
Minister: Humberto Romero

MINISTRY OF PUBLIC HEALTH AND WELFARE
Defensa 120, 1345 Buenos Aires
Tel (1) 30-4322; telex 25064
Minister: Eduardo Bauzá

Secretariat of Health: Defensa 192, 1345 Buenos Aires; tel (1) 34-6650.

MINISTRY OF PUBLIC WORKS AND SERVICES
Avda 9 de Julio 1925, 8, 1332 Buenos Aires
Tel (1) 38-5838; telex 22577; fax (1) 3319967
Minister: José Roberto Dromi

Secretariat of Communications: Sarmiento 151, 4, 1000 Buenos Aires; tel (1) 331-1203; telex 21706; Sec: Raúl José Otero; controls broadcasting, including 30 domestic radio stations.

Subsecretariat of Broadcasting: Sarmiento 151, 4, 1000 Buenos Aires; tel (1) 311-5909; telex 21706; Under-Sec: Alfredo R. Parodi.

Subsecretariat of Planning and Technology: Sarmiento 151, 4, 1000 Buenos Aires; tel (1) 311-5909; telex 21706; Under-Sec: Leonardo José Leibson.

Subsecretariat of Telecommunications: Sarmiento 151, 4, 1000 Buenos Aires; tel (1) 311-5909; telex 21706; Under-Sec: Julio César Guillán.

Secretariat of Energy: Avda Julio A. Roca 651, 1067 Buenos Aires; tel (1) 34-2736; Sec: Julio César Araoz.

Secretariat of the Merchant Navy: Julio A. Roca 734, 1067 Buenos Aires; tel (1) 30-4541; telex 21091; Sec: Luis Alberto Siquot Ferré; oversees merchant marine policy and shipbuilding subsidies, supervises maintenance work in navigable waterways and ports, etc.

Secretariat of Transport: Avda 9 de Julio 1925, 8, 1332 Buenos Aires; tel (1) 38-5838; telex 22577; fax (1) 3319967; oversees policy on terrestrial transport, including road infrastructure.

Subsecretariat of Transport Planning: Avda 9 de Julio 1925, 11, 1332 Buenos Aires; tel (1) 37-2571.

GOVERNMENT AGENCIES AND ORGANIZATIONS

Advisory and Supervisory Body

Consejo Nacional Económico y Social: Maipú 972-974, 1084 Buenos Aires; advisory body for devt planning and economic policy.

Agriculture and the Environment

Instituto Forestal Nacional (IFONA): Avda Pueyrredón 2446, 1119 Buenos Aires; tel (1) 803-3728; telex 21535; f 1948; national forestry commission; responsible to the Secretariat of Agriculture and Livestock; aims to promote balanced devt and exploitation of forest resources.

Junta Nacional de Carnes: Avda San Martín 459, 1004 Buenos Aires; tel (1) 394-5116; telex 24210; fax (1) 322-9357; Pres: Alfredo O. Bigatti; Vice-Pres: Pedro A. Mangieri; f 1933; national meat board; promotion and control of livestock and meat sales.

Junta Nacional de Granos: Avda Paseo Colón 359, 1063 Buenos Aires; tel (1) 30-0641; telex 21793; Pres: Jorge Cort; national grain board; supervises commercial practices and organizes the construction of farm silos and port elevators.

Business and Economy

BANKING

Banco Central de la República Argentina: Reconquista 266, 1003 Buenos Aires; tel (1) 394-8411; telex 1137; Pres: Enrique Eugenio Folcini; f 1935 as central reserve bank; has the right of note issue; all capital is held by the state.

Banco del Chaco: Güemes 102, 3500 Resistencia; tel (722) 24074; telex 71214; Pres: Roberto Salazar; f 1958; provincial bank; 26 brs.

Banco de la Ciudad de Buenos Aires: Florida 302, 1313 Buenos Aires; tel (1) 325-0726; telex 22365; fax (1) 12098; Pres: Saternino Montero Ruiz; f 1878; municipal bank; 37 brs.

Banco Credicoop Cooperativo Ltdo: Maipú 73, 1084 Buenos Aires; tel (1) 34-6719; telex 18245; Chair: Giribaldi Nelson.

Banco de Entre Ríos: Monte Caseros 128, 3100 Paraná; tel (42) 22-3700; telex 45115; Pres: Jorge Heyde; f 1935; provincial bank; 37 brs.

Banco Hipotecario Nacional: Defensa 192, 1065 Buenos Aires; tel (1) 34-2001; Govt Admin: Edgardo Civit; f 1886; mortgage bank.

Banco de Mendoza: Gutiérrez 51, POB 19, 5500 Mendoza; tel (61) 25-1200; telex 55204; Pres: Eduardo del Amor; f 1934; provincial bank; 77 brs.

Banco de la Nación Argentina: Bartolomé Mitre 326, 1039 Buenos Aires; tel (1) 30-1011; telex 21407; Pres: Hugo Santilli; f 1891; national bank; 577 brs.

Banco Nacional de Desarrollo: 25 de Mayo 145, 1002 Buenos Aires; tel (1) 331-2094; telex 9179; Pres: Roberto L. Arana; f 1944; devt bank.

Banco de la Provincia de Buenos Aires: Avda San Martín 137, 1004 Buenos Aires; tel (1) 331-2561; telex 18276; Pres: Eduardo P. Amadeo; f 1822; provincial bank; 322 brs.

Banco de la Provincia de Córdoba: San Jerónimo 166, 5000 Córdoba; tel (51) 42001; telex 51610; Pres: Tito Marcos Battistel; f 1873; provincial bank; 157 brs.

Banco de la Provincia de Corrientes: 9 de Julio y San Juan, 3400 Corrientes; tel (783) 65111; telex 74106; Pres: Ricardo J.G. Harvey; 33 brs.

Banco de la Provincia de Neuquén: Argentina 45, 8300 Neuquén; tel (943) 31-459; telex 84128; Pres: Omar Santiago Negretti; 21 brs.

Banco Provincial de Salta: España 550, 4400 Salta; provincial commercial bank.

Banco de la Provincia de Santa Fé: San Martín 715, 2000 Rosario, Santa Fé; tel (41) 40151; telex 41751; Pres: Emilio Sánchez García; f 1874; provincial bank.

Banco de San Juan: José Ignacio de la Roza 85, Oeste, 5400 San Juan; provincial commercial bank.

Caja Nacional de Ahorro y Seguro: Hipólito Yrigoyen 1770, 1308 Buenos Aires; tel (1) 45-5861; telex 22642; Pres: Jesús L. D'Alessandro; f 1915; national savings bank and insurance institution; 61 brs.

INSURANCE

Instituto Nacional de Reaseguros: Avda Julio A. Roca 694, 1067 Buenos Aires; tel (1) 34-0084; telex 1170; Pres and Man: Feliciano Salvia; f 1947; responsible for reinsurance in all branches except credit.

Superintendencia de Seguros de la Nación: Avda Julio A. Roca 721, 1067 Buenos Aires; tel (1) 30-6653; Supt: Diego Pedro Peluffo; f 1938; supervisory body for the insurance sector.

NATIONALIZED INDUSTRY

Argentine Industrial Steel (Acindar): Avda Paseo Colón 357, 1063 Buenos Aires; tel (1) 33-4531; telex 22352; nationalized steel concern.

Directorio de Empresas Públicas (DEP): Lavalle 1429, 1048 Buenos Aires; Pres: Horacio A. Losoviz; f 1986; holding co for state enterprises.

Petroquímica General Mosconi SAI y C: Perú 103, 1067 Buenos Aires; tel (1) 33-5964; telex 22850; fax (1) 11-2394; Pres: Rubén E. Maltoni; f 1970; state petrochemical industry.

Sindicatura General de Empresas Públicas: Lavalle 1429, 1048 Buenos Aires; tel (1) 40-5200; Pres: Mario J. Truffat; f 1978; exercises external control over wholly- or partly-owned public enterprises.

Defence

Air Force: Edificio Cóndor, Comodoro Pedro Zanni 250, 1104 Buenos Aires; tel (1) 312-9170; Chief of Staff: Brig-Gen Ernesto Crespo.

Army: Edificio Liberador, Azopardo 250, 1328 Buenos Aires; tel (1) 34-3408; telex 22200; Chief of Staff: Gen Isidro Cáceres.

Navy: Edificio Libertad, Comodoro Py y Corbeta Uruguay, 1104 Buenos Aires; tel (1) 312-5001; telex 1388; Chief of Staff: Adm Ramón Arosa.

Development and Planning

Consejo Federal de Inversiones: Avda San Martín 871, 1004 Buenos Aires; tel (1) 313-2034; Sec-Gen: Juan José Ciacera; federal board to regulate domestic and foreign investment.

Instituto de Desarrollo Económico y Social (IDES): Güemes 3950, 1425 Buenos Aires; tel (1) 71-3738; Pres: Torcuato S. DiTella; Sec: Dr Catalina Wainerman; f 1961; promotes social and economic devt.

Instituto Nacional de Planificación Economica: Hipólito Yrigoyen 250, 8, 1310 Buenos Aires; f 1961; national economic planning body; responsible for medium- and long-term forecasts and devt plans.

Legal and Judiciary

Corte Suprema (Supreme Court): Talcahuano 550, 4, 1013 Buenos Aires; tel (1) 40-1540; Pres: Enrique Santiago Petracchi; Attorney-Gen: Andrés d'Alessio; mems appointed by the Executive, with the agreement of the Senate.

Media

BROADCASTING

Argentina Televisora Color LS82 TV Canal 7 (ATC): Avda Figueroa Alcorta 2977, 1425 Buenos Aires; tel (1) 802-6001; fax (1) 802-9878; Dir: Miguel Angel L. Consiglio; state-controlled TV channel.

Comité Federal de Radiodifusión (CFR): Suipacha 765, 1008 Buenos Aires; tel (1) 394-4274; Dir: León Guinsburg; f 1972; controls various technical aspects of broadcasting and transmission of programmes.

LS84 Canal 11: Pavón 2444, 1248 Buenos Aires; tel (1) 941-0091; telex 22780; Dir-Gen: Carlos M. Negri; state-controlled TV channel.

LS85 TV Canal 13: San Juan 1170, 1147 Buenos Aires; tel (1) 27-3661; telex 21762; Dir: Eduardo Metzger; f 1960; state-controlled TV channel.

Servicio Oficial de Radiodifusión (SOR): Ayacucho 1556, 1112 Buenos Aires; tel (1) 30-2121; Dir: Julio E. Maharbiz; official broadcasting organization; runs:

> **Cadena Argentina de Radiodifusión (CAR):** Avda Entre Ríos 149, 3, 1079 Buenos Aires; tel (1) 45-2113; groups all national state-owned commercial radio stations.

> **LRA Radio Nacional:** Ayacucho 1556, 1112 Buenos Aires; tel (1) 803-5555; telex 21250; Dir: Julio E. Maharbiz; f 1937.

> **Radiodifusión Argentina al Exterior (RAE):** Ayacucho 1556, 1112 Buenos Aires; tel (1) 803-2351; Dir-Gen: Luis Romeo Rojas; f 1958; external radio broadcasts in eight languages to all areas of the world.

NEWS AND INFORMATION

Instituto Nacional de Estadística y Censos: Hipólito Yrigoyen 250, 12, Of 1210, 1310 Buenos Aires; tel (1) 33-7872; telex 21952; national statistical office.

Mining and Energy

ENERGY

Agua y Energía Eléctrica Sociedad del Estado (AyEE): Avda Leandro N. Alem 1134, 1001 Buenos Aires; tel (1) 311-6364; telex 21889; Supervisor: Juan C. Derobertis; f 1947; state water and electricity board.

Comisión Nacional de Energía Atómica (CNEA): Avda del Libertador 8250, 1429 Buenos Aires; tel (1) 70-7711; telex 25392; fax (1) 786-9550; Pres: Dr Manuel A. Mondino; f 1950; nuclear power commission.

Consejo Cosultativo Nacional de Energía Atómica: Buenos Aires; f 1987; advises the Pres of the CNEA (see above) in the drawing-up of studies and projects concerned with the reorganization of nuclear activities.

Gas del Estado: Alsina 1169, 1088 Buenos Aires; tel (1) 37-2091; Supervisor: Luis A. Maciel; f 1946; state gas corpn; due to be privatized in 1990 after being merged with other state-owned energy cos.

Hidroeléctrica Norpatagónica SA (Hidronor): Avda Leandro N. Alem 1074, 1001 Buenos Aires; tel (1) 312-6030; telex 18097; Supervisor: Eduardo J. Frigerio; f 1967; state hydro-electric corpn; due to be privatized in 1990 after being merged with other state-owned energy cos.

Instituto Argentino del Petróleo: Maipú 645, Buenos Aires; tel (1) 392-3244; promotes the devt of petroleum exploration and exploitation.

Servicios Eléctricos del Gran Buenos Aires SA (SEGBA): Balcarce 184, 1064 Buenos Aires; tel (1) 33-1901; Supervisor: Bautista J. Marcheschi; f 1958; state electricity enterprise.

Yacimientos Petrolíferos Fiscales Sociedad del Estado (YPF): Avda Roque S. Peña 777, 1364 Buenos Aires; tel (1) 46-7270; telex 21999; Supervisor: Octavio Frigerio; f 1922; public corpn authorized to formulate national petroleum policy; due to be privatized in 1990 after being merged with the other state-run energy cos.

MINING

Yacimientos Carboníferos Fiscales (YCF): Avda Roque S. Peña 1190, 1364 Buenos Aires; Supervisor: Edgardo P. Murguia; f 1958; state coal-mining enterprise.

Yacimientos Mineros de Agua de Dionisio: Avda Julio A. Roca 710, 1067 Buenos Aires; tel (1) 34-8024; Pres: Efraín J. Saadi Herrera; f 1958; state mining enterprise.

Science and Technology

Consejo Nacional de Investigaciones Científicas y Técnicas (CONICET): Rivadavia 1917, 1033 Buenos Aires; tel (1) 953-7230; telex 18052; Pres: Dr Carlos A. Abeledo; f 1958; national council for scientific and technical research.

Tourism

Secretaría de Turismo de la Nación: Calle Suipacha 1111, 21, 1368 Buenos Aires; tel (1) 312-5621; telex 24882; Sec: Raúl Matera; national tourism authority.

Transport and Communications

TELECOMMUNICATIONS

Empresa Nacional de Correos y Telégrafos (ENCOTEL): Sarmiento 151, 1000 Buenos Aires; tel (1) 311-5031; telex 22045; Supervisor: Dr Arlington R. Uliarte; f 1972; postal and telegraph services.

TRANSPORT

Administración General de Puertos: Avda Julio A. Roca 734-42, 1067 Buenos Aires; tel (1) 34-5621; telex 21879; Chair: Ricardo N. Gastaldi; f 1956; state enterprise for direction, admin and exploitation of all national sea and river ports.

Aerolíneas Argentinas: Paseo Colón 185, 1063 Buenos Aires; tel (1) 30-2071; telex 22517; fax (1) 54331; Pres: Eduardo González del Solar; Vice-Pres: Oscar Carbone; f 1950; national carrier, providing passenger, mail and freight services to all internal destinations and airports in North and South America.

Capitanía General del Puerto: Avda Julio A. Roca 734, 2, 1067 Buenos Aires; tel (1) 34-9784; Port Capt: Pedro Taramasco; f 1967; co-ordination of port operations.

Dirección Nacional de Construcciones Portuarias y Vías Navegables: Avda España 221, 4, Buenos Aires; tel (1) 361-5964; Dir: Enrique Casals de Alba; responsible for the maintenance and improvement of waterways and dredging operations.

Dirección Nacional de Transporte Aerocomercial: Avda 9 de Julio 1925, 22, 1332 Buenos Aires; tel (1) 37-8365; telex 28360; fax (1) 38-1472; Dir: Dr Fernando E. Dozo; Dep Dir: Gustavo D. Donisa; responsible for national civil aviation; controlled by the Ministry of Public Works and Services.

Dirección Nacional de Vialidad: Comodoro Py 2002, 1104 Buenos Aires; tel (1) 312-9021; telex 17879; Gen Man: Saúl Martínez; responsible for national highway admin; controlled by the Ministry of Public Works and Services.

Empresa Líneas Marítimas Argentinas SA (ELMA): Avda Corrientes 389, 1043 Buenos Aires; tel (1) 312-8111; telex 21807; Pres: L. A. J. Olaizola; f 1941; state shipping line, operating 50 vessels with services throughout the world.

Ferrocarriles Argentinos (FA): Avda Ramos Mejía 1302, 1302 Buenos Aires; tel (1) 312-1746; telex 22507; Supt: Julio Quevedo; f 1948; autonomous body providing national rail services according to policies controlled by the Ministry of Public Works and Services.

Flota Fluvial del Estado Argentino: Avda Corrientes 389, 3, 1043 Buenos Aires; tel (1) 312-5651; Dir-Gen: Dr Luis Suaréz Herter; f 1958; passenger and cargo services on all principal rivers.

Líneas Aéras del Estado (LADE): Perú 710, 1067 Buenos Aires; tel (1) 361-7174; telex 22040; Dir: Otto A. Ritondale; f 1940; operates through the Argentine Air Force to provide domestic services to 35 southern destinations.

Subterráneos de Buenos Aires: Bartolomé Mitre 3342, 1312 Buenos Aires; tel (1) 89-0631; telex 18979; Pres: José María García Arecha; f 1952; wholly state-owned since 1978; underground railway system for Buenos Aires; controlled by the Municipalidad de la Ciudad de Buenos Aires.

Yacimientos Petrolíferos Fiscales (YPF): Avda Roque S. Peña 777, 1364 Buenos Aires; tel (1) 46-7271; telex 21792; Pres: Héctor J. Fioreli; shipping services, including motor launch, freight and tanker services.

Utilities

Obras Sanitarias de la Nación: Marcelo T. de Alvear 1840, Buenos Aires; tel (1) 41-1081; Supervisor: Luis A. Herrera; f 1973; provides national sanitation services.

AUSTRALIA

Head of State

Australia is a constitutional monarchy. The British monarch is Head of State and is represented locally by a Governor-General. The Governor-General appoints a Prime Minister to head a Federal Executive Council (Cabinet), which administers the country and also advises the Governor-General, and which is responsible to Parliament.

Sovereign: HM Queen Elizabeth II (succeeded to the throne 6 February 1952).

Governor-General: William George Hayden (took office 16 February 1989).

Office of the Governor-General: Govt House, Canberra, ACT 2600; tel (62) 83 3533.

Legislature

Legislative power is vested in the Federal Parliament, which comprises the British sovereign (represented by the Governor-General) and two chambers elected by universal adult suffrage: the Senate, with 76 members, and the House of Representatives (148 members). Each State has a Governor, and its own legislative, executive and judicial system.

Senate: Parliament House, Canberra, ACT 2600; tel (62) 72 1211; telex 62326; fax (62) 73 1380; Pres: Sen Kerry W. Sibraa; Dep Pres and Chair of Committees: Sen D. J. Hamer.

House of Representatives: Parliament House, Canberra, ACT 2600; tel (62) 77 7111; telex 61640; fax (62) 77 2058; Speaker: Joan Child; Dep Speaker and Chair of Committees: Leo B. McLeay.

MINISTRIES AND GOVERNMENT DEPARTMENTS

DEPARTMENT OF THE PRIME MINISTER AND CABINET
3-5 National Circuit, Barton, ACT 2600
Tel (62) 71 5111; telex 61616; fax (62) 71 5414
Prime Minister: Robert J. L. Hawke
Deputy Prime Minister and Minister assisting the Prime Minister for Commonwealth-State Relations: Lionel F. Bowen
Minister assisting the Prime Minister for Multicultural Affairs: Sen Robert F. Ray
Minister assisting the Prime Minister for Public Service Matters: Peter F. Morris
Minister assisting the Prime Minister for Social Justice: Brian L. Howe
Minister assisting the Prime Minister for the Status of Women: Sen Margaret Reynolds

ATTORNEY-GENERAL'S DEPARTMENT
Robert Garran Offices, National Circuit, Barton, ACT 2600
Tel (62) 71 9111; telex 62002; fax (62) 73 3385
Attorney-General: Lionel F. Bowen
Minister for Consumer Affairs: Sen Nick Bolkus
Minister for Justice: Sen Michael Tate

DEPARTMENT OF ABORIGINAL AFFAIRS
MLC Tower, Woden Town Centre, Phillip, ACT 2606
Tel (62) 89 1222; telex 62471; fax (62) 81 0772
Minister: Gerard L. Hand

DEPARTMENT OF ADMINISTRATIVE SERVICES
111 Alinga St, Canberra City;
POB 1920, Canberra City, ACT 2601
Tel (62) 75 3000; telex 62482; fax (62) 75 3819
Minister: J. Stewart West

DEPARTMENT OF THE ARTS, SPORT, THE ENVIRONMENT, TOURISM AND TERRITORIES
Tobruk House, 15 Moore St, Canberra City, ACT 2601;
POB 787, Canberra, ACT 2601
Tel (62) 74 1111; telex 62960; fax (62) 74 1123
Minister: Sen Graham Richardson
Minister for the Arts, Tourism and Territories: A. Clyde Holding
F 1987; formulates and implements Federal Govt policies on matters relating to the arts, sport, recreation, tourism, the environment, conservation and heritage; responsible for Australia's external territories, including the Antarctic.

DEPARTMENT OF COMMUNITY SERVICES AND HEALTH
Alexander and Albermarle Bldgs, Furzer St, Phillip, ACT;
POB 9848, Canberra, ACT 2601
Tel (62) 89 1555; telex 62149; fax (62) 81 6946
Minister: Dr Neal Blewett
Minister for Housing and Aged Care: Peter Staples

DEPARTMENT OF DEFENCE
Russell Offices, Canberra, ACT 2600
Tel (62) 65 9111; telex 62053
Minister: Kim C. Beazley
Minister for Defence, Science and Personnel: David Simmons

DEPARTMENT OF EMPLOYMENT, EDUCATION AND TRAINING
POB 826, Woden, ACT 2606
Tel (62) 83 7777; telex 62116
Minister: John S. Dawkins
Minister for Employment and Education Services:
Peter Duncan

DEPARTMENT OF FINANCE
Newlands St, Parkes, ACT 2600
Tel (62) 63 2222; telex 62639; fax (62) 73 1064
Minister: Sen Peter A. Walsh

DEPARTMENT OF FOREIGN AFFAIRS AND TRADE
Bag 8, Queen Victoria Terrace, Canberra, ACT 2600
Tel (62) 61 9111; telex 62007
Minister: Sen Gareth J. Evans
Minister for Trade Negotiations: Michael J. Duffy

DEPARTMENT OF IMMIGRATION, LOCAL GOVERNMENT AND ETHNIC AFFAIRS
Benjamin Offices, Chan St, Belconnen, ACT 2617
Tel (62) 64 1111; telex 62077; fax (62) 64 2607
Minister: Sen Robert F. Ray
Minister for Local Govt: Sen Margaret Reynolds

DEPARTMENT OF INDUSTRIAL RELATIONS
1 Farrell Place, Canberra City, ACT;
POB 9879, Canberra, ACT 2601
Tel (62) 43 7333; telex 62944
Minister: Peter F. Morris

DEPARTMENT OF INDUSTRY, TECHNOLOGY AND COMMERCE
51 Allara St, Canberra, ACT 2601
Tel (62) 76 1000; telex 62654; fax (62) 76 1111
Minister: Sen John N. Button
Minister assisting the Minister: Michael J. Duffy
Minister for Science, Customs and Small Business:
Barry O. Jones

DEPARTMENT OF PRIMARY INDUSTRIES AND ENERGY
Edmund Barton Bldg, Broughton St, Barton, ACT 2600
Tel (62) 72 3933; telex 62188
Minister: John C. Kerin

Minister assisting the Minister: Michael J. Duffy
Minister for Resources: Sen Peter Cook
F 1987; provides policy advice and administers programmes for aspects of primary and energy industries; undertakes economic and scientific research activities; responsible for the Australian Quarantine and Inspection Service.

DEPARTMENT OF SOCIAL SECURITY
Juliana House, Bowes St, Phillip, ACT 2606;
POB 1, Woden, ACT 2606
Tel (62) 84 4844; telex 62143; fax (62) 82 2677
Minister: Brian L. Howe

DEPARTMENT OF TRANSPORT AND COMMUNICATIONS
cnrs Cooyong St, Northbourne Ave and Mort St, Braddon, ACT;
POB 594, Canberra, ACT 2601
Tel (62) 74 7111; telex 62018; fax (62) 57 2505
Minister: Ralph Willis
Minister for Telecommunications and Aviation Support: Ros Kelly
Minister for Land Transport and Shipping Support:
Bob Brown

Federal Office of Road Safety: address as above; tel (62) 74 7111; fax (62) 74 7922; Dirs: Peter Makeham, Dennis McLennan, Keith Wheatley.

DEPARTMENT OF THE TREASURY
Parkes Place, Parkes, ACT 2600
Tel (62) 63 2111; telex 62372; fax (62) 73 2614
Treasurer: Paul J. Keating
Minister assisting the Treasurer: Peter F. Morris
Minister assisting the Treasurer for Prices:
Sen Nick Bolkus
Secretary: Dr Chris Higgins

DEPARTMENT OF VETERANS' AFFAIRS
MLC Tower, Keltie St, Phillip, ACT 2606;
POB 21, Woden, ACT 2606
Tel (62) 89 1111; telex 62706; fax (62) 82 3120
Minister: Benjamin C. Humphreys
F 1920; provides medical treatment, pensions and other benefits for returned servicemen and women.

GOVERNMENT AGENCIES AND ORGANIZATIONS

Advisory and Supervisory Bodies

Australian Audit Office: Silverton Centre, cnr Moore and Rudd Sts, Canberra City, ACT; POB 707, Canberra, ACT 2601; tel (62) 83 4713; fax (62) 82 2355; Auditor-Gen: John C. Taylor; f 1901; conducts performance and financial statement audits of Govt public sector bodies and reports the results to Parliament, public sector bodies and the community.

Australian Conciliation and Arbitration Commission: Nauru House, 80 Collins St, Melbourne, Vic 3000; tel (3) 653 8200 (Melbourne), (2) 332 0666 (Sydney); Pres: Justice Barry J. Maddern.

Australian Industry and Technology Council: Dept of Industry, Technology and Commerce, 51 Allara St, Canberra, ACT 2601; tel (62) 76 2095; fax (62) 76 2188; Chair: Federal Minister for Industry, Technology and Commerce, Sen John N. Button; Exec Officer: H. Sherwin; mems include State Ministers with responsibility for industry, technology and devt, and an observer from New Zealand.

Australian Loan Council: Dept of the Treasury, Parkes Place, Parkes, ACT 2600; Chair: Paul J. Keating; Sec: D. W. Borthwick;

mems are State Premiers or Ministers with responsibility for finance; sanctions borrowing by Federal and State Govts and semi-governmental authorities.

Australian Manufacturing Council: Industry Councils Secretariat, 9th Floor, Bldg D, World Trade Centre, cnr Flinders and Spencer Sts, Melbourne, Vic; POB 196, World Trade Centre, Melbourne, Vic 3005; tel (3) 611 5200; fax (3) 611 5232; Dir: Bill Mountford; f 1977; responsible to Dept of Industry, Technology and Commerce; tripartite forum for consultation and consideration of policies and issues affecting the manufacturing sector.

Foreign Investment Review Board: Dept of the Treasury, Parkes Place, Parkes, ACT 2600; Chair: Sir Bede Callaghan.

Industries Assistance Commission: Benjamin Offices, Chan St, Belconnen, ACT; POB 80, Belconnen, ACT 2616; tel (62) 64 1144; telex 62283; fax (62) 53 1186; Chair: G. F. Taylor; Head of Office: Dr M. L. Parker; f 1974; provides advice to Govt on industry assistance matters.

National Labour Consultative Council: Dept of Industrial Relations, 1 Farrell Place, Canberra City, ACT; POB 9879, Canberra, ACT 2601; tel (62) 43 7333; telex 62944; Sec: R. A. Fotheringham; mems include the Minister for Industrial

Relations, reps of public authorities as employers, the Confederation of Australian Industry and the Australian Council of Trade Unions.

Trade Practices Commission: Benjamin Offices, Chan St, Belconnen, ACT 2617; POB 19, Belconnen, ACT 2616; tel (62) 64 1166; telex 62626; fax (62) 64 2803; Chair: Prof R. Baxt; Commr: Allan J. Asher; f 1974; administers the 1974 Trade Practices Act.

Agriculture and the Environment

AGRICULTURE

Australian Agricultural Council: Dept of Primary Industries and Energy, Edmund Barton Bldg, Broughton St, Barton, ACT 2600; tel (62) 72 5220; telex 62188; fax (62) 72 4772; Chair: Federal Minister for Primary Industries and Energy, John C. Kerin; Sec: D. C. Ayliffe; f 1934; formed of eight mems comprising the agricultural Ministers of the six States and the Northern Territory and the Federal Minister for Primary Industries and Energy; develops national policies on agricultural production and marketing (excluding forestry and fisheries); promotes the welfare and standards of agricultural industries.

Standing Committee on Agriculture: address as above; Chair: rotates between States annually; Sec: D. C. Ayliffe; f 1934; comprises the State and Northern Territory Dirs of Agriculture and reps of Federal Depts with an interest in agriculture; advises the Australian Agricultural Council; secures co-operation and co-ordination in agricultural research and in quarantine measures relating to pests and diseases of plants and animals.

THE ENVIRONMENT

Australian Environment Council: Dept of the Arts, Sport, the Environment, Tourism and Territories, Tobruk House, 15 Moore St, Canberra City, ACT 2601; POB 787, Canberra, ACT 2601; tel (62) 74 1414; telex 62960; fax (62) 74 1123; Sec: G. T. Hore; f 1972; under the Dept of the Arts, Sport, the Environment, Tourism and Territories; Council consists of Federal, State and Territory Ministers with responsibility for the environment; develops and promotes policies on environmental issues of national and international importance; maintains a trust fund to assist research, policy devt and projects.

Australian National Parks and Wildlife Service: 3rd Floor, Construction House, Northbourne Ave, ACT; POB 636, Canberra, ACT 2601; tel (62) 46 6211; telex 62971; fax (62) 47 3528; Head: Dr Peter Bridgewater.

FISHING

Australian Fisheries Council: Dept of Primary Industries and Energy, Edmund Barton Bldg, Broughton St, Barton, ACT 2600; tel (62) 72 5220; telex 62188; Chair: Federal Minister for Resources, Sen Peter Cook; Sec: I. R. Cottingham; mems include State Ministers with responsibility for fishing.

FORESTRY

Australian Forestry Council: Dept of Primary Industries and Energy, Edmund Barton Bldg, Broughton St, Barton, ACT 2600; tel (62) 71 7370; telex 62188; fax (62) 72 4526; Chair: Minister for Resources, Sen Peter Cook; Sec: L. D. Wood; f 1964; mems are Federal, State and Northern Territory Ministers with responsibility for forestry; promotes the management of Australian forests and associated industries; facilitates consultation and co-ordination between the Federal, State and Territory Govts on forestry matters.

Standing Committee on Forestry: address as above; advises the Council on all matters relating to forestry affairs.

Art and Culture

Australia Council: Northside Gdns, 168 Walker St, North Sydney, NSW; POB 302, North Sydney, NSW 2060; tel (2) 923 3333; telex 26023; Chair: Prof D. R. Horne; Gen Man: M. Bourke; f 1968; fmrly Australian Council for the Arts; promotes devt of the arts through: the Aboriginal Arts Board, the Community Cultural Devt Committee, the Design Board, the Literary Arts Board, the Performing Arts Board and the Visual Arts-Crafts Board.

National Library of Australia: Parkes Place, Canberra, ACT 2600; tel (62) 62 1111; telex 62100; fax (62) 57 1703; Chair: M. L. West; Dir-Gen: Warren M. Horton; f 1960; maintains and develops a national collection of library material.

National Museum of Australia: Yarramundi, Lady Denman Drive, Canberra City, ACT; POB 1901, Canberra, ACT 2601; tel (62) 56 1111; telex 62960; fax (62) 56 1233; Dir (acting): Kaye Dal Bon; Asst Dir: David Lance; f 1980; develops, maintains and exhibits a national collection of historical material; conducts research and disseminates information relating to Australian history.

Business and Economy

BANKING

Australian Resources Development Bank Ltd: 379 Collins St, POB 53, Melbourne, Vic 3000; tel (3) 616 2800; telex 32078; Chair: W. H. Hodgson; Gen Man: A. Locke; f 1967; finances Australian participation in projects of national importance through marshalling funds from local and overseas sources.

Commonwealth Banking Corpn: Pitt St and Martin Place, Sydney, NSW 2000; POB 2719, Sydney, NSW 2001; tel (2) 227 7111; telex 120345; fax (2) 232 6573; Chair: M. A. Besley; Man Dir: D. N. Sanders; f 1960; controlling body for three mem banks:

Commonwealth Bank of Australia: Pitt St and Martin Place, Sydney, NSW 2000; POB 2719, Sydney, NSW 2001; tel (2) 227 7111; telex 120345; fax (2) 235 1653; Chief Gen Mans: B. A. Poulter, C. J. Ker, H. L. Spencer; Chief Exec: D. N. Sanders; f 1912; statutory body established by the Australian Govt; more than 1,200 brs world-wide.

Commonwealth Savings Bank of Australia: Pitt St and Martin Place, Sydney, NSW 2000; POB 2719, Sydney, NSW 2001; tel (2) 227 7111; telex 120345; fax (2) 235 1653; Gen Man: H. L. Spencer; f 1912; subsidiary of the Commonwealth Bank of Australia.

Commonwealth Development Bank of Australia: Prudential Bldg, 39 Martin Place, Sydney, NSW 2000; POB 2719, Sydney, NSW 2001; tel (2) 227 7111; telex 120345; fax (2) 235 1653; Gen Man: J. W. Fletcher; f 1960.

Primary Industry Bank of Australia Ltd: 115 Pitt St, Sydney, NSW 2000; POB 4577, Sydney, NSW 2001; tel (2) 231 5655; telex 23495; Chair: Walter C. Ives; Man Dir: John C. Frearson; f 1978.

Reserve Bank of Australia: 65 Martin Place, Sydney, NSW 2000; POB 3947, Sydney, NSW 2001; tel (2) 234 9333; telex 121636; fax (2) 234 9001; Gov: Bernie Fraser; Dep Gov: M. J. Phillips; f 1911; central bank and bank of issue.

Rural and Industries Bank of Western Australia: 108 St George's Terrace, POB E237, Perth, WA 6001; tel (9) 320 6206;

telex 92417; fax (9) 320 6444; Chair: Dr Ross Garnaut; Man Dir: David P. Fischer; Group Gen Man: Andrew J. Gordon; f 1945; WA govt bank; 109 brs.

State Bank of New South Wales: 52 Martin Place, POB 41, Sydney, NSW 2001; tel (2) 226 8000; telex 74238; Chair: R. F. W. Watson; Man Dir: J. A. O'Neill; f 1933; 295 brs in Australia.

State Bank of South Australia: 91 King William St, Adelaide, SA 5000; POB 399, Adelaide, SA 5001; tel (8) 210 4411; telex 82082; fax (8) 212 3056; Chair: David Simmons; Man Dir: Tim Marcus Clark; f 1984; 186 brs.

State Bank of Victoria: 385 Bourke St, Melbourne, Vic 3000; POB 267D, Melbourne, Vic 3001; tel (3) 604 7000; telex 32910; fax (3) 670 7042; Chair: J. Arnold Hancock; Chief Exec: L. G. C. Moyle; f 1842; 532 brs.

Tasmania Bank: 67 St John St, POB 288, Launceston, Tas 7250; tel (03) 373 444; telex 58579; fax (03) 342 367; Chair: Robert Mather; Man Dir: Don Adams; f 1987 by the merger of the Launceston Bank for Savings (f 1835) and Tasmanian Permanent Building Society; 30 brs.

FINANCIAL AGENCIES

Australian Securities Commission (ASC): Sydney; Chair: Tony Hartnell; f 1990 to replace the National Cos and Securities Commission (NCSC) and the State-level Corporate Affairs Commissions; minimum of three full-time mems.

Australian Taxation Office: 2 Constitution Ave, Canberra, ACT; POB 900, Civic Sq, ACT 2608; tel (62) 75 2222; telex 62187; fax (62) 47 2830; Commr of Taxation: T. P. W. Boucher.

Industries Assistance Commission: Benjamin Offices, Chan St, Belconnen, ACT; POB 80, Belconnen, ACT 2616; tel (62) 64 1144; telex 62283; fax (62) 53 1186; Chair: W. B. Carmichael; Sec: L. F. J. Milkovits; responsible to the Treasury; advises industry on sources of assistance.

Royal Australian Mint: Deakin, ACT 2600; tel (62) 83 3244; Controller: W. F. Sheehan.

INSURANCE

Housing Loans Insurance Corpn: St Martins Tower, cnr Market and York Sts, Sydney, NSW; POB 4617, Sydney, NSW 2001; tel (2) 2 0259; fax (2) 290 2340; Chair and Man Dir (acting): P. M. Bartlett; Head Office Man: W. G. Jenkins.

MARKETING

Australian Dairy Corpn: 1601 Malvern Rd, Glen Iris, Vic 3146; tel (3) 805 3777; telex 30503; fax (3) 885 5885; Chair: John C. Frearson; Man Dir: John L. Gibson; f 1975; promotes local consumption and controls the export of dairy produce.

Australian Meat and Livestock Corpn: Aetna Life Tower, Hyde Park Sq, cnr Elizabeth and Bathurst Sts, Sydney, NSW; POB 4129, Sydney, NSW 2001; tel (2) 260 3111; telex 22887; fax (2) 267 6620; Chair: R. Austen; Man Dir: Dr B. Standen; f 1978; statutory Federal Govt authority; assists the Australian meat and livestock industries in domestic and international trade.

Australian Wheat Board: Ceres House, 528 Lonsdale St, Melbourne, Vic 3000; tel (3) 605 1555; telex 130196; fax (3) 670 2782; Chair: Clinton Condon; f 1939; marketing authority for wheat exportation.

Australian Wool Corpn: Wool House, 369 Royal Parade, Parkville, Vic 3052; POB 4867, Melbourne, Vic 3001; tel (3) 341 9111; telex 30548 (general), 34128 (sales); fax (3) 341 9273; Chair: David Asimus; f 1973; responsible for wool marketing and research; board of 10 mems (chair, four wool growers, four from commerce, one Govt mem).

Wool Council of Australia: POB E10, Queen Victoria Terrace, Canberra, ACT 2600; tel (62) 73 2531; telex 62683; Pres: K. M. Sawers; Exec Dir: S. M. Moore; consists of 20 mems; levies wool tax for research and devt; consults with Australian Wool Corpn on reserve prices; represents wool-growers to Govt and industry; promotes wool marketing.

TRADE

Australian Customs Service: Customs House, Constitution Ave, Canberra, ACT 2601; tel (62) 75 6666; telex 62049; fax (62) 75 6999; Comptroller-Gen: F. I. Kelly; Dep Comptroller-Gen: D. O'Connor; f 1901; responsible to Dept of Industry, Technology and Commerce.

Australian Patent, Trade Marks and Designs Offices: Scarborough House, Phillip, ACT; POB 200, Woden, ACT 2606; tel (62) 83 2211; telex 61517; fax (62) 81 1841; Commr for Patents, Registrar for Trade Marks and Designs: P. A. Smith; grants industrial property rights for patents, trade marks and designs; under the Dept of Industry, Technology and Commerce.

Australian Trade Commission (AUSTRADE): AUSTRADE Centre, cnr Northbourne Ave and Barry Drive, ACT; POB 2386, Canberra, ACT 2601; tel (62) 76 5111; telex 62194; fax (62) 76 5105; Chair: W. D. Ferris; Man Dir: L. T. McAlister; statutory authority charged with the expansion and facilitation of Australian exports and investment; provides a range of insurance, finance and guarantee facilities to Australian exporters and overseas investors.

    Export Finance and Insurance Corpn (AUSTRADE— EFIC): Export House, 22 Pitt St, Sydney NSW 2000; POB R65, Royal Exchange, Sydney, NSW 2000; tel (2) 231 2655; telex 121224; fax (2) 251 3659; Australia's official export credit agency; division of the Australian Trade Commission.

Australian Trade Development Council: Dept of Foreign Affairs and Trade, Admin Bldg, Parkes, ACT 2600; tel (62) 61 2246; fax (62) 61 3998; Chair: Dr B. W. Scott; Exec Officer: Ross Pye; f 1958; advises the Govt on substantive trade policy issues.

Defence

Defence Force Headquarters: Russell Offices, Canberra, ACT 2600; tel (62) 62 2856; Commdr-in-Chief: Sir Ninian Stephen; Chief of the Defence Force Staff: Gen Sir Phillip Bennett.

    Air Force Office: Russell Offices, Canberra, ACT 2600; tel (62) 65 9111; Chief of the Air Staff: Air Marshal J. W. Newham.

    Army Office: Russell Offices, Canberra, ACT 2600; tel (62) 65 9111; telex 62625; fax (62) 65 4205; Chief of the Gen Staff: Lt-Gen P. C. Gration.

    Navy Office: Russell Offices, Canberra, ACT 2600; tel (62) 65 9111; telex 62112; Chief of Naval Staff: Vice-Adm M. W. Hudson.

Australian Federal Police: Police Headquarters, 68 Northbourne Ave, Braddon, ACT; POB 401, Canberra, ACT 2601; tel (62) 49 7444; fax (62) 75 7071; Commr: R. McAulay.

Development and Planning

Aboriginal Development Commission: Bonner House, Neptune St, Woden, ACT; POB 1200, Woden, ACT 2606; tel (62) 89 1666; telex 61686; fax (62) 82 1057; Chair: Shirley A. McPherson; Gen Man (acting): Cedric Wyatt; f 1980; responsible to the Dept of Aboriginal Affairs; furthers the economic and social devt of Aboriginal and Torres Strait Islander people;

promotes devt, self-management and self-sufficiency by assisting Aboriginal bodies with the provision of housing and with funding for Aboriginal enterprises.

Australian Industry Development Corpn: Level 33, AIDC Tower, 201 Kent St, Sydney, NSW 2000; tel (2) 235 5155; telex 23107; fax (2) 235 5195; Chair: Sir Gordon Jackson; Chief Exec: Arthur William O'Sullivan; f 1971; Federal statutory corpn providing finance and financial services including the arrangement of project finance and equity participations to promote the devt of Australian industry; encourages Australian participation in the ownership and control of industries and resources.

REGIONAL DEVELOPMENT

National Capital Development Commission: 220 Northbourne Ave, Braddon, ACT; POB 373, Canberra, ACT 2601; tel (62) 46 8211; telex 62673; fax (62) 47 6980; Commr: M. B. M. Latham; Divisions concerned with town planning, architecture, engineering and construction.

Employment

National Board of Employment, Education and Training: Dept of Employment, Education and Training, 1st Floor, 64 Northbourne Ave, Canberra City, ACT 2601; POB 9880, Canberra City, ACT 2601; tel (62) 76 8111; fax (62) 76 8469; Chair: R. H. T. Smith; Dep Chair: G. A. Ramsey; f 1988; advises the Federal Govt on matters concerning employment, education, training and research.

Health

National Health and Medical Research Council: POB 9848, Canberra, ACT 2601; tel (62) 89 1555; telex 62490; fax (62) 89 8198; Chair: Prof John Chalmers; Sec: Dr John Loy; f 1936; advises the Minister for Health on all health matters; provides funds for medical, biomedical and public health research and devt.

Legal and Judiciary

Director of Public Prosecutions: Hinkler Bldg, 25 Kings Ave, Barton, ACT; POB E370, Queen Victoria Terrace, Canberra, ACT 2600; tel (62) 70 5666; telex 61702; fax (62) 73 1411; Dir of Public Prosecutions: I. D. Temby.

High Court of Australia: Parkes, ACT; POB E435, Queen Victoria Terrace, Canberra, ACT 2600; tel (62) 70 6862; telex 61430; fax (62) 73 3025; Chief Justice: Sir Anthony Frank Mason.

Federal Court of Australia: Law Courts Bldg, Queens Sq, Sydney, NSW 2000; tel (2) 230 8111; fax (3) 223 1906; Chief Judge: Sir Nigel Hubert Bowen.

Media

BROADCASTING

Australian Broadcasting Corpn (ABC): ABC House, 150 William St, POB 9994, Sydney, NSW 2001; tel (2) 339 0211; telex 26506 (corporate), 176464 (radio), 120432 (TV); fax (2) 356 5305; Chair: Robert D. Somervaille; Man Dir: David Hill; f 1932 as Australian Broadcasting Commission; national radio and TV services.

GOVERNMENT PUBLISHER

Australian Government Publishing Service: Govt Printing Office, Wentworth Ave, Kingston, ACT 2604; POB 84, Canberra, ACT 2601; tel (62) 95 4411; telex 62013; fax (62) 95 4455; Govt Printer: R. D. Rubie; Dir of Publishing: F. W. Thompson; f 1970.

NEWS AND INFORMATION

Australian Bureau of Statistics: Cameron Offices, Chandler St, Belconnen, ACT 2616; POB 10, Belconnen, ACT 2616; tel (62) 52 6627; telex 62020; fax (62) 51 6009; Australian Statistician: Ian Castles; provides statistical service; co-ordinates statistical activities across Govt agencies and promotes the use of statistical standards.

Mining and Energy

Australian Minerals and Energy Council: Dept of Primary Industries and Energy, Edmund Barton Bldg, Broughton St, Barton, ACT 2600; tel (62) 71 7020; telex 62188; Sec: A. Free; mems are Federal, State, and Northern Territory Ministers with responsibility for energy and resources.

Joint Coal Board: 1 Chifley Sq, Sydney, NSW; POB 3842, Sydney, NSW 2001; tel (2) 235 9666; telex 25227; fax (2) 223 1896; Chair: J. Wilcox; responsible to the Dept of Primary Industries and Energy.

Research

Industry Research and Development Board: Dept of Industry, Technology and Commerce, Level 1, Bldg 4, 51 Allara St, Canberra City, ACT 2601; POB 2704, Canberra, ACT 2601; tel (62) 76 1000; telex 62654; fax (62) 76 1122; Chair: W. A. Kricker; Chief Exec: Malcolm Farrow; f 1986; responsible for admin of Grants for Industry Research (GIRD) Scheme; encourages research and devt of new products and processes in Australian industry.

National Energy Research, Development and Demonstration Council: NERDDC Secretariat, Dept of Primary Industries and Energy, Edmund Barton Bldg, Broughton St, Barton, ACT 2600; tel (62) 72 3933; telex 62188; fax (62) 72 5161; Chair: J. E. Kolm; f 1978; provides tertiary education institutions, Govt research organizations and private enterprise with funds for energy research, devt and demonstration.

Science and Technology

ANSTO Education and Training Centre: PMB 1, Menai, NSW 2234; tel (2) 543 3111; telex 24562; fax (2) 543 5097; Dir: Peter Nixon; provides short-term intensive courses covering radionuclides in medicine, radioisotope techniques and radiation protection.

Australian Institute of Nuclear Science and Engineering: PMB 1, Menai, NSW 2234; Scientific Sec: Dr R. B. Gammon; supports research and training programmes at university level in all branches of nuclear science and engineering.

Australian Nuclear Science and Technology Organisation (ANSTO): Lucas Heights Research Laboratories, New Illawarra Rd, Lucas Heights, NSW 2234; PMB 1, Menai, NSW 2234; tel (2) 543 3111; telex 24562; fax (2) 543 5097; Chair: Prof R. E. Collins; Exec Dir: Dr David J. Cook; f 1987; promotes nuclear science and technology in industry, medicine and the community.

Australian Science and Technology Council (ASTEC): 3-5 National Circuit, Barton, ACT 2600; POB E439, Queen Victoria Terrace ACT 2600; tel (62) 71 5655; telex 61854; fax (62) 71 5924; Chair: Prof R. L. Martin; Sec: Dr W. J. McG Tegart; f 1979; provides the Govt with independent advice on policies and programmes relating to science and technology within Federal depts and agencies, higher education institutions and private enterprise.

Australian Space Board: Dept of Industry, Technology and Commerce, 51 Allara St, Canberra, ACT; POB 269 Civic Sq, ACT 2608; tel (62) 258 6000; telex 62654; fax (62) 258 6999; Chair: R. D. Somervaille; f 1986; advises the Minister for Industry, Technology and Commerce on Australian space activities.

National Science and Technology Centre: POB E28, Queen Victoria Terrace, Canberra, ACT 2600; tel (62) 70 2800; fax (62) 70 2808; Dir: Dr Michael M. Gore; f 1989; provides science exhibitions, demonstrations and lectures.

Telecommunications

Australian Postal Commission (Australia Post): 71 Rathdowne St, Carlton, Vic; POB 302, Carlton South, Vic 3053; tel (3) 669 7171; telex 34096; fax (3) 663 5250; Chair: R. B. Lansdowne; Exec Officer: E. Morris; Man Dir: D. H. Eltringham.

Australian Telecommunications Commission (Telecom Australia): Communications House, 199 William St, Melbourne, Vic 3000; tel (3) 606 5511; telex 152152; fax (3) 670 0338; Chair: R. W. Brack; Man Dir: M. K. Ward; responsible to the Dept of Transport and Communications.

Overseas Telecommunications Commission Australia: 231 Elizabeth St, Sydney, NSW; POB 7000, Sydney, NSW 2001; tel (2) 287 5000; telex 120591; fax (2) 287 5103; Chief Commr: A. W. Coates; Man Dir: G. F. Maltby.

Tourism

Australian Tourist Commission (ACT): Level 3, 80 William St, Woolloomooloo, Sydney, NSW 2011; POB 2721, Sydney 2001; tel (2) 360 1111; telex 22322; fax (2) 331 6469; Chair: John Haddad; Man Dir: Tony Thirlwell; f 1967; statutory authority established by the Federal Govt to promote tourism to and within Australia.

Transport

Australian Transport Advisory Council: Drakeford Bldg, 72 Northbourne Ave, Braddon, ACT; POB 594, Canberra, ACT 2601; tel (62) 68 7851; telex 62018; fax (62) 57 2505; Sec: T. H. Arrowsmith; f 1946; Mems: Federal Minister for Transport and Communications, State and Territory Ministers of Transport, Roads and Marine and Ports; Observer: the New Zealand Minister of Transport; discusses and reports in order to promote better co-ordinated transport devt; encourages modernization and innovation; promotes research.

State Transit Authority of New South Wales: 100 Mille St, North Sydney, NSW 2060; telex 25702; Chair: J. Landels; Man Dir: J. Brew; co-ordinates bus and ferry services in Sydney, Newcastle and Wollongong; manages publicly-owned bus and ferry services; exercises broad policy control over privately owned public vehicle services in these areas.

CIVIL AVIATION

Australian Airlines Ltd: 50 Franklin St, POB 2806AA, Melbourne, Vic 3000; tel (3) 665 1333; telex 30109; fax (3) 666 3881; Chair: A. E. Harris; Chief Exec: (vacant); f 1946 as Trans-Australia Airlines (TAA); scheduled domestic airline services to all States.

Civil Aviation Authority: Civic Advance Bank Bldg, Allara St, Canberra City, ACT 2600; tel (62) 68 4111; telex 62221; fax (62) 48 5239; Chair: Alaln Woods; Chief Exec: Collin Freeland; f 1988; has responsibility for setting and control of aviation standards; responsible for air traffic control, flight advisory services, communications, navigation and surveillance systems and rescue and fire-fighting services at airports.

Federal Airports Corpn: 1st Floor, 77 Dunning Ave, Roseberry, NSW; POB 150, Roseberry, NSW 2018; tel (2) 697 7474; fax (2) 662 2431; Chair: D. W. Sullivan; Chief Exec: W. A. Swingler.

Qantas Airways Ltd: Qantas International Centre, International Sq, POB 489, Sydney, NSW 2001; tel (2) 236 3636; telex 20113; fax (2) 236 3277; Chair J. B. Leslie; Chief Exec: (vacant); f 1920; services to 42 cities in 24 countries including the UK, Europe, the USA, Canada, Japan, South East Asia, India, the Middle East, Africa and the South West Pacific, including New Zealand.

Australia-Asia Airlines: Sydney; f 1989; a division of Qantas Airways Ltd; operates services between Sydney and Taipei.

RAILWAYS

Australian National: 1 Richmond Rd, Keswick, SA 5035; tel (8) 217 4111; telex 88445; fax (8) 217 4544; Chair: Dr D. G. Williams; Man Dir: R. M. King; f 1975; federal statutory authority providing freight and passenger transport by rail (freight only in Tasmania); ancillary activities in sale and leasing of railway property.

Queensland Railways: Railway Centre, 305 Edward St, Brisbane, Qld 4000; POB 1429, Brisbane, Qld 4001; tel (7) 235 2222; telex 41514; fax (7) 235 1799; Commr: R. T. Sheehy; Dep Commr and Sec: R. W. Dunning; f 1865; operates and maintains the Govt's railway system in Queensland; provides expertise services in railway planning, design, operations and maintenance to developing countries in South East Asia and Africa.

State Rail Authority of New South Wales: 11-31 York St, Sydney, NSW 2000; POB 29, Sydney, NSW 2001; tel (2) 219 8888; telex 25702; Chair and Chief Exec: R. Sayers; administers passenger and freight rail service in NSW.

State Transport Authority (South Australia): 136 North Terrace, Adelaide, SA 5000; POB 2351, Adelaide SA 5001; tel (8) 218 2200; telex 87115; fax (8) 211 7614; Chair: James D. Rump; Gen Man: John V. Brown; f 1974; provides public transport for the Adelaide metropolitan area.

State Transport Authority (Victoria): 589 Collins St, Melbourne, Vic 3000; tel (3) 619 1111; telex 33801; Chair: J. King; Man Dir: K. M. Fitzmaurice; f 1983.

Western Australian Government Railways (Westrail): Westrail Centre, POB S1422, Perth 6001, WA; tel (9) 326 2222; telex 92879; fax (9) 326 2589; Commr: Dr J. I. Gill; f 1879; operates rail freight and passenger services mainly in the south of WA.

SHIPPING

Commonwealth of Australia, Australian National Line (Australian Shipping Commission): 432 St Kilda Rd, Melbourne, Vic 3004; POB 2238T, Melbourne, Vic 3001; tel (3) 269 5555; telex 130584; fax (3) 269 5319; Chair: W. Bolitho; Man

Dir: M. Moore-Wilton; f 1956; shipping agents; coastal trade and coastal and overseas bulk shipping; container management services; container services to Europe and Asia; bulk services to Japan, Asia and New Zealand.

Western Australian Coastal Shipping Commission (Stateships): Port Beach Rd, North Fremantle, WA 6160; POB 394, Fremantle, WA; tel (9) 430 0200; telex 92054; fax (9) 430 4506; Chair and Gen Man: D. F. Wilson; f 1912; shipping.

AUSTRALIAN EXTERNAL TERRITORIES

CHRISTMAS ISLAND

The Government

CHRISTMAS ISLAND ADMINISTRATION
POB AAA, Christmas Island, Indian Ocean 6798
Tel 8501; telex 76678001; fax 8524
Administrator: A. D. Taylor
Manager, Government Services: T. J. White
Administration of the Territory including representation of Commonwealth agencies; functions include radio, television and courts administration, registration of births, deaths and marriages, customs, postal and philatelic office, police port agency, electoral register; responsible for Federal functions including immigration, social security, health and community services, civil aviation, etc.

CHRISTMAS ISLAND ASSEMBLY
Christmas Island, Indian Ocean 6798
Chair: G. Bennett.

Government Agencies

BROADCASTING

Christmas Island Broadcasting: Christmas Island, Indian Ocean 6798; tel 8301; telex 78002; Station Man: Jay Busch; f 1967; owned and operated by the Christmas Island Services Corpn (see below); broadcasts daily by radio in English, Malay and Mandarin.

Christmas Island Television: Station Man: Douglas Maley.

LEGAL AND JUDICIARY

Supreme Court: c/o Govt Offices, Christmas Island, Indian Ocean 6798; tel 8501; telex 78001; Judge: John F. Gallop (non-resident); Additional Judge: Robert S. French (non-resident).

MINING

Phosphate Mining Corpn of Christmas Island (PMCI): Christmas Island, Indian Ocean 6798; tel 8402; telex 78006; f 1981 as the Phosphate Mining Co of Christmas Island; reorganized under present name as Australian Govt statutory authority in 1985; mines, treats and markets Christmas Island phosphates; proposed closure announced in Nov 1987.

UTILITIES

Christmas Island Services Corpn: Christmas Island, Indian Ocean 6798; tel 8269; Dir: R. McLean.

COCOS (KEELING) ISLANDS

The Government

COCOS (KEELING) ISLANDS ADMINISTRATION
Cocos (Keeling) Islands, Indian Ocean 6799
Administrator: A. D. Lawrie.

COCOS (KEELING) ISLANDS COUNCIL
Home Island, Cocos (Keeling) Islands, Indian Ocean 6799
Tel 7587
Chair: Parson bin Yapat.

Government Agencies

BROADCASTING

Radio VKW Cocos: POB 70, Cocos (Keeling) Islands, Indian Ocean 6799; tel 6666; Station Man: D. Williams; Programme Man: R. F. Carey; non-commercial; broadcasts daily services in Cocos Malay and English.

INDUSTRY

Cocos (Keeling) Islands Co-operative Society Ltd: Home Island, Cocos (Keeling) Islands, Indian Ocean 6799; tel 7598; telex 67001; Chair: Medous bin Bynie; f 1979; directs business enterprises of the Cocos Islanders, including boat construction and repairs, copra and coconut production, sail-making and stevedoring.

LEGAL AND JUDICIARY

Supreme Court: Cocos (Keeling) Islands, Indian Ocean 6799; tel 6660; telex 67002; Judge: John F. Gallop (non-resident); Additional Judge: Robert S. French (non-resident).

Magistrates' Court: Special Magistrate: Harold Bingham.

NORFOLK ISLAND

The Government

OFFICE OF THE ADMINISTRATOR
New Military Barracks, Kingston, Norfolk Island 2899
Tel 2152; telex 32025; fax 2681
Administrator: H. B. MacDonald

NORFOLK ISLAND ASSEMBLY
Kingston, Norfolk Island 2899
President: John Terence Brown

MINISTRY OF COMMERCE, TOURISM AND HEALTH
Kingston, Norfolk Island 2899
Minister: Geoffrey James Bennett

MINISTRY OF FINANCE
Kingston, Norfolk Island 2899
Minister: Edward Howard

MINISTRY OF PLANNING
Kingston, Norfolk Island 2899
Minister: William Winton Sanders

Government Agencies

BROADCASTING

Norfolk Island Broadcasting Service: New Cascade Rd, Norfolk Island 2899; tel 2137; fax 2499; Broadcasting Officer: K. M. LeCren; non-commercial; broadcasts 112 hours per week.

LEGAL AND JUDICIARY

Supreme Court: Norfolk Island 2899; Judges: Russell W. Fox (Chief Judge), Trevor R. Morling.

TOURISM

Norfolk Island Government Tourist Board: Burnt Pine, POB 211, Norfolk Island 2899; tel 2147; telex 32010; Chair: Ian W. Kenny.

Norfolk Island Government Visitors' Information Bureau: Burnt Pine, POB 211, Norfolk Island 2899; tel 2147; telex 32010; Chief Exec: Barry J. Schipplock.

AUSTRIA

Head of State

The Federal President is the Head of State, and is elected by popular vote for a six-year term. Re-election for a successive term is permitted only once. Although invested with special emergency powers, the President normally acts on the authority of the Government, which comprises a Federal Chancellor, appointed by the President, a Vice-Chancellor and other Ministers, chosen by the President on the advice of the Chancellor.

Federal President: Dr Kurt Waldheim (took office 8 July 1986)

Office of the Federal President: Hofburg, Ballhausplatz, 1010 Vienna; tel (1) 534-22-0; telex 133484; fax (1) 53-56-512.

Legislature

Legislative power is held by the bicameral Federal Assembly. The first chamber, the Nationalrat (National Council), has 183 members, elected by universal adult suffrage for four years (subject to dissolution) on the basis of proportional representation. The second chamber, the Bundesrat (Federal Council), has 63 members, elected for varying terms by provincial assemblies. For regional government, Austria is divided into nine provinces, each with its own assembly and government.

Nationalrat: Dr Karl-Renner-Ring 3, 1017 Vienna; tel (1) 48-04-0; Pres: Rudolf Pöder; Sec: Dr Robert Fischer.

Bundesrat: Dr Karl-Renner-Ring 3, 1017 Vienna; tel (1) 48-04-0; telex 115231; fax (1) 4804537; Pres: Anton Nigl; Dir: Dr Reinhold Ruckser.

MINISTRIES AND GOVERNMENT DEPARTMENTS

FEDERAL CHANCELLERY
Ballhausplatz 2,1014 Vienna
Tel (1) 53-11-50; telex 1370900
Federal Chancellor: Dr Franz Vranitzky
Vice-Chancellor and Minister of the Federal Chancellery (Federalism and Administrative Reform): Josef Riegler
Minister of the Federal Chancellery (Health and Public Service): Harald Ettl
Secretary of State: Johanna Dohnal

MINISTRY OF AGRICULTURE AND FORESTRY
Stubenring 1, 1010 Vienna
Tel (1) 75-0-00
Minister: Dr Franz Fischler

MINISTRY OF ECONOMIC AFFAIRS
Stubenring 1, 1010 Vienna
Tel (1) 75-0-00; telex 111780
Minister: Dr Wolfgang Schüssel

MINISTRY OF EDUCATION, THE ARTS AND SPORT
Minoritenplatz 5, 1014 Vienna
Tel (1) 53-1-20
Minister: Dr Hilde Hawlicek

MINISTRY OF EMPLOYMENT AND SOCIAL AFFAIRS
Stubenring 1, 1010 Vienna
Tel (1) 71-1-00; telex 111145; fax (1) 713-79-95
Minister: Dr Walter Geppert

MINISTRY OF ENVIRONMENT, YOUTH AND FAMILY
Radetzkystr 2, 1031 Vienna
Tel (1) 71-1-58; telex 3221371
Minister: Dr Marilies Flemming

MINISTRY OF FINANCE
Himmelpfortgasse 4-8B, 1014 Vienna
Tel (1) 51-4-33; telex 111688; fax (1) 512-78-69
Minister: Ferdinand Lacina
Secretary of State: Dr Günther Stummvoll

MINISTRY OF FOREIGN AFFAIRS
Ballhausplatz 2, 1014 Vienna
Tel (1) 53-1-15; telex 01371; fax (1) 63-25-47
Minister: Dr Alois Mock

MINISTRY OF THE INTERIOR
Herrengasse 7, 1014 Vienna
Tel (1) 66-2-60
Minister: Dr Franz Löschnak

MINISTRY OF JUSTICE
Museumstr 7, 1074 Vienna
Tel (1) 96-22-727
Minister: Dr Egmont Foregger

MINISTRY OF THE PUBLIC SECTOR AND TRANSPORT
Radetzkystr 2, 1030 Vienna
Tel (1) 75-76-31; telex 111800
Minister: Dr Rudolf Streicher

MINISTRY OF NATIONAL DEFENCE
Dampfschiffstr 2, 1031 Vienna
Tel (1) 51-5-95; telex 112145
Minister: Dr Robert Lichal

MINISTRY OF SCIENCE AND RESEARCH
Minoritenplatz 5, 1014 Vienna
Tel (1) 53-1-20; telex 111157
Minister: Dr Erhard Busek

GOVERNMENT AGENCIES AND ORGANIZATIONS

Advisory and Supervisory Bodies

Bundeskammer der gewerblichen Wirtschaft (Federal Economic Chamber): Wiedner Hauptstr 63, 1045 Vienna; tel (1) 50-1-05; telex 111871; fax (1) 505-70-07; Pres: Rudolf Sallinger; Sec-Gen: Dr Karl Kehrer; f 1946; promotes international contacts and represents the economic interests of trade and industry on a federal level; comprises six sections: Commerce, Industry, Small-scale Production, Banking and Insurance, Transport and Tourism.

Bundesrechenamt: Hintere Zollamtstr 4, 1030 Vienna; tel (1) 66-23; Dir: Herbert Malek; central auditing body.

Österreichische Glücksspielmonopolverwaltung (Austrian Gaming Board): Mohsgasse 1, 1038 Vienna; tel (1) 78-45-01; Dir: Herbert Kraus; central authority for regulation of gambling.

Rechnungshof (Auditor General's Office): Dampfschiffstr 2, 1033 Vienna; tel (1) 711-71-0; Pres: Dr Tassilo Broesigke; Vice-Pres: Dr Franz Fiedler; supreme audit institution in the sphere of public finance control.

Verwertungsstelle des österreichischen Branntweinmonopols: Schwarzenbergplatz 6, 1037 Vienna; tel (1) 72-41-56; Dir: (vacant); supervisory body for wine and spirit industry.

Agriculture and the Environment

AGRICULTURE

Bundesanstalt für Agrarwirtschaft (Federal Agricultural Office): Schweizertalstr 36, 1130 Vienna; tel (1) 82-36-51; Dir: Hans Alfons; central agricultural organization.

Österreichische Bundesforste: Marxergasse 2, 1030 Vienna; tel (1) 73-15-31; Pres: Edwin Plattner; Chair: Dr Franz Eggl; national forestry commission.

THE ENVIRONMENT

Umweltbundesamt (Federal Environment Office): Radetzkystr 2, 1030 Vienna; tel (1) 75-56-86-0; Dir: Dr Wolfgang Struwe; central environment organization.

Art and Culture

Österreichische Nationalbibliothek (Austrian National Library): Josefsplatz 1, 1015 Vienna; tel (1) 52-16-84; telex 112624; Dir-Gen: Dr Magda Strebl; under the admin of the Ministry of Science and Research.

Österreichisches Staatsarchiv (Austrian State Archives):

Nottendorfergasse 2, 1030 Vienna; tel (1) 78-66-41; Dir-Gen: Dr Kurt Peball; f 1945; preservation of records relating to central state agencies, dissemination of information from such records.

Business and Economy

BANKING

Creditanstalt-Bankverein: Schottengasse 6, 1010 Vienna; tel (1) 531-31-0; telex 133030; fax (1) 531-31-75-66; Chair: Dr G. Schmidt-Chiari; f 1855.

Dorotheum Auktions-, Versatz- und Bank-GmbH: Dorotheergasse 17, 1011 Vienna; tel (1) 515-60-0; state-owned auction, pledge and banking co.

Oesterreichische Nationalbank (Austrian National Bank): Otto Wagner-Platz 3, 1090 Vienna; tel (1) 43-60-0; telex 114778; Pres: Dr Hellmuth Klauhs; Gen Man: Adolf Wala; f 1922; central bank; 7 brs.

Österreichische Investitionskredit AG: Renngasse 10, 1010 Vienna; tel (1) 53-1-35; telex 114495; Chair and Gen Man: Dr Anton Osond; acts as national financing agency.

Österreichische Kommunalkredit AG: Renngasse 10, 1010 Vienna; tel (1) 533-26-77; Chair: Dr Franz Bittermann; industrial financing agency.

Österreichische Kontrollbank AG: Am Hof 4, 1010 Vienna; tel (1) 531-27-0; telex 132747; Chair and Gen Man: Helmut H. Haschek; f 1946; export financing, stock exchange clearing, money market operations.

Österreichische Länderbank AG: Am Hof 2, 1011 Vienna; tel (1) 531-24-0; telex 115561; Chair and Chief Exec: Gerhard Wagner; f 1880; 141 brs.

Österreichische Postsparkasse: Georg-Coch-Platz 2, 1018 Vienna; tel (1) 51-40-00; telex 111663; Gov: Kurt Nößlinger; Vice-Govs: Dr V. Wolf, Dr E. Kampel; f 1883; postal savings bank.

FINANCIAL AGENCIES

Finanzprokurator: Singerstr 17-19, 1010 Vienna; tel (1) 75-76-41; fax (1) 513-89-70; Chair: Dr Gerhard Kubiczek; f 1572; central finance directorate.

Gesellschaft für Bundesbeteiligungen an Industrieunternehmungen (Company for Federal Participation in Industrial Enterprises): Seilergasse 16, 1010 Vienna; tel (1) 52-55-85; Dir: Dr Richard Bock; f 1983; enables federal intervention to provide financial assistance for insolvent industrial concerns; under the administrative jurisdiction of the Ministry of the Public Sector and Transport.

Hauptmünzamt (Central Mint): Am Heumarkt 1, 1031 Vienna;

tel (1) 73-55-25; telex 33880; Chair: (vacant); Vice-Chair: Hans Eckl; production of coins and medals.

INSURANCE

Allgemeine Unfallversicherungsanstalt (General Accident Insurance Institute): Adalbert Stifter-Str 65, 1200 Vienna; tel (1) 33-01; Dir: Dr Ernst Oder.

Sozialversicherungsanstalt der gewerblichen Wirtschaft (Economic and Social Insurance Institute): Wiedner Hauptstr 84-86, 1051 Vienna; tel (1) 55-45-41; Dir: Karl Schneider.

NATIONALIZED INDUSTRY

Austrian Industries: Kantgasse 1, Postfach 99, 1015 Vienna; tel (1) 71-114; telex 132047; fax (1) 71-114-245; Chair, Board of Dirs: Dr Hugo Michael Sekyra; Chair, Supervisory Board: Dr Josef Staribacher; f 1970; renamed in 1990, fmrly Österreichische Industrieholding Aktiengesellschaft (ÖIAG); holding co for all nationalized industries; co-ordinates economic management of the public sector; controls the following concerns and their subsidiaries:

Austria Metall AG: 5280 Braunau am Inn-Ranshofen; tel (7722) 2341; telex 27745; fax (7722) 7741; Chair, Board of Dirs: Dr Robert Ehrlich; Chair, Supervisory Board: Dr Hugo Michael Sekyra; f 1939; aluminium production and processing, copper and copper alloy semi-finished products.

Chemie Holding AG: St Peter-Str 25, Postfach 296, 4021 Linz; tel (732) 5910; telex 21324; fax (732) 52-080; Chair, Board of Dirs: Dr Richard Kirchweger; Chair, Supervisory Board: Dr Oskar Grünwald; f 1939; chemical products.

Elektro- und Elektronik-Industrieholding AG: Penzingerstr 76, 1140 Vienna; tel (1) 89-100-0; telex 112763; fax (1) 82-81-80; Chair, Board of Dirs: Guido Klestil; Chair, Supervisory Board: Hugo Michael Sekyra; f 1988, following the conversion of various depts of Elin Union AG into independent cos; electrical industry.

Maschinen- und Anlagenbau Holding AG: Turmstr, 4031 Linz; tel (732) 585-0; telex 2209222; fax (732) 585-9787; Chair: Othmar Pühringer; Chair, Supervisory Board: Dr Hugo Michael Sekyra; f 1988; contracting, engineering and machine-tool construction.

ÖMV AG: Otto-Wagner-Platz 5, Postfach 15, 1090 Vienna; tel (1) 48-900; telex 114801; fax (1) 48-900-01; Chair, Board of Dirs: Dr Herbert Kaes; Chair, Supervisory Board: Dr Oskar Grünwald; f 1955, partially privatized 1987; exploration, production, import and transport of crude oil, semi-finished products and natural gas.

Voest-Alpine AG: Turmstr 45, 4031 Linz; tel (732) 585; telex 2207450; fax (732) 585-0181; Chair, Board of Dirs: Dr Ludwig von Bogdany; Chair, Supervisory Board: Dr Hugo Michael Sekyra; f 1988; iron and steel works, steel processing, mechanical engineering, design and supply of industrial plant.

TRADE

Bundesamt für Eich- und Vermessungswesen (Office of Weights and Measures): Arltgasse 35, 1163 Vienna; tel (1) 92-16-27; telex 115468; fax (1) 73-79-95; Vice-Pres: Dr Richard Lewisch; f 1923; responsible for legal metrology, maintenance of standards of measurement, pattern approval and verification of measuring instruments; reports to the Ministry of Economic Affairs.

Bundesgremium des Außenhandels (Federal Committee for Foreign Trade): Wiedner Hauptstr 63, 1045 Vienna; tel (1) 6505-3352; telex 111871; Chair: Dr Karl Pisec; Man Dir: Dr Heinrich Kopecky; f 1947.

Österreichische Exportfonds: Gottfried-Keller-Gasse 1, 1030 Vienna; tel (1) 72-61-51; telex 132846; Dirs: Herbert Allwinger, Herbert Niemetz; f 1950; provides finance for exporting cos.

Österreichisches Patentamt (Austrian Patent Office): Kohlmarkt 8-10, 1014 Vienna; tel (1) 53-4-24; telex 136847; fax (1) 53-424-520; Pres: Dr Josef Fichte; Vice-Pres: Dr Norbert Marterer, Dr Otmar Rafeiner; f 1899; responsible for intellectual property; under the jurisdiction of the Ministry of Economic Affairs.

Defence

Armeekommando (Army Command): Kommandogebäude General Körner, Hütteldorfer Str 126, 1141 Vienna; tel (1) 92-66-51; Commdr of the Army: Gen Johann Philipp; Chief of Staff: Commdr Viktor Fortunat; the Federal President is Supreme Commdr of the Armed Forces.

Generaldirektion für die öffentliche Sicherheit (General Directorate for Public Security): Minoritenplatz 9, 1014 Vienna; tel (1) 531-26; responsible for general admin in the field of security; reports to the Ministry of the Interior; oversees the following bodies:

Bundespolizei (Federal Police): Minoritenplatz 9, 1014 Vienna; tel (1) 531-26; Dir: Dr Helmut Zettler.

Gendarmeriezentralkommando (Central Gendarmerie Command): Minoritenplatz 9, 1014 Vienna; tel (1) 531-26; Dir: Dr Erich Bosina.

Legal and Judiciary

Oberster Gerichtshof (Supreme Judicial Court): Museumstr 12, 1016 Vienna; tel (1) 96-22-0; Pres: Dr Walter Melnizky; Vice-Pres: Heribert Harbich, Dr Karl Piska.

Verfassungsgerichtshof (Constitutional Court): Judenplatz 11, 1010 Vienna; tel (1) 531-22; Pres: Dr Ludwig Adamovich; Vice-Pres: Dr Kurt Ringhofer; deals with matters affecting the Constitution, examines the legality of legislation and admin.

Verwaltungsgerichtshof (Administrative Court): Judenplatz 11, 1010 Vienna; tel (1) 531-11; Pres: Dr Ingrid Petrik; Vice-Pres: Dr Wilhelm Zach; deals with matters affecting the legality of admin.

Volksanwaltschaft (Public Attorney's Office): Singerstr 17, Postfach 20, 1010 Vienna; tel (1) 515-05; Chair: Helmuth Josseck; Sec: Heide Schmidt.

Media

BROADCASTING

Österreichischer Rundfunk (ORF): Würzburggasse 30, 1136 Vienna; tel (1) 82-91-0; Dir-Gen: Thaddäus Podgorski; f 1955; national broadcasting co; controls all radio and TV in Austria.

GOVERNMENT PUBLISHERS

Österreichische Staatsdruckerei (Austrian State Printing Office): Rennweg 12A, 1037 Vienna; tel (1) 78-76-310; telex 131805; Dir: Aribert Schwarzmann; f 1804.

Österreichischer Bundesverlag GmbH: Schwarzenbergstr 5, 1015 Vienna; tel (1) 514-05; telex 131159; fax (1) 514-05-210; Dirs: Walter Amon, Dr Robert Sedlaczek; f 1772; national publishing co, producing textbooks, educational periodicals and reference books about Austria.

NEWS AND INFORMATION

Bundespressedienst (Federal Press Service): Ballhausplatz 2, 1014 Vienna; tel (1) 531-15-0; telex 75585; Dir: Dr Herbert Neumayer; under the jurisdiction of the Federal Chancellery.

Österreichisches Statistisches Zentralamt (Austrian Central Statistical Office): Hintere Zollamtsstr 2B, 1033 Vienna; tel (1) 711-28; telex 132600; fax (1) 711-28/7728; Pres: Erich Bader; Vice-Pres: Dr Viktor Lenhart; f 1945; produces censuses and surveys in the entire field of federal statistics; also provides an on-line databank known as ISIS; under the administrative jurisdiction of the Federal Chancellery.

Mining and Energy

ÖAIG Bergbauholding AG: Floragasse 7, 1040 Vienna; tel (1) 505-82-80; fax (1) 505-82-88; Chair: Erich Staska; Chair, Supervisory Board: Dr Erich Wittmann; f 1988; mining.

Österreichische Elektrizitätswirtschafts-AG (Verbundgesellschaft): Am Hof 6A, 1010 Vienna; tel (1) 531-13-0; telex 114234; fax (1) 53113-4197; Chair: Dr Walter Fremuth; Dep Chair: Hannes Zach; f 1947; state undertaking responsible for bulk electricity generation, transmission and national and international interconnection; includes eight subsidiary cos.

Research

Bundesversuchs- und Forschungsanstalt Arsenal (Federal Experimental and Research Institute): Faradaygasse 3, 1031 Vienna; tel (1) 78-25-31; telex 136677; Dir: Heinz Pittner; under the admin of the Ministry of Science and Research.

Österreichisches Forschungszentrum Seibersdorf (Austrian Research Centre at Seibersdorf): 2444 Seibersdorf; tel (2254) 800; telex 14353; Chair: Dr Erich Staska; f 1956; conducts research into nuclear energy; 51%-owned by the Federal Govt.

Science and Technology

Geologische Bundesanstalt (Geological Survey of Austria): Rasumofskygasse 23, Postfach 154, 1031 Vienna; tel (1) 72-56-74; telex 132927; Dir: Dr T. E. Gattinger; Dep Dir: Dr W. Janoschek; f 1849; responsible for geological mapping and surveying, mineral deposits research and exploration and environmental geology; under the jurisdiction of the Ministry of Science and Research.

Zentralanstalt für Meteorologie und Geodynamik (Central Institute for Meteorology and Geodynamics): Hohe Warte 38, Postfach 342, 1191 Vienna; tel (1) 36-44-55; telex 131837; fax (1) 369-12-33; Dir: Dr Peter Steinhauser; Dep Dir: Dr Fritz Neuwirth; f 1851; includes depts of climatology, geophysics and environmental meteorology; under the jurisdiction of the Ministry of Science and Research.

Tourism

Österreichische Fremdenverkehrswerbung (Austrian National Tourist Office): Margaretenstr 1, 1040 Vienna; tel (1) 588-66; telex 3222306; fax (1) 588-66-20; central tourism organization.

Transport and Communications

TELECOMMUNICATIONS

Österreichische Post- und Telegraphenverwaltung: Postgasse 8-10, 1011 Vienna; tel (1) 515-51-0; telex 112300; fax (1) 512-84-14; Dir-Gen: Dr Josef Sindelka; state telecommunications authority; holds the monopoly for postal and telecommunications services.

> **Fernmeldtechnisches Zentralamt** (Telecommunications Central Office): Arsenal Objekt 22, Postfach 111, 1103 Vienna; tel (1) 78-15-11; telex 131722; fax (1) 78-29-16; Dirs: Walter Gruber, Karl Morawetz; f 1947; national organization for telecommunications engineering.

TRANSPORT

Amt für Schiffahrt (Shipping Office): Radetzkystr 2, 1030 Vienna; tel (1) 711-62; telex 111800; Dir: Karl Breitschopf; general admin of the shipping sector; under the jurisdiction of the Ministry of the Public Sector and Transport.

Bundesamt für Zivilluftfahrt (Civil Aviation Department): Schnirchgasse 11, 1030 Vienna; tel (1) 78-05-0; telex 114276; fax (1) 78-05-1206; Dir: Johann Rausch; under the jurisdiction of the Ministry of the Public Sector and Transport.

Österreichische Bundesbahnen (ÖBB) (Austrian Federal Railways): Elisabethstr 9, 1010 Vienna; tel (1) 56-50-0; telex 1377; Dir-Gen: Dr Heinrich Übleis; operates 90% of all railway routes in Austria; main regional offices are located in Innsbruck, Linz and Villach.

Österreichische Luftverkehrs AG (Austrian Airlines): Fontanastr 1, 1107 Vienna; tel (1) 68-35-11; telex 131811; Chair and Dir-Gen: Otto Binder; f 1957; 61% govt-owned; provides passenger and cargo services between five Austrian airports and 55 foreign destinations.

Wasserstraßendirektion (Waterways Directorate): Hetzgasse 2, 1030 Vienna; tel (1) 75-65-11; telex 132135; Dir: Ernst Gantar; under the administrative jurisdiction of the Ministry of Economic Affairs.

THE BAHAMAS

Head of State

The Commonwealth of The Bahamas is a constitutional monarchy, with the British monarch, as Head of State, represented locally by a Governor-General. The Governor-General appoints a Prime Minister and, on the latter's recommendation, the remainder of the Cabinet. The Cabinet advises the Governor-General, and remains responsible to the House of Assembly.

Sovereign: HM Queen Elizabeth II (succeeded to the throne 6 February 1952).

Governor-General (acting): Sir Henry Taylor (took office 26 June 1988).

Office of the Governor-General: POB N-8301, Govt House, Govt Hill, Nassau; tel 322-1875.

Legislature

Legislative power is vested in the bicameral Parliament, consisting of the British monarch (represented by the Governor-General), a Senate of 16 members (nominated by the Governor-General, the Leader of the Opposition and the Prime Minister), and a House of Representatives, with 49 members elected by universal adult suffrage for a five-year term.

Senate: Rawson Sq, Nassau; tel 322-2427; Pres: Edwin Coleby.

House of Assembly: Rawson Sq, Nassau; tel 322-2427; Speaker: Sir Clifford Darling.

MINISTRIES AND GOVERNMENT DEPARTMENTS

CABINET OFFICE
POB N-7147, Churchill Bldg, Rawson Sq, Nassau

OFFICE OF THE PRIME MINISTER
POB N-3733, Rawson Sq, Nassau
Tel 322-2805
Prime Minister: Sir Lynden Oscar Pindling
Deputy Prime Minister: Sir Clement T. Maynard

MINISTRY OF AGRICULTURE, TRADE AND INDUSTRY
POB N-3028, East Bay St, Nassau
Tel 323-1777
Minister: Ervin Knowles

MINISTRY OF CONSUMER AFFAIRS
POB N-3017, Nassau
Tel 328-1774
Minister: Bernard Nottage

MINISTRY OF EDUCATION
POB N-3913, Shirley St, Nassau
Tel 322-8140
Minister: Paul L. Adderley

MINISTRY OF EMPLOYMENT AND IMMIGRATION
POB N-3002, Clarence Bain Bldg, Nassau
Tel 322-8163
Minister: Alfred T. Maycock

MINISTRY OF FINANCE
POB N-3017, Rawson Sq, Nassau
Tel 322-4151; telex 20255
Minister: Sir Lynden Oscar Pindling

MINISTRY OF FOREIGN AFFAIRS
POB N-3746, East Hill St, Nassau
Tel 322-7624; telex 20264
Minister: Edward Charles Carter

MINISTRY OF HEALTH
POB N-3729, Post Office Bldg, East Hill St, Nassau
Tel 322-7425; telex 20516; fax 322-7788
Minister: Dr Norman Gay

MINISTRY OF HOUSING AND NATIONAL INSURANCE
POB N-2306, Boulevard Bldg, Thompson Blvd, Nassau
Tel 322-4415; telex 20164
Minister: George W. Mackey

MINISTRY OF NATIONAL SECURITY
POB N-3002, Clarence A. Bain Bldg, Nassau
Tel 322-8163
Minister: Paul L. Adderley

Immigration Department: POB N-831, Hawkins Hill, Nassau; tel 322-7530.

MINISTRY OF TOURISM
POB N-3701, Bay St, Nassau
Tel 322-7500; telex 20164
Minister of Tourism and Public Personnel:
Sir Clement T. Maynard
Dir-Gen: Baltron Bethel

MINISTRY OF TRANSPORT AND LOCAL GOVERNMENT
POB N-3008, Post Office Bldg, East Hill St, Nassau
Tel 323-7814; telex 20263
Minister: Philip M. Bethel

MINISTRY OF WORKS AND UTILITIES
POB N-8156, J. F. Kennedy Drive, Nassau
Tel 322-4830; telex 20572; fax 326-7344
Minister: Darrell E. Rolle
Responsible for public works, urban and island planning, land use and mining.

MINISTRY OF YOUTH, SPORTS AND COMMUNITY AFFAIRS
POB N-10114, Second Terrace and Collins Ave, Nassau

Tel 322-3140; fax 328-8212
Minister: Peter J. Bethel

OFFICE OF THE ATTORNEY-GENERAL
POB N-3007, East Hill St, Nassau
Tel 322-1141; fax 322-2255
Attorney-General: Sen Sean McWeeney
Dir, Legal Affairs: Ricardo Marques
Solicitor-General: Burton Hall

GOVERNMENT AGENCIES AND ORGANIZATIONS

Advisory and Supervisory Body

Gaming Board for the Commonwealth of The Bahamas: POB N-4565, Nassau; tel 327-7478; fax 327-8864; Chair: Milo B. Butler Jr; Sec: Basil H. Albury; f 1969; regulates casino gambling.

Business and Economy

BANKING

The Bahamas Development Bank: POB N-3034, Bay at Rawson Sq, Nassau; tel 322-8721; telex 20297; fax 322-28721; Chair: Ishmail Lightbourne; Man Dir (acting): Benjamin Rahming; f 1978; devt financing.

Bank of the Bahamas Ltd: POB N-7118, Euro Canadian Centre, George and Marlborough Sts, Nassau; tel 322-1690; telex 20141; Chair: Lord Pritchard; Man Dir: T. R. Kessler; f 1970; jointly owned by the Govt and European Canadian Bank; 3 brs.

The Central Bank of the Bahamas: POB N-4868, Frederick St, Nassau; tel 322-2193; telex 20115; fax 322-4321; Gov: James H. Smith; Dep Gov: Hubert L. Dean; f 1974; central bank and bank of issue.

FINANCIAL AGENCY

Treasury Department: POB N-7524, Churchill Bldg, Nassau; tel 322-4561.

INSURANCE

National Insurance Board: Nassau; tel 322-2005; Chair: B. J. Nottage; Dir: Lenox McCartney.

TRADE

The Bahamas Customs: POB N-155, Nassau; tel 325-65519; fax 325-7409; f 1914.

Defence

Police Department: POB N-458, East Hill St, Nassau; tel 322-4444; Commr: B. K. Bonamy; Dir, Fire Services: Ivan Blackman.

Royal Bahamas Defence Force: Defence Force Headquarters, POB N-3733, Clarence A. Bain Bldg, Nassau; tel 322-1944 (Defence Force Headquarters); 362-1818 (Coral Harbour Base); Commdr, Defence Force: Commodore Leon Smith; Captain, Coral Harbour: Commdr Alan Snell; f 1980; maintains order in conjunction with other law enforcement agencies; patrols the waters of The Bahamas.

Development and Planning

INVESTMENT

Bahamas Agricultural and Industrial Corpn (BAIC): POB N-4940, BAIC Bldg, East Bay St, Nassau; tel 322-3740; telex 20648; fax 322-2123; Chair: Ervin Knowles; f 1971 as Bahamas Development Corpn; encourages investment in all areas of the economy; acts as a clearance agency for devt projects.

Foreign Investment Board (FIB): Nassau; comprises the Prime Minister, Ministers with responsibility for Foreign Affairs and Tourism and others appointed by the Prime Minister; supervises purchase of land by non-nationals and other areas of foreign investment policy.

REGIONAL DEVELOPMENT

Nassau/Cable Beach/Paradise Island Promotion Board: POB N-7799, Dean's Lane, Fort Charlotte, Nassau; tel 322-8381; fax 326-5346; Chair: C. Richard Cook; Exec Vice-Pres: William Yolk; Sec: Michael C. Reckley; f 1970; 30 mems.

Energy

Bahamas Electricity Corpn: POB N-7509, Nassau; tel 325-4101; telex 20396; fax 323-6852; Chair: Leslie Miller; Gen Man: Peter Bethel; f 1956; supply of electricity.

Fishing

Department of Fisheries: POB N-3028, East Bay St, Nassau; tel 393-1777; Dir: Ronald W. Thompson; Dep Dir: Colin L. Higgs; responsible for the admin of the Bahamian fishing industry; under the Min of Agriculture, Trade and Industry.

Health and Welfare

HEALTH

Department of Environmental Health Services: POB N-3729, Nassau; tel 322-2228; telex 23607; Dir: Glenn L. Archer; Dep Dir: Edwin K. Strachan; f 1972; responsible for water quality control, food sanitation and certification, air pollution control and sanitation monitoring; enforces legislation in areas of environment, building control, vector control and solid waste management.

WELFARE

Department of Social Services: POB N-1545, Boulevard Bldg, Thompson Blvd, Nassau; tel 326-0451; Dir: Leila Greene; f 1964; provides social services in areas of public assistance, child welfare, family counselling and education and housing of senior citizens.

Legal and Judiciary

Court of Appeal: POB N-421, Nassau; Pres: Kenneth C. Henry.

Prison Department: POB N-504, Fox Hill, Nassau; tel 324-2994.

Supreme Court: POB N-8167, Nassau; tel 322-3315; Chief Justice (acting): J. C. Gonsalves Sabola; Sen Justice: Sir Denis Malone; Registrar of the Supreme Court: Joseph C. Strachan.

Media

BROADCASTING

Broadcasting Corpn of the Bahamas: POB N-1347, Centreville; tel 322-4623; telex 20253; fax 322-3924; Gen Man: Calsey Johnson; f 1936; Govt-owned commercial service.

Bahamas Television: Programme Dir (acting): R. Simmons; f 1977; broadcasts to New Providence, the Central Bahamas and Nassau.

Radio Bahamas: Programme Dir: A. Foster; f 1950; broadcasts 24 hours per day on three stations.

GOVERNMENT PUBLISHER

Official Gazette: c/o Cabinet Office, POV N-7147, Nassau; tel 322-2805; weekly.

NEWS AND INFORMATION

Department of Statistics: POB N-3904, Clarence A. Bain Bldg, Nassau; tel 325-6511; telex 20255; Dir: J. Egbert Tertullien; Sen Dep Dir: Charles Stuart; f 1968; collects, processes and publishes statistical data.

Tourism

Hotel Corpn: Nassau; tel 327-8395; Chair: Sir Lynden Pindling; Sec and Chief Finance Officer: Loran Carr.

Transport and Communications

TELECOMMUNICATIONS

Bahamas Telecommunications Corpn: Nassau; tel 325-8531; Chair: Edison M. Key.

TRANSPORT

Bahamasair: POB N-4881, Windsor Field, Nassau; tel 327-8451; telex 20239; Exec Chair: Alfred T. Maycock; Chief Operating Officer: Robert Muckleston; f 1973; scheduled services between several domestic airports, the Turks and Caicos Islands and seven US destinations.

Grand Bahama Port Authority: POB F-2666, Pioneers' Way, East Mall, Freeport; tel 352-6711.

New Providence Port Authority: POB N-1417, Prince George Wharf, Nassau; tel 322-8832; regulates principle port of the Bahamas.

Utilities

Water and Sewer Corpn: Nassau; tel 322-4830.

BAHRAIN

Head of State

Bahrain is a traditional Arab monarchy. The Amir, as Head of State, rules the country through an appointed Cabinet, which directs the country's internal and external affairs. In the absence of an elected Assembly, however, the powers of the ruling family are almost absolute.

Amir: Sheikh Isa bin Sulman al-Khalifa (succeeded to the throne 2 November 1961; took the title of Amir 16 August 1971).

Amiri Court: POB 555, Riffa Palace, Manama; tel 661451; telex 8666; Head: Yousuf Rahman al-Dosari.

Crown Prince's Court: POB 28788, Manama; tel 661681; Crown Prince: Sheikh Hamad bin Isa al-Khalifa.

Legislature

According to the 1973 Constitution, legislative power is vested in a National Assembly comprising the members of the Cabinet and 30 members elected by popular vote. However, the National Assembly was dissolved by Amiri decree in 1975; in its place the traditional majlis (assembly) system of petitioning the Amir has been revived.

MINISTRIES AND GOVERNMENT DEPARTMENTS

OFFICE OF THE PRIME MINISTER
POB 1000, Govt House, Govt Rd, Manama
Tel 262266; telex 9336
Prime Minister: Sheikh Khalifa bin Sulman al-Khalifa

MINISTRY OF COMMERCE AND AGRICULTURE
POB 5479, Diplomatic Area, Manama
Tel 531531; telex 9171
Minister: Habib Ahmad Qassim

MINISTRY OF DEFENCE
POB 245, West Rifa'a
Tel 665599; telex 8429
Minister: Maj-Gen Sheikh Khalifa bin Ahmad al-Khalifa

MINISTRY OF DEVELOPMENT AND INDUSTRY
POB 1435, Manama
Tel 291511; telex 8344
Minister: Yousuf Ahmad ash-Shirawi

MINISTRY OF EDUCATION
POB 43, Khalid bin al-Walid Rd, Qudhaibiya, Manama
Tel 258400; telex 9094
Minister: Dr Ali Muhammad Fakhro

MINISTRY OF FINANCE AND NATIONAL ECONOMY
POB 333, Govt House, Govt Rd, Manama
Tel 262400; telex 8933; fax 243655
Minister: Ibrahim Abd al-Karim Muhammad

MINISTRY OF FOREIGN AFFAIRS
POB 547, Govt House, Govt Rd, Manama
Tel 258200; telex 8228
Minister: Sheikh Muhammad bin Mubarak bin Hamad al-Khalifa

MINISTRY OF HEALTH
POB 12, Sheikh Sulman Rd, Manama
Tel 250834; telex 8511
Minister: Jawad Salim al-Arrayedh

MINISTRY OF HOUSING
POB 802, Diplomatic Area, Manama
Tel 533000; telex 8599; fax 245368
Minister: Sheikh Khalid bin Abdullah bin Khalid al-Khalifa

MINISTRY OF INFORMATION
POB 253, Isa Town, Manama
Tel 681555; telex 8399; fax 682777
Minister: Tariq Abd ar-Rahman al-Moayed

MINISTRY OF THE INTERIOR
POB 13, Police Fort Compound, Manama
Tel 254021; telex 8333
Minister: Sheikh Muhammad bin Khalifa bin Hamad al-Khalifa

Directorate of Immigration and Passport Affairs: POB 331, Diplomatic Area, Manama; tel 246000.

MINISTRY OF JUSTICE AND ISLAMIC AFFAIRS
POB 450, Diplomatic Area, Manama
Tel 531333
Minister: Sheikh Abdullah bin Khalid al-Khalifa

Directorate of Land Registration: c/o Ministry of Justice and Islamic Affairs, POB 450, Diplomatic Area, Manama; tel 531333; Dir: Sheikh Sulman bin Abdullah al-Khalifa; responsible for land registration procedures, title deeds and ownership transfers.

MINISTRY OF LABOUR AND SOCIAL AFFAIRS
POB 32333, Isa Town, Manama
Tel 687800; telex 9062
Minister: Sheikh Khalifa bin Sulman bin Muhammad al-Khalifa

MINISTRY OF PUBLIC WORKS, POWER AND WATER
POB 6000, Muharraq Causeway Rd, Manama
Tel 533133; telex 8515; fax 533027
Minister: Majid Jawad al-Jishi

MINISTRY OF STATE FOR CABINET AFFAIRS
POB 1000, Govt House, Govt Rd, Manama
Tel 262266; telex 7424
Minister (acting): Yousuf Ahmad ash-Shirawi

MINISTRY OF STATE FOR LEGAL AFFAIRS
POB 790, Govt House, Govt Rd, Manama
Tel 259990
Minister: Dr Hussain Muhammad al-Baharna

MINISTRY OF TRANSPORT
POB 10325, Diplomatic Area, Manama
Tel 232023; telex 8989
Minister: Ibrahim Muhammad Humaidan

GOVERNMENT AGENCIES AND ORGANIZATIONS

Advisory and Supervisory Bodies

Central Provisional Municipal Committee: POB 53, Govt Rd, opposite Sheikh Mubarak Bldg, Manama; tel 254847; telex 9601; Pres: Sheikh Abdullah bin Mohammad al-Khalifa; Dir: Abdullah Sa'ad al-Sherooqi; responsible for 67 villages in Bahrain; collects municipality tax from rents on properties it owns; funds environmental projects.

Civil Service Bureau: POB 1066, Diplomatic Area, Manama; tel 232626; Head: Sheikh Isa bin Ali al-Khalifa; Exec Dir: Roy C. Mesker; responsible for the centralized admin system.

Agriculture

Directorate of Agriculture: POB 251, Budaiya, Manama; tel 691951; Asst Under-Sec: Siddiq al-Alawi; Dir, Agricultural Projects: Jaffar Habib; Dir, Water Resources Bureau: Ibrahim Lori; Dir, Farmer Services: Hassain Abdul Karim.

General Poultry Co: POB 5472, Manama; tel 631001; telex 8678; Chair: Siddiq al-Alawi; 100% Govt-owned; production of poultry feed and eggs.

Business and Economy

BANKING

Bahrain Housing Bank: POB 5370, Diplomatic Area, Manama; tel 534443; telex 8599; fax 533437; Chair: Sheikh Khalid bin Abdullah bin Khalid al-Khalifa; Gen Man: Isa Sultan al-Dhawadi; f 1979; finance for the construction industry.

Bahrain Monetary Agency (BMA): POB 27, Manama; tel 241241; telex 9144; Gov: Abdullah Hassan Saif; Chair: Sheikh Khalifa bin Salman al-Khalifa; Dep Chair: Ibrahim Abd al-Karim Muhammad; f 1973, in operation from January 1975; central bank controlling currency issue; regulates exchange control and credit policy; organizes and controls banking system and bank credit.

National Bank of Bahrain BSC (NBB): POB 106, Govt Rd, Manama; tel 258800; telex 8242; fax 263876; Chair: Ahmad Ali Kanoo; Gen Man and Chief Exec: Hussain Ali Juma; f 1957; commercial bank with Govt of Bahrain as major shareholder; 19 brs.

MARKETING

Bahrain-Saudi Aluminium Marketing Co (BALCO): POB 20079, Manama; tel 532626; telex 9110; fax 532727; Gen Man: Mahmoud M. A. al-Soufi; Dep Gen Man: Ebrahim Algosaibi; f 1976; owned by the Govt of Bahrain (74.33%) and Saudi Basic Industries Corpn (25.67%); markets aluminium from the ALBA smelter and aluminium powder from Bahrain Atomizers International (see below).

NATIONALIZED INDUSTRY

Aluminium Bahrain BSC (ALBA): POB 570, Manama; tel 752222; telex 8253; fax 662120; Chief Exec: Gudvin K. Tofte; f 1971; operates a smelter owned by the Govts of Bahrain (74.9%) and Saudi Arabia (20%) and Breton Investments.

Arab Shipbuilding and Repair Yard Co (ASRY): POB 50110, Hidd; tel 671111; telex 8455; fax 670236; Chair: Sheikh Daij bin Khalifa al-Khalifa; Gen Man: Antonio J. Machado Lopes; f 1974; ship repairs and steel fabrications.

Bahrain Aluminium Extrusion Co BSC (BALEXCO): POB 1053, Manama; tel 730111; telex 8634; fax 731678; Chair: Dr Abd al-Latif Kanoo; Gen Man: Abd al-Monem Shirawi; f 1976; 100% Govt owned; supplies aluminium profiles in mill finish.

Bahrain Atomizers International: POB 5328, Manama; tel 261158; telex 8253; fax 722319; Chair: Y. Shirawi; f 1973; owned by the Bahrain Govt (51%) and Breton Investments; production of atomized aluminium powder.

Defence

Air Wing: c/o Ministry of Defence, POB 245, West Rifa'a; tel 665599; telex 8429.

Army: c/o Ministry of Defence, POB 245, West Rifa'a; tel 665599; telex 8429; Chief of Bahraini Defence Force: Brig-Gen Sheikh Abdullah bin Sulman bin Khalid al-Khalifa; Chief of Staff: Maj-Gen Sheikh Khalifa bin Ahmad bin Salman al-Khalifa.

Navy: c/o Ministry of Defence, POB 245, West Rifa'a; tel 665599; telex 8429.

Public Security Headquarters: POB 13, Police Fort Compound, Manama; tel 254021; Dir-Gen: Lt-Gen J. S. Bell; Dep Dir-Gen: Maj-Gen Ibrahim bin Mohammed al-Khalifa; responsible for internal and external security; accountable to the Ministry of the Interior.

Energy

Bahrain Directorate of Electricity: POB 2, King Faisal Rd, Manama; tel 533133; Dir: Abdullah Mohammed Jumaa; responsible to the Ministry of Public Works, Power and Water; supplies domestic and industrial power and street lighting.

Bahrain National Gas Co BSC (BANAGAS): POB 29099, Rifa'a; tel 756222; telex 9317; fax 756991; Chair: Sheikh Ibrahim bin Rashid al-Khalifa; Production Man: Ali A. Gindi; f 1979; extracts, processes and markets hydrocarbon liquids from associated gas derived from onshore Bahrain fields; 75% owned by Bahrain Govt, 12.5% by Caltex and 12.5% by Arab Petroleum Investments Corpn (APICORP).

Bahrain National Oil Co (BANOCO): POB 25504, Awali; tel 754666; telex 8670; fax 753203; Chief Exec: Muhammad Saleh Sheikh Ali; f 1976; petroleum and hydrocarbon exploration; refining, transportation, storage, distribution and marketing of petroleum products; international marketing of crude oil and petroleum products; supply of aviation fuels.

Bahrain Petroleum Co BSC (BAPCO): Awali; tel 754444; telex 8214; fax 752924; Chair: Minister of Development and Industry, Yousuf Ahmad ash-Shirawi; Chief Exec: Don F. Hepburn; f 1980; refining co owned by the Bahrain Govt (60%) and Caltex Bahrain (40%).

Health and Welfare

Directorate of Public Health: POB 42, Sheikh Salman Rd, next to the Ministry of Health, Manama; tel 230095.

General Organization for Social Insurance: POB 5319, Manama; tel 532222; telex 9142; Dir-Gen: Sheikh Isa bin Ibrahim al-Khalifa.

Legal and Judiciary

Directorate of Courts: c/o Ministry of Justice and Islamic Affairs, POB 450, Diplomatic Area, Manama; tel 531333.

High Civil Appeals Court: c/o Ministry of Justice and Islamic Affairs, POB 450, Diplomatic Area, Manama; tel 531333; telex 8520; Chief Justice: Sheikh Khalifa bin Mohammad bin Abdullah al-Khalifa.

Law Courts Directorate and Notary Public's Office: c/o Ministry of Justice and Islamic Affairs, POB 450, Diplomatic Area, Manama; tel 222217; attests official papers and contracts on behalf of the public.

Media

BROADCASTING

Bahrain Broadcasting Station: POB 194, Manama; tel 712278; telex 9259; Station Mans: Hassan Salman Kamal (Arabic Service), Ahmad M. Sulaiman (English Service); f 1955; state-owned and -operated enterprise broadcasting in Arabic and English.

GOVERNMENT PUBLISHER

Directorate of Publications: POB 26005, Manama; tel 689077; Dir: Muhammad al-Khozai.

NEWS AND INFORMATION

Central Statistics Organization: POB 5835, Ammar Bldg, Diplomatic Area, Manama; tel 242353; telex 8853; Head: Sheikh Mohammed Atiyatulla al-Khalifa; comprises three areas: computing, statistics and central population registration.

Telecommunications

Bahrain Telecommunications Co BSC (BATELCO): POB 14, Manama; tel 881881; telex 8201; fax 885566; Chair: Ibrahim Muhammad Hassan Humaidan; Gen Man: Brian Wood; f 1981; operates all telecommunications services; owned jointly by Bahrain Govt (60%) and Cable and Wireless PLC (United Kingdom).

Directorate of Posts: POB 121, Ministry of Transport Bldg, Manama; tel 232023; Dir: Ali Ebrahim Matter; responsible to the Ministry of Transport.

Tourism

Bahrain Tourism Co (BTC): POB 5831, Manama; tel 530530; telex 8929.

Directorate of Tourism and Archaeology: Manama; tel 727111; fax 271686; Dir: Sheikh Rashid al-Khalifa.

Transport

CIVIL AVIATION

Bahrain Airport Services (BAS): POB 22285, Manama; tel 320332; telex 8971; Gen Man: K. Zaman; handling agents providing traffic, catering, engineering and cargo services for airline operators.

Directorate of Civil Aviation: POB 586, Bahrain International Airport, Muharraq; tel 321332; telex 9186; Asst Under-Sec: Sheikh Hamad bin Abdullah al-Khalifa; responsible to the Ministry of Development and Industry.

ROADS

Directorate of Public Transport: POB 22500, Muharraq; tel 687979; Dir: Rashid Ali Junaid; responsible to the Ministry of Transport; regulates and maintains the public transport system.

Directorate of Roads and Sewerage: POB 5, Exhibition Rd, Hoora, Manama; tel 273003; Adviser: Jack K. McDade; road maintenance and construction; drainage and sewerage; responsible to the Ministry of Public Works, Power and Water.

Directorate of Traffic and Licensing: POB 13, Public Security, Ministry of the Interior; tel 683999; Dir: Lt-Col Daij Khalifa Daj al-Khalifa; responsible to the Ministry of the Interior; deals with road patrols, licensing and registration of vehicles, driving tests and traffic planning; promotes road safety.

SHIPPING

Directorate of Coastguards: POB 13, Manama; tel 340300; Dir: Lt-Col Adul Aziz A. al-Khalifa; responsible for policing Bahrain national waters.

Directorate of Customs and Ports: POB 15, Manama; tel 243533; telex 8642; Pres of Customs and Ports: Sheikh Daij bin Khalifa al-Khalifa; Port Dir: Eid Abdullah Yousuf; Harbour

Master: Salih Musallam; regulates customs activities and acts as port authority.

Utilities

Directorate of Construction Projects and Maintenance: POB 5, Causeway Rd, Manama; tel 24200; Dir: Kadhem al-Hashmi; carries out building projects; maintains Govt buildings; responsible to the Ministry of Public Works, Power and Water.

Directorate of Water Supply: POB 326, Manama; tel 727009; telex 8515; Dir: Saif Isa al-Bin Ali; Man of Water Services: Khalifa Ibrahim Mansoor; responsible for water supply to all areas except Awal; responsible to the Ministry of Public Works, Power and Water.

BANGLADESH

Head of State

The President is the constitutional Head of State and is elected by universal adult suffrage for a five-year term. The President has supreme control of the armed forces and appoints the Vice-President, Prime Minister and other Ministers and judges. A Council of Ministers, headed by the Prime Minister, advises and aids the President.

President: Lt-Gen (retd) Hossain Mohammad Ershad (assumed power as Chief Martial Law Administrator 24 March 1982; took office as President 11 December 1983, confirmed by referendum 21 March 1985; re-elected 15 October 1986).

Office of the President: Bangabhaban, Dhaka 2; tel (2) 404166.

Vice-President and Minister of Industry and of Law and Justice: Moudud Ahmed.

Legislature

Legislative power is vested in the unicameral Parliament (Jatiya Sangsad) which comprises 300 members directly elected by universal adult suffrage for a term of five years, plus a further 30 women members elected by the other members. For the purposes of regional administration, Bangladesh is divided into 493 sub-districts (upazillas), staffed by civil servants and headed by local chairmen.

Parliament (Jatiya Sansad): Sangsad Bhaban, Sher-e-Bangla Nagar, Dhaka 1207; tel (2) 327433; Speaker: Shamsul Huda Chowdhury; Dep Speaker: M. Riazuddin Ahmed.

MINISTRIES AND GOVERNMENT DEPARTMENTS

PRIME MINISTER'S SECRETARIAT
Gono Bhaban, Sher-e-Bangla Nagar, Dhaka
Tel (2) 328292
Prime Minister and Political Advier to the President:
Kazi Zafar Ahmed
Deputy Prime Minister: Shah Moazzem Hossain

MINISTRY OF AGRICULTURE
Bangladesh Secretariat, Bhaban 4, 2nd Storey, Dhaka
Tel (2) 404282
Minister: Maj-Gen (retd) Mohammad Abdul Munim

MINISTRY OF CIVIL AVIATION AND TOURISM
Bangladesh Secretariat, Bhaban 8, Dhaka
Tel (2) 414425
Minister of State: Lt-Col (retd) H. M. A. Gaffar

MINISTRY OF COMMERCE AND INDUSTRY
Shilpa Bhaban, Motijheel C/A, Dhaka
Telex 642201
Minister of Commerce: M. A. Sattar
Minister of Industry: Moudud Ahmed

MINISTRY OF COMMUNICATIONS
Bangladesh Secretariat, Bhaban 7, 1st 9-Storey Bldg,
8th Floor, Dhaka
Telex 65712
Minister: Anwar Hussain Manzur

Railways Division: Bangladesh Secretariat, Bhaban 7, Dhaka; tel (2) 406223.

Roads and Road Transport Division: Bangladesh Secretariat, Bhaban 7, Dhaka; tel (2) 404165.

MINISTRY OF CULTURAL AFFAIRS
Dhaka
Minister of State: Lt-Col (retd) Zafar Imam

MINISTRY OF DEFENCE
Old High Court Bldg, Dhaka
Tel (2) 259082
Minister: Lt-Gen (retd) Hossain Mohammad Ershad

MINISTRY OF EDUCATION
Bangladesh Secretariat, Bhaban 7, 2nd 9-Storey Bldg,
6th Floor, Dhaka
Minister: Sheikh Shahidul Islam

MINISTRY OF ENERGY AND MINERAL RESOURCES
Bangladesh Secretariat, Bhaban 6, New Bldg,
2nd Floor, Dhaka
Minister: Ziauddin Ahmed Bablu

MINISTRY OF ESTABLISHMENT AND REORGANIZATION
Bangladesh Secretariat, Bhaban 1, Dhaka
Tel (2) 404068
Minister: Lt-Gen (retd) Hossain Mohammad Ershad

MINISTRY OF FINANCE AND PLANNING
Bangladesh Secretariat, Bhaban 7, 1st 9-Storey Bldg,
3rd Floor, Dhaka
Tel (2) 404855; telex 65886
Minister of Finance: Dr Wahidul Huq
Minister of Planning: Air Vice-Marshal (retd) A. K.
Khandakar

MINISTRY OF FISHERIES AND LIVESTOCK
Bangladesh Secretariat, Bhaban 6, Dhaka
Tel (2) 415059
Minister: Sunil Kumar Gupta

MINISTRY OF FOREIGN AFFAIRS
Topkhana Rd, Dhaka
Tel (2) 236020; telex 642200
Minister: Anisul Islam Mahmud

MINISTRY OF FOOD
Bangladesh Secretariat, Bhaban 4, 2nd 9-Storey Bldg,
3rd Floor, Dhaka
Telex 65671
Minister: Maj (retd) Iqbal Hossain Chowdhury

MINISTRY OF HEALTH AND FAMILY PLANNING
Bangladesh Secretariat, Main Bldg, 3rd Floor, Dhaka
Minister: Dr Azizur Rahman

MINISTRY OF HOME AFFAIRS
Bangladesh Secretariat, School Bldg,
2nd and 3rd Floors, Dhaka
Minister: Maj-Gen (retd) M. Mahmudul Hasan

MINISTRY OF INFORMATION
Bangladesh Secretariat, 2nd 9-Storey Bldg, 8th Floor, Dhaka
Tel (2) 235111; telex 675619
Minister: Kazi Zafar Ahmed

MINISTRY OF IRRIGATION, WATER DEVELOPMENT AND FLOOD CONTROL
Bangladesh Secretariat, Bhaban 6, Dhaka
Tel (2) 414440
Minister: A. B. M. Golam Mustafa

MINISTRY OF JUTE AND TEXTILES
Dhaka
Minister of Jute: Mahbubur Rahman
Minister of Textiles: Abdul Malek

MINISTRY OF LABOUR AND MANPOWER
Bangladesh Secretariat, 1st 9-Storey Bldg, 4th Floor, Dhaka
Minister: Shah Moazzem Hossain

MINISTRY OF LAND ADMINISTRATION AND LAND REFORM
Bangladesh Secretariat, Bhaban 4, 2nd 9-Storey Bldg,
3rd Floor, Dhaka
Minister of Land Administration and Land Reform:
Sardar Amzad Hossain

MINISTRY OF LOCAL GOVERNMENT
Bangladesh Secretariat, Bhaban 7, 1st 9-Storey Bldg,
6th Floor, Dhaka
**Minister of Local Government, Rural Development and
Co-operatives:** Mohammad Naziur Rahman

MINISTRY OF PORTS, SHIPPING AND INLAND WATER TRANSPORT
Dhaka
Tel (2) 404345
Minister: M. Korban Ali

MINISTRY OF POSTS AND TELECOMMUNICATIONS
Bangladesh Secretariat, Bhaban 7, Dhaka
Tel (2) 414055
Minister of State: Kazi Feroj Rashid

MINISTRY OF RELIEF AND REHABILITATION
Bangladesh Secretariat, Bhaban 4, Dhaka
Tel (2) 404443
Minister: Serajul Hossain Khan

MINISTRY OF RELIGIOUS AFFAIRS
Bangladesh Secretariat, Bhaban 8, Dhaka
Tel (2) 401442
Minister of State: Nazimuddin Al-Azad

MINISTRY OF SOCIAL WELFARE AND WOMEN'S AFFAIRS
Bangladesh Secretariat, Bhaban 6, New Bldg, Dhaka
Minister of Social Welfare: Mohammad Rezwanul
Haq Chowdhury
Minister of Women's Affairs: Syeda Razia Faiz

MINISTRY OF WORKS
Bangladesh Secretariat, Main Extension Bldg,
2nd Floor, Dhaka
Minister: Mostafa Jamal Haider

MINISTRY OF YOUTH AND SPORTS
Bangladesh Secretariat, Bhaban 3, Dhaka
Tel (2) 401988
Minister: A. B. M. Ruhul Amin Howlader

GOVERNMENT AGENCIES AND ORGANIZATIONS

Agriculture

Bangladesh Fisheries Development Corpn: 24-25 Dilkusha
C/A, Motijheel, Dhaka 1000; tel (2) 259190; telex 255518; Chair:
Brig (retd) Sirajul Haque; f 1964.

Bangladesh Forest Industries Development Corpn: 186
Circular Rd, Motijheel C/A, Dhaka 1000; Chair: M. Atikullah.

Bangladesh Tea Board: 171-172 Baizid Bostami Rd, Nasi-
rabad, POB 876, Chittagong 4210; tel (31) 210491; telex 66304;
Chair: Dr Nazrul Islam; f 1951; regulates, controls and promotes
the cultivation and marketing of tea both in Bangladesh and
abroad.

Business and Economy

BANKING

Agrani Bank: 9D Dilkusha C/A, Motijheel, POB 531, Dhaka
1000; tel (2) 250906; telex 642757; Chair: Imamuddin Ahmed
Chowdhury; Man Dir: Humayun Hamid; f 1972; 859 brs.

Bangladesh Bank: Motijheel C/A, POB 325, Dhaka 1000;
tel (2) 235000; telex 65657; Gov and Chair: Shegufta Bakht
Chaudhuri; Dep Govs: Mahbubur Rahman Khan, A. S. M.
Fakhrul Ahsan; f 1971; central bank; 7 brs.

Bangladesh Krishi Bank: 83-85 Motijheel C/A, POB 357,
Dhaka 1000; tel (2) 240031; telex 642526; Chair: Maj-Gen (retd)

Mahabbat Jan Chowdhury; Man Dir: Dr A. M. M. Shawkat Ali; f 1961; credit for agricultural and rural devt; 823 brs.

Bangladesh Samabaya Bank Ltd (BSBL): 'Sambaya Sadan', 9D Motijheel C/A, POB 505, Dhaka 1000; tel (2) 231129; Chair: Muhammad Hasan Uddin Sarker; Man Dir: Muhammad Nazrul Islam; f 1948; credit for agricultural co-operatives.

Bangladesh Shilpa Bank (BSB) (Industrial Development Bank): Shilpa Bank Bhaban, 8 DIT Ave, POB 975, Dhaka; tel (2) 235151; telex 642950; Chair: K. M. Rabbani; Man Dir: Dr Muhiuddin Khan Alamgir; f 1972; fmrly Industrial Devt Bank; finances industrial devt; 13 brs.

Bank of Small Industries and Commerce (BASIC): Dhaka; Chair: A. K. N. Ahmed; f 1989; joint venture between the Govt and the BBC Foundation; provides devt finance for small-scale and cottage industries.

Grameen Bank: Mirpur-2, Dhaka 1210; tel (2) 381138; telex 642601; Chair: Prof Iqbal Mahmood; Man Dir: Dr Muhammad Yunus; f 1983; credit provision for the landless rural poor; 460 brs.

Janata Bank: 110 Motijheel C/A, Motijheel, POB 468, Dhaka 1000; tel (2) 236216; telex 65840; Chair: Brig (retd) M. Rahman Majumdar; Man Dir: Muhammad Taheruddin; f 1972; 886 brs.

Rupali Bank Ltd: Rupali Bhaban, 34 Dilkusha C/A, POB 719, Dhaka 1000; tel (2) 256021; telex 65635; Chair: A. F. M. Ehsanul Kabir Chowdhury; Man Dir: Qazi Baharul Islam; f 1972; 508 brs.

Sonali Bank: Motijheel C/A, POB 147, Dhaka 1000; tel (2) 252990; telex 642644; Chair: M. Keramat Ali; Man Dir: M. M. Nurul Haque; f 1972; 1,262 brs; 100% Govt-owned.

FINANCIAL AGENCY

Planning Commission: Planning Commission Secretariat, GO Hostel, Sher-e-Bangla Nagar, Dhaka 1207; tel (2) 315011; f 1972; Chair: President Lt-Gen (retd) Hossain Mohammad Ershad; Govt agency; responsible for economic planning and devt; prepares five-year plans and annual devt programmes; promotes savings and investment; compiles statistics and evaluates devt schemes and projects.

INSURANCE

Department of Insurance: 74 Motijheel C/A, Dhaka 1000; attached to the Ministry of Commerce and Industry; Controller of Insurance: Shamsuddin Ahmad; supervises the activities of domestic and foreign insurers.

Jiban Bima Corpn: 24 Motijheel C/A, Dhaka 1000; tel (2) 232047; Man Dir: M. A. Rahim; f 1973; comprises 36 national life insurance cos; life insurance.

Shadharan Bima Corpn: 33 Dilkusha C/A, Dhaka 1000; tel (2) 252026; Man Dir: M. Shamsul Alam; f 1973; general insurance.

MARKETING

Bangladesh Jute Corpn: 14 Topkhana Rd, Dhaka 1000 (Head Office); 139 Motijheel C/A, 2nd Floor, Dhaka 1000 (Sales and Export); tel (2) 412772, (2) 252672 (Sales and Export); telex 642213; Gen Man, Sales and Export: T. I. M. Noor-Un-Nabi; f 1985; purchases raw jute under the price support scheme and markets it abroad.

NATIONALIZED INDUSTRY

Bangladesh Chemical Industries Corpn: Shilpa Bhaban, 2nd Floor, Motijheel C/A, Dhaka 1000; tel (2) 231954; telex 65847; Chair: A. K. M. Mosharraf Hossain.

Bangladesh Jute Mills Corpn: Adamjee Court, Motijheel C/A, Dhaka 1000; tel (2) 238182; telex 65676; fax (2) 412176; Chair: Muhammad Habibur Rahman; f 1972; operates 35 jute mills and two carpet mills.

Bangladesh Small and Cottage Industries Corpn (BSCIC): 137-138 Motijheel C/A, Dhaka 1000; tel (2) 233202; Chair: Muhammad Sirajuddin; f 1957.

Bangladesh Steel and Engineering Corpn: Bangladesh Steel House, Airport Rd, Kawran Bazar, Dhaka; tel (2) 315415; telex 642225; Chair: Nefaur Rahman.

Bangladesh Sugar and Food Industries Corpn: Shilpa Bhaban, Motijheel C/A, Dhaka 1000; tel (2) 258084; telex 642210; Chair: M. Nefaur Rahman; f 1972.

Bangladesh Textile Mills Corpn: Shadharan, Bima Bhaban, 33 Dilkusha C/A, Dhaka 1000; tel (2) 252504; telex 65703; Chair: M. Nurunnabi Chowdhury; f 1972.

TRADE

Bangladesh Export Processing Zones Authority: 222 New Eskaton Rd, Dhaka 1000; tel (2) 405032; telex 642268; Chair: Brig (retd) A. K. M. Azizul Islam; f 1983; manages and controls export processing zones in Bangladesh.

Export Promotion Bureau: 122-124 Motijheel C/A, Dhaka 1000; tel (2) 230500; telex 642204; Vice-Chair: Ruhul Amin Majumder; f 1972; attached to the Ministry of Commerce and Industry; promotes and co-ordinates export devt; monitors export performance and progress; disseminates information on exports; formulates the country's export policies.

Trading Corpn of Bangladesh: 'TCB Bhaban', Kawran Bazar, Dhaka 1215; tel (2) 325030-39; telex 642217; fax (2) 412782; Chair: Brig (retd) M. Habibur Rahman; f 1972; responsible to the Ministry of Commerce and Industry; imports and exports goods and markets them through appointed dealers and agents.

Defence

Armed Forces: Army Headquarters, Dhaka Cantonment, Dhaka; Commdr-in-Chief: Lt-Gen (retd) Hossain Mohammad Ershad.

Air Force: Airport Rd, Dhaka 15; tel (2) 310194; Chief of Air Staff: Air Vice-Marshal Mumtazuddin Ahmed.

Army: Dhaka Cantonment, Dhaka; tel (2) 310341; telex 642200; Chief of Staff: Lt-Gen Muhammad Atiqur Rahman.

Navy: Banani, Dhaka 13; tel (2) 60025; telex 602209; Chief of Naval Staff: Rear-Adm Sultan Ahmed.

Development

Bangladesh House Building Finance Corpn (BHBFC): HBFC Bldg, 22 Purana Paltan, POB 2167, Dhaka 1000; tel (2) 415315; Chair: Hashimuddin Ahmed; Man Dir: Khawja Zahurul Haq; f 1952; provision of low-interest credit for house-building; 20 brs.

Bangladesh Shilpa Rin Sangstha (BSRS) (Industrial Loan Agency): 5th-7th Floors, BIWTA Bhaban, 141-143 Motijheel C/A, POB 473, Dhaka 1000; tel (2) 252016; Chair: Mir Ataul Hoque Khandker; Man Dir: M. Sekandar Ali; f 1972; 4 brs.

Investment Corpn of Bangladesh (ICB): BSB Bldg, 12th-14th Floors, 8 Rajuk Ave, POB 2058, Dhaka 1000; tel (2) 254112; Chair: Maj-Gen (retd) M. A. Matin; Man Dir: Ghiasuddin Ahmed; f 1976; 5 brs.

Legal and Judiciary

Supreme Court: Segunbagicha, Dhaka 2; tel (2) 433585; Chief Justice: Dr F. K. M. Abdul Munim; Attorney-Gen: M. Nurullah.

Media

BROADCASTING

National Broadcasting Authority: NBA House, Shahbag Ave, Dhaka; tel (2) 503342; telex 642228; Chair: Saiful Bari; f 1984 by merger of Radio Bangladesh and Bangladesh Television.

Bangladesh Television (BTV): POB 456, Rampura, Dhaka 1219; tel (2) 400131; telex 65624; Chair: Saiful Bari; Gen Man: Mostafa Kamal Syed; f 1971; daily broadcasts in colour on one channel for 7 hours.

Radio Bangladesh: Chair and Dir-Gen: Enamul Huq; f 1971.

GOVERNMENT PUBLISHERS

Bangladesh Government Press: Tejgaon, Dhaka; tel (2) 603897; f 1972.

Department of Films and Publications: 112 Circuit House Rd, Dhaka 1000; tel (2) 402263.

NEWS AND INFORMATION

Bangladesh Bureau of Statistics: Bldg 8, Room 12, Bangladesh Secretariat, Dhaka; tel (2) 409571; Sec: Abdus Salam; f 1971; responsible to the Ministry of Finance and Planning; publishes statistical yearbooks and monthly bulletins; carries out censuses.

Press Information Department: Bangladesh Secretariat, Bhaban 6, Dhaka 1000; tel (2) 400958; telex 65619.

Mining and Energy

Bangladesh Atomic Energy Commission (BAEC): 4 Kazi Nazrul Islam Ave, POB 158, Dhaka 1000; tel (2) 502600; telex 632203; Chair: Dr M. A. Mannan; Sec: Rafiquel Alam; f 1964; carries out research into atomic energy; runs a nuclear reactor, an atomic energy centre, nuclear medicine centres, and a nuclear power project involving the exploitation of uranium and thorium.

Bangladesh Mineral Exploration and Development Corpn: HBFC Bldg, 8th-9th Floors, 22 Purana Paltan, Dhaka 1000; telex 65737; Chair: M. W. Ali.

Bangladesh Oil, Gas and Mineral Corpn (Petrobangla): 122-124 Motijheel C/A, Chamber Bldg, Dhaka 1000; tel (2) 253131; telex 642765; Chair: Heasum Uddin Ahmed; Sec: Atiqur Rahman; f 1972; responsible to the Ministry of Energy and Mineral Resources; gas, oil and mineral exploration, devt, production and marketing.

Petroleum Corpn: 10 Dilkusha C/A, Dhaka 2; tel (2) 235051; Chair: Abdul Kasem.

Tourism

Bangladesh Parjatan Corpn (National Tourist Organization): 233 Airport Rd, Tejgaon, Dhaka 1215; tel (2) 325155; telex 642206; Chair: Habibur Rahman; Gen Man, Information and Tours: Gazi Sadeq; encourages and develops tourism in Bangladesh; carries out research into various aspects of tourism; runs training institutes for people involved in the tourist industry.

Transport

Bangladesh Inland Water Transport Corpn: 5 Dilkusha C/A, Dhaka 1000; tel (2) 257092; f 1972.

Bangladesh Railway: Railway HQ, Chittagong; tel (31) 500120; telex 66200; Dir-Gen, Railway Div: S. Hasan Ahmad; Gen Man, East Zone: M. Matiur Rahman; Gen Man, West Zone: M. Luftur Rahman; Gen Man, Projects: A. K. M. Amanul Islam Chowdhury; under control of the Railway Division of the Ministry of Communications (see above); divided into East and West zones with HQ at Chittagong and Rajshahi.

Bangladesh Road Transport Corpn: Paribhaban, DIT Ave, Dhaka; f 1961; runs transport services including a truck division; transports Govt foodgrain.

Bangladesh Shipping Corpn: Pine View, 100 Agrabad C/A, POB 641, Chittagong; tel (31) 501855; telex 66277; Chair: Janab M. Korban Ali; Man Dir: Tareck Anis Ahmed; f 1972; maritime shipping.

Biman (Bangladesh Airlines): Biman Bhaban, Motijheeel C/A, Dhaka 1000; tel (2) 240151; telex 642649; Chair: Minister of State for Civil Aviation and Tourism, Lt-Col (retd) H. M. A. Gaffar; Man Dir: Muhammad Faizur Razzaque; f 1972; 100% state-owned; internal services to major towns; international services to Middle- and Far-Eastern destinations and to Europe.

Chittagong Port Authority: POB 2013, Chittagong; tel (31) 505041; telex 66264; Chair: Md Shahadat Hossain; furnishes bunkering and lighterage facilities, ship repair, provisions and drinking water supplies.

BARBADOS

Head of State

Barbados is a constitutional monarchy. The British sovereign, as Head of State, is represented locally by a Governor-General. Government is effectively by the Cabinet, appointed by the Governor-General, which is headed by the Prime Minister and is responsible to Parliament. Provision is also made in the constitution for a Privy Council, presided over by the Governor-General.

Sovereign: HM Queen Elizabeth II (succeeded to the throne 6 February 1952).

Governor-General: Sir Hugh Springer (took office 24 February 1984).

Office of the Governor-General: Govt House, St Michael; tel 429-2946.

Legislature

Legislative power is vested in Parliament, comprising the Senate and the House of Assembly. The 21 members of the Senate are appointed by the Governor-General, while the 27 members of the House of Assembly are elected for a five-year term by universal adult suffrage. Local administration is provided by 11 parishes, controlled by the central Government.

Senate: Parliament Bldg, Bridgetown; tel 426-5331; Pres: Frank Walcott.

House of Assembly: Parliament Bldg, Bridgetown; tel 426-3717; Speaker: Lawson Weekes; Clerk of Parliament: George Brancker.

MINISTRIES AND GOVERNMENT DEPARTMENTS

OFFICE OF THE PRIME MINISTER
Govt Headquarters, Bay St, St Michael
Tel 436-6435
Prime Minister: Lloyd Erskine Sandiford
Deputy Prime Minister: Philip M. Greaves
Minister of State: Sen L. V. Harcourt Lewis
Parliamentary Secretary: Anderson Morrison

MINISTRY OF AGRICULTURE, FOOD AND FISHERIES
POB 505, Graeme Hall, Christ Church
Tel 428-4150
Minister: Warwick O. Franklyn

MINISTRY OF THE CIVIL SERVICE
Govt Headquarters, Bay St, St Michael
Tel 429-8955
Minister: Lloyd Erskine Sandiford

MINISTRY OF EDUCATION AND CULTURE
Jemmott's Lane, St Michael
Tel 427-3272
Minister: Cyril V. Walker
Parliamentary Secretary: Maizie Barker-Welch

MINISTRY OF EMPLOYMENT, LABOUR RELATIONS AND COMMUNITY DEVELOPMENT
Marine House, Hastings, Christ Church
Tel 427-5420; telex 2222
Minister: N. Keith Simmons
Responsible for the Youth and Community Devt Dept, Welfare Dept, Labour Dept, Child Care Board, Women's Bureau, National Assistance Board, National Conservation Commission and the Coastal Conservation Project Unit.

MINISTRY OF FINANCE AND ECONOMIC AFFAIRS
Govt Headquarters, Bay St, St Michael
Tel 436-6435
Minister: Lloyd Erskine Sandiford
Minister of State: Sen Dr Carl Clarke

Energy Division: c/o Ministry of Finance and Economic Affairs, Govt Headquarters, Bay St, St Michael; tel 429-5254; Permanent Sec: E. Griffith; Dir, Petroleum and Natural Gas: Louis de Verteuil; f 1979; administers the Govt's energy policies and programmes.

MINISTRY OF FOREIGN AFFAIRS
1 Culloden Rd, St Michael
Tel 436-2990; telex 2222; fax 429-6652
Minister: Maurice A. King

MINISTRY OF HEALTH
Jemmott's Lane, St Michael
Tel 426-5080
Minister: Brandford M. Taitt

MINISTRY OF HOUSING AND LANDS
Marine House, Hastings, Christ Church
Tel 427-5420
Minister: Harold A. Blackman

MINISTRY OF INTERNATIONAL TRANSPORT, TELECOMMUNICATIONS AND IMMIGRATION
Herbert House, Reef Rd, Fontabelle, St Michael
Tel 427-5163
Minister: Philip M. Greaves

MINISTRY OF LEGAL AFFAIRS
Marine House, Hastings, Christ Church
Tel 427-5420
Attorney-General and Minister: Maurice A. King

MINISTRY OF TOURISM AND SPORTS
PO Bldg, Cheapside, Bridgetown
Tel 436-4830; telex 2222; fax 436-9280
Minister: Wesley W. Hall

MINISTRY OF TRADE, INDUSTRY AND COMMERCE
Savannah Lodge, Garrison, St Michael
Tel 427-5270
Minister: E. Evelyn Greaves

MINISTRY OF TRANSPORT AND WORKS
POB 25, Bridgetown
Tel 429-2191; telex 2203
Minister: Donald Blackman

GOVERNMENT AGENCIES AND ORGANIZATIONS

Business and Economy

BANKING

Barbados Development Bank: POB 50, Level 7, Central Bank Bldg, Church Village, St Michael; tel 436-8870; telex 2295; Gen Man: Richard Leslie; f 1969.

Barbados National Bank: 11 James St, POB 1002, Bridgetown; tel 427-5920; telex 2271; Chair: Sen Amory Phillips; Man Dir: L. G. Francis; f 1978 by the merger of the Barbados Savings Bank, Sugar Industry Agricultural Bank, Agricultural Credit Bank and The Public Officers Housing Loan Fund; 5 brs.

Central Bank of Barbados: POB 1016, Church Village, St Michael; tel 436-6870; telex 2251; fax 427-9559; Gov: Dr Kurleigh King; Gen Man (acting): Calvin M. Springer; f 1972; central bank and bank of issue.

FINANCIAL AGENCIES

Barbados Mortgage Finance Co: Country Rd, St Michael; majority shareholder is the Barbados National Bank; provides financial help for construction and purchase of low- and medium-cost housing; manages savings and deposit accounts.

Office of Inland Revenue: Treasury Bldg, Bridgetown; tel 426-5544; Commr: Gladstone Waithe.

INSURANCE

Insurance Corpn of Barbados: Roebuck St, Bridgetown; tel 427-5590; telex 2317; Chair: John Mayers; Gen Man: David Deane; f 1978.

National Insurance Office: Fairchild St, Bridgetown; tel 436-6335; Chair: Dr Frank Alleyne; Dep Chair: Eric Armstrong; Dir (acting): Grantley Smith; Dep Dir: Oswald Simmons; f 1967; receives contributions from employers and self-employed persons; records investments and prepares financial reports; pays sickness, maternity, invalidity, unemployment, old age and occupational injury benefits and funeral grants.

MARKETING

Barbados Marketing Corpn: POB 703C, Bridgetown; tel 427-5250; telex 2253; Chair: Robert Morris; Gen Man: Clyde King.

NATIONALIZED INDUSTRY

Arawak Cement Co Ltd: Checker Hall, St Lucy; tel 439-9880; telex 2478; fax 439-7976; Chair: Tony Gibbs; Gen Man: Laurence Hawkins; f 1981; joint venture between Trinidad and Barbados; manufacture of bulk cement; marketing and export of cement through co-owned dock to markets in the Caribbean.

Barbados Sugar Industry Ltd: POB 719C, Warrens, St Thomas; tel 425-0010; telex 2418; fax 425-3505; Man Dir: Errie A. B. Deane; Sec: D. H. A. Johnson.

TRADE

Barbados Export Promotion Corpn: Pelican Industrial Park, St Michael; tel 427-5752; telex 2486; fax 427-5867; Exec Dir: Philip A. W. Williams; assists exporters in finding new markets for their products.

Defence

Barbados Defence Force: Headquarters, St Anne's Fort, The Garrison, St Michael; tel 436-6185; Chief of Staff: Brig Rudyard Lewis.

Royal Barbados Police Force: Coleridge St, Bridgetown, St Michael; tel 436-7060; Commr: Orville Durant; Sen Supt: H. D. Rouse; f 1835.

Development

Barbados Agricultural Development Corpn: Fairy Valley, Christ Church; tel 428-0001; Chair: E. R. S. Cumberbatch; Gen Man: G. V. J. Garvey; Sec: Frank B. Taylor; f 1965; responsible for programme of diversification and land reforms.

Barbados Industrial Development Corpn: POB 250, Pelican House, Princess Alice Highway, Bridgetown; tel 427-5350; telex 2295; fax 426-7802; Chair: Frank McConney; Gen Man: Roy Clarke; f 1956; facilitates the devt of the industrial sector, especially in the areas of manufacturing and data-processing; offers free consultancy to investors; provides factory space; administers the Fiscal Incentives Legislation.

Barbados National Housing Corpn: 'The Garden', Country Rd, St Michael; tel 436-6400; Chair: David Bowen; Gen Man: Ivan Gibson; Sec: Cynthia Holder; f 1973; responsible to the Ministry of Housing and Lands; acquires, holds and manages land and other property to sell, let and lease; involved in devt, building, maintenance, etc; provides water, gas, electricity, sewage and other services; executes plans for slum clearance and re-devt.

Legal and Judiciary

Superintendency of Prisons: Station Hill, St Michael; tel 429-2567; Supt: Carl Harewood.

Supreme Court: Judiciary Office, Bridgetown; tel 426-3461; Chief Justice: Sir Denys A. Williams; Puisne Judges: Clifford S. Husbands, John Husband, Elliot F. Belgrave, Errol DaCosta Chase; Registrar: Marie MacCormack; Chief Magistrate: Frank King; the Supreme Court comprises a High Court and a Court of Appeal.

Media

BROADCASTING

Barbados Rediffusion Service Ltd: River Rd, St Michael; tel 426-0820; fax 429-8093; Gen Man: Vic Fernandes; Programme Dir: J. Rogers; f 1935; public co.

Caribbean Broadcasting Corpn (CBC): POB 900, Bridgetown; tel 429-2041; telex 2560; fax 429-4795; Chair: Prof E. R. Walrond; f 1963; administers two radio stations and one TV station in Barbados:

> **CBC Radio:** POB 900, Bridgetown; tel 429-2041; telex 2560; Gen Man: Sam Taitt; Programme Man: C. Graham; f 1963.

> **Radio Liberty FM:** POB 900, Bridgetown; tel 429-2041; telex 2560; f 1984.

> **CBC TV:** POB 900, Bridgetown; tel 429-2041; telex 2560; Programme Man: O. Cumberbatch; f 1964; Channel Nine, operated by Caribbean Broadcasting Corpn.

GOVERNMENT PUBLISHER

Government Printing Office: Bay St, Bridgetown; tel 436-6776; publishes official Govt newspaper twice a week.

NEWS AND INFORMATION

Barbados Statistical Service: National Insurance Bldg, Fairchild St, Bridgetown; tel 427-7841.

Mining and Energy

Barbados National Oil Co Ltd (BNOCL): Woodbourne, St Philip; tel 423-0918; telex 2334; fax 423-0166; Gen Man: Ronald Hewitt; Operations Man: Gordon Worme; f 1982; oil and gas exploration.

National Petroleum Corpn (NPC): Wildey, St Michael; tel 426-5012; Chair: J. Cliviston King; Gen Man (acting): Ronald G. King; f 1951; production, transmission and distribution of natural gas.

Science and Technology

Meteorological Office: Grantley Adams International Airport, Christ Church; tel 428-0910; Dir: Deighton Best.

National Council for Science and Technology: 'Flodden', Culloden Rd, St Michael; tel 426-3870.

Tourism

Barbados Board of Tourism: POB 242, Harbour Rd, Bridgetown; tel 427-2623; telex 2420; Chair: Clevedon Mayers; Dir of Tourism: Patricia Nehaul; f 1958; responsible to the Ministry of Tourism and Sports.

Barbados Tourism Investment Corpn (BTIC): Fontabelle, St Michael; promotes investment in the tourist industry by co-operating with the private sector to construct hotels and leisure facilities, aiding investors to take advantage of tax incentives and co-ordinating tourism-related devt with other Govt bodies.

Caribbean Tourism, Research and Development Centre: Mervre, Marine Gardens, Christ Church; tel 427-5242.

Transport

Barbados Port Authority: Port Authority Bldg, Harbour Rd, St Michael; tel 436-6883; Man: Peter Parker.

Caribbean Air Cargo Ltd (CARICARGO): Grantley Adams International Airport, Christ Church; tel 428-4180; telex 2417; fax 428-0263; Chair: Peter Look Hong; Man Dir: Ian De V. Archer; f 1979; jointly owned by the Govts of Barbados and Trinidad and Tobago; it was announced in August 1989 that Venezuela was also to become a shareholder; services between the Eastern Caribbean, the USA and Puerto Rico.

Utilities

Public Utilities Board: cnr Pine Plantation Rd, Collymore Rock, St Michael; tel 427-5693; Exec Sec: L. A. Chandler; f 1955; five mems; regulates public utilities; supervises the provision of electricity and telephone services by private cos.

BELGIUM

Head of State

Belgium is a constitutional monarchy. Although the monarch is nominally the supreme head of the executive, power is in fact exercised by the Cabinet, headed by a Prime Minister, which is responsible to Parliament. The sovereign has the right to veto legislation, but in practice does not exercise it.

Sovereign: HM King Baudouin (Boudewijn) (took the oath 17 July 1951).

Office of HM the King: Palais Royal/ Koninklijk Paleis, rue de Bréderode, 1000 Brussels; tel (2) 513-07-70; Grand Marshal of the Court: Sylvain Frey.

Legislature

Legislative power is vested in Parliament, comprising the Chambre des Représentants/ Kamer van Volksvertegenwoordigers (Chamber of Representatives), with 212 members, elected by proportional representation by universal adult suffrage for a four-year term, and the Sénat/ Senaat (Senate), with 182 members, chosen by a mixture of direct and indirect election, and also including the heir to the throne. Each linguistic community, and the capital, has regional powers in cultural and economic affairs.

Sénat/Senaat (Senate): Palais de la Nation, 1 place de la Nation, 1000 Brussels; tel (2) 515-82-11; telex 65517; fax (2) 514-06-85; Pres: F. Swaelen; Sec-Gen: H. Nys.

Chambre des Représentants/Kamer van Volksvertegenwoordigers (Chamber of Representatives): Palais de la Nation, 2 place de la Nation, 1000 Brussels; tel (2) 519-81-11; fax (2) 512-65-33; Pres: C. F. Nothomb; Clerk: F. Grulich.

MINISTRIES AND GOVERNMENT DEPARTMENTS

OFFICE OF THE PRIME MINISTER
16 rue de la Loi, 1000 Brussels
Tel (2) 513-80-20; telex 62400
Prime Minister: Dr Wilfried Martens
Deputy Prime Ministers: Willy Claes, Philippe Moureaux, Jean-Luc Dehaene, Melchior Wathelet, Hugo Schlitz.

MINISTRY FOR THE BRUSSELS REGION
21-23 blvd du Régent, 1000 Brussels
Tel (2) 513-82-00; telex 25190
Minister: Philippe Moureaux

MINISTRY OF THE BUDGET AND SCIENTIFIC POLICY
26 rue de la Loi, 1040 Brussels
Tel (2) 237-93-11; telex 22292; fax (2) 237-93-64
Minister: Hugo Schlitz

MINISTRY OF THE CIVIL SERVICE
Lynton Bldg, 31 rue du Commerce, 1040 Brussels
Tel (2) 513-88-40
Minister: Raymond Langendries

MINISTRY OF COMMUNICATIONS AND INSTITUTIONAL REFORMS (FLEMISH SECTOR)
65 rue de la Loi, 1040 Brussels
Tel (2) 237-67-11; telex 25183
Minister: Jean-Luc Dehaene

MINISTRY OF DEVELOPMENT CO-OPERATION
World Trade Center, 162 blvd Emile Jacqmain, 1210 Brussels
Tel (2) 210-19-11; telex 20832; fax (2) 217-33-28
Minister: André Geens

MINISTRY OF ECONOMIC AFFAIRS AND PLANNING
23 square de Meeûs, 1040 Brussels
Tel (2) 511-19-30; telex 21062; fax (2) 514-03-89
Minister: Willy Claes

MINISTRY OF EMPLOYMENT AND LABOUR
51-53 rue Belliard, 1040 Brussels
Tel (2) 233-41-11; telex 22937; fax (2) 233-44-88
Minister: Luc van den Brande

MINISTRY OF FINANCE
12 rue de la Loi, 1000 Brussels
Tel (2) 233-81-11
Minister: Philippe Maystadt

MINISTRY OF FOREIGN AFFAIRS
2 rue des Quatre Bras, 1000 Brussels
Tel (2) 516-81-11; fax (2) 514-30-67
Minister: Mark Eyskens

MINISTRY OF FOREIGN TRADE
2 rue des Quatre Bras, 1000 Brussels
Tel (2) 516-83-11; fax (2) 512-72-21
Minister: Robert Urbain

**MINISTRY OF INSTITUTIONAL REFORMS
(FRENCH SECTOR)**
21-23 blvd du Régent, 1000 Brussels
Tel (2) 513-82-00
Minister: Philippe Moureaux

**MINISTRY OF THE INTERIOR AND FOR THE
MODERNIZATION OF PUBLIC SERVICES AND
NATIONAL SCIENTIFIC AND CULTURAL
INSTITUTIONS**
94 rue Royale, 1000 Brussels
Tel (2) 210-84-11; fax (2) 217-81-26
Minister: Louis Tobback

MINISTRY OF JUSTICE
4 place Poelaert, 1000 Brussels
Tel (2) 513-67-88; telex 62440; fax (2) 514-15-75
Minister: Melchior Wathelet

MINISTRY OF THE MIDDLE CLASSES
61 rue de la Régence, 1000 Brussels
Tel (2) 511-19-48
Minister: Melchior Wathelet

MINISTRY OF NATIONAL DEFENCE
8 rue Lambermont, 1000 Brussels
Tel (2) 512-16-10; telex 61104
Minister: Guy Coëme

**MINISTRY OF NATIONAL EDUCATION
(FLEMISH SECTOR)**
3 rue Ducale, 1000 Brussels
Tel (2) 513-28-90; telex 26750
Minister: Willy Claes

**MINISTRY OF NATIONAL EDUCATION
(FRENCH SECTOR)**
68A rue du Commerce, 1040 Brussels
Tel (2) 511-72-60; telex 24619; fax (2) 511-94-07
Minister: Yvan Ylieff

MINISTRY OF PENSIONS
31 rue du Commerce, 1040 Brussels
Tel (2) 513-63-70
Minister: Alain van der Biest

**MINISTRY OF POSTS AND
TELECOMMUNICATIONS**
56 rue de la Loi, 1040 Brussels
Tel (2) 230-13-30; telex 22681; fax (2) 230-57-02
Minister: Freddy Willockx

MINISTRY OF PUBLIC WORKS
9th Floor, 155 rue de la Loi, 1040 Brussels
Tel (2) 734-91-07; telex 63477; fax (2) 230-99-12
Minister: Paula d'Hondt-van Opdenbosch

MINISTRY OF SOCIAL AFFAIRS
5th Floor, 56 rue de la Loi, 1040 Brussels
Tel (2) 230-01-70; fax (2) 230-38-95
Minister: Philippe Busquin

GOVERNMENT AGENCIES AND ORGANIZATIONS

Advisory and Supervisory Bodies

Directorate of External Markets Administration: 2 rue des Quatre Bras, 1000 Brussels; tel (2) 516-81-11.

Directorate of Overseas Economic and Financial Interests: 9 rue Brédero, 1000 Brussels; tel (2) 513-61-47.

General Administration for Development Co-operation: A. G. Bldg, 5 place du Champs de Mars, BP 57, 1050 Brussels; tel (2) 513-90-60.

General Directorate of Foreign Economic Relations: 2 rue des Quatre Bras; tel (2) 516-81-11.

Price Regulation Commission: 24-26 rue J. A. de Mot, 1040 Brussels; tel (2) 233-61-11.

Business and Economy

BANKING

Banque Nationale de Belgique: 5 blvd de Berlaimont, 1000 Brussels; tel (2) 221-21-11; telex 21355; fax (2) 221-31-01; Gov: Alfons Verplaetse; Vice-Gov: William Fraeys; Exec Dirs: Frans Junius, Jean-Pierre Pauwels, Guy Quaden, Jean-Jacques Rey; f 1850; central bank and bank of issue; supervises the country's external monetary relations; 2 brs.

Caisse Nationale de Crédit Professionnel (CNCP)/Nationale Kas voor Beroepskrediet (NKBK): 16 blvd de Waterloo, 1000 Brussels; tel (2) 513-64-80; telex 22026; fax (2) 514-31-55; Dir-Gen: D. Ponlot; Dirs: F. Jacobs, C. Lejeune; f 1929; financial services for small- and medium-sized businesses, associations of small businesses and the self-employed.

Commission Bancaire: 99 ave Louise, 1050 Brussels; tel (2) 535-22-11; telex 62107; fax (2) 535-23-23; Pres: Jean-Louis Duplat; Man Dirs: P. Dubois, G. Gelders, M. Maes, J. Verteneuil; f 1935; superintends the application of the law relating to the legal status of banks and bankers and to the public issue of securities; responsible for the application of the legal status of common trust funds, of certain non-banking financial enterprises, of holding cos and of the private savings banks.

Crédit Communal de Belgique SA/Gemeentekrediet van België NV: 44 blvd Pachéco, 1000 Brussels; tel (2) 214-41-11; telex 26354; fax (2) 214-40-38; Chair: F. Narmon; Vice-Chair: L. Onclin; f 1860; 1,318 brs.

Gewestelijke Investeringsmaatschappij voor Vlaanderen: 37 Karel Oomstraat, 2018 Antwerp; tel (3) 233-83-83; telex 34167; fax (3) 234-14-87; Pres: R. van Outryve d'Ydewalle; Chief Exec: G. van Acker; f 1980; devt bank; promotes private enterprise; encourages public initiatives; implements the industrial policy of state and regions.

Institut National de Crédit Agricole/Nationaal Instituut voor Landbouwkrediet: 56 rue Joseph II, 1040 Brussels; tel (2) 234-12-11; telex 26863; Pres: J. Detry; f 1937; grants agricultural credits and credits to agricultural associations; finances agricultural products and foodstuffs.

FINANCIAL AGENCIES

Administrator-General of Taxes: 5 ave Galilée, BP 3, 1030 Brussels; tel (2) 219-27-20; responsible to the Ministry of Finance.

Director-General of Budget and Control of Expenditures: Tour Astro, 19 ave de l'Astronomie, 1030 Brussels; tel (2) 219-03-80; under the control of the Ministry of Finance.

Institut de Réescompte et de Garantie (IRG)/Herdisconteringen Waarborginstituut (HWI): 78 rue du Commerce, 1040 Brussels; tel (2) 511-73-30; fax (2) 514-34-50; Chair: Marcel D'Haeze; Gen Man: Willy van Hoeck; f 1935; intervenes in favour of financial intermediaries in case of insolvency; deals with banks, public credit institutions, private savings banks and other financial intermediaries; administers a deposit protection scheme.

Société Nationale de Crédit à l'Industrie (SNCI)/ Nationale Maatschappij voor Krediet aan de Nijverheid (NMKN): 14 ave de l'Astronomie, 1030 Brussels; tel (2) 214-12-11; telex 25996; fax (2) 218-04-78; Chair: K. Dierckx; Gen Man: Alfred Rampen; f 1919; semi-public credit institution; provides long-, medium- and short-term credit for industrial and commercial enterprises; 16 brs.

Treasury: 30 ave des Arts, 1040 Brussels; tel (2) 233-81-11; responsible to the Ministry of Finance.

INSURANCE

Office National du Ducroire (OND)/De Nationale Delcrederedienst: 40 square de Meeûs, 1040 Brussels; tel (2) 509-42-11; telex 21147; fax (2) 513-50-59; Gen Man: Willy Boes; f 1939; insurance cover for credit risks undertaken by exporting cos; insurance of Belgian investments abroad; insurance for certain imports; responsible to the Minister of Economic Affairs.

TRADE

Office Belge du Commerce Extérieur (OBCE): World Trade Center, 162 blvd Emile Jacqmain, 1000 Brussels; tel (2) 219-44-50; telex 21502; Dir: M. A. Hubert; promotes the export of Belgian products; assists Belgian exporting companies.

Defence

Armed Forces: Quartier Reine Elisabeth, rue d'Evere, 1140 Brussels; tel (2) 243-31-11; Commdr-in-Chief: King Baudouin; Chief of Staff: Lt-Gen M. Gysemberg.

Air Force: Quartier Reine Elisabeth, rue d'Evere, 1140 Brussels; tel (2) 243-31-11; Chief of Staff: Lt-Gen Jacques D. M. Lefebvre.

Army: Quartier Reine Elisabeth, rue d'Evere, 1140 Brussels; tel (2) 243-33-80; Chief of Staff: Lt-Gen Jean Berhin.

Navy: Quartier Reine Elisabeth, rue d'Evere, 1140 Brussels; tel (2) 243-31-11; Chief of Staff: Vice-Adm Edmond P. E. H. M. J. Poullet.

Development and Planning

INVESTMENT

Flanders' Investment Opportunities Council (FIOC): 2nd Floor, 100 Trierstraat, 2nd Floor, 1040 Brussels; tel (2) 230-12-25; telex 62073; fax (2) 230-98-34; Man Dir: Josee Mercken; Advisers: Jos Bollen, Fabienne de Vleeschauwer; f 1988; investment office of the Govt of Flanders; assists foreign investors; promotes and markets Flanders as an investment area; offices in the USA, Scandinavia and South East Asia.

Nationale Investeringsmaatschappij (NIM)/Société Nationale d'Investissement (SNI): 63-67 rue Montoyer, 1040 Brussels; tel (2) 237-06-11; telex 25744; Pres: P. Wilmes; f 1962; reconstituted in 1976 as a 100% state-owned holding co; cash-raising powers to muster equity capital; private sector involvement on governing body and investment committee.

Société de Développement Régional de Bruxelles (SDRB) (Brussels Regional Development Agency): 39 ave des Arts, 1040 Brussels; tel (2) 510-39-11; fax (2) 514-29-70; Chair: Luc Bernard; Gen Mans: Camille Deguelle, Jos Crabbe, Marc Pion; f 1974; promotes the economic devt and the urban renovation of the Brussels area.

Société Régionale d'Investissement de Wallonie: 19 place Joséphine-Charlotte, 5100 Jambes; tel (81) 30-64-11; telex 59415; Pres: Bernard Marchand; f 1979; shareholding co; promotes creation, restructuring and extension of private enterprise; stimulates state and provincial industrial policy.

PLANNING

Bureau du Plan (Planning Office): 47-49 ave des Arts, 1040 Brussels; tel (2) 511-23-90; f 1970; co-ordinates economic planning with ministries and committees concerned; promotes national and regional economic devt; promotes employment security and social progress.

General Directorate of Regional and Sectoral Planning: 2 rue des Quatre Bras, 1000 Brussels; tel (2) 516-81-11.

Education and Research

Centre d'Etude de l'Energie Nucléaire (CEN)/Studiecentrum voor Kernenergie (SCK): 1 rue Charles Lemaire, 1160 Brussels; tel (2) 661-08-11; telex 22718; fax (2) 660-75-63; Chair of Board and Man Dir: Ivo van Vaerenbergh; Gen Man: Carl M. Malbrain; f 1952; carries out research into nuclear energy; depts research into materials devt, environment and energy, technology and prototypes, nuclear reactors, nuclear chemistry of fuel cycle, etc.

Institut Interuniversitaire des Sciences Nucléaires/ Interuniversitair Instituut voor Kernwetenschappen: 5 rue d'Egmont, 1050 Brussels; Pres: S. Loccufier; Gen Sec: P. Levaux; f 1947; encourages research in nuclear science and solid state physics in advanced teaching and research establishments.

Legal and Judiciary

Cour de Cassation/Hof van Cassatie (Supreme Court of Justice): Palais de Justice, rue aux Laines, 1000 Brussels; First Pres: M. Chatel; Pres: R. Screvens; Prosecutor-Gen: J. Krings; First Attorney-Gen: J. Velu.

Cours d'Appel/Hoven van Beroep (Civil and Criminal High Courts): Antwerp: fax (3) 216-41-27; First Pres: A. de Man; Prosecutor-Gen: R. van Kamp; Brussels: fax (2) 508-63-50; First Pres: L. Slachmuylder; Prosecutor-Gen: A. van Oudenhove; Ghent: fax (91) 24-02-54; First Pres: M. Couckuyt; Prosecutor-Gen: (vacant); Liège: fax (41) 22-91-22; First Pres: R. Laurent; Prosecutor-Gen: L. Giet; Mons: fax (65) 31-89-16; First Pres: P. Gueritte; Prosecutor-Gen: G. Demanet.

Media

BROADCASTING

Radio-Télévision Belge de la Communauté Culturelle Française (RTBF): 52 blvd Auguste Reyers, 1040 Brussels; tel (2) 737-21-11; telex 21437; fax (2) 736-95-66; Chair: M. van Campenhoudt; Admin-Gen: Robert Stéphane; Dir, Radio Programmes: Philippe Dasnoy; Dir, TV Programmes: Georges Konen; Dir, Information Service (Radio and TV): Pierre Devos.

Belgische Radio en Televisie: Instituut der Nederlandse

Uitzendingen, 52 August Reyerslaan, 1040 Brussels; tel (2) 737-31-11; telex 24216; fax (2) 735-37-04; Chair: Els Witte; Admin-Gen: Casimir Goossens; Dir, Radio Programmes: Piet van Roe; Dir, TV Programmes: Jan Ceuleers; Dir, News Dept: Karel Hemmerechts; Dir, Educational Broadcasting: Lea Martel; Dir, Technical Dept: Michel Gewillig.

NEWS AND INFORMATION

Institut National de Statistique: 44 rue de Louvain, 1000 Brussels; tel (2) 513-96-50.

Mining and Energy

ENERGY

Commissariat à l'Energie Atomique (Atomic Energy Commission): Administration de l'Energie, 30 rue J. A. de Mot, 1040 Brussels; tel (2) 233-61-11; telex 23509; f 1950; responsible for nuclear matters falling within the jurisdiction of the Ministry of Economic Affairs and Planning.

Organisme National des Déchets Radioactifs et des Matières Fissiles (ONDRAF)/Nationale Instelling voor Radioactief Afval en Splijtstoffen (NIRAS): 1 place Madou, BP 24/25, 1030 Brussels; tel (2) 212-10-11; telex 65784; fax (2) 218-51-65; Gen Man: E. Detilleux; Dep Gen Man: F. Decamps; f 1980; responsible for the management of all activities related to radioactive waste collection, transport, treatment, conditioning, storage and disposal.

MINING

Administration of Mines: 28-30 rue J. A. de Mot, 1040 Brussels; tel (2) 233-61-11; Dir-Gen: J. Mendaets.

Institut National des Industries Extractives (INIEX) (National Institute for the Extractive Industries): 200 rue du Chéra, 4000 Liège; tel (41) 52-71-50; telex 41128; Chair: H. Schlitz; f 1967; research, devt and technological demonstration centre working in the areas of extractive industries, energy, the environment, security, electronics, new materials and processing.

Tourism

Office de Promotion du Tourisme de la Communauté Française: 61 rue Marché-aux-Herbes, 1000 Brussels; tel (2) 513-90-90; telex 63245; fax (2) 513-69-50; Dir: José Clossen; f 1981; promotes tourism in the French-speaking areas of Belgium.

Tourist Information Brussels (TIB): Hôtel de Ville, Grand-Place, 1000 Brussels; tel (2) 513-89-40; telex 65206; Pres: Jean Leroy; Dir: E. Puttaert; f 1960; provides guides, press and promotion services, information services, ticket and reservation services, etc.

Tourist Office for Flanders: 61 Grasmarkt, 1000 Brussels; tel (2) 513-90-90; telex 63245; fax (2) 513-69-50; Gen Commr: Urbain Claeys; f 1985; promotes and formulates policies on tourism in the Flemish part of Belgium.

Transport and Communications

TELECOMMUNICATIONS

Régie des Télégraphes et des Téléphones de Belgique (RTT): 42 rue des Palais, 1210; tel (2) 213-41-11; telex 29154; fax (2) 218-82-09; Admin-Gen: L. Eggermont; f 1930; responsible for the public telecommunications infrastructure in Belgium.

TRANSPORT

Hoofdbestuur der Waterwegen (Waterway Administration): Residence Palace, Wetstraat 155, 1040 Brussels; tel (2) 733-96-70; telex 63477; fax (2) 230-32-70; Dir-Gen: J. Demoen; management of waterways; part of the Ministry of Public Works.

Régie Belge des Transports Maritimes/Regie voor Maritiem Transport (Belgian Maritime Transport Authority): 30 rue Belliard, 1040 Brussels; Matiënkaai 5, 8400 Ostend; tel (2) 230-01-80; telex 23851; fax (2) 231-14-80; Gen Man: Paul Muyldermans; overseas shipping services; runs Ostend-Dover lines.

SABENA (Société anonyme belge d'exploitation de la navigation aérienne) (Belgian World Air Lines): 35 rue Cardinal Mercier, 1000 Brussels; tel (2) 723-31-11; telex 21322; fax (2) 509-23-99; Chair of Board and Pres: Carlos van Rafelghem; Vice-Chair and Dep Pres: André Pahaut; f 1923; 54% state-owned; air transport services to most parts of the world.

Sobelair (Société Belge de Transports par Air) NV: 131 ave Frans Courtens, 1030 Brussels; tel (2) 216-21-75; telex 22095; Man Dir: P. Jonnart; Dir: R. Minet; Man: J. Edom; f 1946; subsidiary of SABENA; operates charter and tour flights.

Société Nationale des Chemins de Fer Belges (SNCB)/Nationale Maatschappij der Belgische Spoorwegen (NMBS): 85 rue de France, 1070 Brussels; tel (2) 525-21-11; telex 62925; fax (2) 525-40-45; Gen Man: M. E. Schouppe; f 1926; rail transport.

Société Nationale des Chemins de Fer Vicinaux (SNCV): 14 rue de la Science, 1040 Brussels; tel (2) 237-62-11; fax (2) 237-63-98; Pres: R. Denison; Dir-Gen: Hugo van Wesemael; f 1884; manages public bus and tram services.

BELIZE

Head of State

The British monarch, as Head of State, is represented in Belize by a Governor-General of local citizenship. The Governor-General is appointed on the advice of the Prime Minister and acts on the advice of the Cabinet and the Belize Advisory Council. The Governor-General appoints a Cabinet, headed by the Prime Minister, which is responsible to Parliament.

Head of State: HM Queen Elizabeth II (succeeded to the throne 6 February 1952).

Governor-General: Dame Elmira Minita Gordon (took office 21 September 1981).

Office of the Governor-General: Belmopan; tel (8) 2521; telex 211.

Legislature

Legislative power is vested in the bicameral National Assembly, comprising a Senate, with eight members appointed by the Governor-General, and a House of Representatives, with 28 members elected by universal adult suffrage using a single-member constituency system. The Assembly's normal term is five years, subject to dissolution.

Senate: National Assembly Bldg, Independence Hill, Belmopan; tel (8) 22141; telex 102; fax (8) 2364; President: Jane Usher.

House of Representatives: National Assembly Bldg, Independence Hill, Belmopan; tel (8) 22142; telex 102; fax (8) 2364; Speaker: Robert Swift; Clerk: Alexander E. Johnson.

MINISTRIES AND GOVERNMENT DEPARTMENTS

OFFICE OF THE PRIME MINISTER
Belmopan
Tel (8) 234-6; telex 102; fax (8) 22886
Prime Minister: George Price
Deputy Prime Minister: Florencio Marin

MINISTRY OF AGRICULTURE, FORESTRY AND FISHERIES
West Block, Belmopan
Tel (8) 22166
Minister: Michael Espat

Department of Agriculture: West Block, Belmopan; tel (8) 22332; Chief Agriculture Officer: Liborio González.

Fisheries Department: Princess Margaret Drive, POB 148, Belize City; tel (2) 44552; fax (2) 22409; Permanent Sec: Rodney Neal; Fisheries Admin: Vincent Gillett.

Forestry Department: West Block, Belmopan; tel (8) 22166; Chief Forest Officer: Oscar Rosado; f 1922; responsible for forest admin, national parks, wildlife, conservation matters relating to flaura and fauna, etc.

MINISTRY OF COMMERCE, DEFENCE AND HOME AFFAIRS
Belmopan
Minister: George Price

MINISTRY OF ECONOMIC DEVELOPMENT
Belmopan
Minister: Said Musa

MINISTRY OF EDUCATION
Belmopan
Minister: Said Musa

MINISTRY OF ELECTRICITY, COMMUNICATION AND TRANSPORT
Belmopan
Tel (8) 22692
Minister: Carlos Diaz

MINISTRY OF FINANCE
Belmopan
Minister: George Price

MINISTRY OF FOREIGN AFFAIRS
POB 174, Belmopan
Tel (8) 22322; telex 102
Minister: Said Musa

MINISTRY OF HEALTH AND URBAN DEVELOPMENT
Belmopan
Minister: Dr Theodore Aranda

MINISTRY OF HOUSING AND CO-OPERATIVES
East Block, Belmopan
Tel (8) 23336; fax (8) 23298
Minister: Valdemar Castillo

MINISTRY OF INDUSTRY AND NATURAL RESOURCES
Belmopan
Tel (8) 22249; telex 102
Minister: Florencio Marin

MINISTRY OF LABOUR, PUBLIC SERVICE AND LOCAL GOVERNMENT
Belmopan
Minister: Samuel Waight

Department of Women's Affairs: Albert St, Belize City; tel (2) 77397; Dir: Marilyn Panton.

MINISTRY OF SOCIAL SERVICES AND COMMUNITY DEVELOPMENT
Belmopan
Minister: Remijio Mantejo

MINISTRY OF WORKS
Power Lane, Belmopan
Tel (8) 22136; telex 012
Minister: Leopoldo Briceno

MINISTRY OF TOURISM AND THE ENVIRONMENT AND OFFICE OF THE ATTORNEY GENERAL
Belmopan
Tel (8) 22110
Minister and Attorney-General: Glenn Godfrey

GOVERNMENT AGENCIES AND ORGANIZATIONS

Advisory and Supervisory Bodies

Elections and Boundaries Commission: 38 Queen St, Belize City; tel (2) 45598; Chair: Basil Coleman; f 1978; responsible for the direction and supervision of the registration of voters and the conduct of referendums and general and municipal elections.

Office of the Auditor-General: POB 223, Belize City; tel (2) 77168; Auditor-Gen: O. G. Nicholas; Asst Auditor-Gen: D. I. Gardiner; f 1877; audits and reports on the public accounts of Belize, including accounts of all Govt offices and authorities, commissions and courts of law.

Agriculture

Banana Control Board: c/o Dept of Agriculture, West Block, Belmopan; management of banana industry, responsible to the growers.

Belize Beef Corpn: c/o Dept of Agriculture, West Block, Belmopan; f 1978; semi-governmental organization to aid the devt of the cattle-rearing industry.

Belize Sugar Cane Board: 7 2nd St South, Corozal Town; tel 4-22005; Exec Sec: I. E. Cruz; f 1959; administers the overall production and exportation of sugar and all aspects related to the sugar cane industry.

Citrus Control Board: c/o Dept of Agriculture, West Block, Belmopan; tel (8) 22199; Chair: C. Sosa; f 1966; determines basic quota for each producer, fixes annual citrus prices.

Art and Culture

Government Archives: Unity Blvd, Belmopan; tel (8) 22247; Archivist: Charles Gibson.

National Arts Council: POB 1204, Bliss Institute, Belize City; tel (2) 72110; Exec Dir: Hortense Wade; Chair: Stephanie Anderson; f 1982; develops and promotes the expression of all branches of culture and art in Belize.

Belize Archives Department: 26/28 Unity Blvd, Belmopan; tel (8) 22247; Govt Archivist: Charles A. Gibson; f 1965; collection and preservation of archive material.

Business and Economy

BANKING

Central Bank of Belize: POB 852, Treasury Lane, Belize City; tel (2) 77216; telex 225; fax (2) 77106; Gov: Alan Slusher; Dep Gov: Frank Garbutt; f 1982; regulates and monitors activities of the commercial banks, administers exchange control regulations, analyses and disseminates information on the national economy.

Government Savings Bank: Belmopan.

FINANCIAL AGENCY

Customs and Excise Department: Customs House, POB 146, 12 Fort St, Belize City; tel (2) 77092; Comptroller of Customs: Frank C. Pandy; responsible for the collection of revenue on imported and exported goods and excise tax on local production; also responsible for law enforcement against all forms of contraband.

MARKETING

Marketing Board: POB 479, Belize City; tel (2) 77402; Chair: Santiago Perdomo; f 1948; purchases staple food crops at guaranteed prices, supervises processing, storing and marketing.

TRADE

Belize Export and Investment Promotion Unit: POB 291, 7 Cork St, Belize City; tel (2) 44913; telex 121; fax (2) 30755; Dir: Denton Belisle; f 1986; provides a wide range of services to foreign and local investors, including information on investment sectors and opportunities, sources of funding, assistance to exporters, etc.

Defence

Belize Defence Force: Price Barracks, Ladyville; tel (2) 52171; Chief of Staff: Lt-Col Trevor D. A. Veitch.

Belize Police Force: Office of the Commissioner, POB 284, Belmopan; tel (8) 2221; Commr of Police: B. A. Bevans; Asst Commr of Police: K. A. Haylock.

Security and Intelligence Services: Belmopan; tel (8) 22225; under the administrative jurisdiction of the Ministry of Home Affairs and Local Government.

Development and Planning

Development Finance Corpn: POB 40, Bliss Parade, Belmopan; tel (8) 22350; telex 248; fax (8) 23096; Gen Man: Sandra L. Bedran; Asst Gen Man: Dorla Gill-Leslie; f 1972; provides devt loans for various areas of economic activity.

National Economic Development Council (NEDC):

Belmopan; formulates devt plans according to guidelines set by the Ministry of Economic Development.

Reconstruction and Development Corporation: POB 92, 1 Bliss Promenade, Belize City; tel (2) 77424; f 1962; Gen Man: A. Bryan Card; funding and construction of housing, municipal activities in Belmopan and Ladyville.

Health and Welfare

HEALTH

Medical Department: West Block, Belmopan; tel (8) 22325; Dir of Health Services (acting): Dr José Lopez.

WELFARE

Belize Social Security Board: POB 18, Civic Centre, Belmopan; tel (8) 22163; fax (8) 22366; f 1981; responsible for registration of employers, insurance of employed persons, payment of benefits to claimants, provison of medical care to insured persons, funding social devt programmes, etc.

Social Development Department: 6 Church St, Belize City; tel (8) 22347; Social Devt Officer: Dudley Augustine.

Legal and Judiciary

Magistracy: Paslow Bldg, Belize City; tel (2) 77164; Chief Magistrate: Troadio González.

Office of the Director of Public Prosecutions: Public Bldg, Belize City; tel (2) 77396; Dir of Public Prosecutions: George Singh.

Supreme Court: Supreme Court Bldg, Belize City; tel (2) 72754; Chief Justice: Taufik S. Cotran; Registrar: Hector Knight.

Media

BROADCASTING

Belize Broadcasting Network (BBN): POB 89, Albert Cattouse Bldg, cnr Regent and Bishop Sts, Belize City; tel (2) 77246; telex 157; fax (2) 75040; Dir: René R. Villanueva; f 1937; Govt-operated semi-commercial service; broadcasts in English and Spanish; includes two radio stations and a TV production unit known as BBN Teleproductions.

GOVERNMENT PUBLISHER

Government Printery: Power Lane, Belmopan; tel (8) 22293; f 1871; responsible for printing, binding and engraving requirements of all Govt depts and Ministries; publications include annual Govt estimates, Govt magazines and the official Government Gazette.

NEWS AND INFORMATION

Government Information Service: East Block, Belmopan; tel (8) 22659; telex 138; Chief Information Officer: Manolo Romero; f 1947; disseminates general information on Belize, prepares press releases, arranges press conferences, publishes monthly magazine and newsletter.

Statistical Office of the Ministry of Economic Development: Belmopan; tel (8) 22207; official statistical agency.

Mining and Energy

Belize Electricity Board: 115 Barrack Rd, POB 327, Belize City; tel (2) 77141; telex 272; fax (2) 30891; Chair: Ralph Fonseca; Chief Exec: Louis Lue; f 1958; generation and distribution of national power supply.

Science and Technology

National Meteorological Service: POB 717, Belize City; tel 25-2012; telex 371211; Chief Meteorologist: Carlos Fuller; collects and processes meteorological data, provides forecasts and warnings; under the administrative jurisdiction of the Ministry of Electricity, Communication and Transport.

Tourism

Belize Tourist Bureau: POB 325, 53 Regent St, Belize City; tel (2) 77213; Chair: Minister of Tourism, Glenn Godfrey; Sec (acting): Frank Tillett; f 1964; central tourism body.

Transport and Communications

COMMUNICATIONS

Belize Telecommunications Ltd: St Thomas St, POB 603, Belize City; tel (2) 77085; telex 246; fax (2) 77096; Chief Exec: Ediberto Torres; f 1988; operates national telephone system.

General Post Office: Paslow Bldg, Belize City; tel (2) 77380; f 1830; receipt, delivery and despatch of all mail items.

TRANSPORT

Belize Port Authority: Belize City; tel (2) 2439.

Civil Aviation Department: Philip S. W. Goldson International Airport, Ladyville, Belize District; tel (25) 2013; Chief Civil Aviation Officer: Luigi Zaldivar.

Licensing and Transport Board: POB 833, 3 Goal Lane, Belize City; tel (2) 45838; Sec: Elston R. V. Wade; f 1958; responsible for the regulation of public transport and control of the traffic flow; issues driver and vehicle licences.

Utilities

Belize Water and Sewerage Authority (WASA): POB 150, 44 Regent St, Belize City; tel (2) 77079; telex 117; Chief Exec: Winston W. Michael; Chief Engineer: Denroy A. McCord; f 1971; provides national water and sewer services.

BENIN

Head of State

The President is elected by the National Revolutionary Assembly for a five-year term. Executive power is vested in the National Executive Council, directed by the President as Head of the Military Revolutionary Government, and its Permanent Committee of ministers, including the six provincial Prefects.

President: Mathieu Kérékou (assumed office 27 October 1972; elected President 5 February 1980; re-elected 31 July 1984 and 2 August 1989).

Office of the President: BP 2028, Cotonou; tel 30-00-90; telex 5222; Minister of State without Portfolio, Adviser to the Pres of the Republic: Mamadou Cissé.

Legislature

Legislative power is vested in the Assemblée Nationale Révolutionnaire (National Revolutionary Assembly) comprising 196 People's Commissioners representing socio-professional classes and elected for a five-year term by universal adult suffrage. The Central Committee of the Parti de la Révolution Populaire du Bénin, the only legal political party, plays a leading role in government. Local administration is provided by provincial, town and village councils. It was announced in March 1990 that the Government had resigned, that the National Assembly had been dissolved and the constitution repealed, and that 'Marxist dogma' had been abandoned.

Assemblée Nationale Révolutionnaire (National Revolutionary Assembly): Cotonou; Pres of Permanent Committee: Romain Vilon Guezo.

MINISTRIES AND GOVERNMENT DEPARTMENTS

OFFICE OF THE PRIME MINISTER
Cotonou
Prime Minister: Nicéphore Soglo

MINISTRY OF CULTURE, YOUTH AND SPORTS
BP 65, Porto-Novo
Tel 21-24-30
Minister: Chabi Lafia Yarou

MINISTRY OF DEFENCE
BP 2028, Cotonou
Tel 30-00-90; telex 5222
Minister: Mathieu Kérékou

MINISTRY OF EQUIPMENT AND TRANSPORT
BP 987, Cotonou
Tel 31-46-64
Minister: Martin Dohou Azonhiho

MINISTRY OF FINANCE
BP 302, Cotonou
Tel 31-40-53; telex 5009
Minister: Didier Dassi

MINISTRY OF FOREIGN AFFAIRS AND CO-OPERATION
BP 318, Cotonou
Tel 30-04-00; telex 5200
Minister: Daniel Tawema

MINISTRY OF INDUSTRY AND ENERGY
Cotonou
Minister: Justin Gnidehou

MINISTRY OF INFORMATION AND COMMUNICATIONS
BP 180, Cotonou
Tel 31-43-34; telex 5208
Minister: Ousman Batoko

MINISTRY OF INSPECTION OF STATE-OWNED AND PARASTATAL ENTERPRISES
Cotonou
Tel 31-33-49
Minister: Saliou Aboudou

MINISTRY OF INTERIOR, SECURITY AND TERRITORIAL ADMINISTRATION
Cotonou
Tel 30-11-06
Minister-Delegate to the Presidency: Pancrace Brathier

MINISTRY OF JUSTICE
BP 967, Cotonou
Tel 31-31-46
Minister: Saliou Aboudou

MINISTRY OF LABOUR AND SOCIAL AFFAIRS
BP 907, Cotonou
Tel 31-31-12
Minister: Paul Irenée Zinsou

MINISTRY OF PLANNING AND STATISTICS
BP 342, Cotonou
Tel 30-05-41; telex 5252
Minister-Delegate to the Presidency: Robert Dossou

MINISTRY OF PRE-PRIMARY AND PRIMARY EDUCATION
Porto-Novo
Tel 21-26-51
Minister: Germain Kadja

MINISTRY OF PUBLIC HEALTH
BP 882, Cotonou
Tel 31-26-70
Minister: Rafiatou Karimou

MINISTRY OF RURAL DEVELOPMENT AND CO-OPERATIVE ACTION
BP 34, Porto-Novo
Tel 21-30-53
Minister: Gandouno Kodja

MINISTRY OF SECONDARY AND HIGHER EDUCATION
Cotonou
Tel 30-06-81
Minister: Salifou Alidou

MINISTRY OF TRADE, CRAFTS AND TOURISM
BP 2037, Cotonou
Tel 31-52-58
Minister: Amos Elegbe

OFFICE OF THE PREFECT OF ATACORA PROVINCE
Natitingo
Prefect: Lt-Col Adolphe Biaou

OFFICE OF THE PREFECT OF ATLANTIC PROVINCE
Cotonou
Prefect: Boniface Houegbonou

OFFICE OF THE PREFECT OF BORGOU PROVINCE
Parakou
Prefect: Soulé Mama Sambo

OFFICE OF THE PREFECT OF MONO PROVINCE
Lokossa
Prefect: Gaston Hounkpe

OFFICE OF THE PREFECT OF OUEME PROVINCE
Porto-Novo
Prefect: Moustapha Elegbede

OFFICE OF THE PREFECT OF ZOU PROVINCE
Abomey
Prefect: Leopold Ahoueya

GOVERNMENT AGENCIES AND ORGANIZATIONS

Agriculture

AGRICULTURE

Société Agro-Animale Bénino-Arabe-Libyenne (SABLI): BP 03-1200, Cotonou; tel 31-19-50; telex 5353; Man Dir: Salé Imorou; f 1979; 51% state-owned, 49% Libyan-owned; production of poultry and poultry products.

Société Béninoise de Palmier à Huile (SOBEPALH): ave Victor Regis, BP 12, Porto-Novo; tel 21-29-03; Man Dir: Marius Kokou Quenum; f 1961, nationalized 1975; 100% state-owned; production of palm oil and cottonseed oil.

Société Nationale pour le Développement des Fruits et Légumes (SONAFEL): BP 2040, Cotonou; tel 31-52-34; telex 5031; Man Dir: Joachim Philippe d'Almeida; f 1975; develops production of fruit and vegetables; holds monopoly of export of fruit and vegetable produce.

Société Nationale d'Irrigation et d'Aménagement Hydro-Agricole (SONIAH): BP 312, Porto-Novo; tel 21-34-20; Dir-Gen: Yenakpondji Capochichi; Sec-Gen: Tossa Jérôme Toni; f 1972; devt of irrigation and rice-growing projects.

Société Nationale pour la Promotion Agricole (SON-APRA): BP 933, Cotonou; tel 33-08-20; telex 5248; Pres: Valentin Agbo; Dir-Gen: Robert Tetevi Vinyor; f 1983; marketing of agricultural products.

FISHING

Société Bénino-Arabe-Libyenne de Pêche Maritime (BELIPECHE): BP 1516, Cotonou; tel 31-51-36; Pres: Laurent Fagbohoun; Dir: Saleh Areibi; f 1977; 51% state-owned, 49% owned by Libya; fish and fish products.

FORESTRY

Office National du Bois (ONAB): Akpakpa Pk 3, route de Porto Novo, BP 1238, Cotonou; tel 33-16-32; telex 5160; fax 33-19-56; Man Dir: D. Gabriel Lokoun; f 1983; forest devt and marketing of wood products.

Business and Economy

BANKING

Banque Béninoise pour le Développement (BBD): 2 rue des Cheminots, BP 300, Cotonou; tel 31-34-76; telex 5238; f 1962; devt bank; 3 brs.

Banque Centrale des Etats de l'Afrique de l'Ouest (BCEAO): route de Lomé, BP 325, Cotonou; tel 31-24-66; telex 5211; Gov: Alassane Ouattara; Dir in Benin: Gilbert Medje; f 1955; bank of issue for the seven states of the Union monétaire ouest-africaine (UMOA), comprising Benin, Burkina Faso, Côte d'Ivoire, Mali, Niger, Senegal and Togo; br at Parakou.

Banque Commerciale du Bénin (BCB): rue du Révérend Père Colineau, BP 85, Cotonou; tel 31-37-13; telex 5216; f 1962; conducts all Govt banking business; 22 brs.

FINANCIAL AGENCY

Caisse Centrale de Coopération Economique (CCCE): blvd de France, BP 38, Cotonou; tel 31-35-80; telex 5082; Dir: Didier Mercier.

INSURANCE

Société Béninoise d'Assurance: angle ave Steinmetz et rue du roi Dokodonou, Cotonou; Pres: Valentin Hodonou; f 1974; insurance.

Société Nationale d'Assurance et de Réassurance (SONAR): place des Martyrs, BP 2030, Cotonou; tel 31-16-49; telex 5231; Pres: Raphaël Pollet; Dir-Gen: Mathieu-Aimé Lawson; f 1974; insurance and reinsurance; 8 brs.

MARKETING

Société Béninoise des Matériaux de Construction (SOBEMAC): BP 1209, Cotonou; tel 31-25-93; telex 5262; Pres: Mamoud Moustapha Soule; Man Dir: René Dossa Megniho; f 1975; cement marketing.

Société Nationale de Commercialisation et d'Exportation du Bénin (SONACEB): BP 933, Cotonou; tel 31-28-22; telex 5248; Pres: Armand Alapini; Man Dir: Polycarpe Agossa; f 1972; monopoly of internal marketing of all agricultural produce except palm products, cotton and tobacco; monopoly of cement exports.

Société Nationale d'Equipement (SONAE): BP 2042, Cotonou; tel 31-31-26; telex 5201; Pres: Célestin Zekpa; Man Dir: Nicolas Adagbe; f 1975; import and distribution of capital goods.

NATIONALIZED INDUSTRY

Chambre de Commerce, d'Agriculture et d'Industrie de la République Populaire du Bénin (CCIB): ave du Général de Gaulle, BP 31, Cotonou; tel 31-32-99; Pres: Raffet Loko; Vice-Pres: J-V. Adjovi, M. T. Laleye; Sec-Gen: N. A. Viadenou.

Société d'Alimentation Générale dù Bénin (AGB): 21 route de Porto-Novo, BP 53, Cotonou; tel 33-07-28; telex 5062; Man Dir: Christophe Yebe Semako; f 1978; 100% state-owned; holds monopoly of import and distribution of basic foodstuffs, drink and tobacco; runs chain of supermarkets and wholesale stores.

Société des Ciments d'Onigbolo (SCO): Onigbolo; Pres: Justin Gnidehou; Man Dir: R. J. K. Frymann; f 1975; 51% state-owned, 43% owned by Nigeria; produces and markets cement.

Société de Fabrication des Portes Isolantes (SFPI): route Inter-Etats, quartier Agbocodji, Godomey, BP 52, Cotonou; Pres: Rodolphe Daizo; f 1984; 51% state-owned.

Société Nationale de Boissons (La Béninoise): route de Porto-Novo, BP 135, Cotonou; tel 33-10-61; telex 5275; Pres: Barnabé Midouzo; Dir-Gen: Manassé Ayayi; f 1957, nationalized 1975; manufactures beer, soft drinks and ice.

Société Nationale de Construction et de Travaux Publics (SONACOTRAP): BP 286, Cotonou; tel 30-15-35; Dir-Gen: Théodore Ahoussou; f 1976; construction and public works.

Société Nationale pour l'Industrie des Corps Gras (SONICOG): BP 312, Cotonou; tel 31-33-71; telex 5205; Dir-Gen: Zul-Kifl Salami; f 1962; produces palm oil, palm kernel and groundnut oils and cakes, sheanut butter and soaps.

Defence

Forces Armées Populaires de Bénin (People's Armed Forces of Benin): Cotonou; Chief of Staff: Col Mama Djougou; operational units are as follows:

Forces de Défense Nationale (National Defence Forces).

Forces Maritimes (Navy).

Forces de Sécurité Publique (Public Security Forces): Dir of State Security: Lt François Foulin.

Forces Terrestres (Army): Parakou.

Development and Planning

Mission de Coopération et d'Action Culturelle (Mission Française d'Aide et de Coopération): BP 476, Cotonou; tel 30-08-24; telex 5209; Dir: Bernard Hadjadj; administers bilateral aid from France according to the 1975 co-operation agreement.

Legal and Judiciary

Cour criminelle d'exception (Court of State Security): Cotonou; Chair: Henri Amoussou Kapka; f 1988; holds special jurisdiction over all affairs relating to the internal and external security of the country.

Cour populaire centrale (Central People's Court): BP 330, Cotonou; Chair: Léandre Amlon; responsible to the National Revolutionary Assembly and to the National Executive Council.

Media

BROADCASTING

Office de Radiodiffusion et de Télévision du Bénin: BP 366, Cotonou; tel 31-20-41; telex 5132; Dir-Gen: R. O. Sanni; Dir, Radio: N. J. Sohouenou; Dir, TV: Michèle Badarou; radio broadcasts in French, English and 18 local languages; 12 hours of TV transmissions per week.

GOVERNMENT PUBLISHER

Office National d'Edition, de Presse et d'Imprimerie (ONEPI): BP 1210, Cotonou; tel 30-08-75; Dir-Gen: Boni Zimé Mako; f 1975.

NEWS AND INFORMATION

Agence Bénin-Presse (ABP): BP 72, Cotonou; tel 31-26-55; telex 5221; Dir: Evariste Degla; f 1961; national news agency; section of the Ministry of Information and Communications.

Institut National de la Statistique et de l'Analyse Economique: BP 323, Cotonou; tel 31-40-81; national statistical agency.

Mining and Energy

Communauté Electrique du Bénin: BP 1368, Lomé, Togo; tel 21-61-32; Chair: Emile Nonan; Man Dir: Boukary Alidou; f 1968 as joint venture between Togo and Benin to harness and exploit the energy resources in the two countries; Ghana's Volta dam is currently supplying energy to the two countries.

Société Bénino-Arabe-Libyenne des Mines (BELI-MINES): BP 1913, Cotonou; tel 31-59-24; telex 5128; Pres: André Yoro; Man Dir: Hassan A. Raghi; f 1979; 51% state-owned, 49% Libyan-owned; mining and commercialization of marble.

Société Béninoise d'Electricité et d'Eau (SBEE): BP 123, Cotonou; tel 31-24-10; telex 5207; Man Dir: Emile Louis Paraïso; f 1973; produces and distributes electricity and water.

Société Nationale de Commercialisation des Produits Pétroliers (SONACOP): ave d'Ornano, BP 245, Cotonou; tel 31-22-90; telex 5245; Pres: Richard Adjaho; Man Dir: Edmond-Pierre Amoussou; f 1974; imports and distributes petroleum products.

Tourism

Office National du Tourisme et de l'Hôtellerie (ONATHO): BP 89, Cotonou; tel 31-26-87; telex 5032; Dir: Hilaire Sapondu; f 1974; state tourist agency.

Société Béninoise pour la Promotion du Tourisme (SBPT): BP 1508, Cotonou; tel 30-05-84; telex 5143.

Transport

RAILWAYS

Organisation Commune Bénin-Niger des Chemins de Fer et des Transports (OCBN): BP 16, Cotonou; tel 31-33-80; telex 5210; Dir-Gen: Désiré Ahyi; f 1959; jointly owned by Benin (63%) and Niger (37%); operates passenger and freight rail services.

ROADS

Société de Transit et de Consignation du Bénin (CTCB Express): route de l'Aéroport, BP 7079, Cotonou; Pres: Souléman Koura Zoumarou; f 1986.

SHIPPING

Compagnie Béninoise de Navigation Maritime (COBENAM): BP 2032, Cotonou; tel 31-27-96; telex 5225; Pres: Abder Kader Allal; Man Dir: Nouhoum Assouman; f 1974; owned by Benin (51%) and Algeria (49%); agents for shipping cos from France, Japan, UK and China.

Office Béninois des Manutentions Portuaires (OBEMAP): place des Martyrs, BP 213, Cotonou; tel 30-18-39; telex 5308; Pres: Patrice Vieljeux.

Port Autonome de Cotonou: BP 927, Cotonou; tel 31-28-90; telex 5004; Man Dir: Odon Brice Houncanrin; f 1965.

BHUTAN

Head of State

Bhutan is an absolute hereditary monarchy. Power is shared by the Sovereign (assisted by the Royal Advisory Council), the Council of Ministers, the National Assembly and the Je Khempo (Head Abbot) of Bhutan's 3,000-4,000 Buddhist monks.

Head of State: HM King Jigme Singye Wangchuck (succeeded to the throne July 1972).

Office of HM the King: Tashichhodzong, Thimphu; tel 2590.

Je Khempo (Head Abbot): His Holiness Lopon Kuenley.

Lodoi Tsokde (Royal Advisory Council): Tashichhodzong, Thimphu; tel 2339; Chair: Dasho Kunzang Tangbi.

Legislature

The Tshogdu (National Assembly), which serves a three-year term, has 151 members, including 106 directly elected by adult suffrage. Ten seats in the Assembly are reserved for religious bodies, while the remainder are occupied by officials, ministers and members of the Royal Advisory Council. Both the Royal Advisory Council and the Council of Ministers are responsible to the Assembly.

Tschogdu (National Assembly): Tashichhodzong, Thimphu; tel 2369.

MINISTRIES AND GOVERNMENT DEPARTMENTS

COUNCIL OF MINISTERS
Tashichhodzong, Thimphu
Chair: HM King Jigme Singye Wangchuck
Secretary: Lyonpo Dawa Tsering

MINISTRY OF AGRICULTURE
POB 252, Thimphu
Tel 2545; telex 890221
Minister: (vacant)
Representative of the King: Princess Dechen Wangmo
Wangchuck Dorji

MINISTRY OF FINANCE
Tashichhodzong, Thimphu
Telex 890201
Minister: Lyonpo Dorji Tshering

MINISTRY OF FOREIGN AFFAIRS
Tashichhodzong, Thimphu
Telex 890214
Minister: Lyonpo Dawa Tsering

MINISTRY OF HOME AFFAIRS
Tashichhodzong, Thimphu
Minister: HRH Namgyel Wangchuck

MINISTRY OF SOCIAL SERVICES, COMMUNICATIONS AND TOURISM
Tashichhodzong, Thimphu
Telex 890203
Minister: Lyonpo Dr T. Tobgyal

MINISTRY OF TRADE, INDUSTRIES AND POWER
Tashichhodzong, Thimphu
Telex 890215
Minister: (vacant)

GOVERNMENT AGENCIES AND ORGANIZATIONS

Advisory and Supervisory Body

Royal Civil Service Commission: Tashichhodzong, Thimphu; tel 2491; f 1982; responsible for appointing local Govt officials.

Business and Economy

BANKING

Bank of Bhutan: POB 75, Phuntsholing; tel 225; telex 890304; Chair: Lyonpo Dorji Tshering; Man Dir: Ram Nath; f 1968;

jointly owned by the Bhutan Govt and the State Bank of India, each of which nominates directors; 2 brs.

Royal Monetary Authority (RMA): POB 154, Thimphu; tel 2540; telex 890206; Chair: Princess Sonam Chhoden Wangchuck; Man Dir: Bap Kesang; f 1982; acts as central bank and bank of issue; frames and implements official monetary policy, co-ordinates activities of financial institutions and holds foreign-exchange deposits on behalf of the Govt.

Unit Trust of Bhutan: POB 77, Phuntsholing; tel 434; Gen Man: Sangay Dorji; offers various forms of investment in unit trusts guaranteed by the Govt.

INSURANCE

Royal Insurance Corpn of Bhutan: POB 77, Phuntsholing; tel 309; telex 890305; Chair: Princess Sonam Chhoden Wangchuck; Man Dir: Dasho U. Dorji; f 1975; central insurance organization.

NATIONALIZED INDUSTRY

Bhutan Carbide and Chemicals Ltd: POB 103, Phuntsholing; Gen Man: Nima Dorji; f 1987; joint Govt and private sector undertaking.

Dungsum Cement Project: Nanglam; f 1988; Govt-sponsored industrial project.

TRADE

Food Corpn of Bhutan (FCB): Phuntsholing; tel 241; Man Dir: (vacant); f 1974; responsible for marketing, storage, import and export of agricultural produce; also operates a rural finance scheme to assist farmers.

National Commission for Trade and Industry: Thimphu; tel 403; Chair: HM King Jigme Singye Wangchuck; regulatory body for proposed industrial projects.

State Trading Corpn of Bhutan (STCB): POB 76, Phuntsholing; tel 286; telex 890301; Man Dir: L. B. Rai; Man Dir, Export: D. P. Basnet; procures goods and materials required by the Govt; manages imports and exports on behalf of the Govt.

   Export Development Corpn: Industrial Estate, Phuntsholing; tel 353; telex 890312; operated by STCB; manages export trade on behalf of the Govt.

Defence

Royal Bhutan Army: Tashichhodzong, Thimphu; tel 2306; Chief of Staff: Maj-Gen Lam Dorji.

Development and Planning

Bhutan Development Finance Corpn: c/o Royal Monetary Authority, POB 154, Thimphu; tel 2540; telex 890206; Chief Exec: Pema Tenzin; f 1988; provides long-term devt loans and shorter-term agricultural credit.

Planning Commission: Tashichhodzong, Thimphu; tel 2493; central planning agency; responsible for drawing up economic and social plans.

Legal and Judiciary

Thrimkhang Gongma (High Court): Thimphu; Chief Justice: (vacant); f 1968; the eight High Court Judges serve a five-year term.

Media

BROADCASTING

Bhutan Broadcasting Service (BBS): POB 101, Thimphu; tel 2533; telex 212; Dep Dir: Louise Dorji; f 1973 as Radio National Youth Association of Bhutan (NYAB), present name adopted 1986; short-wave radio station broadcasting three hours daily; under the jurisdiction of the Department of Information and Broadcasting (see below).

NEWS AND INFORMATION

Central Statistical Organization: Thimphu; Govt statistical agency.

Department of Information and Broadcasting: POB 204, Thimphu; telex 890212; official information office; publishes weekly national newspaper.

Tourism

Bhutan Tourism Corpn (BTC): POB 159, Thimphu; tel 2647; telex 890217; Dir: Jigme Tshultim; Sales and Promotion Man: Dago Beda; administers two state-owned hotels.

Transport and Communications

Bhutan Government Transport Service (BGTS): Phuntsholing; tel 2345; Man Dir: Lhendup Dorji; f 1962; operates a fleet of 111 buses.

Druk-Air Corpn (Royal Bhutan Airlines): POB 209, Lower Market, Thimphu; tel 2215; telex 890219; Chair: Princess Sonam Chhoden Wangchuck; Man Dir: Ugyen Namgyal; f 1981; national airline, providing passenger and cargo services between Paro, Calcutta and Dhaka.

Transport Corpn of Bhutan: POB 7, Phuntsholing; tel 476; telex 890305; f 1982; operates coach services between Phuntsholing and Calcutta; owned by the Royal Insurance Corpn of Bhutan.

BOLIVIA

Head of State

Supreme executive power is vested in the President, who is elected by universal adult suffrage for a four-year term. Immediate re-election is prohibited by the Constitution. The President appoints the Cabinet, among other senior officials, and is empowered to issue decrees and initiate legislation by special messages to Congress.

President: Jaime Paz Zamora (took office 6 August 1989).

Office of the President: Palacio de Gobierno, Plaza Murillo, La Paz; tel (2) 371317; telex 5242; Minister of the Presidency: Gustavo Fernández Saavedra; Minister without Portfolio: Guillermo Fortún Suárez.

Vice-President: Luis Ossio Sanjines.

Legislature

Executive power is vested in Congress, comprising a Senate (27 Senators elected at departmental level by universal adult suffrage for a four-year term) and a Chamber of Deputies (130 members elected for a four-year term by universal adult suffrage). For administrative purposes the country is divided into nine departments, which are headed by prefects appointed by the President.

Senado (Senate): La Paz; Pres of Congreso Nacional (National Congress): Julio Garrett.

Cámara de Diputados (Chamber of Deputies): La Paz.

MINISTRIES AND GOVERNMENT DEPARTMENTS

MINISTRY OF AGRICULTURE
Avda Camacho 1407, La Paz
Tel (2) 374260; telex 5242
Minister: Mauro Bertero Gutiérrez

MINISTRY OF AVIATION
Avda Arce 2579, Casilla 6176, La Paz
Tel (2) 374142; telex 3413
Minister: Luis González Quintanilla

MINISTRY OF DEFENCE
Plaza Abaroa esq 20 de Octubre, La Paz
Tel (2) 377130; telex 5242
Minister: Héctor Ormachea Peñaranda

MINISTRY OF EDUCATION AND CULTURE
Avda Arce 2408, La Paz
Tel (2) 373260; telex 3373
Minister: Mariano Baptista Gumucio

MINISTRY OF ENERGY
Avda Mariscal Santa Cruz 1322, La Paz
Tel (2) 374050; telex 5366
Minister: Angel Zannier Claros

MINISTRY OF FINANCE
Calle Bolívar, La Paz
Tel (2) 379240; telex 2617
Minister: David Blanco Zavala

Instituto Nacional de Financiamiento Externo (INDEF): Edif Banco do Brasil, 11, La Paz; advises the Ministry of Finance on foreign debt management and on sources of external financing.

MINISTRY OF FOREIGN AFFAIRS AND WORSHIP
Edif BCB, 6, La Paz
Tel (2) 371152; telex 5242
Minister: Carlos Iturralde Ballivián

MINISTRY OF INDUSTRY, TRADE AND TOURISM
Avda Camacho esq Bueno, Casilla 1372, La Paz
Tel (2) 372044; telex 3259
Minister: Guido Céspedes Argandoña

MINISTRY OF INFORMATION
La Paz
Tel (2) 376350
Minister: Manfredo Kempff Suárez

MINISTRY OF THE INTERIOR, MIGRATION AND JUSTICE
Avda Arce, La Paz
Tel (2) 370460; telex 5437
Minister: Guillermo Capobianco Rivera

MINISTRY OF LABOUR
Calle Yanacocha esq Calle Mercado, La Paz
Tel (2) 374351; telex 5242
Minister: Oscar Zamora Medinacelli

MINISTRY OF MINING AND METALLURGY
Avda 16 de Julio 1769, La Paz
Tel (2) 379310; telex 5564
Minister: Walter Soriana Lea Plaza

MINISTRY OF PLANNING AND CO-ORDINATION
Avda Arce 2147, La Paz
Tel (2) 372060; telex 5321
Minister: Enrique García Rodríguez

MINISTRY OF PUBLIC HEALTH AND SOCIAL SECURITY
Plaza del Estudiante, La Paz
Tel (2) 375460; telex 5242
Minister: Mario Paz Zamora

MINISTRY OF TRANSPORT AND COMMUNICATIONS
Edif La Urbana, Avda Camacho, La Paz
Tel (2) 377220; telex 2648
Minister: Willy Vargas Vacaflor

MINISTRY OF URBAN AFFAIRS
Avda 20 de Octubre esq F. Guachalla, Casilla 5926, La Paz
Tel (2) 372240; telex 5242
Minister: Elena Velasco

GOVERNMENT AGENCIES AND ORGANIZATIONS

Agriculture

Cámara Agropecuaria de La Paz: Calle Santa Cruz 266, Casilla 1620, La Paz; tel (2) 321496; Pres: Fernando Palacios; Gen Man: Héctor Elías Ayoroa.

Cámara Agropecuaria del Oriente: Bolívar 559, Casilla 116, Santa Cruz; tel (33) 31137; telex 4438; fax (33) 22621; Pres: Osman Landivar; Planning Man: Walter Nuñez; Agriculture Man: Jorge Suarez; Livestock Man: Alfonso Roca V.; f 1964; planning and co-ordination of agriculture and livestock production by associations in eastern Bolivia.

Cámara Nacional Forestal: Calle Manuel Ignacio Salvatierra 1055, Casilla 346, Santa Cruz; tel (33) 23996; telex 4330; Pres: Edgar Landívar Landívar; Man: Arturo Bowles O.; f 1971; represents the interests of the timber industry.

Business and Economy

BANKING

Banco Agrícola de Bolivia: Avda Mariscal Santa Cruz esq Almirante Grau, Casilla 1179, La Paz; tel (2) 365876; telex 3278; Pres: Arturo Sornco V.; Gen Man: Víctor G. Rivera; f 1942.

Banco Central de Bolivia: Ayacucho esq Mercado, Casilla 3118, La Paz; tel (2) 374151; telex 3403; Pres: Jacques Trigo; Gen Man: Ricardo Rojas H.; f 1928; bank of issue.

Banco del Estado: Calle Colón esq Mercado, Casilla 1401, La Paz; tel (2) 352868; telex 3267; Pres: Alfredo Buchón; Gen Man: Javier Pantoja Romero; f 1970; state bank incorporating banking dept of Banco Central de Bolivia; 55 brs.

Banco Minero de Bolivia: Calle Comercio 1290, Casilla 1410, La Paz; tel (2) 352168; telex 2568; Gen Man: Rigoberto Pérez; f 1936; provides finance for the private mining industry.

Banco de la Vivienda: Avda Camacho 1336, Casilla 8155, La Paz; tel (2) 343510; telex 2295; Pres: (vacant); Gen Man: José Ramírez Montalva; f 1964; 51% state participation; promotes and finances housing devts.

Superintendencia de Bancos: Edif Banco Central de Bolivia 16, Ayacucho esq Mercado 200, Casilla 3118, La Paz; tel (2) 362679; Man: Luis del Río Chávez; f 1928; banking supervisory authority.

INSURANCE

Superintendencia Nacional de Seguros y Reaseguros: Calle Batallón Colorados 162, 4, Casilla 6118, La Paz; tel (2) 374137; Supt: Alfredo Oporto Crespo; Man: Gabriel Vela Quiroga; f 1975; supervisory authority for insurance industry.

MARKETING

Comité Boliviano del Café (COBOLCA): Avda Villazón 1970, Casilla 21173, La Paz; tel (2) 341553; Gen Man: Alberto Vargas Covarrubias; oversees the export, marketing and growing policies of the coffee industry.

Instituto Boliviano de Promoción de Exportaciones (INBOLPEX): Casilla 5947, La Paz; promotes the growth of export industries; advises exporters on markets and export procedures.

NATIONALIZED INDUSTRY

Cámara Nacional de Industria: Edif Cámara Nacional de Comercio 14, Avda Mariscal Santa Cruz 1392, Casilla 611, La Paz; tel (2) 374478; telex 3533; Pres: Javier Lupo Gamarra; Gen Man: Dr Alfredo Arana Ruck; f 1931; national chamber of industry.

Consejo Directivo Técnico de la Empresa Pública: La Paz; Govt agency co-ordinating policy planning, training and technical assistance for state-owned enterprises.

Corporación de las Fuerzas Armadas para el Desarrollo Nacional (Cofadena): Avda 6 de Agosto 2649, Casilla 1015, La Paz; tel (2) 377305; telex 3286; Gen Man: Crisólogo Rojas Zapata; f 1972; industrial, agricultural and mining holding co and devt organization; owned by the Bolivian armed forces.

Empresa Metalúrgica Vinto (EMV): Casilla 612, Oruro; tel (52) 52857; telex 2255; fax (52) 50458; Pres: Gonzalo Martínez; Gen Man: Alvaro Rejas; smelting of non-ferrous minerals and special alloys.

Defence

Armed Forces: Gran Cuartel General de Miraflores, La Paz; tel (2) 370120; telex 5384; Commdr-in-Chief: Jorgé Rodriguez; Inspector-Gen: Geraldo Peralta Rodo.

Air Force: Avda Montes 734, La Paz; tel (2) 379050; telex 356682; Commdr: Guillermo Escobar Uhry; Chief of Gen Staff: Victor Hugo Baiderrama.

Army: Gran Cuartel General de Miraflores, La Paz; tel (2) 378180; telex 356682; Commdr: Rómulo Mercado Gármica.

Navy: Gran Cuartel General de Miraflores, La Paz; tel (2) 782826; telex 2519; Commdr: Douglas Estremadoiro; Chief of Staff: Luis Azurduv.

Development and Planning

INVESTMENT

Instituto Nacional de Inversiones (INI): Edif Cristal 10, Calle Yanacocha, Casilla 4393, La Paz; tel (2) 375730; Exec Dir: Gastón Murillo; f 1971; promotes new investments and the application of the Investment Law.

PLANNING

Consejo Nacional de Planificación (CONEPLAN): Edif Banco Central de Bolivia 26, La Paz; tel (2) 377115; f 1985; planning; responsible to the Ministry of Planning and Co-ordination.

REGIONAL DEVELOPMENT

Corporación Regional de Desarrollo de La Paz (Cordepaz): Edif Santa Isabel, 2, Bloque A, Avda Arce esq Pinilla, Casilla 6102, La Paz; tel (2) 342325; telex 3256; Pres: Luis Sarmiento Terán; Gen Man: Dr Alberto Muñoz de la Barra; f 1972; decentralized Govt institution to promote the devt of the La Paz area.

Legal and Judiciary

Corte Suprema (Supreme Court): Calle Yanacocha 417, La Paz; tel (2) 377032; telex 2320; Pres: Edgar Oblitas Fernández; 12 mems appointed by Congress for a 10-year term.

Office of the Attorney-General: Sucre; Attorney-Gen: Dr José Hugo Vilar Tufino; the Attorney-General is appointed by the President on the proposal of the Senate.

Media

BROADCASTING

Asociación Boliviana de Radiodifusoras (ASBORA): Potosí 920, Casilla 7958, La Paz; tel (2) 328513; Pres: Miguel A. Dueri; Vice-Pres: Enrique Costas; broadcasting authority for radio.

Empresa Nacional de Televisión: Ayacucho 467, Casilla 900, La Paz; tel (2) 376356; telex 2312; Dir-Gen: J. Barragán; Gen Man: Raúl Novillo Alarcón; f 1969; Govt TV network.

Televisión Universitaria—Canal 13 (University TV Service): Avda 6 de Agosto 2170, Edif 'Hoy', 12 y 13, La Paz; tel (2) 359297; telex 3438; fax (2) 359491; Dir: Carlos Soria Galvarro; f 1980; educational programmes.

NEWS AND INFORMATION

Instituto Nacional de Estadística: Plaza Mario Guzmán Aspiazu No 1, Casilla 6129, La Paz; tel (2) 367444; telex 3505; Exec Dir: Marcelo Mercado Lora; f 1936; statistical office.

Mining and Energy

ENERGY

Empresa Nacional de Electricidad, SA (ENDE): Colombia No 655, esq Falsuri, Casilla 565, Cochabamba; tel (42) 46322; telex 6251; fax (42) 42700; Pres: Minister of Energy, Angel Zannier Claros; Gen Man: Claude Bessé Arce; f 1962; state electricity co.

Instituto Boliviano de Ciencia y Tecnología Nuclear (IBTEN): Avda 6 de Agosto 2905, Casilla 4821, La Paz; tel (2) 356877; telex 2220; Exec Dir (acting): Juan Carlos Méndez Ferry; f 1983; activities include: nuclear engineering, agricultural and industrial application of radio-isotopes, radio-chemical analysis, neutron generating, nuclear physics and dosimetry.

Yacimientos Petrolíferos Fiscales Bolivianos (YPFB): Calle Bueno 185, Casilla 2376, La Paz; tel (2) 356540; telex 2369; Pres: Alfonso Romero; Vice-Pres, Operations: Jorge Flores López; Vice-Pres, Admin and Finance: Dr Mauricio Gonzales; f 1936; petroleum enterprise.

MINING

Cámara Nacional de Minería: Pasaje Bernardo Trigo 429, Casilla 2022, La Paz; tel (2) 350623; Pres: Dr Jorge Gutiérrez del Río; Sec-Gen: Adolfo Castro; f 1953; mining institute.

Comité Boliviano de Productores de Antimonio: Pasaje Bernardo Trigo 429, Casilla 2022, La Paz; tel (2) 350623; Pres: Mario Mercado Vaca Guzmán; f 1978; oversees the marketing, pricing and promotion policies of the antimony industry.

Corporación Minera de Bolivia (COMIBOL): Avda Mariscal Santa Cruz 1092, Casilla 349, La Paz; tel (2) 357979; telex 2420; Gen Man: Gonzalo Barrientos Carreaga; f 1952; state mining corpn; mining and processing.

Empresa Minera Estatal del Oriente (EMEDO): Calle Tarija 55, Casilla 3079, Santa Cruz; tel (33) 27037; telex 4353; Pres: Marcelo Claure; Gen Man: Rolando Ibáñez; mining co.

Fondo Nacional de Exploración Minera (FNEM): Casilla 5796, La Paz; state agency providing credit for privately-owned small and medium-sized mining co.

Tourism

Instituto Boliviano de Turismo (IBT): Calle Mercado 1328, Casilla 1868, La Paz; tel (2) 367463; telex 2534; Exec Dir: Hortensia Romero de Vallotón; f 1977; promotes, plans and co-ordinates tourist activity.

Transport and Communications

TELECOMMUNICATIONS

Dirección General de Telecomunicaciones: Calle Mercado 1115, 5, La Paz; tel (2) 369888; telex 2595; Dir-Gen: Freddy Canavire Pardo; f 1980; administers, finances and regulates telecommunications activity.

Empresa Nacional de Telecomunicaciones (ENTEL): Edif ENTEL, Calle Ayacucho No 267, Casilla 4450, La Paz; tel (2) 355908; telex 3202; Gen Man: Juan José Peralta C.; state telecommunications co.

TRANSPORT

Empresa Nacional de Ferrocarriles (ENFE): Estación Central de Ferrocarriles, Plaza Zalles, Casilla 428, La Paz; tel (2) 327401; telex 2405; Gen Man: Blás Monzón C.; Dep Gen Man: I. Eduardo Villegas; f 1964; administers most of the railways in the country.

Líneas Navieras Bolivianas (LINABOL): Edif Hansa 16,

Avda Mariscal Santa Cruz, Apdo 8695, La Paz; tel (2) 369512; telex 5475; fax (2) 375988; Pres: J. del Carpio Bravo; Vice-Pres: W. Stahlke; ocean shipping.

Lloyd Aéreo Boliviano, SAM (LAB): Casilla 132, Aeropuerto 'Jorge Wilstermann', Cochabamba; tel (42) 5900; telex 6290; fax (42) 29207; Pres: Gen Jaime Niño de Guzman; Gen Man: Fernando Vargas; f 1925; state-owned since 1941; 99.98% Govt-owned; operates internal air services and joint services with other national lines to South American and US destinations.

BOTSWANA

Head of State

Executive power lies with the President, who is also Commander-in-Chief of the Armed Forces. The President, who is elected by the National Assembly for the duration of Parliament, appoints and leads a Cabinet, which comprises a Vice-President and 10 other ministers, and which is responsible to the Assembly.

President: Dr Quett Ketumile Joni Masire (took office 18 July 1980; re-elected 10 September 1984 and 7 October 1989).

Office of the President: Private Bag 001, Gaborone; tel 355434; telex 2414.

Vice-President: Peter S. Mmusi.

Office of the Vice-President: Private Bag 008, Gaborone.

Legislature

Legislative power is vested in Parliament, consisting of the President and the National Assembly. The Assembly includes 34 elected members, a Speaker and the Attorney-General. The Assembly's term of office is five years. Certain legislative matters must be referred to the 15-member House of Chiefs for approval, although this body has no power of veto.

National Assembly: POB 240, Gaborone; tel 373200; telex 2414; fax 313103; Speaker: James G. Haskins.

House of Chiefs: Private Bag 001, Gaborone; Chair: Chief Seepapitso.

MINISTRIES AND GOVERNMENT DEPARTMENTS

MINISTRY OF AGRICULTURE
Private Bag 003, Gaborone
Tel 350500; telex 2543
Minister: Daniel Kwelagobe
Assistant Minister: Geoffrey M. Oteng

MINISTRY OF COMMERCE AND INDUSTRY
Private Bag 004, Gaborone
Tel 353881; telex 2674; fax 371539
Minister: Ponatshengo H. K. Kedikilwe

MINISTRY OF EDUCATION
Private Bag 005, Gaborone
Tel 355294; telex 2944
Minister: Ray Molomo

MINISTRY OF EXTERNAL AFFAIRS
Private Bag 001, Gaborone
Minister: Dr Gaositwe K. T. Chiepe

MINISTRY OF FINANCE AND DEVELOPMENT PLANNING
Private Bag 008, Gaborone
Tel 355272; telex 2401
Minister: Festus G. Mogae
Assistant Minister: D. N. Magang

Department of Supply: POB 80, Gaborone; tel 351321; telex 2548; fax 372557; Dir: P. M. Mokgosana; f 1974; centralized Govt procurement agency, responsible for materials management for the entire public sector.

MINISTRY OF HEALTH
Private Bag 0038, Gaborone
Tel 355557
Minister: Kebathlamang Pitseyosi Morake

MINISTRY OF HOME AFFAIRS
Private Bag 002, Gaborone
Tel 355212
Minister: (vacant)

MINISTRY OF LOCAL GOVERNMENT AND LANDS
Private Bag 006, Gaborone
Tel 354100; telex 2589
Minister: Peter S. Mmusi
Assistant Ministers: Michael R. Tshipinare, Ronald Sebego

Applied Research Unit: Private Bag 006, Gaborone; tel 354100; telex 2589; Dir: Moshe Setimela; f 1980; specialist unit concerned with policy research, formulation and implementation for Ministry of Local Govt and Lands.

Department of Surveys and Lands: Private Bag 0037, Gaborone; tel 353251; telex 2589; Dir: L. J. Howells; Chief Surveyor: B. B. H. Morebodi; f 1969; responsible for surveying, mapping and acquisition of land.

Unified Local Government Service: Private Bag 0052, Gaborone; tel 352091; Sec: P. L. Siele; f 1973; formulates and implements Govt policies, administers local Govt.

MINISTRY OF MINERAL RESOURCES AND WATER AFFAIRS
Private Bag 0018, Gaborone
Tel 352454; telex 2503
Minister: Patrick K. Balopi

MINISTRY OF PRESIDENTIAL AFFAIRS AND PUBLIC ADMINISTRATION
Private Bag 001, Gaborone
Minister: Lt-Gen Mompate Merafe

MINISTRY OF WORKS, TRANSPORT AND COMMUNICATIONS
Private Bag 007, Gaborone
Tel 355303; telex 2743; fax 313303
Minister: Chapson J. Butale

GOVERNMENT AGENCIES AND ORGANIZATIONS

Advisory and Supervisory Body

Office of the Auditor-General: Private Bag 0010, Gaborone; tel 355322; Auditor-General: E. P. S. Letsididi; central financial agency, with powers of audit over all public-sector funds.

Agriculture and the Environment

AGRICULTURE

Botswana Agricultural Marketing Board: Private Bag 0053, Gaborone; tel 351341; telex 2530; fax 352926; Chair: Perm Sec at Ministry of Agriculture; Gen Man: P. R. J. Mulligan; f 1974; buys and sells produce.

Botswana Livestock Development Corpn (Pty) Ltd: POB 455, Gaborone; tel 351949; telex 2543; Gen Man: S. M. R. Burnett; Dep Gen Man: M. Pholoba; f 1973; responsible for livestock marketing, buying cattle from remote areas and selling to other producers.

Botswana Meat Commission (BMC): Private Bag 4, Lobatse; tel 330321; telex 2420; Exec Chair: D. W. Finlay; Gen Man: F. Boakgomo; f 1966; central organization for all aspects of meat production.

THE ENVIRONMENT

Department of Wildlife and National Parks: POB 131, Gaborone; tel 351461; Dir: K. T. Ngwamotsoko.

Business and Economy

BANKING

Bank of Botswana: POB 712, Gaborone; tel 351911; telex 2448; fax 372984; Gov: H. C. L. Hermans; Dep Gov: D. J. Hudson; f 1976; bank of issue.

Botswana Co-operative Bank Ltd: Co-operative Bank House, Broadhurst Mall, POB 40106, Gaborone; tel 371398; telex 2298; Pres: M. L. Setlhare; Gen Man: Dr Harry Tlale; f 1974; central source of credit for registered co-operative societies.

National Development Bank: Development House, The Mall, POB 225, Gaborone; tel 352801; telex 2553; fax 372086; Chair: G. F. Stoneham; Gen Man: B. I. Gasennelwe; f 1964; priority given to agricultural credit for Botswana farmers, and co-operative credit and loans for local business ventures.

FINANCIAL AGENCIES

Department of Taxation: Private Bag 0013; Gaborone; tel 53751; raises Govt revenue through taxation.

Financial Services Company of Botswana (Pty) Ltd: POB 1129, Gaborone; tel 351363; telex 2207; fax 357815; Chair: J. E. Anderson; Gen Man: G. H. Wilson; f 1974; provides hire purchase, mortgage and industrial leasing facilities.

Office of the Accountant-General: Private Bag 0030, Gaborone; tel 350204; telex 2401; fax 356086; Accountant-Gen: E. W. Johwa; Dep Accountant-Gen: M. C. Montshiwa; f 1966; establishment of a proper system of accounts in Govt depts; preparation of annual statement of accounts.

INSURANCE

Botswana Insurance Co (Pty) Ltd: BIC House, POB 336, Gaborone; tel 351791; telex 2359; fax 313290; Gen Man: P. B. Summer.

TRADE

Department of Trade and Investment Promotion: Private Bag 004, Gaborone; tel 353881; telex 2674; fax 371539; Dir: D. T. Tibone; Principal Commercial Officer: R. P. Boikanyo; f 1984; promotes trade and investment by providing consultancy and liaison services; organizes annual trade fair; publishes promotional material and provides trade and investment information services; responsible to the Ministry of Commerce and Industry.

Defence

Botswana Defence Force: Private Bag 061, Sir Seretse Khama Barracks, Mogoditshane; Commdr-in-Chief: President Quett Masire; Defence Force Commdr: Col Mompati Merafe.

Botswana Police Force: Private Bag 0012, Gaborone; Commr of Police: Simon Hirschfield.

Development and Planning

Botswana Co-operative Union: Gaborone; telex 2298; central organization for co-operative societies.

Botswana Development Corpn Ltd: Madirelo House, Mmanaka Rd, POB 438, Gaborone; tel 351811; telex 2251; fax 373539; Chair: the Perm Sec at Ministry of Finance and Development Planning; Gen Man: M. O. Molefane; implements the conditions of national devt plans.

Botswana Enterprise Development Unit (BEDU): Plot No 1269, Lobatse Rd, POB 0014, Gaborone; Dir: J. Lindfors; f 1974; promotes industrialization and rural devt.

Department of Co-operative Development: POB 86, Gaborone; tel 371395; f 1962; promotes co-operative growth, administers the Co-operative Societies Act, supervises and audits co-operative societies.

Department of Town and Regional Planning: Private Bag 0042, Gaborone; tel 351935; telex 2589; f 1972; responsible for physical and natural resources planning; prepares devt plans for settlements, provides environmental advice to Govt and local authorities as well as private bodies.

Legal and Judiciary

High Court: Private Bag 1, Lobatse; tel 330396; Chief Justice: Eben Liveseyluke; Registrar: K. Yoganathas.

Office of the Attorney-General: Private Bag 009, Gaborone; Attorney-Gen: Moleleki D. Mokama.

Media

BROADCASTING

Radio Botswana: Private Bag 0060, Gaborone; tel 352541; telex 2633; Dir: M. Nasha; f 1965; provides radio services in Setswana and English.

TV Association of Botswana: Gaborone; two transmitters relaying TV programmes from South Africa.

GOVERNMENT PUBLISHER

Department of Government Printing and Publishing Services: Private Bag 0081, Gaborone; tel 314441; telex 2414.

NEWS AND INFORMATION

Botswana Press Agency (BOPA): Private Bag 060, Gaborone; tel 313601; telex 2284; f 1981.

Central Statistics Office: Private Bag 0024, Gaborone; tel 52521; official statistics agency.

Department of Information and Broadcasting: Private Bag 0060, Gaborone; tel 352541; telex 2409; publishes official daily newspaper and other material on Botswana.

Mining and Energy

ENERGY

Botswana Power Corpn: Motlakase House, POB 48, Gaborone; tel 352211; telex 2431; fax 373563; Chair: The Dep Perm Sec at Ministry of Mineral Resources and Water Affairs; Chief Exec: E. D. Bell; generation and national distribution of electricity.

MINING

De Beers Botswana Mining Co (Debswana): Botsalano House, The Mall, POB 329, Gaborone; tel 51131; telex 2410; Chair: J. Ogilvie Thompson; jointly owned by Botswana Govt and De Beers; sole diamond-mining interest in Botswana.

Tourism

Botswana Tourism Development Unit: Private Bag 0047, Gaborone; tel 353024; telex 2674; fax 371539; Dir of Tourism: M. K. J. Masisi; Principal Officer: U. S. Mpoloka; f 1980; formulates and implements Govt policies on the devt of tourism; includes sections concerned with marketing and promotion, research and statistics, licensing and inspection, publication and public relations; under the administrative jurisdiction of the Ministry of Commerce and Industry.

Transport and Communications

TELECOMMUNICATIONS

Botswana Telecommunications Corpn: POB 700, Gaborone; tel 358000; telex 2252; fax 313355; Chief Exec: M. T. Curry; f 1980.

TRANSPORT

Air Botswana (Pty) Ltd: POB 92, Gaborone; tel 352812; telex 2413; fax 374802; Chair: M. O. Molefane; Gen Man: Keith Petch; f 1988; owned by the Botswana Development Corpn; domestic services between four airports, connecting with regional services to other African destinations.

Botswana Railways: Private Bag 00125, Gaborone; tel 373185; telex 2980; fax 312305; Gen Man: J. Reeks; f 1987; provides railway transportation services.

Roads Department: Private Bag 0026, Gaborone; tel 55515; responsible for national road network; under the administrative jurisdiction of the Ministry of Works, Transport and Communications.

Utilities

Water Utilities Corpn: Private Bag 00276, Gaborone; tel 352521; telex 2545; fax 373852; Chair: The Perm Sec at Ministry of Mineral Resources and Water Affairs; Chief Exec: T. Waters; f 1970; supply of drinking water to Botswana's urban areas.

Welfare

Botswana Housing Corpn: POB 412, Gaborone; tel 353341; telex 2729; Chair: P. O. Molosi; Gen Man: J. D. Richardson; provides housing for Govt and local authorities; assists with housing schemes and provision of housing for other persons.

Department of Food Resources: POB 96, Gaborone; tel 354124; telex 2589; Admin Officer: M. S. Sehlulane; f 1982; procurement, storage and distribution of food commodities under the Drought Relief Programme.

BRAZIL

Head of State

Executive power is exercised by the President, who is chosen by an electoral college for a five-year term and is not eligible for re-election. A constitutional amendment provides that future Presidents will be elected by direct voting. The President appoints and heads the Cabinet.

President: Fernando Collor de Mello (elected December 1989).

Office of the President: Palácio do Planalto, Praça dos Três Poderes, 70.150 Brasília, DF; tel (61) 223-2714; telex (61) 1451.

Vice-President: Itamar Augusto Cautiero Franco.

Legislature

Legislative power is vested in the bicameral National Congress, comprising the Chamber of Deputies (elected by compulsory universal adult suffrage for a four-year term), and the Federal Senate (elected in rotation for eight years). The number of Deputies is determined by the size of population. On a Federal level, each State has an elected Governor and legislature.

Senado Federal (Federal Senate): Palácio do Congresso, Praça dos Três Poderes, 70.160 Brasília, DF; tel (61) 224-9784; telex (61) 1156; Pres: Sen Nelson Carneiro.

Chamber of Deputies: Palácio do Congresso, Praça dos Três Poderes, 70.160 Brasília, DF; tel (61) 225-2885; telex (61) 1164; Pres: Paes de Andrade.

MINISTRIES AND GOVERNMENT DEPARTMENTS

MINISTRY OF AGRICULTURE
Esplanada dos Ministérios, Bloco D, 8 andar,
70.043 Brasília, DF
Tel (61) 218-2800; telex (61) 1138
Minister: Joaquim Roriz

MINISTRY OF THE AIR FORCE
Esplanada dos Ministérios, Bloco M, 8 andar,
70.045 Brasília, DF
Tel (61) 223-0409; telex (61) 1152; fax (61) 223-0930
Minister: Brig Sócrates da Costa Monteiro

MINISTRY OF THE ARMY
Esplanada dos Ministérios, Bloco 4, 70.042 Brasília, DF
Tel (61) 224-6797; telex (61) 1094
Minister: Gen Carlos Tinoco Ribeiro Gomes

MINISTRY OF CULTURE
SBN, Quadra 2, Bloco F, Edif Central, 70.040 Brasília, DF
Tel (61) 223-5614; telex (61) 1068
Minister: (vacant)

MINISTRY OF EDUCATION
Esplanada dos Ministérios, Bloco L, 70.047 Brasília, DF
Tel (61) 223-7306; telex (61) 9105
Minister: Carlos Chiarelli

MINISTRY OF FINANCE
Esplanada dos Ministérios, Bloco P, 5 andar,
70.048 Brasília, DF
Tel (61) 223-2729; telex (61) 1142
Minister: Zelia Cardoso de Melo

MINISTRY OF FOREIGN AFFAIRS
Palácio do Itamaraty, Esplanada dos Ministérios,
70.040 Brasília, DF
Tel (61) 226-1762; telex (61)1319
Minister: Francisco Rezek

MINISTRY OF HEALTH
Esplanada dos Ministérios, Bloco 11, 70.058 Brasília, DF
Tel (61) 223-8158; telex (61) 1752
Minister: Alcini Guerra

MINISTRY OF INDUSTRIAL DEVELOPMENT, SCIENCE AND TECHNOLOGY
Esplanada dos Ministérios, Bloco 6, 70.053 Brasília, DF
Tel (61) 223-7784; telex (61) 1066
Minister: (vacant)

MINISTRY OF INFRASTRUCTURE
Esplanada dos Ministérios, Bloco R, 70.044 Brasília, DF
Tel (61) 223-4992; telex (61) 1994
Minister: Ozires Silva
Replaced Ministries of Communications, Mines and Energy, and Transport in March 1989.

MINISTRY OF THE INTERIOR
Esplanada dos Ministérios, Bloco 23, 70.054 Brasília, DF
Tel (61) 226-2820; telex (61) 1015
Minister: (vacant)

MINISTRY OF JUSTICE
Esplanada dos Ministérios, Bloco T, 70.064 Brasília, DF
Tel (61) 224-2964; telex (61) 1088
Minister: José Bernardo Cabral

MINISTRY OF LABOUR
Esplanada dos Ministérios, Bloco F, 10 andar,
70.059 Brasília, DF
Tel (61) 224-6864; telex (61) 1158
Minister: António Rogério Magri

MINISTRY OF THE NAVY
Esplanada dos Ministérios, Bloco 3, 70.055 Brasília, DF
Tel (61) 224-3489; telex (61) 1392
Minister: Adm Má César Flores

MINISTRY OF SOCIAL WELFARE
Esplanada dos Ministérios, Bloco U, 70.065 Brasília, DF
Tel (61) 224-3445; telex (61) 1694
Minister: Margarida Maia Procopio

MINISTRY OF URBAN DEVELOPMENT AND ENVIRONMENT
SEPN, Quadra 505, Bloco B, 70.730 Brasília, DF
Tel (61) 272-8413; telex (61) 4220
Minister of Environment: José Lutzemberger

OFFICE OF THE HEAD OF THE NATIONAL INFORMATION SERVICE (SNI)
Brasília
Head: (vacant)

PLANNING SECRETARIAT OF THE PRESIDENCY
Esplanada dos Ministérios, Bloco K, 7 andar,
70.063 Brasília, DF
Tel (61) 224-4114; telex (61) 2207
Minister, Head of the Secretariat for Planning: (vacant)

GOVERNMENT AGENCIES AND ORGANIZATIONS

Advisory and Supervisory Bodies

Comissão de Fusão e Incorporação de Empresa (COFIE): Ministério da Fazenda, Esplanada dos Ministérios, Edif Sede, Ala B, 1 andar, Brasília, DF; tel (61) 225-3405; telex (61) 1539; Pres: Sebastião Marcos Vital; Exec Sec: Edgar Bezerra Leite, Jr; mergers commission; attached to the Ministry of Finance.

Conselho Federal de Desestacização: Brasilía; Sec: Paulo Galleta; f 1988; responsible for proposed privatization of some 70 state cos.

Conselho Nacional de Alcool (CNAL): Esplanada dos Ministérios, Bloco 6, 70.053 Brasília, DF; tel (61) 225-7110.

Agriculture

Conselho Nacional de Desenvolvimento Pecuário (CONDEPE): Brasília, DF; promotes livestock devt.

Empresa Brasileira de Pesquisa Agropecuária (EMBRAPA): Parque SAIN-Final W-3 Norte, 70.770 Brasília, DF; tel (61) 272-4241; telex (61) 1620; Pres: Carlos Magno Campos da Rocha; f 1973; attached to the Ministry of Agriculture; agricultural research.

Instituto do Açúcar e do Álcool (IAA): Largo do Paço 42, Edif Taquara, 20.010 Rio de Janeiro, RJ; tel (21) 224-6463; telex (21) 50201; Pres: Dr José Henrique Turner; f 1933; Govt agency; promotion and devt of the sugar industry; sole exporter of raw sugar.

Instituto Brasileiro do Café (IBC): Av Rodrigues Alves 129, 10 andar, Praça Mauá, 20.081 Rio de Janeiro, RJ; tel (21) 263-5121; telex (21) 23119; Pres: Dr Jório Dauster Magalhães; f 1952; Govt agency; promotes and controls coffee production and commercialization; gives technical advice to producers.

Instituto Brasileiro de Meio Ambiente e Recursos Naturais Renováveis (IBAMA): Setor de Áreas Isoladas Norte, Av L-4 Norte, 70.800 Brasília, DF; tel (61) 321-2324; telex (61) 1711; Pres: Fernando Cezar de Moreira Mesquita; Dir: Marco Antônio Castello Branco; f 1967; under the Ministry of the Interior; responsible for forestry research and devt, endangered animals and fauna, parks and forestry commercialization.

Instituto Nacional de Colonização e Reforma Agrária (INCRA): SBN, Palácio do Desenvolvimento, 14 andar, 70.040 Brasília, DF; f 1970; attached to the Ministry of Agriculture; oversees land settlement and agrarian reform.

Superintendência do Desenvolvimento da Pesca (SUDEPE): Edif da Pesca, Av W-3 Norte, Quadra 506, Bloco C, 70.040 Brasília, DF; tel (61) 272-3229; telex (61) 1179; Supt: Aécio Moura da Silva; attached to the Ministry of Agriculture; promotes the devt of the fishing industry.

Business and Economy

BANKING

Banco da Amazônia (BASA): Av Pres Vargas 800, 16 andar, Belém, PA; tel (91) 224-1055; telex (91) 1093; Pres: Carlos Thadeu de Freitas Gomes; f 1966, nationalized 1969; Govt financial agency promoting the devt of the Amazon region.

Banco do Brasil, SA: Sector Bancário Sul, Lote 32, Quadra 4, CP 562, Brasília, DF; tel (61) 212-2633; telex (61) 8196; Pres: Mário Berard; f 1808; 2,296 brs.

Banco Central do Brasil: Edif Sede, SBS, Conj 7, Bloco A, 70.074 Brasília, DF; tel (61) 214-2000; telex (61) 2098; Pres: Ibrahim Eris; f 1965; central bank and bank of issue; responsible to the Conselho Monetário Nacional (see below).

Banco de Desenvolvimento do Espírito Santo, SA: Av Princesa Isabel 54, CP 1168, 29.000 Vitoria, ES; tel (27) 223-8333; telex (27) 2131; Pres: Odilon Borges, Jr; devt bank.

Banco do Desenvolvimento do Estado da Bahia, SA: Av Tancredo Neves 776, 40.000 Salvador, BA; tel (71) 231-2322; telex (71) 1665; Pres: José Vieira de Santana Neto; f 1937; devt bank.

Banco de Desenvolvimento do Estado do Rio Grande do Sul, SA (BADESUL): Rua 7 de Setembro 666, 90.000 Porto Alegre, RS; tel (51) 21-2655; telex (51) 1159; Pres: James Giacomoni; f 1975; devt bank.

Banco de Desenvolvimento do Estado de São Paulo, SA (BADESP): Av Paulista 1776, 01.310 São Paulo, SP; tel (11) 289-2233; telex (11) 22763; Pres: José Tiacci Kirsten; devt bank.

Banco de Desenvolvimento de Minas Gerais (BDMG): Rua da Bahia 1600, 30.160 Belo Horizonte, MG; tel (31) 222-5008; telex (31) 1343; fax (31) 273-5084; Pres: Dr Carlos Alberto Teixeira de Oliveira; f 1962; implements Govt policies relating to the devt of Minas Gerais; provides loans for manufacturing industries, commerce, agriculture and small businesses.

Banco de Desenvolvimento do Paraná, SA: Av Vicente Machado 445, CP 6042, 80.420 Curitiba, PR; tel (41) 224-9711; telex (41) 5083; Pres: Celso da Costa Sabóia; f 1962; devt bank.

Banco do Estado de Minas Gerais, SA: Rua Rio de Janeiro 471, CP 300, 30.160 Belo Horizonte, MG; tel (31) 224-5882; telex (31) 1181; Pres: José Luiz Rocha; f 1967; 269 brs.

Banco do Estado do Paraná, SA: Rua Máximo João Kopp 274, CP 3331, 80.000 Curitiba, PR; tel (41) 253-8311; telex (41)

6002; Pres: Carlos Antonio de Almeida Ferreira; f 1928; 309 brs.

Banco do Estado do Rio Grande do Sul, SA: Rua Capitão Montanha 177, CP 505, 90.010 Porto Alegre, RS; tel (51) 24-1177; telex (51) 518170; fax (51) 286-473; Pres: Ricardo Russowsky; f 1928; 295 brs.

Banco do Estado do Rio de Janeiro, SA (BANERJ): Av Nilo Peçanha 175, 17 andar, CP 21090, 20.020 Rio de Janeiro, RJ; tel (21) 533-2272; telex (21) 23290; fax (21) 533-1118; Pres: Márcio Fortes; f 1945; taken over by Banco Central do Brasil in March 1987; 2 brs.

Banco do Estado de São Paulo, SA: Praça Antônio Prado 6, CP 30-565, 01.010 São Paulo, SP; tel (11) 36-1448; telex (11) 18647; Chair: Boris Tabacoff; f 1926; 1315 brs.

Banco Nacional de Crédito Cooperativo, SA: SBN, Quadra 01, Bloco C, 2 andar; s/n Edif Palácio do Desenvolvimento-Asa Norte, 70.057 Brasília, DF; tel (61) 224-5515; telex (61) 1370; Pres (acting): Esupério S. de Campos Aguilar; established in conjunction with the Ministry of Agriculture; guaranteed by the Federal Govt to provide co-operative credit; 39 brs.

Banco Nacional do Desenvolvimento Econômico e Social (BNDES): Av República do Chile 100, 20.031 Rio de Janeiro, RJ; tel (21) 291-4442; telex (21) 22466; Pres: Marcio Fortes; f 1952; finances Govt-sponsored devt schemes; supports programmmes for national economic devt.

Banco Nacional da Habitação: SCS, Edif Antônio Venâncio, 6 andar, Brasília, DF; f 1964; provision of credit for construction, improvement and purchase of housing.

Banco do Nordeste do Brasil, SA: Praça Murillo Borges 1, 60.000 Fortaleza, CE; tel (85) 225-6555; telex (85) 1141; Pres: José Pereira e Silva; f 1954; 163 brs.

Banco Regional de Desenvolvimento do Extremo Sul (BRDE): Rua Uruguai 155, CP 139, 90.010 Porto Alegre, RS; tel (51) 221-9200; telex (51) 1229; Dir-Pres: Waldemar Allegretti; f 1961; devt bank for the States of Paraná, Rio Grande do Sul and Santa Catarina; agent for Federal financing agencies; provides finance for small- and medium-sized enterprises; 3 brs.

Conselho Monetário Nacional: SBS, Edif Banco do Brasil, 6 andar, Brasília, DF; Pres: Minister of Finance, Zelia Cardoso de Melo; f 1964; formulates monetary policy and supervises the banking system.

FINANCIAL AGENCY

Conselho Interministerial de Preços (CIP): Av Pres Antônio Carlos 375, 10 andar, 20.020 Rio de Janeiro, RJ; tel (21) 240-2281; telex (21) 33314; Exec Sec: Edgar de Abreu Cardoso; prices commission.

INSURANCE

Conselho Nacional de Seguros Privados (CNSP): Rio de Janeiro, RJ; tel (21) 222-1423; Pres: Minister of Finance, Zelia Cardoso de Melo; Sec: Walter J. Barros Graneiro; f 1966; insurance supervisory authority.

Superintendência de Seguros Privados (SUSEP): Rio de Janeiro, RJ; tel (21) 231-3092; Supt: João Régis Ricardo dos Santos; f 1966; part of the Ministry of Finance; supervisory authority for the insurance industry.

NATIONALIZED INDUSTRY

Aços Finos Piratini, SA: Rua Câncio Gomez 127, Florestas, CP 2118, 90.220 Porto Alegre, RS; tel (51) 22-5611; telex 513126; production of steel, wire, rods, etc.

Comissão Nacional da Indústria de Construção Civil: Rua

Martinez e Barros, 13, 20.270 Rio de Janeiro, RJ; tel (21) 273-2212; construction industry.

Companhia Siderúrgica Nacional, SA (CSN): Av 13 de Maio 13, 8 andar, Centro 20.031 Rio de Janeiro, RJ; tel (21) 297-7177; telex (21) 23025; Pres: Juvenal Osório Gomes; f 1941; production of iron and steel.

Conselho Nacional de Boracha (CNB): Setor de Autarquias Sul, Quadra 5, Lote 5, Bloco H, 70.070 Brasília, DF; tel (61) 223-6155; council of the rubber industry.

Conselho de Não-Ferrosos e de Siderurgia (CONSIDER): Ministério da Indústria e do Comércio, Esplanada dos Ministérios, Bloco 6, 5 andar, 70.053 Brasília, DF; tel (61) 224-6039; telex (61) 1012; Exec Sec: William Rocha Cantal; f 1973; responsible to the Ministry of Industrial Devt, Science and Technology; supervises devt policy in the non-ferrous, and iron and steel industries.

Empresa Brasileira de Aeronáutica, SA (EMBRAER): Av Brigadeiro Faria Lima 2170, CP 343, 01.220 São José dos Campos, SP; tel (123) 25-1000; telex (123) 3589; fax (123) 21-8466; Chief Exec: Ozílio Carlos da Silva; f 1969; aeronautics industry.

Fibase Insumos Basicos: Av Rio Branco 31, 20 andar, 20.090 Rio de Janeiro, RJ; tel (21) 233-1622; telex (21) 22466; raw materials co; promotes the devt of the raw materials industry.

Instituto Nacional de Metalurgia e Qualidade Industrial: Setor de Autarquias Sul, Quadra 2, Lote 2, 70.070 Brasília, DF; tel (61) 225-7556.

Instituto Nacional da Propriedade Industrial (INPI): Praça Mauá 7, 11 andar, 20.081 Rio de Janeiro, RJ; tel (21) 223-4182; telex (21) 22992; Pres: Paulo Afonso Pereira; f 1970.

Siderurgia Brasileira, SA (SIDERBRÁS): SAS, Quadra 2, Bloco E, Edif Siderbrás, 9 andar, 70.070 Brasília, DF; tel (61) 223-9104; telex (61) 1542; Pres: Manoel Moacélio de Aquiar Mendes; f 1974; steel industry.

Usinas Siderúrgicas de Minas Gerais, SA (USIMINAS): Rua Prof Vieira de Mendonça, 3011, CP 806, Engenho Nogueira, 31.310 Belo Horizonte, MG; tel (31) 441-4222; telex (31) 1261; fax (31) 441-7710; Pres: Luiz André Rico Vicente; Dirs: Silvio Bhering, Reginaldo Campos, Uajará Rodrigues; f 1956; production of iron.

TRADE

Carteira de Comércio Exterior (CACEX): Av Pres Vargas 328, 11 andar, 20.091 Rio de Janeiro, RJ; tel (21) 271-7504; telex (21) 23753; Dir: Namir Salek; state foreign trade agency; dept of Banco Central do Brasil.

Conselho Nacional do Comércio Exterior (CONCEX): Fazenda, 5 andar, Gabinete do Ministro, Esplanada dos Ministérios, Bloco 6, 70.048 Brasília, DF; tel (61) 223-4856; telex (61) 1142; Exec Sec: Namir Salek; f 1966; oversees foreign exchange and trade policies; directs export activities.

Instituto Nacional de Metrologia, Normalização e Qualidade Industrial (INMETRO) (Institute for Metrology, Standardizaton and Industrial Quality): Av Nossa Senhora das Graças 50, Xerém, Duque de Caxias, 25.400 Rio de Janeiro; tel (21) 779-1529; telex (21) 30672; fax (21) 779-1507; Pres: Dr Masao Ito; f 1973; institute of standards, weights and measures; linked to the Ministry of Industrial Devt, Science and Technology.

Defence

Armed Forces: Esplanada dos Ministérios, Bloco Q, 70.049 Brasília, DF; tel (61) 225-4605; Chief of the Gen Staff: Adm Valbert Lisieux Medeiros de Figueiredo (mem of the Cabinet).

Air Force: Esplanada dos Ministérios, Bloco M, 6 andar,

70.045 Brasília, DF; tel (61) 225-6405; telex (61) 1152.

Army: SMU, QG Ex, Bloco A, 3 andar, 70.630 Brasília, DF; tel (61) 223-3429; telex (61) 1092.

Navy: Esplanada dos Ministérios, Bloco N, 8 andar, 70.055 Brasília, DF; tel (61) 223-2559; telex (61) 1392.

Development and Planning

Conselho de Desenvolvimento Comercial (CDC): Ministério da Indústria e do Comércio, SCS, Quadra 02, Edif Pres Dutra, 2 andar, Bloco C, Sala 227, Esplanada dos Ministérios, 70.300 Brasília, DF; tel (61) 223-0308; telex (61) 2537; Exec Sec: Dr Ruy Coutinho do Nascimento; commercial devt council.

Conselho de Desenvolvimento Econômico (CDE): Esplanada dos Ministérios, Bloco K, 7 andar, 70.063 Brasília, DF; tel (61) 215-4100; Sec-Gen: Minister, Head of the Secretariat for Planning; f 1974; advises the President on the formulation of economic policy and on the co-ordination of ministerial activities.

Conselho de Desenvolvimento Social (CDS): Esplanada dos Ministérios, Bloco K, 3 andar, 382, 70.063 Brasília, DF; tel (61) 215-4477; Exec Sec: João A. Teles; council for social devt.

Empresa Brasileira de Assistência Técnica e Extensão Rural (EMBRATER): SAIN, Parque Rural, Edif Sede EMBRATER, CP 070530, 70.770 Brasília, DF; tel (61) 274-4650; telex (61) 1916; Pres: Mandelo de Vasconcelos Neto.

Instituto de Planejamento Econômico e Social (IPEA): SBS, Edif BNDE, 6 andar, 70.076 Brasília, DF; tel (61) 225-4350; telex (61) 01979; Pres: Ricardo Santiago; planning institute.

Secretaria Especial de Deseuvolvimento Industrial: Ministério do Deseuvolvimento da Indústria e Comércio, Lotes 2/5-2/8, Bloco G, 8 andar, 70.070 Brasília, DF; tel (61) 225-0822; telex (61) 2225; Exec Sec: Dr Ernesto Carrara; f 1969; industrial devt council; offers fiscal incentives for selected industries and for producers of manufactured goods under the Special Export Programme.

REGIONAL DEVELOPMENT

Companhia de Desenvolvimento do Vale do São Francisco (CODEVASF): SGAN, Quadra 601, Lote 1, Edif Sede, 70.830 Brasília, DF; tel (61) 223-2797; telex (61) 1057; Pres: Eliseu Roberto de Andrade Alves; f 1974; devt co for the São Francisco region.

Instituto de Desenvolvimento Industrial de Minas Gerais (INDI): Av Prudente de Morais 1641, 30.380 Belo Horizonte, MG; tel (31) 344-4466; telex (31) 2040; fax (31) 349-4437; Pres: Accacio Ferreira dos Santos, Jr; Dirs: Oscar Plínio Paschoal Tarquínio, José Alcibíades de Rezende Frota; f 1968; state agency specialising in promoting investment and the setting up of industrial projects.

Superintendência do Desenvolvimento da Amazônia (SUDAM): Av Almirante Barroso 426, Bairro do Marco, 66.000 Belém, PA; tel (91) 226-0044; telex (91) 1117; Supt: Henry Checralla Kayath; f 1966; attached to the Ministry of the Interior; supervises the devt of the Amazon regions of Brazil; oversees industrial, cattle breeding and basic services projects.

Superintendência do Desenvolvimento do Nordeste (SUDENE): Praça Supt João Gonçalves de Souza, Cidade Universitária, 50.000 Recife, PE; tel (81) 271-1044; telex (81) 1245; Supt: Paulo Ganem Souto; f 1959; attached to the Ministry of the Interior; promotes the devt of North East Brazil.

Superintendência do Desenvolvimento da Região Centro Oeste (SUDECO): SAS, Quadra 1, Bloco A, Lotes 9-10, 70-070 Brasília, DF; tel (61) 225-6111; telex (61) 1616; Supt: Ramez Tebet; f 1967; co-ordinates devt projects in the States of Goiás, Mato Grosso, Mato Grosso do Sul, Rondônia and Distrito Federal.

Superintendência do Desenvolvimento da Região Sul (SUDESUL): Rua Caldas Júnior 120, 20 andar, 90.018 Porto Alegre, RS; tel (512) 286-400; telex (51) 1005; Supt: Alceu José Atz; co-ordinates devt in the Staes of Rio Grande do Sul, Santa Catarina and Paraná; attached to the Ministry of the Interior.

Superintendência da Zona Franca de Manaus (SUFRAMA): Rua Ministro João Gonçalves de Souza, Cidade Universitária, Distrito Industrial, 69.000 Manaus, AM; tel (92) 237-3288; telex (92) 2146; Supt: Jadyr Carvalhedo Magalhães.

Legal and Judiciary

Supreme Federal Tribunal: Praça dos Três Poderes, 70.175 Brasília, DF; tel (61) 224-8179; telex (61) 1473; Pres: José Néri da Silveira; Vice-Pres: Aldir G. Passarinho; Procurator-Gen: Aristides Junqueira de Alvarenga; Dir-Gen (Secretariat): Maurício Maranhão de Aguiar.

Media

BROADCASTING

Empresa Brasileira de Comunicação, SA (Radiobrás) (Brazilian Communications Co): SCRN 702-3, Bloco B, No 18, 70.710 Brasília, DF; tel (61) 224-3949; telex (61) 1682; Chair: Antônio Martins de Vasconcelos; f 1988 following merger of Empresa Brasileira de Radiodifusão and Empresa Brasileira de Noticías.

NEWS AND INFORMATION

Fundação Instituto Brasileiro de Geografia e Estatística (IBGE): Av Franklin Roosevelt 166, Castelo, 20.021 Rio de Janeiro, RJ; tel (21) 220-6671; telex (21) 30939; Pres: Charles Curt Mueller; Dir-Gen: David Wu Tai; f 1936; provides information through statistical, geographical, cartographic and demographic surveys and research.

Mining and Energy

ENERGY

Centrais Eléctricas Brasileiras, SA (ELECTROBRÁS): Av Pres Vargas 642, 20.071 Rio De Janeiro, RJ; tel (21) 291-1222; telex (21) 22395; Pres: Mario Penna Bhering; f 1962; Govt holding co (with 6 suibidiary and 23 associated electricity cos), plans, finances and oversees Brazil's electrical energy programme.

Comissão Nacional de Energia Nuclear (CNEN): Rua General Severiano 90, Botafogo, 20.040 Rio de Janeiro, RJ; tel (21) 295-9596; telex (21) 21280; Pres: Rex Nazaré Alves; f 1956; manages the nuclear power programme and nuclear research and engineering institutes.

Concelho Nacional do Petróleo (CNP): SGA Norte, Quadra 603, Módulos H, I, J, 70.830 Brasília, DF; tel (61) 226-0403; telex (61) 1673; Pres: Gen Roberto Franco Domingues; f 1938; directs national policy on petroleum.

Conselho Superior de Política Nuclear (CSPN): Brasília; 1988; determines and supervises the implementation of Brazil's nuclear power programme.

Indústrias Nucleares do Brasil: Brasília; Pres: John Foreman; f 1988; constructs and finances nuclear power plants.

Petróleo Brasileiro, SA (PETROBRÁS): Av República do Chile 65, 20.035 Rio de Janeiro, RJ; tel (21) 534-4477; telex (21) 23335; Pres: Carlos Sant'anna; f 1953; holds monopoly on devt and production of petroleum and petroleum products; the following are subsidiaries of PETROBRÁS:

Petrobrás Comércio Internacional, SA (INTERBRÁS): Rua do Rosário 90, Rio de Janeiro, RJ; tel (21) 296-2033; telex (21) 21709; Pres: Dr Renato Magalhães da Silveira; Vice-Pres: Maurício Alves dos Santos.

Petrobrás Distribuidora, SA: Praça 22 de Abril 36, 8 andar, Castelo, 20.021 Rio de Janeiro, RF; tel (21) 217-8066; telex (21) 21222; Pres: Maximiano Fonseca; Vice-Pres: Luigi Dallolio; f 1971; marketing of all petroleum by-products.

Petrobrás Fertilizantes, SA (PETROFÉRTIL): Praça Mahatma Gandhi 14, 9-13 andares, 20.031 Rio de Janeiro, RJ; tel (21) 217-5335; telex (21) 23880; Pres: Roberto Villa; Vice-Pres: Aurílio Fernandes Lima; f 1976.

Petrobrás Internacional, SA (BRASPETRO): Praça Pio X 119, 20.040 Rio de Janeiro, RJ; tel (21) 297-0102; telex (21) 21889; Pres: Wagner Freire; Vice-Pres: Antônio Seabra Moggi; f 1972; international division with operations in Africa, the Middle and Far East, Latin America, the Caribbean and Europe.

Petrobrás Mineraçao, SA (PETROMISA): Av Pres Vargas 583, 20.076 Rio de Janeiro, RJ; tel (21) 224-7805; telex (21) 32509; fax (21) 224-0596; Pres: José Edilson de Melo Távora; Exec Vice-Pres: Ruben Lahyr Schneider; potassium exploration and non-petroleum mining.

Petrobrás Química, SA (PETROQUISA): Rua Buenos Aires 40, 20.070 Rio de Janeiro, RJ; tel (21) 297-6677; telex (21) 21496; Pres: Paulo Vieira Belotti; Vice-Pres: Tarcisio de Vasconcelos Maia; f 1968; petrochemicals industry; controls 27 affiliated cos and 4 subsidiaries.

Urânio do Brasil: Brasília; f 1988; responsible for fuel-cycle (from extraction of uranium to processing stage).

MINING

Companhia de Pesquisa de Recursos Mineráis: Av Pasteur 404, Urca, 22.292 Rio de Janeiro, RJ; tel (21) 295-5337; telex (21) 22685; f 1970; attached to the Ministry of Infrastructure; prospection and exploitation of mineral deposits in conjunction with the private sector.

Companhia Vale do Rio Doce, SA (CVRD): Av Graça Aranha 26, Bairro Castelo, 20.005 Rio de Janeiro, RJ; tel (21) 272-4477; telex (21) 23162; Pres: Agripino Abranches Viana; f 1942; state-owned mining co; operates the Vitória-Minas railway (see below), the port of Tubarão and the Carajás iron ore project; involved in forestry and pulp production.

Departamento Nacional da Produçao Mineral (DNPM): SAN, Quadra 01, Bloco B, 70.041 Brasília, DF; tel (61) 224-2670; telex (61) 1116; Dir-Gen: José Belfort dos Santos Bastos; f 1934; attached to the Ministry of Infrastructure; plans, co-ordinates and supervises the exploration of mineral resources.

Science and Technology

Conselho Nacional de Desenvolvimento Científico e Tecnológico (CNPq): Av W-3 Norte, Quadra 507, Bloco B, 70.740 Brasília, DF; tel (61) 274-1155; telex (61) 1089; Pres: Dr Crodovaldo Pavan; f 1951; council for the devt of science and technology.

Instituto Nacional de Tecnologia (INT): Av Venezuela 82, 8 andar, 20.081 Rio de Janeiro, RJ; tel (21) 223-1320; telex (21) 30056; Dir: Paulo Roberto Krahe; f 1921; technological assistance; co-operates in national industrial devt.

Telecommunications

Departamento Nacional de Telecomunicações (DENTEL) (National Telecommunications Council): Via NZ, Anexo do Ministério das Comunicações, Esplanada dos Ministérios, Bloco R, 70.066 Brasília, DF; tel (61) 223-3229; telex (61) 1175; Dir-Gen: Roberto Blois Montes de Souza; f 1962; supervises and co-ordinates telecommunications activities.

Empresa Brasileira de Correios e Telégrafos (ECT): Edif Sede, 19 andar, SBN, Conj 3, Bloco A, 70.002 Brasília, DF; tel (61) 224-9262; telex (61) 1119; fax (61) 223-4066; Pres: Joel Marciano Rauber; f 1969; operates post and telegraph services.

Empresa Brasileira de Telecomunicações, SA (EMBRATEL): Av Pres Vargas 1012, CP 2586, 20.071 Rio de Janeiro, RJ; tel (21) 216-7400; telex (21) 22021; Pres: José Eugênio Guisard Ferraz; f 1965; operates national and international telecommunications system.

Tourism

Centro Brasileiro de Informação Turística (CEBITUR): Rua Mariz e Barros 13, 6 andar, Praça da Bandeira, 20.270 Rio de Janeiro, RJ; tel (21) 293-1313; telex (21) 21066; tourist information.

Conselho Nacional de Turismo (CNTUR) (National Tourism Office): Ministério da Indústria e do Comércio, Rua Mariz e Barros 13, 5 andar, 20.270 Rio de Janeiro, RJ; tel (21) 273-0691; Pres: José Eduardo Guinler; Exec Sec: José E. Cassio Teixeira; f 1966.

Divisão de Feiras e Turismo/Departamento de Promoção Comercial: Ministério das Relações Exteriores, Esplanada dos Ministérios, 2 andar, 70.170 Brasília, DF; tel (61) 211-6644; Sec: Edson Maringo Duarte; f 1977; organizes Brazil's participation in trade fairs and commercial exhibitions abroad.

Empresa Brasileira de Turismo (EMBRATUR): Rua Mariz e Barros 13, 12 andar, 20.270 Rio de Janeiro, RJ; tel (21) 273-2212; telex (21) 21066; Pres: Pedro Grossi, Jr; f 1966; studies tourist devt projects.

Transport

Conselho Nacional de Transportes: Ministério dos Transportes, Esplanada dos Ministérios, Bloco 9, 7 andar, 70.062, Brasília, DF; tel (61) 321-8886; telex (61) 1096; Pres: José Reinaldo Carneiro Tavares; Exec José Roberto de Almeida Neves; f 1961; co-ordinates and executes Govt transport policy and the reorganization of railway, road and ports and waterways councils.

Empresa Brasileira de Planejamento de Transportes (GEIPOT): SAN, Quadra 3, Blocos N/O, Edif Núcleo dos Transportes, 70.040 Brasília, DF; tel (61) 226-7335; telex (61) 1354; Dir-Gen: Antônio Alberto Canabrava; f 1973; advises the Govt on transport policy; promotes an integrated modern transport system.

Empresa Brasileira de Transportes Urbanos (EBTU): SAN, Quadra 3, Lote A, 3 andar, 70.040 Brasília, DF; tel (61) 226-7335; telex (61) 1604; Pres: Walter Luiz do Rego Luna; f 1975; administers resources for national urban transportation programmes.

CIVIL AVIATION

Viação Aérea São Paulo, SA (VASP): 04695 Edif VASP, Aeroporto Congonhas, São Paulo, SP; tel (11) 533-7011; telex (11) 56575; Pres: Marcelo G. Antinori; f 1933; controlled by São

Paulo State Govt; due to be 'privatized' in 1990; domestic services covering all Brazil.

RAILWAYS

Carajás Railway: Retorno Itaqui-Pedrinhas, Km 7, BR 135, 65.000 São Luís, MA; tel (982) 222-8844; telex (982) 138; Dir: Romildo Coelho Vello; state-owned; transportation of iron ore, wood and rice.

Companhia Vale de Rio Doce (Vitória-Minas Railway): Av Graça Aranha 26, Bairro Castelo, 20.005 Rio de Janeiro, RJ; tel (21) 272-4477; telex (21) 23162; Pres: Agripino Abranches Viana; f 1942; transportation of iron ore, general cargo and passengers.

FEPASA—Ferrovia Paulista, SA: Praça Julio Prestes 148, 01.218 São Paulo, SP; tel (11) 223-7211; telex (11) 22724; Pres: Antônio Carlos Rios Corral; formed by merger of five failways operated by São Paulo State.

Rêde Ferroviára Federal, SA (RFFSA) (Federal Railway Corpn): Praça Procópio Ferreira 86, 20.221 Rio de Janeiro, RJ; tel (21) 291-2185; telex (21) 21372; fax (21) 263-318; Pres: Fernando Jorge Fagundes Netto; Vice-Pres: Vicente Nardelli; f 1957; holding co for 18 railways; mixed co in which the Govt is the majority shareholder.

Companhia Brasileira de Trens Urbanos (CBTU): Velha da Tijuca 77, Usina, 20.531 Rio de Janeiro, RJ; tel (21) 288-1992; telex (21) 22793; Pres: A. Maia de Vasconcelos Neto; subsidiary of RFFSA responsible for suburban networks and metro systems throughout Brazil; in 1988 CBTU was proposed for transfer to local State govt control.

ROADS

Departamento Nacional de Estradas de Rodagem (DNER) (National Roads Development): Av Pres Vargas 522-534, 20.071 Rio de Janeiro, RJ; tel (21) 233-2493; telex (21) 23535; Dir: Antônio Alberto Canabrava; f 1945; formulates and executes federal road policy; oversees State and municipal roads with the aim of integrating them into the national network.

SHIPPING

Empresa dos Portos do Brasil (Portobrás): Praça Maua 10, Centro, 20.081 Rio de Janeiro, RJ; tel (61) 244-1700; telex (61) 1112; Pres: Carlos Theofilo de S. Mello; f 1975; oversees, manages and develops policies for ports and navigable waterways.

Petróleo Brasileiro SA (Petrobrás)—Frota Nacional de Petroleiros (Fronape): Av República do Chile 65, 12 andar, 20.035 Rio de Janeiro, RJ; tel (21) 580-4581; telex (21) 22286; Pres: S. Ueki; tanker fleet.

Secretaria de Transportes Aquaviáros: Av Rio Branco 115, 14 andar, 20.040 Rio de Janeiro, RJ; tel (21) 221-4015; telex (21) 21652; Sec-Gen: Dr Claudio R. F. Decourt; f 1941; supervisory board of the merchant marine.

Vale do Rio Doce Navegaçâo, SA (DOCENAVE): Rua Voluntários da Pátria 143, Botafogo, 20.000 Rio de Janeiro, RJ; tel (21) 286-8002; telex (21) 22142; Dir: Carlos Auto de Andrade; bulk carrier to Japan, the Persian Gulf, Europe, North America and Argentina.

Welfare

Fundação Nacional do Índio—FUNAI (National Indian Bureau): Sector de Edifícios Utilidade Pública Sul 702, Edif LEX, 70.000 Brasília, DF; Gen Supt: Airton Alcantara Gomes.

BRUNEI

Head of State and Legislature

Supreme executive authority is vested in the Sultan and Yang Di-Pertuan. Since 1962 certain Constitutional provisions have been suspended and the Sultan has ruled by decree, advised and assisted by four Councils: the Religious Council, the Privy Council, the Council of Cabinet Ministers and the Council of Succession. Four administrative districts are headed by a District Officer responsible to the Prime Minister and Minister of Home Affairs.

Sultan and Yang Di-Pertuan: HM Sir Muda Hassanal Bolkiah Mu'izzaddin Waddaulah (succeeded 4 October 1967; crowned 1 August 1968).

Office of HM the Sultan: Bandar Seri Begawan; tel (2) 29988; telex 2727.

MINISTRIES AND GOVERNMENT DEPARTMENTS

OFFICE OF THE PRIME MINISTER
Istana Nurul Iman, Bandar Seri Begawan
Tel (2) 29988; telex 2727
Prime Minister: The Sultan and Yang Di-Pertuan,
HM Sir Muda Hassanal Bolkiah Mu'izzaddin Waddaulah

MINISTRY OF COMMUNICATIONS
Old Airport Rd, Bandar Seri Begawan 1150
Tel (2) 42526; fax (2) 20172
Minister: Awang Zakaria bin Haji Suleiman

MINISTRY OF CULTURE, YOUTH AND SPORTS
Jalan Residency, Bandar Seri Begawan 1200
Tel (2) 40585; telex 2642; fax (2) 41620
Minister: Pehin Jawatan Luar Pekerma Raja Dato Seri
Paduka Haji Awang Hussain

MINISTRY OF DEFENCE
Bolkiah Garrison, Bandar Seri Begawan 1110
Tel (2) 32092; telex 2220
Minister: The Sultan and Yang Di-Pertuan,
HM Sir Muda Hassanal Bolkiah Mu'izzaddin Waddaulah

MINISTRY OF DEVELOPMENT
Lapangan Terbang Lama Berakas, Bandar Seri Begawan
Tel (2) 41911; telex 2722
Minister: Pengiran Dr Ismail

MINISTRY OF EDUCATION
Old Airport, Berakas, Bandar Seri Begawan 1170
Tel (2) 44233; telex 2602; fax (2) 40250
Minister: Dato Seri Paduka Haji Awang Umar

MINISTRY OF FINANCE
Bandar Seri Begawan
Tel (2) 42405; telex 2674
Minister: Pengiran Di-Gadong Pengiran Muda Jefri Bolkiah

Economic Planning Unit: Ministry of Finance, Bandar Seri Begawan; tel (2) 41991; telex 2676.

MINISTRY OF FOREIGN AFFAIRS
Jalan Subok, Bandar Seri Begawan 1120
Tel (2) 41177; telex 2839; fax (2) 24709
Minister: Pengiran Perdana Wazir Pengiran Muda
Mohamad Bolkiah
Deputy Minister: Dato Paduka Haji Mohd Ali bin Haji
Mohd Daud

MINISTRY OF HEALTH
Old Airport, Bandar Seri Begawan 1210
Tel (2) 26640; telex 2421; fax (2) 40980
Minister: Dato Dr Haji Johar

MINISTRY OF HOME AFFAIRS
Bandar Seri Begawan
Tel (2) 23225
Minister and Special Adviser to the Prime Minister:
Pehin Dato Haji Isa

MINISTRY OF LAW
Bandar Seri Begawan
Tel (2) 44872
Minister: Pengiran Bahrin bin Pengiran Haji Abas

MINISTRY OF RELIGIOUS AFFAIRS
Kementerian Hal Ehwal, Agama, Bandar Seri Begawan 1180

Tel (2) 42562; fax (2) 43001
Minister: Pehin Dato Haji Mohd Zain

GOVERNMENT AGENCIES AND ORGANIZATIONS

Business and Economy

BANKING

International Bank of Brunei: Bangunan IBB, Lot 155, Jalan Roberts, POB 2725, Bandar Seri Begawan; tel (2) 20686; telex 2320; Man Dir: Aziz bin Abdul Rahman; f 1981 as Island Development Bank; 25 brs.

FINANCIAL AGENCIES

Brunei Currency Board: Bandar Seri Begawan; tel (2) 22095.

Economic Development Board: Bandar Seri Begawan; tel (2) 40243.

MARKETING

Brunei Shell Marketing Co Bhd: Maya Puri Bldg, 36-37 Jalan Sultan, POB 385, Bandar Seri Begawan; tel (2) 25739; telex 2384; Man Dir: B. P. Randoll; f 1978; jointly owned by the Brunei Govt and Shell; markets petroleum and chemical products in Brunei.

Defence

Royal Brunei Armed Forces: Bandar Seri Begawan; tel (2) 24101; telex 220; Commdr, the Royal Brunei Malay Regiment: Brig-Gen Pahlawan Mohammad Davd.

Muara Base Flotilla Brunei: Bandar Seri Begawan; tel (2) 72442.

Royal Brunei Police: Gadong, Bandar Seri Begawan; tel (2) 42334; telex 2226.

Sixth Queen Elizabeth's Own Gurkha Rifles: Seria Camp; tel (3) 24101; telex 3333.

Energy

Brunei Coldgas Sdn Bhd: Maya Puri Bldg, 36-37 Jalan Sultan, Bandar Seri Begawan 2085; tel (2) 41942; telex 2509; fax (2) 42028; Chief Exec: George Innes; Dep Chief Exec: A. Levine; f 1977; formed by Shell, Mitsubishi Corpn and the Brunei Govt; buys, transports and sells LNG from Brunei LNG Sdn Bhd (see below) to Japan.

Brunei LNG Sdn Bhd: Seria; Man: M. J. Chakko-George; f 1969; owned jointly by the Brunei Govt, Shell and Mitsubishi Corpn; operates liquified natural gas plant.

Brunei Shell Petroleum Co Sdn Bhd: Seria 7082; tel (3-7) 3999; telex 3313; fax (3-7) 2040; Man Dir: George Innes; f 1957; the largest industrial concern in the country and the only oil co at present in production in Brunei; 50% state-owned.

Legal and Judiciary

Supreme Court: Batu 1, Jalan Tutong, Bandar Seri Begawan 2056; tel (2) 25853; fax (2) 41984; Chief Justice: Dato Sir Denys Roberts; Pres, Court of Appeal: Sir Ti-Liang Yang; Chief Registrar: Awang Kifrawi bin Dato Paduka Kifli; f 1963; the Supreme Court consists of the Court of Appeal and the High Court.

Media

BROADCASTING

Department of Broadcasting and Information: Prime Minister's Office, Bandar Seri Begawan 2042; tel (2) 40400; telex 2614; fax (2) 41882; Dir: Pengiran Badaruddin bin Pengiran Ghani; f 1952; attached to the Prime Minister's Office; informs the public about Govt policies; promotes economic, artistic and cultural devt; publishes Govt newspaper.

Jabatan Penyiaran Dan Penerangan (Radio Televisyen Brunei): Jabatan Perdana Menteri, Bandar Seri Begawan 2042, tel (2) 43111; telex 2311; fax (2) 41882; f 1957; attached to the Dept of Broadcasting and Information; radio broadcasts in Malay, local dialects, English, Mandarin and Gurkha; TV service in Malay and English.

GOVERNMENT PUBLISHER

Government Printing Office: Lapangan Terbang Lama, Berakas; tel (2) 44541.

Tourism

Information Bureau: Information Section, Dept of Broadcasting and Information, Prime Minister's Office, Bandar Seri Begawan 2042; tel (2) 40400; telex 2614; fax (2) 41882.

Transport

Department of Civil Aviation: Brunei International Airport, Bandar Seri Begawan 2015; tel (2) 30142; telex 2267; Dir: Job Lim; f 1974.

Land Transport Department: Ministry of Communications, Batu 2.5, Jalan Gadong 2055, Bandar Seri Begawan; tel (2) 23161; telex 2567; fax (2) 24775; Controller: Haji Mohd Kassim bin Haji Johan; f 1960; responsible for the registration of all motor vehicles, licensing drivers, vehicle safety standards and the enforcement of the provisions of the Road Traffic Act.

Royal Brunei Airlines Ltd: RBA Plaza, POB 737, Bandar Seri Begawan 1907; tel (2) 40500; telex 2737; fax (2) 44737; Chair: Prince Jefri Bolkiah; Man Dir: Pengiran Tengah Metassim; services to the Far and Middle East and Australia.

BULGARIA

Head of State

There is no constitutional provision for a Head of State, but certain equivalent functions are exercised by the President of the State Council. The 27-member State Council is elected by the National Assembly to be its permanent organ, and controls the Council of Ministers and the heads of Ministries.

President of the State Council: Petur Mladenov (elected 17 November 1989).

Office of the President: 1000 Sofia, Blvd Dondukov 2; tel (2) 85-01; telex 22272; Sec of the State Council: Nikola Manolov.

First Vice-President: Petar Tanchev

Vice-Presidents: Georgi Dzhagarov, Mitko Grigorev, Yaraoslav Radev.

Legislature

The unicameral National Assembly is the supreme organ of state power, comprising 400 people's representatives, elected (unopposed) for five years by universal adult suffrage. The Assembly elects the State Council and the Council of Ministers (the highest organ of state administration), which is headed by a Chairman. The Bulgarian Communist Party (BCP) relinquished its guaranteed monopoly on political power in January 1990.

Narodno Sobraniye (National Assembly): 1000 Sofia, pl Narodno Sobraniye 3; tel (2) 85-01; telex 22272; Chair: Stanko Todorov; Dep Chairs: Atanas Dimitrov, Milena Stamboliiska, Kiril Zarev.

MINISTRIES AND GOVERNMENT DEPARTMENTS

COUNCIL OF MINISTERS
1000 Sofia, Blvd Dondukov 1
Tel (2) 86-91
Chair: Andrey Lukanov
Deputy Chairs: Choudomir Alexandrov, Belcho Belchev, Konstantin Kosev, Nora Ananieva
Deputy Ministers: Georgi Pirinski, Stoyan Mikhailov
Minister without Portfolio, responsible for Economic Reform: Stefan Stoilov

COMMITTEE FOR STATE AND PEOPLE'S CONTROL
1000 Sofia
Chair: Georgi Georgiev

MINISTRY OF AGRICULTURE AND FORESTRY
Sofia, Blvd Botev 55
Minister: Todor Pandov

MINISTRY OF CONSTRUCTION, ARCHITECTURE AND PUBLIC WORKS
Sofia
Minister: Ivan Krustev

MINISTRY OF CULTURE
Sofia
Minister: (vacant)

MINISTRY OF ECONOMY AND PLANNING
1113 Sofia, Exarch Yosiph St 37
Tel (2) 84-21; telex 22348; fax (2) 88-21-18
Minister: Ivan Tenev

MINISTRY OF FINANCE
Sofia
Minister: Belcho Belchev

MINISTRY OF FOREIGN AFFAIRS
1000 Sofia, Al Zhendov St 2
Telex 22530
Minister: Boyko Dimitrov

MINISTRY OF FOREIGN ECONOMIC RELATIONS
1000 Sofia, Sofiiska Komuna St 12
Tel (2) 88-20-11; telex 22024
Minister: Peter Bashikarov

MINISTRY OF INDUSTRY AND TECHNOLOGY
Sofia
Minister: Krustyu Stanilov

MINISTRY OF THE INTERIOR
Sofia, ul Shesti Septemvri
Tel (2) 87-80-11
Minister: Col-Gen Atanas Semerdzhiev

MINISTRY OF JUSTICE
1000 Sofia, Blvd Dondoukov 2
Tel (2) 867-32-50; telex 23882; fax (2) 867-32-73
Minister: Pencho Penev

MINISTRY OF NATIONAL DEFENCE
1000 Sofia, Levsky St 3
Tel (2) 86-21
Minister: Gen Dobri Dzhurov

MINISTRY OF NATIONAL EDUCATION
Sofia
Minister: Konstantin Kotsev
Minister of Science and Higher Education: Asen Khadzhiolov

MINISTRY OF PUBLIC HEALTH AND SOCIAL WELFARE
1000 Sofia, pl Lenina 5
Tel (2) 86-31; telex 22430
Minister: Prof Ivan Chernozemski

MINISTRY OF TRADE AND PUBLIC UTILITY SERVICES
Sofia
Minister: Ekaterina Marinova

MINISTRY OF TRANSPORT
1000 Sofia, Levsky St 9-11
Tel (2) 87-10-81
Minister: Vesselin Pavlov

STATE COMMITTEE FOR THE PROTECTION OF THE ENVIRONMENT
Sofia
Chair: (vacant)

GOVERNMENT AGENCIES AND ORGANIZATIONS

Advisory and Supervisory Body

Central Co-operative Union: 1000 Sofia, Rakovsky 99, POB 55; tel (2) 84-41; telex 23229; Pres: Ivan Pehlivanov; f 1947; central body of all the co-operative organizations in the country.

Business and Economy

BANKING

Bank for Economic Projects (Mineralbank): 1000 Sofia, Legué St 17, POB 589; tel (2) 80-17-37; telex 23390; Pres: Rumen Georgiyev; f 1980.

Bulgarian Foreign Trade Bank: 1000 Sofia, Sofiiska Komuna St 2; tel (2) 85-51; telex 22031; Pres: Ivan Dragnevsky; f 1964; owned by National Bank of Bulgaria (see below) and other state institutions; co-ordinates foreign trade activities of the other commercial banks.

Bulgarska Narodna Banka (National Bank of Bulgaria): 1000 Sofia, Sofiiska Komuna St 2; tel (2) 85-51; telex 22392; Pres: Vasil Kolarov; First Dep Pres: Ivan Dragnevski; f c 1879; bank of issue; the Pres is a mem of the Cabinet.

State Savings Bank: Sofia, Moskovska 19; f 1951; general individual banking services.

INSURANCE

Bulstrad (Bulgarian Foreign Insurance and Reinsurance Co, Ltd): 1000 Sofia, Dunav St 5; POB 627; tel (2) 8-51-91; telex 22564; Chair: S. Darvingov; f 1961; foreign insurance and reinsurance.

State Insurance Institute: Sofia, Rakovsky St 102; Chair: Toma Tomov; state insurance co.

TRADE

Agrocommerce: 1000 Sofia, Blvd Dondukov 86; tel (2) 80-33-12; telex 23223; Dir-Gen: Vladimir Damiyanov; exports the produce of the mems of the National Agro-Industrial Union (see above); imports and maintains industrial equipment; imports consumer products; utilizes waste products.

Agromachinaimpex: 1040 Sofia, Stoyan Lepoyev St 1; tel (2) 20-03-91; telex 22563; Dir-Gen: Todor Pashaliyev; exports, imports and maintains agricultural equipment.

Balkancarimpex: 1040 Sofia, Blvd Kliment Okhridsky 18; tel (2) 7-53-01; telex 23431; exports trucks, lorries and other vehicles; constructs vehicle parts.

Banimpex: 1113 Sofia, G. Bonchev St 107, POB 98; tel (2) 70-04-11; telex 23688; fax (2) 70-60-63; imports scientific equipment and chemicals; exports software products and chemicals.

Bulgarcoop: 1000 Sofia, Rakovsky St 99; tel (2) 84-41; telex 23429; Gen Man: Nenko Lechev; exports live snails, game and game meat, honey and bee products, nuts, pulses, medicinal plants, rose hips and rose-hip shells, fresh and processed fruit and vegetables, essential oil seeds, onions, mushrooms, natural mineral water, consumer goods.

Bulgarian Chamber of Commerce and Industry: 1040 Sofia, Blvd A. Stamboliisky 11A; tel (2) 87-26-31; telex 22374; Pres: Petur Rusev; promotes economic relations and business contacts between Bulgarian and foreign cos and organizations; runs the international fairs in Plovdiv (see below), and organizes official participation in international fairs; publishes economic works; patents inventions and registers trade marks and industrial designs; arranges foreign trade advertising and publicity; provides legal consultations.

Bulgarplodexport: 1040 Sofia, Blvd A. Stamboliisky 7; tel (2) 88-59-51; telex 23297; fax (2) 89-48-77; Dir-Gen: Alexandur Mirchev; f 1947; production, import and export of fresh and preserved fruit and vegetables; engineering.

Bulgartabac: 1000 Sofia, Blvd A. Stamboliisky 14; POB 96; tel (2) 87-52-11; telex 23288; Dir-Gen: Dimiter Yadkov; production, import and export of raw and manufactured tobacco.

Chimimport: 1000 Sofia, Sofiiska Komuna St 1; tel (2) 88-38-11; telex 22521; Dir-Gen: Belo Belov; import and export of chemicals, fertilizer, plant protection preparations, tyres, synthetic rubber and rubber goods, photographic paper, aniline dyes, crude petroleum and oil products, paraffins, petrochemicals, plastic and plastic products, fuels, etc.

Electroimpex: 1000 Sofia, George Washington St 17; tel (2) 8-61-81; telex 22075; fax (2) 80-33-09; Gen Man: Kiril Tsochev; exports and imports electrical and power equipment and components for the electrical engineering industry.

Energoimpex: 1463 Sofia, Blvd Ernst Thälmann 17A; tel (2) 51-88-67; telex 22669; imports and exports coal and electric power; delivers machines and power equipment.

Hemus: 1000 Sofia, Levsky St 7; tel (2) 80-30-00; telex 22267; fax (2) 80-13-41; Dir-Gen: Ivan Abadjiev; f 1967; imports and exports books, periodicals, posters, printing services, art products, records, compact discs, musical instruments; import of photographic materials.

Hranexport: 1080 Sofia, Alabin St 56; tel (2) 88-22-51; telex 22525; fax (2) 87-74-53; Gen Man: Yovcho Rusev; imports and exports grain, cocoa, sugar, oils, feed, pulses and vegetable oils.

Industrialimport: 1040 Sofia, Pozitano St 3; tel (2) 87-30-21; telex 22092; Gen Man: Angel Angelov; imports and exports cotton, woollen and silk ready-made garments and textiles, knitwear, leather goods, china and glassware, sports equipment.

Intercommerce: 1080 Sofia, pl Lenina 16; POB 676; tel (2) 87-93-64; telex 22067; fax (2) 87-45-29; Gen Man: Ivan Deev; f 1970; imports and exports various goods and raw materials; involved in multilateral, compensation and barter deals, participates in joint venture companies and joint activities in Bulgaria and abroad.

Interpred: 1057 Sofia, Blvd Bulgarosavetska Droujba 16; tel (2) 46-46-46; telex 23284; fax (2) 70-00-06; Chair: Peter Valtchev; represents foreign firms in Bulgaria.

Isotimpex: 1040 Sofia, Chapayev St 51; tel (2) 73-38-1; telex 22731; fax (2) 70-65-86; Pres: Lyubomir Vitanov; f 1968; imports and exports computing and organizational equipment, semiconductors, radio parts, office equipment, materials for computing equipment; maintenance and service of computer systems.

Kintex: 1407 Sofia, Blvd Anton Ivanov 66; tel (2) 66-23-11; telex 22471; fax (2) 65-71-65; Dir-Gen: Ivan Damiyanov; imports and exports sports and hunting goods and explosives for industrial and mining purposes.

Koraboimpex: 9000 Varna, Blvd D. Blagoev 128; tel (52) 88-18-25; telex 77550; Dir-Gen: Kiril Kostov; imports and exports ships, marine and port equipment.

Lessoimpex: 1303 Sofia, Antim I St 17; tel (2) 87-91-75; telex 23407; fax (2) 87-27-65; Dir-Gen: Stefan Stefanov; f 1966; exports furniture, sawn timber, wood panels; imports tropical timber, laminated panels, veneers and furniture fittings.

Machinoexport: 1000 Sofia, Aksakov St 5; tel (2) 88-53-21; telex 23425; Gen Man: Neno Mitev; exports metal-cutting and wood-working machinery, industrial robots, hydraulic and pneumatic products and other equipment, tools and spare parts.

Maimex: 1431 Sofia, Blvd D. Nestorov 15; tel (2) 5-81-01; telex 22712; Dir: Tsoncho Tsonchev; imports and exports specialized medical equipment and pharmaceutical products.

Metalokeramikaimpex: 1113 Sofia, Chapayev St 49; tel (2) 70-00-43; telex 23622; imports and exports products for the cement, machine-building and electrical engineering industries.

Metal Technology: 1574 Sofia, Chapayev St 53; tel (2) 7-14-21; telex 22903; exports and imports machinery and industrial equipment.

Mineralimpex: 1156 Sofia, Blvd Kliment Okhridsky 14; tel (2) 66-19-66; telex 22973; fax (2) 77-13-48; Dir-Gen: Ivan Govedarski; Dep Dir-Gen: Jivko Ivanov; f 1974; imports and exports raw ore materials, drilling and research equipment and machinery for the stone-processing industry.

Pharmachim: 1220 Sofia, Iliyensko chaussée 16; tel (2) 38-50-1; telex 22097; fax (2) 38-81-71; Dir-Gen: Khristo Drashanski; imports and exports drugs, pharmaceutical, microbiological and veterinary products, essential oils, cosmetics and dental materials.

Pirin: 1333 Sofia, Al Samboliiski Blvd 125-2; tel (2) 20-67-11; telex 22761; fax (2) 22-92-68; Dir-Gen: D. Enev; f 1965; manufacture of shoes, leather garments and goods, shoe soles; export and import of shoe, leather goods, equipment; barter and foreign trade deals.

Plovdiv International Fair: Plovdiv, Blvd G. Dimitrov 37; tel (32) 55-31-91; telex 44432; Dir-Gen: Kiril Asparukhov; f 1933; under control of the Bulgarian Chamber of Commerce and Industry (see above); runs international fairs.

Raznoiznos: 1040 Sofia, Tsar Assen St 1; tel (2) 88-02-11; telex 23244; Dir-Gen: Botzho Botev; exports and imports industrial and craft products, timber and paper products, glassware, kitchen utensils, furniture, carpets, toys, sports equipment, musical instruments.

Ribno Stopanstvo: 1000 Sofia, Parchevich St 42; tel (2) 80-10-01; telex 22796; Dir: Khristo Yanev; import and export of fish and fish products.

Rodopaimpex: 1000 Sofia, Gavril Genov St 2; tel (2) 88-26-61; telex 22541; Dir-Gen: Svetoslav Aleksiyev; exports cattle, sheep, breeding animals, meat and dairy products, poultry, eggs; imports meat, equipment for the meat industry, etc.

Rudmetal: 1000 Sofia, Dobrudzha St 1; tel (2) 88-12-71; telex 22027; Dir-Gen: Yosif Yosifov; f 1952; exports and imports metal and metal products, lead, zinc, copper, pure lead, ores, coal, etc.

SPS Corpn—Software Products and System Corpn: 1000 Sofia, Panayot Volov St 2; tel (2) 45-30-37; telex 23149; fax (2) 47-79-68; Pres: Rashko Angelinov; imports and exports information systems, software products and system-engineering services.

Stroyimpex: 1000 Sofia, Triyaditsa St 5; tel (2) 80-30-47; telex 22385; Dir-Gen: Atanas Vlakhov; exports cement, lime, cement slabs, floor tiles and prefabricated wooden houses; imports building materials, machines and equipment.

Technoexportstroy: 1303 Sofia, Antim I St 11; tel (2) 87-85-11; telex 22128; fax (2) 65-81-47; Gen Man: Stoyan Drandarov; designs and constructs public, utility, industrial and infrastructural projects abroad; supplies machines and technical assistance.

Techno-import-export: 1113 Sofia, ul Frédéric Joliot-Curie 20, POB 541; tel (2) 73-81; telex 22193; Dir-Gen: Velimir Dimitrov; imports and exports machines and complete plants in the areas of power generation, metallurgy, mining and construction.

Telecom: 1309 Sofia, Kiril Pchelinsky St 2; tel (2) 2-13-01; telex 22077; Dir-Gen: Nikola Monov; exports and imports radio-electronic equipment and technology for the communications industry.

Transimpex: 1606 Sofia, Blvd Skobelev 65; tel (2) 52-23-21; telex 22123; imports and exports railway equipment, wagons, locomotives, boats and shipping parts.

Vinimpex: 1080 Sofia, Lavele St 19; tel (2) 80-32-39; telex 22467; fax (2) 80-12-99; Dir-Gen: Dimitar Dzhambazov; imports and exports wine and spirits and equipment and spares for the wine industry.

Defence

Armed Forces: c/o Ministry of National Defence, 1000 Sofia, Levsky St 3; tel (2) 86-21.

Air Force: c/o Ministry of National Defence, 1000 Sofia, Levski St 3; tel (2) 86-21.

Army: c/o Ministry of National Defence, 1000 Sofia, Levsky St 3; tel (2) 86-21.

Navy: c/o Ministry of National Defence, 1000 Sofia, Levsky St 3; tel (2) 86-21.

Directorate of the National Police: 1002 Sofia, Blvd Slivnitza 235; tel (2) 31-91-20; telex 24221; Dir of the National Police: Ivan Dimitrov; Head, Criminal Police and Interpol-Sofia: Christo Velichkov; f 1944; law enforcement; protection of citizens' constitutional rights; road traffic control.

Education and Research

Institute for Nuclear Research and Nuclear Energy of the Bulgarian Academy of Sciences: 1784 Sofia, Blvd Lenin 72; tel (2) 75-80-32; telex 23561; Dir: Khr Khristov; f 1973.

National Council for Education, Science and Culture: Sofia.

Energy

Committee on the Use of Atomic Power for Peaceful Purposes: 1574 Sofia, Chapayev St 55A; tel (2) 72-02-17; telex 23383; Chair: Ivan Pandev; Dep Chair: Boris Georgiev; f 1957; ensures the implementation of state policy on the use of atomic energy for peaceful purposes; exercises state control over the safe use of atomic energy and the transport and control of nuclear material.

Legal and Judiciary

Supreme Court: 1000 Sofia, Blvd Vitosha 2, Sudebna Palata; tel (2) 85-71; telex 22977; Pres: Gospodin Gospodinov (with Ministerial rank); Chief Prosecutor: Evtim Stoichkov.

Media

BROADCASTING

Bulgarian Committee for Television and Radio: 1504 Sofia, San Stefano St 29; tel (2) 46-81; telex 22581; Chair: Filip Georgiev.

Bulgarska Televiziya: 1504 Sofia, San Stefano St 29; tel (2) 46-31; telex 22581; daily TV transmissions on two channels.

Bulgarsko Radio: 1421 Sofia, Blvd Dragan Tsankov 4; tel (2) 85-41; telex 22557; radio broadcasts; there are four Home Service Programmes, and a Foreign Service broadcasting in Bulgarian, Turkish, Greek, Serbo-Croat, French, Italian, German, English, Portuguese, Spanish, Albanian and Arabic.

NEWS AND INFORMATION

Central Statistical Office: Council of Ministers, Sofia, Panayot Volov St 2; tel (2) 46-01; telex 22001.

Bulgarska Telegrafna Agentsia (BTA) (Bulgarian Telegraph Agency): 1040 Sofia, Blvd Lenin 49; tel (2) 84-61; telex 22821; Dir-Gen: Boyan Traikov; f 1898; official news agency; publishes weekly surveys of science and technology, international affairs, literature and art.

Jusautor (Bulgarian Copyright Agency): 1463 Sofia, Blvd Ernst Thälmann 17; tel (2) 51-501; telex 23042; Dir-Gen: Yana Markova; Dep Dir-Gen: Alexander Angelov; f 1962; promotes the publishing, production and performance of works of Bulgarian literature and art abroad; grants options and rights for the use of works by foreign publishers; represents foreign authors, publishers and literary and theatrical agencies in Bulgaria.

Tourism

Balkantourist: 1040 Sofia, Blvd Vitosha 1; tel (2) 4-33-31; telex 22583; Dir-Gen: Ivan Milkov; f 1948; state tourist enterprise.

Transport

Autotransport: Sofia, Gurko St 5; tel (2) 87-62-32; telex 22332; Dir-Gen: T. Peyuvsky; f 1965; road transportation.

Balkan Bulgarian Airlines: 1540 Sofia, Sofia Airport; Head Office: Sofia, pl Narodno Sobraniye 12; tel (2) 71-201; telex 22299; fax (2) 79-12-06; Dir-Gen: Kostadin Botev; Dep Dir-Gen: Andon Stoyanov; f 1947; operates scheduled and charter passenger and cargo flights all over the world.

Bulgarian River Shipping Corpn: 7000 Ruse, pl Otets Paisi 2; tel (82) 70-093; telex 62403; fax (82) 70-161; Dir-Gen: Tsonyo Uzunov.

Bulgarian State Railways (BDZ): 1080 Sofia, Ivan Vazov St 3; tel (2) 87-30-45; telex 22423; Chair: Veselin Pavlov; owns and controls all railway transport.

Despred: 1000 Sofia, Slavyanska St 2; tel (2) 87-60-16; telex 23306; fax (2) 80-14-37; Dir-Gen: Traiko Vargov; state forwarding enterprise.

Inflot: 1504 Sofia, Blvd Vl Zaimov 88; 1000 Sofia, POB 634; tel (2) 88-27-71; telex 22376; fax (2) 44-21-18; Dir-Gen: Panayot Vezirev; f 1951; agency for inland and maritime foreign and Bulgarian shipping.

Navigation Maritime Bulgare: 9000 Varna, Blvd Chervenoarmeiski 1; tel (52) 22-24-74; telex 77525; fax (52) 22-24-91; Dir-Gen: Capt Atanas Yonkov; Dep Dirs: D. Mavrov, G. Pavlov; f 1892; runs cargo and passenger services to destinations all over the world; runs Bulcon container service.

Shipping Corpn: Varna, Panagyuriste St 17; tel (52) 22-63-31; telex 77524; fax (52) 22-53-94; Dir-Gen: Nikolai Youchev; f 1969; transportation of cargo and passengers on waterways; handling and forwarding of cargo; research in the field of water transport; repair of Bulgarian and foreign vessels; pilotage.

BURKINA FASO

MINISTRIES AND GOVERNMENT DEPARTMENTS

MINISTRY OF AGRICULTURE AND LIVESTOCK
BP 7005, Ouagadougou
Minister: Albert Djidma
Secretary of State for Livestock: Amadou Maurice Guiao

MINISTRY OF ECONOMIC PROMOTION
Ouagadougou
Tel 30-70-14
Minister: Thomas Sanou
Secretary of State for Mines: Aboubacar Yahya Diallo

MINISTRY OF THE ENVIRONMENT AND TOURISM
BP 7044, Ouagadougou
Tel 33-41-65; telex 5555
Minister: Maurice Dieudonné Bonane

MINISTRY OF EQUIPMENT
BP 7011, Ouagadougou
Minister: Capt Daprou Kambou

MINISTRY OF EXTERNAL RELATONS
BP 7038, Ouagadougou
Telex 5222
Minister: Prosper Vokouma

MINISTRY OF FINANCE
BP 7008, Ouagadougou
Tel 33-40-74; telex 5256
Minister: Bintou Sanogo
Secretary of State in charge of the Budget: Célestin Tiendrébéogo

MINISTRY OF HEALTH AND SOCIAL ACTION
BP 7009, Ouagadougou
Minister: Kanidoua Nabomo
Secretary of State for Social Action: Elie Saré

MINISTRY OF INFORMATION AND CULTURE
BP 7045, Ouagadougou
Tel 33-44-67; telex 5285
Minister: Béatrice Damiba
Secretary of State for Culture: Alimata Salimbéré

MINISTRY OF JUSTICE
BP 526, Ouagadougou
Minister and Keeper of the Seals: Antoine Komi Sambo

MINISTRY OF LABOUR, SOCIAL SECURITY AND THE PUBLIC SERVICE
BP 7006, Ouagadougou
Minister: Salif Sampebogo

MINISTRY OF PEASANT AFFAIRS
Ouagadougou
Minister: Capt Laurent Sedego

MINISTRY OF PLANNING AND CO-OPERATION
BP 7050, Ouagadougou
Telex 5319
Minister: Pascal Zagré

MINISTRY OF POPULAR DEFENCE AND SECURITY
BP 496, Ouagadougou
Telex 5297
Minister: Capt Blaise Compaoré

MINISTRY OF PRIMARY EDUCATION AND MASS LITERACY
BP 7032, Ouagadougou
Telex 5555
Minister: Alice Tiendrébéogo

MINISTRY OF SECONDARY AND HIGHER EDUCATION AND SCIENTIFIC RESEARCH
BP 7130, Ouagadougou
Minister: Mouhoussine Nacro

MINISTRY OF SPORTS
BP 7035, Ouagadougou
Tel 30-72-01
Minister: Lt Kilimité Hien

MINISTRY OF TERRITORIAL ADMINISTRATION
BP 7034, Ouagadougou
Tel 30-71-83
Minister: Jean-Léonard Compaoré

MINISTRY OF TRADE AND POPULAR SUPPLY
BP 365, Ouagadougou
Minister: Frédéric Assomption Korsaga

MINISTRY OF TRANSPORT AND COMMUNICATIONS
BP 7701, Ouagadougou
Minister: Roch Marc Christian Kaboré

MINISTRY OF WATER RESOURCES
Ouagadougou
Tel 30-78-27
Minister: Sabné Koanda

OFFICE OF THE MINISTER DELEGATE TO THE CO-ORDINATING COMMITTEE OF THE POPULAR FRONT

Ouagadougou
Minister-Delegate:: Clément Oumarou Ouedraogo

OFFICE OF THE SECRETARY OF STATE FOR HOUSING AND URBAN AFFAIRS
Ouagadougou
Secretary of State: Joseph Kaboré

OFFICE OF THE SECRETARY-GENERAL
BP 7030, Ouagadougou
Secretary-General of the Revolutionary Committees:
Capt Arsène Yè Bognessan

GOVERNMENT AGENCIES AND ORGANIZATIONS

Advisory and Supervisory Bodies

Caisse de Stabilisation des Prix des Produits Agricoles (CSPPA): BP 1453, Ouagadougou; tel 30-62-13; telex 5202; Dir-Gen: André Emmanuel Yaméogo; f 1964; stabilizes agricultural prices; supervises trade and export of agricultural products such as almonds, cashew nuts, sesame, gum arabic, etc.

Conseil Révolutionnaire Economique et Social: Ouagadougou; Pres: Kader Cissé; f 1985; 38 mems; social and economic advisory body.

Agriculture

Grands Moulins Burkinabè (GMB): BP 64, Banfora; tel 88-00-57; telex 8212; Gen Man: Pierre D. Nare; f 1969; 72.95% state-owned; flour milling and production of animal feed.

Office National des Céréales (OFNACER): BP 53, Ouagadougou; tel 30-26-05; telex 5317; Dir: Goama Henri Kaboré; stabilizes the supply and price of cereals.

Office National de l'Exploitation des Ressources Animales: BP 7058, Ouagadougou; tel 30-66-95; telex 5312; Dir-Gen: Roger Moussa Tall.

Société Burkinabè des Fibres Textiles (SOFITEX): BP 147, Bobo-Dioulasso; tel 99-01-11; telex 8208; Dir: Mathieu Bayala; f 1979; 65% state-owned; cultivation and treatment of fibrous plants.

Union des Coopératives Agricoles et Maraîchères du Burkina (UCOBAM): BP 277, Ouagadougou; tel 30-65-27; telex 5287; Dir-Gen: Issaka Derme; Commercial Dir: André Bicaba; f 1968; comprises 8 regional co-operative unions; markets fruit and vegetables; imports seeds.

Business and Economy

BANKING

Banque Burkinabè-Libyenne pour le Commerce et le Développement (BALIB): BP 1336, Ouagadougou; tel 30-78-78; telex 5501; f 1987; 50% state-owned, 50% Libyan-owned.

Banque Centrale des Etats de l'Afrique de l'Ouest (BCEAO): ave Gamal-Abdel-Nasser, BP 356, Ouagadougou; tel 33-67-15; telex 5205; Gov: Alassane Ouattara; Dir in Burkina Faso: Moussa Koné; f 1955; central bank of issue for the seven states of the Union monétaire ouest-africaine (UMOA), comprising Benin, Burkina Faso, Côte d'Ivoire, Mali, Niger, Senegal and Togo.

Banque pour le Financement du Commerce et des Investissements du Burkina (BFCI-B): 4 rue du Marché, BP 585, Ouagadougou; tel 30-60-35; telex 5269; Pres: M. N'Golo Koné; Dir-Gen: Jean-Baptiste Confé; f 1973; 75% state-owned.

Banque Internationale du Burkina SA (BIB): rue de la Chance angle rue Patrice Lumumba, BP 362, Ouagadougou; tel 31-01-00; telex 5210; fax 31-00-90; Pres: Daouda Bayili; Gen Man: Gaspard Ouedraogo; f 1974; 53% state-owned, 40% owned by BIAO (France); 13 brs.

Banque Internationale pour le Commerce, l'Industrie et l'Agriculture du Burkina SA (BICIA-BF): ave Dr Nkwamé N'Kruma, BP 8, Ouagadougou; tel 30-62-26; telex 5203; Pres: Hamadé Ouedraogo; Man Dir: Augustin Der Somda; f 1973; 51% state-owned; 11 brs.

Banque Nationale de Développement du Burkina Faso (BND): place de la Révolution, BP 148, Ouagadougou; tel 30-60-82; telex 5225; Pres: Bissiri Joseph Sirima; Man Dir: Boukary Ouedraogo; f 1962; 92% state-owned; 6 brs.

Caisse Nationale de Crédit Agricole du Burkina Faso (CNCA-BF): BP 1644, Ouagadougou; tel 30-21-62; telex 5443; Pres: Soulemane Ouedraogo; Dir-Gen: Noël Kaboré; f 1979; 54% state-owned.

Caisse Nationale des Dépôts et des Investissements (CNDI): 4 rue du Marché, BP 585, Ouagadougou; tel 33-41-72; telex 5269; Pres of Admin Council: N'Golo Koné; Dir-Gen: Frédéric Assomption Korsaga; f 1973; 100% state-owned.

Union Révolutionnaire des Banques (UREBA): 2 ave Nelson Mandela, BP 4414; Ouagadougou; tel 33-22-05; telex 5458; Pres: Marcellin Zongo; Man Dir: Kouka Victor Nikiema; f 1984; 51% owned by Govt and provinces.

INSURANCE

Société Nationale d'Assurance et de Réassurance (SONAR): BP 406, Ouagadougou; tel 33-63-43; telex 5294; Man Dir: Bablo Félix Hema; f 1973; 51% state-owned; insurance and reinsurance.

MARKETING

Société de Commercialisation du Burkina 'Faso Yaar': BP 531, Ouagadougou; tel 30-61-28; telex 5274; Pres: Minister of Trade and Popular Supply, Frédéric Assomption Korsaga; Man Dir: Mamadou Karambiri; 99% state-owned; marketing organization with 30 retail outlets.

NATIONALIZED INDUSTRY

Office de Promotion de l'Entreprise (OPE): BP 94, Ouagadougou; f 1970; supervises industrial devt projects.

Société Faso-Fani: BP 105, Koudougou; tel 44-01-33; telex

5250; Man Dir: Jean Claude Bicaba; f 1965; 55% state-owned; weaving, spinning, dyeing and printing of textiles.

Société Sucrière du Burkina Faso (SOSU-BF): BP 13, Banfora; tel 88-00-18; telex 8212; Dir: Urbain Somda; f 1969; 69% state-owned; sugar refining.

TRADE

Groupement Coopératif de Ventes Internationales des Produits du Burkina (Cooproduits): BP 91, Ouagadougou; telex 5224; Man Dir: Kéoulé Nacoulima; agricultural co-operative; export of seeds, nuts and gum arabic.

Office National du Commerce Extérieur (ONAC): BP 389, Ouagadougou; tel 30-62-23; telex 5258; Man Dir: Benoît Zabramba; f 1974; promotes external trade by studying markets and disseminating information on commerce.

Defence

Armed Forces: BP 509, Ouagadougou; tel 30-63-72; telex 5298; Commdr-in-Chief: Maj Jean-Baptiste Boukary Lingani.

Air Force: BP 96, Ouagadougou; tel 30-70-03; Commdr: Augustin Zongo.

Development and Planning

Autorité des Aménagements des Vallées des Voltas (AVV): BP 524, Ouagadougou; tel 30-61-10; telex 5401; Man Dir: Emmanuel Nikiema; f 1974; integrated rural devt and economic and social planning.

Caisse Centrale de Coopération Economique (CCCE): ave Binger, BP 529, Ouagadougou; tel 33-60-76; telex 5271; Dir: François Peyredieu du Charlat.

Legal and Judiciary

High Court of Justice: BP 586, Ouagadougou; tel 30-64-14.

Media

BROADCASTING

Radiodiffusion-Télévision Burkina: BP 7029, Ouagadougou; tel 33-68-05; telex 5132; Dir: Bayer Balawo; f 1959; services in French and 13 vernacular languages.

Télévision Nationale du Burkina (Voltavision): BP 7029, Ouagadougou; tel 33-68-01; telex 5231; Dir: Th S. Balima; f 1963; daily TV transmissions; currently received only in Ouagadougou and Bobo-Dioulasso.

GOVERNMENT PUBLISHER

Imprimerie Nationale du Burkina Faso (INBF): route de l'Hôpital Yalgado, BP 7040, Ouagadougou; tel 33-52-92; Dir: Laty Souleymane Traoré; f 1963.

NEWS AND INFORMATION

Agence Burkinabè de Presse: BP 2507, Ouagadougou; tel 33-28-20; telex 5327; f 1963; state-controlled news agency.

Institut National de la Statistique et de la Démographie: BP 374, Ouagadougou; tel 30-67-98; f 1963; collects, studies and publishes statistical data.

Mining and Energy

Bureau des Mines et de la Géologie du Burkina (BUMIGEB): BP 601, Ouagadougou; tel 30-02-27; telex 5340; Pres: Aly Seye; Man Dir: Kassoum Joseph Kaboré; Dir of Research: G. E. Zoungrana; f 1978; research into geological, mineral and water resources.

Société Minière de Tambao (SOMITAM): BP 587, Ouagadougou; tel 30-67-48; telex 5261; Man Dir: François Ouindélassida Ouedraogo; f 1975; 51% state-owned; exploits manganese deposits at Tambao.

Société Nationale Burkinabè d'Electricité (SONABEL): ave Nelson Mandela, BP 54, Ouagadougou; tel 33-62-05; telex 5208; Dir-Gen: Oumara Idani; f 1968; production and distribution of electricity and water.

Société de Recherches et d'Exploitation Minière du Burkina (SOREMIB): BP 5562, Ouagadougou; tel 30-62-35; telex 5412; Pres: Dieudonné Yameogo; Dir-Gen: Nongodo Joseph Ouedraogo; f 1975; 60% state-owned; prospecting, study and exploitation of minerals, and especially of the gold deposits of Poura.

Tourism

Direction Générale du Tourisme et de l'Hôtellerie: BP 624, Ouagadougou; tel 30-63-96; telex 5555; Dir-Gen: Abdoulaye Sankara; f 1976; promotes tourism; under control of the Ministry of the Environment and Tourism.

Faso Tours: BP 1318 Ouagadougou; tel 30-66-71; telex 5377; Dirs: Mamadou Ouedraogo, Christine Bague; f 1989; runs tours and excursions; vehicle rental.

Transport

Air Burkina: BP 1459, Ouagadougou; tel 30-61-43; telex 203; Man Dir: (vacant); f 1967; 66% state-owned; monopoly of domestic services; flights to and from Mali, Togo, Benin, Niger, Ghana and Côte d'Ivoire.

La Régie du Chemin de Fer Abidjan-Niger (RAN): BP 192, Ouagadougou; tel 33-46-97; telex 5433; Head Office in Côte d'Ivoire; Dir-Gen, Burkina Faso: Grégoire Baboré Bado; f 1904; railway links Ouagadougou with the coast at Abidjan (Côte d'Ivoire); the co was to be reorganized as two independent railways in 1989.

Régie X9 (Régie Nationale des Transports en Commun—RNTC X9): BP 2991, Ouagadougou; tel 33-42-96; telex 5313; Dir-Gen: Nebama Kere; Admin and Finance Dir: Yacouba Hema; f 1984; national and international public transport.

Utilities

Office National de l'Eau et de l'Assainissement (ONEA): BP 170, Ouagadougou; tel 30-60-73; telex 5226; Dir: Victor Wandé Ouedraogo; f 1977; water storage, purification and distribution.

BURUNDI

Head of State

Provision is made in the 1981 Constitution for a President, elected for five years by universal adult suffrage. However, following a coup in September 1987, executive and legislative powers were assumed by a 31-member Military Committee for National Salvation (CMSN) whose Chair became President, and which appointed a civilian Council of Ministers, headed by a Prime Minister.

President: Maj Pierre Buyoya (took office 2 October 1987).

Office of the President: Bujumbura; tel (2) 6063; telex 5049.

Legislature

According to the Constitution, 52 representatives are directly elected to the Assemblée Nationale (National Assembly) by universal adult suffrage every five years, a further 13 representatives being appointed by the President. However, the 65-member Assembly was dissolved following the coup in 1987. For the purposes of local govt, Burundi is divided into 15 provinces.

MINISTRIES AND GOVERNMENT DEPARTMENTS

MINISTRY OF AGRICULTURE AND ANIMAL HUSBANDRY
Bujumbura
Tel (2) 2087
Minister: Jumaine Hussein

MINISTRY OF DEVELOPMENT, TOURISM AND THE ENVIRONMENT
Bujumbura
Minister: Basile Sindaharaye

MINISTRY OF ENERGY AND MINES
Bujumbura
Minister: Gilbert Midende

MINISTRY OF EXTERNAL RELATIONS AND CO-OPERATION
Bujumbura
Tel (2) 2150; telex 5065
Minister: Cyprien Mbonimpa

MINISTRY OF FAMILY AND WOMEN'S DEVELOPMENT AFFAIRS
Bujumbura
Tel (2) 5561
Minister: Pia Ndayiragije

MINISTRY OF FINANCE
BP 1830, Bujumbura
Tel (2) 3988; telex 5135
Minister: Gérard Niyibigira

MINISTRY OF INDUSTRY AND TRADE
Bujumbura
Tel (2) 5330
Minister: Bonaventure Kidwingira

MINISTRY OF INFORMATION
BP 4080, Bujumbura
Tel (2) 4666; telex 56
Minister: Frédéric Ngenzebuhoro

MINISTRY OF INTERNAL AFFAIRS
Bujumbura
Tel (2) 4242
Minister: Aloys Kadoyi

MINISTRY OF JUSTICE
Bujumbura
Tel (2) 2148
Minister: Evariste Niyonkuru

MINISTRY OF LABOUR AND PROFESSIONAL TRAINING
BP 2830, Bujumbura
Tel (2) 5058
Minister: Charles Karikurubu

MINISTRY OF NATIONAL DEFENCE
Bujumbura
Tel (2) 6063; telex 5049
Minister: Maj Pierre Buyoya

MINISTRY OF NATIONAL EDUCATION
Bujumbura
Tel (2) 5112
Minister of Higher Education and Scientific Research: Nicolas Mayugi
Minister of Primary and Secondary Education: Gamaliel Ndaruzaniye

MINISTRY OF PLANNING
Bujumbura
Tel (2) 6063
Prime Minister and Minister of Planning: Adrien Sibomana

MINISTRY OF PUBLIC HEALTH
Bujumbura
Tel (2) 6020
Minister: Dr Norbert Ngendabanyikwa

MINISTRY OF THE PUBLIC SERVICE
Bujumbura
Tel (2) 3514
Minister: Didace Rudaragi

MINISTRY OF PUBLIC WORKS AND URBAN DEVELOPMENT
Bujumbura
Tel (2) 6841; telex 5048
Minister: Evariste Simbarakiye

MINISTRY OF RURAL DEVELOPMENT AND HANDICRAFTS
Bujumbura
Tel (2) 5267
Minister: Gabriel Toyi

MINISTRY OF SOCIAL AFFAIRS
Bujumbura
Tel (2) 5039
Minister: Julie Ngiriye

MINISTRY OF TRANSPORT, POSTS AND TELECOMMUNICATIONS
Bujumbura
Tel (2) 2923; telex 5103
Minister: Maj Simon Rusuku

MINISTRY OF YOUTH, SPORT AND CULTURE
Bujumbura
Tel (2) 6822
Minister: Adolphe Nahayo

OFFICE OF THE SECRETARY OF STATE IN CHARGE OF GOVERNMENT PLANNING
Bujumbura
Secretary of State: Salvator Sahinguvu

OFFICE OF THE SECRETARY OF STATE IN CHARGE OF INTERNATIONAL CO-OPERATION
Bujumbura
Secretary of State: Fridolin Hatungimana

GOVERNMENT AGENCIES AND ORGANIZATIONS

Agriculture

Burundi Coffee Co (BCC): ave de Commerce, Bujumbura; tel (2) 2864; telex 73.

Institut des Sciences Agronomiques du Burundi (ISABU): BP 795, Bujumbura; tel (2) 3384; f 1962; scientific devt of agriculture and livestock.

Minoterie de Muramvya: BP 1110, Bujumbura; tel (2) 6456; telex 5144; f 1980; owned by Burundi Govt and Holding Arabe Libyen du Burundi; imports, processes and markets cereals.

Office du Café du Burundi: Bujumbura; tel (2) 3815; telex 73; Dir-Gen: Salvator Nimubona.

Office des Cultures Industrielles du Burundi (OCIBU): BP 450, Bujumbura; tel (2) 2631; oversees coffee plantations and coffee exports.

Office National du Bois (ONB): BP 1492, Bujumbura; tel (2) 4416; Dir: Lazare Runesa; f 1980; exploitation of local timber resources; importation of foreign timber.

Office du Thé du Burundi (OTB): Bujumbura; telex 5069; f 1979; devt of the the tea industry.

Office de la Tourbe du Burundi (ONATOUR): BP 2360, Bujumbura; tel (2) 6480; telex 48; f 1977; promotes the exploitation of peat bogs.

Société d'Economie Mixte pour l'Exploitation du Quinquina au Burundi (SOKINABU): BP 1783, Bujumbura; tel (2) 3469; telex 81; Man: Raphaël Remezo; f 1975; devt and exploitation of cinchona trees, the source of quinine.

Société Sucrière du Moso (SOSUMO): BP 835, Bujumbura; tel (2) 6576; telex 35; f 1982; develops and oversees sugar cane plantations.

Business and Economy

BANKING

Banque Commerciale du Burundi (BANCOBU): chaussée Prince Louis-Rwagasore, BP 990, Bujumbura; tel (2) 2317; telex 5051; Chair: Jean Berchmans Nsabiyumva; Man Dir: Jacques van Eetvelde; f 1960; reorg 1988; 51% state-owned.

Banque Nationale pour le Développement Economique du Burundi (BNDE): BP 1620, Bujumbura; tel (2) 2888; telex 5091; Chair: Bonus Kamwenubusa; Man Dir: François Barwendere; f 1967; devt bank.

Banque de la République du Burundi (BRB): BP 705, Bujumbura; tel (2) 5142; telex 5071; Gov: Isaac Budabuda; Vice-Gov: Evariste Nibasumba; Dir: Pascal Ntamashimikiro; f 1964; central bank.

Caisse d'Epargne du Burundi (CADEBU): BP 615; Bujumbura; tel (2) 2348; telex 71; Chair: Pasteur Budeyi; Man Dir: Boniface Bagorikunda; f 1964; 100% state-owned.

Holding Arabe Libyen Burundais (HALB): BP 1892; Bujumbura; tel (2) 6635; telex 5090; fax (2) 6485; Pres: Egide Ndahibeshe; Dir-Gen: Muftah el Kekli; Dep Dir-Gen: Ladislas Ncahinyeretse; f 1975; creation and financing of agricultural, commercial, industrial, fishing, and mining research and exploitation projects.

Société Burundaise de Financement (SBF): 13-14 rue de l'Amitié, BP 270, Bujumbura; tel (2) 2126; telex 5080; Chair: Mathias Sinamenye; f 1982; devt bank.

FINANCIAL AGENCY

Caisse Centrale de Mobilisation et de Financement (CAMOFI): 4 ave de l'UJRB, BP 8, Bujumbura; tel (2) 5642; telex 5082; Chair: Minister of Finance, Gérard Niyibigira; Man Dir: Léonard Ntibagirirwa; f 1977; finances public-sector devt projects and businesses.

INSURANCE

Société d'Assurances du Burundi (SOCABU): BP 2440, 14-18 rue de l'Amitié, Bujumbura; tel (2) 6803; telex 5113; Man: Athanase Gahungu; f 1977.

NATIONALIZED INDUSTRY

Complexe Textile de Bujumbura (COTEBU): BP 2890, Bujumbura; tel (2) 32155; telex 5061; f 1978; production and marketing of yarn and clothes.

Office National Pharmaceutique (ONAPHA): BP 2380, Bujumbura; telex 5081; f 1979; manufactures, imports and markets pharmaceutical products.

Office National du Logement (ONL): BP 2480, Bujumbura; tel (2) 6074; telex 48; f 1974; housing construction.

Société Mixte, Minière et Industrielle Roumano-Burundaise (SOMIBUROM): Bujumbura; f 1977; exploits and markets mineral and industrial products.

TRADE

Office National du Commerce (ONC): Bujumbura; f 1973; oversees international commercial dealings between the Govt and other states or private organizations; ensures the import of essential materials; brs in each province.

Office National d'Importation et de Commercialisation des Matériaux de Construction et d'Equipement Domestique (ONIMAC): angle blvd du Port et rue des Marais, BP 1314, Bujumbura; tel (2) 6410; telex 5189; Dirs: Balthazar Mbonimpa, Protais Nzeyimana, Audace Hakizimana, Denis Nahimana, Patrice Harakandi; f 1978; imports and distributes construction materials and domestic equipment; exports cement, steel, joinery and metal-working tools, hardware.

Société de Stockage et de Commercialisation des Produits Vivriers (SOBECOV): Bujumbura; f 1977; stocks and markets agricultural products in Burundi.

Defence

Armed Forces: Bujumbura; tel (2) 6700; Chief of Staff: Maj Michel Mibarurwa.

Development and Planning

Comité de Gérance de la Réserve Cotonnière (COGERCO): Bujumbura; devt of the cotton industry.

Fonds de Promotion Economique: BP 270, Bujumbura; tel (2) 5562; telex 80; Man Dir: Bonaventure Kidwingira; f 1981; promotion and financing of industrial, agricultural and commercial activities.

Legal and Judiciary

Supreme Court: Bujumbura; tel (2) 5442; comprises four chambers: ordinary, cassation, constitutional and administrative.

Media

BROADCASTING

Voix de la Révolution/La Radiodiffusion et Télévision Nationale du Burundi (RTNB): BP 1900, Bujumbura; tel (2) 3742; telex 5119; Dir-Gen: Alexis Ntavyo; Dir, 1st Programme: Christine Ntahe; Dir, 2nd Programme: Antoine Ntamikevyo; Dir, TV: J. Nzononimpa; f 1960; daily radio broadcasts in Kirundi, Swahili, French and English.

GOVERNMENT PUBLISHER

Imprimerie Nationale du Burundi (INABU): BP 991, Bujumbura; tel (2) 4046; telex 80.

NEWS AND INFORMATION

Agence Burundaise de Presse (ABP): 6 ave de la Poste, BP 2870, Bujumbura; tel (2) 5417; telex 5056; news agency.

Tourism

Office National du Tourisme: BP 902, Bujumbura; tel (2) 2202; telex 5030; Dir: André Ndayiragije; f 1972.

Transport and Telecommunications

Office National de Télécommunications (ONATEL): Bujumbura.

Air Burundi: 40 ave du Commerce, BP 2460, Bujumbura; telex 80; Man Dir: Gérard Mugabo; f 1971; internal flights, and external services to Rwanda and Zaire.

CAMBODIA

Head of State

The President of the Council of State is Head of State, and executive power is exercised by the Council of Ministers, which is appointed by the Council of State. The Council of State is the permanent organ of the National Assembly, its members are elected from the National Assembly deputies, and it is responsible to the National Assembly.

President of the Council of State: Heng Samrin.

Council of State: Phnom-Penh; tel 23201; Vice-Pres: Say Phouthang; Sec-Gen: Chan Ven.

Legislature

Legislative power is vested in the National Assembly, comprising 123 members elected for five years by universal adult suffrage. The Assembly elects the Council of State. Local administration is the responsibility of Local People's Committees.

National Assembly: Phnom Penh; tel 23535; Chair: Chea Sim; Vice-Chairs: Ven Tep Vong, Nu Beng, Mat Ly; Sec-Gen: Phlek Piroun.

MINISTRIES AND GOVERNMENT DEPARTMENTS

COUNCIL OF MINISTERS
Phnom-Penh
Chair: Hun Sen
Vice-Chairs: Say Phouthang, Kong Sam-ol, Say Chhum, Tea Banh, Chea Soth, Bou Thang
Minister Assistant to the Chair (Foreign and Judicial): Hor Nam Hong
Minister Assistant to the Chair: Pung Peng Cheng
Dir, Cabinet of the Council of Ministers: Kong Sam-ol
Minister attached to the Council of Ministers: Khun Chhy

CENTRAL ORGANIZATION COMMITTEE
Phnom-Penh
Chair: Say Phonthang

GENERAL DEPARTMENT FOR RUBBER PLANTATIONS
Phnom-Penh
Director: Sam Sarit

MINISTRY OF AGRICULTURE
Phnom-Penh
Minister: Say Chhum
Vice-Minister of Agriculture: Chhung Song
Vice-Minister of Agriculture (Fisheries): Mau Phauk

MINISTRY OF COMMUNICATIONS, TRANSPORT AND POSTS
Phnom-Penh
Minister: Ung Phan
Vice-Ministers: Chhim Seng, Kim Seap

MINISTRY OF EDUCATION
Phnom-Penh
Minister: Pen Navouth
Vice-Minister: Hang Chuon

MINISTRY OF FINANCE
Phnom-Penh
Minister: Chhay Than
Vice-Minister: Bun Sam

MINISTRY OF FOREIGN AFFAIRS
Phnom-Penh
Minister: Hun Sen
Vice-Ministers: Prach Sun, Dith Mounty, Hor Nam Hong

MINISTRY OF FOREIGN TRADE
Phnom-Penh
Minister: Tang Saroem
Vice-Minister of Trade: Thong Chan

MINISTRY OF HEALTH
Phnom-Penh
Minister: Dr Yit Kim Seng
Vice-Ministers: Chea Thang, Chey Kanh Nha

MINISTRY OF INDUSTRY
Phnom-Penh
Minister: Ho Hon
Vice-Ministers: Nuon Sareth, Khlot Vandhi

MINISTRY OF INFORMATION, PRESS AND CULTURE
Phnom-Penh
Minister: Chheng Phon
Vice-Ministers: Chey Sophea, Him Chhem

MINISTRY OF THE INTERIOR
Phnom-Penh
Minister: Sin Song
Vice-Minister: Kim Phon

MINISTRY OF JUSTICE
Phnom-Penh
Minister: Ouk Bun Choeun
Vice-Minister: Chem Snguon

MINISTRY OF NATIONAL DEFENCE
Phnom-Penh
Minister: Tea Banh
Deputy Minister and Chief of Staff: Pol Saroeun
Vice-Ministers: Ke Kimyan, Soy Keo, Pol Saroelin, Di Phin, El Vansarat

MINISTRY OF PLANNING
Phnom-Penh
Minister: Chea Chanto
Vice-Ministers: Ti Yav, Ros Chhum, Keo Samut

MINISTRY OF SOCIAL AFFAIRS AND WAR INVALIDS
Phnom-Penh

Minister: Koy Buntha
Vice-Minister of Social Affairs: Douang Choum

OFFICE OF THE ATTORNEY-GENERAL
Phnom-Penh
Attorney-General: Chan Min

PARTY CENTRAL COMMITTEE'S PROPAGANDA AND EDUCATION COMMISSION
Phnom-Penh
Chair: Ney Pena

STATE AFFAIRS INSPECTORATE
Phnom-Penh
Director: Kong Korm

STATE CONTROL COMMITTEE
Phnom-Penh
Chair: Sim Ka

GOVERNMENT AGENCIES AND ORGANIZATIONS

Business and Economy

BANKING

National Bank of Cambodia: 26 Song Ngoc Minh, Phnom-Penh; Chair: Cha Rieng (mem of the Council of Ministers); f 1980.
  Foreign Trade Bank: Phnom-Penh; f 1980; aims to expand overseas trade.

TRADE

KAMBEXIM: Phnom-Penh; f 1979; handles imports, exports and the receipt of foreign aid.
National Trade Commission: Phnom-Penh; Pres: Tang Saroem.

Defence

Cambodian People's Revolutionary Armed Forces: Phnom-Penh; Commdr-in-Chief: Heng Samrin; Chief of Gen Staff of the Army: Pol Saroeun.

Legal and Judiciary

Supreme People's Court: Phnom Penh; Pres: Khang Sarin.

Media

BROADCASTING

Democratic Kampuchean Television (TVK): 19 rue 242, Donpenh, Phnom-Penh; tel 22349; Chair: Kim Yin; Dep Chair: Vann Sun Heng; opened 1984; broadcasts for 2 hours per day in Khmer; controlled by the KUFNDC (Kampuchean United Front for National Construction and Defence).

Samleng Pracheachon Kampuchea (Voice of the Kampuchean People): 28 ave Sandech Choun Nath, Phnom-Penh; Dir-Gen: Kim Yin; Dep Dir-Gen: Vann Seng Ly; f 1978; home and external radio services; controlled by the KUFNDC (Kampuchean United Front for National Construction and Defence).

NEWS AND INFORMATION

Saporamean Kampuchea—SPK (Kampuchea Information Agency): Phnom-Penh; Dir-Gen: Em Sam An; f 1978; controlled by the KUFNDC (Kampuchean United Front for National Construction and Defence).

Tourism

General Directorate for Tourism: Phnom-Penh; Dir-Gen: (vacant); the Dir-Gen is a mem of the Council of Ministers.

Transport

Air Kampuchea: Phnom-Penh; f 1982; operates routes from Phnom-Penh to Moscow, Ho Chi Minh City (Vietnam) and Vientiane (Laos); charter tours to Angkor Wat.

Chemins de Fer du Cambodge: Moha Vithei Pracheathippatay, Phnom-Penh; tel 25156.

CAMEROON

Head of State

Executive power is vested in the President who, as Head of State, is elected by universal adult suffrage for a five-year term and can be re-elected. The President appoints the Cabinet, makes civil and military appointments and is head of the armed forces.

President: Paul Biya (took office 6 November 1982, following the resignation of Ahmadou Ahidjo; elected 14 January 1984 for a five-year term; re-elected 24 April 1988).

Office of the President: c/o the Central Post Office, Yaoundé; tel 23-40-25; telex 8207; Sec-Gen at the Presidency: Edouard Akame Mfoumou; Ministers at the Presidency in charge of Missions: Ogork Ebot Ntui, Emmanuel Zoa Oloa; Minister Special Adviser to the Pres: Titus Edzoa; Dir, Office of the Pres: Laurent Esso.

Legislature

Legislative power is vested in the unicameral Assemblée Nationale (National Assembly), comprising 180 deputies, elected for five years by universal adult suffrage. For local administration, the country is divided into 10 provinces, each with a Governor appointed by the President.

Assemblée Nationale (National Assembly): Yaoundé; tel 23-02-99; telex 8283; Pres: Lawrence Shang Fonka; Sec-Gen: Efoua Mbozo'o.

MINISTRIES AND GOVERNMENT DEPARTMENTS

MINISTRY OF AGRICULTURE
c/o the Central Post Office, Yaoundé
Tel 23-40-85; telex 8325
Minister: John Niba Ngu
Secretary of State: Tikela Kemonne

MINISTRY OF DEFENCE
c/o the Central Post Office, Yaoundé
Tel 23-40-55; telex 8261
Minister-Delegate at the Presidency in charge of Defence: Michel Meva'a M'Eboutou
Secretary of State: Amadou Ali

MINISTRY OF EXTERNAL RELATIONS
c/o the Central Post Office, Yaoundé
Tel 22-01-33; telex 8252
Minister: Jacques-Roger Booh-Booh

MINISTRY OF FINANCE
BP 18, Yaoundé
Tel 23-40-00; telex 8260
Minister: Sadou Hayatou
Secretaries of State: Ephraim Inoni, Roger Tchoungi

MINISTRY OF HIGHER EDUCATION, SCIENTIFIC RESEARCH AND COMPUTER SCIENCES
BP 1457, Yaoundé
Tel 23-16-50; telex 8418
Minister: Abdoulaye Babale

MINISTRY OF HOUSING AND TOWN PLANNING
c/o the Central Post Office, Yaoundé
Tel 23-22-82; telex 8560
Minister: Ferdinand-Léopold Oyono

MINISTRY OF INDUSTRIAL AND COMMERCIAL DEVELOPMENT AND TRADE
c/o the Central Post Office, Yaoundé
Minister: Joseph Tsanga Abanda
Secretary of State: Louis Abogo Nkono

MINISTRY OF INFORMATION AND CULTURE
BP 1588, Yaoundé
Tel 22-31-55; telex 8215
Minister: Henri Bandolo

MINISTRY OF JUSTICE
c/o the Central Post Office, Yaoundé
Tel 22-01-97; telex 8566
Minister and Keeper of the Seals: Adolphe Moudiki

MINISTRY OF LABOUR AND SOCIAL WELFARE
c/o the Central Post Office, Yaoundé
Tel 22-01-86
Minister: Jean Baptiste Bokam

MINISTRY OF LIVESTOCK, FISHERIES AND ANIMAL HUSBANDRY
c/o the Central Post Office, Yaoundé
Tel 22-33-11
Minister: Hamadjoda Adjoudji

MINISTRY OF MINES, WATER AND ENERGY
c/o the Central Post Office, Yaoundé
Tel 23-34-04; telex 8504
Minister: Francis Wainchom Nkwain

MINISTRY OF NATIONAL EDUCATION
c/o the Central Post Office, Yaoundé
Tel 23-40-50; telex 8551
Minister: Josepoh Mboui
Secretary of State: Paul Enyi Atogo

MINISTRY OF PLANNING AND TERRITORIAL DEVELOPMENT
c/o the Central Post Office, Yaoundé
Telex 8268
Minister: Elizabeth Tankeu
Secretary of State: Ndanga Ndinga Badel

MINISTRY OF POSTS AND TELECOMMUNICATIONS
c/o the Central Post Office, Yaoundé
Tel 23-40-16; telex 8582; fax 22-34-97
Minister: Oumarou Sanda

MINISTRY OF PUBLIC HEALTH
c/o the Central Post Office, Yaoundé
Tel 22-29-01; telex 8565
Minister: Prof Joseph Mbede

MINISTRY OF THE PUBLIC SERVICE AND STATE CONTROL
c/o the Central Post Office, Yaoundé
Telex 8597
Minister: Prof Joseph Owona

MINISTRY OF PUBLIC WORKS AND TRANSPORT
c/o the Central Post Office, Yaoundé
Tel 22-16-22; telex 8653
Minister: Paul Tessa

MINISTRY OF SOCIAL AFFAIRS AND WOMEN'S AFFAIRS
c/o the Central Post Office, Yaoundé
Tel 22-41-48
Minister: Aissatou Yaou

MINISTRY OF TERRITORIAL ADMINISTRATION
c/o the Central Post Office, Yaoundé
Tel 23-40-90; telex 8503
Minister: Ibrahim Mbombo Njoya

MINISTRY OF TOURISM
Yaoundé
Tel 22-44-11; telex 8318
Minister: Benjamin Itoe.

MINISTRY OF YOUTH AND SPORTS
c/o the Central Post Office, Yaoundé
Tel 23-32-57; telex 8568
Minister: Dr Joseph Fofe

GOVERNMENT AGENCIES AND ORGANIZATIONS

Advisory and Supervisory Body

Economic and Social Council: BP 1058, Yaoundé; tel 22-25-97; telex 8275; Pres: Luc Ayang; Sec-Gen: Dr Joseph Simon Epale; state agency; advises Govt on economic and social issues; consists of 85 mems, a permanent secretariat and a pres.

Agriculture

Hévéa-Cameroun (HEVECAM): BP 1298, Douala; BP 174, Kribi; tel (Douala) 42-75-64; telex (Douala) 5880; fax (Kribi) 46-18-30; Dir-Gen: Jean Remy; Dep Dir-Gen: Gaston Mvondo Owoundi; f 1975; devt of rubber plantation.

Mission de Développement des Semences/Cultures Vivrières (MIDEVIV): BP 1682, Yaoundé; tel 23-38-29; Pres: Maxiale Mahi; Dir-Gen: Jean Bernad Abong; Asst Dir: Mulu Tanyi Awa; f 1974; develops and improves seeds and planting materials; produces and distributes foodstuffs for urban centres.

Office Céréalier dans la Province du Nord: BP 298, Garoua; tel 27-14-38; telex 7603; Pres: Fon Fossi Yakum Taw; Dir-Gen: Gilbert Gourlemond; f 1975; stabilization of cereal prices; combating effects of drought in northern areas of Cameroon.

Société Camerounaise de Palmeraies (SOCAPALM): blvd Leclerc, BP 691, Douala; tel 42-81-38; telex 5576; Chair: Jean-Baptiste Yonkeu; Gen Man: Robert Mbella Mbappe; f 1968; 100% state-owned; plans and develops palm oil production; manages palm plantations and production of palm oil and manufactured products.

Société de Développement du Cacao (SODECAO): BP 1651, Yaoundé; tel 22-09-91; telex 8574; Pres: Joseph-Charles Doumba; Dir-Gen: Félix Tonye Mbog; f 1974; devt of cocoa, coffee and food crop production in the Centre-Sud province.

Société de Développement du Coton au Cameroun (SODECOTON): BP 302, Garoua; tel 27-10-80; telex 7617; Pres: Fon Fosi Yakim Niaw; Man Dir: Mohamed Iya; f 1974; 70% state-owned; cotton ginning.

Société de Développement de l'Elevage (SODEVA): BP 50, Kousseri; Dir: Alhadji Oumarou Bakary; devt of animal farming.

Société de Développement et d'Exploitation des Productions Animales (SODEPA): BP 1410, Yaoundé; tel 22-24-28; Man Dir: Etienne Engueleguele; f 1974; devt of livestock and livestock products.

Société de Développement de la Riziculture dans la Plaine des Mbo (SODERIM): BP 12, Santchou; tel 49-15-58; telex 5344; Pres: Siegfrid David Etame Massoma; Dir-Gen: Jean-Baptiste Yonke; f 1977; devt of rice-growing and processing.

Société d'Expansion et de Modernisation de la Riziculture de Yagoua (SEMRY): BP 46, Yagoua; tel 29-62-03; telex 7655; Pres: Albert Ekono Nna; Dir-Gen: Tori Limangana; f 1971; expansion of rice production and commercialization in areas where irrigation is possible.

Business and Economy

BANKING

Banque des Etats de l'Afrique Centrale (BEAC): rue Monseigneur Vogt, BP 1917, Yaoundé; tel 22-25-05; telex 8343; fax 23-33-29; Gov: Casimir Oyé Mba; Dir in Cameroon: Simon Bassilekin; f 1973; central bank of issue for mem states of the Customs and Economic Union of Central Africa (UDEAC), comprising Cameroon, the Central African Republic, Chad, the Congo, Euqatorial Guinea and Gabon; 6 brs in Cameroon.

Banque Unie de Crédit (BUC): Place Elig Essono, BP 122, Yaoundé; tel 23-15-72; telex 8879; Pres and Man Dir: Gustave Lele; f 1976.

Crédit Agricole du Cameroun: Yaoundé; f 1987 to take over activities of Fonds National de Développement Rural; agricultural devt bank.

Crédit Foncier du Cameroun (CFC): BP 1531, Yaoundé; tel 22-03-73; telex 8368; Chair: Edouard Akame Mfoumou; Dir-Gen: André Giannechini; Dep Dir-Gen: Sylvestre Naah Ondoa; f 1977; 70% state-owned; provides financial assistance for social welfare and environment.

Crédit Industriel et Commercial: Yaoundé; f 1987; industrial devt bank.

FINANCIAL AGENCY

Fonds d'Aide et de Garantie des Crédits aux Petites et Moyennes Entreprises Camerounaises (FOGAPE) (Aid and Loan Guarantee Fund for Small- and Medium-Sized Enterprises): BP 1591, Yaoundé; tel 23-16-90; telex 8395; fax 23-12-21; f 1975; Man Dir: Jacques Lamero; grants guarantee loans to small- and medium-sized enterprises; direct loans; promotes mutual guarantee societies.

INSURANCE

Caisse Nationale de Réassurances SA: ave Foch, BP 4180, Yaoundé; tel 22-37-99; telex 8262; fax 23-36-80; Man Dir: Antoine Ntsini; Asst Man Dir: Joachim Foungtcho; f 1965; all forms of reinsurance.

MARKETING

Office National de Commercialisation des Produits de Base (ONCPB): BP 378, Douala; tel 42-67-76; telex 5260; Pres: Luc Ayang; Man Dir: Cyrille Etoundi Atangana; f 1978 to replace the Caisse de stabilisation des prix and the Cocoa Marketing Board; has monopoly of cocoa, coffee, cotton, groundnut and palm kernel marketing; responsible for internal prices for planters, the quality of produce and devt of production; holds 8.3% share in Cameroon Devt Corpn (CAMDEV) (see below).

NATIONALIZED INDUSTRY

Les Grandes Huileries Camerounaises: Zone Industrielle de Bassa, BP 1642, Douala; Pres: Alhadji Bachirou; Man Dir: Eric Jacobsen; f 1982; 50% state-owned; oil-works.

Defence

Armed Forces: Yaoundé; tel 23-36-00; Commdr-in-Chief: Paul Biya; Head, Presidential Guard: Commdr Pierre Minlo Medjo.

Air Force: Yaoundé; tel 23-22-76; telex 5519.

Army: Yaoundé; tel 23-40-55.

Navy: Douala; tel 22-14-50.

Development and Planning

Cameroon Development Corpn (CAMDEV): Bota, Limbe; tel 33-22-51; telex 5242; Chair: Samuel Moka Lifafa Endeley; Gen Man: Peter Mafany Musonge; f 1947, reorganized 1982; 91.7% state-owned; statutory agricultural enterprise; acquires and develops plantations of tropical crops, operates oil mills, banana packing stations, tea and rubber factories; operates in four provinces.

Centre National d'Assistance aux Petites et Moyennes Entreprises (CAPME): BP 1377, Douala; tel 42-58-58; telex 5590; Pres: Dieudonné Tsanga Atangana; Dir: M. Bouba Ardo; f 1970; devt centre for small and medium-sized businesses; advises on industrial techniques and training; undertakes market research.

Centre National de Développement des Entreprises Coopératives (CENADEC): BP 120, Yaoundé; Dir: Jacques Sangue; f 1970; promotes and regulates the co-operative movement; bureaux at BP 43, Kumba and BP 26, Bamenda.

Centre National de Développement des Forêts (CENAD-EFOR): BP 369, Yaoundé; tel 22-51-93; telex 8561; Dir-Gen: Samuel Makon Sehiong; f 1981; devt and protection of forests.

Mission d'Aménagement et d'Equipement des Terrains Urbains et Ruraux (MAETUR): BP 1248, Yaoundé; tel 22-31-13; telex 5725; Pres: Ferdinang Oyono; Dir: August Arcade; f 1977; rural and urban devt.

Société Immobilière du Cameroun (SIC): BP 387, Yaoundé; tel 23-34-11; telex 8577; Pres: Gabriel Louis Djeudjang; Man Dir: André Levy; f 1952; housing construction and devt.

Société Nationale d'Investissement du Cameroun (SNI): Place de la Poste, BP 423, Yaoundé; tel 22-44-22; telex 8205; fax 22-39-64; Chair: Victor Ayissi Mvodo; Dir-Gen: Simon Ngann Yonn; Dep Dir-Gen: Théodore Eyeffa; f 1964; devt bank.

REGIONAL DEVELOPMENT

Mission de Développement de la Province du Nord-Ouest (MIDENO): BP 442, Bamenda; tel 36-13-78; telex 5842; Project Man: Andrew W. Ndonyi; Dep Project Man: Adam D. Fongyen; f 1981; co-ordinates and oversees the implementation of an integrated rural devt project for the North-West province; carries out research and training; provides credit for small farmers; oversees rural water supply and roads.

Société de Développement de la Haute-Vallée du Noun (UNVDA): BP 25, N'Dop; BP 43, Bamenda; Dir-Gen: G. A. Niba; f 1978; devt of rice cultivation.

Legal and Judiciary

High Court of Justice: Yaoundé; Attorney-Gen: Alexis Dipanda Mouelle; consists of nine titular judges and six substitute judges, all elected by the National Assembly.

Supreme Court: Yaoundé; Pres: Remy-Jean Mbaya; comprises a Pres, nine titular and substitute judges, a Procureur Général, an Avocat Général, deputies to the Procureur Général, a Registrar and clerks.

Media

BROADCASTING

Office de Radiodiffusion-Télévision Camerounaise (CRTV): BP 1634, Yaoundé; tel 23-40-88; telex 8888; Pres: Henri Bandolo; Dir-Gen: Gervais Mendo Ze; f 1987; broadcasts in French and English.

Radio Buéa: PMB, Buéa; tel 32-25-25; Man: Peterson Chia Yuh; Head of Station: Gideon Taka; programmes in English, French and 28 local languages.

Radio Douala: BP 986, Douala; tel 42-60-60; Dir: Bruno Djem; Head of Station: Linus Onana Mvondo; programmes in French, English and local languages.

Radio Garoua: BP 103, Garoua; tel 27-11-67; Dir: Bello Malgana; Head of Station: Moussa Epopa; programmes in French, English, Arabic and local languages.

GOVERNMENT PUBLISHER

Imprimerie Nationale: BP 1603, Yaoundé; tel 23-12-77; telex 8403; Dir: Amadou Vamoulke; Dep Dir: Moudjih C. Emmanuel; f 1917.

NEWS AND INFORMATION

Société de Presse et d'Editions du Cameroun (SOPECAM): BP 1218, Yaoundé; tel 23-40-12; telex 8311; Dir-Gen: Joseph-Charles Doumba; Editorial Dir: Abui Mama Eloundou; f 1977; responsible to the Ministry of Information and Culture; book and magazine publishing; printing; news agency.

> **CAMNEWS:** c/o SOPECAM, BP 1218, Yaoundé; Dir: Jean Ngandjeu; news agency.

Direction de la Statistique et de la Comptabilité Nationale: BP 25, Yaoundé; tel 22-07-88; telex 8203; statistical office.

Mining and Energy

Société Nationale d'Electricité du Cameroun (SONEL) (Cameroon National Electricity Co): 63 ave du Général de Gaulle, BP 4077, Douala; tel 42-54-44; telex 5551; Pres: Samuel Obam Mbom; Man: Jean-Paul Boupda; f 1974; took over activities of three previous electricity corpns, EDC, ENELCAM and POWERCAM; 93.1% state-owned; 6.9% held by France's Caisse centrale de coopération économique.

Société Nationale des Hydrocarbures (SNH) (National Hydrocarbons Corpn): BP 955, Yaoundé; tel 22-19-10; telex 8514; Pres: Joseph Zambo; Dir-Gen: Jean Assoumou; f 1980; state oil co; develops and oversees the exploitation of hydrocarbon resources in Cameroon.

Société Nationale de Raffinage (SONARA): BP 365, Cap Limboh, Limbe; tel 33-22-38; telex 5561; Chair: André Botto à Ngon; Man Dir: Bernard Eding; f 1976; 66% state-owned; establishment of petroleum refinery at Cap Limboh.

Tourism

Direction Générale du Développement Touristique (Directorate-General for Development of Tourism): Yaoundé; tel 22-44-11; telex 8318; Dir-Gen: Mohamadou Labarang; Dep Dir-Gen: Rose Zang Nguele; f 1988; promotes tourism; manages hotels, tourist sites and national parks; provides professional training.

Société Camerounaise de Tourisme (SOCATOUR): BP 7138, Yaoundé; tel 23-32-19; telex 8766; Pres of Board of Admin: Dr Abdoulaye Souaibou; Gen Man: Marc Cho Nkwenti; f 1985; promotes tourism; runs travel agencies.

Transport

Cameroon Airlines (CAM-AIR): 3 ave du Général de Gaulle, BP 4092, Douala; tel 42-25-25; telex 5345; Chair: Samuel Eboua; Dir-Gen: Augustin Frédéric Kodock; f 1971; 75% state-owned, 25% by Air France; domestic and international flights to African and European destinations.

Cameroon Shipping Lines SA (CAMSHIPLINES): Centre des Affaires Maritimes, 18 rue Joffre, BP 4054, Douala; tel 42-00-38; telex 5615; Chair: François Sengat Kuo; Man Dir: René Mbayen; f 1975; 67% state-owned; runs vessels trading with Western Europe, USA, Far East and Africa.

Office du Chemin de Fer Transcamerounais: BP 625, Yaoundé; tel 22-44-33; telex 8293; Gen Man: Luc Towa Fotso; oversees the laying of new railway lines and improvements to existing lines; undertakes relevant research.

Office National des Ports/National Ports Authority: 5 blvd Leclerc, BP 4020, Douala; tel 42-01-33; telex 5270; Chair: André-Bosco Cheuoua; Gen Man: Siegfried Dibong.

Régie Nationale des Chemins de Fer du Cameroun (REGIFERCAM): BP 304, Douala; tel 42-60-45; telex 5607; Chair: Samuel Eboua; Dir-Gen: Samuel Minko; f 1947; rail transport and rail supervisory authority.

Société de Transports Urbains du Cameroun (SOTUC): BP 1697, Yaoundé; tel 23-38-07; telex 8330; Dir-Gen: Marcel Yondo; Mans: Jean-Victor Oum (Yaoundé), Gabriel Vasseur (Douala); f 1973; 58% owned by Société Nationale d'Investissement du Cameroun (see above); operates urban transport services in Yaoundé and Douala; rehabilitation programme announced 1989.

Utilities

Direction Générale des Grands Travaux du Cameroon (DGTC): Yaoundé; Chair: Jean Fouman Akame; Man Dir: Michel Kowalzick; f 1988; commissioning, implementation and supervision of public works contracts.

Société Nationale des Eaux du Cameroun (SNEC): BP 157, Douala; tel 42-87-11; telex 5265; Pres: Amadou Ali; Dir-Gen: Clément Oboug Fegue; f 1967; 73% state-owned, 22% by Société Nationale d'Electricité du Cameroun (see above).

CANADA

Head of State

Canada is a federal parliamentary state. The British sovereign is Head of State and is represented locally by a Governor-General. The Governor-General appoints the Prime Minister and, on the latter's recommendation, other ministers to form a Cabinet, which is responsible to the House of Commons.

Sovereign: HM Queen Elizabeth II (succeeded to the throne 6 February 1952).

Governor-General: Ray Hnatyshyn (took office January 1990).

Office of the Governor-General: Government House, 1 Sussex Drive, Ottawa, ON K1A 0A1; tel (613) 993-8200; telex 053-3280; fax (613) 990-7636.

Legislature

Legislative power is vested in the Federal Parliament, which comprises the British sovereign (represented by the Governor-General), a nominated Senate (104 members appointed on a regional basis) and a House of Commons (295 members elected by universal adult suffrage). There are ten provinces (each with a Lieutenant-Governor and a legislature) and two territories.

Senate: Parliament Bldgs, Wellington St, Ottawa, ON K1A 0A4; tel (613) 995-1900; fax (613) 995-0320; Speaker: Guy Charbonneau; Clerk: Charles A. Lussier.

House of Commons: Parliament Bldgs, Wellington St, Ottawa, ON K1A 0A6; Speaker: John A. Fraser.

MINISTRIES AND GOVERNMENT DEPARTMENTS

OFFICE OF THE PRIME MINISTER
Langevin Block, Ottawa, ON K1A OA2
Tel (613) 992-4211; telex 053-3208; fax (613) 995-0101
Prime Minister: Martin Brian Mulroney
Minister of State: Harvie André

OFFICE OF THE DEPUTY PRIME MINISTER AND PRESIDENT OF THE PRIVY COUNCIL
Room 203-S, Centre Block, House of Commons, Ottawa, ON K1A OA6
Tel (613) 957-5657
Deputy Prime Minister and President of the Queen's Privy Council: Donald Frank Mazankowski

DEPARTMENT OF AGRICULTURE
Sir John Carling Bldg, 930 Carling Ave, Ottawa, ON K1A OC5
Tel (613) 995-5222; telex 053-3283; fax (613) 996-9564
Minister: Donald Frank Mazankowski
Minister of State: Pierre Blais
Minister of State, Grains and Oilseeds: Charles Mayer

DEPARTMENT OF COMMUNICATIONS
Journal North Tower, 300 Slater St, Ottawa, ON KIA OC8
Tel (613) 990-4900; telex 053-3342; fax (613) 952-2429
Minister: Marcel Masse

DEPARTMENT OF CONSUMER AND CORPORATE AFFAIRS
Ottawa, ON K1A OC9
Tel (613) 997-2938; telex 053-3694; fax (613) 997-2721
Minister: Pierre Blais

DEPARTMENT OF EMPLOYMENT AND IMMIGRATION
140 promenade du Portage, Ottawa-Hull, ON K1A OJ9
Tel (819) 994-6013; telex 053-3511; fax (819) 994-0116
Minister: Barbara Jean McDougall

Office of the Minister of State for Employment and Immigration: 140 Promenade du Portage, Phase IV, 12th Floor, Hull, PQ K1A 0J9; tel (613) 953-0925; fax (819) 953-0944; Minister of State: Monique Vézina.

Office of the Minister of State for Youth: Room 583, Confederation Bldg, House of Commons, Ottawa, ON K1A OA6; tel (819) 994-2424; Minister of State: Marcel Denis.

DEPARTMENT OF ENERGY, MINES AND RESOURCES
580 Booth St, Ottawa, ON K1A OE4
Tel (613) 995-3065; telex 053-3117; fax (613) 996-9094
Minister: Arthur Jacob Epp

DEPARTMENT OF THE ENVIRONMENT
Les Terrasses de la Chaudière, 10 Wellington St, Ottawa, ON K1A OH3
Tel (819) 997-2800; telex 053-3608; fax (819) 953-6789
Minister: Lucien Bouchard

DEPARTMENT OF EXTERNAL AFFAIRS
Lester B. Pearson Bldg, 125 Sussex Drive, Ottawa, ON K1A OG2
Tel (613) 995-1851; telex 053-3745; fax (613) 996-9288
Secretary of State: Charles Joseph Clark
Minister of External Relations: Monique Landry
Minister of International Trade: John Crosbie

DEPARTMENT OF FINANCE
Esplanade Laurier, 140 O'Connor St, Ottawa, ON K1A OG5
Tel (613) 992-1575; telex 053-3336
Minister: Michael Holcombe Wilson

Office of the Minister of State for Finance: Room 345, Confederation Bldg, Ottawa, ON K1A OA6; tel (613) 996-3170; Minister of State: Gilles Loiselle.

DEPARTMENT OF FISHERIES AND OCEANS
200 Kent St, Ottawa, ON K1A OE6
Tel (613) 993-0600; telex 053-4228
Minister: Bernard Valcourt

DEPARTMENT OF INDIAN AFFAIRS AND NORTHERN DEVELOPMENT
Terrasses de la Chaudière, 10 Wellington St,
Ottawa, ON K1A 0H4
Tel (613) 995-5586; telex 053-3711; fax (613) 997-1587
Minister: Thomas Edward Siddon
Minister of State: Shirley Martin

DEPARTMENT OF INDUSTRY, SCIENCE AND TECHNOLOGY
235 Queen St, Ottawa, ON K1A 1A1
Tel (613) 992-4292; telex 053-4396; fax (613) 952-9073
Minister: Benoît Bouchard
Minister of State: William Winegard

DEPARTMENT OF JUSTICE AND OFFICE OF THE ATTORNEY-GENERAL
Justice Bldg, 239 Wellington St, Ottawa, ON K1A OH8
Tel (613) 957-4222; telex 053-3603; fax (613) 954-0811
Minister and Attorney-General: Kim Campbell

DEPARTMENT OF LABOUR
Place du Portage, 165 Hôtel de Ville St, Ottawa, ON K1A OJ2
Tel (819) 997-2617; telex 053-3640; fax (819) 953-0176
Minister: Jean Corbeil

DEPARTMENT OF NATIONAL DEFENCE
101 Colonel By Drive, Ottawa, ON K1A OK2
Tel (613) 996-4450; telex 053-4218
Minister: William Hunter McKnight
Associate Minister and Minister responsible for the status of Women: Mary Collins

DEPARTMENT OF NATIONAL HEALTH AND WELFARE
Brooke Claxton Bldg, Tunney's Pasture,
Ottawa, ON K1A OK9
Tel (613) 957-2991; telex 053-3270
Minister: Henry Perrin Beatty
Minister of State for Senior Citizens: Monique Vézina

Office of the Minister of State for Fitness and Amateur Sports: Room 274, House of Commons, Ottawa, ON K1A OA6; tel (613) 996-2358; telex 053-4420; Minister of State: Marcel Denis

DEPARTMENT OF NATIONAL REVENUE
Headquarters Bldg, 875 Heron Rd, Ottawa, ON K1A OL8
Tel (613) 995-2960; telex 053-4974
Minister: Otto John Jelinek
Deputy Minister, Customs and Excise: R. Hubbard
Deputy Minister, Taxation: Pierre Gravelle

DEPARTMENT OF PRIVATIZATION AND REGULATORY AFFAIRS
24th Floor, Place Bell Canada, 160 Elgin St,
Ottawa, ON K1A OG5
Tel (613) 996-3170
Minister: (vacant)
Minister of State: John Horton McDermid

DEPARTMENT OF PUBLIC WORKS
Sir Charles Tupper Bldg, Confederation Heights,
Riverside Drive, Ottawa, ON K1A OM2
Tel (613) 736-2400; telex 053-4235; fax (613) 998-9603
Minister: Elmer MacIntosh MacKay
Deputy Minister: Robert Giroux

DEPARTMENT OF REGIONAL INDUSTRIAL EXPANSION
235 Queen St, Ottawa K1A OH5
Tel (613) 995-9001; telex 053-4124; fax (613) 954-1894
Minister: (vacant)

Office of the Minister of State for Small Business and Tourism: Room 656, Confederation Bldg, House of Commons, Ottawa, ON K1A OA6; tel (613) 995-1333; Minister of State: Thomas Hockin.

DEPARTMENT OF STATE
Ottawa, ON K1A OM5
Tel (819) 997-0055; fax (819) 953-5382
Secretary of State and Minister of State for Multiculturalism and Citizenship: Gerry Weiner
Minister of State for Federal-Provincial Affairs:
Lowell Murray
Minister of State for Housing: Alan Redway

DEPARTMENT OF SUPPLY AND SERVICES
11 Laurier St, Ottawa-Hull, ON K1A OS5
Tel (819) 956-2304; telex 053-3703; fax (819) 994-8404
Minister: Paul Wyatt Dick

DEPARTMENT OF TRANSPORT
Transport Canada Bldg, Place de Ville,
330 Sparks St, Ottawa, ON K1A ON5
Tel (613) 990-2309; telex 053-3130; fax (613) 996-9622
Minister: Doug Lewis
Minister of State: Jean Corbeil

DEPARTMENT OF VETERANS' AFFAIRS
POB 7700, Charlottetown, PE C1A 8M9
Tel (902) 566-8888; telex 014-44228; fax (902) 566-8508
Minister: Gerald Stairs Merrithew

DEPARTMENT OF WESTERN ECONOMIC DIVERSIFICATION
Suite 604, Counterpoint Bldg, 10179 105th St,
Edmonton, AB T5J 3N1
Minister: Charles James Mayer

FORESTRY CANADA
351 St Joseph Blvd, Ottawa-Hull, PQ K1A 1G5
Tel (819) 997-1107; fax (613) 953-6905
Minister: Frank Oberle
F 1884; management, protection and utilization of forestry resource.

OFFICE OF THE SOLICITOR GENERAL
Sir Wilfred Laurier Bldg, 340 Laurier Ave,
Ottawa, ON K1A OP8
Tel (613) 991-2857; telex 053-3768; fax (613) 993-6116
Solicitor General: Pierre Cadieux
Chief of Staff: David Near
Responsible for Royal Canadian Mounted Police, Canadian Security Intelligence Service, National Parole Board and Correctional Service of Canada.

TREASURY BOARD
140 O'Connor St, Ottawa, ON K1A OR5
Tel (613) 996-2690; telex 053-3336; fax (613) 957-2400
President: Robert R. de Cotret

GOVERNMENT AGENCIES AND ORGANIZATIONS

Advisory and Supervisory Bodies

Elections Canada: 440 Coventry Rd, Ottawa, ON K1A 0M6; tel (613) 993-2975; telex 053-4267; fax (613) 954-2874; Chief Electoral Officer: J.-M. Hamel; Commr: George Allen; f 1920; administers federal elections.

Emergency Preparedness Canada: Gillin Bldg, 2nd Floor, 141 Laurier Ave West, Ottawa, ON K1A 0W6; tel (613) 992-9988; telex 053-4443; fax (613) 996-1901; Exec Dir: W. B. Snarr; co-ordinates planning aimed at mitigating effects of emergencies and peacetime disasters.

Foreign Claims Commission: 125 Sussex Drive, Box 432, Ottawa, ON K1N 8V5; fax (613) 996-9510; Commr: Peter Hardagan; examines claims of Canadian citizens against countries with which agreements have been negotiated regarding confiscation of property which has been nationalized.

Office of the Auditor-General: 240 Sparks St, Ottawa, ON K1A OG6; tel (613) 995-3766; fax (613) 957-4023; Auditor-Gen: Kenneth M. Dye; Dep Auditors-Gen: Raymond Dubois, Larry Meyers, Edward R. Rowe

Office of the Information and Privacy Commissioners of Canada: Suite 300, Place de Ville, 112 Kent St, Tower B, Ottawa, ON K1A 1H3; tel (613) 995-2410; Commr, Information: Inger Hansen; Commr, Privacy: John W. Grace; f 1983; deals with complaints from individuals who allege Federal Govt has not complied with their rights as laid down in Access to Information Act; oversees Federal Govt's collection, use, handling and disposal of personal information.

Agriculture and Fishing

AGRICULTURE

Agricultural Institute of Canada: Suite 907, 151 Slater St, Ottawa, ON K1P 5H4; tel (613) 232-9459; fax (613) 594-5190; Exec Vice-Pres: Yvan Jacques; f 1920; advances interests and devt of member organizations.

Agricultural Stabilization: Room 3115, Sir John Carling Bldg, 930 Carling Ave, Ottawa K1A 0C5; tel (613) 995-5880; fax (613) 996-9014; Chair: Gilles Lavoie; Man: A. E. Proulx; f 1958; provides support prices for 12 agricultural commodities.

Canadian Dairy Commission: 6th Floor, 2197 Riverside Drive, Ottawa, ON K1A 0Z2; tel (613) 998-9490; telex 053-3634; fax (613) 998-4492; Chair: Roch Morin; Vice-Chair: K. McKinnon; f 1966; administers Govt policy with regard to dairy industry.

Canadian Federation of Agriculture: Suite 1101, 75 Albert St, Ottawa, ON K1P 5E7; tel (613) 236-3633; fax (613) 236-5749; Pres: Don Knoerr; f 1935; represents interests of provincial farm organizations and national and regional commodity groups.

Canadian Horticultural Council: Suite 310, 1101 Prince of Wales Drive, Ottawa, ON K2C 3W7; tel (613) 226-4187; telex 053-3690; fax (613) 226-2984; Exec Vice-Pres: D. Dempster; f 1922.

Farm Credit Corpn Canada (FCCC): Canada Bldg, 434 Queen St, Box 2314, Station D, Ottawa, ON K1P 6J9; tel (613) 996-6606; telex 053-4804; fax (613) 996-8533; Chair: J. J. Hewitt; Vice-Chair: C. G. Penney; f 1959; administers two programmes providing financial assistance to farmers.

Grains and Oilseeds Branch: c/o Management Services Division, Agriculture Canada, Sir John Carling Baldg, 10th Floor, 930 Carling Ave, Ottawa, ON K1A 0C5; tel (613) 995-7127; Man: W. M. Miner; co-ordinating body for diverse Govt and private agencies involved in grains industry; promotes the growth, stability and competitiveness of the industry.

Livestock Feed Board of Canada: Box 177, Snowdon Station, Montréal, PQ H3X 3T4; tel (514) 283-7505; telex 055-67137; fax (514) 283-2754; Chair: Denis Ethier; f 1967; ensures availability of feed grain and stability of grain prices.

National Dairy Council of Canada: Suite 704, 141 Laurier Ave West, Ottawa, ON K1P 5J3; tel (613) 238-4116; telex 053-3952; fax (613) 238-6247; Pres: Kempton L. Matte.

FISHING

Canadian Saltfish Corpn: Torbay Rd, Box 9440, St John's, NF A1C 5XB; tel (709) 772-6080; fax (709) 772-6132; Chair: J. G. Barnes; Pres: W. R. Moyse; f 1970; regulation of inter-provincial and export trade in saltfish.

Fisheries Prices Support Board: Ottawa, ON K1A 0E6; tel (613) 993-2031; telex 053-4228; fax (613) 996-9055; Chair: Harold Collins; recommends action to support fishing prices where necessary.

Art and Culture

ART

National Arts Centre Corpn: Box 1534, Station B, Ottawa, ON K1P 5W1; tel (613) 996-5051; telex 053-3759; fax (613) 996-9578; Chair: Robert Landry; supports initiatives of The Canada Council (see below); promotion of the arts.

The Canada Council: 99 Metcalfe St, Box 1047, Ottawa, ON K1P 5V8; tel (613) 237-3400; telex 053-4573; fax (613) 598-4390; Chair: Allan Gotlieb; Vice-Chair: Jacques E. Lefebvre; promotes and fosters the arts in Canada.

CULTURE

National Archives of Canada: 395 Wellington St, Ottawa, ON K1A 0N3; tel (613) 995-5138; fax (613) 995-6274; Dominion Archivist: J.-P. Wallot.

National Film Board of Canada: Box 6100, Station A, Montréal, QC H3C 3H5; tel (514) 283-9000; fax (514) 496-1895; Commr (acting): Joan Pennefather; Dir, International Distribution: Tom Bindon; f 1939; production, promotion and distribution of Board films.

National Library of Canada: 395 Wellington St, Ottawa, ON K1A 0N4; tel (613) 995-9481; telex 053-4311; fax (613) 996-4424; National Librarian: Marianne Scott; Dirs: Gwynneth Evans, Tom Delsey, Flora Patterson, Louis Forget; to promote knowledge and use of published heritage of Canada; acquisition and preservation, library devt, resource sharing.

National Museums of Canada: Ottawa, ON K1A 0M8; tel (613) 954-4400; Sec-Gen: John Edwards.

Office of the Commissioner of Official Languages: 110 O'Connor St, Ottawa, ON K1A 0T8; tel (613) 996-6368; fax (613) 993-5082; Commr: D'Iberville Fortier.

Business and Economy

BANKING

Bank of Canada: 234 Wellington St, Ottawa, ON K1A 0G9; tel (613) 782-8111; telex 053-4241; fax (613) 782-8655; Gov:

John W. Crow; Sr Dep Gov: Gordon G. Thiessen; f 1934; bank of issue.

Office of the Superintendent of Financial Institutions: 255 Albert St, Kent Sq, Ottawa, ON K1A 0H2; tel (613) 990-7788; fax (613) 952-8219; Supt: Michael A. MacKenzie; f 1987; regulation and supervision of federally regulated banks, other deposit-taking institutions, insurance cos and pension plans.

FINANCIAL AGENCIES

Canada Mortgage and Housing Co (CMHC): 682 Montréal Rd, Ottawa, ON K1A 0P7; tel (613) 748-2000; telex 053-3674; fax (613) 748-6192; Chair: Robert E. Jarvis; Pres: George D. Anderson; f 1946; administers provisions of National Housing Act; advances loans for house purchase and construction projects.

Revenue Canada (Customs and Excise): Connaught Bldg, Mackenzie Ave, Ottawa, ON K1A 0L5; tel (613) 957-8505; telex 053-3330; fax (613) 995-3633; Dep Minister, Customs and Excise: R. Hubbard.

Revenue Canada (Taxation): Headquarters Bldg, 875 Heron Rd, Ottawa, ON K1A 0L8; tel (613) 957-3503; telex 053-4574; fax (613) 957-7476; Dep Minister, Taxation: Pierre Gravelle; f 1927; responsible for the admin of income tax legislation and for co-ordinating Canada's self-assessment system.

Royal Canadian Mint: Ottawa, ON K1A 0G8; telex 053-4454; Pres: Maurice Lafontaine.

Tariff Board: 365 Laurier Ave West, Journal Bldg South, 21st Floor, Ottawa, ON K1A 0G7; tel (613) 990-2452; fax (613) 990-2439; Chair: D. R. Yeomans; First Vice-Chair: J. Bertrand.

INSURANCE

Canada Deposit Insurance Co: Box 2340, Station D, Ottawa, ON K1P 5W5; tel (613) 996-2081; telex 053-3851; fax (613) 996-6095; Chair: R. A. McKinlay; Pres and Chief Exec: Charles C. de Léry; f 1967; provides insurance against loss of deposits held with member institutions.

MARKETING

Canadian Agricultural Export Corpn (CANAGREX): Suite 901, 350 Sparks St, Ottawa, ON K1R 7S8; tel (613) 995-7275; promotes export of agricultural and food products.

Canadian International Grains Institute: 1000-303 Main St, Winnipeg, MB R3C 3G7; tel (204) 983-5344; telex 07-57869; fax (204) 983-2642; Chair: Forest M. Hetland; Exec Dir: Dr Arnold W. Tremere; f 1972; promotes Canadian grains and oilseeds in overseas and domestic markets.

Canadian Wheat Board: 423 Main St, Winnipeg, MB R3C 2P5; tel (204) 983-0239; telex 07-57801; fax (204) 983-3841; Chief Commr: W. E. Jarvis; Asst Chief Commr: Dr R. L. Kristjanson; f 1935; sole marketing agency for Western Canadian wheat, oats and barley.

Freshwater Fish Marketing Corpn: 1199 Plessis Rd, Winnipeg, MB R2C 3L4; tel (204) 949-6483: fax (204) 983-6497; Pres: J. T. Dunn; trading and marketing fish and fish products.

National Farm Products Marketing Council: Box 3430, Station D, Ottawa, ON K1P 6L4; tel (613) 995-2297; telex 053-4188; fax (613) 995-2097; Chair: Ralph Barrie; Vice-Chair: Lise Bergeron; f 1972; enables farmers to form agencies to market their products; advises Minister of Agriculture on issues relating to establishment and operation of marketing agencies under Farm Products Marketing Act.

TRADE

Canadian Commercial Corpn (CCC): Metropolitan Centre, 11th Floor, 50 O'Connor St, Ottawa, ON K1A 0S6; tel (613) 996-0034; telex 053-4359; fax (613) 995-2121; Pres: Hugh J. Mullington; Sr Vice-Pres: O. I. Matthews; f 1946; contractor in Govt-Govt sales transactions.

Canadian International Trade Tribunal: 365 Laurier Ave West, Ottawa, ON K1A 0G7; tel (613) 993-7872; telex 053-4420; fax (613) 998-4783; Chair: John C. Coleman; Vice-Chair: Robert G. Bertrand; f 1988 to replace the Tariff Board, the Canadian Import Tribunal and the Textile and Clothing Board; conducts inquiries, makes determinations and advises the Govt on whether Canadian producers are being injured materially by dumped or subsidized imports; conducts basic trade research.

Directorate of Intellectual Property: Place du Portage, Tower I, Ottawa-Hull, PQ K1A 0C9; tel (819) 997-4418; telex 053-3694; fax (819) 997-2721; Dir: André Gariépy; granting of patents and trademarks; registration of copyrights.

Export Development Corpn (EDC): Box 655, 151 O'Connor St, Ottawa, ON K1P 5T9; tel (613) 598-2500; telex 053-4136; fax (613) 237-2690; Pres and Chief Exec: R. L. Richardson; f 1944 (as Export Credits Insurance Corpn); export credit agency; provides financial services to promote export trade.

Export Trade Development Board: Lester B. Pearson Bldg, 125 Sussex Drive, Ottawa, ON K1A 0G2; tel (613) 996-2947; Chair: Roger E. Hatch; advises Minister of International Trade on export devt.

Standards Council of Canada: Suite 1200, 350 Sparks St, Ottawa, ON K1P 6N7; tel (613) 238-3222; telex 053-4403; fax (613) 995-4564; Pres: Georges Archer; Exec Dir: John R. Woods; f 1970; administers the National Standards System, a federation of organizations that write standards, test products and services, and certify products to specific standards.

Defence

Royal Canadian Mounted Police: Ottawa, ON K1A 0R2; tel (613) 993-1085; fax (613) 993-0216; Commr: N. D. Inkster; f 1873.

Development and Planning

Canada Development Investment Corpn: Suite 4520, 1 First Canadian Place, Box 138, Toronto, ON M5X 1A4; tel (416) 864-0333; fax (416) 864-0289; Chair: W. Darcy McKeough; f 1982; manages Federal Govt investments in business sector.

Canadian Industrial Innovation Centre: 156 Columbia St West, Waterloo, ON N2L 3L3; tel (519) 885-5870; telex 069-55259; fax (519) 885-5729; Chief Exec : Gordon F. Cummer; f 1981; provides assistance in converting new ideas and inventions into commercial products or services.

Canadian Patents and Development Ltd: 275 Slater St, Ottawa, ON K1A 0R3; tel (613) 990-6100; fax (613) 990-8528; Chair: J. A. Léger; Pres: W. D. Gordon; makes available to public information regarding exploitable technology arising from public-funded research and devt.

Defence Construction Canada: Sir Charles Tupper Bldg, Riverside Drive, Ottawa, ON K1A 0K3; tel (613) 998-9548; telex 053-3727; fax (613) 998-1061; Pres: J. R. Lorne Atchison; administers major construction and repair programmes.

Industrial and Regional Development Policy Board: 235 Queen St, Ottawa, ON K1A 0H5; tel (819) 992-2376; Chairs: Shirley Carr, Paul Martin Jr; f 1984; forum through which business and labour leaders can advise Govt on policy and issues relating to industrial devt.

National Capital Commission: 161 Laurier Ave West,

Ottawa, ON K1P 6J6; tel (613) 239-5509; fax (613) 239-5092; Chair: Jean E. Pigott; Gen Man: Graeme M. Kirby; f 1958; responsible for planning, devt and conservation in Ottawa region.

Employment

Canadian Labour Market and Productivity Centre: 116 Albert St, 9th Floor, Ottawa, ON K1P 5G3; tel (613) 234-0505; fax (613) 234-2482; Chairs: Thomas d'Aquino, Shirley Carr, Maryantonett Flumian; f 1984; facilitates consultation between business and labour groups on issues of broad economic and social concern in order to improve operation of labour markets and increase productivity.

Canada Labour Relations Board: C. D. Howe Bldg, 240 Sparks St, 4th Floor, West Tower, Ottawa, ON K1A 0X8; tel (613) 996-9466; telex 053-4426; fax (613) 995-9493; Chair: Marc Lapointe; f 1973; quasi-judicial tribunal dealing with industrial relations, safety rulings and cases of discrimination.

National Joint Council: C. D. Howe Bldg, 240 Sparks St, 7th Floor, West Tower, POB 1525, Station B, Ottawa, ON K1P 5V2; tel (613) 990-1807; fax (613) 990-7071; Chairs: G. Capello, G. Myers; Sec-Gen: D. S. Davidge; f 1944; promotes efficiency of public service and well-being of its employees.

Public Service Commission of Canada: 300 Laurier Ave West, Ottawa, ON K1A 0M7; tel (613) 996-5010; Chair: Huguette Labelle; Commrs: Peter B. Lesaux, Gilbert H. Scott; administers staffing of public service according to merit principle.

Health and Welfare

HEALTH

Canadian Advisory Council on the Status of Women: 110 O'Connor St, 9th Floor, Box 1541, Station B, Ottawa, ON K1P 5R5; tel (613) 992-4975; fax (613) 992-1715; Pres: Sylvia Gould; First Vice-Pres: Sylvia Farrant; advises public and Federal Govt on issues affecting women.

Canadian Centre for Occupational Health and Safety: 250 Main St East, Hamilton, ON L8N 1H6; tel (416) 572-2981; telex 061-8532; fax (416) 572-2206; Pres and Chief Exec: Gordon Atherley; f 1978; provides information on occupational health and safety.

WELFARE

Canadian Human Rights Commission: Suite 400, 90 Sparks St, Ottawa, ON K1A 1E1; tel (613) 995-1151; administers Human Rights Act.

Medical Research Council of Canada: Ottawa, ON K1A 0W9; tel (613) 954-1809; fax (613) 954-1800; Pres: Pierre Bois; assist and promote basic, applied and clinical research in health sciences.

National Advisory Council on Aging (NACA): Jeanne Mance Bldg, Tunney's Pasture, Ottawa, ON K1A 0K9; tel (613) 957-1968; telex 053-3270; fax (613) 957-9869; Pres: Dr Charlotte Matthews; Dir: Susan Fletcher; f 1980; assists and advises Minister of National Health and Welfare and Minister of State for Seniors on all matters concerning quality of life of senior citizens.

Status of Women Canada: 151 Sparks St, 10th Floor, Ottawa, ON K1A 1C3; tel (613) 995-7835; fax (613) 957-3359; Co-ordinator: Kay Stanley; Dep Co-ordinator: Louise B. de Villiers; provides advice and recommendations to ministry responsible for status of women.

International Affairs

Canadian International Development Agency: 200 Promenade du Portage, Ottawa-Hull, PQ K1A 0G4; tel (819) 997-6100; telex 053-4140; fax (819) 953-5469; Pres: Margaret Catley-Carlson; Sr Vice-Pres: Douglas Lindores; f 1968; administers Canadian international devt assistance programmes.

International Boundary Commission: 615 Booth St, Ottawa, ON K1A 0E9; tel (613) 995-4951; telex 053-4328; Commr: Dr Alec C. McEwen; f 1925; maintenance of an effective land and water boundary with the USA.

International Joint Commission: 18th Floor, 100 Metcalfe St, Ottawa, ON K1P 5M1; tel (613) 995-2984; fax (613) 993-5583; Chair: P. A. Bissonnette; Commrs: E. D. Fulton, R. S. K. Welch; jurisdiction over questions arising with the USA involving common boundary.

Immigration and Refugee Board—Documentation Centre (IRBDC): 116 Lisgar St, 2nd Floor, Ottawa, ON K1A 0K1; tel (613) 996-2793; fax (613) 954-1228; Dir: Graham Howell; f 1989; reports on country of origin of refugee claimants.

Legal and Judiciary

Canadian Judicial Council: 450-112 Kent St, Ottawa, ON K1A 0W8; tel (613) 998-5182; fax (613) 998-8889; Chair: Brian Dickson; Exec Sec: Jeannie Thomas; f 1971; judicial council chaired by Chief Justice of Canada; promotion of uniformity and efficiency of judicial service in superior and county courts.

Federal Court of Appeal: Supreme Court of Canada Bldg, Wellington St, Ottawa, ON K1A 0H9; tel (613) 996-6795; fax (613) 952-7226; Chief Justice: Frank Iacobucci; jurisdiction on appeals from Trial Division, Federal Tribunals and Tribunals, and reviews under section 28 of Federal Court Act.

Law Reform Commission of Canada: 7th Floor, Varette Bldg, 130 Albert St, Ottawa, ON K1A 0L6; tel (613) 996-7844; fax (613) 996-8599; Pres: Allen M. Linden; Vice-Pres: Gilles Létourneau; f 1971; reviews and reforms the federal laws of Canada.

National Parole Board: 340 Laurier Ave West, Ottawa, ON K1A 0R1; tel (613) 995-1308; fax (613) 995-4380; Chair and Chief Exec: Fred E. Gibson; f 1959; exclusive jurisdiction over parole for inmates in both federal and provincial prisons.

Supreme Court of Canada: Supreme Court Bldg, Wellington St, Ottawa, ON K1A 0J1; tel (613) 995-4330; fax (613) 996-3063; Chief Justice: Brian Dickson; f 1875; exercises general appellate jurisdiction in civil and criminal cases; judgment of Court is final and conclusive.

Media

BROADCASTING

Canadian Broadcasting Corpn (CBC)/Société Radio Canada (SRC): 1500 Bronson Ave, Box 8478, Ottawa, ON K1G 3J5; tel (613) 724-1200; telex 053-4260; fax (613) 738-6843; Pres: Willam T. Armstrong; Sr Vice-Pres: A. Manera; f 1936; provides national radio and TV service in French and English.

Canadian Radio-Television and Telecommunications Commission: Ottawa, ON K1A 0N2; tel (819) 997-0313; telex 053-4253; fax (819) 994-0218; Chair: Keith Spicer; Vice-Chairs: Monique Coupal, Louis R. Sherman; f 1968; supervises and regulates broadcasting and telecommunications; issues licences to broadcasting stations.

GOVERNMENT PUBLISHER

Canadian Government Publishing Centre: 45 Blvd Sacré-Coeur, Ottawa-Hull, ON K1A 0S9; tel (819) 956-1416; telex 053-4296; fax (819) 997-8863; Dir: Patricia Horner; f 1867; production of books and periodicals on numerous subjects.

NEWS AND INFORMATION

Statistics Canada: R. H. Coats Bldg, Tunney's Pasture, Ottawa, ON K1A 0T6; tel (613) 990-8116; telex 053-3585; fax (613) 951-5116; Chief Statistician: Ivan P. Fellegi; statistical information on economic and social life.

Mining and Energy

ENERGY

Atomic Energy of Canada Ltd: 344 Slater St, Ottawa, ON K1A 0S4; tel (613) 237-3270; telex 053-3126; fax (613) 996-9638; Pres and Chief Exec: James Donnelly; f 1952; devt of nuclear power; research within field of atomic energy; marketing of nuclear reactors.

Atomic Energy Control Board: 270 Albert St, Box 1046, Ottawa, ON K1P 5S9; tel (613) 995-5894; telex 053-3771; fax (613) 995-5086; Pres: Dr R. J. A. Lévesque; Sec: J. G. McManus; f 1946; regulatory control of devt and use of nuclear energy with regard to health, safety and security.

Canartech: 213 Notre Dame Ave, Winnipeg, MB R3B 1N3; tel (204) 949-1160; Pres and Chief Exec: Lorne D. R. Dyke; f 1980; venture capital corpn investing in energy conservation and renewable energy conversion.

Energy Supplies Allocation Board: 580 Booth St, Ottawa, ON K1A 0E4; tel (613) 995-3065; telex 053-3275; fax (613) 996-6424; Chair: H. F. Stevenson; monitors oil supply; reserve powers enable Board to introduce rationing of oil supply in event of national emergency.

National Energy Board: 473 Albert St, Ottawa, ON K1A 0E5; tel (613) 998-7204; telex 053-3791; fax (613) 998-7900; Chair: Roland Priddle; Sec: J. Klenavic; f 1959; licensing of oil, natural gas and electricity exports; setting of tolls and tariffs for oil and gas pipelines.

Petro-Canada: Box 2844, Calgary, AB T2P 3E3; tel (403) 296-8000; telex 03-825753; fax (403) 296-3030; Chair and Chief Exec: W. H. Hopper; Pres: E. M. Lakusta; involved in all aspects of petroleum business.

MINING

Eldorado Nuclear Ltd: Suite 700, 360 Albert St, Ottawa, ON K1R 7X7; tel (613) 238-5222; telex 053-3382; fax (613) 234-8439; Chair: G. N. M. Currie; Pres: N. M. Ediger; mineral exploration; mining and refining of uranium.

Research

Economic Council of Canada: Box 527, Ottawa, ON K1P 5V6; tel (613) 993-1253; fax (613) 991-4904; Corp Sec: W. M. Maidens; f 1963; research into economic devt; provides annual review of economic problems and prospects.

National Research Council of Canada: Montréal Rd, Ottawa, ON K1A 0R6; tel (613) 993-9101; telex 053-3145; fax (613) 952-7928; Pres: Dr Larkin Kerwin; research and devt in natural sciences and engineering.

Natural Sciences and Engineering Research Council: 200 Kent St, Ottawa, ON K1A 1H5; tel (613) 995-6295; telex 053-4228; fax (613) 992-5337; Pres: Arthur W. May; Exec Vice-Pres: Gilles Julien; f 1978; assists and promotes research into natural sciences and engineering other than health sciences.

Social Sciences and Humanities Research Council: 255 Albert St, Box 1610, Ottawa, ON K1P 6G4; tel (613) 992-0682; telex 053-3500; fax (613) 992-1787; Pres: Dr Paule Leduc; Exec Dir; Dr Ralph Heintzman; f 1978; promotion and assistance of research into social sciences and humanities.

Science and Technology

Science Council of Canada: 100 Metcalfe St, Ottawa, ON K1P 5M1; tel (613) 995-6954; fax (613) 995-0115; Chair: Dr Geraldine Kenney-Wallace; Dir, Research: Dr James M. Gilmour; f 1966; advises public and Federal Govt on science and technology policy.

Telecommunications

Canada Post Corpn: Sir Alexander Campbell Bldg, Confederation Heights, Ottawa, ON K1A 0B1; tel (613) 734-8440; fax (613) 734-8814; Chair: Sylvain Cloutier; Pres and Chief Exec: Donald H. Lander.

Tourism

Tourism Canada: Dept of Industry, Science and Technology, 235 Queen St, Ottawa, ON K1A 0H6; tel (613) 954-3935; telex 053-4123; fax (613) 954-1894; Minister of State of Small Businesses and Tourism: Tom Hockin; f 1934 (as Canadian Travel Bureau); devt of tourism.

Transport

Canadian Transport Commission: Ottawa, ON K1A 0N9; tel (819) 997-0677; telex 053-4254; Sec: D. W. Foley.

CIVIL AVIATION

Air Canada: place Air Canada, Montréal, PQ H2Z 1X5; tel (514) 879-7000; telex 062-17537; fax (514) 879-7990; Chair: Claude I. Taylor; Pres and Chief Exec: Pierre J. Jeanniot; f 1937; 55% state-owned; services to cities in USA, Latin America, Europe, Asia and Caribbean.

RAILWAYS

Canadian National Railways: Box 8100, Montréal, PQ H3C 3N4; tel (514) 399-5430; telex 05-25256; fax (514) 399-5586; Pres and Chief Exec: R. E. Lawless; Chair (acting): B. O'N. Gallery; f 1981.

VIA Rail Canada Inc: Suite 400, 2 place Ville Marie, Montréal, PQ H3B 2G6; tel (514) 871-6000; telex 052-68530; fax (514) 861-6463; Chair: Lawrence Hanigan; Pres and Chief Exec: Ronald E. Lawless; manages national passenger rail network.

SHIPPING

Canada Ports Corpn: 99 Metcalfe St, Ottawa, ON K1A 0N6; tel (613) 957-6787; telex 053-4127; fax (613) 995-3501; Pres and

Chief Exec: Jean-Michel Tessier; Exec Vice-Pres: Dr H. J. Ansary; f 1936 (as National Harbours Board); shipping and marine policy and planning.

St Lawrence Seaway Authority: 360 Albert St, Ottawa, ON K1R 7X7; tel (613) 598-4600; telex 053-3322; fax (613) 598-4620; Pres: W. A. O'Neil; Vice-Pres: G. Laniel; control of construction, maintenance and operation of Seaway.

CAPE VERDE

Head of State

Executive power is vested in the President who, as Head of State, is elected by the National People's Assembly for a five-year term. An appointed Council of Ministers, headed by a Prime Minister (nominated by the Assembly) assists the President.

President: Aristides Maria Pereira (took office 5 July 1975; re-elected February 1981 and January 1986).

Office of the President: Presidência da República, Praia, São Tiago; tel 61-26-69; telex 6051.

Legislature

Under the 1980 Constitution, legislative power is vested in the Assembléia Nacional Popular (National People's Assembly), whose 83 deputies are elected by universal adult suffrage for five years. The Partido Africano da Independência de Cabo Verde is the only political party allowed to operate, though it was announced in February 1990 that the November 1990 elections would be multi-party.

Assembléia Nacional Popular (National People's Assembly): Achada Santo António, CP 20A, Praia, São Tiago; tel 61-12-23; telex 6026; Pres: Abílio Augusto Monteiro Duarte.

MINISTRIES AND GOVERNMENT DEPARTMENTS

OFFICE OF THE PRIME MINISTER
Praça 12 de Setembro, CP 16, Praia, São Tiago
Tel 61-25-16; telex 6052; fax 61-30-99
Prime Minister: Gen Pedro Verona Rodrigues Pires
Deputy to the Prime Minister: Cmmdt Herculano Adelaide Vieira
Secretary of State to the Prime Minister: João de Deus Maximiano
Secretary of State for Public Administration: (vacant)

MINISTRY OF AGRICULTURE AND FISHERIES
Rua António Pussich, Praia, São Tiago
Tel 335; telex 6072
Minister: Commdt João Pereira Silva
Secretary of State for Fishing: Miguel Lima

MINISTRY OF THE ARMED FORCES AND SECURITY
Avda Unidade Guiné, Praia, São Tiago
Tel 448; telex 6077
Minister: Col Júlio César de Carvalho

MINISTRY OF EDUCATION AND CULTURE
Avda Amílcar Cabral, CP 111, Praia, São Tiago
Tel 345; telex 6057
Minister of Education: André Corsino Tolentino
Minister of Culture and Sport: Dr David Hopfer Almada

MINISTRY OF FINANCE
107 Avda Amílcar Cabral, CP 30, Praia, São Tiago
Tel 61-41-42; telex 6038
Minister: Gen Pedro Verona Rodrigues Pires
Deputy Minister: Dr Arnaldo Vasconcellos Franca

MINISTRY OF FOREIGN AFFAIRS
Praça 10 de Mayo, CP 60, Praia, São Tiago
Tel 310; telex 6070
Minister: Cmmdt Silvino Manuel da Luz
Secretary of State: Aguinaldo Lisboa Ramos

MINISTRY OF HEALTH, LABOUR AND SOCIAL AFFAIRS
Praça 12 de Setembro, CP 47, Praia, São Tiago
Tel 422; telex 6059
Minister: Dr Ireneu Gomes

MINISTRY OF INDUSTRY AND ENERGY
Avda Amílcar Cabral, Praia, São Tiago
Tel 61-44-44
Minister: Adão Silva Rocha

MINISTRY OF INFORMATION
CP 26, Praia, São Tiago
Tel 564; telex 99352
Minister: Dr David Hopfer Almada

MINISTRY OF THE INTERIOR
Rua Guerra Mendes, Praia, São Tiago
Tel 255; telex 6062
Minister: Cortino Cortes

MINISTRY OF JUSTICE
Praça 12 de Setembro, CP 205, Praia, São Tiago
Tel 336; telex 6025
Minister: Corsino Fortes

MINISTRY OF LOCAL ADMINISTRATION AND TOWN PLANNING
Rua Belem, Praia, São Tiago
Tel 61-44-59
Minister: Tito Livio Santos de Oliveira Ramos

MINISTRY OF PLANNING AND CO-OPERATION
39 Rua Guerra Mendes, CP 217, Praia, São Tiago
Tel 61-15-42; telex 6037
Minister: Gen Pedro Verona Rodrigues Pires
Dep Minister: José Brito

MINISTRY OF PUBLIC WORKS
38 Rua Eduardo Mondlane, Praia, São Tiago
Tel 61-25-23
Minister: Adriano de Oliveira Lima

MINISTRY OF TRANSPORT, TRADE AND TOURISM
46 Rua Guerra Mendes, CP 15, Praia, São Tiago
Tel 61-13-42; telex 6060
Minister: Commdt Osvaldo Lopes da Silva
Secretary of State for the Merchant Navy:
Humberto Morais

GOVERNMENT AGENCIES AND ORGANIZATIONS

ADVISORY AND SUPERVISORY BODY

Instituto Nacional das Cooperativas: CP 218, Praia, São Tiago; tel 61-38-15; telex 6015; Pres: Cândido Santana; f 1978; executes national policy on co-operatives; studies and promotes the co-operative movement; organizes and co-ordinates technical and financial aid to co-operatives.

Agriculture and Fishing

Direcção Nacional das Pescas (DNP) (National Fisheries Authority): Praia, São Tiago; devt of the fishing industry.

Empresa Caboverdeana de Pescas (PESCAVE): CP 59, Mindelo, São Vicente; tel 24-34; telex 3084; f 1987; co-ordinates and equips the fishing industry; manages the harbour; runs ice supply, cold storage facilities and shipping agency.

Empresa de Comercialização de Produtos do Mar, EP (INTERBASE): CP 59, Mindelo, São Vicente; tel 31-23-49; telex 3084; Man Dir: Amadeu Lopes da Silva; f 1979; shipping agency; cold storage; handling of frozen cargo; export of fresh and frozen fish; production of ice.

Empresa Nacional de Avicultura, EP (ENAVI): CP 135, Praia, São Tiago; tel 61-18-59; telex 6072; f 1979; poultry farming.

Secretaria de Estado das Pescas (SEP): CP 30, Praia, São Tiago; tel 61-10-91; telex 6058; Dir-Gen: Vicente Andrade Gomes; f 1983; oversees the devt of the fishing industry.

Sociedade de Comercialização e Apoio à Pesca Artesanal (SCAPA): Praia, São Tiago; oversees small-scale fishing enterprises and promotes modern fishing techniques.

Business and Economy

BANKING

Banco de Cabo Verde: 117 Avda Amílcar Cabral, CP 101, Praia, São Tiago; tel 61-31-53; telex 99350; Gov: Amaro Alexandre da Luz; f 1976; central bank; 8 brs.

FINANCIAL AGENCIES

Fundo de Desenvolvimento Nacional: Praia, São Tiago; channels public investment resources.

Fundo de Solidariedade Nacional: Praia, São Tiago; savings institution.

Instituto Caboverdiano de Solidariedade (ICS): CP 124, Praia, São Tiago; tel 61-13-99; telex 6012; Pres: Maria da Luz Boal; Dir, Projects: Ramiro Azevedo; f 1974; administers non-Governmental aid; professional training.

TRADE

Direcção Geral do Comércio: CP 105, Praia, São Tiago; tel 61-41-59; telex 6060; Dir-Gen: Miguel Costa Monteiro; Dir, Foreign Trade: Aguinaldo Marçal; f 1975; import-export licensing; promotion of exports.

Empresa Nacional de Combustíveis, EP: CP 1, Mindelo, São Vicente; Dir: Rui S. Lopes dos Santos; f 1979; supervises import and distribution of petroleum.

Empresa Nacional de Produtos Farmacêuticos, EP (EMPROFAC): CP 59, Praia; São Tiago; tel 61-14-94; telex 6024; fax 61-37-18; f 1979; imports, exports, produces and markets pharmaceutical products; holds monopoly of local production and medical exports.

Empresa Pública de Abastecimentos (EMPA): CP 107, Praia, São Tiago; tel 61-11-54; telex 6054; Dir-Gen: Orlando José Mascarenhas; f 1975; state provisioning enterprise; oversees imports, exports and domestic distribution.

Defence

Armed Forces: Rua Unidade Guiné-Cabo Verde, Praia, São Tiago; tel 61-13-49; Chief of Staff: Maj António Marino Dias.

Legal and Judiciary

Supremo Tribunal de Justiça: Praça 12 de Setembro, CP 117, Praia, São Tiago; tel 61-23-69; telex 6025; f 1975; highest court; Pres: M. G. Monteiro.

Media

BROADCASTING

Rádio Nacional de Cabo Verde: Praça 12 de Setembro, CP 26, Praia, São Tiago; tel 61-38-89; Head of Station: Carlos Gonçalves; Technical Dir: Francisco Monteiro; f 1985; radio broadcasts in Portuguese and Creole for 18 hours per day.

Televisão Experimental de Cabo Verde (TEVEC): Achada de Santo António, CP 1A, Praia, São Tiago; tel 61-40-80; telex 6030; f 1983; TV broadcasts in Portuguese and Creole for three hours per day.

Voz de São Vicente: CP 29, Mindelo, São Vicente; Dir: Francisco Tomar; f 1974; Govt-controlled radio station.

GOVERNMENT PUBLISHER

Imprensa Nacional: CP 113, Praia, São Tiago.

NEWS AND INFORMATION

National Statistical Service: Avda 12 Setembre, Praia, São Tiago; tel 267.

Statistical Service: Banco de Cabo Verde, 117 Avda Amílcar Cabral, CP 101, Praia, São Tiago; tel 341; telex 99350.

Tourism

Secretaria de Estado de Comércio e Turismo: CP 105, Praia, São Tiago; tel 573; telex 6058.

Transport and Communications

TELECOMMUNICATIONS

Empresa Pública dos Correios e Telecomunicações, EP (CTT): Rua Cesário de Lacerda, CP 220, Praia, São Tiago; tel 61-31-26; telex 6086; f 1982; operates public telecommunications and postal services.

TRANSPORT

Comissão de Gestão dos Transportes Marítimos de Cabo Verde: CP 153, São Vicente; tel 26-52; telex 3031; shipping.

Companhia Nacional de Navegação 'Arca Verde', EP: Rua 5 de Julho, CP 41, Praia, São Tiago; tel 61-10-60; telex 6067; Gen Man: José Cardoso; Shipping Man: Rui Vera-Cruz; Technical Man: Daniel Brito; f 1978; maritime cargo and passenger transport.

Transportes Aéreos de Cabo Verde (TACV): 11-13 Rua Guerra Mendes, CP 1, Praia, São Tiago; tel 339; telex 99365; Gen Man: Valdemar Fortes de Sousa Lobo; f 1955; internal services and weekly services to Portugal and the USA.

Transportes Marítimos de Cabo Verde: Avda Kwame Nkrumah, CP 153, Mindelo, São Vicente; maritime transport; serves African and European destinations.

CENTRAL AFRICAN REPUBLIC

Head of State

Executive power is vested in the President, who is also president of the Rassemblement démocratique centrafricain (RDC), the sole legal political party. The President is elected by universal adult suffrage for a six-year term, and appoints and presides over a Council of Ministers.

President: Gen André Kolingba (assumed power 1 September 1981; elected 21 November 1986).

Office of the President: Palais de la Renaissance, Bangui; tel 61-03-23; telex 5253.

Legislature

Legislative power is vested in the bicameral Congress, comprising the Assemblée Nationale (National Assembly), whose 52 members are elected by universal adult suffrage for a five-year term, and the advisory Conseil Economique et Régional (Economic and Regional Council), half of whose members are appointed by the President, and half elected by the National Assembly.

Assemblée Nationale (National Assembly): Bangui; Pres: Michel Docko; Sec-Gen: Emile Nicaise Mbari.

Consiel Economique et Régional (Economic and Regional Council): Bangui.

MINISTRIES AND GOVERNMENT DEPARTMENTS

MINISTRY OF THE CIVIL SERVICE, LABOUR, SOCIAL SECURITY AND PROFESSIONAL TRAINING
Bangui
Tel 61-01-44
Minister: Daniel Sehoulia

MINISTRY OF COMMUNICATIONS, ARTS AND CULTURE
BP 1290, Bangui
Tel 61-27-66; telex 5301
Minister: Jean Bengue

MINISTRY OF DEFENCE AND WAR VETERANS
Bangui
Tel 61-46-11; telex 5298
Minister: Gen André Kolingba

MINISTRY OF ECONOMY AND FINANCE, PLANNING AND INTERNATIONAL CO-OPERATION
Bangui
Tel 61-08-11; telex 5280
Minister: Dieudonné Wazoua
Secretary of State for Economy and Finance in charge of Budget and Debt Management: Jude Alex Kette
Secretary of State for Planning, Statistics and International Co-operation: Thierry Bingaba

MINISTRY OF ENERGY, MINES, GEOLOGY AND WATER RESOURCES
Bangui
Telex 5243
Minister: Dieudonné Padoudji-Yadjoua
Secretary of State for Energy and Mines: Octave Kossi Oudegbe

MINISTRY OF FOREIGN AFFAIRS
Bangui
Tel 61-15-74; telex 5213
Minister: Michel Gbezera-Bria
Secretary of State: Jules Kouale-Yabro

MINISTRY OF THE INTERIOR AND TERRITORIAL ADMINISTRATION
Bangui
Tel 61-44-77
Minister: Lt-Col Christophe Grelombe
Secretary of State: El-Roosalem Hetman

MINISTRY OF JUSTICE
Bangui
Tel 61-16-44
Minister and Keeper of the Seals: Jean Sillybiro-Sacko

MINISTRY OF NATIONAL AND HIGHER EDUCATION
BP 791, Bangui
Telex 5333
Minister: Jean-Louis Psimhis
Secretary of State: Jean-Marie Bassia

MINISTRY OF POSTS AND TELECOMMUNICATIONS
Bangui
Tel 61-29-46; telex 5304
Minister: Hugues Dobozeindi

MINISTRY OF PUBLIC HEALTH
Bangui
Tel 61-29-01
Minister: Jean Limbassa

MINISTRY OF PUBLIC WORKS AND TERRITORIAL DEVELOPMENT
Bangui
Tel 61-28-00
Minister: Jacques Kitte

MINISTRY OF RURAL DEVELOPMENT
BP 786, Bangui
Tel 61-28-00
Minister: Thomas Matouka
Secretary of State: François Wagoulou

MINISTRY OF TRADE, INDUSTRY AND SMALL- AND MEDIUM-SCALE ENTERPRISES
Bangui
Tel 61-44-88; telex 5215
Minister: Timothée Marboua

MINISTRY OF TRANSPORT AND CIVIL AVIATION
Bangui
Tel 61-06-36; telex 5335
Minister: Pierre Gonifei-Ngaibonanou

MINISTRY OF WATER, FORESTS, WILDLIFE, FISHERIES AND TOURISM
Bangui
Minister: Raymond Mbitikon

OFFICE OF THE MINISTER IN CHARGE OF THE CABINET SECRETARIAT AND OF RELATIONS WITH THE NATIONAL ASSEMBLY
Bangui
Minister: Edouard Franck

OFFICE OF THE SECRETARY OF STATE FOR SOCIAL AFFAIRS
Bangui
Secretary of State: Geneviève Lombilo

GOVERNMENT AGENCIES AND ORGANIZATIONS

Agriculture

Agence de Développement Caféière (ADECAF): BP 1935, Bangui; tel 61-47-30; Dir-Gen: J. J. Nimiziambi; association of coffee producers; assists coffee marketing co-operatives.

La Centrafricaine des Palmiers à Huile (CENTRA-PALM): BP 1355, Bangui; tel 61-49-40; telex 5271; Pres of Board of Admin: Jean-Privat Mbaye; Dir-Gen: Gabriel Ramadhane-Saïd; cultivation, processing and marketing of palm products.

Office National des Forêts (ONF): ave de l'Indépendence, BP 915, Bangui; tel 61-13-51; telex 5217; Dir-Gen: C. D. Songuet; f 1969; reafforestation; devt of forest resources.

Société Centrafricaine de Développement Agricole (SOCADA): ave David Dacko, BP 997, Bangui; tel 61-30-33; telex 5212; Pres: Maurice Methot; Man Dir: Patrice Endjingboma; f 1964; 75% state-owned; cotton ginning; production of cotton and groundnut oil.

Société Centrafricaine d'Exploitation Forestière et Industrielle (SOCEFI): BP 3, M'Bata-Bangui; Man Dir: Pierre Opanzoyen; f 1947; runs sawmill; exports timber; manufactures prefabricated dwellings.

Business and Economy

BANKING

Banque des Etats de l'Afrique Centrale (BEAC): BP 851, Bangui; tel 61-24-00; telex 5236; headquarters in Yaoundé, Cameroon; Gov: Casimir Oyé Mba; Dir in CAR: Alphonse Koyamba; f 1973; central bank of issue for mem states of the Customs and Economic Union of Central Africa (UDEAC), comprising Cameroon, the Central African Republic, Chad, the Congo, Equatorial Guinea and Gabon.

Union Bancaire en Afrique Centrale: rue de Brazza, BP 59, Bangui; tel 61-29-90; telex; 5225; Pres: Henri Maidou; Gen Man: Joseph Koyagbele; f 1962; 60% state-owned.

FINANCIAL AGENCY

Caisse de Stabilisation et de Péréquation des Produits Agricoles (CAISTAB): BP 76, Bangui; tel 61-08-00; telex 5278; Dir-Gen: M. Bounandele-Koumba; oversees pricing and marketing of agricultural products.

INSURANCE

Entreprise d'Etat d'Assurances et de Réassurances (SIRIRI): ave du Président Mobutu, BP 852, Bangui; tel 61-36-55; telex 5306; Pres: Emmanuel Dokouna; Dir-Gen: Jean-Marie Yollot; f 1972; insurance and reinsurance.

NATIONALIZED INDUSTRY

Industrie Centrafricaine du Textile (ICAT): BP 981, Bangui; tel 61-40-00; telex 5215; Man Dir: M. Ngoundoukoua; f 1965; textile complex.

Société Centrafricaine des Tabacs (SCAT): ave Boganda, BP 1042, Bangui; tel 61-17-48; telex 5326; Pres of Board of Admin: Gabriel Dotte-Badekara; Dir-Gen: Casimir Amakpio; f 1984; supervises tobacco production, curing and marketing.

Defence

Forces Armées Centrafricaines (FACA): c/o Ministry of Defence and War Veterans, Bangui; tel 61-26-11; telex 5298; Chief of Staff: Gen André Kolingba.

Gendarmerie Centrafricaine: Bangui; tel 61-22-00; national constabulary.

Police Centrafricaine: Bangui; tel 61-19-44; police force.

Energy

Compagnie Centrafricaine des Pétroles (PETROCA): BP 724, Bangui; tel 61-41-06; telex 5316; 51% state-owned.

Direction Générale de l'Energie Centrafricaine: Bangui;

tel 61-20-22; telex 5241; Dir-Gen: Joseph Gbibri; central office of energy.

Energie Centrafricaine (ENERCA): ave de l'Indépendence, BP 880, Bangui; tel 61-20-22; telex 5241; Man Dir: Lt-Col Dieudonné Molomadon; f 1967; production and distribution of electric power.

Société Centrafricaine des Hydrocarbures (CENTRA-HYDRO): BP 724, Bangui; tel 61-05-88; telex 5243; Dir-Gen: Simon N. Bozanga; 60% state-owned; petroleum distribution and storage

Total Centrafricaine de Gestion (TOCAGES): BP 724, Bangui; tel 61-05-88; telex 5243; Dir: Christian-Dimanche Songuet; f 1950; 51% state-owned; storage, retailing and transport of petroleum products.

Legal and Judiciary

Supreme Court: BP 926, Bangui; tel 61-41-33; Pres: Antoine Grothe; acts as a Court of Cassation in civil and penal cases and as Court of Appeal in administrative cases; comprises four chambers: constitutional, judicial, administrative and financial.

Media

BROADCASTING

Radiodiffusion-Télévision Centrafrique: BP 940, Bangui; telex 2355; Dir: F. P. Zemoniako; f 1958.

GOVERNMENT PUBLISHER

Imprimerie Centrafricaine: BP 329, Bangui; tel 61-00-33; Dir-Gen: Pierre Salamate-Koilet; f 1974.

NEWS AND INFORMATION

Agence Centrafricaine de Presse (ACAP): BP 40, Bangui; tel 61-10-88; telex 5299; Gen Man: Victor Deto Teteya; f 1974 following nationalization of the Bangui branch of Agence France-Presse.

Direction de la Statistique Générale et des Etudes Economiques (DSGEE): BP 696, Bangui; tel 61-45-74; telex 5208; f 1970; statistical office.

Tourism

Office National Centrafricain du Tourisme (OCATOUR): BP 655, Bangui; tel 61-45-66.

Transport

Agence Centrafricaine des Communications Fluviales (ACCF): BP 822, Bangui; tel 61-02-11; telex 5256; Man Dir: Justin Ndjapou; f 1969; devt of inland waterways transport system.

Compagnie Nationale des Transports Routiers (CNTR): BP 330, Bangui; tel 61-46-44; Dir-Gen: Georges Yabada; road transport.

Inter-RCA: BP 1413, Bangui; telex 5239; Man Dir: Jules Bernard Ouande; 52% state-owned, 24% by Air Afrique; extensive internal air services.

Société Centrafricaine de Transports Fluviaux (SOCA-TRAF): BP 1445, Bangui; telex 5256; Man Dir: François Toussaint; f 1980; 51% owned by ACCF (see above).

Utilities

Société Nationale des Eaux (SNE): BP 1838, Bangui; tel 61-12-22; telex 5267; Dir-Gen: Alphonse Kongolo; water co.

CHAD

Head of State

Under the new 1989 Constitution, executive power is vested in the President, who is elected by direct universal suffrage for a seven-year term. The President appoints and leads the Council of Ministers.

President: Hissène Habré (took office 19 June 1982; elected for seven year term 10 December 1989 by national referendum).

Office of the President: N'Djamena; tel 51-44-37; telex 5201.

Legislature

In 1989 legislative power continued to be exercised by the Council of Ministers. The new Constitution envisaged the re-establishment of the National Assembly, to be elected for a five-year term, and also incorporated the principle of a sole ruling party. For administrative purposes, the country is divided into 14 prefectures.

MINISTRIES AND GOVERNMENT DEPARTMENTS

MINISTRY OF AGRICULTURE
N'Djamena
Tel 51-37-52
Minister: Gouara Lassou

MINISTRY OF THE CIVIL SERVICE
N'Djamena
Tel 51-56-56
Minister: Oudalbaye Naham

MINISTRY OF CULTURE, YOUTH AND SPORTS
N'Djamena
Tel 51-44-76
Minister: Djibrine Hisseine Grienky

MINISTRY OF THE ENVIRONMENT AND TOURISM
N'Djamena
Minister: Mbailao Naimbaye Lozimian

MINISTRY OF FINANCE AND DATA PROCESSING
N'Djamena
Tel 51-55-53; telex 5257
Minister: Mbailamdana Ngarnayal

MINISTRY OF FOOD SECURITY AND DISASTER-STRICKEN GROUPS
N'Djamena
Tel 51-36-38
Minister: Seid Bauche

MINISTRY OF FOREIGN AFFAIRS
N'Djamena
Tel 51-50-82; telex 5238
Minister: Acheikh Ibn Oumar

MINISTRY OF INFORMATION AND CIVIC ORIENTATION
BP 748, N'Djamena
Tel 51-56-56; telex 5240
Minister: Adoum Moussa Seif

MINISTRY OF THE INTERIOR AND TERRITORIAL ADMINISTRATION
N'Djamena
Tel 51-46-59
Minister: Djime Togou

MINISTRY OF JUSTICE
N'Djamena
Tel 51-56-56
Minister and Keeper of the Seals: Col Wadal Abdel-Kader Kamougue

MINISTRY OF LABOUR, EMPLOYMENT AND VOCATIONAL TRAINING
N'Djamena
Tel 51-45-26
Minister: Routouang Yoma Golom

MINISTRY OF LIVESTOCK, ANIMAL RESOURCES AND RURAL HYDRAULICS
N'Djamena
Tel 51-59-07
Minister: Mahamat Nour Malaye

MINISTRY OF MINES, PETROLEUM AND ENERGY
N'Djamena
Tel 51-20-96
Minister: Mahamat Senoussi Khatir

MINISTRY OF NATIONAL DEFENCE, VETERANS AND WAR VICTIMS
N'Djamena
Tel 51-58-89
Minister: Hissène Habré

MINISTRY OF NATIONAL EDUCATION
BP 731, N'Djamena
Tel 51-44-76
Minister: Assileck Halata
Minister of Higher Education and Scientific Research: Youssouf Mbodou Mbami

MINISTRY OF PLANNING AND CO-OPERATION
N'Djamena
Tel 51-58-98
Minister: Mahamat Saleh Ibn Oumar

MINISTRY OF POSTS AND TELECOMMUNICATIONS
N'Djamena
Tel 51-42-64; telex 5254
Minister: Kassire Delwa Koumakoye

MINISTRY OF PUBLIC HEALTH
N'Djamena
Tel 51-39-60
Minister: Col Alphonse Kotiga Guerina

MINISTRY OF PUBLIC WORKS, HOUSING AND TOWN PLANNING
N'Djamena
Tel 51-20-96
Minister of Public Works: (vacant)
Minister of Territorial Development, Urbanism and Housing: Bilal Soubiane

MINISTRY OF SOCIAL AFFAIRS AND WOMEN'S PROMOTION
BP 80, N'Djamena
Tel 51-45-26
Minister: Ruth Yaneko Romba

MINISTRY OF TRADE AND INDUSTRY
BP 453, N'Djamena
Tel 51-56-56
Minister: (vacant)

MINISTRY OF TRANSPORT AND CIVIL AVIATION
N'Djamena
Tel 51-56-56
Minister: Gen Djibril Négué Djogo

OFFICE OF THE MINISTER OF STATE WITHOUT PORTFOLIO
N'Djamena
Minister: Djidingar Dono Ngardoum

OFFICE OF THE MINISTER-ADVISER TO THE PRESIDENT
N'Djamena
Tel 51-44-37
Minister: (vacant)

OFFICE OF THE MINISTER-DELEGATE TO THE PRESIDENT IN CHARGE OF GENERAL INSPECTION AND STATE CONTROL
N'Djamena
Tel 51-56-56
Minister: (vacant)

GOVERNMENT AGENCIES AND ORGANIZATIONS

Agriculture

Société Cotonnière du Tchad (COTONTCHAD): rue du Capitaine d'Abzac, BP 1116, N'Djamena; tel 51-41-32; telex 5229, Pres: Elie Romba; Dir-Gen: Tordibaye Adoum Djonouma; f 1971; 75% state-owned; buying, ginning and marketing of cotton; runs cotton gins and a cottonseed oil mill.

Business and Economy

BANKING

Banque de Développement du Tchad (BDT): rue Capitaine Ohrel, BP 19, N'Djamena, tel 51-28-29; Man Dir: Mouta Ali Zezerti; f 1962; 58.4% state-owned; devt bank.

Banque des Etats de l'Afrique Centrale (BEAC): BP 50, N'Djamena; headquarters in Yaoundé, Cameroon; tel 51-41-76; telex 5220; Gov: Casimir Oyé Mba; Dir in Chad: Adam Madji; f 1973; central bank of issue for mem states of the Customs and Economic Union of Central Africa (UDEAC), comprising Cameroon, the Central African Republic, Chad, the Congo, Equatorial Guinea and Gabon; 2 brs.

FINANCIAL AGENCY

Caisse Centrale de Coopération Economique: BP 478, N'Djamena; tel 51-40-71; Dir: François Vincent.

NATIONALIZED INDUSTRY

Société Nationale Sucrière du Tchad (SONASUT): BP 37, N'Djamena; telex 5263; Pres: Ahmat Dadji; Dir-Gen: Ferdinand Volhuis; f 1963; refining of sugar; manufacture of lump sugar and confectionery.

TRADE

Société Nationale de Commercialisation du Tchad (SON-ACOT): N'Djamena; telex 5227; Man Dir: Marbrouck Natroud; f 1965; 76% state-owned; national marketing, distribution and import-export co; has monopoly of purchase and sale of gum arabic in Chad.

Defence

Armed Forces: N'Djamena: Commdr-in-Chief: Allafoza Koni Worimi.

Air Force: N'Djamena; Chief: Lt-Col Zakariah Ouaouei Jahaad.

Army: N'Djamena; Chief of Army Staff: Maj Palomo; Chief of Military Police: Youssouf Galmaye.

Navy: N'Djamena: Chief of Naval Staff: Lt Mornadji Mbaissanebe.

Development

Office National de Développement Rural (ONDR): BP 896, N'Djamena; tel 51-48-64; Dir: Mickael Djibrael; f 1968; rural devt.

REGIONAL DEVELOPMENT

Société pour le Développement de la Région du Lac (SODELAC): BP 782, N'Djamena; tel 51-35-03; telex 5248; Pres: Cherif Abdelwahab; Dir-Gen: Mahamat Moctar Ali; f 1967.

Energy

Société Tchadienne d'Energie Electrique: 11 rue du Col Largeau, BP 44, N'Djamena; tel 51-28-81; telex 5226; Pres: Gomou Mawata Wakang; Dir-Gen: Ismael Mahamat Adoum; f 1968; 81% state-owned; produces and distributes electricity and water.

Media

BROADCASTING

Radiodiffusion Nationale Tchadienne: BP 892, N'Djamena; Dir: Djede Khourtou Gammar; broadcasts in French, Arabic and eight vernacular languages.

Radio Moundou: BP 122, Moundou; Dir: Djamanangar Djaïnta; daily broadcasts in French, Sara and Arabic.

GOVERNMENT PUBLISHER

Government Publishing House: BP 453, N'Djamena.

NEWS AND INFORMATION

Agence Tchadienne de Presse (ATP): BP 670, N'Djamena; tel 51-58-67; telex 5240.

Direction de la Statistique, des Etudes Economiques et Démographiques: BP 453, N'Djamena.

Tourism

Direction du Tourisme, des Parcs Nationaux et Réserves de Faune: BP 86, N'Djamena; tel 51-45-26; Dir: Daboulaye ban-Ymary; f 1962.

Délégation Régionale au Tourisme: BP 88, Sarh; tel 274.

Transport and Communications

TELECOMMUNICATIONS

Office National des Postes et Télécommunications du Tchad (ONPT): N'Djamena; tel 51-42-42; telex 5256; fax 51-58-84; Dir-Gen: Khalil d'Abzac; Dir, Telecommunications: Youssouf Adoum; Dir, Postal and Financial Services: Rosngar Meouro; national telecommunications, postal and financial services.

Société des Télécommunications Internationales du Tchad (TIT): BP 1132, N'Djamena; tel 51-57-82; telex 5200; fax 51-58-84; Man: Khalil d'Abzac; f 1976; 52% state-owned; international telecommunications.

TRANSPORT

Air Tchad: 27 ave du Président Tombalbaye, BP 168, N'Djamena; tel 51-45-64; telex 5345; Dir-Gen: Mahamat Nouri; f 1966; internal and external passenger, freight and charter services.

Coopérative des Transportateurs Tchadiens (CTT): BP 336, N'Djamena; tel 51-43-55; telex 5225; Pres: Saleh Khalifa; road haulage.

CHILE

Head of State

Under the 1981 Constitution, which took full effect in 1989, executive power is vested in the President, who is directly elected for a four-year term. The President is assisted by a Cabinet. There is a National Security Council, comprising the President, the heads of the armed forces and police, and the presidents of the Supreme Court and the Senate.

President: Patricio Aylwin Azócar (took office 11 March 1990).

Office of the President: Palacio de la Moneda, Santiago; tel (2) 221202; Sec to the Presidency: Edgardo Boeninger Kausel.

Legislature

Legislative power is vested in the bicameral National Congress, comprising a Senate of 47 elected and appointed senators serving eight-year terms (all former Presidents are to be senators for life), and a Chamber of Deputies consisting of 120 members elected for four years.

Senado (Senate): Valparaíso; Pres: Gabriel Valdés.

Cámara de Diputados (Chamber of Deputies): Valparaíso; Pres: José Viera Gallo.

MINISTRIES AND GOVERNMENT DEPARTMENTS

MINISTRY OF AGRICULTURE
Teatinos 40, Santiago
Tel (2) 717436; telex 240745
Minister: Juan Agustín Figueroa

MINISTRY OF ECONOMY, DEVELOPMENT AND RECONSTRUCTION
Teatinos 120, Santiago
Tel (2) 725522; telex 240558
Minister of Economy: Carlos Ominami Pascual

MINISTRY OF ENERGY
Teatinos 120, 7, Casilla 14, Correo 21, Santiago
Tel (2) 6981757; telex 240948; fax (2) 6981757
Minister: Jaime Tohá González

National Energy Commission: Teatinos 120, 7, Santiago; tel (2) 6981757; telex 240948; fax (2) 6981757; Pres: Minister of Energy, Jaime Tohá González; f 1978; plans and controls energy investment; regulates prices; advises the President on energy policy.

MINISTRY OF FINANCE
Teatinos 120, 12, Santiago
Tel (2) 6982051; telex 241334
Minister: Alejandro Foxley Rioseco

MINISTRY OF FOREIGN AFFAIRS
Palacio de la Moneda, Santiago
Tel (2) 6982501; telex 40595
Minister: Enrique Silva Cimma

MINISTRY OF HOUSING AND URBAN DEVELOPMENT
Serrano 15, 4, Santiago
Tel (2) 331624; telex 240124
Minister of Housing: Alberto Etchegaray Aubry

MINISTRY OF THE INTERIOR
Palacio de la Moneda, Santiago
Tel (2) 714103; telex 240273; fax (2) 6968740
Minister: Enrique Krauss Rusque

MINISTRY OF JUSTICE
Compañía 1111, Santiago
Tel (2) 6968151; telex 241316
Minister: Francisco Cumplido Cereceda

MINISTRY OF LABOUR AND SOCIAL SECURITY
Huérfanos 1273, 6, Santiago
Tel (2) 7151333; telex 242559; fax (2) 716539
Minister of Labour: René Cortázar Sanz

MINISTRY OF MINES
Teatinos 120, 9, Santiago
Tel (2) 6965872; telex 240948
Minister: Juan Hamilton Depassier

MINISTRY OF NATIONAL DEFENCE
Plaza Bulnes s/n, 4, Santiago
Tel (2) 6965271; telex 40537
Minister: Patricio Rojas Saavedra

MINISTRY OF NATIONAL PLANNING
Ahumada 48, Casilla 9140, Santiago
Tel (2) 722033; telex 341400
Minister: Sergio Molina Silva

Oficina de Planificación Nacional (ODEPLAN): Ahumada 48, 7, Santiago; tel (2) 722895; telex 341400; fax (2) 721879; Dir: Minister of National Planning, Sergio Molina Silva; Dep Dirs: Luis Larraín A., Rodrigo Moncada M.; f 1967; assists the Pres in all matters relating to social and economic planning; evaluates Govt investment projects.

MINISTRY OF NATIONAL PROPERTY
Avda Libertador Bernardo O'Higgins 280, Santiago
Tel (2) 2224669
Minister: Luis Alvarado

MINISTRY OF PRODUCTION DEVELOPMENT (CORFO)
Moneda 921, Casilla 3886, Santiago
Tel (2) 380521; telex 240421
Minister and Vice-Pres of CORFO (see below):
René Abeliuk Manasevich

MINISTRY OF PUBLIC EDUCATION
Avda Libertador Bernardo O'Higgins 1371, Santiago
Tel (2) 6983351; telex 240567; fax (2) 6987831
Minister: Ricardo Lagos Escobar

MINISTRY OF PUBLIC HEALTH
Enrique McIver 541, 1, Santiago
Tel (2) 394001; telex 240136
Minister: Jorge Jiménez de la Jara

MINISTRY OF PUBLIC WORKS
Dirección de Vialidad, Morandé 59, Santiago
Tel (2) 6964839; telex 240777
Minister: Carlos Hurtado Ruiz-Tagle

MINISTRY OF TRANSPORT AND TELECOMMUNICATIONS
Amunátegui 139, Santiago
Tel (2) 726503; telex 240200
Minister: Germán Correa Díaz

OFFICE OF THE COMPTROLLER OF THE REPUBLIC
Teatinos 56, 9, Santiago
Tel (2) 724212; telex 240281
Comptroller-General: (vacant)

SECRETARIAT-GENERAL OF THE GOVERNMENT
Palacio de la Moneda, Plaza de la Constitución s/n, Santiago
Tel (2) 714103; telex 240142; fax (2) 6991657
Secretary-General: Enrique Correa Díaz

GOVERNMENT AGENCIES AND ORGANIZATIONS

Advisory and Supervisory Bodies

Consejo Nacional para la Alimentación y la Nutrición (CONPAN): Ahumada 236, 7, Santiago; advises the Govt on matters relating to the production and supply of basic foodstuffs.

Dirección de Abastecimientos del Estado: Amunátegui 66, Santiago; state supplies authority; purchase, storage and distribution of supplies for Govt depts, agencies, etc.

Sociedad Agrícola y Servicios Isla de Pascua Ltda: Alfredo Lecannelier 1940, Providencia, Santiago; tel (2) 2327497; telex 240690; fax (2) 711058; Gen Man: Fernando Maira Palma; f 1980; administers agriculture and public services on Easter Island.

Agriculture and the Environment

Complejo Forestal y Maderero Panguipulli Ltda: Agustinas 785, Of 560, Santiago; tel (2) 397054; telex 346093; fax (2) 6984127; Gen Man: Manuel F. Izquierdo Fernández; forestry and timber industry; controlled by CORFO (see below).

Corporación Nacional Forestal (CONAF): Avda Bulnes 285, Of 501, Santiago; tel (2) 722724; telex 440138; Exec Dir: Iván Castro Poblete; f 1972; centralizes forestry activities; enforces forestry law, promotes afforestation; administers subsidies for afforestation projects and to develop forest resources; manages National Parks, Natural Monuments and National Reserves; responsible to the Ministry of Agriculture.

Servicio Agricola y Ganadero (SAG): Avda Bulnes 140, Santiago; tel (2) 6982244; telex 242745; fax (2) 721812; Exec Dir: Alejandro Marchant Baeza; f 1967; under Ministry of Agriculture; promotes agricultural devt and marketing of agricultural produce.

Subsecretario de Pesca: Bellavista 168, 16, Valparaíso; tel (32) 212187; telex 230355; fax (32) 212790; Sub-Sec: Roberto Cabezas Bello; f 1976; under Ministry of Economic Affairs; promotes and co-ordinates the fishing industry.

Business and Economy

BANKING

Banco Central de Chile: Agustinas 1180, Santiago; tel (2) 6962281; telex 340315; fax (2) 6985021; Pres: Andrés Bianchi; Vice-Pres: Alfonso Serrano Spoerer; Dir: Brig Enrique Seguel; f 1925; central bank of issue; under Ministry of Finance; 7 brs.

Consejo Monetario: c/o Banco Central, Agustinas 1180, Santiago; monetary council; determines credit and monetary policy.

Banco del Estado de Chile: Avda Libertador Bernardo O'Higgins 1111, Santiago; tel (2) 716001; telex 240481; fax (2) 6983299; Pres: Alvaro Bardón Muñoz; Vice-Pres: Osvaldo Palacios Mery; Exec Gen Man: Osman Flores Araya; f 1953; state bank; 181 brs.

Superintendencia de Bancos e Instituciones Financieras: Moneda 1123, 6, Santiago; tel (2) 6990072; fax (2) 711654; Supt: Guillermo Ramírez Vilardell; f 1925; run by Ministry of Finance; banking supervisory authority.

INSURANCE

Caja Reaseguradora de Chile, SA: Bandera 84, 6, Santiago; tel (2) 6982941; telex 340276; fax (2) 6989730; Pres: Gustavo Dupuis Pinillos; f 1927; reinsurance.

Instituto de Seguros del Estado (ISE): Moneda 1025, 7, Santiago; tel (2) 6964271; telex 240204; fax (2) 6965732; Pres: Gustavo Dupuis Pinillos; f 1953; general insurance.

Superintendencia de Valores y Seguros: Teatinos 120, 6, Casilla 2167, Santiago; tel (2) 6962194; telex 340260; fax (2) 6987425; Supt: Fernando Alvarado Elissetche; f 1931; under Ministry of Finance; insurance supervisory authority.

NATIONALIZED INDUSTRY

Cía de Acero del Pacífico, SA: Casilla 167-D, Santiago; telex 240288; Gen Man: Roberto de Andraca Barbas; f 1946; iron and steel production; controlled by CORFO (see below).

Corporación de Fomento de la Producción (CORFO): Moneda 921, Casilla 3886, Santiago; tel (2) 380521; telex 240421;

fax (2) 711058; Vice-Pres: Minister of Production Development, René Abeliuk Manasevich; Gen Man: Col Eugenio Lavín Hollub; holding group of principal state enterprises; grants loans and guarantees to private sector; responsible for sale of non-strategic state enterprises.

Empresa Nacional de Computación e Informática, SA (ECOM): José Pedro Alessandri 1495, Casilla 14796, Santiago; tel (2) 740076; Pres: Gustavo Ramdohr Vargas; computing; controlled by CORFO (see above).

Empresa Nacional de Explosivos, SA (ENAEX): Agustinas 1350, 3, Casilla 255-V, Santiago; tel (2) 6982148; telex 440069; fax (2) 6982326; Gen Man: Oscar Jadue Salvador; explosives; controlled by CORFO (see above).

Defence

Armada de Chile (Navy): Galvez 45, 7, Santiago; tel (2) 725272; Commdr-in-Chief: (vacant).

Ejército de Chile (Army): Plaza Bulnes, Santiago; tel (2) 83721; Commdr-in-Chief: Gen Augusto Pinochet Ugarte.

Fuerza Aérea de Chile (Air Force): Pedro Aguirre Cerda 5500, Los Cerrillos, Santiago; tel (2) 5570011; telex 5240055; fax (2) 5570238; Commdr-in-Chief: Gen Fernando Matthei Aubel.

Development and Planning

Servicio de Vivienda y Urbanización: Arturo Prat 48, Santiago; housing and town planning agency; appraises housing needs and supply; co-ordinates agencies concerned with town planning and the provision of low-cost housing.

International Affairs

Dirección General de Relaciones Económicas Internacionales (PROCHILE): Pedro de Valdivia 0193, Santiago; tel (2) 2317108; telex 240836; Dir: Guillermo Lunecke Brauning; f 1974; bureau of international economic affairs.

Legal and Judiciary

Corte Suprema: Plaza Montt Varas, Santiago; tel (2) 6980561; Pres: Luis Maldonado Boggiano; Attorney-Gen: René Pica Urrutia; Sec of the Pres: César Deramond Rubio; Sec of the Court: Sergio Mery Bravo; supreme court; comprises 16 mems appointed for life by the Pres of the Republic; the Pres of the Supreme Court is elected by the 16 mems of the Court.

Media

BROADCASTING

Radio Nacional de Chile: San Antonio 220, 2, Casilla 244-V, Correo 21, Santiago; tel (2) 339071; Dir: Roberto Mardones Sáez.

NEWS AND INFORMATION

Instituto Nacional de Estadísticas: Avda Bulnes 418, Casilla 498-3, Correo 3, Santiago; tel (2) 6991441; statistical office.

Mining and Energy

ENERGY

Comisión Chilena de Energía Nuclear: Amunátegui 95, Casilla 188-D, Santiago; tel (2) 6990070; telex 340468; Exec Dir: Víctor Aguilera Acevedo; f 1965; Govt agency; devt of peaceful uses of atomic energy; regulation and control of matters relating to nuclear energy.

Comisión Nacional de Energía: Teatinos 120, 7, Casilla 14, Correo 21, Santiago; tel (2) 6981757; telex 240948; fax (2) 6981758; Pres: Minister of Energy, Jaime Tohá González; Exec Sec: Sebastián Bernstein Letelier; f 1978; establishes energy policy; approves investments in energy-related projects.

Cía Chilena de Electricidad (CHILECTRA): Santo Domingo 789, 2, Casilla 1557, Santiago; tel (2) 391096; telex 40645; Exec Vice-Pres: Rubén Díaz Niera; f 1921; generates, transmits and distributes electricity; controlled by CORFO (see above).

Empresa Nacional de Electricidad, SA (ENDESA): Santa Rosa 76, Casilla 1392, Santiago; tel (2) 2229080; telex 240491; fax (2) 2226328; Chair: Jorge Mardones Acevedo; Gen Man: Mario Zenteno Carvallo; f 1944; controlled by CORFO (see above).

Empresa Nacional del Petróleo (ENAP): Ahumada 341, 3, Casilla 3556, Santiago; tel (2) 381845; telex 240447; fax (2) 391093; Chief Exec: Alejandro Marty; f 1950; devt, exploitation and refining of the country's petroleum resources; attached to the Ministry of Mines.

MINING

Comisión Chilena del Cobre: Agustinas 1161, 4, Casilla 9493, Santiago; tel (2) 726219; telex 645458; Exec Vice-Pres: Patricio Jarpa Yañez; f 1976; attached to Ministry of Mines; provides the Govt, state organizations and institutions with specialized and technical advice on all matters directly and indirectly related to copper and its by-products; supervises the copper industry.

Corporación Nacional del Cobre de Chile (CODELCO—Chile): Huérfanos 1270, Casilla 150-D, Santiago; tel (2) 6988801; telex 240672; Exec Pres: Patricio Contesse; f 1976; attached to Ministry of Mines; copper production.

Empresa Minera de Aysén Ltda: Calle 21, De Mayo 466, 3, Coyhaique; Gen Man: Sergio Araneda Valdivieso; zinc and lead mining; controlled by CORFO (see above).

Empresa Nacional del Carbón, SA (ENACAR): Avda Libertador Bernardo O'Higgins 396, Casilla 271, Concepción; tel (41) 233861; telex 260406; fax (41) 233861; Gen Man: Col Eudoro Quiñones Silva; f 1852; coal production; controlled by CORFO (see above).

Empresa Nacional de Minería (ENAMI): MacIver 459, 2, Casilla 100-D, Santiago; tel (2) 396061; telex 240574; fax (2) 384094; Exec Vice-Pres: Sergio Pérez Hormazábal; f 1960; attached to the Ministry of Mines; promotes the devt of small and medium-sized mines.

Telecommunications

Empresa Nacional de Telecomunicaciones, SA (ENTEL CHILE): Santa Lucía 360, Casilla 4254, Santiago; tel (2) 6902121; telex 240683; Gen Man: Lt-Col Iván van de Wyngard Mellado; f 1964; telecommunications co; operates land satellite stations linked to INTELSAT system.

Tourism

Servicio Nacional de Turismo (SERNATUR): Avda Providencia 1550, Casilla 14082, Santiago; tel 6960474; telex 240137; Dir: Margarita Ducci Budge; f 1975; promotion of tourism.

Transport

RAILWAYS

Empresa de los Ferrocarriles del Estado: Avda Libertador Bernardo O'Higgins 3322, 3, Casilla 134-D, Santiago; tel (2) 790707; telex 242290; Gen Man: Roberto Darrigrandi Chadwick; f 1851; the State Railways are divided between the Ferrocarril Regional de Arica, Ferrocarril Regional del Norte de Chile, Metro Regional de Valparaíso, and the Ferrocarril del Sur.

ROADS

Dirección de Vialidad: c/o Ministry of Public Works, Morandé 59, 2, Santiago; tel (2) 6964839; telex 240777; Dir: Remberto Urrea Muster; Dep Dir: Alberto Bull; f 1836; part of the Ministry of Public Works; responsible for roads.

SHIPPING

Dirección General de Territorio Marítimo y Marina Mercante: Errázuriz 537, 4, Valparaíso; tel (32) 258091; telex 230602; fax (32) 252539; Dir: Rear Adm Fernando Lazcano; f 1848; general directorate for maritime territory and the merchant navy; maritime admin of the coast and national waters; technical and professional control of the merchant navy, etc.

Empresa Marítima, SA (Empremar): Almirante Gómez Carreño 49, Casilla 105-V, Valparaíso; tel (32) 258061; telex 230382; Pres: Alvaro Larenas Letelier; f 1953; international and coastal services.

Empresa Portuaria de Chile (EMPORCHI): Blanco 839, Valparaíso; tel (32) 257167; telex 230313; fax (32) 259937; also Huérfanos 1055, Of 804, Santiago; tel (2) 6982232; telex 240624; fax (2) 6989441; Dir: Vice-Adm (retd) Jorge Baeza Concha; f 1960; ports supervisory authority.

THE PEOPLE'S REPUBLIC OF CHINA

Head of State

The President of the Republic is Head of State and is elected by the National People's Congress (NPC) for a five-year term. Executive power is exercised by the State Council (Cabinet), appointed by the NPC and comprising the Premier, Vice-Premiers, Ministers, the Auditor-General and the Secretary-General.

President: Yang Shangkun (elected by the Seventh National People's Congress on 8 April 1988).

Office of the President: c/o State Council Secretariat, Beijing.

Vice-President: Wang Zhen.

Legislature

The highest body of state power is the National People's Congress (NPC), which in 1988 comprised 2,970 indirectly elected deputies serving five-year terms. The NPC elects a Standing Committee to be its permanent organ, and appoints the State Council and other state functionaries. Political power is effectively held by the Chinese Communist Party (CCP). Local people's congresses and governments are the local organs of state power.

Quanguo Renmin Diabiao Dahui (National People's Congress): Great Hall of the People, Beijing; tel (1) 667380.

Standing Committee of the National People's Congress: Great Hall of the People, Beijing; tel (1) 667380; Chair: Wan Li; Sec-Gen: Peng Chong.

MINISTRIES AND GOVERNMENT DEPARTMENTS

STATE COUNCIL SECRETARIAT
Beijing
State Councillors: Chen Xitong, Li Guixian, Li Tieying, Wang Bingqian, Wang Fang, Qin Jiwei, Song Jian, Zou Jiahua, Chen Junsheng
Secretary-General: Luo Gan

OFFICE OF THE PREMIER
c/o State Council Secretariat, Beijing
Premier: Li Peng
Vice-Premiers: Yao Yilin, Tian Jiyun, Wu Xueqian

MINISTRY OF AERONAUTICS AND ASTRONAUTICS INDUSTRY
Beijing
Minister: Lin Zongtang

MINISTRY OF AGRICULTURE
Hepingli, Dongcheng District, Beijing
Tel (1) 463061
Minister: He Kang

MINISTRY OF CHEMICAL INDUSTRY
Liupukang, Deshengmenwai, Beijing
Tel (1) 446561
Minister: Gu Xiulian

MINISTRY OF CIVIL AFFAIRS
147 Donganmen, Beijing
Tel (1) 551731
Minister: Cui Naifu

MINISTRY OF COMMERCE
45 Fuxingmenwai St, Beijing
Tel (1) 668581
Minister: Hu Ping

MINISTRY OF COMMUNICATIONS
10 Fuxing Rd, Beijing
Tel (1) 8642371; telex 22462
Minister: Qian Yongchang

MINISTRY OF CONSTRUCTION
Baiwanzhuang St, Beijing
Tel (1) 8992833; telex 222302
Minister: Lin Hanxiong

MINISTRY OF CULTURE
Donganmen North St, Beijing
Tel (1) 442131
Minister (acting): He Jingzhi

MINISTRY OF ENERGY RESOURCES
Beijing
Minister: Huang Yicheng

MINISTRY OF FINANCE
South Sanlihe St, Fuxingmenwai, Beijing
Tel (1) 868731; telex 222308
Minister: Wang Bingqian

MINISTRY OF FOREIGN AFFAIRS
225 Chaoyangmennei St, Dongsi, Beijing
Tel (1) 553831
Minister: Qian Qichen

MINISTRY OF FOREIGN ECONOMIC RELATIONS AND TRADE
2 Changan East St, Beijing
Tel (1) 553031; telex 22168
Minister: Zheng Tuobin

MINISTRY OF FORESTRY
Hepingli, Dongchang District, Beijing
Tel (1) 463061; telex 22237
Minister: Gao Dezhan

MINISTRY OF GEOLOGY AND MINERAL RESOURCES
Xisi Yangshi St, Beijing
Tel (1) 668741; telex 22531
Minister: Zhu Xun

MINISTRY OF JUSTICE
2 Nan Shun Cheng Jie, Xi Zhi Men, Beijing
Tel (1) 668971
Minister: Cai Cheng

MINISTRY OF LABOUR
Beijing
Minister: Ruan Chongwu

MINISTRY OF LIGHT INDUSTRY
Fuchengmenwai St, Beijing
Tel (1) 890751
Minister: Zeng Xianlin

MINISTRY OF MACHINE-BUILDING AND ELECTRONICS INDUSTRY
Beijing
Minister: He Guangyuan

MINISTRY OF MATERIALS AND EQUIPMENT
25 Yuetan North St, Beijing
Tel (1) 8391107; telex 200155; fax (1) 8392535
Minister: Liu Suinian
Formulates and implements Govt policies concerning national allocation and distribution of industrial goods such as steel, cement, timber, coal and fuel, cars and trucks, machinery, etc; has depts concerned with each kind of industrial goods.

MINISTRY OF METALLURGICAL INDUSTRY
46 West Dongsi St, Beijing
Tel (1) 557431
Minister: Qi Yuanjing

MINISTRY OF NATIONAL DEFENCE
Beijing
Tel (1) 667343
Minister: Qin Jiwei

MINISTRY OF PERSONNEL
Beijing
Minister: Zhao Dongwan

MINISTRY OF POSTS AND TELECOMMUNICATIONS
13 West Changan St, Beijing 100804
Tel (1) 660540; telex 222187
Minister: Yang Taifang

MINISTRY OF PUBLIC HEALTH
44 Houhaibeiyan, Beijing
Tel (1) 440531; telex 22193
Minister: Chen Minzhang

MINISTRY OF PUBLIC SECURITY
East Changan St, Beijing
Tel (1) 553871
Minister: Wang Fang

MINISTRY OF RADIO, FILM AND TELEVISION
Fuxingmenwai St 2, POB 4501, Beijing
Tel (1) 862753; telex 22236
Minister: Ai Zhisheng

MINISTRY OF RAILWAYS
10 Fuxing Rd, Beijing
Tel (1) 864061
Minister: Li Senmao

MINISTRY OF STATE SECURITY
East Changan St, Beijing
Tel (1) 553871
Minister: Jia Chunwang

MINISTRY OF SUPERVISION
35 Hua Yuan Bei Lu (East Gate), Hai Dian District, Beijing
Tel (1) 2019551
Minister: Wei Jianxing
Responsible for the supervision of Govt depts and their personnel for proper implementation of state policies, laws and statutes; deals with misconduct and offences committed by officials, and maladministration of Govt bodies.

MINISTRY OF TEXTILE INDUSTRY
12 East Changan St, Beijing
Tel (1) 5129542; telex 22661
Minister: Wu Wenying

MINISTRY OF WATER RESOURCES
1 Xiang, Baiguang St, Guanganmen, Beijing
Tel (1) 365563; telex 22466
Minister: Yang Zhenhuai

OFFICE OF THE AUDITOR-GENERAL
Beijing
Auditor-General: Lu Peijian

STATE COMMISSION FOR RESTRUCTURING THE ECONOMY
Beijing
Minister: Li Peng

STATE COMMISSION OF SCIENCE, TECHNOLOGY AND INDUSTRY FOR NATIONAL DEFENCE
Beijing
Minister: Ding Henggao.

STATE EDUCATION COMMISSION
37 Damucang Hutong, Xicheng District, Beijing
Tel (1) 658731
Minister: Li Tieying.

STATE FAMILY PLANNING COMMISSION
Xizhimen South Shuncheng St, Beijing
Tel (1) 668971
Minister: Zou Jiahua.

STATE NATIONALITIES AFFAIRS COMMISSION
252 Taipingqiao St, Beijing
Tel (1) 6016611; telex 222444
Minister: Ismail Amat

STATE PHYSICAL CULTURE AND SPORTS COMMISSION
Chongwai Stadium Rd, Beijing
Tel (1) 757231
Minister: Wu Shaozu.

STATE PLANNING COMMISSION
Beijing
Minister: Yao Yilin
Sec-Gen: Gui Shiyong.

**STATE SCIENTIFIC AND TECHNOLOGICAL
COMMISSION**
52 Sanlihe, Fuxingmenwai, Beijing

Tel (1) 868361; telex 22349; fax (1) 8012594
Minister: Song Jian.

GOVERNMENT AGENCIES AND ORGANIZATIONS

Advisory and Supervisory Bodies

National Administration of State Property: Beijing; Dir: Tang Bingwu.

State Administration of Commodity Prices: Beijing; Dir: Cheng Zhiping; Dep Dirs: Wang Xingjia, Zhang Qi, Ma Kai; operates directly under the State Council; oversees commodity price control at a national level; fixes and adjusts prices of industrial and agricultural products.

Business and Economy

BANKING

Agricultural Bank of China: 25 Fuxing Rd, Beijing; tel (1) 811824; telex 22017; fax (1) 810680; Pres: Ma Yongwei; Vice-Pres: Wang Jingshi; f 1979; functions directly under the State Council; handles state agricultural investments.

Bank of China: Bank of China Bldg, 410 Fuchengmennei St, Beijing; tel (1) 118311; telex 22254; Chair and Pres: Wang Deyan; f 1912; handles foreign exchange and international settlements; 369 brs, 46 abroad.

Bank of Communications: 200 Jiang Xi Zhong Rd, Shanghai; tel (21) 255900; telex 33438; fax (1) 291400; Chair and Pres: Li Xiang Rui; Vice-Chair: Pan Qi Chang; f 1908; functions under the People's Bank of China; handles state investments in the joint state-private enterprises; buys and sells foreign securities and bonds; organizes and participates in loans by international banking groups; handles international and domestic trusts, insurance, investment, leasing and consultancy work.

China Investment Bank: 27-B Wanshou Rd, Beijing; tel (1) 8630273; telex 22537; Chair: Zhou Daojiong; Pres: Lu Xianlin; f 1981; raises foreign funds for domestic investment and credit.

China and South Sea Bank Ltd: 17 Xi Jiao Min Xiang, Beijing; Chair: Cui Ping; f 1921.

China State Bank Ltd: 17 Xi Jiao Min Xiang, Beijing; Gen Man: Li Pinzhou.

Guangdong Provincial Bank: 17 Xi Jiao Min Xiang, Beijing; Gen Man: Cheng Kedong.

Industrial and Commercial Bank of China: 13 Cuiwei Lu, Haidianqu, Beijing; tel (1) 217273; Pres: Zhang Xiao; f 1984; handles industrial and commercial credits.

Kincheng Banking Corpn: 17 Xi Jiao Min Xiang, Beijing; telex 73405; Gen Man: Xiang Kefang; f 1917.

National Commercial Bank Ltd: 17 Xi Jiao Min Xiang, Beijing; Gen Man: Wang Weicai; f 1907.

People's Bank of China: San Li He, West City, Beijing; tel (1) 863907; telex 22612; Gov: Li Guixian (mem of the State Council); Dep Gov: Qiu Qing; f 1948; central bank and bank of issue; 2,204 brs.

People's Construction Bank of China: 6 Wanshou Rd, Beijing; tel (1) 8011166; Pres: Zhou Daojiong; f 1954; payments for capital construction according to plan and budget approval by the state; issues long- and medium-term loans to enterprises and short-term loans to contractors.

The Trust and Investment Corpn of the People's Construction Bank of China: Shou Song Hotel,.6 Xi Wan Shou Rd, Beijing; tel (1) 8212891; telex 222467; fax (1) 8211694; Gen Man: Cui Shu Ling; f 1986; loans, financial leasing, financing of real estate devt, bond issuing agency service, securities business.

Sin Hua Trust, Savings and Commercial Bank Ltd: 17 Xi Jiao Min Xiang, Beijing; Gen Man: Cui Yanxu.

Yien Yieh Commercial Bank Ltd: 17 Xi Jiao Min Xiang, Beijing; Gen Man: Pan Jaw Ling.

FINANCIAL AGENCIES

China International Trust and Investment Corpn (CITIC): 19 Jianguomenwai St, 100004 Beijing; tel (1) 5002633; telex 22305; Chair: Jin Deqin; f 1979; responsible to the State Council; arranges foreign investment in China; engages in joint investment ventures in China and abroad.

State Administration of Exchange Control: Beijing; Dir: Tang Gengyao.

State Administration of Taxation: Beijing; Dir: Jin Xin; Dep Dir: Niu Licheng.

INSURANCE

China Insurance Co Ltd: 22 Xi Jiao Min Xiang, POB 20, Beijing; tel (1) 654231; telex 22102; Man: Song Guo Hua; f 1931; cargo, hull, freight, fire, life, personal accident, industrial injury and motor insurance; reinsurance.

The People's Insurance Co of China (PICC): 410 Fuchengmennei St, Beijing; tel (1) 6016688; telex 22102; Pres: Qin Daofu; Vice-Chairs: Fan Hua, Song Guo Hua; f 1949; hull, marine cargo, aviation, motor, life, fire, accident and liability insurance; reinsurance.

Tai Ping Insurance Co Ltd: 410 Fuchengmennei St, Beijing; tel (1) 6016688; telex 42001; Man: Lin Zhen Feng; marine freight, hull, cargo, fire, life, personal accident, industrial injury and motor insurance; reinsurance.

NATIONALIZED INDUSTRY

China Corpn of Shipbuilding Industry: 10 Yuetan, Beixiaojie, Beijing; tel (1) 895947; telex 22335.

China Great Wall Industry Corpn: POB 847, Beijing; tel (1) 8021202; telex 22651; fax (1) 891809; Pres: Jin An Tang; Vice-Pres: Li Yi Yang; f 1978; international co-operation on commercial satellites and carrier rockets; satellite launching services; import and export of space equipment.

China National Automotive Industry Corpn: 16 Fuxingmenwai St, 100860 Beijing; tel (1) 3063870; telex 22656; fax (1) 3063602; Chair of Board (acting): Cai Shiqing; Vice-Chair: Bo Xiyong; f 1951; co-ordinates production, construction, scientific research in the automotive industry; carries out certain administrative functions for nationwide automotive trade according to the authorization of the State Council.

China National Chemical Construction Corpn: He Ping Li, Dong Cheng Qu, Beijing; tel (1) 55283.

China National Tobacco Corpn (CNTC): 11 Hu Fang Lu, Beijing; tel (1) 3015330; telex 222366; fax (1) 652171; Mans:

Jiang Ming, Ma Erchi, Jin Maoxian, Liu Zhiguang, Guan Zhenglin; f 1982; exercises overall control of all aspects of the tobacco industry: planting of tobacco, purchase and allocation of leaf tobacco, manufacture and distribution of cigarettes, cigars and other tobacco products, import and export of tobacco and tobacco products.

China Road and Bridge Engineering Co: 3 Waihuan Jie, Andingmenwai, Beijing; tel (1) 4213378; telex 22336; fax (1) 4213378; Chair: Wang Zhanyi; Vice-Chairs: Lu Qiu, Ma Jiangda; Pres: Lu Qiu; Vice-Pres: Zhang Jiaxiang, Wu Deliang; f 1979; supervises building of highways, urban roads, bridges, tunnels, industrial and residential buildings, airport runways and parking areas; contracts to do all surveying, designing, pipe-laying, water supply and sewerage.

China State Shipbuilding Corpn: 5 Yuetanjie, Beijing; tel (1) 890971; telex 22335; fax (1) 8313380; Chair of Board: Chai Shufan; Pres: Hu Chuanzhi.

State Administration of Building Materials Industry: Beijing; Dir: Wang Yanmou; Dep Dirs: Zhang Renwei, Li Mingyu, Yang Zhiyuan.

TRADE

All-China Federation of Industry and Commerce: 93 Beiheyan St, Beijing; tel (1) 554231; telex 22044; Chair: Rong Yiren; f 1953; promotes overseas trade relations.

Beijing Foreign Trade Corpn: Bldg 12, Yongan Dong Li, Jian Guomenwai, Beijing; tel (1) 5001843; telex 210064; Dir: Yu Xiaosong; controls import-export trade, foreign trade transportation, export commodity packaging and advertising for Beijing.

China Council for the Promotion of International Trade: 1 Fuxingmenwai St, POB 4509; 100860 Beijing; tel (1) 8013344; telex 22315; fax (1) 8011370; Pres: Zheng Hongye; Sec-Gen: Cui Yushan; f 1952; encourages foreign trade, economic co-operation and foreign investment; arranges and sponsors Chinese exhibitions abroad and foreign exhibitions in China; aids foreigners to apply for patent and trade-mark rights in China; organizes technical exchanges with other countries; provides legal services; publishes trade periodicals.

　China Maritime Arbitration Commission: 1 Fuxingmenwai St, Beijing; tel (1) 8013344; telex 222288; fax (1) 8011369; Chair: Hua Liankuei; Vice-Chairs: Wang Shoumao, Shen Zhicheng, Cheng Wanzhu, Zhu Zenjie, Feng Liqi, Gao Zhunlai; f 1959; settles maritime disputes by means of arbitration.

　Foreign Economic and Trade Arbitration Commission (FETAC): address as above; arbitrates in cases of disputes involving Chinese and foreign investment, foreign investment in China, trade contracts, import of technology, etc.

China Industry and Commerce Development Corpn (INCOMIC): 93 Bei He Yan St, Beijing; tel (1) 554231; telex 22044; Pres: Zou Siyu; f 1985; provides consultancy and promotion of exports and imports in China and internationally.

China International Water and Electric Corpn: Liupukang, Beijing; tel (1) 4015511; telex 22485; Pres: Zhu Jingde; f 1956; exports equipment for, and undertakes projects in the field of water and electrical engineering.

China Metallurgical Import and Export Corpn (CMIEC): 46 Dongsi Xidajie, 100711 Beijing; tel (1) 555515; telex 22461; fax (1) 5123792; Pres: Bai Baohua; f 1980; import of ores, spare parts, automation and control systems; export of metallurgical products, technology and equipment; establishes joint ventures and trade with foreign cos.

China National Aerotechnology Import-Export Corpn: 5 Liangguochang, Dongcheng District, Beijing; tel (1) 445831; telex 22313; fax (1) 4015381; Pres: Sun Zhaoqing; Chair: Mo Wenxiang; exports signal flares, electric detonators, tachometers, parachutes, general purpose aircraft, etc.

China National Animal Breeding Stock Import and Export Corpn (CABS): 10 Dongdan Yangyi Hutong Jia, Beijing; tel (1) 543253; telex 210101; fax (1) 5128694; Pres: Yang Qing; Vice-Pres: Zhang Puze, Li Zhenqing; f 1980; import and export of breeding animals, poultry stock, pasture and turf grass seeds, feed additives, veterinary medicine and vaccines, equipment for animal husbandry.

China National Cereals, Oils and Foodstuffs Import and Export Corpn: 82 Donganmen St, Beijing; tel (1) 555180; telex 22281; fax (1) 551488; Pres: Chen Faxian; Vice-Pres: Cai Peikang, An Jitao, Sun Zhenyu, Sun Zhenchi; f 1952; import and export of cereals, sugar, vegetable oils, meat, eggs, fruit, dairy produce, vegetables, wines and spirits, canned foods and aquatic products; also involved in joint ventures, barter trade and co-operative enterprises.

China National Chemicals Import and Export Corpn: Erligou, Xijiao, Beijing; tel (1) 8311106; telex 22243; Pres: Zheng Dunxun; Chair: Zhu Dazhi; deals in rubber, petroleum, paints, fertilizers, inks, dyestuffs, chemicals and drugs.

China National Coal Import and Export Corpn (CNCIEC): A-3 Huang Si Jie, Andingmenwai, Beijing; tel (1) 4216061; telex 22494; fax (1) 4216327; Pres: Wei Guofu; Chair: Hong Shangqing; import and export of coal and technical equipment for coal industry; involved in joint coal devt and compensation trade.

China National Electric Wire and Cable Export Corpn: Langjia Yuan, Jianguomenwai, Beijing; tel (1) 591163; telex 22614; fax (1) 582714; Gen Man: Han Ke Dong; Dep Gen Mans: Feng Jing Shan, Liu Xue Yong, Cao Qing Yuan, Lei Zhen Huan; f 1981; supplies wire and cable for electrical equipment, power cable, telecommunications cable, etc; imports raw materials for producing electric wires and cables and cable accessories; takes part in joint ventures; provides technical consultancy.

China National Electronics Import and Export Corpn: 9 Fuxing Rd, Beijing; tel (1) 810910; telex 22475; fax (1) 8314387; Pres: Ouyang Zhongmou; Chair: Li Deguang.

China National Foreign Trade Transportation Corpn (SINOTRANS): Import Bldg, Erligou, Xijiao, Beijing; tel (1) 8317733; telex 22153; fax (1) 8311070; Pres: Liu Fulin; Chair: Ping Jian; f 1950; under Ministry of Foreign Economic Relations and Trade; agents for the Ministry's import and export corpns; arranges customs clearance, deliveries, forwarding and insurance for sea, land and air transportation.

China National Machinery and Equipment Import and Export Corpn: 12 Fuxingmenwai, Beijing; tel (1) 362561; telex 22186; fax (1) 362375; Pres: Yao Mingwei; Chair: Wang Ziyi; f 1978; import and export of machine tools, machinery, automobiles, hoisting and transport equipment, electric motors, photographic equipment, etc.

China National Machinery Import and Export Corpn: Erligou, Xijiao, Beijing; tel (1) 891974; telex 22242; fax (1) 8021321; Pres: Li Guangyuan; import and export of machine tools, diesel engines and boilers and all kinds of machinery.

China National Medicines and Health Products Import and Export Corpn: Bldg 12, Jianguomenwai St, Beijing; tel (1) 5003344; telex 210103; Pres: Yan Rudai.

China National Metals and Minerals Import and Export Corpn: Erligou, Xijiao, Beijing; tel (1) 8317733; telex 22241; fax (1) 898996; Pres: Wang Yan; f 1950; import and export of steel, antimony, tungsten concentrates and ferrotungsten, zinc ingots, tin, mercury, pig iron, cement, etc.

China National Packaging Import and Export Corpn: 28 Donghouxiang, Andingmenwai, 100010 Beijing; tel (1) 4214058; telex 22490; fax (1) 4212124; Pres: Xu Jianguo; Vice-Pres: Shi Ying, Li Feng, Zhang Guochen, Feng Ruifang; f 1961; manufacture, import and export of various kinds of packaging materials and products, packaging and printing machinery.

China National Pharmaceutical Foreign Trade Corpn (CPIC): Jia 38, Bei Li Shi Lu, Beijing; tel (1) 8316572; telex 22659; fax (1) 8316571; Pres: Hu Baohua; f 1981; import and export of pharmaceutical products and raw materials; arranges economic and technical co-operation projects, joint ventures, processing of foreign materials, etc.

China National Seed Corpn: 31 Mingfeng Hutong, Xidan, Beijing; tel (1) 652592; telex 22079; fax (1) 651179; Pres: Hu Qinling; f 1978; seed production; import and export of seeds for cereals, cottons, oil crops, sugar crops, vegetables, friut trees, melons, etc.

China National Technical Import Corpn: Erligou, Xijiao, Beijing; tel (1) 8317733; telex 22244; fax (1) 8313584; Pres: Xu Deen; Chair: Chen Xian; f 1952; imports all kinds of complete plant and equipment, acquires modern technology and expertise from abroad, undertakes co-production and joint ventures, technical consultation and updating of existing enterprises.

China National Textiles Import and Export Corpn: 82 Donganmen St, Beijing; tel (1) 553793; telex 22280; fax (1) 5124711; Pres: Zhong Quansheng; Man Dir: Li Tianan; f 1960; imports synthetic fibres, raw cotton, wool, etc; exports cotton yarn, cotton fabric, knitwear, woven garments, etc.

China North Industries Group: 7A Yuetan Nan Jie, Beijing; tel (1) 866898; telex 22339; Chair: Zou Jiahua; Pres: Lai Jinlie; exports mechanical products, light industrial products, chemical products, opto-electronic products, military products, etc.

China Nuclear Energy Industry Corpn (CNEIC): 21 Nanlishi Lu, Beijing; tel (1) 867717; telex 22240; fax (1) 8012393; Pres: Zhang Xinduo; exports air filters, vacuum valves, dosimeters, radioactive detection elements and optical instruments.

Chinese Export Commodities Fair (CECF): Guangzhou Foreign Trade Centre, 117 Lui Hua Rd, Guangzhou; tel (20) 677000; telex 44465; fax (20) 335880; f 1957; organized by the Ministry of Foreign Economic Relations and Trade; two trade fairs a year.

Customs General Administration of the PRC: Beijing; Dir: Dai Jie; Dep Dirs: Su Shifang, Wang Jieping, Wu Naiwen, Zhen Pu; operates under the State Council; oversees customs houses and their supervision of imports and exports.

Shanghai Foreign Trade Corpn: 27 Zhongshan Dong Yi Lu, Shanghai; tel (21) 217350; telex 33034; handles import-export trade, foreign trade transportation, chartering, export commodity packaging, storage and advertising for Shanghai municipality.

Shanghai International Trust Trading Corpn: 521 Henan Rd, POB 3066, Shanghai; tel (21) 3226650; telex 33627; fax (21) 3207412; Dir-Gen: Cai Min; f 1979; handles mail order and foreign trade, drafts contracts, arranges export, customs and deliveries for overseas Chinese, etc.

State Administration for Industry and Commerce: 8 San Li He Dong Lu, Xichengqu, 100820 Beijing; tel (1) 8013300; telex 222431; Dir: Ren Zhonglin; under direct supervision of the State Council; internal trade.

State Bureau of Technology Supervision: Beijing; Dir: Xu Zhijian; Dep Dirs: Li Baoguo, Lu Shaozeng, Bai Jingzhon; depts include: Weights and Measures, Standardization, Quality Supervision and Quality Control.

State Patent Bureau: Beijing; Dir: Jiang Minkuan; First Dep Dir: Gao Lulin.

State Tobacco Monopoly Adminsitration: Beijing; Dir: Jiang Ming; Dep Dirs: Jin Maoxian, Liu Zhiguang.

Culture

State Bureau of Archives: Beijing; Dir: Feng Zizhi.

State Bureau for the Preservation of Cultural Relics: Beijing; Dir: Zhang Deqin; Sec-Gen: Tong Zhenghong.

Defence

Central Military Commission: Beijing; Chair: Jiang Zemin; First Vice-Chair: Yang Shangkun; Sec-Gen: Yang Baibing; directs the armed forces.

Chinese People's Liberation Army (PLA): Gen Staff Headquarters, Beijing; Chief of Gen Staff: Gen Chi Haotian.

  Air Force: Beijing; Commdr: Gen Wang Hai.

  General Logistics Department: Beijing; Head: Zhao Nanqi.

  General Political Department: Beijing; Chief Political Commissar: Yang Baibing.

  Navy: Beijing; Commdr: Rear-Adm Liu Huaqing.

Military Scientific Council: Beijing; Dir: Dr Jian Xuesan.

Chinese People's Armed Police Force: Beijing; Commdr: Lt-Gen Li Lianxiu.

Environment

State Environmental Protection Bureau: Beijing; Dir: Qu Geping; Dep Dirs: Cheng Zhenhua, Jin Jianming.

Legal and Judiciary

Supreme People's Court: Dongjiaomin Xiang, Beijing; tel (1) 550131; Pres: Ren Jianxin; f 1949; highest judicial organ of the state; directs and oversees work of lower courts; Pres is elected by the National People's Congress for a five-year term.

Supreme People's Procuratorate: Donganmen Beiheyan, Beijing; tel (1) 550831; Procurator-Gen: Liu Fuzhi; acts for the National People's Congress; examines Govt depts, civil servants and citizens, to ensure observance of the law; prosecutes in criminal cases; Procurator-Gen is elected by the National People's Congress for a five-year term.

Media

BROADCASTING

Central People's Television Broadcasting Section: Bureau of Broadcasting Affairs of the State Council, Beijing; f 1958; operates three TV channels.

Central People's Broadcasting Station: 2 Fuxingmenwai St, Beijing; Dir: Yang Zhaolin; domestic radio service in several languages; controlled by the Ministry of Radio, Film and Television.

Radio Beijing: 2 Fuxingmenwai St, 100866 Beijing; tel (1) 862691; telex 222271; Dir: Cui Yulin; f 1947; foreign radio service in 38 languages; controlled by the Ministry of Radio, Film and Television.

GOVERNMENT PUBLISHER

People's Communications Publishing House: 8 Hepinglidongjie, Andingmenwai, Beijing; tel (1) 4213713; Vice-Dirs: Mi Zengfu, Gao Zhendu; subordinate unit of the Ministry of Communications; publishes science and technology books, textbooks and laws and specifications of communications.

NEWS AND INFORMATION

China Press and Publications Administration: Beijing; Dir: Song Muwen; Dir, Books Admin: Yang Muzhi; Dir, Newspapers Bureau: Lin Fengsheng; Dir, Periodicals Bureau: Zhang Bohai; administers publishing, printing and distribution under the State Council.

State Statistical Bureau: 38 Yuetan St, Sanlihe, Beijing; tel (1) 8217410; telex 22778; Dir-Gen: Zhan Sai; Dep Dirs-Gen: Zheng Jiaheng, Yu Guangpei, Shao Zongming; Sun Jingxin; Dir, Dept of Foreign Affairs: Wu Hui; f 1952; conducts surveys of national economic and social devts; provides statistical information.

Xinhua (New China) News Agency: 57 Xuanwumen Xi Rd, Beijing; tel (1) 668521; telex 22316; Pres: Mu Qing; Editor-in-Chief: Nan Zhenzhong; f 1931; offices in all Chinese provincial capitals, and about 95 overseas bureaux; news and photographic services.

Zhongguo Xinwen She (China News Agency): POB 1114, Beijing; Dir: Wang Shigu; f 1952; supplies news features, special articles and photographs for newspapers and magazines in Chinese printed overseas.

Mining and Energy

ENERGY

Atomic Research Centre: Tarim Pendi, Xingjiang; Dir: Wang Ganzhang; f 1953.

China National Offshore Oil Corpn (CNOOC): Nansidaokou Rd, Dazhongsi, Beijing; tel (1) 2014653; telex 22611; Pres: Zhong Yiming.

China National Oil Development Corpn: Liupukang, Beijing; tel (1) 444313; telex 22312; Pres: Song Zhenming.

China National Petro-Chemical Corpn (SINOPEC): 24 Xiaoguan St, Andingmenwai, Beijing; tel (1) 4216731; telex 22655; Pres: Chen Jinhua; Chair: Li Renjun; f 1983; under direct control of the State Council; petroleum refining; production of petrochemicals, synthetic fibres, etc; owns 61 subordinate enterprises.

China National Petroleum and Natural Gas Corpn: Liupukang, Beijing; tel (1) 2016107; telex 22312; fax (1) 2018039; Pres: Wang Tao (mem of the State Council).

Institute of Atomic Energy: POB 275, Beijing; tel (1) 868221; telex 222373; Dir: Sun Zuxun; f 1958; research into and devt of nuclear physics, nuclear chemistry and nuclear chemical engineering, reactor engineering, preparation of isotopes, environmental and radiation protection, radiometrology, etc.

Nuclear Safety Administration: Beijing; Dir: Jiang Shengjie; Dep Dir: Shi Guangchang.

State Nuclear Industry Corpn: 1 Sannanxiang Sanlihe, Beijing; tel (1) 8012211; telex 22240; Pres: Jiang Xinxiong (mem of the State Council).

MINING

China National Coal Mine Corpn: 21 Beijie, Hepingli, Beijing; tel (1) 4217766; telex 210277; Pres: Yu Hongen (mem of the State Council).

Science and Technology

Chinese Academy of Space Technology (CAST): 31 Baishigiao Lu, POB 2417, 100081 Beijing; tel (1) 8378237; telex 22473; fax (1) 892250; Pres: Min Guirong; f 1968; designs, develops and manufactures satellites; space devt and research; satellite testing.

State Bureau of Surveying and Cartography: Beijing; Dir: Quan Xiangwen; Dep Dir: Huang Yunkang.

State Meteorological Administration: Beijing; Dir: Zou Jingmeng; Dep Dirs: Zhang Jijia, Luo Jibin.

Tourism

China International Travel Service (CITS): 6 Dongchangan Ave, Beijing; tel (1) 5121122; telex 22350; Gen Man: Wang Erkang; makes travel arrangements for foreign tourists.

Chinese People's Association for Friendship with Foreign Countries: 1 Tai Ji Chang St, 100740 Beijing; tel (1) 5122474; telex 210368; fax (1) 5128354; Pres: Han Xu; Sec-Gen: Xu Qun.

National Tourism Administration: 6 Dongchangan Ave, Beijing; tel (1) 5121122; telex 22350; Dir: Liu Yi.

Transport

Bureau of Water Transportation: Beijing: controls rivers and coastal traffic.

China Ocean Shipping Agency: 6 Dongchangan St, Beijing; tel (1) 5121924; telex 211208; fax (1) 5121924; Pres: Liu Songjin; Vice-Pres: Chen Zhongbao; f 1953; arranges sea passage, booking space, container transportation, ship sale and leasing, etc.

China Ocean Shipping Co (COSCO): 6 Dongchangan St, Beijing; tel (1) 5121188; telex 22264; fax (1) 5122408; Pres: Liu Songjin; runs merchant fleet serving the Far and Middle East, Europe and N. America.

General Administration of Civil Aviation of China (CAAC): 155 Dongsi St, Beijing; tel (1) 550626; telex 22101; f 1949; Gen Man, China Eastern Airways: Yuan Taoyuan; Chair, Shanghai Air Lines: He Pengnian; supervisory agency; controls all civil aviation activities; oversees domestic and external air network of the following airlines: Air China, China Eastern Airways, China Southern Airways, China Southwestern Airways, China Northwestern Airways, China Northeastern Airways, China United Airlines and China Capital Helicopter Service.

Minsheng Shipping Co: 35 Shan Xi Rd, Chongging; tel (811) 45695; telex 62241; fax (811) 47152; Gen Man: Lu Guoji; f 1984; runs barges and tugs.

CHINA (TAIWAN)

Head of State

Under the 1947 constitution the Head of State is the President, who is elected for a six-year term by the National Assembly. The President governs through the Legislative Yuan, and is aided by the Executive Yuan (Council of Ministers) under a Premier.

President: Lee Teng-hui (took office 13 January 1988).

Office of the President: Chiehshou Hall, Chungking South Rd, Taipei 100; tel (2) 311-3731; Sec-Gen: Li Yuan-zu.

Legislature

Legislative power is vested in the five Yuans (governing bodies), the highest legislative organ being the Legislative Yuan, to which the Executive Yuan is responsible. In July 1988 the Legislative Yuan comprised 304 members, many of whom are members for life. The National Assembly meets to vote on constitutional amendments that have been submitted by the Legislative Yuan.

Legislative Yuan: Chungshan South Rd, Taipei 100; tel (2) 321-1531; Pres: Liu Kuo-tsai; Vice-Pres: Liang Su-yung.

National Assembly: Chungshan Hall, 1 Hsiushan St, Taipei 100; tel (2) 331-1986.

MINISTRIES AND GOVERNMENT DEPARTMENTS

OFFICE OF THE PREMIER
1 Chung Hsiao East Rd, Section 1, Taipei 10023
Tel (2) 391-5231; fax (2) 394-8727
Premier and President of the Executive Yuan: Lee Huan
Vice-Premier: Shih Chi-yang
Secretary-General: Wang Chou-ming

CENTRAL PERSONNEL ADMINISTRATION
109 Huaining St, Taipei 100
Tel (2) 311-1720
Director-General: Pu Ta-hai

COUNCIL OF AGRICULTURE
37 Nanhai Rd, Taipei 10728
Tel (2) 331-7541
Chair: Yu Yu-hsien

COUNCIL OF CULTURAL PLANNING AND DEVELOPMENT
Taipei
Chair: Kuo Wei-fan

COUNCIL FOR ECONOMIC PLANNING AND DEVELOPMENT
118 Huaining St, Taipei
Tel (2) 361-0241
Minister and Director-General: Frederick F. Chien

DEPARTMENT OF HEALTH
Aikuo East Rd, 100, 14th Floor, Taipei 105
Tel (2) 321-0151; telex 11707
Director-General: Shih Chun-jen

ENVIRONMENTAL PROTECTION ADMINISTRATION
Taipei
Director-General: Eugene Y. H. Chien

GOVERNMENT INFORMATION OFFICE
3 Chung Hsiao East Rd, Section 1, Taipei
Telex 11636
Director-General: Shaw Yu Ming

MINISTRY OF COMMUNICATIONS
2 Chang-sha St, Section 1, Taipei 10001
Tel (2) 311-2651; fax (2) 311-9611
Minister: Clement C. P. Chang

MINISTRY OF ECONOMIC AFFAIRS
15 Foochow St, Taipei 10722
Tel (2) 393-2307; telex 19884; fax (2) 321-3275
Minister: Chen Li-an

Commission of National Corpns: 109 Hankow St, Section 1, Taipei; tel (2) 371-3161; Chair: Lee Ta-hai; Vice-Chair: Wang Yu-yung.

MINISTRY OF EDUCATION
5 Chung Shan South Rd, Taipei 10040
Tel (2) 351-3111; fax (2) 395-2073
Minister: Dr Mao Kao-wen

MINISTRY OF FINANCE
2 Aikuo West Rd, Taipei
Tel (2) 351-1611; telex 11840
Minister: Shirley W. Y. Kuo

MINISTRY OF FOREIGN AFFAIRS
2 Chiehshou Rd, Taipei 10016
Tel (2) 311-9292; telex 11299
Minister: Lien Chan

MINISTRY OF THE INTERIOR
107 Roosevelt Rd, Section 4, Taipei
Tel (2) 341-5241
Minister: Hsu Shui-teh

MINISTRY OF JUSTICE
130 Chungking South Rd, Section 1, Taipei 10036
Tel (2) 314-6871
Minister: Lu You-wen

MINISTRY OF NATIONAL DEFENCE
Chiehshou Hall, Chungking South Rd, Taipei 10016
Tel (2) 311-7001
Minister: Gen Hau Pei-tsun

**MONGOLIAN AND TIBETAN AFFAIRS
COMMISSION**
109 Roosevelt Rd, Section 4, Taipei
Tel (2) 351-3131
Chair: Wu Hua-peng

NATIONAL SCIENCE COUNCIL
Kwang Po Bldg, 5th and 6th Floors, 2 Canton St, Taipei

Tel (2) 331-7221
Chair: Hsia Han-min

**OFFICE OF THE DIRECTOR-GENERAL OF
BUDGET, ACCOUNTING AND STATISTICS**
1 Chung Hsiao East Rd, Section 1, Taipei 100
Tel (2) 391-5231
Director-General: Yu Chien-min

OVERSEAS CHINESE AFFAIRS COMMISSION
30 Kungyuan Rd, Taipei
Tel (2) 381-0039
Chair: Tseng Kwang-shun

**RESEARCH, DEVELOPMENT AND EVALUATION
COMMISSION**
1 Chung Hsiao East Rd, Section 1, Taipei 10023
Tel (2) 341-2307; fax (2) 392-8133
Chair: Dr Ma Ying-jeou
Vice-Chair: Dr Kao Koong-lian
Directs policy research and planning and evaluates performance of various Govt agencies and state enterprises for Executive Yuan.

GOVERNMENT AGENCIES AND ORGANIZATIONS

Advisory and Supervisory Bodies

Office of the President of the Control Yuan: 2 Chung Hsiao East Rd, Section 1, Taipei 105; tel (2) 341-3183; Pres: Huang Tzuen-chiou; Vice-Pres: Ma Kung-chun; investigates activities of Executive Yuan.

Office of the President of the Examination Yuan: 1 Szuyuan Rd, Mucha, Taipei; tel (2) 936-3081; Pres: Kung Teh-cheng; Vice-Pres: Lin Chin-sheng; supervises civil service examination system.

Agriculture

China Fisheries Corpn: 25 Tung Shan St, Taipei; Pres: P. K. Liu; Gen Man: Y. C. Lee; f 1955.

Council of Agriculture (COA): 37 Nanhai Rd, Taipei 10728; tel (2) 331-7541; Chair: Y. H. Yu; Vice-Chair: H. Y. Chen; f 1984 to replace the Council for Agricultural Planning and Development (CAPD), and the Bureau of Agriculture (BOA); admin of all affairs related to food, crops, forestry, fisheries and the animal industry; promotes technology and provides external assistance.

Business and Economy

BANKING

Bank of Communications: 91 Heng Yang Rd, Taipei 10003; tel (2) 361-3000; telex 11341; Chair: Kuo-shu Liang; Pres: C. Y. Lee; f 1907; 20 brs.

Bank of Taiwan: 120 Chungking South Rd, Section 1, Taipei 10036; tel (2) 314-7377; telex 11021; Chair: Dr I-Shuan Sun; Pres: Pu Chen-ming; f 1946; 67 brs.

Central Bank of China: 2 Roosevelt Rd, Section 1, Taipei; tel (2) 393-6161; telex 21532; Gov: S. C. Shieh; Dep Govs: Chen S. Yu, Paul C. H. Chiu; f 1928; bank of issue.

Central Trust of China: 49 Wu Chang St, Section 1, Taipei

10006; tel (2) 311-1511; telex 11377; Chair: W. S. King; Pres: T. Y. Chu; f 1935; 5 brs.

Chang Hwa Commercial Bank Ltd: 38 Tsuyu Rd, Section 2, Taichung; tel (4) 222-2001; telex 51248; Chair: Liang Kuo-shu; Pres: K. H. Yeh; 51% state-owned; 107 brs.

Co-operative Bank of Taiwan: 77 Kuan Chien Rd, Taipei; tel (2) 311-8811; telex 23749; fax (2) 331-6567; Chair: Hubert M. F. Hsu; Pres: H. P. Liao; f 1946; central bank for co-operatives and major agricultural credit institution; 95 brs.

Export-Import Bank: 3 Nan Hai Rd, 8th Floor, Taipei; tel (2) 321-0511; telex 26044; Chair: P. Y. Pai; Pres: C. S. Lo; f 1979; 1 br.

Farmers Bank of China: 85 Nanking East Rd, Section 2, Taipei 10408; tel (2) 551-7141; telex 21610; Chair: Wilson C. P. Yen; Pres: Richard M. C. Tsai; f 1933; 35 brs.

First Commercial Bank: POB 395, 30 Chungking South Rd, Section 1, Taipei; tel (2) 311-1111; telex 11310; fax (2) 361-0036; Chair: H. A. Chen; Pres: Kenneth B. K. Tsan; f 1899; 74% state-owned; 137 brs.

Hua Nan Commercial Bank Ltd: 38 Chungking South Rd, Section 1, Taipei; tel (2) 371-3111; telex 11307; Chair: Kenneth K. H. Lo; Pres: James Chi Tang-lo; f 1919; 51% state-owned; 98 brs.

International Commercial Bank of China: 100 Chi Lin Rd, Taipei 10424; tel (2) 563-3156; telex 11300; Chair: C. D. Wang; Pres: Theodore S. S. Cheng; f 1912; 32 brs.

Land Bank of Taiwan: 46 Kuan Chien Rd, Taipei 10038; tel (2) 361-3020; telex 14564; Chair: Y. D. Sheu; Pres: T. L. Lin; f 1946; 61 brs.

FINANCIAL AGENCIES

Inspectorate General of Customs: 85 Hsinsheng South Rd, Section 1, Taipei 106; tel (2) 741-3180; Dir-Gen: Chen Chin-ming.

Securities and Exchange Commission: 7F, 49 Kuen Chien Rd, Taipei; tel (2) 341-3101; telex 10864; fax (2) 394-8249; Chair: C. P. Chang; Vice-Chair: Danng-yen Lu; f 1950; supervision and regulation of securities firms and self-regulatory bodies, including stock exchange and Securities Dealer's Association.

Taipei National Tax Administration: 7-1 Peiping East Rd,

Taipei; tel (2) 393-3131; Commr: Hou Po-lieh; Dep Commr: Yang Yu-ming.

NATIONALIZED INDUSTRY

BES Engineering Corpn: 320 Chung Hsiao East Rd, 4th Floor, Section 4, Taipei; tel (2) 752-1111; telex 21985; Chair: Huang Ven-yong; Pres: Ho Chu-shou.

China Petrochemical Development Corpn: 6 Roosevelt Rd, 8th Floor, Section 1, Taipei; tel (2) 392-3111; telex 22240; Chair and Pres: Tung Shih-feng.

China Shipbuilding Corpn: 3 Chung Kung Rd, Hsiao Kang, Kaohsiung; tel (7) 801-0111; Chair: William Y. N. Wei; Pres: Fung Chia-tzeng.

China Steel Corpn: Lin Hai Industrial District, Hsiao Kang, Kaohsiung; tel (7) 801-1111; telex 71108; Chair: King Mou-hui; Pres: Hsiang Chuan-chi.

Chung-Tai Chemical Industries Corpn: 91 Jen Ai Rd, Lane 2, Section 2, Taipei; tel (2) 351-7222; Chair: Yin Chun.

Kaohsiung Ammonium Sulphate Corpn Ltd: 100-2 Chungshan 3rd Rd, Kaohsiung; tel (7) 334-8545; Pres: Chan Teh-hu.

Ret-Ser Engineering Agency (VACRS): 123 Changan East Rd, Section 2, Taipei; tel (2) 541-8641; telex 21531; Pres: Arthur Y. Chen.

Taiwan Aluminium Corpn: 15 Chengkung 11 Rd, Kaohsiung; tel (7) 335-1141; telex 81907; Pres: Chang Tien-to.

Taiwan Chung Hsing Paper Corpn: 35 Kuang Fu South Rd, 10th Floor, Taipei; tel (2) 767-3171; telex 24522; fax (2) 765-9026; Chair and Pres: Yeh Kuo-kuang; f 1958; paper making.

Taiwan Fertilizer Co Ltd: 230 Chung Hsiao East Rd, Section 4, Taipei; tel (2) 773-3411; telex 22386; Chair: Wang Yü-yung; Pres: Jen Lu.

Taiwan Machinery Manufacturing Corpn: 3 Taichi Rd, Hsiao Kang, Kaohsiung; tel (7) 831-0511; telex 81979; Chair: Lay Ying; Pres: Liu Ping-kun.

Taiwan Sugar Corpn: POB 35, Taipei; tel (2) 311-0521; telex 11270; Chair: Wong Yi-ting; Pres: Yuan Shu-sheng.

Tang Eng Iron Works Co Ltd: 65 Kuanchien Rd, Taipei; tel (2) 311-0869; telex 22227; Chair: Chen Ju-keng; Pres: Yen Chien-tai.

TRADE

Board of Foreign Trade: 1 Hukou St, Taipei 10741; tel (2) 351-0271; telex 11434; fax (2) 351-3603; Dir-Gen: Vincent C. Siew.

China External Trade Development Council (CETRA): 333 Keelung Rd, 4th-7th Floors, Section 1, Taipei 10548; tel (2) 738-2345; telex 21676; fax (2) 757-6653; Sec-Gen: Agustin Tingtsu Liu; trade promotion body.

Chinese National Association of Industry and Commerce: 390 Fu Hsin South Rd, 13th Floor, Section 1, Taipei; tel (2) 707-0111; telex 10774; Chair: Koo Chen-fu; Sec-Gen: Wu Tsuping.

Committee of International Technical Co-operation: POB 1366, Taipei; tel (2) 707-3605; Chair: Koh Ching-chao; Exec Sec: Tsai Hai-tu.

Euro-Asia Trade Organization: 1 Hsu Chow Rd, 4th Floor, Taipei; tel (2) 393-2115; telex 25794; fax (2) 3928393; Chair and Sec-Gen: Wellington Y. Tsao; f 1975; initiates trade contacts with European cos, sponsors trade missions and exhibitions, promotes industrial co-operation.

Export Processing Zone Administration (EPZA): 27 Paoching Rd, 5th Floor, Taipei; tel (2) 331-0012; Dir-Gen: Yü Kuang-ya.

International Co-operation Department: 277 Roosevelt Rd, 5th Floor, Taipei; tel (2) 391-8198; Dir: Wu Hsing-chiang.

National Bureau of Standards: 185 Hsin-hai Rd, 3rd Floor, Section 2, Taipei 10637; tel (2) 772-5321; telex 15074; fax (2) 721-5255; Dir-Gen: Wu Hwei-ran; f 1947; issues standards, patents and trademarks.

Taiwan Tobacco and Wine Monopoly Bureau: 4 Nanchang Rd, Section 1, Taipei; tel (2) 321-4567; telex 26494; fax (2) 397-2086; Dir: Chen Shih-ching; f 1947; manufacturing, selling and trading tobacco and wine.

Culture

National Palace Museum: Wai-shuang-hsi, Shih-lin, Taipei; tel (2) 881-2021; fax (2) 882-1440; Dir: Chin Hsiao-yi; f 1925.

Defence

General Staff: Ministry of National Defence, Chiehshou Hall, Chungking South Rd, Taipei 100; tel (2) 311-7001; Chief of the Gen Staff: Gen Hao Pei-tsun.

Air Force: Ministry of National Defence, Chiehshou Hall, Chungking South Rd, Taipei 100; tel (2) 711-1121; Commdr: Gen Kuo Ju-lin.

Army: Ministry of National Defence, Chiehshou Hall, Chungking South Rd, Taipei 100; tel (2) 321-4911; Commdr: Chiang Chung-ling.

Combined Service Forces: Ministry of National Defence, Chiehshou Hall, Chungking South Rd, Taipei 100; tel (2) 761-4121; Commdr: Gen Chiang Wei-kuo.

Navy: Ministry of National Defence, Chiehshou Hall, Chungking South Rd, Taipei 100; tel (2) 594-3811; Commdr: Adm Liu Ho-chien.

Taiwan Garrison General Headquarters: Ministry of National Defence, Chiehshou Hall, Chungking South Rd, Taipei 100; tel (2) 311-1501; Commdr: Gen Chen Shou-shan.

National Police Administration: 7 Chung Hsiao East Rd, Section 1, Taipei 105; tel (2) 321-9011; Dir: Lo Chang; Dep Dir: Lin Yung-hung.

National Security Council: Chiehshou Hall, Chungking South Rd, Taipei 100; tel (2) 311-5687; Chair: Chiang Ching-kuo; Sec-Gen: Chang Wego.

Development and Planning

INVESTMENT

Investment Commission: 7 Roosevelt Rd, 8th Floor, Section 1, Taipei; tel (2) 351-3151; Chair: Hsu Kuo-an; Exec Sec: Wang Chih-kang.

PLANNING

China Development Corpn: CDC Tower, 125 Nanking East Rd, Section 5, Taipei 10572; tel (2) 763-8800; telex 23147; Chair: Yung-Liang Lin; Pres: W. L. Kiang; f 1959; assists in creation, modernization and expansion of private industrial enterprises.

China Productivity Centre: 340 Tun Hua North Rd, 2nd Floor, Taipei; tel (2) 713-7731; telex 22954; fax (2) 717-2178; Pres: Dr Casper T. Y. Shih; f 1955; management consultant; information service; training and education programme activity.

Industrial Development and Investment Centre (IDIC):

7 Roosevelt Rd, Section 1, Taipei 10757; tel (2) 394-7213; telex 10634; fax (2) 392-6835; Dir: John Chang-i Ni; Dep Dir: Lee Ming-yu; f 1959; promotion of planned devt and investment in industrial sector.

Industrial Development Bureau (IDB): 109 Hankow St, Section 1, Taipei; tel (2) 331-7531; Dir: Yang Shih-chien; Dep Dir: Wu Hui-jan; promotion of industrial devt projects under auspices of Ministry of Economic Affairs.

Energy

Atomic Energy Council (AEC): 67 Lane 144, Keelung Rd, Section 4, Taipei 10772; tel (2) 392-4180; telex 26554; Chair: Yen Chen-hsing; Sec-Gen: Liu Kuang-chi; f 1955; promotes advancement of nuclear science and technology; enforces safety requirements.

Chinese Petroleum Corpn: POB 135, Taipei 100; tel (2) 361-0221; telex 11215; Chair: Y. S. Chen; Pres: C. C. Chow.

Institute of Nuclear Energy Research (INER): POB 3, Lung Tan 32500; tel (39) 314-5384; telex 34154; Dir: Jen-chang Chou; f 1968; national nuclear research centre.

Taiwan Power Co: 242 Roosevelt Rd, Section 3, Taipei; tel (2) 396-7777; telex 11520; Chair: Fu Tzu-han; Pres: Chen Chen-hua.

Health and Welfare

HEALTH

Food and Drug Bureau: 161-2 Kunyang St, Taipei 115; tel (2) 785-8283; Dir: Hung Chi-pi.

WELFARE

National Youth Commission: 10 Tsingtao East Rd, Taipei; tel (2) 397-3493; fax (2) 322-2059; Chair (acting): Dr Chiahsing Chiang; Vice-Chair: Huang Kun-huei; f 1966; formulates and implements policies on devt of youth, including vocational training and employment services.

Legal and Judiciary

Administrative Court: 124 Chungking South Rd, Section 1, Taipei 100; tel (2) 311-0142; Pres: Wang Jui-lin; court of final resort in cases brought against Govt agencies.

Committee on the Discipline of Public Functionaries: 124 Chungking South Rd, Section 1, Taipei 100; tel (2) 361-2272; Chair: Fan Kuei-shu; sentences persons impeached by Control Yuan (see above).

Judicial Yuan: 124 Chungking South Rd, Section 1, Taipei 10036; tel (2) 371-3260; Pres: Lin Yang-kang; Vice-Pres: Wang Tao-yuan; f 1928; highest judicial organ; interprets constitution, national laws and ordinances.

Supreme Court: 124 Chungking South Rd, Section 1, Taipei 100; tel (2) 314-1160; Pres: Chu Chien-hung; court of final instance for civil and criminal cases.

Media

BROADCASTING

Broadcasting Corpn of China (BCC): 53 Jen Ai Rd, Section 3, Taipei 106; tel (2) 771-0150; telex 27498; Pres: P. P. Tang; Chair: Kuo Che; f 1928; domestic and external services in 15 languages and dialects.

China Television Co: 120 Chung-yang Rd, Nankang District, Taipei; tel (2) 783-8308; telex 25080; fax (2) 782-6007; Chair: Mah Soo-lay; Pres: Hu-ping Chung; f 1968.

China Television System: 100 Kuang Fu South Rd, Taipei; tel (2) 751-0321; telex 24195; Chair: Yee Chien-chiu; Pres: Wu Shih-sung; f 1971; cultural and educational broadcasts.

Taiwan Television Enterprise Ltd: 10 Pa-te Rd, Section 3, Taipei 10560; tel (2) 771-1515; telex 25714; fax (2) 741-3626; Pres: Walter C. H. Wang; f 1962.

NEWS AND INFORMATION

Central Weather Bureau: 64 Kungyuan Rd, Taipei; tel (2) 371-3181; Dir: Wu Tsung-yao.

Data Processing Centre: 190 Chung Hsiao East Rd, 5th Floor, Section 4, Taipei; tel (2) 721-0222; Dir: Hsü Lin-yun.

Tourism

Taiwan Visitors' Association: 111 Minchuan East Rd, 5th Floor, Taipei; tel (2) 594-3261; telex 20335; Chair: Richard C. C. Chao; f 1956; promotes domestic and international tourism.

Tourism Bureau, Ministry of Communications: 280 Chung Hsiao East Rd, 9th Floor, Section 4, Taipei; tel (2) 721-8541; telex 26408; fax (2) 773-5487; Dir-Gen: Hunter Fu; f 1966.

Transport and Communications

TELECOMMUNICATIONS

Directorate-General of Post: 55 Chin Shan South Rd, Section 2, Taipei 10603; tel (2) 392-1310; telex 12194; fax (2) 351-3310; Dir-Gen: Charles C. Y. Wang; f 1896; national post service.

Directorate-General of Telecommunications: 31 Aikuo East Rd, Taipei 10605; tel (2) 344-3601; telex 21733; fax (2) 397-2254; Dir-Gen: P. Y. Lee; Dep Dir-Gens: C. B. Shiue, Y. Chen; provision of all telecommunications facilities.

TRANSPORT

China Air Lines Ltd (CAL): 131 Nanking East Rd, Section 3, Taipei; tel (2) 715-2626; telex 11346; Chair: Yeuh Wu; Pres: Gen Chi Jung-chun; f 1959; domestic services and international services to USA, the Netherlands and Far East.

Civil Aeronautics Administration: Sungshan Airport, Taipei; tel (2) 712-1212; Dir-Gen: Wang Cheng-yun.

Taiwan Area National Freeway Bureau: POB 75, Sinchwang, Taipei; tel (2) 909-3201; Dir-Gen: C. Genih; f 1970.

Taiwan Highway Bureau: 70 Chung Hsiao West Rd, Section 1, Taipei; tel (2) 311-3456; fax (2) 381-0394; Dir-Gen: Chi-chang Yen; f 1946; highway engineering and motor vehicle admin.

Taiwan Motor Transport Co Ltd: 17 Hsu Chang St, 5th Floor, Taipei; tel (2) 371-5364; Chair: Hsu Jing-yuan; Gen Man: Shu Lung-tan; f 1980; operates national bus service.

Taiwan Railway Administration (TRA): 2 Yen Ping North Rd, Section 1, Taipei; tel (2) 551-1131; telex 21837; Man Dir: Chang Shou-tsen; f 1891; under the provincial govt of Taiwan.

COLOMBIA

Head of State

Executive power is vested in the President, elected by universal adult suffrage for a four-year term. The President appoints a Cabinet and the governors of Departments, Intendencies and Commissaries. A Primer Designado, elected by Congress, acts in the event of a presidential vacancy.

President: Dr Virgilio Barco Vargas (took office 7 August 1986).

Office of the President: Casa de Nariño, Carrera 8A, No 7-26, Bogotá; tel (1) 2843300; telex 44281.

Primer Designado: Dr Víctor Mosquera Chaux.

Legislature

Legislative power is vested in the bicameral Congress, comprising a Senate (112 members) and a House of Representatives (199 members). Members are elected by direct suffrage for a four-year term.

Senate: Capitolio Nacional, Calle 10, Carreras 7 y 8, Bogotá; tel (1) 2817311; Pres: Luis Guillermo Hurtado.

House of Representatives: Capitolio Nacional, Calle 10, Carreras 7 y 8, Bogotá; tel (1) 2817311; Pres: Norberto Morales Ballesteros.

MINISTRIES AND GOVERNMENT DEPARTMENTS

MINISTRY OF AGRICULTURE
Carrera 10A, No 20-30, Bogotá
Tel (1) 2419005; telex 44470
Minister: Gabriel Rosas Vega

MINISTRY OF COMMUNICATIONS
Edif Murillo Toro, Carreras 7A y 8A, Calles 12A y 13, Apdo Aéreo 14515, Bogotá
Tel (1) 2866911; telex 44284; fax (1) 2868668
Minister: Enrique Daníes Rincón

División de Telecomunicaciones: Edif Murillo Toro, Apdo Aéreo 14515, Bogotá; Dir: Minister of Communications, Enrique Daníes Rincón; broadcasting authority.

MINISTRY OF ECONOMIC DEVELOPMENT
Calle 26, No 13-19, 25, 34, 35, Bogotá
Tel (1) 2419030; telex 44508; fax (1) 2811103
Minister: (vacant)
Vice-Minister: Luis Carlos Valenzuela

MINISTRY OF EDUCATION
Centro Administrativo Nacional (CAN), Of 501, Avda Eldorado, Bogotá
Tel (1) 2220029; telex 42456; fax (1) 2220324
Minister: Manuel Francisco Becerra Barney

MINISTRY OF FINANCE AND PUBLIC CREDIT
Carrera 7A, No 6-45, Bogotá
Tel (1) 2863676; telex 44473; fax (1) 845396
Minister: Dr Luis Fernando Alarcón Mantilla

MINISTRY OF FOREIGN AFFAIRS
Palacio de San Carlos, Calle 10A, No 5-51, Bogotá
Tel (1) 2827811; telex 45209
Minister: (vacant)

MINISTRY OF GOVERNMENT (INTERIOR)
Palacio Echeverry, Carrera 8A, No 8-09, Bogotá
Tel (1) 2862324; telex 45406
Minister: Dr Carlos Lemos Simmonds

MINISTRY OF JUSTICE
Calle 26, No 27-48, Bogotá
Tel (1) 2839493
Minister: Roberto Salazar Manrique

MINISTRY OF LABOUR AND SOCIAL SECURITY
Avda 19, No 6-68, Bogotá
Tel (1) 2422007; telex 45445
Minister: María Teresa Forero de Saade

MINISTRY OF MINES AND ENERGY
Centro Administrativo Nacional (CAN), Avda Eldorado, Bogotá
Tel (1) 2222069; telex 45898
Minister: Margarita Mena de Quevedo

MINISTRY OF NATIONAL DEFENCE
Centro Administrativo Nacional (CAN), 2, Avda Eldorado, Bogotá
Tel (1) 2884184
Minister: Gen Oscar Botero Restrepo

MINISTRY OF PUBLIC HEALTH
Calle 16, No 7-39, Of 701, Bogotá
Tel (1) 2820002
Minister: Eduardo Díaz Uribe

MINISTRY OF PUBLIC WORKS AND TRANSPORTATION
Centro Administrativo Nacional (CAN), Of 409, Avda Eldorado, Bogotá
Tel (1) 2223782; telex 45656
Minister: Priscila Ceballos Ordóñez

GOVERNMENT AGENCIES AND ORGANIZATIONS

Advisory and Supervisory Bodies

Registraduria Nacional del Estado Civil: Centro Administrativo Nacional (CAN), Avda Eldorado No 46-20, Of 313, Bogotá; tel (1) 2212200; Registrar: Jaime Serrano Rueda; f 1948; civil register; organizes elections for Pres of the Republic, mayors, etc.

Superintendencia de Sociedades (SUPERSOCIEDADES): Avda El Dorado No 46-80, Apdo Aéreo 4188, Bogotá; tel (1) 2422050; fax (1) 2847659; Supt: Luis Fernando Alvarado Ortiz; oversees activities of local and foreign corpns.

Agriculture and the Environment

AGRICULTURE

Instituto Colombiano Agropecuario (ICA): Calle 37, No 8-43, 4-5, Apdo Aéreo 7984, Bogotá; tel (1) 2855520; telex 44586; Dir: Gabriel Montes Llamas; f 1962; promotes, co-ordinates and implements research into and teaching and devt of agriculture and animal husbandry.

Instituto Colombiano de la Reforma Agraria (INCORA): Avda El Dorado, Apdo Aéreo 151046, Bogotá; tel (1) 2220963; Dir: Carlos Ossa Escobar; f 1962; administers public lands; reclaims land by irrigation and drainage facilities to increase productivity in agriculture and stock-breeding; provides technical assistance and loans; supervises the redistribution of land throughout the country; attached to the Ministry of Agriculture.

THE ENVIRONMENT

Instituto Nacional de los Recursos Naturales Renovables y del Ambiente (INDERENA): Diagonal 34, No 5-18, Apdo Aéreo 13458, Bogotá; tel (1) 2854417; telex 44428; fax (1) 2859987; Dir: Germán García Durán; f 1968; official ecological institute of the Govt; under control of the Ministry of Agriculture; responsible for the protection, conservation and good use of natural renewable resources in Colombia.

Art and Culture

Instituto Colombiano de Cultura (COLCULTURA): Carrera 3A, No 18-24, 5 y 7, Bogotá; tel (1) 2820666; Dir: Dr Liliana Bonilla Otoya; attached to the Ministry of Education; institute of culture; in charge of national library and archives, museums, etc.

Business and Economy

BANKING

Banco de Bogotá: Calle 36, No 7-47, 15, Apdo Aéreo 3436, Bogotá; tel (1) 2881188; telex 44730; Pres: Dr Alejandro Figueroa Jaramillo; f 1870; 251 brs.

Banco Cafetero: Calle 28, No 13-53, Apdo Aéreo 240332, Bogotá; tel (1) 2846800; telex 43422; fax (1) 2835207; Pres: Jorge Humberto Botero Angulo; f 1953; commercial lending institution and devt bank for rural coffee regions; 294 brs.

Banco Central Hipotecario: Carrera 6A, No 15-32, Apdo Aéreo 3637, Bogotá; tel (1) 2813840; telex 45720; fax (1) 2832802;

Gen Man: Arturo Ferrer Carrasco; f 1932; credit for urban housing devt; 137 brs.

Banco de Colombia: Edif San Martín, Calle 30A, No 6-38, Apdo Aéreo 6836, Bogotá; tel (1) 2850300; telex 44744; Pres: Guillermo Villaveces Medina; f 1874; sale of 65% of assets to private sector authorized in 1989; 270 brs.

Banco del Comercio: Calle 13, No 8-52, Apdo Aéreo 4749, Bogotá; tel (1) 2826400; telex 44450; Pres: Hugo Guillermo Díaz Báez; f 1949; sale of 65% of assets to private sector authorized in 1989; 123 brs.

Banco del Estado: Carrera 10A, No 18-15, 9, Apdo Aéreo 11392, Bogotá; tel (1) 2338100; telex 44719; Pres: Dr Hernán Rincón Gómez; f 1884; sale of 65% of assets to private sector authorized in 1989; 61 brs.

Banco Ganadero: Carrera 9A, No 72-21, 11, Bogotá; tel (1) 2170100; telex 45448; Pres: Jesús Enrique Villamizar Angulo; f 1956; provides credit for cattle devt; sale of 65% of assets to private sector authorized in 1989; 123 brs.

Banco Popular: Calle 17, No 7-43, 7, Apdo Aéreo 6796, Bogotá; tel (1) 2815130; telex 45840; fax (1) 2819448; Pres: Florángela Gómez Ordóñez; f 1951; sale of 65% of assets to private sector authorized in 1989; 188 brs.

Banco de la República: Carrera 7, No 14-78, Apdo Aéreo 3531, Bogotá; tel (1) 2831111 telex 44560; Gov: Dr Francisco J. Ortega Acosta; f 1923; central bank of issue; administers financial funds that channel resources to priority sectors; 29 brs.

Caja Agraria: Carrera 8A, No 15-43, 13, Apdo Aéreo 3534, Bogotá; tel (1) 2844600; telex 44738; Gen Man: Carlos Villamil Chaux; f 1931; devt bank; 878 brs.

Junta Monetaria (Monetary Board): Carrera 7, 14-78, Bogotá; Pres: Minister of Finance and Public Credit, Dr Luis Fernando Alarcón Mantilla; oversees banking operations and monetary policy.

Superintendencia Bancaria: Carrera 7, No 4-49, 11, Apdo Aéreo 3460, Bogotá; tel (1) 2800187; telex 41443; fax (1) 800864; Banking Supt: Néstor Humberto Martínez Neira; banking supervisory authority; attached to the Ministry of Finance and Public Credit.

FINANCIAL AGENCIES

Contraloría General de la República: Calle 17, No 9-82, P4, Bogotá; tel (1) 2823549; Controller-Gen: Dr Rodolfo González García; treasury.

Corporación Financiera de Fomento Agropecuario y de Exportaciones, SA (COFIAGRO): Carrera 9, No 72-21, 2, Bogotá; tel (1) 2125711; Pres: Ernesto Burgos Ramírez; Vice-Pres: Mauricio Jaramillo Hoyos, Claudia Balcázar Salamanca; agriculture and export finance; attached to the Ministry of Agriculture.

Corporación Financiera del Transporte, SA (CFT): Calle 49, No 13-33, 8, Bogotá; tel (1) 2851100; telex 41248; fax (1) 2328536; Dir: Ramón Jesurun Franco; f 1964; financing and devt of all kinds of transport; under Ministry of Economic Development.

Financiera Eléctrica Nacional, SA (FEN): Calle 71A, No 6-30, Bogotá; tel (1) 2172100; Pres: Enrique Ruiz Raad; Vice-Pres: Jorge Jiménez, Alberto Rodríguez Hernández; energy financing; attached to the Ministry of Mines and Energy.

Fondo Nacional de Ahorro: Calle 18, No 7-59, Apdos Aéreos 3200 y 11998, Bogotá; tel (1) 2338511; Dir-Gen: Dr Oscar Paredes Zapata; national savings fund; attached to the Ministry of Economic Development.

Instituto de Crédito Territorial (ICT): Carrera 13, No 18-51, Apdo Aéreo 4037, Bogotá; tel (1) 2343560; telex 44826; Gen

Man: Alvaro Pinzón Angel; Sec-Gen: Hugo Puentes Restrepo.

Instituto de Fomento Industrial (IFI): Calle 16, No 6-66, 7-15, Apdo Aéreo 4222, Bogotá; tel (1) 2822055; telex 44642; fax (1) 2838553; Man: Luis Eduardo Robayo Salom; f 1940; finance corpn for the promotion of manufacturing activities.

Superintendencia de Control de Cambios: Carrera 7A, No 32-71, 19-23; Bogotá; tel (1) 2345655; attached to the Ministry of Finance and Public Credit.

INSURANCE

La Previsora, SA: Calle 57, No 8-95, Apdo Aéreo 52946, Bogotá; tel (1) 2176100; telex 41267; fax (1) 2118713; Pres: Rodolfo Jaramillo Ucros; Sec-Gen: Eunice Santos Acevedo; insurance co; attached to the Ministry of Finance and Public Credit.

MARKETING

Instituto de Mercadeo Agropecuario (IDEMA): Carrera 10, No 16-82, Apdo Aéreo 4534, Bogotá; tel (1) 2829911; telex 43315; fax (1) 2831838; Man: Helmut Bickenbach Plata; state enterprise for the marketing of agricultural products.

NATIONALIZED INDUSTRY

Alcalís de Colombia Limitada (ALCO LTDA): Calle 16, No 6-66, 5 y 6, Edif Avianca, Bogotá; tel (1) 2839355; telex 44566; fax (1) 2848197; Pres: Ciro Mendez Buenaventura; production of chemicals; attached to the Ministry of Economic Development.

Artesanías de Colombia, SA: Carrera 3A, No 18-60, Bogotá; tel (1) 2861766; Gen Man: María Cristina Palau de Angulo; handicrafts; attached to the Ministry of Economic Development.

Corporación de la Industria Aeronáutica Colombiana, SA (CIAC): Aeropuerto Internacional Eldorado, Entrada 1 y 2, Apdo Aéreo 14446, Bogotá; tel (1) 4138673; telex 45254; fax (1) 2685326; Man: Maj-Gen Horacio García Rodríguez; f 1956; aeronautics industry; under Ministry of National Defence.

Departamento Administrativo Nacional de Cooperativas (DANCOOP): Carrera 10, No 15-22, 1-7, Bogotá; tel (1) 2819811; telex 42590; Dir: Dr Barlahan Henao Hoyos; f 1981; oversees co-operative societies; plans co-operative devt projects; promotes co-operative economic and social integration.

Superintendencia de Industria y Comercio (SUPERINDUSTRIA): Carrera 13, No 27-00, 5, 7, 8 y 10, Bogotá; tel (1) 2342035; Man: Dr Diego Naranjo Meza; Supt: Fidelia Villamizar de Perez; supervisory authority for industry and commerce; attached to the Ministry of Economic Development.

TRADE

Corporación de Abastos de Bogotá, SA (CORABASTOS): Carrera 86, No 24A-19 Sur, Apdo Aéreo 13205, Bogotá; tel (1) 2644066; attached to the Ministry of Agriculture; supply co.

Corporación de Ferias y Exposiciones, SA: Carrera 40, No 22C-67, Apdo Aéreo 6843, Bogotá; tel (1) 2440141; telex 44553; Man: Oscar Pérez Gutiérrez; f 1954; holds the biannual Bogotá International Fair and the biannual International Agricultural Fair (AGROEXPO).

Dirección General de Aduanas: Carrera 7A, No 6-45, 6, Bogotá; tel (1) 2830468; fax (1) 2865789; Dir-Gen: José Joaquín Palacio Campuzano; Dep Dir-Gen: Jairo Roberto Corredor Rubio; f 1931; customs dept; attached to the Ministry of Finance and Public Credit.

Fondo de Promoción de Exportaciones (PROEXPO): Calle 28, No 13A-15, 35-42, Apdo Aéreo 240092, Bogotá; tel (1) 2690777; telex 44452; Dir: Federico Clarkson; f 1967; acts as consultant to export firms and provides financial aid for export operations to help diversify exports, strengthen the balance of payments and augment the volume of trade; undertakes market studies.

Instituto Colombiano de Comercio Exterior (INCOMEX): Calle 28, No 13A-15, Apdo Aéreo 240193, Bogotá; tel (1) 2833284; telex 44860; Dir: Arturo Saravia Better; sets and executes foreign trade policy.

Defence

Comando General Fuerzas Militares (Military Forces General Command): Centro Administrativo Nacional (CAN), Avda Eldorado, Carrera 52, Bogotá; tel (1) 2669300; Commdr: Gen Oscar Botero Restrepo; Inspector-Gen: Maj-Gen Eduardo Rocca Maichel; Chief of Staff: Maj-Gen Pedro Nel Molano Vanegas.

Comando Armada Nacional (Navy): Centro Administrativo Nacional (CAN), Avda Eldorado, Carrera 52, Bogotá; tel (1) 2669300; Commdr: Vice-Adm Manuel F. Avendaño Galvis.

Comando Ejercito (Army): Centro Administrativo Nacional (CAN), Avda Eldorado, Carrera 52, Bogotá; tel (1) 2669300; Commdr: Gen Nelson Mejia Henao.

Comando Fuerza Aérea Colombiana (Air Force): Centro Administrativo Nacional (CAN), Avda Eldorado, Carrera 52, Bogotá; tel (1) 2669300; Commdr: Maj-Gen Alfonso Amaya Maldonado.

Defensa Civil Colombiana: Calle 55, No 10-46, Bogotá; tel (1) 2122700; fax (1) 129592; Dir-Gen: Maj-Gen Fernando Gómez Barros; f 1967; disasters control and prevention; evacuation, air and aquatic rescue, etc.

Departamento Administrativo de Seguridad (DAS): Bogotá; Dir: Gen Miguel Alfredo Maza Márquez; intelligence agency.

Industria Militar (INDUMIL): Diagonal 40, No 47-75, Apdo Aéreo 7272, Bogotá; tel (1) 2223001; telex 45816; fax (1) 2224889; Man: Adm Tito García Motta; f 1954; attached to the Ministry of Defence; production, importation and supply of arms, munitions and explosives to the military forces and police and other state organizations.

Policia Nacional: Bogotá; tel (1) 2695320; Dir-Gen: Gen José Guillermo Medina Sánchez; Dep Dir-Gen: Maj-Gen Desiderio Vera Jaimes; Inspector-Gen: Brig-Gen Miguel Antonio Gómez Padilla.

Development and Planning

Departamento Nacional de Planeación: Calle 26, No 13-19, Mezanini 17, Bogotá; tel (1) 2822586; telex 45634; fax (1) 2813348; Dir: María Mercedes Cuellar de Martínez; oversees and administers devt projects; approves foreign investments.

Fondo Nacional de Proyectos de Desarrollo (FONADE): Calle 26, No 13-19, 18, 19 y 21, Apdo Aéreo 24110, Bogotá; tel (1) 2829400; telex 45634; fax (1) 2826018; Dir: Diana Cristina Molina Ramírez; f 1968; channels loans towards economic devt projects; works in close association with other official planning organizations; attached to the Departamento Nacional de Planeación.

Instituto Nacional de Fomento Municipal (INSFOPAL): Centro Administrativo Nacional (CAN), Apdo Aéreo 8638, Bogotá; tel (1) 2223177; telex 45328; Gen Man: Jaime Mario Salazar Velásquez.

REGIONAL DEVELOPMENT

Fundación para el Desarrollo Integral del Valle del Cauca (FDI): Calle 8, No 3-14, 17, Apdo Aéreo 7482, Cali; tel (3) 806660; telex 7482; Pres: Gunnar Lindahl Hellberg; Exec Pres: Fabio Rodríguez González; f 1969; industrial devt.

Education and Research

Fondo Colombiano de Investigaciones Científicas y Proyectos Especiales 'Francisco José de Caldas' (COLCIENCIAS): Transversal 9A, No 133-28, Apdo Aéreo 051580, Bogotá; tel (1) 2169800; telex 44305; fax (1) 2744460; scientific research.

Health and Welfare

Instituto Nacional de Salud (INS): Centro Administrativo Nacional (CAN), Apdo Aéreos 80080-80334, Avda Eldorado con Carrera 50, Bogotá; tel (1) 2220577; Dir: Oscar Juliao Ruiz; health institute; under the Ministry of Health.

Legal and Judiciary

Procuraduría General de la Nacion (Attorney-General's Office): Carrera 5a, No 15-80, 2-14, Bogotá; tel (1) 2838609; Attorney-Gen: Alfonso Gómez Méndez; Vice-Attorney-Gen: Omar Henry Velasco Ramírez.

Supreme Court of Justice: Carrera 7A, No 27-18, Edif Banco de Crédito, 15-23, Bogotá; tel (1) 2415009; Pres: (vacant); Vice-Pres: Dr Rodolfo Mantilla Jácome.

    Division of Civil Cassation: Carrera 7A, No 27-18, 22, Bogotá; Pres: Dr Alberto Ospina Botero.

    Division of Constitutional Procedure: Carrera 7A, No 27-18, 23, Bogotá; Pres: Dr Jairo Duque Pérez.

    Division of Criminal Cassation: Carrera 7A, No 27-18, 21, Bogotá; Pres: Dr Guillermo Duque Ruiz.

    Division of Labour Cassation: Carrera 7A, No 27-18, 20, Bogotá; tel (1) 2419024; Pres: Dr Jacobo Pérez Escobar.

Media

BROADCASTING

Federación Nacional de Radio (FEDERADIO): Bogotá; Dir: Libardo Taborda Bolívar; radio association.

Instituto Nacional de Radio y Televisión (INRAVISION): Centro Administrativo Nacional (CAN), Vía del Aeropuerto Eldorado, Bogotá; tel (1) 2414068; telex 43311; Dir: Felipe Zuleta Lleras; Sec-Gen: Juan Carlos Gómez Jaramillo; f 1954; TV and radio broadcasting network; educational and commercial broadcasting; attached to the Ministry of Communications.

RCN (Radio Cadena Nacional, SA): Calle 13, No 37-32, Bogotá; Gen Man: Ricardo Londoño Londoño; official radio network; runs 64 stations.

GOVERNMENT PUBLISHER

Imprenta Nacional de Colombia: Carrera 15 con Avda Primera, Bogotá; tel (1) 2463601; Dir: Evan Suárez Camacho.

NEWS AND INFORMATION

Departamento Administrativo Nacional de Estadística (DANE): Centro Administrativo Nacional (CAN), Avda Eldorado, Apdo Aéreo 80043, Bogotá; tel (1) 2213066; telex 44573; Dir: Alfonso González Caro; statistical office.

Mining and Energy

ENERGY

Empresa Colombiana de Petróleos (ECOPETROL): Carrera 13, No 36-24, Apdo Aéreo 5938, Bogotá; tel (1) 2856400; Pres: Dr Andrés Restrepo Londoño; Sec-Gen: Margarita Mena de Quevedo; f 1951; exploration, production and refining of petroleum.

    ECOPETROL Internacional: Bogotá; f 1988; exploration activities in Peru and other countries in the region.

    Instituto Colombiano de Petróleo: Dir: Dr Medardo Gamboa Maldonado; f 1985; research into all aspects of the hydrocarbon industry.

Instituto de Asuntos Nucleares: Avda Eldorado, Carrera 50, Apdo Aéreo 8595, Bogotá; tel (1) 2220071; telex 42416; fax (1) 2220173; Dir-Gen: Jaime J. Ahumada; Dep Dir: Manuel Montona; Sec-Gen: Carlos Manuel Mahecha; f 1959; researches into the peaceful use of atomic energy and nuclear energy applications; advises the Govt on international atomic energy matters.

Instituto Colombiano de Energía Eléctrica (ICEL): Carrera 13, No 27-00, 3, Apdo Aéreo 16243, Bogotá; tel (1) 2816200; telex 43319; fax (1) 2812890; Man: Diego Otero Prada; Sec-Gen: Germán Rueda Escobar; formulates policy for the devt of electrical energy; constructs systems for the devt, generation, transmission and distribution of electrical energy.

    Compañía de Electricidad y Gas Cundinamarca, SA (CELGAC): Carrera 10A, No 24-49, Apdo Aéreo 12012, Bogotá; tel (1) 2847956; Dir-Gen: Armando Cardenas Ramírez; attached to Instituto Colombiano de Energía Eléctrica; electricity and gas co.

MINING

Carbones de Colombia (CARBOCOL): Carrera 7A, No 31-10, 5, Apdo Aéreo 29740, Bogotá; tel (1) 2873100; telex 45779; fax (1) 2873278; Pres: Sergio Sokoloff Moreno; Sec-Gen: Bernardo Castro Durán; f 1976; state enterprise for the exploration, mining, processing and marketing of coal.

Colombiana de Minería (COLMINAS): Bogotá; Man: Alfonso Rodríguez Kilber; state mining concern.

Empresa Colombiana de Minas (ECOMINAS): Calle 32, No 13-07, Apdo Aéreo 17878, Bogotá; tel (1) 2877136; fax (1) 874606; Gen Man: Vicente Giordanelli Durán; Sec-Gen: Dr Jesús Nivia Quiroga; f 1968; promotes mining devt; administers state resources of emerald, copper, gold, sulphur, gypsum, phosphate rock and other minerals except coal, petroleum and uranium; internal and external trade of minerals.

Empresa Colombia de Níquel (ECONIQUEL): Carrera 7, No 26-20, Bogotá; tel (1) 2323839; telex 43262; Dir: Javier Restrepo Toro; administers state nickel resources.

Empresa Colombiana de Uranio (COLURANIO): Centro Administrativo Nacional (CAN), 4, Ministerio de Minas y Energía, Bogotá; tel (1) 2445440; telex 45898; Dir: Jaime García; f 1977; furthers the exploration, processing and marketing of radio-active minerals.

Instituto Nacional de Investigaciones Geológico Mineras (INGEOMINAS): Diagonal 53, No 34-53, Apdo Aéreo 4865,

Bogotá; tel (1) 2221811; telex 44909; fax (1) 2223597; Dir-Gen: Dr Luis Jaramillo Cortes; f 1968; mineral exploration, prospection and research; geological mapping; hydrogeology.

Sociedad Minera del Guainía (SMG): Bogotá; Pres: Dr Jorge Bendeck Olivella; f 1987; exploration, mining and marketing of gold.

Science and Technology

Instituto Colombiano de Hidrología, Meteorología y Adecuación de Tierras (HIMAT): Carrera 5A, No 15-80, 16-23, Bogotá; tel (1) 2860266; telex 44345; fax (1) 2842402; Dir-Gen: Enrique Sandoval-García; f 1976; under Ministry of Agriculture; hydrology, meteorology and land improvement.

> **Centro Meteorológico Nacional:** Aeropuerto Eldorado, Bogotá; tel (1) 2449365; telex 42539; national meteorological centre; part of HIMAT.

Telecommunications

Administración Postal Nacional (ADPOSTAL): Edif Murillo Toro, Oficinas 701 y 607, Carrera 8, Calles 12A y 13, Bogotá; tel (1) 2412510; telex 44302; fax (1) 2864153; Dir-Gen: Dr Vicente A. Alonso Sereno; f 1963; national postal admin; attached to the Ministry of Communications.

Empresa Nacional de Telecomunicaciones (TELECOM): Calle 23, No 13-49, Bogotá; tel (1) 2694077; telex 44288; fax (1) 2842171; Pres: Emilio Saravia Bravo; f 1947; national and international telecommunications services.

Tourism

Corporación Nacional de Turismo: Calle 28, No 13A-15, 16-18, Apdo Aéreo 8400, Bogotá; tel (1) 2839466; telex 41350; fax (1) 2843818; Gen Man: Fernando Anchique Vaca; attached to the Ministry of Economic Development.

Transport

Instituto Nacional del Transporte (INTRA): Edif Minobras (CAN), 6, Apdo Aéreo 24990, Bogotá; tel (1) 2224100; Dir: Dr Guillermo Anzola Lizarazu; Govt supervisory body; attached to the Ministry of Public Works and Transportation.

CIVIL AVIATION

Departamento Administrativo de Aeronáutica Civil (Aerocivil): Aeropuerto Internacional Eldorado, 4, Bogotá; tel (1) 2669200; telex 44620; fax (1) 2639645; Dir: Yesid Castaño González; f 1938; airports authority.

Servicio Aéreo a Territorios Nacionales (Satena): Aeropuerto Internacional Eldorado, Entrada No 1, Interior No 11, Bogotá; tel (1) 2811739; telex 42332; fax (1) 2862621; Gen Man: Maj-Gen Luis Angel Díz Díz; f 1968; commercial enterprise attached to the Ministry of National Defence; internal air services.

RAILWAYS

Ferrocarriles Nacionales de Colombia: Estación de la Sabana, Apdo Aéreo 29823, Bogotá; tel (1) 2775577; telex 45468; Pres: Dr Luis Fernando Jaramillo Correa; Man Dir: Sergio Hugo Amaya Córdoba; f 1954; national railway system.

ROADS

Fondo Vial Nacional: Bogotá; f 1966; administered by the Ministry of Public Works and Transportation; executes devt programmes in road transport.

SHIPPING

Dirección de Navegación y Puertos: Ministerio de Obras Públicas y Transporte, Centro Administrativo Nacional (CAN), Of 544, Bogotá; tel (1) 2221248; telex 45656; fax (1) 2215150; Dir: Alberto Rodríguez Rojas; f 1972; controls river works and transport.

Empresa Puertos de Colombia (COLPUERTOS): Carrera 10A, No 15-22, 10, Apdo Aéreo 13037, Bogotá; tel (1) 2343701; telex 44770; fax (1) 2811501; Man: Enrique Javier Pucheco Sánchez; f 1959; ports authority.

Servicio Naviero Armada Republica de Colombia (SENARC): Cerrera 25, No 47-36, Bogotá; tel (1) 2455004; Dir: Commdr Roberto Montoya Robledo; f 1984; river and maritime transport of passengers and cargo; under Ministry of National Defence.

THE COMOROS

Head of State

The President of the Republic is Head of State and Head of Government, and is elected for six years by direct suffrage. The President nominates ministers to form the Council of Government. The Governor of each island is nominated by the President for a five-year term.

President of the Republic (acting): Saïd Mohamed Djohar (took office 27 November 1989 following the assassination of President Abdallah; elected 12 March 1990).

Office of the President: BP 521, Moroni; tel 2413; telex 233.

Legislature

Legislative power is vested in the Federal Assembly, with 42 members directly elected for five years. Each island has a degree of autonomy under a Governor and Council. The elections to the Federal Assembly which were held on 22 March 1987 were the first since 1978 in which candidates were officially permitted to stand in opposition to the Union comorienne pour le progrès (Udzima).

Federal Assembly: BP 447, Moroni; tel 73-00-40; telex 233; Pres: Mohamed Taki Abdulkarim.

MINISTRIES AND GOVERNMENT DEPARTMENTS

OFFICE OF THE HEAD OF GOVERNMENT
BP 421, Moroni
Tel 2413; telex 233
Head of Government: Saïd Mohamed Djohar

MINISTRY OF DEFENCE
BP 246, Moroni
Tel 2646; telex 233
Minister: (vacant)

MINISTRY OF FINANCE AND ECONOMY
BP 324, Moroni
Tel 2767; telex 219
Minister: Saïd Ahmed Saïd Ali

MINISTRY OF FOREIGN AFFAIRS, FOREIGN TRADE AND CO-OPERATION
BP 428, Moroni
Tel 2306; telex 219
Minister: Saïd Kafe

MINISTRY OF THE INTERIOR, INFORMATION AND BROADCASTING
BP 520, Moroni
Minister: Omar Tamou
Secretary of State: Abdel Aziz Hamadi

MINISTRY OF JUSTICE
BP 520, Moroni
Tel 2411; telex 219
Minister: Dr Ben Ali Bacar

MINISTRY OF NATIONAL EDUCATION, CULTURE, YOUTH AND SPORTS
BP 446, Moroni
Tel 2420; telex 229
Minister: Salim Idarousse

MINISTRY OF PLANNING, CONSTRUCTION, ENVIRONMENT, URBAN DEVELOPMENT AND HOUSING
BP 12, Moroni
Tel 0000; telex 219
Minister: Mikidache Abdel-Rahim

MINISTRY OF POSTS AND TELECOMMUNICATIONS
Moroni
Secretary of State: Ahmed Ben Daoud

MINISTRY OF PRODUCTION, RURAL DEVELOPMENT, INDUSTRY AND CRAFTS
BP 41, Moroni
Tel 2292; telex 240
Minister: Mohammed Ali

MINISTRY OF PUBLIC ADMINISTRATION, EMPLOYMENT AND PROFESSIONAL TRAINING
BP 109, Moroni
Tel 2098; telex 219
Minister: Dr Ben Ali Bacar

MINISTRY OF PUBLIC HEALTH AND POPULATION
BP 42, Moroni
Tel 2277; telex 219
Minister: Ali Hassan Ali

MINISTRY OF TRANSPORT AND TOURISM
Moroni
Tel 2098; telex 244
Secretary of State: Athoumane Abdou

GOVERNMENT AGENCIES AND ORGANIZATIONS

Business and Economy

BANKING

Banque Centrale des Comores: BP 405, Moroni; tel 73-10-02; telex 213; Pres: Ahmed Dahalani; Dir-Gen: Mohamed Halifa; f 1981; bank of issue.

Banque de Développement des Comores: place de France, BP 298, Moroni; tel 73-08-18; telex 246; Pres: Daroueche Abdallah; Dir-Gen: Caabi Elyachroutu; f 1982; provides loans, guarantees and equity participation for small and medium-scale projects; Banque Centrale des Comores and Comoran Govt hold two-thirds of shares.

TRADE

Chambre de Commerce d'Industrie et d'Agriculture: BP 763, Moroni; chamber of commerce for industry and agriculture.

Office National de Commerce: Moroni; Chair: Saïd Mohamed Djohar; promotion and devt of domestic and external trade.

Defence

Armed Forces: BP 246, Moroni; tel 73-06-45; telex 233; Chief of Staff: Commdt Ahmed Mohamed.

Military Police and National Defence Constabulary: Moroni; tel 73-09-81; Commdr: Captain Abdourazak.

Fishing

Société de développement de la pêche artisanale des Comores (SODEPAC): Moroni; state-operated agency overseeing fisheries devt programme.

Legal and Judiciary

Cour Suprême (Supreme Court): BP 453, Moroni; tel 73-12-38; telex 233; Pres: Haribou Chebani; consists of two mems chosen by the President, two elected by the Federal Assembly, one by the Council of each island, and former Presidents.

Media

BROADCASTING

Radio-Comoros: BP 250, Moroni; tel 73-05-31; telex 241; Technical Dir: Kombo Soulaimana; Govt-controlled since 1975; services in Comoran, French and Arabic.

NEWS AND INFORMATION

Agence Comores Presse (ACP): Moroni.

Tourism

Société Comorienne de Tourisme et d'Hôtellerie (COMOTEL): Itsandra Hotel, Njazidja; tel 2365; national tourist agency.

Transport

Air Comores (Société Nationale des Transports Aériens): BP 544, Moroni; tel 2245; telex 218; Gen Man: Djamaleddine Ahmed; f 1975; services between all the islands.

Société Comorienne de Navigation: Moroni; services to Madagascar.

THE CONGO

Head of State

The Chair of the Central Committee of the Parti congolais du travail (PCT), the sole political party, is President of the Republic and Head of Government, and is elected for a five-year term by the Congress of the PCT. The President chairs a Council of Ministers chosen by the Prime Minister. The PCT effectively holds political power.

President: Col Denis Sassou-Nguesso (appointed President of the Provisional Committee of the PCT 8 February 1979; elected President of the Republic 31 March 1979; re-elected July 1984 and July 1989).

Office of the President: Palais du Peuple, quartier Plateau, Brazzaville; tel 81-07-37; telex 5210.

Legislature

Legislative power is vested in the Assemblée Nationale Populaire (National People's Assembly) comprising 153 members elected for five years by universal adult suffrage. The Assembly is responsible to the Prime Minister, who is responsible to the PCT.

Assemblée Nationale Populaire (National People's Assembly: Brazzaville; Pres: Bernard Combo-Matsiona.

MINISTRIES AND GOVERNMENT DEPARTMENTS

OFFICE OF THE PRIME MINISTER
Palais de la Primature, BP 2096, Brazzaville
Tel 81-11-24; telex 5210
Prime Minister: Alphonse Mouissou Poaty-Souchalaty

MINISTRY OF AGRICULTURE AND FARMING
Brazzaville
Minister: (vacant)

MINISTRY OF CULTURE AND ARTS
quartier Centre-Ville, (face à la Piscine), Brazzaville
Tel 81-08-02; telex 5210
Minister: Jean-Baptiste Tati-Loutard

MINISTRY OF DEFENCE AND SECURITY
quartier Général, Brazzaville
Tel 81-33-65; telex 5210
Minister: Col Denis Sassou-Nguesso

MINISTRY OF EDUCATION
BP 169, Brazzaville
Tel 83-24-60; telex 5210
Minister of Basic Education and Literacy:
Pierre-Damien Bassoukou-Boumba
Minister of Secondary and Higher Education and Scientific Research: Rodolphe Adada

MINISTRY OF EQUIPMENT AND ENVIRONMENT
ave Patrice Lumumba, quartier Plateau, Brazzaville
Tel 81-10-11; telex 5210
Minister: Lt-Col Florent Tsiba

MINISTRY OF FINANCE AND BUDGET
Centre Administratif, quartier Plateau, BP 2093, Brazzaville
Tel 83-06-20; telex 5210
Minister: Edouard Ngakosso

MINISTRY OF FOREIGN AFFAIRS AND CO-OPERATION
BP 2070, Brazzaville
Tel 83-20-28; telex 5210
Minister: Antoine Ndinga Oba
Secretary of State: Pascal Ngayama

MINISTRY OF FORESTRY
Palais de l'Economie Rurale, (face Maternité Blanche Gómez), Brazzaville
Tel 81-29-08
Minister of State: Raymond Damas Ngollo

MINISTRY OF HEALTH AND SOCIAL AFFAIRS
Palais du Peuple, quartier Plateau, Brazzaville
Tel 83-29-35; telex 5210
Minister: Ossebi Douaniam

MINISTRY OF INDUSTRY, TOURISM, FISHERIES AND CRAFTS
Palais du Peuple, quartier Plateau, Brazzaville
Tel 83-51-30; telex 5210
Minister: Hilaire Babassana

MINISTRY OF INFORMATION
BP 2241, Brazzaville
Tel 81-03-83; telex 5291
Minister: Paul Ngatse

MINISTRY OF JUSTICE AND ADMINISTRATIVE REFORMS
Centre Administratif, quartier Plateau, Brazzaville
Tel 81-28-33; telex 5210
Minister: Alphonse Nzoungou

MINISTRY OF LABOUR AND SOCIAL SECURITY
Centre Administratif, quartier Plateau, Brazzaville
Tel 81-28-33; telex 5210
Minister: Jeanne Dambenzet

MINISTRY OF MINES, ENERGY, POSTS AND TELECOMMUNICATIONS
Centre Administratif, quartier Plateau, BP 2120, Brazzaville
Tel 81-44-67; telex 5210
Minister: Aimé-Emmanuel Yoka

MINISTRY OF PHYSICAL CULTURE AND SPORTS
Brazzaville
Minister: Jean-Claude Ganga

MINISTRY OF PLANNING AND ECONOMY
BP 2031, Brazzaville
Tel 83-43-24; telex 5210
Minister of State: Pierre Moussa

MINISTRY OF RURAL DEVELOPMENT AND YOUTH
Palais de l'Economie Rurale, (face Maternité Blanche Gómez), BP 387, Brazzaville
Tel 81-18-13; telex 5210
Minister of State: Justin Lekoundzou Ithi-Ossetoumba

MINISTRY OF TERRITORIAL ADMINISTRATION AND LOCAL GOVERNMENT
Brazzaville
Minister: Celestin Ngoma-Foutou

MINISTRY OF TRADE AND SMALL AND MEDIUM ENTERPRISES
Brazzaville
Tel 83-18-27; telex 5210
Minister: Alphonse Boudenesa

MINISTRY OF TRANSPORT AND CIVIL AVIATION
quartier Plateau, (face au Palais du Peuple), BP 2148 and 2491, Brazzaville
Tel 81-43-34; telex 5210
Minister: François Bita

GOVERNMENT AGENCIES AND ORGANIZATIONS

Agriculture and Forestry

AGRICULTURE

Bureau pour le Développement de la Production Agricole (BDPA): BP 2222, Brazzaville; Govt regulatory body; promotes increase in levels of agricultural production.

Office des Cultures Vivrières (OCV): BP 894, Brazzaville; tel 82-11-03; Dir-Gen: Gilbert Pana; f 1979; production and marketing of agricultural produce except coffee and cacao; under the Ministry of Agriculture and Farming.

Régie Nationale des Palmeraies du Congo (RNPC): BP 8, Brazzaville; tel 83-08-25; Man Dir: René Makosso; f 1966; production of palm oil.

Société Nationale d'Elevage (SONEL): BP 81, Loutété, Massangui; Man Dir: Théophile Bikawa; f 1964; devt of semi-intensive stock-rearing; exploitation of by-products.

Sucrerie du Congo (SUCO): BP 71, Nkayi; tel 92-11-00; telex 8246; Dir: Henri Djombo; f 1978; sugar production.

FORESTRY

Office Congolais des Forêts: BP 839, Pointe-Noire; tel 94-02-79; forestry office; devt of forestry industries.

Société Congolaise Industrielle des Bois d'Ouesso: Ouesso; f 1981; 51% state-owned; extraction of forestry products.

Société Nationale d'Exploitation des Bois (SNEB): BP 1198, Pointe-Noire; tel 94-02-09; Pres: Rigobert Ngoulou; Man Dir: Robert Zinga Kanza; f 1970; production and processing of timber.

Unité d'Afforestation Industrielle du Congo (UAIC): BP 1120, Pointe-Noire; tel 94-04-17; telex 8308; Dir: Yves Laplace; f 1978; eucalyptus plantations providing wood-pulp for export.

Business and Economy

BANKING

Banque Commerciale Congolaise (BCC): ave Patrice Lumumba, BP 79, Brazzaville; tel 83-08-79; telex 5237; Chair: Ambroise Noumazalay; Gen Man: Clément Mouamba; f 1962; 57.8% state-owned; 12 brs.

Banque des Etats de l'Afrique Centrale (BEAC): BP 126, Brazzaville; tel 83-28-14; telex 5200; Headquarters in Yaoundé, Cameroon; Gov: Casimir Oyé Mba; Dir in the Congo: Gabriel Bokilo; f 1973; central bank of issue for mem states of the Customs and Economic Union of Central Africa (UDEAC), comprising Cameroon, the Central African Republic, Chad, the Congo, Equatorial Guinea and Gabon.

Banque Internationale du Congo (BIDC): ave Patrice Lumumba, BP 33, Brazzaville; tel 83-14-11; telex 5339; Pres: Minister of Finance and Budget, Edouard Ngakosso; Gen Man: Mathias Dzon; f 1983; 57% state-owned.

Banque Nationale de Développement du Congo (BNDC): ave Foch, BP 2085, Brazzaville; tel 83-30-13; telex 5312; Pres: Minister of Finance and Budget, Edouard Ngakosso; Man Dir: André Batanga; f 1961; 79% state-owned; financial and technical help for devt projects.

Union Congolaise de Banques SA (UCB): ave Amílcar Cabral, BP 147, Brazzaville; tel 83-10-66; telex 5206; Chair: Ossebi Douaniam; Man Dir: Mathieu Akango; f 1974; 51% state-owned; 12 brs.

FINANCIAL AGENCY

Caisse Congolaise d'Amortissement (CCA): 410 allée du Chaillu, BP 2090, Brazzaville; tel 83-32-41; telex 5294; Dir-Gen: Emile Mabonzo; Administrative and Financial Dir: Laurent Mann; f 1971; ensures servicing of the public debt; formulates Govt policy on public debt in accordance with economic and social devt and financial resources; manages state funds.

INSURANCE

Assurances et Réassurances du Congo (ARC): ave Amílcar Cabral, BP 977, Brazzaville; tel 83-01-71; telex 5236; Dir-Gen: Raymond Ibata; 50% state-owned; f 1973 to acquire the businesses of all insurance cos operating in the Congo.

MARKETING

Office du Café et du Cacao (OCC): BP 2488, Brazzaville; tel 83-19-03; telex 5273; Man Dir: Paul Yora; f 1978; marketing and export of coffee and cocoa.

Office Congolais des Bois (OCB): 2 ave Moe Vangoula, BP 1229, Pointe-Noire; tel 94-22-38; telex 8248; Man Dir: Alexandre Denguet-Attiki; f 1974; holds monopoly of purchase and marketing of all timber products.

Office National de Commercialisation des Produits Agricoles (ONCPA): BP 144, Brazzaville; tel 83-24-01; telex 5273; Dir: Jean-Paul Bockondas; f 1964; marketing of all agricultural products except sugar; promotion of rural co-operatives.

NATIONALIZED INDUSTRY

Minoterie, Aliments de Bétail, Boulangerie (MAB): BP 789, Pointe-Noire; tel 94-19-09; telex 8283; Man Dir: Denis Tempere; f 1978; monopoly importer of cereals; produces flour and animal feed.

Société Nationale de Construction (SONACO): BP 1126, Brazzaville; tel 83-06-54; Man Dir: Denis M'Bomo; f 1979; building works.

Société des Textiles du Congo (SOTEXCO): BP 3222, Brazzaville; tel 81-33-83; Man Dir: M. Kombo-Kitombo; f 1966; operates cotton-spinning mills, dyeing and weaving plants.

Société des Verreries du Congo (SOVERCO): BP 1241, Pointe-Noire; tel 94-19-19; telex 8288; Chair: A. E. Noumazalaye; Man Dir: Ngoyot Ibarra; f 1977; manufacture of glassware.

TRADE

Office National du Commerce (OFNACOM): BP 2305, Brazzaville; tel 83-43-99; telex 5309; Dir-Gen: Valentin Enoussa Ncongo; f 1964; imports and distributes general merchandise; monopoly of imports of salted and dried fish, cooking salt, rice, tomato purée, buckets, enamelled goods and blankets.

Office National d'Importation et de Vente de Viande en Gros (ONIVEG): BP 2130, Brazzaville; tel 82-30-33; telex 5240; Man Dir: Robert Paul Mangouta; f 1975; monopoly importer and distributor of wholesale meats.

Defence

Armed Forces: Brazzaville; telex 5210.

Air Force: Brazzaville; telex 5210.

National People's Army: Brazzaville; telex 5210; Chief of Gen Staff: Col Jean Marie Michel Mokoko.

Navy: Brazzaville; telex 5210.

Legal and Judiciary

Revolutionary Court of Justice: Brazzaville; Pres: (vacant); f 1969; has jurisdiction in cases involving the security of the

state; comprises nine judges, selected by the Central Committee of the PCT.

Supreme Court: Brazzaville; telex 5298; Pres: Charles Assemekang; acts as a Cour de Cassation.

Media

BROADCASTING

Radiodiffusion-Télévision Congolaise: BP 2241, Brazzaville; tel 83-16-76; telex 5299; Dir: Firmin Ayessa.

Télévision Nationale Congolaise: BP 2241, Brazzaville; tel 81-51-52; Dir: Valentin Mafouta; operates for 46 hours per week; programmes in French, Lingala and Kikongo.

La Voix de la Révolution Congolaise: BP 2241, Brazzaville; tel 83-03-83; Dir: Jean-Pascal Mongo-Slym; national radio broadcasting station; programmes in French, Lingala, Kikongo, Subia, English and Portuguese; foreign service in English and vernacular languages.

GOVERNMENT PUBLISHER

Imprimerie Nationale: BP 58, Brazzaville.

NEWS AND INFORMATION

Agence Congolaise d'Information (ACI): ave Patrice Lumumba, BP 2141, Brazzaville; tel 83-05-91; telex 5210; Dir: Augustin Matongo-Aveley; f 1961; news agency.

Centre National de la Statistique et des Etudes Enonomiques: Ministère du Plan, BP 2031, Brazzaville; tel 83-43-94; telex 5210; statistical office; part of the Ministry of Planning.

Mining and Energy

Société Mixte Bulgaro-Congolaise de Recherche et d'Exploitation des Phosphates (SOPHOSCO): Brazzaville; f 1976; 51% state-owned, 49% by Bulgaria; phosphate mining.

Société Nationale d'Energie (SNE): BP 95, Brazzaville; tel 81-38-58; telex 5261; Pres and Man Dir: Louis Issambo; f 1967; energy co.

Société Nationale de Recherches et d'Exploitation Pétrolières (HYDRO-CONGO): BP 2008, Brazzaville; tel 83-40-22; telex 5300; fax 83-12-38; Pres and Dir-Gen: Saturnin Okabe; f 1973; research into, production and refining of petroleum resources; distribution and marketing; production of lubricants.

Tourism

Direction Générale du Tourisme et des Loisirs: BP 456, Brazzaville; tel 83-09-53; telex 5210; fax 83-15-27; Dir-Gen: Jean Félix Taba-Goma; f 1963; formulates and implements Govt policies on the devt of tourism; participates in exhibitions and fairs; acts as travel agency; under Ministry of Tourism, Culture and Arts.

Transport

Agence Transcongolaise des Communications (ATC): BP 711, Pointe-Noire; tel 94-15-32; telex 8345; Man Dir: Minister of Transport and Civil Aviation, François Bita; f 1969; controls nationalization of transport; has three sections: Congo-Océan Railway, inland waterways and general transport facilities, and port control (see below).

CIVIL AVIATION

Agence Nationale de l'Aviation Civile (ANAC): BP 128, Brazzaville; tel 81-09-94; telex 5388; Gen Man: Gilbert M'Fouo-Otsially; f 1970; civil aviation authority.

Lina Congo (Lignes Nationales Aériennes Congolaises): ave Amílcar Cabral, BP 2203, Brazzaville; tel 83-30-66; telex 5243; Man Dir: Jean-Jacques Ontsa-Ontsa; f 1965; operates internal network and external services to Central African Republic and Gabon.

INLAND WATERWAYS

ATC—Direction des Voies Navigables, Ports et Transports Fluviaux: BP 2048, Brazzaville; tel 83-06-27; Dir: Médard Okoumou; waterways authority.

Société Congolaise de Transports (SOCOTRANS): BP 617, Pointe-Noire; tel 94-23-31; Man: Yves Criquet; f 1977.

RAILWAYS

ATC—Chemin de Fer Congo-Océan (CFCO): BP 651, Pointe-Noire; tel 94-11-84; telex 8231; Dir: Noël Bouanga; run by ATC.

ROADS

Régie Nationale des Transports et des Travaux Publics: BP 2073, Brazzaville; tel 83-35-58; Man Dir: Hector Bienvenu Ouamba; f 1965; civil engineering, upkeep of roads and public works.

SHIPPING

ATC—Direction du Port de Brazzaville: BP 2048, Brazzaville; tel 83-00-42; Dir: Jean-Paul Bockondas; port authority for Brazzaville inland port.

ATC—Direction du Port de Pointe-Noire: BP 711, Pointe-Noire; tel 94-00-52; telex 8318; Dir: Alphonse M'Bama; port authority for main port of the Congo.

La Congolaise de Transport Maritime (COTRAM): Brazzaville; f 1984; national shipping co.

Utilities

Société Nationale de Distribution d'Eau (SNDE): ave Sergent Malamine, BP 229 and 365, Brazzaville; tel 83-41-69; telex 5272; Chair and Man Dir: F. S. Sita; f 1967; water supply and sewerage; holds monopoly over wells and import of mineral water.

COSTA RICA

Head of State

Executive power is vested in the President, assisted by two Vice-Presidents and an appointed Cabinet. The President is elected by universal adult suffrage for a four-term, and must receive at least 40% of the votes cast.

President: Oscar Rafael Arias Sánchez (took office 8 May 1986).

President-Elect: Rafael Angel Calderón Fournier (elected 4 February 1990; due to take office 8 May 1990).

Office of the President: Casa Presidencial, Apdo 10.089, 1000 San José; tel 253211; telex 2106.

Vice-Presidents: Victoria Garrón de Doryan, Jorge Manuel Dengo Obregón.

Legislature

Legislative power is vested in a single chamber, the Asamblea Legislativa (Legislative Assembly), which is composed of 57 deputies, who are elected for four years. The Assembly may override the presidential vote by a two-thirds majority vote. The country is divided into seven Provinces, each administered by a Governor who is appointed by the President.

Asamblea Legislativa Nacional (National Legislative Assembly): Apdo 10.162, San José; Pres: Dra Rosemary Kasspinsky de Murillo.

MINISTRIES AND GOVERNMENT DEPARTMENTS

MINISTRY OF AGRICULTURE AND LIVESTOCK
Apdo 10.094, 1000 San José
Tel 329420; telex 3558
Minister: José María Figueres Olsen

MINISTRY OF CULTURE, YOUTH AND SPORT
Apdo 10.227, 1000 San José
Tel 227581
Minister: Carlos Francisco Echeverría Salgado

MINISTRY OF DEVELOPMENT
San José
Minister: Danilo Jiménez Veiga

MINISTRY OF ECONOMY AND TRADE
Apdo 10.216, 1000 San José
Tel 221016; telex 2414
Minister: Antonio Burgues

MINISTRY OF FINANCE
Apdo 5.016, San José
Tel 229122; telex 2277; fax 338267
Minister: Rodrigo Bolanos

MINISTRY OF FOREIGN AFFAIRS
Apdo 10.027, 1000 San José
Tel 237555; telex 2107
Minister: Rodrigo Madrigal Nieto

MINISTRY OF FOREIGN TRADE
La Llacuna 12, Avda Central, Calle 5, San José
Tel 225855; telex 2936
Minister: Luis Diego Escalante Vargas

MINISTRY OF HEALTH
Apdo 10.123, 1000 San José
Tel 230333
Minister: Dr Edgar Mohs Villalta

MINISTRY OF HOUSING AND HUMAN SETTLEMENT
Paseo Estudiantes, Apdo 222, 1002 San José
Tel 332579
Minister: Dr Fernando Zumbado Jiménez

MINISTRY OF INFORMATION
San José
Minister: Guido Fernández Saborío

MINISTRY OF THE INTERIOR AND POLICE
Apdo 10.006, 1000 San José
Tel 214406; telex 3434
Minister: Antonio Alvarez Desanti

MINISTRY OF JUSTICE
Apdo 5.685, 1000 San José
Tel 239739
Minister: Dr Luis Paulino Mora Mora

MINISTRY OF LABOUR AND SOCIAL WELFARE
Apdo 10.133, 1000 San José
Tel 210038
Minister: Edwin León Villalobos

MINISTRY OF NATIONAL PLANNING AND SOCIAL WELFARE
Avda 3 y 5, Calle 4, San José
Tel 219524; telex 2962; fax 31282
Minister: Jorge Monge Aguero

MINISTRY OF NATURAL RESOURCES, ENERGY AND MINES
Avda 8-10, Calle 25, Apdo 10.104, 1000 San José
Tel 334533; telex 2363; fax 570697
Minister: Dr Alvaro Umaña Quesada

MINISTRY OF THE PRESIDENCY
Apdo 520, 2010 Zapote, San José
Tel 246155; telex 2106
Minister: Rodrigo Arias Sánchez

MINISTRY OF PUBLIC EDUCATION
Apdo 10.087, 1000 San José
Tel 220229
Minister: Dr Francisco Antonio Pacheco

MINISTRY OF PUBLIC SECURITY
Apdo 4.768, 1000 San José
Tel 333208; telex 3308
Minister: Hernán Garrón Salazar

MINISTRY OF PUBLIC WORKS AND TRANSPORT
Apdo 10.176, San José
Tel 267311; telex 2478
Minister: Guillermo Constenla Umaña

MINISTRY OF SCIENCE AND TECHNOLOGY
Apdo 10.318, 1000 San José
Tel 244172; telex 3338
Minister: Dr Rodrigo Zeledón Araya

GOVERNMENT AGENCIES AND ORGANIZATIONS

Agriculture

Consejo Nacional de Producción: Calle 36 a 12, Apdo 2.205, San José; tel 236033; telex 2273; fax 339660; Pres: Javier Flores Galagarcía; Man: Horacio Zuñiga Chavarría; f 1948; encourages agricultural and fish production; regulates production and distribution of basic commodities.

Instituto del Café: Calle 1, Avdas 18 y 20, Apdo 37, San José; tel 332888; telex 2279; fax 222838; Pres: Guillermo Canet Brenes; Exec Dir: Mario Fernández Urpí; f 1948; devt of the coffee industry, controls production and regulates marketing.

Instituto de Desarrollo Agrícola (IDA): Apdo 5.054, 1000 San José; tel 246066; Exec Pres: Sergio Quirós Maroto.

Business and Economy

BANKING

Auditoria General de Entidades Financieras: Calle 2, Avdas 4 y 6, San José; tel 235020; telex 2314; Gen Man: Rafael Díaz A.; f 1950; auditing and supervisory body of the banking system.

Banco Anglo-Costarricense: Avda 2, Calles 1 y 3, Apdo 10.038, San José; tel 223322; telex 2132; fax 571845; Pres: Roy McCormick García; Gen Man: José Manuel Peraza; f 1863; responsible for servicing commerce; 10 brs.

Banco Central de Costa Rica: Apdo 10.058, San José; tel 334233; telex 2163; Exec Pres: Dr Eduardo Lizano Fait; Gen Man: Carlos Hernández R.; f 1950; bank of issue and banking supervisory authority.

Banco de Costa Rica: Avdas Central y Segunda, Calles 4 y 6, Apdo 10.035, 1000 San José; tel 551100; telex 2103; fax 553316; Pres: Mario Esquivel V.; Gen Man: (vacant); f 1877; responsible for industry; 55 brs.

Banco Crédito Agrícola de Cartago: Calle 5 y 2, Apdo 297, Cartago; tel 513011; telex 8006; Pres: Raúl Morales Vargas; Gen Man: Roberto Cossani Rivera; f 1918; responsible for housing; 5 brs.

Banco Nacional de Costa Rica: Calles 2 y 4, Avda 1A, Apdo 10.015, San José; tel 232221; telex 02120; fax 552436; Pres: Oscar Auilas; Gen Man: Edgar Avellón Acevedo; f 1914; responsible for the agricultural sector; 13 brs.

Banco Popular y de Desarrollo Comunal: Calle 1, Avda 2 y 4, Apdo 10.190, San José; tel 228122; telex 2844; fax 332350; Pres: Rodolfo Navas Alvarado; Gen Man: Alvaro Ureña Alvarez; f 1969.

INSURANCE

Instituto Nacional de Seguros: Calles 9 y 9B, Avda 7, Apdo 10.061, 1000 San José; tel 235800; telex 2290; fax 553381; Pres: Fernando Zumbado Berry; Gen Man: Gerardo Araúz Montero; f 1924; administers the state monopoly of insurance.

MARKETING

Cámara Nacional de Artesanía y Pequeña Industria de Costa Rica: Calle 11, Avda 1, Apdo 8-6.540, San José; tel 232763; fax 557873; Pres: Mireya Guevara; Exec Dir: Rafael Sáenz Sandí; f 1963; devt, marketing and export for small-scale industries and handicrafts.

Centro de Promoción de Exportaciones e Inversiones (CENPRO): Calle 7, Avda 1 y 3, Apdo 5.418, 1000 San José; tel 217166; telex 2385; fax 235722; Exec Dir: Carlos J. Torres A.; f 1968; encourages investment in export oriented activities and co-ordinates the export of non-traditional goods and services.

Development and Planning

Coalición de Iniciativas para Desarrollo (CINDE): Apdo 7.170, 1000 San José; tel 331711; telex 3514; fax 331946; Pres: Carlos Eduardo Robert Góngora; Man Dir: Federico Vargas P.; f 1983; promotion of foreign investment; provision of training to selected industrial sectors and promotion of the agricultural sector.

Instituto de Fomento y Asesoría Municipal (IFAM): Avda 1, Calle 1 y 3, Apdo 10.187, San José; tel 233714; telex 2871; Exec Pres: Jorge Urbina Ortega; Exec Dir: Harry Jager Contreras; f 1971; municipal devt agency.

Instituto Nacional de Fomento Cooperativo: Apdo 10.103, San José; tel 234355; fax 553835; Pres: Alvaro Chávez Gómez; Exec Dir: Rafael A. Rojas Jiménez; f 1973; promotes the establishment of co-operatives and provides technical assistance and credit facilities.

Instituto Nacional de Vivienda y Urbanismo: Apdo 2.534, San José; tel 215266; telex 2908; Exec Pres: Fernando Cañas Rowson; Dir: José Manuel Aguero; institute of housing and town planning.

Energy

Comisión de Energía Atómica de Costa Rica: Edif Galerias del Este, 3, Curridabat, Apdo 6.681, San José; tel 241591; Pres: Dr Enrique Góngora Trejos; Dir: Solón Contreras Garbanzo; f 1967; atomic energy commission.

Compañía Nacional de Fuerza y Luz SA: Avda 5, Calles Alfredo Volio y 1A, San José; state electricity co.

Instituto Costarricense de Electricidad (ICE): Apdo 10.032, 1000 San José; tel 207720; telex 2140; fax 201555; Exec Pres: Teófilo de la Torre; Gen Man: Rodrigo Suárez Mejido; state power and telecommunications agency.

Refinadora Costarricense de Petróleo (Recope): Apdo 4.351, San José; tel 239611; telex 2215; fax 552049; Dir: Roberto Dobles; f 1961; state petroleum organization.

Legal and Judiciary

La Corte Suprema: Apdo 01, 1000 San José; tel 230666; telex 1548; Pres of the Supreme Court: Miguel Blanco Quirós; 17 mems appointed by the Legislative Assembly for an eight-year term, and automatically re-elected for an equal period unless opposed by a two-thirds majority in the Legislative Assembly.

Media

BROADCASTING

Dirección Nacional de Comunicaciones: Ministerio de Gobernación y Policía, Apdo 8.000, San José; broadcasting control authority.

Control Nacional de Radio: Dirección Nacional de Comunicaciones, Ministerio de Gobernación y Policía, Apdo 8.000, 1000 San José; tel 257364; Dir Warren Murillo Martínez; f 1954; governmental supervisory dept for radio broadcasting.

Sistema Nacional de Radio y Televisión Cultural—RTVE de Costa Rica (SINART): Apdo 7-1.980, San José; tel 310839; telex 2374; Dir-Gen: Nelson Brenes López; f 1979; TV and radio programming.

NEWS AND INFORMATION

Dirección General de Estadística y Censos: Ministerio de Economía y Comercio, Avda 2 y Central, Calle 10, Apdo 10.216, San José; tel 221016; telex 2414; Dir: Marlene Sandoval H.; statistical office.

Tourism

Instituto Costarricense de Turismo: Edif Genaro Valverde, Calles 5 y 7, Avda 4A, Apdo 777, 1000 San José; tel 231733; telex 2281; fax 554997; Exec Pres: Manuel Gutiérrez; Dir Mario Quirós; f 1964.

Transport and Communications

TELECOMMUNICATIONS

Radiográfica Costarricense, SA: Avda 5, Calle 1, San José; state telecommunications co.

TRANSPORT

Cámara Nacional de Transportes: Calle 20, Avda 7, San José; tel 225394; national chamber of transport.

Instituto Costarricense de Ferrocarriles (INCOFER): Apdo 1, 1009 FE al P Estación, Zona 3, San José; tel 260011; telex 2393; Exec Pres: José F. Nicolás Alvarado; state railway co.

Instituto Costarricense de Puertos del Pacífico (INCOP): Calle 36, Avda 3, San José; tel 237111; telex 2793; Exec Pres: Edgar Guardiola Mendoza; state agency for the devt of Pacific ports.

Junta de Administración Portuaria y de Desarrollo Económico de la Vertiente Atlántica (JAPDEVA): Calle 17, Avda 7, Apdo 8-5.330, 1000 San José; tel 335301; telex 2435; Exec Pres: Jorge Arturo Castro Herrera; state agency for the devt of Atlantic ports.

Lineas Aéreas Costarricenses, SA (LACSA): Edif Lacsa, Apdo 1.531, La Uruca, San José; tel 323555; telex 2188; fax 324178; Chair and Chief Exec: Capt Otto Escalante W.; f 1946; state air co.

Utilities

Instituto Costarricense de Acueductos y Alcantarillados: Avda Fg Calle 5 y Avda 10/12, Calle 9, San José; tel 332155; telex 2724; fax 222259; Exec Pres: Eladio Prado; f 1961; water and sewerage authority.

CÔTE D'IVOIRE

Head of State

Executive power is vested in the President, who is elected for a five-year term by direct universal suffrage. The Council of Ministers is appointed by, and directly responsible to the President.

President: Dr Félix Houphouët-Boigny (took office November 1960; re-elected for sixth term of office in October 1985).

Office of the President: blvd Clozel, BP 1354, Abidjan; tel 32-02-22; telex 3754.

Legislature

Legislative power is vested in the unicameral Assemblée Nationale (National Assembly), which is directly elected (using two ballots if necessary) for five years. In 1985 the Assembly comprised 175 members. The ruling Parti démocratique de la Côte d'Ivoire is the only officially-recognized political party.

National Assembly: Palais de l'Assemblée, blvd de la République, BP 1381, Abidjan; tel 32-09-88; telex 2338; Pres: Henri Konan-Bédié.

MINISTRIES AND GOVERNMENT DEPARTMENTS

MINISTRY OF AGRICULTURE, WATER AND FORESTRY RESOURCES
BP V82, Abidjan
Tel 32-08-33; telex 23612
Minister: Vincent Pierre Lokrou

MINISTRY OF ANIMAL HUSBANDRY
01 BP 1249, Abidjan 01
Minister: Cristophe Gboho

MINISTRY OF THE CIVIL SERVICE
BP V93, Abidjan 01
Tel 21-04-00
Minister: Jean-Jacques Bechio

MINISTRY OF COMMUNICATIONS
BP V138, Abidjan
Telex 23501
Minister: Auguste Miremont

MINISTRY OF DEFENCE AND THE NAVY
BP V11, Abidjan
Tel 32-02-88; telex 22855
Minister: Jean Konan Banny

MINISTRY OF ECONOMY AND FINANCE
Immeuble SCIAM, ave Marchand, BP V163, Abidjan
Tel 21-05-66; telex 23747
Minister: Moïse Koumoué Koffi

MINISTRY OF FOREIGN AFFAIRS
BP V109, Abidjan
Tel 32-08-88; telex 23752
Minister: Siméon Aké

MINISTRY OF INDUSTRY AND PLANNING
BP V65, Abidjan
Tel 29-14-68; telex 22638
Minister: Oumar Diarra

MINISTRY OF THE INTERIOR
BP V241, Abidjan
Tel 32-08-88; telex 22296
Minister: Léon Konan Koffi

MINISTRY OF INTERNAL SECURITY AND DRUG CONTROL
BP V241, Abidjan
Tel 29-49-44; telex 23873
Minister: Gen Ioussouf Koné

MINISTRY OF JUSTICE
BP V107, Abidjan
Tel 32-08-99
Minister and Keeper of the Seals: Noël Némin

MINISTRY OF LABOUR
BP V119, Abidjan
Tel 32-06-88
Minister: Albert Vanié Bi Tra

MINISTRY OF MINING
BP V50, Abidjan
Tel 32-50-03; telex 22262; fax 32-53-20
Minister: Yed Esaïe Angoran

MINISTRY OF NATIONAL EDUCATION
BP V120, Abidjan
Tel 21-12-31; telex 23377
Minister, Primary Education: Odette Kouamé N'Guessan
Minister, Secondary and Higher Education:
Dr Balla Kéita
Minister, Scientific Research: Alhassane Salif N'Diaye

MINISTRY OF PUBLIC HEALTH AND POPULATION
BP V4, Abidjan
Tel 29-40-00; telex 42213
Minister: Alain Ekra

MINISTRY OF PUBLIC WORKS, TRANSPORT, CONSTRUCTION, TOWN PLANNING, POSTS AND TELECOMMUNICATIONS
ave Jean Paul II, BP V6, Abidjan 01
Tel 29-13-67; telex 22108
Minister, Public Works, Transport, Construction and Town Planning: Vammoussa Bamba
Minister, Posts and Telecommunications: Vincent Tieko Djédjé

MINISTRY OF TECHNICAL EDUCATION AND VOCATIONAL TRAINING
Cité Administrative, Tour D, Abidjan
Minister: Ange-François Barry-Battesti

MINISTRY OF TOURISM
BP V184, Abidjan
Tel 21-29-92; telex 23438
Minister: Jean-Claude Delafosse

MINISTRY OF TRADE
BP V142, Abidjan
Tel 32-38-16; telex 23704
Minister: Nicolas Kouandi Angba

MINISTRY OF WOMEN'S PROMOTION
Abidjan
Minister: Hortense Aka Anghui

MINISTRY OF YOUTH, SPORTS AND SOCIAL AFFAIRS
BP V124, Abidjan
Tel 32-16-99; telex 23480
Minister: Yaya Ouattara

OFFICE OF THE MINISTERS-DELEGATE AT THE PRESIDENCY
Abidjan
Ministers-Delegate: Paul-Guy Dibo, Guy-Alain Gauze
Ministers of State: Auguste Denise, Mathieu Ekra, Emile Kéï Boguinard

GOVERNMENT AGENCIES AND ORGANIZATIONS

Advisory and Supervisory Body

Conseil Economique et Social: 04 BP 301, Abidjan; tel 21-20-60; Pres: Philippe Grégoire Yacé; Vice-Pres: F. Konian Kodjo, B. Beda Yao, J. Chapman; reconstituted 1982; Govt body overseeing economic and social devt.

Agriculture and Forestry

AGRICULTURE

Compagnie Ivoirienne pour le Développement des Cultures Vivrières (CIDV): 01 BP 2049, Abidjan 01; tel 21-00-79; telex 23347; Man Dir: Benoît N'Dri Brou; f 1963 as Société pour le Développement de l'Exploitation du Palmier à Huile; production of palm oil.

Société Africaine de Plantations d'Hévéas (SAPH): 14 blvd Carde, 01 BP 1322, Abidjan 01; tel 32-18-91; telex 23696; Pres: Laurougnon Guède; Man Dir: Jean-Baptiste Amethier; f 1956; 60.4% state-owned; production of rubber on 24,000 ha of plantations.

Société des Caoutchoucs de Grand-Bereby (SCGB): 12 BP 478, Abidjan 12; tel 32-99-47; telex 23888; Chair and Man Dir: Jean-Baptiste Amethier; f 1979; 94.9% state-owned; production of rubber.

Société pour le Développement de la Motorisation de l'Agriculture (MOTORAGRI): Km 5, route d'Abobo, 01 BP 3745, Abidjan 01; tel 37-16-17; telex 23178; Chair: Minister of Agriculture and Rural Devt, Vincent Pierre Lokrou; Man Dir: Amadou Ouattara; f 1966; state organization for rationalizing machinery use for agricultural devt.

Société pour le Développement des Plantations de Canne à Sucre (SODESUCRE): 16 ave du Docteur Crozet, 01 BP 2164, Abidjan 01; tel 21-04-79; telex 23451; Chair and Man Dir: Joseph Kouamé Kra; f 1971; responsible for sugar plantations and refinery; transfer to private ownership announced in 1989.

Société pour le Développement des Productions Animales (SODEPRA): Ministry of Animal Husbandry, 01 BP 1249, Abidjan 01; tel 21-13-10; telex 22123; Chair: Charles Donwahi; Man Dir: Paul Lamizana; f 1970; responsible for livestock cultivation.

Société pour le Développement de la Production des Fruits et Légumes (SODEFEL): 11 ave Barthe, 01 BP 3032, Abidjan 01; tel 21-63-40; telex 22100; Chair: Felicien Konan Kodjo; Man Dir: Boa Boadou; f 1968; state organization for fruit and vegetable production and marketing.

Société d'Etudes et de Réalisation pour l'Industrie Caféière et Cacaoyère (SERIC): Ministry of Agriculture, 01 BP 4075, Abidjan 01; tel 35-15-22; Chair: P. René Amany; Man Dir: Benoît Kobena; f 1969; responsible for devt of coffee and cocoa industries.

FORESTRY

Société de Développement des Plantations Forestières (SODEFOR): Siège SIS, blvd François Mitterrand, 01 BP 3770, Abidjan 01; tel 44-36-02; telex 26156; Man Dir: Konan Soundele; f 1966; management of plantations, reafforestation and marketing of timber products.

Business and Economy

BANKING

Banque Centrale des Etats de l'Afrique de l'Ouest (BCEAO): ave Terrasson de Fougères, 01 BP 1769, Abidjan 01; tel 32-04-66; telex 3474; Gov: Alassane Ouattara; Dir in Côte d'Ivoire: Charles Konan Banny; f 1955; bank of issue and central bank for the seven states of the Union monétaire ouest africaine (UMOA), comprising Benin, Burkina Faso, Côte d'Ivoire, Mali, Niger, Senegal and Togo; 5 brs.

Banque Nationale pour le Développement Agricole (BNDA): 11 ave Joseph Anoma, 01 BP 2508, Abidjan 01; tel 32-07-57; telex 22298; Chair: Lamine Diabaté; Man Dir: Patrice Kouamé; f 1968; 61% state-owned; 32 brs.

Credit de la Côte d'Ivoire (CCI): 22 ave Joseph Anoma, 01 BP 1720, Abidjan 01; tel 32-03-57; telex 22106; Man (acting): Soungalo Traoré; f 1955; 58.4% state-owned; 5 brs.

FINANCIAL AGENCIES

Caisse de Stabilisation et de Soutien des Prix des Productions Agricoles (CSSPPA): BP V132, Abidjan; tel 32-08-33; telex 23712; Man Dir: René Amani; f 1964; controls price, quality and export of agricultural products.

NATIONALIZED INDUSTRY

Abidjan Industrie: Zone Industrielle de Vridi, Abidjan 01; tel 35-43-60; iron and steel co.

Chocolat de Côte d'Ivoire (Chocodi): Zone Industrielle de Vridi, rue des Pétroliers, Abidjan 01; chocolate co.

Compagnie Ivoirienne pour le Développement des Textiles (CIDT): route de Béoumi, BP 622, Bouaké; tel 63-30-13; telex 69121; fax 63-41-67; Chair: Tidiane Dem; Man Dir: Babacauh Koffi Dongo; f 1974; 70.8% state-owned; devt of cotton production and cotton ginning.

Palmindustrie: 01 BP V239, Abidjan 01; tel 36-93-88; telex 43100; Man Dir: Bernard Dossongui Koné; f 1969; devt of palm, coconut and copra products; transfer to private ownership announced in 1989.

Société Ivoirienne de Construction et de Gestion Immobilière (SICOGI): 01 BP 1856, Abidjan 01; tel 37-03-40; telex 24122; Dir: Koné Banga; f 1965; 65% state-owned; construction and property management.

Société Nationale Ivoirienne de Travaux (SONITRA): route d'Anyama, 01 BP 2609, Abidjan 01; tel 37-13-68; telex 24105; Chair: Fernand Konan Kouadio; Man Dir: Amos Salomon; f 1963; 55% state-owned; building and construction.

Société Nationale d'Opérations Pétrolières de la Côte d'Ivoire (PETROCI): BP V194, Abidjan 12; tel 21-85-58; telex 22135; Pres: Minister of Mining, Yed Esaïe Angoran; Man Dir: Paul Ahui; f 1975; responsible for all aspects of petroleum devt.

Defence

Forces Armées Nationales de la Côte d'Ivoire (FANCI): BP V1, Abidjan; tel 32-03-66; Chief of Staff: (vacant); armed forces.

Groupement Aérien de Transports et de Liaison (GATL): BP 10, Abidjan; tel 36-84-74; telex 727; Commdr: Col Abdoulaye Coulibaly; air force.

Marine Nationale: BP V67, Abidjan; tel 32-06-88; Commdr: Kone Fako; navy.

Legal and Judiciary

Supreme Court: rue Gourgas, BP V30, Abidjan; tel 32-22-45; Pres: (vacant); four chambers: constitutional, judicial, administrative and auditing.

Media

BROADCASTING

Radiodiffusion Ivoirienne: BP V191, Abidjan 01; tel 21-48-00; Dir: Mamadou Berté; f 1962; Govt radio station broadcasting in French, English and local languages.

Télévision Ivoirienne: 08 BP 883, Abidjan 08; tel 43-90-39; telex 22293; Man: Danièle Bonni-Claverie; f 1963; broadcasts in French for 50 hours a week; colour transmissions since 1973.

GOVERNMENT PUBLISHER

Imprimerie Nationale: BP V87, Abidjan; telex 23868.

NEWS AND INFORMATION

Agence Ivoirienne de Presse (AIP): 04 BP 312, Abidjan 04; telex 23781; Dir: Koné Semgué Samba; f 1961; state press agency.

Direction de la Statistique: Ministère de l'Economie et des Finances, 01 BP V55, Abidjan 01; tel 21-15-38; Govt statistical dept.

Mining and Energy

ENERGY

Energie Electrique de Côte d'Ivoire (Electrivoire): BP 1345, Abidjan 01; tel 32-02-33; telex 23738; Man Dir: Lambert Konassi Konan; 92% state-owned; production and distribution of water and electricity.

MINING

Société pour le Développement Minier de la Côte d'Ivoire (SODEMI): 31 blvd André Latrille, 01 BP 2186, Abidjan 01; tel 44-29-94; telex 26162; Pres: Haccandy Kouassi Kouakou; Man Dir: Joseph N'Zi; f 1962; geological and mineral research.

Tourism

Direction de la Promotion Touristique et de l'Artisanat d'Art: BP V184, Abidjan; tel 21-07-33; telex 23438; f 1970; Dir: Dogo Yao; tourist and cultural devt agency.

Transport and Communications

TELECOMMUNICATIONS

Office National des Télécommunications (ONT): 01 BP 1838, Abidjan 01; tel 32-49-85; telex 23758; fax 34-68-65; Dir: Léon Aka Bonny; f 1984; telecommunications office.

TRANSPORT

Air Ivoire: 13 ave Barthe, 01 BP 1027, Abidjan 01; tel 21-34-29; telex 23727; Man Dir: Col Abdoulaye Coulibaly; f 1960; Govt-owned since 1976; internal flights and flights to Mali, Guinea and Burkina Faso.

Port Autonome d'Abidjan: BP V85, Abidjan; tel 21-01-66; telex 22778; Man Dir: Jean-Michel Moulod; f 1950; public undertaking supervised by Ministry of Defence and the Navy.

Port Autonome de San Pedro: BP 339, San Pedro; tel 71-14-79; telex 99102; Man Dir (acting): Ougou Attemane; f 1971.

Société Ivoirienne de Transports Maritimes (SITRAM): ave Lamblin, 01 BP 1546, Abidjan 01; tel 36-92-00; telex 22132; Chair: B. Pegawgnaba; Dir: Commdt Fako Koné; f 1967, nationalized 1976; services between Europe and West Africa; return to private ownership announced in 1989.

Société Ivoirienne de Transports Publics: 01 BP 2949,

Abidjan 01; tel 35-33-68; telex 23685; Chair: Joseph Allou Bright; Dir: Basile Abre; f 1964; road transport.

Société des Transports Abidjanais (SOTRA): 01 BP 2009, Abidjan 01; tel 36-90-11; telex 43101; Chair: Maurice Bahi Zahiri; Dir-Gen: Jean-Baptiste Koffi; 1960; 60% state-owned; urban transport.

CUBA

MINISTRIES AND GOVERNMENT DEPARTMENTS

COUNCIL OF MINISTERS
Havana
President: Dr Fidel Castro Ruz
First Vice-President: Gen Raúl Castro Ruz
Vice-Presidents: Jaime Crombet, Lionel Soto
Secretary: Osmany Cienfuegos Gorriarán
Ministers for Government: José A. Naranjo Morales, Joaquín Benavides

CENTRAL PLANNING BOARD
20 de Mayo y Ayestarán, Plaza de la Revolución, Havana
Tel (7) 79-6115; telex 511158
Minister, President: José López Moreno

COMMISSION FOR THE ECONOMIC MANAGEMENT SYSTEM
Avda 23, No 21425 entre 214 y 222, La Coronela, Havana
Tel (7) 22-0256
President: Joaquín Benavides

MINISTRY OF AGRICULTURE
Avda Independencia, entre Conill y Sta Ana, Havana
Tel (7) 70-1434; telex 511966
Minister: Carlos Pérez León

MINISTRY OF BASIC INDUSTRIES
Avda Salvador Allende, No 666, Havana
Tel (7) 70-7711; telex 511183
Minister: Marcos Portal León

MINISTRY OF COMMUNICATIONS
Plaza de la Revolución 'José Martí', Havana
Tel (7) 70-5581; telex 511657
Minister: Manuel Castillo Rabasa

MINISTRY OF CONSTRUCTION
Avda Carlos M. de Céspedes y Calle 35, Havana
Tel (7) 70-9411; telex 511275
Minister: Homero Crabb Valdés

MINISTRY OF THE CONSTRUCTION MATERIALS INDUSTRY
Calle 0 esq 17, Vedado, Havana
Tel (7) 32-2541; telex 511517
Minister: José Cañete Alvarez

MINISTRY OF CULTURE
Calle 2, No 258, entre 11 y 13, Vedado, Havana
Tel (7) 3-9945; telex 511400
Minister: Dr Armando Hart Dávalos

MINISTRY OF EDUCATION
Obispo No 160, Havana
Tel (7) 31-1302; telex 511188
Minister: José Ramón Fernández Alvarez

MINISTRY OF THE FISHING INDUSTRY
Barlovento, Santa Fe, Havana
Tel (7) 22-7474; telex 511444
Minister: Capt Jorge A. Fernández-Cuervo Vinent

MINISTRY OF THE FOOD INDUSTRY
Calle 41, No 4455, Playa, Havana
Tel (7) 2-6801; telex 511163
Minister: Alejandro Roca Iglesias

MINISTRY OF FOREIGN AFFAIRS
Calzada No 360, Vedado, Havana
Tel (7) 32-3279; telex 511122
Minister: Isidoro Malmierca Peoli
Deputy Ministers: José Viera Linares, Ricardo Alarcón

MINISTRY OF FOREIGN TRADE
Infanta No 16, Vedado, Havana
Tel (7) 70-9341; telex 511174
Minister: Ricardo Cabrisas Ruiz
Deputy Minister: Alberto Betancourt Roa

MINISTRY OF HIGHER EDUCATION
Calle 23, No 565 esq a F, Vedado, Havana
Tel (7) 3-6655; telex 511253
Minister: Fernando Vecino Alegret

MINISTRY OF THE INTERIOR
Plaza de la Revolución, Havana
Minister: Gen Abelardo Colomé Ibarra

MINISTRY OF INTERNAL TRADE
Calle Habana, No 258, Havana
Tel (7) 6-6984; telex 511171
Minister: Manuel Vila Sosa

MINISTRY OF THE IRON AND STEEL AND METALLURGICAL INDUSTRIES
Avda Rancho Boyeros y Calle 100, Havana
Tel (7) 20-4861; telex 511179
Minister: Marcos Lage Coello

MINISTRY OF JUSTICE
Calle 0, No 216 e/23 y Humboldt, Vedado, Havana
Tel (7) 32-6319; telex 511331
Minister: Dr Juan Escalona Reguera

MINISTRY OF LIGHT INDUSTRY
Empedrado No 302, Havana
Tel (7) 31-1280; telex 511141
Minister: Antonio Esquivel Yedra

MINISTRY OF PUBLIC HEALTH
Calle 23, No 201, Vedado, Havana
Tel (7) 32-2561; telex 511149
Minister: Julio Tejas Pérez

MINISTRY OF THE REVOLUTIONARY ARMED FORCES
Plaza de la Revolución, Havana
Minister: Gen Raúl Castro Ruz

MINISTRY OF THE SUGAR INDUSTRY
Calle 23, No 171, Vedado, Havana
Tel (7) 30-6051; telex 511664
Minister: Juan Herrera Machado

MINISTRY OF TRANSPORT
Avda Rancho Boyeros y Tulipán, Havana
Tel (7) 70-7751; telex 511181
Minister: Gen Senén Casas Regueiro

OFFICE OF THE PRESIDENT OF THE ACADEMY OF SCIENCES
Havana
President: Rosa Elena Simeón

STATE COMMITTEE FOR ECONOMIC CO-OPERATION
Calle 1a, No 201, Vedado, Havana
Tel (7) 3-6661; telex 511297
Minister: Ernesto Meléndez Bach

STATE COMMITTEE FOR FINANCE
Obispo esq Cuba, Havana
Tel (7) 62-5770; telex 511101
Minister: Rodrigo García León

STATE COMMITTEE FOR LABOUR AND SOCIAL SECURITY
Calle 23, esq Calle P, Vedado, Havana
Tel (7) 70-4571; telex 511225
Minister: Francisco Linares Calvo

STATE COMMITTEE FOR PRICES
Amistad No 552, Havana
Tel (7) 61-2878
Minister: Arturo Guzmán Pascual

STATE COMMITTEE FOR STANDARDIZATION
Egido No 610 entre Gloria y Apodaca, Havana
Tel (7) 31-1602; telex 511422
Minister: Ramón Darias Rodés

STATE COMMITTEE FOR STATISTICS
Calle 5ta y Paseo, Vedado, Havana
Tel (7) 31-5171; telex 511257
Minister: Fidel Vascos González

STATE COMMITTEE FOR TECHNICAL AND MATERIAL SUPPLIES
Monserrate No 261, Havana
Tel (7) 6-8281; telex 511757
Minister: Sonia Rodríguez Cardona

GOVERNMENT AGENCIES AND ORGANIZATIONS

Agriculture

Instituto Nacional de la Reforma Agraria: Havana; institute of agrarian reform; supervises and aids small-scale agricultural producers; superintends Govt technical aid programmes.

Art and Culture

Fondo Cubano de Bienes Culturales: Muralla 107, esq San Ignacio, Plaza Vieja, La Habana Vieja, Havana; tel (7) 9-5796; telex 993968; fax (7) 512278; Dir-Gen: Nisia Aguero Benitez; f 1979; promotion and commercialization of Cuban plastic arts and crafts; promotion of culture.

Business and Economy

BANKING

Banco Nacional de Cuba (National Bank of Cuba): Cuba 402, esq a Lamparilla, Apdo 736, Havana 1; tel (7) 62-5361; telex 511822; Pres: Héctor Rodríguez Llompart; First Vice-Pres: Osvaldo Fuentes Torres (Domestic), Luis Gutiérrez (International); f 1950; central bank and bank of issue; arranges short- and long-term credits, finances investments and operations with other countries, and acts as the clearing and payments centre; the Pres is a member of the Council of Ministers; 162 brs.

Banco Popular del Ahorro: Calle 16, No 306, entre 5a y 3a Avda, Playa, Havana; tel (7) 22-8240; telex 511608; Pres: Oscar E. Alcalde; f 1983; savings bank; 474 brs.

Banco Financiero Internacional, SA: Calle Línea, No 1,

Vedado, Havana; tel (7) 32-5972; telex 512405; fax (7) 32-5981; Chair: Emilio Bencomo Zurdos; Gen Man: Arnaldo Alayón; f 1984; promotes Cuban exports and banking relations.

INSURANCE

Agencia Internacional de Inspección y Ajuste de Avínas y Servicios Conexos (INTERMAR, SA): Obispo, No 361 entre Habana y Compostela, Havana; Dir-Sec: Horacio Lunán Williams; f 1988; controls the inspection of goods, ship and aircraft breakage.

Empresa del Seguro Estatal Nacional (ESEN): Obispo No 257, 3, Apdo 109, 10100 Havana; tel (7) 62-2963; telex 511185; Dir-Gen: Pedro M. Roche Alvarez; f 1978; state insurance organization.

Seguros Internacionales de Cuba (ESICUBA): Cuba No 314, entre Obispo y Obrapía, Apdo 79, Havana; tel (7) 61-8906; telex 511616; fax (7) 60-4423; Chair and Chief Exec: Salvador Orozco Jhones; f 1963; state insurance organization.

TRADE

Alimport (Empresa Cubana Importadora de Alimentos): Infanta 16, 3, Apdo 7006, Havana; tel (7) 70-2437; telex 511454; Man Dir: Badith Saker Saker; controls import of foodstuffs and liquors.

Autoimport (Empresa Central de Abastecimiento y Venta de Equipos de Transporte Ligero): Galiano 213, entre Concordia y Virtudes, Havana; tel (7) 99-1967; telex 511417; Man Dir: Lorenzo Ortega; imports cars, light vehicles, motor cycles and spare parts.

Aviaimport (Empresa Cubana Importadora y Exportadora de Aviación): Calle 182, No 126 entre 1a y 5a, Reparto Flores, Miramar, Havana; tel (7) 21-8656; telex 511135; Man Dir: Marcos Lagos Martínez; imports aircraft and components.

Cámara de Comercio de la República de Cuba: Calle 21, No 661-701, esq A, Vedado, Apdo 4237, Havana 4; tel (7) 30-3356; telex 511752; Pres: Dr Julio García Oliveras; Vice-Pres: Carlos Lugo Rodríguez; Sec-Gen: Dr Carlos Montalván Mora; f 1963; promotes foreign trade; mems include all Cuban foreign trade enterprises and the most important agricultural and industrial enterprises; responsible for the participation of Cuban enterprises in trade fairs and exhibitions abroad.

Construimport (Empresa Central de Abastecimiento y Venta de Equipos de Construcción y sus Piezas): Carretera de Varona, Km 1.5, Capdevila, Havana; tel (7) 44-7284; telex 511213; Man Dir: Jesús Serrano Rodríguez; controls the import and export of construction machinery and equipment.

Copextel (Corporación Productora y Exportadora de Tecnología Electrónica): Calle 194 y 7a, Siboney, Havana; tel (7) 29-2737; telex 512459; Man Dir: Tirso Luis Joanicot; exports LTEL personal computers and micro-computer software.

Cubacontrol: Havana; trade supervisory agency; oversees and checks import and export of goods via Cuban ports and airports.

Cubaelectrónica (Empresa Importadora y Exportadora de Productos de la Electrónica): Calle 22, No 510 entre 5 y 7, Miramar, Havana; tel (7) 2-6526; telex 512484; Pres: Luis Blanca Fernández; f 1986; import and export of electronic equipment and devices and communications equipment.

Cubaequipos (Empresa Cubana Importadora de Productos Mecánicos y Equipos Varios): Calle 23, No 55, 6, Vedado, Apdo 6052, Havana; tel (7) 79-2212; telex 511371; Man Dir: Porfirio Mederos Paiva; imports machinery for the petroleum, chemical, mining and glass industries; industrial machinery.

Cubaexport (Empresa Cubana Exportadora de Alimentos y Productos Varios): Calle 23, No 55, Vedado, Apdo 6647; Havana; tel (7) 79-1669; telex 511178; Man Dir: Vidal M. Prieto; export of foodstuffs.

Cubafrutas (Empresa Cubana Exportadora de Frutas Tropicales): Calle 23, No 55, Vedado, Apdo 6683, Havana; tel (7) 79-5653; telex 511849; fax (7) 79-5653; Man Dir: Jorge Amaro; controls export of fruits, vegetables and canned foodstuffs.

Cubaindustria (Empresa Cubana Exportadora de Productos Industriales): Calle 15, No 410, entre F y G, Vedado, Havana; tel (7) 32-5522; telex 511677; fax (7) 32-2390; Man Dir: Jorge Reyes González; f 1979; controls export of industrial and agricultural products.

Cubametales (Empresa Cubana Importadora de Metales, Combustibles y Lubricantes): Infanta 16, 4, Vedado, Apdo 6917, Havana; tel (7) 70-4225; telex 511452; Dir: Juan Luis Lozano Birel; controls import of metals, both ferrous and non-ferrous, crude oil and oil products; exports oil products and ferrous and non-ferrous scrap.

Cubaniquel (Empresa Cubana Exportadora de Minerales y Metales): Calle 23, No 55, Vedado, Apdo 6128, Havana; tel (7) 7-8460; telex 511178; Man Dir: Walter S. Leo Tamaján; sole exporter of minerals and metals.

Cubatabaco (Empresa Cubana del Tabaco): Calle O'Reilly No 104, Apdo 6557, Havana; tel (7) 32-1964; telex 511760; fax (7) 92-653; Pres and Man Dir: Francisco Padrón Pérez; f 1962; state monopoly; controls export of leaf tobacco, cigars and cigarettes.

Cubatécnica (Empresa de Contratación de Asistencia Técnica): Avda 1a, No 4, entre 0 y 2, Hotel Sierra Maestra, Miramar, Havana; tel (7) 22-2574; telex 511360; Man Dir: Ramón Soto Recio; controls export and import of technical assistance.

Cubatex (Empresa Cubana Importadora de Fibras, Tejidos, Cueros y sus Productos): Calle 23, No 55, Vedado, Apdo 7115, Havana; tel (7) 70-3269; telex 512361; Dir: Reiner Martín González; controls import of fibres, textiles, hides and by-products and export of fabric and clothing.

Cubazucar (Empresa Cubana Exportadora de Azúcar y sus Derivados): Calle 23, No 55, Vedado, Apdo 6647, Havana; tel (7) 70-3526; telex 511157; fax (7) 37-94303; Asst Dir: Jorge Brioso Domínguez; f 1962; controls export of sugar, molasses and alcohol.

Ecimetal (Empresa Comercial para la Industria Metalurgica y Metal-Mecanica): Calle 1, esq B, Vedado, Havana; tel (7) 30-5581; telex 511555; fax (7) 30-1394; Dir: Raúl Rodríguez Rodríguez; f 1977; import of turn-key or complete plants; technology transfer; technical assistance services; machinery and equipment for erection or modification of plants for the ferrous and non-ferrous metals, metal-mechanical and mining industries.

Emexcon (Empresa Exportadora de la Construcción): Calle 25, No 2606, Miramar, Havana; tel (7) 2-4093; telex 511693; Pres: Eliodoro Pérez; f 1978; consulting engineer services, contracting, import and export of building materials and equipment.

Empresa Cubana de Acuñaciones: Calle 18, No 306, entre 3 y 5, Miramar, Havana; tel (7) 29-6693; telex 511939; fax (7) 22-7771; Man Dir: Guillermo Triana Aguiar; f 1977; controls export of coins, base and precious metals.

Energoimport (Empresa Importadora de Objetivos Electro-energéticos): Calle 7a, No 2602, entre 26 y 28, Miramar, Havana; tel (7) 2-8156; telex 511812; Dir: Lázaro Hernández González; f 1977; controls import of equipment for electricity generation.

Eprob (Empresa de Proyectos para las Industrias de la Básica): Calle 184, No 129, entre Avda 1 y 5, Avda Reparto Flores, Miramar, Apdo 12100, Havana; tel (7) 21-8074; telex 511404; fax (7) 30-1394; Dir-Gen: Antonio Ronda Heredia; f 1967; exports consulting services and processing of engineering construction projects, supplies of complete industrial plants and turn-key projects; feasibility studies and technical assistance for pulp and paper, glass, rubber and tyres, mining and fertilizer industries and ports and port facilities.

Fecuimport (Empresa Cubana Importadora y Exportadora de Ferrocarriles): Avda 7a, No 6209, entre 62 y 66, Miramar, Havana; tel (7) 2-3764; telex 512419; Man Dir: Antonio Conejo Mesa; import and export of railway equipment.

Ferrimport (Empresa Cubana Importadora de Artículos de Ferretería): Calle 23, No 55, 2, Vedado, Apdo 6258, Havana; tel (7) 70-2531; telex 511144; Man Dir: Miguel Sosa Serra; f 1966; import of hardware.

Imexpal (Empresa Importadora y Exportadora de Plantas Alimentarias, sus Completamientos y Derivados): Calle 22, No 313, entre 3a y 5a, Miramar, Apdo 4139, Havana; tel (7) 29-1671; telex 511404; Man Dir: Concepción Bueno Campos; controls import and export of food processing plants and related items.

Maprinter (Empresa Cubana Importadora y Exportadora de Materias Primas y Productos Intermedios): Infanta 16, Vedado, Apdo 2110, Havana; tel (7) 7-4981; telex 511453; Man Dir: Carlos Dantín Acosta; controls import and export of raw materials and intermediate products.

Maquimport (Empresa Cubana Importadora de Maquinarias y Equipos): Calle 23, No 55, Vedado, Apdo 6052, Havana; tel (7) 70-2546; telex 511371; Man Dir: Armando Vera Gil; controls import of machinery and equipment.

Marpesca (Empresa Cubana Importadora y Exportadora de Buques Mercantes y de Pesca): Conill No 580, esq Avda 26, Nuevo Vedado, Havana; tel (7) 30-1971; telex 511687; Man Dir: Reynaldo Luis Cabrera; import and export of ships and port and fishing equipment.

Medicuba (Empresa Cubana Importadora y Exportadora de Productos Médicos): Máximo Gómez 1, esq a Egido, Apdo 6772, Havana; tel (7) 61-1747; telex 511658; Man Dir: Orlando Romero; export and import of medical and pharmaceutical products.

Quimimport (Empresa Cubana Importadora de Productos Químicos): Calle 23, No 55, Vedado, Apdo 6088, Havana; tel (7) 70-8066; telex 511283; Man Dir: Leslie Edward Patterson; controls import of chemical products.

Tecnoimport (Empresa Cubana Importadora y Exportadora de Productos Técnicos): Infanta 16, Apdo 7024, Havana; tel (7) 22-3861; telex 511572; Man Dir: Manuel García Robés; imports technical products.

Tractoimport (Empresa Central de Abastecimiento y Venta de Maquinaria Agrícola y sus Piezas): Avda Rancho Boyeros y Calle 100, Apdo 7007, Havana; tel (7) 20-5154; telex 511162; Man Dir: Manuel Castro del Aguila; f 1960; imports tractors and agricultural equipment; exports pumps and agricultural implements.

Transimport (Empresa Central de Abastecimiento y Venta de Equipos de Transporte Pesados y sus Piezas): Calle 102 y Avda 63, Marianao, Apdo 6665, Havana; tel (7) 20-0325; telex 511150; Man Dir: Jesús Dennes Rivero; f 1962; controls import and export of vehicles and transportation equipment.

Energy

Comisión de Energía Atómica Cuba (CEAC): Apdo 6795, Havana 6; Pres: José R. Fernández; Exec Sec: Fidel Castro Díaz-Balart; f 1980; concerned with the peaceful uses of atomic energy.

Instituto Cubano del Petróleo: Calle 23, No 105, Vedado, Havana; tel (7) 70-6581; petroleum institute; formulates and implements policy towards exploration, production, refining, distribution, etc of petroleum; operates refineries for imported oil.

Empresa Consolidada del Petróleo: Havana; commercial section of Instituto Cubano del Petróleo.

Instituto de Investigaciones Nucleares: Havana; Dir: Raimundo Franco Parellada.

Legal and Judiciary

Office of the Attorney-General: Havana; Attorney-Gen: Dr Ramón de la Cruz Ochoa.

People's Supreme Court: Havana; Pres: Dr José Raúl Amaro Salup; comprises the Plenum, the five courts of Justice in joint session and the Council of Government.

Civil and Administrative Court: Havana; Pres: Andrés Bolaños Gasso; comprises two professional and 12 lay judges.

Court for State Security: Havana; Pres: Dr Everildo Domínguez Domínguez; comprises three professional and 12 lay judges.

Criminal Court: Havana; Pres: Dr Graciela Prieto Martín; comprises eight professional and 12 lay judges.

Labour Court: Havana; Pres: (vacant); comprises three professional and 12 lay judges.

Military Court: Havana; Pres: Col Juan Marino Fuentes Calzado; comprises three professional and 12 lay judges.

Media

BROADCASTING

Empresa Cubana de Radio y Televisión (INTERTV): Calle K, No 352, esq 19, Vedado, Havana; tel (7) 32-1746; telex 511600; Dir: Enrique Soto Rodríguez; radio and TV company.

Instituto Cubano de Radio y Televisión: Televisión Nacional, Calle 23, No 258 entre L y M, Vedado, Havana 4; tel (7) 32-7511; telex 511613; Pres: Ismael González González; Vice-Pres: Gary González Benítez; f 1962.

GOVERNMENT PUBLISHERS

Instituto Cubano del Libro: Palacio del Segundo Cabo, Calle O'Reilly, No 4, esq a Tacón, Havana; tel (7) 6-8341; Pres: Pablo Pacheco López; state printing and publishing house; attached to the Ministry of Culture.

Oficina de Publicaciones: Calle 17 No 552, esq a D, Vedado, Havana; tel (7) 32-1883; Dir: Pedro Alvarez Tabío; attached to the Council of State; publishes speeches and other texts of state and party leaders.

NEWS AND INFORMATION

Agencia de Información Nacional (AIN): Calle 23, No 358 esq a J, Vedado, Havana; tel (7) 32-1269; Dir: Roberto Pavón Tamayo; national news agency.

Prensa Latina (Agencia Informativa Latinoamericana, SA): Calle 23, No 201 esq a N, Vedado, Havana; tel (7) 32-5561; telex 511132; Dir: Pedro Margolles Villanueva; f 1959; news agency.

Tourism

Empresa de Turismo Internacional (Cubatur): Calle 23, No 156, entre N y O, Vedado, Apdo 6560, Havana; tel (7) 32-5088; telex 511143; Dir: Roberto Echevarría García.

Empresa de Turismo Nacional (Viajes Cuba): Calle 20, No 352, entre 21 y 23, Vedado, Havana; tel (7) 30-0587; telex 511366; Dir: Eleuterio Guerra Gómez; f 1981.

Instituto Nacional de Turismo (INTUR): Avda de Malecón y G, Vedado, Apdo 4239, Havana 4; tel (7) 32-0571; telex 511238; Pres: Rafael Sed Pérez; Vice-Pres: Enrique Rodríguez, Orosmán Quintero; f 1959.

Transport

CIVIL AVIATION

Empresa Consolidada Cubana de Aviación (Cubana): Calle 23, No 64, La Rampa, Vedado, Apdo 4249, Havana; tel (7) 7-4961; telex 512273; fax (7) 70-3690; Dir: Ruperto Alvarez Gámez; f 1929; internal and external services.

RAILWAYS

Ferrocarriles de Cuba: Ministerio del Transporte, Avda Rancho Boyeros y Tulipán, Havana; tel (7) 70-7751; f 1960; operates public rail services; under direct management of the Minister of Transport.

SHIPPING

Empresa Consignataria Mambisa: Lamparilla No 2, 2, Apdo 1785, Havana; tel (7) 6-8311; telex 511197; fax (7) 61-0445; Man Dir: Julio Aira Prado; shipping agents, ship-chandlers, bunker suppliers.

Empresa Cubana de Fletes (Cuflet): Calle Oficios No 170, entre Teniente Rey y Amargura, Apdo 6755, Havana; tel (7) 6-4731; telex 512181; Man Dir: Isaac Camacho Aguilera; freight agents for Cuban cargo.

Empresa de Navegación Caribe (Navecaribe): Lamparilla 2, 4, Apdo 1784, Havana; tel (7) 62-3605; telex 511262; Dir: Otto Roca Moralobos; f 1965; operates Cuban coastal fleet.

Empresa de Navegación Mambisa: San Ignacio No 104, Apdo 543, Havana; tel (7) 61-7901; telex 51578; Gen Man: Gumersindo González Feliú; operates dry cargo, reefer and bulk carrier vessels.

Flota Cubana de Pesca: Ensenada de Pote y Atarés, Havana; tel (7) 99-3030; telex 2208; Dir: Emigdio Báez Vigo; f 1962; fishing fleet; transportation of frozen food.

CYPRUS

Republic of Cyprus

Head of State

The 1960 Constitution remains in force, although certain provisions have been altered since the withdrawal of the Turkish members from Government in 1963. Executive power is vested in the President, who is elected by direct universal suffrage for a five-year term. The President appoints and directs the Council of Ministers.

President: Georghios Vassiliou (took office 28 February 1988).

Office of the President: Nicosia; tel (2) 447767.

Legislature

Legislative power is vested in the House of Representatives, comprising 56 members. The representatives are elected by direct universal suffrage for a five-year term.

House of Representatives: Nicosia; tel (2) 403451; telex 5500; fax (2) 366611; Pres: Dr Vassos Lyssarides; Dir-Gen: C. Hadjioannou.

MINISTRIES AND GOVERNMENT DEPARTMENTS

MINISTRY OF AGRICULTURE AND NATURAL RESOURCES
Loukis Akritas Ave, Nicosia
Tel (2) 402171; telex 4660; fax (2) 445156
Minister: Andreas Gavrielides

Department of Fisheries: Aeolou 13, Nicosia; tel (2) 303279; telex 4660; Dir: Andreas Demetropoulos; f 1964; devt and management of fisheries.

Department of Forestry: Loukis Akritas Ave, Nicosia; (2) 302261; Dir: (vacant); f 1879; formulation and implementation of forest policy.

Department of Water Development: Demosthenis Severis Ave, Nicosia; telex 5533; fax (2) 445019.

MINISTRY OF COMMERCE AND INDUSTRY
6 Andreas Araouzous St, Nicosia
Tel (2) 403441; telex 2283; fax (2) 366120
Minister: Takis Nemitsas

Department of the Official Receiver and Registrar: 9 Lord Byron Ave, Nicosia; tel (2) 402133.

MINISTRY OF COMMUNICATIONS AND WORKS
Demosthenis Severis Ave, Nicosia
Tel (2) 402161; telex 3678; fax (2) 465462
Minister: Nakos Protopapas

MINISTRY OF DEFENCE
4A Emmanuel Roides, Ay Omoloyitae Ave, Nicosia
Tel (2) 403595; telex 3553; fax (2) 366225
Minister: Andreas Aloneftis

MINISTRY OF EDUCATION
Gregoris Afxentiou St, Nicosia
Tel (2) 303331; telex 5760; fax (2) 445021
Minister: Andreas Philippou

MINISTRY OF FINANCE
Demosthenis Severis Ave, Nicosia
Tel (2) 303291; telex 3399; fax (2) 366080
Minister: Georghios Syrimis

Department of Customs and Excise: 29 Katsoni St, Ay Omoloyitae Ave, Nicosia; tel (2) 302321; telex 3399; fax (2) 366080; Dir: Thanos Michael; f 1879.

Department of Data Processing Services: Nicosia; tel (2) 302375; telex 3399; fax (2) 366080; Dir: George I. Christoforou; f 1980; responsible for the introduction of computers and information technology into the public service.

Department of Statistics and Research: 13 Lord Byron Ave, Nicosia 162; tel (2) 303286; telex 3399; fax (2) 366080; Dir: Dr E. I. Demetriades; f 1950; responsible for all Govt statistical work.

Department of Stores: St Hilarion St, Kaimakli, POB 2028, Nicosia; tel (2) 403124; telex 4363; Dir: P. Stavrou; f 1950; purchase, store and supply of materials used by all Govt depts.

Inland Revenue Department: Andrea Zakos St, Charalambides Bldg, Engomi, Nicosia; tel (2) 303158; Dir: Andreas Gregoriev.

Public Administration and Personnel Service: Demosthenis Severis Ave, Nicosia; tel (2) 302207; telex 3399; fax (2) 366080; Dir: Andreas X. Koufteros; responsible for organization and management of the civil service.

MINISTRY OF FOREIGN AFFAIRS
Demosthenis Severis Ave, 18-19 Government House, Nicosia
Tel (2) 402307; telex 2366; fax (2) 451881
Minister: Georghios Iakovou

MINISTRY OF HEALTH
11 Byron St, Nicosia
Tel (2) 302009; telex 5734
Minister: Panikos Papageorghiou

Department of Medical and Public Health Services: Medical Headquarters, Nicosia; tel (2) 303178; f 1960; planning, organizing, budgeting and admin in the health sector.

MINISTRY OF THE INTERIOR
Demosthenis Severis Ave, Nicosia
Tel (2) 402423; fax (2) 453465
Minister: Christodoulos Veniamin

Department of Town Planning and Housing: Demosthenis

Severis Ave, Nicosia; tel (2) 402363; Dir: Constantinos P. Ioannides; f 1952; housing management and planning.

Cyprus Fire Service: POB 2011, Nicosia; tel (2) 303412; Chief Fire Officer: D. A. Anastassiades; Asst Chief Fire Officer: S. Poyiadjis; f 1953.

Registration Service: Lord Byron Ave, Nicosia; tel (2) 302115; Dir: Christodoulos Nicolaides; f 1960; registration of inhabitants and civil marriages.

MINISTRY OF JUSTICE
1 Diogenes St, Engomi, Nicosia
Tel (2) 402355; telex 6116; fax (2) 461427
Minister: Christodoulos Chrysanthou

MINISTRY OF LABOUR AND SOCIAL INSURANCE
Lord Byron Ave, Nicosia
Tel (2) 403481; telex 6011; fax (2) 450993
Minister: Takis Christofides

GOVERNMENT AGENCIES AND ORGANIZATIONS

Advisory and Supervisory Bodies

Audit Office: Ex-Secretariat Compound, Nicosia; tel (2) 303127; telex 3399; fax (2) 366080; Auditor Gen: Th. A. Theophilou; Dep Auditor Gen: S. Christou; f 1960; audits and inspects all Govt accounts and the accounts of public corpns and local authorities.

Price Control and Consumers' Protection Service: 64 Araouzos St, Nicosia; tel (2) 403441; telex 2283; fax (2) 366120; Dir: G. Mytides; f 1982; controls prices of basic consumer products; protection of basic consumer rights; implementation of standards.

Public Records Office: Ministry of Justice, Nicosia; tel (2) 403577; telex 6116; fax (2) 461427; Keeper of Public Records: Effy Parparinou; f 1978; maintains public service.

Agriculture

Agricultural Research Institute: Athalassa, Nicosia; tel (2) 303431; telex 4660; fax (2) 445156; Dir: Dr C. S. Serghiou; f 1962; research into field crops, horticulture, soils and water use, plant protection, animal production and agricultural economics.

The Cyprus Carrot and Beetroot Marketing Board: POB 2029, Nicosia; tel (2) 443106; telex 2276; fax (2) 365493; Gen Man: Andreas Savvides; f 1966; sole exporters of carrots and beetroot.

The Cyprus Potato Marketing Board: POB 2029, Nicosia; tel (2) 443107; telex 2276; fax (2) 365493; Gen Man: Andreas Savvides: f 1964; sole exporter of potatoes.

Art and Culture

ART

Department of Antiquities: POB 2024, Nicosia; tel (2) 302191; Dirs: A. Papageorghiou, M. Loulloupis, D. Christou; f 1935; excavations in archaeological sites, restoration and preservation of ancient monuments, provision of information on Cypriot archaeology.

Museum of Struggle: Archbishopric Sq, Nicosia; tel (2) 402465.

State Collection of Contemporary Art: 1 Menandros St, Nicosia; tel (2) 402028.

CULTURE

MAM (House of the Cyprus and Cypriological Publications): Phaneromeni Library Bldg, 46 Phaneromeni St, Nicosia; tel (2) 464698; Dir: Thelma M. Michaelidou; display and promotion of Cypriological publs.

Business and Economy

BANKING

Central Bank of Cyprus: POB 5529, 36 Metochiou St, Nicosia; tel (2) 445281; telex 2424; fax (2) 472012; Gov: A. C. Afxentiou; Sen Mans: E. Ioannou, A. Philippou, H. G. Akhniotis; f 1963; bank of issue, regulation of supply of money and credit, manages international reserves, supervises banks, administers exchange control legislation.

Co-operative Central Bank Ltd: POB 4537, Gregoris Afxentiou St, Nicosia; tel (2) 442921; telex 2313; fax (2) 443088; Chair: B. Baltayian; Gen Man: D. Pitsillides; f 1937; banking and credit facilities to member societies; 5 brs.

The Cyprus Development Bank Ltd: POB 1415, 50 Archbishop Makarios III Ave, Alpha House, Nicosia; tel (2) 457575; telex 2797; fax (2) 464322; Chair: Renos Solomides; Gen Man: John G. Joannides; f 1963; provides medium- and long-term loans for production projects, particularly in manufacturing and processing industries, tourism and agriculture; technical, managerial and administrative assistance and advice; 1 br.

Housing Finance Corpn: POB 3898, 41 Themistoklis Dervis St, Hawaii Tower, Nicosia; tel (2) 452777; telex 4134; Chair: A. Mouskos; Gen Man: A. Papageorgiou; f 1982; provides long-term loans for home buying; provision of building plots; 6 brs.

INSURANCE

Office of the Superintendent of Insurance: Ministry of Finance, Nicosia; tel (2) 403256; telex 2366; f 1969; controls insurance cos, agents and brokers.

NATIONALIZED INDUSTRY

Cyprus Petroleum Refinery Ltd: POB 275, Larnaca; tel (41) 53221; telex 2267; Gen Man: Yiannis Leontis.

TRADE

Cyprus International (State) Fair: POB 3551, Makedonitissa, Nicosia; tel (2) 352918; telex 3344; fax (2) 352316; Gen Man: Stavros Christou; f 1969.

Department of Registrar of Companies, Trade Marks and Patents and Official Receiver: 9 Byron Ave, Nicosia; tel (2) 302133; telex 2866; Dir: Maria A. Kyriacou; f 1945; registers cos, trade marks, patents, copyright and insolvency.

Defence

Cyprus National Guard: Nicosia; tel (2) 402513; Commdr: Lt Gen (retd) Panayioutis Markopoulos.

Cyprus Police Force: Police Headquarters, Nicosia; tel (2) 495888; fax (2) 314198; Chief of Police: Frixos Yiangou; Dep Chief of Police: Andreas Economou; f 1878.

Development and Planning

Cyprus Productivity Centre: Kallipoleos Ave, POB 536, Nicosia; tel (2) 447992; Dir: H. Constantinou; f 1963; assists private and public cos in utilizing human and capital resources with a view to increasing productivity.

Planning Bureau: Apelli St, Nicosia; tel (2) 303282; f 1961; planning and co-ordination of economic and social devt, budget preparation and implementation, technical assistance and multilateral and bilateral economic relations.

Education and Research

EDUCATION

Educational Service Commission: 35 Homer Ave, Nicosia; tel (2) 402322; Chair: Stelios Katsellis.

RESEARCH

Geological Survey Department: Gregoris Afxentiou St (Opp GSP Stadium), Nicosia; tel (2) 302338; telex 4660; Dir: Dr G. Constantinou; f 1952; geological, hydrogeological, mineralogical, geophysical investigations and technical assistance to Govt depts and other bodies.

Employment

Industrial Training Authority of Cyprus: POB 5431, 39 Themostoklis Dervis St, Nicosia; tel (2) 455700; telex 5102; fax (2) 463963; Dir: Lia Mylona; f 1974; assessment of the economy's manpower needs, promotion and provision of industrial training to the island's manpower.

Public Service Commission: Gregoris Afxentiou St (Opp GSP Stadium), Nicosia; tel (2) 302351; Chair: T. Phanos; Mems: L. Xenopoulos, N. Papaxenophontos, C. Hadjiprodromou, C. Christodoulides; f 1960; control of employment within the civil service.

Legal and Judiciary

Attorney-General of the Republic of Cyprus: Apellis St, Ay Omoloyitae Ave, Nicosia; tel (2) 302242; telex 6144; fax (2) 445080; Attorney-Gen: Michalakis Triantafyllides; Dep Attorney-Gen: Loukis Loukaides; f 1960.

Military Court: 19 Parthenon St, Nicosia; tel (2) 402624; Chair: V. Aristodemou.

Office of the Revision and Consolidation of the Cyprus Legislation: 10 P. Nirvanas St, Ay Omoloyitae Ave, Nicosia; tel (2) 402471; Law Commr: G. Stavrinakis.

Prison Department: POB 2014, Nicosia; tel (2) 402525; Dir: I. Iacovides; f 1890.

Rent Control Court: Nicosia; tel (2) 403514; Pres: Andreas Agrotis; f 1983; adjusts rents in all towns which are controlled areas.

Supreme Court: Char Mouskos St, Nicosia; tel (2) 402398; Pres: A. N. Loizou; f 1964; final appellate court; final adjudicator in matters of constitutional and administrative law.

> **Supreme Council of Judicature:** Nicosia; composed of Pres and judges of Supreme Court; responsible for appointment, promotion, etc., of judges exercising civil and criminal jurisdiction in the District Courts and the Assize Courts.

Media

BROADCASTING

Cyprus Broadcasting Corpn (CyBC): POB 4824, Broadcasting House, Nicosia; tel (2) 422231; telex 2333; fax (2) 314050; Chair: Chrysses Demetriades; Dir-Gen: D. Kyprianou; f 1959; state radio and TV co, broadcasting in Greek, Turkish, English, Arabic and Armenian.

GOVERNMENT PUBLISHER

Government Printing Office: Michael Karaoli St, Nicosia; tel (2) 302205; telex 3399; Dir: Dr Chrysostomos Sofianos; f 1878.

NEWS AND INFORMATION

Cyprus News Agency: POB 3947, 97 Ay Omoloyitae Ave, Nicosia; tel (2) 458413; telex 4787; fax (2) 442613; Dir: Ioannis Solomou; f 1976; English and Greek services.

Press and Information Office: Apellis St, Ay Omoloyitae Ave, Nicosia: tel (2) 402617; telex 2526; fax (2) 453730; Dir: Kypros Psyllides; f 1939; deals with foreign and local press.

Mining and Energy

ENERGY

Electricity Authority of Cyprus: POB 4506, 15 Photi Pitta St, Nicosia; tel (2) 462001; telex 2432; fax (2) 457658; Chief Engineer and Gen Man: D. A. Papageorgis; Engineering Controller and Dep Gen Man: Th P. Ergatoudes; f 1952; state electricity co.

MINING

Mines Service: 6 Demetsana St, Nicosia; tel (2) 302209; Dirs: Glafkos Kronides, Savvas Paphites, Charalambos Thrasou; f 1961; processes applications for quarry licences and mining leases; administers mining law.

Science and Technology

Meteorological Service: St George's Hill, Nicosia; tel (2) 302377; telex 4123; fax (41) 52953; Dir: Kleanthis L. Philaniotis; f 1956; weather forecasting and other climatological services.

Tourism

Cyprus Tourism Organization: POB 4535, Zena Bldg, 18 Th Theodotou St, Nicosia; tel (2) 443374; telex 2165; Chair: Stelios Garanis; Dir-Gen: Antonios Andronikou.

Telecommunications

Cyprus Telecommunications Authority: POB 4929, Telecommunications St, Nicosia 142; tel (2) 313111; telex 3288; fax (2) 494155; f 1961; state telecommunications organization.

Transport

CIVIL AVIATION

Cyprus Airways: POB 1903, 21 Alkeou St, Engomi, Nicosia; tel (2) 443054; telex 2225; Chair: K. Lazarides; f 1947; jointly owned by Govt and local interests; flights to Europe and the Middle East.

Department of Civil Aviation: 25 St George's Hill, Nicosia; tel (2) 403200; telex 6055; fax (2) 465462; f 1954.

ROADS

Inland Transport Department: 1 Diogenes St, Engomi, Nicosia; tel (2) 402194; responsible for licensing of all vehicles.

SHIPPING

Cyprus Ports Authority: POB 2007, 23 Crete St, Nicosia; tel (2) 450100; telex 2833; fax (2) 365420; Chair: Andreas Pouyiouros; Gen Man: J. Bayada; f 1973; ownership, operation, commercial running and devt of ports.

Utilities

Water Development Department: Demosthenis Severis Ave, Nicosia; tel (2) 403303; telex 5533; fax (2) 445019; Dir: C. St Lytvas; f 1939; operation and maintenance of water devt works and sewage disposal.

'The Turkish Republic of Northern Cyprus'

Head of State

The President is the Head of State and is elected by universal adult suffrage for a five-year term. No person may be elected President for more than two consecutive terms. The President appoints the Council of Ministers, which is responsible to the Legislative Assembly.

President: Rauf R. Denktaş (assumed office as President of the 'Turkish Federated State of Cyprus' 13 February 1975; became President of the 'Turkish Republic of Northern Cyprus' 15 November 1983; re-elected for a five-year term 9 June 1985).

Office of the President: Lefkoşa, Mersin 10, Turkey; tel (520) 447767; telex 57269; fax (520) 72252.

Legislature

Legislative power is vested in the Legislative Assembly, comprising 50 deputies, elected by universal adult suffrage for a period of five years. A new Constitution was approved by referendum in May 1985. Turkey is the only country to have recognized the 'Turkish Republic of Northern Cyprus'.

Legislative Assembly: Lefkoşa, Mersin 10, Turkey; Speaker: Hakki Atun.

MINISTRIES AND GOVERNMENT DEPARTMENTS

OFFICE OF THE PRIME MINISTER
Lefkoşa, Mersin 10, Turkey
Tel (520) 72141; telex 57444; fax (520) 77518
Prime Minister: Dr Derviş Eroğlu

MINISTRY OF AGRICULTURE AND FORESTRY
Lefkoşa, Mersin 10, Turkey
Tel (520) 73709; telex 57419
Minister: Taşkent Atasayan

MINISTRY OF COMMUNICATIONS, WORKS AND TOURISM
Lefkoşa, Mersin 10, Turkey
Tel (520) 83051; telex 57169; fax (520) 81891
Minister: Nazif Borman

MINISTRY OF THE ECONOMY AND FINANCE
Lefkoşa, Mersin 10, Turkey
Tel (520) 73626; telex 57268; fax (520) 78230
Minister: Mehmet Bayram

MINISTRY OF FOREIGN AFFAIRS AND DEFENCE
Şehit İdris Doğan St, Lefkoşa, Mersin 10, Turkey
Tel (520) 72241; telex 57178; fax (520) 76439
Minister: Dr Kenan Atakol

MINISTRY OF HEALTH AND SOCIAL WELFARE
Lefkoşa, Mersin 10, Turkey
Tel (520) 75229
Minister: Dr Mustafa Erbilen

MINISTRY OF HOUSING
Lefkoşa, Mersin 10, Turkey
Tel (520) 73213
Minister: Mustafa Adaoğlu

MINISTRY OF THE INTERIOR, RURAL AFFAIRS AND ENVIRONMENT
Lefkoşa, Mersin 10, Turkey
Tel (520) 73645
Minister: Olgun Paşalar

MINISTRY OF LABOUR, YOUTH AND SPORT
Lefkoşa, Mersin 10, Turkey
Tel (520) 73611; telex 57178
Minister: Günay Caymaz

MINISTRY OF NATIONAL EDUCATION AND CULTURE
Lefkoşa, Mersin 10, Turkey
Tel (520) 72136; fax (520) 82334
Minister: Salih Coşar

MINISTRY OF TRADE AND INDUSTRY
Lefkoşa, Mersin 10, Turkey
Tel (520) 71341; telex 57174
Minister: Ömer Demir

GOVERNMENT AGENCIES AND ORGANIZATIONS

Agriculture

Cyprus Fruit and Vegetable Enterprises Ltd (Cypfruvex): Ataturk Sq, Guzelyurt, Mersin 10, Turkey; tel (571) 43495; telex 57131; fax (571) 43499; Gen Man: Hasan Ozerdem; f 1974; processing citrus fruits; packing and marketing of fresh fruit.

Business and Economy

BANKING

EFIK Ltd Şti: POB 118, Lefkoşa, Mersin 10, Turkey; banking and insurance.

Turkish Cypriot Co-operative Central Bank Ltd: POB 1861, 49-55 Mahmout Pasha St, Lefkoşa, Mersin 10, Turkey; tel (520) 64257; telex 57216; Gen Man: Dr Tuncer Arifoğlu; banking and credit facilities to mem societies and individuals.

NATIONALIZED INDUSTRY

Turkish Cypriot Industrial Enterprises Holding Co Ltd: POB 445, Lefkoşa, Mersin 10, Turkey; tel (520) 83231; telex 57127; fax (520) 82441; Dir: Hasan Yumuk; f 1974; manufacture of textiles, plastics, chemicals, foodstuffs and a wide range of other products.

KT Tütün Endüstri Ltd (Turkish Cypriot Tobacco Industries Ltd): 27 Atatürk Caddesi, Lefkoşa, Mersin 10, Turkey; manufacture of tobacco products.

TRADE

Eti Ltd: Bedrettin Demirel Caddesi, Lefkoşa, Mersin 10, Turkey; import and distribution of basic foodstuffs.

KT Petrolleri Ltd Şti (Turkish Cypriot Petroleum Co Ltd): Boeros Binasıı, Girne, Mersin 10, Turkey; import and distribution of petrol and petroleum products.

Media

GOVERNMENT PUBLISHER

Devlet Basimevi (Turkish Cypriot Government Printing House): Şerif Arzik St, Lefkoşa, Mersin 10, Turkey; tel (520) 72010; Dir: Sabri Ertürk.

NEWS AND INFORMATION

Enformasyon Dairesi (Public Information Service): Mehmet Akif Caddesi, Lefkoşa, Mersin 10, Turkey; tel (520) 73133; telex 57248; Dir: Oktay Oksuzoğlu.

Türk Ajansı Kıbrıs (TAK)—Turkish News Agency of Cyprus: 9 Server Somuncuoglu St, Lefkoşa, Mersin 10, Turkey; tel (520) 71818; telex 57448; fax (520) 71213; Dir Kemal Âşik; f 1973.

Tourism

KT Turizm İşletmeleri (Turkish Cypriot Tourism Enterprises Ltd): Kordon Caddesi, Kordon Apt, Kat 3, Girne, Mersin 10, Turkey; tel (581) 52071; telex 57128; fax (581) 52073; Gen Man: Mehmet Kiral; Asst Gen Man: Halil Fırket; f 1974.

Transport and Communications

TELECOMMUNICATIONS

Telekomunikasyon Diaresi Mudurlugu (Directorate of Telecommunications): Ministry of Communications and Works, Lefkoşa, Mersin 10, Turkey; tel (520) 73888; telex 57165; admin and operation of telecommunications.

TRANSPORT

Turkish Cypriot Airlines Co Ltd: Bedreddin Demirel Caddesi, Yensehir, Lefkoşa, Mersin 10, Turkey; tel (520) 71901; telex 57350; fax (520) 21462; Chair: Nejat Konuk; f 1975; jointly owned by the Govt and Turkish Airlines Ltd; flights to Turkey, Munich and London.

KT Denizcilik Ltd Şti (Turkish Cypriot Maritime Co Ltd): Girne Caddesi, Adem Kaner Iışhanıı, Lefkoşa, Mersin 10, Turkey; sea transport, cargo and passenger service.

CZECHOSLOVAKIA

Head of State

The President, elected by the Federal Assembly for a five-year term, appoints the Federal Government, the supreme executive organ of State power, which is headed by a Prime Minister. Ministers are responsible to the Federal Assembly. The Federal Government controls external relations, overseas trade, defence, transport and communications, other matters also being the responsibility of the governments of the two constituent republics.

President of the Republic: Václav Havel (took office 29 December 1989).

Office of the President: 119 08 Prague 1; tel (2) 2101.

Legislature

The supreme organ of State power is the bicameral Federal Assembly, comprising the House of the People (200 deputies) and the House of Nations (150 deputies). Deputies serve five-year terms, elected by universal adult suffrage. Each of the two constituent republics has its own government and its own elected National Council.

Federální Shromáždění (Federal Assembly): Vinohradská 1, 110 02 Prague 1; tel (2) 2103; telex 122614; Chair: Alexander Dubček.

Sněmovna lidu (House of the People): Vinohradská 1, 110 02 Prague 1; tel (2) 2103; telex 122614; Chair: Dr Josef Bartončík.

Sněmovna národů (House of Nations): Vinohradská 1, 110 02 Prague 1; tel (2) 2103; telex 122614; Chair: Anton Blažej.

MINISTRIES AND GOVERNMENT DEPARTMENTS

OFFICE OF THE PRIME MINISTER
Prague
Prime Minister: Marián Čalfa
First Deputy Prime Ministers: Valtf Komárek, Jan Čarnogurský
Deputy Prime Minister: František Pitra
Deputy Prime Minister and Premier of the Slovak Socialist Republic: Milan Číč
Deputy Prime Ministers: František Reichel, Dr Vladimír Dlouhy, Josef Hromádka, Oldřich Burský
Minister without portfolio: Robert Martinko

COMMITTEE OF PEOPLE'S CONTROL
Prague
Minister, Chair: Květoslava Kořínková

FEDERAL MINISTRY OF AGRICULTURE AND FOOD
Těšnov 17, 117 05 Prague 1
Tel (2) 282111; telex 121041
Minister: Oldřich Burský

FEDERAL MINISTRY OF CULTURE
Prague
Minister: Milan Lukes

FEDERAL MINISTRY OF FINANCE
Lêtenská 15, 118 10 Prague 1
Tel (2) 532941; telex 121868
Minister: Dr Václav Klaus

FEDERAL MINISTRY OF FOREIGN AFFAIRS
Loretánské nám 5, 125 10 Prague 1
Tel (2) 2193111; telex 121866
Minister: Jiří Dienstbier

FEDERAL MINISTRY OF FOREIGN TRADE
Politických vězňů 20, 112 49 Prague 1
Tel (2) 21261111; telex 121489
Minister: Andrej Barčák

FEDERAL MINISTRY OF FUEL AND ENERGY
Vinohradská 8, 120 70 Prague 2
Tel (2) 2357065; telex 122954
Minister: František Pinc

FEDERAL MINISTRY OF THE INTERIOR
Obráncu miru 85, 170 34 Prague 7
Tel (2) 3801; telex 1204
Minister: Richard Sacher

FEDERAL MINISTRY OF LABOUR AND SOCIAL AFFAIRS
Palackého nám 4, 120 07 Prague 2
Tel (2) 2118; telex 122785
Minister: Petr Miller

FEDERAL MINISTRY OF METALLURGY, MACHINE BUILDING AND ELECTRICAL ENGINEERING
Na Františku 32, 110 15 Prague 1
Tel (2) 2851111; telex 121187
Minister: Ladislav Vodrážka

FEDERAL MINISTRY OF NATIONAL DEFENCE
nám Říjnové Revoluce 1500, 160 01 Prague 6
Tel (2) 330822; telex 121616
Minister: Miroslav Vacek

**FEDERAL MINISTRY OF TRANSPORT AND
COMMUNICATIONS**
Na Příkopě 33, 110 05 Prague 1
Tel (2) 21221111; telex 121096; fax (2) 2368379
Minister: Robert Martinko

FEDERAL PRICE OFFICE
Vinohradská 49, 120 74 Prague 2
Tel (2) 2110; telex 121289
Minister, Chair: Ladislav Dvořák

PEOPLE'S AUDIT COMMITTEE
Jankovcova 63, 170 04 Prague 7
Tel (2) 8734
Minister, Chair: (vacant)
Central authority of the State executive for control and auditing.

**STATE COMMISSION FOR SCIENTIFIC-
TECHNOLOGICAL AND INVESTMENT
DEVELOPMENT**
Prague
Minister, Chair: František Reichel

STATE PLANNING COMMISSION
nábř kpt Jaroše 1000, 170 32 Prague 7
Tel (2) 3802; telex 121404
Chair: Dr Vladimír Dlouhý

GOVERNMENT AGENCIES AND ORGANIZATIONS

Advisory and Supervisory Body

Co-ordination Commission for National Committees: nábř kpt Jaroše 4, Prague 1; oversees admin of national policies at local level; aids community planning and devt; runs training programmes for local govt personnel.

Business and Economy

BANKING

Česká státní spořitelna (Czech State Savings Bank): Václavské nám 42, 113 98 Prague 1; tel (2) 225237; telex 121010; Dir-Gen: Věra Nepimachová; accepts deposits and issues loans.

Československá obchodní banka as (Commercial Bank of Czechoslovakia): Na Příkopě 14, 115 20 Prague 1; tel (2) 2132; telex 122201; fax (2) 2327562; Man Dir: Rostislav Petráš; f 1965; commercial and foreign exchange transactions.

Slovenská státní spořitelna (Slovak State Savings Bank): Leningradská 24, 801 00 Bratislava; telex 93133; Dir: Jozef Cipov.

Státní banka československá (State Bank of Czechoslovakia): Na Příkopě 28, 110 03 Prague 1; tel (2) 2112; telex 121831; Dir: Josef Tosovskýf 1950; bank of issue; grants credits; fixes the exchange rate of the Czechoslovak crown; directs and secures banking economic relations with foreign countries; cash clearing centre.

Živnostenská banka: Na Příkopě 20, 113 80 Prague 1; tel (2) 224346; telex 122313; Gen Man: Jiří Kunert; f 1868.

INSURANCE

Česká státní pojišťovna (Czech State Insurance and Reinsurance Corpn): Spálená 16, 114 00 Prague 1; tel (2) 2148111; telex 121112; fax (2) 299146; Gen Man: Josef Večeřa; controls all insurance; issues life, accident, fire, aviation and marine policies, all classes of reinsurance.

Slovenská štátna poist'ovňa (Slovak State Insurance Corpn): Strakova 1, 815 74 Bratislava; telex 93375; fax (7) 827948; Dir-Gen: Rastislav Haverlik.

TRADE

BVV Trade Fairs and Exhibitions: Výstaviště 1, 602 00 Brno; tel (5) 3141111; telex 62239; fax (5) 333998; Dir: Dr Jaroslav Kučera; f 1959; runs international trade fairs.

Centrotex: POB 49, nám Hrdinů 3, 140 61 Prague 4; tel (2) 415; telex 121130; fax (2) 431829; Dir-Gen: Jiří Koutník; f 1948; exports and imports textile materials and ready-made garments.

Chemapol: Kodaňská 46, 100 10 Prague 10; tel (2) 715; telex 122000; fax (2) 737007; Pres and Dir-Gen: Václav Volf; f 1948; import and export of crude oil and chemical products from crude oil and coal, chemical and pharmaceutical products and raw materials, rubber and plastic materials, organic chemicals and inorganic pigments, organic dyestuffs, inorganic chemicals.

Čechofracht: Na Příkopě 8, 111 83 Prague 1; tel (2) 129111; telex 122221; Dir-Gen: Jiří Kadaník; f 1949; shipping and international forwarding corpn.

Československá obchodní a průmyslová komora (Czechoslovak Chamber of Commerce and Industry): Argentinská 38, 170 05 Prague 7; tel (2) 8724111; telex 121862; Pres: Jaroslav Jakubec; f 1949; its 921 mems are all Czechoslovak foreign trade corpns and the majority of industrial enterprises, banks and research institutes.

Československý Filmexport (Czechoslovak Filmexport): Václavské nám 28, 111 45 Prague 1; tel (2) 2365385; telex 122259; fax (2) 2358432; Dir: Jiří Janoušek; f 1957; export and import of features and shorts; provides location facilities and production services for motion pictures.

Drevounia: Dr V. Clementisa 10, 826 10 Bratislava; tel (7) 229962; telex 93291; fax (7) 236164; Dir-Gen: Jiří Jirava; f 1969; exports and imports furniture, wood products and joinery products.

Exico: Panská 9, 111 77 Prague 1; tel (2) 2368565; telex 122211; fax (2) 263297; Gen Man: František Fremund; f 1966; exports footwear, gloves, leather and fur garments, materials for the shoe industry, bookbinding cloth, artificial leather, etc; imports hides, skins, footwear and leather garments.

Ferromet: Opletalova 27, 111 81 Prague 1; Dir-Gen: Břetislav Sedlák; import and export of metallurgical products.

Inspekta: Na Strži 63, 140 62 Prague 4; tel (2) 4141111; telex 121938; fax (2) 434390; Dir-Gen: Jan Švihel; Dep Dir-Gen: Jan Strnad; f 1951; superintends export and import goods.

Kerametal: Jasikova 2, 829 66 Bratislava; tel (7) 295851; telex 93235; imports mineral ores; exports mineral and ceramic products, including aluminium and aluminium alloys and ferroalloys.

Koospol: Leninova 178, 160 67 Prague 6; Dir-Gen: Jaroslav Říha; import and export of foodstuffs.

Kovo: Jankovcova 2, 170 88 Prague 7; Dir-Gen: Josef Kudrhalt; import and export of precision engineering products.

Ligna: Vodičkova 41, 112 09 Prague 1; Dir-Gen: Miloš Švach; import and export of timber, wood products, musical instruments and paper.

Martimex: Červenej armády 1, 036 65 Martin; tel (842) 33311; telex 75379; fax (842) 39118; Gen Man: Ján Rusnák; f 1970; export and import of engineering technology, passenger and cargo vessels, hydraulic motors, industrial robots, machinery; involved in joint ventures.

Metalimex: Štěpánská 34, 112 17 Prague 1; tel (2) 2359580; telex 121405; fax (2) 2320630; Dir-Gen: Miroslav Hlavička; import and export of metals, natural gas and solid fuels.

Motokov: Na Strži 63, 140 62 Prague 4; Dir-Gen: Andrej Barčák; import and export of vehicles and light engineering products.

Omnia: Dunajska 4, 89932 Bratislava; tel (7) 53155; telex 92226; export and import of precision engineering products, consumer electrical goods, anti-friction bearings, etc.

Omnipol: Nekázanka 11, 112 21 Prague 1; telex 121299; fax (2) 226792; Dir-Gen: František Háva; import and export of sports and civil aircraft.

Petrimex: ul Dr Vl Clementisa 10, 826 08 Bratislava; tel (7) 229962; telex 935259; imports and exports chemicals, raw materials.

Polytechna: POB 834, Panská 9, 112 45 Prague 1; tel (2) 2368065; telex 121585; fax (2) 2321562; Pres: Jiří Mana; Vice-Pres: Alois Dobeš; Commercial Dir: Vladimír Cír; f 1959; export and import of licenses and patents, technical co-operation, consulting and engineering services, software, technical assistance.

Pragoinvest: Českomoravská 23, 180 56 Prague 9; tel (2) 822741; telex 122379; Dir-Gen: Miloslav Kočárek; import and export of machinery and complete plant equipment.

Rempo: Duklianska 25, 812 53 Bratislava; tel (7) 220054; telex 93245; Gen Man: Gabriel Hajdu; Dep Gen Man: Igor Kačáni; f 1984; exports products of the chemical, glass, rubber, textile and clothing industries; barter trade.

Skloexport: tř 1 máje 52, 461 74 Liberec; Dir-Gen: Jaroslav Křivánek; exports glass.

Strojexport: POB 662, Václavské nám 56, 113 26 Prague 1; tel (2) 2357565; telex 121671; fax (2) 269569; Dir-Gen: Josef Levora; f 1953; exports excavators, mining, lifting and warehousing equipment, steel and wooden structures, rail vehicles, geological works and services, drilling of wells.

Strojimport: Vinohradská 184, 130 52; Prague 3; tel (2) 713; telex 122241; fax (2) 777554; Pres: Ivan Capek; Vice-Pres: Rudolf Skuhra; f 1953; export and import of metal-cutting and engineering tools, gauges, finishing equipment, woodworking and processing machines, textile, knitting, tanning and shoe-making machines, industrial sewing machines, needles.

Škodaexport: Václavské nám 56, 113 32 Prague 1; tel (2) 2131; telex 122413; Dir-Gen: Miloslav Mikeš; export and import of power engineering and metallurgical plants, engineering works, electrical locomotives and trolleybuses, tobacco machines.

Tuzex: Rytířská 13, 113 43 Prague 1; telex 121012; Dir-Gen: Antonín Račanský; f 1957; import and export of consumer goods.

Zavody Silnoproude Elektrotechniky (ZSE): Blanicka 28, 120 61 Prague 2; tel (2) 256250; telex 121488; exports and imports motors, cables, conductors, transformers, welding and electric heating equipment, etc.

Culture

Matica Slovenská (Slovak National Library): Novomeského 32, 036 01 Martin; tel (842) 31371; telex 075331; Dir: Dr Viliam Mruškovič; f 1863; central library; central archives of literature and art, contains the Central Slovak Literature Museum and the Centre of Slovak National Bibliography.

Defence

Czechoslovak People's Army: c/o Federal Ministry of National Defence; nám Říjnové Revoluce 1500, 160 01 Prague 6; tel (2) 330822; telex 121616.

Energy

Československá komise pro atomovou energii (ČSKAE) (Czechoslovak Atomic Energy Commission): Slezká 9, 120 29 Prague 2; tel (2) 2151111; telex 121107; Chair: Stanislav Havel; state supervisory authority for nuclear safety; promotes the devt of the peaceful uses of atomic energy.

Legal and Judiciary

Kancelář Generálního Prokurátora (Office of the Procurator-General): nám Hrdinů 1300, 140 04 Prague 4; tel (2) 430551; telex 121154; Procurator-Gen: Dr Pavol Sitár.

Nejvyšši Soud (Supreme Court): nám Hrdinů 1300, 128 13 Prague 4; tel (2) 430841; Chair: Dr Josef Ondřej.

Media

BROADCASTING

Československá televize (Czechoslovak Television): Jindřišska 16, 111 50 Prague 1; tel (2) 221247; telex 121800; Dir-Gen: Miroslav Pavel; f 1953.

Československá televízia na Slovensku (Czechoslovak TV in Slovakia): Asmolovova 28, 845 45 Bratislava; tel (7) 325500; telex 092277; fax (7) 322252; Dir: Dr Jaroslav Hlinický; f 1956.

Československý rozhlas (Czechoslovak Radio): Vinohradská 12, 120 99 Prague 2; tel (2) 2115; telex 121100; fax (2) 2321020; Dir-Gen: Dr Karel Starý; f 1923; federal and national radio network; foreign broadcasts in English, German, French, Spanish, Portuguese, Arabic and Russian.

Český rozhlas (Czech Radio): Vinohradská 12, 120 99 Prague 2; tel (2) 2115; telex 121100; Dir: Dr Jaroslav Hacmac.

Československé zahraniční vysílání (Czechoslovak Foreign Broadcasts): Vinohradská 12, 120 99 Prague 2; tel (2) 2360823; telex 121189; fax (2) 2321020; Dir: Dr Helena Landovská.

Československý rozhlas na Slovensku (Czechoslovak Radio in Slovakia): Mýtna 1, 812 90 Bratislava; tel (7) 47697; telex 93352; fax (7) 48923; Dir: Vasil Bejda; f 1926.

NEWS AND INFORMATION

Československá tisková kancelář (ČTK) (Czechoslovak News Agency): Opletalova 5-7, 111 44 Prague 1; tel (2) 2147; telex 122841; Dir-Gen: Dr Aleš Benda; f 1918; news and photo exchange service; network of foreign correspondents; news service for foreign countries; publishes weekly bulletin in various languages, economic bulletins and documentation surveys.

ČTK—Made in...publicity: Kotorská 16, 140 00 Prague 4; tel (2) 422151; telex 122501; Dir-Gen: Dr Josef Šeda; f 1964; advertises foreign products and services in Czechoslovakia.

Federální statistický úřad (Federal Statistical Office): Sokolovská 142, 186 13 Prague 8; tel (2) 839541; telex 121084; Pres: Vladimír Mička; Vice-Pres: Belo Bosák; f 1969; collects, analyses and presents socio-economic information.

Research

Ústav jaderného výzkumu (Institute of Nuclear Research): 250 68 Řež; tel (2) 896231; telex 122626; Dir: Jan Mrkos; f 1955.

Tourism

Čedok (Travel and Hotels Corpn): Na Příkopě 18, 111 35 Prague 1; tel (2) 2127111; telex 121109; fax (2) 2321656; Pres: Miloslav Holub; official Czechoslovak Travel Agency.

Transport

CIVIL AVIATION

Československé Aerolinie (ČSA) (Czechoslovak Airlines): Ruzyně Airport, 160 08 Prague 6 (Ruznyě); tel (2) 3341111; telex 120338; Dir-Gen: Jiří Nulíček; f 1923; external services to Europe, the Near, Middle and Far East, North and Central America and North Africa.

Slov-Air: Ivanka Airport, 823 12 Bratislava; tel (7) 226172; telex 93270; Dir: Lubomír Kováčik; f 1969; runs domestic scheduled and charter services.

INLAND WATERWAYS

Československá plavba dunajská (Czechoslovak Danube River Shipping): Červena armáda 35, 815 24 Bratislava; tel (7) 57461; telex 92338; fax (7) 59002; Man Dir: Pavol Cibák; f 1922; cargo transport on the Danube and on the Mediterranean and Black seas; repair of river vessels.

Československá plavba labsko-oderská (ČSPLO) (Czechoslovak Elbe-Oder River Shipping): K. Čapka 1, 405 91 Děčín; telex 184241; Man Dir: Karel Adamovský; operates river ports of Prague, Mělník, Kolín, Ustí nad Labem and Děčín; river transport of goods; transfer and storage of goods in Czechoslovak ports.

RAILWAYS

Československé státní dráhy (Czechoslovak State Railways): Na Příkopě 33, 110 05 Prague 1; tel (2) 2122; telex 121096; Dir-Gen: Vladimír Oravec; f 1989; railway transport; building and maintenance of railway lines and transport facilities.

Dopravní podniky hlavního města Prahy (Prague Metropolitan Railway): Bubenská 1, 170 26 Prague 7; tel (2) 878278; telex 122443; Dir-Gen: Ladislav Slepička; f 1897; runs public transport services; maintains roads and pavements in Prague; passenger ship transport.

ROADS

Autoopra: Petrská 31, 116 63 Prague 1; tel (2) 2316030; telex 121892; international motor truck and bus transport.

Československá státní automobilová doprova (ČSAD) (Czechoslovak State Road Transport): Hybernská 32, 111 21 Prague 1; f 1949.

Sdružení československých mezinárodních automobilových dopravců (ČESMAD) (Czechoslovak International Road Transport Enterprises Association): Perucká 5, 120 67 Prague 2; tel (2) 6911920; telex 122303; fax (2) 256273; Chair: Jozef Mrážik; Sec-Gen: Jiří Kladiva; f 1965; organization of goods and personnel transport for 11 mem enterprises; international transport.

SHIPPING

Československá námořní plavba, mezinárodní akciová společnost (Czechoslovak Ocean Shipping, International Joint-Stock Co): Počernická 168, 100 99 Prague 10; tel (2) 778941; telex 122137; fax (2) 773962; Dir-Gen: Antonin Sokolík; Dep Dir-Gen: Jaroslav Stránský; f 1959; shipping co; operation of merchant fleet.

DENMARK

Head of State

Denmark is a constitutional monarchy. Executive power is exercised by the monarch through a Cabinet, headed by the Prime Minister. The Cabinet is responsible to the Folketinget (Parliament).

Sovereign: HM Queen Margrethe II (succeeded to the throne 14 January 1972).

Office of HM The Queen: Amalienborg, 1257 Copenhagen K; tel 33-14-36-28.

Legislature

Legislative power is held jointly by the monarch (who has no personal political power) and the unicameral Folketinget (Parliament) which comprises 179 members, 175 from metropolitan Denmark and two each from the Faeroe Islands and Greenland. Members, elected by universal adult suffrage, serve four-year terms.

Folketinget: Christiansborg Slot; 1240 Copenhagen K; tel 33-37-55-00; telex 21509; fax 33-32-85-36; Pres: Hans Peter Clausen; Sec-Gen: Helge Hjortdal; Clerk: L. E. Hansen-Salby.

MINISTRIES AND GOVERNMENT DEPARTMENTS

OFFICE OF THE PRIME MINISTER
Christiansborg, Prins Jørgens Gård 11, 1218 Copenhagen K
Tel 33-92-33-00; telex 27027
Prime Minister: Poul Schlüter

Greenland Department: Hausergade 3, 1128 Copenhagen K; tel 33-13-68-25; telex 27125; fax 33-93-68-15.

SECRETARIAT OF THE CABINET
Christian VIII's Palace, Amalienborg, 1257 Copenhagen K
Tel 33-14-24-32

MINISTRY OF AGRICULTURE
Slotsholmsgade 10, 1216 Copenhagen K
Tel 33-92-33-01; telex 27157
Minister: Laurits Tørnæs

MINISTRY OF CULTURAL AFFAIRS
Nybrogade 2, 1203 Copenhagen K
Tel 33-92-33-70; telex 27385; fax 33-91-33-88
Minister: Ole Vig Jensen

MINISTRY OF DEFENCE
Slotsholmsgade 10, 1216 Copenhagen K
Tel 33-92-33-20
Minister: Knud Engård

MINISTRY OF ECCLESIASTICAL AFFAIRS
Frederiksholms Kanal 21, 1220 Copenhagen K
Tel 33-92-33-90; fax 33-92-39-13
Minister: Torben Rechendorff
Administers the Lutheran Church in Denmark.

MINISTRY OF ECONOMIC AFFAIRS
Slotsholmsgade 12, 1216 Copenhagen K
Tel 33-92-33-22; telex 16833; fax 33-93-60-20
Minister: Niels Helveg Petersen

MINISTRY OF EDUCATION AND RESEARCH
Frederiksholms Kanal 21-25, 1220 Copenhagen K
Tel 33-92-50-00; telex 16243; fax 33-92-55-47
Minister: Bertel Hårder

MINISTRY OF ENERGY
Slotsholmsgade 1, 1216 Copenhagen K
Tel 33-92-75-00; telex 15505; 33-12-87-07
Minister: Jens Bilgrav-Nielsen

MINISTRY OF THE ENVIRONMENT
Slotsholmsgade 12, 1216 Copenhagen K
Tel 33-92-33-88; telex 31209
Minister: Lone Dybkjær

MINISTRY OF FINANCE
Christiansborg Slotsplads 1, 1218 Copenhagen K
Tel 33-92-33-33; telex 16140; fax 33-32-80-30
Minister: Henning Dyremose

MINISTRY OF FISCAL AFFFAIRS
Slotsholmsgade 12, 1216 Copenhagen K
Tel 33-92-33-66; telex 16939
Minister: Anders Fogh Rasmussen

MINISTRY OF FISHERIES
Stormgade 2, 1470 Copenhagen K
Tel 33-92-65-00; telex 16144; fax 33-92-65-79
Minister: Kent Kirk

MINISTRY OF FOREIGN AFFAIRS
Asiatisk Plads 2, 1448 Copenhagen K
Tel 33-92-00-00; telex 31292; fax 31-54-05-33
Minister: Uffe Ellemann-Jensen

MINISTRY OF HEALTH
Slotsholmsgade 10, 1216 Copenhagen K
Tel 33-92-33-80
Minister: Ester Larsen

MINISTRY OF HOUSING AND BUILDING
Slotsholmsgade 12, 1216 Copenhagen K
Tel 33-92-61-00; telex 31401; fax 33-32-61-04
Minister: Agnete Laustsen

National Housing Agency: Slotsholmsgade 12, 1216 Copenhagen K; tel 33-92-61-00; telex 31401; fax 33-32-34-71; Dir-Gen: H. E. Rasmussen.

National Building Agency: Slotsholmsgade 12, 1216 Copenhagen K; tel 33-92-61-00; telex 31401; fax 33-32-34-71; Dir-Gen: Marius Kjeldsen.

MINISTRY OF INDUSTRY
Slotsholmsgade 12, 1216 Copenhagen K
Tel 33-92-33-50; telex 22373
Minister: Nils Wilhjelm

MINISTRY OF THE INTERIOR AND FOR NORDIC AFFAIRS
Christiansborg Slotsplads 1, 1218 Copenhagen K
Tel 33-92-33-80; fax 33-11-12-39
Minister: Thor Pedersen

MINISTRY OF JUSTICE
Slotsholmsgade 10, 1216 Copenhagen K
Tel 33-92-33-40; telex 15530
Minister: Hans Engell

MINISTRY OF LABOUR
Laksegade 19, 1063 Copenhagen K
Tel 33-92-59-29; telex 19320; fax 33-12-13-78
Minister: Knud E. Kirkegård

MINISTRY OF SOCIAL AFFIARS
Slotsholmsgade 6, 1216 Copenhagen K
Tel 33-92-22-77; telex 27343; fax 33-93-25-18
Minister: Åse Olesen

MINISTRY OF TRANSPORT AND COMMUNICATIONS
Frederiksholms Kanal 25-27, 1220 Copenhagen K
Tel 33-92-33-55; telex 22275; fax 33-12-38-93
Minister of Communications: Torben Rechendorff
Minister of Transport: Knud Øtergård

GOVERNMENT AGENCIES AND ORGANIZATIONS

Advisory and Supervisory Bodies

Department of the Budget: Christiansborg Slotsplads 1, 1218 Copenhagen K; tel 33-92-33-33; telex 16140; fax 33-32-80-30; Permanent Sec: Hans Würtzen; responsible for Govt expenditure policy, the central Govt budget and management of central Govt debt; economic analysis and forecasting; under the Ministry of Finance.

Equal Status Council: Frederiksgade 19-21, 1265 Copenhagen K; tel 33-13-12-77; Chair: Grethe Fenger Møller.

Landsforeningen Dansk Arbejde (National Association for Danish Enterprise): Telegrafvej 5, 2750 Ballerup; tel 44-68-16-22; fax 44-68-16-23.

Rigsrevisionen (National Auditors): St Kongensgade 45, 1264 Copenhagen; tel 33-92-84-00; fax 33-11-04-15; Dir: J. Mohr; f 1976; public auditing; under the Ministry of Economic Affairs.

Agriculture and the Environment

AGRICULTURE

Landbrugsrådet (Agricultural Council): Axelborg, Axeltorv 3, 1609 Copenhagen V; tel 33-14-56-72; telex 16772; Pres: Hans O. A. Kjeldsen; Dir: Kjeld Ejler; f 1919; 32 mems.

National Forestry Agency: Strandvejen 863, Klampenborg; tel 31-63-11-66.

THE ENVIRONMENT

National Agency of Environmental Protection: Strandgade 29, Copenhagen K; tel 31-57-83-10; responsible to the Ministry of the Environment.

National Agency for Physical Planning: Haraldsgade 53, 2100 Copenhagen Ø; tel 39-27-11-00; telex 19092; fax 39-27-12-66; under the Ministry of the Environment.

National Agency for the Protection of Nature, Monuments and Sites: Amaliegade 13, 1256 Copenhagen K; tel 33-11-95-65.

Business and Economy

BANKING

Danmarks Nationalbank: Havnegade 5, 1093 Copenhagen K; tel 33-14-14-11; telex 27051; fax 33-14-59-02; Govs: Erik Hoffmeyer, O. Thomasen, R. Mikkelsen; f 1818; central bank; sole right of issue.

Tilsynet med Banker og Sparekasser (Government Supervision of Banks and Savings Banks): Nørre Voldgade 94, 1358 Copenhagen K; tel 33-15-56-46; telex 19457; fax 33-93-56-46; Dir: Eigil Moelgaard; agency of the Ministry of Industry.

FINANCIAL AGENCIES

Det Økonomiske Råd (Economic Council): Kampmannsgade 1, IV, 1604 Copenhagen V; tel 33-13-51-28; Co-Chair: Prof Arne Larsen, Prof Peder J. Pedersen, Prof C. Vastrup; Sec-Gen: J. Søndergaard; f 1962; observes national economic devt; helps coordinate the actions of economic interest groups; comprises 27 mems representing industry, the Govt and independent economic experts.

The Mortgage Bank and Financial Administration Agency of the Kingdom of Denmark: Landgreven 4, 1301 Copenhagen; tel 33-92-80-00; telex 16323; fax 33-93-77-24; Man Dir: Morten Eskesen; Head, Banking Office: Marianne Ziirsen; f 1906; acts as Govt lending agency; finances investments of public interest; administers Govt assets, guarantees and state subsidies.

INSURANCE

Statsanstalten for Livsforsikring: Kampmannsgade 4, 1645 Copenhagen V; tel 33-15-15-15; telex 15283; fax 33-32-37-32; Dir-Gen: Erik Bonnerup; f 1842; state insurance co.

TRADE

Danmarks Erhvervsfond (Danish Trade Fund): Codanhus, Gl Kongevej 60, 1850 Copenhagen V; tel 31-31-38-25; telex

22910; superintends the Eksportkreditrådet, the Danish export guarantee scheme; promotes Danish exports.

Dansk Standardiseringsråd: Aurehøjvej 12, 2900 Hellerup; tel 31-62-93-15; promotes and maintains Danish standardization procedures.

Direktoratet for Toldvæsenet (Directorate of Customs): Amaliegade 44, 1256 Copenhagen K; tel 33-15-73-00; Dir: C. A. Nielsen; f 1965; central admin of customs; enforcement of customs and excise duties, value added tax, etc.

Erhvervenes Udstillingsudvalg (Industries Board of Trade Fairs): Købmagergade 67, 1150 Copenhagen K.

Export Promotion Denmark: Halmtorvet 20, 1700 Copenhagen V.

Patentdirektoratet (Patents Directorate): Helgeshoej Allé 81, 2630 Taastrup; tel 43-71-71-71; telex 16040; fax 43-71-71-70; Dirs: Per Lund Thoft, Helge Rasmussen, Sten Sterkel; issues patents; registers trademarks and designs.

Culture

National Archives: Rigsdagsgården, 1218 Copenhagen K; tel 33-12-38-78.

Defence

Forsvarskommandoen (Defence Command): POB 202, 2950 Vedbaek; tel 42-89-22-55; telex 40171; Chief of Defence: Adm Sven Eqil Thiede; Chief of Defence Staff: Lt-Gen Joergen Lyng; Chief of Operations: Maj-Gen Poul Thorsen.

Flyvevabnet (Royal Danish Air Force): POB 202, 2950 Vedbaek; tel 42-89-22-55; Inspector-Gen: Maj-Gen Bent Larsen.

Haeren (Royal Danish Army): POB 202, 2950 Vedbaek; tel 42-89-22-55; Inspector-Gen: Maj-Gen Jørgen Essemann.

Sovaernet (Royal Danish Navy): POB 202, 2950 Vedbaek; tel 42-89-22-55; Inspector-Gen: Rear Adm Mogens Telling.

Development and Planning

Direktoratet for Egnsudvikling: Søndergade 25, 8600 Silkeborg; tel 86-82-56-55; telex 366255; fax 86-80-16-29; Dirs: Lilian Trettvik, Torben Nørkær Hansen; f 1967; provides information for foreign investors; encourages planned economic devt in the country's regions.

Education and Research

Danish Polar Centre: Hausergade 3, 1128 Copenhagen K; tel 33-13-68-25; telex 27125; fax 33-13-49-76; Dir (acting): Gunnar Martens; f 1989; under control of Ministry of Education and Research; conveys news and information on Arctic issues and areas with special emphasis on Greenland to research institutions, authorities, trade and industry and the public; helps organize national and international conferences and seminars related to scientific, technological, economic and social issues; evaluates and approves scientific field projects and expeditions; the scientific liaison officer for Greenland is attached to the Centre.

Commission for Scientific Research (KVUG): Hausergade 3, 1128 Copenhagen K; tel 33-13-68-25; telex 27125; fax 33-13-49-76; attached to the Danish Polar Centre.

Risø National Laboratory: Forskningscenter Risø, POB 49, 4000 Roskilde; tel 42-37-12-12; telex 43116; fax 42-36-06-09;

Man Dir: Hans Bjerrum Møller; Technical Dir: Klaus Singer; Research Dirs: Jørgen Kjems, Peter Stranddorf; f 1958; environmental and energy research centre.

Employment

Arbejdstilsynet (Directorate of National Labour Inspection): Landskronagade 33-35, 2100 Copenhagen Ø; tel 31-18-00-88; telex 16149; fax 31-18-35-60; Dir: Erik Andersen; f 1873; ensures that regulations concerning working conditions are complied with.

Energy

Danish Energy Agency: Landemærket 11, 1119 Copenhagen K; tel 33-92-67-00; telex 22450; fax 33-11-47-43; Man Dir: Erik Lindegaard; Dep Man Dir: Jacob E. Holmblad; under Ministry of Energy; funding and co-ordination of energy research; dissemination of information.

Dansk Olie og Naturgas A/S: Agern Allé 24-26, 2970 Hørsholm; tel 42-57-10-22; telex 37322; fax 42-57-17-36; Pres and Chief Exec: Jørgen A. Høy; Chair: Holger Lavesen; Dep Chair: Michael Lunn; f 1972; procures, stores, transports and markets oil, oil products and natural gas in Denmark and abroad; parent of the following cos:

Dansk Naturgas A/S: Agern Allé 24-26, 2970 Hørsholm; tel 42-57-10-22; telex 37322; fax 42-57-17-36; Chief Exec: Søren Guldborg; f 1984; owns and operates natural gas network; superintends the buying, transport and sale of natural gas in Denmark and abroad.

Dansk Olie- og Gasproduktion A/S: Slotsmarken 16, 2970 Hørsholm; tel 42-57-20-44; telex 21259; fax 42-57-28-89; Chief Exec: Hans Jørgen Rasmusen; f 1983; exploration and extraction of oil and natural gas in Danish territory; engineering and construction projects.

Dansk Olierør A/S: Agern Allé 24-26, 2970 Hørsholm; tel 42-57-10-22; telex 37322; fax 42-57-17-36; Chief Exec: Øyvind U. Boldsen; f 1981; owns and operates the oil pipeline system running from the North Sea Fields to Fredericia.

Dansk Olieforsyning A/S: Agern Allé 24-26, 2970 Hørsholm; tel 42-57-10-22; telex 37322; fax 42-57-17-36; Chief Exec: Jørgen A. Høy; f 1980; purchase and resale of Danish oil.

Elektricitetsrådet (Electricity Council):Gothersgade 160, 1123 Copenhagen K; tel 33-11-65-82; fax 33-91-19-50; Dir: H. Kastoft Jansen; f 1907; responsible for general planning, operation and safety of the electricity-supply industry; acts as a law enforcement office in this field.

Health and Welfare

Council on Alcohol and Narcotics: Hovedvagtsgade 6, 4th Floor, 1103 Copenhagen K; tel 35-33-13-44; fax 33-13-54-81; Dir: Mogens Bjørnbak-Hansen; f 1969; assists in the effort to prevent and treat alcohol and drug abuse.

Socialstyrelsen (National Board of Social Welfare): Kristineberg 6, POB 2555, 2100 Copenhagen Ø; tel 31-29-91-22; fax 31-29-84-30; Dir-Gen: Ole Høg; Vice Dirs: S. A. Wurr, Grethe Buss; f 1970; training; child and youth welfare; cash benefits and rehabilitaion; health and social welfare admin; provision of daily cash benefits in case of sickness and pregnancy; social pensions, etc.

International Affairs

DANIDA—Department of International Development Co-operation: Ministry of Foreign Affairs, Asiatisk Plads 2, 1448 Copenhagen K; tel 33-92-00-00; telex 31292; fax 31-54-05-33; Permanent Under-Sec of State: Bent Haakonsen; f 1962; co-ordinates and implements Denmark's devt assistance programme.

Legal and Judiciary

Department of Prisons and Probation: Klareboderne 1, 1115 Copenhagen K; tel 33-13-57-83; telex 19882; Dir-Gen: Anders Troldborg; f 1910; part of the Ministry of Justice; responsible for the prison system; admin of probation and parole.

Højesteret (Supreme Court): Prins Jorgens Gard 13, 1218 Copenhagen K; tel 33-15-66-50; Pres: P. M. Christensen.

Labour Court: Copenhagen; Pres: Johannes Bangert; deals with labour disputes.

Maritime and Commercial Court: Copenhagen; Pres: Emil Frank Poulsen.

Office of the Ombudsman: Copenhagen; Ombudsman: Hans Gammeltoft-Hansen; appointed by Parliament; concerned with defects in the laws of administrative provisions.

Media

BROADCASTING

Danmarks Radio (Radio Denmark): Radio Hus, Rosenørns Allé 22, 1999 Frederiksberg C; tel 31-35-06-47; telex 22965; fax 39-66-12-33; Dir-Gen: Hans Jørgen Jensen; Dir, Radio Programmes: Hans Jørgen Skov; operates a foreign service, 10 regional stations and three national channels.

Danmarks Radio—TV: TV-Byen, 2860 Søborg; tel 31-67-12-33; telex 22695; fax 39-66-12-33; Dir-Gen: Hans Jørgen Jensen; Dir of TV Programmes: Henrik Antonsen.

NEWS AND INFORMATION

Danmarks Statistik: Sejrøgade 11, 2100 Copenhagen Ø; tel 31-29-82-22; telex 16236; fax 31-18-48-01; Dir-Gen: Hans E. Zeuthen; f 1850; statistical office.

Statens Informationstjeneste (State Information Service): Bredgade 20, POB 1103; 1009 Copenhagen K; tel 33-92-92-00; fax 33-92-92-81; Dir: N. Dalum; f 1975; advises and assists Govt offices in the communication of information to the public.

Tourism

Danmarks Turistråd (Tourist Board): Vesterbrogade 6D, 1620 Copenhagen V; tel 33-11-14-15; telex 27586; fax 33-93-14-16; Chair: Stig Bøgh Karlsen; Dir: Jørgen Bertelsen.

Transport and Communications

TELECOMMUNICATIONS

Post- og Telegrafvæsenet: Tietgensgade 37, 1530 Copenhagen V; tel 33-93-24-10; telex 22323; fax 33-11-22-23; Dir-Gen:

Helge Israelsen; Dep Dir-Gen, Posts: Arne Nielsen; Dep Dir-Gen, Telecommunications: Ib Lønberg; directorate-gen for post and telecommunications services; legislation concerning radio and TV activities.

Fyns Kommunale Telefonselskab (FKT): Klingenberg 16, 5100 Odense C; tel 65-90-90-90; telex 59803; fax 66-12-61-09; Dir, Telecommunications: Peer Toftdal; operates domestic telephones in the region of Funen and southern Jutland.

Jydsk Telefon Akteiselskab (JTAS): Sletvej 30, 8310 Århus-Tranbjerg J; tel 86-29-33-66; telex 68647; fax 86-29-33-88; Chair: K. Østergaard; Gen Man: K. Vestergaard; operates telephones on Northern Jutland.

Kjøbenhavns Telefon Aktieselskab (KTAS): Nørregade 21, 1199 Copenhagen K; tel 31-00-19; telex 19791; fax 33-11-80-50; Chair: Mogens Camre; Vice-Chair: Mogens Kierulff; operates telephone service on Zealand, Lolland-Falster and Bornholm.

The Post Office: Østbanegade 83, 2100 Copenhagen Ø; tel 31-42-29-00; telex 22323; fax 35-43-01-85; Dir: Helge Myrvig; Dep Dir: K. B. Pedersen.

Postgiro: Stamholmen 153/6, 2650 Hvidovre; tel 31-78-92-11; fax 36-77-11-09; Dir: Bjarne Wind; Dep Dir: Mogens T. Hansen; in charge of money transfer business, giro inpayments and outpayments as well as account-to-account transfers; admin of funds and overall cash flow management.

South Jutland Telecom: H. P. Ganssens Gade 21, 6200 Åbenrå; tel 74-62-24-11; telex 52158; fax 74-62-01-45; Dir, Telecommunications: P. E. B. Laursen; Dep Dir: Svend Erik Holst.

Telecom Denmark: Telegade 2, 2630 Tåstrup; tel 42-52-91-11; telex 22999; fax 42-52-93-31; Dir, Telecommunications: Jens Kiil; responsible for all telecommunications to and from abroad, maritime telecommunications services, radio and TV broadcasting, etc.

Telecom Inspectorate: Islands Bryge 81, 2300 Copenhagen S; tel 31-54-47-96; telex 31100; fax 31-54-48-30; Dir: Tage M. Iversen; f 1986; licensing and admin of radio frequencies; approval of terminal equipment for connection to the telecommunications network; inspection of radio and antenna systems and terminal equipment, etc.

TRANSPORT

Danish Maritime Authority: Vermundsgade 38 C, POB 2605, 2100 Copenhagen Ø; tel 39-27-15-15; telex 31141; fax 39-27-15-16.

Dansk Internationalt Skibsregister (Danish International Register of Shipping): address as above; Registrar: Arne Raff.

Det Danske Luftfartselskab A/S—DDL (Danish Airlines): Industriens Hus, H. C. Andersens Blvd 18, 1553 Copenhagen V; tel 33-14-13-33; telex 22437; fax 33-14-28-28; Chair: Haldor Topsøe; Man Dir: Fred Ahlgreen Eriksen; f 1918; Danish parent co of the designated national carrier, Scandinavian Airline Systems—SAS and SCANAIR.

DSB (Danish State Railways): Sølvgade 40, 1349 Copenhagen K; tel 33-14-04-00; telex 22225; fax 33-14-04-00; Dir-Gen: Ole Andresen; Gen-Man, Ferries: Peter Langager; f 1847; operates train and car ferry services between the mainland and principal islands.

Farvandsdirektoratet (National Administration of Shipping and Navigation): Overgaden oven Vandet 62B, 1001 Copenhagen K; tel 31-57-40-50; telex 31319; fax 31-57-43-41.

Statens Luftfartsvæsen (Civil Aviation Administration): Luftfartshuset, POB 744, 1850 Copenhagen SV; tel 36-44-48-48; telex 27096; fax 36-44-03-03; Dir-Gen: V. K. H. Eggers.

Vejdirektoratet (Directorate of Roads): Havnegade 27, POB 1569, 1020 Copenhagen K; tel 33-93-33-38; telex 9112233; fax 33-15-63-35; Dir-Gen: Per Milner; Dep Dir-Gen: Johannes Sloth; f 1949; part of the Ministry of Transport; responsible for planning and construction of new main roads, maintaining and improving existing roads; involved in research and devt of road materials; provides consultancy services.

DANISH EXTERNAL TERRITORIES

THE FAEROE ISLANDS

The Government

FØROYA LANDSSTÝRI
POB 64, 110 Tórshavn
Tel 11080; telex 81310; fax 14942
Prime Minister (Løgmadur): Jógvan Sundstein
Deputy Prime Minister: Signar Hansen
Minister of Finance: Finnbogi Ísakson
Minister of Fisheries: Anfinn Kallsberg
Minister of Health, Social Affairs and Agriculture:
Tordur Niclassen
**Minister of Transport, Communications, Church and
Cultural Affairs:** Karl Heri Jønsen

HIGH COMMISSION FOR THE FAEROE ISLANDS
Tórshavn
High Commissioner: Bent Klinte
Representation of the Danish Govt.

Government Agencies

BANKING

Føroya Banki A/S: Niels Finsensgøta 15, POB 14, 110 Tór-
shavn; tel 11350; telex 81227; fax 15850; Chair: Poul Johs
Johansen; Gen Mans: Hans-Jórgen Laursen, Johan Simonsen,
Niels Joel Nattestad; f 1906; 32 brs.

Føroya Sparikassi (Faeroese Savings Bank): POB 34, 110
Tórshavn; tel 14800; telex 81318; fax 18660; f 1832.

Sjóvinnubankin PF (Fisheries Bank): POB 48, 110 Tórshavn;
tel 14900; telex 81229; fax 16950; Chair: Birgir Danielsen; Mans:
Steingirm Nielsen, Regin Olsen; f 1932; 30 brs.

BROADCASTING

Sjónvarp Føroya (Faeroese Television): M. A. Wintersgøta,
POB 21, 3800 Tórshavn; tel (042) 17780; telex 81391; fax 11345;
Man: J. A. Skaale; f 1982.

Útvarp Føroya (Faeroese Broadcasting Corpn): Norðari
Ringvegi, 110 Tórshavn; tel (042) 16566; telex 81226; fax (042)
10471; Man: Niels Juel Arge; f 1957.

FISHING

Fisheries Administration: POB 87, 110 Tórshavn; tel 13098;
telex 81310.

NEWS AND INFORMATION

Faeroe Press Agency: P/f Salvará, Tjarnarðeild 12, Tórshavn;
Man: Jógvan Arge; f 1980; news agency.

TOURISM

Ferðamannamiðstøð Føroya (Faeroe Islands Tourist Board):
Skansavegur 1, 100 Tórshavn; tel 16055; telex 81385; fax 10858;
Chair: Jakob Haraldsen; Man: Jákup Veyhe; f 1984; co-ordinates
tourist activities.

TRADE

Føroya Tollstova (Faeroese Customs Authority): POB 3, 110
Tórshavn; tel 14660; telex 81310.

TRANSPORT

Aviation Authority: Dept of Communications, Govt of the
Faeroe Islands, Tinganes, Tórshavn.

GREENLAND

The Government

GRØNLANDS HJEMMESTYRE
POB 1015, 3900 Nuuk
Tel 23000; telex 90613
**Prime Minister and Secretary for Administration and
the Environment:** Jonathan Motzfeldt
Secretary for the Economy, Trade and Traffic: Emil
Abetsen

**Secretary for Fisheries, Industry and Outlying
Districts:** Kaj Egede
Secretary for Schools, Education and Labour: Jens
Lyberth
Secretary for Social Affairs and Housing: Moses Olsen
Greenland home rule government

HIGH COMMISSION FOR GREENLAND
POB 1030, 3900 Nuuk/Godthåb
Tel 21001; telex 90604; fax 24171
High Commissioner: Torben Hede Pedersen
Deputy High Commissioner: Steen Spore
Danish central Govt's chief representative in Greenland.

Government Agencies

BANKING

Grønlandsbanken A/S: POB 1033, 3900 Nuuk; tel 21380; telex 90611; Man: S. E. Danielsen; f 1967; 5 brs.

BROADCASTING

Kalaallit Nunaata Radioa/Grønlands Radio: POB 1007, 3900 Nuuk; tel 21172; telex 90606; fax 24703; Man Dir: Peter F. Rosing; Admin Dir: Peter Raahøj; Dir of TV: Mike Siegstad; radio programmes in Greenlandic and Danish; TV broadcasts.

TRANSPORT

Grønlandsfly A/S (Greenlandair INC): POB 1012, 3900 Nuuk/Godthå; tel 24488; telex 90602; fax 23888; Chair: Lars Emil Johansen; Pres: Jan K. Rasmussen; f 1960; internal services and external flights to Denmark, Iceland and Canada; subsidiaries are Greenlandair Charter Inc, handling special air transport operations, and Hotel Arctic Illulissat Inc, which provides hotel and catering services.

UTILITIES

NUNA-TEK (Nunatsinni Teknikkikkut Ingerlatsivik) (Greenland Technical Organization): POB 1044, 3900 Nuuk; tel 2-44-66; telex 0503-90434; fax 2-41-11; Man Dir: Gunnar P. Rosendahl; Dep Dirs: Jan Birket-Smith (Nuuk), Hans Oelgaard (Copenhagen); f 1950; operates telecommunications, including telephones, telex, radio and TV transmission, etc; runs energy supply, water supply and central heating plants; directs building and construction work; operates shipyards; carries out mapping and field investigations; regulates mineral activities.

DJIBOUTI

Head of State

Executive power is vested in the President who is directly elected by universal adult suffrage for a six-year term and may serve no more than two terms, under the provisions of the 1981 Constitution. The Council of Ministers, presided over by a Prime Minister, is responsible to the President.

President: Hassan Gouled Aptidon (took office 27 June 1977; re-elected June 1981 and April 1987).

Office of the President: BP 6, Djibouti; tel 350201; telex 5871.

Legislature

Legislative power is vested in the Chambre des Députés (Chamber of Deputies), comprising 65 members elected by universal adult suffrage for five years. Djibouti became a one-party state in October 1981. Political power is held by the Rassemblement populaire pour le progrès (RPP), whose Political Bureau is appointed by the President.

Chambre des Députés (Chamber of Deputies): BP 138, Djibouti; tel 352037; telex 5871; Pres: Abdoulkader Waberi Askar.

MINISTRIES AND GOVERNMENT DEPARTMENTS

OFFICE OF THE PRIME MINISTER
BP 2086, Djibouti
Tel 351494; telex 5871; fax 355049
Prime Minister: Barkad Gourad Hamadou

MINISTRY OF AGRICULTURE AND RURAL DEVELOPMENT
BP 453, Djibouti
Tel 351297; telex 5871
Minister: Muhammad Moussa Chehem

MINISTRY OF THE CIVIL SERVICE AND ADMINISTRATIVE REFORM
BP 155, Djibouti
Tel 351464; telex 5871
Minister: Ismail Ali Youssouf

MINISTRY OF COMMERCE, TRANSPORT AND TOURISM
BP 121, Djibouti
Tel 352540; telex 5871
Minister: Moussa Bourale Roble

MINISTRY OF DEFENCE
BP 42, Djibouti
Tel 352034; telex 5871
Minister: Hussein Barkad Siraj

MINISTRY OF EDUCATION
BP 2102, Djibouti
Tel 351689; telex 5871
Minister: Suleiman Farah Lodon

MINISTRY OF FINANCE AND NATIONAL ECONOMY
BP 13, Djibouti
Tel 353331; telex 5871
Minister: Muhammad Djama Elabe

MINISTRY OF FOREIGN AFFAIRS AND CO-OPERATION
BP 1863, Djibouti
Tel 352471; telex 5871
Minister: Moumin Bahdon Farah

MINISTRY OF HEALTH AND SOCIAL AFFAIRS
BP 296, Djibouti
Tel 353331; telex 5871
Minister: Ougoure Hassan Ibrahim

MINISTRY OF INDUSTRY AND INDUSTRIAL DEVELOPMENT
BP 175, Djibouti
Tel 350137; telex 5871
Minister: Salem Abdou

MINISTRY OF THE INTERIOR, POSTS AND TELECOMMUNICATIONS
BP 33, Djibouti
Tel 350791; telex 5871
Minister: Khaireh Allaleh Hared

MINISTRY OF JUSTICE AND ISLAMIC AFFAIRS
BP 12, Djibouti
Tel 351506; telex 5871
Minister: Elaf Orbiss Ali

MINISTRY OF LABOUR AND SOCIAL WELFARE
BP 170, Djibouti
Tel 350497; telex 5871
Minister: Ahmed Ibrahim Abdi

MINISTRY OF PLANNING AND LAND DEVELOPMENT
BP 2086, Djibouti
Tel 351494; telex 5871
Minister: Barkad Gourad Hamadou

MINISTRY OF PORTS AND MARITIME AFFAIRS
BP 2107, Djibouti
Tel 350105; telex 5871
Minister: Barkad Gourad Hamadou

MINISTRY OF PUBLIC WORKS AND HOUSING
BP 11, Djibouti
Tel 350006; telex 5871
Minister: Ahmed Aden Youssouf

MINISTRY OF YOUTH, SPORTS AND CULTURAL AFFAIRS
BP 2102, Djibouti
Tel 351689; telex 5871
Minister: Omar Chirdon Abass

GOVERNMENT AGENCIES AND ORGANIZATIONS

Business and Economy

BANKING

Banque Nationale de Djibouti: BP 2118, Djibouti; tel 352751; telex 5838; Gov: Luc A. Aden; f 1981; bank of issue.

Caisse de Développement de Djibouti: rue de l'Ethiopie, BP 520, Djibouti; tel 353391; Chair: Luc A. Aden; Man Dir: Nouh Omar Miguil; f 1983; national devt bank; 51% Govt-owned.

TRADE

Office National d'Approvisionnement et de Commercialisation (ONAC): BP 75, Djibouti; tel 350327; responsible for import and distribution of goods; marketing of domestic produce.

Defence

Armed Forces: BP 6, Djibouti; tel 350177; telex 5871; Commdr-in-Chief: President Hassan Gouled Aptidon.

Air Force: Djibouti; telex 5871; Commdr: Hossein Djama.

Army: Djibouti; tel 351156; telex 5871; Chief of Staff: Ali Mehidal Wais.

Navy: Djibouti; telex 5871; Commdr: Yonis Saad.

National Police: Djibouti; telex 5871; Commdr: Hoch Roble Idle.

Media

BROADCASTING

Radiodiffusion-Télévision de Djibouti: BP 97, Djibouti; tel 352294; telex 5863; Dir-Gen: Mohamed Djama Aden; f 1967; programmes in French, Afar, Somali and Arabic.

NEWS AND INFORMATION

Service de Statistique et de Documentation: BP 1846, Djibouti; tel 353331; statistical office.

Tourism

Office National de Tourisme et de l'Artisanat: place du 27 juin, BP 1938, Djibouti; tel 352800; telex 5938; tourism dept.

Transport

CIVIL AVIATION

Air Djibouti (Red Sea Airlines): BP 505, rue Marchand, Djibouti; tel 353651; telex 5820; fax 354363; Gen Man: Paul Botbol; f 1971; 62.5% Govt-owned; internal services and international flights to the Yemen Arab Republic, Somalia, the United Arab Emirates, France, Italy, Egypt, Ethiopia and Saudi Arabia.

RAILWAYS

Compagnie du Chemin de Fer Djibouti-Ethiopien: BP 2116, Djibouti; tel 350353; telex 5953; Pres: Y. Roble; Vice-Pres: Moussa Bourale Roble; Gen Man: Channie Tamiru; f 1908; jointly-owned by the Govts of Djibouti and Ethiopia; plans to grant autonomous status were announced in July 1985.

DOMINICA

Head of State

Executive authority is vested in the President, who is elected for a five-year term by the House of Assembly. In most matters the President is guided by the advice of the Cabinet and acts as a constitutional Head of State. The President appoints the Prime Minister, and (on the Prime Minister's recommendation) other Ministers. The Cabinet is responsible to the House of Assembly.

President: Sir Clarence Seignoret (assumed office 19 December 1983; second term began 20 December 1988).

Office of the President: Morne Bruce, Roseau; tel 82054.

Legislature

Legislative power is vested in the unicameral House of Assembly, composed of 21 Representatives elected for five years by universal adult suffrage, and nine Senators, who are nominated by the President on the advice of the Prime Minister and the Leader of the Opposition.

House of Assembly: Government Headquarters, Kennedy Ave, Roseau; tel 82401; telex 8613; fax 85200; Speaker: Crispin Sorhaidoo; Clerk: Albertha Jno Baptiste.

MINISTRIES AND GOVERNMENT DEPARTMENTS

OFFICE OF THE PRIME MINISTER
Government Headquarters, Kennedy Ave, Roseau
Tel 82406
Prime Minister: Mary Eugenia Charles

MINISTRY OF AGRICULTURE, INDUSTRY, TOURISM, TRADE, LANDS AND SURVEYS
Government Headquarters, Kennedy Ave, Roseau
Tel 82401; telex 8613; fax 85200
Minister: Charles Maynard

MINISTRY OF COMMUNICATIONS, WORKS AND HOUSING
Government Headquarters, Kennedy Ave, Roseau
Tel 82401; telex 8613; fax 85200
Minister: Alleyne J. Carbon

MINISTRY OF COMMUNITY DEVELOPMENT AND SOCIAL AFFAIRS
Government Headquarters, Kennedy Ave, Roseau
Tel 82401; telex 8613; fax 85200
Minister: Heskeith Alexander

MINISTRY OF EDUCATION AND SPORTS
Government Headquarters, Kennedy Ave, Roseau
Tel 82401; telex 8613; fax 85200
Minister: Henry George

MINISTRY OF FINANCE, DEFENCE, FOREIGN AND ECONOMIC AFFAIRS
Government Headquarters, Kennedy Ave, Roseau
Tel 82406
Minister: Mary Eugenia Charles

MINISTRY OF HEALTH, WATER AND SEWAGE
Government Headquarters, Kennedy Ave, Roseau
Tel 82401; telex 8613; fax 85200
Minister: Ronan David

OFFICE OF THE ATTORNEY-GENERAL AND MINISTRY OF LEGAL AFFAIRS, IMMIGRATION AND LABOUR
Government Headquarters, Kennedy Ave, Roseau
Tel 82401; telex 8613; fax 85200
Attorney-General and Minister: Brian G. K. Alleyne

GOVERNMENT AGENCIES AND ORGANIZATIONS

Agriculture and Forestry

AGRICULTURE

Dominica Banana Growers' Association: Hanover St, Roseau; tel 84983; telex 8648; Exec Sec: Jefferson B. Scotland; f 1984; promotes interests of banana growers.

FORESTRY

Forestry Department: Botanic Garden, Roseau; tel 82401; fax 85200; Dir: Felix Gregoire; f 1949; responsible for forestry resource.

Business and Economy

BANKING

Dominica Agricultural, Industrial and Development (AID) Bank: 64 Hillsborough St, POB 215, Roseau; tel 84167; telex 8620; Man: Patricia Charles; f 1971; long-term financing to agricultural, housing, industrial and tourism sectors.

Eastern Caribbean Central Bank (ECCB): POB 89, Basseterre, St Christopher and Nevis; tel 456-2537; telex 6828; Gov: Cecil A. Jacobs; f 1965 as East Caribbean Currency Authority; responsible for issue of currency in East Caribbean islands, including Dominica.

National Commercial Bank of Dominica: 64 Hillsborough St, POB 271, Roseau; tel 84401; telex 8620; fax 83982; Chair: Franklin A. Baron; Gen Man: Lambert V. Lewis; f 1978; financing the devt of commerce, industry, tourism and housing.

MARKETING

Dominica Banana Marketing Corpn (DMBC): cnr Queen Mary St and Turkey Lane, POB 24, Roseau; tel 82671; telex 8684; fax 86445; Chair: Vanoulst Jno Charles; Gen Man: Ambrose V. George; f 1934; restructured 1982; marketing and purchase of bananas for export.

TRADE

Dominica Association of Industry and Commerce (DAIC): King George V St, POB 85, Roseau; tel 82874; Pres: Edward Lambert; Exec Sec: Ferdinand A. Azille; f 1972; promotion of commerce and industry; representation of the business sector.

Dominica Export-Import Agency (Dexia): Charles Ave, POB 173, Roseau; tel 83494; telex 8626; fax 85840; f 1986; export facilitator; importer of essential commodities, particularly rice and sugar.

Defence

Dominica Police Service: Police Headquarters, Roseau; tel 82222; Commr: E. L. Pierre; Dep Commr: J. D. Blanchard.

Development and Planning

National Development Corpn: Valley Rd, Bath Estate, POB 293, Roseau; tel 82045; telex 8642; fax 85840; Chair: Dermot Southwell; Gen Man: W. Ken Alleyne; f 1988 by merger of the Industrial Development Corpn with the Tourist Board; promotion of tourism and investment; industrial and small-business devt.

Employment

Public and Police Services Commissions: Personnel Services Department, Government Headquarters, Roseau; tel 82401; telex 8613; Chair, Public Service Commission: E. P. Munro; Chair, Police Service Commission: H. L. Doctrove; supervision of employment in public and police service.

Energy

DOMLEC: POB 13, Castle St, Roseau; tel 82681; telex 8655; national electricity service.

Media

BROADCASTING

Dominica Broadcasting Corpn: Victoria St, POB 1, Roseau; tel 83283; Chair: Gordon Moreau; Man Dir (acting): J. Pascall; broadcasts in English and French patois.

NEWS AND INFORMATION

Central Statistical Office: Kennedy Ave, Roseau; tel 448-2401; telex 8613; Chief Statistician: Dr Oscar Perez de Tagle; f 1956; collection, analysis and dissemination of statistical information.

Transport

Dominica Ports Authority: POB 243, Roseau; tel 84431; telex 8632; fax 86131; Chair: R. O. P. Armour; Gen Man: O. M. Norris; f 1972; pilotage and cargo handling.

Utilities

Central Water Authority: Roseau; Chair: Donald Boyd; responsible for water supplies and sewerage.

THE DOMINICAN REPUBLIC

Head of State

Executive power is vested in the President, who is elected by direct suffrage for a four-year term. The President appoints a Cabinet containing Secretaries of State, which is responsible to the National Congress.

President: Dr Joaquín Balaguer Ricardo (took office 16 August 1986).

Vice-President: Carlos Morales Troncoso.

Office of the President and of the Vice-President: Palacio Nacional, Moisés García, Santo Domingo, DN; tel 689-1131; telex 346-0011.

Legislature

Legislative power is vested in the bicameral Congreso Nacional (National Congress), with a Senate of 30 members and a Chamber of Deputies of 120 members. Members of both houses are elected by direct suffrage for four years. There are 26 provinces, each administered by an appointed governor, and a Distrito Nacional (DN) containing the capital.

Senado (Senate): Palacio del Congreso, Centro de los Héroes de Constanza, Santo Domingo, DN; tel 533-1334; Pres: Francisco Ortega Canela.

Cámara de Diputados (Chamber of Deputies): Palacio del Congreso, Centro de los Héroes de Costanza, Santo Domingo, DN; tel 533-2633; Pres: Luis José González.

MINISTRIES AND GOVERNMENT DEPARTMENTS

SECRETARIAT OF STATE FOR AGRICULTURE
Centro de los Héroes de Constanza, Santo Domingo, DN
Tel 533-7171; telex 346-0393
Secretary of State: Manuel de Jesús Pina Cacerels

SECRETARIAT OF STATE FOR DEFENCE
Plaza de la Independencia, Avda 27 de Febrero,
Santo Domingo, DN
Tel 533-5131; telex 346-0652
Secretary of State: Manuel Estrada Medina

SECRETARIAT OF STATE FOR EDUCATION AND CULTURE
Avda Máximo Gómez, Santo Domingo, DN
Tel 689-9161
Secretary of State: Nicolás Almanzar

SECRETARIAT OF STATE FOR ENERGY
Santo Domingo, DN
Secretary of State: Celestino Armas

SECRETARIAT OF STATE FOR EXTERNAL RELATIONS
Avda Independencia, Santo Domingo, DN
Tel 533-4121; telex 326-4192
Secretary of State: Joaquín Ricardo García

SECRETARIAT OF STATE FOR FINANCE
Avda México, Santo Domingo, DN
Telex 346-0437
Secretary of State: Rodolfo Rincón

SECRETARIAT OF STATE FOR HEALTH AND SOCIAL WELFARE
Santo Domingo, DN
Secretary of State: Dr Rafael Gautreaux

SECRETARIAT OF STATE FOR INDUSTRY AND COMMERCE
Edif de Oficinas Gubernamentales 7, Avda México,
Santo Domingo, DN
Tel 685-5171
Secretary of State: José Manuel Trullols

SECRETARIAT OF STATE FOR THE INTERIOR AND POLICE
Edif de Oficinas Gubernamentales 3, Avda Leopoldo Navarro
a esq México, Santo Domingo, DN
Tel 689-1979
Secretary of State: Manuel Estrada Medina

SECRETARIAT OF STATE FOR LABOUR
Santo Domingo, DN
Secretary of State: Rafael Emiliano Agramonte

SECRETARIAT OF STATE FOR THE PRESIDENCY
Santo Domingo, DN
Secretary of State: Dr Rafael Bello Andino
Administrative Secretary to the Presidency: Luis Toral
Technical Secretary to the Presidency:
Roberto Martínez Villanueva
Secretaries of State without Portfolio: Manuel Guaroa
Liranzo, Simón Tomás Fernández, Dr Donald Reid Cabral,
Juan Rafael Peralta

**SECRETARIAT OF STATE FOR PUBLIC WORKS
AND COMMUNICATIONS**
Ensanche La Fé, Santo Domingo, DN
Tel 567-4929
Secretary of State: Marcos Subero Sajuín

**SECRETARIAT OF STATE FOR SPORT, PHYSICAL
EDUCATIONAND RECREATION**
Calle Pedro Henríquez Ureña, Santo Domingo, DN
Tel 688-0126; telex 346-0471
Secretary of State: Temistocles Metz

SECRETARIAT OF STATE FOR TOURISM
Avda George Washington, Apdo 497, Santo Domingo, DN
Tel 682-8181; telex 346-0303; fax 682-3806
Secretary of State: Fernando Rainieri Marranzini

GOVERNMENT AGENCIES AND ORGANIZATIONS

Advisory and Supervisory Body

Instituto de Estabilización de Precios (INESPRE): Avda Luperón, Santo Domingo, DN; tel 547-4442; Dir: Katiusca Bobea de Brenes; controls prices of basic commodities.

Agriculture

Consejo Estatal del Azúcar—CEA (State Sugar Council): Calle de los Héroes de Constanza, Apdo 1256/1258, Santo Domingo, DN; tel 533-1161; telex 346-0043; Dir: Manuel Villas Cáceres; f 1966; administers the 12 state sugar mills.

Instituto Agrario Dominicano (IAD): Avda 27 de Febrero, Santo Domingo, DN; tel 566-0141; Dir: Candido Uargas; agricultural institute.

Instituto Azucarero Dominicano (INAZUCAR): Avda Jiménez Moya, Apdo 667, Santo Domingo, DN; tel 532-5571; Dir: Miguel Guerrero; f 1965; sugar institute.

Business and Economy

BANKING

Banco Agrícola de la República Dominicana: Avda George Washington 601, Apdo 1057, Santo Domingo, DN; tel 533-1171; telex 346-0026; Gen Man: Pedro Bretun; f 1945; Govt agricultural devt bank; 31 brs.

Banco Central de la República Dominicana: Calle Pedro Henríquez Ureña a esq Leopoldo Navarro, Apdo 1347, Santo Domingo, DN; tel 689-7121; telex 346-0052; fax 686-7488; Gov: Dr Guillermo Carám (mem of Cabinet); Gen Man: Dr Jorge Matos; f 1947; central bank.

Banco Hipotecario Dominicano, SA: Avda 27 de Febrero a esq Winston Churchill, Apdo 266-2, Santo Domingo, DN; tel 567-7281; telex 4546; fax 541-4949; Pres: Daysi Perello; f 1972; housing devt bank; 5 brs.

Banco Nacional de la Vivienda (BNV): Avda Tiradentes a esq H. Pieter, Ensanche Naco, Apdo 1504, Santo Domingo, DN; f 1962; finances the construction, purchase and improvement of housing.

Banco de Reservas de la República Dominicana: Isabel la Católica 201, Apdo 1353, Santo Domingo, DN; tel 688-2241; telex 346-0012; fax 685-0602; Gen Man: Dr Emilio de Luna Peguero; Business Man: Dr Nicolás Alcides Camilo; f 1941; 36 brs.

Banco de los Trabajadores de la República Dominicana: El Conde a esq Arzobispo Meriño, Apdo 1446, Santo Domingo, DN; tel 688-0181; telex 346-4500; Pres: José A. Rodríguez Espaillat; f 1972; 4 brs.

Superintendencia de Bancos: Avda México a esq Leopoldo Navarro, Apdo 1326, Santo Domingo, DN; tel 685-8141; telex 346-0653; Supt: Dr Emilio de Luna Peguero; banking supervisory body.

FINANCIAL AGENCIES

Cámara de Cuentas de la República Dominicana (National Chamber of Accounts): Autopista Duarte Km 61/2, Santo Domingo, DN; tel 565-5555; telex 346-2549; Pres: Dr Juan Rolando Pimentel; Vice-Pres: Levi A. Disla García; f 1942; accounting body for Govt and state organizations.

Junta Monetaria (Monetary Board): Banco Central, Calle Pedro Henríquez Ureña a esq Leopoldo Navarro, Santo Domingo, DN; forms policy on money supply, credit, interest rates, etc.

Oficina Nacional de Presupuesto (National Budget Office): Secretariado Técnico de la Presidencia, Santo Domingo, DN; studies level and distribution of Govt spending and recommends means for the containment of expenditure, and for the expansion of resources to meet new objectives.

Tesorería Nacional (National Treasury): Santo Domingo, DN; custody of all public funds, reserves and special deposits; receives and releases Govt funds.

INSURANCE

Superintendencia de Seguros: Avda México a esq Leopoldo Navarro, Santo Domingo, DN; tel 688-1245; Supt: Dr Juan Esteban Olivero Feliz; f 1969; supervisory body for insurance cos.

MARKETING

Corporación de Fomento Industrial (CFI): Avda 27 de Febrero, Apdo 1472, Santo Domingo, DN; tel 547-3328; telex 346-0049; Dir: Julio César Pineda; f 1962; promotion of agro-industrial devt.

NATIONALIZED INDUSTRY

Corporación Dominicana de Empresas Estatales (CORDE): Avda Gen Antonio Duvergé, Apdo 1378, Santo Domingo, DN; tel 533-5171; telex 346-0311; Exec Dir: Raúl Barrientos; f 1966; administers and develops state enterprises.

TRADE

Centro Dominicano de Promoción de Exportaciones (CEDOPEX): Plaza de la Independencia, Sección de Herrera,

Apdo 199-2, Santo Domingo, DN; tel 566-9131; telex 346-0351; Dir: José Carlos Isaías; export promotion.

Defence

Air Force: Base Aérea de San Isidro, San Isidro, Santo Domingo, DN; tel 533-0055; Chief of Staff: Héctor Román Torres.

Army: Plaza de la Independencia, Avda 27 de Febrero, Santo Domingo; tel 533-5131; Chief of Staff: Constantino Matos.

Navy: Base Naval 27 de Febrero, Villa Duarte, Santo Domingo, DN; tel 682-2946; Chief of Staff: José Santo Sánchez.

Development and Planning

INVESTMENT

Consejo Promotor de Inversiones (Investment Promotion Council): Avda Abraham Lincoln 2, Santo Domingo, DN; tel 532-3281; fax 533-7029; Pres: Antonio Cáceres Troncoso.

Fondo de Inversión para el Desarrollo Económico—FIDE (Economic Development Investment Fund): Banco Central de la República Dominicana, Avda Pedro Henríquez Ureña a esq Leopoldo Navarro, Santo Domingo, DN; tel 689-7121; Dir: Virgilio Malagon Alvarez; encourages economic devt; authorizes complementary financing to private sector for establishing new industrial and agricultural enterprises and developing existing ones.

Fundación Dominicana de Desarrollo (Dominican Development Foundation): Calle Mercedes 4, Apdo 857, Santo Domingo, DN; Dir: Eduardo La Torre; f 1962; mobilizes private resources for collaboration in financing small-scale devt programmes.

PLANNING

Instituto de Desarrollo y Crédito Cooperativo (IDE-COOP): Centro de los Héroes de Constanza, Santo Domingo, DN; tel 533-8131; Dir: Dr Nelson Eddy Carrasco; f 1963; encourages devt of co-operatives.

Instituto Nacional de la Vivienda: Avda Pedro Henríquez Ureña a esq Leopoldo Navarro, Apdo 1506, Santo Domingo, DN; tel 685-4181; Dir-Gen: Ricardo Canalda; Dep Dir-Gen: Nelly Zeneyda Acosta; f 1962; researches housing needs; provision of low-cost housing.

Oficina Nacional de Planificación: Edif de Oficinas Gubernamentales Juan Pablo Duarte 13, Avda México a esq Leopoldo Navarro, Apdo 20200, Santo Domingo, DN; tel 688-4266; telex 326-4635; f 1962; planning of economic and social devt.

Legal and Judiciary

Corte Suprema (Supreme Court): Centro de los Héroes de Constanza, Santo Domingo, DN; tel 533-3522; Pres: Néstor Coytín Aybar; Attorney-Gen: Semíramis Olivo de Pichardo.

Media

BROADCASTING

Radio Televisión Dominicana: Dr Tejada Florentino 8, Apdo 969, Santo Domingo, DN; tel 689-2121; Dir-Gen: R. A. Font Bernard; Gen Man: Agustín Mercado; two channels.

NEWS AND INFORMATION

Administración General de Bienes Nacionales: Santo Domingo, DN; produces statistical and other information on the assets of the Govt and its agencies.

Oficina Nacional de Estadísticas: Edif de Oficinas Públicas, Avda México a esq Leopoldo Navarro, Santo Domingo, DN.

Mining and Energy

ENERGY

Corporación Dominicana de Electricidad: Avda Independencia, Santo Domingo, DN; tel 533-1131; Man: César Newman Torres; electricity co.

Comisión Nacional de Asuntos Nucleares: Edif de la Defensa Civil, Dr Delgado 58, Santo Domingo, DN; tel 565-5090; telex 346-0461; Pres: Dr Abel González Massenet; commission for nuclear affairs.

MINING

Dirección General de Minería e Hidrocarburos: Edif de Oficinas Gubernamentales 10, Avda México a esq Leopoldo Navarro, Santo Domingo, DN; tel 658-8191; Dir-Gen: Francisco Amezquita; f 1947; mining and hydrocarbon organization.

Transport and Communications

TELECOMMUNICATIONS

Dirección General de Telecomunicaciones: Isabel la Católica 203, Santo Domingo, DN; tel 689-4161; Dir-Gen: Leopoldo Nueñez Santos; telecommunications supervisory body.

TRANSPORT

Dirección General de Tránsito Terrestre: Avda San Cristóbal, Santo Domingo, DN; tel 567-4610; Dir-Gen: Arif Abud Abreu; f 1966; supervisory organization for transport.

Dominicana de Aviación C por A: Avda Jiménez de Moya a esq José Contreras, Apdo 1415, Santo Domingo, DN; tel 532-8511; telex 346-0438; Chair: Manuel Alsina Puello; f 1944; flights to Netherlands Antilles, Aruba, the USA, Haiti, Panama and Venezuela.

Ferrocarril Unidos Dominicanos: Santo Domingo, DN; 142 km of track principally used for the transport of exports.

ECUADOR

Head of State

Executive authority is vested in the President, who is elected by universal adult suffrage for a four-year term and is not eligible for re-election. The President appoints the Cabinet.

President: Dr Rodrigo Borja Cevallos (took office 10 August 1988).

Office of the President: Palacio Nacional, García Moreno 1043, Quito; tel (2) 216-300; telex 23751.

Vice-President: Luis Parodí Valverde.

Office of the Vice-President: Manuel Larrea y Arenas, Edif Consejo Provincial de Pichincha, 21, Quito; tel (2) 503-335; telex 22058; fax (2) 503-379.

Legislature

Legislative power is exercised by the unicameral Cámara Nacional de Representantes which comprises 71 representatives elected for four-year terms. The country consists of 20 provinces, each headed by a Governor appointed by the President. In April 1980 the future formation of an upper chamber was agreed.

Cámara Nacional de Representantes (Chamber of Representatives): Avda Juan Montalvo y Avda 6 de Diciembre, Palacio Legislativo, Quito; tel (2) 230-330; Pres of Congress: Dr Wilfrido Lucero Bolaños; Vice-Pres of Congress: Nicolás Issa Obanbo.

MINISTRIES AND GOVERNMENT DEPARTMENTS

MINISTRY OF AGRICULTURE AND LIVESTOCK
Avda Eloy Alfaro y Avda Amazonas, Quito
Tel (2) 554-122; telex 2291
Minister: Dr Enrique Delgado Copiano

MINISTRY OF DEFENCE
Exposición 208, Quito
Tel (2) 216-150; telex 2703
Minister: Gen (retd) Jorge Félix Mena

MINISTRY OF EDUCATION AND CULTURE
Mejía 348, Quito
Tel (2) 216-224
Minister: Alfredo Vera Arrata

MINISTRY OF ENERGY AND MINES
Santa Prisca 223 y Manuel Larrea, Quito
Tel (2) 239-100; telex 2271
Minister: Diego Tamariz Serrano

MINISTRY OF FINANCE AND PUBLIC CREDIT
Avda 10 de Agosto 1661 y Jorge Washington, Quito
Tel (2) 544-500; telex 2358
Minister: Jorge Gallardo Zavala

MINISTRY OF FOREIGN AFFAIRS
Avda 10 de Agosto y Carrión, Quito
Tel (2) 230-500; telex 2441
Minister: Dr Diego Cordóvez Zégers

MINISTRY OF INDUSTRY, TRADE, INTEGRATION AND FISHERIES
Juan León Mera y Roca, Quito
Tel (2) 524-666; telex 2166
Minister: Jacinto Jouvín

MINISTRY OF THE INTERIOR
Espejo y Benalcázar, Quito
Tel (2) 216-080; telex 2354
Minister of Government and Justice (Interior):
Andrés Vallejo Arco

MINISTRY OF LABOUR AND HUMAN RESOURCES
Ponce y Luis Felipe Borja, Quito
Tel (2) 524-666; telex 2898
Minister: César Verduga Vélez

MINISTRY OF PUBLIC HEALTH
Juan Larrea 446, Quito
Tel (2) 547-329; telex 2677
Minister: Dr Plutarco Naranjo Vargas

MINISTRY OF PUBLIC WORKS AND COMMUNICATIONS
Avda 6 de Diciembre y Wilson, Quito
Tel (2) 242-666; telex 2353
Minister: Juan Neira Carrasco

MINISTRY OF SOCIAL WELFARE
Robles 6, Quito
Tel (2) 540-750; telex 2898
Minister: Rául Baca Carbo

OFFICE OF THE SECRETARY-GENERAL FOR PUBLIC ADMINISTRATION
Palacio Nacional, García Morena 1043, Quito
Tel (2) 515-990
Secretary-General: Washington Herrera

GOVERNMENT AGENCIES AND ORGANIZATIONS

Advisory and Supervisory Bodies

Instituto Nacional Galápagos: Of 6 de Marzo 3507, Guayaquil.

Junta Nacional de la Vivienda: Avda 10 de Agosto 2270 y Cordero, Quito; housing board; takes account of housing need and provision and plans policies accordingly.

Superintendencia de Compañías del Ecuador: Roca 660 y Avda Amazonas, Casilla 1387, Quito; tel (2) 525-022; telex 2595; Pres: Dr Carlos Muños Insua; responsible for the social and economic devt of commercial enterprises.

Agriculture and Fishing

Empresa Pesquera Nacional: Velex 131 y Chile, 5, Guayaquil; tel (4) 524-913; state fishing enterprise.

Instituto Ecuatoriano de Reforma Agraria y Colonización (IERAC): Quito; Dir: Rafael Pérez Reina; f 1973; supervises the Agrarian Reform Law under the auspices and coordination of the Ministry of Agriculture.

Instituto Nacional de Pesca: Letamendi 102 y E, Alfaro, Guayaquil.

Programa Nacional del Banano y Frutas Tropicales: Pichincha 103, Guayaquil; promotes the devt of banana and tropical fruit cultivation.

Business and Economy

BANKING

Banco Central del Ecuador: Avda 10 de Agosto, Plaza Bolívar, Casilla 339, Quito; tel (2) 210-340; telex 2165; Pres: Federico Arteta Rivera; Gen Man: José Morillo Batlle (mem of the Cabinet); f 1927.

Banco de Desarrollo del Ecuador, SA (BEDE): Páez 655 y Ramírez Dávalos, Casilla 373, Quito; tel (2) 551-033; telex 2655; Pres: Gustavo Espinosa Chimbo; Gen Man: Eduardo Valencia; f 1979; finances devt projects through regional govts and devt agencies.

Banco Ecuatoriano de la Vivienda: Avda 10 de Agosto 2270 y Cordero, Casilla 3244, Quito; tel (2) 521-311; telex 2399; Pres: Juan Pablo Moncagatta; Gen Man: Dr Fausto Vásquez Morales; f 1962.

Banco Nacional de Fomento: Ante 107 y 10 de Agosto, Casilla 685, Quito; tel (2) 230-010; telex 22256; Pres: Dr Ignacio Hidalgo Villavicencio; Gen Man: Marcelo Peña Durini; f 1928.

Corporación Financiera Nacional CFN: Juan León Mera 130 y Avda Patria, Casilla 163, Quito; tel (2) 564-900; telex 2193; Pres: Jorge Núñez Dahik; Gen Man: Rodrigo Malo González; f 1964.

Superintendencia de Bancos y Seguros: Avda 12 de Octubre 1561, Apdo 424, Quito; tel (2) 569-526; telex 22148; fax (2) 563-652; Supt: Dr Gonzalo Córdova Galarza; f 1927; banking supervisory authority.

FINANCIAL AGENCIES

COFIEC—Compañía Financiera Ecuatoriana de Desarrollo, SA: Avda Patria y Avda Amazonas, Edif COFIEC, 14, Casilla 411, Quito; tel (2) 546-177; telex 2131; fax (2) 564-224;

Pres: José Luis Alvarez; Exec Pres: César Robalino; f 1966; finance corpn.

Junta Monetaria Nacional (National Monetary Board): Quito; tel (2) 514-833; telex 2182; Pres: Abelardo Pachano Bertero (mem of the Cabinet); f 1927.

NATIONALIZED INDUSTRY

Instituto Ecuatoriano de Recursos Hidráulicos (INEHRI): Quito; Man: Pedro Alava González; irrigation and hydroelectric projects.

TRADE

Empresa Nacional de Almacenamiento y Comercialización de Productos Agropecuarios (ENAC): La Niña 635, Quito; tel (2) 548-500; trades agricultural produce nationally and internationally; market research; promotes Ecuadorean produce abroad.

Empresa de Suministros del Estado: Quito; state purchasing agency; supplies goods and services to Govt.

Fondo de Promoción de Exportaciones (FOPEX): Juan León Mera 130 y Avda Patria, Casilla 163, Quito; tel (2) 562-370; telex 2193; fax (2) 562-519; Dir: Dr Juan Villasis A.; f 1972; financial and technical help to promote exports.

Instituto Ecuatoriano de Normalización (INEN): Baquerizo 454 y 6 de Diciembre, Quito; tel (2) 528-556; standards institute.

Culture

Instituto Nacional de Patrimonio Cultural: Calle Cuenca y Mejia, Quito; tel (2) 512-590; f 1978; anthropological investigation; investigates, conserves, exhibits and promotes Ecuadorean culture.

Defence

Armed Forces: c/o Ministry of Defence, Exposición 208, Quito; tel (2) 218-049; telex 2381; Chief of Staff: Brig-Gen Jorge Andrade Zevallos.

Air Force: address as above; tel (2) 210-080; telex 2706.

Army: address as above; tel (2) 510-902; telex 2703.

Navy: address as above; tel (2) 518-222; telex 2351.

Astilleros Navales Ecuatorianos (ASTINAVE): Vacas Galindo y Viveros, Guayaquil (4) 342-361; telex 3778; fax (4) 441-838; Dir-Gen: Jorge Félix Navarrete; f 1972; construction, maintenance and repair of ships.

Coast Guard: c/o Ministry of Defence, Exposición 208, Quito; tel (2) 518-888.

Development and Planning

DEVELOPMENT

Centro de Desarrollo Industrial del Ecuador (CENDES): Avda Orellana 1715 y 9 de Octubre, Casilla 2321, Quito; tel (2) 527-100; Gen Man: Pablo Durango Vela; f 1962; carries out industrial feasibility studies; supplies technical and administrative assistance to industry; promotes new industries; supervises investment programmes.

Centro Nacional de Promoción de la Pequeña Industria y Artesanía (CENAPIA): Quito; Dir: Mauricio Mier Luna; agency to develop small-scale industry and handicrafts.

Consejo Nacional de Desarrollo (CONADE): Juan Larrea y Arenas, Quito; Chair: Dr Blasco Peñaherrera Padilla; aims to formulate and supervise the execution of a general plan of economic and social devt and to integrate local plans into the national.

Fondo Nacional de Asistencia Técnica: a/c Conade, Juan Larrea y Arenas, Edif Consejo Provincial, Quito; financing of technical aid and training programmes; administered by CONADE.

Organización Comercial Ecuatoriana de Productos Artesanales (OCEPA): Avda República 1527 y Inglaterra, Casilla 2948, Quito; tel (2) 542-045; telex 22062; fax (2) 430-839; Gen Man: Enrique Ponce; f 1964; develops and promotes national arts and crafts.

INVESTMENT

Fondo de Desarrollo Municipal (FODEM): Quito; funds to help municipal authorities complete investment projects approved by Govt planning agencies.

Fondo de Desarrollo del Sector Rural Marginal (FODERUMA): Quito; f 1978; allots funds to rural devt programmes in poor areas.

Fondo Nacional de Desarrollo (FONADE): Quito; f 1973; national devt fund to finance projects as laid down in the five-year plan.

Fondo Nacional de Preinversión (FONAPRE): Jorge Washington 624 y Avda Amazonas, Casilla 3302, Quito; tel (2) 563-261; telex 2772; Pres: Luis Parodi; Exec Dir: Dr Moises Tacle G.; f 1973; promotes and finances social and economic devt projects.

REGIONAL DEVELOPMENT

Centro de Reconversión Económica del Austro (CREA): Bolívar y Cueva, Cuenca; tel (7) 830-799; telex 8610; Dir: Daniel Toral V.; f 1959.

Instituto de Colonización de la Región Amazónica (INCRAE): Quito; f 1978; encourages settlement in and economic devt of the Amazon region.

Programa Regional de Desarrollo del Sur del Ecuador (PREDESUR): 9 de Octubre 275 y Jorge Washington, Quito; tel (2) 230-531; Dir: Jorge Piedra; f 1972; promotes the devt of the southern area of the country.

Energy

Comisión Ecuatoriana de Energía Atómica: Avda Orellana, Casilla 2517, Quito; Exec Dir: Patricio Peñaherrera S.; f 1968; research in the field of nuclear physics radio-isotopes, radiobiology, chemistry and medicine; production and sale of radioactive minerals.

Petroecuador: Avda Colón No 1021, 8, Edif Banco Continental, Casillas 5007-8, Quito; tel (2) 544-939; telex 2861; fmrly Corporación Estatal Petrolera Ecuatoriana (CEPE); Exec Pres: Luis Román; f 1972, reorganized 1989; state petroleum corpn; promotes exploration for and exploitation of petroleum and natural gas deposits by initiating joint ventures with foreign and national cos; acts as agency controlling the concession of onshore and offshore exploration rights; domestic marketing and distribution of petroleum products.

Instituto Ecuatoriano de Electrificación (INECEL): 6 de Diciembre y Orellana, Casilla 565-A y 9076, Suc 7, Quito; tel (2) 237-422; telex 2243; Gen Man: Marcelo Jaramillo A.; f 1961; under control of the Ministry of Energy and Mines; generation, transmission and commercialization of electrical energy.

Health and Welfare

Instituto Ecuatoriano de Seguridad Social: Avda 10 de Agosto y Estrada Ed Parque de Mayo, 4, Quito; tel (2) 566-339; telex 2280; Dir: Dr Mario Paredes-Suárez; f 1937; provides various forms of state insurance; directs the social insurance system; plans and controls medical education and research programmes; plans research and medical education policies at national level; attached to the institute are the Dirección Nacional Medico Social and the Departamento Nacional de Investigación y Docencia (medical and research authorities).

Legal and Judiciary

Office of the Attorney-General: Quito; Attorney-Gen: Jorge Maldonado Renela.

Supreme Court of Justice: Palacio de Justicia, Avda 6 de Diciembre y Piedrahita, Quito; tel (2) 230-200; Pres: (vacant); comprises 15 Judges and two Fiscals.

Media

BROADCASTING

Cadena Ecuatoriana de Televisión: Avda de las Américas, frente al Aeropuerto, Casilla 673, Guayaquil; tel (4) 397-888; telex 3530; Exec Pres: Louis R. Hanna; f 1969.

Corporación Ecuatoriana de Televisión: C. del Carmen, Casilla 10992, Guayaquil; tel (4) 300-150; telex 43409; fax (4) 303-677; Pres: Xavier Alvarado Roca; Gen Man: Francisco Arosemena Robles; f 1967.

NEWS AND INFORMATION

Instituto Nacional de Estadística y Censos: 10 de Agosto 229, Quito; tel (2) 519-597; telex 21421; Dir-Gen: Gaudencio Zurita Herrera; Dep Dir-Gen: Jorge Magaldi Sánchez; f 1976; statistical office.

Secretaria Nacional de Comunicación Social (SENAC): Pasaje Espejo 935 y Guayaquil, Quito; tel (2) 517-544; telex 2180; fax (2) 580-070; Sec-Gen: Dr Gonzalo Ortiz Crespo (mem of the Cabinet); Dir, Dept of Promotion: Gonzalo Guerrero; Dir, Dept of Public Opinion: Del Carmen Burneo; Dir, Dept of Information: Fabian Aguirre; f 1973; register of all communications media; specialized library; publication of official communications; analysis of public opinion.

Science and Technology

Instituto Nacional de Meteorología y Hidrología: Troncal, Daniel Hidalgo 132, Quito; meteorology and hydrology.

Tourism

Asociación Ecuatoriana de Agencias de Viajes y Turismo (ASECUT): Suc 7, Avda Amazonas 2468, Casilla 9377, Quito; tel (2) 552-617; telex 2749; fax (2) 552-916; Pres: Gonzalo Rueda U.; f 1953.

Dirección Nacional de Turismo: Reina Victoria 514 y Roca, Quito; tel (2) 527-002; telex 21158; Exec Dir: Nelson Robelly Lozada; f 1964.

Transport and Communications

TELECOMMUNICATIONS

Empresa Nacional de Correos: Benalcázar 688, Quito.

Instituto Ecuatoriano de Telecomunicaciones (IETEL): Casilla 3066, Quito; telex 2202; Gen Man: Gonzalo Guerrero Jordán.

TRANSPORT

Dirección General de Aviación Civil: Buenos Aires 149 y Avda 10 de Agosto, Quito; tel (2) 238-928; telex 22710; Dir-Gen: Marco Chávez; f 1946; construction and admin of airports; airport control; meteorology.

Empresa Ecuatoriana de Aviación (Ecuadorean Airlines): Avda Reina Victoria y Avda Colón, Torres de Almagro, Casilla 505, Quito; tel (2) 563-003; telex 21143; fax (2) 563-920; Exec Pres: Patricio Avila R.; Exec Vice-Pres: Alfredo Barreiro; Commercial Vice-Pres: Mariano Montenegro M.; f 1974; international passenger, cargo and mail services.

Empresa Nacional de Ferrocarriles del Estado: Calle Bolívar 443, Casilla 159, Quito; tel (2) 216-180; Gen Man: César Felipe Noboa Urresta; railways management.

Flota Bananera Ecuatoriana, SA: Edif Gran Pasaje 9, P. Icaza 437, Casilla 6883, Guayaquil; tel (4) 309-333; telex 43218; Pres: Diego Sánchez; Gen Man: Jorge Barriga; f 1967; shipping.

Flota Petrolera Ecuatoriana (FLOPEC): Edif España 4, Avda Colón y Avda Amazonas, Casilla 535-A, Quito; tel (2) 552-100; telex 2211; Pres: F. Alfaro; Gen Man: M. Villalba; f 1973; shipping.

Transportes Aéreos Nacionales Ecuatorianos (TAME): Casilla 8736, Suc Almagro, Quito; tel (2) 547-304; telex 22567; Gen Man: Lt-Gen (retd) Armando Durán N.; f 1962; domestic scheduled airline services for passengers and freight; charter services abroad.

Utilities

Instituto Ecuatoriano de Obras Sanitarias: Toledo y Lérida, Troncal, Quito.

EGYPT

Head of State

Executive authority is vested in the President, who may appoint one or more Vice-Presidents and appoints all the ministers. The President is nominated by the People's Assembly and elected by popular referendum for a six-year term. The President may be re-elected.

President: Muhammad Hosni Mubarak (confirmed as President by referendum 13 October 1981; re-elected and confirmed by referendum 5 October 1987).

Office of the President: Oruba Palace, Sharia Oruba, Heliopolis, Cairo; tel (2) 830788; telex 331; Presidential Asst: Field-Marshal Muhammad Abd al-Halim Abu Ghazalah.

Vice-President: (vacant).

Legislature

Legislative power is vested in the unicameral Majlis ash-Sha'ab (People's Assembly), which has 458 members: ten nominated by the President and 448 elected by direct suffrage for five years from 48 constituencies. There is also a 210-member advisory assembly, the Shura Council. The country is divided into 26 governorates.

Majlis ash-Sha'ab (People's Assembly): Maglis esh-Sha'ab, Cairo; tel (2) 912888; Speaker: Dr Rifa'at el-Mahgoub; Dep Speakers: Ihab Maqlad (workers), Ahmad Moussa (professions).

MINISTRIES AND GOVERNMENT DEPARTMENTS

OFFICE OF THE PRIME MINISTER
Sharia Maglis esh-Sha'ab, Cairo
Tel (2) 26457; telex 93794
Prime Minister: Dr Atif Muhammad Sidqi
Deputy Prime Ministers: Dr Ahmad Esmat Abd al-Meguid, Dr Kamal Ahmad al-Ganzouri, Dr Yousuf Amin Wali

MINISTRY OF AGRICULTURE
Sharia Wizaret az-Ziraa, Dokki, Gaza
Tel (2) 702677
Minister: Dr Yousuf Amin Wali

Egyptian Documentation and Information Centre for Agriculture (EDICA): Nadi el-Seid St, Dokki, Cairo; tel (2) 3492970; telex 93006; Dir: Ibrahim Zaki; f 1975; collection, analysis and processing of agricultural information and literature.

MINISTRY OF AWQAF (ISLAMIC ENDOWMENTS)
Sharia Sabri Abu Alam, Ean el-Luk, Cairo
Tel (2) 746305
Minister: Dr Muhammad Ali Mahgoub

MINISTRY OF CABINET AFFAIRS
Cairo
Minister: Dr Atif Muhammad Obeid

MINISTRY OF CIVIL AVIATION
Sharia Matar, Heliopolis, Cairo
Tel (2) 969555
Minister: Dr Fouad Sultan

MINISTRY OF COMMUNICATIONS
26 Sharia Ramses, Cairo
Tel (2) 909090
Minister: Sulayman Mutawalli Sulayman

MINISTRY OF CULTURE
110 Sharia al-Galaa, Cairo
Tel (2) 971995
Minister: Farouk Hosni

MINISTRY OF DEFENCE AND MILITARY PRODUCTION
5 Sharia Ismail Abaza, Qasr el-Eini, Cairo
Tel (2) 3553063; telex 92167
Minister: Gen Yusef Sabri Abu Taleb
Minister of State, Military Production: Dr Gamal as-Sayed Ibrahim

MINISTRY OF DEVELOPMENT, NEW COMMUNITIES, HOUSING AND PUBLIC UTILITIES
1 Ismail Abaza, Qasr el-Eini, Cairo
Tel: Development (2) 3540419; New Communities (2) 3540590; Public Utilities (2) 3540110; telex: Development and New Communities 20807; Public Utilities 92188
Minister: Hasaballah Muhammad al-Kafrawi

MINISTRY OF ECONOMY
8 Sharia Adly, Cairo
Tel (2) 907344
Minister: Dr Yusri Ali Mustafa

MINISTRY OF EDUCATION
Sharia el-Falaky, Cairo
Tel (2) 8544805
Minister: Dr Ahmad Fathi Surur

MINISTRY OF ELECTRICITY AND RESEARCH
Nasr City, Cairo
Tel (2) 829565
Minister: Muhammad Mahir Abazah

MINISTRY OF FINANCE
Sharia Maglis esh-Sha'ab, Lazoughli Sq, Cairo
Tel (2) 24857; telex 92169
Minister: Dr Muhammad Ahmad ar-Razzaz

MINISTRY OF FOREIGN AFFAIRS
Tahrir Sq, Cairo
Telex 92220
Minister: Dr Ahmad Esmat Abd al-Meguid
Minister of State: Dr Boutros Boutros Ghali

MINISTRY OF FOREIGN TRADE
Lazoughli Sq, Cairo
Tel (2) 25424
Minister: Dr Yusri Ali Mustafa

MINISTRY OF HEALTH
Sharia Maglis esh-Sha'ab, Cairo
Tel (2) 903939; telex 94107
Minister: Dr Muhammad Ragib Duwaydar

MINISTRY OF INDUSTRY
2 Sharia Latin America, Garden City, Cairo
Tel (2) 3550641; telex 93112
Minister: Muhammad Farag Abd al-Wahhab

MINISTRY OF INFORMATION
Radio and TV Bldg, Corniche en-Nil, Maspiro, Cairo
Tel (2) 974216
Minister: Muhammad Safwat Muhammad
Yousuf ash-Sharif

MINISTRY OF THE INTERIOR
Al-Sheikh Rihan, Bab al-Louk, Cairo
Tel (2) 844900
Minister: Maj-Gen Mohammad Abdul-Halim Moussa

MINISTRY OF INTERNATIONAL CO-OPERATION
9 Sharia Adly, Cairo
Telex 348
Minister: Dr Atif Sidqi
Minister of State: Dr Maurice Makramallah

MINISTRY OF JUSTICE
Justice Bldg, Lazoughli, Cairo
Tel (2) 31176
Minister: Farouk Sayf an-Nasr

MINISTRY OF LAND RECLAMATION
Land Reclamation Bldg, Dokki, Giza
Tel (2) 703011
Minister: Dr Yousuf Amin Wali

MINISTRY OF MANPOWER AND VOCATIONAL TRAINING
Sharia Yousuf Abbas, Nasr City, Abbasia, Cairo
Minister: Asim Abd al-Haq Salih

MINISTRY OF NAVAL TRANSPORT
4 Sharia el-Bataisa, Alexandria
Tel (3) 35763; telex 54147
Minister: Sulayman Mutawalli Sulayman

MINISTER FOR PEOPLE'S ASSEMBLY AND SHURA (ADVISORY) COUNCIL AFFAIRS
Egyptian Cabinet Bldg, Sharia Maglis esh-Sha'ab,
Lazoughli Sq, Cairo
Tel (2) 91288
Minister: Dr Ahmad Salamah Muhammad
Minister of State: (vacant)

MINISTRY OF PETROLEUM AND MINERAL RESOURCES
2 Sharia Latin America, Garden City, Cairo
Tel (2) 3545022; telex 92197
Minister: Abd al-Hadi Muhammad Kandil

MINISTRY OF PLANNING
Sharia Salah Salem, Nasr City, Cairo
Tel (2) 600096
Minister: Dr Kamal Ahmad al-Ganzuri

MINISTRY OF SCIENTIFIC RESEARCH
4 Sharia Ibrahim Nagiv, Garden City, Cairo
Minister: Dr Ahmad Fathi Surur
Minister of State: Dr Adel Abd al-Hamid Izz

MINISTRY OF SOCIAL AFFAIRS
Sharia Sheikh Rihan, Cairo
Telex 94105
Minister: Dr Amal Abd ar-Rahim Osman

MINISTRY OF SOCIAL INSURANCE
3 Sharia el-Alfi, Cairo
Tel (2) 922717
Minister: Dr Amal Abd ar-Rahim Osman

MINISTRY OF SUPPLY AND INTERNAL TRADE
99 Sharia Qasr el-Eini, Cairo
Tel (2) 3552600; telex 93497
Minister: Dr Muhammad Jalal ad-Din Abu adh-Dhahab

MINISTRY OF TOURISM
Misr Travel Tower, Abbasia Sq, Cairo
Tel (2) 2828450; telex 94040
Minister: Dr Fouad Sultan

MINISTRY OF TRANSPORT
Sharia Qasr el-Eini, Cairo
Tel (2) 3557402; telex 92802
Minister: Sulayman Mutawalli Sulayman

MINISTRY OF WORKS AND WATER RESOURCES
Sharia Qasr el-Eini, Cairo
Tel (2) 3552120
Minister: Isam Radi Abd al-Hamid Radi

MINISTRY OF STATE FOR IMMIGRATION AND EGYPTIAN EXPATRIATES
Egyptian Cabinet Bldg, Sharia Maglis esh-Sha'ab,
Lazoughli Sq, Cairo
Minister of State: Dr Fouad Iskandar

GOVERNMENT AGENCIES AND ORGANIZATIONS

Business and Economy

BANKING

Bank of Alexandria, SAE: 6 Sharia Salah Salem, Alexandria; tel (3) 806212; telex 54107; Chair: Abdel Ghani; f 1957; 91 brs.

Bank of Commerce and Development: 13 Midan 26 July, Sphinx, Mohandessin, Cairo; tel (2) 3479461; telex 21607; Chair: Dr Abd al-Aziz Muhammad Hegazi; Vice-Chair and Man Dir: Samir Muhammad Fouad el-Qasri; f 1980; 4 brs.

Banque du Caire, SAE: 30 Sharia Roushdy, POB 1495, Abdin, Cairo; tel (2) 3904554; telex 92022; fax (2) 3908992; Chair: Mahmoud Hassan Abdalla; Dep Chairs: Mahmoud Mohamed Youssef, Mamdouh Said el-Nadoury; f 1952; 109 brs.

Banque Misr, SAE: 151 Sharia Muhammad Farid, Cairo; tel (2) 912711; telex 92242; Chair: Mahmoud Mohammad Mahmoud; f 1920; 300 brs.

Banque Nationale Société Générale, SAE: Evergreen Office Bldg, 3rd Floor, 4 Sharia Talaat Harb, Cairo; tel (2) 770291; telex 93894; Chair: Mahmoud Abd al-Aziz; Gen Man: Jean Dubois; f 1978; 51% owned by the National Bank of Egypt (see below).

Central Bank of Egypt: 31 Sharia Qasr en-Nil, Cairo; tel (2) 751529; telex 92237; Gov and Chair: Dr Mahmoud Salah ed-Din Hamid; f 1961; 3 brs.

Commercial International Bank (Egypt), SAE: Nile Tower Bldg, 21-23 Sharia Giza, POB 2430, Giza; tel (2) 726132; telex 20201; Chair and Man Dir: Ahmad Ismail; f 1975; 51% owned by the National Bank of Egypt (see below); 12 brs.

Crédit Foncier Egyptien: 11 Sharia el-Mashadi, POB 141, Cairo; tel (2) 910197; telex 93863; Chair: Adel Mahmoud Abd al-Baki; Gen Man: Ibrahim Abd al-Halim Khor ed-Din; f 1880; 7 brs.

Egyptian Export Development Bank: Evergreen Bldg, 10 Sharia Talaat Harb, Cairo; tel (2) 777033; telex 20850; Chair: Dr Hazem el-Beblawy; f 1983 to replace National Import-Export Bank.

Egyptian Investment Finance Corpn: Cairo; f 1985; merchant bank.

Housing and Development Bank: 26 Batal Ahmad Abd al-Aziz, POB 234, Dokki, Cairo ; tel (2) 717170; telex 94075; Chair: Mahmoud Nabih el-Minshawi; f 1979; 3 brs.

Islamic International Bank for Investment and Development: 4 Sharia Adly, Mesaha Sq, POB 180, Dokki, Cairo; tel (2) 3489973; Chair: Hassan Ahmad Nagi; Gen Man: Adel Khalifa Tantawi; f 1980; 5 brs.

Misr Iran Development Bank: The Nile Tower, 21 Sharia Giza, POB 219, Giza; tel (2) 727311; telex 22407; Chair: Fathi Muhammad Ibrahim; Man Dir: Al-Motaz Mansour; Gen Man: Dr Ibrahim Moukhtar; f 1975; 5 brs.

Nasser Social Bank: 35 Sharia Qasr en-Nil, POB 2552, Cairo; tel (2) 744377; telex 92754; Chair: Nassif Tahoon; f 1971; interest-free savings and investment bank for social and economic activities, participating in social insurance, specializing in financing co-operatives, craftsmen and social institutions.

National Bank for Development: 5 Sharia el-Borsa el-Gedida, POB 647, Cairo; tel (2) 763528; telex 20878; Chair: Muhammad Ali Z. el-Orabi; Dep Chair and Gen Man: Muhammad Ibrahim Farid; f 1980; there are affiliated National Banks for Development in 16 governorates.

National Bank of Egypt: 24 Sharia Sherif, Cairo; tel (2) 3924143; telex 92238; Chair: Muhammad Nabil Ibrahim; Gen Man: Qasim Barakat; f 1898; handles all commercial bank operations; 182 brs.

National Investment Bank: 8 Sharia Abd el-Meguid ar-Remaly, Bab el-Louk, Cairo; tel (2) 541336; telex 23414; Chair: Gamal al-Ganzouri; Sec-Gen: Muhammad Fahmy; responsible for Govt projects.

Principal Bank for Development and Agricultural Credit: 110 Sharia Qasr el-Eini, POB 11612, Cairo; tel (2) 3551204; telex 93045; Chair: Adel Hussein Ezzi; Gen Man: Abed ar-Raouf Dekhel; f 1976 to succeed former credit organizations.

TRADE

Egyptian Export Promotion Centre (EEPC): 106 Gamiette al-Dawal al-Arabia, Mohohandessin, Giza; tel (2) 3493920; telex 92321; fax (2) 3484142; Dir: Dr Ahmed Adel Rashed; f 1979; organization of trade missions, fairs and exhibitions; dissemination of trade information; organization of training programmes for export promotion activities.

General Organization for Imports and Exports Control: 1 Sharia Ramses, Cairo; tel (2) 756130; telex 93318; Chair: Mr Salah el-Dien Awad; f 1971; quality control for agricultural products before being exported and imported.

Standardization Authority: Ministry of Industry Bldg, 2 Sharia Latin America, Garden City, Cairo; tel (2) 26355; telex 93296; trading standards authority.

Development and Planning

INVESTMENT

General Authority for Investment and Free Zones: 8 Sharia Adly, POB 1007, Cairo; tel (2) 3906804; telex 92235; Dep Chair: Mohi ed-Din el-Ghareb.

PLANNING

Development Planning Authority: 56 Sharia Tahrir, Dokki, Cairo; tel (2) 981703; telex 94025.

General Organization for Industrialization: 6 Sharia Khalil Agha, Garden City, Cairo; tel (2) 20678; Dir: Ibrahim Sharkas.

Education

Documentation and Research Centre for Education (Ministry of Education): 33 Sharia Falaky, Cairo; Dir: Zeinab M. Mehrez; f 1956; produces information and education bulletins.

The Public Organization for Books and Scientific Appliances: Cairo University, Orman, Giza, Cairo; Chair: Kamil Seddik; Vice-Chair: Fathy Labib; f 1965; publisher of academic books; imports books, periodicals and scientific appliances.

Environment

Egyptian General Authority for Coast Protection: Shubra el-Mazalat, Irrigation Bldg, Cairo.

Legal and Judiciary

Supreme Constitutional Court: Ministry of Justice, Justice Bldg, Lazoughli, Cairo; tel (2) 31176; Chief Justice: Ahmad Mamdouh Atteya; highest court in Egypt.

Media

BROADCASTING

Egyptian Radio and Television Corporation (ERTV): Radio and TV Bldg, Sharia Maspiro, Corniche en-Nil, POB 1186, Cairo; tel (2) 757155; telex 92152; Pres: Hussein Enan; f 1928; radio programmes in over 30 languages; three TV channels.

National Authority for Wire and Wireless Communications: 22 Sharia Ramses, Cairo.

NEWS AND INFORMATION

Central Agency for Public Mobilization and Statistics: POB 2086, Nasr City, Cairo; tel (2) 604632; telex 92395; Govt statistical dept.

General Authority for Information: 22 Sharia Talaat Harb, Cairo; tel (2) 756612.

Mining and Energy

ENERGY

Arab Petroleum Pipelines Co (SUMED): 431 el-Geish Ave, Loran, Alexandria; tel (3) 5863139; telex 54295; Chair and Man Dir: Hafez Muhammad el-Sherbini; f 1974; Suez-Mediterranean crude oil transportation pipeline and oil terminal operators.

Atomic Energy Organization: 101 Sharia Qasr el-Eini, Cairo; Chair: Dr Ibrahim Hamouda; Vice-Chair: Dr Saleh Hashish; f 1955.

Belayim Petroleum Co (PETROBEL): Sharia Gharb el-Istad, Nasr City, Cairo; tel (2) 608486; telex 92449; f 1978; capital equally shared between EGPC (see below) and International Egyptian Oil Co, which is a subsidiary of ENI of Italy; oil and gas exploration, drilling and production.

Egyptian General Petroleum Corpn (EGPC): 20 Sharia Osman Abd al-Hafiz, POB 2130, Nasr City, Cairo; tel (2) 837388; telex 92049; Chair: Hamad Ayoub; state supervisory authority generally concerned with the planning of policies relating to petroleum activities in Egypt with the object of securing the devt of the oil industry and ensuring its effective admin.

Egyptian Electricity Authority: 3 Nasr Rd, Nasr City, Abbasia, Cairo; tel (2) 8227071; Chair: Emad el-Sharkawi.

General Petroleum Co (GPC): 8 Sharia Dr Moustafa Abou Zahra, Nasr City, Cairo; f 1957; wholly owned subsidiary of EGPC.

Gulf of Suez Petroleum Co (GUPCO): POB 2400, Cairo; Chair: Dr Hamdi el-Banbi; f 1965; partnership between EGPC and Amoco-Egypt Co, USA.

Nuclear Power Plants Authority: POB 8191, Masaken, Nasr City, 108 Abbasia, Cairo; tel (2) 608291; telex 20761; Chair: Dr A. F. as-Saidi; f 1976.

Western Desert Petroleum Co (WEPCO): POB 412, Alexandria; tel (3) 4928710; telex 54075; Chair: Muhammad Mohi ed-Din Bahgat; f 1967 as partnership between EGPC (50% interest) and Phillips Petroleum (35% interest) and later Hispanoil (15% interest).

MINING

Egyptian Geological Survey and Mining Authority (EGSMA): 3 Sharia Salah Salem, Abbasia, Cairo; tel (2) 829662; telex 22695; Chair: Ahmad Abd al-Halim; supervisory authority concerned with planning of policies relating to mining activities in Egypt.

Science and Technology

General Authority for Meteorology: Cairo Airport Bldg, Heliopolis, Cairo; tel (2) 2451304; Chair: Dr Muhammad el-Saban.

Telecommunications

Post Authority: Ataba Sq, Cairo; tel (2) 910011.

Tourism

Egyptian General Authority for the Promotion of Tourism: Misr Travel Tower, Abbasia Sq, Cairo; tel (2) 823570; telex 20799; Chair: Sayed Moussa.

Egyptian General Co for Tourism and Hotels: 4 Sharia Latin America, Garden City, Cairo; tel (2) 32158; telex 92363; f 1961; affiliated to the Ministry of Tourism.

Transport

CIVIL AVIATION

EgyptAir: Cairo International Airport, Heliopolis, Cairo; tel (2) 455099; telex 22221; Chair: Gen Muhammad Fahim Rayan; f 1932; internal services; external services throughout the Middle East, Far East, Africa, Europe and the USA.

Egyptian Civil Aviation Authority: 31 Sharia 26 July, Cairo; tel (2) 2473950; telex 93044; fax (2) 2470351; Vice-Chairs: Amin Abou el-Magd, Naeem Abdou Salem; f 1945; controls all procedures relating to air safety.

RAILWAYS

Egyptian Railways: Station Bldg, Midan Ramses, Cairo; tel (2) 347600; telex 92616; Chair: Dr Muhammad Maher el-Morsi; f 1851; length 5,355 km.

Alexandria Passenger Transport Authority: 2 Sharia Aflatone, POB 466, Alexandria; tel (3) 5975223; telex 54637; Chair: Muhammad Saleh ed-Din Abd al-Moneim; Technical Dir: Fikry Amin Abd al-Malek; f 1863; controls railways and trams within Alexandria.

Heliopolis Co for Housing and Inhabiting: 28 Sharia Ibrahim el-Lakkany, Heliopolis, Cairo; Gen Man: Abd al-Moneim Seif; 50 km of track.

Lower Egypt Railway: Mansura; f 1898; length 160 km.

ROADS

Egyptian General Organization of Inland Transport for Provinces Passengers: Sharia Qasr el-Eini, Cairo; Pres: Hassan Mourad Kotb.

SHIPPING

Alexandria Port Authority: 106 Sharia el-Hourriya, Alexandria; tel (3) 34321; telex 54147; Chair: Adm Anwar Hegazi.

General Authority for River Transport: 30 Sharia Ramses, Cairo; tel (2) 750144.

Suez Canal Authority (Hay'at Canal as-Suess): Irshad Bldg, Ismailia; tel (64) 20000; telex 63238; Chair: Muhammad Ezzat Adel; f 1956.

Utilities

National Association for Potable Water and Sanitary Drainage (NOPWASD): el-Tahrir Sq, Mogamma Bldg, 6th Floor, Cairo; tel (2) 3557664; telex 93057; fax (2) 3562869; Chair: Mohammed Khaled Mostafa; Vice-Chair: Abdel Salam el-Rafi; f 1981; water and sewerage authority.

EL SALVADOR

Head of State

Executive power is vested in the President assisted by the Vice-President and the Council of Ministers. The President and Vice-President are elected by universal adult suffrage for a five-year term.

President: Alfredo Félix Cristiani Burkard (took office 1 June 1989).

Vice-President: José Francisco Merino López.

Office of the President and of the Vice-President: Casa Presidencial, San Salvador; tel 71-1555; telex 30344.

Legislature

Legislative power is vested in the unicameral Asamblea Nacional (National Assembly), which replaced the National Constituent Assembly in 1985. It comprises 60 members elected by universal adult suffrage for a three-year term.

Asamblea Nacional (National Assembly): San Salvador; tel 21-7201; Pres: Ricardo Alvarenga Valdivieso; First Vice-Pres: Alfonso Arístedes Alvarenga.

MINISTRIES AND GOVERNMENT DEPARTMENTS

MINISTRY OF THE PRESIDENCY
Avda Cuba, Calle Darío González 806, Barro San Jacinto,
San Salvador
Tel 21-8483; telex 20552
Minister: Juan Antonio Martínez Varela

MINISTRY OF AGRICULTURE AND LIVESTOCK
OSPA 31 Avda Sur 627, San Salvador
Tel 23-2598; telex 20228
Minister: Antonio Cabrales

MINISTRY OF DEFENCE AND PUBLIC SECURITY
Km 5, Carretera a Santa Tecla, San Salvador
Tel 23-0233; telex 30345
Minister: Gen Rafael Humberto Larios López

MINISTRY OF ECONOMY
Paseo Gral Escalón 4122, Apdo 0119, San Salvador
Tel 24-3000; telex 20269; fax 98-1965
Minister: José Arturo Zablah

MINISTRY OF EDUCATION
Televisión Educativa, Santa Tecla, San Salvador
Tel 22-8038
Minister: René Eduardo Valiente

MINISTRY OF FINANCE
13 Calle Poniente y 7a Avda Norte, San Salvador
Tel 71-4466; telex 20647
Minister: Rafael Alvarado Cano

MINISTRY OF FOREIGN AFFAIRS
Blvd Dr Manuel Enrique Araújo, Km 6, San Salvador
Tel 23-7145; telex 20179
Minister: Dr José Manuel Pacas Castro

MINISTRY OF THE INTERIOR
Centro de Gobierno, San Salvador
Tel 21-5438
Minister: Col Juan Martínez Varela
Secretary of Information: Mauricio Sandóval

MINISTRY OF JUSTICE
Avda Masferrer Norte 612B, Colonia Escalón, San Salvador
Tel 24-0326
Minister: Dr Oscar Alfredo Santamaría

MINISTRY OF LABOUR AND SOCIAL WELFARE
Edif 2a, Avda Norte 428, San Salvador
Tel 77-1250; telex 20016
Minister: Mauricio González Dubón

MINISTRY OF PLANNING AND CO-ORDINATION OF ECONOMIC AND SOCIAL DEVELOPMENT
Km 1, Carretera a Planes de Renderos, atrás de ALFA,
San Salvador
Tel 71-3266; telex 20809
Minister: Mirna Liévano de Márquez

MINISTRY OF PUBLIC HEALTH AND SOCIAL WELFARE
Calle Arce 827, San Salvador
Tel 21-0966; telex 20704
Minister: Dr Lisandro Vásquez Sosa

MINISTRY OF PUBLIC WORKS
1a Avda Sur 630, 5, San Salvador
Tel 22-2466
Minister: Mauricio Stubig

GOVERNMENT AGENCIES AND ORGANIZATIONS

Agriculture

Instituto Nacional del Azúcar: Paseo Gen Escalón y 87a Avda Norte, San Salvador; tel 24-6044; telex 20430; Pres: Wolf H. von Hundelshausen; national sugar institute.

Instituto Nacional del Café (INCAFE): 6a Avda Sur 133, San Salvador; tel 71-3311; telex 20138; Pres: Dr Robert Suárez Suay; Gen Man: Miguel Angel Aguilar; f 1942; national coffee institute.

Instituto Salvadoreño de Transformación Agraria (ISTA): Km 5, Carretera a Santa Tecla, San Salvador; tel 24-6000; Pres: Ramón Aparacio; f 1976; promotion of rural devt; empowered to buy inefficiently cultivated land.

Business and Economy

BANKING

Banco Agrícola Comercial de El Salvador: Blvd del Hipódromo 803, Colonia San Benito, San Salvador; tel 71-6126; telex 20395; Pres: Rodolfo Santos Morales; f 1955; 17 brs.

Banco Central de Reserva de El Salvador: Calle Rubén Darío y 17 Avda Norte, San Salvador; tel 22-5022; telex 20088; fax 71-0381; Pres: José Roberto Orellana Milla; Man: Armando Barrios; f 1934; nationalized 1961; sole right of note issue.

Junta Monetaria (Monetary Board): San Salvador; responsible for the control of credit and the money supply, and the determination of foreign exchange rates; works mainly through the Banco Central de Reserva.

Banco de Crédito Popular: Avda Olímpica y Pasaje 3, San Salvador; tel 23-2590; telex 20208; Pres: Juan Samuel Quinteros; f 1957; 12 brs.

Banco Cuscatlán: 6a Avda Sur 118, San Salvador; tel 71-1233; telex 20220; Pres: Rafael Edmundo Girón Carballo; Man: José Antonio Manzano; f 1972; 12 brs.

Banco de Fomento Agropecuario: Km 10, Carretera a la Libertad, San Salvador; tel 28-0098; telex 20089; fax 28-2666; Pres: Carlos Antonio Borja Letona; Vice-Pres: Jorge Antonio Zaldívar; Gen Man: Gustavo Adolfo Escobar Tobías; f 1973; provides credit to promote agricultural devt.

Banco Nacional de Fomento Industrial (BANAFI): 1a Calle Poniente 2310, San Salvador; tel 24-6677; telex 20285; Pres: Ernesto Allwoods Lagos; Man: Juan José Manzanares; f 1982; provides credit to promote industrial devt.

Superintendencia del Sistema Financiero: Edif Ex-Quiñonez Hermanos, Carretera a Santa Tecla, Colonia Roma, Apdo 2942, San Salvador; tel 98-0133; telex 20088; Supt: Héctor Edmundo Cuéllar; f 1962; oversees the operations of the Central Bank and all other financial institutions.

FINANCIAL AGENCIES

Financiera Nacional de Tierras Agrícolas (FINATA): Blvd El Hipódromo 643, Colonia San Benito, San Salvador; tel 23-6512; fax 24-4302; Pres: Raúl García Prieto; Man: José Angel Villeda Castillo; financial aid for agricultural devt.

Financiera Nacional de la Vivienda (FNV): San Salvador; tel 23-8822; Pres: Remo Pardi Cevallos; Man: Armando Estrada Valdez; f 1963; improvement of housing facilities through loans and savings associations.

TRADE

Comité Ejecutivo de la Feria Internacional de El Salvador: Avda la Revolución 222, Colonia San Benito, San Salvador; tel 23-6076; telex 20197; preparation and promotion of trade events at a national and international level.

Corporación de Exportadores de El Salvador (COEXPORT): Condomínios del Mediterráneo, Edif A No 23, Colonia Jardines de Guadalupe, San Salvador; tel 23-1888; telex 20235; fax 98-0951; Man: Silvia Cuéllar Sicilia; f 1973; promotion of Salvadorean exports.

Instituto Salvadoreño de Comercio Exterior (ISCE): Paseo Gral Escalón 4122, Apdo 0119, San Salvador; f 1974; information provided to current and potential exporters with the aim of promoting Salvadorean products.

Defence

Armed Forces: Km 5, Carretera a Santa Tecla, Departamento de la Libertad, San Salvador; tel 23-7166; Chief of Staff: Col Rene Emilio Ponce.

Air Force: Ilopango, San Salvador; tel 27-2015; Commdr-in-Chief: Gen Rafael Antonio Villamariona.

Army: Km 5, Carretera a Santa Tecla, Departamento de la Libertad, San Salvador; tel 23-7166.

Navy: Calle Francisco Menéndez, San Salvador; tel 23-3234.

National Guard: Colonia Atlácatl, San Salvador; tel 25-3277.

National Police: San Salvador; tel 21-5500.

Treasury Police: San Salvador; tel 25-5855.

Development and Planning

INVESTMENT

Corporación Salvadoreña de Inversiones (CORSAIN): 1a Calle Poniente entre 43 y 45 Avda Norte, San Salvador; tel 24-4242; telex 20257; Pres: Mario Emilio Redaelli; investment organization.

PLANNING

Fondo de Financiamiento y Garantía para la Pequeña Empresa (FIGAPE): Diagonal Principal y 1a Diagonal, Apdo 1990, San Salvador; tel 25-9466; Pres: Guillermo Funes Araújo; f 1973; assists in devt of small-scale industries.

Instituto Salvadoreño de Fomento Cooperativo (INSAFOCOOP): 43 Avda Sur y 12 Calle Poniente 605, Colonia Flor Blanca, San Salvador; tel 24-6799; Pres: Clara Rico Martínez; promotes the devt of co-operatives.

Education

Fondo de Garantía para el Crédito Educativo (EDUCREDITO): Avda España 726, San Salvador; tel 22-2181; Pres: Juan José Interiano; Dir: Erasmo Sermeño; f 1973; provides funds for educational purposes.

Energy

Comisión Ejecutiva Hidroelectrica del Rio Lempa (CEL): Km 11.5, Calle a la Libertad, Apdo 2669, San Salvador; tel 28-1022; telex 20303; fax 28-1911; Pres: Gen Jaime Abdul Gutiérrez; deals with electricity generation, transmission and distribution, and non-conventional energy sources.

Comisión Nacional del Petróleo (CONAPE): 9a Calle Poniente 950, San Salvador; telex 20301; state petroleum co.

Comisión Salvadoreña de Energía Nuclear (COSEN): Ministerio de Economía, 4a Avda Norte 233, San Salvador; f 1961; atomic energy research institute.

Legal and Judiciary

Office of the Attorney-General: Centro de Gobierno, San Salvador; tel 21-4997; Attorney-Gen: Mauricio Eduardo Colorado Burgos.

Corte Suprema de Justicia (Supreme Court of Justice): Edif de la Corte Suprema de Justicia, Centro de Gobierno, San Salvador; tel 71-3511; fax 71-3379; Pres: Dr Gabriel Mauricio Gutiérrez Castro; f 1824; highest judicial authority.

Media

BROADCASTING

Canal 8 and 10: Avda Robert Baden-Powell, Apdo 4, Nueva San Salvador; tel 28-0973; telex 21046; Dir: Carlos Díaz Chapetón; f 1965.

YSS Radio El Salvador: Dirección General de Medios, 3a Avda Norte y 11 Calle Poniente, San Salvador; tel 21-4376; telex 20145; Dir-Gen: (vacant); cultural station.

NEWS AND INFORMATION

Dirección General de Estadística y Censos: 1a Calle Poniente y 43a Avda Norte, Apdo 2670, San Salvador; tel 71-5011.

Tourism

Buró de Convenciones y Visitantes de la Ciudad de San Salvador: Suite 221-222, Hotel Presidente, Avda la Revolución, Colonia San Benito, Apdo 2124, San Salvador; tel 24-0819; telex 20037; Pres: Alfredo Morales; Exec Dir: Ingrid Tirabischi; f 1973; organizes and promotes conventions and meetings.

Instituto Salvadoreño de Turismo (ISTU): Calle Rubén Darío 619, Apdo 01-115, San Salvador; tel 22-8000; telex 20775; Pres: Carlos Hirlemann; Man Dir: Ricardo Escoto; f 1950; institute of tourism.

Transport and Communications

TELECOMMUNICATIONS

Administración Nacional de Telecomunicaciones (ANTEL): Edif Administrativo ANTEL, Centro de Gobierno, San Salvador; tel 71-7171; telex 20500; Pres: Julio César Gómez; Man: Dr Mauricio Daniel Vides Casanova; f 1963; national organization for telecommunications.

TRANSPORT

AESA Aerolíneas de El Salvador, SA de CV: Centro Comercial Beethoven sobre Paseo Gral Escalón, Apdo (06) 1830, San Salvador; tel 24-6166; Pres: E. Cornejo López; Gen Man: José Roberto Santana; cargo and mail service between San Salvador and Miami.

Comisión Ejecutiva Portuaria Autonoma (CEPA): Edif Torre Roble, Blvd de los Héroes, Apdo 2667, San Salvador; tel 24-1133; telex 20194; fax 24-1355; Chair: Luis Andreu; Gen Man: Arturo Germán Martínez; f 1952; management and maintenance of ports.

Ferrocarriles Nacionales de El Salvador (FENADESAL): Avda Peralta 903, Apdo 2292, San Salvador; tel 22-9000; telex 20194; fax 24-1355; Dir: Oscar Calles; f 1881; network of 602 kms.

Utilities

Administración Nacional de Acueductos y Alcantarillados (ANDA): Calle Rubén Darío 930, San Salvador; tel 21-0622; telex 20432; maintenance of water and sewerage.

Welfare

Fondo Social para la Vivienda (FSV): Edif Magaña, C. Aree y 13a Avda Sur, San Salvador; tel 74-4011; Pres: Edwin Sagrera; f 1973; housing agency.

Instituto de Vivienda Urbana (IVU): Avda Don Bosco, Centro Urbano Libertad, San Salvador; tel 25-3011; Pres: René G. López Canana; Man: Cristobal A. Huezo Nativi; f 1950; oversees the provision of housing for the poorest members of the population.

EQUATORIAL GUINEA

Head of State

The President, serving a seven-year term, is Head of State, and appoints the Council of Ministers. At the expiry of the present President's term, an election by universal adult suffrage is to be held, within the terms of the 1982 constitution. The State Council acts as an electoral college to approve or reject a presidential candidature.

President: Brig-Gen Teodoro Obiang Nguema Mbasogo (assumed office 25 August 1979; elected President 25 June 1989).

Office of the President: Malabo; Minister of State, Sec-Gen at the Presidency: Marcelino Nguema Onguene; Dep Minister Sec-Gen at the Presidency: Martín Nka Esono Nsing.

Legislature

Members of the legislative body, the House of Representatives, should be between 45 and 60 years of age, and are elected for a five-year term. A State Council, comprising 11 members (including the Chair of the House, the President of the Supreme Tribunal and the Minister of Defence), acts as an electoral college to approve or reject a presidential candidature amongst other responsibilities.

Cámara de Representantes del Pueblo (House of Representatives): Malabo.

MINISTRIES AND GOVERNMENT DEPARTMENTS

OFFICE OF THE PRIME MINISTER
Malabo
Prime Minister, in charge of Political and Administrative Co-ordination: Lt-Col Cristino Seriche Bioka Malabo
Deputy Prime Minister: Isidoro Eyi Mosuy Andeme

MINISTRY OF AGRICULTURE, LIVESTOCK, FISHERIES AND FORESTRY
Malabo
Minister: Anatolio Ndong Mba

MINISTRY OF CULTURE, TOURISM AND ARTISANAL PROMOTION
Malabo
Minister-delegate at the Presidency:
Leandro Mbomio Nsue

MINISTRY OF ECONOMIC AND FINANCIAL AFFAIRS
Malabo
Tel 20-43
Minister-delegate at the Presidency:
Antonio Fernando Nve Ngu

MINISTRY OF THE ECONOMY, TRADE AND PLANNING
Malabo
Minister-delegate: Casto Nvono Akele

MINISTRY OF EDUCATION, YOUTH AND SPORT
Malabo
Minister: Isidoro Eyi Mosuy Andeme

MINISTRY OF FOREIGN AFFAIRS AND CO-OPERATION
Malabo
Tel 32-20
Minister-delegate: Santiago Eneme Ovono

MINISTRY OF HEALTH
Malabo
Minister-delegate: Alejandro Masoko Bengono

MINISTRY OF INDUSTRY AND ENERGY
Malabo
Minister: Francisco Pascual Obama Asue

MINISTRY OF JUSTICE
Malabo
Minister: Silvestre Siale Bileka

MINISTRY OF LABOUR AND SOCIAL PROMOTION
Malabo
Minister: Antonio Pascual Oko Ebobo

MINISTRY OF MINES AND HYDROCARBONS
Malabo
Minister-delegate at the Presidency: Juan Olo Mba Nseng

MINISTRY OF MISSIONS
Malabo
Minister of State at the Presidency: Alejandro Evuna Owono Asangono

MINISTRY OF NATIONAL DEFENCE
Malabo
Minister-delegate: Maj Melanio Ebendeng Nsomo

MINISTRY OF PUBLIC WORKS, TOWN PLANNING AND TRANSPORT
Malabo
Minister: Alejandro Envoro Ovono

MINISTRY OF RELATIONS WITH THE ORGANS OF STATE
Malabo

Minister of State at the Presidency:
Eloy Elo Nve Mbengono

MINISTRY OF TERRITORIAL ADMINISTRATION AND COMMUNICATIONS
Malabo
Minister-delegate: Segundo Muñoz Itala

MINISTRY OF WOMEN'S PROMOTION
Malabo
Minister-delegate: Purificanión Angue Ondo

GOVERNMENT AGENCIES AND ORGANIZATIONS

Business and Economy

BANKING

Banco de Crédito y Desarrollo: 1 Avda de la Libertad, Apdo 39, Malabo; tel 35-35; Chair: Carlos Ntutumu Nengono; Man Dir: Dr Manuel E. King Somo; 100% state-owned.

Banque des Etats de l'Afrique Centrale (BEAC): Apdo 501, Malabo; tel 20-10; telex 913111; headquarters in Yaoundé, Cameroon; Gov: Casimir Oyé Mba; Dir in Equatorial Guinea: Martín-Crisanto Ebe Mba; f 1973 as the central bank of issue for mem states of the Customs and Economic Union of Central Africa (UDEAC), comprising Cameroon, the Central African Republic, Chad, the Congo, Equatorial Guinea and Gabon.

TRADE

Empresa Estatal de Comercio Interior y Exterior: Malabo; import and export of agricultural and other goods.

Empresa General de Industria y Comercio (EGISCA): Malabo; f 1986; import-export agency; parastatal body jointly operated with the French Société pour l'Organisation, l'Aménagement et le Développement des Industries Alimentaires et Agricoles (SOMDIA).

Sociedad Anónima de Desarrollo del Comercio (SOADECO-Guinée): Malabo; f 1986; parastatal body jointly operated with the French Société pour l'Organisation, l'Aménagement et le Développement des Industries Alimentaires et Agricoles (SOMDIA); devt of commerce.

Defence

National Guard: Malabo; Supreme Commdr: Col Teodoro Obiang Nguema Mbasogo.

Energy

Empresa Guineano-Española de Petróleos (GEPSA): 33 Avda de la Independencia, Apdo 30, Malabo; tel 23-00; f 1980; owned equally by the Govt and Hispanoil (Spain); petroleum and natural gas exploration.

ENERGE: Malabo; state-owned electricity board.

Total-Guinée Equatoriale: Malabo; Chair of Board of Dirs: Minister of Public Works, Town Planning and Transport, Alejandro Envoro Ovono; f 1984; 50% state-owned, 50% by CFP-Total (France); petroleum marketing and distribution.

Legal and Judiciary

Supreme Tribunal: Malabo; Supreme Tribunal: Julio Ela Ndong; highest court of appeal.

Media

BROADCASTING

Africa 2000: Malabo; f 1988; cultural station; broadcasts in Spanish.

Dirección General de Prensa, Radio y Television de Guinea Ecuatorial: Calle 3 de Agosto s/n, Malabo; Dir-Gen: Maximiliano Mba Ovenga Eyang; f 1968; production of programmes.

Radio Ecuatorial Bata: Apdo 749, Bata; tel 182; Dir: Jesús Obiang Nguema Ndong; programmes in Spanish, French and vernacular languages.

Radio Santa Isabel: Apdo 195, Malabo; tel 382; Dir: Juan Eyene Opkua Nguema; programmes in Spanish, French, Fang, Bubi, Annobonés and Combe.

NEWS AND INFORMATION

Dirección Técnica de Estadística, Secretaría de Estado para el Plan de Desarrollo Económico y Cooperación: Malabo; statistical office.

Transport

Aerolíneas Guinea Ecuatorial (ALGESA): Malabo; f 1982; air services to Cameroon, Gabon and Nigeria.

Empresa Ecuato-Guineano de Aviación (EGA): Malabo; f 1986; 70% state-owned; internal flights and flights to Cameroon and Gabon.

ETHIOPIA

Head of State

Executive power is vested in the President, who is elected by the National Shengo for a five-year term. The President and Vice-President of the country are also, respectively, President and Vice-President of the Council of State. In March 1990 the Marxist-Leninist Workers' Party of Ethiopia (WPE), the only legal political party, was renamed the Democratic Unity Party of Ethiopia (DUPE). Membership of the new party is open to opposition groups.

President: Lt-Col Mengistu Haile Mariam (elected 11 September 1987).

Vice-President: Fisseha Desta.

Office of the President and of the Vice-President: POB 5707, Addis Ababa; tel (1) 113000.

Legislature

Under the new Constitution, adopted in 1987, legislative power is vested in the National Shengo, with 835 members elected by universal adult suffrage for five years. From its members, the National Shengo also elects the Council of State (its permanent organ) and the Council of Ministers, which is headed by a Prime Minister.

National Shengo: Addis Ababa.

MINISTRIES AND GOVERNMENT DEPARTMENTS

OFFICE OF THE CHAIRMAN OF THE COUNCIL OF MINISTERS
POB 1013, Addis Ababa
Tel (1) 123400
Chairman: Lt-Col Mengistu Haile Mariam
Ministers: Feleke Gedle-Ghiorghis, Maj-Gen Kefelegn Yibza, Neguse Wolde Mikael, Maj-Gen Seyoum Mekonen

OFFICE OF THE PRIME MINISTER
POB 1013, Addis Ababa
Tel (1) 123400
Prime Minister (acting): Hailu Yimenu
Deputy Prime Ministers: Ashagre Yigletu, Alemu Agebe, Wole Chekol

COMMISSION FOR HOTELS AND TOURISM
POB 2183, Addis Ababa
Tel 447470; telex 21067
Commissioner: Davit Getachew

COMMISSION FOR RELIEF AND REHABILITATION
POB 5686, Addis Ababa
Tel 153011; telex 21281
Commissioner: Yilma Kasaye

INSTITUTE OF NATIONALITIES
Addis Ababa
Minister and Director: Hailu Amanuel Wolde

MINISTRY OF AGRICULTURE
POB 1223, Addis Ababa
Tel (1) 448040; fax (1) 513042
Minister: Geremew Debele

MINISTRY OF COFFEE AND TEA DEVELOPMENT
POB 3222, Addis Ababa
Tel (1) 518088; telex 21130
Minister: Hambissa Wakoya
Vice-Minister: Dr Birru Abebe

MINISTRY OF CONSTRUCTION
Addis Ababa
Tel (1) 155406
Minister: Kassa Gebre

MINISTRY FOR THE CO-ORDINATION OF REGIONAL AFFAIRS
Addis Ababa
Minister: Tsegaw Ayele

MINISTRY FOR THE CO-ORDINATION OF RELIGIOUS AFFAIRS
Addis Ababa
Minister: Dibekulu Zewde

MINISTRY OF CULTURE, SPORTS AND YOUTH AFFAIRS
POB 1902, Addis Ababa
Tel (1) 446338
Minister: Maj Giram Yilma

MINISTRY OF DEFENCE
POB 125, Addis Ababa
Tel (1) 445555; telex 21261
Minister: (vacant)

MINISTRY OF DOMESTIC TRADE
POB 1769, Addis Ababa
Tel (1) 448200
Minister: Mersha Wodajo

MINISTRY OF EDUCATION
POB 1362, Addis Ababa
Tel (1) 112039
Minister: Dr Yayehrad Kitaw

MINISTRY OF FINANCE
POB 1905, Addis Ababa
Tel (1) 113400; telex 21147
Minister: Tekola Dejene

MINISTRY OF FOREIGN AFFAIRS
POB 393, Addis Ababa
Tel (1) 447345; telex 21050
Minister: Tesfaye Dinka

MINISTRY OF FOREIGN TRADE
POB 2559, Addis Ababa
Tel (1) 151066; telex 21320
Minister: Tadesse Gebre-Kidan

MINISTRY OF HEALTH
POB 1234, Addis Ababa
Tel (1) 157011
Minister: Brig-Gen Dr Gizaw Tsehay

MINISTRY OF HOUSING AND URBAN DEVELOPMENT
POB 3386, Addis Ababa
Tel (1) 150000
Minister: Tadesse Kidane-Mariam
Vice-Minister: Gebre-Mariam Fanta

MINISTRY OF INDUSTRY
POB 704, Addis Ababa
Tel (1) 518025
Minister: Tadewos Harege-Work

MINISTRY OF INFORMATION
POB 1020, Addis Ababa
Tel (1) 111124
Minister: Abdul Hafez Yusuf

MINISTRY OF INTERNAL AFFAIRS
POB 2556, Addis Ababa
Tel (1) 113334
Minister: Col Tesfaye Wolde-Selassie

MINISTRY OF LABOUR AND SOCIAL AFFAIRS
POB 2056, Addis Ababa
Tel (1) 447080
Minister: Shimeles Adugna

MINISTRY OF LAW AND JUSTICE
POB 1370, Addis Ababa
Tel (1) 447390
Minister: Wondayen Mehretu

MINISTRY OF MINES AND ENERGY
POB 486, Addis Ababa
Tel (1) 448250; telex 21448; fax (1) 517874
Minister: Tekize-Shoa Ayitenfisu

MINISTRY OF PLANNING
Addis Ababa
Minister: Mersie Ejigu

MINISTRY OF STATE FARMS
POB 1223, Addis Ababa
Tel (1) 154600
Minister: Yoseph Muleta

MINISTRY OF TRANSPORT AND COMMUNICATIONS
POB 1629, Addis Ababa
Tel (1) 155011; fax (1) 515665
Minister: Assegid Wolde-Ammanuel

GOVERNMENT AGENCIES AND ORGANIZATIONS

Agriculture

Ethiopian Livestock and Meat Corpn: POB 5579, Addis Ababa; tel (1) 159341; telex 21095; f 1984; state trading organization responsible for management of the meat industry.

Ethiopian Oil Seeds And Pulses Export Corpn: POB 5719, Addis Ababa; tel (1) 550047; telex 21133; fax (1) 514396; Gen Man: Ephraim Ambaye; Dep Gen Man: Taye Abebe; f 1975; processing and export of pulses and oil seeds.

Ethiopian Sugar Corpn: POB 133, Addis Ababa; tel (1) 519700; telex 21038; fax 513488.

Business and Economy

BANKING

Agricultural and Industrial Development Bank: Joseph Broz Tito St, POB 1900, Addis Ababa; tel (1) 151188; telex 21173; Gen Man: Tsegaye Asfaw; provides devt finance for industry and agriculture, technical advice and assists in project evaluation; 21 brs.

Commercial Bank of Ethiopia: POB 255, Addis Ababa; tel (1) 515028; telex 21037; Gen Man: Alemu Aberra; f 1943; re-organized 1980; 146 brs.

Housing and Savings Bank: Higher 21, Kebele 04, POB 3480, Addis Ababa; tel (1) 512300; Gen Man: Getachew Yifru; Dep Gen Man: Tassew Demissie; f 1975; provides credit for housing construction; 8 brs.

National Bank of Ethiopia: POB 5550, Addis Ababa; tel (1) 447430; telex 21020; Gov: Bekele Tamirat; f 1964; bank of issue.

INSURANCE

Ethiopian Insurance Corpn: POB 2545, Addis Ababa; tel (1) 156348; telex 21120; Gen Man: Ayalew Bezabeh; f 1976; undertakes all insurance business.

MARKETING

Ethiopian Coffee Marketing Corpn: POB 2591, Addis Ababa; tel (1) 155330; telex 21174; promotion of coffee.

Natural Gums Processing and Marketing Enterprise: POB 62322, Addis Ababa; tel (1) 159930; telex 21336; Man: Yewendwesen Fassil; sole producer, processor, domestic distributor and exporter of natural gum products.

NATIONALIZED INDUSTRY

Ethiopian Beverages Corpn: POB 1285, Addis Ababa; tel (1) 186185; telex 21373.

Ethiopian Cement Corpn: POB 5782, Addis Ababa; tel (1) 122323; telex 21308.

Ethiopian Chemical Corpn: POB 5747, Addis Ababa; tel (1) 184305; telex 21011.

Ethiopian Food Corpn: Higher 21, Kebele 04, Mortgage Bldg, Addis Ababa; tel (1) 158522; telex 21292; fax 513173; f 1975; produces and distributes food items including edible oil, ghee substitute, pasta, bread, maize, wheat flour, etc.

Ethiopian Pharmaceuticals and Medical Supplies Corpn (EPHARMECOR): POB 21094, Addis Ababa; tel (1) 134577; telex 21248; Gen Man: Berhanu Zeleke; f 1981; manufacture, import, export and distribution of pharmaceuticals, chemicals, dressings, surgical and dental instruments, hospital and laboratory supplies.

National Leather and Shoe Corpn: POB 2516, Addis Ababa; tel (1) 517122; telex 21096; fax (1) 513525; f 1975; Gen Man: Yilma Adamu; Dep Gen Man: Girma W. Aregaie; produces and sells semi-processed hides and skins, finished leather, leather goods and footwear.

National Textiles Corpn: POB 2446, Addis Ababa; tel (1) 157316; telex 21129; fax 511955; Gen Man: Bekele Haile; f 1975; production of yarn, fabrics, knitwear, blankets, bags, etc.

TRADE

Ethiopian Chamber of Commerce: POB 517, Addis Ababa; tel (1) 518240; telex 21213; Pres: Bezabih Ayalew; Sec-Gen: Workeneh Mengesha; f 1947; city chambers in Addis Ababa, Asmara, Awassa, Bahir Dar, Dire Dawa, Nazret, Jimma, Gondar and Dessie.

Ethiopian Fruit and Vegetable Marketing Enterprise: POB 2374, Addis Ababa; tel (1) 449192; telex 21106; Gen Man: Hailu Balcha; f 1980; sole wholesale domestic distributor and exporter of fruit and vegetables, spices and floricultural products.

Ethiopian Import and Export Corpn (ETIMEX): POB 2313, Addis Ababa; tel (1) 152400; telex 21009; fax (1) 514396; f 1975; Gen Man: Tesfaye Asfaw; Dep Gen Man: Seyoum Tefera; under the supervision of the Ministry of Foreign Trade; import of building materials, foodstuffs, stationery and office equipment, textiles, clothing, chemicals, general merchandise, capital goods.

Defence

Armed Forces: Ministry of Defence, POB 125, Addis Ababa; tel (1) 445555; Commdr-in-Chief: Lt-Col Mengistu Haile Mariam; Chief of Staff: Lt-Gen Addis Tedla.

Air Force: Ministry of Defence, POB 125, Addis Ababa; tel (1) 445555; Commdr: Brig Alemayehu Agonafir.

Army: Ministry of Defence, POB 125, Addis Ababa; tel (1) 445555; Chief of Staff: Col Embibel Ayele.

Navy: Ministry of Defence, POB 125, Addis Ababa; tel (1) 445555; Commdr: Yehuwalashet Girma.

Police Force: Addis Ababa; Chief of Police: Brig-Gen: Worku Zewde.

Development and Planning

Ethiopian Handicrafts and Small-Scale Industries Development Agency: POB 5758, Addis Ababa; tel (1) 154672; telex 21514; Man: Messeret Shiferaw; f 1977; promotion of small-scale industries.

National Commission for Central Planning (NCCP): POB 1037, Addis Ababa; tel (1) 128800; Commr: Lt-Col Mengistu Haile Mariam.

Education

Commission for Higher Education: POB 30747, Addis Ababa; tel (1) 550088; telex 21452; Dir: Dr Mulugeta Semru; f 1976; planning, organizing and controlling all activities related to higher education.

Employment

Public Service Commission: POB 3240, Addis Ababa; tel (1) 553488; Commr: Masresha Gugsa; Dep Commr: Bekele Gayid; f 1961; processing of recruitments and promotions; general admin of discipline and appeals in the public service.

Energy

Ethiopian Electric Light and Power Authority: POB 1233, Addis Ababa; tel (1) 112263; telex 21023; Gen Man: Tessema Aba Derash.

Ethiopian Petroleum Organization: POB 3375, Addis Ababa; telex 21054; fax 512938; Gen Man: Mamo Gebre Meskel; f 1976; operates Assab petroleum refinery.

Legal and Judiciary

Supreme Court: Addis Ababa; tel (1) 448425; Pres: Asefa Liben; comprises civil, military and criminal sections; in 1987 its jurisdiction was extended to include supervision of all judicial proceedings throughout the country; judges are elected by the National Shengo.

Media

BROADCASTING

Ethiopian Television: POB 5544, Addis Ababa; tel (1) 116701; telex 21429; Dir: Wole Girmu; f 1964; broadcasts over all Ethiopia except for two administrative regions.

GOVERNMENT PUBLISHERS

Addis Ababa University Press: POB 1176, Addis Ababa; tel (1) 119148; telex 21205; Gen Editor: Innes Marshall; f 1968.

Government Printing Press: POB 1241, Addis Ababa.

Kuraz Publishing Agency: POB 30933, Addis Ababa; tel (1) 122588; telex 21512; Gen Man: Tesfa Abebe; f 1979.

NEWS AND INFORMATION

Central Statistical Office: Gen Wingate St, POB 1143, Addis Ababa; tel (1) 553011; Gen Man: Mitik Beyene; f 1960; collection, analysis and dissemination of statistical data.

Ethiopia News Agency (ENA): Patriot's St, POB 530, Addis Ababa; tel (1) 120014; telex 21068.

Science and Technology

Commission for Science and Technology: POB 2490, Addis Ababa; tel (1) 116241; Commr: Abebe Muluneh.

Telecommunications

Ethiopian Telecommunications Authority (ETA): POB 1047, Addis Ababa; tel (1) 510500; telex 21000; fax (1) 515777; Gen Man: Bekele Kebede; f 1952; licence and regulation of all telecommunications facilities.

Tourism

Tourism and Hotels Commission: Revolution Sq, POB 2183, Addis Ababa; tel (1) 447470; telex 21067; Dir: Dawit Getachew (mem of Cabinet); f 1961; devt and promotion of tourist industry.

Transport

CIVIL AVIATION

Civil Aviation Authority: POB 978, Addis Ababa; tel (1) 610277; telex 21162; Gen Man: Col Tsegaye Meshesha; f 1943; air traffic management; airport devt and admin.

Ethiopian Airlines: Bole International Airport, POB 1755, Addis Ababa; tel (1) 152222; telex 21012; fax 611474; Chair: Minister of Transport and Communications, Assegid Wolde-Ammanuel; Gen Man: Capt Muhammad Ahmad; operates regular domestic services and flights to 31 international destinations in Africa, Europe, the Middle East, India and the People's Republic of China.

RAILWAYS

Ethio-Djibouti Railway Co: POB 1051, Addis Ababa; tel (1) 517250; telex 21414; Chair: Minister of Transport and Communications, Assegid Wolde-Ammanuel; Gen Man: Channie Tamiru; f 1908; owned jointly by Ethiopian and Djibouti Govts;

plans to grant autonomous status were announced in July 1985; 781 km of track.

ROADS

Ethiopian Freight Transport Corpn: POB 2538, Addis Ababa; tel (1) 151841; telex 21238; fax (1) 519740; Gen Man: Col Negash Teklemariam; f 1977; truck and tanker operations.

Ethiopian Transport Construction Authority: POB 1770, Addis Ababa; tel (1) 447170; telex 21180; Gen Man: Kelletta Tesfa Michael; f 1951; constructs roads, bridges, airfields, ports and railways, and maintains roads and bridges.

National Public Transport Authority: POB 5780, Addis Ababa; tel (1) 153117; telex 21371; fax (1) 150744; Gen Man: Tesfaye Shenkute; f 1952; urban bus services in Addis Ababa and Jimma, and services between towns.

Road Transport Authority: POB 2504, Addis Ababa; fax (1) 510715; enforcement of road transport regulations, registering of vehicles and issuing of driving licences.

SHIPPING

Ethiopian Shipping Lines Corpn: POB 2572, Addis Ababa; tel (1) 514204; telex 21045; fax (1) 519525; Chair: Min of Transport and Communications, Assegid Wolde-Ammanuel; Gen Man: Tesema Gezaw; f 1964; serves Red Sea, Europe and the Far East.

Marine Transport Authority: POB 1861, Addis Ababa; tel (1) 446448; telex 21280; fax (1) 516015; f 1978; administers and operates the ports of Assab and Massawa; manages inland waterways; handles cargo.

Maritime and Transit Services Corpn: POB 1186, Addis Ababa; tel (1) 510666; telex 21057; fax (1) 514097; f 1979; handles cargoes for import and export; operates shipping agency service.

Utilities

Commission for National Water Resources: POB 486, Addis Ababa; tel (1) 447597; telex 21219; Commr: Alem Alazar.

Welfare

Commission for Pensions and Social Security: POB 1030, Addis Ababa; Commr: Gessese Wolde Kimane.

Commission for Sports: POB 3241, Addis Ababa; tel (1) 445363; Commr: Tesgaw Ayele.

National Children's Commission: POB 1133, Addis Ababa; tel (1) 552200; telex 21524; Dir: Teserawork Shimels; f 1981; caters for and represents children's needs.

FIJI

Head of State

The 1970 Constitution was revoked in 1987 following a coup. According to an interim constitution, executive power is vested in the President of the Republic, who is empowered to make laws by decree.

President: Ratu Sir Penaia Ganilau (took office 6 December 1987).

Office of the President: POB 2513, Govt Bldgs, Suva; tel 315269; telex 2167.

Legislature

A constitution, drafted in 1988 and revised during 1989, which was expected to be promulgated by decree before 1991, provides for a bicameral legislature comprising an elected 64-seat House of Representatives (a majority of seats of which are to be elected by indigenous Fijians), and a Senate of 34 Chiefs appointed by the President.

Senate: Govt Bldgs, Suva; tel 211614; telex 2167; Pres: W. J. Clark.

House of Representatives: Govt Bldgs, Suva; tel 211402; telex 2167; Speaker: Militoni Lewaniqila.

MINISTRIES AND GOVERNMENT DEPARTMENTS

OFFICE OF THE PRIME MINISTER
Govt Bldgs, Suva
Tel 211201; telex 2167
Prime Minister: Ratu Sir Kamisese Mara

MINISTRY OF COMMUNICATIONS, WORKS AND TRANSPORT
4 Ganilau House, Private Bag, Suva
Tel 315133; fax 301198
Minister: (vacant)

MINISTRY OF EDUCATION
Marela House, Thurston St, Suva
Tel 314477
Minister: Filipe Bole

MINISTRY OF EMPLOYMENT AND INDUSTRIAL RELATIONS
POB 2216, Govt Bldgs, Victoria Parade, Suva
Tel 211640
Minister: Taniela Veitata

MINISTRY OF FIJIAN AFFAIRS AND RURAL DEVELOPMENT
POB 2100, Govt Bldgs, Suva
Tel 24086
Minister: Col Vatiliai Navunisaravi

MINISTRY OF FINANCE AND ECONOMIC PLANNING
Govt Bldgs, Suva
Minister: Josefata Kamikamica

MINISTRY OF FOREIGN AFFAIRS
Govt Bldgs, Suva
Minister: Ratu Sir Kamisese Mara

MINISTRY OF FORESTS
Govt Bldgs, Suva
Minister: Ovini Bokini

MINISTRY OF HEALTH
Govt Bldgs, Suva
Minister: Apenisa Kurisaqila

MINISTRY OF HOME AFFAIRS
Govt Bldgs, Suva
Minister: Ratu Sir Kamisese Mara

MINISTRY OF HOUSING AND URBAN DEVELOPMENT
Govt Bldgs, Suva
Minister: Tomasi Vakatora

MINISTRY OF INDIAN AFFAIRS
POB 2444, Govt Bldgs, Suva
Tel 211374; telex 2167
Minister: Irene Jai Narayan

MINISTRY OF INFORMATION, BROADCASTING, TELEVISION AND TELECOMMUNICATIONS
POB 2225, Govt Bldgs, Suva
Tel 211700; telex 2224; fax 300766
Minister: Ratau Inoke Kubuabola

MINISTRY OF INFRASTRUCTURE AND PUBLIC UTILITIES
Govt Bldgs, Suva
Minister: Apisai Tora

MINISTRY OF JUSTICE
POB 2213, Govt Bldgs, Suva
Tel 211580; fax 302404
Attorney-General and Minister: Sailosi Kepa

MINISTRY OF LANDS AND MINERAL RESOURCES
Govt Bldgs, Suva
Minister: Ratu William Toganivalu

MINISTRY OF PRIMARY INDUSTRIES AND CO-OPERATIVES
POB 358, Suva
Tel 311233; telex 2290; fax 302478
Minister: Viliame Gonelevu

MINISTRY OF TOURISM, CIVIL AVIATION AND ENERGY
Govt Bldgs, Suva
Minister: David Pickering

MINISTRY OF TRADE AND COMMERCE
Govt Bldgs, Suva
Minister: Berenado Vunibobo

MINISTRY OF WOMEN'S AFFAIRS AND SOCIAL WELFARE
Govt Bldgs, Suva
Minister: Finau Tabakaucoro

MINISTRY OF YOUTH AND SPORT
POB 2448, Govt Bldgs, Suva
Tel 315800
Minister: Filipe Bole

GOVERNMENT AGENCIES AND ORGANIZATIONS

Advisory and Supervisory Body

Office of the Auditor-General: POB 2214, 7th Floor, Ratu Sukuna House, cnr Victoria Parade and McArthur St, Govt Bldgs, Suva; tel 211560; fax 301741; Auditor-Gen: Ramesh C. Dutt; Dep Auditor-Gen: Isaia Vakabua; f 1969; audits and reports on the audit of Govt depts, statutory bodies and others approved by the Minister of Finance and Economic Planning.

Agriculture

Fiji Pine Commission: POB 521, Lautoka; tel 361511; telex 5294; Gen Man: P. J. Drysdale; Sec: S. D. Sharma; f 1976; devt of forest plantations; marketing of forest products through subsidiary joint venture Forestry Development Service Ltd.

Fiji Sugar Cane Growers' Council: POB 12300, 4th Floor, Dominion House, Thomson St, Suva; tel 314855; telex 2271; fax 301794; Chair: Siddiq Mohidin Koya; Chief Exec: Kalu Karan Singh; Sec: Ratu John D. V. Cavalevu; f 1985; represents growers supplying sugar cane on contract basis to the Fiji Sugar Corpn (see below); protects and develops the sugar industry; markets sugar to overseas markets.

Sugar Commission of Fiji: POB 644, 4th Floor, Dominion House, Thomson St, Suva; tel 315488; fax 301488; Chair: Gerald W. S. Barrack; Sec: M. P. Faktaufon; f 1985; co-ordinates all activities of the Fiji sugar industry.

Business and Economy

BANKING

Fiji Development Bank: POB 104, Devt Bank Centre, 360 Victoria Parade, Suva; tel 314866; telex 2578; fax 314886; Chair: Lyle N. Cupit; Man Dir: Laisenia Qarase; f 1967; provides funds for industry and commerce, agriculture and fishing and equity investments; joint venture participation; 8 brs.

National Bank of Fiji: POB 1166, 107 Victoria Parade, Suva; tel 311999; telex 2135; Chair: Paul Manueli; Chief Man: Visanti Makrava; f 1974; 11 brs.

Reserve Bank of Fiji: POB 1220, Suva; tel 313611; telex 2164; fax 301688; Chair and Gov: Jone Yavala Kubuabola; Dep Gov: H. P. Singh; f 1984 to replace Central Monetary Authority of Fiji; central bank and bank of of issue.

MARKETING

National Marketing Authority: POB 5085, Raiwaqa, Suva; tel 385888; telex 2413; fax 385207; Chair: V. Prasad; Chief Exec: Solomone Makasiale; f 1971; statutory body; processing, marketing, import and export of agricultural and marine products.

Fiji Sugar Marketing Co Ltd: POB 1402, 5th Floor, Dominion House, Thomson St, Suva; tel 311588; telex 2271; Man Dir: John May.

NATIONALIZED INDUSTRY

Fiji Sugar Corpn Ltd: POB 283, 5th Floor, Dominion House, Thomson St, Suva; tel 313455; telex 2119; fax 302685; Chair: Lyle N. Cupit; Man Dir: Rasheed A. Ali; buys sugar cane; manufactures raw sugar.

TRADE

Customs and Excise Department: POB 175, Suva; tel 302322; telex 2121; fax 300834; collection of revenue; law enforcement against drugs, arms and ammunition, prohibited and restricted goods.

The Government Handicraft Centre: POB 2118, Govt Bldgs, Suva; tel 211306; fax 302617; Man: Latileta Makasiale; f 1978; devt and sales of Fijian handicrafts.

Defence

Army: POB 102, Queen Elizabeth Barracks, Maddocks Rd, Nabua; tel 385222; telex 2157; Commdr of the Armed Forces: Maj Gen Sitiveni Rabuka.

Navy: POB 12387, Suva; tel 312397, telex 2157; fax 314783; Commdr: Cmmdr J. V. Bainimarama; f 1975; coast-guard duties; law enforcement in archipelagic waters; emergency medical evacuations; naval control of shipping.

Development and Planning

DEVELOPMENT

Fiji Development Co Ltd: POB 161, Suva; tel 25611; telex 2412; Man: V. W. Yee; f 1960; under the Commonwealth Devt Corpn.

Land Development Authority: c/o Ministry for Primary Industries, POB 358, Suva; tel 311233; telex 2290; fax 302478; Chair: Ratu Sir Josaia Tavaiqia; f 1961; co-ordinates devt plans for land and marine resources.

INVESTMENT

Fijian Development Fund Board: POB 122, Suva; tel 322231; Chair: Ratu Sir Kamisese Mara; Sec: N. Morris; f 1951; funds derived from the sales of copra by indigenous Fijians used for Fijian devt schemes.

Fiji Trade and Investment Board: POB 2303, Velop House, Govt Bldgs, Suva; tel 315988; telex 2355; fax 301783; Chair: Asesela Ravuvu; Dir: Surendra Sharma; f 1980; promotes and stimulates foreign and local economic devt investment.

Legal and Judiciary

Office of the Director of Public Prosecutions: c/o Ministry of Justice, POB 2213, Govt Blgs, Suva; tel 211580; fax 302404; Dir of Public Prosecutions: Isikeli Mataitoga.

Office of the Solicitor-General: c/o Ministry of Justice, POB 2213, Govt Blgs, Suva; tel 211580; fax 302404; Solicitor-Gen: Filimone Jitoko.

Supreme Court: POB 2215, Suva; tel 211335; telex 2167; Chief Justice: Sir Timoci Tuivaga.

Media

BROADCASTING

Fiji Broadcasting Commission—FBC (Radio Fiji): POB 334, Broadcasting House, Suva; tel 314333; telex 2142; fax 301643; Chair: Ratu Joshua Toganivalu; Gen Man: Dr Ali Ahmed; f 1954; programmes in English, Fijian and Hindustani.

Fiji National Video Centre (FNVC): c/o Ministry of Information, Broadcasting, Television and Telecommunications, POB 2225, Govt Bldgs, Suva; video library; production unit established by Govt and Hanns Seidel Foundation (Federal Republic of Germany); educational programmes.

GOVERNMENT PUBLISHER

Printing Department: POB 98, Suva.

NEWS AND INFORMATION

Bureau of Statistics: POB 2221, Govt Bldgs, Suva; tel 315144; telex 2167; f 1967; compiles, analyses and publishes statistical information relating to the economic and general activities and condition of the people of Fiji.

Mining and Energy

Department of Energy: Private Mail Bag, Suva; tel 386677; telex 2330; fax 386864; Dir (acting): D. Kumaran; f 1981; responsible for Fiji's energy resource devt and management; devt of indigenous renewable energy resources and energy efficiency.

Mineral Resources Department: Private Mail Bag, Mead Road, Nabua, Suva; tel 381611; telex 2330; Dir: Abdul Rahiman; Asst Dir: Alfred T. Simpson; f 1972; geological mapping, hydrogeology, geophysics, marine geology, seismology and petroleum geology; admin of mining and petroleum acts; under Ministry of Lands and Mineral Resources.

Tourism

Fiji Visitors Bureau: POB 92, Suva; tel 302433; telex 2180; fax 300970; Chair: Sakeasi Waqanivalagi; Gen Man: Isimeli Bainimara; f 1923.

Transport and Communications

TELECOMMUNICATIONS

Fiji International Telecommunications Ltd (FINTEL): POB 59, 158 Victoria Parade, Suva; tel 312933; telex 2201; provision of international telecommunications services; operates in conjunction with the Fiji Posts and Telecommunications Dept (see below).

Fiji Posts and Telecommunications Department: POB 40, Suva; tel 019; telex 2104; operates telecommunications services in Fiji.

TRANSPORT

Civil Aviation Department: 4th Floor, Devt Bank Centre, Victoria Parade, Suva.

Department of Road Transport: POB 6677, Nasinu Post Office, Suva; tel 392166; Controller, Road Transport and Principal Licensing Authority: M. Vakarewakobau; f 1960; under Ministry of Communications, Works and Transport; responsible for the admin of the Traffic Act and its regulations; vehicle licensing.

   Central Traffic Authority: advises the Minister on all matters relating to road transport and traffic; makes traffic regulations.

   Fiji Road Safety Council: voluntary organisation under the responsibility of the Minister for Communications, Works and Transport.

   Transport Control Board: deals with matters concerning the operation of public service vehicles.

Fiji Air Ltd: POB 1259, 219 Victoria Parade, Suva; tel 322666; telex 2258; fax 300771; Chief Exec: M. C. D. Tyler; domestic airline; international service to Tuvalu; charter operations, aerial photography and surveillance also conducted; partly Govt-owned.

Fiji Sugar Corpn Railway: POB 155, Rarawai Mill, Ba; tel 374044; telex 6248; permanent and temporary track serving cane-growing areas at Ba, Lautoka and Penang on the island of Viti Levu, and Labasa on the island of Vanua Levu.

Welfare

Fiji Housing Authority: Valelevu Regional Centre, Valelevu, Nasinu; tel 392977; fax 411950; Chief Exec: Lionel D. S. Yee; Dep Chief Exec: Fazal Khan; tel 1955; provision of low-cost housing, housing finance and rural housing; site planning; appraisal of housing needs.

FINLAND

Head of State

Executive power is vested in the President, who is elected for a six-year term by direct popular vote. If no candidate wins an absolute majority, an electoral college is convened. The President appoints a Council of State, headed by a Prime Minister, which is responsible to Parliament.

President: Dr Mauno Koivisto (assumed duties 10 September 1981; elected 26 January 1982; re-elected 15 February 1988).

Office of the President: Pohjoisesplanadi 1, 00170 Helsinki; tel (0) 661133; telex 124636.

Legislature

Legislative power is exercised by the unicameral Eduskunta (Parliament) in conjunction with the President. Parliament comprises 200 members elected by universal adult suffrage for four years by proportional representation. Each of Finland's 12 provinces is administered by an appointed Governor.

Eduskunta (Parliament): Mannerheimintie 30, 00102 Helsinki; tel (0) 4321; telex 121464; Speaker: Kalevi Sorsa; First Dep Speaker: Elsi Hetemäki-Olander; Second Dep Speaker: Mikko Pesälä; Sec-Gen: Erkki Ketola.

MINISTRIES AND GOVERNMENT DEPARTMENTS

PRIME MINISTER'S OFFICE
Aleksanterinkatu 3D, 00170 Helsinki
Tel (0) 1601; telex 124636; fax (0) 1602099
Prime Minister: Harri Holkeri
Deputy Prime Minister: Pertti Paasio
Minister in the Council of State: Ilkka Kanerva

MINISTRY OF AGRICULTURE AND FORESTRY
Hallituskatu 3A, 00170 Helsinki
Tel (0) 1601; telex 125621
Minister: Toivo T. Pohjola

MINISTRY OF DEFENCE
Et Makasiinikatu 8A, 00130 Helsinki
Tel (0) 625801; telex 124667
Minister: Ole Norrback

MINISTRY OF EDUCATION
Meritullinkatu 10, POB 293, 00171 Helsinki
Tel (0) 134171; telex 122079; fax (0) 6121335
Minister: Christoffer Taxell
Minister of Culture: Anna-Liisa Piipari

MINISTRY OF THE ENVIRONMENT
Ratakatu 3, POB 399, 00121 Helsinki
Tel (0) 19911; telex 123717; fax (0) 1991499
Minister: Kaj Bärlund

Housing Department: Ratakatu 3, 00120 Helsinki; tel (0) 19911.

Physical Planning and Building Department: Hämeentie 3-5, 00530 Helsinki; tel (0) 1601; fax (0) 1605655.

MINISTRY OF FINANCE
Snellmaninkatu 1A, 00170 Helsinki
Tel (0) 1601; telex 123241; fax (0) 1603120
Minister: Matti Louekoski
Minister of Taxation: Ulla Puolanne

MINISTRY OF FOREIGN AFFAIRS
Merikasarmi, POB 176, 00161 Helsinki
Tel (0) 134151; telex 1000306; fax (0) 629840
Minister: Pertti Paasio

Department for External Economic Relations: Merikasarmi, POB 176, 00161 Helsinki; tel (0) 134151; telex 124636; fax (0) 629840; f 1918.

MINISTRY OF FOREIGN TRADE
Aleksanterinkatu 10, 00170 Helsinki
Tel (0) 1601; telex 124645; fax (0) 1603666
Minister: Pertti Salolainen

MINISTRY OF THE INTERIOR
Kirkkokatu 12, 00170 Helsinki
Tel (0) 1601; telex 123644; fax (0) 1602827
Minister: Jarmo Rantanen

MINISTRY OF JUSTICE
Eteläesplanadi 10, POB 1, 00130 Helsinki
Tel (0) 18251; fax (0) 1825430
Minister: Tarja Halonen

MINISTRY OF LABOUR
Eteläesplanadi 4, 00130 Helsinki
Tel (0) 18561; telex 1856427; fax (0) 121441
Minister: Matti Puhakka

MINISTRY OF SOCIAL AFFAIRS AND HEALTH
Snellmaninkatu 4-6, POB 267, 00171 Helsinki
Tel (0) 1601; telex 125073; fax (0) 650442
Minister of Social Affairs: Mauri Miettinen
Minister of Health: Tuulikki Hamalainen

MINISTRY OF TRADE AND INDUSTRY
Aleksanterinkatu 10, POB 230, 00170 Helsinki
Tel (0) 1601; telex 124645; fax (0) 1603666
Minister: Ilkka Suominen

MINISTRY OF TRANSPORT AND COMMUNICATIONS
Eteläesplanadi 16, POB 235, 00130 Helsinki

Tel (0) 17361; telex 125472; fax (0) 1736270
Minister: Pekka Vennamo

GOVERNMENT AGENCIES AND ORGANIZATIONS

Advisory and Supervisory Body

Valtionyhtiöiden Suunnittelutoimisto (State-Owned Companies Bureau): c/o Ministry of Trade and Industry, Aleksanterinkatu 10, 00170 Helsinki; tel (0) 1601; telex 124645; appraises state-owned cos, their operation and profitability, and makes recommendations on the allocation of state financing.

Agriculture and the Environment

AGRICULTURE

Maatilahallitus (National Board of Agriculture): Mariankatu 23, POB 250, 00171 Helsinki; tel (0) 134211; fax (0) 1352448; Dir-Gen: Dr Kalevi Hemilä; f 1971; under the Ministry of Agriculture and Forestry; administers and supervises agricultural admin; executes Govt policies with regard to the devt of agriculture and rural enterprises.

THE ENVIRONMENT

Environmental Protection Department: Ratakatu 3, 00120 Helsinki; tel (0) 19911; under Ministry of the Environment; divisions concerned with nature conservation, waste management, water management and air pollution control and noise abatement.

National Board of Waters and the Environment: Pohjoinen Rautatiekatu 21B, 00101 Helsinki; tel (0) 40281; telex 126086; fax (0) 6951326; Dir-Gen: Simo Jaatinen; f 1970; public supervisory body under the Ministry of the Environment; administers, manages and protects water and other sections of the environment.

FORESTRY

Metsähallitus (Finnish National Board of Forestry): POB 233, 00121 Helsinki; tel (0) 61631; telex 121132; fax (0) 6163327; Chair and Dir-Gen: Jaakko Piironen; Dir, State Forestry: (vacant); Dir, Gen Forestry: Pentti Takala; f 1859; management, utilization and protection of Govt-owned forests and supervision of other forests.

VAPO Oy: POB 22, 40101 Jyväskylä; tel (41) 617680; telex 28377; peat production, wood industry.

Business and Economy

BANKING

Mortgage Bank of Finland LTD: Eteläesplanadi 8, POB 165, 00130 Helsinki; tel (0) 650066; telex 121840; fax (0) 654740; Chair: Matti Niemi; Man Dir: Ilpo Niitti; f 1956; 100% owned by Postipankki (see below).

Post Office Bank 'Postipankki': Unioninkatu 20, 00007 Helsinki; tel (0) 1641; telex 121698; fax (0) 1643766; Chair and Chief Exec: Seppo Lindblom; Chief Gen Man: Matti Niemi; f

1886; operates through its head office, 66 brs and the 2,912 local post offices.

Suomen Pankki/Finlands Bank (The Bank of Finland): Snellmaninaukio, POB 160, 00171 Helsinki; tel (0) 1831; telex 121224; fax (0) 174872; Gov: Rolf Kullberg; f 1811; bank of issue under the guarantee and supervision of Parliament; 12 brs.

FINANCIAL AGENCIES

National Board of Taxes: Haapaniemenkatu 7-9B, 00530 Helsinki; tel (0) 73111; fax (0) 7311247; Dir-Gen: Lauri Honkavaara; f 1970; oversees and develops the admin of taxation.

Suomen Vientiluotto Oy: Eteläesplanadi 8, POB 123, 00131 Helsinki; tel (0) 131171; telex 121893; fax (0) 174819; f 1963; export credit corpn.

NATIONALIZED INDUSTRY

Alko Ltd: Salmisaarenranta 7, POB 350, 00101 Helsinki; tel (0) 13311; telex 121045; fax (0) 1332784; Chair of Board of Dirs: Heikki Koski; Dep Gen Man and Industrial Dir: Matti Kaukinen; f 1932; production, import, export and sale of alcoholic beverages and spirits; monopoly of retail sale of all alcoholic beverages except medium beer; planning and implementation of alcohol policy; production and marketing of starch, yeasts and enzymes, vinegars, industrial alcohols, animal feeds, etc; 99.9% state-owned.

Confederation of Finnish Industries: Eteläranta 10, POB 220, 00131 Helsinki.

Enso-Gutzeit Oy: Kanavaranta 1, POB 309, 00101 Helsinki; tel (0) 16291; telex 124438; fax (0) 1629471; Pres and Chief Exec: Jukka Härmälä; f 1872; forestry; production of pulp, fine, publication and speciality paper, board, plywood, timber houses, etc; acquires and installs hydro-electric power; 55.2% state-owned.

Kemira Group: Porkkalankatu 3, POB 330, 00101 Helsinki; tel (0) 13211; telex 121191; fax (0) 6946167; Chair of Supervisory Board: Heikki Perho; Chair of Board of Management: Yrjö Pessi; f 1920; fertilizers, agricultural and industrial chemicals, biotechnical products, explosives, safety equipment, man-made fibres, paints, filters and autocatalysts.

Neste Oy: Keilaniemi, 02150 Espoo; tel (0) 4501; telex 124641; Chair of Supervisory Board: Ulf Sundqvist; Chair of Board of Management: Jaakko Ihamuotila; Corporate Vice-Pres, Shipping: Raimo Roos; f 1948; oil refining; production of petrochemicals, plastics, industrial chemicals and lubricants; shipping; natural gas; batteries; 97.96% state-owned.

Outokumpu Oy: POB 280, 00101 Helsinki; tel (0) 4031; telex 124441; Chair of Supervisory Board: Paavo Lipponen; Chair of Board of Dirs and Pres: Pertti Voutilainen; f 1932; exploration, mining, mineral processing, metal refining and processing, equipment manufacture, engineering contracting; 61% state-owned.

Rautaruukki Oy: Kiilakiventie 1, POB 217, 90101 Oulu; tel (81) 327711; telex 32109; Chair of Supervisory Board: Ahti Pekkala; Chair of Board of Management and Pres: Mikko Kivimäki; f 1960; steel processing; 87% state-owned.

Saimaan Kanavalaivat Oy: Pohjoinen Makasiininkatu 7, 00130 Helsinki; holding co.

Oy Sisu-Auto Ab: Ristipellontie 19, 00390 Helsinki; tel (0) 542011; telex 121245; fax (0) 541488; Chair of Supervisory Board: Matti Luttinen; Chair of Board of Management and Chief Exec: Jorma S. Jerkku; f as private co in 1931; state bought 70% of shares in 1975; 99.8% state-owned; manufacture, marketing and maintenance of trucks, terminal tractors and defence vehicles.

Valmet Oy: Punanotkonkatu 2, POB 155, 00131 Helsinki; tel (0) 13291; telex 124427; fax (0) 179677; Chair of Admin Council: Harri Holkeri; Chair of Board of Dirs: Matti Kankaanpää; f 1946; engineering, automation; 79.8% state-owned.

Valvilla Oy: POB 108, 20101 Turku; telex 62156; Chair of Supervisory Board: Bror Wahlroos; Chair of Board of Management: Matti Vainio; f 1978; wool and cotton spinning, weaving and marketing; 99.4% state-owned.

Oy Veikkaus Ab: Karhunkierros 4, 01640 Vantaa; tel (0) 84961; telex 124631; football pools and lotteries.

Veitsiluoto Oy: 94830 Kemi; tel (69) 8141; Chair of Supervisory Board: Jaako Pajula; Chair of Board of Management: Pentti O. Rautalahti; wood processing; 88.8% state-owned.

TRADE

Kulutta Janeuvontaliitto RIJ: Viherniemenkatu 5, 00530 Helsinki; tel (0) 7102744; Chair: Kaj Bärland; Dir: Leena Simonen; f 1979; consumer consulting organization; 70% Govt-funded.

Kuluttaja-asiamies (Consumer Ombudsman): Hietaniemenkatu 7A, 3 krs, POB 1030, 00101 Helsinki; tel (0) 447177; Ombudsman: Erik Mickwitz; f 1978; supervises the legality of marketing and contract terms; assists consumers taking individual matters to court; under Ministry of Trade and Industry.

Kuluttajaneuvosto (Consumer Council): address as above; Sec-Gen: Seija Turtiainen; f 1978; parliamentary committee, making proposals concerning consumer protection and interests; prepares statements to promote legislation, research and education in this area; attached to Ministry of Trade and Industry.

Kuluttajavalituslautakunta (Consumer Complaint Board): address as above; Sec: Marjo-Riitta Lahelma; f 1978; gives recommendations for the settlement of complaints made by consumers concerning the quality of goods or services; under Ministry of Trade and Industry.

National Board of Customs: Erottajankatu 2, POB 512, 00120 Helsinki; tel (0) 6141; telex 121559; fax (0) 6142764; Dir-Gen: Jermu Laine; f 1812; manages the assessment and collection of import and excise duties and customs enforcement; compiles and publishes Finland's foreign trade statistics.

National Board of Patents and Registration: POB 154, 00181 Helsinki; f 1942; under the Ministry of Trade and Industry.

National Board of Trade and Consumer Affairs: POB 5, 00531, Helsinki; tel (0) 7031; fax (0) 7032850; Dir-Gen: Sippo Rautio; Head, Dept of Consumer Affairs: Pirkko Raunemaa; Head, Admin Dept: Pirkko Varpasuo; f 1973; consumer affairs; food control; control of product safety.

Vientitakuulaitos (Export Guarantee Board): Eteläranta 6, POB 187, 00130 Helsinki; tel (0) 661811; telex 12178.

Culture

National Archives: Rauhankatu 17, 00170 Helsinki; tel (0) 176911; Dir: Prof Veikko Litzen; Dep Dir: M. A. Juhani Saarenheimo; f 1869; central administrative authority; supervises the activities of the provincial archives; as the national repository, receives, preserves and makes available official and private records.

Defence

Frontier Guard: Kaikukatu 3, POB 3, 00131 Helsinki; tel (0) 77261; telex 124865; fax (0) 7539698; subordinate to the Ministry of the Interior; guards and controls land and sea borders of the country; enforces customs controls; organized internally along military lines.

General Defence Headquarters: Pääesikunta, et Makasiininkatu 8, POB 919, 00130 Helsinki; tel (0) 1611; telex 124667; fax (0) 1612439; Supreme Commdr of the Defence Forces: Mauno Koivisto; Commdr-in-Chief of the Army: Gen Jaako Valtanen.

  Air Force: POB 30, 41161 Tikkakoski; tel (41) 751322; telex 28231; Commdr-in-Chief: Maj-Gen Pertti Jokinen.

  Navy: Pohjoiskaari 36, 00200 Helsinki; tel (0) 674011; telex 124666; Commdr-in-Chief: Rear-Adm Juha Tikka.

Police Department: c/o Ministry of the Interior, Kirkkokatu 12, 00170 Helsinki; tel (0) 1601; telex 123644; fax 1602827.

Rescue Department: c/o Ministry of the Interior, Kirkkokatu 12, 00170 Helsinki; tel (0) 1601; telex 123275; fax (0) 1604672; in charge of directing, guiding and monitoring fire, rescue services and civil defence admin.

Development and Planning

Kehitysaluerahasto Oy: Haapaniemenkatu 40, POB 127, 70101 Kuopio; tel (71) 124100; telex 42185; regional devt fund.

Teollisen Kehitysyhteistyön Rahasto Oy (Finnfund): Ratakatu 27, POB 391, 00121 Helsinki; tel (0) 641301; telex 125028; fax (0) 603309; f 1980; industrial devt co-operation fund.

Education and Research

EDUCATION

National Board of General Education: Hakaniemenkatu 2, 00530 Helsinki; tel (0) 7061; Dir-Gen: Erkki Aho; Dep Dirs: Erkki Kähkönen, Yrjö Yrjönsuuri; f 1869; administrative board under the Ministry of Education; supervises schools, public libraries and general adult education.

National Board of Vocational Education: Hakaniemenkatu 2, 00530 Helsinki; tel (0) 7061; telex 125548; fax (0) 7062865; Dir-Gen: Dr Jorma Pöyhönen; f 1966; oversees technical and vocational education in Finland.

RESEARCH

The Academy of Finland: Hämeentie 68, POB 57, 00550 Helsinki; tel (0) 77581; telex 123416; fax (0) 7758299; Pres and Chair of the Central Board of Research Councils: Erik Allardt; Admin Dir: Heikki Kallio; Research Dir: Elisabeth Helander; f 1969; central Govt agency for science admin and science policy planning; under the Ministry of Education; comprises the Central Board of Research Councils and seven Research Councils representing the sciences and humanities; funds basic research; advises the Govt on scientific research; co-ordinates international research co-operation.

Valtion Teknillinen Tutkimuskeskus—VTT (Technical Research Centre of Finland): Vuorimiehentie 5, 02150 Espoo; tel (0) 4561; telex 122972; fax (0) 460419; Dir-Gen: Markku

Mannerkoski; f 1942; technological research and devt in the areas of building technology, community devt, manufacturing technology, energy technology and information technology.

Employment

Institute of Occupational Health: Topeliuksenkatu 41A, 00250 Helsinki; tel (0) 47471; telex 121394; fax (0) 414634; Dir-Gen: Jorma Rantanen; Admin Dir: Martti Lehtokangas; Research Dir: Sven Hernberg; f 1945; comprises central unit and six regional institutes; carries out research; provides advisory services, training and information in the field of occupational health and safety.

National Board of Labour Protection: POB 536, 33101 Tampere; tel (31) 608111; telex 22004; fax (31) 530201; Dir-Gen: Jaakko Riikonen; f 1973; labour protection admin.

Health and Welfare

HEALTH

Public Health Institute: Mannerheimintie 166, 00280 Helsinki.

WELFARE

National Board of Social Welfare: Siltasaarenkatu 18C, POB 197, 00530 Helsinki; tel (0) 73191; fax (0) 761307; Dir-Gen: Vappu Taipale; Admin Dir: Sakari Kallio; f 1968; directs welfare; develops new social services and benefits.

Social Insurance Institution: POB 450, 00101 Helsinki.

Legal and Judiciary

Eduskunnan Oikeusasiamies (Parliamentary Solicitor-General): Helsinki; Parliamentary Solicitor-Gen: Olavi E. Heinonen; ombudsman appointed by Parliament to supervise the observance of the law.

Korkein hallinto oikeus (Supreme Administrative Court): Unioninkatu 16, 00130 Helsinki; tel (0) 18531; Pres: Antti Suviranta; f 1918; comprises a Pres and 21 Justices appointed by the Pres of the Republic; highest tribunal for appeals in administrative cases.

Korkein oikeus (Supreme Court): Pohjoisesplanadi 3, 00170 Helsinki; tel (0) 624121; Pres: Olavi Heinonen; consists of a Pres and 21 Justices appointed by the Pres of the Republic; final court appeal in civil and criminal cases; supervises judges and executive authorities; appoints judges.

Office of the Chancellor of Justice: Snellmaninkatu 1A, 00170 Helsinki; tel (0) 1603930; fax (0) 1604006; Chancellor of Justice: Dr Jorma S. Aalto; Dep Chancellor of Justice: Jukka Pasanen; f 1809; responsible for ensuring that authorities and officials comply with the law; chief public prosecutor; acts as counsel for the Govt.

Media

BROADCASTING

Oy Yleisradio Ab—YLE (Finnish Broadcasting Co): Kesäkatu 2, 00260 Helsinki; tel (0) 441141; telex 124735; Dir-Gen: Reino Paasilinna; Dir, Admin and Dep Dir-Gen: Jouni Mykkänen; Dir, Radio: Keijo Savolainen; Dir, TV Programme 1: Arne Wessberg; Dir, TV Programme 2: Tapio Siikala; Dir, Swedish Radio and TV: Bengt Bergman; Dir, Regional Programming: Olavi Peltola; Dir, Engineering: Erkki Larkka; f 1926; management appointed according to the political character of Parliament; radio and TV broadcasting.

GOVERNMENT PUBLISHER

Valtion Painatuskeskus: Hakuninmaantie 2, POB 516, 00101 Helsinki; tel (0) 56601; telex 123458; fax (0) 5660374; Man Dir: Olavi Perilä; f 1859; Govt printing centre.

NEWS AND INFORMATION

National Board of Agriculture Statistical Office: Mariankatu 23, 00170 Helsinki.

Central Statistical Office of Finland: Annankatu 44, POB 504, 00101 Helsinki; tel (0) 17341; telex 1002111; fax (0) 17342279.

Mining and Energy

Atomic Energy Commission: Pohjoinen Makasiinikatu 6, 00130 Helsinki; tel (0) 1605226; telex 125452; fax (0) 1603666; Chair: Prof Jorma Routti; Sec-Gen: Sakari Immonen; Admin Sec: Margit Hovi; f 1988; advisory body operating in the field of nuclear energy; under the Ministry of Trade and Industry.

Finnish Centre for Radiation and Nuclear Safety: POB 268, 00101 Helsinki; tel (0) 70821; telex 122691; fax (0) 7082210; Dir-Gen: Antti P. U. Vuorinen; f 1958; regulates nuclear power plants; supervises radiation protection and nuclear safety.

Finnish Nuclear Society: c/o Technical Research Centre of Finland, Nuclear Engineering Laboratory, Lönnrotinkatu 37, 00180 Helsinki; tel (0) 648931; telex 122972; fax (0) 603626.

Imatran Voima Oy: POB 138, 00101 Helsinki; tel (0) 60901; telex 124608; fax (0) 5666235; Pres: Kalevi Numminen; Chair of Admin Council: Tapani Mörttinen; Exec Vice-Pres: Klaus Ahlstedt; f 1932; electric power, including nuclear energy; 95.6% state-owned.

Kemijoki Oy: POB 457, 00101 Helsinki; tel (0) 6944811; telex 124608; Chair of Supervisory Board: Paavo Väyrynen; Chair of Board of Management: Pertti Kivinen; f 1954; electric power; 77.08% state-owned.

Suomen Malmi Oy (Finnexploration): Juvan teollisuuskatu 16, POB 10, 02921 Espoo; tel (0) 8532422; fax (0) 8533010; Man Dir: Pekka Mikkola; f 1935; contracting and consulting services for mineral exploration and underground construction.

Science and Technology

Finnish Meteorological Institute: Vuorikatu 24, POB 503, 00101 Helsinki; tel (0) 19291; telex 124436; fax (0) 179581; Dir-Gen: E. J. Jatila; f 1838; weather service and climatology; air chemistry and physics; geomagnetism and aeronomy; under the Ministry of Transport and Communications.

Tourism

Matkailun edistämiskeskus (Tourist Board): Asemapäällikönkatu 12B, POB 53, 00521 Helsinki; tel (0) 144511; telex 122690; fax (0) 142306; Chair: Kalervo Hentilä; Dir-Gen: Bengt Pihlström; f 1973; promotes tourism in Finland; co-ordinates the activities of regional, municipal and other tourist organizations;

participates in international co-operative projects.

Transport and Communications

TELECOMMUNICATIONS

General Directorate of Posts and Telecommunications: POB 528, 00101 Helsinki; tel (0) 1954017; telex 124557; fax (0) 1954820; Pres and Dir-Gen: Pekka Vennamo; Sec-Gen: Mauri K. Elovainio; f 1927; postal and telecommunications networks; research and devt of the posts and telecommunications of Finland; international co-operation.

Kokkolan Puhelin Oy: Torikatu 36, POB 36, 67101 Kokkola; tel (68) 15555; fax (68) 20011; f 1912; telephone co.

Post- ja Telelaitos (Posts and Telecommunications of Finland): Mannerheimintie 11A, POB 529, 00101 Helsinki; tel (0) 1951; telex 122695; Dir-Gen: Pekka Tarjanne; f 1638; posts and telecommunications services.

TRANSPORT

Finnair Oy: Mannerheimintie 102, POB 6, 00251 Helsinki; tel (0) 81881; telex 124404; fax (0) 8188736; Chair: Antti Potila; Pres: Risto Ojanen; f 1923; 70% state-owned; domestic and international services to Europe, the Middle East, South East Asia and North America.

Finnaviation Oy (FA): POB 39, 01531 Vantaa; tel (0) 870941; telex 122635; Man Dir: Pekka Välimäki; f 1979; 90% owned by Finnair Oy; scheduled domestic services, also flights to Sweden.

National Board of Aviation: POB 50, 01531 Vantaa.

National Board of Navigation: POB 158, 00141 Helsinki.

Oy Pohjolan Liikenne Ab: Postintaival 3, 00240 Helsinki; tel (0) 143322; telex 121916; f 1940; road transport.

Tie- ja vesirakennushallitus (Roads and Waterways Administration): POB 33, 00521 Helsinki; tel (0) 1541; telex 124589; Dir-Gen: Jouko Loikkanen; f 1799; devt of road and water traffic; planning, construction and maintenance of roads, bridges and ferries, water channels, canals, ports and piers.

Valtionrautatiet (State Railways): Finnish State Railways' Board of Administration, Vilhonkatu 13, POB 488, 00101 Helsinki; tel (0) 7071; telex 301151; fax (0) 7073700; Dir-Gen: Eino Saarinen; Vice Dir-Gen: Panu Haapala; began operating 1862.

FINNISH EXTERNAL TERRITORY

THE ÅLAND ISLANDS

The Government

LANDSKAPSSTYRELSEN
22101 Mariehamn
Lantråd (Provincial Governor): John Sune Eriksson
Deputy Governor: May Valborg Flodin
Members: Göran Bengtz, Holger Eriksson, Karl-Göran
Eriksson, Ragnar Erlandsson, Magnus Lundberg
Executive council, chaired by the Provincial Governor.

LANDSTINGET
POB 69, 22101 Mariehamn
Tel (28) 25000; fax (28) 13302
Talman (Speaker): Sven Olof Jansson
First Deputy Speaker: Jan-Erik H. T. Lindfors
Legislative body comprising 30 members elected for a four-year
term by proportional representation.

Government Agencies

BANKING

Ålandsbanken Ab (Bank of Åland Ltd): Nygatan 2, POB 3,
22101 Mariehamn; tel (28) 29011; telex 63119; fax (28) 29228;
Chair: Folke Woivalin; Chief Gen Man: Folke Husell; f 1919; 21
brs.

Ålands Hypoteksbank Ab: Nygatan 2, 22100 Mariehamn; tel
(28) 29011; telex 63119; Chair: Göran Fagerlund; Chief Man
Dir: Lars Donner; f 1986.

Ålands Sparbank: POB 7, 22101 Mariehamn; tel (28) 16200;
telex 63154; Dirs: Erling Gustavsson, Erik Sundberg, Jan-Erik
Rask.

Andelsbanken för Åland: POB 34, 22101 Mariehamn; tel
(28) 26000; Dirs: Håkan Clemes, Roland Karlsson.

Lappo Andelsbank: 22840 Lappoby; tel (28) 56621; fax (28)
56699; Dir: Torsten Nordberg; f 1925.

BROADCASTING

Mariehamns Centralantenn Ab: Doktorsvillan, 22100
Mariehamn; tel (28) 17122; f 1979; TV broadcasting.

Radio Åland: Ålandsvägen 24, POB 46, 22100 Mariehamn; tel
(28) 26060; fax (28) 26520; Chief Editor: Pernilla Cammert; f
1962; local broadcasting of news and events in Åland.

FRANCE

Head of State

The President holds executive power and is directly elected for a seven-year term by popular vote (using two ballots if necessary). The President appoints a Council of Ministers, headed by a Prime Minister, which administers the country and is responsible to Parliament.

President: François Mitterrand (took office 21 May 1981, re-elected May 1988).

Office of the President: Palais de l'Elysée, 55-57 rue du Faubourg Saint Honoré, 75008 Paris; tel (1) 42-92-81-00; telex 650127.

Legislature

Legislative power is vested in the bicameral Parliament, comprising the Senate (321 members, 296 for metropolitan France, 13 for the overseas possessions and 12 for French nationals abroad, elected for nine years by electoral college, one third being re-elected every three years), and the National Assembly (577 members, 555 for metropolitan France and 22 for the overseas possessions, elected by universal adult suffrage for five years). Departmental and regional assemblies also operate.

Sénat (Senate): Palais du Luxembourg, 15 rue de Vaugirard, 75291 Paris Cedex 06; tel (1) 42-34-20-00; Pres: Alain Poher.

Assemblée Nationale (National Assembly): Palais Bourbon, 126 rue de l'Université, 75700 Paris; tel (1) 42-97-60-00; telex 260420; Pres: Laurent Fabius.

MINISTRIES AND GOVERNMENT DEPARTMENTS

OFFICE OF THE PRIME MINISTER
57 rue de Varenne, 75700 Paris
Tel (1)42-75-80-00; telex 200724
Prime Minister: Michel Rocard
Secretary of State, Environment and the Prevention of Technological and Natural Disasters: Brice Lalonde
Secretary of State, Humanitarian Action: Bernard Kouchner
Secretary of State, Planning: Lionel Stoléru
Secretary of State, without Portfolio: Tony Dreyfus

MINISTRY OF AGRICULTURE AND FORESTS
78 rue de Varenne, 75700 Paris
Tel (1) 45-55-95-50; telex 205202; fax (1) 45-55-95-50
Minister: Henri Nallet

MINISTRY OF THE CIVIL SERVICE AND ADMINISTRATIVE REFORM
69 rue de Varenne, 7500 Paris
Tel (1) 42-75-80-00
Minister: Michel Durafour

MINISTRY OF CO-OPERATION AND DEVELOPMENT
20 rue Monsieur, 75700 Paris
Tel (1) 47-83-10-10; telex 202363; fax (1) 43-06-74-82
Minister: Jacques Pelletier

MINISTRY OF CULTURE AND COMMUNICATIONS AND MAJOR PUBLIC WORKS
3 rue de Valois, 75042 Paris Cedex 01
Tel (1) 40-15-80-00; telex 210293
Minister: Jack Lang
Minister-Delegate, Communications: Catherine Tasca
Secretary of State, Large Projects: Emile Biasini

MINISTRY OF DEFENCE
14 rue Saint Dominique, 75700 Paris
Tel (1) 45-55-95-20; telex 201375; fax (1) 45-52-58-55
Minister: Jean-Pierre Chevènement
Secretary of State: Gérard Renon

MINISTRY OF THE ECONOMY, FINANCE AND THE BUDGET
139 rue de Bercy, 75572, Paris Cedex 12
Tel (1) 42-60-33-00; telex 217068
Minister of State: Pierre Bérégovoy
Minister-Delegate, Budget: Michel Charasse
Secretary of State, Consumer Affairs: Véronique Neiertz

MINISTRY OF EQUIPMENT AND HOUSING
45 ave Georges-Mandel, 75016 Paris
Tel (1) 46-47-31-32; fax (1) 47-20-70-32
Minister of State: Michel Delebarre
Minister-Delegate, Housing: Louis Besson

MINISTRY OF EUROPEAN AFFAIRS
32 ave Raymond Poincaré, 75016 Paris
Minister: Edith Cresson

MINISTRY OF FOREIGN AFFAIRS
37 quai d'Orsay, 75700 Paris
Tel (1) 45-55-95-40; telex 202329
Minister of State: Roland Dumas
Minister-Delegate, Francophone Countries:
Alain Decaux
Minister-Delegate, Foreign Affairs: Edwige Avice
Secretary of State, International Cultural Relations:
Thierry de Beaucé

MINISTRY OF FOREIGN TRADE
41 quai Branly, 75700 Paris
Fax (1) 45-56-34-53
Minister: Jean-Marie Rausch

**MINISTRY OF INDUSTRY, TERRITORIAL
DEVELOPMENT AND TOURISM**
11 ave d'Iéna, 75707 Paris
Tel (1) 45-56-36-36; fax (1) 45-56-36-36
Minister of Industry and Territorial Development:
Roger Fauroux
Minister of Tourism: Olivier Stirn
Minister-Delegate, Territorial Development:
Jacques Chérèque
Minister-Delegate, Commerce and Crafts:
François Doubin

MINISTRY OF THE INTERIOR
place Beauvau, 75800 Paris
Tel (1) 45-22-90-90; telex 290922
Minister: Pierre Joxe
Secretary of State, Territorial Communities:
Jean-Michel Baylet

MINISTRY OF JUSTICE
13 place Vendôme, 75042 Paris Cedex 01
Tel (1) 42-61-80-22; telex 211320; fax (1) 42-61-98-34
Minister and Keeper of the Seals: Pierre Arpaillange

**MINISTRY OF LABOUR, EMPLOYMENT AND
PROFESSIONAL TRAINING**
127 rue de Grenelle, 75700 Paris
Tel (1) 40-56-60-00; fax (1) 40-56-67-60
Minister: Jean-Pierre Soisson
Secretary of State, Professional Training: André Laignel

**MINISTRY OF NATIONAL EDUCATION, YOUTH
AND SPORTS**
110 rue de Grenelle, 75700 Paris
Tel (1) 45-50-10-10; telex 201244
Minister of State: Lionel Jospin
Secretary of State, Technical Education: Robert Chapuis
Secretary of State, Youth and Sports: Roger Bambuck

**MINISTRY OF OVERSEAS DEPARTMENTS AND
TERRITORIES**
27 rue Oudinot, 75700 Paris
Tel (1) 47-83-01-23
Minister: Louis Le Pensec

**MINISTRY OF POSTAL SERVICES,
TELECOMMUNICATIONS AND SPACE**
20 ave de Ségur, 75700 Paris
Fax (1) 45-38-98-96
Minister: Paul Quilès

MINISTRY FOR RELATIONS WITH PARLIAMENT
72 rue de Varenne, 75700 Paris
Tel (1) 42-75-80-00
Minister: Jean Poperen

MINISTRY OF RESEARCH AND TECHNOLOGY
1 rue Descartes, 75005 Paris
Tel (1) 46-34-35-35; fax (1) 46-34-35-35
Minister: Hubert Curien

**MINISTRY OF SOLIDARITY, HEALTH AND
SOCIAL PROTECTION**
127 rue de Grenelle, 75700 Paris
Tel (1) 45-67-55-44; fax (1) 45-67-55-44
Minister and Government Spokesman: Claude Evin
Minister-Delegate, Old People: Théo Braun
Secretary of State, Family Affairs: Hélène Dorlhac
Secretary of State, Handicapped People: Michel Gillibert

MINISTRY OF TRANSPORT AND THE SEA
3 place de Fontenoy, 75700 Paris
Fax (1) 45-82-75-76
Minister: Michel Delebarre
Minister-Delegate, The Sea: Jacques Mellick
Secretary of State, Road Transport and Waterways:
George Sarre

SECRETARIAT OF STATE FOR WAR VETERANS
37 rue de Bellechasse, 75700 Paris
Tel (1) 45-56-80-00
Secretary of State: André Méric

SECRETARIAT OF STATE FOR WOMEN'S RIGHTS
14 blvd de la Madeleine, 75008 Paris
Tel (1) 42-66-57-15
Secretary of State: Michèle André

Mission pour l'Egalité Professionelle: 14 blvd de la Madeleine, 75008 Paris; tel (1) 42-66-57-15; f 1984; promotes equality in work for men and women; applies equality laws.

GOVERNMENT AGENCIES AND ORGANIZATIONS

Advisory and Supervisory Body

Conseil Economique et Social: 1 ave d'Iéna, 75775 Paris Cedex 16; tel (1) 47-23-72-34; Pres: Jean Matteoli; Sec-Gen: François Lavondés; f 1946; consultative assembly on economic and social issues.

Business and Economy

BANKING

Banque de Bretagne: 283 ave du Général Patton, 35000 Rennes Cedex; tel 99-28-36-89; telex 730094; fax 99-28-38-02;

Chair: Xavier Henry de Villeneuve; f 1909; 100 brs.

Banque Française du Commerce Extérieur: 21 blvd Haussmann, BP 265, 75009 Paris Cedex 09; tel (1) 42-47-47-47; telex 660370; fax (1) 45-23-10-56; Pres: Michel Freyche; Dir-Gen: Pierre Antoni; f 1947.

Banque de France: 39 rue Croix des Petits Champs, BP 140, 75001 Paris; tel (1) 42-92-42-92; telex 220932; fax (1) 42-96-04-23; Gov: Jacques de Larosière; First Dep Gov: Philippe Lagayette; Dep Gov: Denis Ferman; f 1800; nationalized from 1946; acts as banker to the Treasury; issues bank notes, controls credit and money supply and administers France's gold and currency assets; the Gov and Dep Governors are nominated by decree of the President of the Republic; 234 offices or brs.

Banque Hervet, SA: 1 place de la Préfecture, 18004 Bourges;

tel 46-40-90-00; telex 620433; fax 46-40-92-77; Chair: Jean Baptiste Pascal; f 1830.

Banque Nationale de Paris, SA: 16 blvd des Italiens, 75009 Paris; tel (1) 40-14-45-46; telex 280605; Chair and Man Dir: René Thomas; f 1966.

Banque Nationale de Paris 'Intercontinentale', SA: 20 blvd des Italiens, BP 315-09, 75009 Paris; tel (1) 40-14-22-11; telex 641419; Chair: René Thomas; f 1940.

Banque Régionale de l'Ain, SA: 2 ave Alsace-Lorraine, 01001 Bourg-en-Bresse; tel 74-32-50-00; telex 310435; Pres: Jean-Noël Reliquet; f 1849; 50 brs.

Banque Régionale de l'Ouest, SA: 7 rue Gallois, 41003 Blois Cedex; tel 54-78-96-28; telex 750408; Chair: Jean de la Chauvinière; f 1913.

Banque de l'Union Européenne: 4 rue Gaillon, BP 89, 75107 Paris Cedex 02; tel (1) 42-66-70-00; telex 210942; fax (1) 42-66-78-90; Pres and Dir-Gen: Paul Alibert; Dir-Gen: Paul d'Abzac; f 1920; 6 brs.

Banque Worms, SA: Le Voltaire, 1 place des Degrés, 92059 Paris La Défense Cedex 58; tel (1) 49-07-50-50; telex 616023; fax (1) 49-07-59-11; Chair: Jean-Michel Bloch-Lainé; f 1928; 32 brs.

Caisse Nationale de Crédit Agricole (CNCA), SA: 91-93 blvd Pasteur, 75015 Paris; tel (1) 43-23-52-02; telex 250971; fax (1) 43-23-44-89; Chair and Man Dir: Philippe Jaffré; f 1920; central institution for 91 regional co-operative banks, the densest banking network in France, with 9,746 domestic branch offices; broad range of banking services with special emphasis on agribusiness; also international network.

Centrale de Banque, SA: 5 blvd de la Madeleine, 75001 Paris; tel (1) 40-15-92-47; telex 210669; fax (1) 42-61-37-40; Chair: Pierre Pichot; f 1880.

Commission Bancaire: 73 rue de Richelieu, 75002 Paris; banking supervisory authority.

Crédit Chimique, SA: 20 rue Treilhard, 75008 Paris; tel (1) 49-53-21-00; telex 650838; fax (1) 42-89-40-40; Chair and Man Dir: Jean-Luc Javal; f 1889; 2 brs.

Crédit Industriel d'Alsace et de Lorraine (CIAL): 31 rue Jean Wenger-Valentin, 67000 Strasbourg; tel 88-37-61-23; telex 890167; fax (1) 88-35-09-70; Chair: Gaston Zerr; f 1919; 151 brs.

Crédit Industriel et Commercial de Paris, SA: 66 rue de la Victoire, 75009 Paris; tel (1) 42-80-80-80; telex 290692; fax (1) 42-80-97-17; Chair: Jean-René Bernard; f 1859; 118 brs.

Crédit Industriel de Normandie, SA: 15 place de la Pucelle d'Orléans, 76000 Rouen; tel 35-08-64-00; telex 770950; Chair and Man Dir: Jean Duramé; f 1932.

Crédit Industriel de l'Ouest, SA: 4 rue Voltaire, 44040 Nantes Cedex 01; tel 40-35-91-91; telex 700590; fax 40-35-92-07; Pres: Bernard Madinier; Chair: Jean-Yves Haberer; Dir-Gen: Jean-Louis Rusterholtz; f 1957.

Crédit Lyonnais, SA: Head Office: 18 rue de la République 69002 Lyon; Central Office: 19 blvd des Italiens, 75002 Paris; tel (1) 42-95-70-00; telex 615310; fax (1) 42-95-11-96; Chair: J. M. Levêque; f 1863; 2,500 brs.

Institut d'Emission des Départements d'Outre-Mer: 1 cité du Retiro, 75008 Paris.

Société Bordelaise de Crédit Industriel et Commercial, SA: 42 cours du Chapeau Rouge, 33001 Bordeaux; tel 56-48-52-90; telex (Foreign Dept) 550850; fax 56-79-08-71; Chair and Man Dir: Bruno Moschetto; f 1880.

Société Lyonnaise de Banque, SA: 8 rue de la République, 69001 Lyon; tel 78-92-02-12; telex 330532; Chair and Man Dir: Henri Moulard; f 1865; 300 brs.

Société Marseillaise de Crédit, SA: 75 rue Paradis, 13006 Marseille; tel 91-54-91-12; telex 430232; fax 91-54-91-12; Chair and Chief Exec: Jean-Paul Escande; f 1865; 190 brs.

Société Nancéienne Varin-Bernier (SNVB): 4 place André Maginot, 5400 Nancy; tel 83-37-65-45; telex 960205; fax 83-34-52-00; Pres: Bernard Yoncourt; f 1881; 176 brs.

FINANCIAL AGENCIES

Caisse Centrale de Coopération Economique: 35-37 rue Boissy d'Anglas, cité du Retiro, 75379 Paris Cedex 08; tel (1) 40-06-31-31; telex 212632; Chair: Jacques Campet; Gen Man: Yves Roland-Billecart; f 1941; 35 brs.

Caisse des Dépôts et Consignations: 56 rue de Lille, 75356 Paris; tel (1) 42-34-56-78; telex 200055; Gen Man: Robert Lion; Dep Gen Mans: Hélène Ploix, Pierre Richard; f 1816.

Commission des Opérations de Bourse (COB): Tour Mirabeau, 39-43 quai André Citroën, 75739 Paris Cedex 15; tel (1) 45-78-33-33; telex 205238; Chair: Jean Saint-Geours; Sec-Gen: Patrick Mordacq; f 1967; stock exchange association; 150 mems.

Crédit d'Equipement des Petites et Moyennes Entreprises: 14 rue du 4 septembre, 75002 Paris; provides credit to small and medium-sized businesses.

INSURANCE

Groupe des Assurances Nationales (GAN): 2 rue Pillet Will, 75448 Paris Cedex 09; tel (1) 42-47-50-00; telex 280006; fax (1) 42-47-57-56; Chair and Chief Exec: François Heilbronner; Gen Mans: Jean-Jacques Bonnaud, Roland Plazen; 85% state-owned.

L'Union des Assurances de Paris (UAP): 9 place Vendôme, 75001 Paris; tel (1) 42-60-33-40; telex 210798; Chair: Jean Peyrelevade; 85.3% state-owned.

NATIONALIZED INDUSTRY

Aerospatiale: 37 blvd de Montmorency, 75781 Paris Cedex 16; tel (1) 45-24-43-21; fax (1) 45-24-43-21; Chair and Gen Man: Henri Martre; Dir: Philippe Couillard; manufactures aircraft, helicopters, strategic missiles, space and ballistic systems.

Orkem: Tour Albert 1er, 65 ave de Colmar, 92507 Rueil Malmaison; Chair: Serge Tchuruk; f 1986, originally part of Charbonnages de France (see below); chemicals.

Péchiney: 23 rue Balzac, 75008 Paris; tel (1) 45-61-61-61; telex 290503; fax (1) 45-61-50-00; Chair and Chief Exec: Jean Gandois; nationalized 1982; 82% state-owned; aluminium, fine metallurgy and advanced materials, ferroalloys and carbon products, copper fabrication.

Régie Nationale des Usines Renault: 34 quai du Point du Jour, BP 103, 92109 Boulogne-Billancourt; tel (1) 46-09-15-30; telex 205677; fax (1) 42-25-18-57; Chair: Raymond Lévy; Dep Man Dir: Philippe Gras; Dep Man Dir and Finance Dir: Louis Schweitzer; Head, RVI (trucks division): Jean-Pierre Capron; nationalized in 1945; manufactures passenger cars and small vans.

Rhône-Poulenc: 25 quai Paul Doumer, 92408 Courbevoie Cedex; tel (1) 47-68-12-34; fax (1) 47-68-19-11; Chair and Chief Exec: Jean-René Fourtou; Man Dir: Jean-Marc Bruel; f 1858; nationalized 1982; chemicals, pharmaceuticals, animal foodstuffs, film, textiles, communications.

Société Nationale d'Etude et de Construction de Moteurs d'Avion (SNECMA): 2 blvd Victor, 75724 Paris Cedex 15; tel (1) 45-54-92-00; telex 202834; Chair and Man Dir: Louis Gallois; f 1905; nationalized 1945; manufactures engines for civil and military aircraft, electronic and meteorological equipment.

Société Nationale d'Exploitation Industrielle des Tabacs et des Allumettes (SEITA): 53 quai d'Orsay, 75007 Paris Cedex 07; tel (1) 45-56-61-50; telex 250604; fax (1) 45-56-62-83; Chair and Man Dir: Bertrand de Galle; Asst Gen Mans: J.

Benassayag, G. Dutreix; f 1959; production and marketing of tobacco and matches in France.

Thomson, SA: 92045 Paris La Défense Cedex 67; tel (1) 49-07-80-00; telex 616780; Chair: Alain Gomez; f 1893; nationalized 1982; holding co for Thomson group; electrical and electronics industry.

Usinor Sacilor: Immeuble 'Ile de France', 4 place de la Pyramide, 92070 Paris la Défense Cedex 33; tel (1) 49-00-60-10; telex 614730; fax (1) 49-00-60-48; Chair and Man Dir: Francis Mer; f 1948 as two cos; Usinor nationalized 1981, Sacilor in 1982, merged 1987; steel production.

TRADE

Centre Français du Commerce Extérieur: 10 ave d'Iéna, 75783 Paris Cedex 16; tel (1) 45-05-30-00; telex 611934; fax (1) 45-05-39-79; Dir-Gen: Claude Blot; Sec-Gen: Maurice Corrèges; f 1943; informs French businesses on foreign markets; promotes French products abroad.

Commissariat à la Normalisation: 10 cité Vaneau, 75700 Paris Cedex 07; tel (1) 45-56-36-36; telex 204231; standards organization.

Conseil National du Commerce: 53 ave Montaigne, 75008 Paris; tel (1) 42-25-01-25; Chair: J. Dermagne; trade council.

Direction Générale des Douanes et Droits Indirects: 8 rue de la Tour des Dames, 75009 Paris; tel (1) 42-80-67-22; telex 660168; fax (1) 48-74-31-58; Dir-Gen: J. Weber; Chief of Statistics: M. F. R. Rivet; customs; publishes statistics of external trade.

Institut National de la Consommation (National Institute for Consumers' Affairs): 80 rue Lecourbe, 75732 Paris Cedex 15; tel (1) 45-67-35-58; telex 270747; Pres: Michel Pain; Dir: Marie-Hélène Dos Reis; f 1968; 50% Govt-funded; public body administered by national consumer organizations to protect and promote the interests of consumers.

Defence

Armed Forces: c/o Ministry of Defence, 14 rue Saint Dominique, 75700 Paris; tel (1) 45-55-92-20; telex 201375; fax (1) 45-52-58-55; Commdr: François Mitterrand; Chief of Staff: Gen Maurice Schmitt; Dep Chief of Staff: Vice-Adm Alain Coapanea; Chief of Staff (Army): Gen Gilbert Forray.

Air Force: 26 blvd Victor, 75996 Paris Armées; tel (1) 45-52-30-30; Commdr: Gen Yves Grousset; Dep Commdr: Lt-Col Lenne.

Navy: 15 rue de Laborde, 75200 Paris Naval; telex 650421; Chief of Staff: Adm Bernard Louzeau.

Direction Générale de la Sécurité Extérieure (DGSE): Paris; Head: Claude Silberzahn; secret service.

Development and Planning

Commissariat Général du Plan: 18 rue de Martignac, 75700 Paris; responsible for planning economic, social and cultural devt.

Institut de Développement Industriel (IDI): 4 rue Ancelle, 92203 Neuilly-sur-Seine; tel (1) 47-58-14-11; telex 630006; Chair: Claude Mandil; f 1970; state agency; assists small and medium-sized businesses by taking equity shares in enterprises and offering advisory services.

Société Centrale d'Aménagement Foncière et d'Equipement Rural (SCAFER): 3 rue de Turin, 75008 Paris; tel (1) 42-93-66-06; fax (1) 43-87-96-56; Pres: Etienne Lapèze; Dir: Roland Baud; f 1960; carries out studies of European land

markets and agricultural economy; statistical studies of French agricultural land market.

Employment

Agence Nationale pour l'Insertion et la Promotion des Travailleurs d'Outre-Mer (ANT): 3 rue de Brissac, 75004 Paris; tel (1) 42-77-60-20; telex 211612; fax 42-77-86-22; Pres: Gérard Beloruey; Dir-Gen: Edmond Lauret; f 1982; helps find workers from French Overseas Possessions employment and housing.

Legal and Judiciary

Conseil d'Etat: Palais-Royal, 75100 Paris; tel (1) 42-61-52-29; Pres: the Prime Minister, Michel Rocard; Vice-Pres: Marceau Long; Sec-Gen: Jean-Pierre Aubert; council of the central power and an administrative tribunal; consultative organ of the Govt, giving opinions in the legislative and administrative domain; judges appeals against excess of power and the application of the law.

Cour d'Appel de Paris: Palais de Justice, blvd de Palais, 75001 Paris; First Pres: Myriam Ezratty; Solicitor-Gen: Pierre Truche; court of appeal.

Cour de Cassation: Palais de Justice, 5 quai de l'Horloge, 75001 Paris; tel (1) 43-29-12-55; First Pres: Pierre Drai; Solicitor-Gen: Pierre Bezio; Chief Clerk of the Court: Daniel Autié; Pres, Council of Advocates at Court of Cassation: Charles Choucroy; higher authority for the proper application of the law; sees that judgments are not contrary either to the letter or the spirit of the law.

Cour des Comptes: 13 rue Cambon, 75100 Paris; tel (1) 42-98-95-00; First Pres: André Chandernagor; Attorney-Gen: Jean Raynaud; Dep Attorneys-Gen: Jean-Pierre Gastinel, Jean-Louis Beaud de Brive; Sec-Gen: Alain Pichon; administrative tribunal; judges the correctness of public accounts; judge of common law of all public accounts laid before it; the judgments of the Court may be annulled by the Conseil d'Etat (see above).

Media

BROADCASTING

Conseil Supérieur de l'Audiovisuel (CSA): 56 rue Jacob, 75272 Paris Cedex 06; tel (1) 42-61-83-18; telex 214214; Pres: Jacques Boutet; f 1989; supervises all French broadcasting; allocates concessions for privatized channels; distributes cable networks and frequencies; appoints heads of state-owned radio and TV cos; oversees telecommunications sectors; monitors programme standards; consists of nine mems, three appointed for eight years, three for six years and three for four years; three nominated by the Pres of the Republic, three by the Pres of the National Assembly and three by the Pres of the Senate.

Institut National de la Communication Audiovisuelle: 4 ave de l'Europe, 94366 Bry sur Marne Cedex; tel (1) 49-83-20-00; telex 262493; fax (1) 43-47-64-00; Pres: Georges Fillioud; f 1975; research and professional training in the field of broadcasting; radio and TV archives.

Radio-Télévision Française d'Outre-Mer (RFO): 5 ave du Recteur Poincaré, 75016 Paris; tel (1) 45-24-71-00; Chair: Jean-Claude Michaud; Dir of DOM-TOM: Claude Lefèvre; Dir of Foreign Affairs: André Brière; controls broadcasting in the French overseas territories.

Société Nationale de Programmes—France Régions 3 (FR3): 116 ave du Président Kennedy, 75790 Paris Cedex 16; tel (1) 42-30-22-22; telex 630720; fax (1) 42-24-63-66; Chair:

Philippe Guilhaume; Pres: Christiane Doré; Dir-Gen: Dominique Alduy; f 1975; production of TV programmes on the third TV channel; responsible for regional and overseas TV.

Société Nationale de Radiodiffusion (Radio France): 116 ave du Président Kennedy, 75790 Paris Cedex 16; tel (1) 42-30-22-22; telex 200002; Chair and Man Dir: Jean Maheu; Dir: Jean Izard; Dirs, France Inter: Pascal Delannoy, Claude Guillaumin; Dir, Programmes: Pierre Bouteiller; Dir, Information: Michel Meyer; Dir, France Culture: Jean-Marie Borzeix; Dir, Programmes and Musical Services: André Jouve; Dir-Gen, Radio France Internationale: André Larquié.

Société Nationale de Télévision en Couleur—Antenne 2 (A2): 22 ave Montaigne, 75387 Paris Cedex 08; tel (1) 42-99-42-42; telex 204068; Chair: Philippe Guillaume; Pres: Christiane Doré; Dir: Jean-Michel Gaillard; Sec-Gen: Louis Bériot; f 1975; production of TV programmes.

Télédiffusion de France (TDF), SA: 21-27 rue Barbès, BP 518, 92542 Montrouge Cedex; tel (1) 46-57-11-15; telex 25738; fax (1) 45-55-35-35; Chair and Chief Exec: Xavier Gouyou Beauchamps; Man Dir: Philippe Levrier; f 1975, partly privatized in 1987; broadcasting and transmission of TV and radio programmes in France and abroad; represents the French TV and radio bodies in international organizatons; promotes French equipment and techniques abroad; organizes and maintains the broadcasting networks.

GOVERNMENT PUBLISHER

La Documentation Française: 29-31 quai Voltaire, 75340 Paris Cedex 07; tel (1) 40-15-70-00; telex 204826; fax (1) 40-15-72-30; Dir: Jean Jenger; f 1947; Govt publisher; publishes ministerial and official reports, books on French and international politics.

NEWS AND INFORMATION

Institut National de la Statistique et des Etudes Economiques (INSEE): 18 blvd Adolphe Pinard, 75675 Paris; under Ministry of the Economy, Finance and the Budget; statistical office.

Mining and Energy

ENERGY

Commissariat à l'Energie Atomique (CEA) (Atomic Energy Commissariat): 31-33 rue de la Fédération, 75752 Paris Cedex 15; tel (1) 40-56-10-00; telex 200671; fax (1) 40-56-25-38; Gen Admin: Philippe Rouvillois; High Commr: Jean Teillac; Sec-Gen: Jean Marmot; f 1945; promotes the uses of nuclear energy in science, industry and national defence; active, either directly or through subsidiaries and participation in private cos in: production of nuclear materials, reactor devt, fundamental research, innovation and transfer of technologies, military applications, bio-technologies, robotics, electronics, new materials, radiological protection and nuclear safety; administered by a 15-member Comité de l'Energie Atomique (Atomic Energy committee), presided over by the Prime Minister and consisting of Govt officials and representatives of sciences and industry; the following are institutes, administrative bodies and research centres overseen by the CEA:

Agence Nationale pour la Gestion des Déchets Radioactifs: 31-33 rue de la Fédération, 75752 Paris Cedex 15; tel (1) 40-56-15-15; Dir: François Chenevier.

Centre d'Etudes Nucléaires de Cadarache (CEN-Ca) (Cadarache Nuclear Research Centre): 13108 Saint-Paul-les-Durance Cedex, Bouches-du-Rhône; tel 42-25-70-00; telex 440678; Dir: Jean Megy; f 1960.

Centre d'Etudes Nucléaires de Fontenay-aux-Roses (Fontenay-aux-Roses Nuclear Research Centre): BP 6, 92265 Fontenay-aux-Roses Cedex; tel (1) 46-54-70-80; Dir: G. Vial; f 1945.

Centre d'Etudes Nucléaires de Grenoble (CEN-G) (Grenoble Nuclear Research Centre): BP 8X, 38041 Grenoble Cedex; tel 76-88-44-00; telex 320323; Dir: François Decool; f 1955; 40 laboratories.

Centre d'Etudes Nucléaires de Saclay (CEN-S) (Saclay Nuclear Research Centre): 91191 Gif-sur-Yvette Cedex; tel 69-08-60-00; telex 604641; Dir: Paul Delpeyroux; f 1949.

Centre d'Etudes Nucléaires de la Vallée du Rhône (CEN-VALHRO) (Rhone Valley Nuclear Research Centre): BP 171, 30205 Bagnols-sur-Cèze Cedex; tel 66-79-60-00; telex 480816; Dir: Albert Teboul.

Groupe ORIS: BP 6, 91192 Gif-sur-Yvette; tel 69-85-70-70; telex 692431; fax 69-85-70-71; Pres and Dir-Gen: Yves le Gallic; f 1987.

Direction des Applications Militaires (Military Applications Division): Paris; Dir: Roger Baleras.

Institut National des Sciences et Techniques Nucléaires (National Institute of Nuclear Science and Technology): CEN Saclay-INSTN, 91191 Gif-sur-Yvette Cedex; tel 69-08-63-14; telex 604641; fax 69-08-79-93; Dir: Yves Chelet; f 1956.

Institut de Protection et de Sûreté Nucléaire (Institute for Nuclear Protection and Security): CEN Fontenay-aux-Roses, BP 6, 92260 Fontenay-aux-Roses; Dir: François Cogne.

Institut de Recherche Fondamentale (Fundamental Research Institute): Orme des Merisiers, 91191 Gif-sur-Yvette Cedex; tel 69-08-75-15; fax 69-08-38-16; Dir: Daniel Cribier.

Institut de Recherche Technologique et de Développement Industriel (Institute of Technological Research and Industrial Development): Centre d'Etudes Nucléires de Saclay, 91191 Gif-sur-Yvette Cedex; tel 69-08-66-16; telex 604641; fax 69-08-79-85; Dir: Jean Chatoux.

Société des Participations du CEA—CEA-Industrie: 31-33 rue de la Fédération, 75752 Paris Cedex 15; tel (1) 40-56-10-00; telex 200671; fax (1) 42-73-32-77; Pres: Philippe Rouvillois; Dir-Gen: Achille Ferrari.

Direction du Gaz, de l'Electricité et du Charbon (DIGEC): 3-5 rue Barbet-de-Jouy, 75700 Paris; tel (1) 45-55-93-00; part of the Ministry of Industry and Territorial Devt; energy organization.

Direction des Hydrocarbures: 3-5 rue Barbet-de-Jouy, 75700 Paris; tel (1) 45-55-93-00; part of the Ministry of Industry and Territorial Devt; energy organization.

Electricité de France: 32 rue de Monceau, 75008 Paris; tel (1) 47-55-94-10; telex 280098; fax (1) 47-64-27-06; Chair: Pierre Delaporte; Man Dir: Jean Bergougnoux; Technical Vice-Pres, with overall resposibility for nuclear operations: Pierre Bacher; established under the Electricity and Gas Industry Nationalization Act of 1946; generates and supplies electricity for distribution to consumers in metropolitan France.

ERAP—Entreprise de Recherches et d'Activités Pétrolières: Tour Elf, 2 place de la Coupole, Paris la Défense 6, Courbevoie; tel (1) 47-44-45-46; telex 615400.

Gaz de France: 23 rue Philibert Delorme, 75840 Paris Cedex 17; tel (1) 47-54-20-20; telex 650483; fax (1) 47-54-21-87; Chair: Francis Gutmann; Dir-Gen: Pierre Gadonneix; established under the Electricity and Gas Industry Nationalization Act of 1946; distributes gas in metropolitan France; about 17.5% of gas is produced in France (Aquitaine) and the rest is imported.

Société Nationale Elf Aquitaine (SNEA): Tour Elf, 2 place de la Coupole, Paris la Défense 6, Courbevoie; tel (1) 47-44-45-46; telex 615400; fax (1) 47-44-69-46; Chair and Chief Exec: Loik Le Floch Prigent; 67% owned by ERAP—Entreprise de Recherches et d'Activités Pétrolières (see above); undertakes exploration for and production of petroleum and natural gas, chiefly in France, Africa, the North Sea and the USA; exploits uranium and non-energy minerals; has subsidiaries in petro-chemicals (ATOCHEM) and pharmaceuticals (SANOFI).

MINING

Charbonnages de France (CdF): Tour Albert 1er, 65 ave de Colmar, 92507 Rueil Malmaison; tel (1) 47-52-92-52; telex 631450; Pres and Dir-Gen: Bernard Pache; established under the Nationalization Act of 1946; coal mining, sales and research in metropolitan France; engineering and informatics divisions.

Direction des Mines: 101 rue de Grenelle, 75700 Paris; tel (1) 45-56-36-36; telex 270257; part of the Ministry of Industry and Territorial Devt; supervises mines and mining activity.

Research

Centre National de la Recherche Scientifique (CNRS): 15 quai Anatole France, 75700 Paris; tel (1) 47-53-15-15; telex 260034; fax (1) 45-51-73-07; f 1939; scientific research; there are nuclear research centres attached to this institution in Strasbourg, Grenoble and Orsay.

Telecommunications

Caisse Nationale des Télécommunications: 20 ave Rapp, 75341 Paris Cedex 07; tel (1) 47-05-94-39; telex 202520; fax (1) 47-05-85-91; Chair: Louis-Joseph Libois; Vice-Chair: Jean-Claude Trichet; state agency; provides loans for cos financing telecommunications.

Direction Générale de la Poste: 20 ave de Ségur, 75700 Paris; tel (1) 45-64-22-22; telex 270496.

Direction Générale des Télécommunications: 20 ave de Ségur, 75700 Paris; tel (1) 45-64-22-22; telex 250310.

France Télécom: 20 ave de Ségur, 75700 Paris Cedex 7; tel (1) 45-64-22-22; telex 250310; Dir-Gen: Marcel Louis Roulet; telecommunications organization.

Tourism

Direction des Industries Touristiques: 2 rue Linois, 75740 Paris Cedex 15; tel (1) 45-75-62-16; Dir: Jean-Luc Michaud; under Ministry of Industry and Territorial Devt.

Maison de la France: 8 ave de l'Opéra, Paris; tel (1) 42-96-10-23; Pres: Jean Marc Janaillac; under Ministry of Industry and Territorial Devt.

Transport

CIVIL AVIATION

Air France: 1 square Max Hymans, 75757 Paris Cedex 15; tel (1) 43-23-81-81; telex 200666; fax (1) 43-23-92-79; Chair: Bernard Attali; Pres: Jean-Didier Blanchet; Sec-Gen: Marc Maugars; f 1933; international, European and inter-continental services.

Air Inter: 1 ave du Maréchal Devaux, 91550 Paray Vieille Poste; tel (1) 46-75-12-12; telex 250932; fax (1) 43-35-39-80; Chair and Man Dir: Pierre Eelsen; f 1954; internal services within metropolitan France; service to Madrid; Air France, Union de Transports Aériens (UTA), a private airline, and the SNCF are the part owners.

Union de Transports Aériens (UTA): 3 blvd Malesherbes, 75008 Paris; tel (1) 40-17-44-44; telex 610692; Chair: René Lapautre; Vice-Pres: Daniel-Charles Richon; f 1963; international air services; 54.6% stake purchased by Air France, Jan 1990.

RAILWAYS

Régie Autonome des Transports Parisiens (RATP): 53 quai des Grands Augustins, BP 70-06, 75271 Paris Cedex 06; tel (1) 40-46-41-41; telex 200000; Chair: Christian Blanc; Gen Man: Michel Rousselot; f 1948; operates the Paris underground and suburban railways and buses.

Société Nationale des Chemins de fer Français (SNCF): 88 rue Saint Lazare, 75436 Paris Cedex 09; tel (1) 42-85-60-00; telex 290936; Pres: Jacques Fournier; Dir-Gen: Jean Costet; f 1937; wholly nationalized 1983.

Réseau Atlantique: 1 place Valhubert, 75013 Paris; tel (1) 45-84-14-18; Dir: Didier Sautter; Atlantic region.

Réseau du Nord-Est: 18 rue de Dunkerque, 75475 Paris Cedex 10; tel (1) 42-80-63-63; Dir: Claude Naud; North Eastern region.

Réseau du Sud-Est: place Louis Armand, 75571 Paris Cedex 12; tel (1) 40-19-60-10; Dir: Claude Arnold; South Eastern region.

SHIPPING

Compagnie Générale Maritime et Financière: Tour Winterthur, 102 Quartier Boieldieu, 92085 Paris la Défense Cedex 18; tel (1) 49-03-70-00; telex 630387; Chair: Claude Abraham; Man Dir: Gilbert Massac; f 1976; 99.9% state-owned; freight services to all continents.

Conseil National des Communautés Portuaires: Pres: 71 ave Foch, 75116 Paris; Gen Secretariat: 244 blvd Saint-Germain, 75007 Paris; tel (1) 47-27-04-84; telex 648700; fax (1) 47-04-95-08; Pres: Jacques Dupuy-Dauby; f 1987; consultative organization of representatives of the harbour industry, ministries concerned and unions; advises Govt on harbour matters.

FRENCH OVERSEAS POSSESSIONS

French Overseas Departments

FRENCH GUIANA

The Government

OFFICE OF THE GOVERNMENT COMMISSIONER (PREFECT)
Cayenne
Government Commissioner (Prefect):
Jean-Pierre Lacroix
French Govt representative.

GENERAL COUNCIL
Cayenne
President: Elie Castor
19 mems elected for six years by universal adult suffrage.

REGIONAL COUNCIL
Cayenne
President: Georges Othily
31 mems elected for six years by universal adult suffrage.

Government Agencies

BANKING

Caisse Centrale de Coopération Economique: 13 rue Louis Blanc, Cayenne; tel 31-41-33; telex 910570; Dir: Hervé Maurice; central bank.

Société Financière de Développement de la Guyane (SOFIDEG): 25 rue F. Arago, Cayenne; tel 30-04-18; telex 910556; Dir: Patrice Pin; f 1982; devt bank.

BROADCASTING

Radio-Télévision Française d'Outre-Mer (RFO): rue du Dr Devèze, BP 336, 97305 Cayenne; tel 31-15-00; telex 910526; Dir: Maurice Grimaud; radio (Radio-Guyane Inter) and TV (Téléguyane) broadcasting.

NEWS AND INFORMATION

Institut National de la Statistique et des Etudes Economiques: 1 rue Maillard Dumesle, BP 6017, 97306 Cayenne; tel 31-12-79; telex 910344; statistical office.

TOURISM

Délégation Régionale au Tourisme pour la Guyane: BP 7008, 973307 Cayenne; tel 31-84-91; telex 910532; fax 30-52-22.

TRADE AND INDUSTRY

Jeune Chambre Economique de Cayenne: 2 bis rue Dr Saint-Rose, BP 1094, Cayenne; Pres: Madeleine Georges.

TRANSPORT

Guyane Air Transport (GAT): Aéroport de Rochambeau, 97307 Matoury; tel 35-65-55; telex 910619; Dir-Gen: Guy Malidor; f 1980.

GUADELOUPE

The Government

OFFICE OF THE GOVERNMENT COMMISSIONER (PREFECT)
rue de Lardenoy, 97109 Basse-Terre
Government Commissioner (Prefect): Jean-Paul Proust
French Govt representative.

GENERAL COUNCIL
Basse-Terre
President: Dominique Larifla
42 mems elected by universal adult suffrage for up to six years.

REGIONAL COUNCIL
Basse-Terre
President: Félix Proto
41 mems elected by universal adult suffrage for up to six years.

Government Agencies

BANKING

Caisse Centrale de Coopération Economique: Faubourg Frébault, BP 160, 97154 Pointe-à-Pitre; tel 83-32-72; telex 919074; central bank.

BROADCASTING

Société Nationale de Radio-Télévision Française d'Outre-Mer (RFO): BP 402, 97163 Pointe-à-Pitre Cedex; tel 90-24-24; Dir: Bernard Joyeux; 24 hours radio and 24 hours TV broadcasting daily.

LEGAL AND JUDICIARY

Cour d'Appel (Court of Appeal): Palais de Justice, 97100 Basse-Terre; tel 81-27-59; telex 919890; fax 81-27-59; First Pres: Jean Levanti; Procurator-Gen: Jerry Sainte-Rose.

NEWS AND INFORMATION

Institut National de la Statistique et des Etudes Economiques: ave Paul Lacavé, BP 96, 97102 Basse-Terre; tel 99-02-50; statistical office.

TOURISM

Bureau Industrie et Tourisme: Préfecture de la Guadeloupe, rue de Lardenoy, 97109 Basse-Terre; tel 81-76-81; telex 919707; Dir: François Vosgien.

Office du Tourisme: 5 square de la Banque, BP 1099, 97181 Pointe-à-Pitre; tel 82-09-30; telex 919715; Dir-Gen: Erick W. Rotin; Pres: Philippe Chaulet.

Syndicat d'Initiative de la Guadeloupe: 28 rue Sadi-Carnot, 97110 Pointe-à-Pitre; Pres: Dr Edouard Chartol.

TRADE AND INDUSTRY

Agence pour la Promotion Industrielle de la Guadeloupe (APRIGA): BP 1229, 97184 Pointe-à-Pitre; tel 83-48-97; telex 919780; fax 90-21-87; Pres: Marius Bade; Dir: Charly Blondeau; f 1979; industrial devt agency.

Centre Technique de la Canne et du Sucre: Morne l'Epingle, 97139 Les Abymes; tel 82-94-70; Pres: Antoine Andreze-Louison; Dir: Philippe Douchel; sugar and sugar cane.

TRANSPORT

Air Guadeloupe: Raizet Airport, 97110 Les Abymes; tel 82-21-61; telex 919008; f 1970; regular flights to Antigua, Dominica, St Martin, St Thomas; connects the various dependent islands.

MARTINIQUE

The Government

OFFICE OF THE GOVERNMENT COMMISSIONER (PREFECT)
97262 Fort-de-France
Government Commissioner (Prefect): Jean-Claude Roure French Govt representative.

GENERAL COUNCIL
Fort-de-France
President: Emile Maurice
45 mems elected by universal adult suffrage for up to six years.

REGIONAL COUNCIL
Fort-de-France
President: Camille Darsières
Vice-President: Louis Crusol
41 mems elected by universal adult suffrage for up to six years.

Government Agencies

BANKING

Caisse Centrale de Coopération Economique: 12 blvd du Général de Gaulle, BP 804, 97200 Fort-de-France; Dir: Jean Brutot; central bank.

BROADCASTING

Radio-Télévision Française d'Outre-Mer (RFO): La Clairère, BP 662, Fort-de-France; tel 71-16-60; Dir: Pierre Girard.

DEVELOPMENT

Agence pour le Développement Economique de la Martinique: 26 rue Lamartine, BP 803, 97244 Fort-de-France; tel 73-45-81; telex 912946; fax 72-41-38; f 1979; promotes industrial devt.

Bureau de l'Industrie de l'Artisanat: Préfecture, 97262 Fort-de-France; tel 71-36-27; telex 029650; Dir: Raphaël Firmin; f 1960; Govt agency; research, documentation, technical and administrative advice on investment in industry and tourism.

Société de Crédit pour le Développement de la Martinique (SODEMA): 12 blvd du Général de Gaulle, BP 575, 97242 Fort-de-France Cedex; tel 60-57-58; telex 912402; fax 63-05-95; Dir-Gen: A. Le Sausse; f 1970; provides finance to promote industrial, economic and social devt.

Société de Développement Régional Antilles-Guyane (SODERAG): 109 rue Ernest Deproge, 97200 Fort-de-France; tel 63-59-78; telex 912343; fax 63-38-88; Dir-Gen: Fernand Lerychard; Sec-Gen: Olympe Francil; regional devt.

LEGAL AND JUDICIARY

Cour d'Appel de Fort-de-France (Court of Appeal): Fort-de-France; tel 70-62-62; telex 912525; Pres: Robert Bosc; Procurator-Gen: Henri Jacquemin; highest court for Martinique and French Guiana.

NEWS AND INFORMATION

Institut National de la Statistique et des Etudes Economiques: Pointe de Jaham Schoëlcher, BP 605, 97261 Fort-de-France; tel 71-71-79; statistical office.

TOURISM

Délégation Régionale au Tourisme: 41 rue Gabriel Péri, 97200 Fort-de-France; tel 63-18-61; Dir: Gilbert Lecurieuk.

Office du Tourisme: Pavillon du Tourisme, blvd Alfassa, BP 520, 97206 Fort-de-France; tel 63-79-60; telex 912678; Pres: Jean-Baptiste Edmond; Dir: Jacques Guannel; f 1938.

Syndicat d'Initiative: BP 299, 97203 Fort-de-France; Pres: M. R. Rose-Rosette.

TRANSPORT

Air Martinique (Compagnie Antillaise d'Affrètement Aérien—CAAA: Aéroport de Fort-de-France, 97232 Le Lamentin; tel 51-08-09; telex 912048; fax 51-53-94; Pres: Michel Ziegler; Dir-Gen: Michel Gouze; f 1981; scheduled and charter services within the lesser Antilles.

Compagnie Générale Maritime: ave Maurice Bishop, BP 574, 97206 Fort-de-France; tel 63-00-40; telex 912049; Rep: Guy Adam; shipping; also represents other passenger and freight lines.

RÉUNION

The Government

OFFICE OF THE GOVERNMENT COMMISSIONER (PREFECT)
Saint-Denis
Government Commissioner (Prefect): Daniel Constantin
French Govt representative.

GENERAL COUNCIL
Saint-Denis
President: Eric Boyer
President of the Economic and Social Committee:
Tony Manglou
44 mems elected by universal adult suffrage for up to six years.

REGIONAL COUNCIL
place Barachois, 97405, Saint-Denis
Presient: Pierre Lagourgue
45 mems elected by universal adult suffrage for up to six years.

Government Agencies

BANKING

Banque Populaire Fédérale de Développement: 33 rue Victor MacAuliffe, 97400 Saint-Denis; tel 21-18-11; telex 916582; Dir: Olivier Devisme; devt bank; 3 brs.

Institut d'Emission des Départements d'Outre-Mer: Office in Réunion: 4 rue de la Compagnie, 97487 Saint-Denis Cedex; tel 21-18-96; Dir: Jacques Pierrat; central bank.

BROADCASTING

Radio France d'Outre-Mer (RFO): place Sarda Garriga, BP 309, 97405 Saint-Denis; tel 21-34-56; Dir: Alain Quintrie-Lamothe; home radio and TV relay services in French; operates two TV channels.

DEVELOPMENT

Association pour le Développement Industriel de la Réunion (ADIR): 18 rue Milius, BP 327, 97468 Saint-Denis Cedex; tel 21-42-69; telex 916666; Pres: Paul Martinel; Engineer Sec: S. Tsakanias; f 1975; advises and gives technical assistance to industries and to industries intending to invest in Réunion.

Secrétariat Général pour les Affaires Economiques: ave de la Victoire, 97405 Saint-Denis; tel 21-86-10; telex 916111.

Direction de l'Action Economique: Secrétariat Général pour les Affaires Economiques, ave de la Victoire, 97405 Saint-Denis; tel 21-86-10; telex 916111.

Société de Développement Economique de la Réunion (SODERE): 26 rue Labourdonnais, 97469 Saint-Denis; tel 20-01-68; telex 916471; Chair: Pierre Peyron; Man Dir: Albert Trimaille; f 1964; economic devt organization.

LEGAL AND JUDICIARY

Cour d'Appel (Court of Appeal): Palais de Justice, 166 rue Juliette Dodu, 97488 Saint-Denis; tel 21-75-39; telex 916149; Pres: Henri Vray.

NEWS AND INFORMATION

Institut National de la Statistique et des Etudes Economiques, Service Régional de la Réunion: Saint-Denis.

TOURISM

L'Agence Régionale du Tourisme et des Loisirs (ARTL): 2 rue de la Victorie, 97400 Saint-Denis; Pres: Bertho Audifax.

Délégation Régionale au Commerce, à l'Artisanat et au Tourisme (DRCAT): Préfecture, Affaires Economiques, DRCAT, 97400 Saint-Denis; tel 40-77-77; telex 916111; fax 41-73-74; Dir: Jean-François Desroches; concerned with commerce, tourism and crafts.

Office du Tourisme: rue Rontaunay, 97400 Saint-Denis; tel 21-24-53; telex 916486; Chair: S. Personné.

TRANSPORT

Air Réunion: BP 611, 97473 Saint-Denis; tel 28-22-60; telex 916236; Gen Man: B. Popineau; f 1975; subsidiary of Air France; scheduled services to Madagascar and the Comoros.

Compagnie Générale Maritime (CGM): 2 rue de l'Est, BP 10, 97420 Le Port; tel 42-00-88; Dir: Henri-Pierre Signeux; shipping agents.

Société de Manutention et de Consignation Maritime (SOMACOM): BP 7, Le Port; shipping agents.

French Overseas Collectivités Territoriales

MAYOTTE

The Government

OFFICE OF THE GOVERNMENT COMMISSIONER (PREFECT)
Dzaoudzi, Mayotte
Government Commissioner (Prefect): Akli Khider
Secretary-General: Philippe Schaefer
The Government Commissioner is the French Govt representative.

GENERAL COUNCIL
Dzaoudzi, Mayotte
President: Youssouf Bamana
17 mems; assists the Government Commissioner in the administration of the island.

Government Agencies

BANKING

Banque Française Commerciale: Mamoudzou, 97600 Mayotte; br at Dzaoudzi.

Institut d'Emission d'Outre-Mer: Dzaoudzi, 97610 Mayotte.

BROADCASTING

Société Nationale de Radio-Télévision Française d'Outre-Mer (RFO)—Mayotte: BP 103, Dzaoudzi, 97610 Mayotte; tel 60-10-17; telex 915822; fax 60-18-52; Regional Dir: Yves Rambeau; Technical Dir: J. Biasco; f 1977; radio broadcasts in French and Mahorian; TV broadcasts.

LEGAL AND JUDICIARY

Tribunal Supérieur d'Appel (Tribunal of Appeal): Dzaoudzi, 97600 Mayotte; tel 61-12-65; fax 61-19-63; Pres: Jean-Baptiste Flori; Procurator: Patrick Brossier.

Tribunal d'Instance: Dzaoudzi, Mayotte; Pres: Arlette Meallonnier-Dugue.

ST PIERRE AND MIQUELON

The Government

OFFICE OF THE GOVERNMENT COMMISSIONER (PREFECT)
97500 Saint-Pierre
Government Commissioner (Prefect):
Jean-Pierre Marquié
President of the Economic and Social Committee:
Rémy Briand
French Govt representative.

GENERAL COUNCIL
Saint-Pierre
President: Marc Plantegenest
19 mems, 15 for Saint-Pierre and four for Miquelon, elected by universal adult suffrage for six years.

Government Agencies

BANKING

Banque des Iles Saint-Pierre-et-Miquelon: rue Jacques-Cartier, Saint-Pierre; tel 41-22-17; telex 914435; fax 41-25-31;
Pres and Gen Man: Charles-Pierre Landry; Man: Guy Roulet; f 1889.

Crédit Saint Pierrais: 20 place du Général de Gaulle, BP 4218, Saint-Pierre; tel 41-22-49; telex 914429; fax 41-25-96; Pres: Marcel Girardin; Man: G. Coquelin.

BROADCASTING

Radio-Télévision Française d'Outre-Mer (RFO): BP 4227, 97500 Saint-Pierre; tel 41-38-24; telex 914443; Dir: Alain Quintrie-Lamotte; radio and TV broadcasting.

LEGAL AND JUDICIARY

Tribunal Supérieur d'Appel (Tribunal of Appeal): Saint-Pierre; Pres: Etienne Diximier.

Tribunal de Première Instance: Saint-Pierre; Pres: (vacant).

TOURISM

Agence Régionale du Tourisme: rue du 11 Novembre, BP 4274, 97500 Saint-Pierre; tel 41-22-22; telex 914437; fax 41-33-55; Pres: Marc Plantegenest; Man: Bernard Vigneau; f 1959.

TRANSPORT

Air Saint-Pierre: 18 rue Albert Briand St Pierre, BP 4225, 97500 Saint-Pierre; tel 41-27-20; telex 914422; Pres: Rémy L. Briand; f 1961; connects the territory with Canada.

French Overseas Territories

FRENCH POLYNESIA

The Government

OFFICE OF THE HIGH COMMISSIONER
Papeete
High Commissioner: Jean Montpezat
Secretary-General: Roger Moser
French Govt representative.

TERRITORIAL ASSEMBLY
Papeete
President: Jean Juventin
Vice-President: Henri Marere
41 mems elected for five years by universal adult suffrage; elects the President of the Council of Ministers.

OFFICE OF THE PRESIDENT OF THE COUNCIL OF MINISTERS
Papeete
President: Alexandre Léontieff
Vice-President: Georges Kelly

MINISTRY OF AGRICULTURE, TRADITIONAL CRAFTS AND THE CULTURAL HERITAGE
Papeete
Minister: Georges Kelly

MINISTRY OF EDUCATION AND TEACHING
Papeete
Minister: Raymond van Bastolaer

MINISTRY OF EMPLOYMENT, TOURISM AND SPORTS
Papeete
Minister: Napoléon Spitz

MINISTRY OF FINANCE AND THE ECONOMY
Papeete
Minister: Louis Savoie

MINISTRY OF FINANCIAL AFFAIRS AND ISLAND DEVELOPMENT
Papeete
Minister: Ioane Temauri

MINISTRY OF HEALTH, THE ENVIRONMENT AND SCIENTIFIC RESEARCH
Papeete
Minister: Jacky Drollet

MINISTRY OF REGIONALIZATION, ISLAND ADMINISTRATION AND POSTS AND TELECOMMUNICATIONS
Papeete
Minister: Emile Vernaudon

MINISTRY OF THE SEA, EQUIPMENT AND ENERGY
BP 2551 Papeete
Tel 42-65-05; fax 41-01-38
Minister: Boris Léontieff

MINISTRY OF SOCIAL AFFAIRS, UNITY, YOUTH, THE FAMILY AND CONSUMER AFFAIRS, AND OFFICE OF THE GOVERNMENT SPOKESPERSON
BP 2551, Papeete
Tel 42-24-40; telex 404; fax 42-24-80
Minister: Huguette Hong-Kiou

Institut Territorial de la Consommation (Institute of Consumer affairs): BP 20500 Papeete; tel 41-33-33; Dir: Pierre Frebault.

Office Territorial de l'Action Sociale et de la Solidarité (Office for Social Action and Unity): BP 3689, Papeete; tel 43-86-03; Dir: Véronique Tumahai.

Service des Affaires Sociales (Social Affairs Section): BP 1707, Papeete; tel 43-80-48; Head: Irène Cathala.

Service des Etablissements Pénitentiaires (Prisons Section): BP 127, Faaa; tel 42-00-15; Head: Tehina Salmon.

Service de la Jeunesse (Youth Section): BP 4249, Papeete; tel 43-97-06; Head: Pierrot Lucas.

MINISTRY OF URBANIZATION, GROUND TRANSPORT AND GENERAL ADMINISTRATION
Papeete
Minister: François Nanai

Government Agencies

BANKING

Banque de Tahiti, SA: Rue Cardella, BP 1602, Papeete; tel 41-70-00; telex 237; fax 42-33-76; Pres: Jean-Claude Duccini; Dirs: Michel Dupieux, Gérard Muller, Gérard E. Seidl; f 1969; 13 brs.

BROADCASTING

Radio-Télé-Tahiti: 410 rue Dumont d'Urville, BP 125, Papeete; tel 43-05-51; telex 290; fax 41-31-55; Dir: Guy Sarthoulet; f 1951 as Radio-Tahiti; TV service began 1965; operated by Société Nationale de Radio-Télévision Française d'Outre-Mer (RFO), Paris; daily programmes in French and Tahitian.

DEVELOPMENT

Association pour la Formation et le Développement en Polynésie (AFODEP): BP 455, Papeete; planning and devt.

LEGAL AND JUDICIARY

Cour d'Appel (Court of Appeal): Papeete; tel 42-01-17; telex 308; Pres: Henri de Labrusse; Attorney-Gen: Paul Marchaud.

Tribunal Administratif (Administrative Tribunal): BP 4522,

Papeete; tel 42-24-82; Pres: Jean Lavoignat; Cllrs: Bernard Leplat, Jean Brenier, Michel Aubert; f 1984; court of administrative law.

Tribunal d'Instance (Court of the First Instance): Papeete; tel 42-01-16; telex 308; Pres: Luc Compain; Procurator: Jean-Yves Duval; Clerk of the Court: Daniel Salmon.

NEWS AND INFORMATION

Institut Territorial de la Statistique: Immeuble Donald, rue Jeanne d'Arc, BP 395, Papeete; tel 43-71-96; fax 42-72-52; Dir: Gérard Baudchon; f 1976; statistical institute.

TOURISM

Office de Promotion et d'Animation Touristiques de Tahiti et ses Iles: Fare Manihini, blvd Pomare, BP 65, Papeete; tel 42-96-26; telex 254; fax 43-66-19; Chair: Minister of Employment, Tourism and Sports, Napoléon Spitz; Dir (acting): Patrick Picard-Robson; f 1966; promotion of tourism.

Service du Tourisme: Fare Manihini, blvd Pomare, BP 4527, Papeete; tel 42-93-30; telex 254; Dir: Gérard Vanizette.

Syndicat d'Initiative de la Polynésie Française: BP 326, Papeete; Pres: Piu Bambridge.

TRANSPORT

Air Moorea: BP 6019, Faaa; tel 42-48-34; telex 314; fax 43-58-97; Pres and Dir-Gen: Marcel Galenou; f 1968; operates internal services between Tahiti and Moorea Island; some inter-territorial services; 90% Govt-owned.

Compagnie Générale Maritime: ave du Général de Gaulle, BP 96, Papeete; tel 42-08-90; telex 259; Dir: (vacant); shipowners and agents; freight services between Europe and many international ports.

NEW CALEDONIA

The Government

OFFICE OF THE HIGH COMMISSIONER
Nouméa
High Commissioner: Bernard Grasset
Secretary-General: Jacques Iékawé
The High Commissioner is the French Govt representative and holds overall executive power.

TERRITORIAL CONGRESS
Nouméa
President: Simon Loueckhote
Formed by the three regional councils (North, South and the Loyalty Islands), elected by direct universal adult suffrage for six years.

Government Agencies

BANKING

Banque Nationale de Paris Nouvelle Calédonie (France): 37 Route Territoriale 13, BP K3, Nouméa; tel 27-55-55; telex 3022; fax 27-79-69; Pres: Jean-Louis Hautcoeur; Gen Man: Christian Faucilhon; f 1969; 8 brs.

Banque de Nouvelle Calédonie (BNC)/Crédit Lyonnais: 25 ave de la Victoire/ave Henri-Lafleur, BP L3, Nouméa Cedex; tel 28-50-69; telex 3091; fax 27-41-47; Pres: Bernard Thiolon; Dir: Guy Javelaud; Dep Dir: Alain Minier; f 1974.

BROADCASTING

Société Nationale de Radio-Télévision Française d'Outre-Mer: BP G3, Nouméa Cedex; tel 27-43-27; telex 3052; fax 28-12-52; Dir: Alain Le Garrec; f 1964; 20 hours of daily radio and TV broadcasts in French.

Télé Nouméa: address as above; f 1965; TV broadcasting.

NEWS AND INFORMATION

Institut Territorial de la Statistique et des Etudes Economiques (ITSEE): BP 823, Nouméa; tel 27-54-81; fax 28-81-48; f 1971; statistical and economic studies.

LEGAL AND JUDICIARY

Cour d'Appel (Court of Appeal): Palais de Justice, BP F4, Nouméa; First Pres: Claude Hanoteau; Procurator-Gen: Gilles Lucazeau.

Tribunal d'Instance (Court of the First Instance): Nouméa; Pres: Didier Marshall; Procurator of the Republic: Robert Finielz.

TOURISM

Office Territorial du Tourisme de Nouvelle Calédonie: Immeuble Manathan 39, 41 rue de Verdun, BP 688, Nouméa; tel 27-26-32; telex 3063; fax 27-46-23; Dir: Michel Doppler; f 1960.

TRANSPORT

Air Calédonie: BP 212, Nouméa; tel 25-23-39; telex 3112; fax 25-44-77; Chair: Franck Wahuzue; Man Dir: Pierre Segui; f 1955; domestic airline.

Air Calédonie International: BP 3736, Nouméa; tel 28-33-33; telex 3177; Chief Exec: Jean-Pierre Varnier; f 1983; services to Australia, New Zealand, Fiji, Wallis Island and Vanuatu.

WALLIS AND FUTUNA ISLANDS

The Government

OFFICE OF THE CHIEF ADMINISTRATOR
Mata-Utu, Uvea, Wallis Islands (par Nouméa)
Chief Administrator: Roger Dumec
French Govt representative.

TERRITORIAL ASSEMBLY
Mata-Utu, Uvea, Wallis Islands (par Nouméa)
President: Falakiko Gata
Assists the Chief Administrator; 20 mems elected for five years by universal adult suffrage.

Government Agencies

BROADCASTING

Radiodiffusion Française d'Outre-Mer (RFO): BP 102, Mata-Utu, Uvea, Wallis Islands (par Nouméa); tel 72-20-20; telex 250500; Man: René Denis; programmes in Wallisian, Futunian and French; TV service transmits for four and a half hours daily.

GABON

<table>
<tr><td>

Head of State

Executive power is vested in the President, who is elected by universal adult suffrage for a seven-year term. The President appoints the Prime Minister, who is Head of Government; he also appoints, and presides over, a Council of Ministers. Gabon became a one-party state in 1968. The Assemblée socialiste démoctratique (PDG) is the only legal party.

President: El Hadj Omar (Albert-Bernard) Bongo (took office 2 December 1967; elected 25 February 1973; re-elected December 1979 and November 1986).

Office of the President: BP 546, Libreville; tel 72-20-30; telex 5211; Sec-Gen at the Presidency: René Radembino Coniquet.

</td><td>

Legislature

Legislative power is vested in the unicameral National Assembly. The Assembly comprises 120 members, of whom 111 are elected by universal adult suffrage and nine are nominated, for a term of five years. The country is divided into nine provinces, each under an appointed Governor, and 37 prefectures.

Assemblée Nationale (National Assembly): BP 29, Libreville; tel 76-09-30; Pres: Augustin Boumah; Sec-Gen: Pierre N'Guema-Mvé.

</td></tr>
</table>

MINISTRIES AND GOVERNMENT DEPARTMENTS

OFFICE OF THE PRIME MINISTER
BP 546, Libreville
Tel 76-15-75; telex 5409
Prime Minister: Léon Mébiame
Ministers without Portfolio, in charge of Government Working Groups: Georges Rawiri, Guy-Etienne Mouvagha-Tchioba, Emile Kassa Mapsi, Simon Essimengane
Minister-Delegate to the Prime Minister, in charge of Finance, Budget and Participation: Paul Toungui
Minister-Delgate to the Prime Minister, in charge of Planning, Development and Economy: Pascal Nze
Minister of State to the Minister-Delegate in charge of Finance, Budget and Participation: Chantal Lidji-Badinga

MINISTRY OF AGRICULTURE, LIVESTOCK AND RURAL DEVELOPMENT
BP 551, Libreville
Tel 76-29-43; telex 5587
Minister: Jules Bourdès-Ogouliguende
Minister of State: Daniel Afome-Nze

MINISTRY OF ENERGY AND HYDRAULIC RESOURCES
BP 576, Libreville
Tel 72-31-96; telex 5629
Minister: Martin Fidele Magnaga

MINISTRY OF FOREIGN AFFAIRS AND CO-OPERATION
BP 2245, Libreville
Tel 76-22-70; telex 5255
Minister: Ali Ben Bongo
Minister of State: Honorine Dossou-Naki

MINISTRY OF INDUSTRY AND CONSUMPTION
Libreville
Minister: Etienne Moussirou

MINISTRY OF INFORMATION, POSTS, TELECOMMUNICATIONS, TOURISM AND LEISURE, REFORM OF PARASTATALS AND RELATIONS WITH THE NATIONAL ASSEMBLY
BP 2280, Libreville
Tel 76-16-92; telex 5361
Minister: Jean Ping

MINISTRY OF JUSTICE
BP 547, Libreville
Tel 72-26-95
Minister: Sylvestre Oyouomi

MINISTRY OF LABOUR, EMPLOYMENT, HUMAN RESOURCES AND PROFESSIONAL TRAINING
BP 371, Libreville
Tel 74-32-18
Minister: Marcel Doupamby Matoka

MINISTRY OF NATIONAL DEFENCE, VETERANS' AFFAIRS, PUBLIC SECURITY AND HYDROCARBONS
BP 546, Libreville
Tel 76-25-95; telex 5453
Minister: Julien Mpouho-Epigat
Minister of State: Samuel Mbaye

MINISTRY OF NATIONAL AND HIGHER EDUCATION, SCIENTIFIC RESEARCH AND TECHNOLOGY
BP 496, Libreville
Tel 72-21-75
Minister: Michel Anchouey
Minister of State: Marcel Kiki

MINISTRY OF PUBLIC HEALTH AND POPULATION
BP 13116, Libreville
Tel 76-30-32; telex 5385
Minister: Dr Adrien Mounguengui Pambo

MINISTRY OF THE ENVIRONMENT, LAND REGISTRATION AND THE LAW OF THE SEA
Libreville
Tel 72-10-39; telex 5545
Minister, Environment: Alexandre Sambat
Minister, Land Registration and Law of the Sea: Henri Minko

MINISTRY OF PUBLIC WORKS, EQUIPMENT, CONSTRUCTION AND TERRITORIAL DEVELOPMENT
BP 371, Libreville
Tel 76-14-87
Minister: Zacharie Myboto
Minister of State: Christian Gondjout

MINISTRY OF SOCIAL AFFAIRS, SOCIAL SECURITY AND NATIONAL SOLIDARITY
BP 13116, Libreville
Tel 72-42-22
Minister: Antoine Mboumbou-Miyakou
Minister of State: Paulin Nguéma Obame

MINISTRY OF STATE CONTROL AND PUBLIC CONTRACTS
BP 178, Libreville
Tel 76-34-62; telex 5711
Minister: Gen Thomas Eyah-Obiang

MINISTRY OF TERRITORIAL ADMINISTRATION, LOCAL COMMUNITIES AND IMMIGRATION
BP 1204, Libreville
Tel 74-00-21; telex 5638
Minister: José-Joseph Amiar Nganga

MINISTRY OF TOWN PLANNING, HOUSING AND HABITATION
Libreville
Minister: Thierry Moussavou
Minister of State: Gustave Bongo

MINISTRY OF TRADE, TRANSFER OF TECHNOLOGIES AND RATIONALIZATION
BP 3906, Libreville
Tel 76-30-55; telex 5347
Minister: Paul Biyogho-Mba

MINISTRY OF TRANSPORT, CIVIL AND COMMERCIAL AVIATION, MERCHANT MARINE AND HUMANITARIAN ACTION
BP 3974, Libreville
Tel 72-11-62; telex 5479; fax 77-33-31
Minister: Mathieu Nguéma

MINISTRY OF WATER RESOURCES, FORESTS AND NATIONAL PARKS
Libreville
Minister: Jean Boniface Assele
Minister of State: Jean Felix Aubame

MINISTRY OF WOMEN'S PROMOTION AND HUMAN RIGHTS
Libreville
Minister of State: Rose Francine Rogombe

MINISTRY OF YOUTH, SPORTS, CULTURE, ARTS, POPULAR EDUCATION AND FRANCOPHONE AFFAIRS
Libreville
Tel 76-35-76; telex 5642
Minister: Victor Afène
Minister of State: Alexandre Chambrier

GOVERNMENT AGENCIES AND ORGANIZATIONS

Advisory and Supervisory Body

Conseil Economique et Social de la République Gabonaise: BP 1075, Libreville; tel 76-26-68; Pres: Edouard Alexis M'Bouy Boutzit; Vice-Pres: M. Richepin Eyogo-Edzang; comprises reps from salaried workers, employers and Govt; commissions on economic, financial and social affairs, and forestry and agriculture.

Agriculture and Forestry

AGRICULTURE

Office Gabonais d'Amélioration et de Production de Viande (OGAPROV): BP 245, Moanda; tel 66-12-67; Pres: Paul Kounda Kiki; Dir-Gen: Vincent Eyi-Ngui; f 1971; devt of private cattle farming; manages ranch at Lekedi-Sud.

Palmiers et Hévéas du Gabon (PALMEVEAS): BP 75, Libreville; f 1956; state co promoting palm-oil devt.

Société de Développement de l'Agriculture au Gabon (AGROGABON): BP 2248, Libreville; tel 76-40-82; telex 5468;

Man Dir: André Le Roux; f 1976; 96% state-owned; agricultural devt agency.

Société de Développement de l'Hévéaculture (HEV-EGAB): BP 316, Libreville; tel 70-03-48; telex 5615; Chair: Emmanuel Ondo-Methogo; Man Dir: Guy de Roquemaurel; f 1981; 99.9% state-owned; devt of rubber plantations.

Société Nationale de Développement des Cultures Industrielles (SONADECI): BP 256, Libreville; tel 76-33-97; telex 5362; Chair: Paul Kounda Kiki; Man Dir: Georges Bekale; f 1978; agricultural devt.

FORESTRY

Compagnie Forestière du Gabon (CFG): BP 521, Port-Gentil; tel 75-20-31; telex 8209; Chair: Emmanuel Nzé Bekale; Man Dir: Martin Rekangalt; 55% state-owned; production of okoumé plywood, veneered quality plywoods and hardwood timber.

Société Nationale des Bois du Gabon (SNBG): BP 67, Libreville; tel 76-26-15; telex 5201; Chair and Man Dir: Mamadou Diop; f 1975; 51% state-owned; has a monopoly of marketing all wood products.

Business and Economy

BANKING

Banque des Etats de l'Afrique Centrale (BEAC): BP 112, Libreville; tel 76-13-52; telex 5215; fax 74-45-63; Gov: Casimir Oyé Mba; Dir in Gabon: Jean-Paul Leyimangoye; f 1973; central bank of issue for mem states of the Customs and Economic Union of Central Africa (UDEAC), comprising Cameroon, the Central African Republic, Chad, the Congo, Equatorial Guinea and Gabon; headquarters in Yaoundé, Cameroon; 2 brs.

Banque Gabonaise de Développement (BGD): rue Alfred Marche, BP 5, Libreville; tel 76-24-29; telex 5430; fax 74-26-99; Pres: Michel Anchouey; Man Dir: Jean-Félix Malamepot; f 1960; 69% state-owned; brs in Franceville, Port-Gentil.

Banque du Gabon et du Luxembourg: blvd de l'Indépendance, BP 3879, Libreville; tel 72-28-62; telex 5344; f 1974; activities temporarily suspended by the Govt.

Banque Nationale de Crédit Rurale (BNCR): ave Bouet, BP 1120, Libreville; tel 72-47-42; telex 5830; Pres: Minister of Planning, Development and the Economy, Pascal Nzé Bie; Man Dir: Jacques Diouf; f 1986; 98% state-owned.

Crédit Foncier du Gabon (CREFOGA): BP 3905, Libreville; tel 72-47-45; telex 5450; Man Dir: Adrien Nkoghe Essingone; 67% state-owned.

Union Gabonaise de Banque SA (UGB): ave du Col Parant, BP 315, Libreville; tel 76-15-14; telex 5232; fax 76-46-16; Pres: Mathieu Nguema; Gen Man: Marcel Doupamby Matoka; f 1962; 6 brs.

NATIONALIZED INDUSTRY

Société Gabonaise du Cellulose (SOGACEL): BP 3986, Libreville; tel 73-26-33; telex 5421; Chair: Jean-François Ntoutoume; Man Dir: G. Avika; f 1969; 62.2% state-owned; construction and management of paper-pulp processing at Kango.

TRADE

Centre Gabonais de Commerce Extérieur (CGCE): BP 3906, Libreville; tel 76-11-67; telex 5347; Man Dir: Michel Leslie Teale; promotion of foreign trade and investment.

Commerce et Développement (CODEV): BP 2142, Libreville; tel 76-06-73; telex 5214; Chair and Man Dir: Jérôme Ngoua-Bekale; 95% state-owned, privatization plans announced 1986; import and distribution of capital goods and food products.

Defence

Armed Forces: BP 2126, Libreville; tel 76-42-43; Commdr-in-Chief, Land and Naval Forces: Maj-Gen André Oyini.

Air Force: BP 10070, Libreville; tel 73-24-75; telex 5348; Chief of Staff: Jacques Mvé.

Army: BP 2126, Libreville; tel 76-41-84; Chief of Staff: Ella Abessolo Paul.

National Police: BP 371, Libreville; tel 76-15-11; Commdr: Gen Jean-Boniface Assélé.

Development and Planning

DEVELOPMENT

Agence Nationale de Promotion de la Petite et Moyenne Entreprise (PROMO-GABON): BP 3939, Libreville; tel 74-31-16; telex 000576; Pres: Simon Boulamatari; Man Dir: Jean-Fidèle Otando; f 1964; promotion of and assistance to small and medium-sized industries.

Société Nationale Immobilière: BP 515, Libreville; tel 76-05-81; Pres and Dir-Gen: Georges Issembe; f 1976; 77% state-owned; devt and improvement of housing.

INVESTMENT

Société Nationale d'Investissements du Gabon (SONADIG): BP 479, Libreville; tel 72-09-22; Pres: Antoine Oyieye; Dir-Gen: Simon Edou-Eyenne; f 1968; state-owned investment co.

Legal and Judiciary

Conseil Supérieur de la Magistrature: Libreville; Pres: Omar Bongo; magistrate's court.

Cour de Sûreté de l'Etat: Libreville; Pres: Florentin Ango; 13 mems; court for the defence of the state.

Cour d'Appel (Court of Appeal): Libreville-Franceville.

High Court of Justice: Libreville; Pres: Gaston Bouckat-Bouziengui; mems appointed by and from the deputies of the National Assembly.

Cour Suprême (Supreme Court): BP 1043, Libreville; tel 76-09-68; Pres: Gen Georges Nkoma; has four chambers: constitutional, judicial, administrative and accounts.

Media

BROADCASTING

Radiodiffusion-Télévision Gabonaise (RTG): BP 150, Libreville; tel 73-20-25; telex 5342; Man Dir: Jacques Adiahenot; Dir, TV: R. Mouyoubi; f 1959; production and broadcast of radio and TV programmes.

GOVERNMENT PUBLISHER

Société Nationale de Presse et d'Edition (SONAPRESSE): BP 3849, Libreville; tel 73-21-84; telex 5391; Pres and Man Dir: Joseph Rendjambe; f 1975.

NEWS AND INFORMATION

Direction Générale de l'Economie: c/o Ministère de la Planification et de l'Economie, Libreville; statistical information dept.

Mining and Energy

ENERGY

Société d'Energie et d'Eau du Gabon (SEEG): ave Félix

Eboué, BP 2187, Libreville; tel 76-72-01; telex 5222; Chair, Admin Council: Paul Malekou; f 1950; 64% state-owned; produces and distributes electricity and drinking water.

Société Gabonaise de Recherches Petrolières (GABOREP): BP 564, Libreville; tel 77-23-86; telex 5829; fax 77-23--85; Chair: Hubert Perrodo; Man Dir: P. F. Lecca; f 1979; prospecting for and exploitation, processing and storage of hydrocarbons; financial and commercial operations relating to the petroleum industry.

MINING

Société Gabonaise de Recherches et d'Exploitation Minières (SOGAREM): blvd de Nice, Libreville; Chair: Arsène Bounguenza; Man Dir: Serge Gassita; research and devt of gold mining.

Telecommunications

Société des Télécommunications Internationales Gabonaises (TIG): BP 2261, Libreville; tel 72-27-56; telex 5200; fax 74-19-09; Man: Thomas Souah; f 1971; controls international telecommunications.

Tourism

Office National Gabonais de Tourisme: BP 161, Libreville; tel 72-21-82.

Transport

CIVIL AVIATION

Compagnie Nationale Air Gabon: BP 2206, Libreville; tel 73-21-97; telex 5213; fax 73-01-11; Chair: Martin Bongo; Dir-Gen: Jean-Claude Laboura; f 1977; 80% state-owned; internal and international cargo and passenger services.

RAILWAYS

Office du Chemin de Fer Transgabonais (OCTRA): BP 2198, Libreville; tel 70-24-78; telex 5307; fax 94-51-45; Chair: Hervé Moutsinga (mem of Cabinet); Man Dir: Charles Tsibah.

ROADS

Société Africaine de Transit et d'Affrètement Gabon (SATAGABON): blvd de l'Indépendance, BP 2258, Libreville; tel 76-11-28; telex 5439; Man Dir: Yves Lerays; f 1961; haulage co.

SHIPPING

Compagnie de Navigation Intérieure (CNI): BP 3982, Libreville; tel 72-39-28; telex 5289; Chair: Jean-Pierre Mengwang me Ngyema; Dir: Mathurin Anotho-Onanga; f 1978; inland waterway transport co.

Office des Ports et Rades du Gabon (OPRAG): BP 1051, Libreville; tel 70-17-98; telex 5319; Man Dir: Marius Foungues; f 1974; national port authority; all port operations.

Société Nationale d'Acconage et de Transit (SNAT): BP 3897, Libreville; tel 72-04-04; telex 5420; fax 70-13-11; Chair: M. Massala-Malonga; Man Dir: Ernest Redombo; f 1976; 51% state-owned; freight transport.

Société Nationale de Transports Maritimes (SONATRAM): BP 3841, Libreville; tel 74-06-32; telex 5289; fax 74-59-67; Man Dir: Raphael Moara Walla; f 1976; 51% state-owned; river and ocean cargo transport.

THE GAMBIA

Head of State

The President is Head of State, and is elected by direct universal suffrage for a five-year term. The President appoints a Vice-President (who is leader of Government business in the House of Representatives) and a Cabinet.

President: Alhaji Sir Dawda Kairaba Jawara (took office 24 April 1970; re-elected 1972, 1977, 1982 and 1987).

Office of the President: State House, Banjul; tel 27208; telex 2204; fax 27034.

Vice-President: Bakary B. Darbo.

Office of the Vice-President: State House, Banjul; tel 27243.

Legislature

Legislative power is held by the unicameral House of Representatives, comprising 50 members (36 directly elected by universal adult suffrage for five years, five Chiefs' Representatives, eight non-voting nominated members and the Attorney-General).

House of Representatives: Independence Drive, Banjul; tel 28305; Speaker: Alhaji Momodou B. N'Jie.

MINISTRIES AND GOVERNMENT DEPARTMENTS

MINISTRY OF AGRICULTURE
The Quadrangle, Banjul
Tel 2147
Minister: Alhaji Omar Amadou Jallow

MINISTRY OF ECONOMIC PLANNING AND INDUSTRIAL DEVELOPMENT
Central Bank Bldg, Banjul
Tel 28229; telex 2293
Minister: Mbemba Jatta

MINISTRY OF EDUCATION, YOUTH, SPORTS AND CULTURE
Bedford Place Bldg, Banjul
Tel 28231
Minister: Bakary B. Darbo

MINISTRY OF EXTERNAL AFFAIRS
The Quadrangle, Banjul
Tel 28291; telex 2351; fax 28060
Minister: Alhaji Omar Sey

MINISTRY OF FINANCE AND TRADE
The Quadrangle, Banjul
Tel 28291; telex 2264
Minister: Alhaji Saihou Sabally

MINISTRY OF HEALTH, LABOUR, SOCIAL WELFARE AND THE ENVIRONMENT
MacCarthy Sq, Banjul
Tel 27223; telex 2263; fax 27122
Minister: Louise N'Jie

MINISTRY OF INFORMATION AND TOURISM
The Quadrangle, Banjul
Tel 28496; telex 2204
Minister: Dr Lamin K. Saho

MINISTRY OF THE INTERIOR
71 Dobson St, Banjul
Tel 28611
Minister: Alhaji Lamin Kitty Jabang

MINISTRY OF JUSTICE
Marina Parade, Banjul
Tel 28181
Minister and Attorney-General: Hassan B. Jallow

MINISTRY OF LOCAL GOVERNMENT AND LANDS
The Quadrangle, Banjul
Tel 28291
Minister: Alhaji Landing Jallow-Sonko

MINISTRY OF NATIONAL DEFENCE
Banjul
Minister: Alhaji Sir Dawda Kairaba Jawara

MINISTRY OF WATER RESOURCES, FORESTRY AND FISHERIES
5 Marina Parade, Banjul
Tel 27431; telex 2204
Minister: Sarjo Touray

MINISTRY OF WORKS AND COMMUNICATIONS
Half-Die, Banjul
Tel 27449
Minister: Momodou Cadi Cham

GOVERNMENT AGENCIES AND ORGANIZATIONS

Business and Economy

BANKING

Central Bank of The Gambia: 1-2 Buckle St, Banjul; tel 28103; telex 2218; fax 26969; Gov: Abdou A. B. Njie; Gen Man: Edward E. Fillingham; f 1971; central bank and bank of issue.

The Gambia Commercial and Development Bank: 3-4 Buckle St, POB 666, Banjul; tel 28651; telex 2221; Chair: M. M. Dibba; Man Dir: (vacant); f 1972; 52% state-owned; 3 brs.

INSURANCE

The Gambia National Insurance Corpn: 6 Leman St, POB 750, Banjul; tel 28412; telex 2268; Man Dir: Sankung S. Fatty; f 1979.

MARKETING

Gambia Produce Marketing Board: Marina Foreshore, Banjul; tel 27572; telex 2205; fax 28037; Chair: M. M. Jallow; Man Dir: Saikou Darammeh.

TRADE

National Trading Corpn of The Gambia Ltd (NTC): 1-3 Wellington St, POB 61, Banjul; tel 28395; telex 2252; Chair and Man Dir: Alieu A. M. Mboge; f 1973; 15 brs; transfer to private ownership pending in 1989.

Defence

Gambia National Army: Yundon; tel 27822; Commdr: Lt-Col M. B. N'dow-N'jie.

Gambia National Gendarmerie: Bakau; tel 95324; Commdr: Lt-Col M. B. N'dow-N'jie.

Police Department: Banjul; tel 27210; Commr: Sidney Riley.

Investment

National Investment Board (NIB): 78 Wellington St, Banjul; telex 2230.

Legal and Judiciary

Supreme Court: Buckle St, Banjul; tel 27743; Chief Justice: Emmanuel Olayinka Ayoola.

The Gambia Court of Appeal: Banjul; Pres: (vacant); Superior Court of Record.

Media

BROADCASTING

Radio Gambia: Mile 7, Banjul; tel 95101; telex 2204; Dir: Marcel Thomasi; f 1962; Govt service of information, education and entertainment broadcasting about 17 hours daily in English, Mandinka, Wolof, Fula, Jola, Serer and Serahuli.

GOVERNMENT PUBLISHER

Government Printer: MacCarthy Sq, Banjul; tel 27399; telex 2204.

NEWS AND INFORMATION

Central Statistics Department: Old Treasury Bldg, Wellington St, Banjul.

Directorate of Information and Broadcasting: 14 Hagan St, Banjul; tel 27230.

Gambia News Agency (GAMNA): Information Office, 14 Hagan St, Banjul; tel 28403; telex 2308.

Transport

Gambia Airways: City Terminal, Wellington St, POB 535, Banjul; tel 26733; Man Dir: Salifou M. Jallow; f 1964; handling agency; operated by Gambian Govt, which holds 60% of shares; 40% owned by British Airways.

Gambia Ports Authority: Wellington St, POB 617, Banjul; tel 27266; telex 2235; fax 27268; Man Dir: Momodou Gaye; administers Banjul port.

Gambia Public Transport Corpn: POB 801, Banjul; tel 932501; telex 2243; fax 92454; Chair: Alhaji A. J. Senghore; Man Dir: Ismailla Ceesay; f 1979; runs fleet of 50 buses.

THE GERMAN DEMOCRATIC REPUBLIC

Head of State

The Council of State is elected by, and is the permanent organ of the Volkskammer (People's Chamber). It functions collectively, and its Chairman is effectively Head of State.

Chairman of the Council of State (acting): Dr Manfred Gerlach

Legislature

The supreme organ of state power is the unicameral Volkskammer (People's Chamber), comprising 500 members directly elected for five years by universal adult suffrage, however in 1990, membership was to be reduced to 400. The Volkskammer appoints a Chairman (Minister-President), who appoints Ministers.

Volkskammer (People's Chamber): Marx-Engels-Platz, 1020 Berlin; tel (2) 238; telex 1152406; Pres: Dr Günther Maleuda; Vice-Pres: Werner Jarowinsky.

MINISTRIES AND GOVERNMENT DEPARTMENTS

COUNCIL OF MINISTERS
Klosterstr 47, 1020 Berlin
Tel (2) 223; telex 1152337
Chair (Minister-President): Hans Modrow
Deputy Chair and Minister of the Economy:
Dr Christa Luft
Deputy Chair and Minister for Local State Bodies:
Dr Peter Moreth
Deputy Chair and Minister for Church Questions:
Lothar de Maizière
Chair of the Economic Committee:
Dr Karl Grünheid
Head of the Press Office and Government Spokesperson:
Wolfgang Meyer
Ministers without Portfolio: Tatiana Boehm, Reiner Eppelmann, Sebastian Pflugbeil, Matías Platzeck, Gerd Poppe, Walter Romberg, Klaus Schlüter, Wolfgang Ullmann

MINISTRY OF AGRICULTURE, FORESTRY AND FOODSTUFFS
Köpenicker Allee 39-57, 1157 Berlin
Tel (2) 25007; telex 112584
Minister: Dr Hans Watzeck

MINISTRY OF CONSTRUCTION AND THE HOUSING ECONOMY
Scharrenstr 2-3, 102 Berlin
Tel (2) 223; telex 61523
Minister: Dr Gerhard Baumgärtel
Minister of Housing: Uta Nickel

MINISTRY OF CULTURE
Molkenmarkt 1-3, 1020 Berlin
Tel (2) 230; telex 115230
Minister: Dr Dietmar Keller

MINISTRY OF EDUCATION AND YOUTH
Unter den Linden 69-73, 1086 Berlin
Tel (2) 232; telex 1152345
Minister: Dr Hans-Heinz Emons

MINISTRY OF ENVIRONMENTAL PROTECTION AND WATER ECONOMY
Schiffbauerdamm 15, 1040 Berlin
Tel (2) 230; telex 1152347
Minister: Dr Peter Diederich

MINISTRY OF FINANCE AND PRICES
Leipziger Str 5-7, 1086 Berlin
Tel (2) 232; telex 1152331
Minister: (vacant)

MINISTRY OF FOREIGN AFFAIRS
Marx-Engels-Platz 2, 1020 Berlin
Tel (2) 220; telex 114621
Minister: Oskar Fischer

MINISTRY OF FOREIGN TRADE
Unter den Linden 44-60, 1080 Berlin
Tel (2) 2330; telex 1152361
Minister: Dr Gerhard Beil

MINISTRY OF HEALTH AND SOCIAL SERVICES
Rathausstr 3, 1020 Berlin
Tel (2) 234
Minister: Dr Klaus Thielmann

MINISTRY OF HEAVY INDUSTRY
Berlin
Minister: Dr Kurt Singhuber

MINISTRY OF INTERNAL AFFAIRS
Mauerstr 29-32, 1086 Berlin
Tel (2) 222; telex 112255
Minister: Lothar Ahrendt

MINISTRY OF JUSTICE
Clara-Zetkin-Str 93, 108 Berlin
Tel (2) 237; telex 113155
Minister: Kurt Wuensche

MINISTRY OF LABOUR AND WAGES
Berlin
Minister: Hannelore Mensch

MINISTRY OF LIGHT INDUSTRY
Leipziger Str 5-7, 1086 Berlin
Tel (2) 232; telex 1152311
Minister: Dr Günter Halm

MINISTRY OF MECHANICAL ENGINEERING
Berlin
Minister: Dr Hans-Joachim Lauck

MINISTRY OF NATIONAL DEFENCE
Schnellerstr 1-4, 1190 Berlin
Tel (2) 6352881; telex 112582
Minister: Adm Theodor Hoffmann

MINISTRY OF POSTS AND TELECOMMUNICATIONS
Mauerstr 69-75, 1066 Berlin
Tel (2) 2312101; telex 112558
Minister: Dr Klaus Wolf

MINISTRY OF SCIENCE AND TECHNOLOGY
Köpenicker Str 325A, 1170 Berlin
Tel (2) 65760; telex 113070
Minister: Dr Peter-Klaus Budig

MINISTRY OF TOURISM
Berlin
Minister: Dr Bruno Benthien

MINISTRY OF TRADE AND SUPPLY
Hans-Beimler-Str 70-72, 1026 Berlin
Tel (2) 235; telex 1152421
Minister: Manfred Flegel

MINISTRY OF TRANSPORT
Voßstr 33, 1086 Berlin
Tel (2) 490; telex 112250
Minister: Heinrich Scholz

GOVERNMENT AGENCIES AND ORGANIZATIONS

Business and Economy

BANKING

Bank für Landwirtschaft und Nahrungsgüterwirtschaft der DDR: Clara-Zetkin-Str 37, 108 Berlin; Pres: Günther Schmidt; Vice-Pres: Hans Wolff; f 1951; credits for agricultural and co-operative organizations.

Deutsche Außenhandelsbank AG: Unter den Linden 24-30, 1080 Berlin; tel (2) 22870; telex 114411; Pres: Dr Werner Polze; Vice-Pres: Dr Friedmar John; f 1966; carries out business connected with export, import and transit trade.

Deutsche Handelsbank AG: Behrenstr 22, 1080 Berlin; tel (2) 2202911; telex 114665; Gen Man: Feodor Ziesche; Dep Gen Mans: Heinrich Gramer, Ingeborg Klein; f 1956; conducts business with regard to import, export and transit trade.

Staatsbank der Deutschen Demokratischen Republik (State Bank of the GDR): Charlottenstr 33-33A, 1086 Berlin; tel (2) 23230; telex 114671; Pres: Horst Kaminsky; Vice-Pres: Hans Taut; f 1948; central bank and bank of issue; it was announced in March 1990 that a new banking group organized as a joint stock co, Deutsche Kreditbank AG, was to be launched in April 1990 and would take over the branch network of the Staatsbank; it was expected to open an additional 200 offices nationwide.

INSURANCE

Auslands- und Rückversicherungs-AG der DDR (DARAG): Inselstr 1B, 1020 Berlin; tel (2) 2700522; telex 114402; fax (2) 2791890; Chair: Günter Hein; Gen Man: L. Thomas; f 1957; marine and general insurances of all kinds, re-insurance, non-payment insurance.

Staatliche Versicherung der DDR: Breite Str 30-31, 1026 Berlin; tel (2) 21620; telex 115043; Gen Man: Günter Hein; f 1952; state organization for property, liability and personal insurance.

NATIONALIZED INDUSTRY

VEB Kombinat Luft- und Kältetechnik: 8080 Dresden; telex 2414; aero-technical plant and equipment.

VEB Kombinat NAGEMA: Breitscheidstr 46-56, 8045 Dresden; tel (51) 22520; telex 2443; Gen Man: R. Grupe; Dir, Sales: R. Balzk; construction, production and distribution of machines and equipment for the food processing industry.

VEB Leuna-Werke 'Walter Ulbricht': 4220 Leuna; telex 4221; chemicals.

VEB Robotron-Messelektronik 'Otto Schön' Dresden: Postfach 211, 8010 Dresden; tel (51) 4870; telex 26068; Dir: Dr A. Jugel.

VEB Schwermaschinenbau-Kombinat 'Ernst Thälmann' Magdeburg (SKET): 3011 Magdeburg; telex 8241; rolling mills, cement, wire and cables, vegetable oil, minerals.

VEB Werkzeugmaschinenkombinat 'Fritz Heckert': Jagdschänkenstr 17, 9030 Karl-Marx-Stadt; tel (71) 8090; telex 07393; machine tools, machining systems, lubricators, fixtures, castings, industrial plants.

TRADE

Baukema Export-Import: Mohrenstr 53-54, 1080 Berlin; tel (2) 2240; telex 112248; fax (2) 2296721; export and import of building machines, cranes, machinery and equipment for the production of building material machines, foundry plant.

Berliner Import-Export-Gesellschaft mbH: Bruno-Taut-Str 8, 1185 Berlin; tel (2) 68120; telex 113284; consumer goods, metal processing industry and building industry products.

Chemieanlagen Export-Import: Storkower Str 120, 1055 Berlin; tel (2) 43520; telex 112916; export of plant and machinery for the chemical industry, equipment for special fields of foodstuffs sector.

Chemie-Export-Import: Storkower Str 133, 1055 Berlin; tel (2) 43220; telex 112171; chemicals, household chemicals and plastics, photographic materials, tyres, etc.

Elektronik Export-Import: Alexanderplatz 6, 1026 Berlin;

tel (2) 2180; telex 114721; time-measuring and meteorological instruments, electronic components, freeze drying.

Elektrotechnik Export-Import: Alexanderplatz 6, 1026 Berlin; tel (2) 2180; telex 115061; fax (2) 2183300; Dir: Manfred Sörgel; electrical installations for industry, radio, railways.

Fischimpex Rostock: Postfach 42, 2510 Rostock 5; tel (81) 8100; telex 31309; export and import of fish and fish products; commercial relations in all fields of the fishing industry, fishing operations, scientific-technical services, licences.

Fortschritt Landmaschinen Export-Import: Bruno-Taut-Str 4, 1185 Berlin; tel (2) 68220; telex 112522; agricultural machinery; machines for the foodstuffs industry.

Fruchtimex: Schicklerstr 7, 1020 Berlin; tel (2) 21480; telex 114684; fresh fruit and vegetables, raw products for children's food.

Genußmittel Import-Export: Mohrenstr 1, 1086 Berlin; tel (2) 22150; telex 112353; fax (2) 2215399; export and import of foodstuffs, spices, brewing malt, wines and spirits; import of coffee, cocoa, tea, tobacco.

GERMED-Export-Import: Glienicker Weg 125-127, 1199 Berlin; tel (2) 6790; telex 112740; fax (2) 2148308; medicines, drugs, dressing materials, plaster, chemicals.

Glas-Keramik: Kronenstr 19-19A, 1080 Berlin; tel (2) 20570; telex 114661; glass and glass products, porcelain, earthenware.

Heim-Electric Export-Import: Storkower Str 97, 1055 Berlin; tel (2) 432010; telex 114158; fax (2) 43201600; f 1960; export of household electrical appliances, kitchen utensils, equipment for engineering, electronics and electric industry, light fittings, electrical equipment for motor vehicles and bicycles.

Holz und Papier Export-Import: Krausenstr 35-36, 1080 Berlin; tel (2) 20375; telex 112235; fax (2) 2004472; exports furniture and upholstery; imports timber, veneers, wicker, cellulose, paper.

Industrieanlagen-Import: Mauerstr 83-84, 1086 Berlin; tel (2) 22890; telex 112214; imports complete plant and processes for chemical industry, metallurgy, power generation, glassware, ceramics, building materials, process instrumentation, control engineering, electronics and telecommunication engineering, automotive industry.

International Leipzig Trade Fair: Leipziger Messeamt, Markt 11-15, Postfach 720, 7010 Leipzig; tel (41) 71810; telex 512294; fax (41) 7181575; Dir-Gen: Siegfried Fischer; holds capital and consumer goods fairs twice a year.

Internationales Handelszentrum (International Trade Centre): Friedrichstr, 1086 Berlin; tel (2) 20960; telex 114381; opened 1978; offices of foreign enterprises accredited in the GDR; seat of the GDR Association of Foreign Trade Agencies and Brokers and its member organizations; provides rooms and services for conferences, symposia and exhibitions; promotes international trade.

Intrac Handelsgesellschaft mbH: Pestalozzistr 5-8, 1100 Berlin; tel (2) 4840; telex 114923; metals, ores, mineral oil and oil products.

Isocommerz GmbH: Robert-Rößler-Str 10, 1115 Berlin; tel (2) 3400111; telex 113148; fax (2) 2821924; Dir: Dr G. Ewald; f 1964; export of radioactive and stable isotopes, phosphors, special inorganic chemicals.

Kali-Bergbau: Otto-Nuschke-Str 55, 1080 Berlin; tel (2) 20450; telex 114471; exports fertilizers, agricultural chemicals and mineral salts; imports barytes, etc.

Kammer für Außenhandel der DDR (Chamber of Foreign Trade of the GDR): Schönholzer Str 10-11, 1100 Berlin; tel (2) 48220; telex 114840; fax (2) 4828408; Pres: Hans-Joachim Semnitzer; f 1952; promotes trade; provides information and advisory services; participates in the work of international organizations; mems are the foreign trade corpns, major industrial enterprises and transport, banking and insurance institutions.

Kohle-Energie Export-Import: Johannes-Dieckmann-Str 26, 1080 Berlin; tel (2) 20450; telex 114470; export and import of coal, natural gas, lignite and mixed fuels, electric energy.

Kombinat VEB Carl Zeiss JENA: Carl-Zeiss-Str 1, 6900 Jena; tel (78) 830; telex 587442; Dir: Dr Wolfgang Biermann; f 1846; exports instruments and instrument systems for industrial research, particularly in optics.

Limex-Bau-Export-Import: Neue Jakobstr 5-7, 1020 Berlin; tel (2) 2737; telex 114968; metal and concrete constructions and building material; responsible for scientific-technological co-operation with socialist and developing countries on the basis of state orders.

Metallurgiehandel: Brunnenstr 188-190, 1054 Berlin; tel (2) 28920; telex 115123; steel and other metals.

MLW Intermed-Export-Import: Schicklerstr 5-7, Postfach 17, 1020 Berlin; tel (2) 21480; telex 114571; medical equipment and supplies, technical education equipment, equipment for industrial and agricultural research.

Nahrung Export-Import: Schicklerstr 5-7, 1020 Berlin; tel (2) 21480; telex 114892; fax (2) 2126925; seeds, sugar, starch, dairy products, meat, fish, live animals.

Polygraph Export-Import: Friedrichstr 61, 1080 Berlin; tel (2) 2000601; telex 112310; fax (2) 2071900; Dir-Gen: T. Schneider; f 1981.

Robotron Export-Import: Friedrichstr 61, 1080 Berlin; tel (2) 5400130; telex 112311; Man Dir: Friedrich Wokurka; export of data-processing systems.

Schienenfahrzeuge Export-Import: Ötztalerstr 5, 1100 Berlin; tel (2) 48040; telex 114322; fax (2) 4728132; passenger coaches, compartment wagons, sleeping-cars, restaurant cars, luggage vans, long distance carriages, etc.

Schiffscommerz: Doberaner Str 44-47, 2500 Rostock; tel (81) 3670; telex 031355; fax (81) 23129; Dir: Dr Claus-D. Junge; f 1968; import and export of ships and shipbuilding services.

SKET Export-Import: Johannes-Dieckmann-Str 7-9, 1086 Berlin; tel (2) 2240; telex 112693; cement plants and equipment, plants for the production of cables and wire ropes.

Spielwaren und Sportartikel Export-Import: Charlottenstr 46, 1080 Berlin; tel (2) 22830; telex 112797; fax (2) 2291331; export and import of boats, camping, sports and fishing equipment, arts and craft products, toys and prams.

TAKRAF Export-Import: Mohrenstr 53-54, 1080 Berlin; tel (2) 2240; telex 112347; cranes, open-cast mining equipment, small lifting appliances.

Technocommerz: Johannes-Dieckmann-Str 11-13, 1086 Berlin; tel (2) 2240; telex 114977; technical equipment including air-conditioning and refrigeration plants, pumps, compressors, diesel engines and diesel-driven generating sets, ventilation, hydraulic sets and equipment, gearings, couplings, fittings and valves for all branches of industry.

Textil Commerz: Unter den Linden 62-68, Postfach 1206, 1080 Berlin; tel (2) 22610; telex 112816; fabrics, clothing, household linen, carpets, upholstery, haberdashery.

TEXTIMA-Export-Import: Johannes-Dieckmann-Str 11-13, 1086 Berlin; tel (2) 2240; telex 114118; machinery and plants for the textile industry.

Transportmaschinen Export-Import: Johannes-Dieckmann-Str 11-13, 1086 Berlin; tel (2) 2240; telex 114494; lorries, cars, motor-cycles, scooters, spare parts, components and accessories.

Union Haushaltgeräte Export-Import: Wilhelm-Külz-Str 46, Postfach 1203, 1080 Berlin; tel (2) 2200101; telex 115193; f 1965; tools, metalware, household appliances.

Verpackung und Bürobedarf Export-Import: Nikolaistr 15-25, Postfach 806, 7010 Leipzig; tel (41) 7974369; telex 512594; fax (41) 281403; Dir-Gen: Dieter Dölding; f 1982; export and import of packing materials, cardboard, paper, foil, wallpapers, labels, stationery, school and office supplies.

WUNEX Wälzlager und Normteile Export-Import: Reichenhainer Str 31-33, Postfach 1045, 9010 Karl-Marx-Stadt; tel (71) 57060; telex 07279; export and import of roller bearings, fasteners and wire products.

Zellstoff und Papier Export-Import: Mauerstr 77, 1080 Berlin; tel (2) 20750; telex 114523; fax (2) 2292401; paper, carton, cellulose.

Zentral-Kommerz GmbH: Pestalozzistr 5-8, 1100 Berlin; tel (2) 4840; telex 114981; agricultural products, foodstuffs, secondary raw materials.

Defence

Armed Forces: c/o Ministry of National Defence, Schnellerstr 1-4, 1190 Berlin; tel (2) 6352881; telex 112582.

Air Force and Air Defence Command: c/o Ministry of National Defence, Schnellerstr 1-4, 1190 Berlin; tel (2) 6352881; telex 112582.

Army: c/o Ministry of National Defence, Schnellerstr 1-4, 1190 Berlin; tel (2) 6352881; telex 112582; Chief of Staff: Manfred Gratz.

Navy: c/o Ministry of National Defence, Schnellerstr 1-4, 1190 Berlin; tel (2) 6352881; telex 112582.

Office of National Security: Normannenstr 22, 113 Berlin; tel (2) 5509991; telex 112726; Dir: Wolfgang Schwanitz; dissolution announced in December 1989.

Energy

Arbeitsstelle für Molekularelektronik (Institute for Molecular Electronics): Königsbrücker Landstr 159, 808 Dresden; Dir: Dr Werner Hartmann; f 1961.

Staatliches Amt für Atomsicherheit und Strahlenschutz der DDR (Board of Nuclear Safety and Radiation Protection of the GDR): Waldowallee 117, 1157 Berlin-Karlshorst; tel (2) 5020; telex 112632; Pres: Dr Georg Sitzlack; f 1962; theoretical problems of radiation protection and nuclear safety; medical, biological and technical research; legislation and licensing; radiation protection monitoring in working areas and medical supervision; environmental protection including radioactive waste processing and disposal; nuclear safeguards; training courses for health physicists and physicians.

VEB Kernkraftwerk (VEB Atomic Power Station): Rheinsberg/Mark; telex 318322; Dir: Prof Karl Ramsbusch; f 1961.

Technical Centre: Görschstr 45-46, Berlin-Pankow; Dir: Gerhard Teichler.

Legal and Judiciary

Generalstaatsanwalt der DDR (Prosecutor-General of the GDR): Hermann-Matern-Str 33-34, 1040 Berlin; Prosecutor-Gen: Hans-Jürgen Joseph.

Oberstes Gericht der DDR (Supreme Court of the GDR): Littenstr 13, 1026 Berlin; tel (2) 2334757; telex 1152352; Pres: (vacant).

Media

BROADCASTING

Berliner Rundfunk: Nalepastr 18-50, 1160 Berlin; tel (2) 6360; telex 112276; Dir: Hannes Potthast; radio broadcasting.

Radio Berlin International: Nalepastr 18-50, 1160 Berlin; tel (2) 6360; telex 112276; Dir: Klaus Fischer; f 1959; external broadcasts in 11 languages.

Radio DDR: Nalepastr 18-50, 1160 Berlin; tel (2) 6360; telex 112276; Dir: Rolf Schmidt; radio broadcasting.

Radio Volga: Menzelstr 5, 15 Potsdam; broadcasts to Soviet forces in the GDR.

Staatliches Komitee für Fernsehen (State Committee for Television Broadcasting): Rudower Chaussee 3, 1199 Berlin-Adlershof; tel (2) 6310; telex 112885; Dir-Gen: Hans Bentzin; supervisory authority; supervises:

Fernsehen der DDR: Rudower Chaussee 3, 1199 Berlin-Adlershof; tel (2) 6310; telex 112885; Programme Dir: Horst Sauer; Technical Dir: Rolf Kramer; Dir of International Relations: Dr Kurt Ottersberg; TV broadcasting.

Staatliches Komitee für Rundfunk beim Ministerrat der DDR (State Committee for Radio Broadcasting): Nalepastr 18-50, 1160 Berlin; tel (2) 6360; telex 112276; Dir-Gen: Manfred Klein; co-ordinating body of all radio organizations in the GDR.

Stimme der DDR: Nalepastr 18-50, 1160 Berlin; tel (2) 6360; telex 112276; Dir: Martin Radmann; radio broadcasting.

GOVERNMENT PUBLISHER

Staatsverlag der DDR: Otto-Grotewohl-Str 17, 1086 Berlin; tel (2) 2230; telex 1152344; Dir: Reiner Tietz; f 1963; publishes official documents of central state organs.

NEWS AND INFORMATION

Allgemeiner Deutscher Nachrichtendienst (ADN): Mollstr 1, 1026 Berlin; tel (2) 230; telex 1146010; fax (2) 2354474; Dir-Gen: Günter Pötschke; f 1946; official news agency of the GDR; offices and additional correspondents abroad; maintains a press photo dept, 'Zentralbild'; provides daily news service in German and radio teletype casts in various languages.

Panorama DDR, Auslandspresseagentur GmbH: Wilhelm-Pieck-Str 49, 1054 Berlin; tel (2) 230; telex 114872.

Staatliche Zentralverwaltung für Statistik (Central State Statistical Office): Hans-Beimler-Str 70-72, 1026 Berlin; tel (2) 2350; telex 114876; Dir: Dr Arno Donda; f 1946.

Research

Institut für Hochenergiephysik der Akademie der Wissenschaften der DDR (Research Institute of High Energy Physics of the GDR Academy of Sciences): Platanenallee 6, 1615 Zeuthen; tel (2) 6858001; telex 158770; Dir: Dr K. Lanius; f 1962; experimental and theoretical high energy and elementary particle physics.

Zentralinstitut für Festkörperphysik und Werkstofforschung der Akademie der Wissenschaften der DDR (Central Institute for Solid State Physics and Materials Research of the Academy of Sciences): Helmholtzstr 20, 8027 Dresden; tel (51) 46590; telex 2131; Dir: Dr Johannes Barthel; f 1969; fundamental and applied research in solid state physics and materials science.

Zentralinstitut für Isotopen- und Strahlenforschung der Akademie der Wissenschaften (Central Institute of Isotope and Radiation Research of the Academy of Sciences): Permoserstr 15, 7050 Leipzig; tel (41) 2392308; telex 512492; Dir: Dr Klaus Wetzel; f 1969.

Zentralinstitut für Kernforschung der Akademie der Wissenschaften (Central Institute for Nuclear Research of the

Academy of Sciences): Postfach 19, 8051 Dresden; tel (51) 5910; telex 2167; Dir: Dr Günter Flach; f 1956.

Tourism

Reisebüro der DDR: Alexanderplatz 5, 1026 Berlin; tel (2) 2150; telex 114652; Dir-Gen: Horst Dannat; f 1958; 120 brs in different towns.

Transport

CIVIL AVIATION

Interflug, Gesellschaft für internationalen Flugverkehr mbH: 1189 Berlin-Schönefeld; tel (2) 6720; telex 112891; fax (2) 6788390; Pres: Dr Klaus Henkes; f 1955; flights throughout Europe and to the Middle, Near and Far East, Africa and Central America; 74% Govt-owned, 26% owned by Deutsche Lufthansa AG (Federal Republic of Germany).

INLAND WATERWAYS

Hauptabteilung Binnenschiffahrt und Wasserstraßen (Dept of Inland Shipping and Waterways): Voßstr 33, 1086 Berlin; tel (2) 490; telex 112250; Dir: Ulrich Tolkmitt; responsible for inland navigation in the DDR.

VE Kombinat Binnenschiffahrt und Wasserstraßen: Alt Stralau 55-58, 1017 Berlin; tel (2) 55230; telex 112703; Dir-Gen: Dr Wolfgang Hettler; affiliated companies:

    Binnenhäfen Berlin: Stralauer Allee 1-16, 1017 Berlin; tel (2) 5800491; telex 112233.

    VEB Binnenhäfen 'Mittelelbe': Wittenberger Str 17, 3010 Magdeburg.

    VEB Binnenhäfen 'Oberelbe': Magdeburger Str 58, 8012 Dresden.

    VEB Binnenhäfen 'Oder': Glashüttenstr, 1220 Eisenhüttenstadt; telex 168444.

    VEB Binnenreederei: Alt Stralau 55-58, 1017 Berlin; tel (2) 55230; telex 112703; inland shipping company.

    VEB Forschungsanstalt für Schiffahrt, Wasser- und Grundbau: Alt Stralau 44, 1017 Berlin; tel (2) 55230; telex 112703; f 1982.

    VEB Schiffsreparaturwerften: Alt Stralau 55-58, 1017 Berlin; shipyards.

    VEB Wasserstraßenbau: Goethestr 16, 1160 Berlin; tel (2) 6352316.

    VEB Wasserstraßenbetrieb und -unterhaltung Eberswalde: Hans-Beimler-Str 1, 1300 Eberswalde/Finow.

    VEB Wasserstraßenbetrieb und -unterhaltung Magdeburg: Wallstr 19-20, 3010 Magdeburg.

Wasserstraßenaufsichtsamt der DDR (Supervisory Board of Inland Navigation and Waterways): Poststr 21-22, 1020 Berlin; telex 114967; Dir: Adolf Meier.

RAILWAYS

Deutsche Reichsbahn: Voßstr 33, 1086 Berlin; tel (2) 490; telex 112250; Dir-Gen: Minister of Transport, Heinrich Scholz; under control of the Ministry of Transport.

ROADS

Hauptverwaltung des Kraftverkehrs (Dept of Public Passenger and Goods Road Transport): Voßstr 33, 1086 Berlin.

Hauptverwaltung Straßenwesen (Dept of Public Roads and Motorways): Voßstr 33, 1086 Berlin.

SHIPPING

DDR-Schiffs-Revision und -Klassifikation (DSRK): Eichenallee 12, 1615 Zeuthen; tel (32982) 2633; telex 158721; Man Dir: Dr Günter Bossow; f 1950; registration, supervision and classification of sea-going ships and inland waterway vessels.

Hauptverwaltung des Seeverkehrs (Dept of Merchant Fleet and Sea-Ports): Voßstr 33, 1086 Berlin.

Seefahrtsamt der DDR (Board of Navigation and Maritime Affairs of the GDR): Patriotischer Weg 120, 2500 Rostock; tel (81) 3832360; telex 31134; fax (81) 3832369; Dir: Capt Gerd Haussmann; f 1953; certification and registration of seafarers; traffic control; supervision of pilotage; combatting water pollution, etc.

Seekammer der DDR (Naval Court of the GDR): Patriotischer Weg 120, 2500 Rostock; tel (81) 3832363; telex 31134; fax (81) 3832369; Chair: Capt Dieter Rapphahn.

Tallierungs-GmbH—Ladungskontrollunternehmen der DDR: 2500 Rostock-Überseehafen; Dir: Margot Reckling; tallying, checking, weighing, surveying, draught measurement, inspection and expertise.

VE Kombinat Deutrans: Leninallee 392, Postfach 407, 1140 Berlin; tel (2) 546020; telex 114631; Dir-Gen: Rainer Schwabe; international forwarding enterprise.

VE Kombinat Seeverkehr und Hafenwirtschaft—Deutfracht/Seereederei: 2540 Rostock-Überseehafen; tel (81) 3660; telex 31381; fax (81) 3666108; Dir-Gen: Artur Maul; f 1952; passenger and cargo shipping and harbour enterprises.

VEB Bagger-, Bugsier- und Bergungsreederei: An der See 14, 2530 Rostock; tel (81) 8152727; telex 31441318; Dir: Wolfgang Soyk; dredging, towage and salvage.

VEB Deutfracht/Seereederei: Postfach 188, 2500 Rostock-Überseehafen; telex 31139; Dir-Gen: Artur Maul; runs bulk carriers, liner ships, cargo trailer ships, refrigeration ships and tankers.

VEB Schiffsmaklerei: Strandstr 25, 2500 Rostock; tel (81) 383365; telex 31265; fax (81) 3666734; Dir: Eduard Zimmermann; f 1958; shipbroker and liner agents.

VEB Schiffsversorgung Rostock: 2540 Rostock-Überseehafen; tel (81) 3667000; telex 31114; fax (81) 3666797; Dir: Gerhard Beckmann; f 1959; gen ship supplies, provisions, technical equipment, nautical charts and handbooks, duty-free goods.

VEB Seehafen Rostock: 2540 Rostock-Überseehafen; tel (81) 31130; telex 31264; fax (81) 21932; Port Dir: Dieter Noll; f 1960; overseas port; handling of all kinds of general cargo, dry bulk goods and liquid bulk cargo.

VEB Seehafen Stralsund: Hafenstr 15, 2300 Stralsund; tel (821) 692360; telex 317350; Dir: Heinz Happ; seaport.

VEB Seehafen Wismar: 2400 Wismar; telex 318882; Dir: Klaus Boddin; seaport.

THE FEDERAL REPUBLIC OF GERMANY AND WEST BERLIN

Head of State

The Federal President, although Head of State, has few constitutional powers. The President is elected by a Federal Convention (Bundesversammlung) for a five-year term; immediate re-election is admissible only once. The President proposes a Federal Chancellor, who is elected by an absolute majority in the Bundestag, to determine the guidelines of policy. Other ministers are appointed by the President on the advice of the Chancellor.

Federal President: Dr Richard von Weizsäcker (took office 1 July 1984; re-elected 23 May 1989).

Office of the Federal President: Kaiser-Friedrich-Str 16, 5300 Bonn 1; tel (228) 2001; telex 886393.

Legislature

Legislative power is vested in the Bundestag (Federal Assembly) and the Bundesrat (Federal Council). The Bundestag, which is the main legislative body, comprises 519 deputies (including 497 elected for four years using a mixed system of proportional representation and direct constituency voting, and 22 members from West Berlin). The Bundesrat has 41 members representing the regional assemblies, plus four deputies from West Berlin. Each of the 10 Länder (federal states), plus West Berlin, has its own constitution, parliament and government.

Bundesrat: Bundeshaus-Nordflügel, Görrestr 15, 5300 Bonn 1; tel (228) 16-1; telex 886841; fax (228) 16-7775; Pres: Björn Engholm.

Bundestag: Bundeshaus, Görrestr 15, 5300 Bonn 1; tel (228) 16-1; telex 886808; fax (228) 16-7775; Speaker: Prof Dr Rita Süssmuth; Sec-Gen: Dr Joseph Bücker.

MINISTRIES AND GOVERNMENT DEPARTMENTS

OFFICE OF THE FEDERAL CHANCELLOR
Adenauerallee 141, 5300 Bonn 1
Tel (228) 561; telex 886750
Chancellor: Dr Helmut Kohl
Vice-Chancellor: Hans-Dietrich Genscher
Minister for Special Tasks and Head of the Federal Chancellery: Rudolf Seiters

MINISTRY OF DEFENCE
Hardthöhe, Postfach 1328, 5300 Bonn 1
Tel (228) 121; telex 886575
Minister: Dr Gerhard Stoltenberg

MINISTRY OF ECONOMIC CO-OPERATION
Karl-Marx-Str 4-6, 5300 Bonn 1
Tel (228) 5351; telex 8869452
Minister: Dr Jürgen Warnke

MINISTRY OF ECONOMICS
Villemombler Str 76, 5300 Bonn 1
Tel (228) 615-1; telex 886747
Minister: Helmut Haussmann
Secretary of State: Otto Schlecht

MINISTRY OF EDUCATION AND SCIENCE
Heinemannstr 2, 5300 Bonn 2
Tel (228) 57-1; telex 228332; fax (228) 572096
Minister: Jürgen W. Möllemann

MINISTRY OF THE ENVIRONMENT, CONSERVATION AND REACTOR SAFETY
Kennedyallee 5, 5300 Bonn 2
Tel (228) 305-0; telex 885790; fax (228) 305-3225
Minister: Dr Klaus Töpfer
Secretary of State: Clemens Stroetmann

MINISTRY OF FINANCE
Graurheindorfer Str 108, 5300 Bonn 1
Tel (228) 682-0; telex 886645
Minister: Dr Theo Waigel

MINISTRY OF FOOD, AGRICULTURE AND FORESTRY
Rochusstr 1, Postfach 140270, 5300 Bonn 1
Tel (228) 529-1; telex 886844; fax (228) 529-4262
Minister: Ignaz Kiechle

MINISTRY OF FOREIGN AFFAIRS
Adenauerallee 99-103, 5300 Bonn 1
Tel (228) 170; telex 886591
Minister: Hans-Dietrich Genscher
Secretary of State: Helmut Schaefer

MINISTRY OF THE INTERIOR
Graurheindorfer Str 198, 5300 Bonn 1
Tel (228) 681-1; telex 886896; fax (228) 681-4665
Minister: Dr Wolfgang Schäuble

Bundesamt für Verfassungsschutz (Federal Office for the Protection of the Constitution): Barthelstr 75, 5000 Cologne 30; tel (221) 4713; Pres: Gerhard Boeden; Vice-Pres: Dr Peter Frisch; aims to protect the fundamental principles of the federal form of govt; gathers information on extremist movements; also responsible for counter-espionage.

Bundesverwaltungsamt (Federal Office of Administration): Barbarastr 1, 5000 Cologne 60; tel (221) 7780-0; telex 8884880; fax (221) 77801291; Pres: Dr Bert Even; Vice-Pres: Dr Ernst Liesner; f 1960; central administrative authority of the Federal Govt; functions include training for the civil service, promotion of sports and cultural activities, citizenship law and refugee affairs.

MINISTRY FOR INTRA-GERMAN RELATIONS
Godesberger Allee 140, 5300 Bonn 2
Tel (228) 306-0; telex 885673
Minister: Dr Dorothee Wilms

MINISTRY OF JUSTICE
Heinemannstr 6, Postfach 200365, 5300 Bonn 2
Tel (228) 581; telex 8869679; fax (228) 584525
Minister: Hans A. Engelhard
Secretary of State: Dr Klaus Kinkel

MINISTRY OF LABOUR AND SOCIAL AFFAIRS
Rochusstr 1, Postfach 140280, 5300 Bonn 1
Tel (228) 5271; telex 886641
Minister: Dr Norbert Blüm

MINISTRY OF POSTS AND TELECOMMUNICATIONS
Heinrich-von-Stephan-Str 1, 5300 Bonn 2
Tel (228) 140; telex 8861101; fax (228) 148872
Minister: Dr Christian Schwarz-Schilling
Secretaries of State: Dr Winfried Florian, Wilhelm Rawe

MINISTRY OF REGIONAL PLANNING, CONSTRUCTION AND URBAN DEVELOPMENT
Deichmannsaue, 5300 Bonn 2
Tel (228) 3371; telex 885462
Minister: Gerda Hasselfeldt

MINISTRY OF RESEARCH AND TECHNOLOGY
Heinemannstr 2, 5300 Bonn 2
Tel (228) 591; telex 885674; fax (228) 593105
Minister: Dr Heinz Riesenhuber

MINISTRY OF TRANSPORT
Kennedyallee 72, 5300 Bonn 2
Tel (228) 3001; telex 885700; fax (228) 800-3428
Minister: Dr Friedrich Zimmermann

MINISTRY OF YOUTH, FAMILY, WOMEN AND HEALTH AFFAIRS
Kennedyallee 105-107, 5300 Bonn 2
Tel (228) 3080; telex 885517; fax (228) 3082221
Minister: Dr Ursula-Maria Lehr

OFFICE OF THE HEAD OF THE PRESS AND INFORMATION OFFICE OF THE FEDERAL GOVERNMENT
Hardthöhe, Postfach 1328, 5300 Bonn 1
Tel (228) 2080
Minister: Hans Klein

GOVERNMENT AGENCIES AND ORGANIZATIONS

Advisory and Supervisory Bodies

Bundeskartellamt (Federal Cartel Office): Mehringdamm 129, 1000 Berlin 61; tel (30) 6901-1; telex 184321; fax (30) 6901-400; Pres: Dr Wolfgang Kartte; f 1958; federal monopolies commission, under the administrative jurisdiction of the Ministry of Economics; responsible for enforcing cartel law.

Bundesrechnungshof (Federal Audit Office): Berliner Str 51, Postfach 2409, 6000 Frankfurt a/M 1; tel (69) 2176-263; telex 412981; fax (69) 2176-248; Pres: Dr Heinz Günter Zavelberg; f 1950; responsible for auditing federal budget, as well as financial monitoring of federal assets and investments and of various schemes based on public funding.

Agriculture and the Environment

AGRICULTURE

Biologische Bundesanstalt für Land- und Forstwirtschaft (Federal Biological Research Centre for Agriculture and Forestry): Messeweg 11-12, 3300 Brunswick; tel (531) 3991; fax (531) 399239; Pres: Prof F. Klingauf; f 1898; federal agency for research in plant protection, and testing and licensing of pesticides.

Bundesamt für Ernährung und Forstwirtschaft (Federal Office for Food and Forestry): Adickesallee 40, 6000 Frankfurt a/M 1; tel (69) 1564403; telex 411165; fax (69) 1564445; Pres: Dr G Drexelius; f 1965; central executive authority responsible for fields of supply, market organization, subsidies and environmental protection.

Bundesforschungsanstalt für Fischerei (Federal Research Centre for Fisheries): Palmaille 9, 2000 Hamburg 55; tel (40) 389050; telex 215716; fax (40) 38905129; Dir: Prof Klaus Tiews; f 1948; advises the Federal Govt on all aspects of the fishing industry; carries out research in related areas.

Bundesforschungsanstalt für Forst- und Holzwirtschaft (Federal Research Centre for Forestry and Forest Products): Leuschnerstr 91, 2050 Hamburg 80; tel (40) 739621; Dir: Prof H. H. Nimz; f 1931; federal agency for research in the forestry sector.

THE ENVIRONMENT

Umweltbundesamt (Federal Environment Agency): Bismarckplatz 1, 1000 Berlin 33; tel (30) 89030; telex 183756; fax (30) 8903-2285; Pres: Dr Heinrich von Lersner; f 1974; central admin of matters dealing with environmental protection; autonomous federal agency under the jurisdiction of the Ministry of the Environment, Conservation and Reactor Safety.

Business and Economy

BANKING

Bayerische Landesbank Girozentrale: Brienner Str 20, 8000 Munich 2; tel (89) 217101; telex 5286270; fax (89) 21713578; f 1972.

Deutsche Bundesbank: Wilhelm-Epstein-Str 14, 6000 Frankfurt a/M 50; tel (69) 1581; telex 414431; fax (69) 5601071; Pres: Karl Otto Pöhl; Vice-Pres: Dr Helmut Schlesinger; f 1957; central bank and bank of issue; advises the Govt on monetary policy; the following regional central banks are included in the central banking system:

Landeszentralbank in Baden-Württemberg: Marstallstr 3, 7000 Stuttgart 1; tel (711) 20741; telex 723512; fax (711) 296225; Pres: Dr Norbert Kloten.

Landeszentralbank in Bayern: Ludwigstr 13, Postfach 201605, 8000 Munich 22; tel (89) 237001; telex 524365; fax (89) 281598; Pres: Lothar Müller; Vice-Pres: Rudolf Ströhlein; f 1957.

Landeszentralbank in Berlin: Leibnizstr 9-10, 1000 Berlin 12; tel (30) 3404-1; telex 181653; fax (30) 3416093; Pres: Dr Dieter Hiß.

Landeszentralbank in Bremen: Kohlhökerstr 29, 2800 Bremen 1; tel (421) 3291-0; telex 244810; Pres: Dr Kurt Nemitz.

Landeszentralbank in der Freien und Hansestadt Hamburg: Ost-West-Str 73, 2000 Hamburg 11; tel (40) 3707-0; telex 21455450; fax (40) 37072205; Pres: Dr Wilhelm Nölling; Vice-Pres: Hans-Jürgen Siegmund; f 1957.

Landeszentralbank in Hessen: Taunusanlage 5, 6000 Frankfurt a/M 1; tel (69) 2388-0; telex 6997404; Pres: Dr Alfred Härtl.

Landeszentralbank in Niedersachsen: Georgsplatz 5, 3000 Hanover; tel (511) 1233-1; telex 922651; Pres: Dr Helmut Hesse.

Landeszentralbank in Nordrhein-Westfalen: Berliner Allee 14, 4000 Düsseldorf; tel (211) 874-1; telex 8582774; Pres: Hans Wertz.

Landeszentralbank in Rheinland-Pfalz: Kaiserstr 50-52, 6500 Mainz; tel (6131) 602-1; telex 4187541; fax (6131) 602224; Pres: Dr Heinrich Schreiner.

Landeszentralbank im Saarland: Keplerstr 18, 6600 Saarbrücken 1; tel (681) 5802-2; telex 4421258; Pres: Hans Gliem.

Landeszentralbank in Schleswig-Holstein: Fleethörn 26, 2300 Kiel; tel (431) 990-0; telex 299803; fax (431) 990119; Pres: Werner Schulz.

Deutsche Genossenschaftsbank: Am Platz der Republik, Postfach 100651, 6000 Frankfurt a/M 1; tel (69) 744701; telex 412291; fax (69) 74471685; Chair: Helmut Guthardt; f 1949; central bank of co-operative banking system.

Deutsche Girozentrale—Deutsche Kommunalbank: Taunusanlage 10, Postfach 110542, 6000 Frankfurt a/M 1; tel (69) 26930; telex 414168; fax (69) 2693-490; Chair: Ernst-Otto Sandvoß; f 1918.

Hamburgische Landesbank Girozentrale: Gerhart-Hauptmann-Platz 50, Postfach 102820, 2000 Hamburg 1; tel (40) 3333-0; telex 2161792; Chair: Dr H. Fahning; f 1938.

Hessische Landesbank Girozentrale: Junghofstr 18-26, Postfach 110833, 6000 Frankfurt a/M 11; tel (69) 132-01; telex 415291-0; fax (69) 291517; Chief Exec: Dr Herbert Kazmierzak.

Kreditanstalt für Wiederaufbau: Palmengartenstr 5-9, Postfach 111141, 6000 Frankfurt a/M 11; tel (69) 7431-0; telex 4152560; fax (69) 7431-2944; f 1948; promotes the economy by granting investment loans and export credits; gives guarantees and extends loans and grants to developing countries on behalf of the Federal Govt.

Landesbank Rheinland-Pfalz Girozentrale: Große Bleiche 54-56, 6500 Mainz; tel (6131) 130; telex 4187858; fax (6131) 132729; Chair: Dr Paul Wieandt.

Norddeutsche Landesbank Girozentrale: Georgsplatz 1, 3000 Hannover 1; tel (511) 103-0; telex 921620; fax (511) 103-2502; Chair: Dr Bernd Thiemann; f 1970 by merger of several North German banks; 224 brs.

Südwestdeutsche Landesbank: Lautenschlagerstr 2, Postfach 106049, D-7000 Stuttgart 10; tel (711) 127-0; telex 721590; fax (711) 127-3278; Chair: W. Schmidt; Vice-Chair: Dr Karl Heidenreich; f 1988 from the merger of the Landesbank Stuttgart and the Badische Kommunale Landesbank.

Westdeutsche Landesbank Girozentrale: Herzogstr 15, Postfach 1128, 4000 Düsseldorf 1; tel (211) 826-01; telex 8588216; fax (211) 826-6120; Chair: F. Neuber; f 1969.

FINANCIAL AGENCY

Bundesamt für Finanzen (Federal Finance Office): Friedhofstr 1, 5300 Bonn 3; tel (228) 4060; responsible to Ministry of Finance.

INSURANCE

Bundesaufsichtsamt für das Versicherungswesen (Federal Supervisory Office for Insurance Matters): Ludwigkirchplatz 3-4, Postfach 150180, 1000 Berlin 15; tel (30) 88-93-0; telex 308743; fax (30) 88-93-494; Pres: Dr Knut Hohlfeld; monitors business operations of insurance cos; approves insurance terms and conditions.

Bundesversicherungsamt (Federal Insurance Agency): Reichpietschufer 72-76, 1000 Berlin 30; tel (30) 26991; telex 184122; responsible to Ministry of Labour and Social Affairs.

TRADE

Bundesamt für Wirtschaft (Federal Office of Economics): Frankfurterstr 29-31, 6236 Eschborn 1; tel (6196) 404-1; telex 4072-666; fax (6196) 404212; Pres: Dr Hans Rummer; Information Officer: Dr Norbert Goworr; law enforcement office responsible for overseeing foreign trade in goods and services, energy supply matters and economic devt; under the jurisdiction of the Ministry of Economics.

Bundesstelle für Außenhandelsinformation (Foreign Trade Promotion Office): Blaubach 13, Postfach 108007, 5000 Cologne 1; tel (221) 2057-1; telex 8882735; Dir: H. D. Dammann; supplies German industry with information on foreign markets; maintains contacts with similar domestic and foreign authorities; reports to Ministry of Economics.

Deutsches Patentamt (German Patent Office): Zweibrückenstr 12, 8000 Munich 2; tel (89) 2195-1; telex 523534; f 1948; protection of commercial rights, issue of patents, registration of trademarks; under the jurisdiction of the Ministry of Justice.

Defence

Bundesnachrichtendienst (Federal Intelligence Agency): Heilmannstr 30, 8023 Pullach; tel (89) 7931567; telex 5212802; Pres: Dr Hans Georg Wieck; Vice-Pres: Dr Paul Muenstermann; central agency for foreign intelligence; under the jurisdiction of the Federal Chancellery.

Bundeswehr (Armed Forces): c/o Ministry of Defence, Hardthöhe, Postfach 1328, 5301 Bonn; tel (228) 121; telex 886575; Inspector-Gen of the Armed Forces: Adm Dieter Wellershoff; Dep Inspector-Gen: Lt-Gen Siegfried Storbeck; the Bundeswehr is divided into separate army, navy and air force branches, each with its own chief-of-staff; supreme military commander is the Minister of Defence.

Führungsstab der Marine (Naval High Command): c/o Ministry of Defence, Hardthöhe, Postfach 1328, BMVG, 5301 Bonn; tel (228) 12-9978; fax (228) 12-6759; Chief of Staff: Vice-Adm Hans Joachim Mann.

Education and Research

Bundesinstitut für Berufsbildung (Federal Institute for Vocational Training): Fehrbelliner Platz 3, 1000 Berlin 31; tel (30) 8683-1; fax (30) 8683-455; Sec-Gen: Dr Hermann Schmidt; f 1970; concerned mainly with in-company training; carries out research into training and advises the Federal Govt.

Bundeszentrale für politische Bildung (Federal Centre for Political Education): Berliner Freiheit 7, 5300 Bonn 1; tel (228) 515-1; telex 886392; fax (228) 515313; Dirs: Franklin Schultheiß, Horst Dahlaus, M. Aurus; f 1952; federal agency to promote general understanding of constitutional democracy; responsible to Ministry of the Interior.

Wissenschaftsrat (Science Council): Marienburger Str 8, 5000 Cologne 51; tel (221) 3776-1; f 1957; primarily concerned with academic affairs; determines the devt of universities and other institutes of higher education.

Employment

Bundesanstalt für Arbeit (Federal Employment Institute): Regensburger Str 104, 8500 Nuremberg 1; tel (911) 17-1; telex 622348; fax (911) 17-2123; f 1952; responsible for career counselling, vocational training and funding, monitoring of labour market; reports to Ministry of Labour and Social Affairs.

Health and Welfare

Bundesgesundheitsamt (Federal Health Office): Thielallee 88-92, Postfach 330013, 1000 Berlin 33; tel (30) 8308-0; telex 184016; f 1952; carries out research in areas of drug safety, health-related consumer protection, etc; administers legal functions regarding drugs, epidemics, food and the general public health system; advises the Govt on scientific and health matters.

Legal and Judiciary

Bundeskriminalamt (Federal Criminal Police Office): Thaerstr 11, Postfach 1820, 6200 Wiesbaden 1; tel (6121) 55-1; telex 4186867; fax (6121) 55-2141; Pres: Dr Heinrich Boge; Vice-Pres: Hans Ludwig Zachert; f 1951; instrument of co-operation and co-ordination between federal and state law-enforcement agencies; central authority for police intelligence.

Bundesgerichtshof (Federal Supreme Court): Herrenstr 45A, 7500 Karlsruhe 1; tel (721) 159-0; telex 7825828; fax (721) 159-606; Pres: Dr Walter Odersky; Vice-Pres: Hannskarl Salger; highest court with jurisdiction in civil and criminal matters.

Bundesverfassungsgericht (Federal Constitutional Court): Schloßbezirk 3, 7500 Karlsruhe; tel (721) 1491; telex 8869679; Pres: Dr Roman Herzog; Vice-Pres: Dr Ernst Gottfried Mahrenholz; f 1951; supreme body in the judicial branch of the Govt; judges are elected by parliament.

Bundesverwaltungsgericht (Federal Administrative Court): Hardenbergstr 31, 1000 Berlin 12; tel (30) 3197-1; fax (30) 3123021; Pres: Dr Horst Sendler; Vice-Pres: Dr Günter Zehner; f 1953; supreme court for administrative affairs.

Generalbundesanwalt (Office of Public Prosecutions): Herrenstr 45A, Postfach 2720, 7500 Karlsruhe 1; tel (721) 159-600; telex 7825828; fax (721) 159-606; Federal Attorney-Gen: Dr Kurt Rebmann; Spokesman: Alexander Prechtel; f 1950; agency responsible for Govt investigations in criminal matters; takes charge of investigative proceedings, issues indictments, presents state cases in court and monitors sentencing.

Media

BROADCASTING

Arbeitsgemeinschaft der öffentlich-rechtlichen Rundfunkanstalten der Bundesrepublik Deutschland—ARD (Association of Public Law Broadcasting Organizations): Bertramstr 8, Postfach 101001, 6000 Frankfurt a/M 1; tel (69) 590607; telex 411127; fax (69) 155-2075; Chair: Dr Hartwig Kelm; f 1950; co-ordinating body for public radio and TV organizations; represents the following regional bodies:

Bayerischer Rundfunk: Rundfunkplatz 1, 8000 Munich 2; tel (89) 5900-01; telex 521070; Chair: Dr Franz Heubl.

Radio Bremen: Heinrich-Hertz-Str 13, 28 Bremen 33; tel (421) 2460; telex 245181; Dir-Gen: Karl-Heinz Klostermeier.

Hessischer Rundfunk: Bertramstr 8, 6000 Frankfurt a/M 1; tel (69) 1551; telex 411127; fax (69) 1552900; Dir-Gen: Dr Hartwig Kelm.

Norddeutscher Rundfunk: Rothenbaumchaussee 132-134, 2000 Hamburg 13; tel (40) 413-0; telex 2198910; fax (40) 4476; Dir-Gen: Dr Peter Schiwy; Dep Dir-Gen: J. Plog; f 1956.

Saarländischer Rundfunk: Funkhaus Halberg, Postfach 1050, 6600 Saarbrücken; tel (681) 6021; telex 4428977; Chair: Franz Schlehofer.

Sender Freies Berlin: Masurenallee 8-14, 1000 Berlin 19; tel (30) 30310; telex 182813; Chair: Helmut Eichmeyer.

Süddeutscher Rundfunk: Neckarstr 230, Postfach 837, 7000 Stuttgart 1; tel (711) 2881; telex 723456; Chair: Walter Ayaß; f 1924.

Südwestfunk: Hans-Bredow-Str, Postfach 820, 7570 Baden-Baden; tel (7221) 2761; telex 787810; Chair: Dr Robert Maus.

Westdeutscher Rundfunk: Appellhofplatz 1, 5000 Cologne 1; tel (221) 2201; telex 8882575; Chair: Reinhard Grätz.

Deutsche Welle: Raderberggürtel 50, Postfach 100444, 5000 Cologne 51; tel (221) 389-0; telex 888485; fax (221) 389-3000; Dir-Gen: Dieter Weirich; f 1953; federally-owned radio station; daily short-wave service in 34 languages.

Deutschlandfunk: Raderberggürtel 40, 5000 Cologne 51; tel (221) 345-1; telex 8884920; fax (221) 380766; Dir: Edmund Gruber; f 1962; federally-owned radio station, broadcasting a 24-hour service for the Federal Republic and Europe.

RIAS Berlin (Rundfunk im amerikanischen Sector): Kufsteiner Str 69, 1000 Berlin 62; tel (30) 8503-0; telex 183790; fax (30) 8503-390; Dir: Dr H. Drück; f 1946; public radio station for West Berlin.

Zweites Deutsches Fernsehen (ZDF): Postfach 4040, 6500 Mainz 1; tel (6131) 701; telex 4187930; fax (6131) 702157; Dir-Gen: Prof Dieter Stolte; Dir, Programmes: Oswald Ring; Editor-in-Chief: Klaus Bresser; Dir, Admin: Rudi Sölch; Dir, Technical: Dr Albrecht Ziemer; f 1961; second public TV channel, controlled by a combined public corpn of the Länder Govts.

GOVERNMENT PUBLISHER

Bundesdruckerei (Federal Printer): Oranienstr 91, 1000 Berlin 61; tel (30) 25981; telex 183706; federal printing agency; under the jurisdiction of the Ministry of Posts and Telecommunications.

NEWS AND INFORMATION

Bundesarchiv (Federal Archives): Am Wöllershof 12, Postfach 320, 5400 Koblenz; tel (261) 339-1; telex 882619; f 1952; preservation of official records; under the jurisdiction of the Ministry of the Interior.

Presse- und Informationsamt der Bundesregierung (Federal Press and Information Office): Welckerstr 11, 5300 Bonn 1; tel (228) 2081; telex 886741; fax (228) 208505; f 1949; provides information on Parliament and the Govt, carries out public relations for the Govt; includes the Office of the Govt Spokesperson.

Statistisches Bundesamt (Federal Statistical Office): Gustav-Stresemann-Ring 11, Postfach 5528, 6200 Wiesbaden; tel (6121) 75-1; telex 4186511; fax (6121) 753425; Pres: Egon Hölder; Vice-Pres: Dr Bürgin; f 1950; compilation of official data, preparation of statistical reports; under the jurisdiction of the Ministry of the Interior.

Mining and Energy

Badenwerk AG: Postfach 1680, 7500 Karlsruhe 1; tel (721) 6921; telex 7825803; main electricity supply co for Baden-Württemberg; over 75% owned by the regional Govt.

Bayernwerk AG: Blutenbergstr 6, Postfach 200340, 8000 Munich 2; tel (89) 12541; telex 523172; electricity supply co for Bavaria; wholly Govt-owned (60% by regional Govt, 40% by Federal Govt).

Berliner Kraft- und Licht AG (BEWAG): Stauffenbergstr 26, 1000 Berlin 30; tel (30) 267-2413; electricity supply co for West Berlin; 58.3% owned by regional Govt.

Energie-Versorgung Schwaben AG (EVS): Kriegsbergstr 32, 7000 Stuttgart 1; tel (711) 20831; telex 723715; publicly-owned electricity supply co for southern-central area.

Hamburgische Elektrizitäts-Werke AG: Überseering 12, Postfach 600960, 2000 Hamburg 60; tel (40) 6361; electricity supply co for the Hamburg region; 73% owned by the regional Govt.

Preussen-Elektra AG (PREAG): Treschkowstr 5, Postfach 4849, 3000 Hanover 91; tel (511) 439-1; telex 922756; Chair: Rudolf von Bennigsen-Foerder; f 1927; electricity supply co for North-East Germany.

Rheinische-Westfälisches Elektrizitätswerk AG (RWE): Kruppstr 5, Postfach 103165, 4300 Essen; tel (201) 185-1; telex 857851; Chair: Dr F. Wilhelm Christians; f 1898; largest electricity supply co in West Germany; accounts for about 35% of total public electricity supply in the country.

Vereinigte Elektrizitätswerke Westfalen AG (VEW): Rheinlanddamm 24, Postfach 105056, 4600 Dortmund 1; tel (231) 438-1; telex 822121; third largest electricity supply co in the country, serving a substantial area of North-Rhine Westphalia.

Science and Technology

Bundesanstalt für Geowissenschaften und Rohstoffe—BGR (Federal Institute for Geosciences and Natural Resources): Postfach 510153, 3000 Hannover 51; tel (511) 643-0; telex 923730; fax (511) 6432304; Pres: Dr Kürsten.

Bundesanstalt für Materialforschung und-Prüfung—BAM (Federal Institute for Materials Research and Testing): Unter den Eichen 87, 1000 Berlin 45; tel (30) 8104-1; telex 183261; fax (30) 8112-029; Pres: Dr Becker.

Deutscher Wetterdienst (German Weather Service): Frankfurter Str 135, 6050 Offenbach a/M; tel (69) 80620; telex 4152817; fax (69) 8062-339; Pres: Dr Heinz Reiser; Dep Pres: Dr Tillmann Mohr; f 1952; central meteorological service; under the jurisdiction of the Ministry of Transport.

Physikalisch-Technische Bundesanstalt—PTB (Federal Institute of Physics and Metrology): Bundesallee 100, 3300 Braunschweig; tel (531) 592-0; telex 09-52822; fax (531) 592-4006; Pres: Dr Kind.

Tourism

Deutsche Zentrale für Tourismus eV: Beethovenstr 69, 6000 Frankfurt a/M 1; tel (69) 75720; telex 6990833; fax (69) 751903; Dir: Günther Spazier; f 1948; Govt-funded central tourism organization.

Transport and Communications

TELECOMMUNICATIONS

Deutsche Bundespost (German Post Office): Postfach 5000, 6100 Darmstadt; tel (6151) 83-1; telex 419511; Pres: Karl-Otto Pöhl; holds monopoly for all postal and telecommunications services in the Federal Republic; under the administrative responsibility of the Ministry of Posts and Telecommunications.

TRANSPORT

Berliner Verkehrs-Betriebe (Berlin Transport Authority): Potsdamer Str 188, 1000 Berlin 30; tel (30) 2561; telex 183329; fax (30) 2164186; Dir: Helmut Döpfer; f 1929; provides public transport services in West Berlin (bus, underground and metropolitan railway).

Bundesanstalt für Straßenwesen (Federal Agency for Road Transport): Brüderstr 53, Postfach 100150, 5060 Bergisch Gladbach 1; tel (02204) 43-0; fax (02204) 43-833; Pres: Dr H. Praxenthaler; Vice-Pres: Dr K. Krell; f 1951; responsible for road infrastructure; reports to Ministry of Transport.

Deutsche Bundesbahn—DB (German Federal Railways): Friedrich-Ebert-Anlage 43-45, 6000 Frankfurt 1; tel (69) 265-1; telex 414087; fax (69) 265-6480; Pres: Dr Reiner Gohlke; f 1949; provides national railway services.

Deutsche Lufthansa AG (Lufthansa German Airlines): Von-Gablenz-Str 2-6, 5000 Cologne 21; tel (221) 8261; telex 8873531; fax (221) 826-3818; Chair, Exec Board: Heinz Ruhnau; Chair, Supervisory Bd: Gerd Lausen; f 1954; national airline, providing domestic and international passenger and cargo services; 65.38% Govt-owned.

Stadtwerke München: Einsteinstr 28, Postfach 202222, 8000 Munich 80; tel (89) 2191-1; telex 522063; fax (89) 2191-2155; Dir: Dieter Buhmann; provides public transport services in Munich.

Verband öffentlicher Verkehrsbetriebe—VöV (Association of Public Transport Authorities): Kamekestr 37-39, 5000 Cologne 1; tel (221) 525064; telex 8881718; fax (221) 514272; Pres: Dr Hans Sattler; f 1895.

Wasser- und Schiffahrtsdirektion Nord (Shipping and Waterways Directorate): Hindenburgufer 247, Postfach 4467, 2300 Kiel 1; tel (431) 385-1; telex 431780; fax (431) 385-348; Pres: G. W. Keil; Dir: R. Reinhardt; maintenance of waterways; under the jurisdiction of the Ministry of Transport.

GHANA

Head of State and Legislature

Upon its accession to power on 31 December 1981, the Provisional National Defence Council (PNDC) dissolved Parliament, abolished the Council of State and suspended the 1979 Constitution. Executive and legislative powers are vested in the PNDC, which rules by decree. Ghana comprises 10 regions, each administered by a Regional Secretary.

Chairman of the Provisional National Defence Council: Flight Lt Jerry Rawlings; mems of the PNDC: Daniel F. Annan, Ebo Tawiah, Iddrisu Mahama, Capt (retd) Kojo Tsikata, P. V. Obeng, Lt-Gen Arnold Quainoo, Maj-Gen W. M. Mensa-Wood, Dr Mary Grnat, Col Jeff Asmah.

Office of the Chairman of the Provisional National Defence Council: The Castle, Osu, POB 1627, Accra; tel (21) 665415.

MINISTRIES AND GOVERNMENT DEPARTMENTS

COMMITTEE OF SECRETARIES
Accra
Chair: P. V. Obeng

SECRETARIAT FOR AGRICULTURE
POB M37, Accra
Tel (21) 665421
Secretary: Cdre (retd) Steve Obimpeh

SECRETARIAT FOR CHIEFTAINCY AFFAIRS
Accra
Secretary: Emmanuel Tanoh

SECRETARIAT FOR DEFENCE
Burma Camp, Accra
Tel (21) 777611; telex 2077
Secretary: Flight-Lt Jerry Rawlings

SECRETARIAT FOR EDUCATION AND CULTURE
POB M45, Accra
Tel (21) 665421
Secretary: K. B. Asante

SECRETARIAT FOR FINANCE AND ECONOMIC PLANNING
POB M40, Accra
Tel (21) 665421; telex 2132
Secretary: Dr Kwesi Botchwey

SECRETARIAT FOR FOREIGN AFFAIRS
POB M53, Accra
Tel (21) 665421; telex 2001
Secretary: Dr Obed Asamoah

SECRETARIAT FOR FUEL AND POWER
POB T40, Stadium-Accra
Tel (21) 667151; telex 2436; fax (21) 668262
Secretary: Ato Ahwoi
Deputy Secretary: Theresa Owusu

SECRETARIAT FOR HEALTH
POB M44, Accra
Tel (21) 665421
Secretary: Nana Akuodo Sarpong

SECRETARIAT FOR INDUSTRY, SCIENCE AND TECHNOLOGY
POB M39, Accra
Tel (21) 662264
Secretary: Col Richard Coomey

SECRETARIAT FOR INFORMATION
POB 745, Accra
Tel (21) 228011; telex 2201
Secretary: Dr Muhammad ben Abdallah

SECRETARIAT FOR INTERNAL AFFAIRS
POB M42, Accra
Tel (21) 665421
Secretary: Nii Okaijo Adamafio

**SECRETARIAT FOR JUSTICE AND OFFICE OF THE
ATTORNEY-GENERAL**
Accra
Secretary and Attorney-General: G. E. K. Aikins

**SECRETARIAT FOR LANDS AND NATURAL
RESOURCES**
POB M212, Accra
Tel (21) 665421
Secretary: Kwame Peprah

**SECRETARIAT FOR LOCAL GOVERNMENT AND
RURAL DEVELOPMENT**
POB M50, Accra
Tel (21) 665421
Secretary: Kwamena Ahwoi

**SECRETARIAT FOR MOBILIZATION AND
PRODUCTIVITY**
POB M84, Accra
Tel (21) 665421
Secretary: D. S. Boateng

SECRETARIAT FOR ROADS AND HIGHWAYS
POB M43, Accra
Secretary: Lt-Col (retd) Mensah Gbedemah

SECRETARIAT FOR TRADE AND TOURISM
POB M47, Accra
Tel (21) 665421; telex 2105
Secretary: Huudu Yahaya

**SECRETARIAT FOR TRANSPORT AND
COMMUNICATIONS**
POB M38, Accra
Tel (21) 665421
Secretary: J. O. Danso

SECRETARIAT FOR WORKS AND HOUSING
POB M43, Accra
Tel (21) 665421
Secretary: Capt Bota

SECRETARIAT FOR YOUTH AND SPORTS
POB M242, Accra
Tel (21) 665421
Secretary: K. Saarah-Mensah

National Sports Council: POB 1272, Accra; tel (21) 663924; telex 2519; Chief Exec: Maj John Addai; f 1961; organization, promotion and devt of sports.

National Youth Organizing Commission: POB 777, State House, Accra; tel (21) 663286; f 1982; co-ordination of Ghanaian youth organizations.

GOVERNMENT AGENCIES AND ORGANIZATIONS

Advisory and Supervisory Body

State Enterprises Commission: POB M393, Accra; tel 229957; telex 2531; Chair: William Adda; responsible for supervision of state privatization programme.

Agriculture and Fishing

AGRICULTURE

Food Production Corpn: POB 1853, Accra; f 1971; state corpn providing employment for youth in large-scale farming enterprises; operates 87 food farms on a co-operative and self-supporting basis, and rears poultry and livestock.

Ghana Cocoa Board (COCOBOD): POB 933, Accra; telex 2082; Chief Exec: David Aninakwa; f 1985 to replace the Cocoa Marketing Board; responsible for purchase, grading and export of coffee, cocoa and shea nuts, and encourages production and scientific research aimed at improving quality and yield of cocoa, coffee and shea nuts.

  The Cocoa Processing Co (GCMB) Ltd: Effia Junction Industrial Estate, POB 218, Takoradi; Gen Man: I. K. van der Puije; f 1964; operates under the control of the Ghana Cocoa Board; processes high-grade cocoa products for export.

Ghana Cotton Co Ltd: POB 4344, Accra; tel (21) 666042; Man Dir, Accra: Tom O. Ankrah; Gen Man: M. T. Abisa-Seidu; f 1985 to replace the Cotton Development Board; production of lint cotton for sale to textile firms; 70% state-owned.

Ghana Food Distribution Corpn: POB 4245, Accra; tel (21) 228428; Man Dir: Dr P. A. Kuranchie; f 1971; buys, stores, preserves, distributes and sells foodstuffs through 10 regional centres.

Grains and Legumes Development Board: POB 4000, Kumasi; tel (51) 4231; f 1970; devt and promotion of foodgrains industry.

State Farms Corpn: Accra; Man Dir (acting): E. N. A.

Thompson; undertakes agricultural projects in all regions but Upper Region.

FISHING

State Fishing Corpn: POB 211, Tema; tel (221) 4081; telex 2043; Chair: Dr Isaac C. N. Morrison; f 1961; management of long-range fishing fleet; production of fish for home consumption and for export; owns eight deep-sea fishing trawlers; due to be privatized in late 1989.

Business and Economy

BANKING

Agricultural Development Bank: C288/3 Ring Rd Central, POB 4191, Accra; tel (21) 228453; telex 2295; Man Dir: Percival Alfred Kuranchie; f 1965; credit facilities for farmers and commercial banking.

Bank of Ghana: Thorpe Rd, POB 2674, Accra; tel (21) 666902; telex 2052; fax (21) 662996; Chair: Dr Godfried Kportufe Agama; f 1957; central bank.

Bank for Housing and Construction (BHC): 24 Kwame Nkrumah Ave, POB M1, Adabraka, Accra; tel (21) 220033; telex 2096; Chair: Gloria Nikoi; Man Dir: Abu Ahmed; f 1973.

Ghana Commercial Bank: POB 134, Accra; tel (21) 664914; telex 2034; Man Dir: Kwame Nini Owusu; f 1953; 148 brs.

Ghana Co-operative Bank: Kwame Nkrumah Ave, POB 5292, Accra-North; tel (21) 228735; telex 2246; Man Dir: A. K. Appiah; f 1970; 49 brs.

National Investment Bank: 37 Kwame Nkrumah Ave, POB 3726, Accra; tel (21) 221312; telex 2161; Chair: John Kobina Richardson; Man Dir: Yaw Osafo Maofo; f 1963; 75% state-owned; provides long-term investment capital and consultancy, joint venture promotion, consortium finance management and commercial banking services.

National Savings and Credit Bank: Private Mail Bag, Ring Rd Central, Accra; tel (21) 228322; telex 2383; Man Dir: J. A. Nuamah; Dep Man Dir: K. K. Mensah; f 1972; savings mobilization.

National Trust Holding Co: Dyson House, Kwame Nkrumah Ave, POB 9563, Airport, Accra; tel (21) 229664; Chair: Joe Donkor; Man Dir: William Cooke; f 1976 to finance acquisitions of indigenous cos by Ghanaians; also assists in their devt and expansion, and carries out trusteeship business.

Social Security Bank Ltd: POB 13119, Accra; tel (21) 221726; telex 2209; Man Dir: Pryce Kojo Thompson; Exec Dir: Nicholas K. Akpebu; f 1976; commercial and devt banking.

FINANCIAL AGENCIES

Ghanaian Enterprises Development Commission: Accra; f 1975; assists the indigenization of the economy, especially small and medium-scale industrial and commercial enterprises, by providing loans and advisory services.

Internal Revenue Service: Kimbu Rd, POB 2202, Accra; tel (21) 664961; Chair and Commr: Dr J. E. A. Mills; collection of direct taxes.

INSURANCE

The State Insurance Co of Ghana: POB 2363, Accra; tel (21) 666961; telex 2171; f 1962; undertakes all classes of insurance; also engages in real estate and other investment.

MARKETING

Timber Export Development Board: POB 515, Takoradi; tel (31) 2921; telex 2189; Chief Exec Officer: (vacant); f 1985 to replace Ghana Timber Marketing Board; promotes the sale and export of timber.

NATIONALIZED INDUSTRY

Bast Fibres Development Board: POB 1992, Kumasi; f 1970; promotes the commercial cultivation of bast fibres and their processing, handling and grading.

Ghana Industrial Holding Corpn (GIHOC): POB 2784, Accra; tel (21) 664998; telex 2109; Chair: J. E. K. Moses; Man Dir: J. K. Williams; manages 26 state enterprises, including the steel, paper, bricks, paint, pharmaceuticals, electronics, metals, canneries, distilleries and boat-building factories; also has three wholly-owned subsidiaries and four joint ventures; in 1979 it was decided to convert all divisions into wholly-owned limited liability cos.

State Construction Corpn: Ring Rd West, Industrial Area, POB 2582, Accra; tel 224041; telex 2392; Man Dir: J. A. Danso Jr; f 1966; construction plans are orientated to aid agricultural production.

State Housing Construction Co: POB 2753, Accra; f 1982 by merger of State Housing Corpn and Tema Development Corpn; oversees Govt housing programme.

TRADE

Department of Co-operatives: POB M150, Accra; tel (21) 666212; Registrar: R. Buachie-Aphram; Sec-Gen: J. M. Appiah; f 1944; responsible for registration, auditing and supervision of co-operative societies.

Ghana Export Promotion Council: Republic House, Tudu Rd, POB M146, Accra; tel (21) 228813; telex 2289; Exec Sec: Kwesi Ahwoi; f 1972; advisory and information service; product devt and adaptation.

Ghana National Trading Corpn (GNTC): POB 67, Accra; tel (21) 664871; f 1961; organizes exports and imports of selected commodities; over 500 retail outlets in 14 admin districts.

Ghana Standards Board: POB M245, Accra; tel (21) 662606; telex 2545; Dir: Dr L. Twum-Danso; Dep Dir, Technical: Sam Boateng; Dep Dir, Admin: F. K. Donkor; f 1967; standardization, quality control, certification and metrology.

Defence

Armed Forces: Burma Camp, Accra; tel (21) 776111; Chief of Defence Staff: Flight-Lt Jerry Rawlings.

Air Force: Burma Camp, Accra; tel (21) 776111; Chief of Staff: Air Cdre A. H. K. Dumashie.

Army: Flagstaff House, Accra; tel (21) 228101; Chief of Staff: Maj-Gen W. N. Mensah-Woode.

Navy: Burma Camp, Accra; tel (21) 776111; Chief of Staff: Rear-Adm Ben Ohene-Kwapong.

Development and Planning

INVESTMENT

Ghana Investment Centre: Central Ministerial Area, POB M193, Accra; tel (21) 665125; telex 2229; fax (21) 663801; Chair: P. V. Obeng; Chief Exec: Dr Kobena G. Erbynn; Dep Chief Exec: N. T. Apotsi; f 1981 to replace the Capital Investments Board; negotiates new investments, approves projects, registers foreign capital and decides extent of Govt participation.

REGIONAL DEVELOPMENT

Ashanti Region Organization: POB 38, Kumasi; tel (51) 6261; Regional Sec: Col (retd) E. M. Osei-Owuso.

Brong Ahafo Region Organization: POB 104, Sunyani; tel (61) 202; Regional Sec: J. H. Owusu-Acheampong; Dep Regional Sec: K. B. Boakye-Boateng; f 1959; political admin and devt.

Central Region Organization: POB 202, Cape Coast; tel (42) 222; Regional Sec: Ato Austin.

Eastern Region Organization: POB 303, Koforidua; tel (81) 2371; Regional Sec: F. Ohene-Kena.

Greater Accra Region Organization: POB M196, Accra; tel (21) 665421; Regional Sec: Lt-Col (retd) W. A. Thompson.

Northern Region Organization: POB 100, Tamale; tel (71) 2212; Regional Sec: John Bawa.

Upper East Region Organization: POB 50, Bolgatanga; tel (72) 431; Regional Sec: Kundab Molbila.

Upper West Region Organization: POB 16, Wa; tel (21) 665421; Regional Sec: Yelibora Antumini.

Volta Region Organization: POB 119, Ho; tel (91) 8301; Regional Sec: Richard Seglah; f 1982; promotion of devt projects.

Western Region Organization: POB 304, Sekondi; tel (31) 6141; Regional Sec: J. R. E. Amenlemah.

Education

Ghana Book Development Council: POB M430, Accra; tel (21) 229178; Exec Dir: S. A. Amu Djoleto; f 1975; promotes and co-ordinates writing, production and distribution of books.

Legal and Judiciary

Court of Appeal: Accra; consists of the Chief Justice and not fewer than five Judges of the Court of Appeal. It has jurisdiction to hear and determine appeals from any judgment, decree or order of the High Court.

High Court: Accra; consists of the Chief Justice and not fewer than 12 Justices of the High Court and has an original jurisdiction in all matters, civil and criminal, other than those for offences involving treason.

Supreme Court: POB 199, Accra; tel (21) 666671; Chief Justice: E. N. P. Sowah; consists of the Chief Justice and not fewer than four other Justices of the Supreme Court. It is the final court of appeal in Ghana and has jurisdiction in matters relating to the enforcement and interpretation of the Constitution.

Media

BROADCASTING

Ghana Broadcasting Co: Broadcasting House, POB 1633, Accra; tel (21) 221161; telex 2114; Dir-Gen: L. W. Fifi-Hesse; Dep Dir-Gen: David Lanaglate; Dir of TV: J. Cromwell; Dir of Radio: Kwasi Amoako.

NEWS AND INFORMATION

Ghana News Agency: POB 2118, Accra; tel (21) 665135; telex 2001; Gen Man: Mawusi Afele; f 1957.

Statistical Service: POB 1098, Accra; tel (21) 66512; f 1948; collection, compilation, analysis and publication of statistical information.

Mining and Energy

ENERGY

Electricity Corpn of Ghana: Accra; f 1966 to replace Govt electricity dept.

Ghana Atomic Energy Commission (GAEC): POB 80, Legon, Accra; tel (21) 221323; telex 2554; Chair: Dr A. K. Ahafia; f 1963; training and devt of staff in nuclear science and technology; application of atomic energy in agriculture, industry and medicine; research and devt in nuclear science and technology.

Ghana National Petroleum Corpn: Private Mail Bag, Accra North; tel (21) 776165; telex 2188; fax (21) 776164; Chair: Tsatsu Tsikata; f 1983; exploration, devt, production and distribution of petroleum.

Ghanaian-Italian Petroleum Co (Ghaip): POB 599, Tema; telex 2011; Man Dirs: P. Adusei Poku, C. C. A. Simpson; f 1963; sole oil refinery in Ghana; state-controlled since 1977.

The Volta River Authority: POB M77, Accra; tel (21) 664941; telex 2022; Chief Exec: Louis Casely-Hayford; operates hydroelectric power station; electricity used for mining and industry, as well as domestic consumption.

MINING

Ashanti Goldfields Corpn (Ghana) Ltd: POB 10, Obuasi; Chair: R. K. Peprah; Gen Man: W. J. Hussey; f 1897; gold mining; leases timber and mining concessions from the Govt, which holds 55% of the shares.

Ghana Bauxite Co Ltd: POB 1, Awaso, Western Region; tel (372) 485; Man Dir: C. F. D. Johnston; f 1940; 55% state-owned; mining, beneficiation and export of bauxite.

Ghana Consolidated Diamond Co Ltd: POB M108, Accra; telex 2058; Chair: Kofi Agyeman; f 1986 to replace Diamond Marketing Corpn; grading, valuing and processing diamonds; promotion of diamond industry.

Ghana National Manganese Corpn: POB M183, Accra; tel 666561; telex 2046; Chair: P. O. Aggrey; Man Dir: Dr A. O. Barnafo; f 1975 following nationalization of African Manganese Co mine at Nsuta.

Minerals Commission: State House, 2nd Floor, 2nd Bay, POB M248, Accra; tel (21) 662986; telex 2545; f 1984; supervises, promotes and co-ordinates the minerals industry.

State Gold Mining Corpn: POB 109, Tarkwa; Accra Office, POB 3634; tel (21) 775376; telex 2348; Chief Exec: F. Awua-Kyerematen; f 1961; manages four gold mines.

Tourism

Ghana Tourist Board: Kwame Nkrumah Conference Centre, 6th Floor, Bay 2, POB 3106, Accra; tel (21) 665461; telex 2105; Exec Dir: Edmund Y. Ofusu-Yeboah; f 1968.

Ghana Tourist Development Co Ltd: POB 8710, Accra; tel (21) 772084; telex 2140; fax (21) 772093; Man Dir: B. A. Akuffo-Amoabeng; f 1974; devt of tourist infrastructure; operation of tourist shops and casinos.

State Hotels Corpn: POB 7542, Accra-North; tel (21) 221424; telex 2112; Man Dir: S. K. A. Obeng; Gen Man: Eben Amoah; f 1957; responsible for all state-owned hotels, restaurants, etc.; also entertainment, banqueting and conference facilities.

Transport and Communications

TELECOMMUNICATIONS

Post and Telecommunications Corpn: Accra-North; tel (21) 221001; telex 3010; fax (21) 665960; Dir-Gen: Col (retd) Kwasi Opong; Dep Dir-Gen, Engineering: J. K. Gyimah; Dep Dir-Gen, Post: F. A. Johnson; f 1974; provision of postal and telecommunications services.

TRANSPORT

Ghana Airways Corpn: POB 1636, Accra; tel (21) 664856; telex 2489; Chair: W. A. Adda; Man Dir: Squad Ldr J. B. Azariah; f 1958; operates domestic services and international routes to West African destinations, Italy, the Federal Republic of Germany and the UK.

Ghana Highway Authority: POB 1641, Accra; tel (21) 666591; telex 2359; Chief Exec: H. O. A. Quaynor; f 1974; devt, admin and maintenance of trunk road network.

Ghana Railway Corpn: POB 251, Takoradi; tel (31) 2181; telex 2297; Man Dir: Amponsah Ababio; Dep Man Dir, Engineering: J. A. K. Baidoo; f 1977; management, maintenance and operation of railways.

State Transport Corpn: Ring Rd West, POB 7384, Accra; tel 221912; telex 2347; Man Dir: C. W. Tachie-Menson; f 1901 as Govt Transport Dept, name changed in 1965; provides road transport for the country.

Utilities

Ghana Water and Sewerage Corpn: POB M194, Accra; tel 666781; Man Dir: T. B. F. Acquah; Dep Man Dir, Operations: E. F. Quashie; Dep Man Dir, Finance and Admin: L. K. Kwakuyi; f 1968; provision, distribution and conservation of water for public, domestic and industrial use, and to establish, operate and control sewerage systems.

GREECE

Head of State

Under the Constitution of 1975, the President is Head of State and is elected by Parliament for a five-year term. The President appoints the Prime Minister and, upon his recommendation, the other members of the Cabinet. In March 1986 Parliament approved a series of constitutional amendments, divesting the President of his executive powers and transferring them to the legislature.

President: Christos Sartzetakis (took office 30 March 1985).

Office of the President: Odos Stissichorou 17, King George B Ave, Athens; tel (1) 72381; Sec-Gen: Leonidas Papakarias.

Prime Minister: Xenofon Zolotas (took office 23 November 1989).

Office of the Prime Minister: Maximos Bldg, Athens; tel (1) 7240654.

Legislature

Legislative power is vested in the unicameral Vouli (Parliament), which has 300 members, elected by universal adult suffrage for four years. Greece is divided into 13 administrative districts.

Vouli (Parliament): Parliament Bldg, Syntagma, Athens; tel (1) 3238434; Pres: Athanassios Tsaldaris.

MINISTRIES AND GOVERNMENT DEPARTMENTS

MINISTRY TO THE PRESIDENT
Odos Zalokosta 10, Athens
Tel (1) 3630911; telex 216325
Minister: (vacant)

MINISTRY TO THE PRIME MINISTER
Leoforos Vassilissis Sophias 15, 106 74 Athens
Tel (1) 3646350; telex 214333
Minister: Nikos Themelis
Deputy Minister: Prokopis Pavlopoulos

MINISTRY OF THE AEGEAN
Leoforos Syngrou 49, Athens
Tel (1) 9237970; telex 210244
Minister: Antonis Foussas

MINISTRY OF AGRICULTURE
Odos Aharnon 2-6, Athens
Tel (1) 3291206; telex 215308
Minister: Georgios Liapis

MINISTRY OF COMMERCE
Kanningos Sq, Athens
Tel (1) 3616251; telex 215282
Minister: Theodhoros Gamaletsos

MINISTRY OF CULTURE
Odos Aristidou 14, 101 86 Athens
Tel (1) 3243015; telex 216412
Minister: Georgios Milonas

MINISTRY OF EDUCATION AND RELIGION
Odos Metropoleos 15, Athens
Tel (1) 3230461; telex 216059
Minister: Konstantinos Dhespotopoulos

MINISTRY OF THE ENVIRONMENT, TOWN PLANNING AND PUBLIC WORKS
Odos Amaliados 17, Athens
Tel (1) 6431461; telex 216374
Minister: Konstantinos Liaskas

MINISTRY OF FINANCE
Odos Karageorgi Servias 10, Athens
Tel (1) 3224071; telex 216373
Minister: Georgios Agapitos

MINISTRY OF FOREIGN AFFAIRS
Odos Zalokosta 2, Athens
Tel (1) 3610581
Minister: Antonis Samaras

MINISTRY OF HEALTH, SOCIAL SERVICES AND WELFARE
Odos Zalokosta 10, Athens
Tel (1) 3630911; telex 21625
Minister: Georgios Merikas

MINISTRY OF INDUSTRY, TECHNOLOGY AND ENERGY
Odos Mighlagpoulou 80, 101 92 Athens
Tel (1) 7700561; telex 215811; fax (1) 7772485
Minister: Pavlos Sakellaridhis

MINISTRY OF THE INTERIOR
Odos Stadiou 27, Athens
Tel (1) 3223521; telex 215776
Minister: Theodoros Katrivanos

MINISTRY OF JUSTICE
Odos Zinonos 12, Athens
Tel (1) 5225903; telex 216352
Minister: Konstantinos Stamatis

MINISTRY OF LABOUR
Odos Pireos 40, Athens
Tel (1) 5233110; telex 216608
Minister: Yannis Koukiadhis

MINISTRY OF MACEDONIA AND THRACE
Odos El Venizelou 48, Thessaloniki
Tel (31) 264321
Minister: Yannis Deliyannis

MINISTRY OF MERCHANT MARINE
Odos Vassilissis Sophias 150, Piraeus
Tel (1) 4121211; telex 211232
Minister: Nikos Pappas

MINISTRY OF NATIONAL DEFENCE
Holargos, Athens
Tel (1) 6465201
Minister: Theodhoros Dheyiannis

MINISTRY OF NATIONAL ECONOMY AND TOURISM
Syntagma Sq, Athens
Tel (1) 3230911; telex 221086
Minister: Georgios Kondoyioryis

MINISTRY OF PUBLIC ORDER
Katehaki 1, 101 77 Athens
Tel (1) 6928510; telex 216353
Minister: Dimitris Manikas

MINISTRY OF TRANSPORT AND COMMUNICATIONS
Leoforos Syngrou 49, Athens
Tel (1) 9233941; telex 216369
Minister: Georghis Mitsopoulos

GOVERNMENT AGENCIES AND ORGANIZATIONS

Agriculture

Hellenic Cotton Board: Leoforos Syngrou 150, 176 71 Athens; tel (1) 9225011; telex 214556; Pres: Anastasios Lekkas; f 1931; responsible for the cotton industry.

Business and Economy

BANKING

Agricultural Bank of Greece: Odos Panepistimiou 23, 105 64 Athens; tel (1) 3230521; telex 222160; fax (1) 3234386; Gov and Chair: Vassilis A. Kafiris; f 1929; state agricultural bank; 420 brs.

Bank of Attica: Odos Omirou 23, 106 72 Athens; tel (1) 3646910; telex 223344; Chair and Gen Man: Costas Kalyvianakis; Vice-Pres: Panayiotis Poulis; f 1925; affiliated to Commercial Bank of Greece; 12 brs.

Bank of Crete SA: Odos Voukourestiou 22, 106 71 Athens; tel (1) 3606511; telex 225624; fax (1) 3644832; First Vice-Chair and Gen Man: Panayotis Vakalis; nationalized in 1989; 36 brs.

Bank of Greece: Odos El Venizelou 21, 102 50 Athens; tel (1) 3201111; telex 215102; fax (1) 3232239; Gov: Demetrios Chalikias; f 1928; central bank; bank of issue; 27 brs.

Commercial Bank of Greece: POB 16, Odos Sophocleous 11, 102 35 Athens; tel (1) 3210911; telex 216545; fax (1) 3252131; Chair and Man Dir: Michael Vranopoulos; Gen Man: George Michelis; f 1907; 293 brs.

Hellenic Industrial Development Bank, SA: Odos El Venizelou 18/20, 106 72 Athens; tel (1) 3237981; telex 215203; fax (1) 3621023; Gov and Chair: Sophoulis Costas; f 1964; state-owned limited liability banking co; major Greek institution in the field of industrial investment.

Ionian and Popular Bank of Greece: Odos Panepistimiou 45, 102 43 Athens; tel (1) 3225501; telex 215269; fax (1) 3223814; Chair: J. Gliniadakis; Gen Man: P. Zacharopoulos; f 1839; 170 brs.

National Bank of Greece, SA: Odos Aeolou 86, Cotzia Sq, 102 32 Athens; tel (1) 3210411; telex 214931; Gov: Prof Dimitrios Germides; f 1841; 479 brs in Greece, 22 abroad.

National Investment Bank for Industrial Development, SA: Leoforos Amalias 14, 102 36 Athens; tel (1) 3242651; telex 216113; fax (1) 3296211; Chair: Stylianos Panagopoulos; Man Dir: Dimitrios K. Varellas; f 1963; long-term loans, equity participation, promotion of co-operation between Greek and foreign enterprises.

National Mortgage Bank of Greece, SA: POB 3667, Odos Panepistimiou 40, 102 10 Athens; tel (1) 3648311; telex 215026; fax (1) 3605683; Gov: Giorgis D. Anomeritis; f 1927; 42 brs.

Postal Savings Bank: Odos Pesmazoglu 2, Athens.

Traders' Credit Bank, SA: Odos Santaroza 3, 105 64 Athens; tel (1) 3212371; telex 222983; Chair: Constantine Sietos; Gen Man: John Papaleventis; f 1924; 14 brs.

TRADE

Directorate of Foreign Commerce: Ministry of Commerce Bldg, Kanningos Sq, Athens; tel (1) 3616251; telex 215282.

Greek Exports, SA: Odos Amerikis, 105 64 Athens; tel (1) 3243111; telex 216732; promotes the export of Greek industrial products.

Hellenic Organization for Standardization (ELOT): Odos Didotou 15, Athens; tel (1) 3609517; telex 219621; promotes standardization in industry.

Defence

Hellenic National Defence: Holargos, Athens; tel (1) 6465201; telex 216780; Chief of Gen Staff: Nikolaos Kouris.

Hellenic Air Force: Holargos, Athens; tel (1) 6428101; Chief of Gen Staff: Nikolaos Stapas; Dep Chief, Gen Staff: Charalambos Starakakis.

Hellenic Army: Holargos, Athens; tel (1) 6465201; Chief of Gen Staff: Stamatis Velidis.

Hellenic Navy: Holargos, Athens; tel (1) 6520401; Chief of Gen Staff: Leonidas Vassilakopoulos; Dep Chief, Gen Staff: Timotheos Massouras.

Development and Planning

PLANNING

Centre of Planning and Economic Research: Odos Hippokratous 22, Athens; preparation of plans for economic and social devt.

Elliniko Kentro Paragogikotitas-ELKEPA (Greek Productivity Centre): Odos Kapodistriou 28, 106 82 Athens; tel (1) 3600411; telex 219416; fax (1) 3640709; f 1953; responsible to the Ministry of National Economy; aims to boost productivity in all sectors.

Public Corpn for Housing and Urban Planning: Odos Dorieleou 10-12, Platia Mavili, Athens; tel (1) 6444734.

REGIONAL DEVELOPMENT

Central Service for Regional Development: Odos Hippokratous 3-5, Athens; planning of regional economic growth and social devt.

Legal and Judiciary

Council of State: Greek Parliament, Constitution Sq, 100 21 Athens; tel (1) 3223830; Pres: V. Botopoulos; the Council of State has appellate powers over acts of the admin upon application by civil servants or other civilians.

Special Supreme Tribunal: Odos Patision 30, Athens; this court has final jurisdiction in matters of constitutionality.

Supreme Court: Leoforos Alexandros 121, Athens; Pres: Yannis Grivas; this is the supreme court, having also appellate powers. It consists of six sections, four Civil and two Penal, and adjudicates in quorum.

Media

BROADCASTING

Elliniki Radiophonia Tileorassi (Hellenic National Radio-Television): Leoforos Messoghion 402, 153 42 Athens; tel (1) 6395970; telex 216066; fax (1) 6390652; Pres and Man Dir: Georges Kontogiorgis; Dir, Radio: Nikos Parikos; state-controlled since 1939.

E. T. 2 (Hellenic Television-Channel 2): Odos Messogion 136, 115 27 Athens; tel (1) 7701911; telex 214439; Pres: (vacant); Dir-Gen: Thanassis Valtinos; f 1967; TV broadcasts from Athens.

GOVERNMENT PUBLISHER

Government Printing House: Odos Kapodistriou 34, 104 32 Athens; tel (1) 5248320.

NEWS AND INFORMATION

National Statistical Service of Greece: Odos Lycourgou 14-16, Athens; tel (1) 3249302; telex 216734.

Mining and Energy

ENERGY

Elliniki Epitropi Atomikis Energias (Greek Atomic Energy Commission): POB 60228, Aghia Paraksevi, 153 10 Athens; tel (1) 6514716; telex 218254; fax (1) 6533939; Pres: Prof Charalambos Proukakis; Vice-Pres: Prof P. Manakos; f 1954; seven-mem administrative committee.

Public Petroleum Corpn of Greece—Exploration and Exploitation of Hydrocarbons SA (DEP—EKY): Kifissias Ave 199, 151 24 Athens; tel (1) 8069301; telex 219415; Pres: G. Frantzeskakis; Man Dir: P. Sivenas; state-owned oil and natural gas co.

Public Power Corpn: Odos Chalcocondylis 30, 102 Athens; responsible for the production and distribution of electricity throughout Greece.

MINING

Eleusis Bauxite Mines, Mining, Industrial and Shipping Inc: POB 19021, Sikelias 18-20, 117 10 Athens; tel (1) 9221411; telex 215433; f 1951; bauxite and manganese mining.

General Directorate of Mines: Odos Xenophontos 13, Athens; tel (1) 7793711.

Hellenic Mining and Metallurgical Co of Laryma SA: Amalias Ave 20, 105 57 Athens; tel (1) 3236011; telex 215047; Dirs: J. Hatzinocolaidis, B. Jenkins; mining and metallurgical co.

Science and Technology

'Demokritos' National Research Centre for Physical Sciences: POB 60228, Aghia Paraskevi, 153 10 Athens; tel (1) 6513110; telex 216199; fax (1) 6519180; Dir: Dr Ion Siotis; institutes for: materials, science, microelectronics, nuclear technology, radiation protection, nuclear physics, biology, physical chemistry, informatics and telecommunications, radioisotopes and radiodiagnostic products.

Tourism

Ellinikos Organismos Tourismou (National Tourist Organization of Greece): Odos Amerikis 2, 105 64 Athens; tel (1) 3223111; telex 215832; fax (1) 3224148; Pres: K. Kyriazis; Sec-Gen: K. Skouras; devt of tourism.

Transport and Communications

TELECOMMUNICATIONS

General Directorate of Post and Telecommunications: Syngrove Ave 49, Athens; tel (1) 9215359; telex 216369; admin of telecommunications.

Organismos Telepikoinonion tes Elladas SA-OTE (Hellenic Telecommunications Organization): Odos Stadiou 15, 102 46 Athens; tel (1) 3227599; telex 215488; Chair: T. Mantelis;

Dir-Gen: T. Tobras; f 1949; state-owned telecommunications authority.

TRANSPORT

Greek Civil Aviation Authority (CAA): POB 73751, 166 04 Helleniko; tel (1) 8947121; telex 214444.

Ilektriki Sidirodromi Athinon-Pireos—ISAP (Athens-Piraeus Electric Railways): Odos Athinas 67, 105 52 Athens; tel (1) 3248311; telex 219998; fax (1) 3223935; Dir-Gen: Konstantinos Kostoylas.

Olympic Airways SA: Leoforos Syngrou 96-100, 117 41 Athens; tel (1) 9292111; telex 216488; fax (1) 9219133; Chair and Dir-Gen: Alexandros D. Akrivakis; Vice-Chair: Dr Dimitriu Bairaktaris; f 1957; domestic services linking principal cities and islands in Greece, and international services to Europe, the Middle East and North America.

Organismos Sidirodromon Ellados-OSE (Hellenic Railways Organization): Odos Karolou 1, 104 37 Athens; tel (1) 5240996; telex 215187; fax (1) 5243290; Pres: Th Rendis; Dir-Gen: D. Karapanos; f 1971; state railway co.

GRENADA

Head of State

Grenada has dominion status within the Commonwealth, and the British sovereign is Head of State, represented locally by a Governor-General. Executive power is effectively held by the Cabinet, appointed by the Governor-General, which is headed by the Prime Minister and is responsible to Parliament.

Sovereign: HM Queen Elizabeth II (succeeded to the throne 6 February 1952).

Governor-General: Sir Paul Scoon (took office 1978).

Office of the Governor-General: Govt House, St George's; tel (440) 2401.

Legislature

Legislative power is vested in the bicameral Parliament, comprising the Senate (13 appointed Senators), and the House of Representatives (15 members elected by universal adult suffrage). The Prime Minister must be a member of the House of Representatives.

Senate: St George's; Pres: John Watts.

House of Representatives: St George's; Speaker: Sir Hudson Scipio.

MINISTRIES AND GOVERNMENT DEPARTMENTS

OFFICE OF THE PRIME MINISTER
Botanical Gdns, St George's
Tel (440) 2255; telex 3457; fax (444) 4116
Prime Minister: Nicholas Brathwaite

MINISTRY OF AGRICULTURE, LANDS, FORESTRY AND FISHERIES
Treasury Bldg, St George's
Tel (440) 2248
Minister: Ben Joseph Jones

MINISTRY OF CARRIACOU AND PETIT MARTINIQUE AFFAIRS
St George's
Minister: Nicholas A. Brathwaite

MINISTRY OF EDUCATION, SOCIAL SERVICES AND LABOUR
St George's
Minister of Labour and Housing: Michael Andrew
Minister of Education: Carlyle Glean

MINISTRY OF FINANCE
Church St, St George's
Tel (440) 2731; telex 3418; fax (440) 2248
Minister: George I. Brizan

MINISTRY OF HEALTH AND COMMUNITY DEVELOPMENT
St George's
Minister: Kenny Lalsingh

MINISTRY OF HOME AND EXTERNAL AFFAIRS
St George's
Minister: Nicholas A. Brathwaite

MINISTRY OF INFORMATION AND ENERGY
Scott St, St George's
Tel (440) 2494; telex 3423
Minister: (vacant)

Government Information Service: Scott St, St George's; tel (440) 2494; telex 3423; Chief Information Officer: Jerome Romain; collects and disseminates Govt news and information.

MINISTRY OF SECURITY
Botanical Gdns, St George's
Tel (440) 2255
Minister: Nicholas A. Brathwaite

MINISTRY OF TOURISM, WOMEN'S AFFAIRS AND CIVIL AVIATION
St George's
Minister: Joan Purcell

MINISTRY OF TRADE, INDUSTRY AND PLANNING
St George's
Minister: George I. Brizan

MINISTRY OF WORKS, COMMUNICATIONS AND PUBLIC UTILITIES
Young St, St George's
Tel (440) 3595
Minister: Phinsley St Louis
Minister of State for Works and Communications: Edzel Thomas

OFFICE OF THE ATTORNEY-GENERAL
St George's
Tel (440) 2050
Attorney-General: Dr Francis R. Alexis

GOVERNMENT AGENCIES AND ORGANIZATIONS

Agriculture and Forestry

Forestry Development Corporation: St George's; f 1979; devt of forestry resources and the establishment of timber industries.

Grenada Co-operative Banana Society: Scott St, St George's; tel (440) 2486; Chair: R. M. Bhola; f 1955; statutory body; co-ordinates production of bananas; arranges for the selection and export of bananas.

Business and Economy

BANKING

Eastern Caribbean Central Bank (ECCB): POB 89, Basseterre, St Christopher and Nevis; tel 465-2537; telex 6828; Grenada Office: 4 Camerhogne House, Church St, St George's; tel (440) 3016; Gov: Cecil A. Jacobs; f 1965 as East Caribbean Currency Authority, expanded responsibilities and changed name in 1983; responsible for issue of currency in Anguilla, Antigua and Barbuda, Dominica, Grenada, Montserrat, Saint Christopher and Nevis, Saint Lucia and Saint Vincent and the Grenadines.

Grenada Development and Agriculture Bank: Treasury Bldg, The Carenage, St George's; tel (440) 2382; Chair: Samuel Graham; Man: Ronald Charles; f 1976 after merger of the Grenada Agricultural Bank and the Grenada Devt Corpn.

National Commercial Bank of Grenada Ltd: cnr Halifax and Hillsborough Sts, POB 57, St George's; tel (440) 3566; telex 3413; fax (444) 4140; Gen Man: M. B. Archibald; f 1979; 5 brs.

MARKETING

Marketing and National Importing Board: Young St, St George's; tel (440) 3191; telex 3435; Chair: Finton George de Bourg; Gen Man: Stephen John; f 1974; import of basic food items, including sugar, rice and milk.

TRADE

Grenada Chamber of Industry and Commerce, Inc: POB 129, Decaul Bldg, Mt Gay, St George's; tel (440) 2937; telex 3469; Pres: Hugh Dolland; First Vice-Pres: Brian Pitt; Second Vice-Pres: Michael Archibald; Exec Dir: Daphne Brown; f 1921; promotes trade; collects and disseminates information on trade, commerce, agriculture and manufacturing; provides training courses, business opportunities and library facilities.

Development and Planning

Grenada Industrial Development Corporation: Archibald Ave, St George's; tel (440) 2857; fax (444) 4135; Chair: Albert Xavier; f 1985.

Energy

Grenada Electricity Services Ltd (Grenlec): POB 381, St George's; tel (440) 2097; telex 3472; Man: G. C. Bowen.

Legal and Judiciary

Grenada Supreme Court: St George's; tel (440) 2030; Chief Justice: Sir Samuel Graham; Puisne Judge: Lyle C. Paul; Registrar: Denise Campbell; Pres, Court of Appeal: Sir Frederick Smith; comprises a High Court of Justice and a two-tier Court of Appeal.

Media

BROADCASTING

Discovery Television Ltd: St George's; Man: Larry Upton; f 1986; bought by majority Govt-owned Grenadan co in 1989.

Radio Grenada: POB 34, St George's; tel (440) 3033; Gen Man: George Grant; f 1972.

NEWS AND INFORMATION

Central Statistical Office: Govt of Grenada, Church St, St George's; tel (440) 3034.

Tourism

Department of Tourism: POB 293, Carenage, St George's; tel (440) 2279; telex 3422; fax (440) 2123; Dir (acting): Diana Taylor; f 1961; under the Ministry of Tourism; promotion of tourism; tourism admin devt of policies and guidelines for the tourism industry.

Grenada Hotel Association: POB 440, Mt Gay, St George's; tel (440) 1590; telex 3425; fax (444) 4124; Pres: Richard Cherman; f 1961.

Transport

Grenada Airports Authority: Point Salines International Airport, St George's; tel (444) 4101.

Grenada Ports Authority: St George's; tel (440) 3013; telex 3418.

GUATEMALA

<table>
<tr><th>Head of State</th><th>Legislature</th></tr>
<tr><td>

Under the 1986 Constitution executive power is vested in the President, who is elected for a five-year term by universal adult suffrage. The President is assisted by a Vice-President and an appointed Cabinet.

President: Mario Vinicio Cerezo Arévalo (took office 14 January 1986).

Office of the President: Palacio Nacional, 6a Calle y 7a Avda, Zona 1, Guatemala City; tel (2) 21212; telex 5325.

Vice-President: Roberto Carpio Nicolle.

Office of the Vice-President: Casa Presidencial, 6a Avda 4-19, Zona 1, Guatemala City; tel (2) 539203; telex 5331.

</td><td>

Legislative power is vested in the unicameral Congreso Nacional (National Congress), comprising 100 members elected for five years by universal adult suffrage. Of the total seats, 75 are filled by direct election and 25 on the basis of proportional representation. For local administration Guatemala is divided into 22 departments.

Congreso Nacional (National Congress): 9a Avda 9-48, Zona 1, Guatemala City; tel (2) 533333; Pres: José Ricardo Gómez Gálvez.

</td></tr>
</table>

MINISTRIES AND GOVERNMENT DEPARTMENTS

MINISTRY OF AGRICULTURE, LIVESTOCK AND FOOD
Palacio Nacional, 6a Calle y 7a Avda, Zona 1, Guatemala City
Tel (2) 86696
Minister: Rodolfo Estrada

MINISTRY OF COMMUNICATIONS, TRANSPORT AND PUBLIC WORKS
Palacio Nacional, 6a Calle y 7a Avda, Zona 1, Guatemala City
Tel (2) 22269; telex 248368
Minister: Mario López Estrada

MINISTRY OF CULTURE AND SPORT
7a Avda 8-92, Zona 9, Guatemala City
Tel (2) 346856; fax (2) 346857
Minister: Marta Regina de Fahsen
Deputy Ministers: Karl Krause, Emilio Goubaud

MINISTRY OF ECONOMY
Palacio Nacional, 6a Calle y 7a Avda, Zona 1, Guatemala City
Tel (2) 80455; telex 6132
Minister: Oscar Humberto Pineda Robles

MINISTRY OF EDUCATION
Palacio Nacional, 6a Calle y 7a Avda, Zona 1, Guatemala City
Tel (2) 20162
Minister: Eduardo Meyer Maldonado

MINISTRY OF ENERGY AND MINES
Diagonal 17, 29-78, Zona 1, Guatemala City
Tel (2) 21212
Minister: Roland Castillo Contoux

MINISTRY OF FINANCE
Centro Cívico, 8a Avda y Calle 21, Zona 1, Guatemala City
Tel (2) 511380; telex 9702
Minister: Francisco Pinto Casarola

MINISTRY OF FOREIGN AFFAIRS
Palacio Nacional, 6a Calle y 7a Avda, Zona 1, Guatemala City
Tel (2) 21212; telex 5321
Minister: Ariel Rivera Irías

MINISTRY OF THE INTERIOR
Palacio Nacional, 6a Calle y 7a Avda, Zona 1, Guatemala City
Tel (2) 21212
Minister: Gen Carlos Morales Villatoro

MINISTRY OF LABOUR AND SOCIAL WELFARE
Palacio Nacional, 6a Calle y 7a Avda, Zona 1, Guatemala City
Tel (2) 21212
Minister: Catalina Soberanis

MINISTRY OF NATIONAL DEFENCE
Palacio Nacional, 6a Calle y 7a Avda, Zona 1, Guatemala City
Tel (2) 80455; telex 248368
Minister: Gen Héctor Alejandro Gramajo Morales

MINISTRY OF PUBLIC HEALTH AND SOCIAL ASSISTANCE
Palacio Nacional, 6a Calle y 7a Avda, Zona 1, Guatemala City
Tel (2) 80258
Minister: Carlos Armando Soto Gómez

MINISTER OF URBAN AND RURAL DEVELOPMENT
15 Avda 9-69, Zona 13, Guatemala City
Tel (2) 21212
Minister: René Armando de León Schlotter

GOVERNMENT AGENCIES AND ORGANIZATIONS

Agriculture and Forestry

AGRICULTURE

Instituto Nacional de Transformación Agraria (INTA): 14 Calle 7-14, Zona 1, Guatemala City; tel (2) 80975; Pres: Jaime González; Vice-Pres: Francisco Morales; f 1962; agrarian research and transformation.

FORESTRY

Instituto Nacional Forestal: 5a Avda 12-31, Zona 9, La Aurora, Guatemala City; tel (2) 319147; Man: Nestor Haroldo Fajardo; national institute of forestry.

Business and Economy

BANKING

Banco de Guatemala: 7a Avda 22-01, Zona 1, Apdo 365, Guatemala City; tel (2) 534053; telex 5231; Pres: Lizardo A. Sosa López; Man: Fabián Pira Arrivillaga; f 1946; central bank.

Banco Nacional de Desarrollo Agrícola (BANDESA): 9a Calle 9-47, Zona 1, Apdo 350, Guatemala City; tel (2) 535222; telex 4122; Pres: Rodolfo Estrada Hurtarte; Man: José Miguel Argueta Bone; f 1971; agricultural devt bank.

Banco Nacional de la Vivienda (BANVI): 6a Avda 1-22, Zona 4, Apdo 2632, Guatemala City; tel (2) 325777; telex 5371; Pres: Rafael Escobar Donis; f 1973; devt bank for housing.

Crédito Hipotecario Nacional de Guatemala: 7a Avda 22-77, Zona 1, Apdo 242, Guatemala City; tel (2) 82041; telex 5192; Pres: Víctor Manuel Moraga Miranda; Gen Man: Ricardo Contreras Cruz; f 1930; state commercial bank; 2 brs.

Superintendencia de Bancos: 7a Avda 22-01, Zona 1, Apdo 2306, Guatemala City; tel (2) 534243; telex 5231; Supt: Gustavo Ayestas Escobar; Sec-Gen: Douglas Borja Vielman; f 1946; banking supervisory body.

FINANCIAL AGENCIES

Corporación Financiera Nacional (CORFINA): 8a Avda 10-43, Zona 1, Guatemala City; tel (2) 83331; telex 5186; Pres: Luis Alfredo Aguilar Aguierre; Gen Man: Sergio René Díaz Izquierdo; f 1973; provides assistance for the devt of industry, mining and tourism.

Dirección Técnica del Presupuesto (DTP): Centro Cívico, Edif del Ministerio de Finanzas Públicas 17, 8a Avda y Calle 21, Zona 1, Guatemala City; tel (2) 537072; f 1956; co-ordinates the preparation of the annual budget and other fiscal and monetary policy.

Instituto de Fomento de Hipotecas Aseguradas (FHA): 6a Avda 0-60, Zona 4, Guatemala City; Pres: Homero Augusto González Barillas; Man: José Salvador Samayoa Aguilar; f 1961; insured mortgage institution for the promotion of house construction.

TRADE

Centro Nacional de Promoción de las Exportaciones (Guatexpro): Torre Profesional 5, 6a Avda 0-60, Zona 4, Guatemala City; provides information on products to potential importers, and advises Guatemalan cos on export procedures and markets.

Comité Permanente de Exposiciones (COPEREX): 8a Calle 2-33, Zona 9, Guatemala City; tel (2) 310388; telex 5971; Pres: Rodolfo Neutze Ay; trade fairs committee.

Zona Libre de Industria y Comercio 'Santo Tomás de Castilla' (ZOLIC): Edif Torre Profesional II, 6a Avda 0-60, Of 301, Zona 4, Guatemala City; tel (2) 352046; Gen Man: Jaime Alfredo Chaluleu Pacheco; f 1973; duty-free commercial zone.

Defence

Armed Forces: c/o Ministry of Defence, Palacio Nacional, 6a Calle y 7a Avda, Zona 1, Guatemala City; tel (2) 21212; Commdr-in-Chief: Gen Héctor Alejandro Gramajo Morales; Dep Commdr: Manuel Antonio Callejas.

Development and Planning

INVESTMENT

Financiera Guatemalteca, SA (FIGSA): 1a Avda 11-50, Zona 10, Apdo 2460, Guatemala City; tel (2) 316051; telex 5896; fax (2) 322879; Pres: Carlos González Barrios; Gen Man: José Roberto Ortega Herrera; f 1962; investment agency.

Financiera Industrial, SA (FISA): Torre No 2 Centro Financiero, 7a Avda 5-10, Zona 4, Apdo 744, Guatemala City; tel (2) 312323; telex 5236; Pres: Carlos Arías Masselli; Man: Carlos Alberto Alpírez Pérez; f 1981.

Financiera de Inversión, SA: 10a Calle 3-17, Zona 10, Guatemala City; tel (2) 311266; telex 3155; Pres: Mario Augusto Porras G.; f 1981; investment agency.

PLANNING

Consejo Nacional de Planificación Económico: Edif Ministerio de Finanzas 12, Palacio Nacional, 6a Calle y 7a Avda, Zona 1, Guatemala City; tel (2) 80264; Sec: Hermes Marroquín; f 1964; prepares and supervises the implementation of the national economic devt plan.

Instituto de Fomento Municipal (INFOM): 8a Calle 1-66, Zona 9, Guatemala City 01009; tel (2) 364489; Pres: Mario Valenzuela; Man: Mario Alvarez; f 1957; technical and financial assistance provided to municipal authorities.

Instituto Nacional de Cooperativas (INACOP): 13 Calle 5-16, Zona 1, Guatemala City; tel (2) 537511; technical and financial assistance in the planning and devt of co-operatives.

Instituto Técnico de Capacitación y Productividad: Calle Mateo Flores 7-51, Zona 5, Guatemala City; tel (2) 313350; telex 5550; Man: Mario Hugo Rosal; institute of planning and productivity.

REGIONAL DEVELOPMENT

Empresa Nacional de Fomento y Desarrollo Económico de El Petén (FYDEP): 11a Avda 'B' 32-46, Zona 5, Guatemala City; tel (2) 316834; telex 6178; Dir: Francisco Angel Castellanos Góngora; f 1959; attached to the Presidency; economic devt agency for the dept of El Petén.

Education

Editorial del Ministerio de Educación: 15a Avda 3-22, Zona 1, Guatemala City; Ministry of Education publisher.

Employment

Instituto Nacional de Administración Pública (INAP): 5a Avda 12-65, Zona 9, Apdo 2753, Guatemala City; tel (2) 66339; Gen Man: Dr Ariel Rivera Irías; f 1964; provides technical experts to assist all branches of the Govt in administrative reform programmes; provides in-service training for local and central Govt staff; has research programmes in admin, sociology, politics and economics; provides post-graduate education in public admin.

Legal and Judiciary

Corte Suprema (Supreme Court): Centro Cívico, 21 Calle y 7a Avda, Guatemala City; tel (2) 84323; Pres: Edmundo Vásquez Martínez.

Office of the Attorney-General: Edif Centroamericano 10, 7a Avda 7-78, Zona 4, Guatemala City; tel (2) 313656; Attorney-Gen: Mario Palencia Lainfiesta.

Media

BROADCASTING

Canal 5, Cultural y Educativo: 4a Calle 18-38, Zona 1, Guatemala City; tel (2) 531961; Dir: Capt Rudy Pozuelos; f 1979; cultural and educational channel.

Dirección General de Radiodiffusión y Televisión: Edif Tipografía Nacional 3, 18 de Septiembre 6-72, Zona 1, Guatemala City; tel (2) 532539; Dir-Gen: Ricardo Gómez Flor; f 1931; supervisory body for media.

Radio Cultural TGN: 4a Avda 30-09, Zona 3, Apdo 601, Guatemala City; tel (2) 714378; Dir: Esteban Sywulka; Man: A. Wayne Berger; f 1950; religious and cultural station; programmes in Spanish, English, Cakchiquel, Kekchí and Mam.

La Voz de Guatemala: 18 Calle 6-70, Zona 1, Guatemala City; Dir: Arturo Soto Echeverría.

NEWS AND INFORMATION

Instituto Nacional de Estadística (INE): Edif América, 8a Calle 9-55, Zona 1, Guatemala City; tel (2) 82587; Dir: Miguel Angel Herrera Saenz; collection, analysis and publication of statistical information.

Mining and Energy

ENERGY

Comisión Nacional de Petróleo: Diagonal 17, 29-78, Zona 11, Guatemala City; tel (2) 460111; f 1983; awards petroleum exploration licences.

Dirección General de Energía Nuclear: Diagonal 17, 29-78, Zona 11, Apdo 1421, Guatemala City; tel (2) 760679; telex 5516; Dir: Raúl Eduardo Pineda González; programmes include the application of nuclear energy in agriculture and industry, nuclear medicine and the control of the import of radioactive materials.

Instituto Nacional de Electrificación (INDE): 6a Avda 2-73, Zona 4, Guatemala City; tel (2) 67991; telex 5324; Exec Pres: Renée de León Escribano; institute controlling electrification of the country.

MINING

Dirección General de Hidrocarburos: Diagonal 17, 29-78, Zona 11, Apdo 1411, Guatemala City; tel (2) 762044; telex 5516; fax (2) 763182; Dir-Gen: Luis Alberto Paz Armas; Dep Dir-Gen: Mario Roberto Cáceres; f 1983; controls all matters dealing with operations regarding the exploitation of hydrocarbons.

Tourism

Guatemala Tourist Commission: Centro Cívico, 7a Avda 1-17, Zona 4, Guatemala City; tel (2) 311333; telex 5532; fax (2) 318893; Dir: Julio César Fonseca; Dep Dir: José Miguel Gaitán; f 1967; policy and planning council: 13 mems representing the public and private sectors.

Transport and Communications

TELECOMMUNICATIONS

Empresa Guatemalteca de Telecomunicaciones (GUATEL): 7a Avda 12-39, Zona 1, Guatemala City; tel (2) 84398; telex 5333; Pres: Mario López Estrada; Man: Francis Ramírez Castillo; state telecommunications co.

TRANSPORT

AVIATECA-Empresa Guatemalteca de Aviación: Avda Hincapié, Aeropuerto 'La Aurora', Zona 13, Guatemala City; tel (2) 310375; telex 5960; Pres: Frederick Melville Novella; Vice-Pres: Andrés Olivero; f 1945; internal services and external services to the USA.

Dirección General de Aeronáutica Civil: Avda Hincapié, Aeropuerto 'La Aurora', Zona 13, Guatemala City; tel (2) 66377; Dir-Gen: Jorge Mario Castillo García; civil aeronautics control body.

Empresa Portuaria 'Quetzal': Edif 74 6, 7a Avda y 4a Calle, Zona 9, Guatemala City; tel (2) 314824; telex 6134; Man: Hugo Francisco Motta Lemus; port and shipping co.

Ferrocarriles de Guatemala (FEGUA): 9a Avda 18-03, Zona 1, Guatemala City; tel (2) 83030; telex 5342; fax (2) 83807; Chair: F. A. Leal Estévez; f 1968; 953 km of track; owns the ports of Barrios (Atlantic) and San José (Pacific).

Welfare

Instituto Guatemalteco de Seguridad Social: 7a Avda 22-72, Zona 1, Guatemala City; tel (2) 26001; Pres: Pietro E. Marroquín; social security institute.

GUINEA

Head of State

Executive power is vested in the President, who is assisted by a Council of Ministers. In December 1984, following a coup earlier in the year, the President became Head of Government. In 1985 an eight-member Comité Militaire de Redressement National (CMRN) Executive Committee was created, to assist the President.

President: Gen Lansana Conté (took office 4 April 1984).

Office of the President: Conakry; tel 44-11-47; telex 623.

Legislature

The 1982 Constitution, providing for a National Assembly elected by universal adult suffrage, was suspended following a coup in April 1984. Legislative power is vested in the Comité Militaire de Redressement National (CMRN-Military Committee for National Recovery), comprising 17 members. Local administration is based on eight provinces, each under the authority of a Governor.

Permanent Secretariat of the CMRN: Conakry; Permanent Sec: Maj Babacar N'Diaye.

MINISTRIES AND GOVERNMENT DEPARTMENTS

MINISTRY OF ADMINISTRATIVE REFORM AND THE PUBLIC SERVICE
Conakry
Minister: Mamouna Bangoura

MINISTRY OF AGRICULTURE AND ANIMAL RESOURCES
BP 576, Conakry
Tel 44-19-66
Minister: Capt Abdourahmane Diallo

MINISTRY OF DEFENCE, SECURITY AND INFORMATION
Conakry
Tel 44-11-47; telex 623
Minister: Gen Lansana Conté

MINISTRY OF ECONOMY AND FINANCE
Conakry
Tel 44-21-62; telex 2199
Minister: Edouard Benjamin

MINISTRY OF FOREIGN AFFAIRS
Conakry
Tel 40-50-55; telex 634
Minister: Maj Jean Traoré

MINISTRY OF FOREST GUINEA (N'ZEREKORE)
Conakry
Minister: Alhoussény Fofana

MINISTRY OF INDUSTRY, TRADE AND CRAFTS
Conakry
Tel 44-38-95; telex 2171
Minister: Dr Ousmane Sylla

MINISTRY OF THE INTERIOR AND DECENTRALIZATION
Conakry
Telex 621
Minister: Maj Mamadou Baldet

MINISTRY OF JUSTICE
Conakry
Tel 44-16-04
Minister: Bassirou Barry

MINISTRY FOR MARITIME GUINEA (KINDIA)
Conakry
Minister: Maj Abou Camara

MINISTRY FOR MIDDLE GUINEA (LABE)
Conakry
Minister: Lt-Col Sory Doumbouya

MINISTRY OF NATIONAL EDUCATION
Conakry
Tel 44-19-01; telex 631
Minister: Maj Jean Kolipé Lama

MINISTRY OF NATURAL RESOURCES AND THE ENVIRONMENT
Conakry
Tel 44-24-26
Minister: Capt Mohammed Lamine Traoré

MINISTRY OF PLANNING AND CO-OPERATION
Conakry
Minister: Ibrahima Sylla

MINISTRY OF POSTS AND TELECOMMUNICATIONS
Conakry
Minister: Lamine Bolivogui

MINISTRY OF THE PRESIDENCY
Conakry
Tel 44-11-47; telex 623
Minister, Economic and Financial Control:
Maj Henri Foula
Minister, Information, Culture and Tourism:
Hervé Vincent Bangoura
Minister, National Defence: Maj Henri Tofani
Minister, Secretary-General of the Presidency:
Alseny René Gomez

MINISTRY OF PUBLIC HEALTH AND POPULATION
Conakry
Minister: Madigbe Fofana

MINISTRY OF SOCIAL AFFAIRS AND EMPLOYMENT
Conakry

Tel 44-33-05
Minister: Saliou Koumbassa

MINISTRY OF TRANSPORT AND PUBLIC WORKS
Conakry
Minister: Maj Faciné Touré

MINISTRY FOR UPPER GUINEA (KANKAN)
Conakry
Minister: Maj Alpha Oumar Diallo

MINISTRY OF URBAN DEVELOPMENT AND HOUSING
Conakry
Minister: Mbaya Sidibe

MINISTRY OF YOUTH AND SPORTS
Conakry
Minister: Capt Joseph Gbago Zoumanigui

GOVERNMENT AGENCIES AND ORGANIZATIONS

Business and Economy

BANKING

Banque Centrale de la République: 12 blvd du Commerce, BP 692, Conakry; tel 44-17-25; telex 22225; Gov: Kerfalla Yansana; f 1960; controls all banking activity; 4 brs.

Banque Internationale pour l'Afrique en Guinée (BIAG): blvd du Commerce, BP 1419, Conakry; tel 44-42-65; telex 22180; Pres: Jean Traoré; Man Dir: Yves J. Durand; f 1985; 51% state-owned; provides 'offshore' banking services.

Société Générale de Banques en Guinée: ave de la République, BP 1514, Conakry 1; tel 44-25-65; telex 22212; Pres: J. M. Le Petit; Man Dir: Hervé Yon; f 1985.

INSURANCE

Société Nationale d'Assurances et de Réassurances de la République de Guinée (SNAR): BP 179, Conakry; Man Dir: Ousmane Sanoko.

TRADE

Entreprise Nationale Import-Export (IMPORTEX): BP 152, Conakry; tel 44-28-13; telex 625; Dir: Mamadou Bobo Dieng; import and export agency.

Defence

Armed Forces: Conakry; tel 44-50-78.

  Air Force: Conakry; tel 46-15-51.

  Army: Conakry; tel 44-16-54.

  Navy: Conakry; tel 44-33-37.

National Militia: Conakry; tel 46-24-81.

Fisheries

Société Guinéenne de Pêche (SOGUIPECHE): Conakry; f 1987; 51% state-owned; fishing and processing of fish products.

Legal and Judiciary

Cour d'Appel (Court of Appeal): Conakry; Pres: Fodé Mamadou Touré.

Media

BROADCASTING

Radiodiffusion-Télévision Guinéenne (RTG): BP 391, Conakry; tel 44-22-05; telex 22341; Man Dir: B. Camara; programmes in French, English, Créole-English, Portuguese, Arabic and local languages.

GOVERNMENT PUBLISHER

Editions du Ministère de l'Education Nationale: Secrétariat à la Recherche scientifique, BP 561, Conakry; general and educational.

NEWS AND INFORMATION

Agence Guinéenne de Presse: BP 1535, Conakry; tel 46-54-14; telex 640; Man Dir: Mohamed Condé.

Service de la Statistique Générale: Bureau du Premier Ministre, Conakry; tel 44-21-48.

Mining and Energy

ENERGY

Office National des Hydrocarbures: Conakry; Dir: Thiero Keita; national petroleum co.

Société Guinéenne des Hydrocarbures (SGH): BP 892, Conakry; tel 46-12-56; telex 776; f 1980; 50% state-owned; research into and exploitation of offshore petroleum reserves.

MINING

Aredor-Guinée, SA: BP 1218, Conakry; tel 44-31-12; telex 22132; Gen Man: Jean-Pierre Moritz; f 1981; 50% state-owned; diamond mining.

Association pour la Recherche et l'Exploitation de l'Or de Kourouassa: Kourouassa; f 1985; 50% state-owned; gold mining.

Office des Bauxites de Kindia (OBK): Conakry; telex 2148; Dir: Mamadou Sylla; receives technical assistance for maintenance from the USSR; bauxite mining at Debelé, 100 km north of Conakry; began production in 1974.

Société Mifergui-Nimba: BP 837, Conakry; telex 622; Chair: El Hadj Sekou Oumar Keita; Gen Man: Arsen Pensa; f 1973; 50% state-owned; devt of high-grade iron deposit at Mt Nimba.

Société Minière de Dinguiraye: Dinguiraye; 50% state-owned; exploitation of gold deposits at Dinguiraye.

Société Minière de Niandan (SMN): Keniéro; f 1986; 50% state-owned; gold and diamond mining.

Société Minière et de Participation Guinée-Alusuisse: Conakry; f 1971; 50% state-owned; mining of bauxite and production of aluminium.

Tourism

Office National du Tourisme et de l'Hôtellerie (ONATHOL): square des Martyrs, BP 1304, Conakry; tel 44-26-06; promotion and co-ordination of the tourist industry.

Transport

CIVIL AVIATION

Air Guinée: ave de la République, BP 12, Conakry; Dir-Gen: Nfa Moussa Diane; f 1960; internal and external flights to Bamako, Dakar, Freetown and Monrovia.

Société de Gestion et d'Exploitation de l'Aéroport de Conakry (SOGEAC): Conakry; f 1987; 51% state-owned; management of Conakry international airport.

RAILWAYS

Office National des Chemins de Fer de Guinée (ONCFG): BP 589, Conakry; tel 44-46-13; telex 22349; Dir-Gen: Fofana M. Kadio; f 1905.

ROADS

Office du Projet Routier: BP 581, Conakry; organization of road rehabilitation and construction projects.

Société Générale des Transports de Guinée (SOGE-TRAG): Conakry; f 1984; bus operator.

SHIPPING

ENTRAT: BP 315, Conakry; Dir-Gen: Daouda Diawara; stevedoring and forwarding co.

Société Navale Guinéenne: BP 522, Conakry; telex 644; Dir-Gen: Naby Sylla; f 1968; shipping co and agency.

SOTRAMAR: Kamsar; f 1971; bauxite export from mines at Boké through the port of Kamsar.

GUINEA-BISSAU

Head of State

The President of the Council of State is Head of State, and is elected for a five-year term by the regional councils. The President of the Council of State is also Head of Government and appoints Ministers and Secretaries of State.

Head of Government and President of the Council of State: Commdr João Bernardo Vieira (assumed power 14 November 1980; elected President of the Council of State 16 May 1984, re-elected 19 June 1989).

Council of State: Bissau; Vice-Pres: Col Iafai Camara; Second Vice-Pres: Vasco Cabral; Permanent Sec: Carlos Correia.

Legislature

Legislative power is vested in the National People's Assembly whose 150 members are chosen by the directly-elected regional councils from among their own members. The Assembly elects a 15-member Council of State to assume legislative functions between its sessions. Political power is effectively held by the Partido Africano da Independência da Guiné e Cabo Verde (PAIGC).

National People's Assembly: Bissau; Pres: Tiago Aleluia Lopes.

MINISTRIES AND GOVERNMENT DEPARTMENTS

MINISTRY OF THE CIVIL SERVICE AND LABOUR
Bissau
Minister: Henriqueta Godinho Gomes

MINISTRY OF DEFENCE AND THE INTERIOR
Bissau
Minister: Commdr João Bernardo Vieira

MINISTRY OF THE EASTERN PROVINCE
Bissau
Minister: Malam Bacai Sanha

MINISTRY OF ECONOMIC PLANNING
CP 6, Bissau
Tel 212626; telex 275
Minister: Bernardino Cardoso

Planning Office: CP 6, Bissau; tel 212626; telex 275; Dir: Ibrahima Dieme; economic and social planning; investment project appraisal and monitoring.

Statistics Office: CP 6, Bissau; tel 212626; telex 275; Dir: Francisco Costa.

MINISTRY OF FINANCE
Bissau
Minister: Vítor Freira Monteiro

MINISTRY OF FOREIGN AFFAIRS
Bissau
Minister: Júlio Semedo

MINISTRY OF INFORMATION AND TELECOMMUNICATIONS
Avda do Brasil, CP 248, Bissau
Minister: Mussa Djassi

MINISTRY OF JUSTICE, PUBLIC HEALTH AND EDUCATION
Bissau
Minister of State: Vasco Cabral

MINISTRY OF NATURAL RESOURCES AND INDUSTRY
Bissau
Minister: Filinto de Barros

MINISTRY OF THE NORTHERN PROVINCE
Bissau
Minister: Mário Cabral

MINISTRY OF SOCIAL INFRASTRUCTURE
Bissau
Minister: Maj Avito da Silva

MINISTRY OF THE SOUTHERN PROVINCE
Bissau
Minister: Dr Luís Oliveira Sanca

MINISTRY OF STATE FOR THE ARMED FORCES
Bissau
Minister of State: Col Iafai Camara

MINISTRY OF STATE FOR ECONOMIC CO-ORDINATION, TRADE AND TOURISM
Bissau
Minister of State: Col Manuel Mário Monteiro dos Santos

MINISTRY OF STATE FOR THE PRESIDENCY IN CHARGE OF FISHERIES
Bissau
Minister of State: Dr Fideles Cabral d'Almada

MINISTRY OF STATE FOR THE PRESIDENCY FOR RURAL DEVELOPMENT AND AGRICULTURE
Bissau
Minister: (vacant)

GOVERNMENT AGENCIES AND ORGANIZATIONS

Business and Economy

BANKING

Banco Nacional da Guiné-Bissau: Avda Amílcar Cabral, CP 38, Bissau; tel 215433; telex 969249; Gov: Dr Pedro A. Godinho Gomes (mem of the Council of Ministers); f 1976; central and commercial bank; 3 brs.

Caixa de Crédito da Guiné: Bissau; Govt savings and loan institution.

Caixa Económica Postal: Avda Amílcar Cabral, Bissau; tel 212999; telex 979; postal savings institution.

NATIONALIZED INDUSTRY

CICER: Bissau; brewery.

Empresa de Automóveis da Guiné: Bissau; car-assembly plant.

Ultramarina: Bissau; wide variety of trading; ship-repairing; agricultural processing; Govt acquired 80% of the capital in 1976.

Defence

People's Revolutionary Armed Forces: Bissau; Commdr-in-Chief: Commdr João Bernardo Vieira; State Commr for the Armed Forces: Maj Umaru Djalo.

Air Force: Bissau; tel 213934.

Navy: Bissau; tel 212556.

Forestry and Fishing

Estrela do Mar: Bissau; fishing co with USSR participation.

GUIALP: Bissau; fishing co with Algerian participation.

SEMAPESCA: Bissau; fishing co with French participation.

Sociedade de Comercialização e Transformação de Madeiras (SOCOTRAM): CP 184, 1011-Codex, Bissau; tel 212308; telex 255; Gen Man: Armando Ramos da Silva; f 1976; wood cutting and processing; logging; marketing of finished products; reafforestation.

Legal and Judiciary

Supreme Court: Bissau; judges are appointed by the Pres of the Council of State.

Media

BROADCASTING

Radiodifusão Nacional da República da Guiné-Bissau: CP 191, Bissau; Dir: Francisco Barreto; broadcasts in Portuguese.

Mining and Energy

Empresa Nacional de Pesquisas e Exploração Petrol-iferas e Mineiras (PETROMINAS): Rua Eduardo Mondlane 58, Bissau; tel 212279; Dir-Gen: Pio Gomes Correia; regulates all mineral prospecting.

Tourism

Centro de Informação e Turismo: CP 294, Bissau; tourism and information service.

Secretaria de Estado do Turismo e Artesanato (SETA): Avda Domingos Ramos, CP 85, Bissau; tel 213282; telex 262; fax 215158; Secretary of State: Alberto Lima Gomes; f 1984; promotion of tourism.

Transport and Communications

TELECOMMUNICATIONS

Secretaria de Estado dos Correios e Telecomunicações: Avda Amílcar Cabral, CP 200, Bissau; tel 213036; telecommunications secretariat.

TRANSPORT

Empresa Nacional de Agências e Transportes Marítimos (Guinémar): Sociedade de Agências e Transportes da Guiné Lda, Rua Guerra Mendes 4-4A, CP 244, Bissau; tel 212675; telex 240; Gen Man: Marcos T. Lopes; Asst Gen Man: Noël Correia; nationalized 1976; shipping agents and brokers.

Transportes Aéreos da Guiné-Bissau (TAGB): Aeroporto Oswaldo Vieira, CP 111, Bissau; telex 268; Dir: Capt Eduardo Pinto Lopes; f 1977; domestic and international services to France, Portugal, Guinea and Senegal.

GUYANA

Head of State

Executive power is vested in the President, who leads the majority party in the National Assembly and holds office for its duration. The President appoints and leads a Cabinet, which includes a Prime Minister, and which is collectively responsible to the National Assembly.

President: Hugh Desmond Hoyte (took office 6 August 1985; sworn in as elected President 12 December 1985).

Minister in the Office of the President: Yvonne Harewood-Benn.

Office of the President: New Garden St, Georgetown; tel (2) 51330; telex 2205; fax (2) 63395; Head of Presidential Secretariat: C. L. Joseph.

First Vice-President: Hamilton Green.

Vice-Presidents: Ranji Chandisingh (in the Office of the President), Viola Burnham (for Culture and Social Development).

Legislature

Legislative power is vested in the unicameral National Assembly, comprising 65 members: 53 elected for five years by universal adult suffrage, on the basis of proportional representation, and 12 regional representatives. Guyana comprises 10 regions, each having a Regional Democratic Council.

National Assembly: Parliament Bldgs, Brickdam, Georgetown; tel (2) 63519; Speaker: Sase Narain.

MINISTRIES AND GOVERNMENT DEPARTMENTS

OFFICE OF THE PRIME MINISTER
Wight's Lane, Kingston, Georgetown
Tel (2) 58821
Prime Minister: Hamilton Green
Deputy Prime Ministers: Viola Burnham, Ranji Chandisingh, William Haslyn Parris, Robert Corbin

MINISTRY OF AGRICULTURE
POB 1001, Regent and Vlissingen Rds, Georgetown
Tel (2) 69154
Senior Minister: Dr Patrick McKenzie
Minister: Vibert Parvattan

MINISTRY OF COMMUNICATIONS AND WORKS
Wight's Lane, Kingston, Georgetown
Tel (2) 56510
Senior Minister: Jules Ranenburg

MINISTRY OF CULTURE AND SOCIAL DEVELOPMENT
Georgetown
Senior Minister: Viola Burnham
Minister of State: Jean Perisco

MINISTRY OF EDUCATION
26 Brickdam, Stabroek, Georgetown
Tel (2) 54163
Senior Minister: Deryck Bernard

MINISTRY OF FINANCE
Main and Urquhart Sts, Georgetown
Tel (2) 67241
Senior Minister: Carl B. Greenidge

MINISTRY OF FOREIGN AFFAIRS
Takuba Lodge, 254 New Garden St and South Rd, Georgetown
Tel (2) 61606; telex 2220
Senior Minister: Rashleigh E. Jackson

MINISTRY OF HEALTH AND PUBLIC WELFARE
Homestretch Ave, D'Urban Park, Georgetown
Tel (2) 65861
Senior Minister: Noel Blackman
Minister, Public Services: Dr Faith Harding

MINISTRY OF HOME AFFAIRS AND PUBLIC INFORMATION
6 Brickdam, Stabroek, Georgetown
Tel (2) 62444
Senior Minister: Hugh Desmond Hoyte
Minister: Stella Odie-Alli

MINISTRY OF JUSTICE AND OFFICE OF THE ATTORNEY-GENERAL
95 Carmichael St, Georgetown
Tel (2) 62616
Senior Minister and Attorney-General:
Keith Stanislaus Massiah

MINISTRY OF LABOUR AND CO-OPERATIVES
Homestretch Ave, D'Urban Park, Georgetown
Tel (2) 57070
Minister: Pandit Chintaman Gowkarran Sharma

MINISTRY OF PLANNING AND DEVELOPMENT
Sophia, Georgetown
Senior Ministers: William Haslyn Parris, Seeram Prashad

MINISTRY OF PUBLIC UTILITIES
Sophia, Georgetown
Tel (2) 71581
Senior Minister: Robert Corbin
Minister: Sharamdheo Sawh

MINISTRY OF REGIONAL PLANNING
1 Water and Cornhill Sts, Stabroek, Georgetown
Tel (2) 56590
Senior Minister: Jeffrey Thomas
Minister: Urmia E. Johnson

MINISTRY OF TRADE AND TOURISM
95 Carmichael St, Georgetown
Tel (2) 62505; telex 2288
Senior Minister: Winston Murray

GOVERNMENT AGENCIES AND ORGANIZATIONS

Agriculture and the Environment

AGRICULTURE

Guyana Rice Board: 1-2 Water St, Georgetown; tel (2) 62480; telex 2266; Exec Chair: Darlene Harris; f 1973; devt of the rice industry and promotion of its export trade.

Guyana Stockfeeds Ltd: Farm, East Bank, Demerara; tel (2) 63402; telex 2203; f 1960; manufacture of poultry feeds.

Guyana Stores Ltd: 22 Church St, POB 10560, Georgetown; tel (2) 66171; telex 2212; Chair: Paul Chan-A-Sue; retailers and wholesalers.

Guyana Sugar Corpn Ltd (Guysuco): 22 Church St, POB 10547, Georgetown; tel (2) 66171; telex 2265; fax (2) 57274; Chair: Harold B. Davis; Sec: C. J. Lawrence; f 1976.

Livestock Development Co Ltd: 58 High St, Georgetown; tel (2) 61601.

Mahaica-Mahaicony-Abary Agricultural Development Authority: Onverwagt, West Coast, Berbice; tel (3) 3117; telex 3055; aims to bring Berbice-Abary region into full agricultural production.

THE ENVIRONMENT

Advisory Environmental Council (AEC): Georgetown; Dir: Jailall Kissoon; f 1988; monitors the environmental impact of the agricultural and industrial sectors.

FISHING

Guyana Fisheries Ltd: Georgetown; tel (2) 58960; telex 2286; Man Dir: Michael Elliot Davis; owners of 26 trawlers, landing and processing facilities.

Guyana-Libya Fishing Co: Houston, East Bank, Demerara; tel (2) 54382; Chair: F. G. Dorway; joint venture between the Govts of Guyana and Libya to develop fishing potential.

Business and Economy

BANKING

Bank of Guyana: 1 Church St and Ave of the Republic, POB 1003, Georgetown; tel (2) 63250; telex 2267; Gov: Patrick E. Matthews; Man: Ivan Hamilton; f 1965; bank of issue.

Guyana Co-operative Agricultural and Industrial Development Bank: Lot 126, Parade and Barracks Sts, Kingston, Georgetown; tel (2) 58808; Man Dir: Cyril K. Hunte; f 1973; 10 brs.

Guyana Co-operative Mortgage Finance Bank: 46 Main St, POB 1083, Georgetown; tel (2) 68415; Man Dir: Alfred E. O. Bobb; f 1973.

Guyana National Co-operative Bank: 1 Lombard and Cornhill Sts, POB 242, Georgetown; tel (2) 57810; telex 2235; fax (2) 60231; Man Dir: Stephen G. Backer; Dep Man Dir: John Alleyne; f 1970; 7 brs.

National Bank of Industry and Commerce: 38-40 Water St, POB 10440, Georgetown; tel (2) 63231; telex 3044; fax (2) 72921; Man Dir: Raymond Ackloo; 1 br.

Republic Bank for Trade and Industry Ltd: Water St, POB 10280, Georgetown; tel (2) 68431; telex 2222; fax (2) 71612; Gen Man: Marguerite Da Silva; f 1990 by merger of Guyana Bank for Trade and Industry and Republic Bank; 2 brs.

INSURANCE

Guyana Co-operative Insurance Service: 47 Main St, Georgetown; tel (2) 68421; telex 2255; Chair: B. Claude Bone; Gen Man: Harold Wilson; f 1976.

MARKETING

Guyana Marketing Corpn: Lombard St, Georgetown; tel (2) 65846; Chair: Dr P. McKenzie; Gen Man: Kelvin Craig.

NATIONALIZED INDUSTRY

Guyana Liquor Corpn: 8-11 Water and Schumaker Sts, Georgetown; tel (2) 64404; telex 2284; fax (2) 58686; Exec Chair: Yesu Persaud; holding co for Demerara Distillers Ltd.

Guyana National Engineering Corpn Ltd: 1-9 Lombard St, Charlestown, POB 10520, Georgetown; tel (2) 63291; telex 2218; Exec Chair: Claude Saul; metal foundry, ship building and repair and shipping agency.

Guyana Pharmaceutical Corpn Ltd: 1 Public Rd, La Penitence, Georgetown; tel (2) 54700; telex 2203; fax (2) 57362; Exec Chair: Wilfred Lee; Finance Dir: Clyde Douglas; manufacture of pharmaceuticals, chemicals and cosmetics.

Defence

Defence Forces: Camp Ayanganna, Thomas Lands, Georgetown; tel (2) 68451; Chief of Staff: Norman Mclean.

Police Headquarters: Eve Leary, Kingston, Georgetown; tel (2) 56940; Commr: Balram Ragubir.

Development and Planning

Guyana Manufacturing and Industrial Development Agency (GUYMIDA): 237 Camp St, Cummingsburg, Georgetown; tel (2) 62434; fax (2) 61492; Exec Dir: C. D. M. Duncan; Man, Industrial Operations: M. Mariano; Man, Admin: C. Wilson; Man, Finance: C. Waddy; f 1984; provision of technical and managerial advice and assistance; devt of entrepreneurial skills; identification of industrial potential.

State Planning Commission: 229 South Rd, Lacytown, Georgetown; tel (2) 68093; fax (2) 72499; Chief Planning Officer: Clyde Roopchand.

Legal and Judiciary

Supreme Court of Judicature: Ave of the Republic and South St, Georgetown; tel (2) 68481; Chancellor of Justice: Kenneth M. George; Chief Justice: Rudolph H. Harper; f 1966; consists of a Court of Appeal and a High Court (both of which are superior courts of record), and a number of Courts of Summary Jurisdiction.

Media

BROADCASTING

Guyana Broadcasting Corpn (GBC): St Phillips Green and High Sts, POB 10760, Georgetown; tel (2) 69231; Exec Chair: J. L. Philadelphia; Gen Man: Ave Brewster; f 1979; formed from the Guyana Broadcasting Service and the Broadcasting Co Ltd (Radio Demerara) when the Govt took over the assets of the latter.

Guyana Television Corpn: Georgetown; limited service.

GOVERNMENT PUBLISHER

Guyana National Printers Ltd: 1 Public Rd, La Penitence, POB 10256, Greater Georgetown; tel (2) 53623; telex 2212; Gen Man: Novear de Freitas; printer and publisher.

NEWS AND INFORMATION

Guyana News Agency: Lama Ave, Bel Air Park, Georgetown; tel (2) 54294; telex 2210; Editor-in Chief: W. Henry Skerret; f 1981.

Guyana Public Communications Agency: 18 Brickdam, Stabroek, Georgetown; tel (2) 72025; telex 2210; fax (2) 60658; Exec Chair: Christopher Nascimento; Dir, Information Services: Kester Alves; Chief Admin Officer: Melissa Humphrey; f 1989; disseminates information about Guyana.

Mining and Energy

ENERGY

Guyana National Energy Authority: Goergetown; formulation and implementation of policy regarding devt of energy sources.

Guyana Natural Resources Agency (GNRA): 41 Brickdam and Boyle Place, Stabroek, Georgetown; tel (2) 66549; telex 3010; fax (2) 71211; Exec Chair: Winston M. King; Dep Chair: Dr Barton Scotland; f 1986; formulates policy for effective natural resource devt, and for the devt of new energy sources and the rational and economic utilization of energy.

Guyana Oil Co Ltd: Providence, East Bank, Demerara; tel (2) 62877; telex 2291.

MINING

Bauxite Industry Development Co Ltd (BIDCO): 71 Main St, Georgetown; tel (2) 57780; telex 2244; fax (2) 67413; Chair: Bernard Crawford; f 1976; holding co of Guyana Mining Enterprise Ltd.

Guyana Mining Enterprise Ltd (Guymine): East Bank, Berbice; tel (3) 22336; telex 2245; Chair: Dunstan Barrow; f 1977 by merger of Guyana Bauxite Co and Berbice Mining Enterprises.

Guyana Agency for the Environment: Georgetown; tel (2) 57523; fax (2) 57524; Dir: Dr Walter Chin; f 1988; monitors, formulates and implements policies on the environment.

Tourism

Guyana Overland Tours: 48 Princes and Russell Sts, Charlestown, POB 10173, Georgetown; tel (2) 69876; Man: John Dalzell; f 1968.

Transport

Guyana Airways Corpn: 32 Main St, POB 10223, Georgetown; tel (2) 68195; telex 2242; Exec Chair: Joseph R. Vieira; f 1939; operates internal scheduled services and flights to the Caribbean, the USA, Brazil and Suriname.

Guyana National Shipping Corpn Ltd: 5-9 Lombard St, La Penitence, POB 10988, Georgetown; tel (2) 66171; telex 2232; Exec Chair: P. A. Chan-A-Sue; shipping agent.

Guyana National Trading Corpn Ltd: 45-47 Water St, POB 10480, Georgetown; tel (2) 61666; telex 2214; Exec Chair: F. A. Griffith; shipping co; due to be privatized in 1990.

Guyana Transport Services Ltd: Nelson Mandela Ave, Industrial Site, Ruimveldt, Greater Georgetown; tel (2) 58261; Gen Man: R. Van Velzen; f 1971; provides road haulage and bus services.

HAITI

Head of State

Following a coup in June 1988 the 1987 Constitution, which provided for an elected President as Head of State, was rejected. In March 1990 a 19-member Council of State was formed in order to preside over elections, which were due to take place no later than February 1991, and to govern the country until that date.

President: Ertha Pascal-Trouillet (took office 11 March 1990).

Office of the President: Palais National, Port-au-Prince; tel (1) 2-4020; telex 0068.

Legislature

The 1987 Constitution provided for a bicameral legislature, comprising a 77-member Chamber of Deputies and a 27-member Senate. The Council of State has announced that legislative elections will be held, after which the newly-elected legislature, acting as a Constituent Assembly, would amend the Constitution.

Assemblée Nationale (National Assembly): blvd Harry Truman, Cité de l'Exposition, Port-au-Prince; tel (1) 2-3212.

MINISTRIES AND GOVERNMENT DEPARTMENTS

COMMISSION FOR OVERSEAS HAITIANS
Port-au-Prince
Head: Gérard Bissainthe

MINISTRY OF ADMINISTRATION AND CIVIL SERVICE
Port-au-Prince
Minister: Remy Mathieu

MINISTRY OF AGRICULTURE, NATURAL RESOURCES AND RURAL DEVELOPMENT
Damien, Port-au-Prince
Tel (1) 2-3457
Minister: Wilner François

MINISTRY OF ECONOMY AND FINANCE
Palais des Ministères, rue Monseigneur Guilloux, Port-au-Prince
Tel (1) 2-1628; telex 0207
Minister: Franck Paultre

MINISTRY OF EDUCATION, YOUTH AND SPORTS
Blvd Harry Truman, Cité de l'Exposition, Port-au-Prince
Tel (1) 2-1036
Minister: Serge Petit-Frere

MINISTRY OF FOREIGN AFFAIRS AND WORSHIP
Blvd Harry Truman, Cité de l'Exposition, Port-au-Prince
Tel (1) 2-1647
Minister: Yvon Perrier

MINISTRY OF HEALTH AND HOUSING
Palais des Ministères, rue Monseigneur Guilloux, Port-au-Prince
Tel (1) 2-1248
Minister: Dr Serge Pinthro

MINISTRY OF INFORMATION AND CO-ORDINATION
300 route de Delmas, Port-au-Prince
Tel (1) 6-3229; telex 0238
Minister: Rosemarie Nazon

MINISTRY OF THE INTERIOR AND NATIONAL DEFENCE
Palais des Ministères, rue Monseigneur Guilloux, Port-au-Prince
Tel (1) 2-1714
Minister: Joseph Maxi

MINISTRY OF JUSTICE
Blvd Harry Truman, Cité de l'Exposition, Port-au-Prince
Tel (1) 2-0718
Minister: Agustin Romain Cème

MINISTRY OF PLANNING AND EXTERNAL CO-OPERATION
Palais des Ministères, rue Monseigneur Guilloux, Port-au-Prince
Tel (1) 2-1027
Minister: Michel Bonnet

MINISTRY OF PUBLIC WORKS, TRANSPORT AND COMMUNICATIONS
Palais des Ministères, rue Monseigneur Guilloux, BP 2002, Port-au-Prince
Tel (1) 2-0300; telex 0353
Minister: Franck Cave

MINISTRY OF SOCIAL AFFAIRS
Rue de la Révolution, Port-au-Prince
Tel (1) 2-2450
Minister: Louis Arnault Guerrier

MINISTRY OF TRADE AND INDUSTRY
Port-au-Prince
Minister: Edmond Dupuy

GOVERNMENT AGENCIES AND ORGANIZATIONS

Art and Culture

Ecole Nationale des Arts: rue Monseigneur Guilloux, Port-au-Prince; Dir-Gen: Michel Philippe Lerebours; national school of the arts.

Business and Economy

BANKING

Banque de la République d'Haïti: angle rue du Magasin de l'Etat et rue des Miracles, BP 1570, Port-au-Prince; tel (1) 2-4700; telex 0394; Dir-Gen: Jean Claude Simon; f 1911; central bank and bank of issue; 12 brs.

Banque Nationale de Crédit: rue des Miracles et rue Américaine, BP 1320, Port-au-Prince; tel (1) 2-0800; telex 0196; Pres: Edouard Racine; f 1979.

Banque Nationale de Développement Agricole et Industriel: rue de Quai, BP 1313, Port-au-Prince; tel (1) 2-1969; telex 0116; Dir-Gen: Yves Lerebours; devt bank for agriculture and industry.

Banque Populaire Haïtienne: Angle rue Américaine et Fort Per, Port-au-Prince; tel (1) 2-1800; telex 0406; Dir-Gen: Senat Mortel; f 1955.

FINANCIAL AGENCIES

Fonds de Développement Industriel: 43 rue des Miracles, BP 2597, Port-au-Prince; tel (1) 2-7852; telex 0432; Dir: Yves Blanchard; f 1981; industrial devt agency.

Société Financière Haïtienne de Développement (SOFIHDES): blvd Harry Truman, BP 1399, Port-au-Prince; tel (1) 2-8628; fax (1) 2-8997; Dir-Gen: Serge Devieux; f 1983; accounting, data processing, management consultancy.

Defence

L'Armée de Terre (Army): Grand Quartier Général, Place des Héros de l'Indépendance, Port-au-Prince; tel (1) 2-3935; telex 0391; Chief of Staff: Maj-Gen Herard Abraham.

Corps d'Aviation (Air Force): ave Somoza, Delmas, Port-au-Prince; tel (1) 2-0231.

Marine Haïtienne (Navy): Garde-Côte, Bizoton; tel 4-0533.

Development and Planning

Société Nationale des Parcs Industriels (SONAPI): BP 2345, Port-au-Prince; tel (1) 6-0099; Exec Man: Max T. Thiesfeld; Gen Man: Wilner G. François; f 1980; responsible for management and devt of an industrial zone near Port-au-Prince; aims to attract foreign investment.

Energy

Electricité d'Haïti: rue Dantes Destouches, Port-au-Prince; tel (1) 2-4600; telex 0113; Dir: Jean-Claude Souriac; electric co.

Legal and Judiciary

Cour de Cassation: blvd Harry Truman, Cité de l'Exposition, 1 Supérieur, Port-au-Prince; tel (1) 2-3212; Pres: Gilbert Austin; law is based on the French Napoleonic Code.

Media

BROADCASTING

Radio Télédiffusion Nationale: rue du Magasin de l'Etat, BP 1143, Port-au-Prince; tel (1) 2-2421; Dir: Dr Georges Michel.

Télévision Nationale d'Haïti: Delmas 33, BP 13400, Port-au-Prince; tel (1) 6-0200; telex 0414; cultural channel; administered by a four-mem board.

NEWS AND INFORMATION

Institut Haïtien de Statistique et d'Informatique (IHSI): blvd Harry Truman, Cité de l'Expostion, Port-au-Prince; tel (1) 2-1011; Man: Carl Jeudy; f 1951; collection, analysis and publication of statistics.

Tourism

Office National du Tourisme d'Haïti: ave Marie-Jeanne, Port-au-Prince; tel (1) 2-1729; telex 0206; Dir: Antonio Fenelon; national tourist office.

Transport and Communications

TELECOMMUNICATIONS

Conseil National des Télécommunications (CONATEL): blvd Harry Truman, Cité de l'Exposition, BP 2002, Port-au-Prince; tel (1) 3-2929; telex 0353; fax (1) 3-0579; Dir-Gen: Alix Lilavois; communications licensing authority.

TRANSPORT

Air Haïti: 35 ave Marie-Jeanne, Port-au-Prince; Gen Man: Ernest Cineas; f 1969; scheduled cargo and mail services from Port-au-Prince to Cap Haïtien, Puerto Rico, the Dominican Republic and the USA.

Autorité Portuaire Nationale: BP 616, Port-au-Prince; national port authority.

HONDURAS

Head of State

Under the terms of the 1982 Constitution executive power is vested in the President, who is elected for a four-year term by a simple majority of the people. No President may serve more than one term.

President: Rafael Leonardo Callejas (took office 27 January 1990).

Office of the President: Casa Presidencial, 6a Avda, 1a Calle, Tegucigalpa; tel 22-8287.

Vice-Presidents: Roberto Martínez Losano, Jacobo Hernández Cruz, Marco Tulio Cruz.

Legislature

Legislative power is vested in the unicameral Asamblea Nacional (National Assembly), comprising 134 members elected by universal adult suffrage for four years. The country is divided into 18 Departments for purposes of local administration.

Asamblea Nacional (National Assembly): Palacio Legislativo, Tegucigalpa; tel 37-2288; Pres: (vacant).

MINISTRIES AND GOVERNMENT DEPARTMENTS

MINISTRY OF COMMUNICATIONS, PUBLIC WORKS AND TRANSPORT
Barrio La Bolsa, Comayagüela, Tegucigalpa
Tel 33-7690
Minister: Mauro Membreño

MINISTRY OF CULTURE, TOURISM AND INFORMATION
Costado Este del Palacio Legislativo, Tegucigalpa
Tel 22-6618
Minister: Sonia Canales de Mendieta

MINISTRY OF DEFENCE AND PUBLIC SECURITY
Palacio de los Ministerios, Tegucigalpa
Tel 22-9521
Minister: Col Francisco Zepeda Andino

MINISTRY OF ECONOMY AND COMMERCE
Edif Salame, 5a Avda, 4a Calle, Tegucigalpa
Tel 22-3251; telex 1396
Minister: Ramón Median Luna
Secretary for Economic Planning: Manilo Martínez

MINISTRY OF FINANCE
Palacio de Hacienda, Avda Cervantes, Tegucigalpa
Tel 22-8452
Minister: Benjamín Villanueva

MINISTRY OF FOREIGN AFFAIRS
Edif Atala, Avda La Paz, Tegucigalpa
Tel 31-4209; telex 1129
Minister: Mario Carías Zapata

MINISTRY OF HEALTH AND SOCIAL SECURITY
4a Avda, 3a Calle, Tegucigalpa
Tel 22-1386
Minister: César Castellanos

MINISTRY OF THE INTERIOR AND JUSTICE
Palacio de los Ministerios 2, Tegucigalpa
Tel 22-8604
Minister: Francisco Cardona

MINISTRY OF LABOUR AND SOCIAL AFFAIRS
2a y 3a Avda, 7a Calle, Comayagüela, Tegucigalpa
Tel 22-8527
Minister: Rodolfo Rosales Abella

MINISTRY OF NATURAL RESOURCES
Blvd Miraflores, Tegucigalpa
Tel 32-3141
Minister: Mario Lucio Gamero

MINISTRY OF THE PRESIDENCY
6a Avda, 1a Calle, Tegucigalpa
Tel 22-8287
Secretary of State: (vacant)

MINISTRY OF PUBLIC EDUCATION
1a Avda, 2a y 3a Calle, No 201, Comayagüela, Tegucigalpa
Tel 22-8573
Minister: Jaime Martínez Guzmán

NATIONAL AGRARIAN INSTITUTE (INA)
Tegucigalpa
Telex 1218
Minister and Director: Juan Ramón Martínez

GOVERNMENT AGENCIES AND ORGANIZATIONS

Agriculture and Forestry

AGRICULTURE

Instituto Hondureño del Café (IHCAFE): POB 40-C, Tegucigalpa; tel 37-3131; telex 1167; Gen Man: Ramiro Rodríguez Lanza; f 1970; coffee devt institute.

Instituto Hondureño de Mercadeo Agrícola (IHMA): POB 727, Tegucigalpa; tel 32-1629; telex 1138; Gen Man: Oscar Roberto Gallardo; agricultural devt agency.

FORESTRY

Corporación Hondureña de Desarrollo Forestal (COHDEFOR): Salida Carretera del Norte, Zona El Carrizal, Comayagüela, Apdo 1378, Tegucigalpa; tel 22-8810; telex 1172; Gen Man: José Segovia I.; f 1974; semi-autonomous organization in charge of forestry management and control of the forestry industry; due to be privatized in 1990.

Business and Economy

BANKING

Banco Capitalizadora Hondureña, SA (BANCAHSA): 5a Avda 501, Apdo 344, Tegucigalpa; tel 22-1171; telex 1162; Pres and Gen Man: Jorge Alberto Alvarado; f 1948; 38 brs.

Banco Central de Honduras (BANTRAL): 6a y 7a Avda, 1a Calle, Apdo 58-C, Tegucigalpa; tel 22-2270; telex 1121; Pres: Ricardo Maduro (mem of Cabinet); Man: Rigoberto Pineda S.; f 1950; central bank and bank of issue; 3 brs.

Banco Centroamericano de Integración Económica: Apdo 772, Tegucigalpa; tel 22-2230; telex 1103; Pres: Dante Gabriel Ramírez; f 1961 to finance the devt of the Central American Common Market and its member countries: Costa Rica, El Salvador, Guatemala, Honduras and Nicaragua.

Banco Municipal Autónomo (BANMA): 6a Avda, 6a Calle, Tegucigalpa; tel 22-5963; Pres: Justo Pastor Calderón; f 1963; 2 brs.

Banco Nacional de Desarrollo Agrícola, SA (BANADESA): 13 Calle, 4-5 Avda Comayagüela, Apdo 212, Tegucigalpa; tel 22-8505; telex 1105; Pres: Adolfo Lionel Sevilla G.; f 1980; agricultural devt bank; 28 brs.

Financiera Nacional de la Vivienda (FINAVI): Apdo 1194, Tegucigalpa; Exec Pres: Elmar Lizardo; f 1975; housing devt bank.

Superintendencia de Bancos: Tegucigalpa; banking regulation and supervision.

FINANCIAL AGENCY

Corporación Financiera de Olancho: Tegucigalpa; Pres: Rafael Calderón López; f 1977 to co-ordinate and manage all financial aspects of the Olancho forests project.

Defence

Fuerzas Armadas (Armed Forces): Cuartel General de las Fuerzas Armadas, Comayagüela, Tegucigalpa; tel 22-3257; Commdr-in-Chief: Humberto Regalado Hernández.

Fuerzas Aéreas (Air Force): Base Aérea HAM, Toncontín, Tegucigalpa; tel 33-6393; Commdr: Edgardo Mejía.

Fuerza Naval de Honduras (Navy): Cuartel General de Fuerzas Armadas, Comayagüela, Tegucigalpa; tel 33-4011; telex 1291; fax 31-2694; Commdr: Capt Arnulfo Cantarero López; Chief of Naval Staff: Capt Cristóbal Cano Sulley; f 1865; maritime law enforcement; illegal drug-trafficking interdiction.

Development and Planning

INVESTMENT

Corporación Nacional de Inversiones (CONADI): Apdo 842, Tegucigalpa; telex 1192; Exec Pres: Eduardo Ramos; Exec Vice-Pres: Lempira Bonilla; f 1974; industrial devt investment corpn; in 1988 managed 62 public-sector corpns of which 20 were to be sold to private investors by 1990.

PLANNING

Centro de Desarrollo Industrial: Avda La Paz 407, Tegucigalpa; prepares industrial devt policy for Ministry of Economy and Commerce.

Secretaría Técnica del Consejo Superior de Planificación Económica (CONSUPLANE): Edif Bancatlán 3, Apdo 1327, Comayagüela, Tegucigalpa; tel 22-8738; telex 1222; Exec Sec: Francisco Figueroa Zúñiga; f 1965; national planning office.

Legal and Judiciary

Corte Suprema (Supreme Court): 10a y 11a Avda, 3a Calle, Tegucigalpa; tel 22-8790; Pres: Salomon Jiménez Castro; Attorney-Gen: Rubén Darío Zepeda Gutiérrez; supreme court has nine judges.

Media

Compañía Televisora Hondureña, SA: Apdo 642, Tegucigalpa; tel 32-7835; telex 1126; Gen Man: José Rafael Ferrari; f 1959; main station is Channel 5; nine relay stations.

Radio Nacional de Honduras: Apdo 403, Tegucigalpa; tel 22-8042; telex 1147; Dir: Tomás Vindel; f 1976.

Mining and Energy

ENERGY

Comisión Hondureña de Energía Atómica: Apdo 104, Tegucigalpa; Pres: Dr Rafael Torres Fiallos; atomic energy commission.

MINING

Dirección General de Minas e Hidrocarburos: Blvd Miraflores, Apdo 981, Tegucigalpa; tel 32-7848; telex 1404; Dir-Gen: José Magin Lanza V.; directorate of mines and hydrocarbons.

Tourism

Secretaria de Cultura y Turismo: Costado Este del Palacio Legislativo, Apdo 154-C, Tegucigalpa; tel 22-6618; telex 1322; Dir-Gen: Tatiana de Pierson; f 1976; national tourism institute.

Transport and Communications

TELECOMMUNICATIONS

Empresa Hondureña de Telecomunicaciones (Hondutel): Apdo 1794, Tegucigalpa; tel 37-9802; telex 1343; Gen Man: Col Mario Leonel Fonseca; telecommunications co.

TRANSPORT

Dirección General de Caminos: Tegucigalpa; highways board.

Empresa Nacional Portuaria: Puerto Cortés, Apdo 18, Cortés; tel 55-0987; telex 8007; fax 55-0367; Dir-Gen: Angel Casanova Borjas; f 1965; has jurisdiction over all ports and port facilities.

Ferrocarril Nacional de Honduras: 1 Calle 0 2, Apdo 496, San Pedro Sula; tel 53-3230; Gen Man: P. R. Romero; f 1870.

Tela Railroad Co: La Lima; tel 56-2018; telex 8305; Pres: Ronald F. Walker; Gen Man: John A. Ordman.

Vaccaro Railway: La Ceiba; Gen Man: D. Dehorenzo.

Líneas Aéreas Nacionales, SA (LANSA): Apdo 35, La Ceiba; Gen Man: Oscar M. Elvir; f 1971; scheduled services within Honduras and to Islas de Bahía.

HUNGARY

Head of State

Executive power is vested in the President, who is elected by universal adult suffrage. The Council of Ministers, the highest organ of state administration, is elected by the Assembly on the recommendation of the President. The leading political role of the Hungarian Socialist Workers' Party was removed in 1989, and a new constitution was due to enter into force in 1990.

President (acting): Mátyás Szürös (elected 18 October 1989).

Office of the President: 1055 Budapest V, Kossuth Lajos tér 1-3; tel (1) 112-2600; telex 22-5547.

Legislature

The highest organ of state power is the unicameral Országgyülés (National Assembly), with 387 members, elected for five years by universal adult suffrage. Multi-party elections for the National Assembly were due to take place in 1990. For local administration Hungary is divided into 19 counties and the capital city.

Országgyülés (National Assembly): 1357 Budapest V, Kossuth Lajos tér 1-3; tel (1) 112-0600; telex 22-3920; fax (1) 153-0533; Pres (acting): István Fodor; Dep Pres: Lajos Horváth, Mária Jakab.

MINISTRIES AND GOVERNMENT DEPARTMENTS

CENTRAL PEOPLE'S CONTROL COMMISSION
1052 Budapest, Apáczai Csere János u 10
Tel (1) 118-8799; telex 22-4308
Chair: László Ballai

COUNCIL OF MINISTERS (SECRETARIAT)
1055 Budapest, Kossuth Lajos tér 1-3
Tel (1) 112-2600; telex 22-5547
Chair: Miklós Németh
Deputy Chair: Péter Medgyessy
Minister of State: Imre Pozsgay

MINISTRY OF AGRICULTURE AND FOOD
1055 Budapest, Kossuth Lajos tér 11
Tel (1) 153-3000; telex 22-5445; fax (1) 153-0518
Minister: Dr Csabo Hütter

MINISTRY OF CULTURE AND NATIONAL EDUCATION
1055 Budapest, Szalay u 10-14
Tel (1) 153-0600; telex 22-5935
Minister: Ferenc Glatz

MINISTRY OF DEFENCE
1055 Budapest, Pálffy Györ u 7-11
Tel (1) 132-2500; telex 22-5424
Minister: Col-Gen Ferenc Kárpati

MINISTRY OF THE ENVIRONMENT AND WATER MANAGEMENT
1394 Budapest, Fő u 44-50, POB 351
Tel (1) 115-8840; telex 22-4879
Minister: (vacant)

MINISTRY OF FINANCE
1051 Budapest, József Nádor tér 2-4
Tel (1) 118-2066
Minister: Dr László Békesi
Deputy Minister: Zsigmond Jarai

MINISTRY OF FOREIGN AFFAIRS
1027 Budapest, Bem rkp 47
Tel (1) 135-0100; telex 22-5571
Minister: Gyüla Horn
Deputy Minister: Ferenc Somogyi

MINISTRY OF INDUSTRY
1024 Budapest, Mártírok u 85
Tel (1) 132-6570; telex 22-5376
Minister: Ferenc Horváth

MINISTRY OF THE INTERIOR
1051 Budapest, József Attila u 2-4
Tel (1) 112-1710; telex 22-5216
Minister (acting): Zoltan Pál

MINISTRY OF JUSTICE
1055 Budapest, Szalay u 16
Tel (1) 132-5330
Minister: Kálmán Kulcsár

MINISTRY OF SOCIAL AFFAIRS AND HEALTH
1361 Budapest V, Arany János u 6-8
Tel (1) 132-3100; telex 22-4337; fax (1) 111-5208
Minister: Dr Judit Csehák

MINISTRY OF TRADE
1880 Budapest, Honvéd u 13-15
Tel (1) 153-0000; telex 22-5578; fax (1) 153-2794
Minister: Tamás Beck

MINISTRY OF TRANSPORT, CONSTRUCTION AND TELECOMMUNICATIONS
1400 Budapest, Dob u 75-81, POB 87
Tel (1) 122-0220; telex 22-5729; fax (1) 122-9831
Minister: András Derzsi
Deputy Minister: Sandor Kalnoki Kiss

NATIONAL PLANNING OFFICE
1051 Budapest, Roosevelt tér 7-8
Tel (1) 111-0200; telex 22-4993
President: Dr Ernő Kemenes

TECHNOLOGICAL DEVELOPMENT COMMITTEE
Budapest
Chair: Pál Tétenyi

GOVERNMENT AGENCIES AND ORGANIZATIONS

Advisory and Supervisory Bodies

Fogyasztási Szövetkezetek Országos Tanácsa—SZÖVOSZ (National Council of Consumer Co-operatives): 1373 Budapest 5, V. Szabadság tér 14, POB 616; tel (1) 153-4222; telex 22-4862; Chair: József Hartmann; Gen Sec: Dr István Szlamenicky; f 1949; safeguards interests of Hungarian consumer, housing and saving co-operative societies; co-owner of co-op foreign trading cos and joint ventures.

Ipari Szövetkezetek Országos Tanácsa—OKISZ (National Council of Industrial Co-operatives): 1443 Budapest, 70 Pf 172; tel (1) 141-5140; telex 22-7576; fax (1) 141-5521; Pres: Lajos Köveskuti; Sec-Gen: Dr István Lendvai; supervisory body for industrial co-operatives.

National Sport Office: 1054 Budapest, Rosenberg u 1; tel (1) 111-9080; telex 227553; fax (1) 153-4226; Pres: Tamás Tibor; Dep Pres: Anna Domonkos, Tamás Keczer; f 1921; co-ordinates policy on physical education and sport.

Országos Szövetkezeti Tanács—OSzT (National Co-operative Council): 1373 Budapest 5, V. Szabadság tér 14; tel (1) 112-7467; telex 22-4862; Pres: József Hartmann; Sec-Gen: Dr József Pál; f 1968; national representative forum for co-operatives.

State Property Agency: Budapest; Commr: János Martonyi; f 1989; supervision of the privatization of state-owned cos.

Agriculture and the Environment

AGRICULTURE

Termelőszövetkezetek Országos Tanácsa—TOT (National Council of Agricultural Co-operatives): 1361 Budapest, Akadémia u 1-3; tel (1) 132-8167; telex 22-6810; Pres: István Szabó; Sec-Gen: Dr János Eleki; f 1967; protection of the interests of agricultural co-operatives.

THE ENVIRONMENT

National Office for Environment and Nature Protection: Budapest XII, Költö u 21; tel (1) 116-6600; Chair: Kálmán Ábrahám.

Business and Economy

BANKING

AGROBANK Rt (Agricultural Innovation Bank Ltd): 1054 Budapest, Széchenyi rkp 6; tel (1) 131-4632; telex 22-3111; fax (1) 131-5740; Man Dir: Miklós Szigethy; Dep Man Dirs: Erika Varga, Gustáv Gehl; f 1984; joint-stock co; investment in agricultural sector; 10 brs.

Állami Fejlesztési Intézet (State Development Institution): 1052 Budapest, Deák F. u 5; tel (1) 118-1200; telex 22-5672; fax (1) 166-8643; Dir-Gen: Dr Borbala Báger; f 1987 to succeed the State Development Bank; management and control of devt projects financed partly from the state budget.

Általános Vállakozási Bank Rt (General Bank for Venture Financing Ltd): 1397 Budapest, POB 525, Stollár Béla u 3A; tel (1) 132-6590; telex 22-3157; fax (1) 131-3181; Gen Man: Elemér Terták; Dep Gen Man: Mihály Németh; f 1985; joint-stock co.

Építőipari Innovációs Bank Rt (Innovation Bank for Construction Industry Ltd): 1063 Budapest, Szív u 53; tel (1) 112-9010; telex 22-3743; fax (1) 132-0567; Man Dir: Tamás Varga; f 1985; joint-stock co.

INNOFINANCE—Általános Innovációs Pénzintézet (General Financial Institution for Innovation): 1365 Budapest, POB 718; tel (1) 138-3366; telex 22-3182; fax (1) 117-7800; Man Dir: Erzsébet Birman; f 1980; joint-stock co.

INVESTBANK—Müszaki Fejlesztési Bank (Bank for Technical Development): 1053 Budapest, Képíró u 9; tel (1) 118-4400; telex 22-3250; fax (1) 118-4400; Dir: Dr Anna Temesi; f 1983.

Ipari Szövetkezeti Fejlesztési Bank (Development Bank of Industrial Co-operatives): Budapest, Gerlóczy u 5; tel (1) 117-6811; telex 22-3042; fax (1) 117-1921; Dir: Bela Seydl; f 1984.

Kisvállalkozási Bank (Bank for Small Ventures): 1876 Budapest, Münnich Ferenc u 16; tel (1) 113-6940; telex 22-4280; Dir: Árpád Bacsóka; f 1986.

Konzumbank (Consumer Co-operatives' Bank): 1052 Budapest, Vitkovics M. u 9; tel (1) 117-2600; telex 22-3305; fax (1) 117-6721; Dir: Dr Gábor Pál; f 1986.

Magyar Külkereskedelmi Bank Rt (Hungarian Foreign Trade Bank Ltd): 1821 Budapest, Szt István tér 11; tel (1) 132-9360; telex 22-6941; fax (1) 132-2568; Chair and Man Dir: Gábor Erdély; f 1950; commercial bank.

Magyar Nemzeti Bank (National Bank of Hungary): 1850 Budapest, Szabadság tér 8-9; tel (1) 153-2600; telex 22-5755; fax (1) 111-7437; Pres: Ferenc Bartha; First Vice-Pres: Imre Tarafas; issue of bank notes; transacts international payments business; supervises banking system; 18 brs.

Mezőbank (National Banking Institution of Agricultural Co-operatives Corpn): 1025 Budapest, Aldás u 5; tel (1) 135-9362; telex 22-7058; Dir: Dr Gyula Kabai; f 1986.

Országos Takarékpénztár—OTP (National Savings Bank): 1051 Budapest, Münnich Ferenc u 16; tel (1) 153-1444; telex 22-4280; fax (1) 112-6858; Gen Man: Dr László Tisza; f 1949; savings bank; long-, medium- and short-term credits for housing construction, foreign currency and exchange operations, capital investments, security operations; 598 brs.

Pénzintézeti Központ (Central Corpn of Banking Cos): 1431 Budapest, Szamuely u 38; tel (1) 117-1255; telex 22-6548; Dir-Gen: Mihály Biró; f 1916; banking, property, rights and interests, deposits, securities and foreign exchange management.

INSURANCE

Állami Biztositó—ÁB (State Insurance Co): 1813 Budapest, Üllői u 1; tel (1) 118-1866; telex 22-4550; Gen Man: Andrea Deák; f 1949; handles life and property insurance, insurance of agricultural plants, co-operatives, foreign insurance etc.

Hungária Biztositó (Hungária Insurance, Reinsurance and Export Credit Insurance Co): 1115 Budapest, Bánk bán u 17/B; tel (1) 175-9211; telex 22-3104; Man Dir: Tamás Uzonyi; f 1986; handles international insurance, insurance of state cos, and car, marine, life, accident and liability insurance.

TRADE

AÉV No 31: 1364 Budapest, POB 83; tel (1) 118-0511; telex 22-4928; f 1951; state building factory; construction of industrial units, power plants, chemical combines, cement plants, etc.; undertakes building work abroad.

Ágker Co Ltd: 1054 Budapest, Akadémia u 1-3; tel (1) 153-4444; telex 22-4415; fax (1) 111-0388; Gen Man: Dr Julianna Berta; Dep Gen Mans: Dr Jenő Rostás, Dr András Bartha; export of agrarian products.

Agrária-Bábolna: 2943 Bábolna; tel (34) 69111; telex 22-6555; fax (34) 69002; f 1789; turn-key poultry and pig farms with breeding stock and feed premixes; hatching eggs, breeding poultry, pigs, sheep and breeding jumping and riding horses; processed chicken; rodent and insect extermination services, etc.

Agrikon: 6001 Kecskemét, Külső-Szegedi u 36, POB 43; tel (76) 27-666; telex 26-495; fax (76) 28-182; Budapest office: 1364 Budapest 4, POB 167; tel (1) 118-9568; telex 22-5517; fax (1) 117-2581; Gen Man: Dr István Kuczik; f 1948; engineering and servicing for agricultural and food processing machines.

Agrimpex: 1392 Budapest, POB 278; tel (1) 111-3800; telex 22-5751; fax (1) 153-0658; Dir-Gen: András Vermes; f 1948; agricultural products.

Agrober: 1502 Budapest, POB 94; tel (1) 162-0640; telex 22-5868; fax (1) 185-0986; Pres and Gen Man: Imre Koncz; Vice-Pres and Dep Gen Man: Imre David; Commercial Man: Pál Saaghy; f 1973; consulting engineers and contractors for the agriculture and food industry.

Agrotek: 1388 Budapest, POB 66; tel (1) 153-0555; telex 22-5651; fax (1) 112-4896; import of agricultural machinery, including machinery for livestock breeding and forestry equipment.

BHG: 1509 Budapest, POB 2; tel (1) 181-3300; telex 22-5933; fax (1) 166-7433; Dir-Gen: Kálmán Kovács; f 1874; manufacture and installation of telecommunications equipment.

Bivimpex: 1046 Budapest, Erzsébet u 2-4; tel (1) 169-3522; telex 22-4279; fax (1) 169-4716; Gen Man: László Vermes; Dir, Commercial: Gábor Kertész; f 1969; trading co of Hungarian tanneries; import of rawhides and skins; export of finished leathers, switch transactions, jobworks, etc.

Bőrker: 1391 Budapest, Pf 215, Paulay Ede u 41; tel (1) 121-0760; telex 22-5543; fax (1) 122-7095; Gen Man: Lajos Alsószentiványi; Dep Gen Man: Dr Iván Berendik; f 1949; export and import of light industry products.

BRG: 1300 Budapest, POB 43; tel (1) 168-2080; telex 22-5928; fax (1) 188-9508; radio engineering.

Budapest International Fairs: Hungexpo, 1441 Budapest, POB 44; tel (1) 157-3555; telex 22-4188; Dir: Ferenc Schriffert; f 1968; technical goods (Spring), consumer goods (Autumn), and other specialized exhibitions and fairs.

Budavox: 1392 Budapest, POB 267; tel (1) 186-8988; telex 22-5077; fax (1) 161-1288; Gen Man: Károly Koncz; f 1956; exports telecommunications equipment and systems.

Chemokomplex: 1389 Budapest, POB 141; tel (1) 132-9980; telex 22-5158; Man Dir: István Kovács; machines and equipment for the chemical industry.

Chemolimpex: 1805 Budapest, POB 121; tel (1) 118-3970; telex 22-4351; Gen Man: Dr Péter Dobrovits; chemicals, agrochemicals, plastics, paints.

Chinoin: 1325 Budapest, POB 110; tel (1) 169-0900; telex 22-4236; pharmaceutical and chemical works.

Cibintra: 1364 Budapest, Váci u 16, POB 170; tel (1) 118-8377; telex 22-6102; fax (1) 118-5777; Man Dir: György Zbedorsky; Dep Man Dir: Michael Graf von Medem; f 1989; owned by the Central European National Bank Ltd; export and import transactions in convertible currency; general trading activity; agency and representation.

Elektroimpex: 1392 Budapest, POB 296; tel (1) 132-8300; telex 22-5771; telecommunications and precision articles.

Elektromodul: 1390 Budapest, POB 158; tel (1) 149-5340; telex 22-5154; fax (1) 140-2583; Gen Man: Gábor Iklody; electrotechnical components.

ERBE: 1361 Budapest, POB 17; tel (1) 111-6460; telex 22-5442; fax (1) 153-4158; power plant investment co.

Factory of Laboratory Instruments Co Ltd: 1450 Budapest, POB 33; tel (1) 133-9708; telex 22-4162; fax (1) 134-0309; Gen Man: K. Varga; f 1899; scientific instruments, laboratory equipment and engineering.

Factory and Machinery Erecting Enterprise: 1394 Budapest, POB 384; tel (1) 132-7360; telex 22-4783.

Ferunion: 1829 Budapest, POB 612; tel (1) 117-2611; telex 22-5054; fax (1) 117-2594; tools, glassware, building materials, hardware.

FMV: 1475 Budapest, POB 215; tel (1) 164-0200; telex 22-4409; precision mechanics.

Folkart: 1364 Budapest, Régisposta u 12, POB 20; tel (1) 118-4844; telex 22-6814; Dir: Dr Judith Lendvai; f 1983; foreign trade office of the Co-operative Enterprise for Folk Art and Handicraft.

Foreign Trade Co for Industrial Co-operation: 1367 Budapest, POB 111; tel (1) 142-4950; telex 22-4435; foreign trade office for co-operation and purchasing of licences in industry.

Gábor Áron Works: 1087 Budapest, Asztalos Sándor u 9-12; tel (1) 133-7970; telex 22-4127; Dir: Sándor Antal; f 1981; production of washing machines and bakery ovens.

Gamma Müvek: 1119 Budapest, Fehérvári u 85; tel (1) 185-0800; telex 22-4946; fax (1) 166-5632; Dir-Gen: János Henz; f 1920; nuclear instruments, complete medical isotope diagnostical laboratories, elements for the instrumentation industry.

Ganz Danubius Shipyard and Crane Factory: Budapest XIII, Váci u 202; tel (1) 149-6370; telex 22-5047; f 1985.

Ganz Electric Works: 1525 Budapest, POB 63; tel (1) 175-3322; telex 22-5363; fax (1) 156-2989; f 1878; electric power generators, transformers, switchgear, electrical vehicles.

Ganz-Hunslet Engineering: Budapest VIII, Vajda Péter u 12; tel (1) 114-0840; telex 22-5576; fax (1) 114-3481; Gen Man: F. Weisz; f 1989; railway rolling stock, locomotives, railbuses, underground trains.

Ganz Measuring Instrument Works: 1701 Budapest, POB 58; tel (1) 127-1025; telex 22-4395; all types of electrical measuring instrument.

Generalimpex: 1518 Budapest, POB 168; tel (1) 126-0200; telex 22-6758; Dir: László Nagy; f 1980; permitted to import or export any product.

Geominco: 1525 Budapest, POB 92; tel (1) 135-4580; telex 22-4442; geological and mining engineering; undertakes exploration and research.

Hungagent Ltd: 1374 Budapest, I. Lajos 11-15, POB 542; tel (1) 188-6180; telex 22-4526; fax (1) 188-8769; Dir: Gábor Szemkeő; f 1961; foreign representations agency; export-import co-operation.

Hungarian Aluminium Corpn (HUNGALU): 1387 Budapest, POB 30; tel (1) 149-4750; telex 22-5471; fax (1) 140-2723; Gen Man: Dr Lajos Dózsa.

Hungarocoop: 1370 Budapest, POB 334; tel (1) 153-1711; telex 22-4859; Hungarian Co-operative Foreign Trading Co; import and export of consumer goods.

Hungarofilm: 1363 Budapest, POB 39; tel (1) 111-6650; telex 22-5768; Sales Man: István Váradi; f 1956; films.

Hungarofruct: 1394 Budapest, POB 386; tel (1) 131-7120; telex 22-5351; fax (1) 132-1378; f 1953; fresh, preserved and dehydrated fruit and vegetables.

Hungarotex: 1804 Budapest, POB 100; tel (1) 117-4555; telex 22-4751; Dir-Gen: Éva Szabó; f 1953; textiles and garments.

Hungexpo (Hungarian Foreign Trade Co for Fairs and Publicity): 1441 Budapest, POB 44; tel (1) 122-5008; telex 22-4525; fax (1) 122-1021; advertising, publicity, public relations; printing, fairs, exhibitions.

IDEX: 1011 Budapest, Fő u 14-18, POB 24; tel (1) 115-9290; telex 22-4541; fax (1) 135-1393; complete factory equipment.

Ikarus: 1630 Budapest, POB 3; tel (1) 183-3550; telex 22-4766; fax (1) 163-6473; Man Dir: András Semsey; Technical Dir: István Lepsényi; f 1895; construction and export of buses in complete state or in sets for assembly.

Industria Ltd: 1117 Budapest, POB 272; commercial representation of foreign firms, technical consulting service, market research etc.

Interag Co Ltd: 1390 Budapest, Rajk László u 11, POB 184; tel (1) 132-6770; telex 22-4776; fax (1) 153-0736; represents foreign firms; conducts general import/export business, after-sale service, domestic trade; operates filling and service stations.

Intercooperation Co Ltd: 1253 Budapest, POB 53; tel (1) 115-2220; telex 22-4242; establishment and carrying out of co-operation agreements, joint ventures and import and export deals.

IPV (Publishing and Promotion Co for Tourism): 1145 Budapest, POB 164; tel (1) 163-3652; telex 22-6074; fax (1) 183-7320; Gen Man: István Fazekas; Dep Gen Man: András Váczi; f 1971; publishing, publicity, film-making, exhibitions, advertising.

KGyV Metallurgical Engineering Corpn: 1553 Budapest, POB 23; tel (1) 111-2274; telex 22-5920; metallurgical engineering.

Komplex: 1807 Budapest, POB 125; tel (1) 111-7010; telex 22-5957; Man Dir: Adolf Féderer; f 1953; agricultural machinery; plant and equipment for food industry.

Konsumex: 1441 Budapest, POB 58; tel (1) 153-0511; telex 22-5151; fax (1) 112-7281; f 1959; consumer goods, household articles etc.

Lampart: 1475 Budapest 10, POB 41; tel (1) 157-0111; telex 22-5365; fax (1) 157-2029; Dir-Gen: Zoltán Réti; Dir, Finance: Imre Dobai; Dir, Commercial: Ildiko Fonyodi; f 1883; glass-lined processing equipment and highly acid-proof glass.

Licencia: 1368 Budapest, POB 207; tel (1) 118-1111; telex 22-5872; fax (1) 138-2304; Dir-Gen: Dr Lajos Vékony; Dir: Ferenc Gebauer; f 1950; purchase and sale of patents and inventions.

Lignimpex: 1393 Budapest, POB 323; tel (1) 112-9850; telex 22-4251; timber, paper and fuel.

Magnesite Industry: 1475 Budapest, POB 11; tel (1) 157-1378; telex 22-5644; Dir: B. Hazai; f 1892; refractory products.

Magyar Gazdasági Kamara (Hungarian Chamber of Commerce): 1389 Budapest, POB 106; tel (1) 153-3333; telex 22-4745; fax (1) 153-1285; Pres: András Gábor; Sec-Gen: László Fodor; f 1948; develops trade with other countries; mediates between cos etc.

Magyar Media Advertising Agency: 1392 Budapest 62, POB 279; tel (1) 132-5176; telex 22-3040.

MAHIR Hungarian Publicity Co: 1818 Budapest, POB 367; tel (1) 118-3444; telex 22-5341; fax (1) 117-9032; advertising agency.

Masped: 1364 Budapest, Kristóf tér 2, POB 104; tel (1) 118-2922; telex 22-4471; fax (1) 118-8343; Gen Man: Kálmán Gelencsér; international forwarding and carriage.

Medimpex: 1808 Budapest; tel (1) 118-3955; telex 22-5477; export and import of pharmaceutical and biological products, veterinary drugs, laboratory chemicals.

Mertcontrol: 1397 Budapest, POB 542; tel (1) 132-5300; telex 22-5777; fax (1) 111-6897; f 1951; quality control of import and export goods.

Metalimpex: 1393 Budapest, POB 330; tel (1) 118-7611; telex 22-5251; metals and metal products.

Metrimpex: 1391 Budapest, POB 202; tel (1) 112-5600; telex 22-5451; fax (1) 111-7212; electronic measuring instruments and equipment.

Mineralimpex: 1062 Budapest, Népköztársaság u 64; tel (1) 111-6470; telex 22-4651; fax (1) 153-1779; Dir-Gen: Dr József Tóth; oils and mining products.

Mirelite Trading Co: 1051 Budapest V, Dorottya u 1; tel (1) 118-6650; telex 22-7141; fax (1) 118-6137; Dir-Gen: Dr László Csaba; Commercial Dir: Gábor Kutrucz; f 1988 to replace Hungarian Deepfreezing Industry; export and import of canned, quick-frozen and fresh fruit and vegetables.

Mogürt (Hungarian Trading Co for Motor Vehicles): 1056 Budapest, Váci u 38; tel (1) 118-6044; telex 22-5357; fax (1) 118-8895; Gen Man: László Pál Tóth; f 1946; export and import of automotive products, accessories and spares.

MOM: 1525 Budapest, POB 52; tel (1) 156-4122; telex 22-4151; f 1876; laboratory and optical instruments.

Monimpex Trader House: 1054 Budapest, V. Tükóry u 4; tel (1) 153-1222; telex 22-5371; fax (1) 111-7263; Gen Man: M. Terelmes; Dep Gen Man: M. Fehér; f 1948; export of wine, confectionery goods, fruit, spirits and beer.

MVMT: 1251 Budapest, POB 34; tel (1) 115-2600; telex 22-4382; electricity.

Nikex: 1016 Budapest, Mészáros u 48-54; tel (1) 156-0122; telex 22-4971; fax (1) 175-5131; Gen Man: Mihály Petrik; f 1948; production of machinery and materials for use in metallurgy, construction, water management and mining.

Novex: 1364 Budapest, POB 62; tel (1) 118-4022; telex 22-6054; Man Dir: Judith Salusinszky; deals with transfer of technology.

Ofotért: 1917 Budapest; tel (1) 120-3669; telex 22-4418; Dir-Gen: Janos Szilágyi; f 1949; optical and photographic articles.

OMIKK Technoinform: 1428 Budapest, POB 12; tel (1) 113-8247; telex 22-4944; technical and economic information services, including translations, studies, conferences, periodicals and documentation, software programmes.

OMKER: 1089 Budapest VIII, Rezső u 5-7; tel (1) 112-3000; telex 22-4683; fax (1) 111-7694; Dir-Gen: Róbert Zentai; f 1951; medical instruments.

ORION: 1475 Budapest, POB 84; tel (1) 128-4830; telex 22-5798; fax (1) 127-2490; Dir-Gen: L. Kovács; f 1913; radios, televisions and electrical goods.

Pannonia (Foreign Trade Co of Cespel Works): 1394 Budapest, POB 354; tel (1) 121-2450; telex 22-5128; metallurgical materials, welding electrodes, cast iron fittings, steel tubes and cylinders, bicycles, industrial sewing and pressing machinery and laundry equipment, complete tube manufacturing plants, bottle plants, etc.

Patentbureau Danubia: 1368 Budapest 5, POB 198; tel (1) 118-1111; telex 22-5872; fax (1) 138-2304; Dir: Dr L. Vékony; f 1951; patent services.

Pharmatrade: 1367 Budapest, POB 126; tel (1) 118-5966; telex 22-6650; fax (1) 118-5346; Man Dir: Dr Lajos Mészáros; f 1983; food and feed additives, medicinal products and cosmetics.

Philatelia Hungarica: 1373 Budapest V, Guszev u 24, POB

600; tel (1) 131-6146; telex 22-6508; fax (1) 111-5421; Gen Man: Imre Biró; Dep Gen Man: László Berzsenyi; f 1950; stamps, wholesale only.

Phylaxia: 1486 Budapest, POB 23; tel (1) 157-5311; telex 22-4549; vaccines, veterinary products.

Precision Fittings Factory: 3301 Eger, POB 2; tel (36) 11-911; telex 63-331.

Prodinform: 1063 Budapest, Munkácsy M. u 16; tel (1) 132-3770; telex 22-7750; fax (1) 122-2245; Gen Man: Dr Pál Simon; f 1982; technical and scientific information, technical consultations, trading of industrial diamond tools, introduction of total quality management systems, organization of language courses.

RÁBA (Hungarian Railway Carriage and Machine Works): 9002 Győr, POB 50; tel (96) 12-111; telex 02-4255; Gen Man: Ede Horváth; f 1896; commercial vehicles, diesel engines, agricultural tractors.

Rekard: 9027 Győr, Kandó Kálmán u 5-7; tel (96) 13-122; telex 24-360; farm equipment.

Tannimpex: 1395 Budapest, POB 406; tel (1) 112-3400; telex 22-4557; hides, leather shoes, gloves, fancy goods and furs.

Tatabánya Mining Co: 2803 Tatabánya, POB 323; tel (34) 10-144; telex 22-6206; fax (34) 11-061; Gen Man: László Vas; f 1894; production of mining equipment and machinery, preparation of industrial and drinking water, purification of waste waters, dewatering of sludges, tunnelling.

Taurus Rubber Works: 1440 Budapest, POB 25; tel (1) 134-1140; telex 22-5312; fax (1) 118-8754; Chief Exec: Dr Ilona Tatai; f 1882; rubber.

Technoimpex: 1390 Budapest, POB 183; tel (1) 118-4055; telex 22-4171; Gen Man: István Mátyás; exports machine tools, specialized machinery, equipment for the oil and gas industry, agricultural equipment; imports machine tools, machines for light industry; organizes barter deals, co-operation, leasing and joint ventures.

Temaforg: 1361 Budapest, POB 8; tel (1) 111-8450; telex 22-4663; textile and synthetic wastes, industrial wipers, geotextiles for agriculture, road and railway construction.

Terimpex: 1825 Budapest, POB 251; tel (1) 117-5011; telex 22-4551; Gen Man: Dr László Ránky; cattle and agricultural products.

TERTA: 1956 Budapest, POB 16; tel (1) 163-4240; telex 22-4087; telecommunications and data transmission equipment.

Tesco: 1367 Budapest, POB 101; tel (1) 111-0850; telex 22-4642; fax (1) 131-6969; Gen Man: István Bene; f 1962; organization for international technical and scientific co-operation.

Transelektro: 1394 Budapest, POB 377; tel (1) 132-0100; telex 22-4571; fax (1) 153-0162; Dir-Gen: Pál Kertész; generators, power stations, cables, lighting, transformers, household appliances, catering equipment, etc.

TSZKER (Trading Co for Agricultural Co-operatives): 1445 Budapest, POB 354; tel (1) 134-0900; telex 22-4147; industrial metal constructions, wine, wood and agricultural products.

TUNGSRAM Co Ltd: 1340 Budapest; tel (1) 169-2800; telex 22-5058; fax (1) 169-2868; Pres: András Gábor; f 1896; light sources, lighting systems, vacuum engineering machinery, vacuum electronics, electronics and components, etc.

Vegyépszer: 1379 Budapest, POB 540; tel (1) 135-1125; telex 22-6930; fax (1) 116-9470; building and assembling of chemical plant, supply of complete equipment.

VEPEX Contractor Ltd: 1370 Budapest, POB 308; tel (1) 142-5535; telex 22-4208; fax (1) 142-5502; vegetable protein extract.

Videoton Rt: 1398 Budapest, POB 557; tel (1) 121-0520; telex 22-4763; Man Dir: István Papp; Gen Man: János Kazsmer; TV sets, tape recorders, computer systems and peripherals, software.

Volánpack: 1475 Budapest, POB 76; tel (1) 148-4300; telex 22-6935; Dir-Gen: Miklós Vajda; forwarding and transport, packaging, warehousing, etc.

Vörös Október Cooperative, ÓCSA: 1734 Budapest, POB 26; tel (1) 157-1355; telex 22-6156; Pres: Rikárd Ledl; Vice-Pres: János Győr; f 1948; agricultural products.

Defence

Army: Budapest V, Ministry of Defence, Pálffy Győr u 7-11; tel (1) 132-2500; telex 22-5424; Chief of Staff: József Pácsek; Dep Chief of Staff: Gyula Remóryi.

Committee of Civil Defence: 1055 Budapest V, Kossuth Lajos tér.

Headquarters of the Commander of the Workers' Militia: 1016 Budapest I, Somloí u 51.

Development and Planning

State Office for Technical Development (OMFB): 1374 Budapest, POB 565; tel (1) 117-5900; telex 22-4233; fax (1) 118-7998; Chair: Dr Pál Tétényi; f 1961; initiation, planning, management and control of technical devt and research activity.

Employment

State Office for Labour and Wages: 1373 Budapest, POB 609; tel (1) 132-2100; telex 22-4993; Pres: Dr Csaba Halmos; Dir: Tamás Marton; f 1981; helps to formulate policy on wages and employment.

Legal and Judiciary

Supreme Court: Budapest I, Fő u 1; tel (1) 116-0075; Pres: Dr Jenő Szilbereky; Chief Public Prosecutor: Dr Károly Szijártó; Pres of the Supreme Court is elected by the National Assembly for a five-year term.

Media

BROADCASTING

Magyar Rádió: 1800 Budapest, Brody Sándor u 5-7; tel (1) 138-8388; telex 22-5188; Pres: István Hajdu; f 1924; three Budapest stations; six regional studios; external broadcasts in English, German, Hungarian, Italian, Spanish and Turkish.

Magyar Televízió: 1810 Budapest 5, Szabadság tér 17; tel (1) 153-3200; telex 22-5568; fax (1) 153-4979; Pres: István Nemeskürty; f 1957; two channels; 100 relay stations.

GOVERNMENT PUBLISHERS

Akadémiai Kiadó: 1054 Budapest, Alkotmány u 21; tel (1) 111-1010; telex 22-6228; Gen Man: György Hazai; Man Dir: Klára Takácsi-Nagy; f 1828; publishes articles and information concerning Hungarian science and research, as well as dictionaries, encyclopaedias and periodicals.

Statistikai Kiadó Vállalat (Statistical Publishing House): 1300 Budapest 3, POB 99; tel (1) 180-3311; telex 22-6699; Man Dir: Benedek Belecz; f 1954; publication of statistical books and journals.

NEWS AND INFORMATION

Cartographia (Hungarian Co for Surveying and Mapping): 1443 Budapest, POB 132; tel (1) 163-4639; telex 22-6218; fax (1) 117-6176; Dir: György Domokos; Man, Technical: János Szép; f 1954; production and trade of cartographical products and services.

Központi Statisztikai Hivatal (Central Statistical Office): 1525 Budapest, POB 51; tel (1) 135-8530; telex 22-4308; Pres: Dr Vera Nyitrai; f 1848; collection, processing, supplying, dissemination, analysis and storage of data.

Magyar Távirati Iroda—MTI (Hungarian News Agency): 1016 Budapest, Fém u 5-7; tel (1) 175-6722; telex 22-4371; Man Dir: Tamás Palos; f 1880; 19 brs in Hungary; 23 bureaux abroad.

Országos Földögyi és Térképészeti Hivatal (National Office of Lands and Mapping): 1860 Budapest 55, Pf 1; tel (1) 131-3736; telex 22-5445; Dir: István Hoffer; f 1952; supervision of all geodetic, cartographic and remote sensing activities; directs all land registration and land protection works.

Mining and Energy

ENERGY

Országos Atomenergia Bizottság (National Atomic Energy Commission): 1374 Budapest, POB 565; tel (1) 121-3000; telex 22-4907; fax (1) 142-7598; Pres: Pál Tétényi; Vice-Pres: Dr György Vajda; f 1955; advises Govt on all matters relating to peaceful use of nuclear energy; regulatory activities in connection with training of personnel and research into nuclear energy.

Paksi Atomerőmű Vállalat—PAV (Paks Nuclear Co): 7031 Paks, POB 71; tel (75) 11-222; telex 14-440; fax (75) 551-332; Dir-Gen: J. Pónya; Dep Dir-Gen: J. Szabó; f 1976; nuclear power production at Paks.

Villamosenergiaipari Kutató Intézet—VEIKI (Institute for Electric Power Research): 1368 Budapest, POB 233; tel (1) 117-2235; telex 22-5744; fax (1) 153-0981; Dir: Dr György Vajda; Dep Dir: Dr Károly Reményi; f 1949; research and devt of electric power resources.

MINING

National Technical Superintendency of Mines: 1055 Budapest V, Markó u 16.

Science and Technology

Budapesti Műszaki Egyetem Nukleáris Technikai Intézet (Institute of Nuclear Technics of the Technical University of Budapest, Training Reactor): 1521 Budapest, POB 91; tel (1) 181-2564; telex 22-5931; fax (1) 166-6808; Dir: Dr G. Csom; Dep Dir: Dr G. Keömley; f 1971; nuclear training, reactor techniques, reactor physics, radiochemistry.

Kossuth Lajos Tudományegyetem Kísérleti Fizikai Intézete (Institute for Experimental Physics of the Kossuth Lajos University): 4001 Debrecen, POB 105; tel (52) 15-222; telex 72-200; fax (52) 14-050; Dir: Dr J. Csikai; f 1923; research in low-energy nuclear physics, neutron gas physics and the application of nuclear methods in science and technology.

Magyar Tudományos Akadémia Atommag Kutató Intézete—ATOMKI (Institute of Nuclear Research of the Hungarian Academy of Sciences): 4001 Debrecen, POB 51; tel (52) 17-266; telex 72-210; fax (1) 16-181; Dir: Prof D. Berényi; Dep Dirs: Dr E. Koltay, Dr D. Varga; f 1954; basic and applied nuclear research.

Magyar Tudományos Akadémia Izotópkutató Intézete (Institute of Isotopes of the Hungarian Academy of Sciences): 1121 Budapest, Konkoly-Thege u 29-33; tel (1) 169-9499; telex 22-5360; fax (1) 156-5045; Dir-Gen: Dr Gábor Földiák; f 1959; research, devt and production of radioisotopes and other clinical diagnostics; national accountancy of fissionable and radioactive materials.

Magyar Tudományos Akadémia Központi Fizikai Kutató Intézete—KFKI (Central Research Institute for Physics of the Hungarian Academy of Sciences): 1525 Budapest, POB 49; tel (1) 169-8566; telex 22-4722; fax (1) 155-3894; Dir-Gen: Dr Ferenc Szabó; f 1950; research in practical and nuclear physics.

Országos 'Frédéric Joliot-Curie' Sugárbiológiai és Sugáregészségügyi Kutató Intézet (National Research Institute for Radiobiology and Radiohygiene): 1775 Budapest, POB 101; tel (1) 730-026; telex 22-5103; Dir: Dr L. B. Sztanyik; f 1957; research on effects of ionizing and non-ionizing radiations.

Telecommunications

Central Administration of the Hungarian PTT: 1540 Budapest; tel (1) 155-0550; telex 22-1193; fax (1) 156-0855; Pres and Gen Man: Zoltán Köteles; provision of all kinds of postal and telecommunications services and facilities.

Tourism

Budapest Tourist: 1051 Budapest, Roosevelt tér 5; tel (1) 118-6663; telex 22-6448; fax (1) 118-1658; Dir: István Kovács; f 1916; runs tours, congresses and cultural programmes; provides accomodation.

COOPTOURIST Travel Agency: 1016 Budapest, Derék u 2; tel (1) 156-8122; telex 22-5399; fax (1) 175-3658; Gen Man: Dr Sandor Sipos; Dep Gen Man: Dr András Tóth; f 1969; general tourism services for groups and individuals.

Danubius Hotel and Spa Co: 1138 Budapest, Margitsziget; tel (1) 112-1000; telex 22-6850; fax (1) 153-1883; Gen Man: István Puskás; f 1972; maintenance of spa hotels.

Express Utazási Iroda (Express Travel Bureau): 1054 Budapest, Szabadság tér 16; tel (1) 153-0660; telex 22-5384; fax (1) 153-1715; Gen Man: Dr Gyula Tarcsi; f 1957; specializes in tours and services for young people.

HungarHotels—Hungarian Hotel and Restaurant Co: 1052 Budapest, Petőfi Sándor u 14, POB 106; tel (1) 118-2033; telex 22-4209; Pres: Dr Gyula Gyökössy; f 1956.

IBUSZ—Idegenforgalmi, Beszerési, Utazási és Szállitási Rt (Hungarian Travel Agency): 1364 Budapest, Felszabadulás tér 5; tel (1) 118-1120; telex 22-4976; fax (1) 117-7723; Pres: Dr Erika Szemenkár; Vice-Pres: Sándor Szür.

Locomotiv Tourist: 1536 Budapest, Szilágyi Dezső tér 1, POB 241; tel (1) 115-9420; telex 22-4249; Dir: Dr Adám Menyhárt.

Malév Air-Tours: 1367 Budapest, Roosevelt tér 2, POB 122; tel (1) 118-3780; telex 22-4954; fax (1) 118-7359; Dir: Tamás Déri.

Máv Tours (Travel Bureau of Hungarian State Railways): 1378 Budapest, Guszev u 1, POB 25; tel (1) 117-3723; telex 22-3251; Man: Dr Katalin Rosztóczy; f 1985.

Országos Idegenforgalmi Hivatal—OIH (Hungarian Tourist Board): 1054 Budapest, Vigadóu 6; tel (1) 118-5694; telex 22-5182; fax (1) 118-5241; Pres: Dr Imre Gellai; f 1978; coordinates policy on tourism, prepares plans for short- and long-term tourist devt, promotes Hungary abroad.

Pannónia—Hotel and Catering Co: 1088 Budapest, Puskin u 6, POB 159; tel (1) 138-3933; telex 22-4561; fax (1) 118-1344; Gen Man: Jenő Somogyi; Dep Gen Man: Gyula Harbula; f 1949; owns 45 hotels; general tourist activities.

Pegazus Tours: 1053 Budapest, Károlyi Mihály u 5; Dir: Mausz Gotthard.

Volántourist: 1066 Budapest, Lenin krt 96; tel (1) 132-2905; telex 22-6722; fax (1) 166-7658; Dir: Lajos Csete; f 1958; promotion of tourism, car rental service.

Transport

CIVIL AVIATION

Légiforgalmi és Repülőtéri Igazgatóság—OIH (Air Traffic and Airport Administration): 1675 Budapest/Ferihegy, POB 53; tel (1) 127-1652; telex 22-7837; fax (1) 147-5741; Dir-Gen: Tamás Erdei; f 1973; air traffic control, airport maintenance and devt.

Légügyi Főigazgatóság (General Directorate of Civil Aviation): 1400 Budapest, Dob u 75-81, POB 87; tel (1) 142-2544; telex 22-5729; Dir-Gen: Ódón Skonda; controls civil aviation.

Magyar Légiközlekedési Vállalat—MALÉV (Hungarian Airlines): 1051 Budapest, Roosevelt tér 2, POB 122; tel (1) 118-9033; telex 22-4954; fax (1) 117-2417; Dir-Gen: Lajos Jahoda; Dep Dir-Gen: Tamás Odor; f 1954; regular services from Budapest to Europe, North Africa and the Middle East.

RAILWAYS

Győr-sopron-ebenfurti vasut—Gysev-ROeEE (Railway of Győr-Sopron-Ebenfurt): 1536 Budapest, Szilágyi Dezső, tér 1, POB 241; tel (1) 115-9420; telex 22-4249; Dir-Gen: László Oroszváry; Hungarian-Austrian owned railway; transport of passengers and goods.

Magyar Államvasutak (MÁV): 1940 Budapest, Népköztarsaság u 73-75; tel (1) 122-0660; telex 22-4342; Dir-Gen: György Onozo; state-owned since 1868; national railway co; total network 8,500km.

ROADS

Hungarocamion: 1442 Budapest, POB 108; tel (1) 157-3811; telex 22-5455; Gen Man: Imre Torma; international road freight transport co; fleet of 1,800 lorries.

Raabersped: 1531 Budapest, POB 33; tel (1) 175-1322; telex 22-5919; Dir: Dr János Berényi; international forwarding agency (rail, road, air and sea).

Volán Vállalatok Köpontja (Centre of Volán Enterprises): 1391 Budapest, Lenin krt 96, POB 221; tel (1) 112-4290; telex 22-5177; Dir: Kálmán Garami; Dep Dir: Elemér Saslics; f 1984; centre of 25 Volán enterprises for inland and international road freight and passenger transport, forwarding, tourism.

SHIPPING

MAFRACHT: 1364 Budapest, Kristóf tér 2, POB 105; tel (1) 118-5276; telex 22-4471; shipping agency.

MAHART—Magyar Hajózási Rt (Hungarian Shipping Co): 1366 Budapest, POB 58; tel (1) 118-1880; telex 22-5258; Dir-Gen: Péter Muradin; carries cargo and passenger traffic on the Danube and Lake Balaton; also Mediterranean and ocean-going services; operates port of Budapest; ship-building and ship-repair services.

ICELAND

Head of State

According to the Constitution, executive power is vested in the President, elected by universal adult suffrage for a four-year term, and the Cabinet, consisting of a Prime Minister and other Ministers appointed by the President. However, real executive power lies with the Cabinet, which is responsible to the Althingi (Parliament).

President: Vigdís Finnbogadóttir (took office 1 Aug 1980; began second term 1 Aug 1984; re-elected for third term beginning 1 Aug 1988).

Office of the President: Stornarráðshúsið, v/ Lækjargötu, 150 Reykjavík; tel (1) 25000.

Legislature

Legislative power is shared by the President and the Althingi (Parliament), which has 63 members elected by universal suffrage for a four-year term. The Althingi chooses 20 of its members to form the Upper House, the other 43 forming the Lower House; both houses sit together for some purposes as the United Althingi.

United Althingi: v/Austurvöll, 101 Reykjavík; tel (01) 11560; Speaker: Gudrún Helgadóttir.

MINISTRIES AND GOVERNMENT DEPARTMENTS

OFFICE OF THE PRIME MINISTER
Stjórnarráðshúsið v/Lækjartorg, 150 Reykjavík
Tel (1) 25000
Prime Minister: Steingrímur Hermansson

MINISTRY OF AGRICULTURE
Rauðarárstígur 25, 150 Reykjavík
Tel (1) 622000; fax (1) 21160
Minister: Steingrímur Sigfússon

MINISTRY OF COMMERCE
Arnarhváli, 150 Reykjavík
Tel (1) 609070; telex 2092; fax (1) 621289
Minister: Jón Sigurðsson

MINISTRY OF COMMUNICATIONS
Hafnarhúsinu við Tryggvagötu, 150 Reykjavík
Tel (1) 609630; fax (1) 621702
Minister: Steingrímur J. Sigfússon

MINISTRY OF CULTURE AND EDUCATION
Hverfisgata 6, 150 Reykjavík
Tel (1) 609000; telex 2111; fax (1) 623068
Minister: Svavar Gestsson

MINISTRY OF FINANCE
Arnarhváli, 150 Reykjavík
Tel (1) 609200; telex 2092; fax (1) 28280
Minister: Ólafur Ragnar Grímsson

MINISTRY OF FISHERIES
Skúlagata 4, 150 Reykjavík
Tel (1) 609000; telex 2342; fax (1) 621853
Minister: Halldór Ásgrímsson

MINISTRY OF FOREIGN AFFAIRS
Hverfisgata 115, 150 Reykjavík
Tel (1) 629000; telex 2050; fax (1) 622373
Minister: Jón Baldvin Hannibalsson

MINISTRY OF HEALTH AND SOCIAL SECURITY
Laugavegur 116, 150 Reykjavík
Tel (1) 609700; fax (1) 19165
Minister: Guðmundur Bjarnason

MINISTRY OF INDUSTRY
Arnarhváli, 150 Reykjavík
Tel (1) 609420; fax (1) 26859
Minister: Jón Sigurðsson

MINISTRY OF JUSTICE AND ECCLESIASTICAL AFFAIRS
Arnarhváli, 150 Reykjavík
Tel (1) 609000; telex 2224; fax (1) 27340
Minister: Halldór Ásgrimsson

MINISTRY OF SOCIAL AFFAIRS
Hafnarhúsinu við Tryggvagötu, 150 Reykjavík
Tel (1) 25000; telex 3000
Minister: Jóhanna Sigurðardóttir

GOVERNMENT AGENCIES AND ORGANIZATIONS

Advisory and Supervisory Body

National Audit Office: Laugavegur 105, 150 Reykjavík; tel (1) 22160; Auditor-Gen: Halldór V. Sigurdsson; Dep Auditor-Gen: Sigurdur Thordarson; f 1987; audits the accounts of the Republic of Iceland, and of state-owned banks and other enterprises.

Business and Economy

BANKING

Búnaðarbanki Íslands (Agricultural Bank of Iceland): Austurstræti 5, 155 Reykjavík; tel (1) 25600; telex 2383; fax (1) 621340; Chair: Stefán Valgeirsson; Man Dirs: Stefán Hilmarsson, Stefán Pálsson, Jón Adolf Guðjónsson; f 1929; state-owned commercial bank; 33 brs.

Idnadarbanki Íslands (Industrial Bank of Iceland): Lækjargata 12, 101 Reykjavík; tel (1) 691800; telex 3003; fax (1) 687784; Gen Mans: Bragi Hannesson, Valur Valsson, Ragnar Önundarson; f 1953; 9 brs.

Landsbanki Íslands (National Bank of Iceland): Austurstræti 11, POB 170, 155 Reykjavík; tel (1) 606600; telex 2030; fax (1) 29882; Gen Mans: Björgvin Vilmundarson, Sverrir Hermannson, Valur Arnthorsson; f 1885; 32 brs.

Seðlabanki Íslands (Central Bank of Iceland): Kalkofnsvegur 1, 150 Reykjavík; tel (1) 699600; telex 2020; Govs: Dr Jóhannes Nordal, Tómas Arnason, Geir Hallgrímsson; f 1961 to fulfil central banking activities previously undertaken by Landsbanki Íslands.

FINANCIAL AGENCIES

Office of Budget and Management: Arnarhváli, 150 Reykjavík; tel (1) 25686; a dept of the Ministry of Finance.

State Treasury: Arnarhváli, v/Lindargötu, 150 Reykjavík; tel (1) 25000.

TRADE

Útflutningsráð Íslands (Export Council of Iceland): Lágmúli 5, POB 8796, 128 Reykjavík; tel (1) 688777; telex 2085; Man Dir: Dr Ingjaldur Hannibalsson; f 1971; provides export promotion and assistance to exporting cos.

Defence

Landhelgisgæzlan (Icelandic Coast Guard): Seljavegur 32, POB 7120, 101 Reykjavík; tel (1) 10230; telex 2048; fax (1) 610240; Dir: Gunnar Bergsteinsson; f 1926; responsible to the Ministry of Justice; polices the ocean around Iceland, both inside and outside territorial waters; assists or salvages boats and ships in difficulty at sea around Iceland; assists in the rescue of persons in danger at sea or in coastal areas; maintains three vessels, one aircraft and two helicopters.

Rannsóknarlögregla Ríkisins (State Criminal Police): Audbrekku, 200 Kópavogur; tel (1) 44000.

Development and Planning

Economic Development Institute: Raudarárstík 31, Reykjavík; conducts research and planning for the devt of Iceland's economy.

Technological Institute of Iceland: Keldnaholt, 112 Reykjavík; tel (1) 687000; telex 3020; fax (1) 687409; f 1978; responsible to the Ministry of Industry; conducts research and planning for the devt of Iceland's industry; provides technical assistance; provides standardization services and maintains standards offices.

Education and Research

National Economic Institute of Iceland: Kalkofnvegi 1, 150 Reykjavík; tel (1) 699500; telex 2020; fax (1) 621802; Dir: Thordur Fridjansson; f 1974; economic forecasts and advisory work for govt and parliament; compiles national accounts and industrial statistics.

Energy

Landsvirkjun (National Power Company): Háaleitisbraut 68, 103 Reykjavík; tel (1) 600700; telex 2054; fax (1) 687469; Gen Man: Halldór Jónatansson; Dep Gen Man: Jóhann Már Maríusson; f 1965; generates, transmits, sells and distributes electric power wholesale to public distribution systems and industrial enterprises.

Orkustofnun (National Energy Authority): Grensásvegi 9, 108 Reykjavík; tel (1) 83600; Dir-Gen: Jakob Björnsson; Geothermal Dir: Guðmundur Pálmason; Hydropower Dir: Haukur Tomasson; f 1967; advises the Minister of Industry on matters concerning energy; studies Icelandic energy resources and energy uses.

Rafmagnsveitur Ríkisins—RARIK (State Electric Power Works): Langavegi 118, 105 Reykjavík; tel (1) 17400; telex 2115; Dir: Kristján Jónsson; f 1947; produces, distributes and sells electric energy.

Fishing

Fiskifélag Íslands (Fisheries Association of Iceland): Hofn við Ingolfsstræti, 101 Reykjavík; tel (1) 10500; telex 8950511; fax (1) 27969; Man: Már Elísson; f 1911; affiliated with the Ministry of Fisheries; technical, consulting and information services to various Govt bodies, and to the fisheries industry; 13 mem orgs.

The Icelandic Fish Quality Institution (IFQI): Noatun 17, 105 Reykjavík; tel (1) 627533; telex 94012078; responsible to the Ministry of Fisheries for the maintenance of quality in Icelandic fish and fish products; issues licences to fishing vessels and to processing and curing facilities.

Icelandic Fisheries Laboratories (Rf): Skúlagata 4, 101 Reykjavík; tel (1) 20240; telex 94013159; fax (1) 623790; f 1965; responsible to the Ministry of Fisheries; conducts research and devt work for the fisheries sector.

Marine Research Institute (MRI): Skúlagata 4, 101 Reykjavík; tel (1) 20240; telex 7400746; fax (1) 623790; f 1965; reports to the Ministry of Fisheries; conducts research on the living resources and environment of the sea around Iceland; operates five branches and three research vessels.

Health and Welfare

HEALTH

Directorate of Public Health: Laugavegur 116, 101 Reykjavík; tel (1) 27555; telex 2050; Dir: Olafsson Olafur, MD; f 1760; supervises all health activities in Iceland.

WELFARE

Tryggingastofnun Ríkisins (State Social Security Institution): Laugavegur 114, 105 Reykjavík; tel (1) 19300; Man Dir: Eggert G. Thorsteinsson; Chair of Tryggingaráð (Social Security Board): Helga Jónsdóttir; f 1936; administers pensions, invalidity, sickness and unemployment insurance, family allowances.

Legal and Judiciary

Supreme Court: Domhúsið, v/Lindargötu, 101 Reykjavík; tel (1) 13936; Chief Justice: Guðmundur Jónsson; Justices of the Supreme Court are appointed by the State President; the Chief Justice is elected by the Justices every two years.

Media

BROADCASTING

Ríkisútvarpið (Icelandic National Broadcasting Service): Efstaleiti 1, 150 Reykjavík; tel (1) 693000; telex 2066; fax (1) 693010; Dir-Gen: Markús Örn Antonsson; Chair of Programme Board: Inga Jóna Thordardóttir; f 1930.

Radio Division: Efstaleiti 1, 150 Reykjavík; tel (1) 693000; telex 2066; fax (1) 693000; Dir: Elfa-Björk Gunnarsdóttir; f 1930; operates Programme 1 and Programme 2.

Rikisútvarpið—Sjónvarp (Icelandic National Broadcasting Service—Television): Laugavegur 176, 105 Reykjavík; tel (1) 693900; telex 2035; fax (1) 693988; Dir: Pétur Guðfinsson; f 1966.

NEWS AND INFORMATION

Hagstofa Íslands (Statistical Bureau of Iceland): Hverfisgata 8-10, 150 Reykjavík; tel (1) 26699; Dir: Hallgrímur Snorrason; Dep Dir: Gunnar H. Hall; f 1914; collects, processes and distributes economic and social statistics; administers the National Registry of Persons, and registers of enterprises and students.

Tourism

Ferðaskrifstofa Íslands (Iceland Tourist Bureau): Skógarhlid 6, 101 Reykjavík; tel (1) 25855; telex 2049; fax (1) 25835; Dir: Kjartan Lárusson; f 1936; encourages all kinds of tourism in Iceland, including foreign visitors and overseas travel by Icelanders; manages the 18-hotel EDDA chain.

Transport and Communications

TELECOMMUNICATIONS

Póst- og Símamalástofnunin (General Directorate of Posts and Telecommunications): við Austurvöll, 150 Reykjavík; tel (1) 26000; telex 2000; fax (1) 28245; Dir-Gen: Ólafur Tómasson; Mans: Bragi Kristjánsson, Guðmundur Björnsson, Thorvadur Jónsson, Thorgeir K. Thorgeirsson; f 1906, merged with post office 1935; administers postal and telecommunication systems of Iceland; operates earth station for satellite telecommunications at Skyggnir.

TRANSPORT

Skipaútgerd Ríkisins (Icelandic Shipping Department): Hafnarhúsinu við, Tryggvagötu, 101 Reykjavík; tel (1) 28822; telex 3008; Gen Man: Guðmundur Einarsson; f 1930; operates passenger and freight services around Iceland.

INDIA

Head of State

The President is the constitutional Head of State, elected for five years by an electoral college comprising elected members of both Houses of Parliament and the state legislatures. The President exercises executive power on the advice of the Council of Ministers, which is responsible to Parliament. The President appoints the Prime Minister and, on the latter's recommendation, other Ministers.

President: Ramaswamy Venkataraman (sworn in 25 July 1987).

Office of the President: Rashtrapti Bhavan, New Delhi 110 004; tel (11) 3016344.

Vice-President: Dr Shankar Dayal Sharma (sworn in 3 September 1987).

Office of the Vice-President: Rashtrapti Bhavan, New Delhi 110 004; tel (11) 3017314.

Legislature

Legislative power is vested in Parliament, consisting of the President and the two Houses. The Rajya Sabha (Council of States) has 245 members, most of whom are indirectly elected by the State Assemblies for six years, the remainder being nominated by the President for six years. The Lok Sabha (House of the People) has 544 members elected by universal adult suffrage for five years. India comprises 25 self-governing states.

Rajya Sabha (Council of States): Parliament House, New Delhi 110 011; tel (11) 389977; Chair: Dr Shankar Dayal Sharma.

Lok Sabha (House of the People): Parliament House, New Delhi 110 011; tel (11) 381825; Speaker: Rabi Ray.

MINISTRIES AND GOVERNMENT DEPARTMENTS

OFFICE OF THE PRIME MINISTER
South Block, New Delhi 110 011
Tel (11) 3012312
Prime Minister: Vishwanath Pratap Singh
Deputy Prime Minister: Devi Lal

MINISTRY OF AGRICULTURE AND RURAL DEVELOPMENT
Krishi Bhavan, Dr Rajendra Prasad Rd, New Delhi 110 001
Tel (11) 382651; telex 3165423
Minister: Devi Lal

MINISTRY OF ATOMIC ENERGY
South Block, New Delhi 110 011
Tel (11) 3011773; telex 3166182
Minister: Vishwanath Pratap Singh

MINISTRY OF CIVIL AVIATION
Sardar Patel Bhavan, New Delhi 110 001
Tel (11) 351700; telex 3165976
Minister: Arif Mohammed Khan

MINISTRY OF COMMERCE
Udyog Bhavan, New Delhi 110 011
Tel (11) 3016664; telex 3165970
Minister: Arun Kumar Nehru

MINISTRY OF COMMUNICATIONS
Sanchar Bhavan, 20 Asoka Rd, New Delhi 110 001
Tel (11) 381209; telex 314422
Minister: K. P. Unnikrishnan

MINISTRY OF DEFENCE
South Block, New Delhi 110 011
Tel (11) 3012380; telex 3162679
Minister: Prof Raja Ramanna

MINISTRY OF ENERGY
Shram Shakti Bhavan, Rafi Marg, New Delhi 110 001
Tel (11) 382966
Minister: Arif Mohammed Khan

MINISTRY OF THE ENVIRONMENT AND FORESTS
Paryavaran Bhavan, CGO Complex Phase II, Lodi Rd, New Delhi 110 003
Tel (11) 360721
Minister: Vishwanath Pratap Singh
Minister of State: Maneka Gandhi

MINISTRY OF EXTERNAL AFFAIRS
South Block, New Delhi 110 011
Tel (11) 3102318; telex 3161880
Minister: Inder Kumar Gujral

MINISTRY OF FINANCE
North Block, New Delhi 110 001
Tel (11) 3012611; telex 3166562
Minister: Prof Madhu Dandavate

MINISTRY OF FOOD AND CIVIL SUPPLIES
Krishi Bhavan, New Delhi 110 001
Tel (11) 382349; telex 3166505
Minister: Nathu Ram Mirdha

MINISTRY OF HEALTH AND FAMILY WELFARE
Nirman Bhavan, New Delhi 110 011
Tel (11) 3018863
Minister: Nilamani Routray

MINISTRY OF HOME AFFAIRS
North Block, New Delhi 110 001
Tel (11) 3011989
Minister: Mufti Mohammed Sayeed

MINISTRY OF HUMAN RESOURCES DEVELOPMENT
Shastri Bhavan, New Delhi 110 001
Tel (11) 381298; telex 3161336
Minister: M. G. K. Menon

MINISTRY OF INDUSTRY
Udyog Bhavan, New Delhi 110 011
Tel (11) 3010221; telex 3166294
Minister: Ajit Singh

MINISTRY OF INFORMATION AND BROADCASTING
Shastri Bhavan, New Delhi 110 001
Tel (11) 382639; telex 3166349
Minister: P. Upendra

MINISTRY OF LABOUR
Shram Shakti Bhavan, Rafi Marg, New Delhi 110 001
Tel (11) 382945; telex 3161131
Minister: Ram Vilas Paswan

MINISTRY OF LAW AND JUSTICE
Shastri Bhavan, Dr Rajendra Prasad Rd, New Delhi 110 001
Tel (11) 384777
Minister: Dinesh Goswami

MINISTRY OF OCEAN DEVELOPMENT
Block 12, CGO Complex, Lodi Rd, New Delhi 110 003
Tel (11) 360874
Minister: Vishwanath Pratap Singh

MINISTRY OF PARLIAMENTARY AFFAIRS
Parliament House, New Delhi 110 001
Tel (11) 3017663
Minister: P. Upendra

MINISTRY OF PERSONNEL, PUBLIC GRIEVANCES AND PENSIONS
North Block, New Delhi 110 001
Tel (11) 3014848
Minister: Vishwanath Pratap Singh

MINISTRY OF PETROLEUM AND CHEMICALS
Shastri Bhavan, New Delhi 110 001
Tel (11) 383501; telex 3166235
Minister: M. S. Gurapadaswamy

MINISTRY OF PLANNING
Sardar Patel Bhavan, Parliament St, New Delhi 110 001
Tel (11) 350150
Minister: (vacant)

MINISTRY OF PROGRAMME IMPLEMENTATION
Sardar Patel Bhavan, Parliament St, New Delhi 110 001
Tel (11) 3012787; telex 3163195
Minister: Maneka Gandhi

MINISTRY OF RAILWAYS
Rail Bhavan, New Delhi 110 001
Tel (11) 384010
Minister: George Fernandes

MINISTRY OF SCIENCE AND TECHNOLOGY
Technology Bhavan, New Mehrauli Rd, New Delhi 110 016
Tel (11) 667373
Minister: Vishwanath Pratap Singh
Minister of State: M. G. K. Menon

MINISTRY OF SPACE
3 Lok Nayak Bhavan, New Delhi 110 003
Tel (11) 698313
Minister: (vacant)

MINISTRY OF STEEL AND MINES
Udyog Bhavan, New Delhi 110 011
Tel (11) 3014096; telex 3161483
Minister: Dinesh Goswami

MINISTRY OF SURFACE TRANSPORT
Transport Bhavan, Sansad Marg, New Delhi 110 001
Tel (11) 384938; telex 3161159
Minister: K. P. Unnikrishnan

MINISTRY OF TEXTILES AND FOOD PROCESSING
Udyog Bhavan, New Delhi 110 011
Tel (11) 3011769
Minister: Sharad Yadav

MINISTRY OF TOURISM
Transport Bhavan, Parliament St, New Delhi 110 001
Tel (11) 383816; telex 3165976
Minister: Arun Kumar Nehru

MINISTRY OF URBAN DEVELOPMENT
Nirman Bhavan, New Delhi 110 011
Tel (11) 3019377
Minister: Murasoli Maran

MINISTRY OF WATER RESOURCES
Shram Shakti Bhavan, Rafi Marg, New Delhi 110 001
Tel (11) 383098; telex 3166568
Minister of State: Manobhai Kotadiya

MINISTRY OF WELFARE
Shastri Bhavan, New Delhi 110 001
Tel (11) 382683; telex 3166256
Minister: Ram Vilas Paswan

GOVERNMENT AGENCIES AND ORGANIZATIONS

Advisory and Supervisory Bodies

Election Commission: Nirvachan Sadan, 1 Ashok Rd, New Delhi 110 011; tel (11) 386552; Commr: Peri Shastri; Sec: R. D. Sharma; electoral supervisory body.

The National Small Industries Corpn Ltd: Laghu Udyog Bhavan, Okhla Industrial Estate, New Delhi 110 020; tel (11) 6837071; telex 3162376; Chair: J. S. Juneja; f 1955; aids, advises, finances, protects and promotes the interests of small industries.

Public Enterprises Bureau: c/o Ministry of Finance, North Block, New Delhi 110 001; monitors progress of state-owned concerns.

Standing Conference on Public Enterprises: 1st Floor, Chandralok, 36 Janpath, New Delhi 110 001; provides support and advice to public sector cos.

Agriculture

Cotton Corpn of India Ltd: Air India Bldg, 12th Floor, Nariman Point, Bombay 400 021; tel (22) 2024363; telex 113463; Chair and Man Dir: M. B. Lal; f 1970; purchase, sale and distribution of home-produced cotton and imported cotton staple fibre; exports long staple cotton.

Food Corpn of India: 16-20 Barakhamba Lane, New Delhi 110 001; tel (11) 3310551; telex 312418; Chair: T. S. Broca; Man Dir: J. M. Lyngdoh; f 1965; trades in food grains on a commercial scale but within the framework of an overall Govt policy; provides farmers with an assured price for their produce; supplies food grains to the consumer at reasonable prices; purchases, stores, sells and distributes food grains and other food-stuffs and arranges imports and handling of food grains and fertilizers at the ports; distributes sugar in a number of states and has set up rice mills.

Jute Corpn of India Ltd: 1 Shakespeare Sarani, Calcutta 700 071; telex 213266; Chair and Man Dir: S. K. Bhattacharya; f 1971; price support operations in respect of raw jute; handles the import and export of raw jute; promotion of trade in jute goods.

National Dairy Development Board (NDDB): POB 40, Anand 388 001; tel (2692) 22121; telex 172207; fax (2692) 22220; Chair: Dr Verghese Kurien; Man Dir: Dr R. P. Aneja; Man Dir, Operations: Dr Amrita Patel; f 1965, replaced the India Dairy Corpn in 1989; aims to promote dairy devt and animal husbandry, agricultural and food products, horticulture and allied industries through co-operative strategy; research and consultancy services in above fields.

National Seeds Corpn Ltd: Beej Bhavan, Pusa, New Delhi 110 012; tel (11) 569721; telex 313705; Man Dir: Dr S. K. Sengupta; f 1963; improvement and devt of the seed industry.

State Farms Corpn of India Ltd: Farm Bhavan, 14-15 Nehru Place, New Delhi 110 019; tel (11) 6413125; Chair: A. R. Mallu; Man Dir: P. S. G. Nair; f 1969; administers central state farms; activities include the production of quality seeds of high-yielding varieties of wheat, paddy, maize, bajra and jowar; advises on soil conservation, reclamation and devt of waste and forest land; consultancy services on farm mechanization.

Tea Board of India: 14 Brabourne Rd, POB 2172, Calcutta 700 001; tel (33) 260210; telex 214527; Chair: Pranab Kumar Bora; provides financial assistance to tea research stations; sponsors and finances independent research projects in universities and technical institutions to supplement the work of tea research establishments; also promotes tea production and export.

Tea Trading Corpn of India Ltd: 7 Wood St, 2nd Floor, Calcutta 700 016; tel (33) 448366; telex 213279; Man Dir: S. S. Ahuja; Sec: P. K. Mitra; f 1971; promotes the export and local sale of tea; owns and manages tea estates; processes and manufactures tea in blended and packaged form; is expanding into export of seafoods and processed fruit and food products.

Business and Economy

BANKING

Allahabad Bank: 2 Netaji Subhas Rd, Calcutta 700 001; tel (33) 209258; telex 217547; Chair and Man Dir: R. L. Wadhwa; f 1865; 1,327 brs.

Andhra Bank: Sultan Bazar, POB 519, Hyderabad 500 195; tel (842) 40141; telex 1556283; Chair and Man Dir: K. R. Nayak; f 1923; nationalized 1980; 1,018 brs.

Bank of Baroda: 3 Walchand Hirachand Marg, Ballard Pier, POB 10046, Bombay 400 038; tel (22) 260341; telex 116345; Chair and Man Dir: Premjit Singh; f 1908; 2,106 brs (worldwide).

Bank of India: Express Towers, Nariman Point, POB 234, Bombay 400 021; tel (22) 2023020; telex 112281; Chair and Man Dir: R. Srinivasan; Gen Man: K. C. Chakrabertti; f 1906; 2,107 brs (worldwide).

Bank of Maharashtra: 'Lokmangal', 1501 Shivajinagar, Pune 411 005; tel (212) 52731; telex 145207; Chair and Man Dir: T. K. K. Bhagawat; f 1935; 1,000 brs.

Benares State Bank Ltd: D52/1 Luxa Rd, Varanasi 221 010.

Bharat Overseas Bank Ltd: 'Oxford House', Anna Salai, POB 4507, Madras 600 006.

Canara Bank: 112 Jayachamarajendra Rd, POB 6648, Bangalore 560 002; tel (812) 76851; telex 845205; Chair and Man Dir: N. D. Prabhu; f 1906; 1,946 brs.

Central Bank of India: Chandermukhi, Nariman Point, Bombay 400 021; tel (22) 2026428; telex 112909; Chair and Man Dir: (vacant); f 1911; 2,720 brs.

Corpn Bank: Mangaladevi Temple Rd, POB 88, Mangalore 575 001; tel (824) 26416; telex 842228; Chair and Man Dir: Y. S. Hedge; Gen Man: K. R. Ramamoorthy; f 1906; nationalized 1980; 431 brs.

Dena Bank: 17 Horniman Circle, Fort, Bombay 400 023; tel (22) 296746; telex 112511; Chair and Man Dir: G. S. Dahotre; f 1938; 1,067 brs.

Export-Import Bank of India: Maker Chambers IV, 8th Floor, 222 Nariman Point, POB 19969, Bombay 400 021.

Indian Bank: 31 Rajaji Salai, POB 1866, Madras 600 001; tel (44) 514151; telex 41307; Chair and Man Dir: M. Gopalakrishnan; Gen Man: K. Subramanian; f 1907; 1,165 brs.

Indian Overseas Bank: 762 Anna Salai, POB 3765, Madras 600 002; tel (44) 82041; telex 416123; Chair and Man Dir: P. S. Gopalakrishnan; f 1937; 1,153 brs (worldwide).

Industrial Development Bank of India (IDBI): Nariman Bhavan, 227 Vinay K. Shah Marg, Nariman Point, Bombay 400 021; tel (22) 214450; telex 116866; Chair and Man Dir: Suresh S. Nadkarni; f 1964; the main financial institution for co-ordinating and supplementing the working of other financial institutions and also for financing and promoting industrial devt.

Jammu and Kashmir Bank Ltd: 2nd Dood Ganga Rd, Karan Nagar, Srinagar 190 010; tel (194) 73018; telex 375224; Chair: Ghulam Hassan; Gen Mans: A. R. Mubarki, M. Y. Kangan; f 1938.

National Bank for Agriculture and Rural Development: Sterling Centre, Dr Annie Besant Rd, Worli, POB 6552, Bombay 400 018; tel (22) 4924306; telex 1173770; Chair: P. R. Nayak; Man Dir: G. P. Bhave; f 1982; provides credit for agricultural and rural devt through commercial, co-operative and regional rural banks.

New Bank of India: 1 Tolstoy Marg, 10th Floor, New Delhi 110 001; tel (11) 3311452; telex 3166920; fax (11) 3320889; Chair and Man Dir: R. C. Suneja; Exec Dir: J. Sethi; f 1936; nationalized 1980; 567 brs.

Oriental Bank of Commerce: Harsha Bhavan, E Block, Connaught Place, POB 329, New Delhi 110 001; tel (11) 3321459; telex 3165462; Chair and Man Dir: S. P. Talwar; Gen Mans: K. K. Saggar, R. C. Kapoor; f 1943; nationalized 1980; 478 brs.

Punjab National Bank: 7 Bhikaiji Cama Place, Africa Ave, POB 274, New Delhi 110 066; tel (11) 602303; telex 3161906; Chair and Man Dir: J. S. Varshneya; f 1895; 2,986 brs (worldwide).

Punjab and Sind Bank: 21 Bank House, Rajendra Place, New Delhi 110 008; tel (11) 5720849; telex 3166456; Chair and Man Dir: M. S. Chahal; f 1908; nationalized 1980; 657 brs.

Reserve Bank of India: Central Office, Shahid Bhagat Singh Rd, Bombay 400 023; tel (22) 2861602; telex 114222; Gov: R. N. Malhotra; f 1935; nationalized 1949; sole bank of issue; 11 brs.

State Bank of India: Madame Cama Rd, POB 10121, Bombay 400 021; tel (22) 2022426; telex 112995; Chair and Man Dir: M. N. Goiporia; f 1955; controls 28 state co-operative banks and

349 district co-operative banks; 34 private-sector banks and 194 regional rural banks; 7,979 brs; subsidiaries:

State Bank of Bikaner and Jaipur: Tilak Marg, POB 154, Jaipur 302 005.

State Bank of Hyderabad: Gunfoundry, Hyderabad 500 177.

State Bank of Indore: 5 Yeshwant Niwas Rd, POB 214, Indore 452 003; tel (731) 7274; telex 0735-264.

State Bank of Mysore: Kempegowda Rd, POB 9727, Bangalore 560 009.

State Bank of Patiala: The Mall, Patiala 147 001.

State Bank of Saurashtra: Darbargadh, POB 51, Bhavnagar 364 001.

State Bank of Travancore: POB 34, Trivandrum; tel (471) 68344; telex 238; Man Dir: J. C. Soares; f 1946.

Syndicate Bank: POB 1, Manipal 576 119; tel 8261; telex 82242; Chair and Man Dir: P. S. V. Mallya; f 1925; 1,475 brs.

UCO Bank (United Commercial Bank): 10 Biplabi Trailokya Maharaj Sarani (Brabourne Rd), POB 2455, Calcutta 700 001; tel (33) 260120; telex 214323; Chair and Man Dir: K. Manmohan Shenoi; f 1943; 1,747 brs.

Union Bank of India: 239 Backbay Reclamation, Nariman Point, Bombay 400 021; tel (22) 2024647; telex 114208; Chair and Man Dir: B. D. Dikshit; f 1919; 1,740 brs.

United Bank of India: 16 Old Court House St, Calcutta 700 001; tel (33) 237741; telex 217387; Chair and Man Dir: J. V. Shetty; f 1950; 1,166 brs.

Vijaya Bank: 41/42 Mahatma Gandhi Rd, Bangalore 560 001; tel (812) 573341; telex 8452428; Chair and Man Dir: K. Sadananda Shetty; f 1931; nationalized 1980; 702 brs.

FINANCIAL AGENCIES

Agricultural Finance Consultants Ltd: Dhanraj Mahal, 1st Floor, Chatrapati Shivaji Maharaj Marg, Bombay 400 039; tel (22) 2028924; telex 115849; Chair: Dr G. V. K. Rao; Man Dir: B. Venkata Rao; f 1968; renamed 1989; a consortium of commercial banks, set up to help member commercial banks participate in agricultural and rural devt projects; provides project consultancy services to commercial banks, Union and State Govts, public sector corpns, the World Bank, etc; undertakes techno-economic and investment surveys in agriculture and agro-industries.

Credit Guarantee Corpn of India Ltd: Bombay; Chair: Dr R. K. Hazari; Man: C. S. Subramaniam; f 1971; promoted by the Reserve Bank of India; guarantees loans and other credit facilities.

Industrial Finance Corpn of India: Bank of Baroda Bldg, 16 Sansad Marg, POB 363, New Delhi 110 001; tel (11) 3322052; telex 3166123; Chair: D. N. Davar; f 1948; provides medium- and long-term finance to cos and co-operatives; promotes industrialization of less developed areas, and sponsors training in management techniques and devt banking.

INSURANCE

Deposit Insurance Corpn: Vidyut Bhavan, Pathakwadi, Bombay 400 002; Chair: K. R. Puri; Man: V. S. Moharir; insures deposits in the 956 banks insured by the corpn.

General Insurance Corpn of India (GIC): Industrial Assurance Bldg, 4th Floor, Churchgate, Bombay 400 020; tel (22) 220046; telex 113833; Man Dir: B. D. Shah; f 1973 by the reorganization of 106 private life and non-life insurance cos as the four groups listed below:

National Insurance Co Ltd: 3 Middleton St, Calcutta 700 071; telex 217074; Chair and Man Dir: G. C. Bhattacharya.

New India Assurance Co Ltd: New India Assurance Bldg, Mahatma Gandhi Rd, Fort, Bombay 400 001; tel (22) 274617; telex 112423; Chair and Man Dir: V. Mony; f 1919.

The Oriental Insurance Co Ltd: Oriental House, A-25/27 Asaf Ali Rd, New Delhi 110 002; tel (11) 279221; telex 3162583; Chair and Man Dir: H. J. Sequeira.

United India Insurance Co Ltd: 24 Whites Rd, Madras 600 014; tel (44) 810061; telex 416141; Chair and Man Dir: M. M. Bhagat.

Life Insurance Corpn of India: Jeevan Bima Marg, Bombay 400 021; tel (22) 2021383; telex 112327; Chair: N. K. Shinkar; Man Dir: G. Chidambar; f 1956; controls all life insurance business.

NATIONALIZED INDUSTRY

Bharat Aluminium Co Ltd: Punj House, 18 Nehru Place, New Delhi 110 019; tel (11) 6432563; telex 3163350; Chair and Man Dir: P. S. Rao; f 1965; operates an integrated aluminium project at Korba (Madhya Pradesh) and a plant for further refining at Bidhanbagh (West Bengal); plans to set up alumina plants in Andhra Pradesh (with USSR aid).

Bharat Electronics Ltd: Jalahalli PO, Bangalore 560 013; telex 845244; Chair and Man Dir: Capt (retd) Subbacao Prabhala; f 1954; manufacturers of electronics and radar equipment and electronic components.

Bharat Heavy Electricals Ltd: Hindustan Times House, 18-20 Kasturba Gandhi Marg, New Delhi 110 001; tel (11) 3313615; telex 312389; Chair and Man Dir: P. S. Gupta; f 1964; integrated global service in power generation, transmission and utilization equipment.

Cement Corpn of India Ltd: Shakuntla Apartments, 59 Nehru Place, New Delhi 110 019; tel (11) 6411691; telex 3165163; Chair and Man Dir: Anand Darbari; f 1965; production and sale of cement.

Fertilizers and Chemicals (Travancore) Ltd: Udyogamandal 683 501, Via Cochin, POB 14, Kerala; tel (481) 856101; telex 885264; Chair and Man Dir: N. B. Chandran; f 1943; manufacturers of fertilizers and chemicals.

Heavy Engineering Corpn Ltd: Plant Plaza Rd, Ranchi 834 004; telex 625204; Chair and Man Dir: P. C. Neogy; f 1956; operates a heavy machine building plant, a foundry forge plant and heavy machine tools plant.

Hindustan Aeronautics Ltd: Indian Express Bldg, POB 5150, Vidhana Veedhi, Bangalore 560 001; telex 845266; Chair and Man Dir: Wing Commdr I. M. Chopra; f 1964; manufacturers of aircraft, helicopters, aero-engines, airborne electronic equipment and accessories; undertakes overhaul of aircraft, etc.

Hindustan Copper Ltd: Industry House, 10 Camac St, POB 16008, Calcutta 700 017; tel (33) 446662; telex 213291; Chair and Man Dir: P. V. Venkatasan; f 1967; responsible for the devt of copper industry.

Hindustan Fertilizer Corpn Ltd: 55 Nehru Place, New Delhi 110 019; tel (11) 6419717; telex 313447; Chair and Man Dir: K. C. Madan; production of fertilizer.

Hindustan Machine Tools Ltd (HMT): 36 Cunningham Rd, Bangalore 560 052; telex 845311; Chair and Man Dir: M. R. Naidu; f 1953; India's largest machine tool manufacturer.

Hindustan Zinc Ltd: 6 New Fatehpura, Udaipur 313 001; tel (141) 23271; telex 33263; Chair and Man Dir: A. C. Wadhawan; f 1966; mining, beneficiation of lead and zinc ore.

The Indian Iron and Steel Co Ltd: Iisco House, 50 Chowringhee Rd, Calcutta 700 071; tel (44) 8371; telex 217372; Man Dir: M. F. Mehta; f 1918; manufacturers of iron and steel products, spun pipes, castings, etc.

Indian Petrochemicals Corpn Ltd: Petrochemicals Township, Vadodara 391 345; tel (265) 72444; telex 175364; fax (265)

73164; Chair and Man Dir: Hasmukh Shah; f 1969; manufacture and marketing of petrochemicals.

Instrumentation Ltd: Kota 324005; tel (141) 24591; telex 305203; Chair and Man Dir: K. Vasudevan; f 1964; manufacturers of industrial process control instruments; designs, build, erects and commissions instrumentation systems.

Neyveli Lignite Corpn Ltd: Neyveli, South Arcot District, Tamil Nadu 607 801; tel (414) 8280; telex 417350; Chair and Man Dir: Mahip Singh; f 1956; activities include lignite mining, power generation, production of urea and carbonized briquettes.

Rashtriya Chemicals and Fertilizers Ltd: Administrative Bldg, Marvali, Chembur, Bombay 400 074; tel (22) 5512854; telex 1171228; Chair and Man Dir: R. Venkatesan.

Steel Authority of India Ltd: Ispat Bhavan, Lodi Rd, POB 3049, New Delhi 110 003; tel (11) 690481; telex 3162689; Chair: V. Krishnamurthy; f 1973; provides co-ordinated devt of the steel industry in both the public and private sectors.

Tungabhadra Steel Products Ltd: Tungabhadra Dam 583 225; tel (8394) 8749; telex 818216; Man Dir: V. Ramanathan; f 1960; manufacture of steel structures, including gates, pylons, etc.

TRADE

Apparel Export Promotion Council: Sahyog Bldg, 58 Nehru Place, New Delhi 110 019; tel (11) 683129; telex 314831; Chair: M. K. Mehthani.

Cashew Corpn of India Ltd: Mahatma Gandhi Rd, POB 1019, Ernakulam, Cochin 682 011; tel (484) 352177; telex 8856202; Chair: P. K. Shunglu; imports raw cashew nuts for distribution to the export-orientated sector of the cashew processing industry; also undertakes exports of cashew kernels.

Handicrafts and Handlooms Exports Corpn of India Ltd: Lok Kalyan Bhavan, 11A Rouse Ave Lane, New Delhi 110 002; tel (11) 3311086; telex 3161522; Chair and Man Dir: K. G. Menon; f 1958; deals in exports of handicrafts, handloom goods, ready-to-wear clothes, carpets and precious jewellery, while promoting exports and trade devt; subsidiary of the State Trading Corpn of India Ltd.

Indian Institute of Foreign Trade: Ashok Bhavan, 93 Nehru Place, New Delhi 110 019; tel (11) 682432; Chair: S. Abid Hussain.

Minerals and Metals Trading Corpn of India Ltd: Scope Complex, Core 1, 7 Lodi Rd, New Delhi 110 003; tel (11) 3319448; telex 3174042; Chair and Man Dir: G. Jhingaran; f 1963; export of iron and manganese ore, ferro-manganese, finished stainless steel products, mica, coal and other minor minerals; import of steel, non-ferrous metals, rough diamonds, fertilizers, etc for supply to industrial units in the country.

Projects and Equipment Corpn of India Ltd: Hansalaya, 15 Barakhamba Rd, New Delhi 110 001; tel (11) 3312673; telex 3165256; fax (11) 3315279; Chair and Man Dir: S. N. Malik; f 1971; export of engineering goods and machinery; also handles industrial projects and civil construction jobs abroad on turnkey basis.

State Trading Corpn of India Ltd: Chandralok, 36 Janpath, New Delhi 110 001; tel (11) 353164; telex 3165180; Chair: I. G. Jhingaran; handles exports and imports.

Trade Development Authority: Bank of Baroda Bldg, 16 Parliament St, POB 767, New Delhi 110 001; tel (11) 3320214; telex 3165155; Chair: A. N. Verma; f 1971; promotes selective devt of exports of high quality products; arranges investment in export-orientated ventures undertaken by India with foreign collaboration.

Trade Fair Authority of India: Pragati Maidan, New Delhi 110 001; tel (11) 804459; telex 3162751; Chair: Mohammad Yunus.

Defence

Air Force: Air House, 23 Akbar Rd, New Delhi 110 001; tel (11) 372517; telex 3132257; Chief of Staff: Air Chief Marshal Surendra Kumar Mehra.

Army: Army House, 4 King George's Ave, New Delhi 110 011; tel (11) 371632; telex 313622; Chief of Staff: Gen Vishwa Nath Sharma.

Navy: 12 King George's Ave, New Delhi 110 011; tel (11) 371400; telex 312872; Chief of Staff: Adm Janyat Ganpat Nadkarni.

Development and Planning

PLANNING

Housing and Urban Development Corpn Ltd: Hudco House, Lodhi Rd, New Delhi 110 003; tel (11) 699534; telex 3161037; Chair and Man Dir: S. K. Sharma; f 1970; financing housing and promoting low cost building technology.

National Co-operative Development Corpn: 4 Siri Institutional Area, Hauz Khas, New Delhi 110 016; tel (11) 669246; telex 3173059; Pres: Bhajan Lal; Man Dir: T. C. A. Srinivasaramanujan; f 1962; planning, initiation, co-ordination, devt and financing of rural economic activities of agro-based co-operatives.

National Industrial Development Corpn Ltd: Chanakya Bhavan, Africa Ave, Chanakyapuri, POB 5212, New Delhi 110 021; tel (11) 670154; telex 3162891; Chair and Man Dir: A. Prasada; Gen Man: A. Kumar; f 1954; consultative engineering services to State and Central Govt, public and private sector enterprises, the United Nations and overseas investors.

National Research Development Corpn: 20-22 Zamroodpur Community Centre, Kailash Colony Extension, New Delhi 110 048; tel (11) 6432121; telex 3171358; Man Dir: N. K. Sharma; f 1953; stimulates devt and commercial exploitation of new inventions with financial and technical aid; finances devt projects to set up demonstration units in collaboration with industry; exports technology.

Projects and Development India Ltd: Siddharth, 96 Nehru Place, New Delhi 110 019; tel (11) 6432550; telex 3166172; Chair and Man Dir: V. R. Joharapurkar; Dir: V. P. Saluja; f 1978; engineering consultancy in the field of fertilizer, chemical, petrochemical and petroleum industries.

REGIONAL DEVELOPMENT

Damodar Valley Corpn: Bhabani Bhavan, Alipore, Calcutta 700 027; tel (33) 451761; telex 217206; f 1948; flood control, irrigation and drainage; production of electricity; navigation; afforestation and control of soil erosion; promotion of public health, agriculture, industry and general economic well-being of the Damodar Valley.

Employment

Rehabilitation Industries Corpn Ltd: 25 Free School St, Calcutta, 700 016; tel (33) 241181; telex 217327; Chair and Man Dir: Rajat Barua; f 1959; creation of employment opportunities through multi-product industries, ranging from consumer goods to engineering products and services, for refugees from Bangladesh and migrants from Pakistan, repatriates from Burma and Sri Lanka, and other immigrants of Indian extraction.

Union Public Service Commission: Dholpur House, 11 Shahjahan Rd, New Delhi; tel (11) 384988; Chair: H. K. L. Cahooe.

Legal and Judiciary

Supreme Court: Tilak Marg, New Delhi 110 011; tel (11) 381635; Chief Justice: Sabyasachi Mukherjee; consists of the Chief Justice and not more than 17 judges appointed by the President; exercises exclusive jurisdiction in any dispute between the Union and the states; has appellate jurisdiction over any judgment, decree or order of the High Court where that Court certifies that either a substantial question of law or the interpretation of the Constitution is involved.

Media

BROADCASTING

All India Radio (AIR): Akashvani Bhavan, Parliament St, New Delhi 110 001; tel (11) 382021; telex 313225; Dir-Gen: A. R. Shinde; broadcasting is controlled by the Ministry of Information and Broadcasting and is govt-financed; operates a network of 96 broadcasting centres.

Doordarshan India (Television India): Mandi House, Doordarshan Bhavan, Copernicus Marg, New Delhi 110 001; tel (11) 382094; telex 3166143; Dir-Gen: Shiv Sharma; f 1976; 18 TV stations and nine relay stations.

GOVERNMENT PUBLISHER

Publications Division: 'A' Block, Patiala House, New Delhi 110 001; tel (11) 387983; Dir: Dr S. S. Shashi; f 1941; culture, art, literature, planning and devt, general; also 21 magazines in English and several Indian languages.

NEWS AND INFORMATION

Central Statistical Organization: Ministry of Planning, Sardar Patel Bhavan, Parliament St, New Delhi 110 001; tel (11) 353626; collection, analysis and publication of statistics.

Directorate of Economics and Statistics: Ministry of Agriculture and Rural Development, Krishi Bhavan, Dr Rajendra Prasad Rd, New Delhi 110 001; collection and analysis of statistics relating to agriculture.

Press Information Bureau: Shastri Bhavan, Dr Rajendra Prasad Rd, New Delhi 110 001; tel (11) 383643; Dir: I. Ramamohan Rao; f 1946; co-ordinates press affairs for the Govt; represents newspaper managements, journalists, news agencies, Parliament; has power to examine journalists under oath and may censor objectionable material.

Registrar of Newspapers for India: Ministry of Information and Broadcasting, West Block 8, Wing 2, Ramakrishna Puram, New Delhi 110 066; tel (11) 698758; Registrar: Krippa Sagar; f 1956; collects press statistics; maintains a register of all Indian newspapers.

Mining and Energy

ENERGY

Atomic Energy Commission: Chhatrapati Shivaji Maharaj Marg, Bombay 400 039; tel (22) 2022543; telex 112355; fax (22) 2048476; Chair: Dr M. R. Srinivasan; Sec: S. Rajgopal; organizes research on the use of atomic energy for peaceful purposes.

Bhabha Atomic Research Centre: Central Complex, Trombay, Bombay 400 085; tel (22) 5514910; telex 1171017; Dir: Dr P. K. Iyengar; f 1954; national centre for research in and devt of nuclear energy for peaceful uses.

Bharat Petroleum Corpn: 4-6 Currimbhoy Rd, Bharat Bhavan, Ballard Estate, POB 688, Bombay 400 088; tel (22) 268281; telex 112468; Chair and Man Dir: M. K. Bagai; f 1952.

Hindustan Petroleum Corpn: Petroleum House, 17 Jamshedji Tata Rd, Bombay 400 020; tel (22) 244151; telex 115096; Chair: R. N. Bhandari.

Indian Oil Corpn: Indian Oil Bhavan, Janpath, New Delhi 110 011; tel (11) 311031; telex 312980; Chair: A. J. A. Tauro; management of six refineries.

Oil India Ltd: Allahabad Bank Bldg, 17 Sansad Marg, POB 203, New Delhi 110 001; tel (11) 310841; telex 3162024; Chair and Man Dir: Shri Surajit Chaliha; f 1959; exploration, transportation and production of crude oil and natural gas.

Oil Industry Development Board (OIDB): 704 Surya Kiran Bldg, 19 Kasturba Gandhi Marg, New Delhi 110 001; tel (11) 3316274; telex 3162008; Chief Consultant: V. K. Ahuja; f 1983; indigenization of imports needed for exploration and exploitation of oil and gas; clearance for imports needed for oil sector.

Oil and Natural Gas Commission: Tel Bhavan, Dehradun 248 001; telex 595206; Chair: S. P. Wahi; f 1956; petroleum exploration and exploitation in India and abroad.

MINING

Coal India Ltd: Coal Bhavan, 10 Netaji Subhas Rd, Calcutta 700 001; tel (33) 209109; telex 217180; fax (33) 2833731; Chair: M. P. Narayanan; Dirs: K. A. Sinha, A. V. Brahma, B. Swaminathan; f 1975; exploration, production and marketing of coal.

Bharat Coking Coal Ltd: Bhuggatdih Bldgs, Jharia 828 111; telex 629205; Chair and Man Dir: P. R. Sinha; f 1972; manages coking coal mines nationalized in 1972.

Central Coalfields Ltd: Darbhanga House, Ranchi 834 001; telex 625201; Chair and Man Dir: S. K. Chowdhary; f 1973.

Eastern Coalfields Ltd: Sanctoria, Dishergarh 713 333; telex 204202; Chair and Man Dir: J. N. Uppal; f 1975.

Western Coalfields Ltd: Bisesar House, Temple Rd, Nagpur 440 001; telex 715219; Chair and Man Dir: S. P. Puri; f 1975.

National Minerals Development Corpn Ltd: Khanij Bhavan, 10-3-311/A Castle Hills, Masab Tank, POB 52, Hyderabad 500 028; tel (842) 222071; telex 1556452; Chair and Man Dir: P. C. Gupta; exploitation of minerals (excluding coal, atomic minerals, lignite, petroleum and natural gas) in public sector; research and devt laboratories and consultancy wing.

Telecommunications

Indian Telephone Industries Ltd: 45/1 Magrath Rd, Bangalore 560 025; tel (812) 566116; telex 8458222; (812) 571288; Chair and Man Dir: U. D. N. Rao; Dir, Finance: B. B. Chaddha; f 1948; manufactures all types of telecommunication equipment.

Punjab Communications Ltd: C-135, Phase VIII, Industrial Area, POB 3, Nagar; tel 87516; telex 395366; Man Dir: Lt Col Inderjit Singh; f 1981; manufacturers of telecommunications equipment.

Videsh Sanchar Nigam Ltd: Videsh Sanchar Bhavan, Mahatma Gandhi Rd, Fort, Bombay 400 001; tel (22) 271819; telex 112429; fax (22) 954321; Chair and Man Dir: T. H. Chowdary; Dirs: G. S. Gundu Rao, V. Babuji; f 1986; planning, operation, maintenance and devt of international telecommunications service.

Tourism

Department of Tourism: Ministry of Tourism, Transport Bhavan, Parliament St, New Delhi 110 001; tel (11) 384111; telex 312827; Dir-Gen: B. K. Goswamy; formulates and administers Govt policy for promotion of tourism; plans the organization and devt of tourist facilities; operates tourist information offices.

India Tourism Development Corpn Ltd: Jeevan Vihar, 3 Sansad Marg, New Delhi 110 001; tel (11) 310923; telex 3163361; Chair and Man Dir: B. K. Goswamy; f 1966; operates hotels, resort accomodation, tourist transport services, duty-free shops and a travel agency, and provides consultancy and management services.

Transport

CIVIL AVIATION

Air India: Air India Bldg, Nariman Point, Bombay 400 021; tel (22) 2024142; telex 112427; fax (22) 2024897; Man Dir: Rajan Jetley; Dir, Finance: S. R. Gupte; Dir, Commercial: B. K. Mangaokar; f 1932; services to 25 countries covering five continents.

Indian Airlines: Airlines House, 113 Gurudwara Rakabganj Rd, Parliament St, New Delhi 110 001; tel (11) 388951; telex 3166110; fax (11) 381730; Chair: Rahul Bajaj; f 1953; regional air carrier of passengers and cargo.

RAILWAYS

Indian Government Administration (Ministry of Railways, Railway Board): Rail Bhavan, Raisina Rd, New Delhi; tel (11) 388931; telex 313561; Chair: Madhavan Narayanan Prasad.

> **Central Railway:** Victoria Terminus, Bombay; tel (22) 4151551; telex 1173819; Gen Man: Y. P. Anand.

Eastern Railway: 17 Netaji Subhas Rd, Calcutta 700 001; tel (33) 226811; Gen Man: R. C. Acharya.

North Eastern Railway: Gorakhpur 273 012; tel (551) 3041; Gen Man: Gauri Shankar.

Northeast Frontier: Maligaon, Guwahati 781 011; tel 88422; telex 2352336; Gen Man: Nikhilesh Mitra.

Northern: Baroda House, New Delhi 110 001; tel (11) 387227; Gen Man: S. M. Vaish.

South Central Railway: Rail Nilayam, Secunderabad 500 371; tel (842) 74848; Gen Man: R. Narasimhan.

South Eastern Railway: Calcutta 700 043; tel (33) 451741; Gen Man: C. M. Khosla.

Southern Railway: Park Town, Madras 600 003; tel (44) 564141; Gen Man: S. P. Jain.

Western Railway: Churchgate, Bombay 400 020; tel (22) 298016; telex 114910; fax (22) 22487; Gen Man: K. Subrahmanyan; f 1951.

SHIPPING

Central Inland Water Transport Corpn Ltd: 4 Fairlie Place, Calcutta; tel (33) 202321; telex 212779; Chair and Man Dir: S. K. Bhose; f 1967; inland water transport services in Bangladesh and the North-East Indian states; also shipbuilding and repairing, general engineering, dredging, lightening of ships and barge services.

Welfare

Employees' Provident Fund Organization: 9th Floor, Mayur Bhavan, Connaught Circus, New Delhi 110 001; tel (11) 3312975; telex 3166190; Commrs: B. N. Som, S. P. Mehrotra; f 1952; provides social security to the working class.

INDONESIA

Head of State

Executive power lies with the President who is elected for five years by the Majelis Permusyawaratan Rakyat (MPR) (People's Consultative Assembly). This is the highest authority of the State, comprising 1,000 members (members of the Dewan and delegates from regions, political and other groups). The Assembly determines the Constitution. Ministers are responsible to the President, who holds effective political power.

President: Suharto (inaugurated 27 March 1968; re-elected March 1973, March 1978, March 1983 and March 1988).

Office of the President: Istana Merdeka, Jarkarta; tel (21) 331097.

Vice-President: Gen Sudharmono.

Office of the Vice-President: Jalan Merdeka Selatan 6, Jakarta; tel (21) 363539.

Majelis Permusyawaratan Rakyat (MPR) (People's Consultative Assembly): Jalan Gatot Subroto 6, Jakarta; tel (21) 5801324; Chair: Kharis Suhud.

Legislature

The legislative branch of the State is the Dewan Perwakilan Rakyat (DPR) (House of Representatives), comprising 500 members, 100 nominated by the President and 400 directly elected. Every statute requires its approval. For local administration Indonesia is divided into 27 provinces.

Dewan Perwakilan Rakyat (DPR) (House of Representatives): Jalan Gatot Subroto 6, Jakarta Pusat; tel (21) 5801324; Speaker: Kharis Suhud.

MINISTRIES AND GOVERNMENT DEPARTMENTS

MINISTRY OF AGRICULTURE
Jalan Harsono Room 3, Ragunan Pasar Minggu, Jakarta Selatan
Tel (21) 783006
Minister: Dr Wardoyo

MINISTRY OF COMMUNICATIONS
Jalan Merdeka Barat 8, Jakarta 10110
Tel (21) 366332; telex 46116
Minister: Azwar Anas

MINISTRY OF CO-OPERATIVES
Jalan H. R. Rasuna Said Kav 3, 4, 5, POB 177, Jakarta 12940
Tel (21) 5204368; telex 62843
Minister: Bustanil Arifin

MINISTRY OF DEFENCE AND SECURITY
Jalan Merdeka Barat 13, Jakarta Pusat
Tel (21) 374408
Minister: Gen L. B. Murdani

MINISTRY OF THE ECONOMY, FINANCE, INDUSTRY AND DEVELOPMENT SUPERVISION
Jalan Lapangan Banteng Timur 4, Jakarta Pusat
Tel (21) 365079
Minister of Finance: Dr Johannes B. Sumarlin
Minister-Co-ordinator: Radius Prawiro

MINISTRY OF EDUCATION AND CULTURE
Jalan Jenderal Sudirman, Senayan, Jakarta Pusat
Tel (21) 581618
Minister: Prof Fuad Hassan

MINISTRY OF FOREIGN AFFAIRS
Jalan Taman Pejambon 6, Jakarta Pusat
Tel (21) 368014
Minister: Ali Alatas

MINISTRY OF FORESTRY
Gedung Pusat Kehutanan, Senayan, Jakarta Selatan
Tel (21) 581820; telex 45996; fax (21) 5700226
Minister: Dr Hasrul Harahap

MINISTRY OF HEALTH
Jalan Hr Rasuna Said Blx 5, Kav 49, Jakarta Pusat
Tel (21) 5201595
Minister: Adhyatma

MINISTRY OF HOME AFFAIRS
Jalan Merdeka Utara 7, Jakarta Pusat
Tel (21) 373908
**Minister, concurrently Chair of the Election
Committee:** Gen Rudini

MINISTRY OF INDUSTRY
Jalan Jenderal Gatot Subroto Kav 52-53, Jakarta
Tel (21) 511661
Minister: Hartarto

MINISTRY OF INFORMATION
Jalan Merdeka Barat 9, Jakarta Pusat
Tel (21) 377408; telex 44264
Minister: Harmoko

MINISTRY OF JUSTICE
Jalan Hr Rasuna Said Kav 4-5, Jakarta Pusat
Tel (21) 513004
Minister: Ismail Saleh

MINISTRY OF MANPOWER
Jalan Jenderal Gatot Subroto, Jakarta Pusat
Tel (21) 515717
Minister: Cosmas Batubara

MINISTRY OF MINING AND ENERGY
Jalan Merdeka Selatan 18, Jakarta Pusat
Tel (21) 360232
Minister: Dr Ginandjar Kartasasmita

MINISTRY OF NATIONAL DEVELOPMENT PLANNING
Jalan Taman Suropati 2, Jakarta Pusat
Tel (21) 336207; telex 61623
**Minister of State, concurrently Chair of the National
Development Planning Board:** Dr Saleh Afif

MINISTRY FOR POPULATION AND THE ENVIRONMENT
Jalan Medan Merdeka Barat 15, Jakarta Pusat
Tel (21) 371295; telex 46143
Minister of State: Dr Emil Salim

MINISTRY OF PUBLIC HOUSING
Jalan Kebon Sirih 31, Jakarta Pusat
Tel (21) 333649
Minister of State: Siswono Judo Husodo

MINISTRY OF PUBLIC WORKS
Jalan Pattimura 20, Kebayoran Baru, Jakarta Selatan 12110
Tel (21) 717564; telex 47247
Minister: Radinal Mochtar

MINISTRY OF RELIGIOUS AFFAIRS
Jalan M. H. Thamrin 6, Jakarta Pusat
Tel (21) 320135
Minister: Haji Munawir Sjadzali

MINISTRY OF RESEARCH AND TECHNOLOGY
Gedung Menara Patra, 3rd Floor, Jalan M. H. Thamrin 8,
Jakarta Pusat
Tel (21) 324767
**Minister of State, concurrently Chair of the Board for
the Study and Application of Technology:**
Dr Bucharuddin Jusuf Habibie

MINISTRY OF SOCIAL AFFAIRS
Jalan Ir H. Juanda 36, Jakarta Pusat
Tel (21) 341329
Minister: Haryati Subadio

MINISTRY FOR STATE ADMINISTRATIVE REFORMS
Jalan Taman Suropati 2, Jakarta
Tel (21) 334811
**Minister of State, concurrently Vice-Chair of the
National Development Planning Board:**
Sarwono Kusumaatmadja

MINISTRY OF TOURISM, POSTS AND TELECOMMUNICATIONS
Jalan Kebon Sirih 36, Jakarta
Tel (21) 346855
Minister: Gen Susilo Sudarman

MINISTRY OF TRADE
Jalan Mohd Ikhwan Ridwan Rais 5, Jakarta
Tel (21) 348667
Minister: Dr Arifin M. Siregar

MINISTRY OF TRANSMIGRATION
Jalan Letjen Haryono MT, Cikoko, Jakarta Selatan
Tel (21) 794682
Minister: Lt-Gen Sugiarto

MINISTRY OF YOUTH AND SPORTS
Jalan Jenderal Sudirman, Senayan, Jakarta Pusat
Tel (21) 581986
Minister of State: Akbar Tanjung

OFFICE OF THE ATTORNEY-GENERAL
Jalan Sultan Hasanuddin 1, Jakarta
Tel (21) 773557
Attorney-General (with the rank of Minister of State):
Sukarton Marmosudjono

OFFICE OF THE CABINET SECRETARY
Jalan Veteran 18, Jakarta Pusat
Tel (21) 3810973
Junior Minister and Cabinet Secretary: Saadilah Mursjid

OFFICE OF CO-ORDINATING MINISTER FOR PEOPLE'S WELFARE
Jalan Merdeka Barat 3, Jakarta Pusat
Tel (21) 353055
Minister-Co-ordinator: Supardjo Rustam

OFFICE OF CO-ORDINATING MINISTER FOR POLITICAL AFFAIRS AND SECURITY
Jalan Merdeka Barat 15, Jakarta
Tel (21) 376004
Minister-Co-ordinator: Adm Sudomo

OFFICE OF THE MINISTER OF STATE FOR THE ROLE OF WOMEN
Jalan Merdeka Barat 15, Jakarta Pusat 10110
Tel (21) 3805563
Minister of State: A. Sulasikin Murpratomo

OFFICE OF THE STATE SECRETARY
Perpustakaan, Dewan Perwakilan Rakyat-R.I., Jalan Jenderal
Gatot Subroto, Senayan, Jakarta Pusat 10270
Tel (21) 5001223
Minister of State and State Secretary:
Maj-Gen Murdiono

GOVERNMENT AGENCIES AND ORGANIZATIONS

Advisory and Supervisory Body

Badan Pemeriksa Keuangan (Supreme Audit Board): Jakarta; controls the accountability of public finance; enjoys investigatory powers and is independent of the Executive; its findings are presented to the House of Representatives.

Art and Culture

Arsip Nasional (National Archives): Jalan Ampera Raya, Cilandak III, Pasar Minggu, Jakarta; tel (21) 781851.

Business and Economy

BANKING

Bank Bumi Daya: Jalan Imam Bonjol 61, POB 106, Jakarta 10002; tel (21) 333721; telex 61117; fax (21) 330153; Pres Dir: H. Surasa; f 1959; commercial and foreign exchange bank; specializes in credits to the plantation and forestry sectors; 82 brs, 17 sub-brs.

Bank Dagang Negara: Jalan M. H. Thamrin 5, POB 338/JKT, Jakarta; tel (21) 321707; telex 61628; fax (21) 323618; Pres: H. M. Widarsadipradja; f 1960; foreign exchange bank; specializes in credits to the mining sector; 127 brs.

Bank Ekspor Impor Indonesia: Jalan Lapangan Setasiun 1, POB 32, Jakarta Kota; tel (21) 673122; telex 42702; fax (21) 674734; Pres: Moeljoto Djojomartono; f 1968; commercial and foreign exchange bank; specializes in credits for manufacture and export; 56 brs.

Bank Indonesia: Jalan M. H. Thamrin 2, Jakarta; tel (21) 372408; telex 44164; Gov: Adrianus Mooy (with the rank of Minister of State); Pres: T. M. Zahirsjah; f 1828; nationalized 1951; central bank since 1953.

Bank Negara Indonesia 1946: Jalan Jenderal Sudirman Kav 1, POB 2955, Jakarta Kota 1110; tel (21) 5701001; telex 45524; fax (21) 5700980; Pres: A. Kukuh Basuki; f 1946; commercial bank; specializes in credits to the industrial sector; 277 domestic brs, 6 overseas brs.

Bank Pembangunan Indonesia—BAPINDO (Development Bank of Indonesia): Jalan Gondangdia Lama 2-4, POB 140, Jakarta 10002; tel (21) 321908; telex 44214; fax (21) 333644; Pres: Subekti Ismaun; f 1960; medium- and long-term investment loans to new and existing business enterprises; equity financing and general banking services; non-financial assistance, industrial research and technical consultancy services; 21 brs.

Bank Rakyat Indonesia: Jalan Jenderal Sudirman Kav 42-43, Jakarta; tel (21) 586111; telex 44728; fax (21) 581363; Pres: Karmady Arief; f 1895; commercial and foreign exchange bank; specializes in credits to co-operatives in agriculture and fisheries, in rural credit generally and international business; 295 brs.

Bank Tabungan Negara (State Savings Bank): Jalan Hr Rasuna Said C-17, Jakarta Selatan; tel (21) 5781210; telex 62313; Pres: Sasonotomo; f 1964; savings bank; 14 brs.

FINANCIAL AGENCIES

Badan Koordinasi Penanaman Modal—BKPM (Investment Co-ordinating Board): Jalan Jenderal Gatot Subroto 44, POB 3186, Jakarta; tel (21) 512008; telex 45651; Chair: Sanyoto Sastrowardoyo; f 1976.

Directorate of Financial Institutions: Ministry of Finance, Jalan Lapangan Banteng Timur 4, Jakarta Pusat.

Insurance Supervisory Authority of Indonesia: address as above; tel (21) 360298; telex 46415; Dir: Dr Bambang Subianto.

Directorate-General of Budget: Jalan Lapangan Banteng Timur 2, Jakarta Pusat; under the Ministry of Finance.

Directorate-General of State Monetary Control: Jalan Lapangan Banteng Timur 2-4, Jakarta Pusat; under the Ministry of Finance.

Directorate-General of Taxation: Jalan Gatot Subroto 4, Jakarta Selatan.

NATIONALIZED INDUSTRY

Association of State-Owned Cos: CTC Bldg, Jalan Kramat Raya 94-96, Jakarta; tel (21) 346071; telex 44208; Pres: Odang; co-ordinates the activities of state-owned enterprises.

National Board of Arbitration (BANI): Jalan Merdeka Timur 11, Jakarta; Chair: Prof R. Subekti; f 1977; resolves co disputes.

PT Dok & Perkapalan 'Tanjung Priok' (PERSERO): Jalan Panambangan, Pelabuhan I, Tanjung Priok, POB 2025, Jakarta 14310; tel (21) 490808; telex 49249; fax (21) 492071; Pres Dir: R. M. S. Wibisono; f 1891; dry dock facilities; shipbuilding and ship repairs; manufacturing and repair of offshore platforms.

PT Nurtanio: BPP Teknologi Bldg, Jalan M. H. Thamrin 8, Jakarta; tel (21) 322395; telex 44331; Chair: Dr B. Jusuf Habibie; aerospace.

TRADE

PT Aneka Tambang: Jalan Bungur Besar 24, POB 2513, Jakarta; tel (21) 410108; telex 49147; Pres: Kosim Gandataruna; f 1968; minerals.

CAFI (Commercial Advisory Foundation in Indonesia): Jalan Probolinggo 5, POB 249, Jakarta 10002; tel (21) 324487; Chair: Dr R. Ng. S. Sosrohadikoesoemo; Man Dir: Benny Sudibjo Pontjosoegito; f 1958; information, consultancy and translation services.

PT Dharma Niaga Ltd: Jalan Abdul Muis 6/8/10, POB 2028, Jakarta 10160; tel (21) 349978; telex 44312; fax (21) 3810434; Pres: Benarto; f 1970; import, export, distribution, installation, after sales service.

Directorate-General of Customs and Excise: Jalan Jenderal A. Yani, Jakarta Timur.

Export Arbitration Board: Jalan Kramat Raya 4-6, Jakarta; Chair: R. M. Sosrohadikusumo; Vice-Chair: Sanusi.

General Management Board of the State Trading Corpns (BPU-PNN): Jakarta; Pres: Col Suhardiman; f 1961.

PT Tjipta Niaga: Jalan Kalibesar Timur IV/1, POB 1314/JAK, Jakarta; tel (21) 673923; telex 42747; Pres: E. Simandjuntak; f 1964; import and distribution of basic goods, bulk articles, sundries, provisions and drinks; export of Indonesian produce.

Defence

Indonesian Armed Forces: Jalan Merdeka Barat 13, Jakarta; tel (21) 366184; Commdr-in-Chief: Lt-Gen Try Sutrisno (with the rank of Minister of State).

Air Force: Jalan Gatot Subroto 72, Jakarta; tel (21) 774055; Chief of Staff: Vice-Marshal Madya Sukardi.

Army: Jalan Merdeka Utara 2, Jakarta; tel (21) 551403; Chief of Staff: Gen Eddy Sudradjat.

Navy: Mabes TNI AL Cilacap, Jakarta; tel (21) 371032; Chief of Staff: Rear-Adm Mohamed Arifin.

Police Headquarters: Jalan Trunojoyo 3, Kebayoran Baru, Jakarta; tel (21) 348537.

Development and Planning

National Development Planning Agency (Bappenas): Jalan Taman Suropati 2, Jakarta; tel (21) 348990; Chair: Dr J. B. Sumarlin; Vice-Chair: Dr Saleh Afiff; formulates national economic devt plans.

Forestry

Perum Perhutani (State Forest Corpn): Gedung Manggala Wanabakti, Blok IV/Lantai 4, Jalan Gatot Subroto, Senayan, POB 19/JKWB, Jakarta; tel (21) 583034; telex 46283; fax (21) 583616; Pres Dir: Hartono Wirjodarmodjo; Marketing Dir: Soedjadi Martodiwirjo; f 1973; production and export of wood and wood products, eg teak, mahogany, pine, gum resin, turpentine oil, etc.

Health and Welfare

Badan Koordinasi Keluarga Berencana Nasional—BKKBN (National Co-ordinating Agency for Family Planning): Jalan Letjen Haryono MT, Kav 9-11, Cawang, Jakarta; tel (21) 8193248.

Legal and Judiciary

Mahkamah Agung (Supreme Court): Jalan Merdeka Utara 13, Jakarta; tel (21) 363709; Chief Justice: Lt-Gen Ali Said; final court of appeal.

Media

BROADCASTING

Radio Republik Indonesia (RRI): Jalan Merdeka Barat 4-5, POB 157, Jakarta 10110; tel (21) 349091; telex 44349; fax (21) 367132; Dir: Arsyad Subik; Dep Dirs: Fachruddin Soekarno (Overseas Service), Suryanta Saleh (Programming), Chairul Zen (Programme Devt), Samsul Muin Harahap (Admin); f 1945; runs 49 stations.

Yayasan Televisi Republik Indonesia (TVRI): TVRI Senayan, Jalan Gerbang Pemuda, Senayan, Jakarta; tel (21) 581125; telex 46154; fax (21) 583122; Dir: Ishadi; f 1962; TV broadcasting.

GOVERNMENT PUBLISHER

Balai Pustaka (State Publishing and Printing House): Jalan Dr Wahadin 1, Jakarta; history, anthropology, politics, philosophy, medical, arts and literature publishing.

NEWS AND INFORMATION

Antara (Indonesian National News Agency): Wisma Antara, 19th and 20th Floors, 17 Jalan Merdeka Seletan, POB 257, Jakarta 10002; tel (21) 344379; telex 44305; Man Dir and Editor-in-Chief: Handjojo Nitimihardjo; f 1937; news agency; brs in Indonesia and overseas; bulletins in Indonesian and English; monitoring service of stock exchanges world-wide; photo service.

Central Bureau of Statistics: 8 Jalan Dr Sutomo, POB 3, Jakarta 10710; tel (21) 372808; telex 45150; fax (21) 357046; Dir-Gen: Azwar Rasjid; Vice Dir-Gen: Soetjipto Wirosardjono; f 1925; carries out statistical activities assigned by the Govt; co-ordinates statistical activities of Govt agencies at central and regional level.

Mining and Energy

Badan Tenaga Atom Nasional—BATAN (National Atomic Energy Agency): Jalan K. H. Abdul Rachim, Kuningan Barat, Mampang Prapatan, POB 85/KBY, Jakarta Selatan; tel (21) 511109; telex 46354; Dir-Gen: Djali Ahimsa; f 1958.

Lembaga Minyak & Gas—LEMIGAS (Oil and Natural Gas Technology Development Centre): Jalan Cipulir, Kebayoran Lama, Jakarta; tel (21) 775994.

PT Perusahaan Pertambangan Minyak & Gas Bumi Negara (PERTAMINA): Jalan Merdeka Timur 1A, POB 12, Jakarta; tel (21) 3031; telex 44152; Pres and Dir: Faisal Abda'oe; f 1957; petroleum and natural gas mining enterprise.

PT Perusahaan Pertambangan Minyak & Gas Bumi Negara—PERTAMINA (tanker services): Directorate for Shipping and Telecommunications, Jalan Jos Sudarso 32-34, POB 265, Tanjung Priok, Jakarta; tel (21) 494309; telex 42753; Pres and Chair: Abdul Rachman Ramly; tanker services.

Perum Tambang Batubara: Jalan Prof Dr Supomo SH 10, Jakarta 12870; tel (21) 8295608; telex 48203; fax (21) 8297642; Pres: Sapari Sutisnawinata; f 1968; coal-mining.

PT Tambang Timah (Persero): Jalan Jenderal Gatot Subroto, Jakarta; tel (21) 510731; telex 62404; Gen Man: Sudjatmiko; tin.

Science and Technology

Badan Koordinasi Survey dan Pemetaan Nasional—BAKOSURTANAL (Co-ordinating Agency for Survey and Mapping): Jalan Dr Wahidin I 11, Jakarta; tel (21) 359766; Chair: Jacub Rais.

Lembaga Ilmu Pengetahuan Indonesia—LIPI (Indonesian Institute of Sciences): Widya Graha LIPI, Jalan Gatot Subroto 10, Jakarta; tel (21) 511831; Chair: Dr D. A. Tisnaamidjaja.

Lembaga Penerbangan dan Antariksa Nasional—LAPAN (National Aeronautics and Outer Space Institute): Jalan Pemuda Persil 1, Jakarta; tel (21) 484744; Chair: R. Ibnoe Soebroto S.

Telecommunications

Directorate-General of Posts and Telecommunications: Jalan Kebon Sirih 37, Jakarta; tel (21) 346000; telex 44407; Dir-Gen: S. Abdulrachman.

Perum Pos dan Giro: Jalan Cilaki 73, Bandung 40115; tel (22) 431050; telex 28174; fax (22) 52717; Chief Exec: Marsoedi; provides postal and giro services.

Perusahaan Umum Telekomunikasi (Perumtel): Jalan Cisanggarung 2, 40114 Bandung; tel (22) 436100; telex 28220;

Chief Exec: W. Moenandir; domestic telecommunications.

PT Indosat: Jalan Merdeka Barat 21, Jakarta 10110; tel (21) 3802614; telex 44383; telecommunications.

Tourism

Direktorat Jenderal Pariwisata (Directorate-General of Tourism): Jalan Kramat Raya 81, POB 409/JKT, Jakarta Pusat 10450; tel (21) 359001; telex 45625; Chair: Hamengku Buwong; Vice-Chair: Sri Budoyo; Dir-Gen: Joop Ave.

Directorate of Conventions and International Relations: Jalan Kramat Raya 81, Jakarta Pusat 10450; tel (21) 3103088; telex 61525; fax (21) 3101146; Dir: Abdoellah Sjamsoeddin; f 1983; joint co-operation with international tourist organizations.

Transport

CIVIL AVIATION

Directorate-General of Air Communications: Jalan Angkasa I/2, Jakarta 10720; tel (21) 416321; telex 49482; Dir-Gen: Sobirin Misbach; under the Ministry of Communications.

PT Garuda Indonesia: Jalan Medan Merdeka Selatan 13, POB 164, Jakarta 10110; tel (21) 3801901; telex 49113; fax (21) 363370; Pres Dir: M. Soeparno; f 1950; state airline; domestic, regional and international services.

PT Merpati Nusantara Airlines: Jalan Angkasa 2, POB

323, Jakarta 10002; tel (21) 413608; telex 49154; Pres: Soeratman; f 1962; subsidiary of PT Garuda Indonesia; domestic and regional services to Australia and Malaysia.

RAILWAYS

Perusahaan Jawatan Kereta Api (Indonesian State Railways): Jalan Perintis Kermedekaan 1, Bandung 40113; tel (22) 58001; telex 28263; Chief Dir: Suharso; controls 6,458 km of track on Java and Sumatra.

ROADS

Directorate-General of Highways: Ministry of Public Works, Jalan Pattimura 20, Kebayoran Baru, 12110 Jakarta Selatan; tel (21) 7203165; Dir: Gen Suryatin Sastromijoyo.

SHIPPING

Directorate-General of Sea Communications: Jalan Medan Merdeka Timur 5, Jakarta; tel (21) 363009; telex 46117; Dir-Gen: J. E. Habibie; under the Ministry of Communciations.

PT Pelayaran Nasional Indonesia (PELNI): Jalan Angkasa 18, POB 115, Jakarta; tel (21) 417817; telex 44301; Pres Dir: Soedharno Mustafa; national shipping co; runs passenger and cargo vessels.

PT Pengembangan Armada Niaga Nasional: Pann Bldg, Jalan Cikini IV/II, Jakarta; tel (21) 322003; telex 46286; Pres: A. Nazahar; shipping co.

IRAN

Head of State

The chief executive of the Islamic Republic of Iran is the President, elected by universal adult suffrage for a four-year term. The Constitution provides for a Wali Faqih (religious leader) who, in the absence of the Imam Mehdi (the hidden Twelfth Imam), carries the burden of leadership.

President: Hojatoleslam Ali Akbar Hashemi Rafsanjani (took office 17 August 1989).

Office of the President: Teheran; tel (21) 6161.

First Vice-President: Dr Hassan Ibrahim Habibi.

Second Vice-President in charge of Judicial and Parliamentary Affairs: Sayed Attaollah Mohadjerani.

Third Vice-President in charge of Executive Affairs: Hamid Merzadeh.

Wali Faqih (Religious Leader): Ayatollah Sayed Ali Khamenei.

Legislature

Legislative power is held by the Majlis (Islamic Consultative Assembly), whose 270 members are elected by universal adult suffrage for a four-year term. The appointed lawyers of the Council of Guardians supervise elections and examine legislation to ensure it accords with the Constitution and Islamic precepts, and the 83 elected clerics of the Council of Experts choose the successor to the Wali Faqih.

Majlis-e-Shura e Islami (Islamic Consultative Assembly): Imam Khomeini Ave, Teheran; tel (21) 6135418; Speaker: Hojatoleslam Mahdi Karrubi; Dep Speakers: Hojatoleslam Hossein Hashemian, Asadollah Bayat.

Council of Experts: Teheran; Chair: Ayatollah Ali Meshkini; Dep Chair: Ayatollah Ibrahim Amini.

Shura-e-Nigahban (Council of Guardians): Teheran; Chair: Ayatollah Muhammad Muhammadi Guilani.

MINISTRIES AND GOVERNMENT DEPARTMENTS

COUNCIL OF MINISTERS
Teheran
President: Dr Hassan Ibrahim Habibi

MINISTRY OF AGRICULTURE
Teheran
Minister: Isa Kalantari

MINISTRY OF COMMERCE
Teheran
Minister: Abdolhssein Vahadji

MINISTRY OF CONSTRUCTION JIHAD
Teheran
Minister: Gholamreza Forouzesh

MINISTRY OF DEFENCE AND LOGISITICS
Teheran
Minister: Akbar Torkan

MINISTRY OF ECONOMIC AFFAIRS AND FINANCE
Teheran
Minister: Mohsen Nourbakhch

MINISTRY OF EDUCATION AND TRAINING
Ekbatan Ave, Baharestan Sq, Teheran
Tel (21) 316577
Minister: Muhammad Ali Najafi

MINISTRY OF ENERGY
Teheran
Minister: Namdar Zanganeh

MINISTRY OF FOREIGN AFFAIRS
Teheran
Minister: Dr Ali Akbar Velayati

MINISTRY OF HEALTH
Teheran
Minister: Iradj Fazel

MINISTRY OF HEAVY INDUSTRY
Teheran
Minister: Muhammad Hadi Nejad Hosseinian

MINISTRY OF HIGHER EDUCATION
Teheran
Minister: Mostapha Mouïne

MINISTRY OF HOUSING AND URBAN DEVELOPMENT
60 Shahid Khoddami St, Vanak Sq, 19944 Teheran
Tel (21) 686802; telex 212117
Minister: Serag ed-Din Kazerouni

Urban Planning and Architecture Research Centre: 12 Laili Alley, Shahik Khoddami St, Vanak Sq, 19946 Teheran; f

279

1987; carries out research on architecture and urban, regional and national planning.

MINISTRY OF INDUSTRIES
Teheran
Minister: Muhammad Reza Neematzadeh

MINISTRY OF INFORMATION
Teheran
Minister: Ali Falahian

MINISTRY OF THE INTERIOR
Teheran
Minister: Abdollah Nouri

MINISTRY OF ISLAMIC GUIDANCE
Teheran
Minister: Hojatoleslam Dr Sayed Muhammad Khatami

MINISTRY OF JUSTICE
Teheran
Minister: Ismaïl Chouchtari

MINISTRY OF LABOUR
Teheran
Minister: Hossein Kamali

MINISTRY OF MINES AND METALS
248 Somayeh Ave, Teheran
Tel (21) 836051; telex 212718
Minister: Hossein Mahloudji

MINISTRY OF OIL
Teheran
Minister: Gholamreza Aqazadeh

MINISTRY OF POSTS, TELEGRAPHS AND TELEPHONES
Teheran
Minister: Sayed Muhammad Gharazi

MINISTRY OF ROADS AND TRANSPORT
49 Taleghani Ave, Teheran
Tel (21) 646770
Minister: Muhammad Sayedikiya

GOVERNMENT AGENCIES AND ORGANIZATIONS

Advisory and Supervisory Bodies

Central Organization for Co-operatives of Iran: Teheran; organizes labour co-operatives and urban non-labour co-operatives.

Central Organization for Rural Co-operatives of Iran (CORC): Teheran; Man Dir: Sayed Hassan Motevalli-Zadeh; f 1963; provides educational, technical, commercial and credit aid to rural co-operative societies and unions.

Plan and Budget Organization: Baharestan Sq, Khiaban Daneshkadeh, 11494 Teheran; tel (21) 3271; telex 212642; Dep Pres and Head: Massoud Zanjani; f 1948; prepares short-, medium- and long-term plans with the co-operation of executive agencies; prepares and compiles the state general budget; conducts devt studies; produces statistics, etc.

Business and Economy

BANKING

Bank Keshavarzi (Agricultural Bank): 129 Patrice Lumumba St, Jalal Al-Ahmad Expressway, POB 14155-6395, Teheran; tel (21) 9121; telex 212058; Man Dir: Dr Ali-Reza Talayi; f 1979 by merger; allocates credit facilities to farmers and agricultural industries and to the general public; 306 brs.

Bank Markazi Jomhouri Islami Iran (Central Bank): Ferdowsi Ave, POB 1136-58551, Teheran; tel (21) 310100; telex 212503; Gov: Muhammad Hossein Adeli; f 1960; central note-issuing bank of Iran; Govt banking.

Bank Maskan (Housing Bank): Ferdowsi Ave, Teheran; tel (21) 675021; telex 213904; Chair and Man Dir: Abdullah Ebtehaj; f 1980; provides mortgage and housing finance; 187 brs.

Bank Mellat (Nation's Bank): Park Shahr, Varzesh Ave, POB 11365-5964, Teheran; tel (21) 891021; telex 213251; Chair and Man Dir: Muhammad Ali Vatani; f 1980 by merger of: International Bank of Iran, Bank Bimeh Iran, Bank Dariush, Distributors' Co-operative Credit Bank, Iran Arab Bank, Bank Omran, Bank Pars, Bank of Teheran, Foreign Trade Bank of Iran, Bank Farhangian; 1209 brs in Iran, 3 brs abroad.

Bank Melli Iran (The National Bank of Iran): Ferdowsi Ave, POB 11365-171, Teheran; tel (21) 33231; telex 212890; Chair and Man Dir: Kazem Najafi Elmi; f 1928; 1,643 brs in Iran, 24 brs abroad.

Bank Refah Kargaran: 125 Ayatollah Shahid Dr Moffateh Ave, POB 111628, Teheran; tel (21) 825000; telex 213786; f 1961; 84 brs.

Bank Saderat Iran (The Export Bank of Iran): 124 Jomhouri Islami Ave, POB 11365-7168, Teheran; tel (21) 670797; telex 213077; fax (21) 674676; Man Dir: Abbas Khafafi; f 1952, reorganized 1979; 2,200 brs in Iran, 18 brs abroad.

Bank Sanat va Madan (Bank of Industry and Mines): 593 Hafiz Ave, POB 11365-4978, Teheran; tel (21) 893271; telex 212816; Chair and Man Dir: Morteza Aramy Parchebaf; f 1979 by merger of: Industrial Credit Bank (ICB), Industrial and Mining Devt Bank of Iran (IMDBI), Devt and Investment Bank of Iran (DIBI), Iranian Bankers Investment Co (IBICO).

Bank Sepah (Army Bank): Imam Khomeini Sq, Teheran; tel (21) 311091; telex 212462; Man Dir: Sassan Manuchehri; f 1925, reorganized 1979; 666 brs in Iran, 5 brs abroad.

Bank Tejarat (Commercial Bank): 130 Taleghani Ave, POB 11365-5416, Teheran; tel (21) 890131; telex 212077; Chair and Man Dir: Muhammad Jafar Eftekhar; f 1979 as merger of: Irano-British Bank, Bank Etebarate Iran, The Bank of Iran and the Middle East, Mercantile Bank of Iran and Holland, Bank Barzagani Iran, Bank Iranshahr, Bank Sanaye Iran, Bank Shahriar, Iranians' Bank, Bank Kar, International Bank of Iran and Japan, Bank Russo-Iran; 667 brs in Iran, brs in London and Paris.

Islamic Economy Organization: Ferdowsi Ave, Teheran; f 1980; fmrly Islamic Bank of Iran; provides interest-free loans; invests in small industry.

FINANCIAL AGENCIES

Teheran Stock Exchange: Taghinia Bldg, 521 South Saadi Ave, 11447 Teheran; tel (21) 311149; Chair of Council: M. Nourbakhsh; f 1966.

INSURANCE

Bimeh Iran (Iran Insurance Co): Saadi Ave, POB 11365-9153, Teheran; tel (21) 304026; telex 212782; Man Dir: Amir Sadeghi Neshat; f 1935; all types of insurance.

Bimeh Markazi Iran (Central Insurance Co): 149 Taleghani Ave, Teheran; Pres: Ahmad Geranmayeh.

Dana Insurance Co Ltd: Enghelab Ane, POB 2868, Teheran; in association with Commercial Union Assurance Co Ltd.

Hafez Insurance Co: Ostad Motahhari Ave, 44 Daraye Noor St, Teheran; Man Dir: K. Helmi; f 1974; most classes of insurance.

Iran-American International Insurance Co: Ave Zohre, Teheran.

Pars, Société Anonyme d'Assurances: Saadi Ave, Teheran; f 1955; fire, marine, motor vehicle, third party liability, personal accident, group, life, contractor's all-risk and medical insurance.

Shirkat Sahami Bimeh Arya (Arya Insurance Co Ltd): 202 Soraya Ave, Teheran; Man Dir: Khalil Karimabadi; f 1952.

Shirkat Sahami Bimeh Asia (Asia Insurance Co Ltd): Asia Insurance Bldg, Taleghani Ave, Teheran; tel (21) 836040; telex 213664; Man Dir: Masoum Zamiri; f 1960.

Shirkat Sahami Bimeh Dan: 315 Enghelab Ave, Teheran; Man Dir: Mansoor Akhwan; f 1974; joint venture between Iranian interests and Commercial Union Insurance Co, London.

Shirkat Sahami Bimeh Iran and America: 8 Apartments Kavah, 20 Mitu Zohra, Mobarezan Ave, Teheran; Man Dir: Khosrow Shabai; f 1974.

Shirkat Sahami Bimeh Melli (The National Insurance Co Ltd): Taleghani Ave, Rasekh St, POB 1786, Teheran; Man Dir: Reza Fatemi; f 1956; all classes of insurance.

Shirkat Sahami Bimeh Omid: Blvd Karimkhan Zand, Kheradniand Jonoubi Ave 99, Teheran; f 1960.

Shirkat Sahami Bimeh Sakhtiman Va Kar (Construction and Labour): Apartments Bank Kar, Khayaban-e-Hafiz; Man Dir: Samad Taheri; f 1964.

Shirkat Sahami Bimeh Teheran: 43 Khayaban Khushbin Villa, Teheran; Man Dir: Eraj Ali Abadi; f 1974.

NATIONALIZED INDUSTRY

National Iranian Drilling Co (NIDC): M. I. S. Rd, POB 61635-138, Ahwaz; tel (61) 40151; telex 612025; fax (61) 42456; Man Dir: S. E. Jalilian; f 1979; drilling and repair of oil and gas wells on and offshore; drilling support services.

National Iranian Industries Organization (NIIO): 133 Dr Fatemi Ave, POB 14155-3579, Teheran; tel (21) 656031; telex 214176; f 1979; owns 500 factories in Iran.

TRADE

Export Promotion Centre of Iran: POB 11-48, Tajrish, Teheran; tel (21) 21911; telex 212896; Pres: Hossein Khabbazan; international trade fairs and exhibitions.

Iran Chamber of Commerce, Industries and Mines: 254 Taleghani Ave, Teheran; tel (21) 836031; telex 213382; supervises the affiliated 20 Chambers in the provinces.

Defence

Armed Forces: c/o Ministry of Defence, Teheran; Commdr-in-Chief (acting): Hojatoleslam Ali Akbar Hashemi Rafsanjani; Chief of Staff and Commdr of the Gendarmerie: Brig-Gen Ali

Shahbazi; Chair, Supreme Defence Council: Hojatoleslam Sayed Ali Khamenei; Chief of Staff, Revolutionaly Guards Corps (Pasdaran): Ali-Reza Afshar; Commdr, Islamic Revolutionary Guards Corps: Mohsen Rezai; Commdr, Basij (Mobilization) War Volunteers Corps: Muhammad Ali Rahmani.

Air Force: c/o Ministry of Defence, Teheran; Commdr: Brig-Gen Mansour Sattari.

Army: c/o Ministry of Defence, Teheran; Commdr: Brig-Gen Hossein Hassani-Saadi.

Navy: c/o Ministry of Defence, Teheran; Commdr: (vacant).

National Security Council: Teheran; Chair: Abdollah Nouri; f 1989 to co-ordinate defence and national security policies, the political programme and intelligence reports, and social, cultural and economic activities related to defence and security; comprises the Chief of the Supreme Command Council of the Armed Forces, the head of the Plan and Budget Organization, two reps appointed by the Wali Faqih, Ministers of Foreign Affairs, Interior and Information, and the Commdr of the Armed Forces.

Education and Research

Isfahan Nuclear Technology Centre (INTC): POB 81465-1589, 81465 Isfahan; tel (31) 58081; telex 212165; f 1979; applied engineering research in areas related to nuclear reactor technology.

Institute of Nuclear Science and Technology (Teheran University Nuclear Centre): POB 2989, Teheran; Dir: Dr J. Moghimi; f 1958; research in nuclear physics, electronics, nuclear chemistry, radiobiology and nuclear engineering; training and advice on nuclear science and the peaceful applications of atomic energy.

Legal and Judiciary

Supreme Court: Teheran; Chief Justice: Hojatoleslam Muhammad Yazdi; Prosecutor-Gen: Hojatoleslam Muhammadi Reyshahri; comprises 16 branches.

Media

BROADCASTING

Islamic Republic of Iran Broadcasting (IRIB): Mossadegh Ave, Jame Jam St, POB 19395-1774, Teheran; tel (21) 21961; telex 212431; Dir-Gen: Hojatoleslam Sayed Muhammad Hashemi; semi-autonomous Govt authority; operates two national TV and three national radio channels, and local provincial radio stations throughout the country.

Radio Network 1 (Voice of the Islamic Republic of Iran): Teheran; broadcasts nationally and internationally on three national radio channels.

NEWS AND INFORMATION

Islamic Republic News Agency (IRNA): 873 Vali Asr Ave, POB 764, Teheran; tel (21) 892050; telex 212827; Man Dir: Houssein Nassiri; f 1936.

Statistical Centre of Iran: Dr Fatemi Ave, cnr Rahiye Moayeri, opposite Sazeman-e-Ab, Teheran 14144; tel (21) 655061; telex 213233.

Mining and Energy

Atomic Energy Organization of Iran: POB 14155-1339, Teheran; tel (21) 61381; telex 213383; Pres: Reza Amrollahi; f 1973; originally set up to produce nuclear power to provide electricity; main aim now is the exploration and exploitation of uranium deposits, to utilize nuclear technology in industry, agriculture and medicine, to provide research and devt work and training for greater national self-sufficiency in nuclear science and technology.

National Iranian Gas Co: Teheran.

National Iranian Oil Co (NIOC): Taleghani Ave, POB 1863, Teheran; tel (21) 6151; telex 212514; Chair of Board and Man Dir: Minister of Oil, Gholamreza Aqazadeh; Dirs: M. Nijad Hossainian (Engineering), A. Salehifrooz (Refining), H. Muhammad Nejad (Distribution and Pipelines), G. Hassantash (Admin), M. Keshavarz (Legal Affairs), S. M. Hedayatzadeh (International Affairs), H. Kheradmand (Corporate Planning Affairs), M. Karbausian (Commercial Affairs), M. Parvinian (Oil Production); state organization controlling all petroleum, petrochemical and natural gas operations in Iran; engages in all phases of oil operations; in 1979 the Ministry of Oil took over control of the NIOC, and the Minister of Oil took over as Chair and Man Dir.

Iranian Offshore Oil Co (IOOC): 339 Dr Beheshti Ave, POB 1434, Teheran; tel (21) 624102; telex 212707; Chair: Muhammad Hadi Nejad Hoseynihan; Man Dir: M. Aghaee; f 1980; devt, exploitation and production of crude oil, natural gas and other hydrocarbons in all offshore areas of Iran in the Persian Gulf.

National Petrochemical Co (NPC): Karimkhan Zand Blvd, POB 7484, Teheran; tel (21) 839060; telex 213520; fax (21) 822087; Man Dir: Mustafa Taheri; f 1964.

Telecommunications

Telecommunications Co of Iran: Teheran.

Transport

CIVIL AVIATION

Iran Air (Airline of the Islamic Republic of Iran): Iran Air Bldg, Mehrabad Airport, Teheran; tel (21) 9111; telex 212975; Man Dir: Muhammad Reza Majidi; f 1962; international flights to the Persian Gulf area, Europe, the Far East and Africa.

Iran Asseman Airlines: Mehrabad Airport, POB 13145-1476, Teheran; tel (21) 6400257; telex 212575; Man Dir: Ali Abedzadeh; Dep Man Dir: H. R. Fekri; f 1979 by merger; scheduled flights; domestic and international charter services.

RAILWAYS

Iranian Islamic Republic Railway: Shahid Kalantary Bldg, Rahe-Ahan Sq, 13185 Teheran; tel (21) 555120; telex 213103; Dir-Gen: Sadegh Afshar; Vice-Pres: Esmail Sheikh Muhammad (Admin and Finance), Nasser Pourmirza (Technical and Operations), Hamidreza Mehrazma (Planning and Technical Studies), Vahab Jamshidi (Construction and Renovation); f 1935; passenger and freight railway traffic.

SHIPPING

Irano-Hind Shipping Co: 3 13th St, Miremad Ave, Dr Beheshti Ave, Teheran; tel (21) 850213; telex 215233; Chair: L. M. S. Rajwar; Vice-Chair: M. H. Dajmar; Man Dir: Ahmad Makhamali; joint venture between the Islamic Republic of Iran and the Shipping Corpn of India.

Islamic Republic of Iran Shipping Lines (IRISL): Arya Bldg, 127 Ghaem Magham Farahani Ave, POB 15875-4646, 15896 Teheran; tel (21) 833061; telex 212794; Chair and Man Dir: Muhammad Hossein Dajmer; f 1967; affiliated to the Ministry of Commerce Jan 1980; liner services between the Persian Gulf and Europe, the Far East and South America.

National Iranian Tanker Co: 67-68 Atefi St, Africa Expressway, POB 16765-947, Teheran; tel (21) 229094; telex 213937; fax (21) 224537; Chair of Board and Man Dir: Muhammad Souri; f 1975; shipping of crude oil and its by-products to international markets.

Ports and Shipping Organization: 751 Enghelab Ave, Teheran; tel (21) 837041; telex 212271; Man Dir: Muhammad Madad.

Welfare

State Welfare Organization: Shahid Fayazbakhsh, POB 11365-9187, Teheran; Tel (21) 673918; Dir: Muhammad Yarigarravesh; f 1980.

IRAQ

Head of State

Executive power is vested in the President and the Revolutionary Command Council (RCC), which comprises nine members. The President and the Vice-President are elected by a two-thirds majority of the Council. Effective political power rests with the Iraq Regional Command of the Baath Party.

President: Saddam Hussain (assumed power 16 July 1979).

Vice-President: Taha Mohi ed-Din Maruf.

Office of the President and the Vice-President: Presidential Palace, Karradat Mariam, Baghdad; telex 212299; Minister of State at the President's Office: Hashim Aqrawi Subhi.

Office of the Chairman of the Revolutionary Council: Presidential Palace, Karradat Mariam, Baghdad; telex 212299; Chair: Saddam Hussain.

Legislature

Legislative responsibility is shared between the Revolutionary Command Council and the National Assembly, with 250 members elected by universal adult suffrage for four years. The country is divided into 15 Provinces and three Autonomous Regions. A Kurdish autonomous area has been set up, with a 50-member Legislative Council.

National Assembly: Baghdad; Chair: Saadi Mahdi Salih.

Chairman of the Kurdish Legislative Council: Ahmad Abd al-Qadir an-Naqshabandi.

MINISTRIES AND GOVERNMENT DEPARTMENTS

OFFICE OF THE PRIME MINISTER
Presidential Palace, Karradat Mariam, Baghdad
Prime Minister: Saddam Hussain
First Deputy Prime Minister: Taha Yassin Ramadan
Deputy Prime Ministers: Dr Sa'adoun Hammadi, Tareq Aziz
Ministers of State: Hashim Hassan, Arshad Ahmed Muhammad az-Zibari

MINISTRY OF AGRICULTURE AND IRRIGATION
Khulafa St, al-Khullani Sq, Baghdad
Tel (1) 887-3251; telex 212222
Minister: (vacant)

MINISTRY OF AWQAF AND RELIGIOUS AFFAIRS
North Gate, St opposite College of Engineering, Baghdad
Tel (1) 888-9561; telex 212785
Minister: Abdullah Faedl-Abbas

MINISTRY OF CULTURE AND INFORMATION
Nr an-Nusoor Sq, fmrly Qasr as-Salaam Bldg, Baghdad
Tel (1) 551-4333; telex 212800
Minister: Latif Nasif al-Jasim

MINISTRY OF DEFENCE
North Gate, Baghdad
Tel (1) 888-9071; telex 212202
Minister: Gen Abd al-Jabbar Khalil ash-Shanshal
Minister of State for Military Affairs: (vacant)

MINISTRY OF EDUCATION
POB 258, Baghdad
Tel (1) 886-0000; telex 212259
Minister: Abd al-Qadir Izzudin Hammudi

MINISTRY OF FINANCE
Khulafa St, Nr ar-Russafi Sq, Baghdad
Tel (1) 887-4871; telex 212459
Minister (acting): Muhammad Mahdi Salih

MINISTRY OF FOREIGN AFFAIRS
Opposite State Organization for Roads and Bridges, Karradat Mariam, Baghdad
Tel (1) 537-0091; telex 212201
Minister: Tareq Aziz
Minister of State: (vacant)

MINISTRY OF HEALTH
Baghdad
Tel (1) 776-1970
Minister (acting): Abd as-Salem Muhammad Saeed

MINISTRY OF HIGHER EDUCATION AND SCIENTIFIC RESEARCH
Baghdad
Tel (1) 39151; telex 212385
Minister: Dr Mundhir Ibrahim

MINISTRY OF HOUSING AND CONSTRUCTION
Salhiya, Baghdad
Tel (1) 23138; telex 212282
Minister: Taher Muhammad Hassoun al-Marzouk

MINISTRY OF INDUSTRY AND MILITARY INDUSTRIALIZATION
Nidhal St, Nr Sa'adoun Petrol Station, Baghdad
Tel (1) 887-2006; telex 212205
Minister: Brig-Gen Hussain Kamel Hassan

MINISTRY OF THE INTERIOR
Baghdad
Minister: Samir Muhammad Abd al-Wahab ash-Shaykhali

MINISTRY OF JUSTICE
Baghdad
Minister: Akram Abd al-Qadr Ali

MINISTRY OF LABOUR AND SOCIAL AFFAIRS
Khulafa St, al-Khullani Sq, Baghdad
Tel (1) 887-1881; telex 212621
Minister: Umeed Madhat Mubarak

MINISTRY OF LOCAL GOVERNMENT
Karradat Mariam, Baghdad
Tel (1) 537-0031; telex 212568
Minister: Ali Hassan al-Hajid

MINISTRY OF OIL
POB 6178, al-Mansour, Baghdad
Tel (1) 541-0031; telex 212216
Minister: Isam Abd ar-Rahim ash-Shalabi

MINISTRY OF PLANNING
Karradat Mariam, ash-Shawaf Sq, Baghdad
Tel (1) 537-0071; telex 212218
Minister: Samal Majid Faraj

MINISTRY OF TRADE
Khulafa St, al-Khullani Sq, Baghdad
Tel (1) 887-2682; telex 212206
Minister: Muhammad Mahdi Salih

MINISTRY OF TRANSPORT AND COMMUNICATIONS
Nr Martyr's Monument, Karradat Dakhil, Baghdad
Tel (1) 776-6041; telex 212020
Minister: Muhammad Hamza az-Zubaidi

MINISTRY OF YOUTH AFFAIRS
Baghdad
Minister: Abd al-Fattah Muhammad Amin

PRESIDENCY DIWAN (PRESIDENTIAL CABINET)
Baghdad
Head: Ahmad Hussain as-Samarrai
Advisers to the President (with status of Minister):
Subhi Yasin Khudair, Abd al-Ghani Abd al-Ghafur, Samir Muhammad Abd al-Wahhab, Abd al-Hasan Rahi Fir'awn, Saadi Mahdi Salih, Mazban Kadr Hadi, Khaled Abd al-Moneim

GOVERNMENT AGENCIES AND ORGANIZATIONS

Advisory and Supervisory Body

Iraqi Federation of Industries: Iraqi Federation of Industries Bldg, al-Khullani Sq, Baghdad; Pres: Hatam Abd ar-Rashid; f 1956.

Agriculture and Fishing

AGRICULTURE

State Enterprise for Sugar Beet: Baghdad; f 1987 by merger of sugar enterprises in Mosul and Sulaimaniya.

FISHING

State Enterprise for Sea Fisheries: POB 260, Basra; telex 7011; Baghdad office: POB 3296, Baghdad; tel (1) 92023; telex 212223.

Business and Economy

BANKING

Agricultural Co-operative Bank of Iraq: Rashid St, POB 5112, Baghdad; tel (1) 888-9081; Dir-Gen: Hdiya H. al-Khayoun; f 1936; 32 brs.

Central Bank of Iraq: Rashid St, POB 64, Baghdad; tel (1) 886-5171; telex 212203; Gov: Subhi N. Frankool; f 1947; sole right of note issue; brs in Mosul and Basra.

Industrial Bank of Iraq: al-Khullani Sq, POB 5825, Baghdad; tel (1) 887-2181; telex 212224; Dir-Gen: Bassima Abdul Haddi al-Dhahir; f 1940; 5 brs.

Rafidain Bank: New Banks' St, POB 11360 Massarif, Baghdad; tel (1) 887-0522; telex 212211; Pres and Chair: Tariq H. al-Khateeb; f 1941; 216 brs.

Rashid Bank: 7177 Haifa St, Baghdad; tel (1) 538-5085; telex 214121; Dir-Gen: Abdel Majid al-Ani; f 1988; 3 brs.

Real Estate Bank of Iraq: Yaffa St, al-Salhiya, POB 14185, Baghdad; tel (1) 537-5165; telex 212635; Dir-Gen: Abdul Razzak Azziz; f 1949; provides loans to assist the building industry; 18 brs.

INSURANCE

Iraq Reinsurance Co: Aqaba bin Nafi's Sq, Khalid bin al-Waleed St, POB 297, Baghdad; tel (1) 719-5131; telex 214407; fax (1) 791-497; Chair and Gen Man: K. M. al-Mudaries; f 1960; transacts reinsurance business on the international market.

Iraqi Life Insurance Co: Aqaba bin Nafi's Sq, Khalid bin al-Waleed St, POB 989, Baghdad; telex 213818; Chair and Gen Man: Abd al-Khaliq Rauf Khalil; f 1959.

National Insurance Co: al-Aman Bldg, al-Khullani St, POB 248, Baghdad; tel (1) 886-0730; telex 212397; Chair and Gen Man: Mowafaq H. Ridha; f 1950; monopoly of all direct non-life insurance.

NATIONALIZED INDUSTRY

Automobile State Enterprise: al-Andalus Sq, POB 3270, Baghdad.

National Co for Manufacturing Oil Equipment: Baghdad; fmrly a State organization; reformed as a co in 1987.

The Rafidain Co for Building Dams: Baghdad; f 1987 to replace the State Organization for Dams.

State Enterprise for Construction Industries: Baghdad; f 1987 by merger of the State organizations for gypsum, asbestos, and the plastic and concrete industries.

State Enterprise for Drinks and Mineral Water: Baghdad; f 1987 by merger of enterprises responsible for soft and alcoholic drinks.

State Enterprise for Textiles: Baghdad; f 1987 to replace the enterprise for textiles in Baghdad, and the enterprise for plastic sacks in Tikrit.

TRADE

Committee for Follow-Up of Oil Affairs and Implementation of Foreign Agreements: National Assembly Bldg, Baghdad; tel (1) 36161; Pres: Saddam Hussain.

Directorate-General of Customs and Excise: Alwiyah nr al-Andalus Sq, Baghdad.

Iraqi Export Co: Sa'adoun St, South Gate, POB 5656, Baghdad.

Iraqi Trading Co: al-Masbah Sq, POB 17, Baghdad.

State Enterprise for Import and Export: Baghdad: f 1987 to replace the five State organizations responsible to the Ministry of Trade for productive commodities, consumer commodities, grain and food products, exports and imports.

Defence

Armed Forces: c/o Ministry of Defence, North Gate, Baghdad; tel (1) 888-9071; telex 212201; Commdr-in-Chief: Saddam Hussain; Chief of Gen Staff: Gen Abd al-Jabbar Shanshal.

Air Force: c/o Ministry of Defence, North Gate, Baghdad; tel (1) 888-9071; Chief of Staff: Lt-Gen Hamid Sha'ban.

Navy: c/o Ministry of Defence, North Gate, Baghdad; tel (1) 888-9071; Commdr: Kaske Rashid Jamil al-Basri.

People's Army: c/o Ministry of Defence, North Gate, Baghdad; tel (1) 888-9071; Commdr: Taha Yassin Ramadan.

Media

BROADCASTING

Baghdad Television: Iraqi Broadcasting and Television Establishment, Salihiya, Karkh, Baghdad; tel (1) 537-1161; telex 212446; Dir-Gen: Dr Majid Ahmad as-Samarrie; f 1956; two channels; there are 23 other regional TV stations.

Iraqi Broadcasting and Television Establishment: Salihiya, Karkh, Baghdad; tel (1) 31151; telex 212446; Dir-Gen: Hamid Said; Dir-Gen, Radio: Adnan Rashid Shukr; Dir-Gen, Engineering and Technical Affairs: Muhammad Fakhri Rashid; f 1936; home service broadcasts in Arabic, Kurdish, Syriac and Turkoman; foreign service in French, German, English, Russian, Swahili, Turkish and Urdu.

State Organization for Broadcasting and Television: Iraqi Broadcasting and Television Establishment, Salihiya, Karkh, Baghdad; tel (1) 537-1161; telex 212246.

GOVERNMENT PUBLISHER

National House for Publishing, Distribution and Advertising: Ministry of Culture and Information, al-Jumhuriya St, POB 624, Baghdad; tel (1) 425-1846; telex 212392; Dir-Gen: M. A. Askar; f 1972; publishes books on politics, economics, education, agriculture, sociology, commerce and science in Arabic and other Middle Eastern languages; sole importer and distributor of newspapers, magazines, periodicals and books; controls all advertising activities, inside Iraq as well as outside.

NEWS AND INFORMATION

Central Statistical Organization: Ministry of Planning, Karradat Mariam, ash-Shawaf Sq, Baghdad; tel (1) 537-0071; telex 212218.

Iraqi News Agency (INA): Zaytoon St, POB 3084, Baghdad; tel (1) 887-5661; telex 212267; Dir-Gen: Taha Yassin Hassan al-Basri; f 1959.

Mining and Energy

ENERGY

Iraq National Oil Co (INOC): al-Khullani Sq, POB 476, Baghdad; tel (1) 887-1115; telex 212204; f in 1964 to operate the petroleum industry at home and abroad; when Iraq nationalized its petroleum, structural changes took place in INOC and it became solely responsible for exploration, production, transportation of Iraqi crude petroleum and petroleum products. INOC was merged with the Ministry of Oil in 1987, and the functions of some of the organizations under its control were transferred to newly created ministerial depts or to cos responsible to the ministry.

National Co for Distribution of Oil Products and Gas: Rashid St, South Gate, POB 3, Baghdad; tel (1) 888-9911; telex 212247; Dir-Gen: Hazim Ali at-Talib; fmrly a State organization; reformed as a co in 1987.

National Co for Oil and Gas Exploration: INOC Bldg, al-Khullani Sq, POB 476, Baghdad; Chair: Dr Hashim al-Khursan; fmrly the State Establishment for Oil and Gas Exploration; reformed as a co in 1987; responsible for exploration and operations in difficult terrain such as marshes, swamps, deserts, valleys and in mountainous regions.

National Co for Oil Projects: as-Sa'adoun St, POB 198, Baghdad; tel (1) 776-3250; telex 212230; Dir-Gen: Rajih Mohi ed-Din; fmrly the State Organization for Oil Projects; reformed as a co in 1987; repsonsible for construction of petroleum projects, mostly inside Iraq through direct execution, and also for design supervision of the projects and contracting with foreign enterprises, etc.

Northern Petroleum Co (NPC): POB 1, at-Ta'meem Governorate; Dir-Gen: Dr Sami Sharif; f 1987 by the merger of the former Northern and Central Petroleum Organizations to carry out petroleum operations in northern Iraq.

Southern Petroleum Co (SPC): POB 240, Basra; fmrly the Southern Petroleum Organization; reformed as the SPC in 1987 to undertake petroleum operations in southern Iraq.

State Enterprise for Gas and Sulphur Extraction: POB 16, Kirkuk.

State Enterprise for Oil Refining in the Central Area: POB 2075, Daura, Baghdad; tel (1) 92081.

State Enterprise for Oil Refining in the Northern Area: POB 7, Kirkuk.

State Enterprise for Oil and Gas Industrialization in the South: f 1988 by a merger of the enterprises responsible for the gas industry and oil refining in the south.

MINING

State Enterprise for Minerals: as-Sa'adoun St, POB 2330, Baghdad.

Telecommunications

State Enterprise for Communications and Post: Karrada Dakhil, Baghdad; tel (1) 718-0400; telex 212002; Dir-Gen: Ghassan A. Mustafa; f 1987 from the State organization for post, telegraph and telephones and its subsidiaries.

Transport

CIVIL AVIATION

National Co for Civil Aviation Services: al-Mansour, Baghdad; tel (1) 551-9443; telex 212662; f 1987 following the abolition of the State Organization for Civil Aviation; responsible for the provision of aircraft, and for airport and passenger services.

RAILWAYS

State Enterprise for Iraqi Railways: Baghdad Central Station Bldg, Damascus Sq, Baghdad; tel (1) 537-3001; telex 212272; Pres: T. T. Abd ar-Razzak; Dir-Gen: Muhammad Y. al-Ahmad; reorganized in 1987; fmrly the Iraqi Republic Railways; under the supervision of the State Organization for Iraqi Railways.

New Railways Implementation Authority: al-Hurriya, POB 17040, Baghdad; tel (1) 537-0021; telex 212906; Sec-Gen: R. A. al-Umari; design and construction of railways to augment the standard-gauge network and to replace the metre-gauge network.

SHIPPING

Iraqi Oil Tankers Co: POB 37, Basra; tel (40) 319990; telex 207007; Dir-Gen: Mohammed A. Mohammed; f 1972; fleet of 17 tankers; training of seamen.

State Enterprise for Iraqi Ports: Maqal, Basra; tel (40) 413211; telex 207008; Pres (acting): Faleh Mahmoud el-Mousa; f 1987 when the State Organization for Iraqi Ports was abolished.

State Enterprise for Water Transport: Ministry of Transport and Communications Bldg, POB 5297, Baghdad; tel (1) 772-3761; telex 212565; f 1952; reformed in 1987; shipping owner, operator and agent.

State Enterprise for Maritime Transport (Iraqi Line): al-Jadiriya al-Hurriya Ave, POB 13038, Baghdad; tel (1) 776-3201; telex 212565; Dir-Gen: Jaber Q. Hassan; Operations Man: M. A. Ali.

IRELAND

Head of State

The constitutional Head of State is the President, elected for seven years by direct popular vote. Executive power is effectively held by the Cabinet headed by the Taoiseach (Prime Minister), who is appointed by the President on the nomination of the Dáil. The Cabinet is responsible to the Dáil.

President: Dr Patrick Hillery (Pádraig Ó hIrighile) (assumed office 3 December 1976; re-elected 21 October 1983).

Office of the President: Áras an Uachtaráin, Phoenix Park, Dublin 8; tel (1) 772815; fax (1) 710529.

Legislature

Legislative power is vested in the Oireachtas (National Parliament) comprising the President and two Houses. The Seanad Éireann (Senate) consists of 60 nominated and indirectly-elected members serving five-year terms. It has no power to veto legislation. The Dáil Éireann (House of Representatives) comprises 166 members elected for five years by universal adult suffrage and proportional representation.

Seanad Éireann (Senate): Leinster House, Kildare St, Dublin 2; tel (1) 789911; Speaker: Tras Honan.

Dáil Éireann (House of Representatives): Leinster House, Kildare St, Dublin 2; tel (1) 789911; Speaker: Sean Treacy.

MINISTRIES AND GOVERNMENT DEPARTMENTS

DEPARTMENT OF THE TAOISEACH (PRIME MINISTER)
Govt Bldgs, Upper Merrion St, Dublin 2
Tel (1) 689333; telex 25800; fax (1) 603281
Taoiseach (Prime Minister): Charles J. Haughey
Tánaiste (Deputy Prime Minister): Brian Lenihan
Minister of State, Govt Chief Whip: Vincent Brady
Minister of State for Heritage Affairs: Brendan Daly
Minister of State, Co-ordinator of Govt policy and EEC Matters: Maire Geoghegan-Quinn

DEPARTMENT OF AGRICULTURE AND FOOD
Kildare St, Dublin 2
Tel (1) 789011; telex 93607; fax (1) 612890
Minister: Michael O'Kennedy
Minister of State for the Food Industry: Joe Walsh
Minister of State for Horticulture: Seamus Kirk

DEPARTMENT OF DEFENCE
Parkgate, Dublin 8
Tel (1) 771881; telex 25250; fax (1) 796097
Minister: Brian Lenihan
Minister of State: Vincent Brady

DEPARTMENT OF EDUCATION
Marlborough St, Dublin 1
Tel (1) 734700; telex 31136; fax (1) 729553
Minister: Mary O'Rourke
Minister of State for Tourism: Denis Lyons
Minister of State for Youth and Sport: Frank Fahey

DEPARTMENT OF ENERGY
25 Clare St, Dublin 2
Tel (1) 715233; telex 90335; fax (1) 773169
Minister: Robert M. Molly

DEPARTMENT OF THE ENVIRONMENT
Custom House, Dublin 1
Tel (1) 793377; telex 31014; fax (1) 742710
Minister: Pádraig Flynn
Minister of State for the Office for the Protection of the Environment: Mary Harney
Minister of State for Urban Renewal: Ger Connolly

DEPARTMENT OF FINANCE
Govt Bldgs, Upper Merrion St, Dublin 2
Tel (1) 767571; telex 30357; fax (1) 789936
Minister: Albert Reynolds
Minister of State: Brendan Daly

DEPARTMENT OF FOREIGN AFFAIRS
80 St Stephen's Green, Dublin 2
Tel (1) 780822; telex 25300; fax (1) 780628
Minister: Gerard Collins
Minister of State for Overseas Aid: Sean Calleary

DEPARTMENT OF THE GAELTACHT
1 Lower Grand Canal St, Dublin 2
Tel (1) 764751; telex 30782; fax (1) 764755
Minister: Charles J. Haughey
Minister of State: Pat the Cope Gallagher
F 1956; promotes the cultural, social and economic welfare of the Gaeltacht (Irish speaking areas); encourages the preservation and extension of the use of Irish as a vernacular language throughout the country.

DEPARTMENT OF HEALTH
Hawkins House, Dublin 2
Tel (1) 714711; telex 33451; fax (1) 711947
Minister: Rory O'Hanlon
Minister of State: Noel Treacy

DEPARTMENT OF INDUSTRY AND COMMERCE
Kildare St, Dublin 2
Tel (1) 614444; telex 93478; fax (1) 762654
Minister: Desmond J. O'Malley
Minister of State for Science and Technology:
Michael Smith
Minister of State for Trade and Marketing: Terry Leyden

DEPARTMENT OF JUSTICE
72-76 St Stephen's Green, Dublin 2
Tel (1) 789711; telex 90495; fax (1) 615461
Minister and Minister for Communications: Ray Burke

DEPARTMENT OF LABOUR
Davitt House, 50-60 Mespil Rd, Dublin 4
Tel (1) 765861; telex 24534; fax (1) 603210
Minister: Bertie Ahern

DEPARTMENT OF THE MARINE
Leeson Lane, Dublin 2
Tel (1) 615666; telex 90253; fax (1) 618214
Minister: John P. Wilson
Minister of State: Michael Noonan

DEPARTMENT OF SOCIAL WELFARE
Áras Mhic Dhiarmada, Dublin 1
Tel (1) 786444; telex 32969; fax (1) 741709
Minister: Dr Michael Woods

DEPARTMENT OF TOURISM AND TRANSPORT
Kildare St, Dublin 2
Tel (1) 789522; telex 91806; fax (1) 763350
Minister: Seamus Brennan

GOVERNMENT AGENCIES AND ORGANIZATIONS

Advisory and Supervisory Bodies

Advisory Council on Development Co-operation: 72-74 Northumberland Rd, Ballsbridge, Dublin 4; tel (1) 680268; Chair: Colm Ó Nualláin; Exec Sec: Paula Clancy; f 1979; mems appointed by Minister for Foreign Affairs; advises Minister for Foreign Affairs on Ireland's devt co-operation policy.

Bord na Gaeilge: 7 Cearnóg Mhuirfean, Baile Átha Cliath 2; tel (1) 763222; fax (1) 616564; Dir: Micheál Grae; Dep Dir: Micheál Ó Gruagáin; f 1978; promotion of the use of Irish as a living language; provides an information service on Irish language matters and a translation, design and editing service.

Clárlann na Talún (Land Registry): Chancery St, Dublin 7; tel (1) 732233; Registrar: John B. Fitzgerald; Dep Registrar: Thomas Moylan.

Companies Registration Office: Lower Castle Yard, Dublin Castle, Dublin 2; tel (1) 614222; Asst Principal: Paul Farrell.

DEVCO—State Agencies Development Co-operation Organization: Elm House, Clanwilliam Court, Lower Mount St, Dublin 2; tel (1) 613616; telex 93370; fax (1) 687521; Chair: Dr Brendan O'Regan; Dir: Breda Howard; association of forty state-sponsored and national bodies; promotes their activities in devt co-operation and training and technical assistance for developing countries.

National Economic and Social Council: Earl Court, Adelaide Rd, Dublin 2; tel (1) 604477; Chair: Padraig O'hUiginn; Sec: Gerry Danager; f 1973; advises the Govt on the devt of the national economy and the achievement of social justice; the Council is representative of the major economic and social interests in society, ie employers, unions and farmers.

Office of the Comptroller and Auditor-General: 72-76 St Stephen's Green, Dublin 2; tel (1) 762797; fax (1) 762797; Comptroller and Auditor-Gen: P. L. McDonnell; audit of accounts of all Govt depts and of certain state-sponsored bodies.

Office of the Ombudsman: 52 St Stephen's Green, Dublin 2; tel (1) 785222; telex 91096; fax (1) 610570; Ombudsman: Michael Mills; f 1980; investigates complaints in relation to Govt depts, local authorities, health boards and postal and telecommunications services.

The Racing Board: 9 Merrion Sq, Dublin 2; tel (1) 61171; fax (1) 611871; Chief Exec: Frank Smyth; Financial Controller: Paddy Walsh; f 1945; operation of Totalisator; control of bookmakers operating at race meetings; grants for prize money at race meetings; carriage of horses competing and improvement of race-courses and amenities.

Údarás na Gaeltachta: Na Forbacha, Gaillimh; tel (91) 92011; telex 50159; fax (91) 92037; encourages the preservation of the Irish language in the Gaeltacht; establishes and develops industries and employment schemes in the Gaeltacht.

Agriculture and Fishing

AGRICULTURE

Agriculture and Food Development Authority (TEAGASC): 19 Sandymount Ave, Dublin 4; tel (1) 688188; telex 30459; fax (1) 688023; Dir: Dr Pierce Ryan; f 1988 by merger of the national agricultural advisory and training body ACOT and the Agricultural Institute; responsible for providing integrated research, and carrying out advisory and training functions for the agriculture and food industry.

Bord na Móna (Irish Peat Board): Lower Baggot St, Dublin 2; tel (1) 688555; telex 30206; fax (1) 601800; Chair: B. Halligan; Man Dir: E. O'Connor; f 1946; devt of peat resources; production of milled peat and machine turf for electricity generation, machine turf and briquettes for gen, industrial and domestic use and horticultural moss peat products for gardeners.

Cómlucht Groighe Naísiúnta na hÉireann Teoranta (Irish National Stud Co Ltd): Tully, Kildare, Co Kildare; tel (45) 21251; telex 60706; fax (45) 22129; Chair: John M. Oxx; Man: John Clarke; f 1945; runs a stud farm for thoroughbred horses at the National Stud; provides the services of first-class stallions; provides advisory service to breeders; carries out farming activities such as raising cattle, hay, etc.

Irish Co-operative Organization Society Ltd: The Plunkett House, 84 Merrion Sq, Dublin 2; tel (1) 764783; telex 30379; Pres: Michael Gibbons; Dir-Gen: John Tyrrell; f 1894 as co-ordinating body for agricultural co-operative movement; mems are 200 co-operatives, approx 140,000 farmers.

FISHING

Bord Iascaigh Mhara (BIM) (Irish Sea Fisheries Board): Crofton Rd, Dún Laoghaire, Co Dublin; tel (1) 841544; telex 93237; fax (1) 841123; Chair: Patrick J. Wright; Chief Exec: Tony Gannon; devt of the fishing industry; provision of financial, technical and educational aid.

Fisheries Research Centre: Abbotstown, Castleknock, Dublin 15; tel (1) 210111; telex 31236; fax (1) 205078; Dir (acting): Eileen Twomey; f 1900; under Dept of the Marine; research into fresh-water and marine fisheries and into water quality.

An Príomh-Bhord Iascaigh (Central Fisheries Board): Mobhi Boreen, Glasnevin, Dublin 9; tel (1) 379206; fax (1) 360060; Chief Officer: M. S. Breathnach; f 1980; co-ordinates the activities of the seven regional fisheries boards in the areas of protection, conservation, management and devt of the country's inland fisheries and sea angling resources.

Art and Culture

The Arts Council: 70 Merrion Sq, Dublin 2; tel (1) 611840; fax (1) 761302; Dir: Adrian Munnelly; f 1951; independent statutory organization promoting and assisting the arts.

National Archives: Four Courts, Dublin 7; tel (1) 733833; Chair of Advisory Council: Justice Niall McCarthy; Dir (acting): David Craig; f 1988 by merger of the Public Record Office and the State Paper Office; preserves records acquired from Govt depts, the courts and other sources and makes them available for public inspection; advises Govt depts and public service organizations on the management and preservation of their records.

National Library of Ireland: Kildare St, Dublin 2; tel (1) 618811; Dir: Dr Patricia Donlon; f 1877; collection of printed, manuscript and pictorial material relating to Ireland.

National Museum of Ireland: Kildare St, Dublin 2; tel (1) 618811; fax (1) 766116; Dir: Dr Patrick F. Wallace; f 1877; collects, conserves, displays and interprets material relating to the national heritage in antiquities, fine arts, ethnography, history, zoology and geology.

Business and Economy

BANKING

Bank Ceannais na hÉireann (Central Bank of Ireland): POB 559, Dame St, Dublin 2; tel (1) 716666; telex 31041; fax (1) 716561; Gov: Maurice F. Doyle; Gen Man: Timothy O'Grady-Walshe; f 1942; sole issuer of Irish currency in the State.

Cuideachta an Cháirde Thionnscail, Teoranta (Industrial Credit Corpn plc): 32-34 Harcourt St, Dublin 2; tel (1) 720055; telex 93220; fax (1) 717797; Chair: J. T. Barton; Man Dir: F. A. Casey; f 1933; provides a range of financial services to businesses.

FINANCIAL AGENCIES

Agricultural Credit Corpn plc (ACC): ACC House, Upper Hatch St, Dublin 2; tel (1) 780644; telex 93512; fax (1) 780723; Chair: D. McGing; Chief Exec: J. McCloskey; f 1927; credit facilities for farmers, the agribusiness and other sectors; promotes savings and investment schemes; the Board is appointed by the Minister for Finance.

Office of the Revenue Commissioners: Dublin Castle, Dublin 2; tel (1) 792777; telex 93479; fax (1) 711826; Chair: Philip F. Curran; Commrs: Liam Réasún, Cathal C. MacDomhnaill; collection and admin of taxes and duties; enforcement of import and export controls; under Ministry of Finance.

MARKETING

Córas Beostoic agus Feola (CBF) (Irish Livestock and Meat Board): Clanwilliam Court, Lower Mount St, Dublin 2; tel (1) 685155; telex 93370; fax (1) 687521; Chair: D. Brosnan; Chief Exec: P. J. Moore; Sec/Dir: S. G. Kenny; f 1969; devt of markets for livestock, meat and meat products.

NATIONALIZED INDUSTRY

Irish Steel Ltd: Haulbowline, Cobh, Co Cork; tel (21) 811731; fax (21) 811347; 25 St Stephen's Green, Dublin; tel (1) 600200; Chair: W. Hugh O'Connor; Chief Exec: L. S. Coughlan; f 1947; steelmaking, rolling and galvanized sheetmaking.

Nitrigin Éireann Teoranta (NET): 60 Northumberland Rd, Dublin 4; tel (1) 689833; telex 93977; Chair: S. MacHale; Man Dir: T. A. Jago; f 1961; production of nitrogenous fertilizers and complete fertilizers.

Siúicre Éireann Cpt (Irish Sugar plc): St Stephen's Green House, Dublin 2; tel (1) 767501; telex 30662; fax (1) 767624; Chair: B. M. Cahill; Man Dir: C. K. Comerford; f 1933; processing of sugar beet grown by 7,000 Irish farmers for domestic and industrial purposes; processing of vegetables for human consumption and formulation of other food products; production of animal feed, manufacture of specialized machinery; production and distribution of ground limestone.

Erin Foods Ltd: St Stephen's Green House, Dublin 2; tel (1) 767501; telex 25352; fax (1) 767624; Group Chair: James E. Fitzpatrick; Man Dir: Maurice Sheehy; f 1958; division of Irish Sugar plc; processing of vegetables; manufacture of soups and formulated products.

TRADE

Córas Tráchtála (Irish Export Board): Merrion Hall, Strand Rd, Sandymount, Dublin 4; tel (1) 695011; telex 93678; fax (1) 695820; Chair: Conor McCarthy; Chief Exec: A. P. McCarthy; f 1959; promotion and devt of exports and aid for Irish exporters; comprehensive service to foreign buyers, financed by a grant-in-aid.

Fair Trade Commission: 50 Upper Mount St, Dublin 2; tel (1) 614255; telex 93478; fax (1) 763148; Chair: Myles K. O'Reilly; Sec: John A. Gleeson; f 1953; independent statutory body whose mems are appointed by the Minister for Industry and Commerce; reports on possible anti-competitive practices in the supply or distribution of goods or the provision of services; also investigates proposed mergers, referred to the Commission by the Minister of Industry and Commerce.

Irish Goods Council: Merrion Hall, Strand Rd, Dublin 4; tel (1) 696011; fax (1) 696251; Chair: Tom Hardiman; Chief Exec: Vivian Murray; market devt and marketing support services for Irish industry; promotion of Irish products on the home market.

Office of Consumer Affairs and Fair Trade: 4th Floor, Shelbourne House, Shelbourne Rd, Dublin 4; tel (1) 613399; fax (1) 606763; Dir: James M. Murray; f 1978; independent statutory office; consumer protection; enforcement of trading standards and competition laws; promotion of codes of practice; provision of information to consumers.

Patents Office: 45 Merrion Sq, Dublin 2; tel (1) 614144; Controller: Sean Fitzpatrick; issues patents and registers trade marks and designs.

Defence

Defence Forces: c/o Dept of Defence, Parkgate, Dublin 8; tel (1) 771881; telex 25250; Chief of Staff: Lt Gen Tadhg M. O'Neill.

Air Corps: address as above; tel (1) 771881; telex 31444; fax (1) 385953; Gen Officer Commanding and Dir, Military Aviation: Brig Gen Brian L. McMahon.

Naval Service: address as above; Flag Officer Commanding and Dir, Naval Service: Cdre William J. Brett.

Garda Síochána: Depot, Phoenix Park, Dublin 8; tel (1) 771156; telex 93909; fax (1) 773205; Commr: E. J. Doherty; national police force; under Ministry of Justice.

Development and Planning

Industrial Development Authority of Ireland (IDA Ireland): Wilton Park House, Wilton Place, Dublin 2; tel (1) 686633; telex 93431; fax (1) 603703; Man Dir: Padraic White; Exec Dir: Kieran McGowan; f 1949; autonomous state-sponsored organization with national responsibility for industrial devt; administers financial incentive schemes for new industrial investment; aims to promote investment in manufacturing and internationally-traded services (including financial services), to develop indigenous industry and to stimulate entrepreneurial and small-scale industries; runs 19 overseas offices.

The National Development Corpn Ltd (NADCORP): Wilton Park House, Wilton Place, Dublin 2; tel (1) 600611; telex 91238; fax (1) 600826; Chair: R. Burrows; Man Dir: G. A. Cashin; Sec: F. Crumlish; f 1986; investment in profitable and efficient enterprises, or enterprises capable of becoming so; all the issued share capital is held by the Minister for Finance.

Education

An tÚdarás um Ard-Oideachas (The Higher Education Authority): 21 Fitzwilliam Sq, Dublin 2; tel (1) 612748; fax (1) 610492; Chair: L. O Laidhin; Sec: J. L. Hayden; f 1971; advisory and funding body for tertiary education.

Employment

Employment Equality Agency: 36 Upper Mount St, Dublin 2; tel (1) 605966; Chief Exec: Sylvia Meehan; Chief Officer: Barbara Cashen; Information Officer: Kevin Foley; f 1977; promotion of legislation towards the elimination of discrimination in employment.

Foras Áiseanna Saothair (FÁS) (The Training and Employment Authority): 27-33 Upper Baggot St, Dublin 4; tel (1) 685777; telex 93313; fax (1) 682691; Dir-Gen: Brendan Leahy; Sec: Arthur O'Reilly; f 1988; runs training and employment programmes, information services and supports co-operative and community enterprises; mems include reps from unions, employers, education and youth interests, and from the Depts of Finance and Labour.

Health and Welfare

HEALTH

Health Research Board: 73 Lower Baggot St, Dublin 2; tel (1) 761176; fax (1) 611856; Chief Exec: Dr J. V. O'Gorman; Sec: John O'Gorman; f 1987; research into health and health services; laboratory research; provision of fellowships and research grants.

The Medical Council: 8 Lower Hatch St, Dublin 2; tel (1) 613622; Pres: Prof P. N. Meenan; Vice-Pres: Dr Dermot Gleeson; Registrar: B. V. Lea; f 1978; establishment of a register of medical practitioners; investigation of the suitability of medical education and training and into the conduct of registered medical practitioners for alleged professional misconduct.

WELFARE

National Pensions Board: Floor 3, Aras Mhic Diarmada, Store St, Dublin 1; tel (1) 786444; Sec: Tim Quirke; advises the Minister for Social Welfare on all aspects of occupational pension schemes.

Legal and Judiciary

Labour Court: Tom Johnson House, Haddington Rd, Dublin 4; tel (1) 608444; fax (1) 608437; f 1946; Chair: John M. Horgan; Dep Chairs: Nicholas Fitzgerald, John O'Connell, Evelyn Owens; investigation of labour disputes; comprises Chair, Dep Chairs and reps of employers and workers.

Office of the Attorney-General: Govt Bldgs, Dublin 2; tel (1) 616944; telex 90879; fax (1) 761806; Attorney-Gen: John L. Murray.

Office of the Chief State Solicitor: The Castle, Dublin 2; tel (1) 784333; fax (1) 784279; Chief State Solicitor: Louis Dockery; Asst Chief State Solicitors: Frank Keane, James Lynch.

Office of the Director of Public Prosecutions: 44-45 St Stephen's Green, Dublin 2; tel (1) 789222; fax (1) 610915; Dir: Eamonn M. Barnes; f 1975.

Supreme and High Courts: Four Courts, Morgan Place, Dublin 7; tel (1) 725555; Chief Justice of the Supreme Court: Thomas A. Finlay; Registrar of the Supreme Court: Ita Heslin; Pres of the High Court: Liam Hamilton.

Media

BROADCASTING

Raidió na Gaeltachta: Casla, Connamara, Co Galway; tel (91) 72235; telex 50815; Controller: Breandán Feiritéar; f 1972; broadcasts a minimum of 53 hours per week for Irish-speaking communities; financed by RTE.

Radio Telefís Éireann (RTE): Donnybrook, Dublin 4; tel (1) 693111; telex 93700; fax (1) 838140; Chair of RTE Authority: James P. Culliton; Sec to the Authority: Tom Quinn; Dir-Gen: Vincent Finn; Dir, TV Programmes: Bob Collins; Dir, Radio Programmes: Kevin Healy; f 1960; autonomous statutory corpn; national broadcasting organization, controlling radio and TV in the Republic; operations are financed by repayable state loans and by the sale of advertising time; governed by Authority of nine, appointed by the Govt.

GOVERNMENT PUBLISHER

Stationery Office: Bishop St, Dublin 8; tel (1) 781666.

NEWS AND INFORMATION

Central Statistics Office: St Stephen's Green House, Earlsfort Terrace, Dublin 2; tel (1) 767531; fax (1) 682221; Dir: Thomas P. Linehan.

Government Information Services: Upper Merrion St, Dublin 2; tel (1) 607555; telex 93938; fax (1) 603281; Govt Press Sec: P. J. Mara; Information Officer: Mairéad Dunne; supplies documents to the press, radio and TV arranges press conferences for Ministers and officials.

Mining and Energy

Bord Gáis Éireann (BGE) (The Irish Gas Board): POB 51, Inchera, Little Island, Co Cork; tel (21) 509199; telex 75087; fax (21) 353487; 24A D'Olier St, Dublin 2; tel (1) 797822; telex 32886; fax (1) 797828; Chair: (vacant); Chief Exec: J. J. Lynch; f 1975; transmission and distribution of natural gas in Ireland; regional subsidiaries are: Dublin Gas, Cork Gas, Limerick Gas, Clonmel Gas, Waterford Gas.

Bord Solathair an Leictreachais (Electricity Supply Board):

27 Lower Fitzwilliam St, Dublin 2; tel (1) 771821; telex 25313; fax (1) 615376; Chair: Prof C. T. G. Dillon; Chief Exec: P. J. Moriarty; f 1927; controls 11 generating stations operating on peat, two oil stations, two oil or gas stations, two gas stations, 10 hydro stations and two coal-fired stations.

Irish National Petroleum Corpn Ltd: Warrington House, Mount St Crescent, Dublin 2; tel (1) 607966; telex 32694; fax (1) 607952; Chief Exec: E. G. Green; f 1979; importation and refining of crude oil; sale of petroleum products.

Mining Board: 25 Clare St, Dublin 2; tel (1) 718756; Chair: Kieran O'Connor; Sec: Martin McDonald; considers applications for the registration of minerals; decides on compensation claims arising from working minerals and petroleum compensation claims; under Dept of Energy.

Science and Technology

Meteorological Service: Glasnevin Hill, Dublin 9; tel (1) 424411; fax (1) 375557; Asst Dir: Willian Wann; Sen Meteorologists: George Callaghan, Declan Murphy, Brendan McWilliams.

An tSaotharlann Stáit (State Laboratory): Abbotstown, Castleknock, Dublin 15; tel (1) 217700; telex 33735; fax (1) 217320; Asst State Chemist: Anne Conroy; f 1924; provision of scientific, analytical and advisory services to central Govt depts; enforcement of acts, eg the Fertilizer, Feeding Stuffs and Mineral Mixtures Act; provision of analytical and advisory services to coroners, state-sponsored bodies, local authorities and the private sector.

Tourism

Bord Fáilte Éireann (Irish Tourist Board): Baggot St Bridge, Dublin 2; tel (1) 765871; telex 93755; fax (1) 764764; Chair and Chief Exec: Martin Dully; Dep Dir-Gen: Matt McNulty; Sec: Niall Reddy; f 1955; develops and promotes tourism in Ireland.

Transport and Communications

TELECOMMUNICATIONS

Bord Telecom Éireann: Merrion House, Merrion Rd, Dublin

4; tel (1) 695444; telex 32713; fax (1) 694829; f 1984; Chair: Dr Michael J. Smurfit; Chief Exec: Fergus McGovern; operation of telecommunications services

Irish Telecommunications Investments plc: 114 St Stephen's Green, Dublin 2; tel (1) 714444; telex 90795; fax (1) 782659; Chair: Maurice Horhan; Gen Man: Martin Keating; f 1981; financing of telecommunications devt through fund-raising from the private sector.

An Post (The Post Office): College House, Townsend St, Dublin 2; tel (1) 728888; telex 33444; fax (1) 795765; Chair: Feargal Quinn; Chief Exec: Gerard P. Harvey; state-owned since 1984; provides national postal, savings and agency services through 2,200 outlets.

TRANSPORT

Aer Lingus plc: POB 180, Dublin Airport, Dublin; tel (1) 370011; telex 31404; fax (1) 420801; Chair: Brian A. Slowey; Chief Exec: David Kennedy; f 1936; regular services to 29 cities in Europe, the USSR and the USA.

Aer Rianta (Irish Airports): Dublin Airport, Dublin; tel (1) 379900; telex 31266; fax (1) 427975; Chair: F. J. Boland; Chief Exec: Martin Dully; management and devt of Dublin, Shannon and Cork airports; main shareholder is the Ministry of Finance; the five-mem board is appointed by the Minister for Tourism and Transport.

B & I Line (British and Irish Steampacket Co plc): POB 19, B & I Ferry Port, Alexandra Rd, Dublin 1; tel (1) 788077; telex 32549; fax (1) 788490; Chair: A. Spain; Chief Exec: J. J. Kennedy; Sec: P. E. M. Ryan; f 1836, purchased by the Irish Govt in 1965; passenger ferry journeys between Ireland, Britain, France and Holland; the Board is appointed by the Minister for Transport.

Córas Iompair Éireann (CIE) (The Irish Transport Co): Heuston Station, Dublin 8; tel (1) 771871; telex 31600; fax (1) 771350; Chair and Chief Exec: G. T. Paul Conlon; f 1950; Govt-appointed; holding co for three operating subsidiaries, Irish Rail, Irish Bus and Dublin Bus; controls railways, inland waterways and road transport services; engaged in tours business, consultancy, advertising and property activities.

ISRAEL

<table>
<tr><td>

Head of State

Executive power is vested in the Cabinet, led by the Prime Minister. The Cabinet takes office after receiving a vote of confidence in the Knesset (Assembly), to which it is responsible. Ministers are usually members of the Knesset, but non-members may be appointed. The President, a constitutional Head of State, is elected by the Knesset for five years.

President: Gen Chaim Herzog (took office 5 May 1983; re-elected 23 February 1988).

Office of the President: 3 Hanassi St, Jerusalem 92180; tel (2) 707211; fax (2) 382273.

</td><td>

Legislature

Legislative power is vested in the Knesset (Assembly), with 120 members elected by universal adult suffrage for four years (subject to dissolution), on the basis of proportional representation. The country is divided into six administrative districts.

Knesset (Assembly): Hakirya, Jerusalem 91000; tel (2) 661211; Speaker: Dov Shilansky.

</td></tr>
</table>

MINISTRIES AND GOVERNMENT DEPARTMENTS

OFFICE OF THE PRIME MINISTER
3 Rehov Kaplan, Hakirya, Jerusalem 91919
Tel (2) 639211
Prime Minister: Itzhak Shamir
Deputy Prime Minister: Moshe Arens
Second Deputy Prime Minister: David Levi
Ministers without Portfolio: Moshe Nissim, Ehud Olmert

MINISTRY OF AGRICULTURE
Hakirya, POB 7011, Tel-Aviv 61070
Tel (3) 255473; telex 361496; fax (3) 268899
Minister: (vacant)

MINISTRY OF COMMUNICATIONS
23 Rehov Yafo, Jerusalem 91999
Tel (2) 230222; telex 26381; fax (2) 240621
Minister: (vacant)

MINISTRY OF DEFENCE
Rehov Kaplan, Hakirya, Tel-Aviv 67659
Tel (3) 205144; telex 337129; fax (3) 217915
Minister: (vacant)

MINISTRY OF ECONOMY AND PLANNING
3 Rehov Kaplan, Kiryat Ben-Gurion, Jerusalem 91950
Tel (2) 535178; telex 26317; fax (2) 789424
Minister: Itzhak Modai

MINISTRY OF EDUCATION AND CULTURE
Hakirya, 14 Klausner St, Tel-Aviv
Tel (3) 414155
Minister: (vacant)

MINISTRY OF ENERGY
234 Rehov Yafo, Jerusalem 91130
Tel (2) 551211; fax (2) 534828
Minister: (vacant)

MINISTRY OF ENVIRONMENTAL QUALITY
Jerusalem
Minister: Ronni Milo

MINISTRY OF FINANCE
1 Rehov Kaplan, Kiryat Ben-Gurion, POB 883, Jerusalem
Tel (2) 558111; telex 25216; fax (2) 558359
Minister: (vacant)
Deputy Minister: Yossi Beilin

MINISTRY OF FOREIGN AFFAIRS
Hakirya, Romema, Jerusalem 91950
Tel (2) 303111; telex 25223; fax (2) 303367
Minister: Moshe Arens

MINISTRY OF HEALTH
2 Ben Tabai St, Jerusalem 93591
Tel (2) 692212; telex 25206; fax (2) 692304
Minister: (vacant)

MINISTRY OF HOUSING AND CONSTRUCTION
2 Clermont-Ganneau St, POB 13198, Jerusalem 91131
Tel (2) 277211; fax (2) 823532
Minister: David Levi

MINISTRY OF IMMIGRATION
1 Rehov Kaplan, Kiryat Ben-Gurion, Jerusalem 91006
Tel (2) 695611
Minister: Itzhak Peres

MINISTRY OF THE INTERIOR
POB 6158, Jerusalem 91061
Tel (2) 660151; telex 26162
Minister: Arie Deri

MINISTRY OF JUSTICE
29 Rehov Salah-a-Din, Jerusalem 91010
Tel (2) 270111; fax (2) 869473
Minister: Dan Meridor

MINISTRY OF LABOUR AND SOCIAL AFFAIRS
2 Rehov Kaplan, Kiryat Ben-Gurion, POB 1260,
Jerusalem 91008
Tel (2) 719081; fax (2) 717564
Minister: Itzhak Shamir

MINISTRY OF POLICE
POB 18182, Jerusalem 91181
Tel (2) 277807; fax (2) 826769
Minister: (vacant)

MINISTRY OF RELIGIOUS AFFAIRS
236 Rehov Yafo, Jerusalem 91130
Tel (2) 551175; fax (2) 551183
Minister: Zevulum Hammer

MINISTRY OF SCIENCE AND TECHNOLOGY
POB 18195, Jerusalem 91181
Tel (2) 811220; telex 26188; fax (2) 820591
Minister: (vacant)

MINISTRY OF TOURISM
24 Rehov King George, POB 1018, Jerusalem 91009
Tel (2) 237311; telex 26115; fax (2) 382148
Minister: Gideon Patt

MINISTRY OF TRADE
30 Rehov Agron, Jerusalem 94190
Tel (2) 210111; telex 25211; fax (2) 245110
Minister: (vacant)

MINISTRY OF TRANSPORT
Klal Bldg, 97 Rehov Yafo, Jerusalem 94342
Tel (2) 229211; fax (2) 229206
Minister: Moshe Katzav

GOVERNMENT AGENCIES AND ORGANIZATIONS

Advisory and Supervisory Bodies

Israel Industries Advisory Co Ltd: 76 Ibn Gvirol St, POB 16266, Tel-Aviv; tel (3) 267049.

Israel Institute of Productivity: 4 Henrietta Szold St, POB 33010, Tel-Aviv; tel (3) 430211; fax (3) 216892; Dir-Gen: Joseph Doreil; Chief Engineer: Joseph Mark; f 1951; training and consulting on management and industrial engineering, quality management, marketing management, industrial relations, etc.

State Comptroller and Public Complaints Commissioner (Ombudsman): 66 Rashi St, Jerusalem; tel (2) 237111; fax (2) 384978; State Comptroller and Ombudsman: Miriam Ben-Porat; Dir-Gen: Y. Hurvitz; f 1949; conducts independent audits of ministries, defence establishments, local authorities, public corpns, universities, etc; deals with complaints of citizens against the public admin.

Agriculture

Israel Citrus Growers Association: 17 Lincoln St, Tel-Aviv 61200; tel (3) 5615587; fax (3) 5612737; Sec-Gen: Glanz Shmuel; f 1936; professional, organizational and economic aid to citrus producers.

Business and Economy

BANKING

Bank of Israel: Kiryat Ben Gurion, POB 780, Jerusalem 91007; tel (2) 552211; telex 25214; fax (2) 528805; Gov: Prof Michael Bruno; f 1954; central bank of Israel; manages currency system, overviews the banking and credit institutions and has responsibility for monetary policy.

FINANCIAL AGENCIES

Israel Securities Authority: 24 Lincoln St, POB 7450, Jerusalem; tel (2) 245288; Chair: Eliezer Shilony.

State of Israel Bonds: 14 Hillel St, Jerusalem; tel (2) 222381; telex 26142; fax (2) 231135; Dir: David Bar-On; f 1951; promotes sales of Israeli bonds, promotes tourism and receives and handles study and investor groups.

INSURANCE

National Insurance Institute: 13 Weizmann Blvd, Jerusalem 91999; tel (2) 559211; Chair and Dir-Gen: Nissim Baruch.

MARKETING

Citrus Marketing Board: 6 Wissotzky St, POB 21371, Tel-Aviv 61213; tel (3) 430711; telex 341601; fax (3) 5468989; Chair: I. Ezra; the growers' institution for the control of the citrus industry; board made up of reps from the Govt and the growers; functions: control of plantations, supervision of picking and packing operations, marketing of the crop overseas and on the home markets; shipping; supply of fertilizers, insecticides, equipment for orchards and packing houses and of packing materials, technical research and extension work; long-term financial assistance to growers.

Cotton Production and Marketing Board: 10 Carlebach St, POB 20206, Tel-Aviv 67132; tel (3) 5613411; telex 32120; fax (3) 5610860; Pres: David Antwerg; Dir, Marketing: David Davidi; f 1955.

NATIONALIZED INDUSTRY

Israel Aircraft Industries Ltd (IAI): Lod; telex 37114; Dir-Gen: Moshe Keret; 96% Govt-owned; designers and manufacturers of military and civil aircraft.

Israel Diamond Exchange Ltd: POB 3222, Ramat-Gan; tel (3) 214211; Pres: Moshe Schnitzer; f 1937; production, import, export and finance facilities.

Israel Government Coins and Medals Corpn Ltd: 5 Ahad Ha'am St, POB 2270, Jerusalem 91022; tel (2) 668105; telex 26326; fax (2) 633167; Man Dir: E. Shiloni; f 1958; sole distributor of the commemorative coins, official uncirculated coin sets and banknotes, issued by the Bank of Israel.

TRADE

Agricultural Export Co (AGROEXCO): Tel-Aviv; Dir-Gen: Amotz Amiad; promotion of agricultural exports.

Israel Export Institute: 29 Hamered St, POB 50084, Tel-Aviv 68125; tel (3) 630830; telex 35613; fax (3) 630902; Dir-Gen: Yossi Genosar; Dep Dir-Gen: Y. Matalon; f 1958; gives advice and financial backing to Israeli exporters.

Patent Office: Clal Centre, 97 Jaffa Rd, POB 767, Jerusalem; tel (2) 209422; Commr: Michael Ohir; grant of patents, registration of trademarks and designs.

Standards Institution of Israel: 42 University St, Tel-Aviv 69977; tel (3) 5454154; telex 35508; fax (3) 419683; Dir-Gen: Miriam Muller; f 1923; standardization, testing, quality assurance.

Defence

Air Force: c/o Ministry of Defence, Rehov Kaplan, Tel-Aviv 61070; tel (3) 212144; telex 33719; Commdr: Maj-Gen Avihu Bin-Nun.

Israeli Defence Forces: c/o Ministry of Defence, Rehov Kaplan, Tel-Aviv 61070; tel (3) 669304; telex 33719; Chief of Staff: Maj-Gen Dan Shomron.

Navy: c/o Ministry of Defence, Rehov Kaplan, Tel-Aviv 61070; tel (3) 212144; telex 33719; Commdr: Rear-Adm Avraham Ben Shoshan.

Education

Council for Higher Education: 12 Hanassi St, POB 4037, Jerusalem 91040; tel (2) 663131; fax (2) 660625; Chair: Minister of Education and Culture, (vacant); Dir-Gen: Simcha Landau; licensing and accrediting authority for higher education.

Energy

Israel Atomic Energy Commission: 26 Rehov Hauniversita, Ramat Aviv, POB 7061, Tel-Aviv; tel (3) 422922; telex 33450; fax (3) 422974; Chair: Prime Minister, Itzhak Shamir; Dir-Gen: Yona S. Ettinger; f 1952; advises the Govt on long-term policies and priorities in the advancement of nuclear research and devt; supervises the implementation of policies approved by the Govt, including the licensing of nuclear power plants and the promotion of technological and industrial applications.

Negev Nuclear Research Centre: POB 9001, Beersheba; Dir: Giora Amir.

Soreq Nuclear Research Centre: Yavne 70600; tel (8) 434211; telex 381455; Dir: G. Frank; f 1954.

Investment

Investment Authority of Israel: POB 883, Jerusalem 91008; tel (2) 705301; telex 25216; fax (2) 537207; Dirs: Dr David Naveh, Aharon Mor, Oded Bonne; f 1960; helps the Govt to formulate policy on investment in various sectors of the economy.

Legal and Judiciary

Supreme Court: 6 Hashin St, Jerusalem 95156; tel (2) 246761; Pres: Meir Shamgar; Vice-Pres: Miriam Ben-Porat; highest judicial instance in the State; it has jurisdiction as an Appellate Court from the District Courts in all matters, both civil and criminal (sitting as a Court of Civil Appeal or as a Court of Criminal Appeal), and as a Court of First Instance (sitting as a High Court of Justice) in matters in which it considers it necessary to grant relief in the interests of justice and which are not within the jurisdiction of any other court or tribunal.

Media

BROADCASTING

Galei Zahal: POB MPO 01005, Zahal; tel (3) 814888; Dir: Nachman Shai; Dir of Engineering: S. Kasif; f 1951; defence forces broadcasting station; broadcasts music, news and other programmes in Hebrew.

Israel Broadcasting Authority-Radio (IBA): POB 6387, Jerusalem; tel (2) 222121; telex 26488; Chair: Micha Yinon; Dir-Gen: Uri Porat; f 1948; radio station in Jerusalem with additional studios in Tel-Aviv and Haifa; broadcasts in 16 languages.

Israel Broadcasting Authority-Television (IBA): POB 7139, Jerusalem 91071; tel (2) 557111; telex 25301; Dir: T. Sa'ar; Dir, Engineering: Yaakov Sviry; f 1968; station in Jerusalem with additional studios in Tel-Aviv; broadcasts in Hebrew and Arabic.

Israel Educational Television: Ministry of Education and Culture, 14 Klausner St, Tel-Aviv; tel (3) 5434343; telex 342325; Gen Man: Yaakov Lorberbaum; Dir, Engineering: A. Kaplan; f 1966; transmits educational programmes for both children and adults.

NEWS AND INFORMATION

Central Bureau of Statistics: POB 13015, Jerusalem 91130; tel (2) 553553; Dir: Prof M. Sicron; f 1948; collection, analysis and publication of all State statistics.

Science and Technology

Israel Academy of Sciences and Humanities: Albert Einstein Sq, Talbieh, POB 4040, Jerusalem 91040; tel (2) 636211; Pres: Efraim Elimelech Urbach.

Israel Meteorological Services: POB 25, Bet Dagan 50250; tel (3) 9682121; telex 381466; fax (3) 9682176; Dir: S. Jaffe; f 1948; meteorological services.

Telecommunications

Israel Telecommunications Corpn Ltd (Bezeq): POB 1088, Jerusalem 91010; tel (2) 695333; telex 25225.

Transport

CIVIL AVIATION

El Al Israel Airlines Ltd: POB 41, Ben Gurion Airport, Lod, Tel-Aviv; tel (3) 9716111; telex 381107; fax (3) 9721442; Chair:

Nachman Perel; Pres: Rafael Har-Lev; f 1948; services to Europe, North America and Africa.

Israeli Airports Authority: Ben Gurion Airport, Lod, Tel-Aviv; tel (3) 9712804; Dir-Gen: Zvi Gov-Ari.

RAILWAYS

Haifa Underground Funicular Railway: 124 Hanassi Ave, Haifa; Man: D. Scharf.

Israel Railways: POB 18085, Tel-Aviv; tel (3) 5421401; telex 371946; fax (3) 258176; Gen Man: Eliahu Barak; Dep Gen Man, Admin: David Guy; Dep Gen Man, Tech: Leon Heyman; f 1948; responsible for passenger and freight services.

SHIPPING

Israel Ports Authority: Maya Bldg, 74 Petach Tikva Rd, POB 20121, Tel-Aviv; tel (3) 338911; telex 33677; Chair: Zvi Keinan; Dir-Gen: Shaul Raziel; f 1961; planning, construction, devt, admin, maintenance and operation of ports.

ZIM Israel Navigation Co Ltd: 7-9 Pal Yam Ave, Haifa 31016; tel (4) 652111; telex 4651; fax (4) 652956; Pres and Chief Exec: M. Morgenstern; f 1945; fleet of 70 vessels calling at ports worldwide.

Welfare

National Housing Corpn for Immigrants Ltd: 39 King Saul Ave, POB 7045, Tel-Aviv.

ITALY

Head of State

Under the 1948 Constitution, the President of the Republic is a constitutional Head of State elected for seven years by an electoral college comprising both Houses of Parliament and 58 regional representatives. Executive power is exercised by the Council of Ministers. The Head of State appoints the President of the Council (Prime Minister) and, on the latter's recommendation, other Ministers. The Council is responsible to Parliament.

President: Francesco Cossiga (took office 3 July 1985).

Office of the President: Palazzo del Quirinale, 00187 Rome; tel (6) 4699; telex 611440.

Legislature

Legislative power is vested in the bicameral Parliament, elected by universal adult suffrage for five years on the basis of proportional representation. The Senate has 315 elected members and seven life Senators. The Chamber of Deputies has 630 members. The two houses have equal power. The country is divided into 20 regions, each with its own executive and legislative powers.

Senato (Senate): Palazzo Madama, 00186 Rome; tel (6) 67061; Pres: Giovanni Spadolini.

Camera dei Deputati (Chamber of Deputies): Piazza Montecitorio, 00186 Rome; tel (6) 6760; telex 612523; Pres: Nilde Jotti.

MINISTRIES AND GOVERNMENT DEPARTMENTS

OFFICE OF THE PRIME MINISTER
Palazzo Chigi, Piazza Colonna 370, 00100 Rome
Tel (6) 6779; telex 613199
Prime Minister: Giulio Andreotti
Deputy Prime Minister: Claudio Martelli

MINISTRY OF AGRICULTURE AND FORESTS
Via XX Settembre, 00187 Rome
Tel (6) 4665; telex 610148
Minister: Calogero Mannino

MINISTRY OF THE BUDGET AND OF ECONOMIC PLANNING
Via XX Settembre 97, 00187 Rome
Tel (6) 47611; telex 626432
Minister: Cirino Pomicino

MINISTRY FOR CULTURAL HERITAGE
Via del Collegio Romano 27, 00186 Rome
Tel (6) 6723; telex 621407
Minister: Ferdinando Facchiano

MINISTRY OF DEFENCE
Palacio Baracchini, Via XX Settembre, 00187 Rome
Tel (6) 4759841; telex 611438
Minister: Mino Martinazzoli

MINISTRY OF EDUCATION
Viale Trastevere 76A, 00153 Rome
Tel (6) 58491; telex 613181
Minister: Sergio Matarella

MINISTRY OF THE ENVIRONMENT
Piazza Venezia 11, 00187 Rome
Tel (6) 6797124
Minister: Dr Giorgio Ruffolo

MINISTRY OF FINANCE
Viale America, EUR, 00144 Rome
Tel (6) 5997; telex 614460
Minister: Salvatore Formica

MINISTRY OF FOREIGN AFFAIRS
Piazzale della Farnesina 1, 00194 Rome
Tel (6) 36911; telex 610611
Minister: Gianni De Michelis

MINISTRY OF FOREIGN TRADE
Viale America 341, EUR, 00144 Rome
Tel (6) 5993; telex 610083
Minister: Dr Renato Ruggiero

MINISTRY OF HEALTH
Piazzale dell'Industria 20, 00144 Rome
Tel (6) 5994; telex 625205; fax (6) 5924774
Minister: Francesco De Lorenzo

MINISTRY OF INDUSTRY
Via Vittorio Veneto 33, 00187 Rome
Tel (6) 4705; telex 622550
Minister: Dr Adolfo Battaglia

MINISTRY OF THE INTERIOR
Piazza Viminale, Palazzo Viminale, Via Depretis, 00184 Rome
Tel (6) 46671
Minister: Antonio Gava

MINISTRY OF JUSTICE
Via Arenula 70, 00186 Rome
Tel (6) 65101; telex 623072
Minister: Prof Giuliano Vassalli

MINISTRY OF LABOUR AND SOCIAL SECURITY
Via Flavia 6, 00187 Rome
Tel (6) 4683; telex 626144
Minister: Carlo Donat-Cattin

MINISTRY OF THE MERCHANT NAVY
Viale Asia 18, EUR, 00144 Rome
Tel (6) 5908
Minister: Carlo Vizzini

MINISTRY OF POSTS AND TELECOMMUNICATIONS
Viale America, EUR, 00187 Rome
Tel (6) 54601; telex 616082
Minister: Dr Oscar Mammì

MINISTRY OF PUBLIC WORKS
Piazza Porta Pia 1, 00198 Rome
Tel (6) 84821
Minister: Giovanni Prandini

MINISTRY OF SCIENTIFIC AND TECHNOLOGICAL RESEARCH
Rome
Minister: Prof Antonio Ruberti

MINISTRY OF STATE PARTICIPATION
Via Sallustiana 53, 00187 Rome
Tel (6) 4750420; telex 614229
Minister: Carlo Francanzani

MINISTRY OF TOURISM AND PERFORMING ARTS
Via della Ferratella in Laterano 51, 00184 Rome
Tel (6) 77321; telex 616400
Minister: Dr Franco Carraro

MINISTRY OF TRANSPORT
Piazza della Croce Rossa 1, 00161 Rome
Tel (6) 84901; telex 613111
Minister: Carlo Bernini

MINISTRY OF THE TREASURY
Via XX Settembre 97, 00187 Rome

Tel (6) 47611; telex 623139
Minister: Guido Carli

OFFICE OF THE MINISTER WITHOUT PORTFOLIO FOR CIVIL DEFENCE
Via Ultiano 11, Rome
Minister without Portfolio: Vito Lattanzio

OFFICE OF THE MINISTER WITHOUT PORTFOLIO FOR EEC AFFAIRS
Via del Tritone 142, 00187 Rome
Tel (6) 4670; telex 613018; fax (6) 4756766
Minister without Portfolio: Prof Pier Luigi Romita

OFFICE OF THE MINISTER WITHOUT PORTFOLIO FOR PUBLIC ADMINISTRATION
Palazzo Chigi, Piazza Colonna 370, 00100 Rome
Minister without Portfolio: Remo Gaspari

OFFICE OF THE MINISTER WITHOUT PORTFOLIO FOR REGIONAL AFFAIRS AND INSTITUTIONAL REFORMS
Piazza della Minerva 38, Rome
Minister without Portfolio: Dr Antonio Maccanico

OFFICE OF THE MINISTER WITHOUT PORTFOLIO FOR RELATIONS WITH PARLIAMENT
Palazzo Chigi, Piazza Colonna 370, 00100 Rome
Minister without Portfolio: Egidio Sterpa

OFFICE OF THE MINISTER WITHOUT PORTFOLIO FOR SOUTHERN DEVELOPMENT
Via Boncompagni 30, Rome
Minister without Portfolio: Ricardo Misasi

OFFICE OF THE MINISTER WITHOUT PORTFOLIO FOR SPECIAL AFFAIRS
Rome
Minister without Portfolio: Rosa Russo Jervolino

OFFICE OF THE MINISTER WITHOUT PORTFOLIO FOR URBAN AREAS
Rome
Minister without Portfolio: Carmelo Conte

GOVERNMENT AGENCIES AND ORGANIZATIONS

Advisory and Supervisory Bodies

Autonomous Administration of State Monopolies: Via della Luce 34A-bis, 00153 Rome; tel (6) 5857.

Consiglio Nazionale dell'Economia e del Lavoro (CNEL): Viale Lubin 2, 00196 Rome; tel (6) 36921; telex 616412; fax (6) 3602867; council for the economy and labour.

Ragioneria Generale dello Stato: Via XX Settembre 97, 00187 Rome; state accounting office.

Business and Economy

BANKING

Associazione Bancaria Italiana: Piazza del Gesù 49, 00186 Rome; tel (6) 67671; telex 622107; Via della Posta 3, 20123 Milan; tel (2) 806689; telex 324195; Pres: Prof Piero Barucci;

Gen Man: Dr Felice Gianani; f 1919; national banking association; comprises public credit institutions, banks of national interest, private banks and bankers, co-operative banks, savings banks, rural banks, agricultural credit institutions, mortgage banks, industrial credit institutions and finance houses.

Banca d'Italia: Via Nazionale 91, 00184 Rome; tel (6) 47921; telex 630045; fax (6) 4747820; Gov: Dr Carlo Azeglio Ciampi; Gen Man: Dr Lamberto Dini; f 1893; since 1926 the bank has has the sole right to issue bank notes.

Banca Nazionale dell'Agricoltura, SpA: Via Salaria 231, 00199 Rome; tel (6) 85881; telex 612121; fax (6) 85883396; Chair: Count Giovanni Auletta Armenise; Man Dirs: Dr Antonio Casella, Ulpiano Quaranta; f 1921; 230 brs incl brs abroad.

Banca Nazionale delle Communicazioni: Via San Martino della Battaglia 4, 00185 Rome; tel (6) 46761; telex 625593; fax (6) 46763555; Pres: Prof Luigi Cappugi; Gen Man: Dr Natale Gilio; f 1927; 17 brs.

Banca Nazionale del Lavoro: Via Vittorio Veneto 119, 00187 Rome; tel (6) 47021; telex 610116; Chair: Giampiero Cantoni;

Man Dir and Chief Gen Man: Prof Paolo Savona; f 1913; 414 brs incl 11 overseas brs.

Banco di Napoli: Via Toledo 177-178, 80132 Naples; tel (81) 7911111; telex 710227; Chair: Prof Luigi Coccioli; Chief Exec: Prof Ferdinando Ventriglia; f 1539; chartered public institution with no shareholders; 494 brs.

Banco di Roma SpA: Viale U. Tupini 180, 00144 Rome; tel (6) 54451; telex 616184; fax (6) 54453154; Chair: Antonio Zurzulo; Man Dirs: Dr Giuseppe Greco, Dr Marcello Tacci; 365 brs.

Banco di Sardegna: Viale Umberto 36, 07100 Sassari; tel (79) 226000; telex 790049; Pres and Chair: Prof Lorenzo Idda; Gen Man: Dr Angelo Giagu de Martini; f 1953; public credit institution; 76 brs.

Banco di Sicilia: Via Generale Magliocco 1, 90141 Palermo; tel (91) 274111; telex 910050; Chair: Prof Giannino Parravicini; Gen Man and Chief Exec: Dr Ottavio Salamone; f 1860; public credit institution; 352 brs.

Credito Italiano SpA: Via San Protaso 3, 20121 Milan; tel (2) 88621; telex 310103; Chair: Prof Natalino Irti; Man Dirs: Lucio Rondelli, Pier Carlo·Marengo; f 1870; 496 brs.

Monte dei Paschi di Siena: Piazza Salimbeni 3, 53100 Siena; tel (577) 294111; telex 572346; fax (577) 294985; Chair: Piero Barucci; Chief Exec and Chief Gen Man: Carlo Zini; Exec Vice-Pres and Gen Man (international): Attilio Bordogna; f 1472; public law credit institution; 469 brs in Italy; offices in London, Cairo, New York, Frankfurt, São Paulo and Singapore.

FINANCIAL AGENCIES

Consorzio di Credito per le Opere Pubbliche (CREDIOP): Via Quintino Sella 2, 00187 Rome; tel (6) 47711; telex 611020; Pres and Chair: Paolo Baratta; Gen Man: Dr Luigi Mazzoni; f 1919; provides loans to industrial, commercial and service cos; medium- and long-term loans to public authorities and their agencies, and export credits.

Istituto Mobiliare Italiano (IMI): Viale dell'Arte 25, 00144 Rome; tel (6) 54501; telex 610256; Pres: Dr Luigi Arcuti; Dir-Gen: Rainer Masera; f 1931; public-law credit institute; specializes in medium- and long-term finance for industry and public utilities, merchant banking, personal finance services and asset management; facilities also availale to foreign concerns willing to make productive investment in Italy or to import Italian-made capital goods; 10 regional offices in Italy.

Istituto per lo Sviluppo Economico dell'Italia Meridionale (ISVEIMER): Via A De Gasperi 71, 80133 Naples; tel (81) 7853111; telex 711020; fax (81) 420042; Pres: Giuseppe Di Vagno; Dir-Gen: Dr Benito Plotino; public credit institution granting medium-term loans in mainland southern Italy; 8 brs.

INSURANCE

Istituto Nazionale delle Assicurazioni (INA): Via Sallustiana 51, 00187 Rome; tel (6) 47221; telex 610336; Chair: (vacant); Gen Man: Dr Mario Fornari; f 1912; National Insurance Institute; state institute with autonomous management.

Sezione Speciale per l'Assicurazione del Credito all'Esportazione (Sace): Rome; Chair: Roberto Ruberti; trade insurance agency.

NATIONALIZED INDUSTRY

Acciaierie di Piombirvo: Viale della Resistenza 2, 57025 Piombino; manufacture of steel products.

Alfa Cavi SpA: Via Caracciano 152, 82011 Airola; manufacture of cables.

Azienda Tabacchi Italiani: Via Cesafe Pascarella 7, 00153 Rome; state tobacco monopoly.

Breda Costruzioni Ferroviarie: Rome; construction of railway locomotives.

Breda Fucine: Viale Sarca 336, 20126 Milan; production of iron and steel.

Breda Meccanica Bresciana: Via Lunga 2, 25126 Brescia; tel (30) 31911; telex 300056; fax (30) 322115; production and devt of automatic and remote controlled weapons including rocket launchers and anti-tank weapons.

Cagiva Commerciale: Via Antonio Cavalieri Ducati 3, 40132 Bologna; tel (51) 405049; telex 510492; fax (51) 406580; Dir: L. D. Giacometti; distribution of motorcycles, accessories and spare parts.

Cementir: Viale Gorizia 24/D, 00198 Rome; production of cement.

Ente Nazionale per la Cellulosa e per la Carta: Viale Regina Margheritta 262, 00198 Rome; tel (6) 84811; responsible for cellulose and paper supply.

Ente Partecipazioni e Finanziamento Industria Manifatturiera (EFIM): Via XXIV Maggio 43/45, 00187 Rome; tel (6) 47101; telex 621381; Pres: Rolando Valiani; f 1962 as a state law agency, managing three holding cos and more than 100 cos; activities including: on-land transports, aeronautics, armaments and defence systems, glass, aluminium and plant engineering.

Ferrosud: Via Appia Antica km 13, 75100 Matera; production of iron products.

Italedil: Via Tanaro 14, 00198 Rome; construction co.

Italimpianti: Viale Liegi 33, 00198 Rome; construction co.

Selenia Industrie Elettroniche: Via Tiburtina km 12,400, 00185 Rome; manufacture of electrical equipment.

Siai Marchetti: Via Indipendenza 2, 21018 Sesto Calende; manufacture of light aircraft.

Sidermontaggi: Via Buttrio 57/B, 33050 Pozzuolo del Friuli; production of steel.

TRADE

Istituto Nazionale per il Commercio Estero (ICE): Via Listz 21, 00144 Rome; tel (6) 59921; telex 610160; Pres: Dr Giuseppe Ratti; Dir-Gen: Dr Massimo Mancini; f 1919; institute of external trade.

Defence

Armed Forces: c/o Ministry of Defence, Palazzo Baracchini, Via XX Settembre, 00187 Rome; tel (6) 4759841; telex 611438; Supreme Commdr of the Armed Forces: President Francesco Cossiga.

Air Force: Viale Università 4, 00185 Rome; tel (6) 4686; telex 611438; Chief of Staff: Gen Franco Pisano.

Army: c/o Ministry of Defence, Palazzo Baracchini, Via XX Settembre, 00187 Rome; tel (6) 47351; telex 611438; Chief of Staff: Gen Ciro Di Martino.

Navy: Piazza della Marina, Via F Corridoni, 00196 Rome; tel (6) 36801; telex 611438; Chief of Staff: Adm Sergio Mayoli.

Development and Planning

PLANNING

Istituto per la Ricostruzione Industriale (IRI): Via Vittorio

Veneto 89, 00187 Rome; tel (6) 47271; Chair: Franco Nobili; f 1933; autonomous agency controlling banking and industrial undertakings; responsible for many State cos.

REGIONAL DEVELOPMENT

Istituto per l'Assistenza allo Sviluppo del Mezzogiorno (IASM): Viale Pilsudski 124, 00197 Rome; tel (6) 84721; telex 680232; Pres: Dr Nino Novacco; f 1962; aids investment to promote economic devt in the South.

Istituto Regionale per il Finanziamento alle Industrie in Sicilia (IRFIS): Via Giovanni Bonanno 47, 90143 Palermo; tel (91) 266200; telex 910332; Pres: Prof Antonio Muccioli; Dir-Gen: Giuseppe Biondo; f 1950; provides credit facilities for business ventures in Sicily; credit for domestic and export trade and for developing tourist facilities.

Forestry

Azienda di Stato per le Foreste Demaniali: Via Carduca 5, 00187 Rome; forestry preservation agency.

Legal and Judiciary

Avvocatura Generale di Stato: Via dei Portoghesi 12, 00186 Rome; tel (6) 65491; telex 625398; fax (6) 6879241; Attorney-Gen: Giorgio Azzariti; Dep Attorneys-Gen: E. Ciardulli, B. Baccari, G. Zagari, L. Siconolfi, G. Mataloni, M. Imponente, I. F. Caramazza; f 1876; represents the central Govt in law courts and gives legal advice to public admins.

Consiglio di Stato: Palazzo Spada, Piazza Capo di Ferro 13, 00186 Rome; tel (6) 650801; Pres: Giorgio Crisco; established in accordance with Article 10 of the Constitution; has both consultative and judicial functions.

Consiglio Superiore della Magistratura (CSM): Piazza dell'Indipendenza 6, 00185 Rome; tel (6) 497981; Pres: President Francesco Cossiga; Vice-Pres: Cesare Mirabelli; f 1958; supervisory body of the judicial system; 33 mems.

Corte dei Conti: Via Baiamonti 25, Rome, and Via Barberini 38, Rome; Pres: Giuseppe Carbone; functions as the court of public auditors for the state.

Corte Costituzionale: Palazzo della Consulta, Piazza del Quirinale 41, 00187 Rome; tel (6) 46981; Pres: Francesco Faja; Vice-Pres: Guglielmo Roherssen; consists of 15 judges, one-third appointed by the President of the Republic, one-third elected by Parliament in joint session, one-third by the ordinary and administrative supreme courts.

Corte Suprema di Cassazione: Palazzo di Giustizia, 00100 Rome; tel (6) 656001; telex 626069; fax (6) 6874170; First Pres: Antonio Brancaccio; Vice-Pres: Fernandino Zucconi Galli Fonseca; supreme court of civil and criminal appeal.

> **Centro Elettronico di Documentazione della Corte Suprema di Cassazione:** Via Damiano Chiesa 24, 00136 Rome; tel (6) 33081; telex 620461; fax (6) 3308338; f 1973; legal information retrieval.

Media

BROADCASTING

Radiotelevisione Italiana (RAI-TV): Viale Mazzini 14, 00195 Rome; tel (6) 3878; telex 61142; Pres: Enrico Manca; Vice-Pres: Prof Giampiero Orsello; Dir-Gen: (vacant); f 1924; a public share capital co; a permanent parliamentary commission

of senators and deputies from all political groups formulates and oversees general guidelines for programmes.

GOVERNMENT PUBLISHER

Istituto Poligrafico e Zecca dello Stato: Piazza Verdi 10, 00198 Rome; tel (6) 85081; Chair: Giuseppe la Loggia; Dir-Gen: Alfredo Maggi; f 1928; art books and reproductions.

NEWS AND INFORMATION

Istituto Centrale di Statistica (ISTAT): Via Cesare Balbo 16, 00184 Rome; tel (6) 46731; telex 610338; fax (6) 464797; Pres: Prof Guido Mario Rey; Dir-Gen: Prof Vincenzo Siesto; f 1926; collection, analysis and publication of information.

Mining and Energy

ENERGY

Comitato Nazionale per la Ricerca e per lo Sviluppo dell'Energia Nucleare e delle Energie Alternative (ENEA): Via Regina Margherita 125, 00198 Rome; tel (6) 85281; telex 610183; fax (6) 85282777; Chair: Umberto Colombo; Vice-Pres: Prof Luigi Noè; Dir-Gen: Dr Fabio Pistella; f 1960; supervises pure and applied research into nuclear power plants; provides technical and economic evaluations and supervision of health and environmental protection; promotes energy saving and the use of renewable energy sources.

Direzione Generale delle Fonti di Energia e delle Industrie di Base (General Directorate of Energy Sources and Primary Industries): Via Vittorio Veneto 33, 00100 Rome; tel (6) 4985; dept of the Ministry of Energy.

Ente Nazionale per l'Energia Elettrica (ENEL): Via Giovanni Battista Martini 3, 00198 Rome; tel (6) 85091; Chair: Franco Viezzoli; f 1962; generation and distribution of electrical power.

Ente Nazionale Idrocarburi (ENI): Piazzale Enrico Mattei 1, 00144 Rome; tel (6) 59001; telex 610082; Chair: Gabriele Cagliari; energy corpn with subsidiaries incl AGIP, AGIP Petroli, AGIP Carbone and SNAM operating in the energy sector; also subsidiaries in chemicals, mining and metallurgy, engineering, machines and instruments, and the financial sector.

MINING

Direzione Generale delle Minerie: Via Vittorio Veneto 33, 00100 Rome; tel (6) 4985; dept of the Ministry of Industry which supervises mining.

Research

Consiglio Nazionale delle Ricerche: Piazzale Aldo Moro 4, 00185 Rome; tel (6) 49931; telex 610072; fax (6) 4957241; Pres: Prof Luigi Rossi Bernardi; Dir-Gen: Dr Bruno Colle; f 1923; devt of scientific and technical research.

Telecommunications

Azienda di Stato per i Servizi Telefonici (ASST): Viale Europa 160, 00100 Rome; tel (6) 5422401; telex 610045; operates toll and international telephones.

Società Italiana per l'esercizio telefonico SpA (SIP): Via San Dalmazzo 15, 10122 Turin; tel (11) 5771; telex 610467; operates, under Govt licence, the telephone system over the entire country except for the intertoll system.

STET: Rome; Chair: Giuliano Graziosi; state telecommunications organization.

Tourism

Ente Nazionale Italiano per il Turismo (ENIT): Via Marghera 2, 00185 Rome; tel (6) 49711; telex 621314; fax (6) 493379; Chair: Dr Marino Corona; Dir-Gen: Armando Foschi; f 1919; promotion of tourism.

Transport

CIVIL AVIATION

Aero Trasporti Italiani SpA (ATI): Aeroporto Capodichino, 80144 Naples; tel (81) 7091111; telex 711005; fax (81) 7093050; Man Dir: Dr Mario Franchi; Gen Man: Dr Gaetano Galia; f 1963; subsidiary of Alitalia; operates scheduled domestic services and charter flights to the Middle East, North Africa, Canary Islands and within Europe.

Alitalia (Linee Aeree Italiane): Palazzo Alitalia, Piazzale Giulio Pastore, 00144 Rome; tel (6) 54441; telex 626211; fax (6) 5914948; Chair: (vacant); Dep Chair: Vittorio Vaccari; Man

Dirs: Maurizio Maspes, Luciano Santoretti; f 1946; international services throughout Europe and to Africa, North and South America, the Middle East, the Far East and Australia.

Registro Aeronautico Italiano: Via del Tritone 169, 00187 Rome; tel (6) 6840457; telex 625229; fax (6) 6781318; f 1938; inspection and certification of civil aircraft manufacture, overhaul, repair and operation.

RAILWAYS

Ente Ferrovie dello Stato: Piazza della Croce Rossa 1, 00161 Rome; tel (6) 84901; telex 622345; fax (6) 8831108; Special Commr: Mario Schimberni; Dir-Gen: Dr Giovanni de Chiara; admin of state railways.

ROADS

Azienda Nazionale Autonoma delle Strade Statali (ANAS): Via Monnzambano 10, 00185 Rome; tel (6) 4957641; Pres: Minister of Public Works, Giovanni Prandini; f 1928, reorganized 1946; responsible for the admin of state roads and their improvement and extension.

Direzione Generale della Motorizzazione Civile e del Trasporti in Concessione: Viale del Policlinico 2, 00100 Rome; tel (6) 859271; telex 616041; Dir-Gen: Gaetano Danese; controls road transport and traffic, and public transport services.

JAMAICA

Head of State

Jamaica is a constitutional monarchy. The British sovereign, as Head of State, is represented locally by a Governor-General. Government is effectively by the Cabinet, appointed by the Governor-General, which is headed by the Prime Minister and is responsible to Parliament. Provision is also made in the constitution for a Privy Council to advise the Governor-General.

Sovereign: HM Queen Elizabeth II (succeeded to the throne 6 February 1952).

Governor-General: Sir Florizel Augustus Glasspole (took office 27 June 1973).

Office of the Governor-General: King's House, Hope Rd, Kingston 10; tel 927-6424.

Privy Council: Kingston; Mems: L. E. Ashenheim, Dr Vernon Lindo, Ewart Forrest, G. Owen, W. H. Swaby, Dr Douglas Fletcher.

Legislature

Legislative power is vested in the bicameral Parliament comprising a Senate of 21 appointed members, and a House of Representatives comprising 60 members elected by universal adult suffrage for five years.

Senate: Gordon House, Duke St, Kingston; tel 922-0200; Pres: Howard Cooke.

House of Representatives: Gordon House, Duke St, Kingston; tel 922-0200; Speaker: Headley Cunningham.

MINISTRIES AND GOVERNMENT DEPARTMENTS

OFFICE OF THE PRIME MINISTER
1 Devon Rd, POB 272, Kingston 6
Tel 927-9941; telex 2398; fax 929-0005
Prime Minister and Minister of Defence: Michael Manley
Deputy Prime Minister: Percival J. Patterson
Minister without Portfolio: Sen Dr Paul Robertson
Minister without Portfolio (Parliamentary Affairs): Dr Ken McNeil

MINISTRY OF AGRICULTURE AND COMMERCE
Hope Gdns, Kingston 6
Tel 927-1731
Minister: Horace Clarke

MINISTRY OF CONSTRUCTION
2 Hagley Park Rd, Kingston 10
Tel 926-1590
Minister: O. D. Ramtallie

MINISTRY OF EDUCATION
2 National Heroes Circle, Kingston 4
Tel 922-1400
Minister: Sen Carlyle Dunkley

MINISTRY OF FINANCE AND PLANNING
30 National Heroes Circle, Kingston 4
Tel 922-8600; telex 2447
Minister of Finance: Seymour Mullings
Minister of Production, Development and Planning: Percival J. Patterson

MINISTRY OF FOREIGN AFFAIRS, FOREIGN TRADE AND INDUSTRY
85 Knutsford Blvd, Kingston 5
Tel 926-4220; telex 2114
Minister of Foreign Affairs and Foreign Trade: Sen David Coore

MINISTRY OF HEALTH
10 Caledonia Ave, Kingston 5
Tel 926-9220
Minister: Easton Douglas

MINISTRY OF INFORMATION AND CULTURE
Kingston
Minister: Paul Robertson

MINISTRY OF JUSTICE
Kingston Mall, 12 Ocean Blvd, Kingston
Tel 922-0080
Attorney-General and Minister: Carl Rattray

MINISTRY OF LABOUR, WELFARE AND SPORT
14 National Heroes Circle, POB 10, Kingston 5
Tel 922-8000
Minister: Portia Simpson

Office of National Insurance: address as above; Dir: Patricia A. Sinclair.

Office of Social Security: address as above; Dir: V. Bell.

MINISTRY OF LOCAL GOVERNMENT
Ocean Blvd, Kingston
Tel 922-1670
Minister: Ralph Brown

MINISTRY OF MINING AND ENERGY
36 Trafalgar Rd, Kingston 10
Tel 926-9170; fax 926-2835
Minister: Hugh Small

MINISTRY OF NATIONAL SECURITY
Kingston Mall, 12 Ocean Blvd, Kingston
Tel 922-0080
Minister: K. D. Knight

MINISTRY OF THE PUBLIC SERVICE
Citibank Bldg, 63-67 Knutsford Blvd, Kingston 5
Tel 926-3235
Minister: Seymour Mullings

**MINISTRY OF PUBLIC UTILITIES AND
TRANSPORT**
2 St Lucia Ave, POB 9000, Kingston 5
Tel 926-8130; fax 929-3375
Minister: Robert Pickersgill

MINISTRY OF TOURISM
Petrojam Bldg, Trafalgar Rd, Kingston 10
Tel 926-9170
Minister: Sen Frank Pringle

**MINISTRY OF YOUTH, CULTURE AND
COMMUNITY DEVELOPMENT**
Kingston Mall, 5th Floor, 12 Ocean Blvd, POB 503, Kingston
Tel 922-1710
Minister: Dr Douglas Manley

GOVERNMENT AGENCIES AND ORGANIZATIONS

Agriculture and the Environment

AGRICULTURE

Agro 21 Corpn Ltd (ADC Group of Cos): Jamaica Conference Centre, 14-20 Port Royal St, POB 552, GPO Kingston, Kingston; tel 922-1470; telex 2341; fax 922-21787; Chair: Cezley Sampson; Man Dir: Claude Stewart; f 1989; monitors activities of Govt-owned commercial agricultural enterprises, including the production of bananas, orchard crops, livestock devt and marketing of local and export agricultural produce; maintains an information centre which provides a wide range of publs on agriculture.

Agricultural Development Corpn: 46 Trinidad Terrace, Kingston; tel 926-9160; Chair: Dr C. L. Bent; Sec: D. Forrester; f 1952.

Cocoa Industry Board: Marcus Garvey Drive, POB 68, Kingston 15; tel 923-6411; telex 3658; Chair: K. A. Haughton; Man: Fitz D. Shaw; Sec: V. V. Wright; f 1957; regulatory and marketing agency; owns and operates four central fermentaries.

Coconut Industry Board: 18 Waterloo Rd, Half Way Tree, POB 204, Kingston 10; tel 926-1770; Chair: R. A. Jones; Gen Man: Roy A. Williams; Sec: James S. Joyles; f 1945; promotes the interests of the coconut industry; promotes the production of, and regulates trade in coconuts.

Coffee Industry Board: Marcus Garvey Drive, POB 508, Kingston 15; tel 923-7211; telex 3578; fax 923-7213; Chair: Keble Munn; Gen Man: John Pickersgill; Sec: Joyce Chang; f 1950; regulation and devt of the coffee industry.

Coffee Industry Development Co: Marcus Garvey Drive, Kingston 15; tel 923-7211; f 1981; implements a coffee expansion programme financed by the Commonwealth Devt Corpn.

Sugar Industry Authority: 5 Trevennion Park Rd, POB 127, Kingston 5; tel 926-5930; telex 2113; fax 926-6149; Exec Chair: Frank G. Downie; Sec: Alvin A. Burnett; f 1970; statutory body under the portfolio of the Ministry of Agriculture; responsible for the regulation and control of the sugar industry and sugar marketing; conducts research through the Sugar Industry Research Institute.

THE ENVIRONMENT

National Resources Conservation Department: 53.5 Malynes Rd, Kingston 10; tel 923-5965; Chair: Cyril Bridge; Principal Dir: S. C. Sinha.

Business and Economy

BANKING

Bank of Jamaica: Nethersole Place, POB 621, Kingston; tel 922-0750; telex 2165; Gov: G. Arthur Brown; f 1960; central bank.

Jamaica Mortgage Bank: 33 Tobago Ave, POB 950, Kingston 5; tel 929-6350; f 1971; became a statutory organization wholly Govt-owned in 1973; established by the Govt and the United States Agency for International Development to function primarily as a secondary market facility for home mortgages and to mobilize long-term funds for housing devts in Jamaica; insures home mortgage loans made by approved financial institutions, thus transferring risk of default on a loan to the Govt.

National Commercial Bank Jamaica Ltd: 'The Atrium', 32 Trafalgar Rd, POB 88, Kingston; tel 929-9053; telex 2139; Chair: Dr Keith S. Panton; Man Dir: Don A. Banks; f 1977; 40 brs and agencies.

National Development Bank of Jamaica Ltd: 11A-15 Oxford Rd, Kingston 5; tel 961-248; telex 2381; fax 929-6996; Chair: Natan Richards; Man Dir: Dr Noel A. Lyon; f 1969; replaced Jamaica Devt Bank; provides funds for medium- and long-term devt-orientated projects in the tourism, industrial, agro-industrial and mining sectors through financial intermediaries.

National Investment Bank of Jamaica: Scotia Bank Centre, cnr Duke and Port Royal Sts, POB 889, Kingston; tel 922-0915; telex 2487; Chair: Mayer Matalon; Man Dir: Charles J. M. Charles.

FINANCIAL AGENCIES

Income Tax Department: 116 East St, POB 476, Kingston; tel 922-3470; Commr: Maizie Distin; f 1919; admin of the Income Tax Act ensuring that persons liable to Income Tax are assessed and that revenue goals are met.

INSURANCE

Jamaica Insurance Advisory Council: 2nd Floor, NEM House, 9 King St, Kingston; tel 922-8710; fax 922-8710; Chair: Leslie Chung; Dep Chair: Errol Ziadie; Man: Denise Y. Cole; f

1963; liaises with insurers and related associations; advises the public.

Office of the Superintendent of Insurance: 51 St Lucia Ave, POB 800, Kingston 5; tel 926-1790; Supt: E. W. Taylor; f 1972; regulates the insurance industry under the provisions of the Insurance Act and Regulations.

NATIONALIZED INDUSTRY

Small Business Association (SBA): 2 Trafalgar Rd, Kingston 5; tel 927-7071; Pres: Errol Dunkley.

TRADE

Bureau of Standards: 6 Winchester Rd, Kingston 10; tel 926-3140.

Customs and Excise Department: Scotia Bank Centre, cnr Duke and Port Royal Sts, Kingston; tel 922-1249; Commr: Victor S. O. Parkin.

Jamaica Commodity Trading Co Ltd: 8 Ocean Blvd, POB 1021, Kingston; tel 922-0971; telex 2318; Chair: David Gaynair; Man Dir: Andree Nembhard; f 1981; successor to the State Trading Corpn; oversees all importing on behalf of the state.

Jamaica Export Trading Co Ltd: 6 Waterloo Rd, POB 645, Kingston 10; tel 929-4390; telex 2233; Dir and Gen Man: Hernal L. Hamilton; Dir, Agricultural Products: Marlene Thomas-Richards; Dir, Industrial Products: Pamela Bruce; f 1977; export trading in non-traditional products, ie spices, fresh produce, furniture, garments, processed foods, etc.

Trade Administration Department: The Office Centre, 12 Ocean Blvd, POB 25, Kingston; tel 922-1840; Admin: Totlyn Grant.

Culture

National Library of Jamaica: 12 East St, POB 823, Kingston; tel 922-0620; fax 922-5567; Dir: Stephney Ferguson; f 1979; national centre for the preservation of publs; national reference library.

Defence

Defence Force: Army Headquarters, UP Park Camp, Kingston 5; tel 926-8121; telex 2359; Chief of Staff: Maj-Gen: Robert J. Neish.

Constabulary Force: Police Headquarters, 101-103 Old Hope Rd, Kingston 6; tel 927-4421; telex 2388; Commr of Police: Herman Rickettes.

Development and Planning

JAMPRO (Jamaica Promotions) Ltd: 35 Trafalgar Rd, Kingston 10; tel 929-7190; telex 2222; fax 924-9650; Chair: Sen Barclay Ewart; Pres: G. E. Tatham; f 1988 by merger of Jamaica Industrial Devt Corpn, Jamaica National Export Corpn and Jamaica National Investment Promotion Ltd; economic devt agency; promotes investment and trade and industry modernization.

Planning Institute of Jamaica: 39-41 Barbados Ave, POB 634, Kingston 5; tel 926-14808; telex 3529; fax 926-4670; Dir-Gen: Dr Omar Davies; f 1955 as the Central Planning Unit, became the Planning Institute of Jamaica in 1984; economic

planning; monitoring of the performance of the economy; publishing of economic surveys.

Town Planning Department: Oxford Bldg, 16 Oxford Rd, Kingston 5; tel 929-7480; Town Planner: Blossom Samuels; Dep Town Planner: Colin Powell; Sec: Alvin Burnett; f 1950; devt, national, regional and urban planning; assesses housing needs, land policy, land use control and settlement policy.

Urban Development Corpn: The Office Centre, 8th Floor, 12 Ocean Blvd, Kingston; tel 922-8310; telex 2281; fax 922-9326; Chair: Dr Vincent Lawrence; Gen Man: Clinton Woodstock; f 1968; responsible for urban renewal and devt within designated areas.

Employment

Human Employment and Resource Training Trust (HEART): 4 Park Blvd, Kingston 5; tel 929-5794; telex 3719; fax 929-6006; Chair: Steadley Webster; Man Dir: Dr Joyce Robinson; f 1982; develops and finances training schemes; provides employment opportunities for trainees; promotes employment projects.

Legal and Judiciary

Court of Appeal: King St, POB 629, Kingston; tel 922-8300; Pres (acting): B. H. Carey.

Judicial Service Commission: Kingston; Chair: Chief Justice, Edward Zacca; mems are the Pres of the Court of Appeal, Chair of the Public Service Commission and three others; advises the Gov-Gen on judicial appointments.

Supreme Court: King St, POB 491, Kingston; Chief Justice: Edward Zacca; Sen Puisne Judge: C. F. B. Orr; Master: L. E. Vanderpump; Registrars: H. Harris, M. K. S. Harrision (acting); Supreme Court includes the Revenue Court and the Gun Court.

Media

BROADCASTING

Educational Broadcasting Service: Multi-Media Centre, 37 Arnold Rd, Kingston 4; tel 922-9370; Pres: Ouida Hylton-Tomlinson; f 1964; radio broadcasts during school term.

Jamaica Broadcasting Corpn (JBC): 5 South Odeon Ave, POB 100, Kingston 10; tel 926-5620; telex 2218; fax 929-1029; Chair: Ian Ramsay; Gen Man (acting): B. C. Barovier; f 1959; statutory corpn; semi-commercial radio and TV; runs 2 radio stations.

Radio Jamaica Ltd (RJR): Broadcasting House, 32 Lyndhurst Rd, POB 23, Kingston 3; tel 926-1100; telex 3661; fax 929-7467; Man Dir: J. A. Lester Spaulding; f 1947; commercial radio broadcasting.

GOVERNMENT PUBLISHER

Government Printing Office: 77 Duke St, Kingston; tel 922-5950; Govt Printer: Earl Brown.

NEWS AND INFORMATION

Jamaica Information Service (JIS): 58A Halfway Tree Rd, POB 2222, Kingston 10; tel 926-3740; telex 2393; fax 926-6715; Exec Dir: Fred Wilmot; Dir, Operations: Ken Williams; Dir, Finance and Admin: Festus Richards; f 1963; organization through which the Govt tells citizens about its policies and programmes and about the activities of its various Ministries and public sector agencies; provides feedback to Govt, and other relevant information for the public, eg in such areas as health, education, social services, laws and regulations, economic activities, etc.

Jampress Ltd: 3 Chelsea Ave, Kingston 10; tel 926-3740; telex 3552; Exec Chair: Ken Chaplin; Editor-in-Chief: Lincoln Robinson; f 1984; official news agency; news gathering and national and international distribution.

Statistical Institute of Jamaica: 25 Dominica Drive, Kingston 5; tel 926-64407; Dir-Gen: V. G. James; f 1946; fmrly Dept of Statistics; collects, compiles, analyses and publishes statistical information relating to commercial, industrial, social, economic and other activities.

Mining and Energy

Bauxite and Alumina Trading Co of Jamaica/Jamaica Bauxite Mining Ltd: PCJ Resource Centre, 36 Trafalgar Rd, Kingston 10; tel 926-4553; telex 2436; fax 929-7165; Man Dir: Audley C. Roberts; f 1975; mining of, and trade in bauxite, alumina and aluminium ingots.

Jamaica Bauxite Institute: Hope Gdns, POB 355, Kingston 6; tel 927-2073; telex 2309; fax 927-1159; Chair: Roy Collister; Exec Dir: Dr Carlton E. Davis; f 1975; research and monitoring organization, provides studies, experiments, tests and other services for mineral and soil-related industries; advises the Govt in the negotiation of agreements; provides consultancy services to clients in the bauxite/alumina and related industries.

Kaiser Jamaica Bauxite Co: 60 Knutsfor Blvd, Kingston; tel 926-4723; Chair: Huntley George Manhertz; bauxite mining, processing and refining.

Petroleum Corpn of Jamaica (PCJ): 36 Trafalgar Rd, POB 597, Kingston 10; tel 929-5380; telex 2356; fax 929-2409; Exec Chair: Eli Matalon; oil co; owns and operates petroleum refinery; holds exploration and exploitation rights to local petroleum and gas reserves.

Telecommunications

Jamaica International Telecommunications Ltd: 15 North St, Kingston; tel 922-6031; telex 112; fax 921-5329; Pres and Chief Exec: Trevor O. Minott; f 1971; external telecommunications.

Post and Telecommunications Department: Central Sorting Office, South Camp Rd, POB 7000, Kingston; tel 922-9430; telex 2133; Postmaster-Gen: Bertram G. Henry; Chief Telecommunications Eng: Roy Humes; operates Postal Service of Jamaica; exercises regulatory responsibility for telecommunications services in Jamaica.

Tourism

Jamaica Hotel and Tourist Association: 2 Ardenne Rd, Kingston 10; tel 926-3635; telex 2426; fax 910-54; Pres: Peter Rousseau; Gen Man: Camille Needham; f 1961; trade association for hoteliers and other cos involved in Jamaican tourism.

Jamaica Tourist Board (JTB): 21 Dominica Drive, POB 360, Kingston 5; tel 929-9200; telex 2140; fax 929-9375; Chair: O. K.

Melhado; Dir of Tourism: Carrole Brady; f 1955; statutory body set up by the Govt to develop all aspects of the tourist industry through marketing, promotional and advertising efforts.

Transport

CIVIL AVIATION

Air Jamaica Ltd: 72-76 Harbour St, Kingston; tel 922-3460; telex 2389; fax 922-0107; Chair: Danny Williams; Pres and Man Dir: Noel A. Hylton; f 1968; fully Govt-owned since 1980; services to Canada, the Cayman Islands, Haiti, Puerto Rico, the USA and the UK (in co-operation with British Airways).

Airports Authority of Jamaica: National Life Bldg, 64 Knutsford Blvd, POB 567, Kingston; tel 926-1622; telex 2441; Chair: Geoffrey Morris; Gen Man (acting): Howard Taylor.

Civil Aviation Department: 9 Trinidad Terrace, Kingston 5; tel 926-9115.

Trans-Jamaican Airlines: POB 218, Montego Bay; tel 952-5401; Chair: Lotse Harvey; Admin Dir: B. G. Osborne; internal air services.

RAILWAYS

Jamaica Railway Corpn (JRC): POB 489 Kingston; tel 922-6621; telex 3509; Chair: Bert Cooper; Gen Man: Owen Crooks; f 1845; autonomous statutory corpn.

SHIPPING

Jamaica Merchant Marine (JMM): Dyoll Bldg, 7th Floor, 40-46 Knutsford Blvd, POB 952, Kingston 5; tel 922-0290; telex 2483; Chair: Noel A. Hylton; Sec: Grantley Stephenson.

Port Authority of Jamaica: 15-17 Duke St, Kingston; tel 922-0290; telex 2386; fax 924-9437; Chair: Noel Hylton; Gen Man: Lucien Rattray; f 1966; Govt's principal maritime agency; responsible for monitoring and regulating the navigation of all vessels berthing at Jamaican ports, for regulating the tariffs on public wharves, and for the devt of industrial Free Zones in Jamaica.

Kingston Free Zone Co Ltd: 27 Shannon Drive, POB 16, Kingston 15; tel 923-5274; telex 2124; fax 923-6023; Chair: Peter C. V. King; Gen Man: Errol Hewitt; f 1976; subsidiary of Port Authority of Jamaica; management and promotion of an export-orientated industrial free trade zone which is home to cos from various countries.

Montego Bay Export Free Zone: c/o Port Authority of Jamaica, 15-17 Duke St, Kingston; tel 922-0290; telex 2386.

Utilities

Metropolitan Parks and Markets Ltd: 12 Ocean Blvd, 6th Floor, Kingston Mall, Kingston; tel 254-459; Chair: Morris Chin; Gen Man: Daphne Hurge; Dep Gen Man: Greta Robinson; f 1985; public cleansing and solid waste management; market admin; parks creation and maintenance.

JAPAN

Head of State

Under the 1947 Constitution, the Emperor is Head of State but holds no governing power. The Emperor appoints the Prime Minister (on designation by the Diet), who heads the Cabinet. The Cabinet is responsible to the Diet.

Emperor: His Imperial Majesty Akihito (succeeded to the throne 7 January 1989).

Imperial Household Agency: 1-1, Chiyoda, Chiyoda-ku, Tokyo 100; tel (3) 213-1111.

Legislature

Legislative power is vested in the bicameral Diet, comprising the House of Representatives or Lower House (512 members elected by universal adult suffrage for a four-year term), and the House of Councillors or Upper House (252 members elected by universal adult suffrage for six years). Japan has 47 prefectures, each administered by an elected Governor.

House of Councillors: 1-7-1, Nagata-cho, Tokyo 100; tel (3) 581-3111; Speaker: Yoshihiko Tsuchiya.

House of Representatives: 1-7-1, Nagata-cho, Chiyoda-ku, Tokyo 100; tel (3) 581-5111; Speaker: Kenzaburo Hara.

MINISTRIES AND GOVERNMENT DEPARTMENTS

OFFICE OF THE PRIME MINISTER
1-6, Nagata-cho, Chiyoda-ku, Tokyo
Tel (3) 581-2361
Prime Minister: Toshiki Kaifu
Cabinet Secretary: Misoji Sakamoto

CABINET LEGISLATION BUREAU
Tokyo
Tel (3) 581-7271
Director: (vacant)

DEFENCE AGENCY
9-7, Akasaka, Minato-ku, Tokyo 107
Tel (3) 408-5211
Director-General: Yozo Ishikawa

ECONOMIC PLANNING AGENCY
3-1, Kasumigaseki, Chiyoda-ku, Tokyo 100
Tel (3) 581-0261
Director-General: Hideyuki Aizawa

Economic Research Institute: Economic Planning Agency, 3-1-1, Kasumigaseki, Chiyoda-ku, Tokyo 100; tel (3) 581-0261; Dir-Gen: Masaru Yoshitomi; f 1958; conducts research on international policy co-ordination; bridges the gap between basic research and the planning of policy.

ENVIRONMENT AGENCY
1-2-2, Kasumigaseki, Chiyoda-ku, Tokyo
Tel (3) 581-3351; telex 33855
Director-General: Ishimatsu Kitagawa

HOKKAIDO DEVELOPMENT AGENCY
3-1-1, Kasumigaseki, Chiyoda-ku, Tokyo 100
Tel (3) 581-9111
Director-General: Shigetami Sunada

MANAGEMENT AND CO-ORDINATION AGENCY
3-1-1, Kasumigaseki, Chiyoda-ku, Tokyo
Tel (3) 581-6361
Director-General: Jun Shiozaki

MINISTRY OF AGRICULTURE, FORESTRY AND FISHERIES
1-2, Kasumigaseki, Chiyoda-ku, Tokyo
Tel (3) 502-8111
Minister: Tomio Yamamoto

MINISTRY OF CONSTRUCTION
1-3, Kasumigaseki 2-chome, Chiyoda-ku, Tokyo 100
Tel (3) 580-4311
Minister: Tamisuke Watanuki

MINISTRY OF EDUCATION
3-2, Kasumigaseki, Chiyoda-ku, Tokyo
Tel (3) 581-4211
Minister: Kosuke Hori

MINISTRY OF FINANCE
3-1-1, Kasumigaseki, Chiyoda-ku, Tokyo
Tel (3) 581-4111; telex 24980
Minister: Ryutaro Hashimoto

MINISTRY OF FOREIGN AFFAIRS
2-2, Kasumigaseki, Chiyoda-ku, Tokyo
Tel (3) 580-3311; telex 22350
Minister: Taro Nakayama

MINISTRY OF HEALTH AND WELFARE
1-2-2, Kasumigaseki, Chiyoda-ku, Tokyo 100
Tel (3) 503-1711
Minister: Yuji Tsushima

MINISTRY OF HOME AFFAIRS
2-1, Kasumigaseki, Chiyoda-ku, Tokyo
Tel (3) 581-5311
Minister: Keiwa Okuda

MINISTRY OF INTERNATIONAL TRADE AND INDUSTRY
1-3, Kasumigaseki, Chiyoda-ku, Tokyo
Tel (3) 501-1511; telex 22916
Minister: Kabun Muto

MINISTRY OF JUSTICE
1-1-1, Kasumigaseki, Chiyoda-ku, Tokyo 100
Tel (3) 580-4111
Minister: Shin Hasegawa

MINISTRY OF LABOUR
2-2, Kasumigaseki 1-chome, Chiyoda-ku, Tokyo
Tel (3) 593-1211
Minister: Shunpei Tsukahara

MINISTRY OF POSTS AND TELECOMMUNICATIONS
3-2, Kasumigaseki 1-chome, Chiyoda-ku, Tokyo 100-90
Tel (3) 504-4411; telex 32538; fax (3) 580-5399
Minister: Takashi Fukaya

MINISTRY OF TRANSPORT
1-3, Kasumigaseki 2-chome, Chiyoda-ku, Tokyo 100
Tel (3) 580-3111
Minister: Akira Ono

NATIONAL LAND AGENCY
1-2-2, Kasumigaseki, Chiyoda-ku, Tokyo 100
Tel (3) 593-3311
Director-General: Moriyoshi Sato

OKINAWA DEVELOPMENT AGENCY
1-6, Nagata-cho, Chiyoda-ku, Tokyo
Tel (3) 581-2361
Director-General: Shigetami Sunada

SCIENCE AND TECHNOLOGY AGENCY
2-2, Kasumigaseki, Chiyoda-ku, Tokyo
Tel (3) 581-5271
Director-General: Tomoji Oshima

GOVERNMENT AGENCIES AND ORGANIZATIONS

Advisory and Supervisory Body

Board of audit: 3-2-1, Kasumigaseki, Chiyoda-ku, Tokyo 100; tel (3) 581-3251; fax (3) 581-8118; Pres: Keiichi Tsuji; f 1880; audit of the accounts of state revenues and expenditures; supervision of accounting activities.

Agriculture

Fisheries Agency: 2-1, Kasumigaseki 1-chome, Chiyoda-ku, Tokyo 100.

Food Agency: 2-1, Kasumigaseki 1-chome, Chiyoda-ku, Tokyo 100.

Forestry Agency: 2-1, Kasumigaseki 1-chome, Chiyoda-ku, Tokyo 100.

Business and Economy

BANKING

The Export-Import Bank of Japan: 4-1, Ohtemachi 1-chome, Chiyoda-ku, Tokyo 100; tel (3) 287-1221; telex 2879539; fax (3) 287-9450; Pres: Takashi Tanaka; Dep Pres: Reiichi Shimamoto; f 1950; supplements and encourages the financing of exports, imports and overseas investment by ordinary financial institutions; provides export credits, import credits, overseas investment credits and overseas project loans, untied direct loans, etc; 2 brs.

The Japan Development Bank: 9-1, Otemachi 1-chome, Chiyoda-ku, Tokyo 100; tel (3) 270-3211; telex 24343; fax (3) 245-1938; Gov: Gen Takahashi; Dep Gov: Shijuro Ogata; f 1951; provides long-term loans for projects in the areas of resources and energy and urban and technology devt; guarantees corporate obligations; issues external bonds and notes; 8 brs.

Nippon Ginko (Bank of Japan): 1-1, Hongoku-cho 2-chome, Nihombashi, Chuo-ku, Tokyo 103; tel (3) 279-1111; telex 22763; Gov: Satoshi Sumita; f 1882; central bank.

Norinchukin Bank (Central Co-operative Bank for Agriculture, Forestry and Fisheries): 8-3, Ohtemachi 1-chome, Chiyoda-ku, Tokyo 100; tel (3) 279-0111; telex 23918; Pres: Osamu Morimoto; Vice-Pres: Teruji Akabane; f 1923; main banker to agricultural, forestry and fisheries co-operatives; receives deposits from individual co-operatives, federations and agricultural enterprises; extends loans to these and to local govt authorities and public corpns; adjusts excess and shortage of funds within co-operative system; issues debentures, invests funds and engages in other regular banking business; 30 brs.

Shoko Chukin Bank (Central Co-operative Bank for Commerce and Industry): 10-17, Yaesu 2-chome, Chuo-ku, Tokyo 104; tel (3) 272-6111; telex 25388; fax (3) 274-3910; Pres: Shiro Miyamoto; Dep Pres: Kenzo Sakai; f 1936; provision of gen banking servies to facilitate finance for smaller enterprise co-operatives and other organizations formed mainly by small- and medium-sized enterprises; issue of debentures; 92 brs.

FINANCIAL AGENCIES

Agriculture, Forestry and Fisheries Finance Corpn: Koko Bldg, 9-3, Ohtemachi 1-chome, Chiyoda-ku, Tokyo 100; tel (3) 270-2261; Pres: Sakue Matsumoto; Vice-Pres: Yasutaka Miyamoto; f 1953; finances plant and equipment investment; 22 brs.

Housing Loan Corpn: 4-10, Koraku 1-chome, Bunkyo-ku, Tokyo 112; tel (3) 812-1111; Pres: Shozo Kono; Vice-Pres: Kazumoto Adachi; f 1950; provides long-term capital for the construction of housing at low interest rates; 14 brs.

Japan Finance Corpn for Municipal Enterprises (JFM): 11-35, Nagata-cho 1-chome, Chiyoda-ku, Tokyo; tel (3) 581-0311; fax (3) 581-0540; Gov: Takayuki Kondo; Exec Dirs: Tokio Ishita, Hideo Asahina, Junya Nakai; f 1957; makes long-term and low-interest loans to municipal enterprises with funds mainly raised through the domestic and overseas issue of Govt-guaranteed bonds.

National Tax Administration Agency: 3-1, Kasumigaseki, Chiyoda-ku, Tokyo 100.

The Overseas Economic Co-operation Fund: Takebashi Godo Bldg, 4-1, Ohtemachi 1-chome, Chiyoda-ku, Tokyo 100; tel (3) 215-1311; telex 28790; fax (3) 201-5982; Chair: Mitsuhide Yamaguchi; Pres: Shouichi Tanimura; f 1961; provides long-term loans or investments for projects in developing countries.

The People's Finance Corpn: Koko Bldg, 9-3, Ohtemachi 1-chome, Chiyoda-ku, Tokyo 100; tel (3) 270-1361; Gov: Hiroshi Yoshimoto; Dep Gov: Hiroshi Kubota; f 1949; provides business funds, particularly to very small enterprises unable to obtain loans from banks and other private financial institutions.

Small Business Finance Corpn: Koko Bldg, 9-3, Ohtemechi 1-chome, Chiyoda-ku, Tokyo 100; tel (3) 270-1261; Gov: Kiichi Watanabe; Vice-Gov: Minoru Harada; f 1953; lends plant and equipment funds and long-term operating funds to small business which are not easily secured from other financial institutions.

TRADE

Fair Trade Commission: 2-2-1, Kasumigaseki, Chiyoda-ku, Tokyo; prevention of unfair business practices.

Japan External Trade Organization (JETRO): 2-5, Toranomon, 2-chome, Minato-ku, Tokyo 105; tel (3) 582-5522; telex 24378; Chair: Shoichi Akazawa; Pres: Masuo Shibata; f 1958; promotion of trade; provision of information on foreign markets for Japanese exporters and on the domestic market for overseas businesses.

Patent Office: 3-4, Kasumigaseki, Chiyoda-ku, Tokyo 100.

Tokyo International Trade Fair Commission: 7-24, Harumi 4-chome, Chuo-ku, CPOB 1201, Tokyo 104; tel (3) 531-3371; telex 2523935.

Defence

National Police Agency: 1-2, Kasumigaseki 2-chome, Chiyoda-ku, Tokyo.

Self Defence Force: c/o Defence Agency, 9-7, Akasaka, Minato-ku, Tokyo 107; tel (3) 408-5211; Chair, Joint Staff Council: Gen Masao Ishii; Chief of Staff, Maritime Self-Defence Force: Adm Mokoto Sakuma.

Energy

Atomic Energy Bureau (AEB): Science and Technology Agency, 2-2-1, Kasumigaseki, Chiyoda-ku, Tokyo 100; tel (3) 581-5271; Dir: Kenjiro Ogata; f 1956; administers and controls research and devt of atomic energy.

Japan Atomic Energy Commission (JAEC): Science and Technology Agency, 2-2-1, Kasumigaseki, Chiyoka-ku, Tokyo 100; tel (3) 581-5271; Chair: Moichi Miyazaki; f 1955; policy board for research, devt and peaceful uses of atomic energy.

Japan Nuclear Safety Commission (JNSC): Science and Technology Agency, 2-2-1, Kasumigaseki, Chiyoda-ku, Tokyo; tel (3) 581-1880; Chair: Hideo Uchida; f 1978; responsible for all matters relating to safety regulations.

Nuclear Safety Bureau (NSB): Science and Technology Agency, 2-2-1 Kasumigaseki, Chiyoda-ku, Tokyo; tel (3) 581-5271; telex 2226720; fax (3) 581-2487; Dir-Gen: Kenichi Murakami; f 1976; promotion of safety measures in devt and utilization of atomic energy.

Health and Welfare

National Public Safety Commission: 2-1-2, Kasumigaseki, Chiyoda-ku, Tokyo 100; tel (3) 581-0141; Chair: Akio Kanagawa.

Legal and Judiciary

Supreme Court: 4-2, Hayabusa-cho, Chiyoda-ku, Tokyo 102; tel (3) 264-8111; Chief Justice: Koichi Yaguchi; f 1947; highest legal authority; determines the constitutionality of laws; comprises a Chief Justice and 14 associate justices.

Media

BROADCASTING

Nippon Hoso Kyokai, NHK (Japan Broadcasting Corpn): Broadcasting Centre, NHK Hoso Centre, 2-2-1, Jinnan, Shibuya-ku, Tokyo 150; tel (3) 465-1234; telex 22377; fax (3) 481-1576; Chair of Board of Govs: Ichiro Isoda; Pres: Y. Ikeda; f 1925; non-commercial public corpn; operates five (two TV and three radio) networks and 2 DBS TV services; TV channels equally divided between general and educational networks; overseas service in 21 languages.

GOVERNMENT PUBLISHER

Government Publications Service Centre: 2-1, Kasumigaseki 1-chome, Chiyoda-ku, Tokyo; tel (3) 504-3885; fax (3) 504-3889; f 1950; distribution of Govt publs.

NEWS AND INFORMATION

Statistics Bureau/Statistics Centre: Management and Co-ordination Agency, 19-1, Wakamatsucho, Shinjukuku, Tokyo 162; tel (3) 202-1111; fax (3) 202-4892; Dir-Gen, Statistics Bureau: Hiroki Tanaka; Dir-Gen, Statistics Centre: Mitsuru Ide; f 1885; planning and co-ordination of the statistical activities of the Govt; censuses and surveys; statistical research.

Research

Japan Atomic Energy Research Institute (JAERI): Fukokuseimei Bldg, 2-2-2, Uchisaiwai-cho, Chiyoda-ku, Tokyo; tel (3) 503-6111; telex 24596; Pres: Tsuneo Fujinami; f 1956; all aspects of nuclear research: water reactor safety, fusion, devt of nuclear-powered maritime vessels, HTR and utilization of radiation.

Power Reactor and Nuclear Fuel Development Corpn (PNC): 1-9-13, Akasaka, Minato-ku, Tokyo; tel (3) 586-3311; telex 26462; Pres: Minoru Yoshida; f 1967; research and devt of FBR, ATR and fuel cycle techologies.

Science and Technology

Institute of Space and Astronautical Science: 4-6-1, Komaba, Meguro-ku, Tokyo 153; telex 24550; Dir: Jun Nishimura.

Meteorological Agency: 3-4, Ohtemachi 1-chome, Chiyoda-ku, Tokyo 100.

National Space Development Agency of Japan: World

Trade Centre Bldg, 2-4-1, Hamamatsu-cho, Minato-ku, Tokyo 105; tel (3) 5470-4111; telex 28424; fax (3) 433-0796; Pres: Hiroyuki Osawa; f 1969; devt, launching and tracking of launch vehicles and satellites; promotion of space experiments.

Science and Technology Agency: 2-2-1, Kasumigaseki, Chiyoda-ku, tokyo 100; tel (3) 581-5271.

Tourism

Department of Tourism: 2-1-3, Kasumigaseki, Chiyoda-ku, Tokyo 100; Dir-Gen: Hirokuni Tsuji; f 1946; a dept of the Ministry of Transport.

Japan National Tourist Organization: Tokyo Kotsu Kaikan Bldg, 2-10-1, Yuraku-cho, Chiyoda-ku, Tokyo; tel (3) 216-1901; telex 24132; Pres: Shunichi Sumita.

JORDAN

Head of State

Jordan is a constitutional monarchy, and executive power is vested in the sovereign, who governs with the assistance of an appointed Council of Ministers, headed by a Prime Minister, which is responsible to the National Assembly.

Sovereign: King Hussein ibn Talal (proclaimed King on 11 August 1952; crowned on 2 May 1953).

Office of HM the King: Royal Palace, Amman; tel (6) 637341; telex 21332; Chief of the Royal Court: Field Marshal Sharif Zaid ibn Shakar.

Legislature

Legislative power is vested in the bicameral National Assembly, comprising a Senate (30 members appointed by the King for four years) and a House of Representatives (80 members elected for four years by universal adult suffrage). There are eight administrative provinces, three of which have been occupied by Israel since 1967.

Senate: POB 72, Amman; tel (6) 664121; Pres: Ahmad al-Louzi.

House of Representatives: POB 926252, Amman; Speaker: Suleiman Arar.

MINISTRIES AND GOVERNMENT DEPARTMENTS

OFFICE OF THE PRIME MINISTER
POB 80, 35216 Amman
Tel (6) 641211; telex 21444
Prime Minister: Mudar Badran
Deputy Prime Ministers: Marwan al-Qassim,
Salem Masadeh
Minister of State for Cabinet Affairs: Abdel-Baqi Gammo

MINISTRY OF AGRICULTURE
POB 2099, Amman
Tel (6) 639391; telex 24176
Minister: Suleiman Arabiyat

MINISTRY OF AWQAF (RELIGIOUS ENDOWMENTS) AND ISLAMIC AFFAIRS
POB 659, Amman
Tel (6) 666141; telex 21559
Minister: Ali Faqir

MINISTRY OF COMMUNICATIONS
POB 71, Amman
Tel (6) 624301; telex 21666
Minister: Ibrahim Ayyoub

MINISTRY OF CULTURE AND INFORMATION
POB 1854, Amman
Tel (6) 641467; telex 21523; fax (6) 648895
Minister of Culture: Khaled al-Karaki
Minister of Information: Ibrahim Izziedin

MINISTRY OF DEFENCE
POB 1577, Amman
Tel (6) 644361; telex 21200
Minister: Mudar Badran

MINISTRY OF EDUCATION
POB 1646, Amman
Tel (6) 669181; telex 21396
Minister: Mohammad Hamdan

MINISTRY OF ENERGY AND MINERAL RESOURCES
POB 140027, Amman
Tel (6) 815615; telex 21259; fax (6) 818336
Minister: Thabet al-Taher

MINISTRY OF FINANCE
POB 85, Amman
Tel (6) 636321; telex 23634
Minister: Basil Jardaneh

MINISTRY OF FOREIGN AFFAIRS
POB 1577, Amman
Tel (6) 644361; telex 21255
Minister: Marwan al-Qassim

Department of Palestinian Affairs: POB 2469, Amman; tel (6) 684455; Dir: Dr Ahmad K. Katanani; f 1987, fmrly Ministry of Occupied Territories Affairs; monitoring and analysis of Palestinian activities at all levels inside and outside the Occupied Territories; supervises people living in camps in Jordan, and oversees trade in Palestinian products.

MINISTRY OF HEALTH
POB 86, Amman
Tel (6) 665131; telex 21595
Minister: Mohammad al-Zaben

MINISTRY OF THE INTERIOR
POB 100, Amman
Tel (6) 663111; telex 23162
Minister: Salem Masadeh

MINISTRY OF JUSTICE
POB 6040, Amman
Tel (6) 663101
Minister: Yousif Mbeideen

MINISTRY OF LABOUR
POB 9052, Amman
Tel (6) 630343
Minister: Qaseem Obeidat

MINISTRY OF MUNICIPAL, RURAL AND ENVIRONMENTAL AFFAIRS
POB 1799, Amman
Tel (6) 641393; fax (6) 672135
Minister: Abdel-Karim al-Dughmi

MINISTRY OF PLANNING
POB 555, Amman
Tel (6) 644466; telex 21319
Minister: Awni al-Masri

MINISTRY OF PUBLIC WORKS AND HOUSING
POB 1220, Amman
Tel (6) 668481; telex 21944
Minister: Abdel-Raouf al-Rawabdeh

MINISTRY OF SOCIAL DEVELOPMENT
POB 6720, Amman
Tel (6) 643838
Minister: Abdel-Majid Shreideh

MINISTRY OF SUPPLY
POB 830, Amman
Tel (6) 602121; telex 21278; fax (6) 604691
Minister: Nabil Abul Huda

MINISTRY OF TOURISM AND ANTIQUITIES
POB 224, Amman
Tel (6) 642311; telex 21741; fax (6) 648465
Minister: Abdul Karim Kabariti

MINISTRY OF TRADE AND INDUSTRY
POB 2019, Amman
Tel (6) 663191; telex 21163; fax (6) 603721
Minister: Zaid Faris

MINISTRY OF TRANSPORT
POB 1929, 35214 Amman
Tel (6) 641461; telex 21541
Minister: Ibrahim Ayyoub

MINISTRY OF WATER AND IRRIGATION
POB 2412, Amman
Tel (6) 666111
Minister: Daoud Khalaf

MINISTRY OF YOUTH
POB 224, Amman
Minister: Ibrahim al-Ghababsheh

GOVERNMENT AGENCIES AND ORGANIZATIONS

Agriculture and the Environment

Agricultural Marketing and Processing Co of Jordan: POB 7314, Amman; tel (6) 819161; telex 23796; Chair and Gen Man: Ghazi Abu Hassan; f 1984.

Natural Resources Authority: POB 2220, Amman; tel (6) 815615; telex 21415.

Business and Economy

BANKING

Arab Jordan Investment Bank: POB 8797, Amman; tel (6) 664126; telex 21719; fax (6) 681482; Chair and Gen Man: Abdul al-Kader al-Qadi; Dep Gen Man and Dir: Jawad Hadid; f 1978; 2 brs.

Central Bank of Jordan: POB 37, King Hussein St, Amman; tel (6) 630301; telex 21250; Gov: Muhammad Said Nabulsi; f 1964; central bank; 2 brs.

Cities and Villages Development Bank: POB 1572, Amman; tel (6) 668151; telex 22476; Gen Man: Muhammad Saleh Hourani; f 1979.

Housing Bank: POB 7693, Police College St, Abdali, Amman; tel (6) 667126; telex 21693; fax (6) 678121; Chair and Dir-Gen: Zuhair Khouri; f 1973; 81 brs.

FINANCIAL AGENCIES

Agricultural Credit Corpn: POB 77, Amman; tel (6) 661105; Chair and Man Dir: Dr Sami Suna'a; f 1959; 18 brs.

Jordan Co-operative Organization: POB 1343, Amman; tel (6) 665171; telex 21835; Chair: Moraiwid at-Tel; f 1968.

Jordan Securities Corpn: POB 926691, Amman; tel (6) 664183; telex 22258; fax (6) 686291; Chair: Zuhair Khouri; Dir: Abd al-Qadir Dweek; f 1979.

Social Security Corpn: POB 926031, Amman; tel (6) 643000; telex 22287; fax (6) 610014; Dir-Gen: Dr M. Mahdi el-Farhan; f 1978.

NATIONALIZED INDUSTRY

Arab Potash Co Ltd: POB 1470, Amman: tel (6) 666165; telex 21683; Chair: Omar Abdullah Daqhan; Dir-Gen: Ali Nsour; f 1956; production of potash and potassium chloride, with a by-product of salt; 51% state-owned.

Defence

Jordanian Armed Forces: Gen Headquarters, Qiadeh; tel 622131; telex 21200; Commdr-in-Chief: Maj-Gen: Fathi Abu Talib; Asst Commdr-in-Chief: Brig Tayseer Zarour; Chief of the Gen Staff: Lt-Gen Abdel Hadi al-Majah; Chief of Staff: (vacant).

Royal Jordanian Air Force: POB 340796 Qiadeh; tel 896351; telex 21305; Commdr: Lt-Gen Ihsan Hamid Shurdum.

Royal Jordanian Coast Guard: c/o General Headquarters, Jordanian Armed Forces, Qiadeh; tel 6042405; telex 21200.

Development

Amman Development Corpn: POB 926621, Amman; tel (6) 629471; telex 22133; Dir-Gen: Sami al-Rashid; f 1979; devt of services in the Amman municipality by constructing and running real estate, industrial and other complexes.

Jordan Valley Authority: POB 2769, Amman; tel (6) 642472; telex 21692; Pres: Muhammad Bani Hani; responsible for the

Jordan Valley Devt Plan of cultivation, roads, housing, schools, health centres, utilities, etc; plans include irrigation and dam projects for the Jordan valley.

Energy

Jordan Electricity Authority: POB 2310, Amman; tel (6) 815615; telex 21507.

Legal and Judiciary

Supreme Court: POB 606, Amman; tel (6) 666101.

Media

BROADCASTING

Jordan Radio and Television Corpn (JRTV): POB 909, Amman; tel (6) 638760; telex 21285; Dir-Gen: Isam Arida; Dir of Programmes (Arabic): S. Mashini; Dir of Programmes (English): J. Zada; Dir (Eng): Radi Alkhas; f 1968; Govt TV station; broadcasts for 90 hours weekly in Arabic and English.

NEWS AND INFORMATION

Department of Statistics: POB 2015, Amman; tel (6) 842171; telex 24117; Dir: Dr Abdulhadi Alawin; Asst Dir: J. Salah; f 1949; conducts economic and social surveys and censuses; disseminates information.

Jordan News Agency (PETRA): POB 6845, Amman; tel (6) 644455; telex 21220; Dir-Gen: Ali Safadi; f 1965.

Science and Technology

Royal Scientific Society: POB 6945, Amman; tel (6) 844700.

Tourism

Tourism Authority: c/o Ministry of Tourism, POB 224, Amman; tel (6) 642311; telex 21741; Dir-Gen: Nasri Atallah; f 1952.

Transport

CIVIL AVIATION

Civil Aviation Authority: POB 7547, Amman; tel (6) 892282; telex 21325; Dir-Gen: Mahmoud J. Balqez; f 1952; responsible for the air worthiness and flight safety of aircraft, training of staff, aeronautical information, ground operations, telecommunications.

Royal Jordanian Airline: POB 302, Housing Bank Commercial Centre, Shmeisani, Amman; tel (6) 672872; telex 21501; fax (6) 672527; Chair of Board: Khaldoun Abu Hassan; Pres and Chief Exec: Hussam Abu Ghazaleh; f 1963; Govt-owned but undergoing privatization; services to the Middle East, North Africa, Europe, USA and Far East.

Arab Wings Co Ltd: POB 341018, Amman; tel (6) 891994; telex 21608; Chair: Ali Ghandour; Man Dir: HE Sharif Ghazi Rakan Nasser; f 1975; subsidiary of Royal Jordanian Airline; executive jet charter service, air ambulances, priority cargo.

RAILWAYS

Aqaba Railway Corpn: POB 50, Ma'an; tel (3) 32114; telex 64003; Dir-Gen: M. Qatamin; f 1972; transport of phosphate; under Ministry of Transport.

Hedjaz-Jordan Railway: POB 1929, Amman; tel (6) 641461; telex 21541; Dir-Gen: A. H. ad-Djazi; f 1902; administered by the Ministry of Transport.

ROADS

Joint Land Transport Co: Amman; joint venture between Govts of Jordan and Iraq; operation of trucks.

SHIPPING

Jordan National Shipping Lines Ltd: POB 5406, Shmeisani, Amman; tel (6) 666214; telex 21730; POB 657, Aqaba; tel (3) 315342; telex 62276; Chair: Wasif Azar; Gen Man: Y. et-Tal; 75% Govt-owned; service from Antwerp, Zeebrugge, Bremen and Sheerness to Aqaba; passenger ferry service to Egypt; land transportation to destinations in Iraq and elsewhere in the region.

KENYA

Head of State

Executive power is vested in the President, who must be a member of the National Assembly and who is elected by direct popular vote for a five-year term. The President appoints, and is assisted by, a Vice-President and a Cabinet.

President: Daniel arap Moi (took office 14 October 1978, returned to office unopposed in August 1983 and February 1988).

Office of the President: Harambee House, Harambee Ave, POB 30510, Nairobi; tel (2) 27411; Ministers of State in the President's Office: Jackson Harvester Angaine, Hussein Maalim Mohammed, Burudi Nabwera.

Vice-President: Prof George Saitoti

Office of the Vice-President: Treasury Bldg, Harambee Ave, POB 30007, Nairobi; tel (2) 338111; telex 22696.

Legislature

Legislative power is vested in the unicameral National Assembly which comprises 188 members elected by universal adult suffrage, 12 members nominated by the President and two ex-officio members, the Attorney-General and the Speaker. All members serve five-year terms, and all must be nominated by the Kenya African National Union (KANU).

National Assembly: Parliament Bldgs, POB 41842, Nairobi; tel (2) 21291; Speaker: Moses arap Keino.

MINISTRIES AND GOVERNMENT DEPARTMENTS

MINISTRY OF AGRICULTURE
Kilimo House, Cathedral Rd, POB 30028, Nairobi
Tel (2) 728370; telex 33042
Minister: Maina Wanjigi

MINISTRY OF COMMERCE AND INDUSTRY
Ufansi House, Haile Selassie Ave, POB 47024, Nairobi
Tel (2) 20866
Minister of Commerce: Arthur K. Magugu
Minister of Industry: Dalmas Otieno Anyango

MINISTRY OF CO-OPERATIVE DEVELOPMENT
Kencom House, POB 30457, Nairobi
Tel (2) 340081
Minister: John Cheruiyot

MINISTRY OF CULTURE AND SOCIAL SERVICES
Reinsurance Plaza, Taifa Rd, POB 45958, Nairobi
Tel (2) 339650
Minister: James Njiru

MINISTRY OF EDUCATION
Jogoo House 'B', POB 30040, Nairobi
Tel (2) 28411
Minister: Peter Aloo Aringo

MINISTRY OF ENERGY AND REGIONAL DEVELOPMENT
Nyayo House, Kenyatta Ave, POB 30582, Nairobi
Tel (2) 331242; telex 23094
Minister of Energy: Nicholas Biwott
Minister of Regional Development: John Okwanyo

MINISTRY OF ENVIRONMENT AND NATURAL RESOURCES
Kencom House, POB 30126, Nairobi
Tel (2) 29261
Minister: Jeremiah Nyagah

MINISTRY OF FINANCE
Treasury Bldg, Harambee Ave, POB 30007, Nairobi
Tel (2) 338111; telex 22696
Minister: Prof George Saitoti

MINISTRY OF FOREIGN AFFAIRS AND INTERNATIONAL CO-OPERATION
Harambee House, POB 30551, Nairobi
Tel (2) 334433; telex 22003
Minister: Wilson Mdolo Ayah

MINISTRY OF HEALTH
Medical HQ, Afya House, Cathedral Rd, POB 30016, Nairobi
Tel (2) 728370
Minister: Mwai Kibaki

MINISTRY OF HOME AFFAIRS AND NATIONAL HERITAGE
Jogoo House, Harambee Ave, POB 30520, Nairobi
Tel (2) 28411
Minister: Davidson Ngibuini Kuguru

MINISTRY OF INFORMATION AND BROADCASTING
Jogoo House, POB 30025, Nairobi
Tel (2) 28411; telex 22244
Minister: Waruru Kanja

Department of Information: POB 8053, Nairobi; tel (2) 23201; telex 22244; Dir: S. J. W. Musandu; f 1963; gathers and disseminates news through Kenya News Agency (see below); operates a Rural Press, the Central Media services, book libraries, mobile cinemas and facilitates accreditation of the press.

MINISTRY OF LABOUR
National Social Security House, POB 40326, Nairobi
Tel (2) 729800
Minister: Peter Okondo
Minister of Manpower Development and Employment: Paul Ngei

MINISTRY OF LANDS, SETTLEMENT AND HOUSING
POB 30450, Nairobi
Tel (2) 728060
Minister: Darius Mbela

MINISTRY OF LIVESTOCK DEVELOPMENT
Kilimo House, Cathedral Rd, POB 34188, Nairobi
Tel (2) 728370
Minister: Elijah Mwangale

MINISTRY OF LOCAL GOVERNMENT AND PHYSICAL PLANNING
Jogoo House 'A', POB 30004, Nairobi
Tel (2) 28411
Minister: William Ole Ntimama

MINISTRY OF PLANNING AND NATIONAL DEVELOPMENT
Treasury Bldg, Harambee Ave, POB 30007, Nairobi
Tel (2) 338111
Minister: Dr Zachary Onyonka

MINISTRY OF PUBLIC WORKS
Transcom House, Ngong Rd, POB 30260, Nairobi
Tel (2) 729200; telex 22174
Minister: Timothy Mibei

MINISTRY OF RECLAMATION AND DEVELOPMENT OF ARID, SEMI-ARID AND WASTE LAND
Nairobi
Minister: George Mutua Ndotto

MINISTRY OF RESEARCH, SCIENCE AND TECHNOLOGY
Utalii House, Uhuru Highway, POB 30623, Nairobi
Tel (2) 336173
Minister: George Muhoho
Minister of Technical Training and Applied Technology: Sam Ongeri

MINISTRY OF SUPPLIES AND MARKETING
Maendaleo House, Loita St, POB 34889, Nairobi
Tel (2) 339266
Minister: Wycliff Musalia Mudavadi

MINISTRY OF TOURISM AND WILDLIFE
Utalii House, Uhuru Highway, POB 30027, Nairobi
Tel (2) 331030
Minister: Noah Katana Ngala

MINISTRY OF TRANSPORT AND COMMUNICATIONS
Transcom House, Ngong Rd, POB 52692, Nairobi
Tel (2) 729200; telex 22272
Minister: Joseph Kamotho

MINISTRY OF WATER DEVELOPMENT
Maji House, Ngong Rd, POB 49720, Nairobi
Tel (2) 723103
Minister: Wilson Ndolo Ayah

OFFICE OF THE ATTORNEY-GENERAL
State Law Office, Harambee Ave, POB 40112, Nairobi
Tel (2) 27461
Attorney-General: Matthew Muli

GOVERNMENT AGENCIES AND ORGANIZATIONS

Advisory and Supervisory Body

Public Service Commission of Kenya: POB 30095, Nairobi; tel (2) 23901; Sec: W. K. K. Kimalat; f 1953; appoints persons to hold office in the public service and in local authorities; exercises disciplinary control over persons holding such offices and has the power to remove them from office.

Agriculture and the Environment

Agricultural Development Corpn: Moi Ave, POB 47101, Nairobi; tel (2) 338530; telex 22856; Man Dir: Walter K. Kilele; Gen Man: Bartholomew I. Muruli; f 1965; agricultural devt; management of national farms for production of certified seed for strategic crops such as hybrid maize, wheat, potatoes, etc; livestock devt.

Horticultural Crops Development Authority: POB 42601, Nairobi; tel (2) 337381; telex 22687; Chair: Kasanga Mulwa; Man Dir: M. A. S. Mulandi; invests in production, dehydration, processing and freezing of fruit and vegetables; exports fresh fruit and vegetables.

Kenya Dairy Board: POB 30406, Nairobi; tel (2) 336070; Exec Officer: J. P. Cheruiyot; f 1958; develops and has a regulatory and advisory role over the dairy industry.

Kenya Fishing Industries Ltd: Nairobi; Man Dir: Abdalla Mbwana.

Kenya Meat Corpn: POB 30414, Nairobi; tel (2) 340750; telex 22150; Chair: H. P. Barclay; f 1953; purchasing, processing and marketing of beef livestock.

Kenya Planters Co-operative Union Ltd: Haile Selassie Ave, POB 72309, Nairobi; tel (2) 28761; telex 22039; Man Dir: Gitonga Chabari; Chair: J. J. Musundi; f 1937; provides co-operatives and plantation coffee farmers with field education on better coffee farming; provides storage, coffee milling, grading, sorting and liquoring facilities before coffee is marketed.

Kenya Sisal Board: Mutual Bldg, Kimathi St, POB 41179, Nairobi; tel (2) 23457; Chief Exec: J. H. Wairagu; f 1946.

Kenya Sugar Authority: Community Bldg, Ngong Rd, POB 51500, Nairobi; tel (2) 720060; Chair: Nehemiah Antipas Ochieng; f 1973.

Kenya Tea Development Authority: POB 30213, Nairobi; tel (2) 21441; telex 22645; Chair: Charles Koinange; Gen Man: (vacant); f 1960; devt of tea growing, manufacturing and marketing among African smallholders; operates factories.

National Cereals and Produce Board: POB 30586, Nairobi; tel (2) 555288; telex 24109; fax (2) 542024; Chair: James Matua;

Man Dir: Maj (retd) S. K. Koitaba; f 1985; marketing; storage; control of agricultural produce throughout the country.

Pyrethrum Board of Kenya: Gen Mathenge Drive, POB 420, Nakuru; tel (37) 40311; Chair: Makone Ombese; Chief Exec: Muigai Wainaina; f 1934; pyrethrum processing and marketing; 14 mems.

The Tea Board of Kenya: Wakulima House, Haile Selassie Ave, POB 20064, Nairobi; tel (2) 20241; Chair: Eliud M. Mahihu; Sec: E. N. K. Wanjama; f 1950; has licensing control over growing, manufacture and export of tea; conducts research into all matters of the tea industry; promotes tea; under Ministry of Agriculture.

Wildlife Department: Nairobi; Head: Dr Richard Leakey; to become semi-autonomous of the Govt.

Business and Economy

BANKING

Central Bank of Kenya: Haile Selassie Ave, POB 60000, Nairobi; tel (2) 26431; telex 22324; Gov: Eric C. Kotut; Dep Gov: Wanjohi Mureithi; f 1966; central bank and bank of issue.

East African Development Bank: Bruce House, POB 47685, Nairobi; tel (2) 340642; telex 22689; Dir-Gen: G. F. Mbowe; f 1967; provides financial and technical assistance to promote industrial devt within Kenya, Uganda and Tanzania, whose Govts each own 30.8% of the equity.

Kenya Commercial Bank Ltd: Kencom House, Moi Ave, POB 48400, Nairobi; tel (2) 339441; telex 23085; Chair: Dr Benjamin E. Kipkorir; Gen Man: A. A. Hamilton; f 1970; 111 brs and sub-brs.

Kenya National Capital Corpn Ltd (KENYAC): POB 73469, Nairobi; tel (2) 336077; telex 22159; Chair: R. Gitau; Gen Man: J. P. Okora; Chief Accountant: I. M. Mworia; f 1974; 60% owned by National Bank of Kenya Ltd, 40% owned by Kenya National Assurance Co (see below); merchant bank.

National Bank of Kenya Ltd (Banki ya Taifa La Kenya Ltd): National Bank Bldg, Harambee Ave, POB 72866, Nairobi; tel (2) 26471; telex 22619; Chair: Raphael Gitau; Gen Man: J. W. Oluga; f 1968; commercial banking services; 11 brs.

Union Bank of Kenya Ltd: Agriculture House, Ground Floor, Harambee Ave, POB 34823, Nairobi; tel (2) 28705; telex 23263; fax (2) 720925; Chair: J. M. Mbaru; Gen Man: S. V. Dabholkar; f 1982; retail and corporate commercial banking; foreign business; 3 brs.

FINANCIAL AGENCIES

Agricultural Finance Corpn: POB 30367, Nairobi; tel (2) 333733; telex 22649; Gen Man: G. K. Toroitich; statutory organization providing agricultural loans.

Housing Finance Co of Kenya Ltd: Rehani House, Kenyatta Ave, POB 30088, Nairobi; tel (2) 333910; Chair: Col Meshack K. Birgen; Man Dir: Walter B. Mukuria; f 1965; promotes financing of home ownership through provision of savings and deposit facilities, admin of provident funds, etc.

Settlement Fund Trustees: POB 30449, Nairobi; administers a land purchase programme involving over 1.2m ha for resettlement of African farmers.

INSURANCE

Kenya National Assurance Co Ltd: POB 20425, Nairobi; tel (2) 338660; telex 23057; Exec Chair: Henry K. Kosgey; Gen Man: E. G. Bunyassi; f 1964; state-owned; all classes of insurance and reinsurance.

MARKETING

Central Province Marketing Board: POB 189, Nyeri.

Coffee Board of Kenya: POB 30566, Nairobi; tel (2) 332896; telex 25706; Chair: (vacant); Gen Man: Patrick M. Katingima; f 1933; coffee marketing.

TRADE

Kenya National Trading Corpn Ltd: Uchumi House, Nkrumah Ave, POB 30587, Nairobi; tel (2) 29141; telex 22298; Chief Exec: S. W. O. Ogessa; f 1965; promotes national control of trade in both locally produced and imported items; exports coffee and sugar.

Defence

Defence Headquarters: Ulinzi House, POB 40668, Nairobi; tel (2) 721100; Commdr-in-Chief of the Armed Forces: President Daniel arap Moi; Chief of Armed Forces Gen Staff: Gen Mahmoud Haji Mohammed.

Air Force Headquarters: Eastleigh, POB 48888, Nairobi; tel (2) 64401.

Army Headquarters: POB 30503, Nairobi; tel (2) 721100.

Navy Headquarters: POB 95350, Mombasa; tel (11) 451351.

Development and Planning

Industrial and Commercial Development Corpn: Uchumi House, Nkrumah Ave, POB 45519, Nairobi; tel (2) 29213; telex 22429; Chair: Charles Rubia; Exec Dir: J. P. N. Simba; f 1954; Govt-financed; facilitates industrial and commercial devt.

Kenya Industrial Research and Develoment Institute: POB 30650, Nairobi; tel (2) 557762; Exec Dir: Dr Robert O. Arunga; f 1942; devt of process and product technologies; design, devt and adaptation of machinery, tools and equipment; setting up of pilot plants; consultancy services.

INVESTMENT

Development Finance Co of Kenya Ltd: Finance House, Loita St, POB 30483, Nairobi; tel (2) 340401; telex 22662; fax (2) 338426; Chair: H. N. K. Arap Mengech; Chief Exec: J. V. Bosse; f 1963; private co with Govt participation.

Investment Promotion Centre: POB 55704, Nairobi; tel (2) 21401; telex 25460; Dir: Silas M. Ita; f 1986; promotes and facilitates private investment in Kenya.

Energy

The Kenya Power Co Ltd: Electricity House, POB 7936, Nairobi; Chair: Amos Ng'ang'a; Sec: A. N. Ngugi; f 1954; bulk generation and importation of electrical energy; operates hydropower stations; sells mostly to the Kenya Power and Lighting Co.

The Kenya Power and Lighting Co Ltd: POB 30099, Nairobi; Chair and Chief Exec: J. K. Gecau; Man Dir: S. K. Gichuru; f 1922; sole distributor of electrical power.

Legal and Judiciary

The High Court of Kenya: Harambee Ave, POB 40112, Nairobi; tel (2) 21221; has unlimited criminal and civil jurisdiction at first instance, and sits as a court of appeal from subordinate courts in both criminal and civil cases; the High Court is a court of admiralty.

The Kenya Court of Appeal: POB 30187, Nairobi; Chief Justice: A. R. W. Hancox; Justices of Appeal: A. A. Kneller, K. D. Potter; Z. R. Chesoni, J. O. Nyarangi, H. G. Platt; final court of appeal in civil and criminal process.

Media

BROADCASTING

Kenya Broadcasting Corpn (KBC): Broadcasting House, POB 30456, Nairobi; tel (2) 334567; telex 25361; Chair: Dr Gikowyo Kiano; Dir of Broadcasting (acting): James Wanjau; f 1989 as state corpn, replacing Voice of Kenya; three radio services; TV services in Kiswahili and English.

GOVERNMENT PUBLISHERS

Government Printing Press: POB 30128, Nairobi.

Kenya Literature Bureau: Ngong Rd, POB 30022, Nairobi; tel (2) 723450; Chair: Leonard Kabetu; Man Dir: S. C. Lang'at; Chief Editor: Gitau S. Githenji; f 1980; parastatal body under Ministry of Education; literary, educational, cultural and scientific books and journals.

NEWS AND INFORMATION

Central Bureau of Statistics: POB 30266, Nairobi; tel (2) 333970; f 1961; collection and compilation of national statistics.

Kenya News Agency: Information House, POB 30025, Nairobi; tel (2) 23201; telex 22244; Dir: S. Musandu; f 1963.

Tourism

Kenya Tourism Marketing Board: Nairobi; Chair: Alexander Furrer; Vice-Chair: Japhet Kiti; f 1984.

Kenya Tourist Development Corpn: POB 42013, Nairobi; tel (2) 330820; telex 23009; Chair: Stanley Kurgat; Man Dir: W. A. Mutsune; f 1965; devt of the tourist industry of Kenya.

Transport

Kenya Airways Ltd: Embakasi, POB 19002, Nairobi; tel (2) 822171; telex 22771; fax (2) 822480; Chair: Bethwel Gechaga; Man Dir: Joseph W. Nyagah; f 1977 following the dissolution of East African Airways; scheduled flights for passengers and cargo; destinations in Africa, the Middle East and Europe; internal services; has charter subsidiary, Kenya Flamingo Airways.

Kenya Directorate of Civil Aviation: POB 30163, Nairobi; tel (2) 822950; telex 25239; Dir: J. N. Kahuki; f 1948 as the East African Directorate of Civil Aviation, under Govt control since 1977; advises Govt on civil aviation activities; air traffic control.

Kenya Ports Authority: POB 95009, Mombasa; tel (11) 312211; telex 21243; Chair: Stephen Mwakisha; Man Dir: Philip Okundi; f 1977.

Kenya Cargo Handling Services Ltd: POB 95187, Mombasa; tel (11) 25955; telex 20047; Man Dir: Joshua Kegode, division of Kenya Ports Authority.

Kenya Railways Corpn: POB 30121, Nairobi; tel (2) 21211; telex 22254; Chair: (vacant); Man Dir: E. J. Mimano; f 1977 following the dissolution of the East African Railways Corpn.

KIRIBATI

Head of State

The Head of State is the Beretitenti (President), who is also Head of Government. The President is elected by direct popular vote. The President governs with the assistance of a Vice-President and Cabinet, whom he appoints from among members of the Maneaba ni Maungatabu (House of Assembly). Executive authority is vested in the Cabinet, which is responsible to the Maneaba.

Beretitenti (President): Ieremia T. Tabai (took office 12 July 1979).

Office of the President: POB 68, Bairiki, Tarawa; tel 21342; telex 77054; fax 21466.

Kauoman-ni-Beretitenti (Vice-President): Teatao Teannaki.

Office of the Vice-President: POB 75, Bairiki, Tarawa.

Legislature

Legislative power is vested in the unicameral Maneaba ni Maungatabu (House of Assembly). It has 39 members elected by universal adult suffrage for four years, one nominated member of the Banaban community and, if not an elected member, the Attorney-General as an ex-officio member.

Maneaba ni Maungatabu (House of Assembly): POB 52, Bairiki, Tarawa; Speaker: Beretitara Neeti.

MINISTRIES AND GOVERNMENT DEPARTMENTS

MINISTRY OF COMMUNICATIONS AND TRANSPORT
POB 487, Betio, Tarawa
Tel 26121
Minister: Uera Rabaua

MINISTRY OF EDUCATION
POB 263, Bikenibeu, Tarawa
Tel 28031; telex 77049
Minister: Ataraoti Bwebwenibure

MINISTRY OF FINANCE
POB 67, Bairiki, Tarawa
Tel 21082; telex 77065
Minister: Teatao Teannaki

MINISTRY OF FOREIGN AFFAIRS
POB 68, Bairiki, Tarawa
Tel 21342; telex 77054; fax 21466
Minister: Ieremia T. Tabai

MINISTRY OF HEALTH AND FAMILY PLANNING
POB 268, Bikenibeu, Tarawa
Tel 28081
Minister: Rotaria Ataia

MINISTRY OF HOME AFFAIRS AND DECENTRALIZATION
POB 75, Bairiki, Tarawa
Tel 21092
Minister: Babera Kirata

MINISTRY OF THE LINE AND PHOENIX GROUPS
Kiritimati Island
Minister: Tekinaiti Kaiteie

MINISTRY OF NATURAL RESOURCES AND DEVELOPMENT
POB 64, Bairiki, Tarawa
Tel 21099; telex 77039
Minister: Taomati Iuta

MINISTRY OF TRADE, INDUSTRY AND LABOUR
POB 69, Bairiki, Tarawa
Tel 21097
Minister: Raion Bataroma

MINISTRY OF WORKS AND ENERGY
POB 498, Betio, Tarawa
Tel 26192; telex 77045
Minister: (vacant)

OFFICE OF THE ATTORNEY-GENERAL
POB 62, Bairiki, Tarawa
Tel 258
Attorney-General: Michael Takabwebwe

GOVERNMENT AGENCIES AND ORGANIZATIONS

Advisory and Supervisory Body

Office of the Director of Audit: POB 63, Bairiki, Tarawa; tel 250; Dir: Iaramako Teoiaki.

Agriculture

The Kiribati Copra Co-operative Society Ltd: POB 489, Betio, Tarawa; tel 26534; telex 77020; Chair: Robati Murdoch; Man: Biromina Awiu; f 1976; sole exporter of copra.

Business and Economy

BANKING

Development Bank of Kiribati: POB 33, Bairiki, Tarawa; tel 21297; Chair: Anote Tong; Gen Man: Uriam Timiti; f 1987; took over the assets of The National Loans Board; provides finance for devt projects; financial advisory service.

TRADE

Abamakoro Trading Ltd: POB 492, Betio, Tarawa; tel 26568; telex 77031; fax 26263; Chair: Teitia Redfern; Dirs: Uriam Timiti, Tom Murdoch, Tekautu Teimarane, Maneta Tekautu; f 1981; import and distribution of goods to retail outlets.

Legal and Judiciary

High Court: POB 501, Betio, Tarawa; tel 26007; Chief Justice: V. O. Maxwell; Puisne Judge: F. Muhammad; superior court of record and has unlimited jurisdiction; all judicial appointments are made by the Beretitenti (President).

Media

BROADCASTING

Radio Kiribati: Broadcasting and Publications Authority, POB 78, Bairiki, Tarawa; tel 21161; telex 77024; fax 21096; Man: Tomasi Kei Tarau; f 1954; programmes in I-Kiribati and English.

NEWS AND INFORMATION

Statistics Office: c/o Ministry of Finance, POB 67, Bairiki, Tarawa.

Transport

Air Tungaru Corpn: POB 274, Bikenibeu, Tarawa; tel 28232; telex 77023; fax 28277; Chair: John I. Tongambeia; Gen Man (acting): Mate T. Moaniba; f 1977; national airline; operates scheduled passenger and cargo services between Tarawa's Bonriki Airport and 15 outer islands; also flights from Tarawa to Fiji and Tuvalu and from Kiritimati to Hawaii.

Shipping Corpn of Kiribati: POB 495, Betio, Tarawa; tel 26195; telex 77030; Man: Tom Murdoch; operates five passenger/freight vessels on inter-island services.

DEMOCRATIC PEOPLE'S REPUBLIC OF KOREA

Head of State

The President, as Head of State, is elected by the Supreme People's Assembly for four years, and is responsible to the Assembly. The Assembly, on the President's recommendation, elects the members of the Central People's Committee, which directs the Government. The Assembly appoints the Premier, and the Committee appoints other Ministers to form the Administration Council, led by the President.

President: Marshal Kim Il Sung (took office 28 December 1972; re-elected December 1977, April 1982, December 1986).

Office of the President: Pyongyang.

Vice-Presidents: Pak Sung Chul, Li Jong Ok.

Central People's Committee: Pyongyang; Sec: Chi Chang Ik.

Legislature

The highest organ of state power is the unicameral Supreme People's Assembly, comprising 655 members elected (unopposed) for four years by universal adult suffrage. Political power is held by the communist Korean Workers' Party (KWP). The country consists of nine provinces and two cities, each with an elected People's Assembly.

Supreme People's Assembly: Pyongyang.

Standing Committee: Pyongyang; Chair: Yang Hyung Sop; Vice-Chairs: Son Song Pil, Ryo Yon Gu; Sec-Gen: Kim Bong Ju.

MINISTRIES AND GOVERNMENT DEPARTMENTS

OFFICE OF THE PREMIER
Pyongyang
Premier: Yon Hyong Muk
Vice-Premiers: Hong Song Nam, Kim Yun Hyok, Chong Jun Gi, Kim Hwan, Kim Yong Nam, Kim Bok Shin, Kim Chang Ju, Kang Hui Won

ADMINISTRATIVE BUREAU OF THE STATE ADMINISTRATION COUNCIL
Pyongyang
Director: Chong Mun San

AGRICULTURAL COMMISSION
Pyongyang
Chair: Kim Chang Ju

EDUCATION COMMISSION
Pyongyang
Chair: Choe Gi Ryong

EXTERNAL ECONOMIC AFFAIRS COMMISSION
Pyongyang
Chair: Kim Dal Hyon

FISHERIES COMMISSION
Pyongyang
Chair: Choe Pok Yon

LIGHT INDUSTRY COMMISSION
Pyongyang
Chair: Kim Bok Sin

MINING INDUSTRY COMMISSION
Pyongyang
Chair: Cho Chang Tok

MINISTRY OF THE ATOMIC INDUSTRY
Pyongyang
Minister: Choe Hak Kun

MINISTRY OF THE CHEMICAL INDUSTRY
Pyongyang
Minister: Kim Hwan

MINISTRY OF CITY MANAGEMENT
Pyongyang
Minister: Li Chol Bong

MINISTRY OF COMMERCE
Pyongyang
Minister: Han Chang Kun

MINISTRY OF COMMUNICATIONS
Pyongyang
Minister: Kim Yong Chae

MINISTRY OF CONSTRUCTION
Pyongyang
Minister: Cho Chol Chun

MINISTRY OF CONSTRUCTION AND BUILDING MATERIALS
Pyongyang
Minister: Chu Yong Hun

MINISTRY OF CULTURE AND ART
Pyongyang
Minister: Li Chang Chol

MINISTRY OF FINANCE
Pyongyang
Minister: Youn Ki Jong

MINISTRY OF FOREIGN AFFAIRS
Pyongyang
Minister: Choe Jong Gun

MINISTRY OF FOREIGN TRADE
Pyongyang
Minister: Kim Dal Hyon

MINISTRY OF FORESTRY
Pyongyang
Minister: Kim Jae Yul

MINISTRY OF JOINT-VENTURE INDUSTRY
Pyongyang
Minister: Choe Hui Chong

MINISTRY OF LABOUR ADMINISTRATION
Pyongyang
Minister: Li Chae Yun

MINISTRY OF LOCAL INDUSTRY
Pyongyang
Minister: Kim Song Ku

MINISTRY OF THE MACHINE INDUSTRY
Pyongyang
Minister: Kye Hong Sun

MINISTRY OF THE METAL INDUSTRY
Pyongyang
Minister: Choe Man Hyon

MINISTRY OF NATURAL RESOURCES DEVELOPMENT
Pyongyang
Minister: Kim Se Yong

MINISTRY OF THE PEOPLE'S ARMED FORCES
Pyongyang
Minister: Vice-Marshal O Jin U

MINISTRY OF PUBLIC HEALTH
Pyongyang
Minister: Li Jong Ryul

MINISTRY OF PUBLIC SECURITY
Pyongyang
Minister: Paek Hak Nim

MINISTRY OF RAILWAYS
Pyongyang
Minister: Pak Yong Sok

MINISTRY OF THE SHIPBUILDING INDUSTRY
Pyongyang
Minister: Li Sok

PHYSICAL EDUCATION COMMISSION
Pyongyang
Chair: Kim Yu Sun

POWER INDUSTRY COMMISSION
Pyongyang
Chair: Li Ji Chan

PUBLIC WELFARE COMMISSION
Pyongyang
Chair: Kong Jin Tae

STATE INSPECTION COMMISSION
Pyongyang
Chair: Yi Yong Mu

STATE PLANNING COMMISSION
Pyongyang
Chair: Hong Song Nam

STATE SCIENTIFIC AND TECHNOLOGICAL COMMISSION
Pyongyang
Chair: Li Cha Pang

TRANSPORT COMMISSION
Pyongyang
Chair: Li Gil Song

GOVERNMENT AGENCIES AND ORGANIZATIONS

Advisory and Supervisory Body

Korean Council of the Central Federation of Consumption Co-operative Trade Union: Pyongyang.

Business and Economy

BANKING

Foreign Trade Bank of the DPRK: Jungsongdong, Central District, Pyongyang; tel 34531; telex 5460; Gov: Kim Ung Chol; Dep Govs: Pak Yang Sok, Kim Jun Chol; f 1959; operates payments with foreign banks and controls foreign currency transactions.

Korea Daesong Bank: Chungsong-dong, Grand Study-House St, Central District, Pyongyang; tel 43002; telex 5479; Pres: Chon Myong Hui; f 1978.

Korean Central Bank: Nammundong, Central District, Pyongyang; Pres: Yon Sung U (mem of the Administration Council); f 1946; bank of issue; supervisory and control bank.

FINANCIAL AGENCY

Korean International General Joint Venture Co: Pyongyang; Dir: Kim Bok Sin; f 1986; promotes joint economic ventures with foreign countries.

INSURANCE

Korea Foreign Insurance Co (Chosunbohom): Potonggang District, Pyongyang; tel 45477; telex 5464; Pres: Pak Yong Nam; f 1957; conducts marine, automobile, aviation and fire insurance, reinsurance of all classes, and all foreign insurance; agencies in foreign ports.

State Insurance Bureau: Central District, Pyongyang; tel 38196; handles life, fire, accident, marine, hull insurance and reinsurance.

NATIONALIZED INDUSTRY

General Central Materials Enterprises: Pyongyang; Chair: Li Pil Song (mem of the Administration Council).

TRADE

Korea Building Materials Export and Import Corpn: Central District, Pyongyang; telex 5467; chemical building materials, woods, timbers, cement, sheet glass, etc.

Korea Chemicals Export and Import Corpn: Central District, Pyongyang; telex 5358; petroleum and petroleum products, raw materials for the chemical industry, rubber and rubber products, fertilizers, etc.

Korea Daesong Trading Corpn: Potonggang District, Pyongyang; telex 5473; machinery and equipment, chemical products, textiles, agricultural products, etc.

Korea Ferrous Metals Export and Import Corpn: Central District, Pyongyang; telex 5491; steel products.

Korea First Equipment Export and Import Co: Central District, Pyongyang; tel 34825; telex 5466; Pres: Chae Won Chol; f 1960; export and import of ferrous and non-ferrous metallurgical plants, geological exploration and mining equipment, communication equipment, machine-building plant, etc; construction of public facilities such as airports, hotels, tourist facilities, etc; joint-venture business in similar projects.

Korea Foodstuffs Export and Import Corpn: Tongdaewon District, Pyongyang; telex 5353; cereals, wines, meat, canned foods, fruits, cigarettes, etc.

Korea Fruit and Vegetables Export Corpn: Central District, Pyongyang; tel 35117; telex 5946; vegetables, fruit and their products.

Korea General Export and Import Corpn: Central District, Pyongyang; telex 5359; plate glass, tiles, granite, locks, medicinal herbs, foodstuffs and light industrial products.

Korea Hyopdong Trading Corpn: Central District, Pyongyang; telex 5614; fabrics, glass products, ceramics, chemical goods, building materials, foodstuffs, machinery, etc.

Korea International Exhibition Corpn: Sosong District, Pyongyang; organizes commodity exhibitions of the DPRK abroad and of foreign producers in North Korea.

Korea Jei Equipment Export and Import Corpn: Sungri St, Central District, Pyongyang; tel 32633; telex 5466; machine plant, agricultural and irrigation equipment, equipment for chemical, mining, food and electronic industries.

Korea Jesam Equipment Export and Import Corpn: Central District, Pyongyang; chemical, textile, pharmaceutical and light industry plant.

Korea Light Industry Products Export and Import Corpn: Juchetab St, Tongdaewon District, Pyongyang; tel 37661; telex 5353; export of silk, cigarettes, canned goods, drinking glasses, ceramics, handbags, pens, plastic flowers, musical instruments, etc; import of chemicals, dyestuffs, machinery, etc.

Korea Machinery and Equipment Export and Import Corpn: Tongdaewon District, Pyongyang; tel 33449; telex 5936; f 1948; metallurgical machinery and equipment, electric machines, building machinery, farm machinery, diesel engines, etc.

Korea Maibong Trading Corpn: Central District, Pyongyang; non-ferrous metal ingots and allied products, non-metallic minerals, agricultural and marine products.

Korea Marine Products Export and Import Corpn: Central District, Pyongyang; telex 5463; canned, frozen, dried, salted and smoked fish, fishing equipment and supplies.

Korea Minerals Export and Import Corpn: Central District, Pyongyang; telex 5469; minerals, solid fuel, graphite, precious stones, etc.

Korea Namheung Trading Co: Tongdaewon District, Pyongyang; fertilizers, rayon yarns and other chemical products.

Korea Ponghwa General Trading Corpn: Central District, Pyongyang; telex 5462; machinery, metal products, minerals and chemicals.

Korea Publications Export and Import Corpn: Yokjondong, Bodnamu St, Central District, Pyongyang; export and import of books, periodicals, postcards, paintings, cassettes, postage stamps and records.

Korea Pyongchon Trading Co: Central District, Pyongyang; telex 5354; axles, springs, spikes, bolts and bicycles.

Korea Pyongyang Trading Co Ltd: Central District, POB 550, Pyongyang; telex 5354; pig iron, steel, magnesia clinker, textiles, etc.

Korea Senbong Trading Corpn: Central District, Pyongyang; ferrous and non-ferrous metals, rolled steels, mineral ores, chemicals, etc.

Korea Somyu Hyopdong Trading Corpn: Oesong District, Pyongyang; telex 5496; clothing and textiles.

Korea Songhwa Trading Corpn: Oesong District, Pyongyang; ceramics, glass, hardware, leaf tobaccos, fruit and wines.

Korea Technical Corpn: Central District, Pyongyang; telex 5466; scientific and technical co-operation.

Korea Unha Trading Corpn: Tongdaewon District, Pyongyang; telex 5492; clothing and fibres.

Korean Committee for the Promotion of International Trade: Central District, Pyongyang; Sec-Gen: Pak Se Chan.

Korean General Merchandise Export and Import Corpn: Pyongyang.

Defence

Armed Forces: Pyongyang; Chief of the Korean People's Army (KPA): Gen Choe Kwang.

Education and Research

Academy of Sciences: Pyongyang; Pres: Kim Kyong Pong (mem of the Administration Council).

Legal and Judiciary

Central Court: Pyongyang; highest judicial organ; supervises the work of all courts.

Central Procurator's Office: Pyongyang; supervises work of procurator's offices in provinces, cities and counties.

Media

BROADCASTING

Korean Central Broadcasting Committee: Pyongyang; telex 5612; Chair: Chu Hyon Ok; Vice-Chairs: Li Jong Nam, Ro Sok Gyu, Cha Sung-su; programmes relayed nationally with local programmes supplied by local radio committees; home broadcasting 22 hours daily; foreign broadcasts in Russian, Chinese, English, French, German, Japanese, Spanish and Arabic; loudspeakers are installed in factories and in open spaces in all towns.

Mansudae Television Station: Mansudae, Pyongyang; telex 5612; f 1983; broadcasts cultural programmes, music and dance, foreign films and news reports at weekends.

NEWS AND INFORMATION

Central Statistics Bureau: Pyongyang; Dir: Sin Kyong Sik (mem of the Administration Council).

Korean Central News Agency (KCNA): Potonggang-dong 1, Potonggang District, Pyongyang; Pres: Kim Gi Ryong; f 1946; sole distributing agency for news in the DPRK; daily bulletins in English, Russian, French and Spanish.

Mining and Energy

State Committee for Atomic Energy: Sosong District, Pyongyang; Chair: Choe Hak Kun; f 1952.

Tourism

Ryohaengsa (Korean International Tourist Bureau): Central District, Pyongyang; Dir: Han Gyong Un; f 1956.

Transport

CIVIL AVIATION

Chosonminhang (Civil Aviation Administration of the DPRK): Sunan District, Pyongyang; telex 5471; Pres: Hwang Ryong Hwan; f 1954; internal services and external flights to the People's Republic of China, the USSR and the German Democratic Republic; charter services are operated to Asia, Africa and Europe.

SHIPPING

Korea Chartering Corpn: Central District, Pyongyang; telex 5357; arranges cargo transportation and chartering.

Korea Foreign Transportation Corpn: Central District, Pyongyang; telex 5498; arranges transportation of export and import cargoes (transit goods and charters).

Korea Tonghae Shipping Co: Oesong District, Pyongyang; telex 5461; arranges transportation by Korean vessels.

Korean-Polish Shipping Co Ltd: Moranbong District, Pyongyang; tel 52534; telex 5480; maritime trade mainly with Polish and DPRK ports.

REPUBLIC OF KOREA

Head of State

Under the 1987 Constitution, executive power is vested in the President, who is elected for one term of five years by universal adult suffrage. The President governs with the assistance of an appointed State Council (Cabinet), led by a Prime Minister.

President: Roh Tae-Woo (took office 25 February 1988).

Office of the President: Chong Wa Dae, 1 Sejong-no, Chongno-ku, Seoul; tel (2) 770-0011.

Legislature

Legislative power is vested in the unicameral National Assembly, popularly elected for a four-year term. The National Assembly has 299 members, of whom 224 are directly elected. Of the remaining 75 seats, 38 are awarded to the party receiving the most votes by direct election, while the other parties share 37, allocated in proportion to seats won directly.

National Assembly: 1-1 Yoido-dong, Youngdungpo-ku, Seoul; tel (2) 782-3211; Speaker: Kim Jai-Son.

MINISTRIES AND GOVERNMENT DEPARTMENTS

OFFICE OF THE PRIME MINISTER
77 Sejong-no, Chongno-ku, Seoul
Tel (2) 720-2006
Prime Minister: Kang Young-Hoon
Deputy Prime Minister: Lee Seung-Yun

ECONOMIC PLANNING BOARD
1 Jungang-dong, Gwachon City, Kyonggi Province
Tel (2) 503-9020; telex 23202
Minister: Lee Seung-Yun

MINISTRY OF AGRICULTURE, FORESTRY AND FISHERIES
1 Jungang-dong, Gwachon City, Kyonggi Province
Tel (2) 503-7209; telex 24759
Minister: Kong Bo-Song

MINISTRY OF COMMUNICATIONS
100 Sejong-no, Chongno-ku, Seoul 110
Tel (2) 750-2811; telex 24819
Minister: Lee Woo-Jae

MINISTRY OF CONSTRUCTION
1 Jungang-dong, Gwachon City, Kyonggi Province
Tel (2) 503-7312; telex 24755
Minister: Kwon Yong-Gack

MINISTRY OF CULTURE AND INFORMATION
82 Sejong-no, Chongno-ku, Seoul
Tel (2) 720-4728; telex 23203
Minister: Choe Byung-Yul

MINISTRY OF EDUCATION
77-6 Sejong-no, Chongno-ku, Seoul
Tel (2) 720-3309; telex 24758
Minister: Chung Won-Shik

MINISTRY OF ENERGY AND RESOURCES
1 Jungang-dong, Gwachon City, Kyonggi Province
Tel (2) 503-9611; telex 23472
Minister: Hee-Il

MINISTRY OF FINANCE
2nd Government Bldg, 1 Jungang-dong, Gwachon City, Kyonggi Province
Tel (2) 503-9211; telex 23243
Minister: Chung Yung-Euy

MINISTRY OF FOREIGN AFFAIRS
77 Sejong-no, Chongno-ku, Seoul
Tel (2) 720-2339; telex 24651
Minister: Choi Ho-Joong
Deputy Minister: Hong Soon Young

MINISTRY OF GOVERNMENT ADMINISTRATION
77 Sejong-no, Chongno-ku, Seoul
Tel (2) 720-4351; telex 24803
Minister: Lee Yun-Taek

MINISTRY OF HEALTH AND SOCIAL AFFAIRS
1 Jungang-dong, Gwachon City, Kyonggi Province
Tel (2) 503-7505; telex 23230
Minister: Kim Jung-Soo

MINISTRY OF HOME AFFAIRS
77 Sejong-no, Chongno-ku, Seoul
Tel (2) 731-2121; telex 24756
Minister: Ahn Eung-Mo

MINISTRY OF JUSTICE
1 Jungang-dong, Gwachon City, Kyonggi Province
Tel (2) 503-7012; telex 24757
Minister: Yi Jong-Nam

MINISTRY OF LABOUR
1 Jungang-dong, Gwachon City, Kyonggi Province
Tel 503-9714; telex 24718
Minister: Choi Young-Choul

MINISTRY OF LEGISLATION
77 Sejong-no, Chongno-ku, Seoul
Tel (2) 720-3554
Minister: Hyun Hong-Choo

MINISTRY OF NATIONAL DEFENCE
101 Huam-dong, Yongsan-ku, Seoul
Tel (2) 754-3843
Minister: Lee Sang-Hoon

MINISTRY OF PATRIOTS' AND VETERANS' AFFAIRS
17-23 Yoido-dong, Youngdungpo-ku, Seoul
Tel (2) 780-9601; fax (2) 784-1087
Minister: Lee Sang-Yon

MINISTRY OF POLITICAL AFFAIRS
77 Sejong-no, Chongno-ku, Seoul
Tel (2) 739-6543
Ministers: Parl Chul-Un, Lee Kye-Soon

MINISTRY OF SCIENCE AND TECHNOLOGY
1 Jungang-dong, Gwachon City, Kyonggi Province
Tel (2) 503-7609; telex 24230
Minister: Chung Kun-Mo

MINISTRY OF SPORTS
77 Sejong-no, Chongno-ku, Seoul
Tel (2) 720-2181; telex 22926
Minister: Chung Dong-Sung

MINISTRY OF TRADE AND INDUSTRY
1 Jungang-dong, Gwachon City, Kyonggi Province
Tel (2) 503-9405; telex 24478
Minister: Park Pil-Soo

MINISTRY OF TRANSPORTATION
168, 2-ka, Bongnae-dong, Seoul
Tel (2) 392-9566; telex 24778
Minister: Kim Chang-Sik

NATIONAL UNIFICATION BOARD
77-6 Sejong-no, Chongno-ku, Seoul 110
Tel (2) 720-2104
Minister: Hong Sung-Chul

GOVERNMENT AGENCIES AND ORGANIZATIONS

Advisory and Supervisory Bodies

Board of Audit and Inspection: 2-26 Samchung-dong, Chongno-ku, Seoul 110-230; tel (2) 732-6305; telex 24628; fax (2) 735-5678; Chair: Young Joon Kim; f 1948; audit of central and local Govt agencies, public enterprises, and other organizations given Govt subsidies, grants, etc.

Office of Monopoly Administration (Tobacco and Ginseng): 112 Inui-dong, Chongno-ku, Seoul; tel (2) 764-5051; telex 24670; Dir-Gen: Lee Kyu-Sung.

Agriculture and the Environment

AGRICULTURE

Agriculture and Fishery Marketing Corpn: 191 Hangang-no, Yongsan-ku, CPOB 3212, Seoul 140; tel (2) 795-8201; telex 23297; Pres: Ahn Kyo-Duck; Exec Vice-Pres: Shin Keun-Ho; f 1967; integrated devt for secondary processing and marketing distribution for agricultural and fisheries products.

Office of Fisheries Administration: 541, 5-ka, Namdaemun-no, Chung-ku, Seoul; tel (2) 23-0810; telex 24719; Dir-Gen: Kim Jong-Soo.

THE ENVIRONMENT

Office of Environment Administration: 5-1 Kongpyong-dong, Chongno-ku, Seoul; tel (2) 720-2619; Dir-Gen: Park Jun-ik.

Office of Forestry Administration: 1 Chongyangni 2-dong, Tongdaemun-ku, Seoul; tel (2) 965-4211; Dir-Gen: Sohn Jong-Ho.

Business and Economy

BANKING

Bank of Korea: 110, 3-ka, Namdaemun-no, Chung-ku, Seoul 100; tel (2) 778-5011; telex 24711; Gov: Kim Kun; Dep Gov: Kim Myung-Ho; f 1950; bank of issue; 15 domestic brs, 8 overseas offices.

Citizen's National Bank: 9-1, 2-ka, Namdaemun-no, Chung-ku, CPOB 815, Seoul 100; tel (2) 754-1211; telex 23481; Pres: Lee Sang-Chul; Dep Pres: Kyrun Jae Min; f 1963.

Export-Import Bank of Korea: 16-1 Yoido-dong, Youngdungpo-ku, CPOB 641, Seoul 150-606; tel (2) 784-1021; telex 26595; fax (2) 784-1030; Chair and Pres: Whang Chang-Ki; Dep Pres: Sung Uk-Ki; f 1976; provision of medium- and long-term export credits, export insurance, investment facilities and advisory services.

Korea Development Bank: 10-2 Kwanchul-dong, Chongno-ku, Seoul 100-600; tel (2) 733-2121; telex 27463; fax (2) 733-4768; Gov: Lee Dong-Ho; Dep Gov: Kim Byong Taek; f 1954; 7 overseas brs.

Korea Exchange Bank: 181, 2-ka, Ulchiro, Chung-ku, Seoul 100; tel (2) 771-46; telex 23141; Pres: Rhee Yong Man; Vice-Pres: Cho Taek-Yung; f 1967.

Korea Housing Bank: 36-3 Yoido-dong, Youngdungpo-ku, Seoul 150-010; tel (2) 784-7711; telex 27879; fax (2) 784-8324; Pres: Chun Young-Soo; Exec Vice-Pres: Kim Jai-Lee; f 1967; 187 brs.

Korea Long-Term Credit Bank: 15-22 Yoido-dong, Youngdungpo-ku, Seoul 150-010; tel (2) 782-0111; telex 26342; Pres: Ham Tae-Yong; Dep Pres and Dir: Kim Yeon-Soo; f 1967; assists in the devt of private enterprise by medium- and long-term financing.

FINANCIAL AGENCIES

Office of the National Tax Administration: 24, 4-ka, Yangpyong-dong, Youngdungpo-ku, Seoul; tel (2) 634-7711; telex 24717; Dir-Gen: Ahn Moo-Hyuk.

TRADE

Korea Exhibition Centre: 159 Samsong-dong, Kangnam-ku, Seoul; tel (2) 550-1114; telex 24594; Pres: Han Bong-Soo; f 1976.

Korea Industrial Property Office: 823 Yeoksam-dong, Kangnam-ku, Seoul; tel (2) 568-8151; telex 28667; fax (2) 553-9584; Commr: Park Hong-Shik; f 1946; promotion of inventive activity, registration of patent applications, resolution of disputes over industrial property.

Korea Trade Promotion Corpn: 10-1, 2-ka, Huehyun-dong, Chung-ku, CPOB 1621, Seoul; tel (2) 753-4180; telex 23659; f 1962; promotion of overseas trade.

Office of Customs Administration: 355 Chunglim-dong, Chung-ku, Seoul; tel (2) 562-7141; telex 24346; Dir-Gen: Kim Uk-Tae.

Defence

Agency for National Security Planning: 70 Sejong-no, Chongno-ku, Seoul; tel (2) 720-2201; Dir: Chang Se-Tong.

Armed Forces: Yongsan-ku, Seoul; tel (2) 3681; Chair, Joint Chiefs of Staff: Gen Chong Chin-Kwan.

Air Force: Daebang-dong, Youngdungpo-ku, Seoul; tel (2) 829-3500; Chief of Staff: Gen So Tong-Yul.

Army: Yongsan-ku, Seoul; tel (2) 792-0100; Chief of Staff: Gen Park Hee Do.

Navy: Daebang-dong, Youngdungpo-ku, Seoul; tel (2) 829-3566; Chief of Naval Operations: Adm Choe Sang-Hwa.

National Police: 77 Sejong-no, Chongno-ku, Seoul; tel (2) 720-2540; Dir-Gen: Kong Min-Chang.

Development and Planning

Office of Industrial Advancement Administration: 94-267 Youngdungpo-dong, Youngdungpo-ku, Seoul; tel (2) 720-4324; Dir-Gen: Kim Hyung-Bae.

Office of Rural Development Administration: 250 Sodun-dong, Suwon; Dir-Gen: Kim Mun-Heon.

Energy

Atomic Energy Bureau: Ministry of Science and Technology, 1 Jungang-dong, Gwachon City, Kyonggi Province; tel (2) 503-7644; telex 24230; Dir-Gen: Han Young-Sung; f 1973, reorganized 1979; admin agency comprising five divisions: Planning, Research and Devt, International Co-operation, Radiation Safety and Reactor Divisions.

Atomic Energy Commission: Ministry of Science and Technology, 1 Jungang-dong, Gwachon City, Kyonggi Province; tel (2) 503-7606; telex 24230; Chair: Cho-Soon; Vice-Chair: Lee Tae-Sup; responsible for fundamental plans and policies, co-ordination of activities, furtherance of research and training of personnel.

Legal and Judiciary

Office of the Prosecutor-General: 88 Sosomun-dong, Chung-ku, Seoul; tel (2) 22-3992; telex 24717; Prosecutor-Gen: Kim Suk Hwi.

Supreme Court: 37 Sosomun-dong, Chung-ku, Seoul; tel (2) 22-4201; Chief Justice: Lee Il-Kyu; highest court; the Chief Justice and the other Justices of the Supreme Court are appointed by the President for six years; receives and decides on appeals against decisions of the Appellate courts in civil and criminal cases; acts as final tribunal to review decisions of courts-martial and to try election cases.

Media

BROADCASTING

Korean Broadcasting System (KBS): 18 Yoido-dong, Youngdungpo-ku, Seoul 150; tel (2) 781-1000; telex 24599; Pres: Chung Ku-Ho; f 1926; overseas radio broadcasts in Korean, English, German, Indonesian, Chinese, Japanese, French, Spanish, Russian and Arabic; 24 local broadcasting and 604 relay stations.

NEWS AND INFORMATION

Korean Overseas Information Service: 1 Sejong-no, Chongno-ku, Seoul; tel (2) 720-4907; telex 23203; Dir-Gen: Yoo Tae-Wan.

National Bureau of Statistics: c/o Economic Planning Board, 90 Gyoungwoon-dong, Chongno-ku, Seoul; tel (2) 725-5371; telex 2350; collection, analysis and publication of statistics.

Tourism

Korea National Tourism Corpn: KNTC Bldg, 10 Ta-dong, Chung-ku, CPOB 903, Seoul 100; tel (2) 757-6030; telex 28555; Pres: Ha Dae-Don; f 1962; promotion of tourism.

Transport

Korea Highway Corpn: 293-1 Geumto-dong, Seongnam-shi, Gyeonggido; tel (2) 234-8141; telex 32212; Pres: Yun Tae-Kyun; f 1969; responsible for construction, maintenance and management of toll roads.

Korea Maritime and Port Authority: 112-2 Inui-dong, Chongno-ku, Seoul 110; tel (2) 744-4030; telex 26528; Admin: Chin Yom; f 1976; supervises all aspects of shipping and port-related affairs.

Korean National Railroads (KNR): 122, 2-ka, Bongnae-dong, Chung-ku, Seoul 100-162; tel (2) 392-0078; telex 24802; fax (2) 392-7105; Admin: Kim Ha Kyeong; f 1963; freight and passenger services.

Seoul Metropolitan Subway Corpn: 447-7 Bangbae-dong, Kangnam-ku, Seoul; tel (2) 582-5892; telex 25172; Pres: Han Jin-Hee; f 1970.

KUWAIT

Head of State

Executive power is vested in the Amir, the Head of State chosen by, and from members of the ruling family. Executive power is exercised by a Council of Ministers, headed by a Prime Minister, who is appointed by the Amir and who recommends the appointment of Ministers. The Amir has ruled by decree since the dissolution of the National Assembly.

Amir: HH Sheikh Jaber al-Ahmad as-Sabah (succeeded on the death of his cousin, 31 December 1977).

Office of the Amir: POB 799, 13008 Safat, Arabian Gulf St, Kuwait City; tel 2439021; telex 22700.

Legislature

The National Assembly, comprising 50 members elected for four years by literate adult male Kuwaiti citizens (excluding members of the armed forces) was dissolved by Amiri decree in July 1986. Some sections of the Constitution, including the stipulation that new elections should be held within two months of dissolving the assembly were suspended.

Majlis al-Umma (National Assembly): Kuwait; tel 2439031.

MINISTRIES AND GOVERNMENT DEPARTMENTS

OFFICE OF THE COUNCIL OF MINISTERS
POB 1397, Safat, Kuwait City
Tel 2455333; telex 22796
Minister of State for Cabinet Affairs: Rashid Abd al-Aziz ar-Rashid
Minister of State for Municipal Affairs: Muhammad as-Sayed Abd al-Mohsin as-Rifa'i
Minister of State for Services Affairs: Isa Muhammad Ibrahim al-Mazidi

OFFICE OF HH CROWN PRINCE AND PRIME MINISTER
POB 4, Safat, Kuwait City
Tel 2441900; telex 44343
Crown Prince and Prime Minister: Sheikh Saad al-Abdullah as-Salim as-Sabah
Deputy Prime Minister: Sheikh Sabah al-Ahmad al-Jaber as-Sabah

MINISTRY OF AMIRI DIWAN AFFAIRS
POB 799, 13008 Safat, Arabian Gulf St, Kuwait City
Tel 2439021; telex 22700
Minister: Sheikh Khalid al-Ahmad al-Jaber

MINISTRY OF AWQAF (RELIGIOUS ENDOWMENTS) AND ISLAMIC AFFAIRS
POB 4, 13001 Safat, al-Morkab St, Ministries Complex, Kuwait City
Tel 2466300; telex 44735
Minister: Khalid Ahmad Saad Al-Jassar

MINISTRY OF COMMERCE AND INDUSTRY
POB 2944, 13030 Safat, Kuwait City
Tel 2463600; telex 22682
Minister: Faisal Abd ar-Razzaq al-Khalid

MINISTRY OF COMMUNICATIONS
POB 16, 13001 Safat, Kuwait City
Tel 4819033; telex 22197
Minister: Abdullah Abd-al Mohsin ash-Sharhan

MINISTRY OF DEFENCE
POB 1170, Safat, Kuwait City
Tel 4819277; telex 22784
Minister: Sheikh Nawaf al-Ahmad al-Jaber as-Sabah

MINISTRY OF EDUCATION
POB 7, 13001 Safat, Hilali St, Kuwait City
Tel 2455454; telex 23166
Minister: Anwar Abdullah an-Nouri
Minister of Higher Education: Dr Ali Abdullah ash-Shamlan

MINISTRY OF ELECTRICITY AND WATER
POB 12, 13001 Safat, Kuwait City
Tel 4896000; telex 30062
Minister: Humud Abdullah ar-Raqubah

MINISTRY OF FINANCE
POB 9, 13001 Safat, al-Morkab St, Ministries Complex, Kuwait City
Tel 2468200; telex 22582
Minister: Jassim Muhammad al-Kharafi

MINISTRY OF FOREIGN AFFAIRS
POB 3, 13001 Safat, Arabian Gulf St, Kuwait City
Tel 2425141; telex 22042
Minister: Sheikh Sabah al-Ahmad al-Jaber as-Sabah
Minister of State: Sa'ud Muhammad al-Usaymi

MINISTRY OF HOUSING
POB 2935, Safat, Kuwait City
Tel 2467300
Minister of State: Nasser Abdullah ar-Rudan

MINISTRY OF INFORMATION
POB 193, 13002 Safat, as-Sour St, Kuwait City
Tel 2415300; telex 46151
Minister: Sheikh Jaber Mubarak al-Hamad as-Sabah

MINISTRY OF THE INTERIOR
POB 11, 13001 Safat, Kuwait City
Tel 4816111; telex 22507; fax 4847734
Minister: Sheikh Salim as-Sabah as-Salim as-Sabah

MINISTRY OF JUSTICE AND LEGAL AND ADMINISTRATIVE AFFAIRS
POB 6, 13001 Safat, al-Morkab St, Ministries Complex, Kuwait City
Tel 2465600; telex 44302
Minister: Dhari Abdullah al-Uthman ar-Rashid

MINISTRY OF LABOUR AND SOCIAL AFFAIRS
POB 563, 13006 Safat, al-Morkab St, Ministries Complex, Kuwait City
Tel 2464500; telex 30329
Minister: Sheikh Nasser Muhammad al-Ahmad al-Jaber as-Sabah

MINISTRY OF OIL
POB 5077, 13051 Safat, Fahd as-Salem St, Kuwait City
Tel 2415201; telex 22363
Minister: Sheikh Ali al-Khalifa al-Athbi as-Sabah

MINISTRY OF PLANNING
POB 15, 13001 Safat, Kuwait City
Tel 2423100; telex 22468
Minister: Dr Abd ar-Rahman Abdullah al-Awadi

MINISTRY OF PUBLIC HEALTH
POB 5, 13001 Safat, Arabian Gulf St, Kuwait City
Tel 2462900; telex 22729
Minister: Dr Abd ar-Razzak Yousuf al-Abd ar-Razzak

MINISTRY OF PUBLIC WORKS
POB 8, 13001 Safat, Mubarak al-Kabir St, Kuwait City
Tel 2449301; telex 22753
Minister: Abd ar-Rahman Ibrahim al-Houti

GOVERNMENT AGENCIES AND ORGANIZATIONS

Advisory and Supervisory Bodies

Audit Bureau: POB 1509, Safat, Kuwait City; tel 2421036; under Ministry of Finance.

Shuaiba Area Authority SAA: POB 4690, 13047 Safat, Kuwait City; POB 10033, Shuaiba; tel 3260903; telex 44205; Dir-Gen: Suleiman K. al-Hamad; f 1964; independent Govt authority to supervise and run the industrial area and Port of Shuaiba; has powers and duties to develop the area and its industries which include an oil refinery, cement factory, fishing plant, power stations and distillation plants, chemical fertilizer and petrochemical industries, sanitary ware factory, asbestos plant and sand lime bricks plant.

Agriculture

Public Authority for Agriculture Affairs and Fish Resources: POB 21422, 13075 Safat, Kuwait City; tel 4711155; telex 30072; fax 4739148; Chair and Dir-Gen: Ibrahim Duaij al-Sabah; Dep Dir-Gen, Technical Affairs: Ahmad Muhammad Sayeed al-Nakib; Dep Dir-Gen, Administrative and Financial Affairs: Ahmad Saleh al-Oqab; f 1983; supervisory activities in the areas of agriculture, landscaping, fisheries and animal wealth.

Art and Culture

Kuwait National Museum: Safat, Kuwait City; tel 2451194.

National Council for Culture, Arts and Literature: POB 23996, Safat, Kuwait City; tel 2455333; telex 44554.

Business and Economy

BANKING

Burgan Bank SAK: POB 5389, 13054 Safat, Ahmad al-Jaber St, Kuwait City; tel 2439000; telex 23309; Chair and Man Dir: Sheikh Ahmad Abdullah al-Ahmad as-Sabah; Gen Man: Muhammad Aqil Tawfiqi; f 1975; 51% owned by the Govt; 49% by Kuwaiti public; 13 brs.

Central Bank of Kuwait: POB 526, 13006 Safat, Abdullah as-Salem St, Kuwait City; tel 2449200; telex 22101; Gov: Sheikh Salem Abd al-Aziz Saud as-Sabah; f 1969.

Savings and Credit Bank: POB 1454, 13015 Safat, al-Hilali St, Kuwait City; tel 2411301; telex 22211; fax 2425516; Chair and Gen Man: Yousef Ali al-Houti; Dep Gen Man: Saleh H. al-Yahya; f 1965.

INSURANCE

Gulf Insurance Co KSC: POB 1040, 13011 Safat, Kuwait City; tel 2423384; telex 22203; Chair: Sulaiman Hamad ad-Dalali; f 1962; 75% Govt-owned; covers all classes of insurance.

NATIONALIZED INDUSTRY

National Industries Co SAK: POB 417, 13005 Safat, Kuwait City; tel 4849466; telex 22165; Chair and Man Dir: Mufarrej I. al-Mufarrej; f 1960; 59.2% Govt-owned, with controlling interest in various construction enterprises.

TRADE

General Directorate of Customs: POB 16, Gamal Abdul Nasir St, Safat, Kuwait City; tel 4817255.

Kuwait Foreign Trading, Contracting and Investment

Co SAK (KFTCIC): POB 5665, 13057 Safat, Omar Bin al-Khattab St, Sharq, Kuwait City; tel 2449031; telex 22021; Chair and Man Dir: Abdullah Ahmad al-Gabandi; f 1965 by Amiri decree; private banking, investments and real estate; 99.2% Govt-owned and 0.8% publicly-owned.

Defence

Armed Forces: c/o Ministry of Defence, POB 1170, Safat, Kuwait City; tel 4819277; telex 22784; Chief of Staff: Maj-Gen Mizayed Abd ar-Rahman as-Sane.

Air Force: address as above; Commdr: Dawoud Shaheen al-Ghanim.

Navy: Safat, Kuwait City; Commdr: Habib al-Meel; consists of a coastguard force administered by the Ministry of the Interior.

Development and Planning

INVESTMENT

Kuwait Fund for Arab Economic Development: POB 2921, 13030 Safat, cnr Mubarak al-Kabir St and al-Hilali St, Kuwait City; tel 2468800; telex 22025; fax 2429063; Chair: Minister of Finance, Jassim Muhammad al-Kharafi; Dir-Gen: Bader M. al-Humaidhi; Dep Dir-Gen, Operations: Abdulwahab al-Bader; Dep Dir-Gen, Admin: Khaled al-Shalfan; f 1961; wholly Govt-owned; under Ministry of Finance; promotes economic devt in Arab and other developing countries by providing loans and technical assistance grants.

Kuwait Investment Co SAK (KIC): POB 1005, Al Manakh Bldg, Mubarak Al Kabir St, 13011 Safat, Kuwait City; tel 2438111; telex 22115; Chair and Man Dir: Hamad Muhammad al-Bahar; Gen Man: Hilal Mishari al-Mutairi; f 1961; 50% Govt-owned and 50% owned by Kuwaiti nationals; investment banking; international banking and investment.

PLANNING

Arab Planning Institute: POB 5834, 13059 Safat, Kuwait City; tel 4843130; telex 22996; Dir: Abdulla Muhammad Ali; Dep Dir: Muhammad el Awad Galaleldin; f 1966; runs short- and medium-term training courses for Govt officials of Arab countries; organizes conferences, seminars, group meetings and discussion sessions; undertakes studies, research and consultancy services in the field of social and economic planning and devt.

Kuwait Planning Board: c/o Ministry of Planning, POB 15, 13001 Safat, Kuwait City; tel 2428200; telex 22468; Dir-Gen: Ahmad Ali ad-Duaij; f 1962; supervises long-term devt plans; publishes information on Kuwait's economic activity through the Central Statistical Office.

Energy

Kuwait Petroleum Corpn (KPC): POB 26565, 13126 Safat, Salhia Complex, Fahed as-Salem St, Kuwait City; tel 2455455; telex 44875; Chair: Minister of Oil, Sheikh Ali al-Khalifa al-Athbi as-Sabah; Dep Chair and Man Dir, Planning, Admin and Finance: Abd ar-Razzaq Muhammad Mulla Hussein; f 1980; 'umbrella' organization to run oil industry; controls cos listed below:

Kuwait Aviation Fuelling Co KSC: POB 1654, Safat, Kuwait City; tel 4749552; telex 23056; Man Dir: Bader ar-Refai.

Kuwait Foreign Petroleum Exploration Co KSC

(KUFPEC): Kuwait City; tel 2455455; telex 244875; Chair: Faisal Kazmawi; f 1981; overseas oil exploration and devt.

Kuwait National Petroleum Co KSC (KNPC): POB 70, 13001 Safat, Ali as-Salem St, Kuwait City; tel 2420121; telex 22006; Chair and Man Dir: Ahmad Abd al-Mohsin al-Mutair; f 1960; oil refining, production of liquefied petroleum gas, and domestic marketing and distribution of petroleum by-products.

Kuwait Oil Co KSC (KOC): POB 9758, 61008 Ahmadi; tel 3989111; telex 44211; Chair and Man Dir: Abd al-Malik M. al-Gharabally; f 1934.

Kuwait Petroleum International Ltd (KPI): 80 New Bond St, London, W1, England; tel (1) 491-4000; Pres: Nader Sultan; marketing division of KPC; controls 4,800 petrol retail stations in Europe, under the trade name 'Q8', and European refineries.

Petrochemical Industries Co KSC (PIC): POB 1084, 13011 Safat, Khalid Bin al-Walid St, Kuwait City; tel 2422141; telex 22024; Chair and Man Dir: Abd al-Baqi an-Nouri; f 1963.

Fertilizer Division: POB 9116, Ahmadi; telex 44212; produces ammonia, urea, sulphuric acid and ammonium sulphate; runs four ammonia plants, three urea plants and one ammonium sulphate plant.

Salt and Chlorine Division: POB 10277, 65453 Shuaiba; tel 3263310; telex 46925; Operations Man: Hamad al-Mishwat; f 1963; produces salt, chlorine, caustic soda, hydrochloric acid, sodium hypochlorite, compressed hydrogen and distilled water.

Health and Welfare

Public Housing Authority: POB 23385, Safat, Kuwait City; tel 2467300.

Public Institution for Social Security (PIFSS): POB 24324, 13104 Safat, Kuwait City; tel 2410170; telex 22804; fax 2418467; Dir-Gen: Fahad M. al-Rajaan; Dep Dir-Gen: Hamad M. al-Humaidhi; f 1976; runs social insurance system.

Legal and Judiciary

Constitutional Court: Safat, Kuwait City; composed of five advisers; interprets the articles of the constitution and judges disputes related to the constitutionality of laws, statutes and by-laws.

Court of Cassation: Safat, Kuwait City; independent dept in the High Court of Appeal, composed of five advisers; considers cases of alleged discrimination.

Court of the First Instance: Safat, Kuwait City; Chief Judge: Ghazi Obaid as-Sammar; its seven divisions consider disputes related to personal, civil, commercial, labour and rent affairs, and also cases of felony and appeals concerning misdemeanours.

Department of Legal Advice and Legislation: POB 5968, Safat, Kuwait City; tel 2442402; telex 44302; under the Ministry of Justice and Legal Affairs.

High Court of Appeal: Safat, Kuwait City; tel 432131; Chief Judge: Muhammad Yousuf ar-Rifa'i; hears appeals against rulings of the Court of the First Instance; its verdicts are passed by three advisers.

Office of the Advocate-General: Safat, Kuwait City; Advocate-Gen: Muhammad Abd al-Haih al-Bannaiy.

Office of the Attorney-General: Safat, Kuwait City; Attorney-Gen: Dhari Abdullah al-Uthman.

Media

BROADCASTING

Kuwait Broadcasting SCE: POB 397, 13004 Safat, Kuwait City; tel 2423774; telex 46285; Dir, Radio: Dr Abd al-Aziz ali Mansour; Dir, Radio Programmes: Abd ar-Rahman Hadi; f 1951; radio broadcasts for 62 hours daily in Arabic, Farsi, English and Urdu.

Kuwait Television: c/o POB 621, 13007 Safat, Kuwait City; tel 2423774; telex 22169; Dir, TV: Salim al-Fahd; Dir, TV Programmes: Badr al-Modaf; f 1961; transmits in Arabic for 86 hours per week.

NEWS AND INFORMATION

Central Statistical Office: c/o Ministry of Planning, POB 26188, 13001 Safat, Kuwait City; tel 2428200; telex 22468.

Kuwait News Agency (KUNA): POB 24063, 13101 Safat, Kuwait City; tel 2412040; telex 22758; Chair and Dir-Gen: Barges Hamoud al-Barges; f 1976; public corporate body; independent; news agency and also publishes research digests on topics of common and special interest.

Public Authority for Civil Information: POB 6634, 32041 Hawalli, Tunis St, Hawalli al-Rehab Complex, Kuwait City; tel 2669111; telex 30876; fax 2634113; Dir-Gen: Faisal Ar al-Sahyji; f 1982; records office; issues identity cards.

Research

Kuwait Institute for Scientific Research (KISR): POB 24885, Safat, Kuwait City; tel 4816988; telex 22299.

Telecommunications

Posts Department: 11045 Safat, General Post Office, Fahd al-Salem St, Kuwait City.

Tourism

Department of Tourism: c/o Ministry of Information, POB 193, 13002 Safat, as-Sour St, Kuwait City; tel 2436644; telex 44041.

Touristic Enterprises Co: POB 23310, 13094 Safat, Kuwait City; tel 5644621; telex 22801; Chair: Muhammad as-Sanoussi; Vice-Chair: Ahmad Hamza; 92% Govt-owned; manages 23 tourist facilities.

Transport

CIVIL AVIATION

Directorate-General of Civil Aviation: POB 17, 13001 Safat, Kuwait City, tel 735599; telex 23038; Dir-Gen: Sheikh Jaber al-Athby as-Sabah.

Kuwait Airways Corpn (KAC): POB 394, 13004 Safat, Kuwait International Airport, Kuwait City; tel 4345555; telex 23036; Chair: Ahmad al-Mishari; Dir-Gen: Ahmad az-Zabin; f 1954; services to 43 destinations in Europe, the Middle and Far East, North Africa and the USA.

ROADS

Kuwait Public Transport Co SAK (KPTC): POB 375, 13004 Safat, Hilali St, Kuwait City; tel 2469420; telex 22246; Chair of Board: Barrak K. al-Marzouk; Man Dir: Abd al-Wahab al-Haroun; f 1962; 100% Govt-owned; provides internal bus service; regular service to Iraq.

Overland Transport Co KSC: POB 24611, 13107 Safat, Sulaibya, Sulaibya Rd, Kuwait City; tel 4673824; telex 23817; fax 4673854; transport; customs clearance.

SHIPPING

Kuwait Oil Tanker Co SAK (KOTC): POB 810, 13009 Safat, as-Salhia Commercial Complex, Blocks 5, 7 and 9, Kuwait City; tel 2455455; telex 22013; Chair and Man Dir: Abd al-Fattah al-Bader; f 1957; controlled by the Kuwait Petroleum Corpn (see above); operates crude oil tankers, LPG and LNG vessels, product carriers; LPG filling and distribution.

Ports Public Authority: POB 3874, 13039 Safat, Kuwait City; tel 4812622; telex 22740; fax 4819714; Dir-Gen: Dr Ibrahim Makki; f 1977.

LAOS

Head of State

The President is the Head of State. Executive power is vested in the Council of Ministers, led by a Prime Minister.

President (acting): Phoumi Vongvichit (took office 29 October 1986).

Office of the President: Vientiane; tel 2315.

Legislature

Under the terms of the 1986 Constitution, which has yet to be approved, legislative power is vested in the Supreme People's Assembly. The Assembly has 79 members elected for five years. Political power is effectively held by the Lao People's Revolutionary Party (LPRP).

People's Supreme Assembly: Vientiane; tel 2516; Chair: Nouhak Phounsavanh; Vice-Chair: Thongsing Thammavong.

MINISTRIES AND GOVERNMENT DEPARTMENTS

OFFICE OF THE CHAIRMAN (PRIME MINISTER)
Vientiane
Tel 3171
Chair: Kaysone Phomvihane
First Vice-Chair: Nouhak Phounsavanh
Vice-Chairs: Gen Phoune Sipraseuth, Gen Khamtai Siphandon, Saly Vongkhamsao
Ministers: Gen Sisavat Keobounphanh, Chanmi Douangboutdi

COMMITTEE FOR ECONOMIC RELATIONS WITH FOREIGN COUNTRIES AND STATE COMMERCE
Vientiane
Chair: Phao Bounaphon

COMMITTEE OF INFORMATION, PRESS, RADIO AND TELEVISION
Vientiane
Chair: Son Khamvanvongsa

MINISTRY OF AGRICULTURE, FORESTRY, IRRIGATION AND AGRICULTURAL CO-OPERATIVES
Vientiane
Tel 2738
Minister: Maj-Gen Inkong Mahavong

MINISTRY OF COMMERCE
Vientiane
Minister: Vanthong Sengmuong

MINISTRY OF CONSTRUCTION
Vientiane
Tel 2587
Minister: Gen Khemphone Phouipaseuth

MINISTRY OF CULTURE
Vientiane
Minister: Thongsing Thammavong

MINISTRY OF EDUCATION, SPORTS AND FINE ARTS
Vientiane
Tel 2050
Minister: Bounthiem Phitsamai

MINISTRY OF FOREIGN AFFAIRS
Vientiane
Tel 2107; telex 317
Minister: Gen Phoune Sipraseuth

MINISTRY OF INDUSTRY AND HANDICRAFT
Vientiane
Tel 2650
Minister: Soulivang Daravong

MINISTRY OF THE INTERIOR
Vientiane
Tel 2225
Minister: Gen Sisavat Kepbounphanh

MINISTRY OF JUSTICE
Vientiane
Tel 2145
Minister: Kou Souvannamethi

MINISTRY OF MATERIALS AND TECHNOLOGY
Vientiane
Minister: Thongsouk Saisangkhy

MINISTRY OF NATIONAL DEFENCE
Vientiane
Tel 2046
Minister: Gen Khamtai Siphandon

MINISTRY OF PUBLIC HEALTH
Vientiane
Tel 2223
Minister: Khamlieng Pholsena

**MINISTRY OF TRANSPORTATION, POSTS AND
TELECOMMUNICATIONS**
Vientiane
Tel 2716
Minister: Oudom Khattigna

**NATIONAL COMMITTEE OF SOCIAL WELFARE
AND WAR VETERANS**
Vientiane
Chair: Khambou Sounisai

NATIONALITIES COMMITTEE
Vientiane
Chair: Nhiavu Lobliayao

PARTY AND STATE INSPECTION COMMITTEE
Vientiane
Chair: Maychantan Sengmani

**STATE ECONOMIC PLANNING AND FINANCE
COMMITTEE**
Vientiane
Tel 2400
Chair: Saly Vongkhamsao

STATE BANK
rue Yonnet, BP 19, Vientiane
Tel 2000; telex 4304
Chair: Nouphan Sitprasai

GOVERNMENT AGENCIES AND ORGANIZATIONS

Agriculture

Central Leading Committee to Guide Agricultural Co-operatives: Vientiane; Chair: Saly Vongkhamsao (mem of Council of Ministers); Dir: Khamsen Vononokeo; f 1978; organization and planning of regulations and policies for co-operatives.

National Office for Agriculture and Livestock: Vientiane; imports and markets agricultural commodities; produces and distributes feed and animals.

Business and Economy

BANKING

Banque du Commerce Extérieur Lao (BCEL): rue Pangkham, BP 19, Vientiane; tel 2646; telex 4301; Dir: Khemvieng; f 1975; acts as executive agent for the central bank in foreign exchange and banking operations.

Banque d'Etat de la RDP Lao: rue Yonnet, BP 19, Vientiane; tel 2000; telex 4304; Chair: Nouphan Sitprasai (mem of Cabinet); Pres: Bousbong Souvannavong; f 1968 as Banque Pathetlao, took over the operations of the Banque Nationale du Laos in 1975; adopted present name in 1982; 115 brs.

NATIONALIZED INDUSTRY

Lao Plywood Co: Km 10, Thadeua Rd, BP 83, Vientiane; tel 2847; telex 4491; Dir: Sykeo Phonphakdy; Vice-Dirs: Bounpheng Phenglamphanh, Phengphanh Douangchak; f 1973; production of plywood and veneers.

TRADE

Société de Commerce Lao: 43-47 ave Lane Xang, Vientiane; tel 2944; telex 4318; Dir: Inhome Phinith.

Defence

Armed Forces: Vientiane; tel 3151; Commdr-in-Chief: Gen Khamtai Siphandon.

Air Force: Vientiane; tel 2027; Chief of Staff: Sithonh Manola.

Army: Vientiane; Chief of Staff: Sisavath Keobounphanh.

National Police Department: Vientiane; tel 2059; Commdr: Khamphonh Bouddakham.

Energy

Electricité du Laos: Vientiane; tel 4311; responsible for production and export of hydroelectricity.

Legal and Judiciary

Supreme Court: Vientiane; Chair: Ounneua Phimmasone.

Media

BROADCASTING

Lao National Radio: BP 310, Vientiane; tel 2457; Dir-Gen: Bouabane Vorakhoun; f 1951; programmes in Lao, French, English, Thai, Khmer and Vietnamese; domestic and international services.

Lao National Television: BP 310, Vientiane; tel 4475; Dir-Gen: Bouabane Vorakhoun; f 1983.

GOVERNMENT PUBLISHERS

Lao Printing Office: rue Samsenthai, Vientiane.

Lao-phanit: Ministry of Education, Bureau des Manuels Scolaires, Vientiane; publishes educational, cookery, art, music, fiction books.

NEWS AND INFORMATION

Khao San Pathet Lao (KPL): BP 310, Vientiane; tel 2758; telex 4328; Dir-Gen: Bounteng Vongsay; f 1968; news agency; organ of the Committee of Information, Press, Radio and Television Broadcasting.

Service Nationale de la Statistique: c/o Direction des Douanes et Régies, Vientiane; tel 2292; collection of foreign trade statistics.

Tourism

Lao National Tourism Department: rue Samsenthai, BP 122, Vientiane.

Transport

Lao Aviation: The National Air Transport Co, 2 rue Pangkham, BP 119, Vientiane; tel 2094; f 1976; operates internal services and international services to Hanoi, Phnom-Penh and Bangkok.

Lao Civil Aviation Department: Vientiane; telex 4310; Dir: Phoun Khammounhuang.

LEBANON

Head of State

Executive power is vested in the President, who is elected for six years by the National Assembly. The President appoints a Prime Minister and other Ministers to form a Cabinet, which is responsible to the Assembly.

President: Elias Hrawi (took office 24 November 1989).

Office of the President: Ba'abda, Beirut; tel (1) 220000; telex 21000.

Legislature

Legislative power is vested in the unicameral Majlis Alnwab (National Assembly), with 99 members elected by universal adult suffrage for four years, on the basis of proportional representation. Seats are allocated on a religious basis, according to 6:5 ratio of Christians to Muslims recorded at the 1932 census. All elections scheduled since 1972 have been postponed.

Majlis Alnwab (National Assembly): Villa Mansour, rue du Musée, Beirut; tel (1) 220040; Pres: Hussain al-Hussaini; Vice-Pres: Albert Mukhaybir.

MINISTRIES AND GOVERNMENT DEPARTMENTS

OFFICE OF THE PRIME MINISTER
Grand Serail, rue des Arts et Métiers, Sanayeh, Beirut
Tel (1) 221000
Prime Minister: Dr Selim al-Hoss
Deputy Prime Minister: Abdullah ar-Rassi

MINISTRY OF AGRICULTURE
rue Sami Solh, Beirut
Tel (1) 380460
Minister: Abd al-Usayran

MINISTRY OF ECONOMY, TRADE, INDUSTRY AND OIL
rue Artois, Beirut
Tel (1) 345051
Minister: (vacant)

MINISTRY OF EDUCATION AND FINE ARTS
Unesco St, Beirut
Tel (1) 30511
Minister: Dr Selim al-Hoss

MINISTRY OF FINANCE
rue de l'Etoile, Beirut
Tel (1) 251600
Minister: (vacant)

MINISTRY OF FOREIGN AND EXPATRIATE AFFAIRS
rue Sursock, Achrafieh, Beirut
Tel (1) 333100; telex 20726
Minister (acting): Dr Selim al-Hoss

MINISTRY OF HOUSING AND CO-OPERATIVES
Grand Serail, rue des Arts et Métiers, Sanayeh, Beirut
Tel (1) 336002
Minister: (vacant)

MINISTRY OF INFORMATION
rue Hamra, Beirut
Tel (1) 345800; telex 20786
Minister: Edmond Rizk

MINISTRY OF THE INTERIOR
Grand Serail, rue des Arts et Métiers, Sanayeh, Beirut
Tel (1) 369135
Minister: Abdullah ar-Rassi

MINISTRY OF JUSTICE
rue Sami Solh, Beirut
Tel (1) 384243
Minister: Nabih Berri

MINISTRY OF LABOUR
Shiah, Beirut
Tel (1) 274140
Minister: Dr Selim al-Hoss

MINISTRY OF NATIONAL DEFENCE
Yarze, Beirut
Tel (1) 452400; telex 20901
Minister: Abd al-Usayran

MINISTRY OF POSTS AND TELECOMMUNICATIONS
rue Sami Solh, Beirut
Tel (1) 240100; telex 20900
Minister: (vacant)

MINISTRY OF PUBLIC HEALTH AND SOCIAL AFFAIRS
rue du Musée, Beirut
Tel (1) 309843
Minister: (vacant)

MINISTRY OF PUBLIC WORKS AND TRANSPORT
Shiah, Beirut
Tel (1) 270225
Minister: Walid Joumblatt

MINISTRY OF TOURISM
rue Banque du Liban, Beirut
Tel (1) 340904; telex 20898
Minister: Walid Joumblatt

**MINISTRY OF STATE FOR AFFAIRS OF THE
SOUTH AND RECONSTRUCTION**
Beirut
Minister of State: Nabih Berri

**MINISTRY OF WATER AND ELECTRICAL
RESOURCES**
Shiah, Beirut
Tel (1) 270256
Minister: Nabih Berri

GOVERNMENT AGENCIES AND ORGANIZATIONS

Advisory and Supervisory Body

Cour des Comptes (Audit Office): Kantari, Beirut; Pres: Seri al-Housami.

Business and Economy

BANKING

Bank of Beirut SAL: POB 11-7354, Gefinor Centre, rue Clémenceau, Beirut; Chair: William S. Kazan; Man Dir: Rida Abujawdeh.

Banque de l'Habitat SAL: Riad as-Solh St, Beirut; Chair and Gen Man: Joseph Sassine; f 1977.

Banque du Liban: POB 5544, rue Masraf Loubnane, Beirut; tel (1) 341230; telex 20744; Gov: Edmond Naim; f 1964 to take over the banking activities of the Banque de Syrie et du Liban in Lebanon; central bank.

Banque Nationale pour le Développement Industriel et Touristique SAL: POB 11-8412, Concorde Bldg, rue Verdun, Beirut; tel (1) 354751; telex 23086; Chair and Gen Man: Dr Talhat al-Yafi; f 1973.

TRADE

Conseil des Relations Economiques Extérieures (CREE): POB 11-5344, Beirut; tel (1) 340944; telex 20898; f 1983; promotion of overseas trade.

Superior Council of Customs: Beirut; tel (1) 810910; Pres: Isam Haydar.

Defence

Armed Forces: c/o Ministry of National Defence, Yarze, Beirut; tel (1) 420400; Commdr-in-Chief: Gen Emile Lahoud.

Air Force: address as above; tel (1) 420400; Commdr: Fahim al-Hajj.

Army: address as above; tel (1) 420400; Chief of Staff: Abu Dirgham.

Navy: address as above; tel (1) 420400; Commdr: Antoine Kreidy.

Development and Planning

Council for Development and Reconstruction: Beirut; Chair: Malik Salim; f 1976; aimed to achieve reconstruction after 1975-76 civil war, is now also dealing with the effects of subsequent inter-communal fighting.

Executive Council for Beirut Projects: Arlequin Area, Kantari St, Beirut; Pres: Mohammed Ghaziri.

Employment

Civil Service Council: rue Thabet, Beirut; tel (1) 306666; Pres: Ibrahim Chouieri.

Energy

Lebanon Electricity Office: Immeuble de l'Electricité du Liban, rue du Fleuve, Beirut; Pres: Elias Nammar.

Legal and Judiciary

Council of State: Beirut; tel (1) 387117; Pres: Yousuf Saavollah el-Khoury; deals with administrative cases; consists of a Pres, Vice-Pres and four Councillors; a Commr represents the Govt.

Cour de Cassation (Superior Court of Appeal): Palais de Justice, Beirut; tel (1) 20744; First Pres: Amin Nassar; four courts, three dealing with civil and commercial cases and the fourth with criminal cases.

Media

BROADCASTING

Lebanese Broadcasting Station: rue des Arts et Métiers, Beirut; tel (1) 346880; telex 20786; Dir-Gen: Qassem Hage Ali; Technical Dir: Louis Rizk; Dir of Programmes: Nizar Mikati; Head of Admin: A. Aoun.

NEWS AND INFORMATION

Direction Centrale de la Statistique: c/o Direction Générale des Douanes, Beirut; collection, analysis and publicaton of statistics.

Tourism

National Council of Tourism in Lebanon (CNTL): POB 11-5344, rue de la Banque du Liban, Beirut; tel (1) 340940; telex 20898; Pres: Samy Maroun; Dir-Gen: Nasser Safieddine;

responsible for the promotion of tourism; overseas offices in London, Paris, Brussels, Rome, Iraq and Cairo.

Transport

Office des Chemins de Fer de l'Etat Libanais et du Transport en Commun de Beyrouth et de sa Banlieue: POB 109, Souk el-Arwam, Beirut; tel (1) 443619; telex 43088; Pres: A. Hamié; Dir-Gen: Abdullah Chehab; since 1961 all railways in Lebanon have been state-owned; only half of the original network is known to be working.

Siège Provisoire de la Commission Portuaire: Immeuble de l'Electricité du Liban, rue du Fleuve, Beirut; port authority.

Welfare

National Social Security Office: UNESCO/Mazraa Area, Beirut; tel (1) 301519; Pres: Georges Khadize.

LESOTHO

<table>
<tr>
<td>

Head of State

According to the Lesotho Order of 1986, executive and legislative powers are vested in the King, who is Head of State, and is assisted by a six-member Military Council and a Council of Ministers. However, in February 1990 the King was deprived of his legislative and executive powers, which were taken over by the Military Council.

Monarch: HM King Moshoeshoe II (succeeded as Paramount Chief 1960; became King at independence, 4 October 1966).

Office of HM the King: POB 524, Maseru 100; tel 322170; telex 433166.

</td>
<td>

Legislature

The Constitution provides for a National Assembly and a Senate. However, the Constitution was suspended in 1970. The 1983 Parliament Act repealing suspension was itself repealed following a military coup, and the National Assembly was dissolved. Lesotho comprises 10 administrative districts, each under an appointed District Co-ordinator.

</td>
</tr>
</table>

MINISTRIES AND GOVERNMENT DEPARTMENTS

OFFICE OF THE CHAIR OF THE MILITARY COUNCIL
Maseru 100
Tel 323004
Chair: Maj-Gen Justin Metsing Lekhanya
Members: Col Elias Ramaema, Brig Benedict Lerotholi, Col Jacob Jane, Col Michael Nkhahle Tsotetsi, Lt-Col Molise Mokete
Minister of State in the Office of the Chair: Anna Matlima Hlalele

MINISTRY OF AGRICULTURE, CO-OPERATIVES AND MARKETING
POB 24, Maseru 100
Tel 322741; telex 4330
Minister: Maj-Gen Justin Metsing Lekhanya

MINISTRY OF DEFENCE AND INTERNAL SECURITY; PUBLIC SERVICE, YOUTH AND WOMEN'S AFFAIRS; FOOD MANAGEMENT UNITS AND CABINET OFFICE
POB 527, Maseru 100
Tel 323861; telex 4330
Minister: Maj-Gen Justin Metsing Lekhanya

MINISTRY OF EDUCATION
POB 47, Maseru 100
Tel 323045; telex 4330
Minister: Dr Lehlohonolo B. B. J. Machobane

MINISTRY OF EMPLOYMENT, SOCIAL SECURITY AND PENSIONS
MINESP, Private Bag A116, Maseru 100
Tel 322564; telex 4330
Minister: Lt Pius Molapo

MINISTRY OF FINANCE
POB 395, Maseru 100
Tel 322961; telex 4330
Minister: Evaristus Retselisitsoe Sekhonyana

MINISTRY OF FOREIGN AFFAIRS
POB 1387, Maseru 100
Tel 323861; telex 4330
Minister: Tom Thabane

MINISTRY OF HEALTH
POB 514, Maseru 100
Tel 324404; telex 4357
Minister: L. Thoahlane

MINISTRY OF HIGHLANDS WATER PROJECT AND ENERGY
Private Bag, Maseru 100
Tel 322491; telex 4253
Minister: M. Habe

MINISTRY OF INFORMATION AND BROADCASTING
POB 36, Maseru 100
Tel 323561; telex 4450; fax 310003
Minister: Tom Thabane

MINISTRY OF THE INTERIOR, CHIEFTAINSHIP AND RURAL DEVELOPMENT
POB 174, Maseru 100
Tel 323771; telex 4330
Minister: Patrick Molapo

MINISTRY OF JUSTICE AND PRISONS
POB 402, Maseru 100
Tel 322683; telex 4330
Minister: A. K. Maope

Administration of courts and their staff, prisons and rehabilitation centres.

MINISTRY OF LAW, CONSTITUTIONAL AND PARLIAMENTARY AFFAIRS, AND GOVERNMENT PRINTING
New Govt Office Complex, POB 33, Maseru 100
Tel 323861; telex 4330
Minister: (vacant)
Represents Govt in legal matters; conducts public prosecutions; manages the Govt printing offices.

MINISTRY OF PLANNING, ECONOMIC AND MANPOWER DEVELOPMENT
POB 630, Maseru 100
Tel 323811; telex 4429
Minister: (vacant)

MINISTRY OF TOURISM, SPORTS AND CULTURE
POB 52, Maseru 100
Tel 323034; telex 4280; fax 310108
Minister: Chief Lechesa Mathealira

MINISTRY OF TRADE AND INDUSTRY
POB 747, Maseru 100
Tel 322802; telex 4384; fax 310121
Minister: Moletsane G. Mokoroane

Trade Promotion Unit: address as above; tel 323414; f 1978; offers technical assistance and advice to the trade sector; publicizes Lesotho products abroad and undertakes market research; identifies Govt policies and other incentives conducive to Lesotho export trade devt.

MINISTRY OF TRANSPORT AND COMMUNICATIONS
POB 413, Maseru 100
Tel 323691; telex 4552; fax 311522
Minister: Lt-Col M. V. Mokoni

MINISTRY OF WATER, ENERGY AND MINING
Maseru 100
Tel 322491; telex 4253
Minister: Col A. L. Jane

MINISTRY OF WORKS
POB 20, Maseru 100
Tel 323761; telex 4330
Minister: Lt-Col M. V. Mokoni

GOVERNMENT AGENCIES AND ORGANIZATIONS

Advisory and Supervisory Body

Registry of Co-operatives: POB 89, Maseru 100; Registrar: P. Moeketsi.

Business and Economy

BANKING

Central Bank of Lesotho: POB 1184, Maseru 100; tel 324281; telex 4367; Gov: Erik L. Karlsson; Gen Man: A. K. Gangopadhyay; f 1980; central bank and bank of issue.

Lesotho Agricultural Development Bank (LADB): POB 845, 58 Kingsway Rd, Maseru 100; tel 323277; telex 4269; Chair: E. R. Sekhonyana; Man Dir: C. S. Molelle.

Lesotho Bank: POB 999, Maseru 100; tel 314333; telex 4366; Chair: E. R. Sekhonyana; Gen Man: P. T. Mafike; f 1972; national devt bank.

INSURANCE

Lesotho National Insurance Co (Pty) Ltd: Private Bag A65, Lesotho Insurance House, Kingsway, Maseru 100; tel 323032; telex 4220.

MARKETING

Livestock Products Marketing Service: POB 800, Maseru 100; telex 4344; Gen Man: S. R. Matlanyane; replaced Livestock Marketing Corpn, f 1973; sole organization for marketing livestock and livestock products; liaises closely with marketing boards in South Africa; projects include an abattoir, a tannery plant, a poultry plant and wool and mohair scouring plants.

Produce Marketing Corpn: Maseru 100; telex 4365; Gen Man: M. Phoofolo; f 1974.

TRADE

Department of Customs and Excise: POB 891, Maseru 100; tel 323796; telex 4292; fax 310157; f 1970; admin of customs and excise duties.

Defence

Royal Lesotho Defence Force: POB 13, Maseru 100; tel 323004; Commdr: Maj-Gen S. K. Molapo.

Royal Lesotho Mounted Police Force: Police Headquarters, POB 13, Maseru 100; tel 323061; telex 4335; fax 310045; f 1857; law enforcement; protection of life and property, etc.

Development and Planning

Lesotho National Development Corpn (LNDC): POB 666, Maseru 100; tel 312012; telex 4341; fax 310038; Chair: Morena Moletsane Mokoroane; Man Dir: A. Moletsane Monyake; f 1967; 90% Govt-owned; runs candle, carpet, tyre-retreading, explosives and furniture factories, potteries, two diamond prospecting operations, a fertilizer factory, an abattoir, a clothing factory, a diamond-cutting and polishing works, a jewellery factory, a housing co, a brewery, an international hotel with a gambling casino, Lesotho Airways Corpn and a training centre for motor mechanics.

Basotho Enterprise Development Corpn (BEDCO): POB 1216, Maseru 100; tel 312094; telex 4370; Man Dir: Tlepu Mahanetsa; f 1977.

Lesotho Co-operatives Handicrafts: Maseru 100; Gen Man: Khotso Matla; f 1978; marketing and distribution of handicrafts.

REGIONAL DEVELOPMENT

Lesotho Highlands Development Authority: POB 7332, Maseru 100; tel 311280; telex 4523; fax 310050; Chief Exec: Masupha Sole; f 1986; supervises the Lesotho Highlands Water Project to divert the water of the Senqu river system for export, being undertaken jointly with South Africa.

Energy

Lesotho Electricity Corpn: POB 423, Maseru 100; tel 322236; telex 4336; Man Dir: T. J. Matsau; f 1969; under the Ministry of Water, Energy and Mining; responsible for the generation and distribution of electricity.

Legal and Judiciary

Court of Appeal: Maseru 100; Pres: I. A. Maisels.

High Court: POB 90, Maseru 100; tel 322183; telex 4330; Chief Justice: Brian P. Cullinan; superior court of record, vested with unlimited original jurisdiction to determine any civil or criminal matter; has appellate jurisdiction to hear appeals and reviews from the subordinate courts.

Media

BROADCASTING

Radio and Television Lesotho: POB 552, Maseru 100; tel 323561; telex 4451; Dir, Broadcasting: T. Ntsane; programmes in Sesotho and English.

GOVERNMENT PUBLISHER

Lesotho Government Printing and Stationery Office: POB 268, Maseru 100; tel 313023; f 1967.

NEWS AND INFORMATION

Bureau of Statistics: POB 455, Maseru 100; tel 323852; f 1965; collection, compilation and dissemination of statistical information.

Lesotho News Agency (LENA): POB 36, Maseru 100; tel 325317; telex 4530; Dir: H. L. Mokhachane; Editor: L. Lejakane; news agency; formed with aid from UNESCO.

Tourism

Lesotho National Tourist Board: POB 1378, Maseru 100; tel 323760; telex 4280; Man Dir: C. M. Mosae; Marketing Man: L. Ntsinyi; Devt Man: P. Mpela; Admin Man: P. Makheth; f 1984; promotion and devt of tourism.

Transport

Lesotho Airways Corpn: POB 861, Maseru 100; tel 312453; telex 4347; Chair: M. P. Sejanamane; Man Dir: S. Machobane; f 1970; scheduled passenger air services linking Lesotho with South Africa, Botswana, Mozambique, Swaziland and Zimbabwe.

Lesotho Freight and Bus Services Corpn: POB 1559, Maseru 100; tel 323535; fax 310014; f 1986; transport of goods and passengers.

LIBERIA

<table>
<tr><td>

Head of State

Executive power is vested in the President, who is elected by universal adult suffrage for a six-year term. The President appoints a Cabinet, to assist in governing the country.

President: Samuel Kanyon Doe (assumed power in military coup 12 April 1980; elected President 15 October 1985, inaugurated 6 January 1986).

Vice-President: Harry Moniba.

Office of the President and of the Vice-President: Executive Mansion, Capitol Hill, POB 9001, Monrovia; tel 224961.

</td><td>

Legislature

Legislative power is vested in the bicameral National Assembly, comprising a Senate, with 26 members, and a House of Representatives, with 64 members. All members of the National Assembly are elected for six years by universal adult suffrage.

Senate: Monrovia; Pres: John G. Rancy.

House of Representatives: Monrovia; Speaker: Samuel D. Hill.

</td></tr>
</table>

MINISTRIES AND GOVERNMENT DEPARTMENTS

OFFICE OF THE DIRECTOR-GENERAL OF THE CABINET
Monrovia
Director-General: Momolu Getaweh
Minister without Portfolio: Peter Naigow

MINISTRY OF AGRICULTURE
POB 9010, Monrovia
Tel 261323; telex 44306
Minister: Maj Scott Gblorzuo Toweh

MINISTRY OF COMMERCE AND INDUSTRY
POB 9041, Monrovia
Tel 222141; telex 44331
Minister: Wisseh McClain

MINISTRY OF DEFENCE
POB 9007, Monrovia
Tel 222303; telex 44351
Minister (acting): Brig-Gen J. Boima Barclay

MINISTRY OF EDUCATION
POB 1545, Monrovia
Tel 221613; telex 44449
Minister: Othello Gonga

MINISTRY OF FINANCE
Broad St, Monrovia
Tel 222231; telex 44221
Minister: Emmanuel Shaw

MINISTRY OF FOREIGN AFFAIRS
POB 9002, Monrovia
Tel 221029; telex 44224
Minister: J. Rudolph Johnson

MINISTRY OF HEALTH AND SOCIAL WELFARE
POB 9009, Monrovia
Tel 261998
Minister: Martha Sendolo Belleh

MINISTRY OF INFORMATION
Capitol Hill, POB 9021, Monrovia
Tel 222229; telex 44249
Minister: J. Emmanuel Z. Bowier

MINISTRY OF INTERNAL AFFAIRS
POB 9008, Monrovia
Tel 222422; telex 44514
Minister: Col Edward K. Sackor

MINISTRY OF JUSTICE
POB 9006, Monrovia
Tel 222342; telex 44286
Minister: Jenkins K. Z. B. Scott

MINISTRY OF LABOUR
Mechlin St/Sekou Touré Ave, POB 9040, Monrovia
Tel 222815
Minister: Momolu Getaweh

MINISTRY OF LANDS, MINES AND ENERGY
POB 9024, Monrovia
Tel 221591; telex 44532
Minister: William Freeman

MINISTRY OF NATIONAL SECURITY
Monrovia
Minister: Sylvester Moses

MINISTRY OF PLANNING AND ECONOMIC AFFAIRS
Randall St, POB 9016, Monrovia
Tel 221971; telex 44374
Minister: Elijah Taylor

MINISTRY OF POSTS AND TELECOMMUNICATIONS
Carey St/McDonald St, Monrovia
Tel 222331; telex 44651
Minister: Momodou Dukalay

MINISTRY OF PRESIDENTIAL AFFAIRS
Executive Mansion, Capitol Hill, POB 9001, Monrovia
Tel 224961
Minister of State: Maj G. Alvin Jones

MINISTRY OF PUBLIC WORKS
POB 9011, Monrovia
Tel 221047
Minister: Yudu S. Gray

MINISTRY OF RURAL DEVELOPMENT
POB 9030, Monrovia
Tel 271092
Minister: Samuel D. Brownell

MINISTRY OF TRANSPORT
Monrovia
Minister: Mrs McLeod Darpoh

MINISTRY OF YOUTH AND SPORTS
Tubman Blvd, POB 90, Monrovia
Tel 262602
Minister: Haven Grigsby

GOVERNMENT AGENCIES AND ORGANIZATIONS

Business and Economy

BANKING

Agricultural and Co-operative Development Bank: Carey and Warren Sts, POB 3585, Monrovia; tel 224385; telex 44535; Pres: Wilson K. Tarpeh; Gen Man: Jerome M. Hodge; short-, medium- and long-term credit to facilitate capital investment in agriculture; 6 brs.

Liberian Bank for Development and Investment (LBDI): Congotown, POB 547, Monrovia; tel 261111; telex 44345; Pres: Philip T. Bowen; f 1961.

National Bank of Liberia: Broad St, POB 2048, Monrovia; tel 222497; telex 44215; Gov: John G. Bestman; Dep Gov: Lindsay M. Haines; central bank.

National Housing and Savings Bank: UN Drive, Waterside, POB 818, Monrovia; tel 221402; telex 44337; Pres: Ignatius N. Clay; f 1972; priority given to low-cost Govt housing programmes.

INSURANCE

National Insurance Corpn of Liberia (NICOL): LBDI Bldg Complex, POB 1528, Sinkor, Liberia; tel 262429; telex 44228; Man Dir: Miatta Edith Sherman; f 1984; sole insurer for Govt and parastatal bodies; also provides insurance for the Liberian-registered merchant shipping fleet.

MARKETING

Liberian Produce Marketing Corpn: POB 662, Monrovia; tel 222447; telex 44590; Man Dir: Aletha Johnson-Francis; f 1961; exports Liberian produce, provides industrial facilities for processing of agricultural products and participates in agricultural devt programmes.

NATIONALIZED INDUSTRY

Mesurado Industrial Complex: POB 142, Monrovia; Pres: P. Bonner Jallah; products include detergents, soap, industrial gases, windows and animal feeds.

TRADE

Liberia Industrial Free Zone Authority: Bushrod Island, POB 9047, Monrovia; Man Dir: Gbai M. Gbala; f 1975.

Defence

Armed Forces: c/o Ministry of Defence, POB 9007, Monrovia; tel 222303; Commdr-in-Chief: Samuel Kanyon Doe.

Navy: address as above; tel 222303.

Forestry

Forestry Development Authority: POB 3010, Monrovia; tel 262250; Man Dir: Shad G. Kaydea; responsible for conservation and management of Liberia's forests.

Legal and Judiciary

People's Supreme Court: Temple of Justice, Capitol Hill, Monrovia; tel 221213; Chief Justice: Emmanuel Gbalazeh.

Media

BROADCASTING

Liberian Broadcasting System: POB 594, Monrovia; tel 271976; telex 44249; Dir-Gen: Alhaji G. V. Kromah; Dep Dir-Gen, Broadcasting: J. Eustace Smith; Dep Dir-Gen, Admin: T. Wellington Toh; controls all broadcasting media.

ELBC: address as above; tel 271976; Asst Dir-Gen for Radio: Tommy Raynes; f 1960; broadcasts 19 hrs daily in English, French and 16 local languages.

ELTV: address as above; tel 271976; telex 44249; Asst Dir-Gen for TV: Sam Bonah; f 1964; broadcasts 6 hrs daily Mon-Fri, 10 hrs daily Sat and Sun.

Liberia Rural Communications Network: POB 2176, Monrovia; tel 271368; Dir: Florida Kweekeh; f 1981; rural devt and entertainment programmes; broadcasts in major Liberian languages.

GOVERNMENT PUBLISHER

Government Printer: Government Printing Office, Ministry of Foreign Affairs, POB 9002, Monrovia.

NEWS AND INFORMATION

Liberian News Agency (LINA): Ministry of Information, Capitol Hill, POB 9021, Monrovia; tel 222229; telex 44249.

Statistics Bureau: c/o Ministry of Planning and Economic Affairs, Randall St, POB 9016, Monrovia; tel 221971; telex 44374; collection, analysis and publication of statistics.

Mining

LAMCO J. V. Operating Co: POB 69, Monrovia; tel 221190; telex 44269; Pres and Gen Man: H. N. Bas Koenen; 63% state-owned; mining of iron ore.

National Iron Ore Co Ltd: POB 548, Monrovia; Gen Man: S. K. Datta Ray; f 1958; 85% state-owned; mining of iron ore at Mano River.

Tourism

Board of Tourism: Sinkor, Monrovia; Dir-Gen: Jallah K. Kamara.

Transport

Air Liberia: POB 2076, Monrovia; telex 44298; Man Dir: James K. Kofa; f 1974; privatization plans were announced in 1986; scheduled passenger and cargo services.

Liberia National Shipping Line (LNSL): Monrovia; f 1987 by Govt and a Federal German shipping co; routes to Europe, including UK and Scandinavia.

National Port Authority: POB 1849, Monrovia; telex 44275; Chair: Sumo Jones; Man Dir: J. Bernard Blamo; f 1967; administers Monrovia Free Port and the ports of Greenville and Harper.

LIBYA

Head of State

The Head of State is the Revolutionary Leader, who is elected by the General People's Congress. Executive power is exercised by the General People's Committee, which comprises 18 Secretaries, each responsible for a Department.

Revolutionary Leader: Col Muammar al-Qaddafi (took office as Chairman of the Revolutionary Command Council on 8 September 1969).

Office of the Leader of the State: c/o Secretariat of the General People's Committee, Tripoli; tel (21) 30777; telex 20032; Sec-Gen of General People's Committee: Omar al-Muntasser.

Legislature

Legislative power is vested in the people through People's Congresses, Popular Committees, Trade Unions, Vocational Syndicates and the 1,112-member General People's Congress, with its General Secretariat. Political power effectively lies with the Arab Socialist Union, which is the only officially-recognized party. The country is divided into three Provinces and 10 Governorates.

General People's Congress: c/o Secretariat of the General People's Congress, Tripoli; tel (21) 30777; telex 20032; Sec-Gen: Dr Muftah al-Usta Omar.

MINISTRIES AND GOVERNMENT DEPARTMENTS

GENERAL SECRETARIAT OF THE GENERAL PEOPLE'S CONGRESS
c/o Secretariat of the General People's Congress, Tripoli
Tel (21) 30777; telex 20032
Secretary-General: Dr Muftah al-Usta Omar
Assistant Secretary-Generals: Salmin Ali al-Uraybi, Ibrahim Bukhizam
Secretary for Affairs of the People's Congresses: Omar Ishkal
Secretary for Affairs of the People's Committees: Sulaiman Sasi ash-Shuhoumi
Secretary for Affairs of the Professional Congresses: Bashir Huwaij Huwaidi

GENERAL PEOPLE'S COMMITTEE FOR COMMUNICATIONS AND TRANSPORT
Sirte
Secretary: Mubarak ash-Shamikh

GENERAL PEOPLE'S COMMITTEE FOR ECONOMY AND TRADE
Benghazi
Secretary: Dr Farhat Sharnanah

GENERAL PEOPLE'S COMMITTEE FOR EDUCATION
Sirte
Secretary: Fatima Abdel-Hafiz al-Mukhtar

GENERAL PEOPLE'S COMMITTEE FOR FOREIGN LIAISON
Tripoli
Tel (21) 41634; telex 20032
Secretary: Jadallah Azouz at-Tali

GENERAL PEOPLE'S COMMITTEE FOR HEALTH
Kufra
Secretary: Dr Mustafa Muhammad az-Zaidi

GENERAL PEOPLE'S COMMITTEE FOR HIGHER EDUCATION
Sirte
Secretary: Ahmad Muhammad Ibrahim

GENERAL PEOPLE'S COMMITTEE FOR INFORMATION AND CULTURE
Tripoli
Secretary: Dr Ragab Muftah Abou Dabbous

GENERAL PEOPLE'S COMMITTEE FOR JUSTICE
Sirte
Secretary: Ezzedine al-Hanchiri

GENERAL PEOPLE'S COMMITTEE FOR LAND MANAGEMENT
Sirte
Secretary: (vacant)

GENERAL PEOPLE'S COMMITTEE FOR LIGHT INDUSTRIES
Sirte
Secretary: Amin Helmi Osman

GENERAL PEOPLE'S COMMITTEE FOR MARINE WEALTH
Sirte
Secretary: Muftah Muhammad Kuaibah

GENERAL PEOPLE'S COMMITTEE FOR MASS MOBILIZATION AND REVOLUTIONARY GUIDANCE
Sirte
Secretary: Ali ash-Shairi

GENERAL PEOPLE'S COMMITTEE FOR PETROLEUM
Sirte
Secretary: Fawzi al-Chakchouki

GENERAL PEOPLE'S COMMITTEE FOR PLANNING
Sirte
Secretary: Dr Muhammad Lutfi Farhat

GENERAL PEOPLE'S COMMITTEE FOR SCIENTIFIC RESEARCH
Sirte
Secretary: Muri al-Faturi al-Madani

GENERAL PEOPLE'S COMMITTEE FOR STRATEGIC INDUSTRIES
Sirte
Secretary: Dr Ahmad Fathi Bin Shatwan

GENERAL PEOPLE'S COMMITTEE FOR THE TREASURY
Sirte
Secretary: Muhammad al-Madani al-Bukhari

GENERAL PEOPLE'S COMMITTEE FOR VOCATIONAL TRAINING
Sirte
Secretary: Maatouq Muhammad Maatouq

GOVERNMENT AGENCIES AND ORGANIZATIONS

Business and Economy

BANKING

Agricultural Bank: 52 Sharia Omar Mukhtar, POB 1100, Tripoli; tel (21) 38666; Chair: Ahmad al-Amin al-Gadamsi; f 1955.

Central Bank of Libya: Sharia al-Malik Seoud, POB 1103, Tripoli; tel (21) 33591; telex 20661; Gov: Muhammad Zaroukh Ragab; f 1955 as National Bank of Libya, name changed to Bank of Libya in 1963, and to Central Bank of Libya in 1977; bank of issue and central bank carrying Govt accounts and operating exchange control; commercial operations transferred to National Commercial Bank in 1970.

Jamahiriya Bank: Sharia Muhammad al-Megharief, POB 3224, Tripoli; tel (21) 33553; telex 20008; Chair: Muhammad H. Nahaisi; Vice-Chair: Omar A. Leyas; Vice-Chair and Gen Man: Gamal Abd al-Malik; f 1969 as successor to Barclays Bank International in Libya; wholly-owned subsidiary of the Central Bank; 35 brs.

Libyan Arab Foreign Bank: Sharia 1 September, POB 2542, Tripoli; tel (21) 41428; telex 20200; fax (21) 42970; Chair and Gen Man: Dr Abd al-Hafid Zelitne; f 1972; offshore bank wholly owned by the Central Bank of Libya.

National Commercial Bank SAL: Shuhada Sq, POB 4647, Tripoli; tel (21) 37191; telex 20169; Chair and Gen Man: Abd al-Hamid N. Raghei; f 1970 to take over the commercial banking division of the Central Bank of Libya and brs of Aruba Bank and Istiklal Bank; 25 brs.

Sahara Bank: 10 Sharia 1 September, POB 270, Tripoli; tel (21) 32771; telex 20009; Chair and Gen Man: Omar Ali Ashabu; f 1964 to take over br of Banco di Sicilia; 20 brs.

Savings and Real Estate Investment Bank: Sharia Haite, POB 2297, Tripoli; tel (21) 49306; telex 20309; Chair and Gen Man: Said Lishani; f 1975; 23 brs.

Umma Bank SAL: 1 Giaddat Omar Mukhtar, POB 685, Tripoli; tel (21) 34031; telex 20256; Chair and Gen Man: Taher A. Hawaisa; f 1969 to take over brs of Banco di Roma; 19 brs.

Wahda Bank: Sharia Gamal Abd an-Naser, POB 452, Benghazi; tel (61) 98918; telex 40011; Chair and Gen Man: Yousuf A. Hassadi; f 1970 to take over Bank of North Africa, Commercial Bank SAL, Nahda Arabia Bank, Société Africaine de Banque, Kafila al-Ahly Bank; 8 brs.

FINANCIAL AGENCY

International Oil Investments Co: Tripoli; Chair: Muhammad al-Jawad; f 1988; acquisition of downstream facilities abroad.

INSURANCE

Libya Insurance Co: Usama Bldg, Sharia 1 September, POB 2438, Tripoli; tel (21) 44151; telex 22018; fax (21) 44178; Chair: K. M. Sherlala; f 1964; all classes of insurance.

MARKETING

Brega Petroleum Marketing Co: Sharia Bashir es-Saidawi, POB 402, Tripoli; tel (21) 40830; telex 20090; Sec of People's Committee: Dr Dokali B. al-Megharief; f 1971.

NATIONALIZED INDUSTRY

National Drilling and Workover Co: 208 Sharia Omar Mukhtar, POB 1454, Tripoli; tel (21) 32411; telex 20332; Chair: Ahmad M. al-Ghaber; f 1987.

Defence

Armed Forces: Tripoli; Commdr-in-Chief: Brig Abu-Bakr Younis Jaber.

Army: Tripoli; Chief of Staff: Brig Mustapha Kharroubi.

Navy: Tripoli; Commdr: Abd al-Latif Ahmad Shakshouki.

Development and Planning

PLANNING

General National Organization for Industrialization: Sharia San'a, POB 4388, Tripoli; tel (21) 34995; telex 200990; f 1970; responsible for the devt of industry.

Industrial Research Centre: POB 3633, Tripoli; tel (21) 691512; telex 20038; fax (21) 690028; Dir-Gen: Dr Abdalla Fadel; f 1970; product testing and preparation of feasibility studies, documentation and industrial information, industrial research.

REGIONAL DEVELOPMENT

Kufra and Sarir Authority: Council of Agricultural Development, Benghazi; f 1972; devt of the Kufra Oasis and Sarir area in South-East Libya.

Energy

Agip (NAME) Ltd—Libyan Branch: POB 346, Tripoli; POB 4120, Benghazi; tel (21) 35135; telex 20282; Chair: H. B. el-Hori; Dirs: A. B. Salama, I. Titone; f 1972; joint venture between Agip SpA (Italy) abd the National Oil Corpn (see below); oil production from onshore and offshore fields.

Arabian Gulf Oil Co: POB 263, Benghazi; telex 40033; Sec of People's Committee: H. A. Layass.

Azzawiya Oil Refining Co: POB 6451, Tripoli; tel (21) 605389; telex 30423; fax (21) 605948; Man Dir: Hammouda M. el-Aswad; Man, Admin: Bedri T. Ayad; f 1979; two refineries and two asphalt plants.

National Oil Corpn: POB 2655, Tripoli; tel (21) 46180; telex 61508; Chair: Abdallah al-Badri; f 1970 as successor to the Libyan General Petroleum Corpn, to undertake joint ventures with foreign cos; to build and operate refineries, storage tanks, petrochemical facilities, pipelines and tankers; to take part in arranging specifications for local and imported petroleum products; to participate in general planning of Libyan oil installations; to market crude oil and to establish and operate oil terminals.

National Petrochemicals Co: Garden City, POB 5234, Benghazi; tel (61) 21361; telex 40059; Chair: A. M. Sahli; f 1979; petrochemicals production.

Oasis Oil Co: POB 395, Tripoli; telex 20158; Sec of People's Committee: Abdullah S. al-Badri.

Ras Lanouf Oil and Gas Processing Co: Ras Lanouf, POB 2323, Tripoli; tel (21) 607924; telex 50661; Chair: Ragab al-Kawafi; f 1978.

Sirte Oil Co: POB 385, Tripoli; tel (21) 602052; telex 50657; Chair: Mansour M. ben Niran; f 1955 as Esso Standard Libya, taken over by Sirte Oil Co in 1982; exploration and production of crude oil and gas, liquefaction of natural gas.

Umm al-Jawaby Petroleum Co: POB 693, Tripoli; Chair and Gen Man: Muhammad Tenttoush.

Zuetina Oil Co: POB 2134, Tripoli; tel (21) 38011; telex 20130; Chair: Dr N. A. Arifi.

Fishing

Aquaculture Project: POB 315, Tripoli; tel (21) 39289; telex 20898; Dir: M. Zorgani; f 1988; implementation and supervision of aquaculture projects.

Legal and Judiciary

Supreme Court: Tripoli; Pres: Abd ar-Razzaq as-Sawsa; hears appeals from the Courts of Appeal in civil, penal, administrative and civil status matters; its judgments are final.

Media

BROADCASTING

Great Socialist People's Libyan Arab Jamahiriya Broadcasting Corpn: POB 3731, Tripoli; POB 119, el-Beida; tel (21) 32451; f 1957 (TV 1968); broadcasts in Arabic and English from Tripoli and Benghazi; from September 1971 special daily broadcasts to Gaza and other Israeli-occupied territories were begun; External Service (Radio) and People's Revolution Broadcasting: POB 333, Tripoli; Dir-Gen, External Service: Abdullah el-Megri.

GOVERNMENT PUBLISHER

General Co for Publishing, Advertising and Distribution: Souf al-Mahmudi, POB 959, Tripoli; tel (21) 45773; telex 20235; general, educational and academic books.

NEWS AND INFORMATION

Census and Statistical Department: General People's Committee for Planning, 40 Sharia Damascus, 2nd Floor, Tripoli; tel (21) 31731; collection, analysis and publication of statistical information.

Jamahiriya News Agency (JANA): Sharia al-Fateh, POB 2303, Tripoli; tel (21) 37106; telex 20012; Dir-Gen: Ibrahim Muhammad al-Bishari; serves Libyan and foreign subscribers.

Tourism

Department of Tourism and Fairs: Sharia Omar Mukhtar, POB 891, Tripoli; tel (21) 32255; telex 20179.

Transport

CIVIL AVIATION

Jamahiriya Air Transport: POB 2792, Tripoli; telex 20621; Pres and Chair: Hadi al-Husumi; f 1982; passenger and cargo charter flights, principally to destinations in Africa and Eastern Europe; took over operations of United African Airlines in 1983.

Libyan Arab Airlines: Sharia Omar Mukhtar, POB 2555, Tripoli; tel (21) 36021; telex 20333; Chair: Ali Aghila Hannoushi; Vice-Chair: Muhammad M. Abrebish; f 1964 as Kingdom of Libya Airlines and renamed in 1969; passenger and cargo services from Tripoli, Benghazi and Sebha to destinations in Europe, the Middle East and North Africa; domestic services throughout Libya.

ROADS

Department of Road Transport and Railways: Sharia az-Zawia, Secretariat of Communications Bldg, Tripoli; tel (21) 609011-30; telex 20401; responsible for maintenance of roads; there are no railways in Libya, although plans have been announced for the construction of a line from Tripoli to Ras Jedir, on the Tunisian frontier.

SHIPPING

General National Maritime Transport Co: 2 Sharia Ahmad Sharif, POB 80173, Tripoli; tel (21) 33155; telex 20208; Chair: Said Milud al-Ahrash; f 1970; handles all projects dealing with maritime trade.

LIECHTENSTEIN

Head of State

The reigning Prince, as Head of State of the hereditary Principality, exercises the legislative right jointly with the Landtag (Parliament). The five members of the Government are nominated by the Prince, on the proposition of the Landtag, and serve for four years.

Ruler: Prince Hans Adam (succeeded 13 November 1989).

Office of the Prince: Schloß Vaduz, 9490 Vaduz; tel 21212; telex 889288.

Legislature

The Constitution provides for a unicameral Landtag (Parliament), comprising 25 members elected for four years on the basis of proportional representation by universal adult suffrage.

Landtag (Parliament): Regierungsgebäude, 9490 Vaduz; tel 66111; telex 889290; Pres: Dr Karlheinz Ritter; Vice-Pres: Josef Büchel.

MINISTRIES AND GOVERNMENT DEPARTMENTS

GOVERNMENT OFFICES
Regierungsgebäude, 9490 Vaduz
Tel 66111; telex 889290; fax 66460
Chief of Government: Hans Brunhart
Deputy Chief of Government: Dr Herbert Wille

OFFICE OF THE COUNCILLOR FOR AGRICULTURE, CULTURE, INTERNAL AFFAIRS AND JUSTICE
Regierungsgebäude, 9490 Vaduz
Tel 66111; telex 889290; fax 66460
Councillor: Herbert Wille

OFFICE OF THE COUNCILLOR FOR EDUCATION AND FOREIGN AFFAIRS
Regierungsgebäude, 9490 Vaduz
Tel 66111; telex 889290; fax 66460
Councillor: Hans Brunhart

OFFICE OF THE COUNCILLOR FOR ECONOMY
Regierungsgebäude, 9490 Vaduz
Tel 66111; telex 889290; fax 66460
Councillor: René Ritter

OFFICE OF THE COUNCILLOR FOR SOCIAL WELFARE AND PUBLIC HEALTH
Regierungsgebäude, 9490 Vaduz
Tel 66111; telex 889290; fax 66460
Councillor: Dr Peter Wolff

OFFICE OF THE COUNCILLOR FOR TRANSPORTATION
Regierungsgebäude, 9490 Vaduz
Tel 66111; telex 889290; fax 66460
Councillor: Wilfried Büchel

GOVERNMENT AGENCIES AND ORGANIZATIONS

Advisory and Supervisory Body

Amt für Volkswirtschaft (Office for National Economy): Kirchstr 7, 9490 Vaduz; tel 66111; telex 889290; fax 66626; Dir: Dr Benno Beck; f 1963; concerned with economics in general, statistics, environmental protection, banking supervision, unemployment, protection of labour and social insurance.

Grundbuchamt (Land Registry): 9490 Vaduz; tel 66111; Registrar: Hubert Kaiser.

Agriculture and the Environment

AGRICULTURE

Landwirtschaftamt (National Agriculture Office): Landesverwaltung, 9490 Vaduz; tel 66111; telex 889290; fax 66460; Dir: Julius Ospelt.

THE ENVIRONMENT

Amt für Gewässerschutz (Office for Water Conservation): 9490 Vaduz; tel 66111; Dir: Theo Kindle.

Landesforstamt (National Forestry Office): 9490 Vaduz; tel 66111; Dir: Dr Felix Näscher.

Art and Culture

Landesarchiv (National Archives): Regierungsgebäude, 9490 Vaduz; tel 66111; Dir: Dr Alois Ospelt; f 1961.

Landesbibliothek (National Library): Regierungsgebäude, 9490 Vaduz; tel 66343; Dir: Dr Alois Ospelt; f 1961.

Landesmuseum (National Museum): Städtle 43, 9490 Vaduz; tel 22310; Dir: Norbert W. Hasler.

Business and Economy

BANKING

Liechtensteinische Landesbank (State Bank): Postfach 384, 9490 Vaduz; tel 68811; telex 889400; Pres: Andreas Vogt; Man: Karlheinz Heeb; f 1861.

FINANCIAL AGENCIES

Steuerverwaltung (Tax Administration): 9490 Vaduz; tel 66111; Tax Admin: Bruno Sprenger.

INSURANCE

Liechtensteinische AHV-IV-FAK (Alters- und Hinterlassenen-Versicherung, Invalidenversicherung, Familienausgleichskasse) (Old Age, Survivors' and Invalidity Insurance, and Family Compensation): Gerberweg 5, 9490 Vaduz; tel 61252; fax 20406; Dir: Gerhard Biedermann; f 1954; state insurance co.

Defence

Amt für Zivilschutz und Landesversorgung (Office for Civil Defence and National Supply): 9490 Vaduz; tel 66111; Dir: Franz Tschugmell.

Fürstlich Liechternstienisches Sicherheitskorps (Police Dept): Regierungsgebäude, 9490 Vaduz; tel 66111; telex 77855; Commr: Vinzenz Batliner.

Energy

Liechtensteinische Gasversorgung: 9490 Vaduz; tel 66268; Dir: Anton Gerner; provision of gas.

Lichtensteinische Kraftwerke: 9494 Schaan; tel 23322; fax 22203; Dirs: Walter Frick, Walter Marxer; power station.

Health and Welfare

Fürsorgeamt (Welfare Office): 9494 Schaan; tel 66111; Dir: Richard Biedermann.

Landesphysikus (National Health Office): 9492 Eschen; tel 31202; Dir: Dr David Büchel.

Legal and Judiciary

Kriminalgericht (Criminal Court): 9490 Vaduz; Presiding Judge: Dr Rainer Amann; bench of five judges.

Landgericht (County Court): 9490 Vaduz; tel 66111; Presiding Judge: Dr Franz Rederer; Court of First Instance.

Obergericht (Superior Court): 9490 Vaduz; Presiding Judge: Max Bizozzero; Court of Second Instance; bench of five judges.

Oberster Gerichtshof (Supreme Court): 9490 Vaduz; Presiding Judge: Dr Karl Kohlegger; Court of Third Instance; bench of five judges.

Schöffengericht (Court of Assizes): 9490 Vaduz; Presiding Judge: Dr Benedikt Marxer; for minor misdemeanours; bench of three judges.

Staatsanwaltschaft (Public Prosecutor's Office): 9490 Vaduz; tel 66111; Public Prosecutors: Dr Gert Frommelt, Dr Gerhard Mislik.

Staatsgerichthof (State Court): 9490 Vaduz; Presiding Judge: Dr Erich Seeger; exists for the protection of Public Law; five mems.

Verwaltungsbeschwerdeinstanz (Administrative Court of Appeal): 9490 Vaduz; Presiding Judge: Harry Gstöhl; appeals against decrees and decisions of the Govt may be made to this court; five mems.

Media

NEWS AND INFORMATION

Presse- und Informationsamt (Press and Information Office): Regierungsgebäude, 9490 Vaduz; tel 66111; telex 889290; fax 66460; Dir: Egon Gstöhl; f 1962; publication of Govt information; advice and information to press officials; press serivces.

Zivilstandsamt (Civil Registry Office): 9490 Vaduz; Registrar: Leo Büchel.

Tourism

Liechtenstein National Tourist Office: Kirchstr 7, Postfach 139, 9490 Vaduz; tel 66288; telex 889488; fax 20806; Dir: Berthold Konrad; f 1972; promotion of tourism; representation in tourism bodies abroad; organization of events relating to tourism.

Transport and Communications

TELECOMMUNICATIONS

Dienststelle für Post und Fernmeldewesen (Service Office for Posts and Telecommunications): 9490 Vaduz; Dir: Theobald Wille.

TRANSPORT

Motorfahrzeugkontrolle (Motor Vehicle Office): 9490 Vaduz; tel 66111; Dir: Manfred Schurti.

LUXEMBOURG

Head of State

Luxembourg is a constitutional monarchy, and executive power is vested in the Grand Duke, but is normally exercised by the Council of Ministers, led by the President of the Government (Prime Minister). The Grand Duke appoints Ministers, who are responsible to the Chamber of Deputies.

Grand Duke: HRH Prince Jean Benoît Guillaume Marie Robert Louis Antoin Adolphe Marc d'Aviano (succeeded to the throne 12 November 1964).

Office of HRH the Grand Duke: Palais Grand-Ducal, rue du Rost, L-2447 Luxembourg; tel 22-60-1; telex 1817.

Legislature

Legislative power is exercised by the unicameral Chambre des Députés (Chamber of Deputies), comprising 60 members elected by universal adult suffrage for five years by proportional representation. Some legislative functions are entrusted to the 21 appointed members of the Council of State, although the Council can be overridden by the Chamber.

Chambre des Députés (Chamber of Deputies): rue du Marché-aux-Herbes, Luxembourg; tel 20-22-2; Pres: Léon Bolendorff.

MINISTRIES AND GOVERNMENT DEPARTMENTS

OFFICE OF THE PRESIDENT OF THE GOVERNMENT (PRIME MINISTER)
Hôtel de Bourgogne, 4 rue de la Congrégation, L-2910 Luxembourg
Tel 478-1; telex 2790; fax 46-17-20
President of the Government (Prime Minister):
Jacques Santer

OFFICE OF THE DEPUTY PRIME MINISTER
5 rue Notre-Dame, L-2240 Luxembourg
Tel 478-1; telex 1702
Deputy Prime Minister: Jacques F. Poos

MINISTRY OF AGRICULTURE, VITICULTURE AND RURAL DEVELOPMENT
15A blvd Joseph II, L-2913 Luxembourg
Tel 478-1; telex 2537
Minister: René Steichen

MINISTRY OF THE ARMED FORCES AND POLICE
Plateau du St Esprit, L-2915 Luxembourg
Tel 478-1; fax 46-26-82
Minister: Jacques F. Poos
Secretary of State: Georges Wohlfart

MINISTRY OF THE CIVIL SERVICE
Plateau du St Esprit, BP 106, L-2915 Luxembourg
Tel 478-1; telex 3404
Minister: Marc Fischbach

MINISTRY OF COMMUNICATIONS
5A rue de Prague, L-2918 Luxembourg
Minister: Alex Bodry

MINISTRY OF CULTURAL AFFAIRS
19-21 rue Goethe, L-2912 Luxembourg
Tel 47-94-1
Minister: Jacques Santer
Assistant Minister of Cultural Affairs and Scientific Research: René Steichen

MINISTRY OF DEFENCE
Plateau du St Esprit, L-2915 Luxembourg
Tel 478-1; telex 60751; fax 46-26-82
Minister: Jacques F. Poos
Secretary of State: Georges Wohlfart

MINISTRY OF THE ECONOMY
19-21 blvd Royal, L-2914 Luxembourg
Tel 478-1; telex 3464
Minister and Minister of Commerce: Robert Goebbels

MINISTRY OF ENERGY
19-21 blvd Royal, L-2917 Luxembourg
Tel 47-94-1
Minister: Alex Bodry

MINISTRY OF THE ENVIRONMENT
5A rue de Prague, L-2918 Luxembourg
Tel 47-88-70; telex 2536; fax 400-410
Minister and Minister for Territorial Administration:
Alex Bodry

MINISTRY OF THE FAMILY AND SOLIDARITY
14 ave de la Gare, L-2919 Luxembourg
Tel 478-1; fax 47-87-14
Minister: Fernand Boden

Service de l'Immigration (Immigration Service): 14 ave de la Gare, L-2919 Luxembourg; tel 47-83-84; Commr: Gaston Raus; f 1972; integration of immigrants and refugees.

MINISTRY OF FINANCE
3 rue de la Congrégation, L-1352 Luxembourg
Tel 478-1; telex 2790; fax 47-52-41
Minister and Minister Responsible for the Budget:
Jean-Claude Juncker

MINISTRY OF FOREIGN AFFAIRS, FOREIGN TRADE AND CO-OPERATION
5 rue Notre Dame, L-2911 Luxembourg
Tel 478-1; telex 3405; fax 231-44
Minister: Jacques F. Poos
Secretary of State: Georges Wohlfart

MINISTRY OF HEALTH
57 blvd de la Pétrusse, L-2320 Luxembourg
Tel 408-01; telex 2546; fax 48-49-03
Minister: Johny Lahure

MINISTRY OF THE INTERIOR, HOUSING AND TOWN PLANNING
19 rue Beaumont, L-1219 Luxembourg
Tel 47-94-1
Minister: Jean Spautz

MINISTRY OF JUSTICE
16 blvd Royal, L-2934 Luxembourg
Tel 47-94-1; fax 27-66-1
Minister: Marc Fischbach

MINISTRY OF LABOUR
26 rue Zithe, L-2939 Luxembourg
Tel 49-92-11; telex 2985; fax 49-92-12-60-9
Minister: Jean-Claude Juncker

MINISTRY OF THE MIDDLE CLASSES AND TOURISM
19-21 blvd Royal, L-2914 Luxembourg
Tel 478-1
Minister: Fernand Boden

MINISTRY OF NATIONAL EDUCATION AND YOUTH
29 rue Aldringen, L-2926 Luxembourg
Tel 46-80-21; fax 46-80-25-73
Minister of National Education: Marc Fischbach
Minister of Youth: Johny Lahure

Secretary of State for Youth: Mady Delvaux-Stehres

MINISTRY OF PHYSICAL EDUCATION AND SPORT
66 route de Trèves, BP 180, L-2916 Luxembourg
Tel 43-60-11; fax 43-45-99
Minister and Minister of Youth: Johny Lahure
Secretary of State: Mady Delvaux-Stehres

MINISTRY OF PUBLIC WORKS
4 blvd F. D. Roosevelt, L-2940 Luxembourg
Tel 478-1; fax 46-27-09
Minister: Robert Goebbels

MINISTRY OF SOCIAL SECURITY
26 rue Zithe, L-2939 Luxembourg
Tel 49-92-11; telex 2985; fax 49-92-1-2609
Minister: Johny Lahure
Secretary of State: Mady Delvaux-Stehres

Administration du Contrôle Médical de la Sécurité Sociale: 125 route d'Esch, BP 1342, L-1013 Luxembourg; tel 49-920-2060; Dir: Dr Marcel Rassel; Dep Dir: Marcel Thill; f 1979; controls medical activites in relation to all social security organizations.

MINISTRY OF STATE
4 rue de la Congrégation, L-2910 Luxembourg
Tel 478-1; fax 46-17-20
Minister: Jacques Santer
Responsible for co-ordination between Govt depts, Govt administration and information

MINISTRY OF TRANSPORT
19-21 blvd Royal, L-2938 Luxembourg
Tel 478-1; telex 1465
Minister: Robert Goebbels

MINISTRY OF THE TREASURY
3 rue de la Congrégation, L-1352 Luxembourg
Tel 478-1; telex 2790; fax 47-52-41
Minister and Minister of Financial Affairs:
Jacques Santer
Director of the Treasury: Yves Mersch

GOVERNMENT AGENCIES AND ORGANIZATIONS

Advisory and Supervisory Bodies

Administration des Bâtiments Publics (Administration of Public Buildings): 10 rue du St Esprit, BP 112, L-2011 Luxembourg; tel 46-19-19-1; fax 46-19-19-323; Dir: Roland Baldauff; Dep Dir: Fernand Otto; f 1945; repair of bldgs belonging to the State; planning, surveying and execution of public bldgs construction projects.

Conseil Economique et Social (Social and Economic Council): 7 rue Alcide de Gasperi, Luxembourg; tel 43-58-51.

Inspection du Travail et des Mines (Labour and Mines Inspectorate): 26 rue Zithe, BP 27, L-2010 Luxembourg; tel 49-92-11; fax 49-14-47; Dir: Arthur Schuster; Asst Dir: Paul Weber; f 1869 (mines), 1902 (labour); implementation and surveillance of labour law and regulations; authorization and surveillance of dangerous and polluting installations; supervision of mines and quarries; under the Ministry of Labour.

Service d'Urbanisme et d'Aménagement Communal (Town Planning and Communal Development Service): 19 rue Beaumont, L-2933 Luxembourg; tel 47-94-515; First Govt Adviser: Edmond Dauphin; Govt Adviser: Daniel Miltgen; application of laws relating to devt of towns; assists communes in the areas of town planning and communal, regional and national devt.

Agriculture and the Environment

AGRICULTURE

Administration des Services Techniques de l'Agriculture (Agricultural Technical Services Administration): 16 route d'Esch, BP 1904, L-1019, Luxembourg; tel 44-32-32; Dir: Thomas Salentiny; f 1883; under the Ministry of Agriculture and Viticulture.

Institut Viti-Vinicole de l'Etat (State Institute of Wine Production): BP 50, Remich; tel 69-12-2; telex 2537; fax 45-01-78; Dir: Jean-Pierre Wagener; f 1925; promotion of the production of quality wines by advising farmers in their choice of grape varieties and in wine-making; professional training for wine farmers.

THE ENVIRONMENT

Administration des Eaux et Forêts (Water and Forest Administration): 67 rue Michel Welter, BP 411, L-2014 Luxembourg; tel 40-22-01; Dir: Paul Decker.

Administration de l'Environnement (Environment Administration): 1A rue Auguste Lumière, L-1950 Luxembourg; tel 49-61-05; telex 60742; fax 48-50-78; Dir: Paul Hansen; implementation of laws relating to the environment, eg atmospheric pollution, noise, waste, etc.

Art and Culture

Archives de l'Etat (National Archives): Plateau du St Esprit, BP 6, L-2010 Luxembourg; tel 47-84-78; under the Ministry of Cultural Affairs.

Bibliothèque Nationale (National Library): 37 blvd F. D. Roosevelt, Luxembourg; tel 2-62-55; under the Ministry of Cultural Affairs.

Fonds Culturel National (National Fund for Culture): 19-21 rue Goethe, Luxembourg; tel 47-83-91; under the Ministry of Cultural Affairs.

Musées de l'Etat (State Museums): Marché-aux-Poissons, Luxembourg; tel 47-93-30.

Service des Sites et Monuments Nationaux (National Sites and Monuments Service): 26 rue Munster, L-2160 Luxembourg; tel 47-89-40; Dir: G. Calteux; f 1977; restoration and conservation of historic buildings.

Business and Economy

BANKING

Banque Générale du Luxembourg SA (BGL): 27 ave Monterey, L-2951 Luxembourg; tel 47-99-1; telex 3401; fax 47-99-25-79; Chair: Georges Arendt; f 1919.

Banque Internationale à Luxembourg SA (BIL): 2 blvd Royal, L-2953 Luxembourg; tel 45-90-1; telex 3626; fax 45-90-26-25; Chair: Gaston Thorn; Man Dir: Albert Dondelinger; f 1856; bank of issue.

Banque de Luxembourg SA: 80 place de la Gare, BP 2221, L-1022 Luxembourg; tel 49-92-41; telex 3425; Chair: Gaston Zerr; Man Dir: Robert Reckinger; f 1936.

Caisse d'Epargne de l'Etat du Grand-Duché de Luxembourg: 1 place de Metz, BP 2105, L-2954 Luxembourg; tel 40-15-1; telex 3417; fax 2-76-87; Chair: Corneille Bruck; Pres of Exec Committee and Chief Exec: Raymond Kirsch; f 1856; all banking and financial operations.

Institut Monétaire Luxembourgeois: 63 ave de la Liberté, L-2983 Luxembourg; tel 40-29-29; telex 2766; fax 49-21-80; Dir-Gen: Pierre Jaans; Dirs: Jean-Nicolas Schaus, Jean Guill; f 1983; represents Luxembourg in international monetary matters; acts as a banking supervisory authority; holds external assets and controls domestic loans; issues bank-notes and coins; manages official reserves; regulates domestic credit; depository institution for Govt funds.

FINANCIAL AGENCIES

Administration de l'Enregistrement et des Domaines: 1-3 ave Guillaume, BP 31, L-2010 Luxembourg; tel 44-90-51; fax 45-42-98; Dir: Jules Pierret; f 1841; responsible for value added tax, stamp and seal taxes, registration and mortgage taxes, inheritance taxes.

Inspection Générale des Finances (General Inspectorate of Finance): 2 rue de la Congrégation, Luxembourg; tel 478-1; under the Ministry of Finance.

Service de la Trésorerie de l'Etat (Treasury): c/o Ministry of the Treasury, 3 rue de la Congrégation, L-1352 Luxembourg; tel 478-1; telex 2790; fax 47-52-41; Dir: Yves Mersch; management of the State's financial assets and debt.

Société Nationale de Crédit et d'Investissement (SNCI): 7 rue du St Esprit, L-1475 Luxembourg; tel 46-19-71-1; telex 60664; fax 46-19-79; Pres: Raymond Kirsch; Vice-Pres: Armand Simon; Gen Man: Georges Bollig; f 1977; finances participations in certain cos, loans cheap investment credit and provides export credit.

INSURANCE

Commissariat aux Assurances (Insurance Commission): Ministry of the Treasury, 3 rue de la Congrégation, L-1352 Luxembourg; tel 478-285; telex 2790; fax 47-52-41; Insurance Commr: Victor Rod; First Inspector: Roger Bellion; f 1984; examines requests for authorization and supervises insurance and reinsurance activities; co-ordinates Govt initiatives concerning insurance.

Office du Ducroire: 7 rue Alcide de Gasperi, L-2981 Luxembourg; tel 43-58-53; telex 60174; fax 43-83-26; Chair: Raymond Kirsch; Sec: Etienne Reuter; f 1961; export credit insurance.

TRADE

Administration des Douanes (Customs Administration): 4-6 rue du St Esprit, Luxembourg; tel 2-09-51; under the Ministry of Finance.

Defence

Armed Forces: 5 rue Auguste Lumière, L-1018 Luxembourg; tel 48-88-36; telex 2912; Commdr: Col Armand Bruck; Asst Commdr: Lt-Col René Alzin.

Direction de la Police: 58 rue Gelsener, BP 1007, L-1630 Luxembourg; tel 4-09-40-1; under the Ministry of the Armed Forces and Police.

Gendarmerie Grand-Ducale (Constabulary): 3-5 rue Auguste Lumière, BP 1202, L-1012 Luxembourg; tel 40-91-91; telex 3310; fax 49-08-28; Commdr: Col Fernand Diederich; Dep Commdr: Lt-Col Charles Bourg; f 1881; law enforcement, public order, crime prevention, etc; under the Ministry of the Armed Forces and Police.

Service National de la Protection Civile (National Service for Civil Protection): 36 rue J. B. Esch, L-1473 Luxembourg; tel 44-51-51; telex 2929; fax 45-37-44; Dir: Léon Jung; f 1936; planning and organization of emergency services; organization of ambulance and rescue services; under the Ministry of the Interior.

Education

Institut Supérieur d'Etudes et de Recherches (Education and Research Institute): BP 2, 7201 Walferdange; tel 33-14-14.

Collège des Inspecteurs: address as above; Inspector-Gen of Education: Jean-Pierre Kraemer; f 1912; co-ordinates education inspection at pre-school, primary and special levels; aids in the production of textbooks.

Energy

Centrales Hydro-Electriques de l'Etat (State Hydro-Electric Power Stations): Centrale d'Esch-sur-Sûre; tel 8-98-85-1; under the Ministry of Energy.

Conseil National de l'Energie Nucléaire (CNEN) (National Nuclear Energy Council): c/o Ministry of Energy, 19-21 blvd Royal, L-2917 Luxembourg; tel 47-94-1; Chair: Minister of Energy, Alex Bodry; f 1956; studies the economic, legal, financial and technical aspects of the use of nuclear energy, particularly when applied to industry; takes part in the work of similar bodies in other countries.

Service de l'Energie de l'Etat (State Energy Service): 34 ave Marie-Thérèse, BP 10, L-2010 Luxembourg; tel 44-20-30; telex 3788; fax 44-20-51; Dir: Jean-Paul Hoffmann; f 1967; under the Ministry of Energy; supervision of energy distributing cos; responsible for electricity production at the state-owned power stations at Esch-sur-Sûre and Rosport.

Health and Welfare

HEALTH

Direction de la Santé (Health Directorate): 57 blvd de la Pétrusse, L-2320 Luxembourg; tel 4-08-01; under the Ministry of Public Health.

WELFARE

Fonds National de Solidarité (National Solidarity Fund): 138 blvd de la Pétrusse, BP 2411, L-1024 Luxembourg; tel 48-31-55; Pres and Dir: Paul-Henri Meyers; f 1960; funds for the seriously handicapped; funds for heating and food; minimum wage; under the Ministry of the Family and Social Solidarity.

Inspection Générale de la Sécurité Sociale (General Inspectorate of Social Security): 26 rue Zithe, BP 1308, L-1013 Luxembourg; tel 49-92-11; telex 2985; fax 49-92-1-2609; Dir: Georges Schroeder;f 1974; co-ordination of social security legislation.

Service National de la Jeunesse (National Youth Service): 1 rue de la Poste, place d'Armes, BP 707, L- 2017, Luxembourg; tel 46-802-335; fax 45-85-50; Dir: Frantz C. Muller; Govt Attaché: Nico Meisch; f 1984; organization of youth activities; acts as intermediary between youth organizations and the Govt; youth information.

Legal and Judiciary

Cour Supérieure de Justice (Superior Court of Justice): Bâtiment de Justice, 12 Côte d'Eich, L-1450 Luxembourg; tel 47-59-81-1; Chief Justice: Prosper Jacques; includes both a court of appeal, hearing decisions made by District Courts, and a Cour de Cassation.

Direction Générale des Etablissements Pénitentiaires et des Maisons d'Education (General Directorate for Prisons and Reform Schools): Bâtiment de Justice, 12 côte d'Eich, L-1450 Luxembourg; tel 47-59-81-1; fax 47-05-50; State Prosecutor: Camille Wampach; Advocate-Gen, delegate of the State Prosecutor: Pierre Schmit; f 1964; under the Ministry of Justice.

Office of the Attorney-General: Bâtiment de Justice, L-1450 Luxembourg, tel 47-59-81-1; Attorney-Gen: Camille Wampach.

Media

GOVERNMENT PUBLISHER

Service Central de Législation: 34 rue du Marché-aux-Herbes, L-1728 Luxembourg; tel 478-1; First Govt Advisor: Raymond Weydert; f 1959; produces the official journal of the Grand-Duchy, containing new laws, notices of the admin and publs prescribed by law for commercial cos; publishes law books; under the Ministry of State.

NEWS AND INFORMATION

Service Central de la Statistique et des Etudes Economiques (STATEC): 19-21 blvd Royal, BP 304, L-2013 Luxembourg; tel 47-94-27-3; Dir: Georges Als; f 1962; statistical office; under the Ministry of Economy.

Service Central VideoSTATE (Videotex): 10 blvd F. D. Roosevelt, L-2450 Luxembourg; tel 47-86-58; fax 20-09-0; f 1986; information on Videotex on Ministries, public offices and services of the Luxembourg Govt.

Service Information et Presse: 10 blvd F. D. Roosevelt, L-2450 Luxembourg; tel 47-82-24; telex 1727; fax 20-09-0; Head of the Press and Information Dept: Lex Roth; f 1944; responsible for Govt information and domestic and foreign press relations; publishes gen information booklets; provides general information on the Grand Duchy; acts as public relations dept of the Govt.

Science and Technology

Administration du Cadastre et de la Topographie (National Survey and Topohraphic Office): 54 ave Gaston Diderich, L-1420 Luxembourg; tel 44-90-11; Dir: Emile Schlesser; Dep Dir: René Wagner; f 1945; surveying and land information.

Centre Informatique de l'Etat (CIE) (State Computer Science Centre): 1 rue Mercier, L-2144 Luxembourg; tel 49-92-51; telex 60482; Dir: Félix Schumacher; f 1974; promotes, administers and co-ordinates computing activities in the public sector.

Tourism

Office National du Tourisme: 77 rue d'Anvers, BP 1001, L-1010 Luxembourg; tel 48-79-99; telex 2715; Pres: Raymond Frisch; Man: Georges Hausemer; f 1931; promotion of tourism; 155 mems.

Transport and Communications

TELECOMMUNICATIONS

Administration des Postes et Télécommunications (Posts and Telecommunications Administration): Hôtel des Postes, L-2020 Luxembourg; tel 47-65-1.

TRANSPORT

Administration des Ponts et Chaussées (Roads and Bridges Administration): 38 blvd de la Foire, BP 243, Luxembourg; tel 45-05-91; fax 45-32-98; Dir: Pierre Reiff; under the Ministry of Public Works; plans and oversees road construction and maintenance.

Cargolux Airlines International SA: Aéroport de Luxembourg, BP 591, L-2015 Luxembourg; tel 43-60-21-1; telex 2272; fax 43-54-46; Pres and Chief Exec: Sten Grotenfelt; f 1970; cargo air services.

Luxair SA (Société Luxembourgeoise de Navigation Aérienne): Aéroport de Luxembourg, L-2987 Luxembourg; tel 47-98-1; telex 2372; fax 43-24-82; Chair of Board of Dirs: Gust Graas; Pres: Roger Sietzen; f 1961; passenger flights; tour operator; handling agent for Luxembourg Airport.

Société Nationale des Chemins de Fer Luxembourgeois: 9 place de la Gare, Luxembourg; tel 49-90-1; telex 2288; Pres of Admin Council: Jeannot Schneider; Dir-Gen: Romain Kugener; railways.

MADAGASCAR

Head of State

Executive power is vested in the President, as Head of State, who is elected for a seven-year term by universal adult suffrage. The President is also Chairman of a Supreme Revolutionary Council (SRC), an advisory body which acts as 'the guardian of the Malagasy Socialist Revolution'. Its members are chosen by the President. The President appoints a Prime Minister and, on the latter's recommendation, the other members of the Council of Ministers.

President: Didier Ratsiraka (took office as President of the Supreme Revolutionary Council 15 June 1975; sworn in as President of Madagascar 4 January 1976; re-elected for further seven-year terms on 7 November 1982 and 12 March 1989).

Office of the President: Ambohitsorohitra, 101 Antananarivo; tel (2) 27474; telex 22339.

Legislature

According to the 1975 Constitution supreme legislative authority is vested in the Assemblée Nationale Populaire (National People's Assembly), with 137 members elected for five years by universal adult suffrage. Local government has a four-tier structure, based on traditional village assemblies (fokonolona).

Assemblée Nationale Populaire (National People's Assembly): Tsimbazaza, 101 Antananarivo; tel (2) 21637; telex 22339; Pres: Honoré Rakotomanana.

MINISTRIES AND GOVERNMENT DEPARTMENTS

SUPREME REVOLUTIONARY COUNCIL
Ambohitsorohitra, 101 Antananarivo
Tel (2) 27474; telex 22339
President: Didier Ratsiraka

OFFICE OF THE PRIME MINISTER
Mahazoarivo, 101 Antananarivo
Tel (2) 25258; telex 22339
Prime Minister: Lt-Col Victor Ramahatra

MINISTRY OF AGRICULTURAL PRODUCTION AND AGRARIAN REFORM
Anosy, 101 Antananarivo
Tel (2) 24710; telex 22508
Minister: José Michel Andrianoelison

MINISTRY OF ANIMAL HUSBANDRY, WATER AND FORESTS
Anosy, 101 Antananarivo
Tel (2) 28208
Minister: Joseph Randrianasolo

MINISTRY OF THE CIVIL SERVICE AND LABOUR
Tsaralalana, 101 Antananarivo
Tel (2) 24911; telex 22339
Minister: Georges Ruphin

MINISTRY OF COMMERCE
Antaninarenina, 101 Antananarivo
Tel (2) 27292; telex 22378
Minister: Georges Solofoson

MINISTRY OF DEFENCE
101 Antananarivo
Tel (2) 22211
Minister: Gen Christopher Raveloson-Mahasampo

MINISTRY OF FINANCE AND ECONOMY
Antaninarenina, BP 61, 101 Antananarivo
Tel (2) 21632; telex 22489
Minister: Pascal Rakotomavo
Special Adviser to the President on Economic Affairs: Nirina Andriamanerasoa

MINISTRY OF FOREIGN AFFAIRS
Anosy, 101 Antananarivo
Tel (2) 21198; telex 22236
Minister: Jean Bemananjara

MINISTRY OF HEALTH
Ambohidahy, 101 Antananarivo
Tel (2) 23697
Minister: Jean-Jacques Séraphin

MINISTRY OF HIGHER EDUCATION
Tsimbazaza, 101 Antananarivo
Tel (2) 27185
Minister: Ignace Rakoto

MINISTRY OF INDUSTRY, ENERGY AND MINES
BP 527, 101 Antananarivo
Tel (2) 25515; telex 22540
Minister: José Rakotomavo

MINISTRY OF INFORMATION AND IDEOLOGICAL GUIDANCE
rue Ratsimilaho, Antaninarenina, BP 491, 101 Antananarivo
Tel (2) 21125; telex 22506
Minister: Simon Pierre

MINISTRY OF THE INTERIOR
Anosy, 101 Antananarivo
Tel (2) 23084
Minister: Ampy Augustin Portos

MINISTRY OF JUSTICE
Faravohitra, BP 231, 101 Antananarivo
Tel (2) 24030
Minister: Joseph Bedo

MINISTRY OF POPULATION, SOCIAL AFFAIRS, YOUTH AND SPORTS
BP 723, 101 Antananarivo
Tel (2) 23129
Minister: M. Badhroudine

MINISTRY OF POSTS AND TELECOMMUNICATIONS
Antaninarenina, 101 Antananarivo
Tel (2) 26121; telex 22250
Minister: M. Rakotovao-Andriantiana

MINISTRY OF PUBLIC WORKS
Anosy, 101 Antananarivo
Tel (2) 24224; telex 22343
Minister: Andrianaivomanana Razafindramisa

MINISTRY OF REVOLUTIONARY CULTURE AND ART
BP 305, 101 Antananarivo
Tel (2) 27092
Minister: Gisèle Rabesahala

MINISTRY OF SCIENTIFIC RESEARCH AND TECHNOLOGICAL DEVELOPMENT
27 rue Fernand Kassanga, BP 6224, 101 Antananarivo
Tel (2) 33288; telex 22539
Minister: Antoine Zafera Rabesa

MINISTRY OF SECONDARY AND BASIC EDUCATION
Anosy, BP 267, 101 Antananarivo
Tel (2) 21325
Minister: Charles Zeny

MINISTRY OF TRANSPORT, METEOROLOGY AND TOURISM
Anosy, 101 Antananarivo
Tel (2) 24604; telex 22301
Minister: Commdt Jean-Emile Tsaranazy

GOVERNMENT AGENCIES AND ORGANIZATIONS

Advisory and Supervisory Bodies

Caisses et Bureau de Commercialisation et de Stabilisation des Prix du Café, de la Vanille et du Girofle: rue Pierre Rajaonah, BP 804, 101 Antananarivo; sets the prices for coffee, vanilla and cloves; promotion of these products.

Office Militaire National pour les Industries Stratégiques (OMNIS): 21 làlana Razanakombana, BP 1 bis, 101 Antananarivo; tel (2) 24439; telex 22370; Dir-Gen: Capt Roland Ratsimandresy; f 1976; oversees the management of major industrial organizations, oil and mining exploration.

Agriculture

Société d'Intérêt National Malgache des Produits Agricoles (SINPA): rue Fernand Kassanga, Tsimbazaza, BP 754, 101 Antananarivo; tel (2) 20558; telex 22309; fax (2) 20665; Chair: Yves Ramelison; Gen Man: Alphonse Ralison; f 1973; purchase and distribution of all cash and food crops.

Société Malgache de Produits Laitiers SA: km 7,500, route de Majunga, Ambohidroa, BP 4126, 101 Antananarivo; tel (2) 44266; telex 22341; Dir-Gen: Ramanoelina Bodololao; promotion and devt of the dairy-products industry.

Business and Economy

BANKING

Bankin'ny Indostria (BNI): 74 rue du 26 juin 1960, BP 174, 101 Antananarivo; tel (2) 23951; telex 22205; Pres: Pascal Rakotomavo; Gen Man: Tantely Andrianarivo; f 1976 by merger of Banque pour le Commerce et l'Industrie de Madagascar and Banque Nationale Malgasy de Développement; 14 brs.

Bankin'ny Tantsaha Mpamokatra (BTM): place de l'Indépendance, BP 183, 101 Antananarivo; tel (2) 20251; telex 22208; Dir-Gen: Jean-Marie Henri; Dep Dir-Gen: Jean Pouillard; f 1977; fmrly Banque Malgache d'Escompte et de Crédit; specializes in rural devt; 43 brs.

Banky Fampandrosoana ny Varotra (BFV): 14 làlana Jeneraly Rabehevitra, BP 196 & 440, 101 Antananarivo; tel 26424; telex 22264; fax (2) 34535; Gen Man: Jean Clariel Ramasinaivo; Dep Gen Man: Paul Razafindrakoto; f 1977; short-, medium- and long-term credit for devt in all sectors of the economy.

Banque Centrale de la République Malgache: ave de la Révolution Socialiste Malgache, BP 550, 101 Antananarivo; tel (2) 21751; telex 22329; Gov: Blondin Razafimanjato; Dir-Gen: Renée Razafintsamala; f 1973 to replace the Institut Malgache d'Emission as bank of issue.

INSURANCE

ARO (Assurances Réassurances Omnibranches): Antsahavola, BP 42, 101 Antananarivo; tel (2) 20154; telex 22265; Dir-Gen: Pascal Rakotomavo; Dep Dir-Gen: Bruno Rabary.

Assurance France-Madagascar: 7 rue Rainitivo, BP 710, 101 Antananarivo; tel (2) 23024; telex 22321; Pres: Guy Sabouret; Dir: Isabelle Ratsira; f 1951; all classes of insurance.

Compagnie Malgache d'Assurances et de Réassurances: Immeuble 'Ny Havana', Zone des 67 Ha, BP 3881, 101 Antananarivo; tel (2) 26760; telex 22377; Dir-Gen: Panoël Rakotovao; f 1968.

Mutuelle d'Assurances Malagasy (MAMA): 1F, 12 bis, rue Rainibetsimisaraka, Ambalavao-Isotry, BP 185, 101 Antananarivo.

Société Malgache d'Assurances, Faugère, Jutheau et Cie: 13 rue Patrice Lumumba, BP 673, 101 Antananarivo; tel (2) 23162; telex 22247; Dir: Raymond Rajohnson; f 1952.

NATIONALIZED INDUSTRY

Société Siramamy Malagasy (SIRAMA): Impasse rue de Belgique, Isoraka, BP 1633, 101 Antananarivo; tel (2) 25235; telex 22372; Dir-Gen: Roland M. Rasamoely; f 1949; refining of sugar.

TRADE

Société Nationale de Commerce (SONACO): BP 3187, 101 Antananarivo; telex 55623; Dir-Gen: Andriamaniraka Ralison; f 1973; handles all imports and exports.

Defence

Armed Forces: 101 Antananarivo; tel (2) 21414; telex 22339; Chief of Staff: Claude James Rasamoely.

Army: 101 Antananarivo; tel (2) 21414; telex 22339.

Navy: 101 Antananarivo; tel (2) 21414; telex 22339; Commdr: Robert Rabemanantsoa.

Development and Planning

General Directorate for Planning: Antaninarenina, 101 Antananarivo; tel (2) 21345; telex 22339; Dir-Gen: Jean Robiarivony.

Société d'Etude et de Réalisation pour le Développement Industriel (SERDI): 43 SIAG, rue Rabezavana, BP 3180, 101 Antananarivo; telex 22453; Dir-Gen: David Rafidison; f 1966; industrial devt agency.

Legal and Judiciary

Cour Suprême (Supreme Court): Palais de Justice, Anosy, 101 Antananarivo; tel (2) 20381; telex 22339; Pres: Sylvain Randrianahinoro; Attorney-Gen: Olivier Ratovondriaka.

Haute Cour Constitutionnelle (Constitutional High Court): 101 Antananarivo; tel (2) 20020; telex 22339; Pres: Honoré Rakotomanana; interprets the Constitution and rules on constitutional issues; seven mems.

Media

BROADCASTING

Radio Madagasikara: BP 1202, 101 Antananarivo; tel (2) 22381; Dir: D. Ranaivoharisoa; broadcasts in French and Malagasy.

Radio Télévision Malagasy (RTM): Anosy, BP 442, 101 Antananarivo; tel (2) 23137; telex 22506; Dir: Gabriel Rabesahala; f 1931; TV began 1968; radio broadcasts in French, Malagasy and English; TV broadcasts in French and Malagasy.

GOVERNMENT PUBLISHER

Imprimerie Nationale: BP 38, 101 Antananarivo; tel (2) 23675; Dir: Samuël Ramaroson; all official publs.

NEWS AND INFORMATION

Agence Nationale d'Information 'Taratra' (ANTA): 3 rue du R. P. Callet, Behoririka, BP 386, 101 Antananarivo; tel (2) 21171; telex 22395; Man Dir: Elisabeth Harinoro Andriamarolahy-Robinson; f 1977; state news agency.

Direction Générale de la Banque des Données de l'Etat: Anosy, BP 485, 101 Antananarivo; tel (2) 20070; Dir-Gen: Armand Roger Randrianarivony; f 1963; collection and analysis of economic statistics.

Mining and Energy

ENERGY

Jiro dy Rano Malagasy (JIRAMA): 149 rue Rainandriamampandry, 101 Antananarivo; f 1975; controls production and distribution of electricity and water.

Société Malgache de Raffinage: BP 433, 501 Toamasina; Dir-Gen: Jacques Glantenet; 51% state-owned; refinery for petroleum imported from the Middle East, chiefly Iran; production from offshore petroleum in Madagascar is planned.

MINING

Kraomita Malagasy (KRAOMA): BP 936, Antananarivo; Dir-Gen: Hubert Razafinjato; f 1966; 100% state-owned; chrome mining and concentration.

Société Malgache Commerciale et Minière (SMCM): 13 rue Patrice Lumumba, BP 432, 101 Antananarivo; tel (2) 22883; Dir-Gen: Evariste Marson; f 1973; mining and import and export of mining products.

Science

Laboratoire National des Travaux Publics et du Bâtiment (LNTPB): BP 1151, 101 Antananarivo; tel (2) 42188; telex 22541; Dir: Herbert Razanakoto; f 1954; study of soil structure, foundations for buildings, construction materials, proposed routes for devt of communications, etc.

Tourism

Direction du Tourisme de Madagascar: rue Fernand Kassanga, Tsimbazaza, BP 610, 101 Antananarivo; tel (2) 26298; fax (2) 34479; Dir: Rakotomanana Razanamanana; f 1975; regulation and promotion of tourism.

Transport and Communications

TELECOMMUNICATIONS

Société des Télécommunications Internationales de Madagascar: Alarobia, BP 763, 101 Antananarivo; tel (2) 22402; national telecommunications co.

TRANSPORT

Air Madagascar: 31 ave de l'Indépendance, BP 437, 101 Antananarivo; tel (2) 22222; telex 22232; fax (2) 33760; Pres: N. Andriamanerasoa; Gen Man: R. Rasata Rainiketamanga; f 1962;

89.58% state-owned; extensive internal routes connecting all principal towns; external services to France, Djibouti, Kenya, Mauritius and Réunion.

Compagnie Générale Maritime (CGM): BP 69, 501 Toamasina; tel (5) 32312; telex 22231; Rep: J. P. Bergerot; f 1976 by merger of Messageries Maritimes and Compagnie Générale Transatlantique.

Compagnie Malgache de Navigation (CMN): rue Toto Radona, BP 1621, 101 Antananarivo; tel (2) 25516; telex 22263; fax (2) 30358; Man Dir: Lucien Zasy; f 1960; shipping line.

Réseau National des Chemins de Fer Malagasy (RNCFM): 1 ave de l'Indépendance, Gare Soarano, BP 259, 101 Antananarivo; tel (2) 20521; telex 22233; fax (2) 22288; Gen Man: Samuel Razanamapisa; f 1909; operation of railway network.

Société Nationale Malgache des Transports Maritimes (SMTM): 6 rue Indira Gandhi, BP 4077, 101 Antananarivo; tel (2) 27342; telex 22277; Chair: J. Bemananjara; Man Dir: Andrianaho Rakotondramboa; f 1963; shipping services to Europe.

Solitany Malagasy (SOLIMA): 2 ave Grandidier, BP 140, 101 Antananarivo; tel (2) 20633; telex 22222; Chair: Justin Rarivoson; Dir-Gen: Jean-Baptiste René; f 1976; transports refined petroleum and its products.

MALAWI

Head of State

The Head of State is an elected President, whose term of office is five years, though the present incumbent became President for life in 1971, as a result of a constitutional amendment. Executive power is vested in the President, who appoints Ministers to form a Cabinet, which is responsible to him.

Life President: Ngwazi Dr Hastings Kamuzu Banda (took office 6 July 1966; President for life from 6 July 1971).

Office of the President: Private Bag 301, Capital City, Lilongwe 3; tel 731199; telex 44389; Sec: Justin Malewezi.

Legislature

Legislative power is vested in the unicameral National Assembly. The 112 members are elected for five years. The President is empowered to appoint an unlimited number of members to the Assembly. Effective political power resides with the Malawi Congress Party (MCP), the only legal party in the country. The country is divided into three regions and 24 districts.

National Assembly: Paliament Bldg, POB 80, Zomba; tel 2627; Speaker: Malani Mordecai Lungu.

MINISTRIES AND GOVERNMENT DEPARTMENTS

MINISTRY OF AGRICULTURE
POB 30134, Capital City, Lilongwe 3
Tel 733300; telex 4648
Minister: Dr Hastings Kamuzu Banda

MINISTRY OF COMMUNITY SERVICES
Private Bag 330, Capital City, Lilongwe 3
Tel 732222; telex 44361
Minister: Katola Phiri

MINISTRY OF EDUCATION AND CULTURE
Private Bag 328, Capital City, Lilongwe 3
Tel 733922; telex 4636
Minister: Michael Mlambala

MINISTRY OF EXTERNAL AFFAIRS
POB 30315, Capital City, Lilongwe 3
Telex 4833
Minister: Dr Hastings Kamuzu Banda

MINISTRY OF FINANCE
POB 30049, Capital City, Lilongwe 3
Tel 731311; telex 4407
Minister: Louis Chimango

MINISTRY OF FORESTRY AND NATURAL RESOURCES
Private Bag 350, Capital City, Lilongwe 3
Minister: Stanford Demba

MINISTRY OF HEALTH
POB 30377, Capital City, Lilongwe 3
Telex 4558
Minister: Edward Bwanali

MINISTRY OF JUSTICE
Private Bag 333, Capital City, Lilongwe 3
Telex 4766
Minister: Dr Hastings Kamuzu Banda

MINISTRY OF LABOUR
Private Bag 344, Capital City, Lilongwe 3
Minister: Wadson Deleza

MINISTRY OF LOCAL GOVERNMENT
POB 30312, Capital City, Lilongwe 3
Tel 732555; telex 45073
Minister: Mfunjo Mwakikunga

MINISTRY OF TRADE, INDUSTRY AND TOURISM
POB 30366, Capital City, Lilongwe 3
Minister: Robson Watayachanga Chirwa

MINISTRY OF TRANSPORT AND COMMUNICATIONS
Private Bag 322, Capital City, Lilongwe 3
Tel 730122
Minister: Dalton Katopola

MINISTRY OF WORKS AND SUPPLIES
Private Bag 316, Capital City, Lilongwe 3
Tel 733188; telex 4285
Minister: Dr Hastings Kamuzu Banda

GOVERNMENT AGENCIES AND ORGANIZATIONS

Agriculture and the Environment

AGRICULTURE

Agricultural Development and Marketing Corpn (ADMARC): POB 5052, Limbe; tel 640044; telex 44121; fax 640486; Gen Man: J. S. Magombo; f 1971; statutory trading organization which markets the agricultural crops grown by small-holder farmers; sole exporter of confectionery groundnut kernels, cotton lint, maize, rice, cassava and sunflower seed; primary marketing of tobacco, also handles wheat, arabica coffee and a wide variety of beans, peas, pulses and other seeds and vegetables; co-operates with commercial cos in the growing and processing of agricultural and horticultural produce.

THE ENVIRONMENT

Department of Forestry: POB 30048, Capital City, Lilongwe 3; tel 734144; telex 4465; f 1891; protection, management and control of forestry resource.

Department of National Parks and Wildlife: POB 30131, Capital City, Lilongwe 3.

FISHING

Department of Fisheries: POB 593, Lilongwe.

FORESTRY

Wood Industries Corpn Ltd: POB 30359, Chichiri, Blantyre 3; tel 670144.

Business and Economy

BANKING

Commercial Bank of Malawi Ltd: POB 1111, Blantyre; tel 620144; telex 4340; Chair: J. Z. U. Tembo; Gen Man and Chief Exec: D. G. Lawrence; f 1970 to encourage Malawian participation in business; 14 brs; agencies throughout Malawi.

Investment and Development Bank of Malawi Ltd (Indebank): POB 358, Delamere House, Victoria Ave, Blantyre; tel 620055; telex 4735; Chair: C. Barrow; Gen Man: C. L. Mphande; f 1972; provides loans on a joint-financing basis to statutory corpns and to private enterprises in the agricultural, industrial, tourism, transport and commercial sectors.

National Bank of Malawi: POB 945, Blantyre; tel 620622; telex 44318; fax 620606; Chair: C. E. Freyer; Chief Exec: J. R. Gilbert; f 1971; 14 brs; agencies throughout Malawi.

Reserve Bank of Malawi: POB 30063, Capital City, Lilongwe 3; tel 732488; telex 4788; Gov: Hans Joachim Lesshafft; Gen Man: H. M. Mapondo; f 1965; central bank and bank of issue; br in Blantyre.

TRADE

Department of Customs and Excise: Private Bag 20, Blantyre; tel 620288; telex 44804; fax 620048; f 1892; admin of customs laws, collection and accounting of revenue.

Malawi Bureau of Standards: POB 946, Blantyre; tel 670488; f 1972; preparation of standards; testing, inspection and certification of products.

Malawi Export Promotion Council: Delamere House, POB 1299, Blantyre; tel 620499; telex 4589; Gen Man: J. B. L. Malange.

Culture

National Archives of Malawi: POB 62, Zomba; tel 522922; Archivist: K. M. Mtapiko; f 1964; collection and preservation of public archives, records management services, library services.

Defence

Army: Kamuzu Barracks, Lilongwe; tel 732900; Commdr: Gen M. M. Khanga.

Police: Police Headquarters, Private Bag 305, Capital City, Lilongwe 3; tel 731999; Inspector-Gen: Mc. J. Kamwana.

Development and Planning

INVESTMENT

Malawi Development Corpn (MDC): Development House, Henderson St, POB 566, Blantyre; tel 620100; telex 4146; Chair: Prof C. Chipeta; Gen Man: Wolfgang Ulbrich; f 1964; equity loans and management advice to commerce and industry; investments in 20 subsidiary and associate cos in 1987.

REGIONAL DEVELOPMENT

Capital City Development Corpn (CCDC): POB 30139, Lilongwe; tel 731177; telex 4175; supervises the growth of Lilongwe as an industrial and commercial centre.

Department of Housing and Physical Planning: Convention Drive, Ekistics House, POB 30385, Capital City, Lilongwe; tel 733666; Sec: D. A. Kachimanga; Commr (Physical Planning): J. J. Matope; f 1948; preparation of physical devt plans at national, regional, district and local level.

Legal and Judiciary

High Court: POB 30244, Chichiri, Blantyre 3; tel 30244; Chief Justice: F. L. Makuta; consists of the Chief Justice and four puisne judges; unlimited jurisdiction in civil and criminal matters.

Media

BROADCASTING

Malawi Broadcasting Corpn: POB 30133, Chichiri, Blantyre 3; tel 671222; telex 4425; Gen Man: Tony Kandiero; Head of Production: Henry Chirwa; Editor-in-Chief: Kafumbi Njewa; semi-commercial, semi-state-financed; domestic radio service in English and Chichewa.

GOVERNMENT PUBLISHER

Government Printer: POB 37, Zomba; tel 523155.

NEWS AND INFORMATION

Department of Information: POB 494, Blantyre; collection, analysis and publication of statistics.

Malawi News Agency (MANA): Mzuza; tel 636122; telex 4234; Man Editor: (vacant); f 1966.

Mining and Energy

ENERGY

Electricity Supply Commission of Malawi: Escom Rd, POB 768, Lilongwe; tel 721788.

MINING

Mining Investment and Development Corpn Ltd: POB 565, Lilongwe; tel 722466; telex 44427; Gen Man: S. M. Kalyati; Admin Man: G. M. Musaya; f 1985; mining co.

Tourism

Department of Tourism: POB 30366, Capital City, Lilongwe 3; tel 620300; telex 4645; Chief Tourism Officer: Mike M. Matola; responsible for Malawi tourist policy, administers Govt rest houses, sponsors training of hotel staff.

Tourism Development and Investment Co (TIDC): Blantyre; f 1988 by Malawi Development Corpn to run hotels and tours.

Transport and Communications

TELECOMMUNICATIONS

Department of Posts and Telecommunications, Postal Division: POB 30500, Capital City, Lilongwe 3.

TRANSPORT

Air Malawi Ltd: POB 84, Blantyre; tel 620177; telex 44245; Gen Man: I. Walker; Dep Gen Man: Capt L. Mbilizi; f 1967; international services to Kenya, Mozambique, South Africa, Zambia and Zimbabwe; domestic services to Karonga, Lilongwe, Mangochi and Mzuzu; charter flights are also operated.

Civil Aviation Dpartment: Private Bag 322, Capital City, Lilongwe 3.

Malawi Railways: POB 5144, Limbe; tel 640844; telex 4810; Chair: C. Barrow; Gen Man (acting): W. L. Gillman; links with the ports of Beira and Nacala in Mozambique.

Utilities

Blantyre Water Board: POB 30369, Chichiri, Blantyre 3; tel 672000; telex 44455; Gen Man: P. H. Bray; f 1929; supplies water to Blantyre.

Lilongwe Water Board: Aquarius House, City Centre, POB 96, Lilongwe; tel 732766; telex 44517; fax 732957; supplies water to Lilongwe.

MALAYSIA

Head of State

The Yang di-Pertuan Agong (King or Supreme Sovereign) is the Supreme Head of Malaysia, elected (with a Deputy Head of State) for a five-year term, by and from the hereditary rulers of nine of the Malaysian States. The Head of State appoints the Prime Minister to head a Cabinet which is responsible to Parliament.

HM the Yang di-Pertuan Agong (Supreme Head of State): HM Paduka Seri Sultan Azlan Muhibbuddin Shah ibni Al-Marhum Sultan Yusuff Izzuddin Ghafarullahu-Lahu Shah (Sultan of Perak) (succeeded 26 April 1989).

Office of HM the Supreme Head of State: Istana Negara, 50500 Kuala Lumpur; tel (3) 2388332.

Timbalan Yang di-Pertuan Agong (Deputy Supreme Head of State): HRH Tuanku Ja'afar ibni Al-Marhum Tuanku Abdul Rahman (Sultan of Negri Sembilan).

Legislature

Legislative power is vested in the bicameral Parliament, comprising the Dewan Negara (Senate) of 26 elected and 42 appointed members, and the Dewan Rakyat (House of Representatives) of 177 members elected for five years by universal adult suffrage. Malaysia is a federation of 13 States, and the capital, Kuala Lumpur, is a separate Federal Territory.

Dewan Negara (Senate): Parliament House, 50680 Kuala Lumpur; tel (3) 2321955; telex 20241; fax (3) 2300986; Speaker: Tan Sri Benedict Stephens; Clerk: Mohamad Salleh bin Abu Bakar; Asst Clerks: Abdullah A. Wahab; Ghazali A. Hamid.

Dewan Rakyat (House of Representatives): Parliament House, 50680 Kuala Lumpur; tel (3) 2321955; Speaker: Tan Sri Mohamad Zahir Ismail.

MINISTRIES AND GOVERNMENT DEPARTMENTS

PRIME MINISTER'S DEPARTMENT
Jalan Dato' Onn, 50502 Kuala Lumpur
Tel (3) 2301957; telex 33099
Prime Minister: Datuk Seri Dr Mahathir Mohamad
Deputy Prime Minister: Encik Abdul Ghafar Baba
Ministers in the Prime Minister's Department:
Datuk Dr Mohd Yusof Mohamad Nor, Dato' Dr Haji Sulaiman bin Haji Daud

MINISTRY OF AGRICULTURE
Wisma Tani, 5th Floor, Jalan Sultan Salhuddin, 50632 Kuala Lumpur
Tel (3) 2982011; telex 33045; fax (3) 2986363
Minister: Datuk Seri Sanusi Junid

MINISTRY OF CULTURE AND TOURISM
POB 5-7, Menara Dato' Onn, Putra World Trade Centre, 50694 Kuala Lumpur
Tel (3) 2980088
Minister: Datuk Haji Sabbaruddin Chik

MINISTRY OF DEFENCE
Jalan Padang Tembak, 50634 Kuala Lumpur
Tel (3) 2921333; telex 30289
Minister: Tunku Datuk Ahmad Rithauddeen

MINISTRY OF EDUCATION
Bangunan Bank Pertanian, 9th-25th Floors, Leboh Pasar Besar, 50604 Kuala Lumpur
Tel (3) 2922066
Minister: Encik Anwar Ibrahim

MINISTRY OF ENERGY, TELECOMMUNICATIONS AND POSTS
Wisma Damansara, Ground Floor, Jalan Semantan, 50688 Kuala Lumpur
Tel (3) 2546677; telex 30777
Minister: Dato' S. Samy Vellu

MINISTRY OF FINANCE
Block 9, Kompleks Pejabat Pejabat Kerajaan, Jalan Duta, 50592 Kuala Lumpur
Tel (3) 2546066; telex 30242
Minister: Encik Daim Zainuddin

MINISTRY OF FOREIGN AFFAIRS
Wisma Putra, Jalan Wisma Putra, 50602 Kuala Lumpur
Tel (3) 2488088; telex 30310
Minister: Datuk Abu Hassan Omar

MINISTRY OF HEALTH
Jalan Cenderasari, 50590 Kuala Lumpur
Tel (3) 2985077
Minister: Encik Ng Cheng Kiat

MINISTRY OF HOME AFFAIRS
Jalan Dato' Onn, 50546 Kuala Lumpur
Tel (3) 2309344
Minister: Datuk Seri Dr Mahathir Mohamad

MINISTRY OF HOUSING AND LOCAL GOVERNMENT
46 Jalan Dungun, Damansara Heights, 50644 Kuala Lumpur
Tel (3) 2547033
Minister: Encik Lee Kim Sai

MINISTRY OF INFORMATION
Angkasapuri, Bukit Putra, 50614 Kuala Lumpur
Tel (3) 2745333; telex 31383
Minister: Datuk Mohamad Rahmad

MINISTRY OF JUSTICE
Kernenterian Kehakiman, 21st-22nd Floors, Bangunan
Kuwasa, Jalan Raja Laut, 50506 Kuala Lumpur
Tel (3) 2935733; telex 33548
Minister: Haji Sulaiman bin Haji Daud

MINISTRY OF LABOUR
Block B, Level 5, Pusat Bandar Damansara,
50532 Kuala Lumpur
Tel (3) 2557200; fax (3) 2554700
Minister: Lim Ah Lek

MINISTRY OF LAND AND REGIONAL DEVELOPMENT
Medan MARA, 4th Floor, Jalan Raja Laut,
50574 Kuala Lumpur
Tel (3) 2921566; fax (3) 2918641
Minister: Kasitah bin Gaddam

MINISTRY OF NATIONAL AND RURAL DEVELOPMENT
Bangunan Bank Rakayat, 1st Floor, Jalan Tangsi,
50606 Kuala Lumpur
Tel (3) 2910255
Minister: Encik Abdul Ghafar Baba

MINISTRY OF PRIMARY INDUSTRIES
Menara Daya Bumi, 6th-8th Floors, Jalan Sultan
Hishamuddin, 50654 Kuala Lumpur
Tel (3) 2747511; telex 30808; fax (3) 2745014
Minister: Datuk Dr Lim Keng Yaik

MINISTRY OF PUBLIC ENTERPRISES
Wisma PKNS, 3rd Floor, Jalan Raja Laut,
50652 Kuala Lumpur
Tel (3) 2985022; telex 33069
Minister: Puan Napsiah Omar

MINISTRY OF PUBLIC WORKS AND UTILITIES
Jalan Sultan Salahuddin, 50580 Kuala Lumpur
Tel (3) 2919011; telex 30415
Minister: Dato' Leo Moggie Anak Arok

MINISTRY OF SCIENCE, TECHNOLOGY AND ENVIRONMENT
Wisma Sime Darby, 14th Floor, Jalan Raja Laut,
50662 Kuala Lumpur
Tel (3) 2938917; telex 28154
Minister: Datuk Amar Stephen Yong Kuet Tze

MINISTRY OF TRADE AND INDUSTRY
Block 10, Govt Offices Complex, Jalan Duta,
50622 Kuala Lumpur
Tel (3) 2546022; telex 30634
Minister: Datin Paduka Rafidah Aziz

MINISTRY OF TRANSPORT
Jalan Dungun Bukit Damansara, 5th-7th Floors,
50616 Kuala Lumpur
Tel (3) 2548122; telex 30999
Minister: Datuk Dr Ling Liong Sik

MINISTRY OF WELFARE SERVICES
Wisma Shen, 6th-16th Floors, Jalan Masjid India,
50562 Kuala Lumpur
Tel (3) 2925011
Minister: Datuk Mustaffa Mohamad

MINISTRY OF YOUTH AND SPORTS
Block K, 7th Floor, Pusat Bandar, Damansara,
50570 Kuala Lumpur
Tel (3) 2552255
Minister: Datuk Seri Najib Tun Razak

GOVERNMENT AGENCIES AND ORGANIZATIONS

Advisory and Supervisory Bodies

Anti Corruption Agency: POB 6000, Pesiaran Duta, 50988 Kuala Lumpur; tel (3) 2551982; fax (3) 2554914; f 1967; investigates corruption cases and malpractice and prosecutes offenders.

Department of Industrial Relations: Level 7, Block B South, Jalan Satu, Damansara Town Centre, Damansara Heights, 50536 Kuala Lumpur; tel (3) 2557222; fax (3) 2554700; Dir-Gen: Ahmad bin Mohd Idrus; f 1972; settlement of trade disputes through conciliation; settlement of claims for reinstatement.

Election Commission: Wisma Tong Ah, 3rd-11th Floors, Jalan P. Ramlee/Tun Perak, 50250 Kuala Lumpur; tel (3) 2614011.

Jabatan Imigeresen (Immigration Department): Bangunan Bukota, Jalan Pantai Baru, 50550 Kuala Lumpur; tel (3) 7578155.

National Institute of Public Administration (INTAN): Bukit Kiara, Jalan Damansara, Kuala Lumpur; tel (3) 2552400; telex 31858; fax (3) 2561403; Dir: Johari bin Mat; f 1972; training of Govt personnel in the field of public management in human and economic resources devt.

Pusat Daya Pengeluaran Negara (National Productivity Centre): POB 64, off Jalan Sultan, 46904 Petaling Jaya, Selangor; tel (3) 7557266; telex 36312; fax (3) 7578068; Dir: Ir Haji Arshad bin Haji Marsidi; f 1962; management training; research and consultancy; productivity promotion.

Registry of Companies: Kuwasa Bldg, 16th-20th Floors, Jalan Raja Laut, 50350 Kuala Lumpur; tel (3) 2933768; fax (3) 2911157; Dir: Zainun Bte Ali; f 1940; administers and enforces laws pertaining to cos and securities industry; facilitates research into corporate information.

Agriculture and the Environment

AGRICULTURE

Fisheries Development Authority (Malaysia) (MAJUIKAN): Bangunan PKNS, 7th Floor, Jalan Raja Laut,

50350 Kuala Lumpur; tel (3) 2924044; telex 31560; Chair: Datuk Arshad bin Ayub.

Institut Penyelidikan dan Kemajuan Pertanian Malaysia (Malaysian Agricultural Research and Development Institute): POB 12301, General Post Office, 50774 Kuala Lumpur; tel (3) 9486601; telex 37115; fax (3) 9483664; Dir-Gen: Dato' Dr Haji Mohamad Yusof bin Hashim; Dep Dirs: Dr Haji Hashim bin Haji Wahab, Dr Mohamad Shariff bin Ahmad; f 1968; conducts scientific, technical, economic and sociological research into the production, utilization and processing of all crops (except rubber and palm oil) and livestock.

Jabatan Pertanian (Department of Agriculture): Jalan Mahameru, 50632 Kuala Lumpur; tel (3) 2982011.

Kumpulan FIMA Bhd (Food Industries of Malaysia): Kompleks FIMA, Subang-Kuala Lumpur International Airport, Subang, Selangor; tel (3) 7462199; telex 37933; Man Dir: Dato' Mohd Noor bin Ismail; f 1972; Govt corpn to promote food and related industry through investment or by co-ventures with local or foreign entrepreneurs; oil palm, cocoa and fruit plantation devts; manufacturing and packaging, trading, supermarkets and restaurants.

Lembaga Padi dan Beras Negara (National Paddy and Rice board): Bangunan Perkim, 13th-17th Floors, Jalan Ipoh, 51200 Kuala Lumpur; tel (3) 2934122; telex 30992.

Lembaga Perindustrian Kayu Malaysia (Malaysian Timber Industry Board): Bangunan Sateras, Wisma DNP, 5th-6th Floors, Jalan Ampang, POB 10887, 50450 Kuala Lumpur; tel (3) 2486233; telex 30993; fax (3) 2418416; Chair: Tan Sri Dato' Wong Kum Choon; Dir-Gen: Dato' Baharuddin bin Haji Ghazali; f 1968; promotes and regulates the export of timber and timber products; mems of the Board are appointed by the Minister of Primary Industries and are federal, state and trade reps.

Lembaga Tembakau Negara (National Tobacco Board): Kubang Kerian, POB 198, 15720 Kota Bharu, Kelantan; tel (9) 922933.

The Malayan Pineapple Industry Board: Jalan Skudai, 5th Floor, POB 35, 80200 Johore Bahru; tel (7) 361211; Exec Sec: Tuan Haji Azman bin Saidin.

Malaysia Rubber Development Corpn (MARDEC): Bangunan MARDEC, Jalan Kerja Air Lama, Ulu Kelang, Peti Surat 10546, 50716 Kuala Lumpur; tel (3) 4567055; telex 30950.

Malaysian Rubber Research and Development Board (MRRDB): Bangunan Getah Asli, 15th-18th Floors, 148 Jalan Ampang, 50450 Kuala Lumpur; tel (3) 2614422; telex 30953; fax (3) 2613139; Chair and Controller of Rubber Research: Ahmad Farouk bin Haji S. M. Ishak; f 1959; overall control of the research, technical devt and promotion of the rubber industry; determines policies of research and devt.

Palm Oil Registration and Licensing Authority (PORLA): Block A, 5th-7th Floors, Damansara Town Centre, Damansara Heights, POB 12184, 50770 Kuala Lumpur; tel (3) 2547122; telex 31823; fax (3) 2551520; Dir-Gen: Rahim Zain; f 1977; promotes marketing of palm oil products; monitors devt of palm oil industry; licenses and regulates all those involved in the palm oil trade.

Palm Oil Research Institute of Malaysia (PORIM): 6 Persiaran Institusi, Bandar Baru Bang, 43000 Kajang, Selangor; tel (3) 8259155; telex 31609; fax (3) 8259446; Dir: Datuk Prof Augustine S. H. Ong; f 1979; research and devt of palm oil and palm oil products.

Rubber Industry Smallholders Development Authority (RISDA): 4.5 miles, Jalan Ampang, 50450 Kuala Lumpur; tel (3) 4564022; telex 30369; Dir-Gen: Encik Mohd Zain bin Haji Yahya.

THE ENVIRONMENT

Department of Wildlife and National Parks: Km 10, Jalan Cheras, 56100 Kuala Lumpur; tel (3) 9052872; fax (3) 9052873; Dir-Gen: Mohd Khan B. Momin Khan; f 1937; wildlife management and research; habitat protection and maintenance; law enforcement; education and training.

Federal Department of Forestry: Jalan Mahameru, 50660 Kuala Lumpur; tel (3) 2988244; under Ministry of Primary Industries.

Federal Land Consolidation and Rehabilitation Authority (FELCRA): Bangunan MISC, 1st Floor, Jalan Conlay, 50450 Kuala Lumpur; tel (3) 2931048; telex 31789.

Art and Culture

National Archives: Jalan Duta, 50568 Kuala Lumpur; tel (3) 2543244.

National Library: Wisma Sachdev, Jalan Raja Laut, 50350 Kuala Lumpur; tel (3) 2923144; telex 30092.

Business and Economy

BANKING

Bank Bumiputra Malaysia Bhd: Menara Bumiputra, Jalan Melaka, POB 10407, 50913 Kuala Lumpur; tel (3) 2981011; telex 30445; fax (3) 2934667; Exec Chair: Tan Sri Dato' Haji Basir Ismail; Exec Dir: Mohamad Taufik Dato' Abdullah; f 1965; commercial bank; 90% owned by Petroliam Nasional Bhd (see below), 10% by Ministry of Finance.

Bank Kemajuan Perusahaan Malaysia Bhd (Industrial Development Bank of Malaysia): Wisma Lee Rubber, 15th Floor, Jalan Melaka, 50100 Kuala Lumpur; tel (3) 2929088; telex 31546; Chair: Tan Sri Dato' Sallehuddin bin Mohamad; Gen Man: Saleh Ghazali; f 1979; finances long-term, high-technology projects, shipping and shipyards, engineering (metal-based, electrical and electronic) and export credit industries.

Bank Negara Malaysia: Jalan Kuching, POB 10922, 50929 Kuala Lumpur; tel (3) 2988044; telex 30201; Gov: Tan Sri Datuk Jaffar Hussein; Dep Gov: Dr Lin See Yan; f 1959; bank of issue; 9 brs.

Development Bank of Malaysia: Bangunan MOCCIS, 17 Jalan Melaka, 50100 Kuala Lumpur; tel (3) 2320633; telex 30058.

Perwira Habib Bank Malaysia Bhd: Wisma SPK, 3rd Floor, Jalan Sultan Ismail, POB 10459, 50915 Kuala Lumpur; tel (3) 2432000; telex 30488; Chair: Gen Tan Sri Dato' Zain Hashim; Exec Dir: Raja Aman Ahmad; f 1975; partly-owned by Bank Negara Malaysia; 25 brs.

Sabah Development Bank Bhd: SDB Tower, Block A, Wisma Tun Fuad Stephens, POB 12172, 88824 Kota Kinabalu, Sabah; tel (88) 58522; telex 80214; fax (88) 222852; Chair: Datuk Simon Sipaun; Man Dir: Jimmy Duis; Gen Man: Francis Lu; f 1977; wholly owned by State govt of Sabah; devt banking.

United Asian Bank Bhd: Menara UAB, 6 Jalan Tun Perak, POB 10753, 50724 Kuala Lumpur; tel (3) 2931722; telex 30454; Gen Man: Abdul Rahman bin Ramli; f 1973; partly-owned by Bank Negara Malaysia; 32 brs.

FINANCIAL AGENCIES

Amanah Saham Nasional Bhd: Balai PNB, 201A, Jalan Tun Razak, Peti Surat 12443, 50945 Kuala Lumpur; tel (3) 2618544; telex 30522; fax (3) 2618259; Gen Man: Dato' Abdul Khalid Ibrahim; f 1979; promotes and mobilizes savings among indigenous people through unit trust schemes; manages and markets unit trust schemes.

Department of Inland Revenue: 14th-16th Floors, Blok 8, Kompleks Pejabat Kerajaan, Jalan Duta, 50600 Kuala Lumpur; tel (3) 2549066.

Employees Provident Fund: Jalan Gasing, 46598 Petaling Jaya, Selangor Darul Ehsan; tel (3) 7565333; telex 37650; fax (3) 7553709; Gen Man: Abdul Rahim Haji Din; f 1952; compulsory savings scheme for workers with the objective of providing social security benefits during their old age; privatization plans announced in 1989.

Jabatan Odit (Audit Department): Jalan Cenderasari, 50518 Kuala Lumpur; tel (3) 2986422.

Malaysian Industrial Development Finance Bhd: 195A Jalan Tun Razak, POB 12110, 50939 Kuala Lumpur; tel (3) 2610066; telex 30534; Chair: Tun Tan Sri Ismail bin Mohamad Ali; Gen Man: Encik Darwis bin Mohd Daek; f 1960 by the Govt, banks and insurance cos; industrial financing, advisory services, project devt, joint venture and information services and analysis.

National Land Finance Co-operative Society Ltd: Bangunan UMBC, 20th Floor, 2 Jalan Suleiman, POB 12133, 50768 Kuala Lumpur; tel (3) 2307044; Chief Exec: K. R. Somasundram; f 1960 to raise funds form rubber industry workers and others to purchase rubber estates; 65,000 mems; owns rubber, tea, oil palm, cocoa and coconut plantations.

Jabatan Pegawai Pemegang Harta dan Pegawai Penerima (Official Assignee and Official Receiver): Bangunan Bank Rakyat, 9th-10th Floors, Jalan Tangsi, 50516 Kuala Lumpur; tel (3) 2923077.

MARKETING

Federal Agricultural Marketing Authority (FAMA): Bangunan KUWASA, 5th-8th Floors, Jalan Raja Laut, 50350 Kuala Lumpur; tel (3) 2932622; telex 31669; Chair: Encik Haji Yahya Haji Shafie; Dir-Gen: Encik Othman Rijal; f 1965; supervises, co-ordinates and improves existing markets and methods of marketing agricultural produce; promotes new markets and outlets for agricultural produce.

Sarawak Pepper Marketing Board: Tanah Putih, POB 1653, 93916 Kuching, Sarawak; tel (82) 331811; telex 70987; fax (82) 336877; Chair: Michael Pilo ak Gangga; Gen Man: Mohamad Shariff Abdul Aziz; f 1972; statutory grading of all Sarawak pepper for export; licensing of pepper dealers and exporters; devt and promotion of pepper grading, storage and processing facilities; provision of market information; direct trading; market promotion and establishment of trade contacts.

NATIONALIZED INDUSTRY

Heavy Industries Corpn of Malaysia (HICOM): Wisma Yeng Chong, 6th-9th Floors, Jalan Punchak, 50250 Kuala Lumpur; tel (3) 2325133; telex 31217.

Syarikat Limbungan Kapal dan Kejuruteraan Malaysia Sdb Bhd (Malaysia Shipyard and Engineering Bhd): Wisma MISC, Jalan Conlay, 50450 Kuala Lumpur; tel (3) 242026; telex 30281.

TRADE

Commodities Trading Commission (CTC): Podium Daya Bumi, 5th Floor, Jalan Sultan Hishamuddin, 50050 Kuala Lumpur; tel (3) 2936644; telex 20234; fax (3) 2748330; Chair: Tun Ismail bin Muhamad Ali; Commr: Ismail bin Haji Ahmad; f 1980; under Ministry of Primary Industries; independent statutory body responsible for regulating and supervising commodity futures trading.

Malaysia Export Credit Insurance Bhd: Wisma Damansara, 2nd Floor, Kuala Lumpur; tel (3) 24957; Gen Man: Tasaduk bin Haji Kamarally; joint Govt and private sector venture to provide insurance for exporters of locally manufactured products.

Royal Customs and Excise Department: Blok 11, 1st-6th Floors, Kompleks Pejabat Pejabat Kerajaan, Jalan Duta, 50596 Kuala Lumpur; tel (3) 2546088; telex 30928.

Defence

Armed Forces: c/o Ministry of Defence, Jalan Padang Tembak, 50634 Kuala Lumpur; tel (3) 2921333; telex 30289; Chief of Staff: Gen Tan Sri Datuk Mohamad Ghazali Haji Che Mat.

Air Force: c/o Ministry of Defence, Jalan Padang Tembak, 50634 Kuala Lumpur; tel (3) 2921333; telex 30289; Chief of Staff: Lt-Gen Dato' Mohamad bin Ngah Said.

Army: c/o Ministry of Defence, Jalan Padang Tembak, 50634 Kuala Lumpur; tel (3) 2921333; telex 30289; Chief of Staff: Dato' Mohamad Hashim Mohamad Ali.

Navy: c/o Ministry of Defence, Jalan Padang Tembak, 50634 Kuala Lumpur; tel (3) 2921333; telex 30289; Chief of Staff: Vice-Adm Dato' Abdul Wahab bin Haji Nawi.

Police Department: Jalan Bukit Aman, 50560 Kuala Lumpur; tel (3) 2924444; telex 30469.

Development and Planning

Department of Co-operative Development: Jalan Mahameru, 50608 Kuala Lumpur; tel (3) 2989033.

Federal Land Development Authority (FELDA): Jalan Maktab, 50400 Kuala Lumpur; tel (3) 2936066; telex 30219; Chair: Raja Tan Sri Mohamad Alias; Dir-Gen: Alladin Hashim; f 1957; quasi-Govt corpn formed to raise the productivity and income of low income groups and to eradicate rural poverty; involved in rubber, oil palm, cocoa and sugar cane cultivation.

Majlis Amanah Rakyat (MARA) (Trust Council for the People): MARA Bldg, 26th Floor, Jalan Raja Laut, 50609 Kuala Lumpur; tel (3) 2915111; telex 30316; fax (3) 2913620; Chair: Ismail Said; Dir-Gen: Mohamad Ridzuan bin Abdul Halim; f 1966; promotes, facilitates and undertakes economic and social devt; encourages, trains and assists natives to enable them to participate in small and medium-scale commercial and industrial enterprises; participates in industrial and commercial undertakings and joint ventures.

Malaysian Handicraft Development Corpn: Wisma Kraftangan, 11th Floor, Jalan Tun Perak, 50050 Kuala Lumpur; tel (3) 2925322; telex 28203; fax (3) 2934858; Dir-Gen: Sulaiman Othman; f 1979; production, promotion and advisory services; training; trade promotion; design and product devt.

Malaysian Industrial Development Authority (MIDA): Wisma Damansara, 3rd-6th Floors, Jalan Semantan, POB 10618, 50720 Kuala Lumpur; tel (3) 2553633; telex 30752; fax (3) 2557970; Chair: Tan Sri Dato' Zainal Abidin bin Sulong; Dir-Gen: N. Sadasivan; f 1967.

Urban Development Authority (UDA): Perbadanan Pembangunan Bandar, Bukit Bintang Plaza, 126 Jalan Bukit Bintang, POB 80, 50990 Kuala Lumpur; tel (3) 2428022.

PLANNING

Federal Department of Town and Country Planning: Jalan Cenderasari, 50646 Kuala Lumpur; tel (3) 2989211; fax (3) 2929994; Dir: Datuk Mohamad Ishak B. Haji Mohamad

Ariff; f 1921; advises the Ministry of Housing and Local Government on all matters relating to town and country planning.

National Economic Planning Unit: Jalan Dato Onn, 50502 Kuala Lumpur; tel (3) 2300133; telex 30098.

REGIONAL DEVELOPMENT

Borneo Development Corpn SDN Bhd: Electra House, Top Floor, POB 342, 93704 Kuching, Sarawak; tel (82) 244241; telex 70188; fax (82) 428786; Gen Man: Salleh Haji Sulaiman; f 1958; housing and industrial devt; loan financing; shareholders are state govts of Sarawak and Sabah, Sarawak Economic Devt Corpn.

Muda Agricultural Development Authority (MADA): MADA HQ, Ampang Jajar, 05990 Alor Setar, Kedah; tel (4) 728255; telex 42106; Chair: Dato Seri Syed Nahar Shahabuddin.

Sarawak Economic Development Corpn: Menara SEDC, 6th-11th Floors, Jalan Tunku Abdul Rahman, POB 400, 93100 Kuching, Sarawak; tel (82) 416777; telex 70063; fax (82) 424330; Exec Chair: Effendi Norwawi; Exec Dir: Leslie Marjoribanks; f 1972; promotion of commerce and industry; promotion of investments by foreign and local investors; responsible for the management and devt of industrial estates.

Employment

Department of Labour: Blok B, Level 5, Pusat Bandar Damansara, 50532 Kuala Lumpur; tel (3) 2557200; fax (3) 2554700; Dir-Gen: Y. M. Tengku Omar bin Tengku Bot.

Jabatan Kilang dan Jentera (Factories and Machinery Department): Wisma Perdana, 10th Floor, Jalan Dungun, Damansara Heights, 50534 Kuala Lumpur; tel (3) 2542355; Dir-Gen: Abdul Jalil Mahmud; Dep Dir-Gen: Harminder Singh; promotes industrial health and safety in factories, building operations and engineering construction works, and also in respect of petroleum related activities such as storage and transportation of petroleum products.

Legal and Judiciary

Federal Judicial Department: High Court Bldg, Jalan Raja, 50506 Kuala Lumpur; tel (3) 2939011.

High Court: High Court Bldg, Jalan Raja, 50506 Kuala Lumpur; tel (3) 2939011; Chief Justice in Peninsular Malaysia (acting): Tan Sri Hashim Yeop Sani; Chief Justice in Sabah and Sarawak: Tan Sri Datuk Lee Hun Hoe.

Supreme Court: High Court Bldg, Jalan Raja, 50506 Kuala Lumpur; tel (3) 2939011; Lord Pres: Tan Sri Abdul Hamid Omar.

Media

BROADCASTING

Department of Broadcasting: c/o Ministry of Information, Angkasapuri, Bukit Putra, POB 11272, 50614 Kuala Lumpur; tel (3) 2745333; telex 30283.

Radio Malaysia: Dept of Broadcasting, Ministry of Information, Angkasapuri, Bukit Putra, POB 11272, 50614 Kuala Lumpur; tel (3) 2745333; telex 30283; Controller of Programmes: Yap Swee Choon; f 1946; domestic service; operates six networks; broadcasts in Bahasa Malaysia, English, Chinese (Mandarin and other dialects), Tamil and Aborigine (Temiar and Semai dialects).

Suara Malaysia (Voice of Malaysia): address as above; tel (3) 2744976; Head of Overseas Service: Mohamad Safian Abdul Ghani; f 1963; overseas service in Arabic, Burmese, English, Indonesian, Chinese (Mandarin), Bahasa Malaysia, Tagalog and Thai.

Radio Television Malaysia: Dept of Broadcasting, Ministry of Information, Angkasapuri, Bukit Putra, POB 11272, 50614 Kuala Lumpur; tel (3) 2745333; telex 30283 (Radio), 31383 (TV); Dir-Gen: Jaafar Kamin; Dep Dir-Gen: Tamimuddin Abdul Karim; f 1946; supervises radio and TV broadcasting.

Radio Television Malaysia (Sabah): Jalan Tuaran, 88614 Kota Kinabalu, Sabah; tel (88) 52711; telex 80061; Dir of Broadcasting: Tamimuddin Abdul Kauim; f 1955; dept of RTM; broadcasts 259 hours a week in Malay, English, Chinese (two dialects), Kadazan, Murut, Dusun and Bajau.

Radio Television Malaysia (Sarawak): Broadcasting House, Jalan Satok, Kuching, Sarawak; tel (82) 53442; telex 70084; Dir of Broadcasting: Salleh Pateh Akhir; f 1954; dept of RTM; broadcasts 483 hours per week in Malay, English, Chinese, Iban, Bidayuh, Melanau, Kayan/Kenyah, Bisayah and Murut.

Television Malaysia: Dept of Broadcasting, Ministry of Information, Angkasapuri, Bukit Putra, POB 11272, 50614 Kuala Lumpur; tel (3) 445333; telex 31383; Controller of Programmes Ahmad Noor; operates three national networks.

GOVERNMENT PUBLISHER

National Printing Department (Publications Branch): Ketua Pengarah, Jabatan Percetakon Negara, Jalan Chan Sow Lin, 50554 Kuala Lumpur; tel (3) 2212022.

NEWS AND INFORMATION

Bernama (Malaysian National News Agency): Wisma Bernama, 28 Jalan 1/65A, off Jalan Tun Razak, POB 10024, 50700 Kuala Lumpur; tel (3) 2939933; telex 30461; Gen Man: Muhamad ali Ismail; Editor-in-Chief: Ahmad Rejal Arbee; f 1967; news agency; gen and foreign news, economic features and photo services, public relations wire, screen information and data service, stock market on-line monitor service, real-time commodity and monetary information services; daily output in Malay and English.

Department of Information: c/o Ministry of Information, Angkasapuri, Bukit Putra, POB 11272, 50614 Kuala Lumpur; tel (3) 2745333; telex 30223.

Department of Statistics: Wisma Statistik, Jalan Cenderasari, 50514 Kuala Lumpur; tel (3) 2922133; Chief Statistician: Khoo Teik Huat; f 1948; collects, compiles and analyses data required for the implementation of the New Economic Policy and for overall macro-economic planning; advises and assists Ministries and agencies in the compilation of special statistics required in the formulation of policies and programmes.

Mining and Energy

ENERGY

National Electricity Board: 129 Jalan Bangsar, 59200 Kuala Lumpur; tel (3) 2745566; privatization plans announced in 1989.

Nuclear Energy Unit (UTN): Kompleks Puspati, Bangi, 43000 Kajang; tel (3) 8250510; telex 31619; fax (3) 8258262; Dir-Gen: Datuk Dr Muhamad Ghazali bin Haji Abd Rahman; f 1971; responsible for introducing and encouraging peaceful use of nuclear science and technology in such fields as agriculture, industry, medicine and education; oversees and co-ordinates all matters relating to the use of nuclear technology in the country.

Petroliam Nasional Bhd (PETRONAS): Menara Daya Bumi, Kompleks Daya Bumi, Jalan Sultan Hishamuddin, POB 12444, 50778 Kuala Lumpur; tel (3) 2743833; telex 31123; fax (3) 2740217; Chair: Tan Sri Dato' Haji Basir bin Ismail; Pres and Chief Exec: Tan Sri Datuk Azizan bin Azinul Abidin; f 1974; national oil co; oil and gas exploration; marketing of petroleum and petroleum products.

MINING

Department of Mines: Bangunan Ukur, Jalan Gurney, 50656 Kuala Lumpur; tel (3) 2924436; under Ministry of Primary Industries.

Mines Research Institute: POB 1016, Lorong Harimau, 30820 Ipoh; tel (5) 557100.

Tin Industry Research and Development Board: Ming Bldg, 9th Floor, Jalan Bukit Nanas, POB 12560, 50782 Kuala Lumpur; tel (3) 2328461; Chair: Ibrahim Menudin; Sec: Mohamad Nor Mohamad.

Research

Institute of Medical Research: Jalan Pahang, 50588 Kuala Lumpur; tel (3) 2986033.

Science and Technology

Department of Survey and National Mapping: CAMS Bldg, Jalan Semarak, 50578 Kuala Lumpur; tel (3) 2925311; telex 28148; fax (3) 2917457; Dir-Gen: A. Majid Mohamad; tel 1885; cadastral survey and topographic mapping.

Geological Survey of Malaysia: Tabong Haji Bldg, 19th-20th Floors, Jalan Tun Razak, POB 11110, 50736 Kuala Lumpur; tel (3) 2611033; telex 30808; Dir-Gen: Yin Ee Heng; f 1903; geological mapping, mineral exploration, engineering geology, hydrogeology, cartography; provides analytical services, national mineral data bank and consultancy services.

Malaysian Meteorological Service: Jalan Sultan, 46667 Petaling Jaya, Selangor; tel (3) 7569422; telex 37243; Dir-Gen (acting): P. Markandan; f 1946; information and services in the fields of climatology, agrometeorology, marine meteorology and oceanography, aviation meteorology, air pollution and seismology.

Standards and Industrial Research Institute of Malaysia (SIRIM): Persiaran Dato' Menteri, Seksyen 2, POB 35, 40700 Shah Alam, Selangor Darul Ehsan; tel (3) 5591630; telex 38672; fax (3) 5508955; Controller: Dr Ahmad Tajuddin Ali; f 1975; promotes standardization and quality; technology devt; technical services.

Telecommunications

Department of Postal Services: Podium, Kompleks Daya Bumi, Jalan Sultan Hishamuddin, 50670 Kuala Lumpur; tel (3) 2741122; telex 30677.

Jabatan Telekom Malaysia (JTM): Wisma Damansara, Jalan Semantan, 50668 Kuala Lumpur; tel (3) 2556687; telex 28020; fax (3) 2557901; Dir-Gen of Telecommunications: Norizan Baharin; f 1987; under the Ministry of Energy, Telecommunications and Posts; regulatory authority for telecommunications.

Tourism

Sabah Tourist Association: POB 946, Kota Kinabalu, Sabah; tel (88) 211484; Chair: Albert Teo; Exec Sec: Agnes Ho; f 1962; 55 mems; parastatal promotional organization.

Sarawak Tourist Association: c/o Sarawak Tourist Information Centre, Main Bazaar, 93000 Kuching, Sarawak; POB 887, 93718 Kuching, Sarawak; tel (82) 240620; Chair: Datuk Amar Leonard Linggi Jugah; Hon Sec: Peter E. Mueller; f 1964.

Tourist Development Corpn of Malaysia: Menara Dato' Onn, Putra World Trade Centre, 24th-27th Floors, 45 Jalan Tun Ismail, 50480 Kuala Lumpur; tel (3) 2935188; telex 30093; fax (3) 2935884; Chair: Raja Tan Sri Mohar bin Raja Badiozaman; Dep Chair and Dir-Gen: Encik Badri bin Masri; f 1972; co-ordinates the activities of the tourism industry in Malaysia; promotes tourism.

Transport

CIVIL AVIATION

Department of Civil Aviation: Terminal 2, Subang-Kuala Lumpur International Airport, 47200 Subang, Selangor; tel (3) 7461844; telex 37960; Dir-Gen: Zolkipli bin Abdul; f 1947; supervision of air transport.

RAILWAYS

Pentadbiran Keretapi Tanah Melayu (KTM) (Malayan Railways): Jalan Sultan Hishamuddin, 50621 Kuala Lumpur; tel (3) 2749422; telex 32925; Gen Man: Encik Sulaiman Hashim; f 1885; privatization plans announced in 1989.

Sabah State Railways: 88200 Kota Kinabalu, Sabah; tel (88) 54611; Gen Man: Mohamad Tahir Jaafar; f 1896; goods and passenger services.

ROADS

Public Works Department (Sabah): 88582 Kota Kinabalu, Sabah; tel (88) 244333; telex 80339; fax (88) 237234; Dir: Datuk Michael Wong Chen Ying; maintains a network of roads; builds bridges, airports, public bldgs, drainage and sewerage facilities; promotes economic and social devt.

Public Works Department (Sarawak): Jalan Simpang Tiga, Kuching, Sarawak; tel (82) 51011; telex 70112; Dir: Fung Chee Ping; Dep Dir: Michael Parker; roads maintenance.

SHIPPING

Johore Port Authority: POB 66, 81707 Pasir Gudang, Johore; tel (7) 512601; telex 60717.

Kelang Port Authority: POB 202, Jalan Pelabuhan, 42005 Port Kelang, Selangor; tel (3) 3688211; telex 39524; fax (3) 3670211; Gen Man: Hashir H. Abdullah; f 1963.

Kuantan Port Authority: Tanjung Gelang, POB 161, 25720 Kuantan, Pahang Darul Makmur; tel (9) 433200; telex 50234; fax (9) 433866; Gen Man: Dato' Tik Mustaffa; Dep Gen Man: Tuan Haji Mohamad Awang Tera; f 1974.

Kuching Port Authority: POB 530, Jalan Pelabuhan, Pending, 93710 Kuching, Sarawak; tel (82) 482144; telex 70420; f 1961.

Penang Port Commission: POB 143, 10710 Penang; tel (4) 612211; telex 40157; fax (4) 613336; Chair: Tuan Syed Mohamad Aidid; Gen Man: Abdullah Alias; f 1956; cargo handling and ferry services between the island and the mainland.

Rajang Port Authority: 96000 Sibu, Sarawak; tel (84) 319009; telex 72121.

Sabah Ports Authority: Bangunan Ibu Pejabat LPS, Jalan Tun Fuad, Tanjung Lipat, 88617 Kota Kinabalu, Sabah; tel (88) 56155; telex 80074.

Welfare

Department of Social Welfare: Bangunan Wisma Shen, Jalan Masjid India, 50564 Kuala Lumpur; tel (3) 2925011.

National Population and Family Development Board: Bangunan LPPKN, 12B, Jalan Raja Laut, Peti Surat 10416, 50712 Kuala Lumpur; tel (3) 2937555; telex 31911; fax (3) 2921357; Dir-Gen: Annuar bin Ma'Aruf; f 1966; planning and co-ordination of population and family devt programmes in the country.

Social Security Organization: Block A, Level 2-4, Jalan Damanlela, Pusat Bandar Damansara, 50538 Kuala Lumpur; tel (3) 2558800; Dir: Seow Ewe Hoe; f 1969; provides social security protection to all workers employed under a contract of service against the contingencies of industrial accident, occupational disease and invalidity.

MALDIVES

Head of State

Executive power is vested in the President, elected by popular vote (on nomination by the Majilis) for five years. The President governs with the assistance of an appointed Cabinet, which is responsible to the Majilis.

President: Maumoon Abdul Gayoom (took office 11 November 1978; re-elected 30 September 1983 and 23 September 1988).

Office of the President: Marine Drive (North), Malé 20-05; tel 323701; telex 66013.

Legislature

Legislative power is vested in the unicameral Majilis (Citizens' Council), with 48 members. Of these, 40 are elected for five years by universal adult suffrage and eight appointed by the President. The country has 20 administrative districts: the capital is under direct central administration while the 19 atolls are each under an atoll chief (verin), appointed by the President.

Majilis (Citizens' Council): Naadi, Ameer Ahmed Magu, Malé 20-05; tel 322617; Speaker: Abdulla Hameed.

MINISTRIES AND GOVERNMENT DEPARTMENTS

MINISTRY OF ATOLLS ADMINISTRATION
Faashana Bldg, Malé 20-05
Tel 322826
Minister: Abdulla Hameed

MINISTRY OF DEFENCE AND NATIONAL SECURITY
Badeyrige, Malé 20-05
Tel 322118; telex 66056
Minister: Maumoon Abdul Gayoom

MINISTRY OF EDUCATION
Ghaazee Bldg, Ameer Ahmed Magu, Malé 20-05
Tel 323261; telex 66032
Minister: Mohamed Zahir Hussain

MINISTRY OF FINANCE
2nd Floor, Ghaazee Bldg, Ameer Ahmed Magu, Malé 20-05
Tel 322262; telex 66032; fax 324432
Minister: Maumoon Abdul Gayoom
Minister of State: Ismail Fathy

MINISTRY OF FISHERIES AND AGRICULTURE
Ghaazee Bldg, Ameer Ahmed Magu, Malé 20-05
Tel 322622; telex 77033
Minister: Abdulla Jameel

MINISTRY OF FOREIGN AFFAIRS
Marine Drive (North), Malé 20-05
Tel 323405; telex 66008
Minister: Fathulla Jameel

MINISTRY OF HEALTH AND WELFARE
Ghaazee Bldg, Ameer Ahmed Magu, Malé 20-05
Tel 323216
Minister: Abdul Sattar Moosa Didi

MINISTRY OF HOME AFFAIRS AND SPORTS
Huravee Bldg, Ameer Ahmed Magu, Malé 20-05
Tel 323821; telex 77039
Minister: Umar Zahir

MINISTRY OF JUSTICE
Ghaazee Bldg, Ameer Ahmed Magu, Malé 20-05
Tel 323820
Minister: Mohamed Rasheed Ibrahim

MINISTRY OF PUBLIC WORKS AND LABOUR
Marine Drive (North), Malé 20-05
Tel 323234; telex 77071
Minister: Abdulla Kamaludheen

MINISTRY OF STATE FOR PRESIDENTIAL AFFAIRS
Malé
Minister of State: Abdul Rasheed Hussain

MINISTRY OF STATE FOR RELIGIOUS AFFAIRS
Fareedhi Bldg, Malé 20-05
Tel 322266
Minister of State: Ahmed Shathir

MINISTRY OF TOURISM
Ghaazee Bldg, Ameer Ahmed Magu, Malé 20-05
Tel 323224; telex 66019
Minister: Ahmed Mujuthaba

MINISTRY OF TRADE AND INDUSTRIES
Ghaazee Bldg, Ameer Ahmed Magu, Malé 20-05
Tel 323668; telex 77076
Minister: Ilyas Ibrahim

MINISTRY OF TRANSPORT AND SHIPPING
Huravee Bldg, Ameer Ahmed Magu, Malé 20-05
Tel 323991; telex 77066
Minister: Abbas Ibrahim

OFFICE OF THE ATTORNEY-GENERAL
Huravee Bldg, Ameer Ahmed Magu, Malé 20-05
Tel 323802
Attorney-General: Ahmed Zaki

GOVERNMENT AGENCIES AND ORGANIZATIONS

Advisory and Supervisory Bodies

Department of Immigration and Emigration: Huravee Bldg, Ameer Ahmed Magu, Malé 20-05; tel 323913; Dir: K. Ahmed Manik.

Elections Division: Ghaazee Bldg, Ameer Ahmed Magu, Malé 20-05; tel 322241; Commr: Abdul Sattar Ahmed Didi; supervision of elections.

Maldivian Audit Office: 3rd Floor, Huravee Bldg, Ameer Ahmed Magu, Malé 20-05; tel 323930; Auditor-Gen: Abdul Rasheed; f 1951; examination of Govt revenues and expenditures; control of Govt's general accounts.

Art and Culture

National Centre for Linguistic and Historical Research: Malé 20-05; tel 323206; Chair (acting): Abdulla Hameed; Dirs: Mohamed Ibrahim Luthfi, Mohamed Waheed; f 1982; promotion and preservation of Maldivian language, history and culture.

National Library: 59 Billoorijehige, Malé 20-04; tel 323945; Dep Dir: Habeeba Zubair; f 1945; promotion and preservation of library facilities.

Business and Economy

BANKING

Bank of Maldives Ltd (BML): 11 Marine Drive, Malé 20-05; tel 323091; telex 77030; Chair: Ahmed Mujuthaba; Gen Man and Chief Exec: Shafaat Ahmed Siddiky; f 1982; 60% state-owned, 40% owned by International Finance Investment and Commerce Bank Ltd (Bangladesh); 2 brs.

Maldives Monetary Authority (MMA): Majeedee Bldg, Marine Drive, Malé 20-02; tel 322290; telex 66055; fax 323892; Gov: President Maumoon Abdul Gayoom; Vice-Gov: Ismail Fathy; Gen Man: Maizan Adam Maniku; f 1981; bank of issue; supervises foreign exchange dealings and advises the Govt on banking and monetary matters.

INSURANCE

Allied Insurance Co of Maldives Ltd: 'Stardust', SEK No 2, Chandhanee Magu, Malé; tel 324612; telex 77063; Man Dir: Ilyas Ibrahim; Dir of Admin: Ibrahim Shafeeg; f 1985; all classes of non-life insurance; operated by the State Trading Organization (see below).

TRADE

State Trading Organization (STO): STO Bldg, 7 Haveeree Higun, Malé 20-02; tel 323640; telex 66006; Man Dir: Ilyas Ibrahim; Dirs: Moosa Ismail, Ibrahim Shakeeb; f 1964; state-sponsored commercial and financial organization; imports staple foods and other consumer items and distributes them to the public; handles more than 50% of the country's imports; exports goods on behalf of the Govt; handles all the commercial fisheries projects and many infrastructural and devt projects for the Govt; operates the following subsidiaries:

Felivaru Tuna Processing Plant: Felivaru; Gen Man: Nasrullah Kamaluddeen; Man: Mohamed Ahmed.

Fisheries Projects Implementation Department: Huravee Bldg, Ameer Ahmed Magu, Malé 20-02; tel 323831; telex 77014; fax 323955; f 1984; export of marine products; implementation and management of all fisheries projects.

JSM/STO Maldives Ltd: Malé; telex 66082.

Silverline Garments (Maldives) Ltd: c/o STO, 'Golden Sunbeam', Haveeree Higun, Malé 20-03; tel 323276; telex 66023; manufacture and export of ready-made garments.

Development and Planning

Addu Development Authority: Dhoshimeynaa Bldg, Ameer Ahmed Magu, Malé 20-05; tel 323101; Chair: Abdullah Hameed.

Education

Educational Development Centre: H. Windy Rest, Sosun Magu, Malé 20-06; tel 323243; Dir: Mohamed Latheef; f 1976; responsible for the devt of the school curricular and teaching/learning materials, providing educational media services, assisting the island communities in upgrading of schools.

Energy

Maldives Electricity Board: Majeedi Magu, Malé 20-03; tel 323271; Dir: Abdul Shakoor.

Health and Welfare

HEALTH

Allied Health Services Training Centre: Sosun Magu, Malé 20-06; tel 323119; Dir: Aminath Rasheeda; f 1972; training of mid-level health workers, in-service education, public health education, promotion of traditional medicine.

WELFARE

Department of Women's Affairs: Fareedhee Bldg, Malé; tel 323687; Dir-Gen: Fathimath Jameel; f 1979; women's devt activities.

Pensions and Social Welfare Division: Marine Drive (North), Malé 20-02; tel 322238; Dir: Ahmed Islam.

Legal and Judiciary

High Court: Moonlight Higun, Malé 20-06; tel 323082; Chief Justice: Moosa Fathuy; f 1980.

Prisons Division: Dhoshimeynaa Bldg, Ameer Ahmed Magu, Malé 20-05; tel 322242; Dir: Ibrahim Mohamed Manik.

Media

Department of Information and Broadcasting: 3rd Floor, Huravee Bldg, Ameer Ahmed Magu, Malé 20-05; tel 323830;

telex 66085; Dir-Gen: Ibrahim Manik; Dir: Abdulla Rasheed; Dep Dir: Ahmed Saleem; f 1978.

Television Maldives: Buruzu Magu, Galolhu, Malé; tel 323106; telex 66120; fax 325371; Dir: Ali Shareef; Dep Dir: Hussain Mohamed; f 1978.

Voice of Maldives: Moonlight Higun, Malé; tel 325577; telex 66085; Dir, Programmes: Badrul Naseer; Dir, Engineering: Maizan Ahmed Manik; f 1962; home service in Dhivehi and English.

Telecommunications

Department of Posts and Telecommunications: Marine Drive (North), Malé 20-02; tel 323453; telex 66005; Dir-Gen: Riluwan Shareef; Dir: Hussain Shareef.

Tourism

Tourist Information Unit: Marine Drive (North), Malé 20-05; f 1987.

Transport

CIVIL AVIATION

Air Maldives: KUM Bldg, Marine Drive, Malé; tel 322434; telex 77053; Dir: Anbaree Abdul Sattar; f 1984, as Maldives Airways, by the Govt-owned Maldives Aviation Co Ltd (the majority shareholder) and foreign investors; domestic flights.

Civil Aviation Authority: Dhoshimeynaa Bldg, Ameer Ahmed Magu, Malé 20-05; tel 323507; telex 66034; Dir: Mohamed Shareef.

Maldives Airports Authority: Dhoshimeynaa Bldg, Ameer Ahmed Magu, Malé 20-05; tel 322210; telex 66123; fax 325034; Dir: Mohamed Ibrahim; Dep Dir: Ahmed Shihab; f 1988; devt and admin of airports in the country.

ROADS

Maldives Transport and Contracting Co Ltd: Ship Plaza, Orchid Magu, POB 2063, Malé; tel 323522; telex 77038; Man Dir (acting): Mohamed Zahir; Dir, Operations: Adam Saleem; f 1981; 60% state-owned.

SHIPPING

Maldives National Ship Management Ltd: MSL Bldg, Orchid Magu, Malé; tel 322021; telex 66001; Man Dir: Ali Umar Manik; Dir: Ahmed Mujuthaba; f 1965 as Maldives Shipping Ltd; 100% state-owned.

Maldives Ports Authority: Malé Commercial Harbour, Malé 20-02; tel 325681; telex 66109; Man Dir: Abdulla Kamaluddeen; Dir: Mohamed Zaki; f 1986; responsible for loading, unloading and releasing of cargo at Malé commercial harbour.

Utilities

Maldives Water and Sanitation Authority: Marine Drive (North), Malé 20-01; tel 323710; telex 77047; Dir: M. Ibrahim; Dep Dir: M. Rasheed; f 1973; provision of drinking water and sewerage facilities.

MALI

Head of State

The President, elected for a six-year term by universal adult suffrage, is Head of State and Head of Government. The President appoints a Council of Ministers, which is responsible to the Assemblée Nationale (National Assembly).

President: Gen Moussa Traoré (assumed power 19 November 1968; elected President 19 June 1979; re-elected 9 June 1985).

Office of the President: BP 1463, Bamako; tel 22-24-61; telex 2521; Minister Sec-Gen of the Presidency: Django Cissoko.

Legislature

Legislative power is vested in the Assemblée Nationale (National Assembly), with 82 members, directly elected for a three-year term from a list of candidates chosen by the single political party, the Union Démocratique du Peuple Malien (UDPM). Mali has seven administrative regions, and a district Government in Bamako.

Assemblée Nationale (National Assembly): Bamako; Pres: Sidki Diarra.

MINISTRIES AND GOVERNMENT DEPARTMENTS

MINISTRY OF AGRICULTURE
BP 61, Bamako
Tel 22-29-79
Minister: Moulaye Mohamed Haidara

MINISTRY OF DEFENCE
BP 215, Bamako
Tel 22-26-17
Minister: Gen Moussa Traoré
Minister-delegate to the Minister:
Gen Abdoulaye Ouologuem

MINISTRY OF THE ENVIRONMENT AND ANIMAL HUSBANDRY
BP 1676, Bamako
Tel 22-60-24
Minister: Morifing Koné

MINISTRY OF FINANCE AND TRADE
BP 234, Koulouba, Bamako
Tel 22-56-87; telex 2559
Minister: Tiénan Coulibaly

MINISTRY OF FOREIGN AFFAIRS AND INTERNATIONAL CO-OPERATION
Koulouba, Bamako
Tel 22-54-89; telex 2560
Minister: N'Golo Traoré

MINISTRY OF INDUSTRY, HYDRAULICS AND ENERGY
BP 238, Bamako
Tel 22-35-47
Minister: Amadou Demé

MINISTRY OF INFORMATION AND TELECOMMUNICATIONS
BP 116, Bamako
Tel 22-26-47; telex 2421
Minister: Niamonto Diarra

MINISTRY OF JUSTICE
BP 97, Bamako
Tel 22-24-36
Minister: Mamadou Sissoko

MINISTRY OF LABOUR AND CIVIL SERVICE
BP 80, Bamako
Tel 22-59-51
Minister: Diallo Lalla Sy

MINISTRY OF NATIONAL EDUCATION
BP 71, Bamako
Tel 22-24-50
Minister: Gen Sékou Ly

MINISTRY OF PLANNING
Koulouba, Bamako
Tel 22-57-80; telex 2412
Minister: Souleymane Dembélé

MINISTRY OF PUBLIC HEALTH AND SOCIAL AFFAIRS
Koulouba, Bamako
Tel 22-53-01
Minister: Abdoulaye Diallo

MINISTRY OF PUBLIC WORKS, URBAN PLANNING AND CONSTRUCTION
BP 78, Bamako
Tel 22-39-37
Minister: Cheikh Oumar Doumbia

MINISTRY OF SPORTS, ARTS AND CULTURE
BP 88, Bamako
Tel 22-32-10
Minister: Bakary Traoré

**MINISTRY OF TERRITORIAL ADMINISTRATION
AND BASIC DEVELOPMENT**
Bamako
Tel 22-42-12
Minister: Col Issa Ongoiba

**MINISTRY OF TRANSPORT,
TELECOMMUNICATIONS AND TOURISM**
Bamako
Minister: Zéini Moulaye

GOVERNMENT AGENCIES AND ORGANIZATIONS

Agriculture

Compagnie Malienne pour le Développement des Textiles (CMDT): BP 487, Bamako; tel 22-24-62; telex 2554; Man Dir: Dr Boubacar Sada Sy; f 1975; 60% state-owned; cotton cultivation and ginning, promotion of other crops.

Huilerie Cotonière du Mali: c/o CMDT, BP 487, Bamako; tel 22-24-62; telex 2554; Dir: Fagnamana Koné; f 1979; 80% state-owned; production and marketing of cottonseed oil.

Office de Développement Intégré des Productions Arachidières et Céréalières (ODIPAC): square Lumumba, BP 72, Bamako; tel 22-57-59; Man Dir: Zana Vincent Dembélé; devt of diversified forms of agricultural production.

Office du Niger: BP 160, Ségou; tel 32-01-43; Dir-Gen: Moussa Léo Sidibe; f 1932; taken over from the French Govt in 1958; responsible for irrigation projects involving the Niger river with a view to enlarging cultivable areas; also operates a number of research stations, four rice-processing plants, a cotton-ginning factory, two sugar refineries and a distillery.

Office des Produits Agricoles du Mali: BP 132, Bamako; tel 22-31-48; telex 2509; Dir-Gen: Abdoulaye Sall; Dep Dir-Gen: C. A. Tidjani Touré; f 1965; storage and distribution of cereals; information service and assistance to private producers.

Société d'Exploitation des Produits Oléagineux du Mali (SEPOM): BP 15, Koulikoro; tel 26-20-24; telex 2545; Man Dir: Brahima Bocoum; f 1962; production of groundnut oil, cottonseed oil, karité butter, beauty creams, soap and cattle cake.

Société Libyo-Malienne de Développement, de l'Elevage et d'Exploitation du Bétail (SOLIMA): ave Kassé Keïta, Bamako; telex 2438; Dir: Moulay Bocoum; f 1978; 60% state-owned, 40% owned by Libya; livestock devt.

Business and Economy

BANKING

Banque Centrale des Etats de l'Afrique de l'Ouest (BCEAO): BP 206, Bamako; tel 22-37-56; telex 1674; Gov: Alassane Ouattara; Dir in Mali: Younoussi Touré; headquarters in Dakar, Senegal; took over functions of Banque Centrale du Mali in 1984; bank of issue and central bank for the seven states of Union monétaire ouest-africaine (UMOA), comprising Benin, Burkina Faso, Côte d'Ivoire, Mali, Niger, Senegal and Togo.

Banque Malienne du Crédit et de Dépôts SA (BMCD): ave du Fleuve, BP 45, Bamako; tel 22-53-36; telex 2572; Chair and Man Dir: Ismaïla Kanoute; f 1961 to take over Mali brs of Crédit Lyonnais; 50.02% state-owned, 49.98% owned by Crédit Lyonnais.

Banque Nationale de Développement Agricole (BNDA): Immeuble Caisse Autonome d'Amortissement, BP 2424, Bamako; tel 22-64-64; telex 2638; Pres: Minister of Finance and Trade, Tiéna Coulibaly; Man Dir: Bakary Traoré; f 1981; 53% state-owned; 2 brs.

Société de Crédit Agricole d'Equipement Rural (SCAER): rue Karamoko, Diaby, BP 787, Bamako; tel 22-31-43; telex 2578; Man Dir: Yaya Coulibaly.

FINANCIAL AGENCY

Caisse Centrale de Coopération Economique (CCCE): BP 32, Bamako; tel 22-28-42; telex 2502; Dir: Philippe Renard; devt agency.

INSURANCE

Caisse Nationale d'Assurance et de Réassurance (CNAR): BP 568, Bamako; tel 22-64-54; telex 2549; Man Dir: Mamadou Drame; 5 brs.

NATIONALIZED INDUSTRY

Abattoir Frigorifique de Bamako: Zone Industrielle, BP 356, Bamako; tel 22-24-67; telex 2992; Man Dir: El Hadj Youssouf Camara; f 1965.

Compagnie Malienne des Textiles (COMATEX): route de Markala, BP 52, Ségou; tel 32-01-83; telex 2584; Man Dir: Lassana Sacko; majority state-owned; production of unbleached fibre and textiles.

Industrie Textile du Mali (ITEMA): BP 299, Bamako; tel 22-29-05; telex 2504; Man Dir: Régis Pollot; majority state-owned; textile complex at Bamako.

Société des Ciments du Mali (SOCIMA): BP 3, Diamou (Kayes); Man Dir: Diatrou Diakité; f 1969; majority state-owned; production of cement and quicklime at Diamou; marble quarry at Korofina.

Société Nationale des Tabacs et Allumettes du Mali (SONATAM): route du Sotuba, BP 59, Bamako; tel 22-49-65; telex 2537; Man Dir: Boubacar Dembélé; f 1968; production of cigarettes and matches.

TRADE

Société Malienne d'Importation et d'Exportation (SOMIEX): BP 182, Bamako; tel 22-39-27; telex 2585; Dir-Gen: Mohamed Habibou Coulibaly; f 1960; majority state-owned; has monopoly of imports of consumer goods and of exports of agricultural products.

Defence

Armed Forces: BP 10, Bamako; tel 22-26-58; Chief of Staff: Gen Moussa Traoré.

Air Force: BP 56, Bamako; tel 22-57-38; Chief of Staff: Lt-Col Mamadou Coulibaly.

Army: BP 10, Bamako; tel 22-26-58; Chief of Staff: Lt-Col Ousmane Coulibaly.

Health and Welfare

Pharmacie Populaire du Mali (PPM): BP 277, Bamako; tel 22-46-25; telex 2523; Man Dir: Abdoulaye Diallo; f 1960; majority state-owned; import and marketing of medicines and pharmaceutical products.

Legal and Judiciary

Cour Suprême (Supreme Court): BP 7, Bamako; tel 22-24-06; Pres: Bekaye N'Diaye; f 1969; 19 mems; judicial section comprises three civil chambers and one criminal chamber; administrative section deals with appeals and fundamental rulings.

Special Court of State Security: Bamako; Chief Justice: Mele Diakité; f 1976, reorganized 1978; comprises four civilian magistrates, 22 army officers and NCOs and three regional governors; adjudicates in offences against state property, especially embezzlement.

Media

BROADCASTING

Radiodiffusion-Télévision Malienne: BP 171, Bamako; tel 22-24-74; Man Dir: Younous Hamaye Dicko; f 1957; radio programmes in French, English, Bambara, Peulh, Sarakolé, Tamachek, Sonrai, Moorish, Wolof; two hours weekly of colour TV broadcasting.

GOVERNMENT PUBLISHER

Editions Imprimerie du Mali (EDIM): BP 21, Bamako; tel 22-20-41; f 1972.

NEWS AND INFORMATION

Agence Malienne de Presse (AMAP): BP 116, Bamako; tel 22-26-47; telex 2421; f 1977; national news agency.

Direction de la Statistique et de l'Informatique: c/o Ministry of Planning, Koulouba, Bamako; tel 22-57-80; telex 2412; responsible for the formulation of economic devt plans and collection, analysis and publication of statistics.

Mining and Energy

Société Minière de Loulo (SOMILO): Loulo; f 1987; Chair: Mamadou Touré; Dir-Gen: Jean-Marie Bouffière; 51% state-owned, 49% by Bureau des Recherches Géologiques et Minières (France); exploitation of gold deposits.

Société Nationale de Recherches et d'Exploitation des Ressources Minières du Mali (SONAREM): BP 2, Kati; tel 27-20-42; Man Dir: Makan Kayentao; exploration and exploitation of mining resources.

Transport

Air Mali: BP 27, Bamako; tel 22-35-36; telex 2568; f 1960, reorganized 1987; domestic services; backing from USSR.

Compagnie Malienne de Navigation (CMN): BP 10, Koulikoro; tel 26-20-34; Man Dir: Amadou Dem; f 1968; shipping co.

Compagnie Malienne de Transports Routiers (CMTR): BP 208, Bamako; tel 22-33-64; telex 2539; Dir-Gen: Mamadou Touré; f 1970; road haulage co.

Régie du Chemin de Fer du Mali (RCFM): rue Kassé Keïta, BP 260, Bamako; tel 22-29-57; telex 2586; Dir-Gen: Noumoucounda Savane; f 1960; state railways co.

MALTA

<table>
<tr><td>

Head of State

Under the 1974 Constitution, the President is Head of State, elected for a five-year term by the House of Representatives. Executive power is exercised by a Cabinet, headed by the Prime Minister, who is appointed by the President. The Cabinet is responsible to the House.

President: Dr Vincent (Censu) Tabone (took office 4 April 1989).

Office of the President: The Palace, Valletta; tel 221221; telex 1100; fax 227822.

</td><td>

Legislature

Legislative power is vested in the unicameral House of Representatives whose members are elected by universal adult suffrage for five years on the basis of proportional representation. A party which receives more than 50% of the total votes cast in a general election obtains a majority of seats.

House of Representatives: The Palace, Valletta; tel 221221; telex 1100; Speaker: Dr Lawrence Gonzi.

</td></tr>
</table>

MINISTRIES AND GOVERNMENT DEPARTMENTS

OFFICE OF THE PRIME MINISTER
Auberge de Castille, Valletta
Tel 623026; telex 1531; fax 234494
Prime Minister: Dr Edward Fenech-Adami

OFFICE OF THE DEPUTY PRIME MINISTER AND OF THE MINISTER OF THE INTERIOR AND OF JUSTICE
The Palace, Valletta
Tel 225401; telex 1471
Deputy Prime Minister and Minister:
Prof Guido de Marco

MINISTRY OF EDUCATION
Beltissebh, Floriana
Tel 231393; telex 1114
Minister: Dr Ugo Mifsud Bonnici

MINISTRY OF FINANCE
St Calcedonius Sq, Floriana
Tel 220437; telex 1100; fax 234494
Minister: Dr George Bonello du Puis

MINISTRY OF FOREIGN AFFAIRS
Palazzo Parisio, Merchants St, Valletta
Tel 222407; telex 1497; fax 227822
Minister: Dr Edward Fenech-Adami

MINISTRY FOR GOZO
St Francis Sq, Victoria, Gozo
Tel 556482; telex 1715; fax 557755
Minister: Anton Tabone
Co-ordinates the activities of the various ministries in Gozo; helps draw up and implement a devt plan for the island of Gozo.

MINISTRY OF HEALTH
15 Merchants St, Valletta
Tel 224071
Minister: Dr George Hyzlar

MINISTRY OF INDUSTRY
Auberge d'Aragon, Independence Sq, Valletta
Tel 229898; telex 1111
Minister: John Dalli

MINISTRY OF INFRASTRUCTURE DEVELOPMENT
Block B, Beltissebh, Floriana
Tel 229939; telex 1861
Minister: Michael Falzon
Parliamentary Secretary for Water and Energy:
Ninu Zammit
Formulates and implements Govt policies on public works, water, energy, telephone and telecommunications, and postal services.

MINISTRY OF PRODUCTIVE DEVELOPMENT
3A Old Mint St, Valletta
Tel 225236; telex 1790
Minister: Lawrence A. Gatt
Formulates and implements Govt policies on industrial devt, parastatal industries, manufacturing industry and exports, co-operatives, agriculture, fisheries, export promotion and credit, science and technology; responsible for Malta Devt Corpn (see below).

MINISTRY OF SOCIAL POLICY
310 Republic St, Valletta
Tel 232286; telex 1893; fax 623017
Minister: Dr Louis Galea
Parliamentary Secretary for the Elderly:
Dr John Rizzo Naudi
Parliamentary Secretary for Housing: Dr Joe Cassar

MINISTRY OF TERTIARY SECTOR DEVELOPMENT
Palazzo Verdelin, 111 Archbishop St, Valletta
Tel 623071; telex 1107
Minister: Dr Emanuel Bonnici
Parliamentary Secretary for Maritime Affairs and Offshore Activities: Dr Joe Fenech
Formulates and implements Govt policies on tourism, imports

and internal trade, insurance, Air Malta and Sea Malta (see below), shipping, ports, price control and consumer protection.

MINISTRY OF TOURISM
Republic St, Valletta
Tel 224444; telex 1105; fax 220401
Minister: Dr Michael Refalo
OFFICE OF THE PARLIAMENTARY SECRETARY FOR

POSTS AND TELECOMMUNICATIONS
Lascaris
Tel 620901; telex 1108; fax 620761
Parliamentary Secretary for Posts and Telecommunications: Pierre Muscat
Formulates policy of posts and telecommunications; responsible for the Dept of Posts and Telemalta Corpn.

GOVERNMENT AGENCIES AND ORGANIZATIONS

Advisory and Supervisory Bodies

Electoral Commission: Evans Bldg, St Elmo Sq, Valletta; tel 226380; telex 1100; fax 227822; Chief Electoral Commr and Electoral Registrar: Carmel R. Callus; f 1921; conduct of general elections; revision of electoral boundaries; publication of the Electoral Register every six months; constitutional body whose mems are appointed by the Pres of Malta.

Public Service Commission: The Palace, Valletta; tel 222063; telex 1471; Chair: Dr Albert G. Camilleri; Sec: Nicholas Scicluna; advises and submits recommendations to the Prime Minister with regard to appointments, promotions and discipline in the Public Service; mems appointed by the Pres of Malta.

Business and Economy

BANKING

Bank of Valletta Ltd: 58 Zachary St, Valletta; tel 623261; telex 1235; fax 230894; Chair: Joseph N. Tabone; f 1974; commercial bank; 60% Govt-owned; 44 brs.

Central Bank of Malta: Calstille Place, Valletta; tel 607480; telex 1262; fax 623051; Gov: Anthony P. Galdes; Dep Gov: Henry C. de Gabriele; f 1968; central bank; advises the Govt on economic and financial matters and implements monetary policy; custodian of foreign exchange reserves and administers exchange control; operates a clearing house.

Investment Finance Bank Ltd: 168 Strait St, Valletta; tel 232017; telex 1744; fax 622014; Chair: V. E. Ragonesi; Gen Man: J. C. Caruana; f 1976; provides medium- and long-term finance for business and service industries.
Mid-Med Bank Ltd: 233 Republic St, POB 428, Valletta; tel 625281; telex 1370; fax 230406; Chair: Dr Riccardo Farrugia; Gen Man: f. R. Flynn; f 1975; 46 brs.

FINANCIAL AGENCY

Treasury: St Calcedonius Sq, Floriana; tel 220437; telex 1100; fax 234494; Accountant-Gen: Charles Portelli.

INSURANCE

Middle Sea Insurance Co Ltd: Middle Sea House, POB 337, Floriana; tel 626262; telex 1862; Man Dir: Mario V. Grech; f 1981.

NATIONALIZED INDUSTRY

Department of Industry: 90 West St, Valletta; tel 229898; telex 1111; Dir: John Camilleri-Brennan; f 1964; maintains a regular surveillance of the performance of established private industries; aids devt of local, especially small-scale industry;

ensures high quality of manufactured goods both imported and locally-made; protects and fosters typical Maltese handicrafts; runs crafts villages and craft centres; assists in marketing and monitors latest achievements in international technology.

Malta Drydocks: The Docks, POB 581, Valletta; tel 822451; telex 1211; fax 800021; Chair: S. Meilaq; Gen Man: L. V. Farrugia; f 1959; ship repairing and shipbuilding; heavy industrial work; operates seven dry docks and nine deep-water berths.

Manoel Island Yacht Yard: Manoel Island; tel 334453; telex 1310; Man: Albert Borg; yacht and small craft repairs; boat park.

Malta Shipbuilding Co Ltd: Marsa Shipyard, Marsa; POB 5, Valletta; tel 231335; telex 1963; fax 620930; Chair and Chief Exec: Saviour G. Brincat; Man Dir: Philip Buhagiar; f 1976; shipbuilding facilities; structural steel fabrication; other projects in the oil offshore field industries, eg single buoy moorings and specialized bldgs; 61% Govt-owned, 30% by Libyan and 9% by Algerian interests.

TRADE

Customs Department: Customs House, Vittoriosa.

Department of Trade: Lascaris, Valletta; tel 224411; telex 1106; Dir: John F. X. Muscat; f 1955; functions include import, export, trade licensing, consumer protection, price enforcement, bulk buying of essential supplies, foreign trade relations and the registration of partnerships, trade marks, patents and designs.

Malta Countertrade Co Ltd: Kingsway Palace, 3rd Floor, Door 40, POB 130, Republic St, Valletta; tel 623234; telex 1799; Dep Chair: Victor Galea Pace; Exec Dir and Sec: Robert V. Ferrante; f 1985; encourages, monitors and assists both buyers and sellers in all countertrade operations; assists potential investors in setting up cos or entering into joint ventures; helps foreign cos identify fields of activities in which to trade with their Maltese counterparts.

Malta Export Trade Corpn Ltd (MEICO): Middle Sea House, Floriana; tel 235351; telex 1966; fax 235253; Chair: Dr John Grech; Man Dir: Alexander Agius Cesareo; f 1989; export promotion and international trade; provides trade information service to the commercial sector and other forms of direct assistance to exporters; advises Govt on the formulation of trade agreements.

Defence

Armed Forces: Luga Barracks, Luga; tel 824213; telex 1100; Commdr: Brig John Spiteri; Dep Commdr: Col Maurice Calleja.

Police General Headquarters: Floriana; tel 224002; telex 1899; fax 235467; Commr of Police: Alfred A. Calleja; Dep Commr: Anthony Mifsud-Tommasi; f 1814.

Development and Planning

Malta Development Corpn: House of Catalunya, Marsamxetto Rd, Valletta; tel 227052; telex 1275; fax 606407; Chair: Michael Soler; Dep Chair: Louis Farrugia; f 1967; statutory body responsible for administering the Govt's programme of investment inducements; liaises between industry and Govt; assists foreign cos; promotes exports; under Ministry of Productive Devt.

INVESTMENT

Libyan-Maltese Investment Co: Valletta; tel 20982; f 1972; owned by Malta Devt Corpn and Libyan Arab Foreign Investment Co; investment in industry, agriculture, fisheries, tourism and other devt projects.

Malta Investment Management Co Ltd (MIMCOL): UB 14/15, San Gwann Industrial Estate, B'Kara; tel 497970; telex 960; fax 499568; Chair: Alfred Mallia; Chief Exec: George Papagiorcopulo; f 1988; manages and monitors the investments acquired by the Malta Devt Corpn (see above) and the Govt.

Energy

Enemalta Corpn: Central Admin Bldg, Church Wharf, Marsa; tel 225822; telex 1735; fax 623055; Chair: Lawrence C. Ciantar; Dep Chair: Joseph f. Grima; f 1977; state energy corpn; acquires petroleum products and steam coal for electricity generation; electricity transmission and distribution; distribution of petroleum products and gas.

Oil Exploration Division: Office of the Prime Minister, Auberge de Castille, Valletta; tel 227921; telex 1458; fax 603015; Dir: Roger Scotto; f 1971; assists the Govt in the formulation and execution of petroleum exploration programmes.

Legal and Judiciary

Constitutional Court and Court of Appeal: Courts of Justice, Republic St, Valletta; tel 113281; telex 1100; Chief Justice and Pres: Hugh William Harding; Registrar of the Courts of Malta and Gozo: Emanuel Grech.

Office of the Attorney-General: The Palace, Valletta; Attorney-Gen: C. Testa.

Media

BROADCASTING

Malta Broadcasting Authority: National Rd, Blata I-Bajda; tel 221281; telex 1100; Chair: Dr Joseph Micallef Stafrace; Chief Exec: Antoine J. Ellul; Sec: Harry Zammit Cordina; f 1961; supervises and controls radio and TV services; a constitutional body whose members are appointed by the President of Malta.

Xandir Malta: POB 82, Valletta; tel 225051; telex 1443; fax 624601; Head: Manni Spiteri; Dep Head: Maurice Tanti Burlo; f 1935; division of the Telemalta Corpn (see below); provides a cable radio service on a two-channel network with a combined output of 34 programme-hours a day and a wireless service; TV service (Television Malta) broadcasts programmes in Maltese and English for eight hours per evening.

GOVERNMENT PUBLISHER

Government Printing Press: Dept of Information, Auberge de Castille, Valletta; tel 224901; telex 1448.

NEWS AND INFORMATION

Central Office of Statistics: Auberge d'Italie, Merchants St, Valletta; tel 224597; telex 1800.

Department of Information: Auberge de Castille, Valletta; tel 224901; telex 1448; Dir of Information: Edward Sammut.

Tourism

National Tourism Organization—Malta (NTOM): Republic St, Valletta; tel 224444; telex 1105; fax 220401; Chair: Norman Mifsud; Chief Exec: Alfred Cassar-Reynaud; f 1984; statutory body responsible for tourism promotion; publishes tourist information brochures and hotel lists.

Transport and Communications

TELECOMMUNICATIONS

Telemalta Corpn: Spencer Hill, Marsa; tel 607770; telex 1286; fax 330441; Chair: John A. Scicluna; Gen Man: Anthony Debono; f 1975; state telecommunications corpn.

TRANSPORT

Air Malta Co Ltd: Head Office, Luqa; tel 824330; telex 1389; fax 773241; Chair: Albert Mizzi; Vice-Chair: Nicholas de Giorgio; f 1973; national airline in which Govt has a 96.4% shareholding; carriage of passengers and cargo on flights to various European destinations; extensive charter operations throughout Europe; tour operations, tourist accommodation, in-flight supplies.

Civil Aviation Department: Luqa Airport; tel 784321; telex 1313.

Malta Freeport Corpn Ltd: Europa Centre, Floriana; tel 603096; telex 1522; fax 603094; Chair: Marin Hili; f 1988; agency responsible for the devt and management of the Malta Freeport in Malta's second harbour, Marsaxlokk.

Public Transport Authority: Auberge de Castille, Valletta; tel 224901; telex 1100; fax 234494; Chair: Francis Stivala; Dep Chair: Edmund Grech; f 1989; promotion and devt of an integrated, safe, economical and efficient public transport system.

Sea Malta Co Ltd: Sea Malta Bldg, Flagston Wharf, Marsa; tel 232230; telex 1321; fax 225776; Chair: Carmel J. Mallia; Man Dir: Joseph Curmi; Sec: J. T. Apps; f 1977; national shipping line; liner services, trade shipping services; roll-on/roll-off services.

Utilities

Water Works Department (WWD): Auberge d'Italie, 229 Merchants St, Valletta; tel 221901; Man: Charles A. Delia; Asst Mans: Joseph E. Cardona, Albert A. Palmier; f 1801; provides potable water to all localities in the Maltese islands.

MAURITANIA

Head of State and Legislature

After the coup in July 1978, the National Assembly was suspended. The Constitution was replaced by a Charter which granted legislative and executive power to the Comité militaire de salut national (Military Committee for National Salvation). The CMSN is headed by the President, and has 24 members. The President is assisted by an appointed Council of Ministers. All political parties are illegal. The country is divided into 12 regions, each with an appointed Governor.

President of the Republic, Chairman of the Military Committee for National Salvation and Prime Minister: Col Maawiya Ould Sid'Ahmed Taya (took office 12 December 1984).

Office of the President and of the Chairman of the Military Committee for National Salvation: La Présidence de la République, BP 184, Nouakchott; tel 523-17; telex 580; Permanent Secretary: Commdt Mohamed Lemine Ould N'Diaye.

MINISTRIES AND GOVERNMENT DEPARTMENTS

MINISTRY OF THE CIVIL SERVICE, ADMINISTRATIVE TRAINING, LABOUR, YOUTH AND SPORTS
BP 193, Nouakchott
Tel 529-43
Minister: Mohamed Ould Haimer

MINISTRY OF CULTURE AND ISLAMIC ORIENTATION
BP 223, Nouakchott
Tel 511-30; telex 585
Minister: Sidi Ould Benahi Mohamed Salem Ould Abdel Addoud

MINISTRY OF DEFENCE
BP 184, Nouakchott
Tel 520-20; telex 566
Minister: Col Maawiya Ould Sid'Ahmed Taya

MINISTRY OF ECONOMY AND FINANCE
BP 183, Nouakchott
Tel 513-65; telex 540
Minister: Mohamed Ould Nani

MINISTRY OF EQUIPMENT
BP 237, Nouakchott
Tel 521-57; telex 585
Minister: Lt-Col Oumar Dieng Harouna

MINISTRY OF FISHERIES AND MARINE ECONOMY
BP 137, Nouakchott
Tel 524-76; telex 595
Minister: Col Mohamed Sidina Ould Sidya

MINISTRY OF FOREIGN AFFAIRS AND CO-OPERATION
BP 230, Nouakchott
Tel 520-20; telex 585
Minister: Maj Cheikh Sid'Ahmed Ould Baba

MINISTRY OF HEALTH AND SOCIAL AFFAIRS
BP 177, Nouakchott
Tel 518-58
Minister: Maj N'Diaye Kane

MINISTRY OF INFORMATION
BP 233, Nouakchott
Tel 520-20
Minister: Mohamed Lemine Ould Ahmed

MINISTRY OF THE INTERIOR
BP 195, Nouakchott
Tel 529-34; telex 844
Minister: Lt-Col Djibril Ould Abdallahi
Secretary of State for Maghreb Affairs:
Ahmedou Ould Sidi
Secretary-General of the Government: Barou Abdoulaye
Assistant Secretary-General of the Government:
Ba Alassane Yero

MINISTRY OF JUSTICE
BP 350, Nouakchott
Tel 510-83
Minister: Cheikh Mohamed Salem Ould Mohamed Lemine

MINISTRY OF MINES AND INDUSTRY
BP 183, Nouakchott
Tel 513-18
Minister: Ahmed Ould Jiddou

MINISTRY OF NATIONAL AND HIGHER EDUCATION
BP 387, Nouakchott
Tel 518-98
Minister: Ba Aliou Ibra Hasni Ould Didi
Secretary of State for Literacy and Basic Education:
Mohamed Lemine Ould Ahmed

MINISTRY OF PLANNING AND EMPLOYMENT
Nouakchott
Minister: Mostefa Ould Oubayed Rahman

MINISTRY OF RURAL DEVELOPMENT
BP 366, Nouakchott
Tel 520-20
Minister: Hamoud Ould Ely

MINISTRY OF STATE CONTROL
Nouakchott
Minister: Ethmane Sid'Ahmed Yessa

MINISTRY OF TRADE AND TRANSPORT
BP 238, Nouakchott
Tel 520-63
Minister: Hamdi Samba Diop

MINISTRY OF WATER AND ENERGY
BP 1255, Nouakchott
Tel 533-51
Minister: Mohamed Lemine Ould Abdi Soumare Oumar

MINISTRY OF WOMEN'S AFFAIRS, ARTISANAL AFFAIRS AND TOURISM
Nouakchott
Minister: M'Barek Ould Maoulou Khadijetou Abderrahmane

GOVERNMENT AGENCIES AND ORGANIZATIONS

Agriculture and Fishing

AGRICULTURE

Office Mauritanien des Céréales (OMC): BP 368, Nouakchott; tel 528-30; telex 513; Pres: Waly N'Dao; Dir: Mohamed Bocoum; f 1975; cereals agency.

Société Arabe Mauritano-Libyenne de Développement Agricole (SAMALIDA): 42 ave Gamal-Abdel-Nasser, BP 658, Nouakchott; tel 537-15; telex 854; Dir-Gen: Abderrahmane Liman; f 1980; 51% state-owned, 49% owned by Libya.

FISHING

Société Algéro-Mauritanienne des Pêches (ALMAP): BP 321, Nouadhibou; tel 45-148; telex 424; Dir: Brahim Ould Boidaha; f 1974; 51% state-owned, 49% owned by Algeria; fishing, processing of fishery products.

Société Arabe Libyenne-Mauritanienne des Ressources Maritimes (SALIMAUREM): BP 75, Nouadhibou; tel 452-41; telex 452; Chair: Ahmed Ould Ghnahalla; Dir-Gen: Sala Mohamed Aribi; 50% state-owned, 50% owned by Libya; fishing and fish processing; freezer factory.

Société Arabe Mauritano-Irakienne de Pêche (SAMIP): BP 289, Nouadhibou; telex 431; f 1979; fishing and related activities.

Société Mauritanienne de Commercialisation du Poisson (SMCP): BP 259, Nouadhibou; tel 45-281; telex 420; Pres: Mohamed Salem Ould Lekhal; Dir-Gen: Cheikh el Afia Ould Mouhamed Khouna; f 1984; monopoly of exporting demersal fish and crustaceans.

Société Mixte de Pêche: Nouakchott; f 1978; 51% state-owned, 49% by Iraq; fishing and related activities.

Business and Economy

BANKING

Banque Centale de Mauritanie (BCM): ave de l'Indépendance, BP 623, Nouakchott; tel 522-06; telex 532; Gov: Ahmed Ould Zein; f 1973; central bank; 3 brs.

Société Mauritanienne de Banque SA (SMB): ave Gamal-Abdel-Nasser, BP 614, Nouakchott; tel 526-02; telex 567; Chair: Camara Ali Gueladio; Man Dir: Abdel Majid Kamil; 55% state-owned; 3 brs.

Union des Banques de Développpement (UBD): Immeuble Afarco, ave Gamal-Abdel-Nasser, BP 648, Nouakchott; tel 530-58; telex 840; Chair: Michel Ould Mohamedou; Man Dir: Diagana Djime; f 1987 following merger of Banque Mauritanienne pour le Développement et le Commerce and Fonds National de Développement.

INSURANCE

Société Mauritanienne d'Assurances et de Réassurances (SMAR): 12 ave Gamal-Abdel-Nasser, BP 163, Nouakchott; tel 526-50; telex 527; fax 518-18; f 1974; state insurance monopoly.

NATIONALIZED INDUSTRY

Société Arabe des Industries Métallurgiques Mauritano-Koweïtienne (SAMIA): BP 1248, Nouakchott; tel 526-41; telex 508; Chair: Mohamed Yehdih Ould el Hacen; Man Dir: Ahmed Wafi; 50% state-owned, 50% by Kuwaiti interests; copper refining.

Société Mauritanienne des Industries du Sucre (SOMIS): BP 671, Nouakchott; tel 527-22; telex 861; Chair: Mamadou Cissoko; Dir-Gen: El Hadj Amadou Wone; 63% state-owned; sugar production.

TRADE

Bureau d'Achats pour la République Islamique de Mauritanie (BARIM): ave du Président J. F. Kennedy, BP 272, Nouakchott; tel 510-57; telex 810; Dir-Gen: D. Diabira; f 1969; importer and exporter.

Société Nationale d'Importation et d'Exportation (SONIMEX): BP 290, Nouakchott; tel 514-72; telex 561; Pres: Dewahi Mohamed Saleck; Dir-Gen: Moussa Fall; f 1966; 62% state-owned; monopoly importer of consumer goods such as rice, tea, sugar; monopoly exporter of gum-arabic.

Defence

Army: c/o Ministry of Defence, BP 184, Nouakchott; tel 533-51; Chief of Staff: Lt-Col Ahmed Ould Minnih.

Garde Nationale (National Guard): address as above; tel 533-51; Commdr: Brahim Ould Alioune N'Diaye.

Gendarmerie Nationale (National Police): Nouakchott; Chief of Staff: Lt-Col De Ould Ne.

Groupement Aérien de la République Islamique de Mauritanie (Air Force): c/o Ministry of Defence, BP 184, Nouakchott; tel 533-51; Commdr: Hamadi Demba.

Navy: address as above; tel 533-51; Commdr: Vaisseau Abderrahman Ould Lekouar.

Development and Planning

Société Mauritanienne de Développement Rural (SOMADER): BP 321, Nouakchott; tel 521-61; telex 807; Dir: Youba Ould Cheikh Benani; rural devt agency.

Legal and Judiciary

Cour Suprême (Supreme Court): Palais de Justice, BP 350, Nouakchott; tel 521-20; Pres: Ahmedou Ould Abdelkader; f 1961; intended to ensure the independence of the judiciary; the court is competent in juridical, administrative and electoral matters.

Special Court of Justice: Nouakchott; Pres: Col Cheikh Ould Boyda; f 1978; 13 mems; investigates offences against the security of the state.

Media

BROADCASTING

Office de Radiodiffusion et Télévision de Mauritanie (ORTM): BP 200, Nouakchott; tel 521-64; telex 515; Dir: Sidi Ould Cheikh; f 1958; broadcasts in French, Arabic, Wolof, Toucouleur and Sarakolé.

GOVERNMENT PUBLISHER

Imprimerie Nationale: BP 618, Nouakchott; Pres: Moustapha Saleck Ould Ahmed Brihim.

NEWS AND INFORMATION

Agence Mauritanienne de Presse (AMP): BP 371, Nouakchott; tel 529-70; telex 525; Dir: Rachid Ould Saleh; news agency.

Direction de la Statistique et des Etudes Economiques: BP 240, Nouakchott; tel 514-77; collection, analysis and publication of statistics and economic studies.

Mining and Energy

ENERGY

Société Mauritanienne de Commercialisation des Produits Pétroliers (SMCPP): BP 679, Nouakchott; tel 526-61; telex 849; Dir-Gen: Sid'Ahmed Ould Babou; f 1980; importer of petroleum products.

Société Nationale d'Eau et d'Electricité (SONELEC): ave de l'Indépendance, BP 355, Nouakchott; tel 523-08; telex 587; Dir-Gen: Capt Mohamed Ould Boueïda; f 1968; production and distribution of electricity and water.

MINING

Complexe Minier du Nord (COMINOR): BP 1260, Nouadhibou; tel 451-74; telex 426; Operations Man (at Zouérate): M. Milliotte; fmrly MIFERMA, nationalized 1974; iron ore mining.

Société Nationale Industrielle et Minière—Société d'Economie Mixte (SNIM—SEM): BP 42, Nouadhibou; tel 451-90; telex 426; Chair: Abdel Aziz Ould Ahmed; Man Dir: Mohamed Saleck Ould Heyine; f 1972; 71% state-owned; national co for state intervention in research, exploitation and processing of minerals.

Tourism

Direction du Tourisme: BP 246, Nouakchott; tel 533-37; Dir: M'Boye Ould Arafa; f 1988; to organize and promote tourism.

Société Mauritanienne de Tourisme et d'Hôtellerie (SMTH): BP 552, Nouakcott; tel 533-51; Man Dir: Moustapha Teffahi; f 1969; 50% owned by Air Afrique; promotes tourism, manages hotels and organizes tours.

Transport

CIVIL AVIATION

Air Mauritanie: BP 41, Nouakchott; tel 522-11; telex 573; Dir-Gen: Sidi Ould Zein; f 1974; 60% state-owned; has monopoly of scheduled domestic passenger and cargo services from Nouakchott and Nouadhibou; also operates international services to Mali, the Canary Islands and Senegal.

RAILWAYS

SNIM—Direction du Chemin de Fer et du Port: BP 42, Nouakchott; tel 451-74; Gen Man: Mohamed Saleck Ould Heyine; Dir: A. Taleb Mohamed; also the directorate of ports; operated by SNIM-SEN (see Mining and Energy).

ROADS

Société des Transports Publics de Nouakchott: BP 342, Nouakchott; tel 529-53; Pres: Cheikh Malainine Robert; Dir-Gen: Mamadou Souleymane Kane; responsible for public transport in Nouakchott.

SHIPPING

Compagnie Mauritanienne de Navigation Maritime (COMAUNAM): 36 ave Gamal-Abdel-Nasser, BP 799, Nouakchott; tel 536-34; telex 862; fax 525-04; Dir-Gen: Abdel Kader Kamil; f 1974; 51% state-owned, 49% owned by Algeria; shipping co.

Port de l'Amitié de Nouakchott: BP 267, Nouakchott; tel 514-53; telex 538; Dir-Gen: Koné Ould Mahmoud; deep water port.

Port Autonome de Nouadhibou: BP 236, Nouadhibou; tel 451-34; telex 441; Pres: Habib Ely; Dir-Gen: Amar Ould H'Moïdha; f 1973.

Port Autonome de Nouakchott: Nouakchott; f 1986.

MAURITIUS

Head of State

Executive power is vested in the British sovereign as Head of State, who is represented locally by a Governor-General. Government is effectively by the Council of Ministers, appointed by the Governor-General, which is headed by the Prime Minister and is responsible to the Legislative Assembly.

Sovereign: HM Queen Elizabeth II (succeeded to the throne 6 February 1952).

Governor-General: Sir Veerasamy Ringadoo (took office 17 January 1986).

Office of the Governor-General: Le Réduit, Port-Louis; tel 543021; telex 4249.

Legislature

Legislative power is vested in the unicameral Legislative Assembly, which comprises a Speaker, 62 elected and up to eight 'additional' members and the Attorney-General (if not an elected member). Rodrigues returns two members, one of whom is Minister for the island.

Legislative Assembly: Hôtel du Gouvernement, Port Louis; tel 085331; telex 4249; Speaker: C. Daby.

MINISTRIES AND GOVERNMENT DEPARTMENTS

OFFICE OF THE PRIME MINISTER
Hôtel du Gouvernement, Port Louis
Tel 011001; telex 4249
Prime Minister: Aneerood Jugnauth
Deputy Prime Ministers: Sir Satcam Boolell, Seetanah Lutchmeenaraidoo, Dr Beergoonath Ghurburrun

MINISTRY OF AGRICULTURE, FISHERIES AND NATURAL RESOURCES
Hôtel du Gouvernement, Port Louis
Tel 011403; telex 4249
Minister: Murlidas Dulloo

MINISTRY OF CIVIL SERVICE AFFAIRS AND EMPLOYMENT
Port-Louis
Minister: France Roussety

MINISTRY OF CO-OPERATIVES
Hôtel du Gouvernement, Port Louis
Tel 088319
Minister: Vishwanath Sajadah

MINISTRY OF DEFENCE AND INTERNAL SECURITY
Hôtel du Gouvernement, Port Louis
Tel 011001; telex 4249
Minister: Aneerood Jugnauth

MINISTRY OF ECONOMIC PLANNING AND DEVELOPMENT
Registrar General Bldg, Port Louis
Tel 011576; telex 4249
Minister: Dr Beergoonath Ghurburrun

MINISTRY OF EDUCATION, ARTS AND CULTURE
3rd Floor, New Govt Centre, Port Louis
Tel 012346; telex 4249
Minister: Armoogum Parsuramen

MINISTRY OF ENERGY, WATER RESOURCES AND POSTAL SERVICES
5th Floor, New Govt Centre, Port Louis
Tel 011087; telex 4249
Minister: Mahyendrah Utchanah

MINISTRY OF EXTERNAL AFFAIRS AND EMIGRATION
5th Floor, New Govt Centre, Port Louis
Tel 011416; telex 4249; fax 088087
Minister: Sir Satcam Boolell

MINISTRY OF FINANCE
Hôtel du Gouvernement, Port Louis
Tel 011145; 4249
Minister: Seetanah Lutchmeenaraidoo

MINISTRY OF HEALTH
Registrar General Bldg, Port Louis
Tel 011910; telex 4249
Minister: Jagdishwar Goburdhun

MINISTRY OF HOUSING, LANDS AND THE ENVIRONMENT
Edith Cavell St, Port Louis
Tel 011944; telex 4249
Minister: Sir Ramesh Jeewoolall

MINISTRY OF INDUSTRY
New Govt Centre, Port Louis
Tel 011022; telex 4249
Minister: Clarel Malherbe

MINISTRY OF INFORMATION AND INTERNAL AND EXTERNAL COMMUNICATIONS
Forest Side, Port Louis
Telex 4230
Minister: Aneerood Jugnauth

MINISTRY OF JUSTICE AND OFFICE OF THE ATTORNEY-GENERAL
Hôtel du Gouvernement, Port-Louis
Tel 011001; telex 4249
Minister and Attorney-General: Sir Satcam Boolell

MINISTRY OF LABOUR AND INDUSTRIAL RELATIONS, WOMEN'S RIGHTS AND FAMILY WELFARE
Hôtel du Gouvernement, Port Louis
Tel 011195; telex 4249
Minister: Sheilabai Bappoo

MINISTRY OF LOCAL GOVERNMENT
Hôtel du Gouvernement, Port Louis
Tel 011215; telex 4249
Minister: Regis Finette

MINISTRY OF RODRIGUES AND THE OUTER ISLANDS
Sir William Newton St, Port Louis
Tel 011323; telex 4249

Minister of the Outer Islands: Aneerood Jugnauth
Minister for Rodrigues: Louis Serge Clair

MINISTRY OF SOCIAL SECURITY, NATIONAL SOLIDARITY AND REFORM INSTITUTIONS
Astor Court, 13 Lislet Geoffroy St, Port Louis
Tel 081232; telex 4249
Minister: Dineshwar Ramjuttun

MINISTRY OF TOURISM
Hôtel du Gouvernement, Port Louis
Tel 011604
Minister: Michael Glover

MINISTRY OF TRADE AND SHIPPING
4th Floor, New Govt Centre, Port Louis
Tel 011067; telex 4249
Minister: Dwarkanath Gungah

MINISTRY OF WORKS
Treasury Bldg, Port Louis
Tel 080281; telex 4249
Minister: Ramduthsing Jaddoo

MINISTRY OF YOUTH AND SPORTS
Emmanuel Anquetil Bldg, Jules Koenig St, Port Louis
Tel 011242; telex 4249
Minister: Michael Glover

GOVERNMENT AGENCIES AND ORGANIZATIONS

Business and Economy

BANKING

Bank of Mauritius: Sir William Newton St, POB 29, Port Louis; tel 084154; telex 4803; fax 089204; Gov: Indurduth Ramphul; Man Dir: Ranapartab Tacouri; f 1967; central bank and bank of issue.

Development Bank of Mauritius Ltd (DBM): La Chaussée, POB 157, Port Louis; tel 080241; telex 4248; fax 088498; Chair: Madhukarlall Baguant; Man Dir: S. M. Chitnis; Asst Man Dir: K. K. Gujadhur; f 1964; provides financial assistance to industry, agriculture, tourism and other activities relevant to the country's economic devt.

State Bank of Mauritius: Chancery House, Lislet Geoffroy St, Port Louis; tel 088909; telex 4910; fax 088209; Man Dir: T. Muni Krishna Reddy; f 1973; 42 brs.

INSURANCE

State Insurance Corpn of Mauritius (SICOM) Ltd: Sir Celicourt Antelme St, Port Louis; tel 24899; telex 496; Chair: D. Manraj; Man Dir: Percy Jacques Blackburn; f 1974; insurance.

TRADE

State Trading Corpn: 3rd Floor, Fon Sing Bldg, 12 Edith Cavell St, Port-Louis; tel 080181; telex 4537; fax 088359; Gen Man: B. Ghoorah; f 1982; fmrly Dept of Supplies; imports, exports, markets and distributes rice, flour, petroleum products and cement; under Ministry of Trade and Shipping.

Defence

Mauritius Police Force: Line Barracks, Port Louis; tel 081212; Commr of Police: B. Kowlessur; Dep Commr: A. Feillafé; Dir-Gen, National Intelligence Unit: G. Burrumdoyal.

Development and Planning

INVESTMENT

Mauritius Development Investment Trust Co (MDITC): Port Louis; Man Dir: Georges Leung Shing; investment co.

Mauritius Export Development and Investment Authority (MEDIA): 2nd Floor, Jamalacs Bldg, Old Council St, Port Louis; tel 087750; telex 4597; Chair: Benoît Arouff; Chief Exec: Chand Bhadain; f 1986; promotes exports of goods and services and encourages export-orientated investment.

State Investment Corpn Ltd (SIC): 2nd Floor, Fon Sing Bldg, 12 Edith Cavell St, Port Louis; tel 081577; telex 4635; fax 088948; provides support for new investment and transfer of technology in agriculture, industry and tourism.

REGIONAL DEVELOPMENT

Outer Islands Development Corpn: Jade House, Jummah Mosque St, Port Louis; tel 084061; Chair: S. Balgobin; Gen Man: K. Sooknah; Sec: P. Davay; f 1983; responsible for the management and devt of the outer islands forming part of Mauritius.

Energy

Central Electricity Board: Poudrière St, Port Louis; Gen Man: Jules Labat.

Legal and Judiciary

Supreme Court: Jules Koenig St, Port Louis; tel 20275; telex 4249; Chief Justice: Sir Victor Glover; Senior Puisne Judge: R. Lallah; comprises the Chief Justice and eight other Judges who are also Judges of the Court of Criminal Appeal and the Court of Civil Appeal, the Intermediate Court, the Industrial Court and 10 District Courts; final appeal is to the Judicial Committee of the Privy Council in the UK.

Media

BROADCASTING

Mauritius Broadcasting Corpn: Broadcasting House, Louis Pasteur St, Forest Side, Port Louis; tel 65001; telex 4230; Dir-Gen: Dhanjay Callikan; Dep Dir-Gen: D. Suraj-Bali; f 1964; national radio and TV service.

NEWS AND INFORMATION

Central Statistical Office: Rose Hill; tel 42088.

Tourism

Mauritius Government Tourist Office: Emmanuel Anquetil Bldg, Sir Seewoosagur Ramgoolam St, Port Louis; tel 011703; telex 4249; fax 086776; f 1958; Gen Man: Cyril Vadamootoo; Dep Gen Man: K. Bhuckory; devt of tourism; provision of tourist facilities; co-ordination of tourist promotion activities in the public and private sectors; sales support materials.

Transport

Air Mauritius: Rogers House, 5 President John F. Kennedy St, POB 60, Port Louis; tel 087700; telex 4415; Chair and Man Dir: Harry Krishan Tirvengadum; f 1967; 51% state-owned; internal and international services.

Mauritius Marine Authority: Port Admin Bldg, POB 379, Mer Rouge, Port Louis; tel 080415; telex 4238; fax 080856; Chair: H. Ramnarain; Dir-Gen: J. H. Nagdan; f 1976; port authority.

MEXICO

Head of State

Under the 1917 Constitution, executive power is vested in the President, who is elected by universal adult suffrage for a six-year term. The President governs with the assistance of an appointed Cabinet.

President: Carlos Salinas de Gortari (took office 1 December 1988).

Office of the President: Los Pinos, México, DF; tel (905) 5153353; telex 1760010; Chief of Staff: Brig-Gen Arturo Cardona Marino; Sec: Andrés Massieu Berlanga; Dir-Gen of Legal Affairs: Rubén Valdés Abascal.

Legislature

Legislative power is vested in the bicameral Congreso de la Unión (National Congress). The Cámara de Senadores (Chamber of Senators) has 64 members elected by universal adult suffrage for six years. The Cámara de Diputados (Chamber of Deputies) has 500 members directly elected for three years. Under legislation passed in 1989, at future elections the winning party will receive an absolute majority in the Chamber of Deputies, provided it wins at least 35% of the vote. The country comprises 31 States and a Federal District, each of which is administered by a Governor and an elected Chamber of Deputies.

Cámara de Senadores (Chamber of Senators): Xicoténcatl 9, Avda Zaragoza y Calle Corregidora, 06018 México, DF; tel (5) 5218046; telex 1760172; Pres: Emilio M. González.

Cámara de Diputados (Chamber of Deputies): Avda Congreso de la Unión, Palacio Legislativo, Col de Parque, 15969 México, DF; tel (5) 7957044; Pres: Guillermo Jiménez Morales.

MINISTRIES AND GOVERNMENT DEPARTMENTS

DEPARTMENT OF THE FEDERAL DISTRICT
Plaza de la Constitución y Pino Suárez, 1°, 06068 México, DF
Tel (5) 5850187
Attorney-General of the Federal District:
Ignacio Morales Lechuga

OFFICE OF THE ATTORNEY-GENERAL
Eje Lázaro Cárdenas 9, 06058 México, DF
Tel (5) 5213725; telex 1772701
Attorney-General: Enrique Alvarez del Castillo

OFFICE OF THE COMPTROLLER-GENERAL
Insurgentes Sur 1735, 10°, 01020 México, DF
Tel (5) 5592690; telex 1764014
Comptroller-General: María Elena Vázquez Nava

SECRETARIAT OF STATE FOR AGRARIAN REFORM
Bolívar 145, 6°, 06088 México, DF
Tel (5) 7610266; telex 1772505
Secretary of State: Víctor Cervera Pacheco

SECRETARIAT OF STATE FOR AGRICULTURE AND WATER RESOURCES
Insurgentes Sur 476, 13°, 06038 México, DF
Tel (5) 5840066; telex 1775890
Secretary of State: Jorge de la Vega Domínguez

SECRETARIAT OF STATE FOR COMMERCE AND INDUSTRIAL DEVELOPMENT
Alfonso Reyes 30, México, DF
Tel (5) 2861823; telex 1775718
Secretary of State: Dr Jaime Serra Puche

SECRETARIAT OF STATE FOR COMMUNICATIONS AND TRANSPORT
Anexo Torre de Telecomunicaciones, 2°, México, DF
Tel (5) 5387946; telex 170972
Secretary of State: Andrés Caso Lombardo

SECRETARIAT OF STATE FOR ENERGY, MINES AND FEDERAL INDUSTRY
Insurgentes Sur 552, 3°, 06769 México, DF
Tel (5) 5649789; telex 1775690
Secretary of State: Fernando Hiriart Balderrama

SECRETARIAT OF STATE FOR FINANCE AND PUBLIC CREDIT
Palacio Nacional, 1 Patio Mariano, 06066 México, DF
Tel (5) 5182060; telex 1776397
Secretary of State: Dr Pedro Aspe Armella

SECRETARIAT OF STATE FOR FISHERIES
Avda Alvaro Obregón 269, 6°, 06700 México, DF
Tel (5) 5119278; telex 1777483
Secretary of State: María de los Angeles Moreno Iruegas

SECRETARIAT OF STATE FOR FOREIGN AFFAIRS
Ricardo Flores Magón 1, Tlatelolco, 06995 México, DF
Tel (5) 2775470; telex 1763478
Secretary of State: Fernando Solana Morales

SECRETARIAT OF STATE FOR HEALTH AND WELFARE
Lieja 7, Col Juárez, 06696 México, DF
Tel (5) 5536967; telex 1771769
Secretary of State: Dr Jesús Cumate Rodríguez

SECRETARIAT OF STATE FOR THE INTERIOR
Bucareli 99, 10°, 06699 México, DF
Tel (5) 5351513; telex 1774375
Secretary of State: Fernando Gutiérrez Barrios

SECRETARIAT OF STATE FOR LABOUR AND SOCIAL SECURITY
Anillo Periférico Sur 4271, Edif A, Nivel 9, 14140 México, DF
Tel (5) 6520636
Secretary of State: Arsenio Farell Cubillas

SECRETARIAT OF STATE FOR THE MERCHANT MARINE
Revillagigedo 11, 06050 México, DF
Tel (5) 5122457; telex 1773646
Secretary of State: Mauricio Scheleske Sánchez

SECRETARIAT OF STATE FOR NATIONAL DEFENCE
Avila Camacho e Industria Militar, Lomas de Sotelo, 11640 México, DF
Tel (5) 5574500; telex 1776312
Secretary of State: Gen Antonio Riviello Bazán

SECRETARIAT OF STATE FOR PLANNING AND FEDERAL BUDGET
Palacio Nacional, 1 Patio Mariano, 06067 México, DF
Tel (5) 5121616; telex 1777552; fax (5) 5186912
Secretary of State: Dr Ernesto Zedillo Ponce de León
Deputy Secretaries of State: Dr Pascual García Alba, Dr Rogelio Gasca Neri, Carlos Rojas Gutiérrez

SECRETARIAT OF STATE FOR PUBLIC EDUCATION
República de Argentina y González Obregón 28, 06029 México, DF
Tel (5) 5103029
Secretary of State: Manuel Bartlett Díaz

SECRETARIAT OF STATE FOR TOURISM
Avda Presidente Masaryk 172, Col Polanco, 11587 México, DF
Tel (5) 2508555; telex 1777566
Secretary of State: Prof Carlos Hank González

SECRETARIAT OF STATE FOR URBAN DEVELOPMENT AND ECOLOGY
Avda Constituyentes 947, Col Belén de las Flores, 01110 México, DF
Tel (5) 2710365; telex 1771198
Secretary of State: Patricio Chirinos Calero

TECHNICAL CABINET SECRETARIAT
México, DF
Director-General: Dr José Córdoba Montoya

GOVERNMENT AGENCIES AND ORGANIZATIONS

Advisory and Supervisory Bodies

Comisión Electoral: México, DF; f 1989; electoral commission.

Comisión Nacional de Precios: Avda Juárez 101, 17°, México 1, DF; tel (5) 5100436; Dir-Gen: Jesús Sánchez Jiménez; f 1977; national prices commission.

Comisión Nacional de Salarios Mínimos: Avda Cuauhtémoc 14, Col Doctores, 06720 México, DF; tel (5) 7616030; Pres: Norma Samaniego de Villarreal; Technical Dir: Basilio González Núñez; f 1963; tripartite organization that formulates and establishes the general and professional minimum salaries with the participation of the Govt, employers' and employees' reps.

Instituto Nacional del Consumidor: Insurgentes Sur 1228, Col Tlacoquemecatl del Valle, 03210 México, DF; tel (5) 5592478; fax (5) 5590123; Dir-Gen: José Marino Mañón; f 1976; research consumer problems related to price, quality and availability; conducts comparative product testing, informs consumers on their rights.

Procuraduría Federal del Consumidor: Dr Carmona y Valle 11, Col Doctores, 06720 México, DF; tel (5) 7613021; Dir: Ignacio Pichardo Pagaza; f 1975; protection of consumer interests.

Agriculture and Fishing

AGRICULTURE

Azúcar, SA de CV: Insurgentes Sur 1079, Col Nochebuena, 03910 México, DF; tel (5) 5637100; telex 1772554; Dir: Eduardo A. MacGregor Beltrán; f 1983; responsible for devt of the sugar industry.

Comisión Nacional del Cacao (Conadeca): Calle Tlaxcala 208, Col Hipódromo, 06100 México, DF; tel (5) 2869495; telex 1771397; Dir-Gen: Julio Derbez del Pino; f 1973; promotes the cultivation, industrialization and marketing of cocoa.

Comisión Nacional de Fruticultura (Conafrut): Allende 8 Sur, Querétaro, 76007 Qro; tel (463) 5702499; telex 1776351; Dir: Francisco Merino Rábago; f 1961; responsible for the devt of the production, industrialization and marketing of fruit.

Comisión Nacional de las Zonas Aridas: México, DF; tel (5) 5259360; Dir: José Ignacio Navarro González; f 1970; co-ordinates the devt and use of arid areas.

Compañía Nacional de Subsistencias Populares (CON-ASUPO): Avda Insurgentes 489, 4°, Col Roma Sur, 01600 México, DF; tel (5) 2641236; telex 173372; Dir: José Ernesto Costemalle Botello; f 1965; protects the income of small farmers; improvement in the marketing of basic farm commodities and supervision of the operation of rural co-operative stores.

Instituto Mexicano del Café: Carretera Jalapa-Veracruz Km 4, Campo Experimental Garnica, Jalapa, Ver; Lago Merú 32,

Col Granada, México, DF; tel (5) 2505543; telex 15536; Dir: Mario Alberto Zubieta; f 1958; sponsors cultivation to boost domestic and foreign sales of coffee.

Instituto Nacional de Investigaciones Forestales y Agropecuarios—INIFAP (National Forestry and Agricultural Research Institute): Apdo 6-882, 06600 México, DF; Exec Dir: Dr Manuel R. Villa Issa; f 1985; conducts research into plant genetics, management of species and conservation.

FISHING

Instituto Nacional de Pesca: Alvaro Obregón 269, 10°, Col Roma, 06700 México, DF; tel (5) 2110063; Dir: Alfredo Laguarda Figueras; f 1962; national institute for fisheries.

Business and Economy

BANKING

Banca Confía, SNC: Paseo de la Reforma 450, México, DF; tel (5) 2070197; telex 1776494; Dir-Gen: Héctor Reyes Retana; f 1977, fmrly Banco de Industria y Comercio; 121 brs.

Banca Cremi, SNC: Paseo de la Reforma 93, 15°, México, DF; tel (5) 7030333; telex 1771214; Dir-Gen: Octavio Gómez G.; f 1978; multiple bank; merged with Fomento y Promoción in 1985; 130 brs.

Banca Promex, SNC: Avda La Paz 865, 44180, Guadalajara, Jal; tel (36) 134916; telex 17681847; Chief Exec: Carlos Magaña Rojas; f 1940; multiple bank; merged with Banco Refaccionario de Jalisco in 1985; 162 brs.

Banca Serfín, SNC: Avda 16 de Septiembre 38, Col Centro, 06000 México, DF; tel (5) 7097644; telex 1762020; fax (5) 7097644; Dir-Gen: Dr José Juan de Olloqui; f 1864; merged with Banco Continental Ganadero in 1985; 625 brs.

Banco del Atlántico, SNC: Avda Hidalgo 128, Coyoacán, México 21, DF; tel (5) 6892911; telex 1772456; Dir-Gen: Francisco Vizcaya Canales; f 1952; merged with Banco Monterrey in 1985; 204 brs.

Banco BCH, SNC: Paseo de la Reforma 364, Col Juárez, 06694 México, DF; tel (5) 5532277; telex 1776230; Dir-Gen: Alfonso García Macías; f 1941; merged with Banco Sofimex in 1985; 130 brs.

Banco del Centro, SNC: Venustiano Carranza 235, San Luis Potosí, SLP; tel (481) 21316; telex 13819; Dir-Gen: Ignacio Alcalá de León; f 1935; merged with Banca de Provincias in 1985; 98 brs.

Banco de Crédito y Servicio, SNC: Paseo de la Reforma 116, 18°, México, DF; tel (5) 5352685; telex 1774564; Dir-Gen: Carlos Elías Rincón; f 1976; 75 brs.

Banco Internacional, SNC: Paseo de la Reforma 156, 17°, México, DF; tel (5) 5662800; telex 1776341; Dir-Gen: Jaime Corredor Esnaola; f 1976; 371 brs.

Banco Mexicano Somex, SNC: Paseo de la Reforma 211, México, DF; tel (5) 5911611; telex 1772789; Dir-Gen: Francisco Suárez Dávila; f 1981 from merger of Banco Somex and Banco Mexicano; multiple bank; 293 brs.

Banco de México: Avda 5 de Mayo 2, Apdo 98 bis, 06059 México, DF; tel (5) 7090044; telex 1773821; Dir-Gen: Miguel Mancera Aguayo; f 1925; currency issuing authority; controls monetary policy incuding bank reserve requirements and interest rates; responsible for exchange rates and national and international reserves; legal Govt agent within international financial institutions and fiscal agent; 9 brs.

Banco Nacional de Comercio Exterior, SNC: Camino a Santa Teresa 1679, Col Jardines del Pedregal, 01900 México, DF; tel (5) 5682122; telex 1764393; fax (5) 6521557; Dir-Gen:

Dr Humberto Soto Rodríguez; Dep Dir-Gens: Juan Manuel Romero, Humberto Molina Medina; f 1937; devt bank; 3 brs.

Banco Nacional de Crédito Rural, SNC: Agrarismo 227, 3°, Col Escándon, 11800 México, DF; tel (5) 2718132; telex 1764346; fax (5) 2715519; Dir-Gen: Jaime de la Mora Gómez; f 1975; provides credit for low-paid farmers; 370 brs.

Banco Nacional del Ejército, Fuerza Aérea y Armada, SNC: Avda Industria Militar 1053, 2°, Lomas de Sotelo, 11800 México, DF; tel (5) 5579188; telex 1763307; Dir-Gen: Col Enrique Lendo Pérez; f 1947; devt bank; 11 brs.

Banco Nacional de México, SNC (Banamex): Isabel la Católica 43, 06089 México, DF; tel (5) 7090920; telex 1772611; Dir-Gen: Antonio Ortiz Mena; f 1884; 738 brs.

Banco Nacional de Obras y Servicios Públicos, SNC: Insurgentes Norte 423, 22°, Apdo 71-33, 06900 México, DF; tel (5) 5830022; telex 1772619; Dir-Gen: Fernando del Villar Moreno; f 1933; 43 brs.

Banco del Noreste, SNC: Obregón y Angel Flores, Culiacán, Sin; tel (671) 57100; telex 665882; Dir-Gen: Francisco Gurria Lacroix; f 1939; merged with UNIBANCO IN 1985; 81 brs.

Banco de Oriente, SNC: Avda 2 Oriente 10, 72000 Puebla, Pue; tel (22) 416752; telex 178209; Dir-Gen: Rafael Murillo Pérez; f 1944; 36 brs.

Banco del Pequeño Comercio del DF, SNC: Paseo de la Reforma 262, México, DF; tel (5) 5336095; telex 1760119; Dir-Gen: Roberto Diéguez Armas; f 1943; devt bank; 101 brs.

Bancomer, SNC: Centro Bancomer, Avda Universidad 1200, Apdo 9 bis, 03339 México, DF; tel (5) 5340034; telex 1775781; Dir-Gen: Héctor Hernández Cervantes; f 1932; multiple bank; 734 brs.

Banpaís, SNC: Insurgentes Sur 1443, 03900 México, DF; tel (5) 5637459; telex 3823225; Dir-Gen: Sergio Martínez M.; f 1892 as Banco de Nueva León, present name 1978; merged with Banco Latino in 1985; 99 brs.

Comisión Nacional Bancaria y Comisión Nacional de Seguros y Fianzas: República del Salvador 47, Col Centro, 06080 México, DF; tel (5) 7097924; Pres: Alfredo A. Luengas Garibay; f 1924; Govt commission controlling all financial and insurance institutions.

Crédito Mexicano, SNC: Insurgentes Sur 1931, 8°, México, DF; tel (5) 5484043; telex 1772577; Dir-Gen: Roberto Molina Pasquel; f 1945; 97 brs.

Multibanco Comermex, SNC: Plaza Comermex, Blvd Manuel Avila Camacho 1, Col Chapultapec Palanco, 11560 México, DF; tel (5) 5578622; telex 1775837; fax (5) 2025264; Dir-Gen: Guillermo Prieto Fortun; Dir, International: Rafael González Calvillo; f 1934; 339 brs.

Multibanco Mercantil de México, SNC: Montes Urales 620, 3°, México, DF; tel (5) 2590113; telex 1775837; Dir-Gen: Jaime Sánchez Montemayor; f 1977; merged with Bancam in 1985; 84 brs.

Multibanco Mercantil del Norte, SNC: Zaragoza Sur 920, 64000 Monterrey, NL; tel (83) 429200; telex 382378; Dir-Gen: Francisco Patiño Leal; f 1899; merged with Banco Regional del Norte in 1985; 114 brs.

Nacional Financiera, SNC (NAFINSA): Insurgentes Sur 1971, 01020 México, DF; tel (5) 5506911; telex 1775629; Dir-Gen: Juan José Páramo; f 1934; Govt industrial devt bank; provides loans, guarantees and investments; contracts and handles devt loans from abroad; 60 brs.

FINANCIAL AGENCIES

Fideicomiso Instituído en la Relación con la Agricultura (FIRA): México, DF; tel (5) 5507011; Dir: Antonio Baca Díaz; a group of funds to aid agricultural financing, comprising:

Fondo Especial de Asistencia Técnica y Garantía para Créditos Agropecuarios (FEGA): f 1972.

Fondo Especial para Financiamientos Agropecuarios (FEFA): f 1965.

Fondo de Garantía y Fomento para la Agricultura, Ganadería y Avicultura (FOGAGA): f 1954.

Fondo de Equipamiento Industrial (FONEI): México, DF; tel (5) 5598702; Dir: Jesús Villaseñor G.; f 1971; finances industrial investment projects.

Fondo para el Fomento de las Exportaciones de Productos Manifacturados (FOMEX): Camino a Santa Teresa 1679, Col Jardines del Pedregal, Del Alvaro Obregón, 01900 México, DF; tel (5) 5594481; Dir: Fernando Villareal y Puga Colmenares; f 1962; finances the devt of the export of manufactured goods.

Fondo de Garantía y Fomento a la Industria Mediana y Pequeña (FOGAIN): Insurgentes Sur 1480, 4°, Col Insurgentes Mixcoac, México, DF; tel (5) 5351974; telex 1773363; Dir: Héctor Arangua Morales; f 1953; supplies credit and encourages the devt of small- and medium-sized industries.

Fondo Nacional de Fomento Industrial (FOMIN): Paseo de la Reforma 295, 9°, Col Cuauhtémoc, 06500 México, DF; tel (5) 5142430; Dir: Gustavo Varela Ruiz; f 1972; promotes industrial and initiative with venture capital.

Fondo de Operación y Financiamiento Bancario a la Vivienda (FOVI): Ejército Nacional 180, 8°, Col Anzures, 11590 México, DF; tel (5) 2554199; Dir-Gen: Manuel Zepeda Payeras; Dep Dir-Gen: Mario J. Hernández Gallardo; f 1963; promotes the construction of low-cost housing through savings and credit schemes.

Instituto Nacional del Fondo Nacional de la Vivienda para los Trabajadores (INFONAVIT): Barranca del Muerto 280, México 20, DF; tel (5) 6519400; Dir: Emilio Gamboa Patrón; f 1972; promotes the construction of low-cost housing for the working classes.

NATIONALIZED INDUSTRY

Comisión Coordinadora de la Industria Siderúrgica: México, DF; Dir-Gen: Alfredo Ade Tomasini; f 1972; co-ordinating commission for the devt of the iron and steel industries.

Siderúrgica Mexicana, SA de C (SIDERMEX): Yucatán 15, Col Roma, México, DF; tel (5) 2110085; telex 1773818; Dir: Dr Guillermo Becker Arreola; f 1978 by the amalgamation of the three important steel producing companies: Ahmsa, Fundidora de Monterrey and Sicartsa; the three cos continued to operate autonomously but under a single state management (Fundidora de Monterrey was closed down by the Govt in 1986).

Tabacos Mexicanos, SA de CV (TABAMEX): Avda Ejército Nacional 862, Col Chapultapec de los Morales, Del Miguel Hidalgo, 11510 México, DF; tel (5) 3955477; telex 1773904; fax (5) 3956836; Dir-Gen: Gustavo Carvajal Moreno; Commercial Dir: Marco Vinicio Martínez Guerrero; f 1972; responsible for production, semi-industrialization and commercialization of tobacco industry.

Uranio Mexicano (URAMEX): Insurgentes Sur 1079, 3°, México, DF; tel (5) 5637100; telex 349702; Dir-Gen: Alberto Escoget Artigas; supervises the use of uranium.

TRADE

Asociación Nacional de Importadores y Exportadores de la República Mexicana (ANIERM): Monterrey 130, Col Roma-Cuauhtémoc, 06700 México, DF; tel (5) 5648618; telex 1772443; Pres: Carlos Viveros Figueroa; Dir: Humberto Simoneen Ardila; f 1944; association of importers and exporters.

Consejo Nacional de Comercio Exterior del Noreste, AC: Edif de las Instituciones, 7°, Ocampo 250 Pte, Apdo 2674,

Monterrey, NL; tel (83) 422143; telex 383050; fax (83) 428207; Pres: José R. Treviño Salinas; Dir-Gen: Guillermo Díaz de la Garza; f 1962; promotion of exports.

Instituto Mexicano de Comercio Exterior: Alfonso Reyes 30, Col Condesa, México 11, DF; promotes the export of goods.

Defence

Ejército Mexicano (Army): Avila Camacho e Industria Militar, Lomas de Sotelo, 11640 México, DF; tel (5) 5574500; telex 1776312; Commdr: Juan Arévalo Gardoqui.

Fuerza Aérea Mexicana (Air Force): Avila Camacho e Industria Militar, Lomas de Sotelo, 11640 México, DF; tel (5) 5573310; Commdr: Miguel Mendoza Márquez.

Marina Nacional (Navy): Revillagigedo 11, 3°, 06050 México, DF; tel (5) 5122457; telex 1776312; Commdr: Miguel Angel Gómez Ortega.

Development and Planning

Comisión Nacional de Inversiones Extranjeras: Blvd Manuel Avila Camacho 1, 11°, Col Lomas de Chapultepec, Del Miguel Hidalgo, 11000 México, DF; tel (5) 5401426; telex 1763158; fax (5) 2861551; Exec Sec: Dr Fernando Sánchez Ugarte; Dep Exec Sec: Carlos Camacho Gaos; f 1973; commission to co-ordinate foreign investment.

Dirección General de Política e Inversiones Industriales: México, DF; Dir-Gen: Vladimiro Brailovsky F.; directs industrial policy and allocates industrial investment.

Laboratorios Nacionales de Fomento Industrial: Avda Industria Militar 261, Col Lomas de Sotelo, 11200 México, DF; tel (5) 5890199; telex 1771996; Dir: José Antonio Esteva Marbota; f 1948; conducts scientific research for industrial devt.

International Affairs

Dirección General de Relaciones Internacionales: Brazil 31, Puerta 135, Col Centro, 06029 México, DF; tel (5) 5216542; Dir-Gen: Miguel Messmacher; f 1921; establishes links with international organizations and other countries.

Legal and Judiciary

Suprema Corte de la Justicia de la Nación (Supreme Court): Pino Suárez 2, 2°, Col Centro, Del Cuauhtémoc, 06065 México, DF; tel (5) 5220096; Pres: Carlos del Río Rodríguez.

Media

BROADCASTING

Cámara Nacional de la Industria de Radio y Televisión: Avda Horacio 1013, Col Polanco, 11550 México, DF; tel (5) 2502577; telex 1777272; Pres: Casio Carlos Narváez Lidolf; Gen Man: César Hernández Espejo; f 1942; national agency for TV and radio agency.

Dirección General de Radio, Televisión y Cinematografía: Atletas 2, Col Country Club, Del Coyoacán, 04220 México, DF; tel (5) 5443768; telex 1760298; Dir-Gen: Jesús Hernández Torres; directorate for radio, TV and cinema.

Dirección de Normas de Radiofusión: Eugenia 197, 1°,

03020 México, DF; tel (5) 5904372; Dir: Marco Antonio Hernández Ramírez; licence issuing authority.

Televisión Cultural de México: Secretaría de Comunicaciones y Transportes, Comisión de Radiodifusión, Torre de Comunicaciones, Insurgentes Sur, México, DF; transmits a selection of programmes from all stations.

NEWS AND INFORMATION

Instituto Nacional de Estadística, Geografía e Informática (INEGI): Patriotismo 711, Col San Juan Mixcoac, Del Benito Suárez, 03910 México, DF; tel (5) 5988241; telex 1772298; fax (5) 5368093; f 1983; directs and organizes economic, geographic and cartographic studies.

Mining and Energy

ENERGY

Comisión Federal de Electricidad (CFE): Río Rodano 14, México 5, DF; tel (5) 5337133; telex 171031; Dir-Gen: Joaquín Carrión Hernández; federal commission for the electricity industry.

Comisión Nacional de Energéticos: Francisco Márquez 160, Col Condesa, México, DF; Exec Sec: A. Lajous Vargas; f 1973; commission to control energy planning and policy.

Comisión Nacional de Seguridad Nuclear y Salvaguardias (CNSNS): Insurgentes Sur 1806, Col Florida, Del Alvaro Obregón, 01030 México, DF; tel (5) 5341401; telex 1773280; fax (5) 5341405; Dir-Gen: Miguel Medina Vaillard; f 1979; fixes standards for the devt of the nuclear industry and guarantees its safety.

Comisión Petroquímica Mexicana: México,DF; tel (5) 5249285; Technical Sec: Juan Antonio Bargés Mestres; promotes the devt of the petrochemical industry.

Instituto Mexicano del Petróleo (IMP): Avda Eje Central Central Lázaro Cárdenas 152, Apdo 14-805, México 14, DF; tel (5) 5676600; telex 1773116; Dir: José Luis García Luna; f 1966; fosters the devt of the petroleum, chemical and petrochemical industries.

Instituto Nacional de Investigaciones Nucleares (ININ): Insurgentes Sur 1079, Apdo 18-1027, 03720 México, DF; tel (5) 5219402; telex 1773824; Dir-Gen: Carlos Vélez Ocón; f 1979 to plan research and devt of nuclear science and technology, as well as the peaceful uses of nuclear energy, for the social, scientific and technological devt of the country.

MINING

Comisión de Fomento Minero: Puente de Tecamachalco 26, Lomas de Chapultepec, 11000 México, DF; tel (5) 5409206; telex 1771382; Dir: Luis de Pablo Serna; f 1934; promotes the devt of the mining sector.

Consejo Nacional de Recursos Minerales: Avda Niños Héroes 139, 06720 México, DF; tel (5) 5686112; Dir: Fernando Castillo Nieto; f 1957; promotes the devt of mineral resources.

Siderúrgica Lázaro Cárdenas Las Truchas, SA: Yucatán 15, Col Roma, 06700 México, DF; telex 1773147; Pres: Francisco Labastida Ochoa; mining co.

Tourism

Fondo Nacional de Fomento al Turismo (FONATUR): Insurgentes Sur 800, 17°, Col del Valle, 03100 México, DF; tel (5) 6872697; telex 1777636; Dir-Gen: Dr Kemil A. Rizk; f 1956 to finance and promote the devt of tourism.

Transport and Communications

TELECOMMUNICATIONS

Dirección General de Telecomunicaciones: Lázaro Cárdenas 567, 11°, Ala Norte, 03020 México, DF; tel (5) 5303492; Dir-Gen: Enrique Luengas Hubp; telecommunications authority.

TRANSPORT

Cámara Nacional de Transportes y Comunicaciones: Pachuca 158 bis, Col Condesa, 06140 México, DF; tel (5) 5539856; Pres: Isidoro Rodríguez Ruiz; Sec-Gen: Oscar Aguirre López; transport and telecommunications authority.

Comisión Nacional Coordinadora de Puertos: Insurgentes Sur 617, 3°, Col Nápoles, 03810 México, DF; tel (5) 6877207; telex 1160079; Exec Dir: Jaime Luna Traill; f 1970; co-ordinates all maritime port operations.

Dirección General de Transporte Terrestre: Calzada de las Bombas 411, Col los Girasoles, 04920 México, DF; tel (5) 6840752; telex 1771121; Dir-Gen: Alejandro Peniche Alvarez; f 1928; co-ordination and control of the country's bus services.

Ferrocarriles Nacionales de México: Centro Administrativo, Avda Jesús García 140, 13°, Ala 'A', Col Buenavista, 06358 México, DF; tel (5) 5479060; telex 1773999; Dir-Gen: Andrés Caso Lombardo; f 1873; Govt-owned since 1937; national railways co.

Mexicana (Compañía Mexicana de Aviación, SA de CV): Xola 535, 30°, Apdo 12813, Col del Valle, 03100 México, DF; tel (5) 6604433; telex 1771247; Pres: Manuel Sosa de la Vega; Chair: Daniel Díaz Díaz; f 1921; operated as a private co until July 1982, when the Govt took a 58% share; flights to Central America, the Caribbean and the USA; domestic services.

Petróleos Mexicanos (PEMEX): Avda Marina Nacional 329, México 17, DF; tel (5) 5316053; telex 1773986; Man: Enrique Vázquez Domínguez; shipping agency, primarily oil tankers.

Sistema de Transporte Colectivo: Delicias 67, 06070 México, DF; tel (5) 5218620; telex 1774267; Dir-Gen: Gerardo Ferrando Bravo; f 1967; combined underground and surface railway system in Mexico City.

Welfare

Instituto Mexicano del Seguro Social: Roma Sur, Del Cuauhtémoc, Apdo 107-090, 06725 México, DF; institute of social security.

MONACO

Head of State

The Prince, as hereditary ruler, is Head of State, and exercises executive power jointly with the Council of Government, which is headed by a Minister of State (a French civil servant chosen by the Prince).

Ruler: HSH Prince Rainier III (succeeded 9 May 1949).

Office of HSH the Prince: Palais de Monaco, BP 518, MC 98015 Monaco Cedex; tel (93) 30-18-31; telex 469920.

Legislature

Legislative power is held jointly by the Prince and the unicameral Conseil National (National Council) with 18 members elected by universal adult suffrage for five years. The electorate comprises only Monégasque citizens aged 21 years or over.

Conseil National (National Council): 2 rue Col Bellando de Castro, MC 98000 Monaco; tel (93) 30-41-50; Pres: Jean-Charles Rey; Vice-Pres: Dr Pierre Crovetto.

MINISTRIES AND GOVERNMENT DEPARTMENTS

OFFICE OF THE CHIEF OF THE CABINET
BP 522, MC 98015 Monaco Cedex
Tel (93) 30-19-21; telex 469942
Chief of the Cabinet: Charles Ballerio

OFFICE OF THE MINISTER OF STATE
BP 522, MC 98015 Monaco Cedex
Tel (93) 30-19-21; telex 469942
Minister: Jean Ausseil

OFFICE OF THE GOVERNMENT COUNCILLOR FOR THE INTERIOR
BP 522, MC 98015 Monaco Cedex
Tel (93) 30-19-21; telex 469942
Government Councillor: Michael Eon

OFFICE OF THE GOVERNMENT COUNCILLOR FOR FINANCE AND ECONOMIC AFFAIRS
BP 522, MC 98015 Monaco Cedex
Tel (93) 30-19-21; telex 469942
Government Councillor: Jean Pastorelli

OFFICE OF THE GOVERNMENT COUNCILLOR FOR PUBLIC WORKS AND SOCIAL AFFAIRS
BP 522, MC 98015 Monaco Cedex
Tel (93) 30-19-21; telex 469942
Government Councillor: Bernard Fautrier

GOVERNMENT AGENCIES AND ORGANIZATIONS

Advisory and Supervisory Body

Conseil Economique: 8 rue Louis Notari, Monte-Carlo; tel (93) 30-20-82; Pres: René Clerissi; Vice-Pres: Henri Bronne, André Morra; consultative organization in six sections dealing with all aspects of Monaco's economy; comprises 30 mems who represent, in equal proportions, employers, workers and the Govt; named by the Head of State every three years from all nationalities, but Pres must be Monégasque national.

Business and Economy

BANKING

Banque Centrale Monégasque de Crédit à Long et Moyen

Terme: 15 ave d'Ostende, MC 98000, Monaco; tel (93) 30-92-95; telex 469623; Pres: Jean Deflassieux; Dir-Gen: Pierre David; f 1969.

Defence

Sûreté Publique (Police): Monaco; Commr: Maurice Alberin.

Legal and Judiciary

Palais de Justice: rue Col Bellando de Castro, BP 513, MC 98025 Monaco Cedex; tel (93) 30-19-21; Dir of Judicial Services: Noël Museux.

Tribunal Suprême (Supreme Tribunal): Palais de Justice, rue Col Bellando de Castro, BP 513, MC 98025 Monaco Cedex; tel (93) 30-19-21; Pres: Paul Reuter; deals with infringements of the rights and liberties provided by the Constitution, and with legal action aiming at the annulment of administrative decisions or abusive exercise of power.

Cour de Révision Judiciaire (High Court of Appeal): Palais de Justice, rue Col Bellando de Castro, BP 513, MC 98025 Monaco Cedex; tel (93) 30-19-21; Pres: Jean Bel.

Media

BROADCASTING

Radio Monte-Carlo SAM (RMC): 16 blvd Princesse Charlotte, BP 128, MC 98080 Monaco; tel (93) 50-52-52; telex 469511; Pres: César Charles Solamito; Dir-Gen: Hervé Bourges; f 1942; programmes in French and Italian; programmes may be backed by commercials or by sponsors; the French Govt has a shareholding in the co.

> **Société Monégasque d'Exploitation et d'Etudes de Radiodiffusion (SOMERA):** 16 blvd Princesse Charlotte, MC 98000 Monaco; Pres: César Charles Solamito; Dir-Gen: Pierre Casalta; broadcasts in French and Arabic.

Société Spéciale d'Entreprises Télé Monte-Carlo: 16 blvd Princesse Charlotte, BP 279, MC 98090 Monaco Cedex; tel (93) 50-59-40; telex 469823; Pres: César Charles Solamito; f 1954; TV broadcasting.

Tourism

Académie Internationale du Tourisme: 9 rue Princesse Marie de Lorraine, Monte-Carlo; tel (93) 30-97-68; Pres: Mario Grego; Treas: Louis Nagel; f 1951 under the patronage of Prince Rainier III; promotes the devt of tourism; 108 mems.

Direction du Tourisme et des Congrès: 2A blvd des Moulins, MC 98030 Monaco Cedex; tel (93) 30-87-01; telex 469760; fax (93) 50-92-80; Man Dir: Gilles Noghes; f 1972; tourist and convention authority.

Société des Bains de Mer (SBM): place du Casino, BP 309, MC 98007; tel (93) 50-80-80; telex 469925; Chair: Raoul Biancheri; f 1863; Govt holds a 69% interest; controls the entertainment facilities of Monaco, including the casino and numerous hotels, clubs, restaurants and sporting facilities.

MONGOLIA

Head of State

The Head of State is the Chair of the Presidium, the body elected by the People's Great Hural (Assembly) to be its permanent organ. The highest executive body is the Council of Ministers, appointed by, and responsible to the Assembly.

Chair of the Presidium of the People's Great Hural: Punsalmaagiyn Ochirbat (elected 21 March 1990).

Deputy Chair of the Presidium: Tserendashiyn Namsray.

Presidium of the People's Great Hural: Ulan Bator; Sec: Tsedendambyn Gotov.

Legislature

The supreme organ of state power is the People's Great Hural (Assembly), whose deputies are elected by universal adult suffrage for five years. The communist Mongolian People's Revolutionary Party (MPRP) relinquished its monopoly on power in March 1990. For local administration, Mongolia is divided into 18 provinces and three municipalities with elected local assemblies.

People's Great Hural (Assembly): Ulan Bator; Chair of the People's Great Hural: Lodongiyn Rinchin; Chair of the Executive Committee of the Parliamentary Group: Lodongiyn Tüdev.

MINISTRIES AND GOVERNMENT DEPARTMENTS

COUNCIL OF MINISTERS
Ulan Bator
Chair: Sharavyn Gunjaadorj
Deputy Chairs: Dashiin Byambasuren, Puntsagiyn Jasray, Myatavyn Peljee, Choynoryn Süren, Sharavyn Gungaadorj, Bat-ochiryn Altangerel
Director of Administration: Dzunduyn Saaral

COMMISSION FOR CMEA AFFAIRS
Ulan Bator
Chair: Myatavyn Peljee

MINISTRY OF AGRICULTURE AND THE FOOD INDUSTRY
Ulan Bator
Minister: Sharavyn Gungaadorj

MINISTRY OF COMMUNAL ECONOMY AND SERVICES
Ulan Bator
Minister: Tümengiyn Demchigdorj

MINISTRY OF COMMUNICATIONS
Ulan Bator
Telex 237
Minister: Byambajavyn Baatar

MINISTRY OF CULTURE
Ulan Bator
Minister: Budyn Sum'yaa

MINISTRY OF DEFENCE
Ulan Bator
Minister: Lt-Gen Luvsangombyn Molomjamts

MINISTRY OF ENERGY, MINING INDUSTRY AND GEOLOGY
Baga Toirog 6, Ulan Bator 11
Tel 20437
Minister: Sodovyn Bathuyag

MINISTRY OF EXTERNAL ECONOMIC RELATIONS AND SUPPLY
Sambuu St, Ulan Bator 11
Tel 23454
Minister: Punsalmaagiyn Ochirbat

MINISTRY OF FINANCE
Ulan Bator
Minister: Demchigjavyn Molomjamts

MINISTRY OF FOREIGN AFFAIRS
Ulan Bator
Tel 21870; telex 245
Minister: Tserenpiliyn Gombosüren

MINISTRY OF HEALTH
Ulan Bator
Minister: Choyjiljavyn Tserennadmid

MINISTRY OF LAW AND ARBITRATION
Ulan Bator
Minister: Origiyn Jambaldorj

MINISTRY OF LIGHT INDUSTRY
Ulan Bator
Minister: Nyam-Osoryn Dagvadorj

MINISTRY OF PUBLIC EDUCATION
Barilgachdiin Talbai 13, Ulan Bator
Tel 22480
Minister: Byambyn Davaasüren

**MINISTRY FOR PROTECTION OF NATURE AND
THE ENVIRONMENT**
Ulan Bator
Minister: Uthany Mavlyet

MINISTRY OF PUBLIC SECURITY
Ulan Bator
Minister: Lt-Gen Agvaanjantsangiyn Jamsranjav

MINISTRY OF ROADS AND TRANSPORT
Ulan Bator
Minister: Dogoyn Yondonsüren

MINISTRY OF TRADE AND PROCUREMENT
Ulan Bator
Minister: Badarhiyn Sharavsambuu

**STATE COMMITTEE FOR INFORMATION, RADIO
AND TELEVISION**
POB 365, Ulan Bator
Tel 21624
Chair: Choydoryn Tümendelger

**STATE COMMITTEE FOR PHYSICAL CULTURE
AND SPORT**
Ulan Bator
Chair: Galsangiyn Dashdzeveg

**STATE COMMITTEE FOR PLANNING AND THE
ECONOMY**
Ulan Bator
Chair: Puntsagiyn Jasray
First Deputy Chair (Minister): Tömöriyn Namjim

**STATE COMMITTEE FOR SCIENCE, TECHNOLOGY
AND HIGHER EDUCATION**
Kolarov St 49, Ulan Bator 11
Tel 23934; telex 236
Chair: Mönhdorjiyn Dash
First Vice-Chair: B. Enkhtuvshin
F 1971; formulates and implements state policies on the devt
of science and technology and higher and special secondary
education.

STATE CONSTRUCTION COMMITTEE
Ulan Bator
Chair: Luvsanbaldangiyn Nyamsambuu

GOVERNMENT AGENCIES AND ORGANIZATIONS

Agriculture

**Federation of Agricultural Production Associations (Co-
operatives):** Ulan Bator; Chair of Council: Minister of Agriculture and the Food Industry, Sharavyn Gungaadorj; administers
the 255 agricultural co-operatives throughout the country.

Business and Economy

BANKING

State Bank of the Mongolian People's Republic: Oktya-
briyn Gudamj 6, Ulan Bator; tel 22847; telex 241; Chair of Board:
Gochoogiyn Hüderchuluun (mem of the Council of Ministers); f
1924; central bank; 320 brs.

INSURANCE

Mongoldaatgal (State Directorate for Insurance of the Ministry of Finance): Ulan Bator; tel 51981; telex 222; Dir-Gen: Ts.
Achitsayhan; national insurance and reinsurance enterprise.

TRADE

Avtonefteimport: Ministry of External Economic Relations
and Supply, Sambuun St, Ulan Bator 11; Dir: S. Dzorigt; import
of motor vehicles, fuels and lubricants.

**Chamber of Commerce and Industry of the Mongolian
People's Republic:** J. Sambuugyn Gudamj, Ulan Bator 11; tel
24620; telex 221; Chair: J. Gölgöö; Sec-Gen: Gombyn Dolgor; f
1960; responsible for establishing economic and trading
relations, contacts between trade and industrial organizations
both at home and abroad and for generating foreign trade;
organizes commodity inspection, press information and international exhibitions and fairs at home and abroad.

Horshoololimpex: Ministry of Communal Economy and Services, Ulan Bator; Dir: N. Dash-Öldziy; trade with foreign co-
operative societies, export of waste for recycling.

Kompleksimport: Ministry of External Economic Relations
and Supply, Sambuu St, Ulan Bator 11; Dir: D. Sanchin; imports
sets of equipment for the mining industry and power stations
and production lines for light and food industry enterprises.

Mongolilgeemj: Ulan Bator 11; tel 27781; telex 221; f 1977;
foreign parcel trade, sale and purchase of consumer goods,
establishment of business contacts with foreign cos, intermediary services on foreign trade and commodity exchange.

Mongolimpex: Ulan Bator 11; tel 26081; telex 231; Pres: Dz.
Tseveenregdzen; Vice-Pres: H. Gungaajav, S. Tömör; f 1984;
import and export of goods in convertible currencies, philatelic
exports.

Mongolnom: Ulan Bator; tel 21512; export of Mongolian publs.

Mongolraznoimport: Ministry of External Economic
Relations and Supply, Sambuu St, Ulan Bator 11; tel 715639;
import of consumer goods, postage stamps and medicines, philatelic exports.

Mongoltekhnikimport: J. Sambuugyn Gudamj, Ulan Bator
11; tel 22892; import of industrial machinery and equipment,
raw materials, chemicals and dyestuffs, other than motor
vehicles, agricultural machinery, fuels and lubricants.

Defence

Defence Council: Ulan Bator; Chair: Gombojavyn Ochirbat
(Sec-Gen of the Mongolian People's Revolutionary Party—
MPRP); supreme political control of military affairs.

Mongolian People's Army: Ulan Bator; Chief of Staff: Lt-
Gen Shagalyn Jadambaa.

Legal and Judiciary

Office of the Procurator of the Republic: Ulan Bator; Procurator: Jügderiyn Baljinnyam; appointed by the People's Great Hural for a term of five years.

Supreme Court: Ulan Bator; Chair: Luvsandorjiyn Renchin; Chair and mems are elected by the People's Great Hural for a term of five years.

Media

BROADCASTING

Mongoltelevidz: Hasbaatar St, Ulan Bator 11; Dir of TV: Yundengiyn Erdenetuyaa; f 1967; daily transmissions, comprising locally-originated material and/or relays of Soviet programmes.

Ulan Bator Radio: State Committee for Information, Radio and Television, POB 365, Ulan Bator; tel 21624; Head of Foreign Relations Dept: Lhagvasurengiyn Lhagvadulam; programmes in Mongolian, Russian, Chinese, English, French and Kazakh.

GOVERNMENT PUBLISHER

Sühbaatar Publishing House: Ulan Bator; produces 70% of Mongolia's printed matter, including 12 central newspapers, 32 magazines and books.

NEWS AND INFORMATION

Mongolpress: POB 1514, Ulan Bator 13; tel 24699; Editor-in-Chief: M. Bayartogtoh; f 1986; fortnightly news bulletins in Russian, English and French.

Montsame (Mongol Tsahilgaan Medeeniy Agentlag) (Mongolian Telegraph Agency): Sühbaataryn Talbay 9, Ulan Bator 13; tel 23801; Dir-Gen: Choydoryn Tümendelger; f 1957.

State Central Statistical Bureau: Ulan Bator.

Science and Technology

Academy of Sciences: Ulan Bator 11; Pres: Namsaryn Sodnom (mem of the Council of Ministers).

Tourism

Zhuulchin: Ulan Bator; tel 20246; telex 232; Dir: G. Sanj; f 1954; the official foreign tourist service bureau, managed by the Ministry of External Economic Relations and Supply.

Transport

Mongolian Civil Air Transport (MIAT): Ulan Bator; tel 20221; Dir of Civil Aviation: Darjaagiyn Sürenhorloo; f 1956; internal services to most provincial and many county centres; service from Ulan Bator to Irkutsk (USSR) and Beijing.

Ulan Bator Railway: Ulan Bator; Dir: A. I. Dolgiy; First Dep Dir: Sosorbaramyn Bold; connects with the Trans-Siberian Railway and Beijing; branches serving coalfields and mines.

MOROCCO

Head of State

Morocco is a constitutional monarchy, with an hereditary King as Head of State. Executive power is vested in the King, who appoints the Prime Minister and other members of the Cabinet. The King is empowered to dissolve the Chamber of Representatives.

King: HM Hassan II (acceded 3 March 1961).

Office of HM the King: Palais Royal, Rabat; tel (7) 60122; Minister of Royal Protocol: Gen Moulay Abd al-Hafid Alaoui; Royal Advisers: Ahmad Reda Guedira, Ahmad ben Souda, Muhammad Aouad.

Legislature

Legislative power is vested in the unicameral Chamber of Representatives, which comprises 306 members elected for six years (206 directly elected by universal adult suffrage and 100 chosen by an electoral college).

Majlis an-Nuwab (Chamber of Representatives): ave Muhammad V, Quartier Administratif, Rabat; tel (7) 60311; telex 31937; Pres: Ahmad Osman.

MINISTRIES AND GOVERNMENT DEPARTMENTS

OFFICE OF THE PRIME MINISTER
Palais Royal, Rabat
Tel (7) 64554; telex 31008
Prime Minister: Dr Az ad-Dine Laraki
Minister Attached to the Prime Minister's Office in charge of Administrative Affairs: Abd ar-Rahim ben Abd al-Jaul
Minister Attached to the Prime Minister's Office in charge of Economic Affairs: Moulay Zine Zahidi
Minister Attached to the Prime Minister's Office in charge of Planning: Rachid Ghazouani
Minister Attached to the Prime Minister's Office in charge of Relations with the EEC: Muhammad Saqat
Minister Attached to the Prime Minister's Office in charge of Saharan Affairs: Khali Henna Ould ar-Rachid
Ministers of State without Portfolio:
Muhammad Bahnini, Moulay Ahmad Alaoui
Secretary-General of the Government: Abbes Kaissi

MINISTRY OF AGRICULTURE AND AGRARIAN REFORM
Quartier Administratif, Rabat
Tel (7) 60993; telex 31038
Minister: Othmane Demnati

MINISTRY OF CULTURAL AFFAIRS
rue Gandhi, Rabat
Tel (7) 66054
Minister: Muhammad Benaissa

MINISTRY OF ENERGY AND MINES
ave Maa al-Ainane, Rabat
Tel (7) 74758; telex 32761
Minister: Muhammad Fettah

MINISTRY OF FINANCE
ave Muhammad V, Quartier Administratif, Rabat
Tel (7) 62171; telex 31820
Minister: Muhammad Berrada

MINISTRY OF FOREIGN AFFAIRS AND CO-OPERATION
ave Franklin Roosevelt, Rabat
Tel (7) 62841; telex 31007
Minister: Abd al-Latif Filali

MINISTRY OF HANDICRAFTS AND SOCIAL AFFAIRS
ave des Héros, Agdal, Rabat
Tel (7) 70141; telex 32840
Minister: Muhammad Labied

MINISTRY OF HEALTH
335 ave Muhammad V, Rabat
Tel (7) 61121; telex 31642
Minister: Tayeb ben Cheikh

MINISTRY OF HOUSING
Quartier Administratif, Rabat
Tel (7) 602363; telex 32744
Minister: Abd ar-Rahman Boufettass

MINISTRY OF INFORMATION
place de la Poste Centrale, Rabat
Tel (7) 66016; telex 31015
Minister: Driss Basri

MINISTRY OF THE INTERIOR
Quartier Administratif, Rabat
Tel (7) 64718; telex 31710
Minister: Driss Basri

MINISTRY OF JUSTICE
485 blvd Muhammad V, Rabat
Tel (7) 60041; telex 31888
Minister: Moulay Mustafa Belarbi Alaoui

MINISTRY OF LABOUR
Quartier Administratif, Rabat
Tel (7) 60521; telex 31057
Minister: Hassan Abbadi

MINISTRY OF NATIONAL EDUCATION
place de la Victoire, Rabat
Tel (7) 71822; telex 31016
Minister: Tayeb Chkili

MINISTRY OF OCEAN FISHERIES AND THE MERCHANT NAVY
63 blvd Moulay Youssef, Rabat
Tel (7) 63366; telex 32679
Minister: Ben-Salem Smili

MINISTRY OF POSTS AND TELECOMMUNICATIONS
ave Moulay Hassan, Rabat
Tel (7) 62091; telex 31001
Minister: Mohand Laenser

MINISTRY OF PUBLIC WORKS, VOCATIONAL TRAINING AND EXECUTIVE TRAINING
Quartier Administratif, Rabat
Tel (7) 63688; telex 31613; fax (7) 63779
Minister: Muhammad Kabbaj

MINISTRY OF RELATIONS WITH PARLIAMENT
27 rue Oqbais, Rabat
Tel (7) 75170
Minister (attached to the Prime Minister's Office):
Abd as-Slam Baraki

MINISTRY OF WAQFS (RELIGIOUS ENDOWMENTS) AND ISLAMIC AFFAIRS
Enceinte du Palais Royal, Rabat
Tel (7) 62703; telex 31771
Minister: Abd al-Kaebir Alaoui M'Daghri

MINISTRY OF TOURISM
Quartier Administratif, Rabat
Tel (7) 65513; telex 31641
Minister: Moussa Saadi

MINISTRY OF TRADE AND INDUSTRY
Quartier Administratif, Rabat
Tel (7) 65996; telex 32968
Minister: Abdallah al-Azmani

MINISTRY OF TRANSPORT
rue Maa al-Ainane, Casier Officiel, Rabat-Chellah
Tel (7) 73486; telex 31626
Minister: Muhammad Bouamoud

MINISTRY OF YOUTH AND SPORTS
485 blvd Muhammad V, Rabat
Tel (7) 60041; telex 32652
Minister: Abd al-Latif Semlali

GOVERNMENT AGENCIES AND ORGANIZATIONS

Agriculture and Fishing

Office du Développement de la Coopération: 7 rue Moulay Rachid, BP 1297, Rabat; tel (7) 22999; telex 32867; Dirs: Omar el-Alaoui el-Mdarhri, Driss Nait Bach; f 1962; devt and promotion of co-operatives.

Office National Interprofessionnel des Céréales et des Légumineuses: 25 ave Hassan I, BP 154, Rabat; tel (7) 61735; telex 31930; Dir-Gen: Muhammad Guerraoui; f 1937; office for cereals and vegetables.

Office National des Pêches: 13/15 rue Chevalier Bayard, BP 21, Casablanca; tel 24-05-51; telex 25708; Man Dir: Abd al-Aziz el-Belgheti; f 1969; state fishing organization.

Société de Développement Agricole (SODEA): prolongement rue Abd ar-Rahman al-Ghafiki-Agdal, BP 6280, Rabat; tel (7) 70813; telex 31675; Man Dir: Mustafa Kazouz; f 1972; state agricultural devt organization.

Société de Gestion des Terres Agricoles (SOGETA): 35 rue Daïet-Erroumi, BP 731, Rabat-Agdal; tel (7) 72834; telex 31704; Man Dir: Omar al-Gebil; f 1973; oversees use of agricultural land.

Société Nationale de Commercialisation des Semences (SONACOS): 30 rue Moulay Ali Cherif, BP 67, Rabat; tel (7) 61464; telex 21728; Dir: Abdelhaï Bouzoubaa; f 1975; import, export and commercialization of cereal seeds, potatoes, sugar beet, maize, etc.

Business and Economy

BANKING

Banque al-Maghrib: 277 ave Muhammad V, BP 445, Rabat; tel (7) 63009; telex 31006; Gov: Muhammad Sekkat; f 1959 as Banque du Maroc; central bank and bank of issue.

Banque Marocaine du Commerce Extérieur SA: 140 ave Hassan II, BP 13425, Casablanca; tel 27-60-27; telex 21055; Chair and Chief Exec: Abd al-Latif Jouahri; Man Dir: Driss Gueddari; f 1959; 58.73% state-owned; 115 brs.

FINANCIAL AGENCIES

Caisse de Dépôt et de Gestion: Shat Moulay Hassan, BP 408, Rabat; tel (7) 22438; telex 31072; Dir-Gen: Muhammad Fadel Lahlou; f 1959; finances small-scale projects.

Caisse Marocaine des Marchés (Marketing Fund): Résidence El Manar, blvd Abd al-Moumen, Casablanca; tel 25-91-18; telex 24740; Man: Hassan Kissi; f 1950.

Caisse Nationale de Crédit Agricole (Agricultural Credit Fund): 2 rue d'Alger, BP 49, Rabat; tel (7) 32555; telex 31657; Dir-Gen: Moulay Rachid Haddaoui; f 1961; finances agriculture, forestry and fishing, crafts, tourism in rural areas, rural commerce, young entrepreneurs, etc.

INSURANCE

Société Marocaine d'Assurances à l'Exportation: angle blvd d'Anfa et rue de Nièvre, Casablanca; Pres and Dir-Gen: Abd al-Hamid Jouahri; Asst Dir-Gen: Abd el-Kader Driouache; insurance for exporters in the public and private sectors; assistance for export promotion.

NATIONALIZED INDUSTRY

Cimenterie de l'Oriental (CIOR): 2 rue Ali Chouaïb Eddoukali, BP 1291, Rabat; tel (7) 24594; telex 31677; f 1976; cement production; under ODI (see below).

Compagnie Sucrière Marocaine et de Raffinage SA (COSUMAR): 8 rue el Mouatamid Ibnou Abbad, BP 30098, Casablanca; tel 24-73-45; telex 25032; Chair: Fouad Filali; Gen Man: Muhammad al-Baz; f 1967; sugar refining and trading.

Complexe Textile de Fès (COTEF): Quartier Sidi Brahim, route de Sefrou, BP 2267, Fez; tel (6) 41309; telex 51606; Dir-Gen: Abd al-Hamid Seddiki; 99% state participation; production of yarns and textiles.

Office Chérifien des Phosphates (OCP): blvd de la Grande Ceinture, route d'el Jadida, Casablanca; tel 36-00-25; telex 21630; Dir-Gen: Muhammad Karim Lamrani; f 1921; state co producing and marketing rock phosphates and derivatives.

> **Maroc-Chimie:** route du Djorf el-Youdi, BP 219, Safi; tel (46) 3089; telex 71057; manufacture and marketing of phosphate fertilizer.

Régie des Tabacs: 53 blvd My-Idriss I, Casablanca; tel 28-41-09; telex 21090; monopoly of purchase, production and marketing of tobacco; 100% state-owned.

Société Marocaine de Constructions Automobiles (SOMACA): km 12, autoroute de Rabat, BP 2628, Casablanca; tel 35-39-24; telex 25825; Pres: Mehdi ben Bouchta; Dir-Gen: Muhammad A. Belarbi; f 1959; assembly of motor vehicles; owned by Moroccan Govt, Fiat, Simca and SNI.

Société Nationale de Sidérurgie (SONASID): ave Yousuf ibn Tachfine, rue No 2, BP 151, Nador; tel (60) 4028; telex 65787; Dir-Gen: Abdallah Souibri; f 1974; iron and steel projects.

TRADE

Centre Marocain de Promotion des Exportations: 23 blvd Girardot, BP 10937, Casablanca; tel 30-22-10; telex 27847; fax 30-17-93; Dir-Gen: Muhammad Guedira; Sec-Gen: Abdelhamid Boumediene; f 1981; promotion and devt of exports.

Defence

Air Force: Des Far, Rabat; tel (7) 60710; telex 32977.

Army: ave Muhammad V, Rabat; tel (7) 64511; telex 31887; Commdr-in-Chief: HM King Hassan II.

General Office of National Security: Zankat Soekarno, Rabat; tel (7) 24011.

National Defence Administration: 6 bis, rue Patrice Lumumba, Rabat; tel (7) 62731; telex 31987.

Navy: blvd Sour Jdid, Casablanca; tel 27-84-51.

Development and Planning

Office pour le Développement Industriel (ODI): 10 rue Gandhi; BP 211, Rabat; tel (7) 68460; telex 31053; Man Dir: Muhammad Belkhayat; f 1973; state agency to develop industry.

INVESTMENT

Société Nationale d'Investissement (SNI): 43 rue Aspirant Lafuenté, BP 38, Casablanca; tel 22-30-81; telex 22736; Pres: Muhammad Bargach; Dir-Gen: Abdallah Belkziz; f 1966.

Legal and Judiciary

Supreme Court: place du Golan, Rabat; tel (7) 31016; First Pres: Muhammad Larbi al-Majboub; responsible for the interpretation of the law and regulates the jurisprudence of the courts and tribunals of the Kingdom; sits at Rabat and is divided into six Chambers.

Office of the Attorney-General: Rabat; Attorney-Gen: Ahmad Zeghari.

Media

BROADCASTING

Radiodiffusion Télévision Marocaine: 1 Zenkat el-Brihi, BP 1042, Rabat; tel (7) 64871; telex 31010; Dir-Gen: Muhammad Tricha; Dir, TV: Muhammad Lissari; Dir, Radio: Abd ar-Rahman Achour; Dir, Foreign Service: Ahmad Rayane; radio networks in Arabic, French, Berber, Spanish and English; Foreign Radio Service in Arabic, French and English; TV broadcasting 45 hours weekly in French and Arabic.

GOVERNMENT PUBLISHER

Imprimierie Officielle: Rabat-Chellah; tel (7) 65025.

NEWS AND INFORMATION

Direction de la Statistique: Ministère du Plan, BP 178, Rabat; tel (7) 73606; telex 32714.

Wikalat al-Maghreb al-Arabi (WMA): ave Allal ben Abdallah, BP 1049, Rabat; tel (7) 61672; telex 31044; Man Dir: Abd al-Jalil Fenjiro; f 1959; news agency; information in Arabic, French, English and Spanish.

Mining and Energy

Bureau de Recherches et de Participations Minières (BRPM): 5 charia Moulay Hassan, BP 99, Rabat; tel (7) 63035; telex 31066; Gen Man: Assou Lhatoute; Sec-Gen: Ali Bennani; state agency conducting exploration, exploitation and valorization of mineral resources.

Office National de l'Electricité: 65 rue Aspirant Lafuenté, BP 498, Casablanca; tel 22-41-65; telex 22780; Dir-Gen: Ahmad Tazi; state electricity authority.

Société d'Exploitation des Mines du Rif (SEFERIF): 30 Abou-Faris el-Marini, BP 436, Rabat; tel (7) 66350; telex 31708; Man Dir: Muhammad Harrak; nationalized 1967; open and underground mines producing iron ore for export and for the projected Nador iron and steel complex.

Telecommunications

Société Nationale de Télécommunications (SNT): 43 Zankat al Mansour Addahbi, BP 1067, Rabat; tel (7) 63333; telex 31789; fax (7) 62633; telecommunications; f 1964.

Tourism

Office National Marocain du Tourisme: 22 ave d'Alger, BP 19, Rabat; tel (7) 21252; telex 32019; fax (7) 20325; Dir: Abd ar-Raouf Hajji; Sec-Gen: Omar Rihani; f 1918; promotion of tourism.

Société Immobilière pour le Développement Touristique du Sud Atlas (SIDETSA): 9 rue Larache, Rabat; tel (7) 61027; telex 31641; Dir: Taoufik Berrada; f 1975; study, promotion and co-financing of tourist enterprises.

Transport

Office National des Transports: rue al-Fadila, Quartier Industriel, BP Rabat-Chellah; tel (7) 97842; telex 31090; Man Dir: Driss Arjouj; f 1985.

CIVIL AVIATION

Royal Air Maroc: Aéroport de Casablanca-Anfa; tel 36-16-20; telex 21880; Chair: Muhammad Mekouar; Man Dir: Said ben Ali Yaala; f 1957; 93% Govt-owned; domestic flights and services to Europe, the USA, Canada, Brazil, North and West Africa, the Canary Islands and the Middle East.

RAILWAYS

Office National des Chemins de Fer du Maroc (ONCFM): rue Abd ar-Rahman al-Ghafiki, Rabat-Agdal; tel (7) 74747; telex 31669; fax (7) 74480; Pres: Minister of Transport, Muhammad

Bouamoud; Dir-Gen: Moussa Moussaoui; f 1963; runs Moroccan railways.

ROADS

Compagnie de Transports au Maroc 'Lignes Nationales' (CTM—LN): 23 rue Léon l'Africain, Casablanca; tel 31-20-61; telex 28962; Man Dir: Muhammad al-Alj; road transport co.

SHIPPING

Compagnie Marocaine d'Agences Maritimes (COMARINE): 65 ave des Forces Armées Royales, BP 60, Casablanca; tel 31-19-41; telex 21851; Pres: Ahmad el-Ouali el-Alami; Dir-Gen: Muhammad el-Ouali el-Alami; f 1969.

Compagnie Marocaine de Navigation (COMANAV): 7 blvd de la Résistance, BP 628, Casablanca; tel 30-30-12; telex 26093; Pres and Dir-Gen: M. A. Alaoui Kacimi; f 1946; regular lines to Mediterranean, North West European, Middle Eastern and West African ports; tramping.

Utilities

Office National de l'Eau Potable (ONEP): 6 bis rue Patrice Lumumba, Rabat; tel (7) 21281; telex 31982; Dir: Houcine Tijani; responsible for drinking-water supply.

MOZAMBIQUE

Head of State

The 1975 Constitution proclaims that the Frente de Libertação de Moçambique (Frelimo) is the directing power of the state and of society. Executive power is vested in the President, who is Head of State and President of Frelimo. The President governs with the assistance of an appointed Council of Ministers. The Permanent Commission of the Assembly, chaired by the President, carries out the functions of the Council of Ministers between meetings.

President: Joaquim Alberto Chissano (took office 6 November 1986).

Office of the President: Avda Julius Nyerere 1780, Maputo; tel 741121; telex 6243.

Legislature

Legislative power is vested in the Assémbleia Popular (People's Assembly), with a maximum of 250 members, mostly Frelimo Party officials, who are indirectly elected by provincial assemblies. District administrators have overall responsibility for the functions of Government within each district, and city councils.

Assémbleia Popular (People's Assembly): Sala do Quarto Congresso, Avda 24 de Julho 3673, CP 1516, Maputo; tel 400826; telex 6473; fax 400711; Pres: Marcelino dos Santos; Sec-Gen: David Sibambo.

MINISTRIES AND GOVERNMENT DEPARTMENTS

OFFICE OF THE PRIME MINISTER
Avda Mário da Graça Machungo, Maputo
Tel 741081; telex 6154
Prime Minister: Mário da Graça Machungo

MINISTRY OF AGRICULTURE
Praça dos Heróis Moçambicanos, Maputo
Tel 21071; telex 6209
Minister: Alexandre José Zandamela

MINISTRY OF CONSTRUCTION AND WATER
Avda Karl Marx 606, CP 268, Maputo
Tel 30028; telex 6572
Minister: João Mário Salomão

MINISTRY OF CO-OPERATION
Avda Ahmed Sekou Touré 21, Maputo
Tel 741966
Minister: Maj-Gen Jacinto Soares Veloso

MINISTRY OF CULTURE
Avda Patrice Lumumba 1217, CP 1742, Maputo
Tel 32073; telex 6621
Minister: Luís Bernardo Honwana

MINISTRY OF EDUCATION
Avda 24 de Julho 167, Maputo
Tel 742006
Minister: Ancieto dos Muchangos

MINISTRY OF FINANCE
Praça de Marinha Popular, CP 272, Maputo
Tel 25071; telex 6569
Minister: Abdul Magid Osman

MINISTRY OF FOREIGN AFFAIRS
Avda Julius Nyerere 4, Maputo
Tel 744061; telex 6418
Minister: Pascoal Manuel Mocumbi

MINISTRY OF HEALTH
Avdas Eduardo Mondlane e Salvador Allende, Maputo
Tel 30814; telex 6239
Minister: Leonardo Simão

MINISTRY OF INDUSTRY AND ENERGY
Avda 25 de Setembro 1218, Maputo
Tel 27239; telex 6235
Minister: António José Lima Rodrigues Branco

MINISTRY OF INFORMATION
Avda Francisco Orlando Magumbué 780, Maputo
Tel 741080; telex 6487
Minister: Teodato Mondim da Silva Hunguana

MINISTRY OF THE INTERIOR
Avda Anchieta 46/48, Maputo
Tel 20130; telex 6419
Minister: Col Manuel José António

MINISTRY OF JUSTICE
Avda Julius Nyerere 33, Maputo
Tel 744646; telex 6594
Minister: Ossumane Ali Dauto

MINISTRY OF LABOUR
Avda 24 de Julho 2351-2365, CP 281, Maputo
Tel 21051; telex 6392
Minister: Aguiar Real Mazula

MINISTRY OF MINERAL RESOURCES
Avda Fernão de Magalhães 34, Maputo
Tel 29353
Minister: João Kachamila

MINISTRY OF NATIONAL DEFENCE
Avda Mártires de Mueda, Maputo
Tel 742081; telex 6331
Minister: Gen Alberto Joaquim Chipande
Deputy Minister and Chief of General Staff of the Armed Forces: Gen António Hama Thai

MINISTRY OF THE NATIONAL PEOPLE'S SECURITY SERVICE
Avda Ahmed Sekou Touré 810, Maputo
Tel 31832
Minister: Maj-Gen Mariano de Araújo Matsinhe

MINISTRY OF PLANNING
Avda Ahmed Sekou Touré 21, Maputo
Tel 741054; telex 6398
Minister: Mário da Graça Machungo

MINISTRY OF STATE FOR THE PRESIDENCY
Avda Julius Nyerere, Maputo
Tel 741081; telex 6485
Minister for Administration: José Oscar Monteiro
Minister without Portfolio: Feliciano Gundana

MINISTRY OF TRADE
Praça 25 de Junho, CP 1831, Maputo
Tel 26091; telex 6374
Minister: Daniel Gabriel Tembe

MINISTRY OF TRANSPORT AND COMMUNICATIONS
Avda Eduardo Mondlane 123/127, Maputo
Tel 743131; telex 6595
Minister: Lt-Gen Armando Emílio Nuno Guebuza

GOVERNMENT AGENCIES AND ORGANIZATIONS

Agriculture and Fishing

AGRICULTURE

Comércio Grossista de Produtos Alimentares (COGROPA): Avda 25 de Setembro 874-896, CP 308, Maputo; tel 424161; telex 6370; Dir: B. Amaral; Dir, Commercial: C. Cangi; f 1975; wholesale and distribution of food supplies.

Companhia do Cajú do Monapo, SARL: Avda do Trabalho 2106, CP 1248, Maputo; tel 732507; telex 6484; Dirs: António José Ribeiro da Mota, Dr Manuel Jorge Gouveia e Soeiro; f 1971; cashew nut processing and exportation.

Companhia da Zambézia, SARL: Avda Samora Machel 245, 4° Andar, CP 617, Maputo; tel 26195; telex 6380; Dir: Venancio Mondlane; responsible for agricultural production in the Zambézia region.

Empresa Moçambicana de Chá (EMOCHÁ): Avda Zedequias Manganela 250, CP 4123, Maputo; tel 425514; telex 6458; Dir: Marcos Basto; f 1978; tea production and export.

Empresa Nacional de Cajú (CAJÚ): Rua Joaquim Lapa 192, CP 124, Maputo; tel 22954; telex 6326; Dir: Peixoto Ferreira; cashew nuts.

Fábricas Associadas de Óleos (FASOL), SARL: Avda de Namaacha, CP 1128, Maputo; tel 723186; telex 6470; Dir: Carlos Costa; production of oils.

Fondo de Desenvolvimento Agrícola e Rural: Maputo; f 1988; provides credit for small farmers and rural co-operatives.

Sena Sugar Estate Lda: Maputo; telex 6422; Dir: José Paulo N'Chumali; fmrly British-owned, administered by Govt since 1978; plantations and mills in Sofala and Zambézia provinces.

FISHING

State Secretariat of Fisheries: Avda Mao Tse Tung 250, 15° Andar, Maputo; tel 741978; telex 6497; Sec of State: Joaquim José Tenreiro de Almeida.

Business and Economy

BANKING

Banco de Moçambique: Avda 25 de Setembro 1695, CP 423, Maputo; tel 28151; telex 6244; Gov: Eneias da Conceicão Comiche; f 1975; bank of issue; 20 brs and agencies.

Banco Popular de Desenvolvimento: Avda 25 de Setembro 1184, CP 757, Maputo; tel 21011; telex 6250; fax 23470; Chair: Hermenegíldo Cepeda Gamito; f 1977.

INSURANCE

Empresa Moçambicana de Seguros, EE (EMOSE): Avda 25 de Setembro 1383, CP 1165, Maputo; tel 22095; telex 6280; Dir-Gen: Luís F. T. Neves; f 1977 as state insurance monopoly.

NATIONALIZED INDUSTRY

Companhia Industrial de Fundição e Laminagem (CIFEL), SARL: Avda de Oua 485, CP 441, Maputo; tel 732181; telex 6262; Dir: Evaristo J. Vílanculo; production of steel goods.

Companhia Industrial do Monapo, SARL: Avda do Trabalho 2106, CP 1248, Maputo; tel 732507; telex 6484; Dirs: António José Ribeiro da Mota, Dr Manuel Jorge Gouveia e Soeiro; f 1946; soap and food oil processing.

Empresa de Assistência Técnica ao Equipamento Agrícola (MECANAGRO): Rua Consiglieri Pedroso 301, Maputo; tel 24579; telex 6344; Dir: Ragendra de Sousa; production of agricultural machinery.

Empresa de Construções Matálicos (ECOME): Avda das Industrias-Machava, CP 1358, Maputo; tel 752282; Dir: Justino Lucas; production of agricultural equipment.

Empresa Estatal de Maquinaria Agrícola (AGRO-ALFA): Avda 24 de Julho 2755, CP 1318, Maputo; tel 422928; telex 6405; fax 30889; Dir: José Alves; Commercial Dir: Friedrich Rakar; f 1978; production of agricultural equipment.

Empresa Metalúrgica de Moçambique, SARL: Avda de Moçambique Km 1.5, CP 1316, Maputo; tel 475189; telex 6499;

fax 475149; Dir: António Maciel; f 1951; production of metallurgical goods.

Empresa Moçambicana de Malhas (EMMA), SARL: CP 2896, Maputo; tel 25513; telex 6219; Admin: Joaquim Meque; textiles production.

Empresa Nacional de Calçado e Têxteis (ENCATEX): Avda 24 de Julho 2969, CP 67, Maputo; tel 731251; telex 6421; Dir: António Munguambe; production of footwear and textiles.

A Forjadora Fábrica de Equipamentos Industriais, Lda: Avda de Angola 2850, CP 3078, Maputo; tel 733841; Gen Man: Adelino Carrilho; production of metal structures.

Indústria Moçambicana de Aço (IMA), SARL: Avda 24 de Julho 2373, 12° Andar, CP 2566, Maputo; tel 21141; telex 6323; Dir: António Francisco S. de Maciel; steel products.

Moçambique-Industrial, SARL: Rua Aruangua 39, 1° Andar, CP 432, Maputo; tel 22123; telex 7352; Dir: Arnaldo Ascensão Santos; production of oils.

Química-Geral, SARL: Língamo-Matola, CP 15, Maputo; tel 723077; telex 6448; Dir: Alfredo Baduru; production of fertilizers.

Texlom, SARL: Avda Filipe Samuel Magaia 514, CP 194, Maputo; tel 21198; telex 6289; Dir: Célia Lorena; textile production.

TRADE

Câmara de Comércio de Moçambique: Rua Mateus Sansâo Mutemba 452, CP 1836, Maputo; tel 741970; telex 6498; Pres: Américo Magaia; Sec-Gen: João Albasini; chamber of commerce.

Cimentos de Moçambique: Avda Fernâo de Magalhâes 34, 2° Andar, CP 270, Maputo; tel 24061; telex 6336; Dir: Helder Rodrigues; trade in cement.

Citrinos de Maputo, EE: Avda 25 de Setembro 1509, 6° Andar, CP 1659, Maputo; tel 21857; telex 6538; Dir: António Augusto Cabral; exports of citrus fruits.

Companhia Industrial de Cordoarias de Moçambique (CICOMO), SARL: Avda Zedequias Manganhela 514, 4° Andar, CP 4113, Maputo; tel 27272; telex 6347; Dir: Carlos Ferreira; exports of sisal.

Distribuidora de Materias de Construção, EE (DIMAC): Avda Zedequias Manganhela 520, 11° Andar, CP 222, Maputo; tel 28453; telex 6269; Dir: Rui Fernandes; import and distribution of construction and building materials.

Emopesca: CP 2290, Maputo; exports of fish and fish products.

Empresa de Citrinos de Manica: Avda 25 de Setembro, CP 15, Chimoio; tel 2219; telex 7314; Dir: Osias M. Manjate; f 1980; export of citrus fruits.

Empresa de Comércio Externo de Equipamentos Industriais (INTERMÁQUINA): Rua Consiglieri Pedroso 165, CP 808, Maputo; tel 24056; telex 6543; Dir: Kong Lam; trade in industrial equipment and accessories.

Empresa Distribuidora de Equipamento Eléctrico e Electrónico e Componentes (INTERELECTRA): Avda Samora Machel 162, CP 1159, Maputo; tel 427091; telex 6203; Dirs: Francisco Paulo Cuche, Jorge Ernesto Massingue, Lourenço Silvestre Uamusse; f 1985; importers and distributors of electrical materials and communications and telecommunications equipment.

Empresa Distribuidora e Importadora de Metais (INTERMETAL): Rua Vladimir Lénine 605, CP 1162, Maputo; tel 22770; telex 6372; Man Dir: Jorge Silvestre Luís Guinda; trade in metals and metal products.

Empresa Estatal de Importação e Exportação de Medicamentos (MEDIMOC): Avda Julius Nyerere 500, 1° Andar, CP 600, Maputo; tel 744045; telex 6260; Dir-Gen: Aranda Correia; trade in pharmaceuticals, medical equipment and supplies.

Empresa Moçambicana de Apetrechamento da Indústria Pesqueira (EQUIPESCA): Rua Tavares de Almeida 30, CP 2342, Maputo; tel 27630; telex 6284; Dir: Eduardo B. Salia; trade in fishing equipment.

Empresa Moçambicana de Hidráulica (HIDROMOC): Avda do Trabalho 1501, CP 193, Maputo; tel 732033; telex 6234; Dir: Frederico Martins; f 1952; trade in irrigation equipment and chemicals for water treatment.

Empresa Moçambicana de Importação e Exportação de Produtos Pesqueiros (PESCOM International): Rua Consiglieri Pedroso 343, 4° Andar, CP 1570, Maputo; tel 21568; telex 6409; fax 24961; Man Dir: Felisberto Manuel; Dir, Commercial: Salvador Ganhane; f 1978; imports and exports of fish products, particularly prawns.

Empresa Moçambicana de Importação e Exportação de Produtos Químicos e Plastícos (INTERQUÍMICA): Rua de Bagamoyo 333, CP 2268, Maputo; tel 23167; telex 6274; Dir-Gen: Aurélio Ricardo Chiziane; Dir, Commercial: Milton Jossias; f 1978; trade in chemicals, fertilizers, pesticides, plastics, papers.

Empresa Nacional de Carvão de Moçambique (CARBOMOC): Rua Joaquim Lapa 108, Maputo; tel 24251; telex 6491; Dir: Miquelina Menezes; export and extraction of minerals.

Empresa Nacional de Exportação (ENACOMO): Avda Samora Machel 285, 1° Andar, Maputo; tel 30172; telex 6387; fax 28484; Gen Man: Carlos Pacheco Faria; Dir, Marketing: K. Patel; f 1976; import and export of agricultural commodities.

Empresa Nacional de Importação e Exportação de Veículos Motorizadas (INTERMECANO): Avda Revolução de Outubro 290, CP 1280, Maputo; tel 30221; telex 6505; Dir: Rodrigo de Oliveira; import and export of motor vehicles, construction plant, agricultural machinery, spare parts.

Importadora de Bens de Consumo (IMBEC): Rua da Mesquita 33, 2° Andar, Maputo; tel 20326; telex 6350; fax 23650; Dir-Gen: Carlos Cossa; Dir, Finance: Paulino Bernardo; Dir, Commercial: Augusto Mazoka; f 1982; importer of consumer goods.

Lojas Rancas de Moçambique (INTERFRANCA): Rua Timor Leste 106/108, CP 1206, Maputo; tel 31043; telex 6403; Dir-Gen: Carlos E. N. Ribeiro; Man, Finance: Jorge Moiana; f 1978; trade in tobacco, alcohol, food and consumer goods.

Pescom Internacional: CP 1570, Maputo; tel 21734; telex 6409; fax 24961; export of fish and prawns.

Riopele Téxteis de Moçambique, SARL: Rua Joaquim Lapa 21, CP 1658, Maputo; tel 31331; telex 6371; Dir: Carlos Ribeiro; trade in textiles.

Defence

Mozambican Armed Forces-People's Force for the Liberation of Mozambique (FAM-FPLM): Avda Mártires de Mueda, Maputo; tel 742081; telex 6331; Commdr-in-Chief: President Joaquim Alberto Chissano; Chief of Gen Staff: Gen António Hama Thai.

Legal and Judiciary

Office of the Attorney-General: Avda Julius Nyerere 15, Maputo; tel 741014; Attorney-Gen: Eduardo Mulembue.

Supreme Court of Appeal: Avda Vladimir Lenine 103, Maputo; tel 26642; Presiding Judge: Victor Serraventoso.

Media

BROADCASTING

Rádio Moçambique: CP 2000, Maputo; tel 34041; telex 6317; Dir-Gen: Manuel Toué; Dir, Admin: António Fonseca; f 1975; programmes in Portuguese, English and vernaculars.

Televisão Experimental de Moçambique (TVE-M): Avda Julius Nyerere 942, Maputo; tel 491395; telex 6346; Dir: António Júlio Botelho Moniz; f 1981; transmissions on Wednesday, Thursday, Saturday and Sunday only.

GOVERNMENT PUBLISHER

Imprensa Nacional de Moçambique: CP 275, Maputo.

NEWS AND INFORMATION

Agência de Informação de Moçambique (AIM): CP 896, Maputo; tel 30795; telex 6430; Dir: Ricardo Malate; Dir, Admin: Eugenio Gerente; f 1975; daily reports in Portuguese and English.

Direcção Nacional de Estatística: Commissão Nacional do Plano, Avda Ahmed Sekou Touré 21, CP 493, Maputo; tel 743117; collection, analysis and distribution of statistics.

Mining and Energy

ENERGY

Electricidade de Moçambique: Avda Agostinho Neto 70, CP 2447, Maputo; tel 742011; telex 6555; Dir: Fernando Ramos Julião; production and distribution of electric energy.

Empresa Nacional de Hidrocarbonetos de Moçambique (ENHM): Avda Fernão de Magalães 34, CP 2904, Maputo; tel 29676; telex 6491; Dir: Mario Marques; controls concessions for petroleum exploration and production.

Empresa Nacional de Petróleos de Moçambique (PETROMOC): Praça dos Trabalhadores 9, CP 417, Maputo; tel 27191; telex 6382; Dir: Manuel da Cruz Viola; f 1978 to take over the Sonarep oil refinery and its associted distribution co; state dirctorate for liquid fuels, including petroleum products passing through Mozambique to inland countries.

MINING

Minas Gerais de Moçambique (MAGMA): Avda 24 de Julho 1895, 2° Andar, Maputo; tel 27692; telex 6413; Dir-Gen: Estevão Tomas Rafael; Dir, Commercial: Juvenal A. Mabote; produces metallic and non-metallic ore, copper concentrate and marble.

Tourism

Empresa Nacional de Turismo (ENT): Avda 25 de Setembro 12011, CP 2446, Maputo; tel 425011; telex 6303; Dir-Gen: Marechal David Nhavoto; f 1985; national tour operator.

Transport

CIVIL AVIATION

Empresa Nacional de Transporte e Trabalho Aéreo, EE (TTA): Aeroporto Internacional de Maputo, CP 2054, Maputo; tel 732141; telex 6539; Dir: Jerónimo Albino Parruque; scheduled services to 35 destinations, air taxi services, aerial photography, agricultural and special aviation services.

Linhas Aéreas de Moçambique (LAM): Aeroporto Internacional de Maputo, CP 2060, Maputo; tel 731688; telex 6386; Chair and Dir-Gen: José Ricardo Zuzarte Viegas; took over the functions of DETA in 1980; operates domestic services and international flights within Africa and to Europe.

RAILWAYS

Direcção Nacional dos Portos e Caminhos de Ferro de Moçambique (CFM): Rua dos Mártires de Inhaminga 336, CP 276, Maputo; tel 24228; telex 6208; Dir: Fernando Ferreira Mendes; f 1929; there are five main railway systems linking ports in Mozambique with other southern African countries.

Empresa dos Caminhos de Ferro de Moçambique (CFM), SARL: Praça dos Trabalhadores, CP 2158, Maputo; tel 27173; telex 6208; Dir: Fernando Ferreira Mendes; national railway co.

SHIPPING

Agência Nacional de Frete e Navegaçao (ANFRENA): Rua Consiglieri Pedroso 396, Maputo; tel 28111; telex 6258; Dir: Ferdinand Wilson; national freight and shipping co.

Companhia Nacional de Navegação: CP 2064, Maputo; telex 6237; national shipping co.

Empresa Moçambicana de Cargas (MOCARGO): Avda Consiglieri Pedroso 430, CP 888, Maputo; tel 31022; telex 6581; fax 33106; Dir-Gen: Rafique Jusob; Dirs: Manuel Amarel, Calisto Suaze; f 1984; shipping, chartering, air and road transportation.

Navique, EE (Empresa Moçambicana de Navegação): Rua de Bagamoyo 336, CP 145, Maputo; tel 31470; telex 6524; Man Dir: Jorge de Sousa Coelho; shipping co.

MYANMAR

Head of State and Legislature

Following the military coup of 18 September 1988, all state organs were abolished by the State Law and Order Restoration Council. The Chair of the Council became Head of State. Ministers are chosen by the Council. Elections were promised in May 1990, after which a new legislative body was to be formed.

Chair of the State Law and Order Restoration Council: Gen Saw Maung (took office 18 September 1988).

State Law and Order Restoration Council: Yangon; First Sec: Brig-Gen Khin Nyunt; Second Sec: Col Tin U.

MINISTRIES AND GOVERNMENT DEPARTMENTS

OFFICE OF THE PRIME MINISTER
Ministers' Office, Yangon
Tel (1) 83742
Prime Minister: Gen Saw Maung

MINISTRY OF AGRICULTURE AND FORESTS
Ministers' Office, Yangon
Tel (1) 75080
Minister: Maj-Gen Chit Swe

MINISTRY OF CONSTRUCTION
Ministers' Office, Yangon
Tel (1) 76773
Minister: Brig-Gen Aung Ye Kyaw

MINISTRY OF CO-OPERATIVES
259-263 Bogyoke Aung San St, Yangon
Tel (1) 77096
Minister: Brig-Gen Aung Ye Kyaw

MINISTRY OF CULTURE
26-42 Pansodan St, Yangon
Tel (1) 81321
Minister: Maj-Gen Phone Myint

MINISTRY OF DEFENCE
Signal Pagoda Rd, Yangon
Tel (1) 71611; telex 21316
Minister: Gen Saw Maung

MINISTRY OF EDUCATION
Ministers' Office, Yangon
Tel (1) 78597
Minister: Dr Pe Thein

MINISTRY OF ENERGY
74-80 Minye Kyawswa Rd, Yangon
Tel (1) 21060; telex 21307
Minister: Rear-Adm Maung Maung Khin

MINISTRY OF FOREIGN AFFAIRS
Prome Court, Prome Rd, Yangon
Tel (1) 83333; telex 21313
Minister: Gen Saw Maung

MINISTRY OF HEALTH
Ministers' Office, Yangon
Tel (1) 72075
Minister: Dr Pe Thein

MINISTRY OF HOME AND RELIGIOUS AFFAIRS
Ministers' Office, Yangon
Tel (1) 71952
Minister: Maj-Gen Phone Myint

MINISTRY OF INDUSTRY (No 1)
192 Kaba Aye Pagoda Rd, Yangon
Tel (1) 50701; telex 21513
Minister: Maj-Gen Sein Aung

MINISTRY OF INDUSTRY (No 2)
Ministers' Office, Yangon
Tel (1) 78142; telex 21500
Minister: Maj-Gen Sein Aung

MINISTRY OF INFORMATION
Ministers' Office, Yangon
Tel (1) 71409
Minister: Maj-Gen Phone Myint

MINISTRY OF LABOUR AND SOCIAL WELFARE
Ministers' Office, Yangon
Tel (1) 78350
Minister: Maj-Gen Tin Tun

MINISTRY OF LIVESTOCK BREEDING AND FISHERIES
Ministers' Office, Yangon
Tel (1) 80398
Minister: Maj-Gen Chit Swe

MINISTRY OF MINES
Ministers' Office, Yangon
Tel (1) 73996
Minister: Rear-Adm Maung Maung Khin

MINISTRY OF PLANNING AND FINANCE
Ministers' Office, Yangon
Tel (1) 76066
Minister: Col David Abel

MINISTRY OF TRADE
228-240 Strand Rd, Yangon
Tel (1) 73613; telex 21338
Minister: Col David Abel

MINISTRY OF TRANSPORT AND COMMUNICATIONS
Ministers' Office, Yangon
Tel (1) 78438
Minister: Maj-Gen Tin Tun

GOVERNMENT AGENCIES AND ORGANIZATIONS

Advisory and Supervisory Bodies

Election Commission: Yangon; Chair: U Ba Htay.

Socialist Economic Planning Committee: Yangon; f 1967; 10 mems.

Agriculture

Agriculture Corpn: 72-74 Shwedagon Pagoda Rd, Yangon; tel (1) 83480; telex 21311; Man Dir: U Tin Hlaing.

Central Co-operative Society (CCS) Council: 334/336 Strand Rd, Yangon; tel (1) 74550; Chair: U Than Hlang; Sec: U Tin Latt.

Forest Department: 62 Pansodan St, Yangon; tel (1) 81367.

Myanma Fisheries Enterprise: 654 Merchant St, Yangon; telex 21310; Man Dir: U Han Tun; f 1973; marine fishing; fish and prawn farming and farming of other marine animals; processing and marketing.

Foodstuff Industries Corpn: 523 Merchant St, Yangon; tel (1) 844944; telex 21500; Man Dir: Col Soe Lwin.

Livestock Breeding Corpn: Veterinary Institute Estate, Insein, POB 1457, Yangon; tel (1) 40726; telex 21310; Man Dir: U Khin Latt.

Timber Corpn: POB 206, Ahlone, Yangon; tel (1) 83933; telex 21312; Man Dir: U Khin Maung Gyi; f 1948; extraction, processing, and main exporter of Burma teak and other timber, veneers, plywood and other forest products.

Art and Culture

National Archives Department: 114 Pyidaungsu Yeiktha Rd, Yangon; tel (1) 81670.

Business and Economy

BANKING

Myanma Agricultural Bank: 1-7 Latha St, Yangon; tel (1) 73018; Man Dir: U Sein Bann; provides agricultural credit for farmers.

Myanma Economic Bank: 564 Merchant St, Yangon; tel (1) 81819; telex 21213; Man Dir: U Maung Maung Than; provides savings and credit facilities and extends loans to state economic organizations, municipal bodies and co-operatives.

Myanma Foreign Trade Bank: 80-86 Maha Bandoola Gdn St, POB 203, Yangon; tel (1) 84911; telex 21300; Man Dir: U Maung Maung Than; Dep Gen Mans: U Mya U, U Khin Maung Kyi; f 1976; handles all foreign exchange and international banking transactions.

Union of Myanmar Bank: 24-26 Sule Pagoda Rd, Yangon; tel (1) 85300; telex 21213; Chair: U Maung Maung Han; f 1976; central bank and bank of issue.

FINANCIAL AGENCIES

Central Account Office: 35 Lower Kemmendine Rd, Yangon; tel (1) 84779.

Internal Revenue Department: 554 Merchant St, Yangon; tel (1) 83055.

INSURANCE

Myanmar Insurance Corpn: 163-167 Pansodan St, Yangon; tel (1) 84466; telex 21203; Man Dir: U Maung Maung Than; f 1975.

NATIONALIZED INDUSTRY

Construction Corpn: 60 Shwedagon Pagoda Rd, Yangon; tel (1) 80955; telex 21336; Man Dir: U Khin Maung Yin.

General Industries Corpn: 192 Kaba Aye Pagoda Rd, Yangon; tel (1) 56055; telex 21500; Man Dir: Saw Myint.

Industrial Planning Department: 192 Kaba Aye Pagoda Rd, Bahan PO, Yangon; tel (1) 56313; telex 21500; Dir-Gen: Col Aung Koe; f 1976; promotes the devt of manufacturing industries by co-ordinating the activities of the industrial establishments under the Ministry of Industry (No 1) with other Ministries and with international aid agencies and foreign businessmen; consultancy services.

Metal Industries Corpn: 354 Prome Rd, Yangon; tel (1) 31518; telex 21500; Man Dir: U Myo Thant.

Myanma Gems Enterprise: 66 Kaba Aye Pagoda Rd, POB 1397, Yangon; tel (1) 60905; telex 21533; Man Dir: Col Hlaing Win; f 1976; production and export of gems, jade, pearl and jewellery.

Myanma Heavy Industries Corpn: 56 Kaba Aye Pagoda Rd, POB 370, Yangon; tel (1) 61769; telex 21503; Man Dir: Lt-Col Than Shwe; Dir, Planning: Lt-Col Sein Htoon; f 1962;

manufacture of heavy and light vehicles, agricultural machinery, electrical home appliances, electronic products, bicycles, tyres, electric cables, etc.

Pharmaceuticals Industries Corpn: 192 Kaba Aye Pagoda Rd, Yangon; tel (1) 56740; telex 21500; Man Dir: U Ba Nyunt.

Textiles Industries Corpn: 192 Kaba Aye Pagoda Rd, Yangon; tel (1) 56333; telex 21500; Man Dir: U Mya Soe Nyein.

TRADE

Customs Department: 132 Strand Rd, Yangon; tel (1) 84533; Dir-Gen: U Tun Shwe; f 1867; assessment and collection of customs duties on imports and exports; prevention and detection of illegal trade; collection of data for compilation of statistics on foreign trade.

Inspection and Agency Corpn: Yangon; Man Dir: U Win Kyi; works on behalf of state-owned enterprises to promote business with foreign cos.

Myanma Agricultural Produce Trading: 70 Pansodan St, Yangon; tel (1) 84044; telex 21227; Man Dir: U Toe Kyi.

Myanma Export-Import Corpn: 577 Merchant St, Yangon; tel (1) 80260; telex 21305; Man Dir: U Aung Kyi.

Defence

Armed Forces: Siganl Pagoda Rd, Yangon; tel (1) 81611; Chief of Staff: Gen Saw Maung; Dep Chief of Staff: Lt-Gen Than Shwe.

Legal and Judiciary

Council of the People's Justices: Maha Bandoola Gdn St, Yangon; tel (1) 72249; functioned as the central Court of Justice; ceased to operate following the imposition of military rule in September 1988; in November 1988 it was announced that all courts would be closed until April 1989.

Media

BROADCASTING

Myanma Broadcasting Service (MBS): Yangon Taing, POB 1432, Yangon; tel (1) 31355; telex 21360; Dir-Gen: U Kyaw Minn; Dir of Broadcasting: U Aung Kyi; Dir of TV (acting): U Ko Ko Gyi; f 1946; broadcasts in Burmese, Arakanese, Mon, Shan, Karen, Chin, Kachin, Kayah and English; colour TV transmissions.

GOVERNMENT PUBLISHER

Printing and Publishing Corpn: 228 Theinbyu St, Yangon; tel (1) 81033; Man Dir: Col Maung Maung Khin.

NEWS AND INFORMATION

News Agency of Myanmar (NAM): 212 Theinbyu St, Yangon; tel (1) 70893; Chief Editors: U Ye Tint (domestic section), U Kyaw Min (external section); news agency.

Mining and Energy

ENERGY

Electric Power Corpn: 197-199 Lower Kemmendine Rd, Yangon; tel (1) 85366; telex 21306; Man Dir: U Khin Maung Thein.

Myanma Oil and Gas Enterprise: 74-80 Minye Kyawswa Rd, Yangon; tel (1) 21049; telex 21307; Man Dir: U Aung Min; nationalized 1963; fmrly Burma Oil Co.

Petrochemical Industries Corpn: 23 Prome Rd, Yangon; tel (1) 22822; telex 21329; Man Dir: U Hlaing Myint San; f 1975.

Petroleum Products Supply Corpn: 74-80 Minye Kyawswa Rd, Yangon; tel (1) 82011; telex 21307; Man Dir: Col Myint Soe.

Union of Myanmar Atomic Energy Department: Central Research Organization, 6 Kaba Aye Pagoda Rd, Yangon; Chair: Dr Maung Maung Gale; f 1955.

MINING

No 1 Mining Corpn: 226 Maha Bandoola St, Yangon; tel (1) 74711; telex 21307; Man Dir: U Myo Nyunt; fmrly Myanma Bawdwin Corpn; devt and mining of non-ferrous metals.

No 2 Mining Corpn: Kanbe, Yankin, Yangon; tel (1) 50166; telex 21511; Man Dir: U Nyan Lin; fmrly Myanma Tin Tungsten Devt Corpn; devt and mining of tin, tungsten and antimony.

No 3 Mining Corpn: Kanabe, Yankin PO, Yangon; tel (1) 57444; telex 21511; Man Dir: U Hla Thein; production of pig iron, carbon steel, steel grinding balls, coal, barytes, gypsum, limestone and various clays, etc.

Science and Technology

Geological Survey and Mineral Exploration Department: Kanbe Rd, Yangon; tel (1) 52099.

Tourism

Hotel and Tourist Corpn (Tourist Burma): 77-91 Sule Pagoda Rd, Yangon; tel (1) 78376; telex 21330; Gen Man: U Myo Lwin; Man: U Minn Oo; f 1965; runs retail travel agency; manages all hotels, tourist offices, diplomatic stores and duty-free shops.

Myanmar Travels and Tours: 77-91 Sule Pagoda Rd, Yangon; tel (1) 78376; telex 21330; sole tour operator and travel agent; handles all travel arrangements for groups and individuals.

Transport and Communications

TELECOMMUNICATIONS

Posts and Telecommunications Corpn: 43 Bo Aung Gyaw St, Yangon; tel (1) 85499; telex 21222; Man Dir: U Tin.

TRANSPORT

Inland Water Transport Corpn: 50 Pansodan St, Yangon; tel (1) 83244; Man Dir: U Khin Maung Thein; operates cargo and passenger services throughout Myanmar.

Myanma Airways (MA): 104 Strand Rd, Yangon; tel (1)

72911; telex 21204; Man Dir: Col Kyaw Thein; f 1948; internal network operates services to 25 airports; external services to Bangkok, Calcutta, Dhaka, Kathmandu and Singapore.

Myanma Five Star Shipping Corpn: 132-136 Theinbyu Rd, POB 1221, Yangon; tel (1) 80022; telex 21210; Man Dir: U Shwe Than; Gen Man: U Kyaw Zaw; f 1959; cargo services to the Far East, South East Asia and Europe; runs coastal and ocean-going vessels.

Myanma Port Authority: 10 Pansodan St, POB 1, Yangon; tel (1) 83122; telex 21208; Man Dir: U Tin Maung Soe; Gen Man: U Tin Oo; f 1880; gen port and harbour duties.

Myanma Railways Corpn: Bogyoke Aung San St, POB 118, Yangon; tel (1) 84455; telex 21361; Man Dir: Col Win Sein; Gen Man: U Saw Clyde; f 1972.

Road Transport Corpn: 375 Bogyoke Aung San St, Yangon; tel (1) 82252; Man Dir: (vacant); f 1963 to carry out phased nationalization of passenger and freight road transport; operates haulage trucks and passenger buses.

NAMIBIA

Head of State and Legislature

Under the terms of the constitution, which was passed by a directly-elected Constituent Assembly in February 1990, Namibia was due to become a multi-party republic with an independent judiciary, a bill of fundamental human rights and an executive President, who may serve a maximum of two five-year terms. The new Government was due to be formed at independence on 21 March 1990.

Constituent Assembly: Windhoek 9000; Chair: Hage Geingob.

President-Elect: Sam Nujoma (elected by the Constituent Assembly 16 February 1990.

Office of the President: Windhoek 9000.

GOVERNMENT AGENCIES AND ORGANIZATIONS

Agriculture and Fishing

AGRICULTURE

Department of Agriculture and Nature Conservation: Private Bag 13184, Windhoek 9000; tel (61) 3029111; telex 908-3109; fax (61) 224566; Sec: Dr H. Schneider; f 1981; research, management and control of agriculture, forestry, nature conservation and veterinary services.

FISHING

Directorate of Sea Fisheries: Private Bag 13184, Windhoek 9000; tel (61) 3029111; telex 908-3109; fax (61) 224566; Dir: Dr J. D. Jurgens; f 1982; research, management and control of sea fisheries.

Banking

South African Reserve Bank: Göring St, POB 2882, Windhoek 9000; tel (61) 226401; telex 710; central bank.

Bank of South West Africa/Namibia Ltd: POB 1, Windhoek 9000; tel (61) 3039111; telex 908-898; fax (61) 224417; Chair: J. A. Bruckner; Man Dir: E. Krause; f 1973.

Development and Planning

Development Co-ordination Directorate: Private Bag 12025, Windhoek 9000; co-ordination of devt activities and initiatives.

First National Development Corpn (ENOK): Private Bag 13252, Windhoek 9000; tel (61) 306911; telex 908-570; fax (61) 33943; Exec Chair: H. A. R. Meiring; Gen Man: H. J. Champion; f 1978; promotion of investment and private entrepreneurship, and thus promote commercial, industrial, mining and agricultural devt.

Energy

Namibian Water and Eelctricity Corpn: Windhoek 9000; fmrly South West Africa Water and Electricity Corpn, transferred to Namibian Govt in 1986.

Media

South West Africa Broadcasting Corpn: POB 321, Windhoek 9000; tel (61) 291911; telex 622; fax (61) 291156; Dir-Gen: P. J. Venter; Dep Dir-Gens: P. A. van der Smith, P. J. B. Coetzer; f 1979; broadcasts in 13 languages.

Transport

Namib Air (Pty) Ltd: POB 731, Eros Airport, Windhoek 9000; tel (61) 38220; telex 657; Chair: G. F. Greebe; Gen Man: F. Uys; f 1959; owned by interim Govt; domestic flights and services to Botswana and South Africa.

NAURU

Head of State

Executive authority is vested in a Cabinet which consists of the President of the Republic, who is Head of State and elected by Parliament, and Ministers appointed by the President. The Cabinet is responsible to Parliament.

President: Bernard Dowiyogo (elected December 1989).

Office of the President: Govt Offices, Yaren; tel 3100; telex 33081; Minister Assisting the Pres: Vinson Detenamo.

Legislature

Legislative power is vested in the unicameral Parliament, comprising 18 members elected by (compulsory) universal adult suffrage for up to three years.

Parliament: Nauru; tel 3180; telex 33081; Speaker: Nimes Ekwona.

MINISTRIES AND GOVERNMENT DEPARTMENTS

MINISTRY OF FINANCE
Civic Centre, Nauru
Tel 3140; telex 33081
Minister: Kinza Godfrey Clodumar

MINISTRY OF HEALTH AND EDUCATION
Govt Offices, Yaren
Tel 3350; telex 33081
Minister: Vinci Clodumar

MINISTRY OF INTERNAL AND EXTERNAL AFFAIRS
Govt Offices, Yaren
Tel 3300; telex 33081
Minister: Bernard Dowiyogo

MINISTRY OF ISLAND DEVELOPMENT AND INDUSTRY
Govt Offices, Yaren

Tel 3320; telex 33081
Minister: Bernard Dowiyogo

MINISTRY OF JUSTICE
Govt Offices, Yaren
Tel 3320; telex 33081
Minister: Kennan Ranibok Adeang

MINISTRY OF WORKS AND COMMUNITY SERVICES
Govt Offices, Yaren
Tel 3165; telex 33081
Minister: Vinson Detenamo

MINISTRY OF PUBLIC SERVICE
c/o Chief Secretary's Dept, Govt Offices, Yaren
Tel 3300; telex 33081
Minister: Bernard Dowiyogo

GOVERNMENT AGENCIES AND ORGANIZATIONS

Business and Economy

BANKING

Bank of Nauru: POB 289, Nauru; tel 3238; telex 33085; fax 3202; Chair: Bernard Dowiyogo; Gen Man and Sec: N. Goswami; Mans: N. K. Sarin, R. Garoa; f 1976; state bank.

FINANCIAL AGENCY

Nauru Agency Corpn: POB 300, Aiwo; tel 3347; telex 33090; Vice-Chair: Kenas Aroi; Gen Man: M. N. Khushu; functions as a merchant bank to assist entrepreneurs in the registration of

holding and trading corpns and the procurement of banking, trust and insurance licences.

INSURANCE

Nauru Insurance Corpn: POB 82, Nauru; tel 3346; telex 33088; f 1974; sole licensed insurer and reinsurer in Nauru.

TRADE

Nauru Corpn: Civic Centre, Nauru; Chair: Hammer DeRoburt; Gen Man: Theodore Moses; f 1925; operated by the Nauru Local Govt Council; the major retailer in Nauru.

Fishing

Nauru Fishing Corpn: Aiwo; Chair: Hammer DeRoburt; f 1979; owned by Nauru Local Govt Council.

Legal and Judiciary

Supreme Court: Nauru; tel 3365; telex 333081; exercises both original and appellate jurisdiction; presided over by the Chief Justice.

    Chief Justice's Chambers: 50th Floor, Nauru House, 80 Colling St. Melbourne, Vic, Australia; tel (3) 653 5709; telex 31158; Chief Justice: Sir Gaven Donne (non-resident).

Media

BROADCASTING

Nauru Broadcasting Service: Nauru; tel 3095; Station Man: Millicent Aroi; Broadcasts Officer: R. Tsitsi; f 1968; Govt-owned and non-commercial; radio broadcasts in English and Nauruan.

Mining

Nauru Phosphate Corpn: Aiwo; tel 4180; telex 33082; fax 4111; Chair: Ruben Kun; Gen Man: James Stewart; f 1969; operates the phosphate industry and several public services of the Rep of Nauru on behalf of the Nauruan people; mining and export of phosphate deposits.

Transport

Directorate of Civil Aviation: Govt Offices, Yaren; tel 3310; telex 33081.

Air Nauru: c/o Directorate of Civil Aviation, Govt Offices, Yaren; tel 3310; telex 33081; Dir: G. F. Vae'au; f 1972; operates international air services in the region.

Nauru Pacific Line: Civic Centre, Nauru; tel 4581; telex 33083; Man Dir: Hammer DeRoburt; f 1969; owned by Nauru Local Govt Council; runs six vessels; operates services to ports in Australia, New Zealand, Asia, the Pacific and the west coast of the USA.

NEPAL

Head of State

Nepal is a constitutional monarchy, and executive power is vested in the King as Head of State. On the recommendation of the Prime Minister, the King appoints a Council of Ministers, which is responsible to the National Assembly.

Sovereign: HM King Birendra Bir Bikram Shah Dev (succeeded to the throne 31 January 1972; crowned 24 February 1975).

Office of HM the King: Narayanhity Royal Palace, Durbar Marg, Kathmandu; tel 212396.

Legislature

Legislative power is vested in the unicameral Rashtriya Panchayat (National Assembly), which is presided over by the King and comprises 140 members (112 directly elected every five years, and 28 nominated by the King). The Assembly elects the Prime Minister. Provision is made in the Constitution for a Raj Sabha (State Council) to watch over political affairs and advise the King in times of emergency.

Rashtriya Panchayat (National Assembly): Singha Durbar, Kathmandu; tel 212690.

Raj Sabha (Council of State): Singha Durbar, Kathmandu; tel 215318.

MINISTRIES AND GOVERNMENT DEPARTMENTS

OFFICE OF THE PRIME MINISTER
Cabinet Secretariat, Singha Durbar, Kathmandu
Tel 211555
Prime Minister: Marich Man Singh Shrestha

MINISTRY OF AGRICULTURE
Singha Durbar, Kathmandu
Tel 215832
Minister: Krishna Charan Shrestha

MINISTRY OF COMMERCE
Babar Mahal, Kathmandu
Tel 215064
Minister: (vacant)

MINISTRY OF COMMUNICATIONS
Singha Durbar, Kathmandu
Minister: (vacant)

MINISTRY OF DEFENCE
Singha Durbar, Kathmandu
Tel 216089
Minister: Marich Man Singh Shrestha

MINISTRY OF EDUCATION AND CULTURE
Kaiser Mahal, Kathmandu
Tel 414054
Minister: Parasu Narayan Chaudhari

MINISTRY OF FINANCE
Bagdurbar, Kathmandu
Tel 215099; telex 2249
Minister: Bharat Bahadur Pradhan

MINISTRY OF FOREIGN AFFAIRS
Singha Durbar, Kathmandu
Tel 215906; telex 2224
Minister: Shailendra Kumar Upadhayaya

MINISTRY OF HEALTH
Teku, Kathmandu
Tel 212733
Minister: Shushila Thapa

MINISTRY OF HOUSING AND PHYSICAL PLANNING
Singha Durbar, Kathmandu
Tel 227280
Minister: Prakash Chandra Lohani

MINISTRY OF INDUSTRY
Tripureshwor, Kathmandu
Tel 213492
Minister: (vacant)

MINISTRY OF LABOUR AND SOCIAL SERVICES
Singha Durbar, Kathmandu
Tel 215969
Minister: Lila Raj Bista

MINISTRY OF LAND REFORM AND MANAGEMENT
Singha Durbar, Kathmandu
Tel 212054
Minister: (vacant)

MINISTRY OF LAW AND JUSTICE
Babar Mahal, Kathmandu
Tel 220621
Minister: Badri Prasad Mandal

MINISTRY OF LOCAL SUPPLY
Kathmandu
Minister: (vacant)

MINISTRY OF PANCHAYAT AND LOCAL DEVELOPMENT
Shri Mahal, Lalitpur, Paten
Tel 521329
Minister: Prakash Bahadur Singh

MINISTRY OF ROYAL PALACE AFFAIRS
Kathmandu
Minister: Marich Man Singh Shrestha

MINISTRY OF TOURISM
Tripureshwar, Kathmandu
Tel 211286
Minister: Muhammad Mohsin

MINISTRY OF WATER RESOURCES
Babar Mahal, Kathmandu
Tel 215046; telex 2312
Minister: Hari Bahadur Basnet

MINISTRY OF WORKS AND TRANSPORT
Babar Mahal, Kathmandu
Tel 226537
Minister: (vacant)

OFFICE OF THE MINISTER OF STATE FOR FORESTS
Singha Durbar, Kathmandu
Tel 220160
Minister of State: Gagan Bahadur Singh

OFFICE OF THE MINISTER OF STATE FOR GENERAL ADMINISTRATION
Harihar Bhawan, Lalitpur, Patan
Tel 521083
Minister of State: Buddhi Man Tamang

OFFICE OF THE MINISTER OF STATE FOR HOME AFFAIRS
Singha Durbar, Kathmandu
Tel 215349
Minister of State: Niranjan Thapa

GOVERNMENT AGENCIES AND ORGANIZATIONS

Advisory and Supervisory Bodies

Election Commission: Bahadur Bhawan, Kathmandu; tel 226092; supervises elections.

Nepal Resettlement Co: Kathmandu; f 1963; engaged in resettling people from the densely-populated hill country to the western Terai plain.

Office of the Auditor-General: Babar Mahal, Kathmandu; tel 211035; Auditor-Gen: Nara Kanta Adhikary; Asst Auditor-Gen: Yadav Ranjan Baral; f 1959; audits the accounts of all Govt offices and fully Govt-owned corporate bodies.

Agriculture

Agriculture Inputs Corpn: Teku, Kuleswor, POB 195, Kathmandu; Chair: Prithu Narshing Rana; Gen Man: Narayan Bahadur Shrestha; Planning Chief: Amrit Man Tamrakar; f 1972; sole supplier of inputs for agricultural devt (procuring and distribution of chemical fertilizers, improved seeds, agricultural tools and plant protection material) at national level; operates seeds multiplication programmes (paddy, wheat, maize and vegetable); runs seed processing plants.

Dairy Development Corpn: Lainchaur, POB 838, Kathmandu; tel 411710; telex 2238; Gen Man: Dr Durga D. Joshi; f 1969; production and marketing of milk and milk products.

Jute Development and Trading Corpn: Old Airport, Biratnagar; tel 22208; telex 3010; Exec Chair: L. L. Shrestha; f 1974; jute devt and trading.

Business and Economy

BANKING

Agricultural Development Bank: Ramshah Path, Kathmandu; tel 211744; telex 2267; Chair and Gen Man: S. Krishna Upadhyaya; f 1968; 74% state-owned, 21% owned by the Nepal Rastra Bank (see below), and 5% by co-operatives and private individuals; specialized agricultural credit institution providing credit for agricultural devt to co-operatives, individuals and associations; receives deposits from individuals, co-operatives and other associations to generate savings in the agricultural sector; acts as Govt's implementing agency for small farmers' group devt project, assisted by the Asian Devt Bank and financed by the UN Devt Programme; operational networks include 14 zonal offices, 37 brs, 92 sub-brs, 52 depots and 160 small farmers' devt projects, 3 zonal training centres and 2 Appropriate Technology Units.

Nepal Bank Ltd: Dharma Path, Juddha Rd, POB 36, Kathmandu; tel 211185; telex 2220; Chair: Ishwori Lall Shrestha; Gen Man (acting): Biswambher Man Singh Pradhan; f 1937; 51% state-owned; 228 brs.

Nepal Rastra Bank: Lalita Niwas, Baluwatar, Kathmandu; tel 410158; telex 2207; Gov and Chair: Ganesh Bahadur Thapa Shrestha; f 1956; central bank and bank of issue; 9 brs.

Rastriya Banijya Bank (National Commercial Bank): Tangal, Kathmandu; tel 413884; telex 2247; Chair: Damodar Pd Gautam; Gen Man: Dr Laxman Bahadur Hamal; f 1966; 100% state-owned; 193 brs, 4 regional offices.

FINANCIAL AGENCY

Nepal Industrial Development Corpn (NIDC): NIDC Bldg, Durbar Marga, POB 10, Kathmandu; tel 228322; telex 2369; Gen Man: Ajit Narayan Singh Thapa; f 1959; holds investments in industrial enterprises; offers financial and technical assistance to private sector industries; grants loans.

INSURANCE

Rastriya Beema Sansthan (National Insurance Corpn): POB 527, Kathmandu; telex 2219; Gen Man: Nara Pratap; f 1967; sole insurer operating in Nepal.

NATIONALIZED INDUSTRY

Bansbari Leather and Shoe Factory Ltd: Bansbari, POB 227, Kathmandu; tel 414561; telex 2550; f 1965; production and sales of leather shoes, leather goods; hide tanning.

Brick and Tile Factory Ltd: Harisiddhi, Lalitpur, Kathmandu; tel 522776; telex 2524; Gen Man: J. P. Sharma; f 1969; manufacture of machine-made roofing and flooring tiles.

National Construction Co Ltd: POB 37, Kathmandu; tel 222326; Gen Man: Dr Ratna Lall Shreshtha; Dep Gen Mans: Lakshman Prasad Sharma (Technical), Keshab Kumar Subedi (General); f 1961; construction of highways, airports, bridges, dams, buildings, irrigation canals, etc.

TRADE

National Trading Ltd: Teku, POB 128, Kathmandu; tel 211962; telex 2211; Chair: Sher B. Pandey; Gen Man: G. M. Maskey; f 1962; imports and distributes construction materials and raw materials for industry, machinery, vehicles and consumer goods; operates bonded warehouse, duty-free shop and related activities; brs in all major towns.

Trade Promotion Centre: Pulchowk, Lalitpur, POB 825, Kathmandu; tel 524771; telex 2302; Gen Man: Bindu Dhoj Adhikary; f 1971; promotes exports to traditional and new markets abroad; carries out market research and product survey and devt; organizes participation in international trade fairs and exhibitions; information network.

Defence

Prahari Pradhan Karlaya (Police Headquarters): Naxal, Kathmandu; tel 411210.

Shahi Nepal Jangi Adda (Royal Nepalese Army): Tundikhel, Kathmandu; tel 211173; Chief of Staff: Gen Satchit Shumshere Rana.

Development and Planning

National Planning Commission (NPC): Singha Durbar, POB 1284, Kathmandu; tel 215936; Chair: the Prime Minister, Marich Man Singh Shrestha; Vice-Chair: Mohan Man Sainju; Sec: Dr Debya Deo Bhatt.

Legal and Judiciary

Office of the Attorney-General: Supreme Court Bldg, Ram Shah Path, Kathmandu; tel 211544; Attorney-Gen: Maghraj Bahadur Bista.

Sarbochha Adalat (Supreme Court): Supreme Court Bldg, Ram Shah Path, Kathmandu; tel 211811; Chief Justice: Dhanendra Bahadur Singh; holds appellate as well as original jurisdiction, and may function as a court of review; protects the fundamental rights of the people and guarantees the rule of law.

Media

BROADCASTING

Nepalese Television Corpn: Singha Durbar, POB 3826, Kathmandu; tel 228134; telex 2548; Gen Man: Neer Bikram Shah; Dep Gen Man: Rabindra S. Rana, f 1985; broadcasts four and a half hours daily; concentrates on programmes dealing with education, preservation of the national heritage, tradition, conservation and the protection of the environment.

Radio Nepal: Dept of Broadcasting, HM Govt of Nepal, Singha Durbar, POB 634, Kathmandu; tel 215773; telex 2590; Dir-Gen: B. P. Shah; Man Dir: P. M. S. Pradhan; f 1951; broadcasts in Nepali and English.

NEWS AND INFORMATION

Department of Information: Ministry of Communications, Singha Durbar, Kathmandu.

Mining and Energy

Nepal Bureau of Mines: Lainchour, Kathmandu.

Nepal Electricity Corpn: Tudikhel, Kathmandu.

Nepal Oil Corpn: Babar Mahal, POB 1140, Kathmandu; tel 214600; telex 2246; Chair: H. S. Shrestha; Gen Man: D. Thapa; Dep Gen Mans: J. P. Khanal, T. P. Pradhan; f 1971; import, storage and marketing of all kinds of petroleum products throughout Nepal.

Tourism

Department of Tourism: HM Govt of Nepal, Tripureshor, Kathmandu; tel 211293; Dir-Gen: Dipendra Purush Dhakal.

Transport and Communications

TELECOMMUNICATIONS

Nepal Telecommunications Corpn: Singha Durbar, Kathmandu; tel 215444; telex 2201; fax 226260; Gen Man: S. K. Pudasaini; Dep Gen Mans: R. Nepali, G. S. Bora, V. B. Bajracharya; f 1975; telecommunications services.

TRANSPORT

Nepal Government Railway: Birganj; Man: B. P. Pandey; f 1927; 48 km linking Raxaul to Amlekhganj.

Nepal Yatayat Sansthan (Nepal Transport Corpn): Teku, POB 309, Kathmandu; tel 222547; Chair: Govinda Prasad Ranjitkar; Gen Man: Anand Bahadur Shrestha; f 1965; controls the operation of road transport facilities, railways, ropeway, trucks, trolley buses and container services.

Royal Nepal Airlines Corpn: RNAC Bldg, Kanti Path, POB 401, Kathmandu; tel 220757; telex 2212; Exec Dir: T. B. Prasai; Gen Man: A. S. J. B. Rana; f 1958; 100% state-owned; scheduled services and charters to 37 domestic airfields and international flights.

THE NETHERLANDS

Head of State

The Netherlands is a constitutional and hereditary monarchy. The monarch, as Head of State, has mainly formal prerogatives, and executive power is exercised by the Council of Ministers, led by the Prime Minister, which is responsible to the Staten Generaal (States-General). The monarch appoints the Prime Minister and, on the latter's recommendation, other Ministers.

Queen of The Netherlands: HM Queen Beatrix Wilhelmina Armgard (succeeded to the throne 30 April 1980).

Office of the Queen: Paleis Noordeinde, POB 30412, 2500 GK The Hague.

Legislature

Legislative power is vested in the bicameral Staten Generaal (States-General). The Eerste Kamer (First Chamber) has 75 members indirectly elected for six years (half retiring every three years) by members of the 12 Provincial Councils. The Tweede Kamer (Second Chamber) has 150 members directly elected for four years on the basis of proportional representation. Each of the 12 provinces is administered by an appointed Governor and an elected council.

Eerste Kamer (First Chamber): Binnenhof 22, POB 20017, 2500 EA The Hague; tel (70) 62-45-71; Pres: Dr P. A. J. M. Steenkamp.

Tweede Kamer (Second Chamber): Binnenhof 1A, POB 20018, 2500 EA The Hague; tel (70) 18-22-11; telex 32653; Chair: Dr D. Dolman.

MINISTRIES AND GOVERNMENT DEPARTMENTS

OFFICE OF THE PRIME MINISTER
Binnenhof 20, POB 20001, 2500 EA The Hague
Tel (70) 61-40-31; telex 32473
Prime Minister: Rudolph Lubbers
Deputy Prime Minister: Wim Kok

MINISTRY OF AGRICULTURE AND FISHERIES
POB 20401, 2500 EK The Hague
Tel (70) 79-39-11; telex 32040
Minister: Gerrit Braks

MINISTRY OF DEFENCE
Plein 4, POB 20701, 2500 ES The Hague
Tel (70) 18-81-88; telex 31337
Minister: Relus ter Beek
State Secretary: Berend-Jan van Voorst

MINISTRY OF DEVELOPMENT CO-OPERATION
Bezuidenhoutseweg 67, POB 20061, 2500 EB The Hague
Tel (70) 48-64-86; telex 31326
Minister: Jan Pronk

MINISTRY OF ECONOMIC AFFAIRS
Bezuidenhoutseweg 30, POB 20101, 2500 EC The Hague
Tel (70) 79-89-11; telex 31099
Minister: Koos Andriessen
Secretary of State for Foreign Trade: Piet Bukman

MINISTRY OF EDUCATION AND SCIENCE
Europaweg 4, POB 25000, 2700 LZ Zoetermeer
Tel (79) 53-19-11; telex 32636; fax (79) 51-26-51
Minister: Dr J. M. M. Ritzen
Secretary of State: Jacques Wallage

MINISTRY OF EMPLOYMENT
Zeestraat 73, POB 20801, 2500 EN The Hague
Tel (70) 46-94-70; telex 31250
Minister: Bert de Vries

MINISTRY OF FINANCE
Korte Voorhout 7, 2511 VB The Hague
Tel (70) 76-77-67; telex 33141
Minister: Wim Kok
Secretary of State: Marius van Amelsvoort

MINISTRY OF FOREIGN AFFAIRS
Bezuidenhoutseweg 67, POB 20061, 2500 EB The Hague
Tel (70) 348-64-86; telex 31326; fax (70) 48-48-48
Minister: Hans van den Broek
Secretary of State for Europe: Piet Dankert

MINISTRY OF HOME AFFAIRS
Schedeldoekshaven 200, POB 20011, 2500 EA The Hague
Tel (70) 71-79-11; telex 32109
Minister: Ien Dales
Secretary of State: Dieuwke de Graaff-Nauta

MINISTRY OF HOUSING, PHYSICAL PLANNING AND THE ENVIRONMENT
Van Alkemadelaan 85, 2597 AC The Hague
Tel (70) 26-42-01; telex 34429
Minister: Hans Alders
Secretary of State for Housing: Enneüs Heerma

MINISTRY OF JUSTICE
Schedeldoekshaven 100, 2511 EX The Hague
Tel (70) 70-79-11; telex 34554; fax (70) 64-77-02
Minister: Ernst Hirsch Ballin
Secretary of State: Aad Kosto

MINISTRY OF SOCIAL AFFAIRS AND THE NETHERLANDS ANTILLES
Zeestraat 73, POB 20801, 2518 AA The Hague
Tel (70) 71-59-11; telex 31250
Minister: Bert de Vries
Secretary of State for Social Affairs: Elske ter Veld

MINISTRY OF TRANSPORT AND PUBLIC WORKS
Plesmanweg 1, POB 20901, 2500 EX The Hague
Tel (70) 51-61-71; telex 32562
Minister: Hanja Maij-Weggen

MINISTRY OF WELFARE, PUBLIC HEALTH AND CULTURAL AFFAIRS
Sir Winston Churchillaan 368, POB 5406, 2280 HK Rijswijk
Tel (70) 40-79-11; telex 31680; fax (70) 20-17-03
Minister: Hedy d'Ancona
Secretary of State for Public Health: Hans Simons

GOVERNMENT AGENCIES AND ORGANIZATIONS

Advisory and Supervisory Bodies

National Ombudsman: POB 29729, 2502 The Hague; tel (70) 89-89-89; fax (70) 60-75-72; Dirs: M. Oosting, N. A. M. Schipper; f 1982; acts as a control on the power of the state with regard to abuse of rights of the individual.

Social and Economic Council: Bezuidenhoutseweg 60, 2594 AW The Hague; tel (70) 49-94-99; telex 32377; fax (70) 83-25-35; Chair: Th. Quené; Sec-Gen: B. N. J. Pompen; f 1950; stimulates new devts in the economy, advises on social and economic policy.

Art and Culture

General State Archives of the Netherlands: POB 90520, 2509 LM The Hague; tel (70) 81-43-81; Chief Archivist: Dr F. C. J. Keklaar; f 1802; responsible for keeping central and local Govt records.

Business and Economy

BANKING

Bank voor Nederlandsche Gemeenten (BNG): Koninginnegracht 2, POB 30305, 2500 GH 's-Gravenhage; tel (70) 48-39-91; telex 31046; bank for the municipalities.

De Nationale Investeringsbank: Carnegieplein 4, 2517 HJ The Hague; telex 31368; f 1945; provides medium- and long-term credit for industrial and agricultural projects.

De Nederlandsche Bank NV: Westeinde 1, POB 98, 1000 AB Amsterdam; tel (20) 52-49-111; telex 11355; Pres: Dr W. F. Duisenberg; Sec: T. de Swaan; f 1814; nationalized 1948; bank of issue; 12 brs.

FINANCIAL AGENCIES

Netherlands Development Finance Co: Bezuidenhoutseweg 62, POB 93060, 2509 AB The Hague; tel (70) 41-96-41; telex 33042; fax (70) 47-17-33; Gen Man: Dr L. B. M. Mennes; f 1970; medium- and long-term loans and financing of technical assistance programmes through subsidies.

Rijks Munt (Royal Mint): Leidseweg 90, POB 2407, 3500 GK Utrecht.

TRADE

Centrale Dienst voor In- en Uitvoer (Commission for Imports and Exports): Engelse Kamp 2, POB 30003, 9700 RD Groningen; tel (50) 23-91-11.

Economische Voorlichtingsdienst—EVD (Netherlands Foreign Trade Agency): Bezuidenhoutseweg 151, 2594 AG The Hague; tel (70) 79-89-33; telex 31099; export promotion dept of the Ministry of Economic Affairs.

Interdepartementale Commissie voor Normalisatie en Certificatie (Commission for Standardization and Certification): Bezuidenhoutseweg 20, POB 20101, 2500 EC The Hague; tel (70) 79-66-25; telex 31099; fax (70) 47-40-81; Chair: C. Lemckert; Sec: T. W. A. Hummelink; f 1975; co-ordinates policy on standardization and certification.

Octrooiraad—Bureau voor de Industrieele Eigendom (Netherlands Patent Office): Patentlaan 2, POB 5820, 2280 HV Rijswijk; tel (70) 90-76-16; f 1912; responsible for the supervision and issue of patents.

Defence

Netherlands Defence Staff: Plein 4, The Hague; tel (70) 72-27-22; telex 31337; Chief of Defence Staff: C. de Jager.

Koninklijke Marine (Royal Netherlands Navy): Koningin Marialaan 17, 2595 GA The Hague; tel (70) 81-42-61; telex 31335; Chief of Staff: J. H. Hushof.

Landmachtstaf (Royal Netherlands Army): Thérèse Schwartzestraat 15, 2509 LS The Hague; tel (70) 73-57-35; Chief of Staff: J. G. Roos.

Royal Netherlands Air Force: Binckhorstlaan 135, POB 20703, 2500 ES The Hague; tel (70) 49-35-91; telex 31540; Chief of Staff: C. Baas.

Development and Planning

Central Planning Bureau: Van Stolweg 14, 2585 JR The Hague; tel (70) 51-41-51; fax (70) 50-58-47; Dir: Dr G. Zalm; f 1947; policy-oriented research of economic devts on macro-economic and sectoral level; forecasting activities.

Directoraat-Generaal voor Industrie en Regional Beleid: POB 20101, 2500 EC The Hague; tel (70) 79-89-11; telex 31099; fax (70) 79-75-47; Dir-Gen: M. C. van der Harst; promotion of Dutch industry and industrial policy.

Rijksplanologische Dienst (National Physical Planning Agency): POB 90618, 2509 LP The Hague; tel (70) 26-42-01; fax (70) 24-27-84; Dir-Gen: J. Witsen; preparation of national spatial policy.

Energy

Directoraat-General voor Energie: Bezuidenhoutseweg 30, POB 20101, 2500 EC The Hague; tel (70) 81-40-11; telex 31099; part of the Ministry of Economic Affairs; responsible for gas and electricity supply, and for nuclear power.

Elektriciteitsraad: Bezuidenhoutseweg 6, 2594 AV The Hague; tel (70) 81-40-11; electricity council; part of the Ministry of Economic Affairs.

Interdepartmental Committee on Nuclear Energy (ICK): Bezuidenhoutseweg 30, POB 20101, 2500 EC The Hague; tel (70) 79-89-11; telex 31099; f 1964; preparation of policy with regard to the peaceful use of nuclear energy.

Netherlands Energy Research Foundation (ECN): The Hague; tel (70) 51-45-81; telex 31459; Chair and Man Dir: Dr R. W. R. Dee; Scientific Dir: Dr J. F. V. D. Vate; research concerned with the whole field of energy supply.

The Environment

General-Directorate for Environmental Protection: Stamstraat 2, POB 450, 2260 MB Leidschendam; tel (70) 20-93-67; telex 32362; fax (70) 27-98-68; f 1972.

Health and Welfare

HEALTH

Directoraat-Generaal van de Volksgezondheid (General-Directorate for Public Health): POB 5406, 2280 HK Rijswijk; tel (70) 40-79-11; telex 31680; fax (70) 40-73-40.

Gezondheidsraad (Health Council of The Netherlands): POB 90517, 2509 LM The Hague; tel (70) 47-14-41; fax (70) 83-71-09; Pres: Dr L. Ginjaar; Vice-Pres: Dr E. Borst-Eilers; f 1901; advises the Govt on health care and environmental protection.

Nationale Raad voor de Volksgezondheid (National Council for Public Health): Gebouw Meerhorst III, Boerhaavelaan 1, POB 7100, 2701 AC Zoetermeer; tel (79) 51-76-44; fax (79) 51-08-81; Chair: J. P. M. Hendriks; Sec-Gen: Dr J. P. M. van der Wolf; f 1982; provides advice and information on health matters.

WELFARE

Directoraat-Generaal van de Volkshuisvesting (National Office of Housing Affairs): POB 3001, 2700 KA Zoetermeer; tel (79) 27-91-11; telex 31729; fax (79) 51-00-20; Dir: R. Spreekmeester: f 1988.

Ziekenfondsraad (ZFR): Prof J. H. Bavincklaan 2, 1123 AT Amsterdam; tel (20) 54-78-911; fax (20) 47-34-94; Chair: L. de Graaf; Sec-Gen: E. Brouwer; f 1949; sickness insurance council; supervises and controls the health boards; advises the Govt on health insurance.

International Affairs

Directoraat-Generaal Internationale Samenwerking (General Directorate for International Co-operation): Bezuidenhoutseweg 67, POB 20061, 2500 EB The Hague; tel (70) 48-64-86; telex 31326; fax (70) 48-48-48; Dir-Gen: Dr N. H. Biegman; Dep Dir-Gen: J. J. A. M. van Gennip; f 1964; formulation and implementation of policy on international devt co-operation.

Legal and Judiciary

De Hoge Raad der Nederlanden (Supreme Court): Kazernestraat 52, POB 20303, 2500 EH 's-Gravenhage; tel (70) 61-13-11; fax (70) 61-74-84; Chief Justice: Sjoerd Royer; Procurator-Gen: Jan Remmelink; Sec: W. J. C. M. van Nispen tot Sevenaer; f 1838; for appeals in cassation against decisions of courts of lower jurisdiction; as a court of first instance it tries offences committed in their official capacity by mems of the States-General and Ministers.

Raad van State (Council of State): Binnenhof 1, POB 20019, 2500 EA The Hague; tel (70) 62-48-71; fax (70) 65-13-80; Vice-Pres: W. Scholten; f 1531; ensures quality, balance and harmony in legislation and safeguards the legal status of the citizen against Govt interference.

Media

BROADCASTING

Nederlandse Omroepprogramma Stichting (NOS): POB 444, 1200 JJ Hilversum; tel (35) 77-92-22; telex 43312; Chair: J. P. van der Reijden; Vice-Chair: A. H. van den Hoevel; transmission of programmes of general interest and promotion of Dutch broadcasting interests.

GOVERNMENT PUBLISHER

Staatsdrukkerij-en Uitgeveribedrijf: Christoffel Plantijnstraat 2, POB 20014, 2515 TZ 'S Granenhage; tel (70) 378-99-11; telex 32486; fax (70) 385-27-89; Dirs: C. H. J. Peters, D. Koger; f 1988.

NEWS AND INFORMATION

Netherlands Central Bureau of Statistics: POB 959, 2270 AZ Voorburg; tel (70) 369-43-41; telex 32692; fax (70) 387-74-29; Dir-Gen: Dr W. Begeer; f 1899; collection, analysis and publication of statistics.

Science

Nationaal Instituut voor Kernfysica en Hoge-Energiefysica—NIKHEF (National Institute for Nuclear Physics and High-Energy Physics): Ooster Ringdijk 18, POB 4395, 1009 AJ Amsterdam; tel (20) 59-29-111; telex 11538; Man Dir: Dr J. Langelaar; Scientific Dir: Dr G. van Middelkoop.

Tourism

Nederlands Bureau voor Toerisme (Netherlands Board of Tourism): Vlietweg 15, 2266 KA Leidschendam; tel (70) 70-57-05; telex 32588; Dir-Gen: J. A. T. Cornelissen; f 1969.

Transport

Directorate-General of Maritime Affairs: Bordewijkstraat 4, 2288 EB Rijswijk; tel (70) 94-94-20; telex 31040; fax (70) 99-62-74; Dir-Gen: Dr J. van Tiel; f 1980; safeguards the competitive position of ships sailing under the Dutch flag, ensuring safety and regard for the environment; oversees the safety and smooth operation of marine traffic.

Nederlandse Spoorwegen: Moreelsepark 1, 3511 EP Utrecht; tel (30) 35-91-11; telex 47257; fax (30) 33-24-58; Pres: Dr L. F. Ploeger; f 1938; national railway co.

NETHERLANDS DEPENDENCIES

ARUBA

The Government

OFFICE OF THE GOVERNOR
Oranjestad
Governor: Felipe Tromp
The Governor, appointed by the crown, represents the monarch of the Netherlands and holds responsibility for external affairs and defence.

STATEN (PARLIAMENT)
Oranjestad
Speaker: (vacant)
The legislature is a unicameral Staten (Parliament) of 21 members, elected by universal adult suffrage for four years.

OFFICE OF THE PRIME MINISTER
Oranjestad
Prime Minister: Nelson O. Oduber
Deputy Prime Minister: Pedro P. Kelly
Executive power in domestic affairs is vested in a Council of Ministers (led by a Prime Minister), responsible to the Staten (Parliament).

MINISTRY OF ECONOMIC AFFAIRS, COMMERCE AND INDUSTRY
L. G. Smith Blvd 15, Oranjestad
Tel (8) 21181; telex 5191; fax (8) 34494
Minister: Daniel I. Leo

MINISTRY OF FINANCE
Oranjestad
Tel (8) 23237
Minister: Guillermo P. Trinidad

MINISTRY OF GENERAL AFFAIRS
Oranjestad
Minister: Nelson O. Oduber

MINISTRY OF JUSTICE
Oranjestad
Minister: Hendrik S. Croes

MINISTRY OF PUBLIC WORKS AND HEALTH
Oranjestad
Tel (8) 28355
Minister: Pedro P. Kelly

MINISTRY OF SOCIAL AFFAIRS AND EDUCATION
Oranjestad
Tel (8) 23360
Minister: Fredis J. Refunjol

MINISTRY OF TRANSPORT AND COMMUNICATIONS
Oranjestad
Minister: Euladio D. Nicolaas

OFFICE OF THE MINISTER PLENIPOTENTIARY OF ARUBA
Paleisstraat 6, 2519 JA The Hague, The Netherlands
Tel (70) 659824
Minister: Roland H. Laclé
Represents the Aruban Govt in the Govt of the Kingdom.

Government Agencies

ADVISORY AND SUPERVISORY BODY

Department of Economic Affairs, Trade and Industry: Blvd Center, Oranjestad; tel (8) 21181; telex 5191; fax (8) 34494; Dir: Humphrey van Trikt.

ART AND CULTURE

Biblioteca Nacional: Madurostraat 13, Oranjestad; tel (8) 21580; Dir: Alice von Romondt; national library.

BANKING

Aruban Investment Bank NV: Middenweg 20, Oranjestad; tel (8) 27327; telex 5053; fax (8) 27461; Pres: H. Mehran; Vice-Pres: L. Wong; f 1987; support of long-term investment, provision of investment banking services.

Centrale Bank van Aruba: Havenstraat 2, Oranjestad; tel (8) 23032; telex 5045; fax (8) 32251; Pres: E. den Dunnen; Exec Dir: J. H. G. Driessen; f 1985; central bank; supervisory body for banking system.

INTERNATIONAL AFFAIRS

Directie Buitenlandse Betrekkingen (Department of Foreign Affairs): Zoutmanstraat z/n, Oranjestad; tel (8) 34705; fax (8) 34660; Dir: Henry Baarh; f 1986; advises the Prime Minister on foreign affairs, promotes co-operation with other countries and international agencies.

INVESTMENT

Aruba Foreign Investment Agency: Ennia Bldg, Oranjestad; tel (8) 26070; telex 5010; fax (8) 22745; Dir: Dr Peter Palmen.

TOURISM

Aruba Tourism Authority: L. G. Smith Blvd 172, Oranjestad; tel (8) 23777; telex 5006; fax (8) 34702; Dir: Rory Arends; offices in North America, Latin America, Europe and Japan.

TRANSPORT

Aruba Ports Authority NV: L. G. Smith Blvd 68, Oranjestad; tel (8) 26633; telex 5120; Dir: M. H. Henríquez; Harbourmaster: P. C. Martinus; f 1981.

Compania Arubiano di Bus (Arubus) NV: Sabana Blanco 67, Oranjestad; tel (8) 27089; fax (8) 28633; Dir: E. Bremer; f 1979; public transport services.

NETHERLANDS ANTILLES

The Government

OFFICE OF THE GOVERNOR
Fort Amsterdam 2, Willemstad, Curaçao
Tel (9) 612000
Governor: Dr Rene A. Römer
The Governor, appointed by the Crown, represents the monarch of the Netherlands and has executive powers in external affairs, which he exercises in co-operation with the Council of Ministers.

STATEN (PARLIAMENT)
Wilhelminaplein 4, Curaçao
Tel (9) 612025
Speaker: J. A. O. Bikker
The Staten has 22 members elected by universal adult suffrage for four years. The administration of each island is conducted by an Island Council, an Executive Council and a Lieutenant-Governor.

OFFICE OF THE PRIME MINISTER
Fort Amsterdam 17, Willemstad, Curaçao
Tel (9) 613988; telex 1079
Prime Minister: Maria Ph. Liberia-Peters
Deputy Prime Minister: Louis Gumbs
Executive power in internal affairs is vested in the Council of Ministers, led by the Prime Minister, which is responsible to the Staten (Parliament).

OFFICE OF THE LIEUTENANT-GOVERNOR OF THE ISLAND TERRITORY OF BONAIRE
Bestuurskantoor, Kralendijk, Bonaire
Tel (7) 8330; telex 1292
Lieutenant-Governor: George Soleano

OFFICE OF THE LIEUTENANT-GOVERNOR OF THE ISLAND TERRITORY OF CURAÇAO
Concordiastraat 24, Willemstad, Curaçao
Tel (9) 612900; telex 1064
Lieutenant-Governor: Elmer Wilsoe

OFFICE OF THE LIEUTENANT-GOVERNOR OF THE ISLAND TERRITORY OF SABA
The Bottom, Saba
Tel (4) 3311; fax (4) 3274
Lieutenant-Governor: Wycliffe S. Smith

OFFICE OF THE LIEUTENANT-GOVERNOR OF THE ISLAND TERRITORY OF ST EUSTATIUS
Bestuurkantoor, Philipsburg, St Maarten
Tel (5) 2213; telex 8009
Lieutenant-Governor: G. R. Sleeswijk

OFFICE OF THE LIEUTENANT-GOVERNOR OF THE ISLAND TERRITORY OF ST MAARTEN
Administration Bldg, Clem Labega Sq, Philipsburg, St Maarten
Tel (5) 22233; telex 8009; fax (5) 24884
Lieutenant-Governor: Ralph R. H. Richardson

MINISTRY FOR DEVELOPMENT AND CO-OPERATION
Ansinghstraat 1, Curaçao
Tel (9) 611866; telex 1035; fax (9) 611268
Minister: Franklin Christiaan

MINISTRY OF ECONOMIC AFFAIRS
De Rouvilleweg 7, Willemstad, Curaçao
Tel (9) 626400; telex 123; fax (9) 627590
Minister: Cornelius Smits

MINISTRY OF EDUCATION
Schouwburgweg 24-26, Curaçao
Tel (9) 616033; fax (9) 618941
Minister: Ellis Woodley

MINISTRY OF FINANCE
Pietermaai 4-4A, Willemstad, Curaçao
Tel (9) 612052
Minister: Gilbert de Paula

MINISTRY OF HEALTH
Heelsumstraat, Willemstad, Curaçao
Tel (9) 614555
Minister: Louis Gumbs

MINISTRY OF JUSTICE
Fort Amsterdam, Willemstad, Curaçao
Tel (9) 612494; telex 1079
Minister: Ivo Knoppel

MINISTRY OF SOCIAL AND LABOUR AFFAIRS
Fort Amsterdam 17, Willemstad, Curaçao
Tel (9) 613988
Minister: Stanley Inderson

MINISTRY OF TRANSPORT AND COMMUNICATIONS
Fort Amsterdam 17, Willemstad, Curaçao
Tel (9) 613988; telex 1079
Minister: Louis Gumbs

OFFICE OF THE MINISTER PLENIPOTENTIARY FOR THE NETHERLANDS ANTILLES
Antillenhuis, Badhuisweg 173-175, 2597 JP The Hague, The Netherlands
Tel (70) 51-28-11
Minister: Edsel Jesurun
Represents the Antilles in the Govt of the Kingdom.

Government Agencies

BANKING

Bank van der Nederlandse Antillen (Bank of the Netherlands Antilles): Breedestraat 1, Willemstad, Curaçao; tel (9) 613600; telex 1155; Chair: D. Bakhuis; Pres: V. Servage; Dir: S. Betrian; f 1828; central bank; br in Philipsburg, St Maarten.

Ontwikkelingsbank van de Nederlandse Antillen: Willemstad, Curaçao; f 1981; provides long-term credit for export-orientated devt projects.

DEFENCE

Air Force: Curaçao; tel (9) 81622; Commdr: D. G. G. Margadant.

Marine Corps: Curaçao; tel (9) 641222; Commdr and Chief of Staff: W. H. W. van den Born.

National Guard: Van Leeuwenhoekstraat 11, Willemstad, Curaçao; tel (9) 623262; Commdr: G. H. Raven.

Navy: Parera, Curaçao; tel (9) 614222; Commdr: J. B. C. Clocquet.

INTERNATIONAL AFFAIRS

Department of Foreign Relations: Fort Amsterdam 4, Willemstad, Curaçao; tel (9) 613933; telex 1440; fax (9) 617123; Dir: Dr Eric Kleinmoedig; f 1973; deals with diplomatic and consular affairs, organization of protocol, co-ordinates activity with regard to the Caribbean Corpn.

LEGAL AND JUDICIARY

Joint High Court of Justice: Wilhelminaplein 4, Willemstad, Curaçao; tel (9) 634111; Chief Justice: Dr J. M. Saleh; the Chief Justice of the Joint High Court of Justice, its mems (a maximum of 20) and the Attorneys-General of the Netherlands Antilles and of Aruba are appointed for life by the monarch, after consultation with the Govts of the Netherlands Antilles and Aruba.

MEDIA

Antillaanse Televisie Mij NV (Antilles Television Co): Berg Arraret, POB 415, Willemstad, Curaçao; tel (9) 611288; telex 3332; Gen Man: J. Rofina; f 1960; operates Tele-Curaçao and cable service.

NEWS AND INFORMATION

Central Bureau of Statistics: Fort Amsterdam, Willemstad, Curaçao; tel (9) 611031; telex 1079; fax (9) 612348; Dir: S. H. Tecla; Dep Dir: R. Ph. Romer; f 1980; responsible for information on official statistics.

TOURISM

Bonaire Government Tourist Board: Kaya Simón Bolívar 12, Kralendijk, Bonaire; tel (7) 8322; telex 1292; fax (7) 8408; Dir: P. N. Tromp.

Curaçao Government Tourist Board: Schouwburgweg z/n, Willemstad, Curaçao; tel (9) 77232; telex 1185; Dir: Rafaelito C. Hato.

Saba Tourist Office: Windwardside, POB 527, Saba; tel (4) 62231; telex 8006; fax (4) 63274; Dir: Glenn Holm.

St Eustatius Tourist Bureau: Emmweg z/n, Oranjestad, St Eustatius, tel (3) 2433; telex 8080; Dir: James E. Maduro; Sec: Maxine A. J. Suares.

St Maarten Tourist Board: Cyrus Wathey Sq, Philipsburg, St Maarten; tel (5) 22337; Dir: Cornelius de Weever.

TRADE

Curaçao Chamber of Commerce and Industry: Kaya Junior Salas 1, POB 10, Curaçao; tel (9) 611451; telex 1055; fax (9) 615652; Pres: Robert G. Willems; Exec Sec: Michael A. A. Hellburg; f 1884; trade information and representation of industry and commerce.

Curaçao Industrial and International Trade Development Co (CURINDE) NV: Emancipatie Blvd 7, Landhuis Koningsplein, Curaçao; tel (9) 76000; telex 1459; fax (9) 371336; Man Dir: Dr C. J. T. Römer; Dep Dir: E. Smeulders; f 1980; evaluation of feasibility studies and devt of advisory recommendations; information service.

TRANSPORT

Antilliaanse Luchvaart Maatschappij—ALM (Antillean Airlines): Aeropuerto Internashonal Hato, Curaçao; tel (9) 81322; telex 1114; Pres: Kitland Chong; f 1964; internal services between Bonaire, Curaçao and St Maarten; external services to Aruba, Latin America, the Caribbean and the USA.

Windward Islands Airways International (WIA—Winair) NV: POB 288, Princess Juliana Airport, St Maarten; tel (5) 42568; fax (5) 44229; Pres: I. G. Romer; Chair: N. C. Wathey; f 1962; scheduled flights to Lesser Antilles and charter flights throughout eastern Caribbean.

Curaçao Drydock Co (CDM): Dokweg 1, Koningsplein, POB 3012, Willemstad, Curaçao; tel (9) 78333; telex 1107; fax (9) 79950; f 1959; ship repairs and conversions.

Curaçao Port Services NV: Curaçao Container Terminal, Rijks Eenheid Blvd, POB 170, Curaçao; tel (9) 615177; telex 3053; fax (9) 616536; Man Dir: K. J. O. Aster; Operations Man: C. R. Muskus; f 1982; national stevedores and terminal operators in the ports of Cuarçao.

NEW ZEALAND

Head of State

Executive power is vested in the British monarch, as Head of State, who is represented by a Governor-General. The Governor-General appoints the Prime Minister and, on the latter's recommendation, other Ministers. The Executive Council (Cabinet) advises the Governor-General and is responsible to the House.

Sovereign: HM Queen Elizabeth II (succeeded to the throne 6 February 1952).

Governor-General and Commander-in-Chief: Most Rev Sir Paul Alfred Reeves (took office 20 November 1985); to be replaced by Dame Catherine Tizard (20 November 1990).

Office of the Governor-General: Private Bag, Govt House, Wellington; tel (4) 898-055.

Legislature

Legislative power is vested in the Crown and the unicameral House of Representatives, comprising 97 members (including four Maoris) elected by universal adult suffrage for a three-year term.

House of Representatives: POB 18041, Wellington; tel (4) 719-199; Speaker: T. Kerry Burke; Chair of the Committees: John Terris.

MINISTRIES AND GOVERNMENT DEPARTMENTS

OFFICE OF THE PRIME MINISTER
Executive Wing, Parliament House, Wellington
Tel (4) 719-998; fax (4) 711-345
Prime Minister: Geoffrey W. R. Palmer
Minister Assisting the Prime Minister: Annette King
Ministers without Portfolio: Noel Scott, F. Gerbic, Ralph Maxwell

OFFICE OF THE DEPUTY PRIME MINISTER
Executive Wing, Parliament House, Wellington
Tel (4) 749-997
Deputy Prime Minister: Helen Clark

DEPARTMENT OF CONSERVATION
POB 10420, Wellington
Tel (4) 710-726; fax (4) 711-082
Minister: Philip T. E. Woollaston

DEPARTMENT OF HEALTH
POB 5013, Wellington
Tel (4) 727-627; telex 3571
Minister: Helen Clark
Associate Ministers: Dr Michael Cullen, Ken Shirley

DEPARTMENT OF JUSTICE
Private Bag, Wellington
Tel (4) 725-980; fax (4) 710-165
Minister: William P. Jeffries
Associate Ministers: Philip T. E. Woollaston, P. F. Dunne

DEPARTMENT OF LABOUR
POB 3705, Wellington
Tel (4) 737-800; telex 3441
Minister: Helen Clark
Associate Ministers: Dr Michael Cullen, Clive Matthewson

DEPARTMENT OF LANDS
POB 12162, Thorndon, Wellington
Tel (4) 710-828; fax (4) 725-816
Minister and Minister of Survey and Land Information: Peter W. Tapsell
Director-General (acting): I. D. Campbell

DEPARTMENT OF SCIENTIFIC AND INDUSTRIAL RESEARCH
POB 1578, Wellington
Tel (4) 729-979; telex 2553; fax (4) 724-025
Minister of Research, Science and Technology: Margaret Austin
Director-General: M. A. Collins
Advances, maintains and applies scientific and technical knowledge for the benefit of the country's economic and social devt

Ross Dependency Research Committee (RDRC): address as above; Chair: R. G. Norman; Sec: K. Carpinter; f 1958; advises the Minister of Research, Science and Technology on the organization and admin of New Zealand's activities in the Antarctic; co-ordinates and supervises these activities with reference to the country's scientific and technical research programme.

DEPARTMENT OF SOCIAL WELFARE
Private Bag 21, Wellington
Tel (4) 727-666; telex 025; fax (4) 726-873
Minister and Minister in charge of War Pensions: Dr Michael Cullen
Director-General: John Grant

DEPARTMENT OF STATISTICS
POB 2922, Wellington
Tel (4) 729-119; telex 31313
Minister: Margaret Shields

MINISTRY OF AGRICULTURE AND FISHERIES
101-103 the Terrace, POB 2526, Wellington
Tel (4) 720-367; telex 31532; fax (4) 744-244
Minister of Agriculture: J. R. Sutton
Minister of Fisheries: Ken Shirley
Associate Ministers of Agriculture: Ralph Maxwell,
Ken Shirley

MINISTRY OF ARTS AND CULTURE
Parliament Bldgs, Wellington
Telex 31042; fax (4) 725-924
Minister: Margaret Austin

MINISTRY OF BROADCASTING
Parliament Bldgs, Wellington
Telex 31042; fax (4) 725-924
Minister and Minister of Communications:
Jonathan L. Hunt

MINISTRY OF COMMERCE
Bowen State Bldg, Bowen St, POB 2847, Wellington
Tel (4) 720-030; telex 31530; fax (4) 712573
Minister: David J. Butcher
Associate Minister: Clive Mattewson

MINISTRY OF CONSUMER AFFAIRS
POB 1473, Wellington
Tel (4) 742-750; telex 31530
Minister: Margaret Shields

MINISTRY OF DEFENCE
Stout St, Wellington
Tel (4) 726-499; telex 3513; fax (4) 711-528
Minister: Peter W. Tapsell

MINISTRY OF DISARMAMENT AND ARMS CONTROL
Parliament Bldgs, Wellington
Telex 31042; fax (4) 725-924
Minister: Fran Wilde

MINISTRY OF EDUCATION
Private Box 1379, Wellington
Tel (4) 735-499; telex 31586; fax (4) 712-106
Minister: Philip B. Goff
Associate Ministers: Margaret Shields, Noel Scott

MINISTRY OF EMPLOYMENT
Parliament Bldgs, Wellington
Telex 31042; fax (4) 725924
Minister: Annette King
Associate Minister: Noel Scott

MINISTRY OF ENERGY
Lambton House, 152-172 Lambton Quay,
POB 2337, Wellington
Tel (4) 727-044; telex 31488; fax (4) 739-930
Minister: David J. Butcher
Associate Minister: Clive Matthewson

MINISTRY FOR THE ENVIRONMENT
84 Boulcott St, POB 10362, Wellington
Tel (4) 734-090; fax (4) 710-195
Minister: Geoffrey W. R. Palmer
Associate Minister: P. F. Dunne

MINISTRY OF EXTERNAL RELATIONS AND TRADE
Parliament Bldgs, Wellington
Telex 31042; fax (4) 725-924
Minister and Minister of Overseas Trade and Marketing: Michael K. Moore
Associate Ministers: Fran Wilde, Ralph Maxwell

MINISTRY OF FINANCE
POB 3724, Wellington
Tel (4) 722-733; telex 31198
Minister: David F. Caygill
Associate Minister and Minister of Revenue:
Peter Neilson

MINISTRY OF FOREIGN AFFAIRS
Private Bag, Wellington
Tel (4) 728-877; telex 3441
Minister: Michael K. Moore
Associate Minister: Fran Wilde

MINISTRY OF FORESTRY
POB 1610, Wellington
Tel (4) 721-569; fax (4) 722-314
Minister: J. R. Sutton
Associate Minister: Ken Shirley

MINISTRY OF HOUSING
Parliament Bldgs, Wellington
Telex 31042; fax (4) 725-924
Minister: Jonathan L. Hunt

MINISTRY OF INTERNAL AFFAIRS, LOCAL GOVERNMENT AND CIVIL DEFENCE
POB 805, Wellington
Tel (4) 738-699; telex 31134; fax (4) 711-914
Minister of Internal Affairs and Civil Defence:
Margaret Austin
Minister of Local Government: Philip T. E. Woollaston

Department of Internal Affairs: address as above; tel (4) 738-699; telex 31134; fax (4) 499-0544; Dir: Peter Boag; f 1840; constitutional, cultural, community and specialist commercial activities.

MINISTRY OF MAORI AFFAIRS
Parliament Bldgs, Wellington
Telex 31042; fax (4) 725-924
Minister: Koro T. Wetere

MINISTRY OF PACIFIC ISLAND AFFAIRS
35 Pipitea St, POB 833, Wellington
Tel (4) 734-493; fax (4) 734-301
Minister: Richard W. Prebble

MINISTRY OF POLICE AND IMMIGRATION
Parliament Bldgs, Wellington
Telex 31042; fax (4) 725-924
Minister of Police: Richard W. Prebble
Minister of Immigration: Annette King
Associate Minister of Immigration: F. Gerbic

MINISTRY OF RAILWAYS
Parliament Bldgs, Wellington
Telex 31042; fax (4) 725-924
Minister: Stanley J. Rodger

MINISTRY OF RECREATION AND SPORT
Parliament Bldgs, Wellington
Telex 31042; fax (4) 725-924
Minister: Peter W. Tapsell

MINISTRY OF REGIONAL DEVELOPMENT
Parliament Bldgs, Wellington
Telex 31042; fax (4) 725-924
Minister: P. F. Dunne

MINISTRY OF SCIENCE
Parliament Bldgs, Wellington
Telex 31042; fax (4) 725-924
Minister: Clive Matthewson

MINISTRY OF STATE OWNED ENTERPRISES
Parliament Bldgs, Wellington
Telex 31042; fax (4) 725-924
Minister: Richard W. Prebble
Associate Minister: Peter Neilson

MINISTRY OF STATE SERVICES
Parliament Bldgs, Wellington
Telex 31042; fax (4) 725-924
Minister: Clive Matthewson

MINISTRY OF TRANSPORT
38-42 Waring Taylor St, POB 3175, Wellington
Tel (4) 721-253; fax (4) 733-697
Minister and Minister of Civil Aviation and Meteorological Services: William P. Jeffries
Associate Minister of Transport, Civil Aviation and Meteorological Services: F. Gerbic

Air Transport Division: Aviation House, 1 Market Grove, Lower Hutt; tel (4) 600-400; fax (4) 692-024; Gen Man: Brian Lynch.

Land Transport Division: 225 Willis St, POB 27459, Upper Willis St, Wellington; tel (4) 828-300; fax (4) 737-902; Gen Man: Tim Sanger.

Maritime Transport Division: 275-281 Upper Cuba St, POB 27006, Wellington; tel (4) 828-198; fax (4) 829-065; Gen Man: Kevin Ward.

MINISTRY OF WOMEN'S AFFAIRS
32 the Terrace, POB 10049, Wellington
Tel (4) 734-112; fax (4) 720-961
Minister: Margaret Shields

MINISTRY OF WORKS AND DEVELOPMENT
Wellington
Minister: Peter Neilson

MINISTRY OF YOUTH AFFAIRS
Parliament Bldgs, Wellington
Telex 31042; fax (4) 725-924
Minister: Annette King

NEW ZEALAND TOURIST AND PUBLICITY DEPARTMENT
POB 95, Wellington
Tel (4) 728-860; telex 3491; fax (4) 781-736
Minister: Fran Wilde
Gen Man: W. N. Plimmer
Acts as New Zealand's national travel office; administers Govt assistance for tourism.

GOVERNMENT AGENCIES AND ORGANIZATIONS

Advisory and Supervisory Bodies

Audit Office: POB 3928, Wellington; tel (4) 724-979; fax (4) 712-929; f 1842; audits the financial statements of Govt depts, local authorities and most Govt-controlled corpns, boards and cos.

Government Property Services Ltd: POB 1690, Wellington; tel (4) 734-740; fax (4) 710-093; Chair: John Hodgetts; Gen Man: N. Sanders-Francis.

Higher Salaries Commission: 178-182 Willis St, POB 27024, Wellington; tel (4) 856-125; Chair: Prof J. Dunmore; Exec Officer: L. A. Shanks; Mems: J. T. F. Francis; G. L. Jackson; f 1974; determines salaries, allowances and superannuation rights of mems of Parliament and of the Judiciary, remuneration of statutory officers and of Chief Execs of local authorities; determines annual allowances payable to certain mayors and to Chairs of local authorities.

Iwi Transition Agency: Massey House, 126-132 Lambton Quay, Private Bag, Wellington; tel (4) 720-588; fax (4) 721-138; Minister in charge: Koro T. Wetere; Gen Man: Wira Gardiner; Asst Gen Mans: John Paki, Joan Fleming; f 1989; formed to transfer the functions of the now defunct Dept of Maori Affairs to the Maori tribal authorities.

Office of the Ombudsman: 4th Floor, Digital House, 163 The Terrace, POB 10152, Wellington; tel (4) 739-533; fax (4) 712-254; Chief Ombudsman: John F. Robertson; Ombudsman: Nadja Tollemache; f 1962; investigation of complaints involving central, local and regional Govt.

Parliamentary Service: Parliament Bldgs, Wellington; tel (4) 719-999; fax (4) 711-225; Gen Man: D. G. Brooks; Dep Gen Man: M. G. Gianotti; f 1985; replaced Legislative Dept; provides administrative and support services to Parliament.

Public Trust Office: POB 5024, Wellington; tel (4) 727-377; fax (4) 711-990; Public Trustee: W. B. R. Hawkins.

Securities Commission: POB 1179, Wellington 1; tel (4) 729-830; fax (4) 728-076; Chair: C. I. Patterson; Exec Dir: J. Farrell; f 1979; supervision of cos and securities markets.

Services Corpn New Zealand Ltd: POB 12041 Wellington.

State Services Commission: 100 Molesworth St, POB 329, Wellington; tel (4) 725-639; fax (4) 725-979; Chief Commr: D. Hunn; Commr: D. Swallow; f 1912; reviews the performance of Govt depts and Chief Execs; recommends the most suitable candidates for Chief Exec posts; advises on industrial relations and personnel policies.

Valuation New Zealand: Commercial Union House, 142 Featherston St, POB 5098, Wellington; tel (4) 738-555; fax (4) 738-552; Valuer-Gen: H. F. McDonald; Dep Valuer-Gen: K. J. Cooper; Asst Valuer-Gen: A. P. Pegler; f 1896; provides Govt valuations of every individual property in New Zealand on a three-yearly basis to be used by local authorities for rating and by the Inland Revenue Dept for taxation purposes; undertakes commercial market valuations for state and local Govt agencies and provides information and advice on the property market.

Agriculture and Fishing

AGRICULTURE

Land Corpn Ltd: POB 1790, Wellington; tel (4) 710-400; fax (4) 734-966; Chief Exec: G. McMillan; Sec: G. Muirhead; f 1987; established to own and manage previous Crown farms; provides services for investment and management of commercial, urban and rural properties; extensive farming operations.

New Zealand Dairy Board: Pastoral House, Lambton Quay, POB 417, Wellington 1; tel (4) 718-300; telex 3348; Chair: D. T. Spring; Sec: J. Murray; f 1961; statutory board of 14 mems.

New Zealand Forestry Corpn Ltd: The Terrace, POB 10310, Wellington 1; tel (4) 710-210; fax (4) 711-231; Man Dir: A. Kirkland; Sec: T. G. Simeoniois; f 1987; forest management; sawmilling; seed production; log exports; forest consultants.

New Zealand Kiwifruit Marketing Board: Downtown House, 21-29 Queen St, POB 3742, Auckland 1; tel (9) 799-913; telex 60058; Chief Exec: G. Simon M. Caughey.

New Zealand Pork Industry Board: POB 4048, Wellington;

tel (4) 728102; Chair: D. H. Lepper; Gen Man: D. J. Dobson; f 1937.

New Zealand Wool Board: 10 Brandon St, POB 3225, Wellington; tel (4) 726-888; telex 3472; Chair: P. G. Morrison; Man Dir: Dr J. E. Sinclair; assists research, devt, production and marketing of wool.

FISHING

New Zealand Fishing Industry Board: Private Bag, Manners St PO, Wellington; tel (4) 854-005; fax (4) 852-727; Chair: R. W. Stannard; Chief Exec: R. W. Dobson; f 1963; promotes the fishing industry and acts as a co-ordinator for the industry trade associations; represents the industry to Govt, Govt depts and other commercial and public bodies.

New Zealand Fishing Industry Inspection and Certification Council (FIICC): c/o New Zealand Fishing Industry Board, Private Bag, Manners St PO, Wellington; tel (4) 854-005; fax (4) 852-727; Chair: B. Cunningham; Man: A. R. Branson; f 1988; tripartite organization of industry, Fishing Industry Board and Govt which identifies and establishes industry-agreed standards for a variety of products and processes.

New Zealand Mussel Industry Council: c/o New Zealand Fishing Industry Board, Private Bag, Manners St PO, Wellington; tel (4) 854-005; fax (4) 854-005; Chair: A. R. Branson; Exec Sec: E. J. Phipps; f 1985; monitors the industry and makes recommendations on promotion, marketing and biological research requirements; promotes co-operation and communication between all sectors of the industry.

Art and Culture

National Library of New Zealand: 70 Molesworth St, POB 1467, Wellington; tel (4) 743-000; telex 30076; fax (4) 743-035; National Librarian: P. G. Scott; f 1965; collects, preserves and makes available recorded knowledge, particularly that relating to New Zealand.

Queen Elizabeth II Arts Council of New Zealand: Advisorcorp House, 131-137 Lambton Quay, POB 3806, Wellington; tel (4) 730-880; fax (4) 712-865; Chair: I. W. Cochrane; Dir: P. J. Quin; f 1963; promotion and research of the arts; provides training in, and finance for, the practice and appreciation of the arts.

Business and Economy

BANKING

Bank of New Zealand: BNZ Centre, 1 Willis St, POB 2392, Wellington; tel (4) 746-999; telex 3344; Chair: S. D. Pasley; Group Chief Exec and Man Dir: Lyndsay C. Pyne; f 1861; 87% Govt-owned, but became public co in March 1989.

Bank of New Zealand Savings Bank Ltd: BNZ Centre, 1 Willis St, POB 2392, Wellington; tel (4) 746-999; telex 3344; f 1964.

DFC New Zealand Ltd: POB 3090, Wellington; tel (4) 716-400; telex 30316; Man Dir: Murray R. Smith; Exec Dir: Keith G. Sutton; f 1964 as the Devt Finance Corpn of New Zealand; present name adopted in 1987; 80% owned by National Provident Fund, 20% by Salomon Brothers, New York; provides selected financial services to, and trade with, major corpns, businesses, Govts, banks and other financial institutions in New Zealand and abroad.

Reserve Bank of New Zealand: 2 The Terrace, POB 2498, Wellington 1; tel (4) 722-029; telex 3368; fax (4) 738-554; Gov: Dr Donald Brash; Dep Gov: R. L. Knight; Sec to Treasury: G. C.

Scott; central bank; advises Govt on monetary policy, banking, credit and overseas exchange; implements Govt monetary policy; acts as banker to the Govt; bank of issue.

Overseas Investment Commission: 2 The Terrace, POB 2498, Wellington 1; tel (4) 722-029; telex 3368; fax (4) 738-238; Sec: P. Tindill; Chair: R. W. Stannard; f 1973; considers whether overseas investment proposals are in the national interest and are compatible with Govt policy; advises Govt on matters relating to foreign investment in the country.

Rural Banking and Finance Corpn of New Zealand: 34-42 Manners St, POB 5046, Wellington; tel (4) 828-188; telex 31840; fax (4) 828-191; Chair: K. J. Macdonald; Man Dir: M. J. Bolton; f 1974; principal financier of the primary sector; offers investment facilities; money market operations.

FINANCIAL AGENCY

Inland Revenue Dept: 12-22 Hawkestone St, POB 2198, Wellington; tel (4) 721-032; fax (4) 732-817; Commr: David Henry; f 1953; administers the Inland Revenue Acts.

National Provident Fund: POB 606, Wellington; tel (4) 732-752; fax (4) 733-993.

Treasury: 1 The Terrace, POB 3724, Wellington; tel (4) 722-733; telex 31198; fax (4) 730-982; advises Govt on economic and financial matters; manages the Crown's flows of revenue and expenditure, public debt and overseas reserves held by the Treasury.

New Zealand Debt Management Office: POB 3724, Wellington; tel (4) 715-076; telex 30414; fax (4) 723-791; Treasurer: P. J. Duignan; f 1988; manages the fixed income portfolio of the Govt; manages the cash flow of the core public sector.

INSURANCE

State Insurance Office: Lambton Quay, POB 5037, Wellington 1; tel (4) 720-265; telex 31239; fax (4) 725-824; Gen Man: J. F. Stirton; f 1905.

MARKETING

Market Development Board: POB 10341, Wellington; tel (4) 734-452; telex 31825; fax (4) 733-193.

TRADE

Commerce Commission: POB 2351, Wellington; tel (4) 710-180; fax (4) 710-771; Chair: J. G. Collinge; f 1986; administers the Commerce and Fair Trading Acts which prevent restrictive trade practices, scrutinize mergers and takeovers, consolidate laws on misleading advertising, prohibit deceptive or misleading conduct and false representations about the provision of goods and services, prohibit certain unfair trading practices, etc.

Customs Department: POB 2218, Wellington; tel (4) 736-099; telex 31213; fax (4) 721-092; Minister: Peter Neilson; Comptroller of Customs: M. W. Taylor; f 1840; admin of customs tariff; protection of borders; collection of customs and excise duties.

Export Import Corpn of New Zealand: POB 11332, Wellington; tel (4) 738-110; telex 31081; fax (4) 731-714; Chair: A. P. van Heeren; Chief Exec: Alistair M. S. Davis.

New Zealand Patent Office: Levin House, 330 High St, Private Bag, Lower Hutt; tel (4) 694-400; Commr of Patents: H. Burton; f 1883; administers Patents, Trade Marks and Designs Acts.

New Zealand Trade Development Board: Pastoral House, 25 The Terrace, POB 10341, Wellington 6001; tel (4) 499-2244;

telex 31507; fax (4) 733-193; Chair: Peter Shirtcliffe; Chief Exec: Eric Millar; f 1988; fosters the devt and expansion of foreign exchange earnings by maintaining a network of trade commrs in significant overseas markets; works with sectoral groupings of cos on co-operative market devt programmes; provides strategic input and analysis into planning export business activity.

Standards Association of New Zealand: Private Bag, Wellington; tel (4) 842-108; telex 3850; fax (4) 843-938; Chair: G. B. Tait; Chief Exec: D. R. M. Pinfold; f 1932; national standards body.

Defence

New Zealand Fire Service Commission: Willbank House, 57 Willis St, POB 2133, Wellington; tel (4) 724-969; fax (4) 781-603; Chair: Fraser Colman; Fire Commrs: B. F. Hyland, B. S. Armstrong; f 1975; controls the New Zealand Fire Service.

New Zealand Police: Police National Headquarters, POB 3017, Wellington; tel (4) 749-499; telex 3550; fax (4) 732-699; Commr of Police: M. T. Churches; Dep Commr: J. J. Jamieson; f 1886.

Royal New Zealand Air Force: Defence Headquarters, Private Bag, Wellington; tel (4) 726-499; telex 3513; fax (4) 711-528; Chief of Staff: Air Vice-Marshal David Manson Crooks.

Royal New Zealand Army: Defence Headquarters, Private Bag, Wellington; tel (4) 726-499; telex 3513; fax (4) 711-528; Chief of the Defence Staff: Air Marshal Sir David Ewan Jamieson; Chief of Staff: Maj-Gen John Airth Mace.

Royal New Zealand Navy: Defence Headquarters, Private Bag, Wellington; tel (4) 726-499; telex 3152; fax (4) 726-499; Chief of Staff: Rear-Adm Cedric John Steward.

Development and Planning

Maori Development Corpn: POB 9845, Newmarket, Auckland; tel (9) 50682; Chair: W. Ward-Holmes; Chief Exec: R. E. Mead; f 1987 to provide finance for Maori-owned enterprises.

New Zealand Planning Council: 107 Customhouse Quay, POB 5066, Wellington; tel (4) 724-250; fax (4) 732-514; Chair: Prof Gary Hawke; Dep Chair: Jill Holt; Dir: Peter J. Rankin; f 1977; monitors economy, population, income distribution, social policy, Maori devt, forecasting, employment and the environment.

Health and Welfare

HEALTH

Alcoholic Liquor Advisory Council: National Insurance House, 119-123 Featherston St, POB 5023, Wellington; tel (4) 720-997; fax (4) 730-890; Chair: A. C. Shailes; Chief Exec: K. R. Evans; f 1977; promotes moderation in the use of alcohol; advises on the effects of alcohol use and misuse and encourages devts in health education, treatment and research in relation to alcohol use.

WELFARE

Accident Compensation Corpn: Shamrock House, cnr Molesworth and Hawkestone St, POB 242, Wellington; tel (4) 738-775; fax (4) 711-688; Chair: C. A. N. Beyer; Man Dir: J. T. Chapman; Dep Man Dirs: V. M. Morel, S. J. Anderson; f 1974; administers a comprehensive, no-fault social insurance scheme for victims of unintentional injury; promotes injury prevention throughout the country and helps injured persons by providing

them with rehabilitation assistance and financial compensation.

Housing Corpn of New Zealand: POB 5009, Wellington; tel (4) 721-294; telex 31665; fax (4) 723-152; Dir-Gen: Robert A. Carter; f 1974; advises the Govt on housing and implements Govt policies; helps provide acceptable and affordable housing; largest combined home lender, property developer and landlord.

Human Rights Commission: Lambton Quay, POB 5045, Wellington; tel (4) 739-981; fax (4) 710-858; Chief Commr: Margaret Mulgan; f 1977; set up under the Human Rights Commission Act to promote, by education and publicity, respect for and observance of human rights in New Zealand and to deal with complaints of discrimination.

Legal and Judiciary

Court of Appeal: cnr Molesworth and Aitken Sts, Wellington; tel (4) 727-307; fax (4) 734-147; Pres: Sir Robin Brunskill Cooke.

Crown Law Office: POB 5012, Wellington; tel (4) 721-719; fax (4) 733-482; Solicitor-Gen: John McGrath.

High Court: POB 1091, Wellington; tel (4) 727-307; fax (4) 734-537; Chief Justice: Sir Thomas Eichelbaum; Registrar and Sheriff: J. D. Earles; Attorney-Gen: David R. Lange.

Media

BROADCASTING

Radio Frequency Service: c/o Ministry of Commerce, Bowen State Bldg, Bowen St, POB 2847, Wellington; advisory role; advises Govt on frequency allocations.

Radio New Zealand Ltd: Aurora House, The Terrace, POB 2092, Wellington; tel (4) 741-500; telex 31031; fax (4) 741-440; Chief Exec: Beverley A. Wakem; f 1988; operates three non-commercial networks and 32 commercial community stations in New Zealand, and directs a service to the South Pacific.

Television New Zealand Ltd: Television Centre, cnr Hobson and Victoria Sts, POB 3819, Auckland; tel (9) 770630; telex 60056; Dir-Gen and Chief Exec: Julian Mounter; f 1980; responsible for the production of programmes for the two TV networks and for the sale of all local productions; both networks transmit morning, afternoon and evening, seven days a week.

GOVERNMENT PUBLISHER

Government Printing Office: Private Bag, Wellington; tel (4) 737-320; telex 31370; fax (4) 734-943; Govt Printer: V. R. Ward; Dir of Publs: J. F. Seymour; f 1864; printing, binding, publishing, stationery supplies.

NEWS AND INFORMATION

Information Authority: POB 10351, Wellington; tel (4) 725-639; Chair: Alan Danks; Chief Exec: A. J. Salt.

Mining and Energy

Coal Corpn of New Zealand Ltd: 17-21 Dixon St, POB 439, Wellington; tel (4) 856-784; telex 31341; fax (4) 854-703; Chief Exec: Ron Janes; f 1987; coal mining and marketing.

Electricity Corpn of New Zealand Ltd: Rutherford House, 23 Lambton Quay, POB 930, Wellington; tel (4) 723-550; telex 3592; fax (4) 737-091; Chair of Board: John Fernyhough; Chief Exec: Dr Roderick Deane; f 1987, fmrly Electricity Division of

Ministry of Energy until it became a state-owned enterprise; electricity supply, production, transmission and marketing.

Research

Medical Research Council: POB 5541, Auckland; tel (9) 798-227; fax (9) 779-988.

Science and Technology

Department of Survey and Land Information: POB 170, Wellington; tel (4) 735-022; fax (4) 722-244; Dir-Gen and Surveyor-Gen: W. A. Robertson; f 1987; computer mapping, photogrammetry, surveying, draughting and land information products and services.

GCS Ltd: Equicorp House, South Tower, 68-86 Jervois Quay, POB 3055, Wellington; tel (4) 738-821; fax (4) 711-223; Chief Exec: Mike Foden; Sec: Brian Chapman; f 1988, fmrly Govt Computing Service; software devt, communication services, consultancy services, financial management systems, etc.

Tourism

Tourist Hotel Corpn of New Zealand: Level 28, Plimmer City Centre, Plimmer Lane, Wellington 1; tel (4) 729-179; telex 3488; fax (4) 734-844; Chief Exec: Mike Hoy; f 1955; resort and city hotel operators.

Transport and Communications

TELECOMMUNICATIONS

New Zealand Post Ltd: 7-27 Waterloo Quay, Wellington; tel (4) 738-498; fax (4) 710-468; Man Dir: Harvey C. Parker; f 1987; operates letter and parcel mail delivery services nationally and internationally; issues postage stamps and conducts a philatelic business.

Telecom Corpn of New Zealand Ltd: POB 570, Wellington; tel (4) 823-333; fax (4) 846-377.

TRANSPORT

Airways Corpn New Zealand Ltd: Airways House, POB 294, Wellington; tel (4) 711-888; fax (4) 710-395; Chief Exec: Frank Baldwin; Sec: Terry O'Regan; f 1987; statutory monopoly to provide air traffic advisory services in national and international (Oceanic) airspace, encompassing area control, approach control and flight information services.

National Roads Board: Vogel Bldg, Aitken St, POB 12446, Wellington; tel (4) 717-351; fax (4) 733-339; Chair: Minister of Transport, William P. Jeffries; Dir: Ron Fisher; f 1953; construction, maintenance and control of state highways and motorways; subsidizes road works; 10 mems nominated to represent various interests; advised by District Roads Councils.

New Zealand Railways Corpn: Private Bag, Wellington; tel (4) 725-599; telex 3996; fax (4) 712-491; Chief Exec: K. O. Hyde; f 1982; provides a network of freight and passenger services throughout the North and South Islands of New Zealand; also operates a rail ferry service between the two islands.

NEW ZEALAND'S ASSOCIATED TERRITORIES

COOK ISLANDS

The Government

OFFICE OF THE QUEEN'S REPRESENTATIVE
Avarua, Rarotonga
Queen's Representative: Sir Tangaroa Tangaroa
Official representative of the Head of State, the British monarch.

**OFFICE OF THE NEW ZEALAND
REPRESENTATIVE**
Avarua, Rarotonga
New Zealand Representative: Adrian Sincock
Representative of the New Zealand Govt.

HOUSE OF ARIKI
Avarua, Rarotonga
President: Pa Tepaeru Ariki (Lady Davis)
Comprises up to 15 mems who are hereditary chiefs; can advise the Govt, but has no legislative powers.

PARLIAMENT
Avarua, Rarotonga
Speaker: David Hosking
Formed of 24 mems, elected by universal adult suffrage every five years.

**OFFICE OF THE PRIME MINISTER, AND
MINISTRY OF FINANCE, FOREIGN AFFAIRS,
TOURISM, CUSTOMS, INLAND REVENUE,
DEVELOPMENT PLANNING, CROWN LAW,
PUBLIC WORKS, LEGISLATIVE SERVICE AND
ARTS AND CULTURE**
Avarua, Rarotonga
Prime Minister: Geoffrey A. Henry
Deputy Prime Minister: Inatio Akaruru

**MINISTRY OF AGRICULTURE, MARINE
RESOURCES, TRADE, LABOUR, INDUSTRY AND
TRANSPORT**
Avarua, Rarotonga
Minister: Vaine Tairea

**MINISTRY OF EDUCATION, CIVIL AVIATION,
CORRECTIVE SERVICES AND THE PUBLIC
SERVICE COMMISSION**
Avarua, Rarotonga
Minister: Ngereteina Puna

**MINISTRY OF ENERGY, IMMIGRATION, THE
POLICE AND THE ELECTORAL OFFICE**
Avarua, Rarotonga
Minister: Inatio Akaruru

**MINISTRY OF HEALTH, INTERNAL AFFAIRS,
LOCAL GOVERNMENT AND HOUSING**
Avarua, Rarotonga
Minister: Kura Strickland

**MINISTRY OF POST AND
TELECOMMUNICATIONS, CONSERVATION AND
FOR THE HOUSE OF ARIKI AND KOUTU NUI**
Avarua, Rarotonga
Minister: Teanua Kamana

**MINISTRY OF YOUTH, SPORTS, INFORMATION
SERVICES, SURVEY AND JUSTICE**
Avarua, Rarotonga
Minister: Tiki Matopo

Government Agencies

BANKING

Cook Islands Development Bank: POB 113, Rarotonga; tel 29341; telex 62080; Gen Man: Unakea Kauvai; f 1978 to replace National Devt Corpn and Housing Corpn; finances devt projects in all areas of the economy and helps islanders establish small businesses and industries by providing loans and management advisory assistance.

BROADCASTING

Cook Islands Boradcasting Corpn: POB 126, Avarua, Rarotonga; f 1989 to operate new TV service and radio service of former Broadcasting and Newspaper Corpn.

Cook Islands TV: f 1989; programmes provided by Television New Zealand.

Radio Cook Islands: tel 20100; Gen Man: Arthur Taripo; broadcasts in English and Maori.

CIVIL AVIATION

Cook Islandair: Rarotonga; tel 26304; fax 23300; owned by Air New Zealand and the Cook Islands Govt; operates an internal cargo and passenger service between Rarotonga, Mauke, Aitutaki, Mitiaro, Mangaia and Atiu.

Cook Islands International: 50 King St, Sydney, NSW 2000, Australia; telex 20143; Chair: Tuingariki Short; Man: Ted Krasek; f 1986; owned by Cook Islands Govt, but operated by Anselt Airlines (Australia).

LEGAL AND JUDICIARY

Department of Justice: POB 111, Avarua, Rarotonga; tel 29410; fax 29610; Chief Justice of the High Court: Sir Clinton Marcus Roper; the High Court exercises jurisdiction in respect of civil, criminal and land titles cases; the Court of Appeal hears appeals against decisions of the High Court.

NEWS AND INFORMATION

Cook Islands News: POB 126, Avarua, Rarotonga; tel 21907; telex 62006; Editor: Alexander Sword; f 1954; Govt-owned daily.

Statistics Office: POB 125, Rarotonga; tel 29390.

TOURISM

Cook Islands Tourist Authority: POB 14, Rarotonga; tel 29436; telex 62054; fax 21435; Dir: Chris Wong; f 1968; national tourist office; tourism policy and planning; licensing of all accommodation and restaurants.

NIUE

The Government

OFFICE OF THE NEW ZEALAND REPRESENTATIVE
Govt Bldg, Main St, Alofi
New Zealand Representative: John Springford
Represents New Zealand Govt.

OFFICE OF THE PREMIER
Govt Bldg, Main St, Alofi
Premier: Sir Robert Rex

MINISTRY OF AGRICULTURE AND FISHERIES
Govt Bldg, Main St, Alofi
Minister: Dr Enetama Lipitoa

MINISTRY OF EDUCATION, COMMUNITY AFFAIRS AND HEALTH
Govt Bldg, Main St, Alofi
Minister: Frank Fakaotimanava Lui

MINISTRY OF FINANCE
Govt Bldg, Main St, Alofi
Minister: Dr Enetama Lipitoa

MINISTRY OF PUBLIC SERVICES AND POLICE
Govt Bldg, Main St, Alofi
Minister: Sir Robert Rex

MINISTRY OF WORKS, ADMINISTRATIVE SERVICES, POSTS AND TELECOMMUNICATIONS
Govt Bldg, Main St, Alofi
Minister: Robert R. Rex, Jr

OFFICE OF ECONOMIC AFFAIRS
Govt Bldg, Main St, POB 42, Alofi
Tel 131; telex 67014
Minister for Economic Affairs: Sir Robert Rex
Director: Toke T. Talagi
F 1984; promotes and develops tourism; assists with the devt of local and overseas markets; promotes the devt and establishment of business activities; advises Govt on aviation and shipping policies.

Government Agencies

BROADCASTING

Radio Sunshine and Television Niue: Broadcasting Corpn of Niue, POB 23, Alofi; telex 67014; Chief Exec: Hima Douglas; broadcasts in Niuean and English.

NEWS AND INFORMATION

Tohi Tala Niue: Broadcasting Services, Dept of Community Affairs, POB 23, Alofi; telex 67014; weekly; English and Niuean.

TOKELAU

The Government

OFFICE OF THE ADMINISTRATOR
Tokelau
Administrator: H. H. Francis
Administration of Tokelau is the responsibility of the Minister of Foreign Affairs of New Zealand, who is empowered to appoint an Administrator to the territory.

OFFICE FOR TOKELAU AFFAIRS
POB 865, Apia, Western Samoa
Tel 20822
Official Secretary: Casimilo J. Perez

Most of the Administrator's powers are delegated to the Official Secretary.

Government Agencies

UTILITIES

Tokelan Public Service: Tokelau; services the islands.

NICARAGUA

Head of State

Executive power is vested in the President, who is elected by universal adult suffrage for a six-year term. The President is assisted by a Vice-President and an appointed Cabinet.

President: Commdr Daniel Ortega Saavedra (took office 10 January 1985).

President-Elect: Violeta Barrios de Chamorro (elected 25 February 1990; due to take office 25 April 1990).

Vice-President: Dr Sergio Ramírez Mercado.

Office of the President and of the Vice-President: Casa de Gobierno, Apdo 2398, Managua, JR; tel (2) 27381.

Legislature

Legislative power is vested in the 96-member Asamblea Nacional (National Assembly). Its members are elected by universal adult suffrage, on the basis of proportional representation, for six years.

Asamblea Nacional (National Assembly): Frente al Parque Luis Alfonso Velasquez, Apdo 4659, Managua, JR; tel (2) 25939; telex 1214; fax (2) 25789; Pres: Commdt Carlos Núñez Téllez; Sec-Gen: Rafael Solís Cerda; f 1985.

MINISTRIES AND GOVERNMENT DEPARTMENTS

MINISTRY OF AGRICULTURAL DEVELOPMENT AND AGRARIAN REFORM
Km 8, Carretera a Masaya, Managua, JR
Tel (2) 97211
Minister: Commdr Jaime Wheelock Román

MINISTRY OF CONSTRUCTION, TRANSPORT AND HOUSING
Km 5, Carretera Norte, Managua, JR
Tel (2) 43104
Minister: Commdr Mauricio Valenzuela Sotomayor

MINISTRY OF ECONOMY, INDUSTRY AND COMMERCE
Frente a Camino de Oriente, Apdo 2412, Managua, JR
Tel (2) 70176; telex 2410; fax (2) 70095
Minister: Commdr Luis Carrión Cruz

MINISTRY OF EDUCATION
Complejo Cívico 'Camilo Ortega Saavedra', Managua, JR
Tel (2) 50051
Minister: Padre Fernando Cardenal Martínez

MINISTRY OF FINANCE
Palacio de Héroes y Mártires de la Revolución, Apdo 28, Managua, JR
Tel (2) 27231; telex 1213; fax (2) 27714
Minister: William Huper Argüello

MINISTRY OF FOREIGN AFFAIRS
Detrás de 'Los Ranchos', Managua, JR
Tel (2) 96563
Minister: Padre Miguel d'Escoto Brockmann

MINISTRY OF FOREIGN CO-OPERATION
Apdo 4595, Managua, JR
Tel (2) 61796; telex 1367
Minister: Commdr Henry Ruiz Hernández

MINISTRY OF HEALTH
Complejo Cívico 'Camilo Ortega Saavedra', Managua, JR
Tel (2) 50039
Minister: Dora María Téllez Argüello

MINISTRY OF THE INTERIOR
Apdo 68, Managua, JR
Tel (2) 27531
Minister: Commdr Tomás Borge Martínez
First Deputy Minister: Lenin Cerna Suárez

MINISTRY OF LABOUR
Frente donde fue la Cruz Roja, Managua, JR
Tel (2) 25729
Minister: Benedicto Meneses Fonseca

MINISTRY OF NATIONAL DEFENCE
'El Chipote', Complejo Germán Pomares, Managua, JR
Tel (2) 27261; telex 1369
Minister: Gen Humberto Ortega Saavedra
Deputy Minister: Maj-Gen Joachim Cuadra

MINISTRY OF PLANNING
Entrada Colegio 'Rigoberto López Pérez', Apdo 4596, Managua, JR
Tel (2) 75206
Minister: Alejandro Martínez Cuenca

MINISTRY OF THE PRESIDENCY
Casa de Gobierno, Managua, JR
Minister: René Núñez Téllez

MINISTRY OF PRESS AND INFORMATION
Managua, JR
Minister: Manuel Espinoza Hernández

MINISTRY OF SOCIAL WELFARE
Km 7, Carretera Sur, Managua, JR
Tel (2) 50161
Minister: Reinaldo Antonio Téfel

MINISTRY OF TOURISM
Avda Bolívar Sur, Apdo 122, Managua, JR
Tel (2) 24334; telex 1299; fax (2) 25314
Minister: Herty Lewites
Deputy Minister: Octavio Caldera

GOVERNMENT AGENCIES AND ORGANIZATIONS

Agriculture and the Environment

AGRICULTURE

Empresa Nacional de Agromecanización (AGROMEC): Apdo 323, Managua, JR; mechanization of agriculture.

Instituto Nicaragüense de Reforma Agraria (INRA): Km 8, entrada a Sierrita Santo Domingo, Managua, JR; tel (2) 73210; Dir: Minister of Agricultural Development and Agrarian Reform, Jaime Wheelock Román; agency promoting agrarian reform.

THE ENVIRONMENT

Dirección de Recursos Naturales y del Ambiente (DIRENA): Km 12, Carretera Norte, Managua; tel (2) 31110; telex 1328; fax (2) 31274; Dir: Jairo Rodríguez Blandino; f 1979; conservation and devt of natural resources.

FISHING

Corporación Nicaragüense de la Pesca (Nicaraguan Fishing Corpn): Km 6, Carretera Sur, Managua; tel (2) 52017; telex 1309; fax (2) 52000; Exec Pres: Francisco Lacayo Barbarena; Dir, Commercial: Felix Parrales S.; f 1980; processing of lobster and prawns, promotion of fish products.

Business and Economy

BANKING

Banco de América (BAMER): Avda Sandino y 4a Calle Sur Este, Apdo 285, Managua, JR; tel (2) 26100; telex 1040; Exec Dir: Antonio Medrano B.; f 1952; 47 brs.

Banco Central de Nicaragua: Carretera Sur, Km 7, Apdos 2252/3, Managua, JR; tel (2) 50500; telex 2460; fax (2) 52272; Pres: Joaquín Cuadra Chamorro; Vice-Pres: Roberto Gutiérrez H.; f 1961; bank of issue and Govt fiscal agent.

Banco Inmobiliario (BIN): Calle Principal Colonia Centroamérica, Apdo 1162, Managua, JR; Exec Dir: Luis Angel Montenegro E.; f 1980; savings bank and housing funding.

Banco Nacional de Desarrollo (BND): Km 3, Carretera a Masaya, Apdo 328, Managua, JR; tel (2) 71771; telex 1067; Pres: Anredo Alaniz Downing; Exec Dir: Porfirio J. Gómez; f 1912; 108 brs.

Banco Nicaragüense (BANIC): Centro Financiero Oscar Pérez Cassar, Km 5, Carretera a Masaya, Apdo 549, Managua, JR; tel (2) 72730; telex 1305; Exec Dir: Angel Enrique Ramírez Gómez; f 1953; 27 brs.

Banco Popular: Contiguo Parque El Carmen, Apdo 3904, Managua, JR; tel (2) 666648; fax (2) 22238; Exec Dir: Jaime García G.; f 1972 as autonomous state institution to promote

savings and provide bank loans to small enterprises and low income workers and employees.

FINANCIAL AGENCIES

Contraloría General de la República: Palacio de la Revolución, Apdo 48, Managua; tel (2) 26466; telex 1213; Comptroller-Gen: Emilio Baltodano Pallais; f 1979; supervises and controls the use of public funds; took over the functions of the Superintendencia de Bancos in 1981.

Corporación Financiera de Nicaragua (CORFIN): Edif Oscar Pérez Cassar 1°, Km 4, Carretera a Masaya, Apdo 53, Managua, JR; tel (2) 72107; telex 1090; Dir-Gen: Fernando Guzmán Cuadra; f 1980; Nicaraguan Finance Corpn.

INSURANCE

Instituto Nicaragüense de Seguros y Reaseguros (INISER): Centro Comercial Camino de Oriente, Km 6, Carretera a Masaya, Apdo 1147, Managua, JR; tel (2) 72280; telex 2045; Chief Exec: Dr Leonel Argüello Ramírez; f 1979 to assume the activities of all the pre-revolution national private insurance cos.

NATIONALIZED INDUSTRY

Cámara Nicaragüense de la Construcción (CNC): Segundo Callejón, Casa 239, Col Mántica, Managua, JR; tel (2) 666525; Pres: Alfonso Delgado M.; Exec Sec: Felipe Lau G.; f 1961; promotes the devt of the construction industry.

TRADE

Cámara de Comercio de Nicaragua: Frente a Lotería Popular, Apdo 135, CC Managua, JR; tel (2) 70718; Pres: León José Ruiz Amador; Gen Man: Orestes Romero Rojas; national chamber of commerce.

Corporación Comercial del Pueblo (CORCOP): Plaza España, Managua, JR; tel (2) 660232; telex 1043; fax (2) 661029; Exec Pres: Domingo Toruño M.; f 1979; promotes commercial devt at all levels.

Empresa Nicaragüense del Algodón (ENAL): Contiguo al Banco Inmobiliario, Colonia Centroamérica, Apdo 3684, Managua, JR; tel (2) 72226; telex 2216; fax (2) 70758; Exec Dir: Juan Carrión Calero; f 1979; responsible for the sale and export of cotton and sesame seeds.

Empresa Nicaragüense de Alimentos Básicos (ENABAS): Apdo 1041, Salida a Carretera Norte, Managua, JR; tel (2) 26183; telex 1314; Dir: Commdr William Ramírez Solorazano; f 1979; controls trading in basic foodstuffs.

Empresa Nicaragüense del Azúcar (ENAZUCAR): Ministerio de Defensa, 2 c abajo, Apdo 3245, Managua, JR; tel (2)

72229; telex 2273; Dir: Noel Chamorro Cuadra; f 1979; controls sugar trading.

Empresa Nicaragüense del Banano (BANANIC): Edif Málaga, Plaza España, Apdo 3433, Managua, JR; tel (2) 74491; Dir: Noel Chamorro Cuadra; f 1979; controls banana trading.

Empresa Nicaragüense del Café (ENCAFE): Plaza de Compras, Contiguo al Banco de Londres, Colonia Centroamérica, Apdo 2482, Managua, JR; tel (2) 70122; telex 2336; Dir: Dr Armando Jarquín Sequiera; controls coffee trading.

Empresa Nicaragüense de la Carne (ENCAR): Frente al Edif Pérez Cassar, Apdo C-11, Managua, JR; tel (2) 70519; telex 2033; fax (2) 70621; Exec Dir: Orlando N. Bonilla; f 1979; responsible for meat production and export of meat and by-products.

Empresa Nicaragüense de Importaciones (ENIMPORT): Contiguo al Ministerio de Comercio Exterior, antiguo Centro Comercial 'Los Portales', Apdo 2793, Managua, JR; tel (2) 75793; telex 2366; Dir: Wilfredo Delgado C.; national import agency.

Empresa Nicaragüense de Insumos Agropecuarios (ENIA): Distribuidora Vicky 2 c Oeste, Apdo C-11, Managua, JR; tel (2) 71724; telex 2301; Dir: Eduardo Fonseca Fábregas; f 1979; agricultural investment goods board.

Empresa Nicaragüense de Productos del Mar (ENMAR): Frente al Cine Aguerri, Apdo 356, Managua, JR; tel 23572; telex 1009; Dir: Franklin Mendieta Medina; f 1979; controls trading in all seafood products.

Empresa Nicaragüense de Promoción de Exportaciones (ENIPREX): Costado este del Centro Financiero Oscar Pérez Cassar, Apdo 1449, Managua, JR; tel (2) 70733; telex 2062; Dir: Rodolfo Zelaya Rivas; export promotion.

Defence

Armed Forces: 'El Chipote', Complejo Germán Pomares, Managua, JR; tel (2) 27161; telex 1369; Chief of Staff: Gen Humberto Ortega Saavedra; Dep Chief of Staff: Maj-Gen Joachim Cuadra.

Sandinista Air Force: Km 10, Carretera Norte, Managua, JR; tel (2) 3601; Chief of Staff: Gen Emmett Lang.

Development and Planning

Consejo Nacional de Planificación (National Planning Council): Managua, JR; Chair: President, Commdr Daniel Ortega Saavedra; f 1985; co-ordinates economic planning.

Fondo Nicaragüense de Inversiones: Km 4, Carretera a Masaya, Apdo 316, Managua, JR; tel (2) 73995; telex 75620; Exec Dir: Silvio Lanuza M.; Dep Exec Dir: Julio Mayorga P.; f 1983; provides finance for devt projects and investigates the feasibility of proposed projects.

Fondo Internacional para la Reconstrucción de Nicaragua (FIR): Managua, JR; f 1979; promotes, co-ordinates and channels international aid and co-operation towards repairing war damage and restructuring the economy.

Fundación Nicaragüense de Desarrollo (FUNDE): De Montoya 1c al lago 1c abajo, Apdo 2598, Managua 3, JR; tel (2) 666066; Exec Sec: Carlos Antonio Noguera P.; f 1969; promotes improvement in living standards through the devt of the co-operative system.

Legal and Judiciary

Corte Suprema (Supreme Court): Ciudad Jardín, Managua, JR; tel (2) 43562; Pres: Alejandro Serrano Caldera; deals with both civil and criminal cases, acts as a Court of Cassation, appoints Judges of First Instance, and generally supervises the legal admin of the country.

Media

BROADCASTING

La Voz de Nicaragua: Detrás de Telcor de Villa Panamá, Managua, JR; tel (2) 72330; Dir-Gen: Eustasio Sánchez; f 1979.

Sistema Sandinista de Televisión (SSTV): Km 3, Carretera Sur, Contiguo a la gasolinera Shell, Las Palmas, Apdo 1505, Managua, JR; tel (2) 660879; telex 1226; fax (2) 666522; Dir: Iván García C; Dir, Programming: Medardo Mendoza; f 1979; state commercial TV station; due to return to private ownership following the takeover of the new Govt in April 1990.

GOVERNMENT PUBLISHER

Editorial Nueva Nicaragua: Paseo Salvador Allende, Km 3, Carretera Sur, Apdo 073, Managua, JR; telex 1033; Pres: Dr Sergio Ramírez Mercado; Dir-Gen: Roberto Díaz Castillo; f 1981.

NEWS AND INFORMATION

Agencia Nicaragüense de Noticias (ANN): Managua, JR; Dir-Gen: Roberto García; news agency.

Instituto Nacional de Estadísticas y Censos (INEC): c/o Ministry of Planning, Entrada Colegio 'Rigoberto López Pérez', Apdo 4596, Managua, JR; tel (2) 75206; collection, analysis and publication of statistics.

Mining and Energy

ENERGY

Empresa Nicaragüense del Petróleo: Del Restaurante Terraza, 1c abajo, 1c al Sur, Managua, JR; petroleum organization.

Instituto Nicaragüense de Energía (INE): Apdo 55, Managua, JR; tel (2) 74103; telex 2344; fax (2) 72686; Dir: Emilio Rappaccioli B.; f 1979; national energy institute; responsble for planning, organization, management, admin, research and devt of energy resources.

MINING

Condemina: Frente Casa Nazareth, Apdo 195, Managua, JR; tel (2) 50645; Dir: Antonio Arellano; state mining agency.

Instituto Nicaragüense de Minas (INMINE): Pista de la Resistencia, Antiguo Centro Comercial El Punto, Apdo 195, Managua, JR; tel (2) 52071; telex 2146; fax (2) 51043; Dir: Ramiro Bermúdez Mallol; f 1979; extraction and processing of metallic and non-metallic minerals.

Tourism

Instituto Nicaragüense de Turismo: Avda Bolívar Sur, Apdo 122, Managua, JR; tel (2) 24334; telex 1299; fax (2) 25314; Dir: Dr Francisco Olivas; f 1979; promotion of tourism.

Transport and Communications

TELECOMMUNICATIONS

Dirección de Telecomunicaciones (Telcor): Apdo 2264, Managua, JR; Dir: Nelba Cecilia Blandón; telecommunications supervisory body.

TRANSPORT

Administración Portuaria de Corinto: Frente al Ferrocarril del Pacífico, Apdo 11, Corinto; tel (342) 211; f 1956; port authority at Corinto.

Aerolíneas Nicaragüenses (AERONICA): Contiguo Aeropuerto Internacional Augusto C. Sandino, Apdo 3688, Managua, JR; tel (2) 31801; Gen Man: Julio Rocha; f 1981; domestic services and services to the rest of Central America.

Ferrocarril de Nicaragua: Plantel Casimiro Sotelo, Apdo 5, Managua, JR; tel (2) 22806; telex 1239; Gen Man: Isaac Ruiz Borge; f 1881.

Ferrocarril del Pacífico de Nicaragua: Plantel Central Casimiro Sotelo, Del Parque San Sebastián, 4c al Lago, Apdo 5, Managua, JR; telex 1239; Pacific railway co.

Naviera Nicaragüense, SA (NANICA): CST 8s al Sur, 150 varas abajo, Apdo 909, Managua, JR; tel (2) 26861; telex 1011; Man Dir: Marlon Valdivia Argüello; regular services between Central America, Mexico, Panama and Europe.

Utilities

Instituto Nicaragüense de Acueductos y Alcantarillados—INAA (Nicaraguan Aquaducts and Sewerage Co): Km 5, Carretera Sur Oeste, Managua, JR; tel (2) 51063; telex 2144; fax (2) 51858; Dirs: Ottoniel Argüello, Carlos Espinosa, Francisco Solorzano; f 1900; maintenance of the water supply.

Welfare

Instituto Nicaragüense de Previsión Social: Managua, JR; Dir: Minister of Social Welfare, Reinaldo Antonio Téfel; social security dept.

NIGER

Head of State

According to the Constitution adopted in 1989, the President is Head of State and is elected to serve a seven-year term. The President cannot serve more than two successive terms. The President appoints and presides over the Council of Ministers.

President: Brig Ali Saïbou (elected 10 December 1989).

Office of the President: Niamey; tel 72-23-81; telex 5214; Minister-Delegate to the Pres in charge of Admin Reform: Mahamane Boukari.

Legislature

The Constitution, adopted in 1989, provides for a National Assembly of 93 members elected from a single parliamentary list nominated by the ruling Mouvement National de la Société de Développement (MNSD).

National Assembly: Niamey; Speaker: Moutari Moussa.

MINISTRIES AND GOVERNMENT DEPARTMENTS

OFFICE OF THE PRIME MINISTER
Niamey
Prime Minister: Aliou Mahamidou
Secretary-General of the Government in charge of Relations with Institutions: Seydou Amadou

MINISTRY OF AGRICULTURE AND ANIMAL RESOURCES
BP 12091, Niamey
Tel 73-35-41; telex 5386
Minister: Adamou Souna
Secretary of State for Agriculture: Ibrahim Koussou
Secretary of State in charge of Co-operative Development: Mamane Boulama

MINISTRY OF THE CIVIL SERVICE, LABOUR AND PROFESSIONAL TRAINING
Niamey
Tel 72-25-01; telex 5283
Minister of Civil Service and Labour: Mamadou Dagra

MINISTRY OF ECONOMICS
BP 235, Niamey
Tel 72-34-67; telex 5203
Minister: Nassirou Sabou

MINISTRY OF EQUIPMENT
Niamey
Tel 72-25-01; telex 5283
Minister: Commdr Ousmane Issaka

MINISTRY OF FINANCE
BP 720, Niamey
Tel 72-20-22; telex 5337
Minister: Wassalke Boukari
Secretary of State: Ibrahim Koussou

MINISTRY OF FOREIGN AFFAIRS AND CO-OPERATION
BP 396, Niamey
Tel 72-29-07; telex 5200
Minister: Mahamane Sani Bako
Secretary of State in charge of Co-operation: Issaka Diamballa

MINISTRY OF HIGHER EDUCATION, RESEARCH AND TECHNOLOGY
Niamey
Tel 72-36-60; telex 5214
Minister: Aboubakar Adamou

MINISTRY OF THE INTERIOR
Niamey
Tel 72-21-76; telex 5214
Minister: Lt-Col Tanja Mamadou

MINISTRY OF JUSTICE AND SECURITY
Niamey
Tel 72-20-94; telex 5214
Minister and Keeper of the Seals: Ali Bandiere

MINISTRY OF MINES AND ENERGY
Niamey
Tel 72-27-75; telex 5214
Minister: Abdou Insa

MINISTRY OF NATIONAL DEFENCE
Niamey
Tel 72-28-40; telex 5291
Minister: Brig Ali Saïbou

MINISTRY OF NATIONAL EDUCATION
Niamey
Tel 72-20-26; telex 5214
Minister: Lt-Col Issa Amsa

MINISTRY OF PLANNING
Niamey
Tel 72-22-33; telex 5463
Minister: Almoustapha Soumeila
Secretary of State: Douramane Moussa

MINISTRY OF POSTS AND TELECOMMUNICATIONS
Niamey
Tel 72-21-35; telex 5206
Minister: Khamed Abdoulaye

MINISTRY OF PUBLIC HEALTH
Niamey
Tel 72-35-87; telex 5214
Minister: Lt-Col Ousmane Gazere

MINISTRY OF SOCIAL AND WOMEN'S AFFAIRS
Niamey
Minister: Aissata Moumouni

MINISTRY OF TRANSPORT AND TOURISM
BP 12130, Niamey
Tel 73-43-82; telex 5467
Minister: Capt Amadou Moussa Gros

MINISTRY OF WATER RESOURCES AND ENVIRONMENT
Niamey
Minister: Karagi Ayarga
High Commissioner for the Kandaji Dam Project (with the rank of Minister): Amadou Mamadou

MINISTRY OF YOUTH, SPORTS AND CULTURE
Niamey
Tel 72-24-89; telex 5214
Minister: Capt Abdoul Rahamane Seydou

GOVERNMENT AGENCIES AND ORGANIZATIONS

Advisory and Supervisory Bodies

Caisse de Stabilisation des Prix des Produits du Niger (CSPPN): BP 480, Niamey; telex 5286; Dir: Ibrahim Koussou; price control office for Niger goods.

Conseil National de Développement (CND) (National Development Council): c/o Ministry of Planning, Niamey; tel 72-22-33; telex 5214; Pres: Moussa Moutari; f 1974; oversees all aspects of the economy; drafted new constitution; was to become a consultative body following the legislative elections in December 1989.

Agriculture

Office du Lait du Niger (OLANI): BP 404, Niamey; tel 73-23-69; Pres: Dr Abdoua Kabo; Dir: Dr Pierre Inne; f 1971; Govt bureau for devt and marketing of milk products.

Office des Produits Vivriers du Niger (OPVN): BP 474, Niamey; telex 5323; Dir: Adamou Souna; Govt bureau for developing agricultural and food production.

Riz du Niger (RINI): BP 476, Tellabéry, Niamey; tel 72-35-06; Dir-Gen: Mahamane Brah; f 1967; 99% state-owned; devt and marketing of rice.

Business and Economy

BANKING

Banque Arabe-Libyenne Nigérienne pour le Commerce Extérieur et le Développement (BALINEX): BP 11363, Immeuble El Nasr, Niamey; tel 73-39-14; telex 5292; Chair and Man Dir: Ibrahim Fteis; f 1978; 50% state-owned; 50% owned by Libyan Arab Foreign Bank.

Banque Centrale des Etats de l'Afrique de l'Ouest (BCEAO): BP 487, Rond-Point de la Poste, Niamey; tel 72-24-91; telex 5218; Gov: Alassane Ouattara; Dir in Niger: Mamadou Diop; f 1955; headquarters in Dakar, Senegal; bank of issue for the seven states of the Union monétaire ouest-africaine (UMOA), comprising Benin, Burkina Faso, Côte d'Ivoire, Mali, Niger, Senegal and Togo.

MARKETING

Société Nigérienne de Commercialisation de l'Arachide et du Nièbe (SONARA): BP 473, Niamey; tel 72-31-07; telex 5216; Chair: Amadou Salifou; Man Dir: Mamadou Sourghia; f 1962; 91% owned by state and parastatal organizations; production and marketing of groundnuts and cowpeas.

NATIONALIZED INDUSTRY

Office National des Produits Pharmaceutiques et Chimiques (ONPPC): BP 11585, Niamey; tel 73-27-81; telex 5231; Dir: Dr Maidana Saidou Djermakoye; f 1962; pharmaceutical and chemical products.

Société Nigérienne de Cimenterie (SNC): BP 03, Malbaza; tel 01-02; telex 8216; Chair: Saidou Mamane; Man Dir: Aboubacar Kada Labo; f 1963; 59% state-owned; production of cement at Malbaza; monopoly of cement marketing.

Société Nigérienne de Produits Céramiques (SONICERAM): BP 10536, Niamey; tel 73-23-62; f 1966; manufacture and commercialization of ceramic goods; 93% state-owned.

Société Nigérienne de Tannerie (SONITAN): BP 144, Maradi; tel 41-02-86; f 1969; 72% state-owned; tannery.

TRADE

Chambre de Commerce, d'Agriculture et d'Industrie du Niger: BP 209, Niamey; tel 73-22-10; telex 5242; Pres: Adamou Souna; Sec-Gen: Iro Mayaki; f 1954; 40 elected mems, 20 official mems.

Société Nationale de Commerce et de Production du Niger (COPRO-Niger): BP 615, Niamey; telex 5222; Man Dir: Ali Halidou; f 1962; monopoly importer of selected products; 81% state-owned.

Defence

Armed Forces: Niamey; tel 72-25-11; Chief of Staff: Col Toumba Boubacar.

Escadrille Nationale Nigérienne (Air Force): Niamey; tel 72-21-77; telex 5214.

National Security Force: Niamey; Dir-Gen of National Security: Moussa Harouna; tel 72-28-40; telex 5214.

Legal and Judiciary

Court of Appeal: Niamey; Attorney-Gen: Bazeye Salifou.

Court of State Security: Niamey; Pres: Mamadou Mallam Aouami; Solicitor-Gen: Soli Abdourahamane; replaced Supreme Court following the coup of April 1974; martial court for criminal offences.

Media

BROADCASTING

Office de Radiodiffusion-Télévision du Niger (ORTN): BP 309, Niamey; tel 72-31-63; telex 5229; Dir-Gen: Djibrill Hanounou; Technical Dir (Radio and TV): Zoudi Issouf; state broadcasting authority.

Télé-Sahel: BP 309, Niamey; tel 72-31-53; telex 5229; Dir: Maitourare Abdou Saleye; TV service broadcasting four days a week.

La Voix du Sahel: BP 361, Niamey; tel 72-22-72; Dir: Aboubacar Kio Koudize; radio station; programmes in French, Hausa (Haoussa), Djerma (Zarma), Kanuri, Fulfuldé, Tamajak, Toubou, Gourmantché and Arabic.

GOVERNMENT PUBLISHER

L'Imprimerie Nationale du Niger (INN): BP 61, Niamey; tel 73-47-98; telex 5312; Dir: E. Wohlrab; f 1962.

NEWS AND INFORMATION

Agence Nigérienne de Presse: BP 11158, Niamey; tel 74-08-09; telex 5497; Dir: Boureima Magagi; f 1987 by Govt decree; collection and dissemination of information; two publs.

Service de la Statistique et de la Mécanographie: Commissariat Général au Développement, Niamey.

Mining and Energy

Office National de l'Energie Solaire (ONERSOL): BP 621, Niamey; tel 73-45-05; Dir: Albert Wright; Govt bureau for research and devt, with capacity of commercial production or exploitation of solar devices.

Office National des Ressources Minières (ONAREM): BP 12716, Niamey; tel 73-59-26; telex 5300; Dir-Gen: Ousmane Gaouri; f 1976; research, exploitation and commercialization of mineral and fossil substances, eg uranium, gold, phosphates, steel, platinum, chrome, iron, coal, lithium, etc.

Société Minière du Niger (SMDN): BP 12443, Niamey; tel 73-45-82; telex 5300; Chair: Amani Issaka; Man Dir: Mamadou Saadou; f 1941; 71% state-owned, 10% by Benin Govt; cassiterite mining at El Mecki and Tarrouadji.

Société Nigérienne du Charbon d'Anou Araren (SON-ICHAR): BP 51, Agadez; tel 44-10-20; telex 8246; Chair: Ali Sabo; Man Dir: Mahamadou Ouhoumoudou; f 1975; 61.4% state-owned, 10% owned by the Islamic Devt Bank, 23.7% owned by COMINAK, SMTT and SOMAIR; exploitation of coal reserves at Anou Araren and production of electricity.

Société Nigérienne d'Electricité (NIGELEC): BP 11202, Niamey; tel 72-26-92; telex 5224; Man Dir: Amadou Mayaki; f 1968; 95% state-owned; production and distribution of electricity and water.

Société Nigérienne de Produits Pétroliers (SONIDEP): BP 11702, Niamey; tel 73-33-34; telex 5343; Man Dir: Abdou Insa; f 1977; Govt bureau for the distribution and marketing of petroleum products.

Tourism

Direction du Tourisme et de l'Hôtellerie: c/o Ministry of Transport and Tourism, BP 12130, Niamey; tel 73-23-85; telex 5467; Dir: Mato Ali.

Office National du Tourisme (ONT): BP 612, ave du Président H. Luebke, Niamey; tel 73-24-47; telex 5467; fax 227; f 1959; promotion of tourism.

Société Nigérienne d'Hôtellerie (SONHOTEL): BP 11040, Niamey; tel 73-23-87; telex 5239; Dir-Gen: Habi Abdou; f 1977; state-owned hotel corpn.

Transport and Communications

TELECOMMUNICATIONS

Société des Télécommunications Internationales de la République du Niger (STIN): BP 616, Niamey; tel 72-23-91; f 1981; 77.19% state-owned; telecommunications.

TRANSPORT

Trans-Niger: Niamey; f 1989, following liquidation of Air Niger; 52% state-owned; weekly flights to Benin, Burkina Faso, Mali and Togo.

Organisation Commune Bénin-Niger des Chemins de Fer et des Transports (OCBN): BP 38, Niamey; tel 31-33-80; BP 16, Cotonou, Benin; f 1959; manages the Benin-Niger railway project in which Niger has a share; there are as yet no railways in Niger, but plans to extend the Cotonou-Parakou line from Benin to Niamey were under discussion in the late 1980s.

Société Nigérienne des Transports Fluviaux et Maritimes (SNTFM): BP 802, Niamey; tel 73-39-69; telex 5265; Man Dir: Bertrand Dejean; river and sea transport organization; 99% state-owned.

Utilities

Office des Eaux du Sous-Sol (OFEDES): BP 734, Niamey; tel 73-23-44; telex 5313; Dir: Adou Adam; Govt bureau for the maintenance and devt of wells and boreholes.

NIGERIA

Head of State and Legislature

Executive and legislative power are vested in the Armed Forces Ruling Council (AFRC), which includes the President as Head of State. The President is assisted by the Chief of General Staff (whose functions are not military, but are confined to political administration). The AFRC appoints a National Council of Ministers, headed by the President, which is responsible for federal administration. Each of the 21 states has a military Governor, who appoints and presides over a state executive council.

President: Gen Ibrahim Babangida (took power 27 August 1985).

Office of the President and of the Armed Forces Ruling Council: Dodan Barracks, Ikoyi, Lagos.

MINISTRIES AND GOVERNMENT DEPARTMENTS

OFFICE OF THE CHIEF OF GENERAL STAFF
Lagos
Chief of General Staff: Vice-Adm Augustus Aikhomu

MINISTRY OF AGRICULTURE, WATER RESOURCES AND RURAL DEVELOPMENT
Abuja
Tel (1) 681896; telex 22605
Minister: Alhaji Ismaila Mamman

MINISTRY OF AVIATION
New Federal Secretariat Bldgs, Bedwell Rd, Ikoyi, Lagos
Tel (1) 652120
Minister: T. O. Graham-Douglas

MINISTRY OF COMMUNICATIONS
Lagos
Minister: Col David Mark

MINISTRY OF DEFENCE
Independence Bldg, Tafawa Balewa Sq, Lagos
Tel (1) 633994; telex 22610
Minister: Gen Ibrahim Babangida

MINISTRY OF EDUCATION
Ahmadu Bello Way, Victoria Island, PMB 12573, Lagos
Tel (1) 619906
Minister: Babs Fafunwa

MINISTRY OF EMPLOYMENT, LABOUR AND PRODUCTIVITY
PMB 12576, Lagos
Tel (1) 681643
Minister: Alhaji Abubakar Umar

MINISTRY OF EXTERNAL AFFAIRS
23 Marina, PMB 12600, Lagos
Tel (1) 601320; telex 21444
Minister: Alhaji Rilwan Lukman
Minister of State: Eyoma Ita Eyoma

MINISTRY OF THE FEDERAL CAPITAL TERRITORY
15B Awolowo Rd, SW Ikoyi, Lagos
Tel (1) 684372
Minister: Maj-Gen Mohammed Gado Nasko

MINISTRY OF FINANCE AND ECONOMIC DEVELOPMENT
Abuja
Minister: Olu Falae

MINISTRY OF HEALTH
New Federal Secretariat Bldgs, Bedwell Rd, Ikoyi, Lagos
Tel (1) 684405
Minister: Prof Olikoye Ransome-Kuti

MINISTRY OF INDUSTRY
Abuja
Minister: Air Vice-Marshal Mohammed Yahaya

MINISTRY OF INFORMATION AND CULTURE
15 Awolowo Rd, SW Ikoyi, Lagos
Tel (1) 610836; telex 22649
Minister: Prince Tony Momoh

MINISTRY OF INTERNAL AFFAIRS
Abuja
Minister: Lt-Gen Domkat Bali

433

MINISTRY OF JUSTICE
New Federal Secretariat Bldgs, Bedwell Rd, Ikoyi, Lagos
Tel (1) 684414
Minister: Prince Bola Ajibola

MINISTRY OF MINES, POWER AND STEEL
6 Storey Bldg, Broad St, Lagos
Tel (1) 600240; telex 21126
Minister: Air Vice-Marshal Nura M. Imam

MINISTRY OF PETROLEUM RESOURCES
Lagos
Minister: Jibril Aminu

MINISTRY OF SCIENCE AND TECHNOLOGY
New Federal Secretariat Bldgs, Bedwell Rd, Ikoyi, Lagos
Tel (1) 614250
Minister: Gordian Ezekwe

MINISTRY OF SPECIAL DUTIES
Dodan Barracks, Lagos
Tel (1) 684379

Minister: Air Vice-Marshal (retd) Hamza Abdullahi

MINISTRY OF TRADE
Abuja
Minister: S. J. Ukpanah

MINISTRY OF TRANSPORT
Old Secretariat Bldgs, Marina, Lagos
Tel (1) 652120; telex 21535
Minister: Lt-Gen (retd) Alani Akinrinade

MINISTRY OF WORKS AND HOUSING
Tafawa Balewa Sq, PMB 12635, Lagos
Tel (1) 631926
Minister: Maj-Gen Mamman T. Kontagora

MINISTRY OF YOUTH, SPORTS AND SOCIAL DEVELOPMENT
5 Kofo Abayomi Rd, Victoria Island, Lagos
Tel (1) 619747
Minister: Cdre A. Ikazobor

GOVERNMENT AGENCIES AND ORGANIZATIONS

Advisory and Supervisory Body

National Electoral Commission: Lagos; f 1987; appointed to supervise the selection of political parties for the elections due to be held in 1992.

Agriculture

Anambra State Agricultural Development Corpn: Garden Ave, PMB 1024, Enugu.

Co-operative Federation of Nigeria: c/o Co-operative Dept, Ministry of Employment, Labour and Productivity, PMB 12576, Lagos; tel (1) 681463.

Cross River State Agricultural Development Corpn: PMB 1024, Calabar.

Ogun State Agricultural Credit Corpn: PMB 2029, Abeokuta; f 1976.

Rubber Research Institute of Nigeria: PMB 1049, Benin City; telex 41190; Dir: Dr E. K. Okaisabor; Dep Dir: Dr Ayoola B. Fasina; f 1961; conducts research into the production and products of rubber and other latex products of economic importance.

Business and Economy

BANKING

Allied Bank of Nigeria Ltd: Elephant House, 16th Floor, 214 Broad St, PMB 12785, Lagos; tel (1) 662976; telex 21512; Chair: Malam M. W. Gadzama; Man Dir: Mallam Muhtar Bello; f 1962 as Bank of India; 33 brs.

Central Bank of Nigeria: Tinubu Sq, PMB 12194, Lagos; tel (1) 660100; telex 21350; Gov: Alhaji Abdul Kadir Ahmed; f 1958; bank of issue; 11 brs.

Federal Mortgage Bank of Nigeria: 11 Breadfruit St, POB 2078, Lagos; tel (1) 662662; telex 21840; Chair: Chief Emmanuel Adiele; Man Dir: G. A. Onabule; f 1977; loans to individuals and mortgage institutions; 52 brs.

Federal Savings Bank: 23 Awolowo Rd, PMB 12512, Ikoyi,

Lagos; tel (1) 686071; telex 23671; Gen Man: I. T. Udo; Dep Gen Man: T. A. T. Samaiye; f 1886; 51% state-owned.

First Bank of Nigeria Ltd: 35 Marina, POB 5216, Lagos; tel (1) 665900; telex 21231; Chair: Alhaji Mohammedu Danmadami; Man Dir: Wole Adeosun; f 1894 as Bank of British West Africa; 268 brs.

International Bank for West Africa Ltd (IBWA): 94 Broad St, PMB 12021, Lagos; tel (1) 664135; telex 21345; Man Dir: Abubaker A. Dalil; f 1969; 64 brs.

International Merchant Bank (Nigeria) Ltd: IBM Plaza, 1 Akin Adesola St, PMB 12028, Victoria Island, Lagos; tel (1) 612204; telex 21169; Chair: Walter G. Ollor; Man Dir: Mohammed A. Kollere; f 1974; 5 brs.

National Bank of Nigeria Ltd: 82-86 Broad St, PMB 12123, Lagos; tel (1) 661561; telex 21348; Chair: Prof Ayo Ogunsheye; Man Dir: Chief 'Luyi Rotimi; f 1933; nationalized 1961; 100 brs.

Nigeria Merchant Bank Ltd: 6 Broad St, POB 2413, Lagos; tel (1) 631476; telex 21475; Chair: S. Miner; Man Dir: A. K. Belgore; 3 brs.

Nigeria-Arab Bank Ltd: 96-102 Broad St, PMB 12807, Lagos; tel (1) 661955; telex 21973; Chair: Etim J. Umoren; Vice-Chair: M. Fahoum.

Nigerian Agricultural and Co-operative Bank Ltd (NACB): Hospital Rd, PMB 2155, Lagos; tel (1) 201000; telex 71115; Chair: Group-Capt (retd) Usman Jibrin; Man Dir: Malam Hammam Bello Mohammed; f 1973; provides funds to farmers and co-operatives to improve production techniques.

Nigerian Bank for Commerce and Industry: 26 Idejo St, Victoria Island, POB 4424, Lagos; tel (1) 617665; telex 21917; fax (1) 614880; Man Dir: G. C. Akwaeze; Gen Man: J. O. Amao; f 1973; loans to small- and medium-sized industries, merchant banking, promotion of industrial devt.

Nigerian Industrial Development Bank Ltd: NIDB House, 63-71 Broad St, Lagos; tel (1) 663470; telex 21701; Man Dir: Alhaji Abubakar Abdulkadir; Exec Dirs: M. S. Udom, E. A. Egonminan; f 1964; provides medium- and long-term finance to industry, manufacturing, non-petroleum mining and tourism; encourages foreign investment in partnership with Nigerians; 5 brs.

Savannah Bank of Nigeria Ltd: 62-66 Broad St, POB 2317, Lagos; tel (1) 600470; telex 21876; Chair: Dr W. Ollor; Man Dir: G. C. Okonkwo; f 1976; 25 brs.

Union Bank of Nigeria Ltd: 40 Marina, PMB 2027, Lagos;

tel (1) 665439; telex 21222; Chair: Alhaji Abdulrahman Okene; Man Dir: Paul Ogwuma; f 1969 as Barclays Bank of Nigeria Ltd; 201 brs.

United Bank for Africa (Nigeria) Ltd: 97-105 Broad St, POB 2406, Lagos; tel (1) 667410; telex 21247; fax (1) 660844; Man Dir: Alhaji Sulaiman S. Baffa; f 1961; 180 brs.

FINANCIAL AGENCIES

Securities and Exchange Commission (SEC): Mandilas House, 96-102 Broad St, PMB 12638, Lagos; Dir, Admin: S. S. Akingbohungbe; f 1979 to regulate and develop the capital market; responsible for supervision of stock exchange operations.

INSURANCE

American International Insurance Co (Nigeria): 200 Broad St, Lagos.

Law Union and Rock Insurance Co of Nigeria Ltd: 88-92 Broad St, POB 944, Lagos; tel (1) 663526; Chair: Col S. Bello; fire, accident and marine; 6 brs.

Lion of Africa Insurance Co Ltd: St Peter's House, 3 Ajele St, POB 2055, Lagos; tel (1) 600950; telex 23536; Man Dir: M. J. S. Bedi; f 1952; all classes of insurance.

National Insurance Corpn of Nigeria: 5 Customs St, POB 1100, Lagos; tel (1) 666012; telex 22651; Man Dir: Yinka Lijadu; Gen Man, Technical: B. A. Lawson; Gen Man, Admin: L. O. Sotimehin; f 1969; all classes of insurance; 23 brs.

Nigeria Reinsurance Corpn: Bookshop House, 50-52 Broad St, PMB 12766, Lagos; tel (1) 634141; telex 21092; Man Dir: Chief J. O. Irukwu; all classes of reinsurance; since 1978 all insurance cos have been required to reinsure 20% of the sum insured with the Nigeria Reinsurance Co.

United Nigeria Insurance Co Ltd: 53 Marina, POB 588, Lagos; tel (1) 663130; Man Dir: F. C. Nwokolo; f 1965; all classes except life; 17 brs.

West African Provincial Insurance Co: Wesley House, 21 Marina, POB 2013, Lagos; tel (1) 636433; telex 21613; Man Dir: A. A. Akintunde; all classes except life.

MARKETING

Anambra State Co-operative Produce Marketing Association Ltd: Ministry of Trade, Enugu; Pres: J. U. Agwu; Vice-Pres: S. O. Iheanacho; co-operative co.

National Oil and Chemical Marketing Co: 38-39 Marina, PMB 2052, Lagos; Chair: Halil I. Said; Man Dir: M. O. Akanbi; markets petroleum, petroleum products and chemicals.

NATIONALIZED INDUSTRY

Ajaokuta Steel Co Ltd: PMB 1000, Ajaokuta, Kwara State; tel 400450; telex 36390; Chief Exec: M. M. Inuwa.

Delta Steel Co Ltd: Ovwian-Aladja, PMB 1220, Warr, Bendel State; tel (53) 621001; telex 43456; Gen Man: Tachia Jooji; f 1982; manufacture of steel and related products.

Gaskiya Corpn Ltd: PMB 1033, Zaria, Kaduna State; tel (69) 322033; Chief Exec: Labo U. Yari; f 1945; printing and publishing co.

Nigerian Cement Co Ltd: Nkalagu, POB 331, Enugu-Awambra State; tel (42) 335794; telex 51113; Chair: Col L. O. Ihenacho; Gen Man: S. N. Okereke; f 1954; manufacture of cement.

Nigerian Engineering and Construction Co Ltd (NECCO): Km 14, Badagry Expressway (opposite International Trade Fair Complex), PMB 12684, Lagos; tel (1) 880591; telex 21836; Chair: Ehioze Ediae; building, civil, mechanical and electrical engineers; furniture makers and steel fabricators.

TRADE

Nigerian Export Promotion Council: 103 Lewis St, Lagos; Dir: George Niyi; f 1977.

Nigerian National Supply Co Ltd: 29 Burma Rd, PMB 12662, Lagos-Apapa; Chair: Brig J. I. Onoja; Gen Man: Maj A. Dahiru; import organization.

Defence

Armed Forces: c/o Ministry of Defence, Independence Bldg, Tafawa Balewa Sq, Lagos; tel (1) 633994; telex 22610; Commdr-in-Chief: Gen Ibrahim Babangida; Chief of General Staff: Vice-Adm Augustus Aikhomu.

> **Air Force:** address as above; tel (1) 635557; telex 22613; Chief of Staff: Air Marshal Ibrahim Alfa.

> **Army:** address as above; tel (1) 632204; telex 22609; Chief of Staff: Lt-Gen Sanni Abacha.

> **Navy:** address as above; tel (1) 635664; Chief of Staff: Vice-Adm Patrick Koshoni.

Police Affairs Office: 7 Okotie-Eboh Rd, SW Ikoyi, Lagos; tel (1) 603080; Inspector-Gen: Alhaji Muhammadu Gambo; f 1984; oversees and administers the police.

Development and Planning

INVESTMENT

Kaduna State Investment Co Ltd: Investment House, 27 Ali Akilu Rd, PMB 2230, Kaduna; tel (62) 211018; telex 71319; Chief Exec: Alhaji Saminu Dalhatu; f 1977; devt finance institution.

Kwara State Investment Co: PMB 1344, Ilorin.

New Nigerian Development Co Ltd: 18/19 Ahmadu Bello Way, Ahmed Talib House, PMB 2120, Kaduna; tel (62) 210909; telex 71108; Chair: Maj Gen (retd) M. D. Jega; f 1968; investment/financial institution owned by the Govts of 11 northern States.

Northern Nigeria Investments Ltd: POB 138, Kaduna; Man Dir: Kassim M. Bichi; f 1959 to identify and invest in industrial and agricultural projects in 11 northern States.

Odu'a Investment Co Ltd: Cocoa House, PMB 5435, Ibadan; tel (22) 417710; telex 31225; Man Dir: O. A. Iyowu; f 1976 to succeed the Western State Industrial Investment Corpn; jointly owned by Ogun, Ondo and Oyo States.

Ondo State Investment Corpn: Adekunle Ajasin Rd, PMB 700, Akure; tel (34) 231589; telex 32518; Dir: Chief F. O. Mogaji; f 1976 to investigate and promote both agricultural and industrial projects on a commercial basis in the State.

Trans Investments Co Ltd: 6 Bale Oyewole Rd, PMB 5085, Ibadan; tel (22) 416000; telex 31122; Man Dir and Chief Exec: M. A. Adesiyun; f 1986; initiates and finances industrial and agricultural schemes.

PLANNING

Federal Institute of Industrial Research, Oshodi (FIIRO): Murtala Mohammed Airport, Ikeja, PMB 21023, Lagos; Dir: Dr O. A. Koleoso; f 1956; plans and directs industrial research and provides technical assistance and information to Nigerian industry; specializes in foods, minerals, textiles, natural products, industrial intermediates and others.

Projects Development Institute (PRODA): 3 Independence Layout, POB 609, Enugu, Anambra State; tel (42) 337691; telex 51120; Dir: Prof G. O. Ezekwe; Dep Dirs: E. O. Kaine, L. K. Nwosu, Harry Okolo; f 1970; promotes the establishment of new industries and develops industrial projects utilizing local raw materials.

REGIONAL DEVELOPMENT

Chad Basin Development Authority: PMB 1130, Maiduguri, Borno State; tel (76) 232015; Chair; Mohammed Abali; Gen Man: Alhaji Bunu S. Musa; f 1973; devt of irrigation and agriculture-allied industries.

Federal Capital Development Authority: PMB 24, Abuja; tel (9) 2341483; telex 71495; Permanent Sec: Alhaji Abubakar Koko; f 1976; state agency for the design, construction and management of Abuja.

Gongola State Housing Corpn: Yola; Chair: Dominic M. Mapeo.

Hadejia Jama'are Basin Development Authority: Bauchi State; Gen Man: Alhaji Ahmadu Rufai; f 1976; began building four dams for irrigation and hydroelectric power in 1980.

Imo State Housing Corpn: Uratta Rd, PMB 1224, Owerri, Imo State; tel (83) 230733; Gen Man: .O. A. Kalu; Sec: E. Nwankwo; f 1976; devt of housing estates in Imo State.

Lagos State Development and Property Corpn: Ilupeju Industrial Estate, Ikorodu Rd, PMB 1050, Ikeja; POB 907, Lagos; Gen Man: G. B. Jinadu; f 1972; planning and devt of Lagos.

New Nigeria Development Co (Properties) Ltd: 18-19 Ahmadu Bello Way, PMB 2040, Kaduna; housing devt agency.

Nigerian Enterprises Promotion Board: 72 Campbell St, PMB 12553, Lagos; Chair: Minso Gadzama; f 1972; promotes indigenization in industry.

Ogun State Housing Corpn: PMB 2077, Ibara, Abeokuta; (37) 231303; Gen Man: Adewunmi Tade; f 1977; develops housing and industrial estates; grants finance for house purchase and operates a savings plan.

Ondo State Housing Corpn: PMB 693, Akure; tel (34) 230993; Dir-Gen: J. G. Adeyanju; Sec: R. J. Aliki; f 1976 to develop house-building and industrial estates, grant mortgages and loans for house purchase; also operates a savings scheme.

Plateau Housing Corpn: Murtala House, 37 Murtala Mohammed Way, PMB 2109, Jos, Plateau State; tel (73) 56518; f 1987; provides housing to the public, office and factory space to industry and a loan and grants service for the purpose of building and purchasing housing; undertakes architectural and engineering consultancy services.

Rivers State Development Corpn: Port Harcourt; f 1970.

Rivers State Housing and Property Development Authority: Moscow Rd, PMB 5044, Port Harcourt; tel (84) 301090; f 1985; Gen Man: Sunday A. Adirimo; housing and property devt.

Urban Planning and Development Authority: Hospital Rd, PMB 2202, Yola; tel (75) 25771; f 1986; town and country planning in the Gongola State region.

Employment

Federal Civil Service Commission: New Federal Secretariat Bldgs, Bedwell Rd, Ikoyi, Lagos; Permanent Sec: A. M. Magali; controls the appointment of mems of the public service.

Industrial Training Fund: 8th Floor, Federal Secretariat, PMB 2199, Jos; tel (73) 55297; telex 81154; Dir-Gen and Chief Exec: Alhaji Lawal Tudun Wada; f 1971; promotes and encourages the acquisition of skills in industry and commerce with a view to generating sufficient trained manpower to meet the needs of the economy.

Legal and Judiciary

Supreme Court: Tafawa Balewa Sq, Lagos; Chief Justice: Mohammed Bello; consists of a Chief Justice and up to 15 Justices, appointed by the Armed Forces Ruling Council. It has original jurisdiction in any dispute between the Federation and a State, or between States, and hears appeals from the Federal Court of Appeal.

Media

BROADCASTING

Federal Radio Corpn of Nigeria (FRCN): Broadcasting House, Ikoyi, PMB 12504, Lagos; tel (1) 603010; telex 21484; Dir-Gen: Alhaji Mohammed Ibrahim; f 1978 to replace the Nigerian Broadcasting Corpn; controlled by the Federal Govt and divided into five zones: Lagos, Kaduna, Ibadan, Enugu and external services.

Nigerian Television Authority (NTA): Television House, Ahmadu Bello Way, Victoria Island, PMB 12036, Lagos; tel (1) 615154; telex 22536; Chair: Mamman Daura; Dir-Gen: S. I. Wigwe; f 1976; responsible for all aspects of TV broadcasting.

GOVERNMENT PUBLISHER

Government Press: PMB 2020, Kaduna; tel (62) 213812.

NEWS AND INFORMATION

Federal Office of Statistics: 36-38 Broad St, PMB 12528, Lagos; tel (1) 635005; f 1947; collection, analysis and publication of statistics; training of statisticians.

News Agency of Nigeria (NAN): c/o National Theatre, Iganmu, PMB 12756, Lagos; tel (1) 832832; telex 22648; Chair: (vacant); Gen Man: Dr Nwabu Mgbemena; f 1978.

Mining and Energy

ENERGY

National Electric Power Authority: 24/25 Marina, PMB 12030, Lagos; tel (1) 651370; telex 21212; Man Dir: David Adeyemi Oyelele; Dep Man Dirs: George Egere, Hamzat Ibrahim; f 1972; generation, transmission, distribution and sale of electricity.

Electricity Corpn of Nigeria: address as above; chief authority for the generation, transmission and distribution of electric power.

Niger Dams Authority: PMB 12605, Lagos; Chair: Alhaji

Ahmadu Danbaba; f 1962; operates and maintains hydroelectric plant, transmission lines and substations.

Nigerian National Petroleum Corpn: Falom Office Complex, PMB 12701, Ikoyi, Lagos; tel (1) 603100; telex 23436; Chair: Minister of Petroleum Resources, Alhaji R. Rilwanu Lukman; Man Dir: Godwin Adams; f 1977; merged with Nigerian Petroleum Refining Co in 1985; holding corpn for Govt interests in the oil cos; restructured in 1988 to cover three areas of responsibility (Corporate Services, Operations and National Petroleum Investment Management Services), with 11 subsidiary cos.

Nigerian Petroleum Refining Co Ltd (NRPC): 21-25 Broad St, Lagos.

Shell Petroleum Development Co of Nigeria Ltd: Freeman House, 21-22 Marina, PMB 2418, Lagos; tel (1) 601600; telex 21235; Man Dir: Hein Hooykaas; 80% state-owned; largest oil operator in Nigeria; responsible for onshore and offshore exploration and production.

MINING

Nigerian Coal Corpn: 29 Okpara Ave, Enugu, Anambra State; tel (1) 335314; telex 51115; Gen Man: F. N. Ugwu; Dep Gen Man: M. O. Ozoani; f 1916; mining and sale of coal.

Nigerian Mining Corpn: Federal Secretariat, 7th Floor, PMB 2154, Jos; Chair: Alhaji Mohammed Inuwa Morrow; f 1972; exploration, production, processing and marketing of minerals.

Nigerian Tin Mining Co Ltd: PMB 2036, Jos; tel (73) 80632; Chair: E. A. Ifaturoti; Gen Man: Alhaji M. A. Ibrahim; f 1986 by merger of Amalgamated Tin Mines of Nigeria Ltd and four other mining cos operating on the Jos plateau; owned by the Nigerian Mining Corpn (see above) and the former non-national shareholders in the four cos; production of tin concentrate from alluvial tin ore and separation of columbite, zircon and monazite.

Tourism

Nigerian Tourist Board: Trade Fair Complex, Badagry Expressway, POB 2944, Lagos; tel (1) 883364; Chair: R. A. Folami; Dir-Gen: Alhaji Garba Adamu Gumel; f 1976.

Transport and Communications

TELECOMMUNICATIONS

Nigerian Telecommunications Ltd (NITEL): Marina, Lagos; tel (1) 634200; Man Dir: Patrick C. Uchiduno.

TRANSPORT

National Freight Co Ltd: PMB 2175, Kaduna; Chair: M. B. Ahmed; f 1976.

National Maritime Authority: 15 Louis Solomon Close, Victoria Island, Lagos; tel 618388; telex 23891; fax 617173; Dir-Gen: Adebisi Akinfie; f 1987; administers maritime affairs, allocates routes, shares cargoes amongst shipping operators.

Nigerian Airports Authority: Lagos; Chair: Sa'ad Asad Mohammed; Man Dir: Air Cdre N. Yusuf.

Nigeria Airways: Airways House, Murtala Muhammed Airport, PMB 1024, Ikeja; tel (1) 900470; telex 22646; Chair: Air Vice-Marshal (retd) A. D. Bello; Man Dir (acting): Capt W. M. Atabo; f 1958; scheduled domestic and international cargo and passenger services throughout Africa, and to Europe, the USA and Saudi Arabia.

Nigerian National Shipping Line Ltd: Development House, 21 Wharf Rd, POB 326, Lagos-Apapa; tel (1) 877262; telex 21253; Chair: Vice-Adm (retd) A. Adelanwa; Man Dir: Rear-Adm Sunday Uguna; f 1959; operates cargo and limited passenger services between West Africa, the United Kingdom, the Mediterranean, North America and the Far East.

Nigerian Ports Authority: 26-28 Marina, PMB 12588, Lagos; tel (1) 655020; telex 21500; Chair: Maj-Gen (retd) Martin Adamu; Gen Man: Brig M. B. Halidu; f 1955.

Nigerian Railway Corpn: Ebute Metta, Lagos; tel (1) 802000; telex 26584; Chair: Maj-Gen (retd) Mohammed Shuwa; Gen Man: N. C. U. Okoro; f 1898; transport of goods and passengers.

Nigerian Road Federation: c/o Ministry of Transport, Old Secretariat Bldgs, Marina, Lagos.

Utilities

Plateau State Water Resources Development Board: Jos; incorporates the former Plateau River Basin Devt Authority and Plateau State Water Resources Devt Board.

NORWAY

Head of State

Norway is a constitutional monarchy, and executive power is nominally vested in the Head of State, the King, though it is effectively exercised by the Statsråd (State Council) headed by the Prime Minister. The Council is appointed by the monarch, in accordance with the will of the Storting, to which the Council is responsible.

Sovereign: HM King Olav V (succeeded to the throne 21 September 1957).

Office of HM the King: Det Kgl Slott, Oslo 1; tel (2) 44-19-20.

Legislature

Legislative power is held by the unicameral Storting (Parliament), comprising 157 members elected for four years by universal adult suffrage, on the basis of proportional representation. For the consideration of legislative proposals, the Storting divides itself into the Lagting (Upper House) and the Odelsting (Lower House). Norway comprises 19 fylker (counties).

Storting (Parliament): Karl Johansgt 22, Oslo 1; tel (2) 31-30-50; Pres: Jo Benkow, Reiulf Steen.

MINISTRIES AND GOVERNMENT DEPARTMENTS

OFFICE OF THE PRIME MINISTER
Akersgt 42, POB 8001 Dep, 0030 Oslo 1
Tel (2) 34-90-90; telex 21565
Prime Minister: Jan P. Syse

MINISTRY OF AGRICULTURE
Akersgt 42, POB 8007 Dep, 0030 Oslo 1
Tel (2) 34-90-90; telex 72969; fax (2) 34-95-55
Minister: Anne Vik

MINISTRY OF CHURCH AND EDUCATION
Akersgt 42, POB 8119 Dep, 0032 Oslo 1
Tel (2) 34-90-90; telex 21428; fax (2) 34-95-40
Minister of Church Affairs: Eleonore Bjartveit
Minister of Education: Einar Steensnæs
Formulates policies relating to the Church and the clergy, and to primary, secondary and adult education.

MINISTRY OF COMMUNICATIONS
Møllergt 1-3, POB 8010 Dep, 0030 Oslo 1
Tel (2) 34-90-90
Minister of Transportation and Communications: Lars Gunnar Lie

MINISTRY OF CONSUMER AFFAIRS AND THE FAMILY
Akersgt 42, POB 8004 Dep, 0030 Oslo 1
Tel (2) 34-90-90
Minister: Solveig Sollie

MINISTRY OF CULTURAL AFFAIRS
Akersgt 42, POB 8030 Dep, Oslo 1
Tel (2) 34-90-90; telex 21428; fax (2) 34-95-50
Minister: Eleonore Bjartveit

MINISTRY OF DEFENCE
Myntgt 1, POB 8126 Dep, 0032 Oslo 1
Tel (2) 40-20-00; telex 21605; fax (2) 40-23-23
Minister: Per Ditlev-Simonsen

MINISTRY OF DEVELOPMENT CO-OPERATION
Victoria terrasse 7, POB 8142 Dep, 0033 Oslo 1
Tel (2) 31-40-55
Minister: Tom Vraalsen

MINISTRY OF ENVIRONMENT
Myntgt 2, POB 8013 Dep, 0030 Oslo 1
Tel (2) 34-90-90; telex 21480; fax (2) 34-95-60
Minister: Kristin Hille Valla

MINISTRY OF FINANCE
Akersgt 42, POB 8008 Dep, 0030 Oslo 1
Tel (2) 34-90-90; telex 21444; fax (2) 34-95-05
Minister: Arne Skauge

Department of Customs and Excise: address as above; Dir-Gen: Thorbjørn Wiig.

Economic Affairs Department: address as above; Dir-Gen: Svein Gjedrem.

Finance Department: address as above; Dir-Gen: Odd Solbraa.

Petroleum Department: address as above; Dir-Gen: Leif K. Ervik.

Planning Department: address as above; Dir-Gen: Per Schreiner.

Tax Legislation Department: address as above; Dir-Gen: Thorbjørn Gjølstad.

MINISTRY OF FISHERIES
Øvre Slottsgt 2, POB 8118 Dep, 0032 Oslo 1
Tel (2) 34-90-90; telex 21499
Minister: Svein M. Munkejord

MINISTRY OF FOREIGN AFFAIRS
7 juni plassen 1, POB 8114 Dep, 0032 Oslo 1
Tel (2) 34-36-00; telex 71004; fax (2) 34-95-80
Minister of Foreign Affairs: Kjell Magne Bondevik
Minister of Trade and Shipping: Kaci Kullmann Five
Merged with Ministry of Trade and Shipping in 1988.

MINISTRY OF HEALTH
Akersgt 42, POB 8011 Dep, 0030 Oslo 1
Tel (2) 34-90-90
Minister: Wenche Frogn Sellæg

MINISTRY OF INDUSTRY
Akersgt 42, POB 8014 Dep, 0030 Oslo 1
Tel (2) 34-90-90
Minister: Petter Thomassen

Travel and Tourism Section: Pløensgt 8, POB 8014 Dep, 0030 Oslo 1; tel (2) 34-67-80; telex 21428; fax (2) 34-95-25; Dir-Gen: Anna Bale; Asst Dir-Gen: Tore Bjerke; f 1978; co-ordination cf a national strategy for tourism; devt of tourism on a commercial basis; international co-operation.

MINISTRY OF JUSTICE
Akersgt 42, POB 8005 Dep, 0030 Oslo 1
Tel (2) 34-90-90
Minister: Else Bugge Fougner

MINISTRY OF LOCAL GOVERNMENT AND LABOUR
Møllergt 43, POB 8112 Dep, 0030 Oslo 1
Tel (2) 34-90-90 telex 21414; fax (2) 34-95-45
Minister of Labour: Kristin Clemet
Minister of Local Government: Johan J. Jakobsen

MINISTRY OF PETROLEUM AND ENERGY
Pløensgt 8, POB 8148 Dep, Oslo 1
Tel (2) 34-90-90; telex 21486; fax (2) 34-95-65
Minister: Eivind Reiten

GOVERNMENT AGENCIES AND ORGANIZATIONS

Business and Economy

BANKING

Norges Bank (Bank of Norway): Bankplassen 2, 0107 Oslo 1; tel (2) 31-60-00; telex 71369; fax (2) 41-31-05; Chair of Supervisory Board: K. Asdahl; Gov: Hermod Skånland; Dep gov: Kjell Storvik; f 1816; central bank; holds the exclusive right of note issue.

FINANCIAL AGENCY

Kredittilsynet (Banking, Securities, Insurance and Exchange Commission): c/o Ministry of Finance, POB 8008 Dep, 0030 Oslo 1; Chair: Erling Selvig; finance inspectorate.

NATIONALIZED INDUSTRY

Hydro Aluminium A/S: Drammensveien 134, POB 245, Skøyen, 0212 Oslo 2; tel (2) 45-15-15; fax (2) 45-18-18; Pres: Dag Flaa; Vice-Pres: Per Ivar Abyholm; f 1986 by a merger between Ardal og Sunndal Verk A/S and Norsk Hydro; production of aluminium.

Norsk Forsvarsteknologi A/S (NFT): POB 1003, 3601 Kongsberg; tel (3) 73-82-50; telex 71491; fax (3) 73-85-86; Pres: Jan T. Jørgensen; Vice-Pres: Arne Solberg; Bjoern Wiggo Bjune; f 1814; fmrly Kongsberg Våpenfabrikk; 100% state-owned; manufacture of defence equipment for army, navy and air force; devt, evaluation and production of defence products; maintenance of defence products, eg anti-ship missiles, fighter planes, helicopters and land-based command and control systems.

Norsk Jern Holding A/S: POB 308, 1301 Sandvika; tel (2) 51-50-80; telex 76070; fax (2) 51-50-88; Pres: Øistein Smith Larsen; Man Dir: Einar J. Berg; f 1988; 100% state-owned; steel production and trading; distribution of steel products; production of tin plate, ferrochrome, chrome-rich pig iron and iron concentrates.

Norsk Koksverk A/S: POB 203, 8601 Mo; tel (87) 51-555; telex 55235; Chair: Ragnar Skaudal; Gen Man: Arne Bottolfsen; f 1961; coke and liquid ammonia; 100% state-owned.

A/S Olivin: 6146 Åheim; tel (70) 24-016; telex 42307; Pres: John M. Kleven; Gen Man: Ola Øverlie; f 1948; 99.95% state-owned; sand and stone.

TRADE

Export Council of Norway: Drammensvn 40, 0255 Oslo 2; tel (2) 43-77-00; telex 78532; fax (2) 55-26-28.

Styret for det industrielle rettsvern (Norwegian Patent Office): POB 8160 Dep, 0033 Oslo 1; tel (2) 46-19-00; telex 19152; fax (2) 60-98-43; Dir-Gen: Arne G. Gerhardsen; national office for patents, trademarks, designs and hallmarks.

Defence

Norwegian Armed Forces: c/o Ministry of Defence, Myntgt 1, POB 8126 Dep, 0032 Oslo 1; tel (2) 40-20-00; telex 21605; fax (2) 40-23-23; Supreme Commdr-in-Chief: King Olav V; Chief of Defence Staff: Gen V. Eide.

Norwegian Air Force: address as above; Inspector-Gen: Maj-Gen O. F. Aamoth.

Norwegian Army: address as above; Inspector-Gen: Maj-Gen D. Danielsen.

Norwegian Home Guard: address as above; Inspector-Gen: Maj-Gen T. Sletten.

Norwegian Navy: address as above; Inspector-Gen: Rear-Adm Bjarne H. Grimstvedt.

Development

Distriktenes Utbyggingsfond (Regional Development Fund): Fr Selmers Vei 4, Oslo 6; tel (2) 63-40-00.

Legal and Judiciary

Høyesterett (Supreme Court): Grubbegaten 1, Oslo 1; tel (2) 33-27-90; Pres: Erling Sandene; decides cases in the last instance; composed of five judges appointed by the Crown and is competent to try all factual and legal aspects of cases in civil and criminal cause; in criminal cases, however, the competence of the Court is limited to questions concerning the application of the law, the nature of the penalty, and procedural errors of the lower courts.

Media

BROADCASTING

Norsk Rikskringkasting—NRK (Norwegian Broadcasting Corpn): Bj Bjørnsons plassen 1, 0340 Oslo 3; tel (2) 45-90-50; telex 76820; fax (2) 45-74-40; Chair of Govs: Halvor Stenstadvold; Dir-Gen: Einar Førde.

Teledirektoratet (Broadcasting Authority): St Olavs plassen, POB 6701, 0130 Oslo 1; tel (2) 48-89-90; telex 71203.

GOVERNMENT PUBLISHER

Statens Trykningskontor—STK (Government Printing Office): Mollergt 19, POB 8129 Dep, 0032 Oslo 1; tel (2) 34-98-00; fax (2) 34-95-95; Govt Printer: Per Mjelva; f 1904; publication of Bills, Acts, Regulations, all Govt printing; sale and marketing of Govt information.

NEWS AND INFORMATION

Statistisk Sentralbyrå (Central Bureau of Statistics): Skippergt 15, POB 8131 Dep, 0033 Oslo 1; tel (2) 41-38-20; fax (2) 33-32-64; Dir-Gen (acting): Gisle Skancke; f 1876; preparation of official statistics; carries out economic and social research and analyses.

Mining and Energy

Fosdalens Bergverks A/S: 7720 Malm; Pres: Kåre Gisvold; Gen Man: Snorre Tessem; f 1912; iron ore concentrates (magnetite), pyrites, calchopyrites; 100% state-owned.

Institutt for Energiteknikk—IFE (Institute for Energy Technology): POB 40, 2007 Kjeller; tel (6) 80-60-60; telex 74573; fax (6) 81-63-56; Man Dir: N. G. Aamodt; Technical Dir: J. O. Berg; f 1948; national institute for energy research; carries out research into nuclear power, isotope production and irradiation services, petroleum technology, materials technology, industrial energy technology, etc.

Norges Energiverkforbund (Federation of Norwegian Energy Utilities): Gaustadalléen 30D, POB 74 Blindern, 0314 Oslo 3; tel (2) 69-58-70; Man Dir: Robert Heiberg Kahrs; f 1901; about 300 mems.

Norsk Hydro A/S: Bygdøy Allé 2, 0257 Oslo 2; tel (2) 43-21-00; telex 78350; Chair: E. Abrahamsen; Pres: T. Aakvaag; f 1905; 51% state-controlled; large industrial conglomerate with gas and petroleum interests.

Norwegian Water Resources and Energy Administration: Middelthunsgt 29, 0301 Oslo 3; tel (2) 99-59-59-5; telex 79397; fax (2) 95-90-01; Chief Exec Dir: Erling Diesen; f 1920; planning of hydroelectric power; handles applications for licences to construct and operate gas-fired power plants; presents recommendations to the Ministry of Petroleum and Energy.

Oljedirektoratet (Norwegian Petroleum Directorate): Prof Olav Hanssensvei 10, POB 600, 4001 Stavanger; tel (4) 87-60-00; telex 42863; fax (4) 55-15-71; Dir-Gen: Fredrik Hagemann;

f 1973; admin of Norwegian petroleum resources; ensures the licencee administers petroleum resources in an efficient manner; advises the Ministry of Petroleum and Energy and the Ministry of Local Govt and Labour and informs the public.

Statkraft (Norwegian State Power Board): Middelthuns Gate 29, Majorstva, Oslo 3; tel (2) 46-98-00; telex 8180403; fax (2) 60-67-58; Gen Man: Gunnar Vatten; Dir, Planning: Ingvald S. Haga; f 1913; planning, building and operation of all state-owned power stations and main transmission lines in Norway.

Statoil (Den norske stats oljeselskap A/S): POB 300, 4001 Stavanger; tel (4) 80-80-80; telex 73600; fax (4) 80-70-42; Chair: Jan Erik Langangen; Pres: Harald Norvik; f 1972; integrated oil co; 100% state-owned; has 14 subsidiaries in which Statoil owns a controlling interest of at least 50%.

Norwegian Underwater Technology Centre A/S (Nutec): POB 6, 5034 Laksevåg; tel (5) 34-16-00; telex 42892.

A/S Sydvaranger: POB 405, 9901 Kirkenes; tel (85) 91-40-1; telex 64108; fax (85) 91-99-5; Dirs: Oddmund Husum; Tarald Husaas; f 1906; iron ore co.

Tourism

NORTRA (Norwegian Tourist Board): Head Office, Havnelageret, Langkaia 1, POB 499 Sentrum, 0105 Oslo 1; tel (2) 42-70-44; telex 78582; fax (2) 33-69-98; Man Dir: Torbjørn Frøysnes; f 1903; tourism marketing organization; provides information.

Transport and Communications

TELECOMMUNICATIONS

Televerket (Norwegian Telecommunications Administration): St Olavs plassen, POB 6701, 0130 Oslo 1; tel (2) 48-89-90; telex 71203; Dir-Gen: Kjell Holler; telecommunications operating co.

TRANSPORT

Civil Aviation Authority: POB 8124, 0032 Oslo 1; tel (2) 42-92-80; telex 71032.

Sjøfartsdirektoratet (Maritime Directorate): Thorvald Meyersgt 7, POB 8123 Dep, Oslo 1; tel (2) 35-02-50.

Norges Statsbaner (Norwegian State Railways): Storgt 33, 0184 Oslo 1; tel (2) 36-80-00; telex 71168; Gen Man: Robert F. Nordén; f 1854.

Det Norske Luftfartselskap A/S—DNL (Norwegian Airlines): 1330 Oslo Lufthavn; tel (2) 59-63-99; telex 76797; fax (2) 58-08-20; Pres: Torstein Ljøstad; f 1946; partner in Scandinavian Airline Systems—SAS (see under Sweden, Transport section) and SCANAIR.

Norwegian Public Roads Administration: POB 6390, Etterstad, 0604 Oslo 6; tel (2) 63-95-00; telex 21542; fax (2) 63-97-68; Dir-Gen: Eskild Jensen; f 1864; construction and maintenance of public roads and bridges; roads authority.

NORWEGIAN DEPENDENCY

SVALBARD

The Government

OFFICE OF THE GOVERNOR
9170 Longyearbyen
Tel (80) 21-400
Sysselmann (Governor): Leif Eldring

Government Agencies

BROADCASTING

Svalbard Radio: Longyearbyen; operates the regional telephone system as well as broadcasting a local radio and TV service.

MINING

Office of the Commissioner of Mines: Longyearbyen; Commr: Johannes Vik.

Store Norske Spitsbergen Kulkompani A/S: Longyearbyen; Admin Dir: Gunnar R. Christiansen; state-owned coal-mining co.

OMAN

MINISTRIES AND GOVERNMENT DEPARTMENTS

OFFICE OF THE DEPUTY PRIME MINISTER FOR FINANCIAL AND ECONOMIC AFFAIRS
POB 506, Muscat
Tel 738201; telex 5333
Deputy Prime Minister: Qais bin Abd al-Munim az-Zawawi

OFFICE OF THE DEPUTY PRIME MINISTER FOR LEGAL AFFAIRS
POB 721, Muscat
Tel 738520; telex 5575
Deputy Prime Minister: Sayed Fahd bin Mahmoud as-Said

OFFICE OF THE DEPUTY PRIME MINISTER FOR SECURITY AND DEFENCE
POB 113, Muscat
Telex 3228
Deputy Prime Minister: Sayed Fahar bin Taimour as-Said

OFFICE OF THE SPECIAL REPRESENTATIVE OF HM THE SULTAN
POB 875, Muscat
Tel 736222
Special Representative: Sayed Thuwaini bin Shibab as-Said

DIWAN OF ROYAL COURT AFFAIRS
POB 949, Muscat
Tel 736621; telex 5016
President: Sayed Saif bin Hamad Bin Saud

MINISTRY OF AGRICULTURE AND FISHERIES
POB 467, Ruwi
Tel 696300; telex 3503
Minister: Sheikh Muhammad bin Abdullah bin Zahir al-Hana'i

MINISTRY OF THE CIVIL SERVICE
Muscat
Minister: Ahmad bin Abd an-Nabi Mekki

MINISTRY OF COMMERCE AND INDUSTRY
POB 550, Muscat
Tel 799500; telex 3665
Minister: Col Salim bin Abdullah al-Ghazali

MINISTRY OF COMMUNICATIONS, CIVIL AVIATION, PORTS AND ROADS
POB 684, Muscat
Tel 702233; telex 7616
Minister: Sheikh Hamoud bin Abdullah al-Harthy

MINISTRY OF DEFENCE
POB 113, Muscat
Tel 704096; telex 3228
Minister: Sultan Qaboos bin Said
Minister of State: Brig al-Mutasim bin Hamoud bin Nasr al-Bousaidi

MINISTRY OF EDUCATION AND YOUTH AFFAIRS
POB 3, Ruwi
Tel 775202; telex 3369
Minister: Yahya bin Mahfouz al-Munziri

MINISTRY OF ELECTRICITY AND WATER
POB 4491, Ruwi
Tel 603800; telex 3358
Minister: Khalfan bin Nasir al-Wahaibi

MINISTRY OF ENVIRONMENT AND WATER RESOURCES
POB 323, Muscat
Tel 696444; telex 5711
Minister: Sayed Shabib bin Taimour bin Faisal as-Said

MINISTRY OF FINANCE
POB 506, Muscat
Tel 738201; telex 5333
Minister: Sultan Qaboos bin Said
Minister of State: Muhammad Ridha Musa

MINISTRY OF FOREIGN AFFAIRS
POB 252, Muscat
Tel 699532; telex 3337
Minister: Sultan Qaboos bin Said
Minister of State: Yousuf bin al-Alawi bin Abdullah

MINISTRY OF HEALTH
POB 393, Muscat
Tel 602177; telex 5294
Minister: Ali bin Muhammad bin Mousa

MINISTRY OF HOUSING AND MUNICIPALITIES
POB 173, Muscat
Tel 703366; telex 3694
Minister: Malek bin Sulaiman al-Muammari

MINISTRY OF INFORMATION
POB 600, Muscat
Tel 603888; telex 6265
Minister: Abd al-Aziz bin Muhammad ar-Rowas

MINISTRY OF THE INTERIOR
POB 3127, Ruwi
Tel 602244; telex 5650
Minister: Sayed Badr bin Saud bin Hareb

MINISTRY OF JUSTICE, AWQAF (RELIGIOUS ENDOWMENTS) AND ISLAMIC AFFAIRS
POB 3354, Ruwi
Tel 702233
Minister: Sayed Hilal bin Saud bin Hareb al-Bousaidi

MINISTRY OF NATIONAL HERITAGE AND CULTURE
POB 668, Muscat
Tel 602555; telex 5649
Minister: Sayed Faisal bin Ali as-Said

MINISTRY OF PETROLEUM AND MINERALS
POB 551, Muscat
Tel 603333; telex 5280; fax 696972
Minister: Said bin Ahmad bin Said ash-Shanfari

MINISTRY OF POSTS, TELEGRAPHS AND TELEPHONES
POB 3338, Muscat
Tel 697888; telex 3237
Minister: Ahmad bin Sowaidan al-Baluchi

MINISTRY OF PUBLIC WORKS
POB 215, Muscat
Tel 704280; telex 3359
Minister: Dr Asim al-Jamali

MINISTRY OF REGIONAL AND MUNICIPAL AFFAIRS
POB 3461, Ruwi
Tel 701947; telex 3842
Minister: Muhammad bin Ali al-Qatabi

MINISTRY OF SOCIAL AFFAIRS AND LABOUR
POB 560, Muscat
Tel 602353; telex 5002
Minister: Sheikh Mustahil bin Ahmad al-Ma'shini

OFFICE OF THE MINISTER OF STATE AND WALI OF DHOFAR
POB 18040, Salalah
Tel 290000; telex 7620; fax 294269
Minister of State and Governor: Musallam bin Ali al-Bousaidi

OFFICE OF THE PRESIDENT OF THE PALACE OFFICE
POB 5227, Ruwi
Tel 600631; telex 3267
President: Ali bin Majid al-Maamari

OFFICE OF THE PRESIDENT OF THE STATE CONSULTATIVE ASSEMBLY
POB 5361, Ruwi
Tel 510444; telex 5117
President: Muhammad bin Ali al-Qatabi

OFFICE OF THE VICE-CHANCELLOR OF SULTAN QABOOS UNIVERSITY
POB 32500-Al Khod, Ruwi
Tel 513333; telex 5602
Vice-Chancellor: Sheikh Amer bin Ali bin Omeir al-Marhoubi

OFFICE OF THE WALI OF MUSCAT
POB 927, Muscat
Tel 798100
Governor: Sayed Sultan Muhammad bin Hilal as-Sammar

GOVERNMENT AGENCIES AND ORGANIZATIONS

Advisory and Supervisory Bodies

Oman Tender Board: POB 6868, Ruwi; tel 708881; telex 3728; Chair: Assim al-Jamali; responsible for inviting, receiving and assessing tenders for public works contracts.

Public Authority for Stores and Food Reserves: POB 5955, Ruwi; tel 707538; telex 3030; Dir-Gen: Mahmoud bin Muhammad bin Ali al-Jarwani.

Business and Economy

BANKING

Central Bank of Oman: POB 4161, Ruwi; tel 702222; telex 3794; Chair: (vacant); Dep Chair and Pres: Dr Abd al-Wahab Khayata; f 1974; 2 brs.

Oman Bank for Agriculture and Fisheries SAO: POB 6077, Ruwi; tel 701761; telex 3046; Chair: Sheikh Muhammad bin Abdullah bin Zaher al-Hinai; Gen Man: Saad bin Musa al-Jenaibi; f 1981; short-, medium- and long-term finance for all activities in the public sector related to agriculture and fisheries; 12 brs.

Oman Housing Bank: POB 5555, Ruwi; tel 704444; telex 3077; Chair: Malik bin Sulaiman bin Said al Ma'mari; Gen Man: Hamoud bin Sangour bin Hashim; f 1977; 60.9% state-owned; medium- and long-term finance for housing devt; 8 brs.

FINANCIAL AGENCIES

State General Reserve Fund: DGF Bldg, POB 188, Muscat.

INSURANCE

Oman National Insurance Co SAO (ONIC): POB 5254, Ruwi; tel 795020; telex 3111; Gen Man: Jack McRobbie; f 1978.

MARKETING

Al Omaneya Advertising Marketing Co: POB 6303, Ruwi; tel 707849; telex 3758; Gen Man: Hamad bin Muhammad al-Rashdy.

Public Authority for Marketing of Agricultural Produce: POB 1392, CPO Seeb; tel 591540; telex 5676; Exec Chair: Said bin Nasser al-Kousaibi.

NATIONALIZED INDUSTRY

Government Clothing Factory: POB 5527, Ruwi; tel 590307; telex 5542; Dir: Joy Silva.

Oman Cement Co SAO: POB 3560, Ruwi; tel 626626; telex 5139; Chair: Dr al-Yaqdhan bin Taleb bin Ali al-Hinai; Vice-Chair and Gen Man: Dr Ali bin Moosa; f 1977; devt and production of cement.

Oman Flour Mills Co Ltd SAO: POB 3566, Ruwi; tel 711155; telex 5422; Chair: Dr al-Yaqdhari bin Taleb bin Ali al-Hinai; f 1976; 60% state-owned; production of flour and animal feed.

TRADE

Authority for the Settlement of Commercial Disputes: POB 6363, Ruwi; tel 703291; telex 3185; Pres: Ali bin Daud.

Oman Exhibition Centre: Seeb Airport, POB 1117, Muscat; tel 510900; telex 5511; fax 510055; Gen Man: Jean Jacques Deutsch; Operations Man: Hassan Mosafer; f 1985; exhibitions, fairs, conferences, shows.

Defence

Armed Forces: c/o Ministry of Defence, POB 113, Muscat; tel 704096; telex 3228; Chief of Staff: Lt-Gen Hamid bin Said al-Oufi.

> **Sultan of Oman Air Forces:** POB 1772, CPO Seeb; telex 5592.
>
> **Sultan of Oman Land Forces:** POB 1720, CPO Seeb; telex 5445.
>
> **Sultan of Oman Navy Forces:** POB 1723, CPO Seeb; telex 5593.

Royal Oman Police: POB 2, Muscat; tel 560099; telex 5442.

Development and Planning

Development Council: POB 881, Muscat; tel 698900; telex 5384; Sec-Gen: Sharif Lofty.

Musandam Development Committee: POB 5286, Ruwi; tel 704599; telex 3103; Chair: Hamoud bin Abdullah al-Harthy.

Regional Development Committee: POB 6255, Ruwi; tel 561923; telex 5204; Chair: Sheikh Bader bin Saud bin Harib al-Bousaidi.

Rusayl Industrial Estate Auhtority (RIEA): POB 42002, Rusayl; tel 626080; telex 5001; Chair: Ahmad bin Abdul Nabi Makki.

Education

Sultan Qaboos University Council: POB 32500-Al Khod, Ruwi; tel 513333; telex 5602; Vice-Chancellor: Sheikh Amer bin Ali bin Omeir al-Marhoubi.

Employment

Civil Service Council: POB 229, Muscat; tel 736158; Chair: Sayed Faisal bin Ali al-Said; responsible for appointments within the civil service.

The Environment

Council for the Conservation of the Environment and Water Resources: POB 5310, Ruwi; tel 704344; telex 3590; Dep Chair: Sayyid Shabib bin Taimur.

Fishing

Oman National Fisheries Co: POB 5900, Ruwi; tel 714129; telex 5092; fax 714765; Gen Man: Muhammad M. al-Alawi; f 1980; responsible for the commercial devt of fishing, and processing and marketing of marine products; operates 7 deep-sea trawlers and a processing and freezing plant.

Media

BROADCASTING

Radio Oman: Ministry of Information, POB 600, Muscat; tel 603888; telex 6265; Dir-Gen: Ali bin Abdullah al-Mujeni; f 1970; transmits in Arabic and English.

NEWS AND INFORMATION

Oman Directorate-General of National Statistics: Development Council, POB 881, Muscat; tel 698900; telex 5384; collection, analysis and publication of statistics.

Oman News Agency: c/o Ministry of Information, POB 600, Muscat; tel 696970; telex 6265; Dir-Gen: Muhammad bin Salim al-Marhoon.

Oman Newspaper House: POB 6002, Ruwi; tel 701555; telex 3638; Chair: Abdul Aziz bin Muhammad al-Rowas.

Mining and Energy

ENERGY

Directorate-General of Electricity: POB 3015, Ruwi.

Mina al-Fahal Oil Terminal: POB 81, Mina al-Fahal, Qurm, Muscat.

National Gas Co SAO: POB 1350, CPO Seeb International Airport; tel 626073; Gen Man: L. N. Goculdas; f 1979; bottling of liquefied petroleum gas.

Oman National Electric Co SAO: POB 4393, Mutrah; tel 796353; telex 3328; Chair: Saud Ali al-Khalili; Gen Man (acting): M. Osman Baig.

Oman Refinery Co LLC: POB 6568, Ruwi; tel 561200; telex 5123; Man Dir: James J. Prichard; production of light petroleum products.

Petroleum Development Oman LLC (PDO): POB 81, Mina al-Fahal, Qurm, Muscat; tel 678111; telex 5212; Man Dir: M. Pink; 60% state-owned; incorporated in Sultanate of Oman since 1980 by royal decree as limited liability co.

MINING

Oman Mining Co Ltd LLC: POB 758, Muscat; tel 603501; telex 5492; Chair: Mohsin Haider Darwish; f 1978; 100% state-owned; devt of copper mines.

Transport and Communications

TELECOMMUNICATIONS

General Telecommunications Organization (GTO): POB 3789, Ruwi; tel 696844; telex 5600; Exec Pres: Noor bin Muhammad bin Noor.

TRANSPORT

Directorate-General of Civil Aviation: POB 204, Muscat; tel 519210; telex 5418; Dir-Gen: Tariq bin Muhammad al-Mantheri.

Directorate-General of Roads: POB 7027, Mutrah; tel 701577; Dir-Gen: Sheikh Muhammad bin Hilal al-Khalili.

Gulf Air Co: POB 138, Manama, Bahrain; tel 531166; telex 8255; fax 530385; Pres and Chief Exec: Ali Ibrahim al-Malki; Exec Vice-Pres: Ali Muhammad al-Jasim; f 1978; jointly owned by the Govts of Oman, Bahrain, Qatar and Abu Dhabi; services throughout the Middle East, and to Europe and the Far East.

Oman Aviation Services Co (SAO): POB 1058, CPO Seeb International Airport; tel 519223; telex 5424; fax 510805; Gen Man: Riadh bin Abdullah al-Bousaidi; Dep Gen Mans: Hamoud M. al-Behlany, Saud bin Dawood al-Raisy; f 1981; domestic airline; also provides ground handling, engineering maintenance and catering services to the airlines using Seeb Airport.

Oman National Transport Co SAO: POB 620, Muscat; tel 590046; telex 5018; fax 590152; Chair: Sali bin Ali bin Nasser Assiyabi; Man Dir: Suleiman bin Muhana al-Adawi; f 1984; public bus and express coach operators.

Port Services Corpn: POB 133, Mina Qaboos, Muscat; tel 714000; telex 5233; Chair: Sheikh Hamoud bin Abdullah al-Harthi; Pres: Awad bin Salim ash-Shanfari; f 1976; jointly owned by Govt and private shareholders.

Utilities

Public Authority for Water Resources: POB 5575, Ruwi; tel 704188; telex 3629.

PAKISTAN

Head of State

The President is Head of State and is elected at a joint sitting of the Federal Legislature to serve a five-year term. The President must be a Muslim. The President acts on the advice of the Prime Minister.

President: Ghulam Ishaq Khan (assumed power 17 August 1988; elected 12 December 1988).

Office of the President: Constitution Ave, Islamabad; tel (51) 65971.

Legislature

The Federal Legislature comprises the President, a National Assembly and a Senate. The National Assembly consists of 207 members elected directly for five years by universal adult suffrage, plus 20 women members and 10 members representing minorities. The Senate comprises 87 indirectly-elected members serving six-year terms. Pakistan comprises four provinces (with appointed Governors and provincial governments), the federal capital of Islamabad and federally administered 'tribal areas'.

Senate: Parliament House, Islamabad; Chair: Wasim Sajjad Jan.

National Assembly: Parliament House, Islamabad; Speaker: Malik Meraj Khalid.

MINISTRIES AND GOVERNMENT DEPARTMENTS

OFFICE OF THE PRIME MINISTER
Islamabad
Prime Minister: Benazir Bhutto
Minister with responsibility for Kashmir:
Mohammad Hanif Khan
Minister without portfolio: Begum Nusrat Bhutto

MINISTRY OF COMMERCE
Block A, Pakistan Secretariat, Islamabad
Tel (51) 825078; telex 5859
Minister: Syed Faisal Saleh Hayat

MINISTRY OF COMMUNICATIONS
Block D, Pakistan Secretariat, Islamabad
Tel (51) 826277; telex 5713
Minister: Makhdoom Fahim Amin

MINISTRY OF CULTURE AND TOURISM
College Rd, Shalimar 7/2, Islamabad
Tel (51) 824702
Minister of Culture: Agha Tariq Khan
Minister of Tourism: Yusuf Raza Gilani

MINISTRY OF DEFENCE
Pakistan Secretariat, No 11, Rawalpindi
Tel (51) 63329; telex 5779
Minister: Benazir Bhutto

MINISTRY OF EDUCATION
Block D, Pakistan Secretariat, Islamabad
Tel (51) 825001
Minister: Syed Ghulam Mustafa Shah

MINISTRY OF THE ESTABLISHMENT
Islamabad
Minister: Benazir Bhutto

MINISTRY OF FINANCE AND ECONOMIC AFFAIRS
Block Q, Pakistan Secretariat, Islamabad
Tel (51) 820928
Minister: Benazir Bhutto

Economic Affairs Division: Block C, Pakistan Secretariat, Islamabad; tel (51) 821876.

MINISTRY OF FOOD, AGRICULTURE AND CO-OPERATIVES
Block B, Pakistan Secretariat, Islamabad
Tel (51) 821905; telex 5844
Minister: Rao Sikandar Iqbal

MINISTRY OF FOREIGN AFFAIRS
Constitution Ave, Islamabad
Tel (51) 812470; telex 5800
Minister: Sahabzada Yaqub Khan

MINISTRY OF HEALTH, SPECIAL EDUCATION AND SOCIAL WELFARE
Block C, Pakistan Secretariat, Islamabad
Tel (51) 824960
Minister: Syed Amir Hyder Kazmi

MINISTRY OF HOUSING AND WORKS
Block B, Pakistan Secretariat, Islamabad
Tel (51) 825941
Minister: Mohammad Hanif Khan

MINISTRY OF INDUSTRIES
Block A, Pakistan Secretariat, Islamabad
Tel (51) 822164; telex 5774
Minister: Ali Nawaz Shah

MINISTRY OF INFORMATION AND BROADCASTING
Block M, Pakistan Secretariat, Islamabad
Tel (51) 821626; telex 5782
Minister: Benazir Bhutto

MINISTRY OF THE INTERIOR
Block R, Pakistan Secretariat, Islamabad
Tel (51) 820641
Minister: Aitazaz Ahsan

MINISTRY OF LAW AND JUSTICE
Islamabad
Tel (51) 823397
Minister: Syed Iftikhar Hussain Gilani

MINISTRY OF LABOUR AND MANPOWER
Block B, Pakistan Secretariat, Islamabad
Tel (51) 823686
Minister: (vacant)

MINISTRY OF LOCAL GOVERNMENT AND RURAL DEVELOPMENT
Islamabad
Tel (51) 820902
Minister: Syed Faisal Saleh Hayat

MINISTRY OF NARCOTICS
Pakistan Secretariat, Islamabad
Minister of State: Muzaffar Shah

MINISTRY OF PAKISTANI AFFAIRS
Islamabad
Minister: Mukhtar Ahmad Awan

MINISTRY OF PARLIAMENTARY AFFAIRS
Islamabad
Minister: Khwaja Tariq Rahim

MINISTRY OF PETROLEUM AND NATURAL RESOURCES
Block A, Pakistan Secretariat, Islamabad
Tel (51) 821220; telex 5851
Minister: Jehangir Badar

MINISTRY OF PLANNING AND DEVELOPMENT
Block P, Pakistan Secretariat, Islamabad
Tel (51) 829442; telex 5717
Minister: (vacant)

MINISTRY OF PRODUCTION
Block D, Pakistan Secretariat, Islamabad
Tel (51) 822175; telex 5579
Minister of State: Raja Shahid Zafar

MINISTRY OF RAILWAYS
Islamabad
Tel (51) 827650; telex 5714
Minister: Zafar Ali Leghari

MINISTRY OF RELIGIOUS AFFAIRS AND MINORITIES' AFFAIRS
Plot 20, Markaz G-6, Civic Centre, Islamabad
Tel (51) 828411; telex 54047
Minister: Khan Bahadur Khan

MINISTRY OF SCIENCE AND TECHNOLOGY
Block S, Pakistan Secretariat, Islamabad
Tel (51) 825208
Minister of State: Javed Jabbar

MINISTRY OF STATE FOR THE ENVIRONMENT AND URBAN AFFAIRS
Islamabad
Minister of State: Syed Qasim Ali Shah

MINISTRY OF STATE FOR SPORTS
Islamabad
Minister: Chaudhry Qadir Bakhsh Mela

MINISTRY OF STATE FOR WOMEN'S DIVISION
Islamabad
Minister of State: Begum Khakwani

MINISTRY OF STATES AND FRONTIER REGIONS
Block R, Pakistan Secretariat, Islamabad
Tel (51) 820672
Minister: Mohammad Hanif Khan

MINISTRY OF WATER AND POWER
Block A, Pakistan Secretariat, Islamabad
Tel (51) 851041
Minister: Sardar Farooq Ahmad Khan Leghari

GOVERNMENT AGENCIES AND ORGANIZATIONS

Advisory and Supervisory Bodies

Council of Islamic Ideology: House 30, St 48, F-8/4, Islamabad; tel (51) 858273; f 1962; makes recommendations to Parliament and provincial assemblies on ways of enabling and encouraging the Muslims of Pakistan to order their lives in accordance with the principles of Islam; advises on whether laws are compatible with Islamic law.

Election Commission of Pakistan: Block S, Pakistan Secretariat, Islamabad; tel (51) 820415; telex 5847; fax (51) 825402; Dep Sec: Ch. Basrir Ahmed; f 1956; prepares and revises electoral rolls for elections to the National and Provincial Assemblies; organizes elections; appoints election tribunals to rule on election disputes.

National Economic Board: Karachi; Chair: Dr Mahbubul Haq; Vice-Chair: Ghulam Ishaq Khan; f 1979; advisory body; reviews and evaluates the state of the economy and makes proposals, especially to further the socio-economic principles of Islam.

National Economic Council: Karachi; Chair: Benazir Bhutto; supreme economic body; mems are governors and chief ministers of the four provinces and Federal Ministers in charge of economic ministries; senior Federal and provincial officials in the economic field are also associated.

Office of the Federal Ombudsman: Benevolent Fund Bldg, Zero Point, Islamabad; tel (51) 854191.

Agriculture

Cotton Board: Dr Abbasi Clinic Bldg, 76 Strachan Rd, Karachi 1; Chair: Hamid D. Habib; Dep Sec: Sifatullah Khan; f 1950.

Ghee Corpn of Pakistan Ltd: LDA Plaza, 5th Floor, Egerton Rd, Lahore; Chair: Sadiq Saeed.

Punjab Seed Corpn: 4 Lytton Rd, Lahore; tel (42) 311280; Dep Man Dir: Mohammad Hassan Chaudhry; f 1976; seed production, processing, storage, packing, marketing, etc.

Sind Sugar Corpn Ltd: Shaikh Sultan Trust Bldg, 6th Floor, Beaumont Rd, Karachi 3; Chair: Saeed Ahmad Siddiqi.

Business and Economy

BANKING

Agricultural Development Bank of Pakistan: Faisal Ave, POB 1400, Islamabad; tel (51) 824135; telex 5618; Chair: Chaudhry Ahmad Saeed; f 1961; provides credit facilities to agriculturists and cottage industrialists in the rural areas and for allied projects; promotes agricultural devt by providing loans and supervised credit programme; 42 regional offices and 250 field offices.

Allied Bank of Pakistan Ltd: 3rd Floor, New Jubilee Insurance House, I. I. Chundrigar Rd, Karachi 2; tel (21) 2417011; telex 2681; Pres: S. Amjad Ali; f 1942; 689 brs in Pakistan and 2 brs overseas.

Bankers Equity Ltd: State Life Bldg No 3, Dr Ziauddin Ahmed Rd, Karachi 4; tel (21) 514017; telex 24646; Man Dir: Abdul Karim Lodhi; f 1980; devt bank; provides financing for industrial projects in the private and mixed sector.

Federal Bank for Co-operatives: State Bank Bldg, G-5, POB 1218, Islamabad; tel (51) 826994; telex 5878; Chair: Muhammad Aslam; f 1976; owned jointly by the Federal Govt, provincial govts and the State Bank of Pakistan; provides credit facilities to each of four provincial co-operative banks and regulates their operations; they in turn provide credit facilities through co-operative socs; supervises policy of provincial co-operative banks and of multi-unit co-operative socs; assists Federal and provincial govts in formulating schemes for devt and revitalization of co-operative movement; carries out research on rural credit, etc; 4 brs.

Habib Bank Ltd: 11 Habib Bank Plaza, I. I. Chundrigar Rd, Karachi 2; tel (21) 219111; telex 2786; Pres: Safdar Abbas Zaidi; Exec Vice-Pres: Waheed A. Kidwai; f 1941; 1,815 brs in Pakistan and 65 brs overseas.

Industrial Development Bank of Pakistan: State Life Bldg, 2 Wallace Rd, off I. I. Chundrigar Rd, POB 5082, Karachi 2; tel (21) 228535; telex 23722; Man Dir: Masood Akhtar; f 1961; provides credit facilities for small- and medium-sized industrial enterprises in the private sector; 10 brs.

Muslim Commercial Bank Ltd: Adamjee House, I. I. Chundrigar Rd, Karachi 2; tel (21) 224091; telex 2887; Pres: Muhammad Ibrahim Gurwara; f 1948; 1,261 brs in Pakistan and 5 brs overseas.

National Bank of Pakistan (NBP): NBP Bldg, I. I. Chundrigar Rd, POB 4937, Karachi 2; tel (21) 2416780; telex 23733; fax (21) 2416769; Pres: D. M. Quraishi; f 1949; c 1,400 brs in Pakistan and 23 brs overseas.

State Bank of Pakistan: Central Directorate, I. I. Chundrigar Rd, POB 4456, Karachi 2; tel (21) 234141; telex 23730; Gov: I. A. Hanafi; Dep Gov: I. H. Qarni; f 1948; central bank and bank of issue; controls and regulates currency and foreign exchange; 14 brs.

United Bank Ltd: State Life Bldg, I. I. Chundrigar Rd, Karachi; tel (21) 2417100; telex 2834; fax (21) 2413483; Pres: Maqbool A. Soomro; f 1959; 1,559 brs in Pakistan and 25 brs overseas.

INSURANCE

Department of Insurance: Hajra Mansion, Zaibun-Nisa St, Saddar, Karachi; tel (21) 514410; Controller of Insurance: A.

M. Khalfe; f 1948; Govt dept attached to the Ministry of Commerce; regulates insurance business.

Pakistan Insurance Institute: Shafi Court, 2nd Floor, Mereweather Rd, Karachi 4; Chair: Mahmood Hashmi; f 1951 to encourage insurance education.

Postal Life Insurance Organization: Tibet Centre, M. A. Jinnah Rd, Karachi; tel (21) 723804; Gen Man and Chief Exec: Dr Salahuddin Ahmad; f 1884; life and group insurance.

State Life Insurance Corpn of Pakistan: State Life Bldg No 9, Dr Ziauddin Ahmed Rd, POB 5725, Karachi 4; tel (21) 523236; telex 2779; Chair: Iqbal M. Qureshi; f 1972 by merger of all life insurance cos and the life depts of composite cos; life and group insurance and pension schemes.

NATIONALIZED INDUSTRY

Federal Chemical and Ceramics Corpn Ltd: PNSC Bldg, 15th Floor, Moulvi Tamizuddin Khan Rd, POB 4180, Karachi; tel (21) 551021; telex 23541; Chair: Saadat Hussain Khan.

Karachi Shipyard and Engineering Works Ltd: West Wharf, Dockyard Rd, POB 4419, Karachi; tel (21) 202760; telex 2706; fax (21) 2415952; Man Dir: M. Naeem Beg; f 1956; building and repairing ships, general engineering (sugar and cement plant, petro-chemical plant, boilers, cranes, pressure vessels, steel structures, etc).

National Engineering Services (Pakistan) (NESPAK): Karachi; Pres and Man Dir: Amjad Agha; f 1973; consulting co for engineering projects, including irrigation, power stations, roads and town planning; operates in Pakistan and abroad.

National Fertilizer Corpn of Pakistan (Pvt) Ltd: Alfalah Bldg, Shahrah-e-Quaid-e-Azam, POB 1730, Lahore; tel (42) 302904; telex 44726; Chair: A. M. Shah.

National Motors Ltd: Hub Chowki Rd, SITE, POB 2706, Karachi 28; telex 25105; Man Dir: Azhar Elahi Jafri; manufactures trucks; assembles buses, jeeps and land cruisers.

National Petrocarbon Ltd: National Bank Bldg, 1st Floor, Sharea Faisal, POB 8911, Karachi 29; tel (21) 43966.

Pakistan Automobile Corpn (PACO): PNSC Bldg, 6th Floor, Karachi 2; tel (21) 551056; telex 2865; Chair: Kunwar Idris; f 1972.

Pakistan Steel Mills Corpn Ltd: Bin Qasim, POB 5429, Karachi; tel (21) 737321; telex 23804; Chair: Maj-Gen Shujat Ali Bokharee; Man Dir: Dr M. Akram Shaikh; f 1973; production of coke, pig iron, steel billets, hot and cold rolled sheets, coils, galvanized sheets and coil, coal tar, ammonium sulphate, oxygen, etc.

State Cement Corpn of Pakistan (Pvt) Ltd: PEC Bldg, 97-A/B-D Gulberg III, Lahore; tel (42) 870341; telex 44636; Chair: Dr Imriaz Ahmad Khan; f 1973; operates public-sector cement plants; distributes cement.

State Engineering Corpn Ltd: PNSC Bldg, 10th Floor, Karachi 2; tel (21) 552061; telex 24744; Chair: M. Saeed Khan; f 1979.

Pakistan Engineering Co Ltd (PECO): 6 Ganga Ram Trust Bldg, Shahrah-e-Quaid-e-Azam, Lahore; tel (42) 320225; telex 44750; Man Dir: Maj-Gen Muhammad Ikram Cheema; f 1950; machine tools, diesel engines, centrifugal, turbine and submersible pumps, power looms, concrete mixers, rerolled material, electric motors and bicycles.

TRADE

Cotton Export Corpn of Pakistan (Pvt) Ltd: State Life Bldg No 3, Dr Ziauddin Ahmed Rd, POB 3738, Karachi; tel (21) 516056; telex 2628; Chair: Dr Muhammad Arshad Malik; Sec: Fasihuddin; f 1973; raw cotton exports in both the public sector and private sector.

Export Promotion Bureau: National Press Trust House, I. I. Chundrigar Rd, Karachi; tel (21) 210505; telex 23877; Chair: Shaikh Inaam-ul-Haque; f 1963; devt of Pakistan's exports; collection, maintenance, analyses and dissemination of export information; guides the Govt on various issues concerning exports.

Rice Export Corpn of Pakistan: State Life Bldg No 1, 3rd Floor, I. I. Chundrigar Rd, Karachi; tel (21) 221063; telex 23706; Chair: Naseer Muhammad Shah; f 1974; procures, mills, cleans, stores, packs and markets standard quality rice for export on monopoly basis.

Trading Corpn of Pakistan: Press Trust House, I. I. Chundrigar Rd, Karachi; tel (21) 210515; telex 2784; Chair: Ali Khan Junejo; f 1967; sole importer of Pakistan's total requirements in bulk; special-quality billets, coal, hessian, iron and steel pipes; major importer of edible oils and non-ferrous metals and exporters of goods of Pakistani origin (urea, cotton, textiles, dried dates, etc) except rice.

Defence

Armed Forces: Joint Staff Headquarters, Chaklala, Rawalpindi; tel (51) 63350; Chair, Joint Chiefs of Staff Committee: Adm Iftikhar Ahmad Sirohey; Chief of Gen Staff: Lt-Gen Shamim Alam Khan.

Air Force: Air Headquarters, Peshawar; tel (521) 76430; Chief of Staff: Air Vice-Marshal Hakimullah Khan.

Army: General Headquarters, Rawalpindi; tel (51) 61600; telex 623; Chief of Staff: Gen Mirza Aslam Beg.

Navy: Naval Headquarters, Islamabad; tel (51) 829061; Chief of Staff: Vice-Adm Yasurul Haq Malik.

Inter Services Intelligence (ISI): Karachi; Head: Lt-Gen Hamid Gul; f 1948; military's intelligence wing.

Development and Planning

DEVELOPMENT

Development Advisory Centre: Karachi; tel (21) 218129.

Pakistan Industrial Development Corpn (PIDC): PIDC House, Dr Ziauddin Ahmad Rd, Karachi; Chair: (vacant); f 1962; parastatal body; manufacture of woollen and cotton textiles, carpets, sugar; gas distributors.

Pakistan Industrial Technical Assistance Centre (PITAC): Shahrah Moulana Jalal-Ud-Din-Roomi, Lahore 54600; tel (42) 864171; Gen Man: M. A. Jabbar Khan; Sen Mans: Ehsan Ali Khan, Ch. Aftab Yousaf; f 1962; provides technical assistance to industry for productivity promotion through training; design, production of dyes, moulds, fixtures, machine parts, prototypes, etc; dissemination of modern technical know-how through consultancy, seminars, publs, etc; productivity promotion activities in the Asian and Pacific Region.

INVESTMENT

Investment Advisory Centre of Pakistan: State Life Bldg No 3, Dr Ziauddin Ahmed Rd, POB 7534, Karachi 74400; tel (21) 511542; telex 25101; Dir: Reza H. Syed; f 1963; industrial research and management consultancy organization; provides guidance to prospective investors, promotes joint ventures, etc.

Investment Corpn of Pakistan: NBP Bldg, 5th Floor, I. I. Chundrigar Rd, POB 5410, Karachi 2; tel (21) 225861; telex 2879; Chair: Ghulam Faruque; Man Dir: Mutiur Rahman; f 1966 by the Govt to encourage and broaden the base of investments and to develop the capital market; 9 brs.

Investment Promotion Bureau: Godrej Kandawala Bldg, M. A. Jinnah Rd, Karachi 74400; tel (21) 718819; telex 23137; Chair: Syed Mohibullah Shah; Dir-Gen: Sayed Muzafar Ali Shah; f 1947; promotes foreign private investment; disseminates information about investment opportunities in Pakistan; employs foreign national in Pakistan.

National Development Finance Corpn: PNSC Bldg, Moulvi Tamizuddin Khan Rd, POB 5094, Karachi; tel (21) 551076; telex 23842; Chair: M. W. Memon; f 1973; sanctions loans for industrial devt; 16 brs.

National Investment (Unit Trust) Ltd: NBP Bldg, 6th Floor, I. I. Chundrigar Rd, POB 5671, Karachi; tel (21) 222056; telex 24476; Chair and Man Dir: S. M. A. Ashraf; f 1962; mobilizes domestic savings to meet the requirements of growing economic devt and enables investors to share in the industrial and economic prosperity of the country.

Pakistan Kuwait Investment Co Ltd: Sultan Trust Bldg, Beaumont Rd, Karachi; telex 24396; Man Dir: Adnan Ahmed Ali; joint venture between the Govt and Kuwait to promote investment in industrial and agro-based enterprises.

Pak-Libya Holding Co (Pvt) Ltd: Shaikh Sultan Trust Bldg No 2, 3rd Floor, 10 Beaumont Rd, POB 10425, Karachi; tel (21) 527407; telex 25763; Man Dir and Chief Exec: Haji Ali Muhammad Shaikh; Dep Man Dir: Nagmeddin H. Mokhtar; f 1978; joint venture between the Govt and Libya; devt finance institution established to promote industrial financing in Pakistan.

Saudi Pak Industrial and Agricultural Investment Co: 44 East, 2nd Floor, Blue Area, Islamabad; tel (51) 815001; telex 56635; fax (51) 815005; Gen Man and Chief Exec: S. M. Yusuf; f 1981 jointly by Saudi Arabia and Pakistan; provides medium- and long-term finance to industrial and agro-based industrial projects in the private sector; provides direct equity support.

REGIONAL DEVELOPMENT

Baluchistan Development Authority: Civil Secretariat, Block 7, Quetta; tel (81) 71780; Chair: Abu Shahmim M. Ariff; created for economic and industrial devt of Baluchistan; exploration and exploitation of mineral resources; establishment of industries, devt of infrastructure, water resources, etc.

Education

University Grants Commission: H-9, Islamabad; tel (51) 856071; telex 5591; f 1974; promotion and co-ordination of university education; determination and maintenance of teaching, examination and research standards; orientation of university programmes to national needs; provides grants; institutes fellowships, scholarships, etc; advises Federal and provincial Govts.

Employment

Overseas Employment Corpn (Pvt) Ltd: Red Crescent Bldg, Dr Daud Pota Rd, POB 15541, Karachi; tel (21) 524794; telex 25475; Exec Dir: S. A. Qarni; f 1976; labour recruitment for foreign countries.

Legal and Judiciary

Supreme Court: Peshawar Rd, Rawalpindi; tel (51) 62091; Chief Justice: Muhammad Abdul Haleem; Chief Justice, Federal Shari'a Court (acting): Gul Muhammad Khan; Chief Justice, High Court of Baluchistan: Abdul Qadeer Chaudhry; Chief Justice, High Court of North West Frontier Province: Sardar Fakhre Alam; Chief Justice, High Court of Punjab: Abdus Shakur Salam; Chief Justice, High Court of Sind: Muhammad Ajmal Mian.

Media

BROADCASTING

Pakistan Broadcasting Corpn: National Broadcasting House, Constitution Ave, Islamabad; tel (51) 829021; telex 5816; Chair: Rashid Latif; Dir-Gen: Agha Nasir; f 1947 as Radio Pakistan; home service 240 hrs daily in 21 languages; external services 30 hrs daily in 15 languages.

Pakistan Television Corpn Ltd: Federal TV Complex, Constitution Ave, POB 1221, Islamabad; tel (51) 810051; telex 5833; Chair: Aslam Azhar; Man Dir: Hamid Qureshi; f 1967; daily transmissions form 07.00 to 08.30 and from 16.30 to 23.30; extended transmissions on Fridays.

GOVERNMENT PUBLISHER

Government Publications: Central Publications Branch, Govt of Pakistan, Block University Rd, Karachi.

Mining and Energy

ENERGY

Karachi Electricity Supply Corpn: Abdullah Haroon Rd, Karachi; telex 25601; Chair: Lt-Gen Ghulam Safdar Butt; Man Dir: T. H. Naqvi; provides electricity supplies to Karachi.

National Power Construction Corpn (Pvt) Ltd: 46 Main Gulberg, Lahore 54660; tel (42) 877094; telex 44825; Man Dir: Muhammad Ajaz Malik; Chief Eng: Tauqir Ahmad Sharifi; f 1974; turnkey handling of power engineering projects, ie high voltage transmission lines, distribution networks, sub-stations, power generation plants, industrial electrification and external lighting of housing complexes, civil and building works, etc.

Oil and Gas Development Corpn: Masood Mansion, F-8 Markaz, Islamabad; tel (51) 853974; telex 5692; Chair: Dr Gulfaraz Ahmed; Admin Dir: M. Mohsin Khan; f 1961.

Pakistan Atomic Energy Commission: POB 1114, Islamabad; tel (51) 811030; telex 5725; Chair: Munir Ahmad Khan; f 1955; responsible for harnessing nuclear energy for the devt of peaceful nuclear power programme; operates power station and research centre; promotes peaceful applications of atomic energy in agriculture, medicine and hydrology; searching for indigenous nuclear mineral deposits; trains project personnel.

Pakistan Institute of Nuclear Science and Technology (PINSTECH): PO Nilore, Islamabad; tel (51) 843496; telex 5725; Dir: Dr Iqbal H. Qureshi; f 1963; centre for nuclear studies and research; controlled by the Pakistan Atomic Energy Commission.

Pakistan State Oil Co Ltd: Dawood Centre, Moulvi Tamizuddin Khan Rd, POB 3983, Karachi 4; tel (21) 513570; telex 2824; fax (21) 510215; Man Dir: S. Amjed Husain; f 1976; import, export, storage, distribution, marketing and blending of all kinds of petroleum products and chemicals.

State Petroleum, Refining and Petro-Chemical Corpn Ltd (PERAC): Karim Chambers, 4th Floor, Mereweather Rd, Karachi; tel (21) 515071; telex 24546; Chair: Dr M. H. Chaudhry.

MINING

Gemstone Corpn of Pakistan: 5 Marghuz House, Shaheen Town, Jamrud Rd, POB 25140, Peshawar; tel (521) 40626; telex 52321; Man Dir: Bashir Ahmad Saleemi; f 1979; gem exploration, mining, cutting and polishing; jewellery manufacturing and marketing.

Pakistan Mineral Development Corpn: PIDC House, Dr Ziauddin Ahmed Rd, Karachi 4; Chair: Jawaid Ahmad Mirza; Man: A. A. Malik.

Tourism

Pakistan Tourism Development Corpn Ltd: House No 2, St 61, F-7/4, Islamabad; tel (51) 811001; telex 23823; fax (51) 54356; Chair: Syed Yousaf Raza Gilani; Man Dir: Syed Ayaz Shah Rashdi; f 1970; promotion of tourism; maintenance of tourist information centres; tour operations within the country and abroad; operation of hotels and motels in Pakistan.

Transport

Civil Aviation Authority: 19 Liaquat Barracks, Karachi; tel (21) 529681; Dir-Gen: Air Marshal (retd) Shabbir H. Syed; controls all the civil airports.

National Tanker Co (Pvt) Ltd: Phase 1, Defence Officers Housing Authority, 35B, North Circular Ave, Karachi; tel (21) 541933; telex 23844; Chair: Vice-Adm Saeed M. Khan; Chief Exec: Rear Adm I. H. Khan; Gen Man: Turab Ali Khan; f 1981; transportation of crude oil from Arabian Gulf ports to Karachi.

Pakistan International Airlines Corpn (PIA): PIA Bldg, Karachi Airport; tel (21) 412011; telex 2832; Chair: Air Marshal (retd) Muhammad Azim Daudpota; f 1954; merged with Orient Airways in 1955; 62% Govt-owned; operates domestic services to 32 destinations and international services to 40 destinations in 37 countries.

Pakistan National Shipping Corpn: PNSC Bldg, Moulvi Tamizuddin Khan Rd, POB 5350, Karachi 2; tel (21) 551081; telex 2723; fax (21) 2412363; Chair: Vice-Adm Saeed M. Khan; f 1979; transportation of goods and pilgrims.

Pakistan Railways: Lahore; tel (42) 306186; telex 44672; Chair and Gen Man: H. A. Majeed; comprises seven divisions (Karachi, Lahore, Multan, Quetta, Rawalpindi, Peshawar and Sukkur).

Utilities

Pakistan Water and Power Development Authority: WAPDA House, Shahrah-e-Quaid-e-Azam, Lahore; tel (42) 69911; telex 44869; Chair: Lt-Gen Zahid Ali Akbar Khan; f 1958; devt of irrigation, water supply and drainage; building of replacement works under the World Bank-sponsored Indo-Pakistan Indus Basin Treaty; flood-control and watershed management; reclamation of waterlogged and saline lands; inland navigation; generation, transmission and distribution of hydroelectric and thermal power.

PANAMA

Head of State

Executive power is vested in the President, who is elected by universal adult suffrage for a five-year term. The President is assisted by two elected Vice-Presidents and an appointed Cabinet. Following a coup in December 1989 the Electoral Tribunal recognized the results of the election held in May 1989, which the Tribunal had previously suspended. Subsequently a new Government was formed.

President: Guillermo Endara (elected 7 May 1989; took office 27 December 1989).

Office of the President: Palacio Presidencial, Panamá 1; tel 27-4062; telex 2770.

First Vice-President: Ricardo Arias Calderón.

Second Vice-President: Guillermo Ford.

Office of the Vice-Presidents: Palacio Presidencial, Panamá 1; tel 66-4419; telex 2770.

Legislature

Legislative authority is vested in the Asamblea Legislativa (Legislative Assembly), with 67 members elected for five years by universal adult suffrage. Panama is divided into nine provinces and three autonomous Indian reservations.

Asamblea Legislativa (Legislative Assembly): Apdo 3346, Panamá 4; tel 62-6091.

MINISTRIES AND GOVERNMENT DEPARTMENTS

MINISTRY OF AGRICULTURAL DEVELOPMENT
Apdo 5390, Panamá 5
Tel 69-3122; telex 2994
Minister: Ezequiel Rodríguez

MINISTRY OF COMMERCE AND INDUSTRY
Apdo 9658, Panamá 4
Tel 27-4283; telex 2256
Minister: Juan Chevalier

MINISTRY OF EDUCATION
Apdo 2440, Panamá 3
Tel 62-2645
Minister: Ada de Gordon

MINISTRY OF FINANCE AND THE TREASURY
Central Postal Balboa, Ancón, Apdo 5245, Panamá 5
Tel 25-3431; telex 2352
Minister: Mario Galindo

MINISTRY OF FOREIGN AFFAIRS
Panamá 4
Tel 27-0013; telex 2771
Minister: Julio Linares

MINISTRY OF HOUSING
Apdo 5228, Panamá 5
Tel 62-5960
Minister: Rauúl Figueroa

MINISTRY OF THE INTERIOR AND JUSTICE
Apdo 1628, Panamá 1
Tel 22-8973; telex 2746
Minister: Ricardo Arias Calderón
Deputy Minister: Ramón Lima

MINISTRY OF LABOUR AND SOCIAL WELFARE
Apdo 2441, Panamá 3
Tel 62-1627
Minister: Jorge Rubén Rosas

MINISTRY OF PLANNING AND ECONOMIC POLICY
Edif Ooawa, 3°, Vía España, Apdo 2694, Panamá 3
Tel 69-2169; telex 3683; fax 69-6822
Minister: Guillermo Ford

MINISTRY OF THE PRESIDENCY
Valija 50, Apdo 53, Panamá 1
Tel 22-0520; telex 3720
Minister: René Orillac

MINISTRY OF PUBLIC HEALTH
Apdo 2048, Panamá 1
Tel 25-6080
Minister: José Trinidad Castillero

MINISTRY OF PUBLIC WORKS
Panamá 1
Tel 32-5572; telex 3438
Minister: René Orillac

OFFICE OF THE COMPTROLLER-GENERAL
Panamá
Comptroller-General: (vacant)

GOVERNMENT AGENCIES AND ORGANIZATIONS

Advisory and Supervisory Bodies

Controlaría de la República (National Auditing Office): Avda Balboa y Federico Boyd, Apdo 5213, Panamá; tel 64-3734; receives and certifies the accounts of all Govt depts; controls the State Organization for Statistics and the Census.

Tribunal Electoral (Electoral Tribunal): Panamá; Pres: Yolanda Púlice.

Agriculture

Corporación Azucarera La Victoria: Calle II Juegos Centroamericanos, Apdo 1228, Panamá 1; tel 33-3833; telex 2601; Dir: Prof Alejandro Vernaza; state sugar corpn.

Corporación para el Desarrollo Integral del Bayano: Avda Balboa, al lado de la estación del tren, Apdo 6-3802, Estafeta El Dorado, Panamá 2; tel 32-6160; Dir: José María Chaverri; f 1978; state agriculture, forestry and cattle-breeding corpn.

Art and Culture

Instituto Nacional de Cultura: Apdo 662, Panamá 1; national institute of culture.

Business and Economy

BANKING

Banco de Desarrollo Agropecuario (BDA): Apdo 5282, Panamá; telex 2406; Pres: Minister of Agricultural Development, Ezequiel Rodríguez; f 1973; agricultural and livestock credit organization.

Banco General, SA: Calle 34 y Avda Cuba, Apdo 4592, Panamá 5; tel 27-3200; Exec Vice-Pres: Raúl Alemán; f 1955; 16 brs.

Banco Hipotecario Nacional: Edif Peña Prieta, Avda Bilboa y Calle 40 Bella Vista, Apdo 222, Panamá 1; tel 27-0055; telex 3776; Pres: Minister of Housing, Raúl Figueroa; Gen Man: Jaime E. Simons B.; f 1973.

Banco Institucional Patria (BIP): Panamá; Pres: (vacant); Gen Man: Simón Vega; f 1989; owned by the Benevolent Society of the National Defence Forces.

Banco Nacional de Panamá: Torre Banconal, Vía España, Apdo 5220, Panamá 5; tel 63-5151; telex 2136; Gen Man: Rafael Arosemena; f 1904; 47 brs.

Banco Panameño de la Vivienda: Edif Elaga, Vía España con Calle 50, Apdo 8639, Panamá 5; tel 64-9353; telex 3391; Gen Man: Mario L. Fabrega Arosemena; f 1981.

Caja de Ahorros: Vía España y Calle Thais de Pons, Apdo 1740, Panamá 1; tel 63-6233; telex 2417; Dir: Jaime E. Simons; f 1963; 12 brs.

Comisión Bancaria Nacional (National Banking Commission): Edif Hatillo, Avda Justo Arosemena, Calle 35 y Calle 36, Apdo 1686, Panamá 1; tel 27-3753; telex 2464; Exec Dir: Mario de Diego, Jr; f 1970; license and control of banking activities; 7 full mems including two Ministers, Gen Man of Banco Nacional de Panamá and three reps of private banking.

Primer Banco de Ahorros, SA: Avda Justo Arosemena y Calle 32, Apdo 7322, Panamá 5; tel 27-2225; telex 2766; Gen Man: Joaquín de la Guardia; f 1963; 12 brs.

FINANCIAL AGENCY

Corporación Financiera Nacional (COFINA): Apdo 6-2191, Estafeta El Dorado, Panamá; telex 2583; Dir: Pedro Sotomayor; f 1976 to develop state and private undertakings in productive sectors.

TRADE

Colón Free Zone (CFZ): Avda Roosevelt, Apdo 1118, Colón; tel 45-1035; telex 8677; Gen Man: Veyra Remón; f 1948 to manufacture, import, handle and re-export all types of merchandise; 786 cos were established by 1976.

Instituto Panameño de Comercio Exterior (Panamanian Institute of Trade Development): POB 1897, Zona 6, El Dorado; tel 64-7211; telex 3499; fax 69-0091; Chief Exec: Luis A. Barletta; Dep Chief Exec: Rubén Dario Ortega Vieta; f 1984; promotion of exports and investment.

Defence

Fuerzas Públicas de Panamá—FPP (Public Forces of Panama): Apdo 3434, Panamá 1; tel 28-1475; telex 2736; Commdr-in-Chief: Col Eduardo Herrera Hassan Morena; Air Force Commdr: Maj Augusto Villalaz.

Development and Planning

Centro de Desarrollo y Productividad Industrial (Centre for Development and Industrial Production): Apdo 7639, Panamá 5; research and advice on industrial expansion and innovation, and devt strategies.

Consejo Nacional de Inversiones (CNI): Edif Banco Nacional de Panamá, Apdo 2350, Panamá; tel 64-7211; telex 3499; Exec Dir: Julio E. Sosa; f 1982; national investment council; promotes private local and foreign investment.

Departamento de Cooperación Técnica Internacional: Edif Prosperidad, Vía España, 2°, Apdo 2694, Panamá 3; tel 69-1016; Dir: Alfredo Broce; f 1973; co-ordinating body for international devt projects in the country.

Dirección General de Industrias: Edif de la Lotería, 19°, Apdo 9658, Panamá 4; tel 27-4403; Dir-Gen: Carlota Marisín Bieberach; Dep Dir-Gen: Inola Mapp; undertakes feasibility studies, analyses and promotions in order to develop Panamanian industry.

Legal and Judiciary

Corte Suprema (Supreme Court): Palacio de Justicia, Calle 1a Catedral, Apdo 1770, Panamá 1; tel 28-8117; Pres: Marisol Reyes de Vásquez; Attorney-Gen: Rogelio Cruz; nine judges appointed for a ten-year term.

Media

BROADCASTING

Asociación Panameña de Radiodifusión: Panamá; tel 63-5252; Pres: Fernando Eleta Casanova; Panamian radio service.

Dirección Nacional de Medios de Comunicación Social: Avda 7a Central y Calle 3a, Apdo 1628, Panamá 1; tel 22-9410; telex 2746; Dir: Osvaldo Gudiño Aguilar; co-ordinating organization for media.

GOVERNMENT PUBLISHER

Editorial Mariano Arosemena: Instituto Nacional de Cultura, Apdo 662, Panamá 1; tel 22-3233; Dir: Esther Urieta de Real; f 1974; literature, anthropology, social sciences, archaeology.

NEWS AND INFORMATION

Dirección de Estadística y Censo: c/o Contraloría General de la República, Avda Balboa y Federico Boyd, Apdo 5213, Panamá 5; tel 64-3734; Dir: Amílcar Villarreal L.; f 1941; collection, analysis and publication of statistics.

Mining and Energy

ENERGY

Instituto de Recursos Hidráulicos y Electrificación (IRHE): Edif Poli, Avda Justo Arosemena y 26 Este, Apdo 5285, Panamá 5; tel 62-6272; telex 2158; Dir-Gen: Lt-Col Ricardo Garibaldo; responsible for the national public electricity supply.

MINING

Codemín: Vía España, Edif Banco Nacional, 1a Torre, 12°, Panamá; tel 63-7475; Dir: Jaime Roquebert; state mining organization.

Tourism

Instituto Panameño de Turismo (IPAT): Centro de Convenciones Atlapa, Vía Cincuentenario, Apdo 4421, Panamá 5; tel 26-7000; telex 3359; Dir-Gen: Bernardo Domínguez; f 1970; tourism institute.

Transport and Communications

TELECOMMUNICATIONS

Instituto Nacional de Telecomunicaciones: Apdo 659, Panamá 9; tel 23-8620; telex 2667; Dir: Luis Blanco.

TRANSPORT

Autoridad Portuaria Nacional: POB 8062, Panamá 7; tel 69-5444; telex 2765; Dir-Gen: Capt José Santos Motta; national port authority.

Chiriquí Land Co: Apdo 6-2637, Estafeta El Dorado, Panamá; tel 78-8240; telex 2292; Gen Man: Robert Walker; railway co purchased by the Govt in 1978.

Dirección de Aeronaútica Civil: Apdo 7615, Panamá 5; tel 27-0211; telex 2618; Dir: Mayor Pascual González; directorate for civil aviation.

Dirección General Consular y de Naves: c/o Ministerio de Hacienda y Tesoro, Apdo 5245, Panamá 5; tel 25-9277; telex 2597; Dir-Gen: Dr Hugo Torrijos Richa; general consular and shipping directorate.

Panama Railroad: Ferrocarril de Panamá, Apdo 2023, Balboa; Gen Man: Maj Enrique Williams; operates mainly as a tourist attraction and for cargo transport.

PAPUA NEW GUINEA

Head of State

Executive power is vested in the British monarch, represented locally by a Governor-General, who is appointed on the recommendation of the Prime Minister and acts on the advice of the National Executive Council (the Cabinet), led by the Prime Minister. The normal term of office for the Governor-General is six years.

Sovereign: HM Queen Elizabeth II (suceeded to the throne 6 February 1952).

Governor-General: Vincent Eri (took office February 1990).

Office of the Governor-General: POB 79, Port Moresby; tel 214466; telex 22275.

Legislature

Legislative authority is vested in the unicameral National Parliament, with 109 members elected by universal adult suffrage for a term of five years. For local administration there are provincial Governments in each of the 20 provinces.

National Parliament: Parliament House, POB 596, Waigani; tel 277410; telex 22374; Speaker: Dennis Young; Dep Speaker: Christopher Sambre.

MINISTRIES AND GOVERNMENT DEPARTMENTS

OFFICE OF THE PRIME MINISTER
POB 6605, Boroko
Tel 276715; telex 22388; fax 214861
Prime Minister: Rabbie Namaliu
Minister of State: Ted R. Diro

OFFICE OF THE DEPUTY PRIME MINISTER
Haus Tomakala, PO Wards Strip, Waigani
Tel 271799; telex 22144
Deputy Prime Minister: Akoka Doi

MINISTRY FOR ADMINISTRATIVE SERVICES
POB 1207, Boroko
Tel 272525; fax 259757
Minister: Theodore Tuya

MINISTRY FOR AGRICULTURE AND LIVESTOCK
POB 417, Konedobu
Tel 214699; telex 22143; fax 211337
Minister: Galen Lang

MINISTRY FOR CIVIL AVIATION
POB 7144, Boroko
Tel 272521
Minister: Bernard Vogae

MINISTRY FOR COMMUNICATIONS
POB 1279, Boroko
Tel 276681; telex 22237; fax 252298
Minister: Bown Sinamoi
First Secretary: Timothy Komane
Second Secretary: Yanopa Kai

MINISTRY FOR CORRECTIONAL SERVICES
Brian Bell Plaza, POB 5097, Boroko
Tel 277549
Minister: Melchior Pep

MINISTRY FOR CULTURE AND TOURISM
POB 7144, Boroko
Tel 277519
Minister: Gerard Beona Motawiya

MINISTRY FOR DEFENCE
Murray Barracks, PB Boroko
Tel 242270; telex 256117
Minister: Benias Sabumei

MINISTRY FOR EDUCATION
PSA Haus, Independence Drive, Waigani
Tel 251133; telex 22193; fax 254648
Minister: Jack Genia

MINISTRY FOR ENVIRONMENT AND CONSERVATION
POB 6601, Boroko
Tel 271692; telex 22327
Minister: Jim Yer Waim

MINISTRY FOR FINANCE AND PLANNING
Central Govt Offices, Kumul Ave, PO Wards Strip, Waigani
Tel 271739; telex 22218; fax 213826
Minister: Paul Pora

Economic Policy Unit: c/o Dept of Finance and Planning, Central Govt Offices, Kumul Ave, PO Wards Strip, Waigani; tel 271739; telex 22218; fax 213826; advises on and formulates economic policy.

MINISTRY FOR FISHERIES AND MARINE RESOURCES.
POB 165, Konedobu
Tel 213911
Minister: Allan Ebu
First Secretary: Barney Rongap

MINISTRY FOR FOREIGN AFFAIRS
Central Govt Offices, Kumul Ave, PO Wards Strip, Waigani
Tel 271311; telex 22136; fax 277710
Minister: Michael Somare

MINISTRY FOR FORESTS
Frangipani St, Hohola; POB 5055 Boroko
Tel 277800; telex 22360; fax 254433
Minister: Karl Stack

MINISTRY FOR HEALTH
POB 3991, Boroko
Tel 248600; telex 22151; fax 213821
Minister: Robert Suckling

MINISTRY FOR HOME AFFAIRS AND YOUTH
Maori Kiki Haus, 2nd Floor, POB 7354, Boroko
Tel 254967; telex 23226
Minister: Timothy Bonga

MINISTRY FOR HOUSING
POB 5245, Boroko
Tel 258490; telex 22327; fax 213749
Minister (acting): Fr John Momois
Secretary: Jack Bagita

MINISTRY FOR JUSTICE
Central Govt Offices, Kumul Ave, PO Wards Strip, Waigani
Tel 271915; 22144
Minister: Bernard Narakobi

Law and Order Foundation: Justice Dept, Central Govt Offices, Kumul Ave, PO Wards Strip, Waigani; tel 271502; Chair: Bernard Narakobi; promotion of law and order, advises the Govt on legal policy, trains officers.

MINISTRY FOR LABOUR AND EMPLOYMENT
POB 5644, Boroko
Tel 272262; telex 22375; fax 276679
Minister: Peter Garong

MINISTRY FOR LANDS AND PHYSICAL PLANNING
Marea Haus, Melanesian Way, Waigani; POB 5665, Boroko
Tel 272572
Minister: Kala Swokin

MINISTRY FOR MINERALS AND ENERGY
POB 352, Konedobu
Tel 214011; telex 22211; fax 213701
Minister: Patterson Lowa

Minerals and Energy Policy Division: address as above; tel 214011; telex 22211; fax 213701; policy analysis, project evaluation and programme management in minerals and energy sector.

MINISTRY FOR POLICE
POB 85, Konedobu
Tel 226183; telex 22113; fax 226113
Minister: Mathias Ijape

MINISTRY FOR PROVINCIAL AFFAIRS
Central Govt Offices, Kumul Ave, PO Wards Strip, Waigani
Tel 271787; telex 22141; fax 211623
Minister: Fr John Momis

MINISTRY FOR PUBLIC SERVICE
Haus Tomakala, PO Wards Strip, Waigani
Tel 271799; telex 22322; fax 271222
Minister: Akoka Doi

MINISTRY FOR TRADE AND INDUSTRY
Central Govt Offices, Kumul Ave, PO Wards Strip, Waigani
Tel 271094; telex 23310; fax 214158
Minister: John Giheno

Department of Trade and Industry: address as above; tel 271111; fax 242503; Secs: Peter Ipu Peipul, Sam Abal; f 1985; formulation and implementation of Govt policy in the area of trade and industrial devt.

MINISTRY FOR TRANSPORT
POB 457, Konedobu
Tel 211866; telex 22203; fax 217310
Minister: Anthony Temo

MINISTRY FOR WORKS AND SUPPLY
POB 1108, Boroko
Tel 241124; telex 22114; fax 241610
Minister: Paul Wanjik

GOVERNMENT AGENCIES AND ORGANIZATIONS

Advisory and Supervisory Body

Industrial Advisory Council: Port Moresby; f 1984; 15 mems, including representatives of commerce, banking and labour; advises the Govt on social and economic aspects of major industrial devts.

Agriculture and Forestry

AGRICULTURE

Cocoa Board of Papua New Guinea: POB 532, Rabaul; tel 921354; telex 92935; fax 921794; Chair: Jack Ockley; Chief Exec: Mark Ivarami; f 1975; control and regulation of the cocoa industry.

Higaturu Oil Palm Pty Ltd: POB 28, Popondetta; tel 297177; telex 29188; fax 297137; Man Dir: C. Warn; Sec: J. McIndoe; f 1976; jointly owned by the Govt and the Commonwealth Development Corpn (UK); producer of palm oil and cocoa.

New Britain Palm Oil Development Ltd: Kimbe, West New Britain; tel 935177; telex 93128; Dir: James Montgomerie; f 1967; jointly owned by the Govt and Harrisons and Crossfield (London); major producer of palm oil and coffee and supplier of high quality oil palm seed.

Papua New Guinea Coffee Industry Board: POB 137, Goroka; tel 721266; telex 72647; fax 721431; Chief Exec: Ron G. Ganarafo; f 1976; control and regulation of the coffee industry.

FORESTRY

Forest Industries Council: Waigani Drive, POB 1829, Port Moresby; tel 256399; telex 22226; fax 212911; Exec Dir: Imari Trawa; Dep Exec Dir: Andrew Aopo; f 1973; promotion and devt of forest products' industries.

Business and Economy

BANKING

Agriculture Bank of Papua New Guinea: POB 6310,

Boroko; tel 259255; telex 22295; Chair: Frederick Reiher; Man Dir: Vai Reva; f 1967.

Bank of Papua New Guinea: Douglas St, POB 121, Port Moresby; tel 212999; telex 22128; fax 227259; Gov: Sir Henry ToRobert; Dep Gov: Nick Bokas; central bank and bank of issue since 1975.

Papua New Guinea Banking Corpn: POB 78, Port Moresby; tel 229729; telex 22160; fax 211954; Chair: Ubum Makarai; Man Dir: Mekere Morauta; Dep Man Dir: H. T. Fabila; 21 brs.

MARKETING

Copra Marketing Board of Papua New Guinea: Port Moresby; telex 22135; Chair: Sir John Guise; markets all copra in Papua New Guinea.

Food Marketing Corpn: Port Moresby; f 1976; encourages the production and distribution of fruit and vegetables.

Niugini Produce Marketing Pty Ltd: POB 1811, Lae; telex 42409; f 1982; handles distribution of fruit and vegetables.

NATIONALIZED INDUSTRY

Pita Lus National Silk Institute: Kagamuga, Mt Hagen; f 1978; silk-producing project.

Defence

Papua New Guinea Defence Force: Headquarters, Murray Barracks, Free Mail Bag, Boroko; Commdr: Brig-Gen Ken Noga.

Development and Planning

Investment Corpn of Papua New Guinea: Hunter St, POB 155, Port Moresby; tel 212855; telex 22354; f 1975; supports local enterprise and purchases shares in foreign businesses operating in Papua New Guinea.

National Investment and Development Authority (NIDA): POB 5053, Boroko; tel 258777; telex 22123; Chair: Wep Kanawi; Exec Dir: Stephen Mark; f 1975; promotion, supervision and regulation of foreign investment; contributes to planning for investment and recommends priority areas for investment to the Govt; also co-ordinates investment proposals.

Legal and Judiciary

Supreme Court of Papua New Guinea: POB 7018, Boroko; tel 257099; telex 23371; fax 257732; Chief Justice: Sir Buri Kidu;

Dep Chief Justice: Sir Mari Kapi; f 1946; highest judicial authority; deals with all matters involving interpretation of the Constitution, and with appeals from the National Court.

Media

BROADCASTING

National Broadcasting Commission of Papua New Guinea: POB 1359, Boroko; tel 255233; telex 23083; Chair: Kedea Uru; f 1973; broadcasts in English, Melanesian, Pidgin, Motu and 30 vernaculars.

NEWS AND INFORMATION

National Statistical Office: Central Govt Offices, Kumul Ave, PO Wards Strip, Waigani; tel 271705; telex 22144; fax 255057; Dirs: Nick Suvulo, Siddiquer Rahman, Taua Magaru, Henry Korim; f 1960; collection of data and the compilation, dissemination and analysis of statistics.

Tourism

National Tourist Office: POB 7144, Boroko; tel 251269; telex 23472; fax 259447; Dir: Daniel Oreke; f 1966; promotion of tourism.

Transport and Communications

TELECOMMUNICATIONS

Department of Post and Telecommunications: POB 1279, Boroko; tel 274388.

TRANSPORT

Air Niugini: POB 7186, Boroko; tel 273200; telex 22225; Chair: Michael Bromley; Gen Man: Dieter Seefeld; f 1973; operates scheduled internal cargo and passenger services within Papua New Guinea and international services to Australia, Indonesia, the Solomon Islands, Vanuatu, the Philippines and Singapore.

> **Douglas Airways Pty Ltd:** POB 1179, Boroko; tel 253499; telex 22145; Man Dir: Dennis Douglas; f 1961; a subsidiary of Air Niugini since 1987; domestic services and a service to Indonesia.

PARAGUAY

Head of State

Executive power is held by the President, who is Head of State, and is elected for five years at the same time as the National Congress. The President governs with the assistance of an appointed Council of Ministers.

President: Gen Andrés Rodríguez (assumed power 3 February 1989; elected President 1 May 1989).

Office of the President: Palacio de Gobierno, Asunción; tel (21) 41940; telex 411.

Vice-President: Dr Luis María Argaña.

Legislature

Legislative power is held by the bicameral National Congress. The 36 members of the Senate and the 72 members of the Chamber of Deputies are elected by universal adult suffrage and serve five-year terms. The party receiving the largest number of votes is allocated two-thirds of the seats in each Chamber, the remaining seats being divided proportionately among other contending parties. Paraguay comprises 19 departments, each administered by a governor appointed by the President.

Senado (Senate): Palacio Legislativo, Asunción; tel (21) 48100.

Cámara de Diputados (Chamber of Deputies): Palacio Legislativo, Asunción; tel (21) 49089.

MINISTRIES AND GOVERNMENT DEPARTMENTS

MINISTRY OF AGRICULTURE AND LIVESTOCK
Ptde Franco 472, Asunción
Tel (21) 49385; telex 324
Minister: Hernando Bertoni

MINISTRY OF EDUCATION AND RELIGION
Chile, Humaitá y Piribebuy, Asunción
Minister: Dr Dionisio González Torres

MINISTRY OF FINANCE
Chile 128 esq Palmas, Asunción
Minister: Enzo Debernardi Orillier

MINISTRY OF FOREIGN AFFAIRS
Palacio de Gobierno, Asunción
Telex 111
Minister: Dr Luis María Argaña

MINISTRY OF INDUSTRY AND COMMERCE
Avda España 323, Asunción
Tel (21) 204693; telex 259
Minister: Antonio Zuccolillo Moscarda

MINISTRY OF THE INTERIOR
Estrella y Montevideo, Asunción
Telex 153
Minister: Gen Orlando Machuca Vargas

MINISTRY OF JUSTICE AND LABOUR
G.R. de Francia y Estados Unidos, Asunción
Minister: Dr Alexis Fruitos Vaesken

MINISTRY OF NATIONAL DEFENCE
Avda Mcal López y Vice-Pdte Sánchez, Asunción
Telex 762
Minister: Gen Juan Angel Souto

MINISTRY OF PUBLIC HEALTH AND SOCIAL WELFARE
Avda Pettirossi y Brasil, Asunción
Minister: Dr Cinthya Prieto

MINISTRY OF PUBLIC WORKS AND COMMUNICATIONS
Oliva y Alberdi, Asunción
Tel (21) 41530; telex 162
Minister: Brig-Gen (retd) Porfirio Pereira Ruiz Díaz

OFFICE OF THE MINISTER WITHOUT PORTFOLIO
Asunción
Minister: Dr Juan Ramón Chávez

GOVERNMENT AGENCIES AND ORGANIZATIONS

Advisory and Supervisory Body

Consejo Nacional de Coordinación Económica: Presidencia de la República, Paraguayo Independiente y Juan E. O'Leary, Asunción; Sec: Fulvio Monges Ocampos; responsible for overall economic policy.

Agriculture

Consejo Nacional para el Desarrollo de la Ganadería: Asunción; tel (21) 290939; f 1964; Govt council representing public and private bodies in the cattle industry.

Business and Economy

BANKING

Banco Central del Paraguay: Avda Pablo VI y Sgto Marecos, Asunción; tel (21) 68015; telex 134; Pres: Crispiniano Sandoval; Gen Man: Dr Augusto Colmán Villamayor; f 1952; central bank.

Banco de Desarrollo del Paraguay, SA (COMDESA): Haedo entre Nuestra Señora de la Asunción e Independencia Nacional, Casilla 1531, Asunción; tel (21) 91717; telex 656; Pres: Juan Antonio Sosa Gautier; Gen Man: Julio E. Sauca; f 1970; devt bank.

Banco Nacional de Fomento: Independencia Nacional y Cerro Corá, Asunción; tel (21) 44440; telex 130; Pres: Dr Julio Regis Sanguina; f 1961 to supply short-, medium- and long-term industrial and agricultural credits; 41 brs and 16 agencies throughout the country.

Superintendencia de Bancos: Edif Banco Central del Paraguay, Avda Pablo VI y Sgto Marecos, Asunción; tel (21) 45416; telex 134; Supt: Dr Oscar Estigarribia; suprevisory authority.

Crédito Agrícola de Habilitación: Caríos y Primera, Asunción; Pres: Estéban Medina Santacruz.

FINANCIAL AGENCY

Fondo Ganadero: Cerro Corá e Independencia Nacional, Asunción; tel (21) 47463; Pres: Epifanio Salcedo; livestock fund.

NATIONALIZED INDUSTRY

Acero del Paraguay (ACEPAR): Asunción; Sec-Gen: Jacinto Santa María; national steel co.

Siderurgia Paraguaya (SIDEPAR): Azara 197 6°, esq Yegros, Casilla 2441, Asunción; tel (21) 95963; telex 287; Pres: Brig-Gen Roberto Knopfelmacher; Gen Man: Rolando González Murdoch; f 1974; state steel co.

TRADE

Centro de Promoción de las Exportaciones (CEPEX): Avda España 374, Asunción; tel (21) 444231; telex 259; Exec Dir: Dr Segundo Udagawa; f 1969; participates in international fairs and exhibitions; organizes commercial missions; holds training courses for entrepreneurs and civil servants; disseminates trade information to exporters.

Instituto Nacional de Tecnología y Normalización (INTN) (National Institute of Technology and Standardization): Avda Artigas y Gral Roa, Casilla 967, Asunción; tel (21) 290160; telex 306; f 1963; national standards institute; carries out chemical analyses; technological investigation of wood, leather, textiles, construction materials, food, etc.

Defence

Armed Forces: Asunción; tel (21) 204966.

Aeronáutica Militar (Air Force): Campo Grande, Asunción; tel (21) 290883.

Armada Nacional (Navy): Asunción; tel (21) 46102.

Development and Planning

Consejo Nacional de Desarrollo Industrial (National Council for Industrial Development): Asunción; national planning institution.

Secretaría Técnica de Planificación de la Presidencia de la República: Iturbe 175 esq Eligio Ayala, Asunción; tel (21) 48074; Govt body responsible for overall economic and social planning.

Energy

Administración Nacional de Electricidad (ANDE): Avda España 1268, Asunción; tel (21) 22713; telex 142; Pres: (vacant); national electricity board.

Comisión Nacional de Energía Atómica: Ministerio de Relaciones Exteriores, Palacio de Gobierno, Asunción; Pres: Dr José Danilo Pecci; f 1960; atomic energy commission; maintains no laboratories or installations.

Petróleos Paraguayos (PETROPAR): Oliva 299 4°, Casilla 571, Asunción; tel (21) 95117; telex 5153; Pres: Dr Julio Cosme Gutiérrez; f 1981; national petroleum co.

Legal and Judiciary

The Supreme Court: Palacio de Justicia, Asunción; tel (21) 84383; telex 290; Pres: (vacant); composed of five judges chosen by the Pres with the approval of the Council of State.

Media

BROADCASTING

Radio Nacional del Paraguay: Oliva y Alberdi 6°, Asunción; Dir: Alejandro Cáceres Almada; medium- and short-wave and FM.

NEWS AND INFORMATION

Dirección General de Estadística y Censos: Humaitá 473, Asunción; tel (21) 47900.

Undersecretariat of Information and Cultural Affairs: Palacio de Gobierno, Asunción; tel (21) 47454; telex 411; responsible to the Office of the Pres.

Tourism

Dirección General de Turismo: Ministerio de Obras Públicas y Comunicaciones, Oliva y Alberdi, Asunción; tel (21) 441530; telex 162; Pres and Dir-Gen: Dr Jorge Patricio Escobar Genes; Sec-Gen: Carlos Rubén Turitich Marín; f 1940; promotion of tourism; participation in international fairs and congresses.

Transport and Communications

TELECOMMUNICATIONS

Administración Nacional de Telecomunicaciones (ANTELCO): Administración General 4°, Alberdi y Gral Díaz, Casilla 84, Asunción; tel (21) 44001; telex 110; Chair of Board and Gen Man: Col (retd) Miguel Cirilo Guanes; f 1926.

TRANSPORT

Administración Nacional de Navegación y Puertos (National Shipping and Ports Department): Colón e Isabel la Católica, Asunción; tel (21) 92846; f 1965; responsible for ports services and maintaining navigable channels in rivers and for improving navigation on the River Paraguay.

Ferrocarril del Norte: Concepción; service to Horqueta 56 km east.

Ferrocarril Presidente Carlos Antonio López: México 145, Casilla 453, Asunción; tel (21) 43273; Pres: Miguel Angel Barrios Arce; Man: Ramón Ayala; f 1854; control passed from UK co to Paraguayan Govt in 1961; 441 km open; service to Encarnación and Buenos Aires three times a week.

Flota Mercante Del Estado: Estrella 672-686, Casilla 454, Asunción; tel (21) 446010; telex 159; Pres: O. V. Johannsen; runs boats and barges on Paraguay and Paraná rivers; cold storage ships for use between Asunción-Buenos Aires-Montevideo.

Líneas Aéreas Paraguayas (LAP): Oliva 455-467, Asunción; tel (21) 95261; telex 5230; Chair: Gen Gerardo Johanssen; Pres: Gen Raúl Calvet; f 1962; services to South and North American and European destinations.

Utilities

Corporación de Obras Sanitarias: José Berges y Brasil, Asunción; tel (21) 25001; telex 172; responsible for public water supply, sewage disposal and drainage.

Welfare

INDI (National Indian Institute): Asunción; tel (21) 93802; Pres: Minister of National Defence, Gen Juan Angel Souto; Dir: Col Machucha Godoy; responsible for welfare of the Indian population.

Instituto de Bienestar Rural (IBR): Tacuary 276, Asunción; tel (21) 43930; Pres: Juan Manuel Frutos; responsible for rural welfare and colonization.

Instituto de Previsión Social: Constitución y Luis A. de Herrera, Casilla 437, Asunción; tel (21) 23141; telex 848; f 1943; responsible for employees' welfare and health insurance scheme.

PERU

Head of State

Executive power is vested in the President, who is Head of State. The President is elected by universal adult suffrage for five years, and governs with the assistance of an appointed Council of Ministers.

President: Alan García Pérez (sworn in 28 July 1985).

Office of the President: Palacio de Gobierno, Plaza de Armas s/n, Lima 1; tel (14) 271366; telex 20167.

First Vice-President: Dr Luis Alberto Sánchez.

Second Vice-President: Dr Luis Alva Castro.

Legislature

Legislative power is vested in the bicameral Congreso (National Congress), consisting of a Senate (comprising 60 Senators elected on a regional basis, and former Presidents of constitutional Governments as life Senators) and a Chamber of Deputies (180 members elected by proportional representation). Deputies and Senators serve five-year terms.

Senado de la República (Senate): Plaza Bolívar 139, Lima 1; tel (14) 283119; telex 20002; Pres: Armando Villanueva del Campo.

Cámara de Diputados (Chamber of Deputies): Plaza Bolívar 139, Lima 1; tel (14) 287980; telex 25311; Pres: Dr Luis Alva Castro.

MINISTRIES AND GOVERNMENT DEPARTMENTS

OFFICE OF THE PRIME MINISTER AND MINISTRY OF FOREIGN AFFAIRS
Ucayali 363, Lima
Tel (14) 273860; telex 20467
Prime Minister and Minister: Guillermo Larco Cox

MINISTRY OF AGRICULTURE AND FOOD
Avda Salaverry s/n, Edif M. de Trabajo, Lima
Tel (14) 324040; telex 25835
Minister: Juan Coronado Balmaceda

MINISTRY OF DEFENCE
Lima
Minister: Gen Julio Velasquez Giacarini

MINISTRY OF ECONOMY AND FINANCE
Cuadra Avda Abancay 5, Lima
Tel (14) 289590; telex 20187
Minister: César Vásquez Bazán

MINISTRY OF ENERGY AND MINES
Avda Las Artes s/n, San Borja, Apdo 2600, Lima 100
Tel (14) 410065; telex 25731
Minister: Mario Samame Boggiora

Dirección General de Hidrocárburos: address as above; tel (14) 417674; formulates policy on the exploitation of hydrocarbons.

MINISTRY OF FISHERIES
Avda Javier Prado Este 2465, San Luis, Lima
Tel (14) 362630; telex 21058
Minister: Juan Carpio Rebaza

MINISTRY OF HEALTH
Cuadra Avda Salaverry 8, Jesús María, Lima
Tel (14) 323535; telex 20433
Minister: Paul Caro Gamarra

MINISTRY OF HOUSING
D. Cueto 120, Jesús María, Lima
Tel (14) 716070; telex 25158
Minister: Antenor Orrego Stelucín

MINISTRY OF INDUSTRY, COMMERCE, TOURISM AND INTEGRATION
Calle 1 Oeste, Corpac, San Isidro, Lima 27
Tel (14) 407120; telex 20194
Minister: Carlos Raffo Dasso

Vice Ministerio de Turismo: Ministry of Industry, Commerce, Tourism and Integration, Calle 1 Oeste, Corpac, San Isidro, Lima 27; tel (14) 406119; telex 20194; Vice Minister: Alfonso Salcedo Rubio; devt and promotion of tourism.

MINISTRY OF THE INTERIOR
Plaza 30 de Agosto 150, San Isidro, Lima
Tel (14) 416990
Minister: (vacant)

MINISTRY OF JUSTICE
Edif del Banco Continental, 7°, esq de la Avda Emancipación y Jirón Lampa, Lima
Tel (14) 278181
Minister: María Angélica Bockos Heredia

MINISTRY OF LABOUR AND SOCIAL RELATIONS
Avda Salaverry s/n, Jesús María, Lima
Tel (14) 322510
Minister: Wilfredo Chao Villanueva

MINISTRY OF THE PRESIDENCY
Centro Cívico, 4°, Avda Garcilaso de la Vega 1351, Lima 1
Tel (14) 320298
Minister: Rodolfo Beltrán Bravo

MINISTRY OF PUBLIC EDUCATION
Instituto Nacional de Cultura, Jirón Ancash 390,
Apdo 5247, Lima

Tel (14) 275680; telex 25803
Minister: Efrain Obregoso Rodriguez

MINISTRY OF TRANSPORT AND COMMUNICATIONS
Avda 28 de Julio 800, Lima
Tel (14) 237800; telex 25211
Minister: Osvaldo Moran

GOVERNMENT AGENCIES AND ORGANIZATIONS

Advisory and Supervisory Body

Sociedad Nacional de Industrias (SNI) (National Industrial Association): Los Laureles 365, Apdo 632, San Isidro, Lima 27; tel (14) 408700; telex 21030; fax (14) 403395; Pres: Salvador Majluf Poza; Gen Man: Gabriel Ferrer Wurst; f 1896; comprises permanent commissions covering various aspects of industry including labour, integration, fairs and exhibitions, industrial promotion; its Small Industry Committee groups over 2,000 small enterprises; 2,500 mems; 60 sectorial committees.

Business and Economy

BANKING

Banco Agrario del Perú: Jirón Junín 319, Apdo 2683, Lima 1; tel (14) 276140; telex 20377; Pres: Alfredo García Llosa; Gen Man: Carlos Lecca Arrieta; provides loans to farmers for agricultural devt; 22 brs.

Banco Central Hipotecario del Perú: Jirón Carabaya 421, Lima 1; tel (14) 273352; telex 25827; fax (14) 329677; Chair of Board: Miguel Estremadoyro Lindow; Gen Man: Dr Augusto Hermoza Alarcón; f 1929; 24 brs.

Banco Central de Reserva del Perú: Jirón Antonio Miró Quesada 441, Lima 1; tel (14) 276250; telex 20169; Pres: Pedro Coronado Labo; Gen Man: Santiago B. Antúñez de Mayolo Morelli; f 1922; refounded 1931; central bank; 6 brs.

Banco Continental: Avda República de Panamá 3050-3065, Apdo 3849, San Isidro, Lima 27; tel (14) 726065; telex 21281; Pres: Rómulo León Ramírez; Gen Man: Benedicto Cigüeñas Guevara; f 1951; 4 brs.

Banco de Crédito del Perú: Jirón Lampa 401-499, Apdo 225, Lima 1; tel (14) 275600; telex 20018; Chair: Dionisio Romero Seminario; Pres and Chief Exec: Juan Francisco Raffo Novelli; f 1889; designated a self-managing institution by the Govt in March 1988; 248 brs.

Banco de Desarrollo (BANDESCO): Jirón Camaná 700, Lima 1; tel (14) 286360; telex 20437; Pres: Moisés Woll Dávila; Gen Man: Giovanni Castoldi Castillo; f 1980; 18 brs.

Banco Industrial del Perú: Jirón Lampa 535, Apdo 1230, Lima 100; tel (14) 288080; telex 20092; fax (14) 282213; Chair: Carlos Massa Rodríguez; Gen Man: María Eugenia Tuesta; f 1936; 42 brs.

Banco Internacional del Perú (Interbanc): Jirón de la Unión 600, Plaza de la Merced, Apdo 148, Lima; tel (14) 273850; telex 25270; fax (14) 273203; Chair: Aaron Morales; Gen Man: Alfredo Saldaña; f 1897; provides advice to industry on commercial opportunities.

Banco Latino de Fomento de la Construcción (BANCON): Jirón Carabaya 341, Lima 1; tel (14) 326347; telex 25531; fax (14) 327124; Chair of Board: Jorge Picasso Salinas; Gen Man: John Bayly Llona; f 1982; 1 br.

Banco Mercantil del Perú: Calle Ricardo Rivera Navarrete 641, esq con Dean Valdivia, Apdo 5926, San Isidro, Lima 100; tel (14) 428000; telex 21245; Pres: Francisco Pardo Mesones; Gen Man: Valdemaro Mendoza Urquiaga; f 1984; 1 br.

Banco Minero del Perú: Avda Garcilaso de la Vega 1472, Apdo 2565, Lima; tel (14) 329535; telex 20133; Pres: Roger Arévalo Ramírez; Gen Man: Victor Rivas Gómez; f 1941; 13 brs.

Banco de la Nación: Avda Javier Prado Este 2465, Apdo 1835, Lima 100; tel (14) 362630; Pres: Adán Seminario Esquerra; Gen Man: José Carlos Caballero Araujo; f 1966; carries out all commercial banking operations of official Govt agencies; 19 brs.

Banco Popular del Perú: Jirón Haullaga 380, Apdo 143, Lima 1; tel (14) 289680; telex 20033; Pres: Roberto Carrión Pollit; Gen Man: Dr Rodolfo Abram Cavelerino; f 1899; 54 brs.

Banco de la Vivienda del Perú: Jirón Camaná 616, Apdo 5425, Lima 100; tel (14) 276655; telex 20077; Chair: Antenor Orrego Stelucin; Gen Man: Oscar Bauer Cotrina; f 1962; 9 brs.

Superintendencia de Banca y Seguros: Jirón Huancavelica 240, Lima; tel (14) 288210; telex 25807; Supt: Hugo García Salvatecci; f 1931; supervisory authority.

FINANCIAL AGENCY

Corporación Financiera de Desarrollo (Cofide): Camino Real 390, Lima 27; tel (14) 422550; telex 21515; fax (14) 423384; Pres: José Salaverry Llosa; Gen Man: Sidney Poppe Bravo; f 1971; directs investments in state enterprises; gives technical and financial help to private cos.

NATIONALIZED INDUSTRY

Siderperú (Empresa Siderúrgica del Perú): Avda Tacna 543, 9°-12°, Lima; tel (14) 283450; telex 20270; fax (14) 276156; Pres: (vacant); Gen Man: Dr Antonio Martínez González; f 1958; iron and steel production.

TRADE

Enci (Empresa Nacional de Comercialización de Insumos): Bernardo Monteagudo 210, Lima 17; tel (14) 629049; telex 25892; Gen Man: Eduardo de la Rosa Cárdenas; f 1974; controls the import, export and national distribution of agricultural and basic food products.

Instituto de Comercio Exterior (ICE): Bernardo Monteagudo 210, Lima 17; Apdo 3544, Lima 1; tel (14) 617094; telex 25301; Pres: (vacant); f 1986; responsible for supervision and promotion of foreign trade.

Minpeco, SA (Empresa Comercializadora de Productos Mineros): Jirón Scipión Llona 350, Miraflores, Apdo 180274, Lima; tel (14) 473561; telex 20360; fax (14) 402840; Chair: F. H. Bustamante; Gen Man: Mario Mesia; f 1974; marketing of metals and minerals; has divisions concerned with iron ore, copper, lead and zinc, precious metals, etc.

Culture

Instituto Nacional de Cultura: Jirón Ancash 390, Lima 1; Dir: Germán Peralta Rivera.

Defence

Comando Conjunto de las Fuerzas Armadas (Armed Forces Joint Command): Avda Arequipa 29, Lima; tel (14) 320640; Pres of Joint Command of the Armed Forces: Lt-Gen Pablo Varela Novella (mem of the Council of Ministers).

Ejército (Army): Comandancia General del Ejército, Ministerio de Guerra, Avda Boulevard s/n, Chacarilla, Lima; tel (14) 369778; telex 25438.

Fuerza Aérea del Perú (Air Force): Cuartel General de la FAP, Campo de Marte s/n, Lima 11; tel (14) 325540; telex 20125.

Marina (Navy): Comandancia General de la Marina, Cdra 24, Avda Salaverry, Lima 11; tel (14) 635151; telex 20143.

Development and Planning

DEVELOPMENT

Consejo Nacional de Desarrollo (CONADE): Avda Garcilaso de la Vega 1456, Lima; Chair: José Palomino; national devt council.

Instituto Nacional de Planificación: Calle Siete 229, Rinconada Baja, La Molina, Apdo 2027, Lima 1; tel (14) 358141; Dir: Javier Tantaleán Arbulú; f 1962; national planning institute.

INVESTMENT

Proinversión: Lima; Pres: Roberto Dañino; Exec Dir: Drago Kisic; f 1981; agency to supervise public investment projects.

REGIONAL DEVELOPMENT

Comisión Nacional de Desarrollo Regional (National Regional Development Commission): Lima; Pres: the Prime Minister, Guillermo Larco Cox; f 1975 to promote economic and social devt in the eleven administrative regions.

Fishing

Epsep (Empresa Peruana de Servicios Pesqueros): Lima; tel (14) 362630; telex 25498; Pres: Antonio Hudtwalcker Texeira; Gen Man: Antonio Romano Thantawatae; edible fish.

Pescaperú (Empresa Nacional de Pesca): Avda Petit Thoars 119, Apdo 4682, Lima 1; tel (14) 238901; telex 25601; Pres: Juan Rebaza Carpio; f 1973; took over Epchap in 1979; fishmeal and fish production and export.

Legal and Judiciary

Corte Suprema: Palacio de Justicia, 2°, Avda Paseo de la República, Lima 1; tel (14) 283690; Pres: Dr Oscar Alfaro Alvarez; Attorney-Gen: Hugo Dengri Cornejo; consists of a Pres and 12 mems.

Ministerio Público-Fiscalía de la Nación (Office of the Public Prosecutor): Las Torres de Lima, Centro Civico s/n, Lima 1; tel (14) 314620; telex 21297.

Media

BROADCASTING

Empresa de Cine, Radio y Televisión Peruana, SA (RTP): Avda José Gálvez 1040, Santa Beatriz, Lima; tel (14) 715570; telex 25029; Exec Pres: Carlos Guillén Bringas; part of the Sistema Nacional de Comunicación Social (SINACOMS); operates 29 radio stations and 27 TV channels.

Radio Nacional del Perú: Avda Petit Thouars 447, Santa Beatriz, Lima; Dir: Jorge Florian Alvarado; f 1937; Govt radio station.

Radiodifusión del Perú: Lima.

NEWS AND INFORMATION

Instituto Nacional de Estadística: Avda 28 de Julio 1056, Lima 1; tel (14) 279552; Dir: Dr Ulises Robles Freyre; Technical Dir: Carmen Reyes Hiuguay; f 1975; national statistical office.

Mining and Energy

ENERGY

Dirección General de Hidrocárburos: Avda Javier Prado esq Avda Aviación, Edif Sol Gas, 5°, Lima 34; tel (14) 352996; telex 25731; hydrocarbons authority; formulates Govt policy on exploitation of hydrocarbons; under Ministry of Energy and Mines.

Electroperú: Centro Cívico, Paseo de la República 144, Lima 1; tel (14) 310644; telex 25680; Exec Pres: Eduardo Caillaux Angulo; Gen Man: Humberto Zelaya Sotomayor; electricity.

Instituto Peruano de Energía Nuclear (IPEN): Avda Canadá 1470, San Borja, Apdo 1687, Lima 41; tel (14) 723136; telex 25746; Pres: Guillermo Flórez Pinedo; Exec Dir: Brig-Gen Alvaro Santiváñez Villalobos; promotes, co-ordinates, advises and represents the devt of nuclear energy and its applications in Peru.

Petroperú (Empresa de Petróleos del Perú): Paseo de la República 3361, San Isidro, Apdo 3126/1081, Lima 27; tel (14) 411919; telex 20303; Pres: (vacant); Gen Man: Augusto Morales Zevallos; f 1969; petroleum.

Petróleos del Mar (Petromar): Lima; Pres: Alberto Vera La Rosa; f 1986, following the nationalization of the US co, Belco Petroleum; state petroleum prospecting co.

MINING

Centromín, SA (Empresa Minera del Centro del Perú): Avda Javier Prado Este s/n, Edif Solgas, Apdo 2412, San Borja, Lima 34; tel (14) 365924; telex 21238; fax (14) 358782; Exec Pres: Jaime Cenzano; Gen Man: J. Ortiz; Supt of Railways (acting): V. Zuñiga; f 1904; mining corpn; railway transportation of ores, concentrates, oils, etc.

Empresa Minera del Hierro del Perú (HIERRO PERÚ): Paseo de la República 3587, San Isidro, Lima 1; tel (14) 410636; telex 20001; fax (14) 412330; Pres of Board: Samuel Suárez O.; Gen Man: Dr Franklin Rivas A.; f 1953; fmrly Marcona Mining Co; iron ore mining, transportation and beneficiation (crushing, grinding, magnetic separation, flotation of sulphides and pelletizing).

Minero Perú (Empresa Minera del Perú): Bernardo Monteagudo 222, Apdo 4332, Lima 17; tel (14) 620740; telex 25598; Pres: Manuel Lescano Rivera; Gen Man: Carlos Philipps Jaramillo; f 1970; mining co.

Research

Centro Superior de Estudios Nucleares (CSEN): Avda Canadá 1470, San Borja, Apdo 1687, Lima; tel (14) 723639; Dir: Ignacio Frisancho Pineda; f 1956; specialist centre for nuclear sciences and technology; uses the research facilities of IPEN (see above) and co-operates with various universities.

Telecommunications

Dirección General de Comunicaciones: Avda 28 de Julio 800, 2°, Lima; tel (14) 230752; telex 25511; Dir-Gen: Carlos A. Romero Sanjines; telecommunications directorate.

Entelperú (Empresa Nacional de Telecomunicaciones, SA): Las Begonias 475, San Isidro, Apdo 2600, Lima 27; tel (14) 423553; telex 25522; Pres: Julio Jiménez Castro; Gen Man: Carlos Chian Chong; f 1969; telecommunications.

Tourism

Empresa Nacional de Turismo (ENTURPERU): Avda Javier Prado Oeste 1358, San Isidro, Lima; tel (14) 404630; telex 20393; Gen Man: Luis Osorio Coello; f 1964.

Fondo de Promoción Turística del Perú (FOPTUR): Col Andrés Reyes 320, San Isidro, Lima; tel (14) 414700; telex 21363; fax (14) 429280; Pres: Adolfo Dammert Ludowieg; Gen Man: Alvaro de Romaña Amorós; f 1979; promotion of tourism.

Transport

CIVIL AVIATION

Corpac (Corporación Peruana de Aeropuertos y Aviación Comercial, SA): Aeropuerto Internacional Jorge Chávez, Avda Elmer Faucett, Lima; tel (14) 529570; telex 26055; Pres: Dr Augusto Valquí Malpica; Gen Man: Marco Aurelio González Perriggo; commercial aviation.

RAILWAYS

Empresa Minera del Centro del Perú, SA—División Ferrocarriles (Centromín-Perú SA): Avda Javier Prado Este s/n, Edif Solgas, Apdo 2412, San Borja, Lima 34; tel (14) 355467; telex 21231; Pres: E. de la Vega; Supt: Raúl Benites P.; fmrly Cerro de Pasco Railway.

Empresa Nacional de Ferrocarriles del Perú (Enafer-Perú): Ancash 207, Apdo 1379, Lima; Gen Man: Erwin Ludman Paredes; f 1972; 1,650 km open; operates the following lines:

Ferrocarril del Centro del Perú (Central Railway of Peru): Ancash 201, Apdo 301, Lima; Man: David San Román; 493 km open.

Ferrocarril del Sur del Perú ENAFER, SA (Southern Railway): Avda Tacna y Arica 200, Apdo 194, Arequipa; tel (54) 215350; telex 51071; Man: Gino Olcese Gargurevich; 1,095 km open; also operates steamship service on Lake Titicaca.

Tacna-Arica Ferrocarril (Tacna-Arica Railway): Avda Albarracín 484, Tacna; 62 km open.

Ferrocarril Pimentel: Pimentel, Chiclayo; Pres: R. Montenegro; Man: Luis de la Piedra Alvizuri; 56 km open; owned by Empresa Nacional de Puertos (see below); cargo services only.

SHIPPING

Comisión Nacional de Marina Mercante: Ministerio de Marina, Avda Salaverry s/n, Jesús María, Lima; Sec-Gen: Capt Carlos Badani Souza Peixoto; f 1962; promotes the devt of the merchant navy.

Compañía Peruana de Vapores: Gamarra 680, Chucuito, Apdo 208, Callao; tel 659510; telex 20103; Pres and Gen Man: Juan Manuel Ontaneda Meyer; f 1906; operates regular services to North America, the Far East, Europe, South America and Australasia.

Empresa Nacional de Puertos, SA (Enapu): Terminal Marítimo del Callao, Edif Administrativo, 3°, Grau 1199, Apdo 260, Callao; tel 290355; telex 26010; Chair: Commdr Oscar Lezameta B.; f 1970; Govt agency administering all coastal, river and lake ports.

Oficina Naviera Comercial: Avda Salaverry s/n, Jesús María, Lima; tel (14) 638000; runs 10 vessels.

THE PHILIPPINES

Head of State

Executive power is vested in the President, who is Head of State. The President is elected by universal adult suffrage for a six-year term, and is not eligible for re-election. The President appoints a Cabinet and other officials, with the approval of the Commission on Appointments (drawn from members of both chambers of Congress). The President cannot prevent the enactment of legislative proposals if they are approved by a two-thirds majority vote in Congress.

President: Corazon Aquino (inaugurated 25 February 1986).

Vice-President: Salvador Laurel.

Office of the President and of the Vice-President: Premiere Guest House, Malacañang Palace Compound, J. P. Laurel St, San Miguel, Metro Manila; tel (2) 521-2301; telex 40213.

Legislature

Legislative power is vested in the bicameral Congress, comprising a Senate, with 24 members elected by universal adult suffrage (initially for a five-year term, thereafter to be extended to six years under the 1987 Constitution), and a House of Representatives, with a maximum of 250 members, 200 of whom are directly elected (also initially for five years and thereafter for six), while a further 50 may be appointed by the President from minority groups, for a three-year term. Local government is by Barangays (citizens' assemblies).

Senate: Metro Manila; Pres and Chair of the Commission on Appointments: Jovito Salonga; Senate Pres pro tempore: Teofisto Guingona.

House of Representatives: Metro Manila; Speaker: Ramon Mitra.

MINISTRIES AND GOVERNMENT DEPARTMENTS

DEPARTMENT OF AGRARIAN REFORM
PTA Bldg, Diliman, Quezon City, Metro Manila
Tel (2) 99-70-31
Secretary: Florencio Abad

DEPARTMENT OF AGRICULTURE
Elliptical Rd, Diliman, Quezon City, Metro Manila
Tel (2) 99-70-11; telex 27726; fax (2) 97-81-83
Secretary: Senen Bacani

DEPARTMENT OF THE BUDGET AND MANAGEMENT
Administration Bldg, Malacañang, Metro Manila
Tel (2) 40-75-85
Secretary: Guillermo N. Carague
Undersecretary for Administration: Jesus C. Beringuela
Undersecretary for Budget Operations: Benjamin E. Diokno
Undersecretary for Management Services: Nazario S. Cabuquit

DEPARTMENT OF EDUCATION, CULTURE AND SPORTS
Palacio del Gobernador, cnr Gen Luna and Aduana Sts, Intramuros, Metro Manila
Tel (2) 40-29-49
Secretary: Isidro Carino

DEPARTMENT OF THE ENVIRONMENT AND NATURAL RESOURCES
Visayas Ave, Diliman, Quezon City, Metro Manila
Tel (2) 97-66-26
Secretary: Fulgencio Factoran

DEPARTMENT OF FINANCE
Agrifina Circle, Ermita, Metro Manila
Tel (2) 58-67-19
Secretary: Jesús Estanislao

DEPARTMENT OF FOREIGN AFFAIRS
PICC Bldg, Roxas Blvd, Metro Manila
Tel (2) 832-0309; telex 14654
Secretary: Raul Manglapus

DEPARTMENT OF GENERAL SERVICES
Philcomcen Bldg, Mandaluyong, Metro Manila
Tel (2) 77-25-63
Secretary and Cabinet Secretary: José de Jesús

DEPARTMENT OF HEALTH
San Lazaro Hospital Compound, Rizal Ave, Santa Cruz, Metro Manila
Tel (2) 711-6080
Secretary and Government Chief Negotiator: Alfredo R. A. Bengzon

DEPARTMENT OF JUSTICE
Padre Faura St, Metro Manila
Tel (2) 59-92-71; telex 4194
Secretary: Franklin M. Drilon

DEPARTMENT OF LABOUR AND EMPLOYMENT
Gen Luna St, cnr San José St, Intramuros, Metro Manila
Tel (2) 47-02-64; telex 40386
Secretary: Franklin M. Drilon

DEPARTMENT OF LOCAL GOVERNMENT
PNCC Complex, EDSA cnr Reliance St, Mandaluyong, Metro Manila
Tel (2) 77-40-11
Secretary: Luis Santos

DEPARTMENT OF MUSLIM AFFAIRS
117 Ablaza Bldg, E. Rodriguez Ave, Quezon City, Metro Manila
Tel (2) 731-4574
Secretary: (vacant)

DEPARTMENT OF NATIONAL DEFENCE
Camp Emilio Aguinaldo, Quezon City, Metro Manila
Tel (2) 78-98-96
Secretary: Gen (retd) Fidel V. Ramos
Undersecretary: Maj-Gen (retd) Fortunato U. Abat
Undersecretary for Civilian Relations:
Leonardo A. Quisumbing
Undersecretary for Reserve Affairs: Lt-Gen (retd)
Eduardo R. Ermita

DEPARTMENT OF PUBLIC WORKS AND HIGHWAYS
Bonifacio Drive, Port Area, Metro Manila
Tel (2) 47-93-11; telex 2335
Secretary: Fiorello R. Estuar

DEPARTMENT OF SCIENCE AND TECHNOLOGY
Bicutan, Taguig, POB 3596, Metro Manila
Tel (2) 822-0961
Secretary: Cerefino Follosco

DEPARTMENT OF SOCIAL WELFARE AND DEVELOPMENT
IBP Complex, Constitution Hills, Quezon City, Metro Manila
Tel (2) 96-31-41
Secretary: Dr Mita Pardo de Tavera

DEPARTMENT OF TOURISM
T. M. Kalaw St, Rizal Park, Metro Manila
Tel (2) 59-90-31; telex 40183; fax (2) 522-2194
Secretary: Peter D. Garrucho, Jr
Undersecretary: Rafael Alunan

DEPARTMENT OF TRADE AND INDUSTRY
Trade and Industry Bldg, 385 Sen Gil J. Puyat Ave, Makati, Metro Manila
Tel (2) 818-1831; telex 45555; fax (2) 819-1887
Secretary: José S. Concepcion, Jr
Undersecretary: Tomas I. Alcantara

DEPARTMENT OF TRANSPORTATION AND COMMUNICATIONS
Philcomcen Bldg, Ortigas Ave, Pasig, Metro Manila
Tel (2) 721-3781; telex 42219
Secretary: Oscar Orbos

NATIONAL ECONOMIC AND DEVELOPMENT AUTHORITY (NEDA—DEPARTMENT OF ECONOMIC PLANNING)
NEDA Bldg, Amber Ave, Pasig 1600, Metro Manila
Tel (2) 673-5031; telex 29058
Director-General and Secretary: Vicente Jayme

NATIONAL INTELLIGENCE CO-ORDINATING AGENCY
Metro Manila
Director-General: Gen Mariano Adalen

OFFICE OF THE CABINET
Malcañang, Metro Manila
Tel (2) 521-2301
Executive Secretary: Catalino Macaraig
Governor of the Central Bank: José Cuisia
Military Adviser to the President: Maj-Gen José Magno

OFFICE OF THE PRESS SECRETARY (DEPARTMENT OF INFORMATION)
Kalayaan Hall, Malacañang, Metro Manila
Tel (2) 49-79-47; telex 40213; fax (2) 731-1325
Press Secretary (acting): Adolfo Azcuna
Undersecretaries: G. Noel Tolentino, Felix B. Bautista
Formulation and implementation of an integrated programme of information and developmental communication that will present the work of the Presidency.

Philippine Information Agency: Visayas Ave, Quezon City, Metro Manila; tel (2) 921-79-41; fax (2) 922-65-43; Dir-Gen: Undersec G. Noel Tolentino; f 1986; provision of information to assist in decision-making, identification of opportunities and improvement in quality of life.

PRESIDENTIAL COMMISSION ON CUSTOMS
Metro Manila
Director: Lt-Gen Salvador Mison

PRESIDENTIAL COMMISSION OF GOOD GOVERNMENT
Philcomcen Bldg, 6th Floor, Ortigas Ave, Pasig, Metro Manila
Tel (2) 78-09-51
Director: Mateo T. Caparas

PRESIDENTIAL COMMISSION ON HUMAN RIGHTS
Metro Manila
Director: Mary Concepcion Bautista

PRESIDENTIAL COMMISSION ON URBAN POVERTY
Metro Manila
Director: (vacant)

GOVERNMENT AGENCIES AND ORGANIZATIONS

Agriculture and the Environment

AGRICULTURE

Agricultural Training Institute (ATI): BAex Bldg, Diliman, Quezon City, Metro Manila; tel (2) 97-73-97; Dir: Segundo C. Serrano.

Bureau of Agricultural Co-operatives Development (BACOD): Arcadia Bldg, Quezon City, Metro Manila; tel (2) 99-26-41; Dir: Clemente Terso.

Bureau of Agricultural Research (BAR): BAex Bldg, Diliman, Quezon City, Metro Manila; tel (2) 99-49-07; Dir: William D. Dar.

Bureau of Animal Industry (BAI): Visayas Ave, Diliman,

Quezon City, Metro Manila; tel (2) 96-68-83; Dir: Romeo N. Alcasid.

Bureau of Plant Industry (BPI): San Andres, Malate, Metro Manila; tel (2) 59-11-32; Dir: Nerius Roperos.

Fertilizer and Pesticide Authority (FPA): Raha Sulayman Bldg, 6th Floor, Benavidez St, Legaspi Village, Makati, Metro Manila; tel (2) 818-51-15; Admin: Luis T. Villareal.

Fibre Development Authority (FIDA): Philfinance Bldg, Benavidez St, Legaspi Village, Makati, Metro Manila; tel (2) 818-73-47; Admin: Joaquin M. Teotico.

Livestock Development Council (LDC): DA Compound, Elliptical Rd, Diliman, Quezon City, Metro Manila; tel (2) 98-87-41; Exec Dir: Lino E. Nazareno.

National Agricultural and Fisheries Council (NAFC): DA Compound, Elliptical Rd, Diliman, Quezon City, Metro Manila; tel (2) 98-86-08; Undersec: Dante Q. Barbosa.

National Food Authority (NFA): Matimyas Bldg, E. Rodriguez Blvd, Quezon City, Metro Manila; tel (2) 712-17-19; Admin: Pelayo Gabaldon.

National Irrigation Administration: Epifanio de los Santos Ave, Quezon City, Metro Manila; tel (2) 97-60-71; Chair: Jesus Hipolito.

National Meat Inspection Commission: BAex Bldg, 3rd Floor, Elliptical Rd, Quezon City, Metro Manila; tel (2) 97-11-84; Exec Dir: Bernardo Resoso.

National Post Harvest Institution: ECCOI Bldg, 4th Floor, 947 E. Rodriguez Blvd, Quezon City, Metro Manila; tel (2) 711-27-01; Exec Dir: Frank Tua.

National Sugar Trading Corpn: Traders Royal Bank Bldg, Aduana St, Intramuros, Metro Manila; tel (2) 40-86-67; Chair: R. S. Benedicto.

National Tobacco Administration (NTA): Consolacion Bldg, Cubao, Quezon City, Metro Manila; tel (2) 921-21-56; Admin: Alonzo Q. Ancheta.

Philippine Coconut Authority (PCA): PCA Bldg, Elliptical Rd, Diliman, Quezon City, Metro Manila; tel (2) 96-76-75; telex 66296; Chair: José V. Romero.

Philippine Cotton Corpn (PCC): JJACIS Bldg, 4th Floor, 31 Shaw Blvd, Pasig, Metro Manila; tel (2) 673-14-76; Pres: Patricio L. Lim; Vice-Pres, Operations: Alfonso D. Merca; Vice-Pres, Finance and Admin: Louis D. Sese; f 1973; promotion of cotton growing; assists in organization of farmer cooperatives; disseminates technical guidelines.

Philippine Dairy Corpn (PDC): Philsucom Bldg, North Ave, Quezon City, Metro Manila; tel (2) 99-87-41; Pres: Conrado C. Gozun.

Philippine Rice Research Institute (PRRI): UP College, Los Baños, Laguna; tel (93) 3515; Exec Dir: Santiago R. Obien.

Sugar Regulatory Administration (SRA): Philsucom Bldg, North Ave, Quezon City, Metro Manila; tel (2) 922-39-07; Chair: Arsenio B. Yula, Jr.

THE ENVIRONMENT

Bureau of Soils and Water Management (BSWM): Sunvesco Bldg, Taft Ave, Manila; tel (2) 521-13-50; Dir: Godofredo N. Alcasid.

FISHING

Bureau of Fisheries and Aquatic Resources (BFAR): Arcadia Bldg, Quezon Ave, Quezon City, Metro Manila; tel (2) 96-54-98; Dir: Juanito B. Malig.

Philippine Fisheries Development Authority (PFDA): Bookman Bldg, 3rd Floor, Quezon Ave, Quezon City, Metro

Manila; tel (2) 711-43-69; Gen Man: Malcolm M. Sarmiento.

Business and Economy

BANKING

Central Bank of the Philippines: A. Mabini St cnr Vito Cruz St, Malate, Metro Manila; tel (2) 50-70-51; telex 27550; fax (2) 522-39-87; Gov and Chair of Monetary Board: José Cuisia (mem of Cabinet); Senior Dep Gov: Gabriel C. Singson; f 1949; regulation of money, credit and foreign exchange operations; fiscal agent, banking and financial advisor of the Govt; supervision and examination of banking institutions and non-bank financial intermediaries; sole right and authority to issue currency.

Monetary Board: c/o Central Bank of the Philippines, A. Mabini St cnr Vito Cruz St, Malate, Metro Manila; economic policy-making body; consists of Gov of Central Bank, the Prime Minister, and reps appointed from the private and public sectors.

Development Bank of the Philippines: POB 800, Makati Central PO, Makati, Metro Manila 3117; tel (2) 818-95-11; telex 22197; Chair: Jesús Estanislao; Vice-Chair: Roberto F. de Ocampo; f 1946 as Rehabilitation Finance Corpn; provides long-term loans for agricultural and industrial devt; 57 brs.

Land Bank of the Philippines: BF Condominium Bldg, 6th Floor, Aduana St, Intramuros, Metro Manila; tel (2) 48-47-51; telex 2252; Chair: (vacant); Pres: Deogracias N. Vistan; provides financial support in all phases of the Govt's agrarian reform programme; 23 brs.

Philippine Amanah Bank: La Purisima St, Plaza Pershing, Zamboanga City; Chair: César C. Zalamea; Pres: Michael O. Mastura; f 1974; operates on Islamic banking principles; promotes the socio-economic devt of Mindinao; 8 brs.

Philippine National Bank (PHILNABANK): PNB Bldg, POB 1844, Escolta, Metro Manila 1099; tel (2) 40-20-51; telex 63292; Pres: Edgardo B. Espiritu; Chair: Joker Arroyo; f 1916; scheduled for privatization in July 1990; 190 brs.

United Coconut Planters Bank: UCPB Bldg, Makati Ave, Makati, Metro Manila; tel (2) 818-8361; telex 23068; Chair: Ramon Y. Sy; Pres: Enrique M. Herbosa; f 1963; nationalized 1986; 96 brs.

FINANCIAL AGENCIES

Agricultural Credit Policy Council (ACPC): Central Bank of the Philippines Bldg, 19th Floor, cnr Mabini and Vito Cruz Sts, Metro Manila; tel (2) 521-5825; Exec Dir: Bruce J. Tolentino.

National Home Mortgage Finance Corpn: Allied Bank Centre, Makati, Metro Manila; tel (2) 815-8251.

Philippine Export and Foreign Loan Guarantee Corpn (PHILGUARANTEE): Executive Bldg Centre, 5th Floor, Sen Gil J. Puyat cnr Makati Ave, Makati; Metro Manila; tel (2) 818-03-16; telex 23053; Pres: Victor C. Macalincag; Exec Vice-Pres: Jesús M. Tañedo; f 1977; guarantees loans to exporters and overseas contractors with approved service contracts abroad; provides counter-guarantees to financial institutions issuing standby letters of credit or letters of guarantee for the performance of service contracts of Philippine contractors.

Quedan Guarantee Fund Board (QGFB): 102 Manlili Bldg, E. Rodriguez Ave, Metro Manila; tel (2) 732-2312; Exec Dir: Galo B. Garchitorena.

INSURANCE

Philippine Crop Insurance Corpn: VAG Bldg, Ortigas Ave, Greenhills, San Juan, Metro Manila; tel (2) 721-5461; telex 2542; Pres: Jorge C. Abada; f 1978; provides insurance cover for agricultural produce and for agricultural loans not covered by crop insurance.

Philippine Deposit Insurance Corpn: 229 Salcedo St, Legaspi Village, Makati, Metro Manila; tel (2) 810-4901; telex 22164; Pres: Vitaliano N. Nañagas II; Vice-Pres: Isayas G. Peneyra; f 1963; insurance of bank deposits.

NATIONALIZED INDUSTRY

National Steel Corpn: 377 Sen Gil J. Puyat Ave Ext, Makati, Metro Manila; tel (2) 816-2036; telex 22524; Pres: José Ben R. Laraya; Chair: José S. Concepcion, Jr; f 1974.

Philippine Cement Corpn (Philcemcor): Cocho-Gonzales Bldg, Makati, Metro Manila.

Philippine National Construction Corpn: Epifanio de los Santos (EDSA), cnr Reliance St, Mandaluyong, Metro Manila; tel (2) 77-40-11; telex 64148; fax (2) 721-6584; Chair: Eduardo B. Espiritu; Pres: Eduardo B. Olaguer; f 1966; national and international construction projects.

Wenagro Industrial Corpn: 92 Mindanao Ave, Quezon City, Metro Manila; Man Dir: Francisco C. Wenceslao; producer and exporter of Philippine products; took over Philippine Exporters Trading Co in 1980.

TRADE

Bureau of Patents, Trademarks and Technology Transfer: Trade and Industry Bldg, 361 Sen Gil J. Puyat Ave, Makati, Metro Manila.

Export Processing Zones Authority (EPZA): 300 Legaspi Tower, 4th Floor, Vito Cruz C. Roxas Blvd, Metro Manila; tel (2) 50-75-88; telex 40723; promotes designated areas of the Philippines as transit depots for international trading cos by use of incentives.

Philippine International Trading Corpn (PITC): Philippines International Centre, Tordesillas St, Salcedo Village, Makati, Metro Manila 3116; tel (2) 818-9801; telex 63745; Pres: Raul A. Boncan; f 1973; conducts international marketing of general merchandise, industrial and construction goods, raw materials, semi-finished and finished goods, and bulk trade of agri-based products.

Defence

Armed Forces: Fort Bonifacio, Metro Manila; Chief of Staff of the Armed Forces: Gen Renato de Villa; Chief of Staff (Army): Maj-Gen Manuel Cacanando; Chief of Staff (Navy): Cdre Serapio C. Martillano; Chief of Staff (Air Force): Brig-Gen José de Leon.

National Bureau of Investigation: Taft Ave, Ermita, Metro Manila; tel (2) 59-24-51; Dir: Brig-Gen Alfredo Lim; Asst Dir: Epimaco A. Velasco; f 1947; criminal investigation, drug treatment and rehabilitation.

National Police Commission: 391 Alco Bldg, 391 Sen Gil J. Puyat Ave, Makati, Metro Manila.

Development and Planning

INVESTMENT

Board of Investments: Trade and Industry Bldg, 385 Sen Gil J. Puyat Ave, Makati, Metro Manila; tel (2) 818-1831; telex 45555; fax (2) 819-1887; Chair: Secretary for Trade and Industry, José S. Concepcion, Jr; Vice-Chair: Undersecretary for Trade and Industry, Tomas I. Alcantara; f 1968; regulates and promotes investment in the Philippines.

PLANNING

Construction and Development Corpn of the Philippines (CDP): TFC Bldg, 355 Sen Gil J. Puyat Ave, Makati, Metro Manila; tel (2) 87-60-61; telex 45538; f 1966; became 90% state-owned in 1983; devt of the construction sector.

National Development Co (NDC): Goodland Bldg, 377 Buendia Ave Ext, Makati, Metro Manila; Chair: Secretary for Trade and Industry, José S. Concepcion, Jr; Gen Man: Antonio A. Henson; f 1919; engages in the organization, financing and management of subsidaries and corpns, including commercial, industrial, mining, agricultural and other enterprises assisting national devt.

Private Development Corpn of the Philippines (PDCP): PDCP Bldg, 6758 Ayala Ave, Makati, Metro Manila; tel (2) 85-06-86; telex 45055; Chair and Chief Exec: Rodrigo de los Reyes; f 1963 with World Bank assistance; provides medium- and long-term foreign currency; provides small business term loans, equity investment and guarantees, funds mobilization, underwriting and private placements, external funds management, insurance brokerage; business consultancy.

REGIONAL DEVELOPMENT

Southern Philippines Development Authority (SPDA): 1515 Vito Cruz C. Roxas Blvd, Ermita, Metro Manila; promotion of economic devt in southern regions.

Energy

National Electrification Administration: Capitol Bldg, Quezon Ave, Quezon City, Metro Manila; tel (2) 99-87-81; Admin: Pedro Dumol.

National Power Corpn: Agham Rd, East Triangle, Diliman, Quezon City, Metro Manila; tel (2) 921-3541; Pres: Gabriel Itchon; Sr Vice-Pres: Mamerto S. Bocanegra, Conrado del Rosario; f 1936; supplies electric and hydroelectric power.

Philippine National Oil Co (Petrophil): 7901 Makati Ave, Makati, Metro Manila; tel (2) 85-90-61; telex 22259; fax (2) 815-3094; Chair: Catalino Macaraig, Jr; Pres: Manuel Estrella; f 1973; national oil co; involved in marketing, refining, exploration and devt of oil industry; also coal mining, oil transport, shipbuilding and ship repair.

Health and Welfare

HEALTH

National Nutrition Council (NNC): Nichols Interchange, South Superhighway, Metro Manila; tel (2) 818-7398; Exec Dir: Bernardo Resoso.

WELFARE

Human Settlement Development Corpn: University of Life, Pasig, Metro Manila; tel (2) 77-48-11; concerned with the improvement and devt of living conditions, particularly in rural and under-developed regions.

National Housing Authority: Elliptical Rd, Diliman, Quezon City, Metro Manila; tel (2) 99-45-61; Gen Man: Raymundo R. Dizon, Jr; Asst Gen Man: Col Antonio A. Fernando; f 1975; engaged in direct shelter production.

Legal and Judiciary

Office of the Solicitor-General: 134 Amorsolo St, Legaspi Village, Makati, Metro Manila; tel (2) 817-6405; Solicitor-Gen: Francisco Chavez.

Supreme Court: Taft Ave cnr Padre Faura St, Ermita, Metro Manila; tel (2) 50-91-41; Chief Justice: Marcelo B. Fernan; comprises a Chief Justice and 14 Associate Justices; Justices are appointed by the President from a list of a minimum of three nominees prepared by a Judicial and Bar Council; sole judge of disputes relating to presidential and vice-presidential elections.

Media

BROADCASTING

Maharlika Broadcasting System: Media Centre, Sgt Esguerra Ave, Quezon City, Metro Manila 3005; tel (2) 922-0880; telex 42220; Dir: Antonio Barriero; jointly operated by the Bureau of Broadcasts and the National Media Production Centre.

Philippines Broadcasting Service (PBS): Bureau of Broadcasts, Office of the Press Sec, PTV-4 Complex, Sgt Esguerra Ave, Quezon City, Metro Manila; tel (2) 96-96-12; telex 42220; overseas service of the Bureau of Broadcasts and the Office of Media Affairs.

NEWS AND INFORMATION

Bureau of Agricultural Statistics (BAS): Ben-Lor Bldg, Quezon Ave, Quezon City, Metro Manila; tel (2) 99-84-50; Dir: Generoso de Guzman.

National Census and Statistics Office: c/o National Economic and Development Authority, Amber Ave, Pasig 1600, Metro Manila; tel (2) 673-5031; telex 29058; collection, analysis and publication of statistical information.

Science and Technology

Philippine Nuclear Research Institute: Don Marino Marcos Ave, Diliman, Quezon City, Metro Manila; Dir: Quirino Navarro; Dep Dir: Guillermo C. Corpus; f 1958; deals with nuclear energy activities under the auspices of the Dept of Science and Technology; grants licences and regulates the production, transfer and utilization of nuclear and radioactive substances; provides technical services utilizing nuclear techniques to research agencies, educational institutions and hospitals; its research centre conducts studies in agriculture, biology, medicine, chemistry, physics and nuclear engineering.

Telecommunications

Bureau of Posts: Liwasang Bonifacio, Metro Manila; tel (2) 48-15-78; Postmaster-Gen: José Roilo S. Golez.

Bureau of Telecommunications: A. Roces Ave, Quezon City, Metro Manila; tel (2) 96-43-91; Dir: C. R. Carreon.

National Telecommunications Commission: Vibal Bldg, cnr Times St, EDSA, Quezon City, Metro Manila; tel (2) 99-89-11; telex 63912; Commr: José Luis A. Alcuaz; f 1981; telecommunications regulatory body.

Philippine Telegraph and Telephone Corpn: PT&T Spirit of Communication Centre, 106 Alvarado St, Legaspi Village, Makati, Metro Manila.

Tourism

Philippine Convention and Visitors Corpn (PCVC): Legaspi Towers, 4th Floor, Suite 10-17, 300 Roxas Blvd, Metro Manila; tel (2) 57-50-31; telex 40604; fax (2) 521-6165; Exec Dir: Undersecretary Mina T. Gabor; Dep Exec Dirs: Victor B. Bernardino, José Jesús F. Roces; f 1976; organization of conventions and services to foreign visitors.

Tourism Council of the Philippines: Manila; Pres: Ermin Garcia, Jr.

Transport

CIVIL AVIATION

Bureau of Air Transportation: Manila International Airport, Pasay City, Metro Manila; tel (2) 832-3047; Dir: Victorino G. Palpal-Latoc; implements policy for the devt and operation of a safe and efficient aviation network.

Philippine Airlines Inc (PAL): PAL Bldg, Legaspi St, Legaspi Village, Makati, POB 954, Metro Manila; tel (2) 818-0111; telex 22475; fax (2) 810-9214; Pres and Chief Exec: Dante Santos; Exec Vice-Pres: Leslie W. Espino; f 1941; 99.7% state-owned; domestic and international services within the Far East, to Europe, Australia, the Middle East and the USA.

RAILWAYS

Light Rail Transit Authority (Metrorail): Adm Bldg, LRTA Cpd, Aurora Blvd, Pasay City, Metro Manila; tel (2) 832-0423; telex 64614; managed by Light Rail Transit Authority (LRTA) and operated by Meralco Transit Organization (METRO); electrically-driven mass transit system in the Manila region.

Philippine National Railways: Tutuban Station, 943 Claro M. Recto Ave, Metro Manila; tel (2) 20-93-75; Chair: H. Perez; Gen Man: S. B. Arrastia; f 1887; over 1,000 km of track.

ROADS

Land Transportation Office: East Ave, Quezon City, Metro Manila; tel (2) 922-90-61; Asst Sec: Manuel N. Sabalza; f 1954; registration of motor vehicles, issue of driving licences, enforcement of traffic laws and regulations.

SHIPPING

Maritime Industry Authority: PPL Bldg, 1000 United Nations Ave, Ermita, Metro Manila; tel (2) 58-27-10; telex

27267; Admin: Philip S. Tuazon; Dep Admin for Operations: Reynaldo Q. Marquez; f 1974; promotion, devt, supervision and regulation of the maritime industry.

Philippine Ports Authority (PPA): Marsman Bldg, 22 Muelle de Francisco St, South Harbour, Metro Manila; tel (2) 47-92-04; telex 40404; Gen Man: Rogelio A. Dayan; f 1977; supervises all national, municipal and private ports.

Utilities

National Water Resources Board: NIA Bldg, 8th Floor, Epifanio de los Santos Ave, Quezon City, Metro Manila; tel (2) 99-23-65; Chair: Dr Fiorello R. Estuar; Exec Dir: Luis M. Sosa; f 1974; co-ordinates and integrates all activities related to water resources to achieve a scientific and orderly devt and management.

POLAND

Head of State

The state President is Head of State and has absolute authority in foreign and defence policy, a right of veto over Sejm legislation and has the power to introduce a state of emergency and dissolve the Sejm. The President nominates a Prime Minister, who appoints the Council of Ministers. In 1989, the President was chosen by the two chambers of the National Assembly, but at the end of the first six-year term, popular elections were envisaged.

President: Gen Wojciech Jaruzelski (elected 19 July 1989).

Office of the President: ul Wiejksa 10, 00-902 Warsaw.

Legislature

Legislative power is held by the bicameral National Assembly, comprising the Sejm (lower house), with 460 deputies, which holds supreme authority of legislative power, and the Senate, with 100 senators, which has right of veto over the Sejm. The Assembly was to draft a new Constitution. Both houses were to be elected, after the first four-year term, by free direct popular elections, though in 1989 65% of the Sejm seats were reserved for approved political parties and Catholic organizations.

Senate: Warsaw.

Sejm PRI: ul Wiejska 4-6, 00-902 Warsaw; tel (22) 285927; telex 813559; Speaker: Mikolaj Kozakiewicz.

MINISTRIES AND GOVERNMENT DEPARTMENTS

COUNCIL OF MINISTERS
Al Ujazdowskie 1-3, 00-583 Warsaw
Tel (22) 284471; telex 813466
Chairman and Prime Minister: Tadeusz Mazowiecki
Deputy Chairs: Leszek Balcerowicz, Czesław Janicki, Jan Janowski, Czesław Kiszczak
Minister, Head of the Office of the Council of Ministers: Jacek Ambroziak
Minister, Member of the Council of Ministers (Chair of the Economic Council): Witold Trzeciakowski
Minister, Member of the Council of Ministers (Responsible for Co-operation with Political Organizations and Associations): Aleksander Hall
Minister, Member of the Council of Ministers (Responsible for the Co-ordination of Social and Civilizational Affairs in Rural Areas): Artur Balazs
Minister, Member of the Council of Ministers (Responsible for Media Policy): Jerzy Urban
Minister, Member of the Council of Ministers (to prepare the organization of the Ministry of Communications): Marek Kucharski
Minister (Responsible for Privatisation): Dr Kristof Lis

CENTRAL PLANNING OFFICE
Pl Trzech Krzyży 5, 00-507 Warsaw
tel (22) 210321; telex 814698
Minister-Director: Jerzy Osiatyński

MINISTRY OF AGRICULTURE, FORESTRY AND FOOD ECONOMY
ul Wspólna 30, 00-930 Warsaw
Tel (22) 210251; telex 814597
Minister: Czesław Janicki

MINISTRY OF CULTURE AND ART
ul Krakowskie Przedmieście 15-17, 00-071 Warsaw
Tel (22) 265750; telex 813762
Minister: Izabella Cywińska

MINISTRY OF ENVIRONMENTAL PROTECTION AND NATURAL RESOURCES
ul Wawelska 52-54, 00-922 Warsaw
Tel (22) 250001; telex 812816
Minister: Bronisław Kamiński
Protects and develops the environment, manages inland waterways, flood control, oversees meteorology, hydrology and geology.

MINISTRY OF FINANCE
ul Świętokrzyska 12, POB 20, 00-916 Warsaw
Tel (22) 200311; telex 815592; fax (22) 266670
Minister: Leszek Balcerowicz

MINISTRY OF FOREIGN AFFAIRS
Al I Armii WP 23, 00-580 Warsaw
Tel (22) 288451; telex 814301; fax (22) 280906
Minister: Krzysztof Skubiszewski

MINISTRY OF FOREIGN ECONOMIC CO-OPERATION
ul Wiejska 10, 00-489 Warsaw
Tel (22) 210331; telex 814501
Minister: Marcin Święcicki

MINISTRY OF HEALTH AND SOCIAL WELFARE
ul Miodowa 15, 00-246 Warsaw
Tel (22) 313441; telex 813864
Minister: Andrzej Kosiniak-Kamysz

MINISTRY OF INDUSTRY
ul Wspólna 4, 00-926 Warsaw
Tel (22) 210351; telex 814261
Minister: Tadeusz Syryjczyk

MINISTRY OF INTERNAL AFFAIRS
ul Rakowiecka 2B, 00-904 Warsaw
Tel (22) 210251; telex 813681
Minister: Czesław Kiszczak

MINISTRY OF INTERNAL MARKET
Pl Powstańców Warszawy 1, 00-950 Warsaw
Tel (22) 269041; telex 814291
Minister: Aleksander Mackiewicz

MINISTRY OF JUSTICE
Al Ujazdowskie 11, 00-950 Warsaw
Tel (22) 284431; telex 813891
Minister: Aleksander Bentkowski

MINISTRY OF LABOUR AND SOCIAL POLICY
ul Nowogrodzka 1-3-5, 00-513 Warsaw
Tel (22) 289041; telex 814710
Minister: Jacek Kuroń

MINISTRY OF NATIONAL DEFENCE
ul Klonowa 1, 00-909 Warsaw
Tel (22) 210261; telex 813370
Minister: Gen Florian Siwicki

MINISTRY OF NATIONAL EDUCATION
Al I Armii WP 25, 00-918 Warsaw
Tel (22) 297241; telex 813523
Minister: Henryk Samsonowicz

MINISTRY OF PHYSICAL PLANNING AND CONSTRUCTION
ul Wspólna 2, 00-926 Warsaw
Tel (22) 210351; telex 814411; fax (22) 285887
Minister: Aleksander Paszyński
Deputy Minister: Lucjan Mieczkowski
Physical planning, urban devt, cartography and housing; co-ordinates the activity of about 300 cos.

MINISTRY OF TRANSPORT AND MARITIME ECONOMY
ul Chałubińskiego 4-6, 00-928 Warsaw
Tel (22) 284902; telex 816651; fax (22) 265343
Minister: Franciszek Adam Wielądek
Deputy Minister: Bogusław Liberadzki

OFFICE FOR RELIGIOUS AFFAIRS
ul Krakowskie Przedmieście 50, 00-325 Warsaw
Tel (22) 285557; telex 817881
Minister: (vacant)

OFFICE FOR SCIENTIFIC-TECHNOLOGICAL PROGRESS AND IMPLEMENTATION
ul Wspólna 1-3, 00-926 Warsaw
Tel (22) 217557; telex 816440
Minister and Head: Jan Janowski

GOVERNMENT AGENCIES AND ORGANIZATIONS

Business and Economy

BANKING

Bank Gospodarki Żywnościowej (Bank of Food Economy): Świętokrzyska 12, 00-916 Warsaw; tel (22) 271327; telex 813869; Pres: Janusz Cichosz; Vice-Pres: Tadeusz Wyszomirski; Dir, Office for Int Co-operation: Stefan Kobyliński; f 1975; provides credit for agriculture and food economy, clears foreign exchange within Poland.

Bank Handlowy (Export Development Bank): ul Wiejska 10, POB P22, 00-950 Warsaw; tel (22) 297934; telex 817119; fax (22) 287850; Pres: Krzysztof Szwarc; f 1986; the main shareholder is the Ministry of Foreign Economic Co-operation; finances and promotes foreign trade, provides foreign exchange facilities.

Bank Handlowy w Warszawie SA: ul Chałubińskiego 8, POB 129, 00-950 Warsaw; tel (22) 303000; telex 814811; fax (22) 300113; Pres: Tadeusz Barłowski; f 1870; commercial bank; finances export-oriented industries; provides foreign exchange.

Bank Polska Kasa Opieki (PKO) SA: ul Traugutta 7-9, POB 1008, 00-950 Warsaw; tel (22) 269211; telex 813441; Pres: Edmund Zawadzki; Chair: Andrzej Dorosz; f 1929; state savings bank; involved in domestic and foreign business; 21 brs and about 80 offices throughout Poland, also Paris and Tel-Aviv.

Narodowy Bank Polski (National Bank of Poland): ul Świętokrzyska 11-21, POB 10-11, 00-950 Warsaw; tel (22) 200321; telex 813324; Pres: Zdzisław Pakuła; Vice-Pres: Andrej Olechowski; f 1945; state central bank.

INSURANCE

Państwowy Zakład Ubezpieczeń (PZU) (Polish National Insurance): ul Traugutta 5, 00-916 Warsaw 51; tel (22) 200311; telex 814487; fax (22) 269743; Pres: Anatol Adamski; f 1803; state insurance co.

Towarzystwo Ubezpieczeń i Reasekuracji Warta SA (Warta Insurance and Reinsurance Co Ltd): ul Traugutta 5A, 00-916 Warsaw; tel (22) 272625; telex 813549; Pres: Jerzy Chyliński; f 1920; marine, air, motor, fire, illness, luggage, technical and credit insurance; responsible for all foreign insurance business.

NATIONALIZED INDUSTRY

Budimex Co Ltd: ul Marszalkowska 82, 00-926 Warsaw; tel (22) 284251; telex 813756; fax (22) 213853; Gen Man: Grzegorz Tuderek; f 1968; industrial construction; power engineering; construction of chemical plants, food industry works, warehouses, water treatment plants; general and public utility construction; assembly of industrial appliances, steel structures; technological, electric, land reclamation and irrigation schemes.

Energopol: ul Nowogrodzka 21, POB 367, 00-950 Warsaw; tel (22) 298081; telex 813663; fax (22) 299997; Dir-Gen: Bogdan Woś; Dir of Foreign Activities: Janusz Górzny; Dir of Finance: Wacław Achler; f 1974; constructs pipelines, inland and maritime hydro-engineering projects, and water and sewage plants.

TRADE

Agromet-Motoimport: Przemysłowa 26, POB 990, 00-950 Warsaw; tel (22) 285071; telex 813511; fax (22) 261595; Dir-Gen: Andrzej Michejda; f 1950; exports agricultural machinery.

Agros: Chałubińskiego 8, POB 41, 00-950 Warsaw; tel (export) (22) 300602, (import) (22) 300616; telex 814391; fax (export) (22) 300792, (import) (22) 300791; Man Dir: Zofia Gaber; f 1966; exports and imports alcoholic drinks, tobacco products, frozen foods, fruit and preserves, pharmaceutical raw materials, coffee, cocoa beans and confectionery.

Animex: ul Chałubińskiego 8, 00-613 Warsaw; tel (22) 300810; telex 814491; fax (22) 300537; Chair and Man Dir: Witold Pereta; First Dep Man Dir: Henryk Poniewierski; f 1983; export and import of meat and meat products, poultry and poultry products, game, feathers and down, cattle, calves, sheep, etc.

Baltona: Pułaskiego 6, 81-963 Gdynia; tel (58) 202357; telex 054361; fax (58) 203825; Pres and Dir-Gen: Jerzy Mrozowicki; f 1946; exports and imports foodstuffs and industrial products, supplies duty-free shops, airlines and diplomatic corps.

Befama: Powstańców Śląskich 6, 43-300 Bielsko Biała; tel (30) 23061; telex 035333; fax (30) 21293; Gen Man: Andrzej Jeremienko; f 1851; produces and exports textile machinery, imports equipment for textile machinery.

Centrozap: ul Mickiewicza 29, 40-085 Katowice; tel (32) 513401; telex 0315771; Dir-Gen: Henryk Kalita; import and export of complete plants, machines and equipment for the metallurgical, foundry and mining industries, air conditioning, etc.

Cepelia: ul Łucka 11, POB 1014, 00-950 Warsaw; tel (22) 205001; telex 813671; Gen Man: Wiesław Winiarski; f 1983; exports artistic and folk handicraft goods such as leather goods, regional dresses, fabrics and ceramics.

Ciech: Jasna 12, POB 271, 00-950 Warsaw; tel (22) 269001; telex 814561; Dir: Władysław Szczepankowski; import and export of organic and inorganic chemicals, dye-stuffs, fertilizers, paints, varnishes, enamels, cosmetics, petroleum products, rubber and synthetic rubber products, plastics, sulphur and pharmaceutical products.

Elektrim: ul Chałubińskiego 8, 00-950 Warsaw; tel (22) 301000; telex 814351; fax (22) 300841; Dir-Gen: Dr Andrzej Skowroński; f 1945; imports and exports power technology, transmission, electrical and telecommunications equipment.

Film Polski Ltd: Mazowiecka 6-8, 00-480 Warsaw; tel (22) 268455; telex 813640; fax (22) 275784; Dir: Ryszard Pospieszyński; f 1964; exports and imports films and film concept-to-completion services; distributes films; provides services for journalists, film festivals; publishes advertising materials.

C. Hartwig: Poznańska 15, 00-950 Warsaw; tel (22) 296031; telex 814601; fax (22) 291401; Dir-Gen: Zygmunt Kordecki; f 1858; international forwarding agents, by rail, road and air.

Hortex: ul Warecka 11, 00-034 Warsaw; tel (22) 265281; telex 816611; fax (22) 270522; Dir-Gen: Ludwik Olejarz; f 1958; foreign trade enterprise of the Union of Horticultural and Apicultural Co-operatives; export of fresh, frozen and processed fruit and vegetables, honey, flowers, fruit wines and meads; import of fresh and processed fruit and vegetables, tools; harvesting, processing and storage of fruit and vegetables.

Impexmetal: Łucka 7-9, POB 62, 00-842 Warsaw; tel (22) 200201; telex 814371; fax (22) 200544; Dir: Wojciech Opalko; import and export of non-ferrous metals and metal products, ball and roller bearings, electrical conductors and accessories, mine construction and smelting.

Intraco: ul Stawki 2, POB 812, 00-950 Warsaw; tel (2) 6352521; telex 812341; fax (2) 6355418; Man Dir: Jerzy Pietrula; f 1974; exports and imports tool spare parts and equipment, rents offices, offers building services and interior design services.

Kolmex: Mokotowska 49, POB 236, 00-950 Warsaw; tel (22) 282291; telex 813270; fax (22) 295879; Dir: Aleksander Gudzowaty; export and import of electric and diesel locomotives, railway rolling-stock and containers, equipment for track construction and maintenance, and medical equipment.

Kopex: Grabowa 1, POB 245, 40-952 Katowice; tel (32) 581631; telex 315681; fax (32) 580040; Man Dir: Dir-Gen: Eugeniusz Kuczka; export and import of machinery, equipment and appliances for mining, drilling and other industries.

Labimex: Ul Krakowskie Przedmieście 79, POB 261, 00-950 Warsaw; (22) 266431; telex 814230; fax (22) 262835; Dir-Gen: Jerzy Rychter; Dep Dir-Gen: Kazimierz Kimszal; f 1973; import and export of laboratory apparatus and equipment, scientific

research and optical apparatus; school teaching aids, laboratory furniture and glassware, etc.

BHZ Locum: ul Marchlewskiego 13, 00-828 Warsaw; tel (22) 201599; telex 816237; Commercial Dir: T. Wanago; imports hydraulic and electrical tools, drill, hammers, etc.

Minex: Chałubińskiego 8, POB 1002, 00-950 Warsaw; tel (22) 300500; telex 814401; fax (22) 300448; Dir: Józef Kostera; f 1949; import and export of minerals, cement, glass and ceramics.

Mundial Import-Export: ul Czerniakowska 58, 00-957 Warsaw; tel (22) 416086; telex 813689; fax (22) 402006; Man Dir: K. Pisz; f 1965; represents foreign cos selling in Poland.

Navimor Spółka z oo: ul Heweluisza 11, 80-890 Gdańsk; tel (58) 316821; telex 0512453; fax (58) 314497; Gen Man: Romuald Jaskulecki; f 1971; exports and imports marine industrial services and products; carries out ship repairs, shipbuilding, hydrotechnical works and consulting services.

Paged: Pl Trzech Krzyży 18, POB 991, 00-950 Warsaw; tel (22) 295241; telex 814221; fax (22) 281396; Dir: Henryk Prodomski; import and export of timber, paper, furniture, boards and machines and equipment for the wood and paper industry.

Pewex: Al Jerozolimskie 65/79, 00-697 Warsaw; tel (22) 300170; telex 812688; f 1974; import and export of textiles, clothing, consumer goods.

Pezetel: Al Stanów Zjednoczonych 61, 00-991 Warsaw 44; tel (22) 108001; telex 812815; Dir: Jerzy Kręźlewicz; import and export of aircraft, helicopters, sailplanes, turbo-shaft, jet and radial-piston aircraft engines, diesel engines, generators, air equipment, electric carts, pneumatics, hydraulics, motor cycles, aviation and agricultural services.

Polcargo: ul Żeromskiego 32, POB 223, 81-963 Gdynia; tel (58) 205371; telex 054247; Dir-Gen: Ryszard Jagiełło; Dep Dir-Gen: Henryk Jurkiewicz; f 1949; tests machinery and technical equipment, carries out laboratory tests, analyses and quality inspections, gives consultations and assistance on technical matters.

Polcomex: ul Marszałkowska 140, POB 478, 00-950 Warsaw; tel (22) 266810; telex 813452; Man Dir: Dr Andrzej Onacik; f 1960; represents foreign firms in Poland.

Polcoop: Kopernika 30, POB 199, 00-950 Warsaw; tel (22) 262363; telex 814705; Man Dir: Kazimierz Pracki; f 1957; export of fresh, pre-cooled and deep-frozen fruit and vegetables, fruit semi-products, fruit and vegetable preserves, mushrooms, rabbit, goose and duck meat, dairy products, etc; compensation and barter transactions.

Polcotex: Mysia 3, 00-950 Warsaw; tel (22) 213660; telex 815364; Dir-Gen: Zygmunt Karpiński; Commercial Dir: Witold Kowalski; Economic Man: Ryszard Brust; f 1985; exports garments.

Polexpo: Łopuszańska 38, 02-232 Warsaw; tel (22) 460401; telex 813633; fax (22) 464591; Gen Man: Henryk Usakowski; consultation services; designing and construction of stands at fairs and exhibitions.

Poliglob: ul Stawki 2, POB 40, 00-950 Warsaw; tel (2) 6353689; telex 813557; Man Dir: Ryszard Jaroszyński; f 1959; represents foreign firms in Poland, initiates and develops commercial contacts, co-operation agreements, exhibitions and technical symposia.

Polimar: ul Stawki 2, 00-193 Warsaw; tel (2) 6350187; telex 814895; fax (2) 6355943; Man Dir: Walerian Chryszczanowicz; Vice-Dir: Tadeusz Krzemiński; f 1972; assists foreign-owned manufacturing enterprises established in Poland conduct export-import business; represents foreign cos on the Polish market; consignment stores for different products, eg used cars, textile fabrics, kitchen and bath equipment.

Pol-Mot Ltd: Stalingradzka 23, POB 5, 03-370 Warsaw; tel (2) 111093; telex 813901; fax (2) 111907; Man Dir: Andrzej Zarajczyk; Commercial Dir: Józef Korono; f 1968; export and import of passenger cars, delivery vans, trucks, buses, specialized vehicles, trailers, service stations, garage equipment, car acessories, assembly plants.

Polservice: Chałubińskiego 8, 00-613 Warsaw; tel (22) 300522; telex 813539; fax (22) 300076; Dir: Leszek Święch; provides consulting, engineering and technical services.

Polska Izba Handlu Zagranicznego (Polish Chamber of Foreign Trade): Trębacka 4, POB 361, 00-950 Warsaw; tel (22) 260221; telex 814361; Pres: Tadeusz Żyłkowski; f 1949; organizes international trade fairs in Poland and promotes Poland at fairs abroad; publishes information on trade, foreign market possibilities and trade regulations, initiates co-operation with foreign firms.

Poltel: J P Woronica 17, POB 211, 00-950 Warsaw; tel (22) 478191; telex 816203; fax (22) 440206; Dir-Gen: Lew Rywin; Commercial Dir: Piotr Łaszcz; f 1984; represents Polish radio and TV abroad, purchases TV programmes, represents the interests of artists, orchestras, music groups and choirs.

Poznań International Fair: ul Głogowska 14, 60-734 Poznań; tel (61) 692592; telex 413251; fax (61) 665827; Dir: Stanisław Laskowski; f 1921; organizes international trade fairs.

Remex: ul Bracka 25, 00-950 Warsaw; tel (22) 276021; telex 815387; fax (22) 274472; Dir-Gen: Lech Wójcik; f 1977; export of handicraft products and technical services.

Rolimpex: Chałubińskiego 8, POB 364, 00-613 Warsaw; tel (22) 301000; telex 814341; fax (22) 302911; Dir: Roman Młyniec; export and import of sugar and vegetable products.

Shipcontrol: ul Polska 21, 81-336 Gdynia; tel (58) 207096; telex 054271; Dir: Zbigniew Nowakiewicz; f 1963; provides services for shipowners and charterers; tallies, weighs and gauges cargo and inspects containers.

Skórimpex: Piotrkowska 148-150, POB 133, 90-950 Łódź; tel (42) 363833; telex 885251; fax (42) 364229; Dir: Ryszard Winiarski; exports leather garments, footwear and leather goods.

Spedrapid: ul Zgoda 8, POB 201, 81-364 Gdynia; tel (58) 216085; telex 054321; fax (58) 216614; Dir: Witold Górski; f 1949; Polish-Czech forwarding co.

Timex SA: ul Stawki 2, 00-193 Warsaw; tel (22) 6356202; telex 813678; fax (22) 6356018; Dir: Stanisław Leszkowicz; f 1947; represents foreign cos on the Polish market; marketing of vehicles, building machines, machines for the mining, steelwork, textile and telecommunications industries, tyres, spare parts, chemicals, pharmaceuticals, glues, etc.

Unitra: ul Nowogrodzka 50, 00-950 Warsaw; tel (22) 289411; telex 814878; fax (22) 295038; Dir: Jan Brukszo; f 1972; imports and exports electronic equipment.

Universal: Al Jerozolimskie 44, POB 370, 00-950 Warsaw; tel (22) 262011; telex 814431; fax (22) 278312; Dir-Gen: Dariusz Przywieczerski; f 1959; exports and imports consumer and technical goods, and foodstuffs.

Węglokoks: ul A. Mickiewicza, 40-185 Katowice; tel (32) 582431; telex 0315641; Dir: Lucjan Gajda; import and export of coal, coke and gas.

Defence

National Defence Committee: Al Ujazdowskie 1-3, 00-583 Warsaw; tel (22) 284471; telex 813446; Chair and Supreme Commdr of the Armed Forces: Gen Wojciech Jaruzelski.

Air Force: ul Kościuszki 92-98, 60-928 Poznań; tel (61) 250441.

Army: ul Rakowiecka 4, 02-519 Warsaw; tel (22) 21006.

Navy: Dowództwo Marynarki Wojennej, 81-912 Gdynia; tel (58) 207870; telex 054489; Commdr: Rear-Adm Piotr Kołodziejczyk; Chief of Staff: Rear-Adm Romuald Waga; f 1918.

Energy

Instytut Energii Atomowej (Institute of Atomic Energy): 05-400 Otwock-Świerk; tel (22) 793888; telex 813244; Dir: Dr hab Jerzy Stanisław Michalik; f 1983 (fmrly Institute of Nuclear Research); reactor technology, gas-cooled power reactors, nuclear heating plants, electronic reactor systems, raw materials and fuel for reactor power industry, nuclear safety, waste disposal, etc.

Panstwowa Agencja Atomistyki (State Atomic Energy Agency): ul Krucza 36, 00-921 Warsaw; tel (22) 280281; telex 816915; Pres: Mieczysław Sowiński; f 1982; co-ordinates and supervises the use of nuclear energy; participates in international co-operation in the field of nuclear energy.

Fishing

Przediębiorstwo Połowów Dalekomorskich i Usług Rybackich Gryf: Pl Batorego 4, 70-952 Szczecin; tel (91) 533772; telex 0425491; fax (91) 47989; Man Dir: Jerzy Neja; f 1958; deep-sea fishing and fish-processing.

Legal and Judiciary

Office of the Public Prosecutor-General: Krakowskie Przedmieście 25, 00-071 Warsaw; Prosecutor-Gen: Józef Żyta; protects social property.

Supreme Court of the Polish People's Republic: ul Ogrodowa 6, 00-896 Warsaw; tel (22) 203975; Pres: Dr Adam Łopatka; f 1917; highest judicial body; supervises the activity of all other courts, gives directives on interpretation of the law and on judicial practice.

Media

BROADCASTING

Polskie Radio i Telewizja (Polish Radio and Television): Komitet do Spraw Radia i Telewizji, ul Woronicza 17, POB 35, 00-950 Warsaw; tel (22) 478501; telex 815331; fax (22) 437408; Pres: Andrzej Drawicz; Vice-Pres (TV): Jerzy Słabicki; Vice-Pres (Radio): Józef Królikowski; Chair of the Radio and Television Committee: Jerzy Urban; production of programmes; broadcasting.

NEWS AND INFORMATION

Centralna Agencja Fotografczna—CAF (Press-Photo Agency—CAF): ul Foksal 16, 00-372 Warsaw; tel (22) 265221; telex 814801; Editor-in-Chief and Dir: Michał Gardowski; f 1951; supplies photographs to Polish and foreign press agencies, publishing houses and advertising agencies.

Główny Urząd Statystyczny (Central Statistical Office): Al Niepodległości 208, 00-925 Warsaw; tel (22) 252431; telex 814581; fax (22) 251525.

Polska Agencja Interpress (Polish Agency Interpress): ul Bagatela 12, 00-585 Warsaw; tel (22) 285740; telex 814775; fax (22) 284651; Editor-in-Chief: Jan Grzelak; f 1967; provides multilingual books, magazines, bulletins, news, films, feature and photographic services on Polish culture, foreign policy and economics.

Polska Agencja Prasowa—PAP (Polish Press Agency): Al Jerozolimskie 7, 00-950 Warsaw; tel (22) 280001; telex 812509; Pres and Editor-in-Chief: Bogdan Jachacz; f 1944; transmits information abroad in English, French, Russian and Spanish.

Research

Instytut Problemów Jądrowych (Institute for Nuclear Studies): 05-400 Otwock-Świerk; tel (22) 793481; telex 813244; fax (22) 793481; Dir: Dr Wojciech Ratyński; Dep Dirs: Dr Andrzej Budzanowski, Dr Andrzej Jasiński; f 1983; carries out research in areas such as nuclear physics and radiation.

Science and Technology

Henryk Niewodniezański Institute of Nuclear Physics: ul Radzikowskiego 152, 31-342 Kraków; tel (12) 370222; telex 03222461; fax (12) 333438; Dir: Dr Zbigniew Bochnacki; f 1956; high and low energy nuclear physics, structural investigations and applied physics.

Instytut Chemii i Techniki Jadrowej (Institute of Nuclear Chemistry and Technology): ul Dorodna 16, 03-195 Warsaw; tel (22) 110656; telex 813027; Dir: Dr Janusz Leciejewicz; f 1983.

Tourism

ORBIS: ul Bracka 16, 00-028 Warsaw; tel (22) 260221; telex 814761; Pres: Marek Manowiecki; f 1920; national tourist enterprise operating domestic and foreign tours and tourist hotels.

Polskie Towarzystwo Turystyczno-Krajoznawcze (Polish Tourist and Country-Lovers' Society): ul Senatorska 11, 00-075 Warsaw; tel (22) 265735; telex 812441; Pres: Andrzej Gordon; Sec-Gen: Zdzisław Łysio; f 1950; involved in the promotion and devt of tourism; runs hostels, chalets and camping sites; promotes the preservation of nature and of historic monuments.

Transport

CIVIL AVIATION

Polskie Linie Lotnicze (LOT) (Polish Airlines): ul 17

Stycznia 39, 00-906 Warsaw; tel (22) 225546; telex 813552; Dir-Gen: Jerzy Słowiński; f 1929; provides domestic services and international air services to the Middle East, Africa, Asia, Canada, the USA, Australia and throughout Europe.

ROADS

PKS/Państwowa Komunikacja Samochodowa (Polish Motor Communications): ul Grójecka 17, 00-973 Warsaw; tel (22) 220011; telex 816598; f 1945; organizes inland road transport for passengers and goods.

Pekaes Enterprise (International Road Co): ul Świętokrzyska 30, 00-950 Warsaw; tel (22) 242813; telex 813509; f 1958; organizes freight road transport to all European countries, and operates tourist circuits to East and West Europe.

SHIPPING

Polskie Linie Oceaniczne—PLO (Polish Ocean Lines): ul 10 Lutego 24, 81-364 Gdynia; tel (58) 201901; telex 54231; fax (58) 278537; Dir-Gen: K. Misiejuk; f 1951; world-wide shipping operations.

Polska Żegluga Morska—PZM (Polish Steamship Co): ul Małopolska 44, 70-515 Szczecin; tel (91) 305011; telex 422135; fax (91) 39764; Chair and Dir-Gen: Mieczysław Andruczyk; f 1951; world-wide tramping.

Żegluga Polska Spółka Akcyjna: ul Małopolska 43-44, 70-515 Szczecin; tel (91) 305011; telex 0422136; Pres: Ryszard Karger; f 1982; world-wide tramping.

Zjednoczenie Żeglugi Śródlądowej (United Inland Navigation and River Shipyards): Wita Stwosza 28, 50-149 Wrocław 2; responsible for five inland navigation enterprises and eight inland shipyards.

PORTUGAL

Head of State

The President is Head of State and is elected by popular vote for a five-year term. The President appoints the Prime Minister and, on the latter's proposal, other members of the Government, principally the Council of Ministers. A consultative body, the Council of State (comprising 17 members in 1988) is presided over by the President.

President: Dr Mário Alberto Nobre Lopes Soares (took office 9 March 1986).

Office of the President: Presidência da República, Palácio de Belém, Lisbon; tel (1) 637141; telex 16733.

Legislature

Legislative power is vested in the unicameral Assembly, comprising 250 members (including four representing Portuguese abroad), elected by universal adult suffrage for four years, subject to dissolution. The Azores and Madeira (integral parts of the Portuguese Republic) were granted autonomy in 1976.

Assembléia da República (Assembly of the Republic): Largo das Cortes, 1200 Lisbon; tel (1) 660141; Pres: Vítor Crespo.

MINISTRIES AND GOVERNMENT DEPARTMENTS

OFFICE OF THE PRIME MINISTER
Presidência do Conselho de Ministros, Rua da Imprensa 8, 1300 Lisbon
Telex 12176
Prime Minister: Prof Aníbal Cavaco Silva
(Assistant) Minister of Youth: António Couto dos Santos

MINISTRY OF AGRICULTURE, FISHERIES AND FOOD
Praça do Comércio, 1100 Lisbon
Tel (1) 363151; telex 13517
Minister: Arlindo Cunha

MINISTRY OF DEFENCE
Rua Gomes Teixeira, 1300 Lisbon
Tel (1) 677001; telex 42530
Minister: Dr Joachim Fernando Nogueira

MINISTRY OF EDUCATION
Av 5 de Outubro 107, 1051 Lisbon Codex
Tel (1) 731603; telex 18428; fax (1) 764119
Minister: Roberto Carneiro

MINISTRY OF EMPLOYMENT AND SOCIAL SECURITY
Praça de Londres, 1000 Lisbon
Tel (1) 544560; telex 63425
Minister: Dr José da Silva Peneda

MINISTRY OF ENVIRONMENT
Praça du Comercio, 1100 Lisbon
Tel (1) 320593
Minister: Prof Fernando Real

MINISTRY OF FINANCE
Rua da Alfândega, 1100 Lisbon
Tel (1) 877555; telex 12143
Minister: Miguel Couceiro Pizarro Beleza

MINISTRY OF FOREIGN AFFAIRS
Largo do Rilvas, 1354 Lisbon Codex
Tel (1) 601028; telex 12276
Minister: Prof João de Deus Pinheiro

MINISTRY OF HEALTH
Av João Crisóstomo 9, 1093 Lisbon Codex
Tel (1) 544560; telex 15655
Minister: Arlindo de Carvalho

MINISTRY OF INDUSTRY AND ENERGY
Rua da Horta Seca 15, 1200 Lisbon
Tel (1) 734049; telex 13567
Minister: Luís de Mira Amaral

MINISTRY OF THE INTERIOR
Praça do Comércio, 1194 Lisbon Codex
Tel (1) 364521; telex 16765
Minister: Manuel Pereira

MINISTRY OF JUSTICE
Praça do Comércio, 1194 Lisbon Codex
Tel (1) 360786; telex 42998
Minister: Alvaro Lucio

MINISTRY OF PLANNING
Lisbon
Telex 12566
Minister: Prof Luís Valente de Oliveira

MINISTRY OF PARLIAMENTARY AFFAIRS
Presidência do Conselho de Ministros, Rua Gomes Teixeira,
1300 Lisbon
Tel (1) 677001
Minister: Manuel Dias Loureiro

MINISTRY OF PUBLIC WORKS, TRANSPORT AND COMMUNICATIONS
Praça do Comércio, 1194 Lisbon Codex
Tel (1) 879541; telex 13461
Minister: João Maria Leitão de Oliveira Martins

MINISTRY OF TERRITORIAL ADMINISTRATION
Rua da Alfaandega, 1100 Lisbon
Tel (1) 877555
Minister: Prof Luís Valente de Oliveira

MINISTRY OF TRADE AND TOURISM
Av da República 79, 1000 Lisbon Codex
Tel (1) 730412; telex 13455
Minister: Joaquim Ferreira do Amaral

GOVERNMENT AGENCIES AND ORGANIZATIONS

Agriculture

Administração Geral do Açúcar e do Álcool (AGA), EP:
Rua Castilho 14-C-5°, 1200 Lisbon; tel (1) 563361; telex 16688;
Pres: Dr José Nunes dos Santos; imports raw sugar for the
national refining industry; ethyl alcohol trade.

Instituto do Vinho do Porto: Rua S. Pedro de Alcântara, 45
r/c, 1200 Lisbon; tel (1) 323307; Pres: Dr Leopoldo Mourão; an
official body dealing with quality control and the promotion of
port wine; also gives technical advice to exporters.

Business and Economy

BANKING

Banco Borges e Irmão: Rua Sá da Bandeira 20, 4001 Porto
Codex; tel (2) 324517; telex 26899; Pres: Dr António Carlos
Magalhães Tato; f 1884; to be adopted by the Banco de Fomento
Nacional and Caixa Geral de Depositos (see below); 114 brs,
incl 9 in France.

Banco Comercial dos Açores: Apdo 1379, 9503 Ponta Delgada, Azores Codex; tel (96) 27501; telex 82111; fax (96) 27004;
Chair: Raul Gomes dos Santos; f 1912; commercial bank.

Banco Espírito Santo e Comercial de Lisboa: Av da Liberdade 195, 1200 Lisbon; tel (1) 578005; telex 12191; Pres: Dr
Alexandre Vaz Pinto; f 1875; merger between Banco Comercial
de Lisboa and Banco Espírito Santo in 1987; 144 brs.

Banco de Fomento Nacional (BFN): Av Casal Ribeiro 59,
1000 Lisbon; tel (1) 562021; telex 64752; Pres: Dr João Salgueiro;
f 1959; investment bank; 22 brs.

Banco Fonsecas e Burnay: Rua Do Comércio 132, Apdo
2231, 1106 Lisbon Codex; tel (1) 874081; telex 12210; Pres: Dr
Almerindo da Silva Marques; f 1967 by merger; 103 brs.

Banco Nacional Ultramarino: Rua Augusta 24, Apdo 2419,
1111 Lisbon Codex; tel (1) 369981; telex 13305; Chair and Pres:
Dr João Costa Pinto; f 1864; to be adopted by the Banco de
Fomento Nacional and Caixa Geral de Depositos; 156 brs, incl
2 in Madeira, 2 in the Azores and 5 in Macau.

Banco Pinto e Sotto Mayor: Av Fontes P. de Melo 7-5°, 1000
Lisbon; tel (1) 542078; telex 12516; Chair: Dr António José
Nunes Loureiro Borges; f 1914; Banco Intercontinental Portu-
guês merged in 1977; 163 brs, incl 22 in France and 1 in Macau.

Banco de Portugal: Rua do Comércio 148, 1101 Lisbon Codex;
tel (1) 3462931; telex 16554; fax (1) 3464843; Gov: José Alberto
Tavares Moreira; Vice-Gov: António Carlos Palmeiro Ribeiro;
f 1846, reorganized 1931 with sole right to issue notes in Continental Portugal and adjacent islands (Madeira, Azores); nationalized 1974; central bank; chief br Porto, with 22 others including
Madeira and Azores.

Banco Português do Atlântico: Praça D. João I, 4001 Porto
Codex; tel (2) 381494; telex 22720; Pres: Dr João dos Santos

Oliveira; f 1919; plans to privatize at least 49% were announced
in 1989; 155 brs incl 9 abroad.

Banco Totta e Açores: Rua Aurea 88, 1100 Lisbon; tel (1)
369421; telex 12266; Pres: Dr Alípio Pereira Dias; f 1970 by
merger; 49% privatized in 1989; 132 brs in Portugal and 5
abroad.

Sociedade Financeira Portuguesa: Rua Alexandre Herculano 50-5°, 1296 Lisbon Codex; tel (1) 533113; telex 65952; fax
(1) 540516; Board Member (International): Dr E. Farinha; Man,
Financial Dept: Dr H. Castanheira; f 1969; merchant banking.

União de Bancos Portugueses SA: Praça D. João I 80, 4000
Porto; (2) 20961; telex 26061; Pres: Dr António de Almeida; f
1978 by merger; 51% state-owned, 49% by public-sector enterprises; 125 brs.

FINANCIAL AGENCIES

Caixa Geral de Depositos: Largo do Calhariz, 1109 Lisbon
Codex; tel (1) 361981; telex 18481; fax (1) 327476; Chair: Dr
Alberto A. Oliveira Pinto; Vice-Chair: Dr José Pires Lourenço;
f 1876; state credit institution; source of long-term and non-
commercial short-term credit; handles credits for agriculture,
industry, building, housing, central and local admin, energy and
other purposes; administers the pension funds of the civil and
defence services; 370 brs.

Crédito Predial Português: Campo Pequeno 81, 1000 Lisbon;
tel (1) 734024; telex 62533; Pres: Dr José Manuel Ferreira Neto;
f 1864 to further building devt for industrial, commercial and
residential purposes; 60 brs.

INSURANCE

Aliança Seguradora, EP: Rua Gonçalo Sampaio 39-6°, 4100
Porto; tel (2) 62930; telex 25819; Pres: Dr Manuel Oliveira
Marques; f 1980 from merger of five cos; all branches of
insurance and reinsurance; 49% privatized in 1989.

Companhia de Seguros Açoreana, EP: Largo da Matriz 45-
52, Apdo 186, 9500 Ponta Delgada, San Miguel, Azores; tel (96)
27481; telex 82279; Pres: Dr António Carlos Ribeiro; f 1892; all
branches of insurance and reinsurance.

Companhia de Seguros Bonança, EP: Av José Malhoa 9,
Apdo 4287, 1507 Lisbon Codex; tel (1) 7266195; telex 12776;
Pres: Dr Jerónimo Campos do Espírito Santo; f 1808; all bran-
ches of insurance and reinsurance except credit.

Companhia de Seguros Império, EP: Rua Garrett 62, 1200
Lisbon; tel (1) 362921; telex 16644; Pres: Dr Tomé Pinho Gil; f
1980 from merger of two cos; all branches of insurance and
reinsurance.

Companhia de Seguros Mundial Confiança, EP: Largo do
Chiado 8, 1200 Lisbon; tel (1) 360191; telex 15065; Pres: Dr
Pedro Rogério de Azevedo Seixas Vale; f 1980; all branches of
insurance and reinsurance.

Cosec—Companhia de Seguros de Créditos, EP: Av da República 58, 1094 Lisbon Codex; tel (1) 760131; telex 12885; Pres: Dr Alberto Heleno do Nascimento Regueira; f 1969; domestic and export credit insurance; bond insurance.

Fidelidade—Grupo Segurador, EP: Largo do Corpo Santo 13, 1200 Lisbon; tel (1) 360321; telex 16483; Pres: Dr António José Barata Alves Caetano; f 1980 from merger of four cos; all branches of insurance and reinsurance.

Instituto de Seguros de Portugal (ISP): Av 5 de Outubro 17, 1094 Lisbon Codex; tel (1) 579596; telex 15398; fax (1) 579546; Pres: Dr Armando Francisco da Silva Almeida; f 1982.

Tranquilidade Seguros, EP: Av da Liberdade 242, 1200 Lisbon; tel (1) 538866; telex 12164; Pres: Dr Luís Frederico Redondo Lopes; f 1980 from merger of three cos; all branches of insurance and reinsurance; 49% privatized in 1989.

NATIONALIZED INDUSTRY

Centralcer—Central de Cervejas, EP: Av Almirante Reis 115, 1100 Lisbon; tel (1) 536841; telex 13749; Pres: Baltazar António de Morais Barroco; f 1934; production and marketing of malt, beer and soft drinks; marketing of mineral waters and whisky.

Cimpor—Cimentos de Portugal, EP: Rua Alexandre Herculano 35, Apdo 2211, 1200 Lisbon; tel (1) 526070; telex 12433; Pres: Vergílio Teixeira Lopo; f 1976; cement; plans to privatize at least 49% were announced in 1989.

Companhia Nacional de Petroquímica (CNP): Av Eng Duarte Pacheco 1-2°, 1092 Lisbon Codex; tel (1) 656071; telex 65524; Pres: Jorge Gonçalves; f 1976; petro-chemical industry.

Conselho Nacional da Indústria (CNI): Lisbon; f 1985; under the Min istry of Industry and Energy; advises on industrial and technological policy.

Estaleiros Navais de Viana Do Castelo, EP: Av do Restelo 37, 1400 Lisbon; tel (1) 610219; telex 13526; Pres: António Duarte Silva; f 1944; ship-building and repairing.

Fábrica Escola Irmãos Stephens, EP: Praça Stephens, 2431 Marinha Grande Codex; tel (44) 52021; telex 18636; fax (44) 53149; Pres: Vítor Carvalho; Vice-Pres: Carlos Poço; f 1769; blown glass and lead crystal.

Instituto das Participações do Estado, SA—IPE (Institute of State Participation): Av Júlio Dinis 11, 1000 Lisbon; tel (1) 761536; telex 14176; Pres: Sousa Gomes; state holding co.

Instituto dos Têxteis: Rua Vale do Pereiro 4, 1200 Lisbon; tel (1) 655521; telex 15380; Pres: Bartolomeu Monteiro; institute of textiles.

Portucel—Empresa de Celulose e Papel de Portugal, EP: Rua Joaquim António de Aguiar 3-2° a 8°, 1092 Lisbon Codex; tel (1) 538857; telex 12140; Pres: Dr António Celeste; f 1976; pulp, paper, forestry, packaging.

Quimigal—Química de Portugal, EP: Av Infante Santo 2, 1399 Lisbon Codex; tel (1) 604040; telex 12426; Pres: Alberto Justiniano; f 1977; fertilizers and pesticides, products for livestock, inorganic and organic chemicals, industrial gases, non-ferrous metals, plastics, margarines, edible oils, soaps, glycerines, home textiles.

Setenave—Estaleiros Navais de Setúbal: Apdo 135, 2902 Setúbal Codex; tel (65) 20101; telex 16171; Pres: Oscar Napoleão Mota; f 1972; ship-building and repairing.

Siderurgia Nacional, EP: Rua Braamcamp 7, 1297 Lisbon Codex; tel (1) 533151; telex 12229; fax (1) 535051; Pres: Dr José Almeida Serra; f 1954, nationalized 1975; privatization plans announced in 1990; metallurgical industry.

Tabaqueira—Empresa Industrial de Tabacos, EP: Rua Alexandre Herculano 51-6°, 1200 Lisbon; tel (1) 686131; telex 16657; fax (1) 689476; Pres: Dr Lucena Ival; f 1975; tobacco industry.

Culture

Instituto de Cultura e Língua Portuguesa: Praça do Príncipe Real 74-1°, 1200 Lisbon; tel (1) 364508; fax (1) 373997; Pres: Dr Fernando Cristóvão; promotes the Portuguese language and culture abroad in foreign universities; under the Ministry of Education.

Defence

Armed Forces: Av Ilha da Madeira, 1400 Lisbon; tel (1) 610001; Chief of Staff: Gen José Lemos Ferreira.

Air Force: Av Leite de Vasconcelos, 2700 Amadora Alfagide, Lisbon; tel (1) 972383; telex 12110; Chief of Staff: Gen Jorge M. Brochado Miranda.

Army: Rua Museu de Artilharia, 1100 Lisbon; tel (1) 867131; telex 22223; Chief of Staff: Gen Mario Firmino Miguel.

Navy: Praça do Comércio, Lisbon; tel (1) 368960; Chief of Staff: Adm António Manuel Andrade e Silva.

Development and Planning

PLANNING

Cedintec—Centro para o Desenvolvimento e Inovação Tecnológicos (Centre for Technological Development and Innovation): Rua de S. Domingos à Lapa 117-2° Dt°, 1200 Lisbon; tel (1) 609473; fax (1) 661203; Pres: Dr Pedro Homem e Sousa; Vice-Pres: Dr Luís Palma Féria; f 1983; promotes the devt of industry through the allocation of financial resources obtained from the management of securities, portfolios and from the Govt.

Gabinete de Estudos e Planeamento: Av Conselheiro Fernando de Sousa 11-12°, 1092 Lisbon Codex; tel (1) 659161; telex 13567; fax (1) 658685; Dir: Alberto Moreno; f 1977; planning and research board; industrial economics.

INVESTMENT

Instituto de Apoio às Pequenas e Médias Empresas Industriais (IAPMEI): Rua Rodrigo da Fonseca 73, 1297 Lisbon Codex; tel (1) 525419; telex 15657; Pres: Gaspar Prata Dias; financial and technical aid to small and medium-sized industrial enterprises; under the Ministry of Industry and Energy.

Instituto Financeiro de Apoio ao Desenvolvimento da Agricultura e Pescas (IFADAP): Av João Crisóstomo 11, 1000 Lisbon; tel (1) 574337; telex 64138; fax (1) 558030; Chair: Dr Henrique Manuel Fusco Granadeiro; f 1977; provides loans for agriculture and fisheries.

REGIONAL DEVELOPMENT

Gabinete da Área de Sines (GAS): Rua Artilharia Um 33, 1297 Lisbon Codex; tel (1) 655540; telex 12572; Chair: Almeida Viana; co-ordinates and promotes the devt of the Sines port and industrial area.

Education and Research

EDUCATION

Direcção-Geral do Ensino Básico e Secundário: Av 24 de

Julho 138, 1300 Lisbon; tel (1) 677181; Dir-Gen: Dr Pereira Neto; responsible for pedagogical orientation, methods and techniques, the training of teachers, etc in the fields of elementary and secondary education; under the Ministry of Education.

Direcção-Geral do Ensino Superior: Av 5 de Outubro 107, 8°, 1000 Lisbon; tel (1) 731291; fax (1) 760984; Dir-Gen: Dr Lynce de Faria; implements Govt policies concerning higher education; controls the quality of teaching and is responsible for the University Entrance General Examination; under the Ministry of Education.

Direcção-Geral de Extensão Educativa: Av 5 de Outubro 35, 7°, 1000 Lisbon; tel (1) 534964; Dir-Gen: Dr Maria Helena Valente Rosa; promotes and co-ordinates private and co-operative educational institutions, Portuguese schools abroad and adult education; under the Ministry of Education.

Gabinete de Estudos e Planeamento: Av Miguel Bombarda 20, 1000 Lisbon; tel (1) 736095; telex 62553; fax (1) 734538; Dir-Gen: Dr Valadares Tavares; formulates general policy on education for the Govt; under the Ministry of Education.

Inspecção-Geral de Ensino: Av 24 de Julho 138, 1300 Lisbon; tel (1) 677181; Inspector-Gen: Dr René Rodrigues da Silva; inspects and supervises teachers and educational institutions at primary and secondary level; under the Ministry of Education.

RESEARCH

Instituto Nacional de Investigação Científica: Av Elias Garcia 137, 6°, 1000 Lisbon; tel (1) 774541; telex 63413; fax (1) 773330; Pres: Dr Britaldo Rodrigues; promotes the devt of science and research activities and policies at higher education level; under the Ministry of Education.

Laboratório Nacional de Engenharia e Tecnologia Industrial—LNETI (National Laboratory for Engineering and Industrial Technology): Azinhaga dos Lameiros, à Estrada do Paço do Lumiar, 1699 Lisbon Codex; tel (1) 7586141; telex 42486; fax (1) 7580901; Pres: Prof José Veiga Simão; Vice-Pres: Dr Mario de Abreu, Dr António Homem de Sousa; f 1979; industrial and technological research; implements Govt policy on energy; under the Ministry of Industry and Energy.

Legal and Judiciary

Procuradoria-Geral da República (Office of the Attorney-General): Lisbon; Attorney-Gen: Dr José Narciso da Cunha Rodrigues.

Supremo Tribunal de Justiça (Supreme Court): Praça do Comércio, 1100 Lisbon; tel (1) 366236; Pres: Victor Coelho; the highest organ of the judicial system; has jurisdiction over Metropolitan Portugal, the Azores, Madeira and Macau; comprises a president and 29 judges.

Tribunal Constitucional (Constitutional Court): Rua do Século 111, Lisbon; tel (1) 360024; Pres: Prof Armando Marques Guedes; rules on matters of constitutionality according to the terms of the Constitution of the Portuguese Republic; exercises jurisdiction over all Portuguese territory; consists of 13 judges.

Media

BROADCASTING

RDP—Radiodifusão Portuguesa, EP: Av Eng Duarte Pacheco 5, 1000 Lisbon; tel (1) 654041; telex 15649; Pres: Dr Arlindo de Carvalho; Dir, Non-Commercial Programmes: José Manuel Nunes; Dir, Commercial Programmes: J. David Nunes; Dir, External Relations: Dr Duarte Guedes Vaz; f 1975 after the nationalization of nine radio stations and their merger with the

existing national broadcasting co; home and international radio services; regional services as follows:

Central Zone (RDP/Centro): Rua Dr José Alberto dos Reis (Celas), 3000 Coímbra; tel (39) 76623; telex 52280; Dir: Domingos Grilo.

Northern Zone (RDP/Norte): Rua Cândido dos Reis 74-1°, 4099 Porto; tel (2) 20163; telex 22449; Dir: Rui Pereira.

RDP Açores: Rua Aristides da Mota 33, 9500 Ponta Delgada, San Miguel, Azores; tel 22045; telex 82139; fax 27996; Regional Dir: José ALberto Rolão Bernardo; f 1941.

RDP Madeira: Rua dos Netos 27, 9000 Funchal, Madeira; tel 29155; telex 72111; Dir: João Afonso de Almeida.

Southern Zone (RDP/Sul): Campo da Sra da Saúde, 8000 Faro; tel (89) 25031; telex 56512; Dir: Carlos Moita.

RTP—Radiotelevisão Portuguesa, EP: Av 5 de Outubro 187, Apdo 2934, 1000 Lisbon; tel (1) 760031; telex 1427; Chair: Dr João Coelho Ribeiro; Technical Dir: J. M. Franco Dias; f 1956, nationalized in 1975; TV broadcasting network.

GOVERNMENT PUBLISHER

Imprensa Nacional—Casa de Moeda: Rua D. Francisco Manuel de Melo 5, 1000 Lisbon; tel (1) 685684; telex 15328; Man Dir: Dr Américo Farinha de Carvalho; Portuguese literature, arts, philosophy, history, geography, sociology, economics, encyclopaedias, dictionaries.

NEWS AND INFORMATION

Instituto Nacional de Estatística: Av António José de Almeida, 1078 Lisbon Codex; tel (1) 802080; telex 63738; fax (1) 889480; f 1935; statistical office.

Mining and Energy

ENERGY

Direcção-Geral de Energia (Directorate-General of Energy): Rua da Beneficência 241, 1600 Lisbon; tel (1) 771091; telex 14755; fax (1) 730667; Dir-Gen: C. A. Migunes; energy planning, pricing, legislation and regulation; energy conservation incentives; devt of renewable sources of energy.

Divisão de Energia Nuclear: Av da República 45-8° Esq, 1000 Lisbon; tel (1) 770060; telex 14755; Head Eng: Hélio Vieira; f 1968; under the Ministry of Industry and Energy.

Electricidade de Portugal, EDP: Av José Malhoa, Lote A-13, 1000 Lisbon; tel (1) 7263013; telex 16550; Pres of Board of Dirs: José Manuel Castro Rocha; f 1976; responsible for the generation, transmission and distribution of electrical energy.

Gabinete de Protecção e Segurança Nuclear: Av da República 45-6°, 1000 Lisbon; tel (1) 736135; telex 14344; fax (1) 773482; Dir-Gen: António Francisco Marques de Carvalho; Dep Dir: Isabel Roriz; f 1977; nuclear safety regulation; environmental radio-activity surveillance; under the Ministry of Industry and Energy.

Petrogal—Petróleos de Portugal, EP: Rua das Flores 7, Apdo 2539, 1113 Lisbon Codex; tel (1) 328035; telex 12521; Pres: António da Silva Pinto; f 1976; oil and petrochemicals; exploration, refining, transport, marketing, etc.

Petroquímica e Gás de Portugal, EP: Av António Augusto de Aguiar 104-4°, Apdo 1933, 1004 Lisbon Codex; tel (1) 538801; telex 12864; Pres: F. David de Moura; f 1979; incorporates Empresa de Petroquímica e Gás, EP, and Petrofibras, EP; manufactures anhydrous ammonia, city gas, hydrogen, nitrogen, carbon dioxide, phthalic anhydride and plasticizers.

MINING

Direcção Geral da Geologia e Minas: Rua António Enes 7-5°, Lisbon; tel (1) 549108; mining and geology directorate; part of the Ministry of Industry and Energy.

Empresa de Desenvolvimento Mineiro (EDM), EP: Rua Sampaio e Pina 1-7°, 1000 Lisbon; tel (1) 659121; telex 42637; fax (1) 656344; Pres: Fernando Alves da Silva; Vice-Pres: Belarmino A. F. C. Silva; f 1979 as Empresa Mineira e Metalúrgica do Alentejo; mining co; holds majority shareholding in Somincor, SA, Pirites Alentejanas, SA, Empresa Carbonífera do Douro, SA, Nordareias, Lda, Segurmina, Lda; investigation and devt of mining projects.

Empresa Nacional de Urânio, EP: Urgeiriça, 3525 Canas de Senhorim, Nelas; tel (32) 67242; telex 53562; Pres and Chair: Armindo Torres Lopes; f 1977; uranium mining and concentration.

Ferrominas: Rua Sampaio e Pina, 1000 Lisbon; tel (1) 659121; telex 42637; Pres: António Santiago Baptista; iron ore- and coal-mining.

Telecommunications

Correios e Telecomunicações de Portugal (CTT): Rua de S. José 20, 1000 Lisbon; tel (1) 370051; telex 13351; fax (1) 320936; f 1880; post office and telecommunications.

Direcção-Geral de Telecomunicaçãoes—DGT: Av Fontes Pereira de Melo 40, 1089 Lisbon Codex; tel (1) 540020; telex 65722; Dir-Gen: Iriarte Esteves; telecommunications admin and operation.

Telefones de Lisboa e Porto (TLP): Rua de S. José 20, 1000 Lisbon; tel (1) 370051; telex 13351; fax (1) 320936; f 1969; telecommunications services in Lisbon and Oporto.

Tourism

Direcção-Geral do Turismo: Av António Augusto de Aguiar 86, 1099 Lisbon Codex; tel (1) 575086; telex 13408; Dir-Gen: João Strecht Ribeiro.

Instituto de Promoção Turística: Rua Alexandre Herculano 51-2° Dt°, 1127 Lisbon Codex; tel (1) 681174; telex 64999; fax (1) 659782; Pres: Dr José Valle; Vice-Pres: Dr Luís Rodrigues; f 1986; promotion of tourism through local and regional offices and national tourist offices abroad.

Instituto Nacional de Formação Turística: Rua Duque de Palmela 2-2°, 1200 Lisbon; tel (1) 562261; telex 65740.

Transport

CIVIL AVIATION

Ana, EP—Empresa Pública Aeroportos e Navegação Aérea: Rua D, Edifício 120, Aeroporto de Lisboa, 1700 Lisbon; tel (1) 808044; telex 14738; fax (1) 803547; Dirs: Henrique Risques Pereira, Rogério Lameira, Manuel Joaquim Maia Gonçalves, Damião Martins de Castro; f 1978; study, planning, construction, devt and operation of airport and air navigation infrastructures.

Serviço Açoreano de Transportes Aéreos, EP (SATA): Head Office: Av Infante D. Henrique 55-2°, 9500 Ponta Delgada, Azores; tel 27220; telex 82276; fax 25027; Pres: José Pacheco de Almeida; f 1947; runs scheduled air services for passengers and cargo within the Azores islands; owned by the regional Govt of the Azores.

TAP—Air Portugal, EP: Aeroporto de Lisboa, Apdo 5194, 1704 Lisbon Codex; tel (1) 899121; telex 12231; fax (1) 805030; Pres: Dr João de Lencastre; f 1945; international services to Europe, Africa, North and South America; tour operations and hotel and restaurant management.

LAR—Ligações Aéreas Regionais, SA: address as above; Pres: José Eduardo Vilar Queiroz; f 1985 to replace TAP—Regional.

Air Atlantis: Aeroporto de Faro, Faro; tel (89) 28277; telex 56227; Pres: Dr João H. Medeiros Norte; Man Dir: Francisco A. Matos; Dep Man Dir: Sebastião Balixa; f 1985; subsidiary of TAP—Air Portugal; operates air charter services to more than 40 European destinations.

RAILWAYS

Caminhos de Ferro Portugueses, EP (CP): Calçada do Duque 20, 1294 Lisbon Codex; tel (1) 363181; telex 13334; Pres: João Nuno Voulain Carvalho Carreira; f 1856, nationalized 1975; incorporated Sociedade Estoril Caminhos de Ferro from Cais do Sodré to Cascais in 1977.

Metropolitano de Lisboa, EP (ML-EP): Av Fontes Pereira de Melo 28, 1098 Lisbon Codex; tel (1) 575457; telex 15681; Pres: José Manuel da Costa Monteiro Consiglieri Pedroso; f 1948, nationalized 1975; operates underground system.

ROADS

Junta Autónoma de Estradas (JAE): Praça da Portagem, 2800 Almada; tel (1) 2956040; telex 12688; fax (1) 2951997; Pres: Mário Pinto Alves Fernandes; f 1927; under the Ministry of Public Works, Transport and Communication; responsible for national road and bridge planning, construction and maintenance.

Rodoviária Nacional, EP (RN): Av Columbano Bordalo Pinheiro 86, Lisbon; tel (1) 7267123; telex 15028; Pres: António Brito da Silva; f 1975 by incorporating the nationalized transportation enterprises; national bus co; passenger and goods transport.

SHIPPING

Portline—Transportes Marótimos Internacionais, SA: Rua Actor António Silva 7, 1600 Lisbon; tel (1) 7854553; telex 62053; Chair: Dr José António da Luz Varela Pinto; Pres: Dr Norberto da Cunha J. Fernandes Félix Pilar; f 1984; 100% state-owned; passenger and goods transport; agencies throughout the world.

PORTUGUESE OVERSEAS TERRITORY

MACAU

The Government

OFFICE OF THE GOVERNOR
Macau
Governor: Carlos Melancia
The Governor is nominated (after the local population is consulted, through the Legislative Assembly) and dismissed by the President of Portugal, to whom he is responsible; the Governor has a rank similar to that of a Minister of Govt in Portugal; the Cabinet comprises five secretaries appointed by the President of Portugal on the Governor's advice; there is a Consultative Committee of ex-officio and nominated mems representing the Chinese community.

LEGISLATIVE ASSEMBLY
Macau
President: (vacant)
Comprises 17 members, five appointed by the Governor, six elected directly and six indirectly; members serve three-year terms.

MINISTRY OF ADMINISTRATION AND JUSTICE
Macau
Secretary: Dr Magalhães e Silva

MINISTRY OF ECONOMY, FINANCE AND TOURISM
Macau
Secretary: Dr António Galhardo Simões

MINISTRY OF EDUCATION, SOCIAL AFFAIRS AND HEALTH
Macau
Secretary: Dr Francisco Murteria Nabo

MINISTRY OF MAJOR PUBLIC WORKS
Macau
Secretary: Luis Pinto de Vasconceles

MINISTRY OF PUBLIC WORKS AND HOUSING
Macau
Secretary: Joaquim Rosha Cabral

Government Agencies

BANKING

Monetary Authority of Macau: Macau; to replace Instituto Emissor de Macau, EP (IEM); Chair of Co-ordinating Council: Sec for Economy, Finance and Tourism, Dr António Galhardo Simões; f 1989; reinforces the role of the Banco Nacional Ultramarino (see under Portugal) as the Govt's agent for issuing Macau's currency until 1999.

BROADCASTING

Teledifusão de Macau, SARL: 157A Rua Francisco Xavier Pereira, CP 446, Macau; tel 550129; telex 88309; fax 595029; Man Dir: Dr Kwok Kwong Leung; f 1988; 50.5% Govt-owned; two radio channels, one Portuguese, one Chinese; TV and radio broadcasting in Portuguese and Chinese.

FINANCIAL AGENCY

Macao Economic Services-Industry Dept: 24th Floor, 1-3 Rua Dr Pedro José Lobo, Luso International Bldg, CP 122, Macao; tel 388527; telex 88413; fax 590309.

NEWS AND INFORMATION

Boletim Oficial: CP 33, Macau; tel 573822; telex 88540; Dir: António de Vasconcelos Mendes Liz; f 1838; Govt weekly.

Direcção dos Serviços de Estatística e Censos: Rua de Inácio Baptista 4D-6, CP 3022; tel 550935; fax 561884; Dir: Alberto Manuel Sarmento Azevedo Soares; Dep Dirs: Sérgio Correia Cortes, Maria Suzete das Neves Saraiva; f 1984; statistical office.

Gabinete de Comunicação Social (Government Information Bureau): Rua de S. Domingos 1, Macau; tel 332886; telex 88329; fax 336372; Dir: Miguel Lemos; f 1981; public information.

TOURISM

Direcção dos Serviços de Turismo: Travessa do Paiva 1, CP 3006, Macau; tel 77218; telex 88338; fax 510104; Dir: João Manuel Costa Antunes; f 1957; Govt body responsible for promoting tourism in Macau.

TRADE

Departamento de Promoção de Exportações (Export Promotion Department/Macau Economic Services): Edif Luso International 8°, Rua Dr Pedro José Lobo 1-3, Macau; tel 378221; telex 88413; fax 590309; Dir: António Leça da Veiga Paz; f 1982; export promotion.

QATAR

Head of State and Legislature

Qatar is an absolute monarchy, with full powers vested in the Amir as Head of State. A provisional constitution took effect in 1970. Executive power is exercised by the Council of Ministers, which is appointed by the Head of State, who is also Prime Minister. An Advisory Council was formed in 1972, with 20 nominated members, was expanded to 30 members in 1975, and to 35 members in 1988. Qatar has no legislature or political parties.

Amir: Sheikh Khalifa bin Hamad ath-Thani (assumed power 22 February 1972).

Office of the Amir: POB 923, Doha; tel 415888; telex 4297.

Advisory Council: Doha; telex 25211; Speaker: Abd al-Aziz bin Khalid al-Ghanem.

MINISTRIES AND GOVERNMENT DEPARTMENTS

OFFICE OF THE PRIME MINISTER
POB 923, Doha
Tel 415888; telex 4297
Prime Minister: Sheikh Khalifa bin Hamad ath-Thani
Adviser: Issa Ghanim al-Kawari

MINISTRY OF DEFENCE
Qatar Armed Forces, POB 37, Doha
Tel 334111; telex 4153
Minister: Maj-Gen Sheikh Hamad bin Khalifa ath-Thani

MINISTRY OF THE ECONOMY AND TRADE
POB 1968, Doha
Tel 434888; telex 4488
Minister: Sheikh Hamad bin Jassim Hamad ath-Thani

MINISTRY OF EDUCATION, CULTURE AND YOUTH
POB 80, Doha
Tel 413444; telex 4316
Minister: Abd al-Aziz Abdullah Turki

MINISTRY OF ELECTRICITY AND WATER
POB 41, Doha
Tel 494444; telex 4478; fax 426608
Minister: Mubarak Ali al-Khatir

Department of Electricity and Water: address as above; Dir: M. Y. al-Ali; f 1953; production, distribution and transmission of electricity and water.

MINISTRY OF FINANCE AND PETROLEUM
POB 83, Doha
Tel 413120; telex 4315
Minister: Sheikh Abd al-Aziz bin Khalifa ath-Thani

Customs Department: POB 218, Doha; tel 23971.

Department of Financial Affairs: address as above; tel 325181; telex 4572.

State Purchasing Department: POB 1908, Doha; tel 328502; telex 4499.

Supply Department: POB 925, Doha; tel 325763.

MINISTRY OF FOREIGN AFFAIRS
POB 250, Doha
Tel 410000; telex 4252
Minister: Abdullah bin Khalifa al-Attiyyah
Minister of State: Sheikh Ahmad bin Saif ath-Thani

MINISTRY OF INDUSTRY AND PUBLIC WORKS
POB 1966, Doha
Tel 412525; telex 4096
Minister: Ahmad Muhammad Ali as-Subaie

MINISTRY OF INFORMATION AND CULTURE
POB 1836, Doha
Tel 831333; telex 4229; fax 831518
Minister: Sheikh Hamad bin Suhaim ath-Thani

Department of Engineering: address as above; Asst Undersecretary and Dir: Shaheen Abdulrahman al-Kawari.

MINISTRY OF THE INTERIOR
POB 2433, Doha
Tel 330000; telex 4532
Minister: Sheikh Abdullah bin Khalifa ath-Thani

MINISTRY OF JUSTICE
POB 2377, Doha
Tel 325844
Minister: Sheikh Ahmad bin Seif ath-Thani

MINISTRY OF LABOUR, SOCIAL AFFAIRS AND HOUSING
POB 201, Doha
Tel 321955; telex 4227
Minister: Abd ar-Rahman Saad ad-Dirhem

MINISTRY OF MUNICIPAL AFFAIRS AND AGRICULTURE
POB 2727, Doha

Tel 413535; telex 4476
Minister: Sheikh Hamad bin Jassim bin Jaber ath-Thani

MINISTRY OF PUBLIC HEALTH
POB 42, Doha
Tel 441555; telex 4261
Minister: Sheikh Khalid bin Muhammad bin ath-Thani

MINISTRY OF TRANSPORT AND COMMUNICATIONS
POB 3416, Doha
Tel 324101; telex 4800
Minister: Abdullah bin Salih al-Manna

GOVERNMENT AGENCIES AND ORGANIZATIONS

Advisory and Supervisory Bodies

Gulf Organization for Industrial Consulting (GOIC): POB 5114, Doha.

Immigration, Passports and Naturalization Administration: 'C' Ring Rd, Gemco Bldg, POB 122, Doha.

Agriculture and Fishing

AGRICULTURE

Qatar General Poultry Establishment: POB 3606, Doha; tel 740042; telex 4348; Dir: Ismail Faiti al-Ismail.

Sheep Farm Project: POB 1966, Abu Samra.

FISHING

Qatar National Fishing Co: Doha.

Art and Culture

Department of Culture and Arts: POB 3332, Doha; tel 321227.

National Library: POB 205, Doha; tel 429955; telex 4743; Dir: M. H. al-Nassr; f 1961; provision of library services, collection and preservation of manuscripts, holding book fairs, training of librarians.

Qatar National Museum: Corniche Rd East, al-Salata, POB 879, Doha.

Business and Economy

BANKING

Qatar Monetary Agency: POB 1234, Doha; tel 321150; telex 4335; Pres and Chair: Sheikh Abd al-Aziz bin Khalifa ath-Thani; Dir-Gen: Majid Muhammad al-Majid as-Saad; f 1966 as Qatar and Dubai Currency Board; became Qatar Monetary Agency in 1973 when Qatar issued its own currency; central bank and bank of issue.

Qatar National Bank SAQ: POB 1002, Doha; tel 413511; telex 4212; Chair: Sheikh Abd al-Aziz bin Khalifa ath-Thani; Gen Man: Abdullah Khalid al-Attiyah; f 1965; acts as Govt

bank; jointly owned by Govt and Qatari nationals; 11 brs in Qatar; 3 brs overseas.

INSURANCE

Qatar Insurance Co SAQ: POB 666, Doha; tel 831555; telex 4216; Gen Man: Khalifa A. as-Sobai; Govt has a majority shareholding; brs in Dubai and Riyadh.

NATIONALIZED INDUSTRY

Qatar Flour Mills Co SAQ: POB 1444, Doha; tel 770452; telex 4285; Chair: Sheikh Ahmad bin Abdullah ath-Thani; Gen Man: Ghazi Abd al-Halim as-Salimi; f 1968.

Qatar National Cement Co (QNC Manufacturing Co) SAQ: POB 1333, Doha; tel 412691; telex 4337; Chair: Ahmad A. Rahman al-Mana; Man Dir: Rashid M. al-Mannai; f 1965.

Qatar Steel Co (QASCO): POB 50090, Steel Mill, Umm Said; tel 770011; telex 4606; Chair: Ahmad Muhammad Ali as-Subaie; Man Dir: Nasser Muhammad al-Mansouri; f 1978; 70% state-owned.

Defence

Qatar Armed Forces (QAF): POB 37, Doha; tel 334111; telex 4153; Commdr-in-Chief: Minister of Defence, Maj-Gen Sheikh Hamad bin Khalifa ath-Thani.

Qatar Sea Arm (QSA): POB 37, Doha; tel 22088.

Qatari Amiri Air Force (QAAF): POB 37, Doha; tel 851389.

Qatar State Police Force: POB 920, Doha; tel 321111.

Development and Planning

Industrial Agencies Corpn: POB 229, Doha; telex 4656.

Industrial Development Technical Centre (IDTC): POB 2599, Doha; tel 832121; telex 4323; Dir-Gen: Sheikh Abd ar-Rahman Muhammad bin Jaber ath-Thani; conducts research, devt and supervision of new industrial projects.

Qatar Industrial Development Corpn: POB 5165, Doha; telex 4744.

Energy

Qatar General Petroleum Corpn (QGPC): POB 3212, Doha; tel 491491; telex 4343; Chair: Minister of Finance and Petroleum, Sheikh Abd al-Aziz bin Khalifa ath-Thani; Man Dir (acting): Jaber A. al-Marri; f 1974; the State of Qatar's interest in cos active in petroleum and related industries has passed to the Corpn. In line with OPEC policy, the Govt agreed a participation agreement with the Qatar Petroleum Co and Shell Co of Qatar in 1974 to secure Qatar's interest and obtained a 60% interest in both. In late 1976, under two separate agreements, the Govt secured a 100% interest in both cos. The Qatar Petroleum Producing Authority (QPPA) was established in 1976 as a subsidiary, wholly owned by the Corpn, to carry out all operations previously conducted by the two cos. In February 1980 the QPPA was merged with the Corpn. The QGPC wholly or partly owns the following cos:

National Oil Distribution Co (NODCO): POB 2244, Umm Said; tel 776555; telex 4324; Gen Man: Mahmoud H. al-Hifnawi; operates two refineries; responsible for the nationwide distribution of petroleum products; wholly owned by QGPC.

Qatar Fertilizer Co (QAFCO) SAQ: POB 2131, Umm Said; tel 770252; telex 4215; Chair: Fouad al-Mahmoud; Man Dir: Arnt Almentingen; QGPC holds 75% share, Norsk Hydro holds the remaining 25%.

Qatar Liquefied Gas Co (QATARGAS): POB 2954, Doha; tel 86252; telex 4500; Chair: Minister of Finance and Petroleum, Sheikh Abd al-Aziz Khalifa ath-Thani; f 1984; QGPC has a 77.5% share.

QGPC (Onshore Operations): Doha; tel 343287; telex 4253; Gen Man: Jaber al-Marri; Dep Exec Man: Ajlan al-Kuwari; produces and exports crude petroleum from the Dukham oilfield and processes and exports natural gas liquids from the onshore and offshore oilfields in Qatar; also responsible for the internal distribution of fuel gas.

QGPC (Offshore Operations): POB 47, Doha; tel 402437; telex 4201; Man Dir: Jaber A. al-Marri; Exec Man: Ajlan Ali al-Kawari; offshore gas/oil exploration and production.

Qatar Petrochemical Co (QAPCO) SAQ: POB 756, Doha; tel 321105; telex 4361; Gen Man: Bernard Martinot; f 1974; QGPC has an 84% share; operation of petrochemical plant at Umm Said (tel 770111; telex 4871).

Legal and Judiciary

Presidency of Shari'a Courts and Islamic Affairs: POB 232, Doha; tel 321044; telex 5115; Pres: Sheikh Abdul bin Said al-Mahmoud; Chief Justice: Al-Fateh Awouda; Shari'a Court decides on all issues regarding the personal affairs of Muslims, specific offences where the defendant is Muslim, and civil disputes where the parties elect to have them adjudicated upon, by recourse to Islamic Law of the Holy Quran and the Prophet's Sunna or tradition. Non-Muslims are invariably tried by a court operating codified law.

Media

BROADCASTING

Qatar Broadcasting Service (QBS): POB 3939, Doha; tel 894444; telex 4597; Dir: Abd ar-Rahman Seif al-Madhadi; f 1968; broadcasts in Arabic, English, French and Urdu.

Qatar Television: POB 1944, Doha; tel 894444; telex 4040; Dir: Mana al-Hajri; Controller of Programmes: Muhammad Jassim al-Ali; f 1970; transmissions throughout the Gulf on eight channels.

GOVERNMENT PUBLISHER

Qatar National Printing Press: POB 355, Doha; tel 423680; telex 4072; Propr: Khaled bin Nasser as-Suwaidi; Dir: Abd al-Karim Dib.

NEWS AND INFORMATION

Press and Publications Department: c/o Ministry of Information and Culture, POB 1836, Doha; tel 831333; telex 4229; publication of statistical information.

Qatar News Agency (QNA): POB 1836, Doha; tel 322725; telex 4394; Dir and Editor-in-Chief: Ali Saeed al-Kawari; f 1975.

Tourism

Tourism and Antiquities Department: POB 2777, Doha; tel 327286.

Transport and Communications

TELECOMMUNICATIONS

Department of Posts: POB 3416, Doha; tel 325566; telex 4111.

Qatar Public Telecommunications Corpn (Q-Tel): POB 217, Doha; tel 400400; telex 4468; fax 413904; Gen Man: Saleh al-Mohannadi; Dep Gen Man: Abdullah al-Mannai; f 1987; provision of private and public telecommunications service.

TRANSPORT

Department of Civil Aviation: POB 3000, Doha; tel 852852; telex 4306; fax 852274; Dir: Omran I. al-Kawari; f 1973; supervision of civil aviation and the regularization of its aspects in accordance with the standards and procedures of the International Civil Aviation Organization and for the preservation of aviation safety.

Department of Ports: POB 313, Doha; tel 414626; telex 4378; Dir: Abd ar-Rahman Jaber al-Muftah.

Welfare

Supreme Council for Youth Welfare: POB 2511, Doha; tel 453333; telex 4590; Sec-Gen: Sheikh Muhammad bin Eid al-Thani; Dir of Public Relations and Information: Sultan M. al-Mohannadi; f 1979.

ROMANIA

Head of State and Legislature

Following a revolution in December 1989 the Executive and Legislature were united under the authority of the Provisional Council of National Unity, which was established in February 1990. The Council comprises 180 members, half coming from the 30 political parties established since the coup and half coming from the country's various regions and public figures who played a prominent part following the coup. Multi-party elections were scheduled to take place in May 1990 after which the Executive and Legislature was to be reformed.

President: Ion Iliescu (took office as Provisional President on 26 December 1989).

Office of the President: Bucharest, Calea Victoriei 49-53; tel (0) 148110.

MINISTRIES AND GOVERNMENT DEPARTMENTS

OFFICE OF THE PRIME MINISTER
Bucharest, Str Academiei 34
Tel (0) 150200
Prime Minister: Petre Roman
Deputy Prime Ministers: Mihai Draganescu, Gelu Voican

CENTRAL DEPARTMENT OF GEOLOGY
Bucharest, Str Mendeleev 36
Tel (0) 132208
Chief Exec: (vacant)

GENERAL TRADE UNION CONFEDERATION
71724 Bucharest, Str Stefan Georghiu 14
Tel (0) 334060; telex 10844
Chair: (vacant)

MINISTRY OF AGRICULTURE
70030 Bucharest, Bd Republicii 24
Tel (0) 144020; telex 11217
Minister: Stefan Nicolae

MINISTRY OF CHEMICAL AND PETROCHEMICAL INDUSTRY
Bucharest, Splaiul Independenţei 202
Tel (0) 497275; telex 11171
Minister: Gheorghe Caranfil

MINISTRY OF CULTURE AND TECHNOLOGY
Bucharest, Piaţa Scînteii 1
Tel (0) 176010
Minister: Andrei Plesu

MINISTRY OF EDUCATION AND INSTRUCTION
Bucharest, Str Nuferilor 30
Tel (0) 142680; telex 11637
Minister: (vacant)

MINISTRY OF ELECTRIC POWER
Bucharest, Bd Magheru 33
Tel (0) 596000; telex 11279
Minister: Adrian Georgescu

MINISTRY OF ELECTRICAL ENGINEERING
Bucharest, Calea Victoriei 133
Tel (0) 504090
Minister: (vacant)

MINISTRY OF FARM CONTRACTING AND ACQUISITION
Bucharest
Minister: (vacant)

MINISTRY OF FINANCE
Bucharest, Str Doamnei 8
Tel (0) 132000
Minister: (vacant)
Deputy Minister: Theodor Stolojan

MINISTRY OF FOOD INDUSTRY
Bucharest, Str Valter Mărăcineanu 1-3
Tel (0) 134610
Minister: Stefan Nicolae

MINISTRY OF FOREIGN AFFAIRS
Bucharest, Piața Victoriei 1
Tel (0) 166850; telex 11220
Minister: Sergiu Celac

MINISTRY OF FOREIGN TRADE AND INTERNATIONAL ECONOMIC CO-OPERATION
Bucharest, Bd Republicii 14
Tel (0) 145680; telex 10533
Minister: (vacant)
Deputy Minister: Ioan Aurel

MINISTRY OF HEALTH
Bucharest, Str Ilfov 6
Tel (0) 134230; telex 11468
Minister: Prof Dan Enachescu

MINISTRY OF INDUSTRIAL CONSTRUCTION
79519 Bucharest 3, Str Scaune 1-3
Tel (0) 154050; telex 11727
Minister: (vacant)
Deputy Minister: Ion Militaru

Department for Overseas Construction: address as above; tel (0) 130016; telex 11490; Chief Exec: Dep Minister of Industrial Construction, Ion Militaru; Dir: Paul Jugănaru; f 1981; assists, supervises and co-ordinates the activities of Romanian enterprises involved in overseas construction projects.

MINISTRY OF INTERNAL AFFAIRS
Bucharest, Str Eforie 3
Tel (0) 160080
Minister: Lt-Gen Mihai Ghitac
Deputy Minister: Jean Moldoveanu

MINISTRY OF INTERNAL TRADE
Bucharest, Str Doamnei 12
Tel (0) 334050; telex 10369
Minister: (vacant)

MINISTRY OF JUSTICE AND OFFICE OF THE ATTORNEY-GENERAL
Bucharest, Bd Gheorghe Gheorghiou-Dej 33
Tel (0) 144400
Minister and Attorney-General: Gheorghe Robu

MINISTRY OF LABOUR
Bucharest, Str Stefan Gheorghiu 14
Tel (0) 334060
Minister: (vacant)

MINISTRY OF LIGHT INDUSTRY
Bucharest, Str Ion Ghica 13
Tel (0) 162310; telex 10556
Minister: (vacant)

MINISTRY OF MACHINE BUILDING INDUSTRY
Bucharest, Calea Victoriei 133
Tel (0) 504090; telex 11222
Minister: (vacant)

MINISTRY OF METALLURGICAL INDUSTRY
Bucharest, Str Mendeleev 21
Tel (0) 156460; telex 11669
Minister: (vacant)

MINISTRY OF MINING
Bucharest, Str Mendeleev 36
Tel (0) 502183; telex 11263
Minister: (vacant)

MINISTRY OF NATIONAL DEFENCE
Bucharest, Intrarea Drumul Tabarei 9
Tel (0) 314150
Minister: Lt-Gen Victor Anastasie Stanculescu
Deputy Minister: Gen Vasile Ionel

MINISTRY OF NATIONAL ECONOMY
Bucharest, Str Academiei 34
Tel 170160
Chair: Lt-Gen Victor Anastasie Stanculescu

MINISTRY OF OIL
Bucharest, Calea Victoriei 109
Tel (0) 502256
Minister: (vacant)

MINISTRY OF SPORT
Bucharest
Minister: Mircea Anghelescu

MINISTRY OF TECHNICAL AND MATERIAL SUPPLY AND FOR FIXED ASSETS MANAGEMENT CONTROL
Bucharest, Calea Victoriei 152
Tel (0) 505020; telex 10640
Minister: (vacant)

MINISTRY OF TOURISM
Bucharest, Bd Magheru 7
Tel (0) 145160; telex 11278
Minister: (vacant)

MINISTRY OF TRANSPORT AND TELECOMMUNICATIONS
Bucharest, Bd Dinicu Golescu 38
Tel (0) 177140; telex 11372
Minister: (vacant)

Directorate of Roads: address as above; tel (0) 173914; telex 10835; Dir: Dr Mihai Boicu; road management and maintenance.

MINISTRY OF WATER, FORESTS AND ENVIRONMENT
Bucharest 3, Str Radu Calomfirescu 8
Tel (0) 150936; telex 10455
Minister: Simion Hincu

MINISTRY OF WOOD PROCESSING AND BUILDING MATERIALS
Bucharest, Calea Grivitei 21
Tel (0) 506430; telex 11495
Minister: (vacant)

MINISTRY OF YOUTH PROBLEMS
Bucharest, Str Onesti 6-8
Minister: (vacant)

NATIONAL COMMITTEE FOR SCIENCE AND TECHNOLOGY
71202 Bucharest 1, Piața Victoriei 1
Tel (0) 337660; telex 11312
First Vice-Pres: (vacant)
Co-ordinates scientific research and technological devt.

NATIONAL COUNCIL FOR SCIENCE AND EDUCATION
Bucharest
Chair: (vacant)

NATIONAL UNION OF PRODUCER CO-OPERATIVE FARMS
Bucharest, Bd Balescu 17-19
Tel (0) 170160
Chair: (vacant)

NATIONAL WOMEN'S COUNCIL
Bucharest, Str Stefan Gheorghiu 14
Chair: (vacant)

STATE COMMITTEE FOR NUCLEAR ENERGY
Bucharest, Platforma Măgurele
Tel (0) 807040; telex 11397
Chair: (vacant)

STATE COMMITTEE FOR PRICES
Bucharest, Str Doamnei 8-12

Tel (0) 132200; telex 11387
Chair: (vacant)

GOVERNMENT AGENCIES AND ORGANIZATIONS

Business and Economy

BANKING

Banca pentru Agricultură și Industrie Alimentară (Bank for Agriculture and Food Industry): Bucharest, Str Smîrdan 3; tel (0) 130410; telex 11622; Pres: (vacant); f 1968; organizes and effects the financing and crediting of the food industry enterprises, state agricultural co-operatives and private farmers.

Banca de Investiții (Investment Bank): Bucharest, Str Doamnei 4; tel (0) 134640; telex 11289; Pres: Gheorghe Popescu; First Vice-Pres: Octavian Cezarie; f 1948; finances and gives long-term credits for investments by state enterprises, the Central Unions of the handicraft and consumers' co-operatives and other state institutions; gives short credits for building enterprises, geological prospecting and research, and project organization.

Banca Națională a RSR (National Bank of the SRR): Bucharest 3, Str Lipscani 25; tel (0) 130410; telex 11136; Gov: Florea Dumitrescu; Vice-Pres: Horia Tatu, Valeriu Moșoeanu; f 1880; central bank and bank of issue; participates in the elaboration and implementation of state policy in the monetary, financial, credit and foreign exchange fields.

Banca Româna de Comerț Exterior (Romanian Bank for Foreign Trade): Bucharest, Calea Victoriei 22-24; tel (0) 149190; telex 11235; Pres: Teodor Gheorghe Barbulescu; Dep Chair: Gheorghe Crainiceanu; f 1968; organizes and effects payments in foreign currency and lei for import and export services, tourism, etc; receives and supplies credits to and from abroad.

Casa de Economii și Consemnațiuni—CEC (Savings and Consignation Bank): Bucharest, Calea Victoriei 13; tel (0) 154810; Pres: Mircea Popovici; f 1864; handles deposit savings on behalf of the people; handles other operations established by law.

INSURANCE

Administația Asigurărilor de Stat—ADAS (Administration of State Insurance): 79118 Bucharest, Str Smîrdan 5; tel (0) 147748; telex 11209; Pres: (vacant); f 1952; covers all types of insurance, reinsurance and insurance services.

TRADE

Agroexport: Bucharest, Bd Republicii 12; tel (0) 137172; telex 11141; Dir: Florica Gurscă; import and export of grains.

Arcif (Romanian Construction Co for Overseas Land Reclamation): Bucharest 3, Str Scaune 1-3; tel (0) 130016; telex 11490; Dir-Gen: Vasile Berbeci; Dep Dir-Gens: Corneliu Pascu, Gogu Stanciu; Financial Dir: Nicu Ciucă; f 1982; land reclamation works, well drilling, water course improvements, water treatment plants.

Arcom: 70448 Bucharest, Str Scaune 1-3; tel (0) 130016; telex 11490; Dir: Ionel Mocanu; f 1969; civil and industrial constructions, mechanical and electrical installations, engineering and technical assistance services.

Arpimex: Bucharest 3, Str Lipscani 19, POB 1-130; tel (0) 145464; telex 11472; Dir-Gen: Mișu Negrițoiu; export of footwear, leather goods, leather and fur garments, gloves; import of raw hides, organic dyes, chemical auxiliaries.

Artexim: 70055 Bucharest, Piața Scînteii 1; tel (0) 171313; telex 11191; Dir: Constantin Voiculescu; world-wide distribution of Romanian films for cinema, TV, cable TV and video; imports foreign films; organizes international co-operation ventures.

Autoexportimport: 2200 Brașov, Str Poenelor 5; tel (21) 27222; telex 61268; Dir-Gen: Ovidiu Barbu; import and export of trucks and special purpose vehicles.

Auto-Dacia: Pitești, 0300 Colibași; tel (76) 34800; telex 16296; Gen Man: Ion Stamatescu; export and import of road and special purpose vehicles.

Bucharest International Fair: Bucharest, Bd Bălcescu 22; tel (0) 147535; telex 11374; Dir: Octavian Moracăș; f 1970; general trade fair held annually in October.

Centrul National Aeronautic (CNA): 70185 Bucharest, Bd Dacia 13, POB 22-149; tel (0) 118213; telex 10660; Dir-Gen: Dumitru Stănescu; import and export of aircraft, helicopters, gliders, assemblies, equipment, spare parts, ground facilities, technical assistance, services, etc.

Chamber of Commerce and Industry: 79501 Bucharest, Bd Nicolae Bălcescu 22, POB 1-875; tel (0) 139883; telex 11374; Pres: Nicolae Andrei; f 1868.

Chimica: Bucharest, Spaiul Independenței 202A; tel (0) 495060; telex 11489; exports fertilizers, pharmaceuticals, paints, soaps, paper, etc.; imports phosphorites, pulp, paper, etc.

Comturist: Bucharest, Str Gabriel Péri 7-9; tel (0) 136160; telex 11173; Dir: Ilie Moraru; import and export against payment in foreign currency of goods bought by tourists.

Confex: Bucharest, Bd Armata Poporului 5-7; tel (0) 313751; telex 11195; Dir: Nicolae Popîrlan; exports ready-made clothes and knitwear.

Contransimex: 79511 Bucharest, Bd Dinicu Golescu 38, POB 2006; tel (0) 180042; telex 11606; Man Dir: Alfons Irimescu; civil engineering and construction projects; import and export of transport and telecommunications equipment and installations.

Danubiana: Bucharest, Bd Republicii 10; tel (0) 156051; telex 11184; Dir: Mircea Negoescu; import and export of petrochemicals and chemicals.

Dunărea: Bucharest, Str Varsovia 4, POB 63124; tel (0) 331681; telex 10435; fax (0) 337333; Dir: Constantin Gavril; f 1982; exports transport equipment, farm machinery, electrical and electronic products, machine tools, light industry, metallurgical and chemical products, furniture and building materials, synthetic diamonds and diamond tools.

Electroexportimport: Bucharest, Calea Victoriei 216, tel (0) 502175; telex 11388; Dir-Gen: Mircea Ionescu; f 1950; export and import of electric motors, cables, conductors, high and low voltage equipment, electrical equipment, transformers, household electrical appliances, scientific equipment, bicycles, etc.

Electronum: Bucharest, Bd Magheru 28-30; tel (0) 137081; telex 11547; Dir: Anghel Stan; exports computing technique, telecommunication equipment, radio receivers, TV sets, components, etc.; imports electronic components, TV equipment, etc.

Fructexport-Agroexport: 70714 Bucharest, Str Brezoianu 43, POB 790; tel (0) 136563; telex 10963; Dir-Gen: Eduard Vasiliu; f 1950; exports fruit and vegetable produce, wine, spirits, medicinal herbs, aromatic seeds, technical assistance; imports agricultural products, veterinary supplies, etc.

Icecoop-Ilexim: Bucharest, Str Decembrie 13, POB 1-136; tel (0) 148530; telex 11226; Dir: Bujor Ursulescu; Dep Dir: Mihail

Popescu; exports carpets, toys, basketware, furniture, handicrafts, ready-made clothes, metal and rubber goods, interior decoration items, wooden articles, foodstuffs and agricultural products, cultural goods and books, records, films, etc.

ICE Tehnoforestexport: Bucharest, Piaţa Rosetti 4; tel (0) 136317; telex 10330; Dir-Gen: Eduard Vasiliu; Dep Dir-Gen: Mihalache Neacşu; f 1948; exports wide range of wooden finished products.

Industrialexportimport: Bucharest, Bd Republicii 32; tel (0) 131009; telex 10930; Pres and Gen Man: Nicolae Constantin; exports oilfield and mining equipment, complex chemical, petrochemical oil refining and food industry plants and equipment, grain silos, pumps, and industrial valves and fittings.

Maşinexportimport: 70433 Bucharest, Bd Republcii 2; tel (0) 137596; telex 11206; Dir-Gen: Ion Bălănuță; sole exporter and importer of machine tools for metal-working; also exports woodworking and textiles machinery.

Mecanoexportimport: 79522 Bucharest, Str Mihai Eminescu 10, POB 22-107; tel (0) 119855; telex 10269; Dir-Gen: Stelian Postelnicu; imports and exports construction equipment, diesel engines, air compressors, lifting and conveying equipment, rolling stock.

Mercur: Bucharest, Calea Victoriei 118; tel (0) 596880; telex 11366; Dir-Gen: Marin Pariş; exchange of consumer goods.

Metalexportimport: Bucharest, Str Mendeleev 21-25; tel (0) 596825; telex 11515; Dir: Ghita Constantin; exports and imports rolled steel products, welded and seamless tubes, ferro-alloys, non-ferrous metals.

Mineralimportexport: 7000 Bucharest 3, Bd Republicii 16, POB 92; tel (0) 139167; telex 11873; fax (0) 136927; Dir-Gen: Geormaneanu Dan; Dep Dir-Gen: Petrescu Constantin; Economic Dir: Voinea Filoteea; f 1962; import and export of raw materials and finished products for siderurgical and aluminium industries.

Navlomar: Bucharest, Bd Republicii 16; tel (0) 132279; telex 11783; Man Dir: Viorel Covrig; shipbrokers, chartering agents, ship agents and ship-chandlers.

Petrolexportimport: Bucharest, Bd Magheru 1-3; tel (0) 131249; telex 11519; Dir: Florian Stoica; export of petroleum products; import of raw materials for petrochemical industry.

Prodexport: Bucharest, Str Valter Mărăcineanu; tel (0) 161660; telex 11527; Dir: Gheorghe Bela; f 1948; exports and imports livestock, meat, sugar, vegetable oils, tobacco, spices, food additives, etc.

Radioteleviziunea Română—Export-Import Board: Bucharest, Calea Dorobanţilor 191; telex 10182; Dir: Alexandru Jojea; export and import of films and magnetic tape recordings for TV and radio programmes.

Romagrimex: Bucharest, Bd Republicii 24; tel (0) 149747; telex 11522; Dir: Vasile Ichim; export of seeds, seedlings, breeding livestock, agricultural equipment, veterinary medicines, technical assistance in all fields of agriculture.

Românoexport: 70014 Bucharest, Str Doamnei 17-19, POB 594; tel (0) 133699; telex 11186; fax (0) 131841; Man Dir: Petru Crişan; f 1948; exports fabrics, knitwear, carpets and blankets; imports wool, cotton, jute, dyestuffs, felt, etc.

Romelectro: Bucharest, Calea Dorobanţilor 60; tel (0) 112170; telex 10449; Dir: Corneliu Lazăr; export and import of power equipment, electrical appliances, spare parts, etc.

Romenergo: 71101 Bucharest, Calea Victoriei 194; tel (0) 506682; telex 11525; Gen Man: Alexandru Pârvescu; import and export of power generation equipment for hydro, thermal and nuclear power projects, boilers, turbines, generators; studies, training, service, etc.

Rompetrol-Geomin: Bucharest, Calea Victoriei 109; tel (0) 594325; telex 10155; Gen Man: Stelian Tănăsescu; carries out abroad: geological excavations, design, surveys, engineering and technical assistance in the field of petroleum and gas extraction; construction of oilfields, petroleum pipelines, oil and natural

gas bulk plants and distribution facilities; participation in joint ventures for hydrocarbon devt and production.

Romproiect: 70704 Bucharest 1, Str Matei Millo 13; tel (0) 154237; telex 11490; Dir-Gen: Ioan Militaru; f 1969; direct technical assistance, consultancy engineering services, design for building contractors and investors.

Romsit: Bucharest, Str Ion Ghica 13; tel (0) 156821; telex 11836; fax (0) 131841; Man Dir: Valentin Dimitriuc; f 1972; exports glassware, porcelain, household and decorative earthenware, household stoneware, lead crystal items, glass fibres, etc.

Romtrans: 75260 Bucharest, Calea Rahovei 196; tel (0) 236040; telex 11346; Dir: Ion Mirica; f 1952; international forwarding agency.

Tehnoimportexport: Bucharest, Str Doamnei 5; tel (0) 152653; telex 10254; Dir-Gen: Mircea Borteş; imports and exports bearings and technical goods, aircraft, helicopters, spare parts, etc.

Terra: Bucharest, Bd Republicii 16; tel (0) 167293; telex 11571; fax (0) 138483; Gen Man: Ionel Dumitrescu; Mans: Aurel Dusan, Adriana Fleschiu; Financial Man: Petru Stefanut; f 1969; export and import of goods in its own name or jointly with specialized cos; feasibility studies, design, transfer of technology, consultancy services, exchange of goods between central supply bodies; took over the functions of Romconsult foreign trade co in 1989.

Universal-Autotractor: 2200 Braşov, Str Turnului 5; tel (21) 62661; telex 61335; Dir (acting): Guta Pascu; exports and imports tractors and farming machinery.

Uzinexportimport: 70033 Bucharest, Bd Republicii 32; tel (0) 132959; telex 11214; Man Dir: Vasile Stevoiu; export and import of complex installations and basic equipment for the machine-building industry and food processing and cement industries, metallurgical and steel plants.

Vitrocim—Forexim: 70416 Bucharest, Str Doamnei 2; tel (0) 131638; telex 11330; fax (0) 142412; Dir-Gen: Victor Ionescu; f 1970; import and export of building materials, woodworking machinery, pulp and paper equipment, research studies, technical assistance and complete plants.

Defence

Air Force: Bucharest, Intrarea Drumul Tagarei 9; Commdr: Gheorghe Zărnescu.

Army: Bucharest, Intrarea Drumul Taberei 9; tel (0) 317010; Chief of Staff: Gen Vaile Ionel.

Navy: Bucharest, Intrarea Drumul Tagarei 9; tel (0) 460111; Commdr: Vice-Adm Vasile Musaf.

Legal and Judiciary

Supreme Court: Bucharest, Str Rahovei 2; tel (0) 132040; Chair: Ioan Sălăjan; exercises general control over the judicial activity of all courts, by passing judgement on certain appeals and by studying judicial practices; issues rulings to ensure uniform application of the law; exercises original jurisdiction in certain cases. The members of the Supreme Court are professional magistrates elected by the Grand National Assembly.

Media

BROADCASTING

Radioteleviziunea Romania Liberă (Romanian Radio and Television): Bucharest, Calea Dorobanţilor 191, POB 63-1200; tel (0) 331092; telex 11251; Pres: (vacant); reorganized 1990.

Radiodifuziunea Română: Bucharest, Str Nuferilor 60-62, POB 1-111; tel (0) 162080; f 1929; foreign broadcasts on one medium-wave and eight short-wave transmitters in Arabic, English, French, German, Greek, Italian, Persian, Portuguese, Romanian, Russian, Serbian, Spanish and Turkish.

Televiziunea Română—Telecentrul Bucureşti (Romanian Television—Bucharest TV Centre): Bucharest, Calea Dorobanţilor 191, POB 63-1200; tel (0) 331092; telex 11251; f 1956; daily transmissions.

GOVERNMENT PUBLISHER

Întreprinderea de Stat pendru Imprimate şi Administrarea Publicaţiilor (State Enterprise for Printed Matter and Periodicals): 71341 Bucharest, Piaţa Scînteii 1; Dir: Ludovic Tarnovschi; f 1951; general publications.

NEWS AND INFORMATION

Agentia Română de Presa (Agerpres): 71341 Bucharest, Piaţa Scînteii; tel (0) 182030; telex 11272; Dir-Gen: Alexandru Ionescu; Dep Dir-Gen: Nicolae Puicea; f 1949; news agency; service in Arabic, English, French, Russian and Spanish.

Centrala Editorială (Publishing Centre): 79715 Bucharest, Piaţa Scînteii; tel (0) 181255; Man Dir: Gheorghe Trandafir; f 1962; co-ordinates book production and distribution throughout Romania, as well as the economic and financial activities of the publishing houses; organizes the import and export of books and other cultural goods.

Consiliul Ziariştilor din Republica Socialistă Româania (Journalists' Council of the SRR): 71341 Bucharest, Piaţa Scînteii 1, POB 33; tel (0) 184293; telex 11272; Pres (acting): Nicolae Dragoş; Sec: Ion Puţinelu; f 1955; represents and supervises those involved in journalism in Romania.

Direcţia Centrală de Statistică (Central Statistical Board): Bucharest, Str Stavropoleos 6; tel (0) 158200; telex 111153; collection, analysis and publication of statistical data.

Research

Romanian Ocean Research Institute: Constanţa, Bd Lenin 300; tel (16) 43288; telex 14286; Gen Man: Vaile Tomescu.

Tourism

National Tourist Office, Carpaţi: Bucharest 1, Bd Magheru 7; telex 11270; Gen Man: Ilie Moraru.

National Tourist Office, Carpaţi-Braşov: Braşov, Carpaţi Hotel; Gen Man: Dumitru Burtea.

National Tourist Office, Litoral: Mamaia Constanţa, Hotel Bucharest; Gen Man: Petre Ariton.

Transport

Căile Ferate Române-CFR (Departamentul Căilor Ferate): c/o Ministry of Transport and Telecommunications, Bucharest 1, Bd Dinicu Golescu 38; tel (0) 184020; Dir: (vacant); Romanian railways board.

Direcţia Drumurilor (Directorate of Roads): c/o Ministry of Transport and Telecommunications, Bucharest 1, Bd Dinicu Golescu 38; tel (0) 173914; telex 10835; Man: Dr Mihai Boicu.

Liniile Aeriene Române—LAR: Otopeni Airport, Bucharest; Man Dir: Toma Mihaj; f 1975; operates passenger charter service.

NAVROM (Romanian Shipping Co): 8700 Constanţa; telex 14237; Dir: (vacant); organizes sea transport; routes to Mediterranean, North West Europe, West Africa, Persian Gulf, Far East.

Transporturile Aeriene Române—TAROM (Romanian Air Transport): Otopeni Airport, Bucharest; telex 11491; Gen Man: Vasile Petrariu; f 1954; services throughout Europe, Asia, Africa and the USA and extensive internal services.

RWANDA

Head of State

Executive power is exercised by the President, who is Head of State and President of the Mouvement révolutionnaire national pour le développement (MRND), the sole legal party. The President is elected by universal adult suffrage for a five-year term and appoints and presides over the Council of Ministers.

President: Maj-Gen Juvénal Habyarimana (assumed power 5 July 1973; elected President 24 December 1978; re-elected 19 December 1983, and 19 December 1988).

Office of the President: BP 15, Kigali; tel 75432; telex 22517; Minister at the Presidency: Siméon Nteziryayo.

Legislature

Legislative power is held by the President in conjunction with the National Development Council, which comprises 70 members elected by universal adult suffrage for a five-year term. The country is divided into 10 Prefectures and 143 communes or municipalities, administered by appointed Governors, assisted by elected councils of local inhabitants.

Conseil National de Développement (National Development Council): BP 352, Kigali; tel 83985; Pres: Dr Théodore Sindikubwabo; Vice-Pres: Immaculée Nyiuabizeyimana; Sec: Cyprien Munyampundu.

MINISTRIES AND GOVERNMENT DEPARTMENTS

COUNCIL OF MINISTERS
Kigali
President: Maj-Gen Juvénal Habyarimana

MINISTRY OF AGRICULTURE, LIVESTOCK AND FORESTS
BP 621, Kigali
Tel 75324
Minister: Anastase Ntezilyayo

MINISTRY OF THE CIVIL SERVICE AND VOCATIONAL TRAINING
BP 403, Kigali
Tel 86578
Minister: François Habiyakare

MINISTRY OF COMMERCE AND CONSUMPTION
BP 476, Kigali
Tel 73875
Minister: Juvénal Uwiringiyimana

MINISTRY OF FINANCE
BP 158, Kigali
Tel 75410; telex 22502
Minister: Benoît Ntigulirwa

MINISTRY OF FOREIGN AFFAIRS AND INTERNATIONAL CO-OPERATION
BP 179, Kigali
Tel 75257
Minister: Dr Casimir Bizimungu

MINISTRY OF HEALTH
BP 84, Kigali
Tel 76681
Minister: Dr Placide Ngendahayo

MINISTRY OF HIGHER EDUCATION AND SCIENTIFIC RESEARCH
BP 624, Kigali
Tel 85422
Minister: Charles Nyandwi

MINISTRY OF INDUSTRY AND CRAFTS
BP 73, Kigali
Tel 75465
Minister: Col Aloys Nsekalije

MINISTRY OF INSTITUTIONAL RELATIONS
BP 790, Kigali
Tel 73481
Minister: Antoine Ntashamaje

MINISTRY OF THE INTERIOR AND OF COMMUNITY DEVELOPMENT
BP 446, Kigali
Tel 86708
Minister: Jean-Marie Vianney Mugemana

MINISTRY OF JUSTICE
BP 160, Kigali
Tel 866626
Minister: Théoneste Mujyanama

MINISTRY OF NATIONAL DEFENCE
BP 23, Kigali
Tel 75160; telex 22578
Minister: Maj-Gen Juvénal Habyarimana

MINISTRY OF PLANNING
BP 46, Kigali
Tel 75513
Minister: Calixte Nzabonimana

MINISTRY OF PRIMARY AND SECONDARY EDUCATION
BP 622, Kigali
Tel 85422
Minister: Daniel Mbangura

MINISTRY OF PUBLIC WORKS, ENERGY AND WATER
BP 24, Kigali
Tel 86649
Minister: Joseph Nzirorera

MINISTRY OF TRANSPORT AND COMMUNICATIONS
BP 720, Kigali
Tel 72424; telex 22573; fax 76574
Minister: André Ntagerura

MINISTRY OF YOUTH AND THE ASSOCIATED MOVEMENT
BP 1044, Kigali
Tel 5861; telex 22502
Minister: Lt-Col Augustin Ndindiliyimana

GOVERNMENT AGENCIES AND ORGANIZATIONS

Agriculture

Institut des Sciences Agronomiques du Rwanda (ISAR): BP 138, Butare; Dir: Léopold Gahamanyi; f 1962; devt of subsistence and export agriculture.

Office des Cafés (OCIR-Café): BP 104, Kigali; tel 75004; telex 22513; Dir: Fabien Neretse; f 1978; devt of coffee and other new agronomic industries; maintains a coffee stabilization fund.

Office du Pyrèthre du Rwanda (OPYRWA): BP 79, Ruhengeri; tel 46306; Dir: Augustin Bizimana; f 1978; devt of pyrethrum.

Office du Thé (OCIR-Thé): BP 1244, Kigali; Dir: Michel Bagaragaza; devt and marketing of tea.

Société Rwandaise pour la Production et la Commercialisation du Thé (SORWATHE), SARL: Kigali; tel 75461; telex 22548; Dir: Cyohaha-Rukeri; f 1978; production and marketing of tea.

Business and Economy

BANKING

Banque Nationale du Rwanda: BP 531, Kigali; tel 75249; telex 22508; Gov: Augustin Ruzindana; f 1964; central bank.

Banque Rwandaise de Développement, SARL (BRD): BP 1341, Kigali; tel 75079; telex 22563; Chair: François Kanimba; Man Dir: Emmanuel Ndahimana; f 1967; devt bank.

Banques Populaires du Rwanda (Banki Z'Abaturage Mu Rwanda): BP 1348, Kigali; tel 73559; telex 22584; Chair: Augustin Bizimana; Gen Man: Bernard Taillefer; devt bank.

Caisse d'Epargne du Rwanda: BP 146, Kigali; tel 75231; telex 22553; Dir-Gen: Juvénal Ndisanze; f 1963; savings bank; 16 brs and 23 sub-brs.

INSURANCE

Société Nationale d'Assurances du Rwanda (SONARWA): BP 1035, Kigali; tel 72101; telex 22540; fax 72052; Dir-Gen: Joseph Sibomana; f 1975; all types of insurance.

Société Rwandaise d'Assurances (SORAS): BP 924, Kigali; tel 73716; telex 22571; Dir-Gen: Jean de Curton; Dir: Charles Mporanyi; f 1984.

NATIONALIZED INDUSTRY

BRALIRWA: BP 131, Kigali; f 1959; manufactures and bottles beer in Gisenyi and soft drinks in Kigali.

TRADE

Chambre de Commerce et d'Industrie du Rwanda: BP 319, Kigali; tel 72319; telex 22504; Pres: Silas Majyambere; Sec-Gen: Martin Ayirwanda; f 1982; co-ordinates commerce and industry on national scale.

Culture

Bibliothèque Nationale: c/o Minesupres, BP 624, Kigali; tel 72730; Dir: Michel Niyibizi; f 1989; national library; co-ordination and promotion of national documentation; conservation of documents; publication of national bibliography.

Defence

Army: BP 85, Kigali; tel 75158; Commdr-in-Chief: Maj-Gen Juvénal Habyarimana.

Development and Planning

Bureau National d'Etudes de Projets (BUNEP): BP 1337, Kigali; tel 72121; telex 22502; f 1978; surveillance and evaluation of economic devt projects; research and planning.

Legal and Judiciary

Conseil d'Etat (State Council): c/o Ministry of Justice, BP 160, Kigali; tel 866626; administrative jurisdiction.

Cour de Cassation (Court of Cassation): c/o Ministry of Justice, BP 160, Kigali; tel 866626; Pres: Joseph Kavaruganda.

Cour des Comptes (Court of Accounts): BP 32, Nyabisindu; tel 33152; f 1962; Pres: Marcel Munyangabe; examines all public accounts; reports on the budget to Parliament.

Media

BROADCASTING

Radiodiffusion de la République Rwandaise: BP 83, Kigali; tel 75665; telex 22557; Chief of Programmes: Paul Mbaraga; Dir: Laurent Mulindabigwi; f 1961; daily radio broadcasts in Kinyarwanda, Swahili and French.

GOVERNMENT PUBLISHERS

Imprimerie Nationale du Rwanda: BP 351, Kigali; tel 75350; Dir: Dominique Munyangoga; f 1967.

Imprimerie Scolaire du Rwanda (Imprisco): BP 622, Kigali; tel 85819.

NEWS AND INFORMATION

Office Rwandais d'Information: BP 83, Kigali; tel 75665.

Mining

Régie d'Exploitation et de Développement des Mines: Kigali; f 1988; state organization for mining tin and tungsten (replacing Société des Mines du Rwanda, bankrupt in 1985 after closure of mines, owing to decline in world prices).

Tourism

Office Rwandais du Tourisme et des Parcs Nationaux (ORTPN): BP 905, Kigali; tel 76514; telex 22542; fax 76512; Dir: Laurent Habiyaremye; f 1973; tourism promotion and conservation of nature; transfer to the private sector of hotels previously managed by the ORTPN was announced in 1988.

Transport and Communications

TELECOMMUNICATIONS

General Directorate of Posts: BP 4, Kigali; tel 75652.

General Directorate of Telecommunications: BP 1332, Kigali; tel 76777; telex 22573; fax 73110; Chair: Assumani Bizimana; f 1930; national and international telecommunications services; runs public telephone and telex network.

TRANSPORT

Air Rwanda (Société Nationale de Transports Aériens du Rwanda): BP 808, Kigali; tel 73093; telex 22554; Chair: Jean Damascene Hategekimana; Gen Man: Isidore Jean-Baptiste Rukira; Man Dir: Dr Damien Bambanza Muhamyankaka; f 1975; operates domestic passenger and cargo services and international cargo flights to African and European destinations.

Office National des Transport en Commun (ONATRACOM): BP 720, Kigali; tel 75064; Dir: Denis Ntirugilimbabazi; road transport.

SAINT CHRISTOPHER AND NEVIS

Head of State

The Federation of Saint Christopher and Nevis is a constitutional monarchy, and executive power is vested in the British sovereign, as Head of State, represented locally by a Governor-General. The Governor-General acts in accordance with the advice of the Cabinet, headed by a Prime Minister. Government is effectively by the Cabinet, which is responsible to Parliament.

Sovereign: HM Queen Elizabeth II (succeeded to the throne 6 February 1952).

Governor-General: Sir Clement Arrindell (took office 19 September 1983).

Office of the Governor-General: Govt House, Basseterre; tel 465-2315; telex 6820.

Legislature

Legislative power is vested in Parliament, comprising the monarch and a National Assembly composed of the Speaker, three (or, if a nominated member is Attorney-General, four) nominated Senators and 11 Representatives, elected by universal adult suffrage for up to five years. The Nevis Island legislature comprises the Nevis Island Assembly and the Nevis Island Administration headed by the British sovereign, represented locally by the Deputy Governor-General.

National Assembly: Chambers, Govt Headquarters, Church St, POB 186, Basseterre; tel 465-2521; telex 6820; Clerk: Alphonso Lewis.

Office of the Speaker: Govt Headquarters, Church St, POB 186, Basseterre; tel 465-2521; telex 6820; Speaker: Ivan Buchanan.

Nevis Island Assembly Nevis; tel 469-5521.

MINISTRIES AND GOVERNMENT DEPARTMENTS

GOVERNMENT HEADQUARTERS
Church St, POB 186, Basseterre
Tel 465-2521; telex 6820
Prime Minister: Dr Kennedy Alphonse Simmonds
Deputy Prime Minister: Michael O. Powell

NEVIS ISLAND ADMINISTRATION
Nevis
Tel 469-5521
Premier: Simeon Daniel

MINISTRY OF AGRICULTURE, LANDS, HOUSING AND DEVELOPMENT
Kittstoddarts, Basseterre
Tel 465-2220
Minister: Hugh C. Heyliger
Special Assistant in the Ministry of Agriculture: Roosevelt Caines

MINISTRY OF COMMUNICATION, WORKS AND PUBLIC UTILITIES
Govt Headquarters, Church St, POB 186, Basseterre
Tel 465-2521; telex 6820
Minister: Sidney Morris
Adviser with special responsibility for Communications and Transport: Uhral Swanston
Assistant to the Minister: Royden Benjamin

MINISTRY OF EDUCATION, YOUTH AND COMMUNITY AFFAIRS
Cavon St, POB 333, Basseterre
Tel 465-2521
Minister: Sidney Morris
Assistant to the Minister: Royden Benjamin

MINISTRY OF FINANCE
Govt Headquarters, Church St, POB 186, Basseterre
Tel 465-2612
Minister: Dr Kennedy Alphonse Simmonds
Minister in the Ministry of Finance: Richard Caines

MINISTRY OF HOME AND FOREIGN AFFAIRS
Govt Headquarters, Church St, POB 186, Basseterre
Tel 465-2521; telex 6820
Minister: Dr Kennedy Alphonse Simmonds

MINISTRY OF LABOUR AND TOURISM
Govt Headquarters, Church St, POB 186, Basseterre
Tel 465-2521; telex 6820
Minister: Michael O. Powell

MINISTRY OF TRADE AND INDUSTRY
Govt Headquarters, Church St, POB 186, Basseterre
Tel 465-2302
Minister: Fitzroy Jones

MINISTRY OF WOMEN'S AFFAIRS AND HEALTH
Govt Headquarters, Church St, POB 186, Basseterre
Tel 465-2521; telex 6820
Minister: Constance V. Mitcham

OFFICE OF THE ATTORNEY-GENERAL
Govt Headquarters, Church St, POB 186, Basseterre
Tel 465-2521; telex 6820
Attorney-General: S. W. Tapley Seaton

GOVERNMENT AGENCIES AND ORGANIZATIONS

Advisory and Supervisory Body

Audit Office: Basseterre; Dir of Audit: Wendell Lawrence.

Business and Economy

BANKING

Eastern Caribbean Central Bank (ECCB): POB 89, Basseterre; tel 465-2537; telex 6828; Gov: Cecil A. Jacobs; f 1965 as East Caribbean Currency Authority, expanded responsibilities and changed name in 1983; responsible for issue of currency in Anguilla, Antigua and Barbuda, Dominica, Grenada, Montserrat, Saint Christopher and Nevis, Saint Lucia and Saint Vincent and the Grenadines.

St Kitts-Nevis Development Bank: Church St, Basseterre; tel 462-4041; Man: Auckland Hector.

St Kitts-Nevis-Anguilla National Bank Ltd: Church St, POB 343, Basseterre; tel 465-2204; telex 6826; Chair: William Liburd; Gen Man: E. Pistana; majority Govt-owned; br on Nevis.

FINANCIAL AGENCIES

Office of the Accountant-General: Basseterre; Accountant-Gen: Eustace John.

Office of the Comptroller of Inland Revenue: Basseterre; Comptroller: Douglas Richardson.

MARKETING

Central Marketing Corpn (CEMACO): Ponds Pasture, Basseterre; tel 465-2326; Man: Morris Browne.

NATIONALIZED INDUSTRY

St Kitts Sugar Manufacturing Corpn: POB 96, Golden Rock; tel 465-8099; telex 6812; fax 465-1059; Man Dir: Peter van Hamel; Agricultural Man: Christopher Walwyn; Chief Eng: George Thomas; f 1911; growing of sugar cane and manufacture of sugar; transport of sugar cane and sugar by railway.

TRADE

Office of the Comptroller of Customs: Basseterre; Comptroller of Customs: Winston Warner.

Defence

Police Headquarters: Basseterre; Commr of Police: Stanley V. Franks.

Development and Planning

Frigate Bay Development Corpn: POB 315, Basseterre; tel 465-8339; promotes tourist and residential devts.

Education

Office of the Chief Education Officer: Basseterre; Chief Education Officer: Joseph Halliday.

Employment

Office of the Labour Commissioner: Basseterre; Labour Commr: Aubrey York.

Health and Welfare

Office of the Chief Medical Officer: Basseterre; Chief Medical Officer: Dr Franklyn Lloyd.

Office of the Director of Social Security: Bay Road, Basseterre; tel 462-2535; Dir: Robert E. Manning.

Legal and Judiciary

Eastern Caribbean Supreme Court: POB 1093, Castries, Saint Lucia; tel 22573; Chief Justice: Sir Lascelles Robotham; Puisne Judge: Lloyd Williams; f 1967; based in Saint Lucia; jurisdiction extends to Anguilla, Antigua and Barbuda, the British Virgin Islands, Dominica, Montserrat, Saint Christopher and Nevis, Saint Lucia and Saint Vincent and the Grenadines; consists of a Court of Appeal and a High Court; one of the seven puisne judges is responsible for St Christopher and Nevis and presides over the Court of Summary Jurisdiction.

Office of the Superintendent of Prisons: Basseterre; Supt: Norman Gill.

Media

BROADCASTING

ZIZ Radio and Television: Springfield, POB 555, Basseterre; tel 465-2621; telex 6820; Gen Man (acting): Claudette Manchester; f 1961.

Tourism

St Kitts-Nevis Tourist Board: Treasury Pier, POB 132, Basseterre; tel 465-4040; Main St, Nevis; Chair: Colin Pereira.

Transport and Communications

TELECOMMUNICATIONS

Office of the Postmaster: Basseterre; Postmistress: Dorothy Ferguson.

TRANSPORT

St Kitts Sugar Railway: St Kitts Sugar Manufacturing Corpn, POB 96, Golden Rock; tel 465-8099; telex 6812; fax 465-1059; Man Dir: Peter van Hamel; Railway Supt: Lionel Trotman; f 1911; narrow-gauge railway serving the sugar plantations.

Utilities

Office of the Director of Public Works: Basseterre; Dir: Lionel Gamon.

SAINT LUCIA

Head of State

Saint Lucia is a constitutional monarchy, and executive power is vested in the British sovereign, as Head of State, represented locally by a Governor-General, appointed on the advice of the Prime Minister. Government is effectively by the Cabinet, headed by a Prime Minister appointed by the Governor-General. The Cabinet is responsible to the House.

Sovereign: HM Queen Elizabeth II (succeeded to the throne 6 February 1952).

Governor-General: Stanislaus A. James (took office in an acting capacity on 10 October 1988).

Office of the Governor-General: Govt House, The Morne, Castries; tel 22481.

Legislature

Legislative power is vested in Parliament, comprising the monarch, a 17-member House of Assembly, elected for up to five years by universal adult suffrage, and a Senate of 11 members appointed by the Governor-General.

Senate: Govt Bldgs, Laborie St, Castries; Pres: Henry Giraudy.

Parliament Office and House of Assembly: Govt Bldgs, Laborie St, Castries; tel 23856; telex 6394; Speaker: W. St Clair Daniel; Clerk: Doris Bailey.

MINISTRIES AND GOVERNMENT DEPARTMENTS

OFFICE OF THE PRIME MINISTER
Conway, Castries
Tel 23980; telex 6394; fax 22506
Prime Minister: John G. M. Compton
Deputy Prime Minister: W. George Mallet

MINISTRY OF AGRICULTURE, LANDS, FISHERIES, FORESTRY AND CO-OPERATIVES
Manoel St, Castries
Tel 22526; telex 6394; fax 22506
Minister: Ferdinand Henry
Minister of State: Gregory Avril

MINISTRY OF COMMUNICATIONS, WORKS AND TRANSPORT
Micoud St, Castries
Tel 21128; telex 6394; fax 27427
Minister: Desmond Fostin

MINISTRY OF EDUCATION AND CULTURE
Govt Bldgs, Laborie St, Castries
Tel 31218
Minister: Louis George

MINISTRY OF FINANCE, STATISTICS AND DEVELOPMENT
Govt Bldgs, Laborie St, Castries
Tel 25315
Minister: John G. M. Compton

Department of the Accountant-General: Govt Bldgs, Laborie St, Castries; tel 22397; Accountant-Gen: Gregory St Helene; Dep Accountant-Gen: Joseph Lawrence; accounts for and reports on all Govt revenues and expenditure.

MINISTRY OF FOREIGN AFFAIRS
Brazil St, Castries
Tel 21178; telex 6394
Minister: Neville Cenac

MINISTRY OF HEALTH, HOUSING, LABOUR, INFORMATION AND BROADCASTING
Chaussee Rd, Castries
Tel 22827
Minister: Romanus Lansiquot

MINISTRY OF HOME AFFAIRS
Conway, Castries
Tel 23980; telex 6394; fax 22506
Minister: John G. M. Compton

MINISTRY OF LEGAL AFFAIRS
Bridge St, Castries
Tel 23622
Attorney-General and Minister: Parry Husbands

MINISTRY OF PLANNING, PERSONNEL, ESTABLISHMENT AND TRAINING
New Govt Bldg, John Compton Highway, Castries
Tel 23688; telex 6243; fax 22560
Minister of Planning: John G. M. Compton
Formulation, implementation and evaluation of economic, social and physical plans and projects; devt and admin of the manpower resources of the public sector.

MINISTRY OF TRADE, INDUSTRY AND TOURISM
Govt Headquarters, Castries
Tel 22627; telex 6243; fax 22506
Minister: W. George Mallet

**MINISTRY OF YOUTH, COMMUNITY
DEVELOPMENT, SOCIAL AFFAIRS AND SPORTS**
New Govt Bldg, John Compton Highway, Castries

Tel 23688; telex 6394
Minister: Stephenson King

GOVERNMENT AGENCIES AND ORGANIZATIONS

Agriculture

Saint Lucia Agriculturists' Association Ltd: POB 153, Castries; tel 22494; Chair: Christopher Alcindor; Man and Sec: Rene R. Raveneau; f 1950; agricultural membership co; markets agricultural produce, mainly cocoa; imports agricultural implements and tools, building hardware, etc.

Saint Lucia Banana Growers' Association: 7 Manoel St, POB 197, Castries; tel 22251; Chair (acting): Charles Cadet; Gen Man: Michael Lansiquot; f 1953; became a statutory corpn in 1967; 8,000 mems.

Saint Lucia Coconut Growers' Association: 13 Manoel St, POB 259, Castries; tel 23230; telex 6378; fax 31499; Chair: Johaness Leonce; looks after the interests of coconut farmers; has controlling interest in Copra Manufacturers Ltd which produces edible oils, margarines and soap.

Business and Economy

BANKING

Eastern Caribbean Central Bank (ECCB): POB 89, Basseterre, St Christopher and Nevis; tel 465-2537; telex 6828; Gov: Cecil A. Jacobs; f 1965 as East Caribbean Currency Authority, expanded responsibilities and changed name in 1983; responsible for issue of currency in Anguilla, Antigua and Barbuda, Dominica, Grenada, Montserrat, Saint Christopher and Nevis, Saint Lucia and Saint Vincent and the Grenadines.

Government Savings Bank: Treasury, Castries.

National Commercial Bank of Saint Lucia: Bridge St, POB 1031, Castries; tel 23562; telex 6300; Man: McDonald Dixon; f 1981; 3 brs.

Saint Lucia Co-operative Bank Ltd: 21 Bridge St, POB 168, Castries; tel 22881; telex 6308; Pres: Francis J. Carasco; Man: E. A. Throdore; incorporated 1937; br at Vieux Fort.

Saint Lucia Development Bank: Bridge St, POB 368, Castries; tel 23561; telex 3600; Man Dir: George Theophilus; Dep Man Dir and Sec: Daniel Girard; f 1980; merged with former Agricultural and Industrial Development Bank; provides finance for and promotes economic devt; makes loans and advances for education, industry, tourism, housing and agricultural projects.

FINANCIAL AGENCY

Saint Lucia Mortgage Finance Co Ltd (SMFC): Brazil St, POB 455, Castries; tel 23464; telex 6222; fax 20064; Chief Exec: Rupert O. Martyr; Chair: Leslie C. Gullan; Sec: Augustus C. Fricot; f 1968; provides loans for the purchase, construction or extension of private dwelling houses.

MARKETING

Saint Lucia Fish Marketing Corpn Ltd: Sans Soucis, POB 891, Castries; tel 21341; fax 28141; Chair: Dunstan du Boulay; Gen Man: Martin Fevrier; f 1985; processing and marketing of seafood.

Saint Lucia Marketing Board: Conway, POB 441, Castries; tel 23214; telex 6221; Chair: (vacant); Man: M. B. Toussaint.

Defence

Royal Saint Lucia Police Force: Castries; tel 22855.

Development and Planning

National Development Corpn (NDC): 27 Brazil St, POB 495, Castries; tel 23614; telex 6387; fax 21841; Gen Man: Cromwell R. Goodridge; Sec and Accounts and Admin Man: Eulalie Scobie-Henry; f 1971; promotes the devt of trade, industry and tourism; implements Govt's policy in regard to land use for industrial estates and residential devts; maintains overseas office in New York, USA, to promote investment; manages four industrial estates.

Legal and Judiciary

Eastern Caribbean Supreme Court: POB 1093, Castries; tel 22573; Chief Justice: Sir Lascelles Robotham; f 1967; jurisdiction extends to Anguilla, Antigua and Barbuda, the British Virgin Islands, Dominica, Montserrat, Saint Christopher and Nevis, Saint Lucia and Saint Vincent and the Grenadines; comprises a High Court of Justice and a Court of Appeal; High Court is composed of the Chief Justice and seven Puisne Judges; the Court of Appeal is presided over by the Chief Justice and includes two other Justices of Appeal.

Media

BROADCASTING

Saint Lucia Broadcasting Corpn: Morne Fortune, POB 660, Castries; tel 22337.

Radio Saint Lucia (RSL): Morne Fortune, POB 660, Castries; tel 22337; Chair: Hollis D. Bristol; Man: W. Springer; English and Creole services.

Tourism

Saint Lucia Hotel and Tourism Association: Pointe Seraphine, POB 545, Castries; tel 25978; fax 31121; Exec Vice-Pres: Joseph A. Bergasse; Exec Sec: Eileen Paul; f 1963; represents all sectors concerned with tourism.

Saint Lucia Tourist Board: Pointe Seraphine, POB 221, Castries; tel 25968; telex 6380; fax 31121; Chair: Stephen McNamara; Dir: Nicholas Thomas; marketing and promotion of tourist industry; three brs overseas.

Transport

Saint Lucia Air and Sea Ports Authority: POB 651, Castries; tel 22893; telex 6355.

Welfare

Housing and Urban Development Corpn: cnr Chisel and High St, POB 299, Castries; tel 23801; Chair: Peter P. Philip; Gen Man: Adrian Dolcy; f 1971; develops housing programmes and projects for low and middle income groups including upgrading and the installation of all infrastructure; carries out urban devt programmes.

SAINT VINCENT AND THE GRENADINES

Head of State

Saint Vincent and the Grenadines is a constitutional monarchy, and executive power is vested in the British sovereign, as Head of State, represented locally by a Governor-General, appointed on the advice of the Prime Minister. Government is effectively by the Cabinet, headed by a Prime Minister, appointed by the Governor-General. The Cabinet is responsible to the House.

Sovereign: HM Queen Elizabeth II (succeeded to the throne 6 February 1952).

Governor-General: Henry H. Williams (took office in an acting capacity 29 February 1988).

Office of the Governor-General: Govt House, Kingstown; tel 61401.

Legislature

Legislative power is vested in Parliament, comprising the Governor-General and a House of Assembly composed of 21 members: six Senators appointed by the Governor-General and 15 Representatives, elected for up to five years by universal adult suffrage.

House of Assembly: Kingstown; tel 71872; telex 7351; Speaker: Emmanuel F. Adams; Clerk: Theresa Adams.

MINISTRIES AND GOVERNMENT DEPARTMENTS

OFFICE OF THE PRIME MINISTER
Kingstown
Tel 61111; telex 7531
Prime Minister: James F. Mitchell

MINISTRY OF AGRICULTURE, INDUSTRY AND LABOUR
Kingstown
Minister: Allan C. Cruickshank

MINISTRY OF COMMUNICATIONS AND WORKS
Halifax St, Kingstown
Tel 71962; telex 7531; fax 72943
Minister: Jeremiah C. Scott
Supervises and controls postal and telecommunications services, sea and river defence, Govt works, roads, Electrical Inspectorate, and to a lesser extent the Port Authority and the General Equipment and Services Corpn.

MINISTRY OF EDUCATION, YOUTH, WOMEN'S AFFAIRS AND SPORT
Kinstown
Tel 71607
Minister: John A. Horne

MINISTRY OF FINANCE AND FOREIGN AFFAIRS
Halifax St, Kingstown
Tel 61111; telex 7531
Minister: James F. Mitchell

MINISTRY OF HEALTH AND THE ENVIRONMENT
Kingstown
Tel 71892
Minister: Burton B. Williams

MINISTRY OF HOUSING AND COMMUNITY DEVELOPMENT
Kingstown
Tel 61080
Minister: Louis Jones

MINISTRY OF JUSTICE, INFORMATION AND CULTURE
Kingstown
Tel 61189
Attorney-General and Minister: Parnel R. Campbell

MINISTRY OF TOURISM
Kingstown
Minister: Herbert B. Young

MINISTRY OF TRADE
Kingstown
Tel 61410
Minister: Herbert B. Young

GOVERNMENT AGENCIES AND ORGANIZATIONS

Agriculture

Saint Vincent Banana Growers' Association: Sharpe St, POB 10, Kingstown; tel 71605; telex 7545; fax 62585; Gen Man: R. L. M. Eustace; f 1954; purchases bananas from registered banana farmers and sells them in the UK; provides extension services to banana farmers; stocks and sells agricultural tools; over 7,000 mems.

Business and Economy

BANKING

Eastern Caribbean Central Bank (ECCB): POB 89, Basseterre, Saint Christopher and Nevis; tel 465-2537; telex 6828; Gov: Cecil A. Jacobs; f 1965 as East Caribbean Currency Authority, expanded responsibilities and changed name in 1983; responsible for issue of currency in Anguilla, Antigua and Barbuda, Dominica, Grenada, Montserrat, Saint Christopher and Nevis, Saint Lucia and Saint Vincent and the Grenadines.

National Commercial Bank of Saint Vincent: cnr Halifax and Egmont Sts, POB 880, Kingstown; tel 71844; telex 7522; Chair: Richard Joachim; Man: Beverly Brisbane; f 1977; 4 brs.

MARKETING

Saint Vincent Marketing Corpn: Upper Bay St, POB 872, Kingstown; tel 71603; telex 7528; fax 62673; Gen Man: L. S. Rose; f 1959; dealers and exporters of tropical and exotic produce such as fruit and vegetables; importers of raw and refined sugar, edible oils and commodities.

Development and Planning

Saint Vincent Agricultural Development Corpn: Upper Bay St, Kingstown; tel 71574; Chair: Herbert Young; f 1975 to stimulate agricultural devt and to manage Govt estates.

Saint Vincent Development Corpn: POB 841, Kingstown; tel 71358; telex 7566; Chair: Samuel Goodluck; Man: Claude M. Leach; f 1970; finances industry, agriculture, fisheries and tourism.

Legal and Judiciary

Eastern Caribbean Supreme Court: POB 1093, Castries, St Lucia; tel 22573; Chief Justice: Sir Lascelles Robotham; f 1967; jurisdiction extends to Anguilla, Antigua and Barbuda, the British Virgin Islands, Dominica, Montserrat, Saint Christopher and Nevis, Saint Lucia and Saint Vincent and the Grenadines; comprises a High Court of Justice and a Court of Appeal; High Court is composed of the Chief Justice and seven Puisne Judges; the Court of Appeal is presided over by the Chief Justice and includes two other Justices of Appeal.

Supreme Court: Kingstown; tel 71424; Puisne Judge: Satrohan Singh; Registrar (acting): A. Cato; justice is administered by the Eastern Caribbean Supreme Court.

Media

BROADCASTING

National Broadcasting Corpn of Saint Vincent and the Grenadines: Richmond Hill, POB 705, Kingstown; Chair: G. Ferrari; controls:

Radio 705: Richmond Hill, POB 705, Kingstown; tel 71111; telex 7473; Man: Bernard John; commercial.

SVG Television: Dorsetshire Hill, POB 617, Kingstown; tel 61078; cable service.

NEWS AND INFORMATION

Statistical Unit: Ministry of Trade, Industry and Agriculture, Kingstown.

Statistical Office: Ministry of Finance and Planning, Kingstown.

Tourism

SVG Department of Tourism: Egmont St, POB 834, Kingstown; tel 71502; telex 7531; fax 72152; Admin Man: Janet Woods; Sen Marketing Officer: Yvette Murray; Sen Product Devt Officer: Branson Thomas; f 1951 as Saint Vincent Tourist Board; management and control of tourism industry; promotion and marketing of tourism; creation of incentives for hotel devt; training of tourism personnel; compilation of statistical data; dissemination of information.

SAN MARINO

Head of State

The two Capitani Reggenti (Captains-Regent) act jointly as Head of State and Government, and are elected for six months at a time (ending in March and September) by the Great and General Council. The Captains-Regent preside over the Congress of State comprising 10 members elected by the Council for the duration of its term, and which holds executive power. The Congress has three Secretaries of State and seven Ministers of State.

Captains-Regent: Leo Achilli, Gloriana Ranocchini (October 1989-March 1990).

Executive Office of the Captains-Regent: Palazzo Pubblico, 47031 San Marino; tel 992345; telex 303.

Legislature

Legislative power is vested in the unicameral Great and General Council, comprising 60 members elected by universal adult suffrage for five years (subject to dissolution). San Marino is divided into nine 'Castles' corresponding to the original parishes of the republic, and each 'Castle' is governed by a Castle-Captain, who holds office for two years, and an Auxiliary Council, holding office for five years.

Consiglio Grande e Generale (Grand and General Council): Palazzo Pubblico, 47031 San Marino; tel 991385.

MINISTRIES AND GOVERNMENT DEPARTMENTS

MINISTRY OF COMMERCE
47031 San Marino
Minister of State: Clelio Galassi

MINISTRY OF EDUCATION AND CULTURE
Contrada Omerelli, 47031 San Marino
Tel 992813; telex 330; fax 992018
Minister of State: Dottssa Fausta Simona Morganti

MINISTRY OF THE ENVIRONMENT AND AGRICULTURE
47031 San Marino
Minister of State: Fernando Bindi

MINISTRY OF HEALTH AND SOCIAL SECURITY
47031 San Marino
Minister of State: Renzo Ghiotti

MINISTRY OF INDUSTRY AND HANDICRAFT
47031 San Marino
Minister of State: Giuseppe Amici

MINISTRY OF LABOUR AND CO-OPERATION
Contrada Omerelli 38, 47031 San Marino
Tel 991089
Minister of State: Pierro Natalino Mularoni

MINISTRY OF TRANSPORT, COMMUNICATIONS, TOURISM AND SPORT
47031 San Marino
Minister of State: Gastone Pasolini

SECRETARIAT OF STATE FOR FINANCE AND THE BUDGET
Palazzo Begni, Contrada Omerelli, 47031 San Marino
Tel 992345; telex 330; fax 992018
Secretary of State: Dr Clara Boscaglia

SECRETARIAT OF STATE FOR FOREIGN AND POLITICAL AFFAIRS
Palazzo Begni, Contrada Omerelli, 47031 San Marino
Tel 992345; telex 330
Secretary of State: Gabriele Gatti

SECRETARIAT OF STATE FOR INTERNAL AFFAIRS
Palazzo Pubblico, Piazza della Libertà, 47031 San Marino
Tel 992896
Secretary of State for Internal Affairs and Justice: Alvaro Selva

GOVERNMENT AGENCIES AND ORGANIZATIONS

Business and Economy

BANKING

Cassa di Risparmio della Repubblica di San Marino: Piazetta Titano 2, 47031 San Marino; tel 991011; telex 337; fax 991657; Pres: Dott Tito Masi; Dir: Primo Cecchini; f 1882; 12 brs.

Cassa Rurale di Depositi e Prestiti di Faetano: Strada La Croce, 47031 Faetano; tel 996015; Pres: Sergio Zanotti; Dir: Marcello Malpeli; 4 brs.

Legal and Judiciary

Commissario della Legge: 47031 San Marino; deals with civil and criminal cases where the sentence does not exceed three years' imprisonment.

Consiglio dei XII: 47031 San Marino; has authority as a Supreme Court of Appeal.

Giudici di Appello: 47031 San Marino; deal with both civil and criminal appeal cases.

Tourism

Ufficio di Stato per il Turismo (State Tourist Board): Contrada Omagnano 20, 47031 San Marino; tel 882400; telex 282; fax 990388; Dir: Edith Tamagnini; f 1949; responsible for tourist promotion, congresses, tourist packages, sport and cultural events, tourist material.

SÃO TOMÉ AND PRÍNCIPE

Head of State

Executive power is held by the President, who is Head of State and is elected for five years by universal adult suffrage on the proposal of the Movimento de Libertação de São Tomé e Príncipe (MLSTP). The President is assisted by a Council of Ministers, including a Prime Minister who is appointed by the President.

President: Dr Manuel Pinto da Costa (took office 12 July 1975; re-elected 30 September 1985).

Office of the President: Praga do Pouo, São Tomé; tel 21020.

Legislature

The supreme organ of the state is the National People's Assembly, comprising 40 members, (nominated by the MLSTP or standing as 'independents'), elected by universal adult suffrage to serve a five-year term.

Assembléia Popular Nacional (National People's Assembly): São Tomé; tel 22764; Pres: Alda Neves Graça do Espírito Santo; Vice-Pres: Maj Raul Wagner Bragança Neto; Sec: Leovegildo Barbosa Neto.

MINISTRIES AND GOVERNMENT DEPARTMENTS

OFFICE OF THE PRIME MINISTER
São Tomé
Prime Minister: Celestino Rochas da Costa
Minister-Delegate to the Prime Minister's Office for Príncipe Island: Manuel Quaresma Costa
Minister-Delegate, Secretary-General of the Government: Manuel Vaz Afonso Fernandes

MINISTRY OF AGRICULTURE AND FISHERIES
São Tomé
Tel 22714
Minister: Óscar Aguiar do Sacramento e Souza

MINISTRY OF CO-OPERATION
CP 111, São Tomé
Tel 22105; telex 238
Minister: Guilherme Posser da Costa

MINISTRY OF DEFENCE AND INTERNAL SECURITY
São Tomé
Tel 21092
Minister: Maj Raul Wagner Bragança Neto Gomez

MINISTRY OF ECONOMY AND FINANCE
CP 168, São Tomé
Tel 22142; telex 225
Minister of Economy and Finance, in charge of Planning and Trade: Agapito Mendes Dias

MINISTRY OF EDUCATION AND CULTURE
São Tomé
Tel 21571
Minister: Ligia do Espírito Santo Costa

MINISTRY OF EQUIPMENT AND ENVIRONMENT
São Tomé
Tel 21571
Minister of Equipment and Environment, in charge of Transport and Communications: Carlos Ferreira

MINISTRY OF FOREIGN AFFAIRS
São Tomé
Tel 21446; telex 211
Minister: Carlos da Graça

MINISTRY OF HEALTH, LABOUR AND SOCIAL SECURITY
São Tomé
Tel 22182
Minister: Armindo Vaz de Almeida

MINISTRY OF INFORMATION
CP 112, São Tomé
Tel 21538; telex 217
Minister: (vacant)

MINISTRY OF JUSTICE AND PUBLIC AFFAIRS
São Tomé
Tel 22020
Minister: Francesco Fortunato Pires

GOVERNMENT AGENCIES AND ORGANIZATIONS

Business and Economy

BANKING

Banco Nacional de São Tomé e Príncipe: Praça da Independência, CP 13, São Tomé; tel 22407; telex 204; Gov: Nazaret Mendes; f 1975; central bank and bank of issue.

Caixa Popular de São Tomé e Príncipe: CP 13, São Tomé; telex 204; savings; loans for housing.

INSURANCE

Caixa de Previdência dos Funcionários Públicos: São Tomé; insurance fund for civil servants.

Empresa Nacional de Seguros e Resseguros 'A Compensadora': Rua Patrice Lumumba, CP 190, São Tomé; tel 22796; telex 215; Dir: Dr Jorge da Costa Coelho; f 1980.

Defence

Armed Forces: Bairro Militar, São Tomé; tel 21092; Commdr-in-Chief: Dr Manuel Pinto da Costa; Chief of Staff: Capt João Bexigas.

National Police Department: Rua Ex-João de Deus, São Tomé.

Media

BROADCASTING

Rádio Nacional de São Tomé e Príncipe: Avda Marginal de 12 de Julho, CP 44, São Tomé; tel 22704; Dir: João Fernando Barbosa Neto; f 1958; home service in Portuguese.

Transport

Equatorial Airlines of São Tomé and Príncipe: Avda Marginal de 12 de Julho, CP 45, São Tomé; tel 21160; telex 216; Pres: C. R. G. Hellinger, G. W. Conolly; Gen Man: J. Portugal; f 1986 (replacing fmr nat airline, Linhas Aéreas de São Tomé); jointly owned by São Tomé Govt and International Aircraft Services (Guernsey) Ltd; operates services between the islands of São Tomé and Príncipe, and thrice-weekly flights between São Tomé and Libreville (Gabon).

Welfare

Direcção de Segurança Social: CP 35, São Tomé; tel 21382; Dir: Carlos Sequeira; f 1979; social security payments.

SAUDI ARABIA

Head of State and Legislature

Saudi Arabia is an absolute monarchy, with no legislature or political parties. Constitutionally, the King rules in accordance with the Shari'a, the sacred law of Islam. He appoints and leads a Council of Ministers, which serves as the instrument of royal authority in both legislative and executive matters. Decisions of the Council are reached by majority vote, but require royal sanction.

Monarch: King Fahd ibn Abd al-Aziz as-Sa'ud (acceded to the throne 13 June 1982).

Office of the HM the King: Riyadh; tel (1) 402-0245.

MINISTRIES AND GOVERNMENT DEPARTMENTS

COUNCIL OF MINISTERS
Murabba, Riyadh 11121
Tel (1) 404-4200; telex 401039
Prime Minister: King Fahd ibn Abd al-Aziz as-Sa'ud
First Deputy Prime Minister: Crown Prince Abdullah ibn Abd al-Aziz
Second Deputy Prime Minister: Prince Sultan ibn Abd al-Aziz
Minister without Portfolio: Fayez Badr

MINISTRY OF AGRICULTURE AND WATER
Airport Rd, Riyadh 11195
Tel (1) 401-2666; telex 401108
Minister: Dr Abd ar-Rahman ibn Abd al-Aziz ibn Hasan ash-Sheikh

MINISTRY OF COMMERCE
POB 1774, Airport Rd, Riyadh 11162
Tel (1) 401-2222; telex 401057
Minister: Dr Sulaiman Abd al-Aziz as-Sulaim

MINISTRY OF COMMUNICATIONS
Airport Rd, Riyadh 1117
Tel (1) 404-3000; telex 401616
Minister: (vacant)

MINISTRY OF DEFENCE AND CIVIL AVIATION
Airport Rd, Riyadh 11165
Tel (1) 477-7777; telex 401188
Minister: Prince Sultan ibn Abd al-Aziz
Deputy Ministers: Gen Othman al-Humaid, Prine Abd ar-Rahman ibn Abd al-Aziz

MINISTRY OF EDUCATION
Airport Rd, Riyadh 11148
Tel (1) 404-2888; telex 401673
Minister: Dr Abd al-Aziz al-Abdullah al-Khuwaiter

MINISTRY OF FINANCE AND NATIONAL ECONOMY
Airport Rd, Riyadh 11177
Tel (1) 405-0080; telex 401021
Minister: Sheikh Muhammad Ali Aba al-Khail

MINISTRY OF FOREIGN AFFAIRS
Nasseriya St, Riyadh 11134
Tel (1) 406-7777; telex 403360
Minister: Prince Sa'ud al-Faisal ibn Abd al-Aziz

MINISTRY OF HEALTH
Airport Rd, Riyadh 11176
Tel (1) 401-2220; telex 401628
Minister: Faisal ibn Abd al-Aziz al-Hejailan

MINISTRY OF HIGHER EDUCATION
King Faisal Hospital St, Riyadh 11153
Tel (1) 464-4444; telex 401481
Minister (acting): Dr Abd al-Aziz al-Abdullah al-Khuwaiter

MINISTRY OF INDUSTRY AND ELECTRICITY
POB 5729, Omar bin al-Khatab St, Riyadh 11127
Tel (1) 477-6666; telex 401154; fax (1) 477-5476
Minister: Abd al-Aziz az-Zamil
Deputy Minister for Industrial Affairs: Mubarak al-Khafrah
Deputy Minister for Electrical Affairs: Abdullah al-Tasan
Deputy Minister for Finance and Administration: Abdullah al-Qarawy
Assistant Deputy Minister for Industrial Affairs: Muhammad al-Musallam

MINISTRY OF INFORMATION
POB 570, Nasseriya St, Riyadh 11161
Tel (1) 401-4440; telex 402640
Minister: Ali Hassan ash-Shaer

Department of Engineering Affairs: POB 3949, Riyadh 11481; tel (1) 402-4370; telex 401040; fax (1) 404-0480; Dir: Asst Dep Minister for Engineering Affairs, Fouad A. Taher; f 1960; supervision and commissioning of all projects for the Ministry; frequency co-ordination; maintenance, operation and supply of spare parts.

MINISTRY OF THE INTERIOR
POB 2933, Airport Rd, Riyadh 11134
Tel (1) 401-1111; telex 401622
Minister: Prince Nayef ibn Abd al-Aziz
Deputy Minister: Prince Ahmad ibn Abd al-Aziz

MINISTRY OF JUSTICE
Riyadh 11137
Tel (1) 405-8692; telex 404450
Minister (acting): Sheikh Muhammad ibn Ibrahim al-Jubair

MINISTRY OF LABOUR AND SOCIAL AFFAIRS
Omar bin al-Khatab St, Riyadh 11157
Tel (1) 477-1480; telex 401043
Minister: Muhammad al-Ali al-Fayez

MINISTRY OF MUNICIPAL AND RURAL AFFAIRS
Nasseriya St, Riyadh 11136
Tel (1) 441-5434; telex 401063
Minister: Ibrahim ibn Abdullah al-Anqari

MINISTRY OF PETROLEUM AND MINERAL RESOURCES
POB 247, King Abd al-Aziz Rd, Riyadh 11191
Tel (1) 478-1661; telex 400997; fax (1) 476-5058
Minister: Sheikh Hisham Mohi ed-Din Nazer

MINISTRY OF PILGRAMAGE (HAJJ) AFFAIRS AND AWQAF (RELIGIOUS ENDOWMENTS)
Omar bin al-Khatab St, Riyadh 11183
Tel (1) 404-3003; telex 400189
Minister: Sheikh Abd al-Wahhab Ahmad Abd al-Wasi

MINISTRY OF PLANNING
POB 1358, University St, Riyadh 11183
Tel (1) 401-3333; telex 401075
Minister (acting): Sheikh Hisham Mohi ed-Din Nazer

MINISTRY OF POSTS, TELEGRAPHS AND TELECOMMUNICATIONS
Sharia al-Ma'azer, Intercontinental Rd, Riyadh 11112
Tel (1) 463-1152; telex 401220
Minister: Dr Alawi Darwish Kayyal

MINISTRY OF PUBLIC WORKS AND HOUSING
Washem St, Riyadh 11151
Tel (1) 402-2036; telex 400415
Minister: Prince Mutaib ibn Abd al-Aziz

MINISTRY OF TRANPORT
Riyadh
Minister: Sheikh Hussein Ibrahim al-Mansouri

OFFICE OF THE GOVERNOR OF EASTERN PROVINCE
Asir
Governor: Prince Muhammad ibn Fahd ibn Abd al-Aziz

OFFICE OF THE GOVERNOR OF MECCA
Jeddah
Tel (2) 653-0022
Governor: Prince Majid ibn Abd al-Aziz

OFFICE OF THE GOVERNOR OF MEDINA
Medina
Tel (4) 24641
Governor: Prince Abd al-Majid ibn Abd al-Aziz

OFFICE OF THE GOVERNOR OF RIYADH
Riyadh
Tel (1) 402-5300
Governor: Prince Salman ibn al-Aziz

OFFICE OF THE MINISTERS OF STATE
c/o Council of Ministers, Murabba, Riyadh 11121
Tel (1) 404-4200; telex 401039
Ministers of State: Sheikh Muhammad Ibrahim Masoud, Dr Muhammad Abd al-Latif Milhim, Omar Abd al-Qader Faqih, Dr Fayez bin Ibrahim Badr, Muhammad ibn Abd al-Aziz ibn Zaraa, Turki ibn Khalid as-Sudairi

YOUTH WELFARE ORGANIZATION
POB 4143, Sama Bldg, South Tower, Airport Rd, Riyadh
Tel (1) 477-4002; telex 201065
President: Prince Faisal ibn Fahd ibn Abd al-Aziz

GOVERNMENT AGENCIES AND ORGANIZATIONS

Agriculture and Fishing

AGRICULTURE

Agricultural Research Centre: POB 2579, Jeddah; tel (2) 642-7840; Dir: Salem Bamufleh.

Grain Silos and Flour Mills Organization (GSMFO): POB 3402, Riyadh 11471; tel (1) 464-3500; telex 404510; fax (1) 463-1943; Dir-Gen: Saleh M. al-Sulaiman; Dep Dir-Gen: Dr Muhammad al-Bisher; f 1973; storage of wheat and barley, production of animal feed and flour; marketing of wheat and GSMFO products.

National Agricultural Development Co (NADEC): POB 2557, Riyadh 11461; tel (1) 478-3488; telex 403681; fax (1) 478-4127; Chair: Minister of Agriculture and Water, Dr Abd ar-Rahman ibn Abd al-Aziz ibn Hasan ash-Sheikh; Dir-Gen: Muhammad A. Abu-Butain; f 1981; devt of crop and livestock production, food processing.

Saudi Arabian Agriculture and Dairy Co Ltd: POB 10525, Riyadh 11443; tel (1) 495-1400; telex 402356; fax (1) 495-4927;

Dir-Gen: Abd al-Latif al-Ajaji; Commercial Man: Ghazi Gelidan; f 1976; fresh dairy production, processing, packing and distribution.

FISHING

Saudi Fisheries Co (SFC): POB 6535, Damman 31452; tel (3) 857-3979; telex 802020; Chair: Minister of Agriculture and Water, Dr Abd ar-Rahman ibn Abd al-Aziz ibn Hasan ash-Sheikh; Gen Man: Dr Nasser Otham as-Saleh.

Business and Economy

BANKING

National Commercial Bank (NCB): POB 3555, Jeddah 21481; tel (2) 644-6644; telex 605571; Chair and Gen Man: Sheikh Salim Ahmad bin Mahouz; f 1938; more than 200 brs including international offices.

Riyad Bank Ltd: POB 22622, King Abd al-Aziz St, Riyadh 11416; tel (1) 401-3030; telex 407490; Chair: Sheikh Abdullah bin Adwan; Man Dir: Sheikh Ahmad Abd al-Latif; Gen Man: Sheikh Ibrahim M. S. Shams; f 1957; 154 brs.

Saudi Arabian Agricultural Bank (SAAB): POB 11126, Riyadh; tel (1) 402-2361; telex 201184; Controller-Gen: Abdullah Saad al-Mengash; Gen Man: Abd al-Aziz Muhammad al-Manqur; f 1963; 71 brs.

Saudi Arabian Monetary Agency (SAMA): POB 2992, Riyadh 11169; tel (1) 463-3000; telex 401734 (English), 401466 (Arabic); Gov: Sheikh Hamad Sa'ud as-Sayari; f 1952; central bank; 10 brs.

Saudi Credit Bank: POB 3401, Riyadh; tel (1) 402-9128; Chair: Osama Jaafar Faqith; f 1973; provides interest-free loans for specific purposes to Saudi citizens of moderate means.

Saudi Investment Bank (SAIB): POB 3533, Riyadh 11481; tel (1) 477-8433; telex 401170; Chair: Dr Abd al-Aziz O'Hali; Gen Man: Robert S. Wilcox; f 1976; provides a comprehensive range of traditional and specialized banking services to business and individuals.

FINANCIAL AGENCIES

Directorate-General of Zakat and Income Tax: Airport Rd, Riyadh; tel (1) 404-4375; Dir-Gen: Hussein Abd al-Latif.

General Investment Fund (Public Investment Fund): c/o Ministry of Finance and National Economy, Airport Rd, Riyadh 11177; tel (1) 405-0000; telex 401021; Chair: Minister of Finance and National Economy, Sheikh Muhammad Ali Aba al-Khail; Sec-Gen: Suleiman Mandil; f 1970; provides Govt's share of capital to mixed capital cos.

Saudi Fund for Development (SFD): POB 1887, Riyadh 11441; tel (1) 403-8268; telex 401145; Chair: Sheikh Muhammad Ali Aba al-Khail; Vice-Chair and Man Dir: Muhammad A. as-Sugair; f 1974 to help finance projects in developing countries.

Saudi Industrial Development Fund (SIDF): POB 4143, Riyadh 11149; tel (1) 477-4002; telex 401065; Chair: Sheikh Hamad Sa'ud as-Sayari; Dir-Gen: Saleh Abdullah an-Naim; f 1974; supports and promotes industrial and electrical devt in the private sector, providing long-term interest-free loans to industry; also offers marketing, technical, financial and administrative advice.

INSURANCE

National Co for Co-operative Insurance: Jeddah; f 1985 by royal decree; owned by three Govt agencies.

NATIONALIZED INDUSTRY

Al-Jubail Fertilizer Co (Samad): POB 10046, Jubail 31961; tel (3) 341-6488; telex 832024; Pres: Ahmad A. al-Ahmad; f 1980; joint venture with Taiwan Fertilizer Co.

Al-Jubail Petrochemical Co (Kemya): POB 10084, Jubail 31961; tel (3) 357-6000; telex 832058; Pres: Robert D. Wotring; Exec Vice-Pres: Khalil I. al-Gannas; f 1980; production of polythene; joint venture with Exxon Corpn (USA).

Arabian Petrochemical Co (Petrokemya): POB 10002, Jubail 31961; tel (3) 357-7126; telex 832053; fax (3) 358-4480; Chair: Ibrahim A. bin Salamah; Exec Vice-Pres: Nabil A. Mansouri; f 1981; production of ethylene, polystyrene and butene; wholly-owned subsidiary of SABIC (see below).

Eastern Petrochemical Co (Sharq): POB 10035, Jubail 31961; tel (3) 357-5000; telex 832037; fax (3) 358-0383; Chair: Dep Minister for Industrial Affairs, Mubarak al-Khafrah; Pres: Ahmad M. al-Nekhilan; f 1981; production of polyethylene and ethylene glycol; joint venture with Japanese consortium.

Jeddah Steel Rolling Mill (Sulb): POB 1826, Jeddah; tel (2) 636-7462; telex 602127; Pres: Ian Smith; f 1981; production of steel rods and bars.

National Industrial Gases Co (Gas): POB 10110, Jubail 31961; tel (3) 341-1992; telex 832082; Dir-Gen: Saad H. al-Ghurairi; production of oxygen and nitrogen; joint venture with private sector.

National Methanol Co (Ibn Sina): POB 10003, Jubail 31961; tel (3) 340-5500; telex 832033; Pres: K. S. Rawaf; production of chemical-grade methanol; joint venture of SABIC with Hoechst AG (FRG), Celanese (USA) and Texas Eastern (USA).

National Plastic Co (Ibn Hayyan): POB 10002, Jubail 31961; tel (3) 357-7000; telex 832123; fax (3) 358-4736; Pres: Ibrahim S. al-Sheweir; f 1983; production of plastics; joint venture with Lucky Group (South Korea).

Qassim Cement Co: POB 345, Buraydah, Qassim; tel (6) 323-6811; telex 301202; Hon Chair: Prince Abdullah al-Faisal as-Sa'ud; Chair: Prince Sultan al-Abdullah al-Faisal as-Sa'ud; production of cement.

Saudi Arabian Fertilizer Co (SAFCO): POB 553, Damman 31421; tel (3) 857-5011; telex 870117; fax (3) 8574311; Gen Man: Hussein Eid al-Jubeihi; Asst Gen Man: Saleh I. Quraidis; f 1965; production of fertilizer, melamine and sulphuric acid.

Saudi Basic Industries Corpn (SABIC): POB 5101, Riyadh 11422; tel (1) 401-2033; telex 401177; Chair: Minister of Industry and Electricity, Abd al-Aziz az-Zamil; Vice-Chair and Man Dir: Ibrahim bin Salamah; f 1976 to foster the petrochemical industry and other hydro-carbon based industries through joint ventures with foreign partners, and to market their products.

Saudi-European Petrochemical Co (Ibn Zahr): POB 10330, Jubail 31961; tel (3) 341-5060; telex 832157; Pres: Abd ar-Rahman A. al-Gawari; f 1985; production of ether; SABIC has a 70% share.

Saudi Iron and Steel (Hadeed): POB 136, Jubail; tel (3) 341-7500; telex 832011; Pres: G. Yung; production of steel reinforcing rods and bars.

Saudi Methanol Co (ar-Razi): POB 10065, Jubail 31961; tel (3) 341-6396; telex 832023; Pres: Abd al-Aziz A. at-Turki; Exec Vice-Pres: Gyosuke Shigeno; f 1979; production of methanol; joint venture with a consortium of Japanese cos.

Saudi Petrochemical Co (Sadaf): POB 10025, Jubail 31961; tel (3) 357-3000; telex 832032; Pres: R. M. Kingsbury; production of ethylene, ethylene dichloride, styrene, crude industrial ethanol and caustic soda; Shell (Pecten) has a 50% share.

Saudi Yanbu Petrochemical Co (YANPET): POB 555, Yanbu; tel (4) 432-13850; telex 662359; Pres: J. G. Griffith; production of ethylene and polythene; joint venture with Mobil.

Yanbu Cement Co: POB 5330, Jeddah; POB 467, Yanbu; tel (4) 322-6652; Chair: Prince Mehsal bin Abd al-Aziz.

TRADE

Customs Department: POB 3483, Riyadh; tel (1) 401-3334; telex 201626; fax (1) 404-3412; Man: Hamad Ibrahim al-Rashudi; f 1929; control of import and export customs procedures.

Saudi Arabian Standards Organization: POB 3437, Riyadh 11471; tel (1) 479-3332; telex 401610; fax (1) 479-3046; Dir-Gen: Dr Khaled Youssef al-Khalaf; Dep Dir-Gen: Nabil Amin Molla; f 1972; responsible for formulation and adoption of national standards for all commodities and products, methods of sampling and testing; sets the rules for granting certificates of conformity and quality marks as well as regulating their issue and use.

Saudi Corpn for International Exhibitions and Fairs (Saudiexpo): POB 1252, Jeddah 21431; tel (2) 651-1212; telex 603908; fax (2) 653-0869; organization and promotion of international and local exhibitions and trade fairs.

Defence

Armed Forces: c/o Ministry of Defence and Civil Aviation, Airport Rd, Riyadh 11165; tel (1) 477-7777; telex 401188; Chief of the Gen Staff: Maj-Gen Muhammad as-Salah al-Hammad.

Air Force: Riyadh; tel (1) 402-7966; telex 201661; Commdr: Maj-Gen Ahmad Ibrahim al-Buhayri.

Army: c/o Ministry of Defence and Civil Aviation, Airport Rd, Riyadh 11165; tel (1) 477-7777; telex 401188; Commdr: Maj-Gen Abd al-Muhsin Ali al-Amran.

Navy: Damman; Chief of Staff: Muhammad Oun Sharaf al-Barakat.

Coast Guard: c/o Ministry of the Interior, POB 2833, Airport Rd, Riyadh 11134; tel (1) 401-1111; telex 401622; Dir: Muhammad bin Hilal.

Frontier Force: c/o Ministry of the Interior, POB 2833, Airport Rd, Riyadh 11134; tel (1) 401-1111; telex 401622.

National Guard: Riyadh; tel (1) 402-4600; telex 201064; Commdr: Prince Abdullah bin Abd al-Aziz.

Public Security Forces: c/o Ministry of the Interior, POB 2833, Airport Rd, Riyadh 11134; tel (1) 401-1111; telex 401622; Dir-Gen: Brig-Gen Abdullah ibn ash-Sheikh.

Development and Planning

Royal Commission for Jubail and Yanbu: POB 5964, Riyadh 11432; tel (1) 479-4445; telex 401386; fax (1) 477-5404; Sec-Gen: Prince Abdullah bin Faisal bin Turki Alsaud; Dep Sec-Gen: Rashad Fouad Reda; f 1975; design, construction, operation and maintenance of new industrial cities of Jubail and Yanbu.

Directorate-General for Jubail: Jubail Industrial Complex, POB 121, Jubail 31961; tel (3) 341-5905; telex 631280.

Directorate-General for Yanbu: POB 31, Yanbu; tel (4) 321-6000; telex 430303.

Saudi Consulting House (SCH): POB 1267, Riyadh 11431; tel (1) 448-4533; telex 401152; Chair: Minister of Industry and Electricity, Abdullah az-Zamil; Vice-Chair and Man Dir: Ahmad Saleh at-Twaijri; f 1979; engineering, economic, industrial and management consultants.

Employment

Civil Service Commission: POB 18367, Washeem St, Riyadh 11114.

Institute of Public Administration: POB 205, Riyadh 11141; tel (1) 476-8888; telex 401160; fax (1) 479-2136; Dir-Gen: Dr Muhammad al-Tawail; Dep Dir-Gen: Abdulrahman al-Shakawy; f 1961; in-service training of Govt employees; pre-service training of graduates who will later join the public and private sectors; commissioned consultations in admin and organization; research and studies in admin science and allied fields; collection and organization of public documents.

Legal and Judiciary

Supreme Coucil of Justice: Riyadh; tel (1) 435-1155; consists of 11 mems and supervises work of the courts; reviews legal questions referred to it by the Minister of Justice and expresses opinions on judicial questions; reviews sentences of death, cutting and stoning.

Media

BROADCASTING

Gulfvision: POB 6802, Riyadh 11452; tel (1) 403-2912; telex 402118; fax (1) 403-7459; Dir-Gen: Saud Abdel Hamid Dahlawi; f 1977; co-ordination of co-operation between the TV authorities in the Gulf region.

Saudi Arabian Broadcasting Service: c/o Ministry of Information, POB 570, Nasseriya St, Riyadh 11161; tel (1) 401-4440; telex 401040; Dir-Gen: Khalid H. Ghouth; 43 medium-wave stations broadcasting in Arabic and English; 23 FM stations; overseas service in Urdu, Indonesian, Farsi, French, Somali and Swahili.

Saudi Arabian Television: POB 57137, Riyadh 11574; tel (1) 404-3353; telex 201030; fax (1) 403-3026; Dir: Dr Ali M. Najai; f 1964; responsible for all TV affairs, including admin and programme activities.

Foreign Affairs Department: POB 53051, Riyadh 11583; tel (1) 401-4213; telex 201030; fax (1) 403-3026; Dir: Abdul-Rahman M. Ghulaigah; f 1964; responsible for contacts with organizations outside Saudi Arabia.

NEWS AND INFORMATION

Central Department of Statistics: POB 3735, Riyadh; tel (1) 402-3355; collection, analysis and publication of statistical information.

Saudi Press Agency: c/o Ministry of Information, POB 570, Nasseriya St, Riyadh 11161; tel (1) 402-3065; telex 401074; Dir-Gen: Abdullah Hilail; f 1970.

Mining and Energy

ENERGY

General Electricity Organization (ELECTRICO): POB 1185, Riyadh; tel (1) 402-9252; telex 201052; Gov: Mahmoud Taiba.

Saudi Arabian Marketing and Refining Co (SAMAREC): POB 757, Riyadh 11189; tel (1) 478-1328; telex 402802; Chair: Sheikh Hisham Mohi ed-Din Nazer; Pres: Hussein A. Linjawi; f 1989, previously known as the General Petroleum and Mineral Organization (PETROMIN); responsible for petroleum refining, domestic marketing and distribution of petroleum products, and some exports of petroleum and LPG.

Arabian Drilling Co: POB 708, Damman 31421; telex 871212; Man Dir: Sulaiman al-Amri; f 1964; SAMAREC shareholding 51%, remainder French private capital; undertakes contract drilling for oil (onshore and offshore), minerals and water, both inside and outside Saudi Arabia.

Arabian Geophysical and Surveying Co (ARGAS): POB 2109, Jeddah 21451; tel (2) 671-0087; telex 601786; Man Dir: Fadlullah Farouq; Technical Dir: Yves Serres; SAMAREC shareholding 51%; geophysical exploration for oil, minerals and ground water, as well as all types of land, airborne and marine surveys.

Arabian Marine Petroleum Co (MARINCO): POB 50, Dhahran Airport 31932; tel (3) 891-3831; telex 870047; Chair: Ali I. ar-Rubaishi; f 1968; SAMAREC shareholding 51%; undertakes marine construction work (pipelines, rigs, sea terminals, etc).

Jeddah Oil Refinery Terminal (JORC): POB 1604, Jeddah 21441; tel (2) 636-7811; telex 601867; Chair: Ali I. ar-Rubaishi; Man Dir: Muhammad H. Ajaj; f 1968; SAMAREC shareholding 75%, remainder held by the Saudi Arabian

Refining Co (SARCO); responsible for distribution in the Western Province.

Petromin—Jet: POB 7550, Jeddah 21472; tel (2) 685-7592; telex 603402; Chair and Chief Exec Asst (acting): Abdullah O. Attas; f 1979; wholly owned by SAMAREC; supplies petroleum products, in particular jet fuel, to King Abd al-Aziz International Airport.

Petromin Lubricating Oil Co (PETROLUBE): POB 1432, Jeddah 21431; tel (2) 651-0909; telex 606175; fax (2) 651-2500; Pres and Chief Exec: Ahmad al-Muhammad al-Khereiji; f 1968; SAMAREC shareholding 71%, Mobil Oil Investment owns 29%; processing, manufacture, marketing and distribtion of lubricating oils and other related products.

> **Petromin Lube Oil Blending and Grease Manufacturing Plant (SAUDI LUBE):** POB 10382, Jubail 31961; tel (3) 341-1209; telex 832168; Man Dirs: Baddah S. as-Sebai'e (Finance and Trade), Abd ar-Rahman M. al-Cabbani; f 1987; wholly owned by PETROLUBE; production and marketing of lubricants and grease.

Petromin Lubricating Oil Refining Co (LUBEREF): POB 5518, Jeddah 21432; tel (2) 660-3232; telex 606218; fax (2) 665-6343; Chair and Exec Man Dir: Bakr A. Khoja; f 1975; SAMAREC shareholding 70%, 30% owned by Mobil.

Petromin Marketing (PETMARK): POB 50, Dhahran Airport; tel (3) 891-3883; telex 870009; Exec Man Dir (Marketing Affairs): S. S. Abu al-Jadayil; f 1967; wholly owned by SAMAREC; operates the installations and facilities for the distribution of petroleum products in the Eastern, Central, Southern and Northern provinces of Saudi Arabia.

Petromin Mobil Refinery: POB 30078, Yanbu; tel (4) 396-4000; telex 662325; Chair: Abd al-Aziz at-Turki; f 1984; operated by SAMAREC and Mobil.

Petromin Riyadh Refinery (PRR): POB 3946, Riyadh 11199; tel (1) 498-0995; telex 401015; Exec Man Dir: Muhammad S. Mufarrih; f 1974; wholly owned by SAMAREC.

Petromin Services Department (PERTOSERVE): POB 2329, Jeddah 21451; tel (2) 636-6309; telex 601867; Pres: Hussain A. Lingawi; f 1968; operates all types of services with regard to medical care, social and sports activities, telecommunications, computers, housing, security and training.

Petromin-Shell Refinery Co: POB 10088, Jubail 31961; tel (3) 357-2023; telex 832060; Chair: Dr Faisal Bashir; operated by SAMAREC and Shell; exports began in 1985.

Petromin Tankers and Mineral Shipping Co (PETROSHIP): POB 1600, Jeddah 21441; tel (2) 647-7200; telex 607016; fax (2) 647-3762; Chair and Exec Man Dir: Abd al-Latif A. Sultan; Asst Gen Man, Operations: Abd ar-Razzak Hassim Almadani; Asst Gen Man, Admin: Faiz Awad Khalil; f 1968; wholly owned by SAMAREC; operation and charter of sea-going vessels for the transportation of oil.

Petromin Yanbu Refinery: POB 30021, Yanbu; tel (4) 321-8000; telex 662337; Exec Dir: Yahya A. az-Zaid; f 1983.

Saudi Arabian Oil Co (Saudi Aramco): POB 58521, Riyadh 11515; tel (1) 464-1055; telex 401084; Chair: Sheikh Hisham Mohi ed-Din Nazer; Dir-Gen: Ali I. Naimi; f 1933, previously known as Arabian-American Oil Co (Aramco): holds the principal working concessions in Saudi Arabia.

MINING

Directorate-General of Mineral Resources: POB 345, Jeddah 21191; tel (2) 667-4800; telex 601157; fax (2) 667-2265; Dir-Gen: Minister of Petroleum and Mineral Resources, Sheikh Hisham Mohi ed-Din Nazer; f 1960; basic geological and city mapping, mineral exploration, prospect evaluation, mining devt, participation in feasibility studies.

Science and Technology

King Abd al-Aziz City for Science and Technology (KACST): POB 6086, Old Airport Rd, Nr al-Khaleej Bridge, Riyadh; tel (1) 478-8000; telex 404017; fax (1) 478-7305; Pres: Dr Saleh Abdulrahman al-Athel; Vice-Pres: Dr Abdullah al-Kadhi; f 1978; formulates national policy for science and technology devt, conducts scientific research programmes to further devt, awards scholarships to develop necessary skills of individuals and grants to institutions to undertake applied research work.

Meteorology and Environmental Protection Agency: POB 1358, Jeddah.

Telecommunications

Directorate-General of Posts: Airport Rd, Riyadh 11142.

Gulf Postal Organization: POB 135, Riyadh 11141.

Saudi Telex Co: POB 361, Riyadh.

Tourism

Saudi Hotels and Resort Areas Co: POB 5500, Riyadh 11422; tel (1) 465-7177; telex 401173; fax (1) 465-7177; Chair: Dr Faisal al-Bashir; Dir-Gen: Abd al-Aziz al-Ambar; Dep Dir-Gen: Osama A. Kamakhi; f 1976; ownership and management of hotels, resort areas and amusement parks.

Transport

CIVIL AVIATION

International Airports Projects Office: POB 6326, Jeddah; tel (2) 685-4200; telex 401521; approves work on new international airports.

Presidency of Civil Aviation (PCA): POB 887, Jeddah; tel (2) 667-3664; telex 600171 (English), 401093 (Arabic); Pres: Nasir al-Assaf.

Saudia—Saudi Arabian Airlines: POB 620, Saudia Bldg, Jeddah 21231; tel (2) 686-0000; telex 601007; Chair: Minister of Defence and Civil Aviation, Prince Sultan ibn Abd al-Aziz; Dir-Gen: Sheikh Ahmad Mattar; Exec Vice-Pres (Finance and Admin): Ahmad Boubshait; f 1945 and began operations in 1947; regular services to 23 domestic destinations; international services throughout the Middle East, and to Africa, Europe, the Far East and the USA.

RAILWAYS

Saudi Railways Organization: POB 36, Damman 31241; tel (3) 871-3001; telex 801050; fax (3) 871-2293; Pres: Faisal M. ash-Shehail; Vice-Pres: Abdul Mohsin Bashawari; f 1951; passenger and cargo link between Damman and Riyadh.

ROADS

National Transport Co of Saudi Arabia: POB 7280, Jeddah; Man Dir: A. D. Blackstock; Operations Man: I. Croxson; specializes in inward clearance, freight forwarding, general and heavy road haulage, re-export, charter air freight and exhibitions.

SHIPPING

Saudi National Shipping Co: POB 8931, Riyadh 11492; tel (1) 478-5454; telex 405625; fax (1) 477-8036; Chief Exec: Muhammad al-Jarbou; Vice-Chair, Finance and Admin: Hazza B. al-Qahtani; Vice-Chair, Lines: Muhammad al-Ahmad; Vice-Chair, Technical: Abd al-Aziz Toyan; f 1979; purchase, charter and operation of vessels for the transportation of cargo, passengers, etc.

Seaports Authority (SEAPA): POB 5162, Riyadh 11188; tel (1) 405-0005; telex 401158; f 1976; admin and devt of ports and port infrastructure.

Utilities

Saline Water Conversion Corpn: POB 5968, Riyadh 11432; tel (1) 463-1111; telex 400097; fax (1) 465-0852; Gov: Abdullah M. al-Gholaikah; Vice-Gov, Technical Affairs and Projects: Abdullah Abd al-Aziz Abanmy; Vice-Gov, Operation and Maintenance: Abdullah al-Hussein; Vice-Gov, Admin and Finance: Abd ar-Rahman al-Khamis; f 1965; conversion of sea water into drinking water, provision of water by pipeline and generation of electricity in some of its plants.

Welfare

General Organization for Social Insurance (GOSI): POB 2963, Airport Rd, Riyadh 11461; tel (1) 478-5721.

SENEGAL

Head of State

Executive power is held by the President, who is Head of State, directly-elected by universal adult suffrage to serve a five-year term at the same time as the National Assembly. The President appoints and leads a Council of Ministers.

President: Abdou Diouf (took office 1 January 1981; elected President on 27 February 1983; re-elected 28 February 1988).

Office of the President: ave Roume, BP 168, Dakar; tel 23-10-88; telex 258; Minister of State and Secretary-General of the Presidency of the Republic: Jean Collin.

Legislature

Legislative power rests with the unicameral National Assembly, comprising 120 members elected for five years by universal adult suffrage. Senegal consists of 10 regions, each with an appointed Governor, an elected local assembly and a separate budget.

Assemblée Nationale (National Assembly): place Tascher, Dakar; tel 23-10-99; Pres: Abdoul Aziz Ndaw; Sec-Gen: Dam Ndiaye.

MINISTRIES AND GOVERNMENT DEPARTMENTS

MINISTRY OF CULTURE
Immeuble Administratif, Dakar
Tel 23-10-88; telex 482
Minister: Moustapha Kâ

**MINISTRY OF THE CIVIL SERVICE,
EMPLOYMENT AND LABOUR**
BP 403, Dakar
Tel 23-10-88; telex 482
Minister: Moussa N'Doye

MINISTRY OF COMMUNICATIONS
Immeuble Radio-Sénégal, Dakar
Tel 23-10-65; telex 236
Minister: Robert Sagna

MINISTRY OF DEFENCE
BP 176, Dakar
Tel 23-10-88; telex 482
Minister: Médoune Fall

MINISTRY OF ECONOMY AND FINANCE
Centre Peytavin, rue Charles Laisné et ave Carde,
BP 462, Dakar
Tel 21-06-99; telex 3203
Minister: Serigne Lamine Diop
Minister-Delegate for Economic and Financial Affairs:
Moussa Touré

Direction de la Prévision et de la Conjoncture: 70 rue du Dr Thèze, Dakar; tel 21-33-98; telex 3203; f 1980; economic and financial programmes; studies economic situation and perspectives; makes short-term economic projections.

MINISTRY OF EQUIPMENT
Immeuble Communal, blvd du Général de Gaulle, Dakar
Tel 21-42-01; telex 3151
Minister: Alexandre N'Diali N'Diaye

MINISTRY OF FOREIGN AFFAIRS
place de l'Indépendance, Dakar
Tel 21-62-84; telex 482
Minister: Ibrahima Fall

MINISTRY OF HOUSING AND URBAN AFFAIRS
blvd Franklin Roosevelt, Dakar
Tel 23-10-88; telex 482
Minister: Mamadou Abbas Ba

**MINISTRY OF INDUSTRIAL DEVELOPMENT AND
CRAFTS**
route de Ouakam, Dakar
Tel 23-00-00; telex 482
Minister: Famara Ibrahima Sagna

MINISTRY OF THE INTERIOR
Rond-point de la République, Dakar
Tel 21-41-51; telex 3351
Minister: André Sonko

MINISTRY OF JUSTICE
BP 784, Dakar
Tel 23-10-88; telex 482
Minister and Keeper of the Seals: Seydou Madani Sy

MINISTRY OF NATIONAL EDUCATION
rue Calmette et René Ndiaye, BP 699, Dakar
Tel 22-12-28; telex 482
Minister: Ibrahima Niang
Minister of Higher Education: Sahir Thiam

MINISTRY OF PLANNING AND CO-OPERATION
BP 411, Dakar
Tel 23-10-88; telex 3133
Minister: Djibo Kâ

MINISTRY OF PUBLIC HEALTH
Immeuble Administratif, Dakar
Tel 23-10-88; telex 482
Minister: Thérèse King

MINISTRY OF RURAL DEVELOPMENT
Immeuble Administratif, Dakar
Tel 23-10-88; telex 3151
Minister: Cheikh Abdoul Khadre Cissokho
Minister-Delegate in charge of Animal Resources:
M'Baye Diouf
**Minister-Delegate in charge of the Protection of
Nature:** Moctar Kébé

MINISTRY OF SOCIAL DEVELOPMENT
Immeuble Administratif, Dakar
Tel 23-10-88; telex 482
Minister: Ndioro N'Diaye

MINISTRY OF TOURISM
ave André Peytavin, BP 4049, Dakar
Tel 21-94-49
Minister: El Hadj Malick Sy

MINISTRY OF TRADE
Centre Peytavin, rue Charles Laisné et ave Carde,
BP 439, Dakar
Tel 22-14-44; telex 482
Minister: Oumar Seidina Sy

MINISTRY OF WATER RESOURCES
Immeuble Communal, blvd Général de Gaulle, Dakar
Tel 22-37-78
Minister: Samba Yéla Diop

MINISTRY OF YOUTH AND SPORTS
ave du Barachois, Dakar
Minister: Abdoulaye Makhtar Diop

OFFICE OF THE MINISTER-DELEGATE IN CHARGE OF RELATIONS WITH THE NATIONAL ASSEMBLY
Dakar
Minister-Delegate: Farbo Lo

OFFICE OF THE MINISTER-DELEGATE FOR EMIGRATION
Dakar
Minister-Delegate: Fatou N'Dongo N'Diang

GOVERNMENT AGENCIES AND ORGANIZATIONS

Advisory and Supervisory Bodies

Commission for State Disengagement: Dakar; Dir: El Hadj Malik Sy; in charge of selling certain cos in which the state has partial and in some cases majority holdings.

Conseil Economique et Social: Dakar; Pres: Mamba Guirassy.

Agriculture

Société d'Exploitation des Ressources Animales du Sénégal (SERAS): BP 14, Dakar; tel 22-31-78; telex 256; Dir: Dr Mamadou S. Diallo; f 1962; livestock devt; 97% state-owned.

Business and Economy

BANKING

Assurbank: 31 ave Albert Sarraut, BP 3872, Dakar; tel 23-80-29; telex 61140; fax 22-95-22; Chair of Board: Abdoulaye Sow; Gen Man: Doumbaly Camara; f 1986; took over activities of Banque Commerciale du Sénégal; 30% owned by Assurances Générales Sénégalaises; financing of small-scale enterprises and exports; involved in gold business.

Banque Centrale des Etats de l'Afrique de l'Ouest (BCEAO): ave du Barachois, BP 3108, Dakar; tel 21-16-15; telex 21875; Commercial Branch: ave Georges Pompidou, BP 3159, Dakar; tel 22-53-84; telex 536; Gov: Alassane Ouattara; f 1955; Dir in Senegal: Djebril Sakho; bank of issue and central bank for states of the Union monétaire ouest africaine (UMOA), comprising Benin, Burkina Faso, Côte d'Ivoire, Mali, Niger, Senegal and Togo; 2 other brs.

Banque Nationale de Développement du Sénégal (BNDS): 7 ave Roume, BP 319, Dakar; tel 22-34-86; telex 3283; Pres: Cheikhou Faye; Man Dir: Abdoulaye Seye; f 1964; 73% state-owned; devt bank; 7 brs.

Caisse Nationale de Crédit Agricole du Sénégal (CNCAS):

45 ave Albert Sarrault, BP 3890, Dakar; tel 22-74-31; telex 61345; Pres: Alassane Fall; Dir-Gen: Samicidine Dieng; f 1984; 68% state-owned; 4 brs.

Union Sénégalaise de Banque pour le Commerce et l'Industrie (USB): 17 blvd Pinet-Laprade, BP 56, Dakar; tel 23-10-08; telex 21678; f 1961; undergoing reorganization in 1989.

FINANCIAL AGENCY

Société Nationale de Garantie et d'Assistance de Crédit (SONAGA): 15 allée Robert-Delmas, BP 3374, Dakar; tel 22-05-94; f 1971; 90.74% state-owned; guarantees and supports commercial enterprises.

NATIONALIZED INDUSTRY

Société Electrique et Industrielle du Baol (SEIB): BP 5, Diourbel; tel 71-10-52; telex 7780; Chair and Man Dir: Yaya Kane; f 1920; 57% state-owned; processing and marketing of groundnuts; manufactures oils, margarine, perfumes, alcoholic drinks, ice, vinegar, chemicals.

Société Industrielle des Applications de l'Energie Solaire A. Daguerre (SINAES A. DAGUERRE): 21A Zone B, BP 1277, Dakar; tel 21-12-08; telex 661; f 1976; 50% state-owned; production and marketing of solar and wind energy systems.

TRADE

Centre International du Commerce Extérieur du Sénégal (CICES): route de l'Aéroport, BP 8166; Dakar-Yoff; tel 20-14-54; telex 31512; fax 35-07-12; Dir-Gen: Ibrahima Diagne; f 1986; promotes exports; runs Foire Internationale de Dakar (international trade fair).

Zone Franche Industrielle de Dakar (ZFID): Immeuble Excellence, rue Carnot, ave Roume, BP 3298, Dakar; tel 22-68-69; telex 3330; promotion of exporting industries.

Defence

Office of the Chief of Staff to the General Armies: Immeuble Administratif, Dakar; tel 23-10-71; telex 482; Chief of the Gen Staff: Gen Mamadou Mansour Seck.

Development and Planning

DEVELOPMENT

Société de Développement Agricole et Industriel du Sénégal (SODAGRI): 23 ave Roume, BP 222, Dakar; tel 22-18-18; telex 477; Dir-Gen: Kassimou Dia; agricultural and industrial projects.

Société de Développement des Fibres Textiles (SODE-FITEX): km 4.5, route de Rufisque, BP 3216, Dakar; tel 22-47-80; telex 280; Dir-Gen: Falilou Mbacke; f 1974; 70% state-owned; responsible for planning and devt of cotton industry.

Société de Développement et de Vulgarisation Agricole (SODEVA): 92 rue Moussé Diop (ex rue Blanchot), BP 3234, Dakar; tel 23-16-78; telex 51638; Dir-Gen: Bakary Djileh Coly; f 1968; devt of intensive farming methods and diversified livestock breeding.

Société Nationale d'Etudes et de Promotion Industrielle (SONEPI): ave Bourguiba Prolongée, derrière Résidence Seydou Nourou Tall, BP 100, Dakar; tel 25-21-30; telex 61178; fax 24-65-65; Pres and Dir-Gen: Sheikh Tidiane Sakho; f 1969 by the Senegal Govt in collaboration with the private sector; studies industrial projects, agro-industry, etc; provides consultancy and assistance services to national and foreign economic operators; promotes investment.

Société Nouvelle des Etudes de Développement en Afrique (SONED—Afrique): 142 rue de Bayeux, BP 2084, Dakar; tel 21-22-31; telex 464; Pres: Latyr N'Diaye; Man Dir: Oumar Souleymane Thiaw; f 1974; 61% state-owned.

Société Sénégalaise pour la Promotion de l'Artisanat d'Art (SOSEPRA): BP 3162, Dakar; tel 21-59-76; f 1975; runs craft village of Soumbédioune.

REGIONAL DEVELOPMENT

Société Nationale d'Aménagement et d'Exploitation des Terres du Delta du Fleuve Sénégal et des Vallées du Fleuve Sénégal et de la Falémé (SAED): route de Khor, BP 74, Saint-Louis; tel 61-15-33; telex 75124; fax 61-14-63; Pres and Man Dir: Sidy Moctar Keita; Sec-Gen: Mamadou Sambe; f 1965; rural devt; controls the agricultural devt of 30,000 ha around the Senegal river delta.

Legal and Judiciary

Court of Appeal: Dakar; Pres: Gilbert Anché.

High Court of Justice: Dakar; f 1962; composed of mems of the National Assembly.

High Council of the Magistrature: Dakar; Pres: President Abdou Diouf; Vice-Pres: Alioune Badara Mbengue; f 1960.

Supreme Court: Dakar; tel 22-37-78; Pres: Ousmane Camara; Sectional Pres: Menoumbé Sar, Laïty Niang; f 1960.

Media

BROADCASTING

Office de Radiodiffusion-Télévision du Sénégal (ORTS): BP 1765, Dakar; Man Dir: Marcel Ndione; Dir (Radio): Pathe Fall Dieye; state radio broadcasting authority.

Office de Radiodiffusion-Télévision du Sénégal (ORTS): BP 2375, Dakar; tel 21-56-89; telex 634; Man Dir: Marcel Ndione; Dir, TV: S. Dieng; state TV broadcasting authority.

GOVERNMENT PUBLISHER

Société Sénégalaise de Presse et de Publications (SSPP): route du Service géographique, BP 92, Dakar; tel 21-46-92; telex 431; Pres: Bara Diouf; f 1970; 62% Govt-owned.

NEWS AND INFORMATION

Agence de Presse Sénégalaise: 72 blvd de la République, BP 117, Dakar; tel 23-14-27; telex 51520; Dir: Amadou Dieng; f 1959; Govt-controlled; news agency.

Direction de la Statistique: Point E, BP 116, Dakar; tel 24-03-01; Dir, Documentation and Publs: Jean Ndong; statistical office.

Mining and Energy

Compagnie Sénégalaise des Phosphates de Taïba (CSPT): 19 rue Parchappe, BP 1713, Dakar; tel 21-00-81; telex 21834; fax 22-12-56; Chair: Andien Senghor; Man Dir: Mouhamadou Sy; Asst Man Dir: Bernard F. d'Andon; f 1957; 50% state-owned; extraction and marketing of high-grade calcium phosphate.

Société Nationale d'Electricité (SENELEC): 28/30 rue Vincens, BP 93, Dakar; tel 21-72-82; telex 21845; Pres: André Guillabert; Man Dir: Samba Diallo; f 1973; 67% state-owned; production and distribution of electricity.

Société Nationale des Pétroles du Sénégal (PETROSEN): 2 rue Malan, blvd Pinet Laprade, Dakar; f 1981; 90% state-owned.

Société des Pétroles du Sénégal: BP 2076, Dakar; tel 22-04-44; telex 3249; 90% state-owned; exploration and production of petroleum.

Société Sénégalaise des Phosphates de Thiès (SSPT): 14 ave Borgnis-Desbordes, BP 241, Dakar; tel 22-32-83; telex 21683; Chair: Abdoulaye Diack; Man Dir: Daniel Ducret; f 1948; 50% state-owned; production of phosphates and attapulgite; manufactures phosphate fertilizers and animal feed.

Transport and Communications

TELECOMMUNICATIONS

Société Nationale des Télécommunications du Sénégal (SONATEL): 6 rue Wagane Diouf, BP 69, Dakar; tel 23-10-23; telex 1296; fax 22-14-92; Dir, Commercial Affairs and External Relations: Pape Gorgui Toure; f 1985; telecommunications.

TRANSPORT

Air Sénégal—Société Nationale des Transports Aériens du Sénégal: BP 8010, Dakar-Yoff; tel 20-09-13; telex 31513; fax 20-00-33; Gen Man: Modou Khaya; f 1971; 50% state-owned, 40% owned by Air Afrique; extensive national and international flights.

Port Autonome de Dakar (PAD): blvd de la Libération, BP 3195, Dakar; tel 21-29-22; telex 21404; Pres: Issa Diop; Dir-Gen: Soulaye Sall; f 1865; port authority.

Régie des Chemins de Fer du Sénégal (RCFS): Cité Ballabey, BP 175, Thiès; tel 51-10-13; telex 7789; Dir-Gen: Ibrahima Niang; railway transport.

Société pour le Développement de l'Infrastructure de Chantiers Maritimes du Port de Dakar (DAKAR MARINE): blvd de l'Arsenal, BP 438, Dakar; tel 23-36-88; telex 61104; fax 23-83-99; Chair: Gorgui Ibrahima Sene; f 1981; 90.5% state-owned; transfer to private ownership announced in 1987; ship-building and ship repairs; repair and maintenance of super-tankers and other large vessels.

Société des Transports en Commun du Cap-Vert (SOTRAC): 16 rue Emile Zola, angle Bayeux, BP 4036, Dakar; tel 21-14-43; telex 276; f 1971; public transport in the Dakar area.

Utilities

Société Nationale d'Exploitation des Eaux du Sénégal (SONEES): 97 ave André Peytavin, BP 400, Dakar; tel 21-28-65; telex 3137; Pres: Abdoul Magib Seck; Man Dir: Abdoulaye Bouna Fall; f 1972; 97% state-owned; waterworks and supplies.

Société Nationale de Forages (SONAFOR): km 4, route de Rufisque, BP 2703, Dakar; tel 22-13-18; telex 268; f 1973; 74.31% state-owned; study and exploitation of underground water sources.

SEYCHELLES

Head of State

Executive power is vested in the President, who is Head of State and Head of Government. The President is elected for a five-year term by direct popular vote. The President appoints and leads the Council of Ministers, and also appoints the holders of certain public offices, and the judiciary.

President: France Albert René (assumed power 5 June 1977; elected President 26 June 1979, re-elected 18 June 1984 and 12 June 1989).

Office of the President: State House, POB 655, Victoria, Mahé; tel 24391; telex 2217.

Legislature

Under the terms of the 1979 constitution, Seychelles is a one-party state. The Seychelles People's Progressive Front (SPPF) holds total political power. The legislature is the unicameral National Assembly, with 25 members: 23 directly elected for four years and two appointed by the President to represent the Inner and Outlying Islands.

National Assembly: POB 56, Victoria, Mahé; tel 24041; telex 2260; fax 24200; Chair: Francis MacGregor; Clerk: F. Shroff; f 1979.

MINISTRIES AND GOVERNMENT DEPARTMENTS

DEPARTMENT OF ADMINISTRATION AND MANPOWER
National House, POB 56, Victoria, Mahé
Tel 24041; telex 2260
Minister: Joseph Belmont

DEPARTMENT OF DEFENCE AND INDUSTRY
State House, POB 646, Victoria, Mahé
Tel 22011
Minister: France Albert René

DEPARTMENT OF FINANCE
Central Bank Bldg, Independence Ave, POB 313, Victoria, Mahé
Tel 21790; telex 2363
Minister: James Michel

Department of Audit: State House, POB 655, Victoria, Mahé; tel 24391; telex 2217.

DEPARTMENT OF INFORMATION, SPORTS AND CULTURE
POB 321, Victoria, Mahé
Tel 24220; telex 2320
Minister: Sylvette Frichot

DEPARTMENT OF LEGAL AFFAIRS AND OFFICE OF THE ATTORNEY-GENERAL
National House, POB 58, Victoria, Mahé
Tel 24041; fax 25063
Attorney-General: (vacant)

DEPARTMENT OF MANAGEMENT SERVICES
National House, POB 56, Victoria, Mahé
Tel 24041; telex 2333
Director-General: A. A. Lucas
Responsible for management audits, overseeing of public enterprises.

DEPARTMENT OF PLANNING AND EXTERNAL AFFAIRS
National House, POB 56, Victoria, Mahé
Tel 24041; telex 2260
Minister: Danielle de St Jorre

MINISTRY OF AGRICULTURE AND FISHERIES
Victoria, Mahé
Minister: Jeremie Bonnelame

MINISTRY OF COMMUNITY DEVELOPMENT
POB 463, Victoria, Mahé
Tel 22881; telex 2312
Minister: Esmé Jumeau

MINISTRY OF EDUCATION AND YOUTH
POB 48, Mont Fleuri
Tel 21330; telex 2305
Minister: Simone Testa

MINISTRY OF HEALTH, EMPLOYMENT AND SOCIAL SERVICES
POB 52, Botanical Gdns, Victoria, Mahé
Tel 24400; telex 2302; fax 24792
Minister, Health: Ralph Adam
Minister, Employment and Social Services: William Herminie
Principal Sec: Dr Conrad Shamlaye

MINISTRY OF INTERNAL AFFAIRS
Independence Ave, Victoria, Mahé
Tel 24222
Minister: (vacant)

MINISTRY OF TOURISM AND TRANSPORT
Independence House, Independence Ave, POB 92, Victoria, Mahé
Tel 22881; telex 2275; fax 21612
Minister: Jacques Houdoul

GOVERNMENT AGENCIES AND ORGANIZATIONS

Agriculture and Fishing

AGRICULTURE

Seychelles Agricultural Development Co Ltd (SADECO): POB 172, Victoria, Mahé; tel 24644; Exec Chair: Antoine R. Young; f 1980.

FISHING

Seychelles Fishing Authority (SFA): POB 49, Victoria, Mahé; tel 24597; telex 2289; Man Dir: P. Michaud; Resource Man: J. Nageon; Research Man: G. Lablache-Carrara; f 1984; fisheries management, research, management of fishing port.

Art and Culture

Seychelles National Archives and Museums: POB 720, La Bastille, Mahé; tel 24777; Asst Dir: Alain Daniel Lucas; f 1964; preservation of archival holding and dissemination of information to public; preservation and exhibition of museum objects; provides a forum for scientific research pertaining to exhibits.

Business and Economy

BANKING

Central Bank of Seychelles (CBS): Independence Ave, POB 701, Victoria, Mahé; tel 21580; telex 2301; Chair: Guy Morel; Gen Man: O. Scott; f 1983 to replace Seychelles Monetary Authority.

Development Bank of Seychelles: POB 217, Victoria, Mahé; tel 24471; telex 2348; fax 24274; Man Dir (acting): G. Troian; f 1978; provision of loans for devt projects in various economic sectors.

Seychelles Savings Bank: Independence Ave, POB 531, Victoria, Mahé; tel 21921; telex 2260; Man Dir: E. Domingue; operates deposit, savings and current accounts.

FINANCIAL AGENCIES

National Provident Fund: Oceangate House, POB 350, Victoria, Mahé.

INSURANCE

State Assurance Corpn of Seychelles (SACOS): Pirates Arms Bldg, POB 636, Victoria, Mahé; tel 21219; telex 2331; Man Dir: Omar B. Y. Dibba; f 1980; insures Govt property and personnel; all local insurance cos must reinsure with SACOS.

MARKETING

Seychelles Marketing Board (SMB): Oceangate House, POB 516, Victoria, Mahé; tel 24444; telex 2368; Chair: President, France Albert René; Man: Jacques Garcin; f 1984; state trading organization for food production and processing, agro-industries, with subsidiaries in fisheries devt and toiletries.

NATIONALIZED INDUSTRY

Seychelles Timber Co: Grand Anse, POB 372, Victoria, Mahé; tel 78343; Dir: Mukesh Valabhji; Man: Claude Marimba; joinery activities, logging, construction.

TRADE

Seychelles National Commodity Co (Seycom): Independence Ave, POB 252, Victoria, Mahé; tel 21190; telex 2328; f 1980; operates Govt's commodity import business; provides information to traders, retailers and wholesalers.

Defence

Seychelles People's Progressive Front: POB 154, Victoria, Mahé; tel 22618; Commdr-in-Chief: President, France Albert René.

Development

Seychelles Industrial Development Corpn (SIDEC): POB 537, Victoria, Mahé; tel 23325; telex 2312; fax 21787; industrial promotion, property devt and engineering services; management consultancy and financial services.

Investment

Seychelles National Investment Corpn: Central Bank Bldg, Independence Ave, POB 574, Victoria, Mahé; tel 21790; telex 2201; Chair: Guy Morel; Gen Man: David Workman; f 1979; holding co for state-owned enterprises and Govt investments.

Legal and Judiciary

Supreme Court: Victoria, Mahé; Chief Justice: Dr E. E. Seaton; Pres of the Court of Appeal: A. Mustafa; Justices of Appeal: H. Goburdhun, C. D'Arifat, Telford P. Georges, V. Floissac; Puisne Judges: I. K. Abban, E. Georges; the Court of Appeal hears appeals from the Supreme Court in both civil and criminal cases; the Supreme Court is a Court of Appeal from the Magistrates Court as well as having jurisdiction at first instance.

Media

BROADCASTING

Radio-Television Seychelles (RTS): POB 321, Victoria, Mahé; tel 24161; telex 2320; fax 24914; Dir-Gen: Patrick Nanty; Asst Dir of Productions: Miggie Mermitte; Asst Dir of News: Ibrahim Afif; Chief Engineer: Jude Rene; f 1983; operates national radio and TV services; programmes in Creole, English and French.

Central Information Service: address as above; tel 24161; telex 2320; fax 21006; Asst Dir: René Morel; f 1988; supplies information to foreign bodies, deals in advertising, helps with publs.

NEWS AND INFORMATION

Information System's Division: POB 206, Victoria, Mahé; tel 24041; telex 2333; fax 21739; Dir-Gen: Errol A. Dias; Principal Statistician: Hendrick Gappy; Principal Analyst Programmer: Wilson Quilindo; collects, provides and analyses data, provision of computer services, maintains national databases.

Tourism

Seychelles Tourist Board: Independence House, Independence Ave, POB 56, Victoria, Mahé; tel 22881; telex 2275; Man: (vacant).

Transport

Air Seychelles: Victoria House, POB 386, Victoria, Mahé; tel 21400; telex 2289; fax 23989; Exec Chair: C. Benoiton; Vice-Pres: M. Harewood; f 1979; operates scheduled passenger services from Mahé to Praslin and Frigate Islands and charter flights to Bird and Denis Islands; international flights to Europe and Singapore.

Port and Marine Services Division: POB 47, Victoria, Mahé; tel 24701; telex 2329; fax 24004; Dir-Gen: S. A. G. Andrade; Harbour Master: Capt R. R. Morgan; responsible for ports and port-related services, maritime safety, rescue, salvage, etc.

SIERRA LEONE

Head of State

The Head of State is the President. The presidential candidate is endorsed by the National Delegates' Conference of the All-People's Congress (APC), the only authorized political party, and is elected for a seven-year term. The President appoints and leads the Cabinet, which includes two Vice-Presidents. A 16-member Defence Council, chaired by the President, advises the President on military policy.

President: Maj-Gen Joseph Saidu Momoh (took office 28 November 1985).

Office of the President: State House, Independence Ave, Freetown; tel (22) 22202; telex 3230.

First Vice-President: Abubaker Kamara.

Office of the First Vice-President: Tower Hill, Freetown; tel (22) 23884; telex 3218.

Second Vice-President: Salia Jusu-Sheriff.

Office of the Second Vice-President: Youyi Bldg, 9th Floor, Brookfields, Freetown; tel (22) 41500; telex 3218.

Legislature

Legislative power is vested in the unicameral House of Representatives, comprising 105 members elected for five years by universal adult suffrage, 12 Paramount Chiefs (one from each District), and 10 members appointed by the President. The country is divided into four regions administered through the Ministry of the Interior, and divided into 147 Chiefdoms, each controlled by a Paramount Chief and a Council of Elders, known as the Tribal Authority.

House of Representatives: House of Parliament, Tower Hill, Freetown; tel (22) 23911; telex 3218; Speaker: William Niaka Stephen Conteh.

MINISTRIES AND GOVERNMENT DEPARTMENTS

MINISTRY OF AGRICULTURE, NATURAL RESOURCES AND FORESTRY
Youyi Bldg, Brookfields, Freetown
Tel (22) 3418
Minister: Mohamed O. Bash-Taqi

MINISTRY OF CULTURAL AFFAIRS AND SPORT
Freetown
Minister: Dr Moses Dumbaya

MINISTRY OF DEFENCE
Tower Hill, Freetown
Tel (22) 23884; telex 3218
Minister: Maj-Gen Joseph Saidu Momoh

MINISTRY OF EDUCATION
New England, Freetown
Tel (22) 40846
Minister: Dr Moses Dumbaya

MINISTRY OF ENERGY AND POWER
Electricity House, 4th Floor, Siaka Stevens St, Freetown
Tel (22) 22669
Minister: Dr Sheku Sesay

MINISTRY OF FINANCE
Secretariat Bldg, George St, Freetown
Tel (22) 26911; telex 3363
Minister: Hassan Gbassay Kanu

MINISTRY OF FOREIGN AFFAIRS
Gloucester St, Freetown
Tel (22) 24778; telex 3218
Minister: Alhaji Abdul Karim Koroma

MINISTRY OF HEALTH
Youyi Bldg, 4th Floor, Brookfields, Freetown
Tel (22) 41500
Minister: Dr Wiltshire Johnson

MINISTRY OF INFORMATION AND BROADCASTING
Youyi Bldg, 8th Floor, Brookfields, Freetown
Tel (22) 40034; telex 3218
Minister: Victor J. V. Mambu

MINISTRY OF INTERNAL AFFAIRS
State Ave, Freetown
Tel (22) 23447
Minister: Ahmed Sesay

MINISTRY OF JUSTICE
Guma Bldg, Lamina Sankoh St, Freetown
Tel (22) 23498
Attorney-General and Minister: Dr Abdulai O. Conteh

Law Officers' Department: address as above; principal officers are the Solicitor-Gen and the Dir of Public Prosecutions; advises Govt on all legal matters.

MINISTRY OF LABOUR
Freetown
Minister: M. Lamin Sidique

MINISTRY OF LANDS, HOUSING AND THE ENVIRONMENT
New England, Freetown
Tel (22) 40426
Minister: Dominic Musa

MINISTRY OF MINES
Youyi Bldg, 5th Floor, Brookfields, Freetown
Tel (22) 41500
Minister: Birch Conté

MINISTRY OF NATIONAL DEVELOPMENT AND ECONOMIC PLANNING
Ministerial Bldg, George St, Freetown
Tel (22) 25211
Minister: Sheka Kanu

MINISTRY OF PUBLIC SERVICES
Freetown
Minister: Maj-Gen Joseph Saidu Momoh

MINISTRY OF RURAL DEVELOPMENT, SOCIAL SERVICES AND YOUTH
Freetown
Minister: Musa Kabia

MINISTRY OF TOURISM
Govt Wharf, Freetown
Tel (22) 23772; telex 3218
Minister: Abdul Iscandri

MINISTRY OF TRADE AND INDUSTRY
Ministerial Bldg, George St, Freetown
Tel (22) 25211; telex 3218
Minister of Trade: Joseph Bandala Dauda
Minister of Industry and State Enterprises: Ben Kanu

MINISTRY OF TRANSPORT AND COMMUNICATIONS
Ministerial Bldg, 5th Floor, George St, Freetown
Tel (22) 25211
Minister: Philipson Kamara

MINISTRY OF WORKS
New England, Freetown
Tel (22) 40401
Minister: J. E. Laverse

OFFICE OF THE COMMANDER OF THE ARMED FORCES AND MINISTER OF STATE
Freetown
Commander of the Armed Forces and Minister of State: Maj-Gen Mohamed Sheku Tarawali

OFFICE OF THE INSPECTOR-GENERAL OF POLICE AND MINISTER OF STATE
Freetown
Inspector-General of Police and Minister of State: James B. Kamara

OFFICE OF THE LEADER OF THE HOUSE OF REPRESENTATIVES AND MINISTER OF STATE
Freetown
Leader of the House and Minister of State: Ernest R. Ndomahina

OFFICE OF THE MINISTER OF STATE FOR PARTY AFFAIRS
Freetown
Minister of State: E. T. Kamara

GOVERNMENT AGENCIES AND ORGANIZATIONS

Business and Economy

BANKING

Bank of Sierra Leone: Siaka Stevens St, POB 30, Freetown; tel (22) 26501; telex 3232; Gov: Abdul R. Turay; Dep Gov: J. K. E. Cole; f 1964; central bank.

National Development Bank Ltd: Leone House, 21-23 Siaka Stevens St, Freetown; tel (22) 26791; telex 3589; Chair of Board: J. K. E. Cole; Man Dir: J. Sanpha Koroma; f 1969; provides capital for industrial and agricultural devt investment through devt banking and commercial banking services.

Sierra Leone Commercial Bank Ltd: 20-31 Siaka Stevens St, Freetown; tel (22) 25264; telex 3275; Chair: G. C. C. Jarrett; Man Dir: C. J. Smith; f 1973; 7 brs.

INSURANCE

National Insurance Co Ltd: 18-20 Walpole St, PMB 84, Freetown; tel (22) 22819; telex 3344; Chair: Manilius Garber; Man Dir (acting): S. G. Kamara; f 1972.

MARKETING

Government Gold and Diamond Office (GGDO): c/o Bank of Sierra Leone, Siaka Stevens St, POB 30, Freetown; Man Dir: (vacant); f 1985 to succeed Precious Metals Marketing Co (PMMC) as country's purchaser and exporter of diamonds and gold; combats smuggling.

Sierra Leone Produce Marketing Board (SLPMB): POB 508, Cline Town, Freetown; telex 3211; Chair: Paramount Chief M. J. Kutubu; Man Dir: Y. T. Sesay; f 1949 to manage the marketing of Sierra Leone produce and to stimulate agricultural devt; took over control of the Rice Corpn in 1979, and set up two subsidiaries: SLAPCO (coffee and cocoa production) and NAPCO (groundnuts, ginger and chillies).

TRADE

National Trading Co: 2 Howe St, POB 15, Freetown; tel (22) 22237; f 1971; imports essential consumer products for wholesale and distribution; acts as agent and broker for manufactures; involved in export trade.

Defence

Armed Forces: Military Headquarters, Murray Town Barracks, Freetown; tel (22) 30826; telex 3350; Commdr: Maj-Gen Mohamed Sheku Tarawali.

Police Force: Freetown; Inspector-Gen of Police: James B. Kamara.

Legal and Judiciary

Supreme Court: Guma Valley Bldg, Lamina Sankoh St, Freetown; tel (22) 22848; telex 3218; Chief Justice: S. M. F. Kutubu; highest and final judicial tribunal; has supervisory jurisdiction over all other courts and any adjudicating authority in Sierra Leone, and original jurisdiction in all matters relating to the interpretation or enforcement of any provision of the Constitution.

Media

BROADCASTING

Sierra Leone Broadcasting Service: New England, Freetown; tel (22) 40403; telex 3334; Dir-Gen: M. J. Tunis; Chief Eng: Fennel Greene; f 1934; programmes mainly in English and the four main Sierra Leonean vernaculars, Mende, Limba, Temne and Krio; weekly broadcast in French; TV service established 1963.

GOVERNMENT PUBLISHER

Government Printer: New England, Freetown; tel (22) 41146.

NEWS AND INFORMATION

Sierra Leone News Agency (SLENA): Wallace Johnson St, Freetown; tel (22) 40344; telex 3218; Dir: Rod Mac-Johnson; f 1980.

Mining and Energy

National Diamond Mining Co (Sierra Leone) Ltd (DIMINCO): Charlotte St, POB 11, Freetown; Chair: Victor Strasser-King; Man Dir: Jon M. Kamanda; f 1970; 51% state-owned.

Sierra Leone Electricity Corpn: Freetown; supplies all electricity in Sierra Leone.

Sierra Leone Petroleum Refining Co Ltd: PMB, Kissy Dockyard, Freetown; 50% state-owned; operates a refinery.

Tourism

Tourist and Hotel Board: 28 Siaka Stevens St, Freetown.

Transport

Directorate of Civil Aviation: c/o Ministry of Transport and Communications, Ministerial Bldg, 5th Floor, George St, Freetown; tel (22) 25211; Dir: J. A. Johnson.

Marampa Mineral Railway: Delco House, POB 735, Freetown; tel (22) 22556; telex 3460; Gen Man: Dr O. Kortan; 84 km of track linking iron ore mines at Marampa with Pepel port; mining operations at Marampa have been suspended since 1985.

Sierra Leone Airlines: Leone House, 21-23 Siaka Stevens St, POB 285, Freetown; telex 3242; Chair: Alhaji M. S. Mustapha; Man Dir: Capt K. Yusufuddin; f 1982 to succeed Sierra Leone Airways; 60% of shares owned by Sierra Leone Govt; 20% by Aer Lingus (Republic of Ireland) and 20% by private interests; domestic services and international flights to West Africa, France and the UK; suspended operations in 1987.

Sierra Leone National Shipping Co Ltd: 45 Cline St, POB 935, Freetown; tel (22) 50824; telex 3212; f 1972; shipping, clearing and forwarding agency; represents foreign lines.

Sierra Leone Ports Authority: Queen Elizabeth II Quay, PMB 386, Cline Town, Freetown; tel (22) 50989; telex 3262; Gen Man: Capt Renato Slobec; f 1964; Govt parastatal body supervised by the Ministry of Transport and Communications; operates the port of Freetown, which has full facilities for ocean-going vessels; stevedoring operations.

Sierra Leone Road Transport Corpn: POB 1008, Freetown; tel (22) 50000; telex 3395; Chair: George Gobio Lamin; Gen Man: Abdul-Rahman Sessay; f 1964; operates road transport services throughout the country.

Utilities

Guma Valley Water Co: Guma Bldg, 13-14 Lamina Sankoh St, POB 700, Freetown; tel (22) 25887; f 1961; responsible for all existing water supplies in Freetown and surrounding villages, including the Guma dam and associated works.

SINGAPORE

Head of State

The President is elected by Parliament to serve a four-year term as a constitutional Head of State. Effective executive authority rests with the Cabinet, led by the Prime Minister, which is appointed by the President and is responsible to Parliament.

President: Wee Kim Wee (elected 30 August 1985; re-elected 31 August 1989).

Office of the President: Istana, Orchard Rd, Singapore 0922; tel 7375522.

Legislature

Legislative power is vested in the unicameral Parliament, with 81 members elected by universal adult suffrage for five years (subject to dissolution) in single- and multi-member constituencies. A 21-member Presidential Council, chaired by the Chief Justice, examines material of racial and/or religious significance to see whether it differentiates between racial or religious communities or contains provisions inconsistent with the fundamental liberties of Singapore citizens.

Parliament: Parliament House, Empress Place, Singapore 0617; tel 3368811; Speaker: Tan Soo Khoon.

MINISTRIES AND GOVERNMENT DEPARTMENTS

OFFICE OF THE PRIME MINISTER
Istana Annexe, Istana, Singapore 0923
Tel 7375133
Prime Minister: Lee Kuan Yew
First Deputy Prime Minister: Goh Chok Tong
Second Deputy Prime Minister: Ong Teng Cheong
Minister of State: Dr Yeo Ning Hong

MINISTRY OF COMMUNICATIONS AND INFORMATION
460 Alexandra Rd, PSA Bldg 39-00, Singapore 0511
Tel 2707988; telex 25500
Minister: Dr Yeo Ning Hong

MINISTRY OF COMMUNITY DEVELOPMENT
512 Thomson Rd, MCD Bldg, Singapore 1129
Tel 2589595; telex 34361
Minister: Wong Kan Seng

MINISTRY OF DEFENCE
Tanglin Rd, Singapore 1024
Tel 4741155; telex 21373
Minister: Goh Chok Tong
Second Minister (Policy): Dr Yeo Ning Hong
Second Minister (Services): Brig-Gen (retd) Lee Hsien Loong

MINISTRY OF EDUCATION
Kay Siang Rd, Singapore 1024
Tel 4739111; telex 34366
Minister: Dr Tony Tan Keng Yam

MINISTRY OF THE ENVIRONMENT
40 Scotts Rd, Environment Bldg, Singapore 0922
Tel 7327733
Minister: Dr Ahmad Mattar

MINISTRY OF FINANCE
8 Shenton Way, 43rd, 45th, 46th and 50th Storey, Treasury Bldg, Singapore 0106
Tel 2259911; telex 34371
Minister: Dr Richard Hu Tsu Tau

MINISTRY OF FOREIGN AFFAIRS
250 North Bridge Rd, Raffles City Tower 07-00, Singapore 0617
Tel 3361177; telex 21242
Minister: Wong Kan Seng
Senior Minister of State (Foreign Affairs): Yeo Cheow Tong
Minister of State: George Yong-Boon Yeo

MINISTRY OF HEALTH
16 College Rd, College of Medicine Bldg, Singapore 0316
Tel 2237777; telex 34360; fax 2241677
Minister (acting): Yeo Cheow Tong

MINISTRY OF HOME AFFAIRS
Phoenix Park, Tanglin Rd, Singapore 1024
Tel 2359111; telex 34363; fax 7344420
Minister: Prof S. Jayakumar

MINISTRY OF LABOUR
Havelock Rd, Singapore
Tel 5336141; telex 34364; fax 5344840
Minister: Lee Yock Suan

MINISTRY OF LAW
250 North Bridge Rd, Raffles City Tower 21-00, Singapore 0617
Tel 3378191; telex 34374
Minister: Prof S. Jayakumar

MINISTRY OF NATIONAL DEVELOPMENT
Telok Ayer St, 5th Storey, MND Bldg Annexe B,
Singapore 0106
Tel 2221211; telex 34369
Minister: Suppiah Dhanabalan

MINISTRY OF TRADE AND INDUSTRY
8 Shenton Way, Treasury Bldg 48-01, Singapore 0106
Tel 2259911; telex 24702
Minister: Brig-Gen (retd) Lee Hsien Loong
Minister of State: Mah Bow Tan

GOVERNMENT AGENCIES AND ORGANIZATIONS

Agriculture

Malayan Pineapple Industry Board: 10 Collyer Quay, Ocean Bldg 24-05, Singapore 0104; tel 5338827; Chair: Mohd Rusli bin Haji Hussein; f 1957; controls pineapple cultivation, canning and marketing.

Rubber Association of Singapore: 14 Collyer Quay, Singapore Rubber House 13-00, Singapore 0104; tel 5353333; telex 205544; Chair: Ling Lee Hua; Exec Sec: Gnoh Chong Hock; f 1968 to regulate, promote, develop and supervise the rubber market in Singapore, including the establishment and dissemination of official prices for all grades and types of rubber; provides clearing facilities; endorses certificates of origin and licences for packers, shippers and manufacturers.

Business and Economy

BANKING

Board of Commissioners of Currency: 79 Robinson Rd 01-01, Singapore 0106; tel 2222211; telex 24722; fax 2257671; Chair: Dr Richard Hu Tsu Tau; Dep Chair: Lee Ek Tieng; Gen Man: Lau Kim Boo; f 1967; sole currency issuing authority.

Government of Singapore Investment Corpn Pte Ltd (GSIC): 250 North Bridge Rd, Raffles City Tower 33-00, Singapore 0617; tel 3363366; telex 20484; Chair: Lee Kuan Yew; Dep Chair: Dr Goh Keng Swee; Man Dir: J. Y. Pillay; f 1981.

Monetary Authority of Singapore (MAS): 10 Shenton Way, MAS Bldg, Singapore 0207; tel 2255577; telex 28174; Chair: Dr Richard Hu Tsu Tau; Dep Chair: Dr Goh Keng Swee; Man Dir: J. Y. Pillay; regulates monetary system; performs all functions of a central bank, except the issuing of currency.

Post Office Savings Bank: 73 Bras Basah Rd, POSB Centre, Singapore 0718; tel 3393333; telex 25450; Chair: Chua Kim Yeow; Gen Man: Bertie Cheng; Govt statutory body.

FINANCIAL AGENCY

Central Provident Fund Board: 79 Robinson Rd, CPF Bldg, Singapore 0106; tel 2202422; telex 20896; fax 2290598; Gen Man: Lim Han Soon; Dep Gen Man: Chay Yee; f 1955; national provident fund.

INSURANCE

Export Credit Insurance Corpn of Singapore Ltd: 460 Alexandra Rd, 18-00 PSA Bldg, Singapore 0314; tel 2728866; telex 21524; fax 2786351; Man Dir: Foo Kok Swee; Gen Man: Kwah Thiam Hock; f 1975; 50% state-owned, 47.5% by commercial banks, 2.2% by insurance cos and 0.3% by others; provides credit insurance for trade and capital goods exports, unconditional guarantees to banks and bond issue support; subsidiaries, International Factors (Singapore) Pte Ltd and International Factors Marine (Singapore) Pte Ltd, provide financing such as factoring, hire-purchase, leasing and factory loans.

NATIONALIZED INDUSTRY

Keppel Corpn: 51 Pioneer Sector 1, Singapore 2262; state-linked co; shipbuilding and repairing.

TRADE

Customs and Excise Department: Maxwell Rd, Custom House, Singapore 0106.

Registry of Trade Marks and Patents: Colombo Court 03-02, Singapore 0617; tel 3307596; telex 28005; fax 3390252; Registrar: Ibrahim B. Burhan; f 1939; registration of trade marks and patents.

Singapore Institute of Standards and Industrial Research (SISIR): 1 Science Park Drive, SISIR Bldg, Singapore Science Park, Singapore 0511; tel 7787777; telex 28499; fax 7780086; Gen Man: Liew Mun Leong; f 1973; national standards body and research and devt organization using industrial technology to assist local industries; helps cos develop, test and refine concepts and technologies; identifies problem areas in industry, improves processes and develops new products.

Singapore Trade Development Board: 1 Maritime Sq, 10-40 (lobby D) World Trade Centre, Telok Blangah Rd, Singapore 0409; tel 2719388; telex 28617; fax 2740770; Chief Exec: Yeo Seng Teck; Dep Chief Exec: Lee Ying Cheun; Dir-Gen (Special Duties): Ridzwan Dzafir; f 1983; national agency to promote international trade; provides assistance to local and foreign cos using Singapore as trading base for activities such as third-world trade, entrepot trade, countertrade, etc; regional warehousing and distribution.

Defence

Commercial and Industrial Security Corpn (CISCO): CISCO Centre, 20 Jalan Afifi, Singapore 1440; tel 7472888; telex 50898; fax 7472275; f 1972; statutory board under the Ministry of Home Affairs; security consultancy services; security management; valuables and bullion transfer; armed escorts and patrols, etc.

Defence Forces: Singapore; Chief of Gen Staff: Col Boey Tak Hap.

Development and Planning

DEVELOPMENT

Housing and Development Board: Maxwell Rd, National Devt Bldg, POB 702, Singapore 9014; tel 2254444; telex 22020; Chair: Hsuan Owyang; f 1960; public housing authority.

Jurong Town Corpn: 5 Pulau Samulun, Jurong Town, Singapore 2260; tel 5600056; telex 35733; Chair: Yeo Seng Teck; Gen Man: Francis Mak; f 1968; statutory body responsible for developing and maintaining industrial estates.

INVESTMENT

Singapore Economic Development Board: 250 North Bridge Rd, 24-00 Raffles City Tower, Singapore 0617; tel 3362288; telex 26233; fax 3396077; Chair: Philip Yeo; Dep Chair: Chan Chin Bock; Gen Man: Tan Chin Nam; f 1961; planning, devt and co-ordination of investment in manufacturing and services; devt of local, small- and medium-sized enterprises.

Legal and Judiciary

Supreme Court: St Andrew's Rd, Supreme Court Bldg, Singapore 0617; tel 3360644; Chief Justice: Wee Chong Jin; Attorney-Gen: Tan Boon Teik; consists of the High Court, the Court of Appeal and the Court of Criminal Appeal; the Chief Justice is appointed by the Pres, acting on the advice of the Prime Minister; there are eight judges, including the Chief Justice.

Media

BROADCASTING

Singapore Broadcasting Corpn: Caldecott Hill, Andrew Rd, Singapore 1129; tel 2560401; telex 39265; fax 2538808; Chair: Dr Cheong Choong Kong; Dep Chair: Goh Kim Leong; Gen Man: Wong-Lee Siok Tin; f 1980; statutory body; collects radio and TV licence fees; runs six radio services and three TV channels.

> **SBC—Radio Singapore:** Farrer Rd, POB 60, Singapore 9128; tel 2560401; telex 39265; Gen Man: Wong-Lee Siok Tin; Dir: Chua Foo Yong; f 1936; operates six services, one for each of the official languages in English, Chinese (Mandarin), Malay and Tamil, an English-Chinese arts and culture service and a 24-hour popular music service; broadcasts 818 hours per week.

> **SBC—Television Singapore:** Farrer Rd, POB 60, Singapore 9128; tel 2560401; telex 39265; Gen Man: Wong-Lee Siok Tin; f 1963; three channels; total weekly average of 163 hours; education service of 6 hours weekly; programmes in Malay, Chinese (Mandarin), Tamil and English.

GOVERNMENT PUBLISHER

Singapore National Printers (Pte) Ltd: Publishing Sales Division, 10 Anson Rd, International Plaza 01-29, Singapore 0207; tel 22308340.

NEWS AND INFORMATION

Department of Statistics: 8 Shenton Way 10-01, Maxwell Rd, POB 3010, Singapore 0106; tel 2259911; telex 20826.

Science and Technology

Meteorological Service: POB 8, Changi Airport, Singapore 9181; tel 5457190; telex 50345; fax 5425026; meteorological services.

Tourism

Singapore Tourist Promotion Board: 250 North Bridge Rd, Raffles City Tower 36-04, Singapore 0617; tel 3396622; telex 33375; fax 3399423; Chair: Leong Chee Whye; Dir: Pek Hock Thiam; f 1964; promotion of tourism and conventions; licenses travel agents and tour guides.

Singapore Convention Bureau: 250 North Bridge Rd, Raffles City Tower 36-04, Singapore 0617; tel 3396622; telex 33375; fax 3399423; Convention Dir: Kelvin Leong; Asst Convention Dir: Polly Leong; f 1974; a division of the Singapore Tourist Promotion Board; promotes conferences, conventions, exhibitions, etc.

Transport and Communications

TELECOMMUNICATIONS

Telecommunication Authority of Singapore: Exeter Rd, Comcentre 31, Singapore 0923; tel 7343344; telex 33311; provides telecommunications and postal services; regulatory and licensing authority for telecommunications in Singapore.

TRANSPORT

Civil Aviation Authority of Singapore: Changi Airport, Singapore 1781.

Marine Department: 1 Maritime Sq 09-66, Singapore 0409; tel 2785611; telex 50287; fax 2790231; registration and surveys of ships; examination of seafaring officers; mercantile marine functions.

Mass Rapid Transit Corpn: 25K Paterson Rd, Singapore 0923; tel 7324433; telex 39954; Chair: M. Fam.

National Maritime Board: 120 Cantonment Rd, Maritime House, Singapore 0208; tel 2227311; telex 28735; fax 2227311 ext 8405; Chair: M. Coomaraswamy; Dir: Chua Lian Ho; f 1973; training, empolyment and welfare of seamen.

Neptune Orient Lines Ltd: 456 Alexandra Rd, PDS 06-00 NOL Bldg, Singapore 0511; tel 2789000; telex 51168; Chair: H. R. Hochstadt; Man Dir: Lua Cheng Eng; f 1968; liner containerized services on the Far East/Europe, Far East/North America, Straits/Australia, South Asia/Europe and South East Asia, Far East/Mediterranean routes; tankers, bulk carriers and dry cargo vessels on charter.

Port of Singapore Authority: 460 Alexandra Rd, PSA Bldg, Singapore 0511; tel 2747111; telex 21507; fax 2744677; Chair: Lim Kim San; Exec Dir: Ng Kiat Chong; Dep Exec Dir: Goon Kok Loon; f 1964; statutory board under the Ministry of Communications and Information; responsible for the provision and maintenance of port facilities and services.

Singapore Airlines Ltd (SIA): 25 Airline Rd, Airline House, Singapore 1781; tel 5423333; telex 21241; Chair: J. Y. Pillay; Man Dir: Cheong Choong Kong; f 1972; passenger services to 56 cities in 37 countries.

Utilities

Parks and Recreation Department: 7 Maxwell Rd, 5th Storey, MND Bldg Annexe B, Singapore 0106; tel 2221211; telex 22603; fax 2296422; Commr: Dr S. E. Chua; f 1976; provides and maintains parks and open spaces; undertakes tree and shrub planting; has divisions responsible for the design and devt of new parks; manages plant nurseries; botanical and horticultural research and training.

Public Works Department: Maxwell Rd, 11th Storey, MND Bldg, Singapore 0106; tel 2220044; telex 27194; fax 2220044; Dir-Gen: Dr Tan Swan Beng; f 1870; Govt's engineering authority; under the Ministry of National Development; develops and manages public works; plans, designs, constructs and manages public facilities such as roads, bridges, schools, airports, hospitals and Govt bldgs; controls the devt, construction and maintenance of bldgs in the private sector.

SOLOMON ISLANDS

Head of State

Executive authority is vested in the British monarch, as Head of State, and is exercisable by the monarch's representative, the Governor-General, who is appointed on the advice of Parliament and acts on the advice of the Cabinet. The Cabinet is composed of the Prime Minister, elected by Parliament, and other Ministers appointed by the Governor-General on the Prime Minister's recommendation. The Cabinet is responsible to Parliament.

Sovereign: HM Queen Elizabeth II (succeeded to the throne 6 February 1952).

Governor-General: Sir George Lepping (took office in July 1988; formally appointed June 1989).

Office of the Governor-General: Government House, Honiara; tel 22222; telex 66201.

Legislature

Legislative power is vested in the unicameral National Parliament, comprising 38 members elected by universal adult suffrage for four years (subject to dissolution) in single-member constituencies. The country comprises four Districts, within which there are eight local government councils, elected by universal adult suffrage.

National Parliament: National Parliament Offices, POB G19, Honiara; tel 22732; telex 66311; Speaker: Waeta Ben.

MINISTRIES AND GOVERNMENT DEPARTMENTS

OFFICE OF THE PRIME MINISTER
POB G1, Honiara
Tel 21863; telex 66311
Prime Minister: Solomon Mamaloni
Deputy Prime Minister: Danny Philip

MINISTRY OF AGRICULTURE AND LANDS
POB G13, Honiara
Tel 21621 (Agriculture), 21511 (Lands); telex 66417
Minister: Abraham Kapei

MINISTRY OF COMMERCE AND PRIMARY INDUSTRIES
POB G26, Honiara
Tel 21140; telex 66311
Minister: Edmund Andresen

MINISTRY OF EDUCATION AND HUMAN RESOURCES DEVELOPMENT
POB 584, Honiara
Tel 23900
Minister: Albert Bakele Laore

MINISTRY OF FINANCE AND ECONOMIC PLANNING
POB 26, Honiara
Tel 23700; telex 66337
Minister: Christopher Columbus Abe

MINISTRY OF FOREIGN AFFAIRS AND TRADE RELATIONS
POB G10, Honiara
Tel 22223; telex 66311
Minister: Sir Baddeley Devesi

MINISTRY OF HEALTH AND MEDICAL SERVICES
POB 349, Honiara
Tel 23600
Minister: Nathaniel Supa

MINISTRY OF HOME AFFAIRS AND PROVINCIAL GOVERNMENT
POB G11, Honiara
Tel 22262
Minister (Home Affairs): Danny Philip
Minister (Provincial Government): Nathaniel Waena

MINISTRY OF HOUSING AND GOVERNMENT SERVICES
POB G29, Honiara
Minister: Allan Qurusu

MINISTRY OF NATURAL RESOURCES
POB G24, Honiara
Tel 22944; telex 66306
Minister: Allen Paul

MINISTRY OF POLICE AND JUSTICE
POB G3, Honiara
Tel 22915; telex 66358
Minister: Allen Kemakeza

MINISTRY OF POSTS AND COMMUNICATIONS
POB G25, Honiara
Tel 21281; telex 66310
Minister: Ben Gale

MINISTRY OF TOURISM AND AVIATION
Honiara
Minister: Victor Ngele

MINISTRY OF TRANSPORT, WORKS AND UTILITIES
POB G8, Honiara
Tel 21141; telex 66352
Minister: Michael Maena

OFFICE OF THE ATTORNEY-GENERAL
Honiara
Attorney-General: Frank Kabui

GOVERNMENT AGENCIES AND ORGANIZATIONS

Agriculture and Fishing

AGRICULTURE

Livestock Development Authority (LDA): POB 525, Honiara; Gen Man: Richard Namo; f 1977.

Rural Services Project: POB 24, Honiara; tel 21200; telex 66417; Dir: Ezekiel Walaodo; f 1983; establishes support facilities for agricultural devt, including research, training, marketing and transport infrastructure.

FISHING

National Fisheries Development Ltd: POB 717, Honiara; telex 66341; Gen Man: Milton Sibisopere.

Business and Economy

BANKING

Central Bank of Solomon Islands: POB 634, Honiara; tel 21791; telex 66320; Gov: A. V. Hughes; Dep Gov: R. N. Hou; f 1983; sole bank of issue.

Development Bank of Solomon Islands: POB 760, Honiara; tel 21595; telex 66427; Man Dir: Philip Wong; f 1978; promotes rural devt.

FINANCIAL AGENCIES

Solomon Islands National Provident Fund: POB 619, Honiara.

TRADE

Commodities Export Marketing Authority: POB 54, Honiara; telex 66316; Gen Man: Solomon Ilala; sole exporter of copra; agencies at Honiara and Yandina.

Customs and Excise Division: POB G26, Honiara.

Solomons Trading Co Ltd: Mendana Ave, POB 114, Honiara.

Investment

Commercial Investment Committee: POB 64, Honiara.

Investment Corpn of Solomon Islands: POB 570, Honiara; tel 22511; telex 66337; fax 21263; Chair: Mathias Pepena; Gen Man: Eric Mason; f 1988; management of Govt investment in commercial sector; promotion and support of investment in enterprises of strategic importance, and achievement of national devt plans.

Legal and Judiciary

High Court and Court of Appeal: POB G21, Honiara; tel 21632; Pres of Court of Appeal: Peter David Connolly; Chief Justice of High Court: Gordon Roy Ward; Chief Magistrate and Registrar: Kim Stanford-Smith; appeals from the High Court go to the Court of Appeal, the members of which are senior judges from Australia, New Zealand and Papua New Guinea.

Media

BROADCASTING

Solomon Islands Broadcasting Corpn: POB 654, Honiara; tel 20051; telex 66406; fax 23159; Gen Man: Patteson Mae; f 1977; daily radio transmissions are mainly in Pidgin with some English news bulletins and programmes; a radio telecommunications system is being established in collaboration with Cable and Wireless.

GOVERNMENT PUBLISHER

Government Printing Office: POB G14, Honiara; tel 22642; telex 66337; fax 21353; Dir: P. B. O'Callaghan; f 1966.

NEWS AND INFORMATION

Statistics Office: POB G6, Honiara; tel 20354; telex 66337; collection, analysis and publication of statistical information.

Mining

Association of Mining and Exploration Cos: Honiara; Pres: Nelson Greg Young; f 1988.

Tourism

Solomon Islands Tourist Authority: POB 321, Honiara; tel 22442; telex 66436; fax 23986; Gen Man: Wilson C. Maelaua; Product Devt Man: Pye Robert Kuve; f 1970; provides tourist information, technical assistance to tourist-linked businesses, formulates and implements Govt policy.

Transport and Communications

TELECOMMUNICATIONS

Solomon Islands International Telecommunications Ltd:
POB 148, Honiara.

TRANSPORT

Solomon Islands Airlines: POB 23, Honiara; tel 20031; telex 66312; Gen Man (acting): John Baura; f 1968; internal scheduled and charter services to 27 airstrips, and scheduled services to Papua New Guinea and Vanuatu.

Solomon Islands Ports Authority: POB 307, Honiara; tel 22646; telex 66348; Chair: B. Kinika; Gen Man: Ngenomea Kabui; f 1956.

SOMALIA

Head of State

The President of the Republic, who is also Secretary-General of the Somali Revolutionary Socialist Party (SRSP), is Head of State and directs the Government with the assistance of an appointed Council of Ministers. The President is elected for a seven-year term by universal adult suffrage. The SRSP is the only legal party.

President: Maj-Gen Mohamed Siad Barre (assumed power 21 October 1969; elected President by the People's Assembly on 26 January 1980; re-elected President by popular vote on 23 December 1986).

Office of the President: People's Palace, Mogadishu; tel (1) 723.

Vice-Presidents: Lt-Gen Mohamed Ali Samater, Maj-Gen Hussein Kulmia Afrah.

Legislature

Legislative power is vested in the People's Assembly, comprising 177 members: six nominated by the President and 171 elected by universal adult suffrage for five years.

People's Assembly: People's Palace, Mogadishu; tel (1) 720; Chair of the Standing Committee: Mohamed Ibrahim Ahmed.

MINISTRIES AND GOVERNMENT DEPARTMENTS

OFFICE OF THE PRIME MINISTER
Mogadishu
Prime Minister: Lt-Gen Mohamed Ali Samater
Deputy Prime Minister: Ahmed Mohamoud Farah

MINISTRY OF AGRICULTURE
Mogadishu
Tel (1) 80716
Minister: Mohamoud Mohamed Ulusow

MINISTRY OF CIVIL AVIATION AND TRANSPORT
Mogadishu
Tel (1) 23025
Minister: Mohamed Sheikh Osman Jawar

MINISTRY OF COMMERCE AND INDUSTRY
Mogadishu
Tel (1) 33089
Minister: Bashir Farah Kahiye

MINISTRY OF DEFENCE
Mogadishu
Tel (1) 710; telex 726
Minister: Hussein Abd ar-Rahman Mattan

MINISTRY OF EDUCATION
Mogadishu
Tel (1) 35042
Minister: Abdullahi Mohamed Mireh

MINISTRY OF FINANCE AND THE TREASURY
Mogadishu
Tel (1) 33090
Minister: Mohamoud Geleh Yusuf

MINISTRY OF FISHERIES AND MARINE RESOURCES
Mogadishu
Tel (1) 32056; telex 727
Minister: Mohamed Saed Gees

MINISTRY OF FOREIGN AFFAIRS
Mogadishu
Tel (1) 721; telex 639
Minister: Ahmed Jama Abdulleh

MINISTRY OF HEALTH
Mogadishu
Tel (1) 31055; telex 776
Minister: Dr Mohamed Sheikh Ali Munasar

MINISTRY OF INFORMATION AND TOURISM
POB 1748, Mogadishu
Tel (1) 24058; telex 621
Minister: Farah Dahir Afey

MINISTRY OF INTERNAL AFFAIRS
Mogadishu
Minister: Abdulkadir Haji Mohamed

MINISTRY OF JUBA VALLEY DEVELOPMENT
POB 2945, Mogadishu
Tel (1) 80614
Minister: Ahmed Habib Ahmed
Director-General: Abdi Ali Moallin

MINISTRY OF JUSTICE AND RELIGIOUS AFFAIRS
Mogadishu
Tel (1) 36062
Minister: Sheikh Mohamed Guled

MINISTRY OF LABOUR, SOCIAL AFFAIRS AND SPORTS
Mogadishu
Tel (1) 33086
Minister: Abde Warsame Isaaq

MINISTRY OF LIVESTOCK, FORESTRY AND RANGE
Mogadishu
Tel (1) 80541
Minister: (vacant)

MINISTRY OF MARINE TRANSPORT, SEA AND PORTS
Mogadishu
Tel (1) 35064
Minister: Mohamed Saed Gees

MINISTRY OF NATIONAL PLANNING
Mogadishu
Tel (1) 80384; telex 715
Minister: Mohamed Godah Barre

MINISTRY OF POSTS AND TELECOMMUNICATIONS
Mogadishu
Tel (1) 29005; telex 615
Minister: Abukar Hassan Wehe

MINISTRY OF PUBLIC WORKS AND HOUSING
Mogadishu
Tel (1) 21051; telex 700
Minister: Mohamed Said Morgan

MINISTRY OF WATER DEVELOPMENT AND MINERAL RESOURCES
Mogadishu
Tel (1) 80980
Minister: Abdirizak Ali Elmi

GOVERNMENT AGENCIES AND ORGANIZATIONS

Agriculture

Agricultural Development Corpn: POB 930, Mogadishu; telex 713; Dir-Gen: Mohamed Farah Anshur; f 1971 by merger of previous agricultural and machinery agencies and grain marketing board; supplies farmers with equipment and materials at reasonable prices; buys Somali growers' cereal and oil seed crops.

Livestock Development Agency: POB 1759, Mogadishu; Dir-Gen: Hassan Weli Scek Hussein; brs throughout Somalia.

Somali Co-operative Movement: Mogadishu; Chair: Hassan Hawadle Madar.

Business and Economy

BANKING

Central Bank of Somalia: Corso Somalia 55, POB 11, Mogadishu; tel (1) 725; telex 604759; Gov: Omar Ahmed Omar; f 1960; bank of issue; brs in Hargeisa and Kismayu.

Commercial and Savings Bank of Somalia: Place Lagarde, POB 2004, Mogadishu; tel (1) 351252; telex 5879; Pres: Osman Haji Youssouf; Vice-Pres: Abdullahi Ahmed Afra; f 1975; 33 brs.

Somali Development Bank: Via Primo Luglio, POB 1079, Mogadishu; tel (1) 21800; telex 635; Pres: Abdulkadir Adan Mahmud; f 1968; 4 brs.

INSURANCE

Cassa per le Assicurazioni Sociali della Somalia: POB 123, Mogadishu; Dir-Gen: Hassan Mohamed Jama; f 1950; workers' compensation; 9 brs.

State Insurance Co of Somalia: POB 992, Mogadishu; telex 710; Gen Man: Abdullahi Ga'al; f 1974; brs throughout Somalia.

TRADE

National Agency of Foreign Trade: POB 602, Mogadishu; Dir-Gen: Jam aw Muse; major foreign trade agency with over 150 brs throughout the country.

Defence

Armed Forces: Mogadishu; tel (1) 710; Commdr-in-Chief: President of the Republic, Maj-Gen Mohamed Siad Barre; Chief of Staff: Adan Abdullahi Nur.

  Air Force: Mogadishu; tel (1) 80852; Commdr: Mohamed Nur Dudi.

  Army: Mogadishu; tel (1) 710.

  Navy: Mogadishu; tel (1) 31009; Commdr: Said Abdullah Omar.

National Security Service: Mogadishu; tel (1) 724; Commdr: Mohamed Jibril.

Development and Planning

State Planning Commission: POB 1742, Mogadishu; tel (1) 80385; telex 715.

Energy

Ente Nazionale Petroli (National Petroleum Agency): Via Kaml al-Din, POB 920, Mogadishu; tel (1) 605; Gen Man: Mohamed Noor Abukar.

Legal and Judiciary

Supreme Court: Mogadishu; Chair: Sheikh Ahmad Hasan; highest judicial organ, with ultimate jurisdiction in civil, criminal, administrative and auditing matters.

Media

BROADCASTING

Somali Broadcasting Service: Ministry of Information and National Guidance, POB 1748, Mogadishu; tel (1) 20947; telex 621; Dir: M. Ismail; broadcasts in Somali, English, Italian, Arabic, Swahili, Amharic, Galla and Afar.

Radio Hargiesa: POB 14, Hargiesa; Dir of Radio: Idris Egal Nur; serves the northern region; broadcasts in Somali, and relays Somali and Amharic transmissions from Radio Mogadishu.

Radio Mogadishu: Mogadishu; tel (1) 712; telex 621; Dir: Mohamed Farax Halane.

NEWS AND INFORMATION

Central Statistical Department: c/o State Planning Commission, POB 1742, Mogadishu; tel (1) 80385; telex 715; collection, analysis and publication of statistical data.

Economic, Research and Statistics Department: c/o Central Bank of Somalia, Corso Somalia 55, POB 11, Mogadishu; tel (1) 725; telex 604759; research and statistical projects.

Somali National News Agency (SONNA): POB 1748, Mogadishu; tel (1) 24058; telex 621; Dir: Mohamed Hasan Kahin.

Transport

Somali Airlines: Via Medina, POB 726, Mogadishu; tel (1) 81533; telex 3619; Pres: Mohamoud Mohamed Gulaid; Vice-Pres: Abdullahi Mohamoud Dirshe; f 1964; operates internal passenger and cargo services and international flights within Africa, to Europe and the Middle East.

Utilities

Water Development Agency: POB 525, Mogadishu; Dir-Gen: Khalif Hagi Farah.

SOUTH AFRICA

Head of State

Executive power is vested in the State President, acting on the advice of the Ministers' Council, and in consultation with the Cabinet, which is composed of Ministers appointed by the President. The President, who is also Prime Minister, is elected by an electoral college, presided over by the Chief Justice and composed of 88 members of Parliament, a majority of these members coming from the House of Assembly, which represents the white population. The black population is excluded from participation in central government.

President: Frederik Willem de Klerk (sworn in as Acting State President 15 August 1989; took office as State President 14 September 1989).

Office of the President: Union Bldgs, Private Bag X83, Pretoria 0001; tel (12) 212222; telex 322158.

Legislature

Legislative power is vested in the State President and a tricameral Parliament, consisting of the House of Assembly (178 members representing the white population), the House of Representatives (85 members representing the Coloured population), and the House of Delegates (45 members representing the Indian population). The duration of Parliament is five years. Each House is solely responsible for the legislation deemed by the President to be the 'own' affairs of its particular population group, although all legislation is subject to the final approval of the President. The country is divided into four provinces, each with an Administrator, who is appointed by the President for five years.

Parliament: Cape Town; tel (12) 403-2911; telex 520869; Speaker: Louis le Grange.

House of Assembly: Private Bag X723, Pretoria 0001; tel (12) 314-5911; telex 321424; fax (12) 323-3982.

House of Representatives: Private Bag 9114, Cape Town 8000; tel (21) 403-6911; fax (21) 419567.

House of Delegates: Malgate Bldg, Smith St, Private Bag 54330, Durban 4000; tel (31) 327-0495; telex 622344.

MINISTRIES AND GOVERNMENT DEPARTMENTS

MINISTRY OF ADMINISTRATION AND PRIVATIZATION
Private Bag X121, Pretoria 0001
Tel (12) 214411; fax (12) 322152
Minister: Dr W. J. de Villiers

MINISTRY OF AGRICULTURE
Private Bag X250, Pretoria 0001
Tel (12) 323-0924; telex 322150; fax (12) 206-3066
Minister: Jacob de Villiers

MINISTRY OF CONSTITUTIONAL DEVELOPMENT
Union Bldgs, Private Bag X645, Pretoria
Tel (12) 282665; telex 322418
Minister: Dr Gerrit van Niekerk Viljoen

MINISTRY OF DEFENCE
Armscor Bldg, 224 Visagie St, Pretoria
Tel (12) 266717; telex 320502
Minister: Gen Magnus de M. Malan

MINISTRY OF EDUCATION AND DEVELOPMENT AID
Private Bag X212, Pretoria 0001
Tel (12) 312-5911; telex 320953; fax (12) 216770
Minister: Dr Stoffel van der Merwe
Responsible for the education of all citizens who are classified as non-white by the Govt.

MINISTRY OF ENVIRONMENT AND WATER AFFAIRS
Private Bag X447, Pretoria 0001
Tel (12) 310-3911; telex 527241; fax (12) 322-2682
Minister: G. J. Kotze

Department of Water Affairs: Private Bag X313, Pretoria 0001; tel (12) 299-9111.

MINISTRY OF FINANCE
240 Vermeulen St, Pretoria
Tel (12) 260261; telex 320153
Minister: Barend J. du Plessis

MINISTRY OF FOREIGN AFFAIRS
Union Bldgs, Private Bag X152, Pretoria
Tel (12) 286912; telex 321348
Minister: Roelof F. Botha

MINISTRY OF HOME AFFAIRS AND COMMUNICATIONS
Post Office HQ Bldg, cnr Vermeulen and Bosman Sts, Private Bag X741, Pretoria 0001
Tel (12) 293-1911; telex 350013
Minister: Gene Louw

Department of Posts and Telecommunications: Private Bag X425, Pretoria 0001; tel (12) 293-1811.

MINISTRY OF JUSTICE
Sanlam Centre, 252 Andries St, Pretoria
Tel (12) 323-8581; telex 321347
Minister: Hendrik J. Coetsee

MINISTRY OF LAW AND ORDER
Civitas Bldg, Struben and Andries Sts, Pretoria 0001
Tel (12) 323-8880
Minister: Adriaan Vlok

MINISTRY OF MANPOWER
Laboria Bldg, Paul Kruger St, Pretoria
Tel (12) 267731; telex 322765
Minister: Eli Louw

MINISTRY OF MINERAL AND ENERGY AFFAIRS AND PUBLIC ENTERPRISES
Sinodale Sentrum, Visagie St, Private Bag X59, Pretoria 0001
Tel (12) 325-3700; telex 321398
Minister: Dr Dawie de Villiers

MINISTRY OF NATIONAL EDUCATION
Private Bag X122, Pretoria 0001
Tel (12) 314-6134; telex 350192; fax (12) 282849
Minister: Dr Gerrit van Niekerk Viljoen
Dir-Gen: Dr J. G. Garbers
Responsible for the education of all citizens who are classified as white by the Govt.

MINISTRY OF NATIONAL HEALTH AND POPULATION DEVELOPMENT
Civitas Bldg, Struben and Andries Sts, Private Bag X399, Pretoria 0001
Tel (12) 284773; telex 321366; fax (12) 325-5706
Minister: Dr Rina Venter

MINISTRY OF PLANNING AND PROVINCIAL AFFAIRS
Pretoria
Minister: Hermanus Kriel

MINISTRY OF TRADE, INDUSTRY AND TOURISM
Legal and General Bldg, Struben and Andries Sts, Private Bag X84, Pretoria 0001
Tel (12) 285500; telex 321353
Minister: Kent Durr

MINISTRY OF TRANSPORT, PUBLIC WORKS AND LAND AFFAIRS
Private Bag X483, Pretoria
Tel (12) 322-1343; fax (12) 294-2693
Minister: George S. Bartlett

Department of Public Works and Land Affairs: Private Bag X65, Pretoria 0001; tel (12) 205-9111.

GOVERNMENT AGENCIES AND ORGANIZATIONS

Advisory and Supervisory Bodies

Central Economic Advisory Service: Private Bag X455, Pretoria 0001; tel (12) 325-1545; fax (12) 325-1569; Chief Exec: J. P. Dreyer; Chief Economists: Dr E. Calitz, Dr D. Mullins; f 1960; co-ordinated and comprehensive economic policy analysis and planning.

Commission for Administration: Private Bag X121, Pretoria 0001; tel (12) 214411; fax (12) 322152; Chair: Dr P. J. van der Merwe; f 1912; responsible for Govt organization and public personnel admin.

National Productivity Institute: POB 3971, Pretoria 0001; tel (12) 341-1470; telex 320485; Exec Dir: Dr J. H. Visser; f 1968.

Office of the Auditor-General: Old Mutual Centre, Andries St, POB 446, Pretoria 0001; tel (12) 218320.

Procurement Administration: Private Bag X49, Pretoria 0001; tel (12) 324-1560; telex 350233; fax (12) 323-4669; Chief Dir and Chair of State Tender Board: J. C. Coetzer; f 1968; invites tenders and price quotations, submission of recommendations and other requests to the State Tender Board; conveys decisions made by the Board to all concerned and admin of contracts.

Registrar of Companies: Zanza Bldg, POB 429, Pretoria 0001.

Business and Economy

BANKING

Development Bank of Southern Africa: POB 1234, Halfway House 1685; tel (11) 313-3911; telex 425546; Chair: Dr S. S. Brand.

Land and Agricultural Bank of South Africa: Paul Kruger and Visagie Sts, POB 375, Pretoria 0001.

South African Reserve Bank: POB 427, Pretoria 0001; tel (12) 313-3911; telex 322136; fax (12) 313-3197; Gov: C. L. Stals; Senior Dep Gov: A. S. Jacobs; Dep Gov, Admin: B. P. Groenewald; Dep Gov, Foreign Functions and Economic Services: J. A. Lombard; central bank; controls the money supply and the availability of credit.

NATIONALIZED INDUSTRY

Armscor: Private Bag X337, Pretoria 0001; tel (12) 292-9111; telex 320217; fax (12) 322-0183; Exec Chair: J. G. J. van Vuuren; f 1977; 10 directly-owned subsidiaries; armaments manufacturer, arms purchaser.

TRADE

Directorate of Customs and Excise: Frans du Toit Bldg, Private Bag X47, Pretoria 0001.

Registrar of Patents, Designs, Trademarks and Copyright: Private Bag X400, Pretoria 0001; tel (12) 325-2350; telex

350168; fax (12) 323-4257; Dir: A. P. Geyser; f 1893; registration and maintenance of patents, designs, trademarks and copyright.

South African Bureau of Standards: Dr Lategan Rd, Private Bag X191, Groenkloof, Pretoria; tel (12) 481311; f 1945; responsible for the admin of national standards procedures.

Defence

South African Defence Force: Private Bag X161, Pretoria 0001; tel (12) 291-9111; telex 3721; Commdr-in-Chief: President of the Republic, Frederik Willem de Klerk; Head of Defence Forces: Gen C. L. Viljoen; Chief of Staff: Gen Jan Klopper.

Air Force: Private Bag X199, Pretoria 0001; tel (12) 269941; telex 3761; Chief: Lt-Gen J. P. B. van Loggerenberg.

Army: Private Bag X172, Pretoria 0001; tel (12) 291-2012; telex 3721; Head: Lt-Gen J. J. Geldenhuys.

Navy: Private Bag X104, Pretoria 0001; tel (12) 214911; telex 577946; Chief: Adm Glen Syndercombe.

Development and Planning

PLANNING

Board of Trade and Industry: Private Bag X753, Pretoria 0001; tel (12) 322-8244; telex 350167; fax (12) 322-0149; Chair: Dr L. P. McCrystal; Chief Exec: M. R. Heyns; f 1921; promotes economic devt in the Republic.

Industrial Development Corpn of South Africa Ltd: POB 780455, Sandton 2146; tel (11) 883-1600; telex 427174; Pres: M. T. de Waal; Man Dir: P. J. van Rooy; f 1940; provides medium- and long-term loans to assist existing enterprises, or to establish new industrial devts.

Small Businesses Development Corpn: 5 Wellington Rd, Parktown 2001; POB 4300, Johannesburg.

South African Development Trust Corpn: Karel Schoeman Bldg, 179ᴀ Skinner St, POB 213, Pretoria 0002; tel (12) 325-3300; telex 322125; fax (12) 325-3329; Chair: G. v. d. Wall; Man Dir: F. P. Weyer; f 1984; devt assistance in agricultural, mining, commerce, industry and transport sectors.

REGIONAL DEVELOPMENT

Kwazulu Finance and Investment Corpn Ltd: POB 2801, Durban; tel (31) 907-1055; telex 624406; fax (31) 907-5350; Exec Dir: Dr M. Spies; f 1978; promotion of economic devt of Kwazulu.

Lebowa Development Corpn: POB 951, Pietersburg 0700; tel (1521) 72221; telex 311021; fax (1521) 72151; Man Dir: Johan Koster; Dep Man Dir: F. Rabe; Man, Public Relations: N. G. Hulley; f 1976; industrial, commercial, economic and mining devt in Lebowa.

Qwagwa Development Corpn: Ontwikkelings Korp BPK, Phuthaditjhaba, Witsiesjoek.

Legal and Judiciary

Commissioner of Prisons: Private Bag X136, Pretoria 0001; tel (12) 285417; Commr: Gen W. H. Willemse.

Supreme Court: Private Bag 258, Bloemfontein 9300; tel (51) 472631; Chief Justice (acting): Michael Corbett; consists of an appellate division and provincial and local divisions.

Media

BROADCASTING

South African Broadcasting Corpn (SABC): Private Bag X1, Auckland Park 2006; tel (11) 714-9111; telex 424116; Chair: Prof H. C. Viljoen; Dir-Gen: Wynand J. J. Harmse; f 1936; receives revenue from advertising and licences; operates 23 radio services broadcasting in 19 languages, and four TV channels broadcasting in seven languages.

External Radio Services: POB 4559, Johannesburg 2000; tel (11) 714-2600; telex 424116; fax (11) 714-6377; Dir: Fanus Venter; f 1966; international shortwave broadcasting in 12 languages to Africa, Europe, Far East, Middle East, and North and South America.

SABC-Television: Private Bag X41, Auckland Park 2006; tel (11) 714-9111; telex 424116; transmissions began in 1976; operates TV services in seven languages over four channels.

NEWS AND INFORMATION

Bureau of Information: Private Bag X745, Pretoria 0001; tel (12) 314-9211; sole authorized source of information on matters relating to, and arising from, the state of emergency declared by the Govt in 1985.

Central Statistical Service: Private Bag X44, Pretoria 0001; tel (12) 310-8911; telex 320450; fax (12) 322-2769; f 1910; compilation and publication of national statistics.

Directorate of Publications: Pleinpark Bldg, 12th Floor, Plein St, Private Bag 9069, Cape Town 8000; tel (21) 456518; telex 521667; Dir: Dr A. Coetzee; f 1974; undertakes censorship of films and video cassettes and the examination of publs submitted to it for adjudication.

Mining and Energy

ENERGY

Atomic Energy Corpn of South Africa Ltd (AEC): POB 582, Pretoria 0001; tel (12) 324-2811; telex 321047; Chief Exec: Dr J. W. L. de Villiers; f 1982; incorporates Nuclear Development Corpn of South Africa (Pty) Ltd and Uranium Enrichment Corpn of South Africa (Pty) Ltd; conducts research into nuclear materials, nuclear power economics, reactor systems, and radio-isotopes and their applications.

Council for Nuclear Safety: POB 7106, Hennopsmeer 0046; tel (12) 663-5500; telex 320246; fax (12) 663-5512; Chair: Prof J. B. Martin; Chief Exec and Gen Man: J. O. Tattersall; f 1988; regulatory control over nuclear installations and activities involving radioactive material.

MINING

South African Coal, Oil and Gas Corpn (SASOL): POB 1, Sasolburg 9570; tel (16) 688-9111; telex 487938.

Tourism

South African Tourist Board: Menlyn Park Office Block, cnr Atterbury Rd and Menlyn Drive, Private Bag X164, Pretoria 0001; tel (12) 348-9521; telex 320457; fax (12) 348-9293; Exec Dir: Spencer V. F. Thomas.

Transport

National Transport Commission: Private Bag X193, Pretoria 0001; tel (12) 290-2506; telex 321195; fax (12) 290-2040; Commr: J. J. Smit; responsible for location, planning, design, construction and maintenance of national roads and transport services.

Safair Lines (Pty) Ltd: D. F. Malan Airport, 7525 Cape Town; tel (21) 934-0344; telex 520246; fax (21) 934-08796; Chair: Dr P. J. van Aswegen; Gen Man: G. A. Nortje; f 1962; scheduled and charter services.

South African Airways: S. A. Airways Centre, POB 7778, Johannesburg 2000; telex 425020; Chief Exec: G. D. van der Veer; f 1934; internal passenger services linking all the principal towns; regional services to other southern African countries; intercontinental services to Europe, the Far East and South America; some international services have been disrupted as a result of economic sanctions against South Africa.

THE BANTU HOMELANDS

BOPHUTHATSWANA

The Government

OFFICE OF THE PRESIDENT
Mafikeng

President: Kgosi (Chief) Lucas Manyane Mangope (took office 6 December 1977; re-elected 11 November 1984). Executive power resides in the President, who is directly elected by general suffrage. The President appoints, and acts on the advice of, an Executive Council. The Republic of Bophuthatswana has not been recognized by any Government other than that of South Africa.

LEGISLATIVE ASSEMBLY
Mafikeng

Speaker: Rev O. J. Kgaladi

Legislative power is vested in the Legislative Assembly, which is unicameral and comprises 108 members, of whom 72 are elected by popular vote, 24 are nominated by regional authorities, and 12 are designated by the President.

MINISTRY OF AGRICULTURE AND NATURAL RESOURCES
Mafikeng

Minister: P. H. Moeketsi

MINISTRY OF DEFENCE
Mafikeng

Minister: (vacant)

MINISTRY OF ECONOMIC AFFAIRS
Mafikeng

Minister: B. E. Keikelame

MINISTRY OF EDUCATION
Mafikeng

Minister: S. M. Nkau

MINISTRY OF FINANCE
Private Bag X2060, Mmabatho 8681
Tel (140) 293251; fax (140) 293268

Minister: L. G. Young
Secretary: J. P. Vermaak

MINISTRY OF FOREIGN AFFAIRS
Private Bag X2012, Mafikeng
Tel (140) 293150; telex 3068; fax (140) 23846

Minister: S. L. L. Rathebe
Secretary: I. M. Mehong

MINISTRY OF HEALTH AND SOCIAL WELFARE
Mafikeng

Minister: Dr Khaole

MINISTRY OF INTERNAL AFFAIRS
Mafikeng

Minister: Kgosi Suping

MINISTRY OF JUSTICE
Mafikeng

Minister: S. G. Mothibe

MINISTRY OF MANPOWER AND CO-ORDINATION
Mafikeng

Minister: Rev S. M. Seodi

MINISTRY OF PARLIAMENTARY AFFAIRS, LOCAL GOVERNMENT AND HOUSING
Garona Govt Bldg, Private Bag X2099, 8681 Mmabatho
Tel (140) 292238; telex 3063; fax (140) 292219

Minister: Hendrick F. Tlou
Secretary: P. H. Masibi

MINISTRY OF POPULATION DEVELOPMENT
Mafikeng

Minister: T. M. Molatlhwa

MINISTRY OF POSTS AND TELECOMMUNICATIONS
Private Bag X2001, Mmabatho 8681
Tel (140) 292101; telex 3208; fax (140) 22781

Minister: K. C. V. A. Sehume

MINISTRY OF PUBLIC WORKS
Private Bag X2037, Mmabatho 8681
Tel (140) 292939; telex 3061; fax (140) 292574

Minister: S. C. Kgobokoe

MINISTRY OF STATE AFFAIRS AND CIVIL AVIATION
Mafikeng

Minister: Rowan Cronje

MINISTRY OF WATER AFFAIRS
Mafikeng

Minister: T. M. Tlhabane

Government Agencies

BANKING

Bophuthatswana Agricultural Bank: Private Bag X2105, Mmabatho 8681; tel (140) 22123; telex 3074; fax (140) 24746; Man Dir: Willie Maree; f 1981; loan financing for the agricultural sector.

DEFENCE

Defence Force: Private Bag X2014, Mmabatho 8681; tel (140) 22141; telex 3026; fax (140) 22141; Chief of Defence: Maj-Gen H. S. Turner; Chief Support Services: Brig N. Jacobs; Chief Combat Services: Brig J. L. Jordaan; Chief of Air Force: Col M. P. van Rensburg; f 1979.

DEVELOPMENT

Bophuthatswana National Development Corpn: POB 3011, Mmabatho 8681; tel (140) 22151; telex 3055; Chair: Beau

Sutherland; Man Dir: Johan Maree; f 1975; promotes economic devt through investment in business enterprises.

MEDIA

Bophuthatswana Broadcasting: Private Bag X540, Mmabatho 8681; tel (140) 28911; telex 3049; Dir-Gen: Jonathan Proctor; operates two channels broadcasting in English and Setswana.

Bophuthatswana Pioneer: Ministry of Foreign Affairs, Private Bag X2012, Mafikeng 8670; tel (140) 292465; telex 3169; monthly English language newspaper.

Bophuthatswana Television: Private Bag X2150, Mafikeng 8670; tel (140) 22041; telex 3017; Dir: R. R. Minton; programmes in English and Setswana.

CISKEI

The Government

OFFICE OF THE COUNCIL OF STATE
Bisho
President: Brig Josh Gqozo (took office 4 March 1990). Following a military coup in March 1990, executive control was taken over by a four-person military council, which is assisted in government by a Council of State. The Republic of Ciskei has not been recognized by any Government other than that of South Africa.

NATIONAL ASSEMBLY
Bisho
The National Assembly consists of 50 members, who are elected by universal adult suffrage, and 37 hereditary chiefs.

MINISTRY OF AGRICULTURE AND WATER AFFAIRS
Bisho
Minister: V. H. Mafani

MINISTRY OF DEFENCE
Bisho
Minister: Chief D. N. Mavuso

MINISTRY OF EDUCATION
Bisho
Minister: H. Nabe

MINISTER OF FINANCE AND ECONOMIC DEVELOPMENT
Private Bag X0029, Bisho
Tel (401) 91145; fax (401) 992356
Minister: Chief M. E. P. Malefane

MINISTRY OF FOREIGN AFFAIRS
Private Bag X0014, Bisho
Tel (401) 91166; telex 250786
Minister: B. N. Pityi

MINISTRY OF HEALTH
Bisho
Minister (acting): D. M. Takane

MINISTRY OF INTERNAL AFFAIRS
Bisho
Minister: L. B. Williams

MINISTRY OF JUSTICE
Bisho
Minister: D. M. Takane

MINISTRY OF MANPOWER UTILIZATION
Private Bag X0031, Bisho
Tel (401) 999111
Minister: G. M. Mpepo

MINISTRY OF POSTS AND TELECOMMUNICATIONS
Bisho
Minister: A. A. Hoyana

MINISTRY OF PUBLIC WORKS
Bisho
Minister: Chief D. M. Jongilanga

MINISTRY OF RURAL DEVELOPMENT
Bisho
Minister: W. M. Boqwana

MINISTRY OF SOCIAL WELFARE AND PENSIONS
Bisho
Minister: A. M. Tapa

MINISTRY OF TRANSPORT
Bisho
Minister: R. R. Mali

MINISTRY OF YOUTH AFFAIRS
Bisho
Minister: V. G. Ntshinga

Government Agencies

AGRICULTURE

Ciskei Agricultural Marketing Board: POB 59, Bisho; tel (401) 92191; telex 250458; Chair: L. Ngoma; Man Dir: V. Ngcakani.

Ciskei Rural Development Council: Private Bag X501, Zwelitsha 5608; Chair: Minister of Rural Development, W. M. Boqwana.

BANKING

Ciskei People's Development Bank Ltd: Independence Blvd, POB 66, Bisho; tel (401) 92011; telex 250134; fax (401) 91442; Chair: Dr P. K. Hoogendyk; Man Dir: J. M. Sondiyazi; f 1983; promotes economic devt especially in fields of commerce and industry.

MEDIA

Ciskei Broadcasting Service: Ministry of Foreign Affairs, Private Bag X0014, Bisho; tel (401) 91166; telex 250786; Station Man: D. Tuswa; services in Xhosa, English and Afrikaans.

TRANSKEI

The Government

OFFICE OF THE PRESIDENT
Umtata
President: Paramount Chief Tutor Nyangelizwe Vulinolela Ndamase (elected 19 February 1986).
The Constitution was suspended by the Military Council following the overthrow of the civilian Government in December 1987. Political power effectively resides in the President and the Military Council until new elections are arranged for the National Assembly. The Republic of Transkei has not been recognized by any Government other than that of South Africa.

MILITARY COUNCIL
Umtata
Chair: Maj-Gen Bantu Holomisa
Secretary-General: T. M. Mbambisa
Councillors: Col Mfundiso Mordecai Ndeleleni, Lt-Col Paul Tobia, Brig E. R. G. Keswa, Maj V. P. Makhalali

MINISTER IN THE OFFICE OF THE MILITARY COUNCIL, MINISTER OF DEFENCE AND AUDIT
Umtata
Minister: Maj-Gen Bantu Holomisa

MINISTRY OF AGRICULTURE AND FORESTRY
Umtata
Minister: Chief J. M. N. Matanzima

MINISTRY OF COMMERCE, INDUSTRY AND TOURISM
Umtata
Minister: D. Mgudlwa

MINISTRY OF EDUCATION, YOUTH, CULTURE AND SPORT
Umtata
Minister: P. N. Tshaka

MINISTRY OF FINANCE AND OF THE PUBLIC SERVICE COMMISSION
Umtata
Minister (acting): M. Titus

MINISTRY OF FOREIGN AFFAIRS AND INFORMATION
Umtata
Minister: Brig E. R. G. Keswa

MINISTRY OF HEALTH
Private Bag X5005, Umtata
Tel (471) 249544
Minister: Prof Xaba-Mokoena
Director-General: G. Sineke

MINISTRY OF THE INTERIOR
Umtata
Minister: Chief B. M. Dumalisile

MINISTRY OF JUSTICE AND PRISONS
Umtata
Minister: Chief P. Ndamase

MINISTRY OF LOCAL GOVERNMENT AND LAND TENURE
Umtata
Minister (Local Government): S. A. Indazwe
Minister (Land Tenure): Chief D. D. Mlindazwe

MINISTRY OF MANPOWER PLANNING AND UTILIZATION
Umtata
Minister: Chief Z. Z. Sigcau

MINISTRY OF POLICE
Umtata
Minister: Col Mfundiso Mordecai Ndeleleni

MINISTRY OF POSTS AND TELECOMMUNICATIONS
Umtata
Minister: G. S. K. Nota

MINISTRY OF TRANSPORT
Umtata
Minister: S. P. Kakudi

MINISTRY OF WELFARE AND PENSIONS
Private Bag X6000, Umtata 5100
Tel (471) 24781
Minister: E. T. Katshunungwa

MINISTRY OF WORKS AND ENERGY
Umtata
Minister: M. Titus

Government Agencies

BANKING

Bank of Transkei Ltd: POB 30, Umtata; tel (471) 23361; telex 720; Chair: J. L. J. van Vuuren; Man: T. N. G. Boshoff.

DEVELOPMENT

Transkei Development Corpn: Private Bag X5028, Umtata; tel (471) 26881; telex 711; Chair: K. M. Mdleleni; Man Dir: M. Swann; f 1976; invests in commercial and industrial devts in partnership with local and foreign investors.

DEFENCE

Transkei Defence Force: Private Bag X5024, Umtata 5100; tel (471) 26525; telex 726; fax (471) 25946; Commdr (acting): Brig T. T. Matanzima; Chief of Staff (acting): Col M. M. Ndleleni; Staff Officer Operations and Training: Col G. T. Madikiza; Staff Officer Planning: Col D. M. Tshiki; f 1975.

LEGAL AND JUDICIARY

Transkei Supreme Court: Private Bag X5017, Umtata; Chief Justice: T. H. van Reenen; Puisne Judge (acting): D. J. Lombard; f 1976; jurisdiction over all persons and matters in Transkei.

MEDIA

Radio Transkei: POB 794, Umtata; tel (471) 2373; Man Dir: T. Mcinga; Programme Man: O. S. Maya; broadcasts in Xhosa and English.

Transkei News Agency: Umtata; telex 710.

TRANSPORT

Transkei Airways Corpn (TAC): POB 773, Matanzima Airport, Umtata; tel (471) 24451; telex 727; Chair: K. A. Fauré;

Man Dir: M. S. Pike; f 1976; services to Mzamba, Johannesburg and Durban.

VENDA

The Government

OFFICE OF THE PRESIDENT
Sibasa

President: Gota Vho-Frank N. Ravele (took office in October 1988).

Executive power is vested in the President, who is elected by the members of the National Assembly and holds office for a period not exceeding the five-year life of the Assembly. The President appoints a Cabinet of Ministers, who must all be members of the Assembly. The Republic of Venda has not been recognized by any Government other than that of South Africa.

NATIONAL ASSEMBLY
Sibasa

The unicameral Assembly normally consists of 45 members elected by popular vote, six presidential appointees, 28 mahosi (chiefs) and 15 members designated by Venda's five regional councils.

MINISTRY OF AGRICULTURE, WATER AFFAIRS AND FORESTRY
Sibasa
Minister (Agriculture and Forestry): Khosi Vho-A. M. Madzivhandila
Minister (Water Affairs): Khosi Vho-C. N. Makuya

MINISTRY OF EDUCATION AND CULTURE
Sibasa
Minister: Gota Vho-R. R. Sumbana

MINISTRY OF FINANCE, COMMERCE, INDUSTRY AND TOURISM
Sibasa
Minister: Gota Vho-E. R. B. Nesengani

MINISTRY OF FOREIGN AFFAIRS, INFORMATION AND BROADCASTING
Private Bag X2319, Sibasa
Tel (15581) 21248; telex 331583; fax (15581) 23172
Minister: Khosi Vho-C. A. Nelwamondo

MINISTRY OF HEALTH, WELFARE AND PENSIONS
Sibasa
Minister: Khosi Vho-T. A. Mulima

MINISTRY OF INTERNAL AFFAIRS AND MANPOWER
Sibasa
Minister: Khosi Vho-J. R. Rambuda

MINISTRY OF JUSTICE AND VENDA PRISONS
Private Bag X2246, Sibasa

Tel (15581) 21310; telex 331583
Minister: Khosi Vho-N. A. Mashila

MINISTRY OF TRANSPORT, PUBLIC WORKS, POSTS AND TELECOMMUNICATIONS
Sibasa
Minister: Khosi Vho-G. M. Ramabulana

MINISTRY OF URBAN AFFAIRS AND LAND TENURE
Sibasa
Minister: Khosi Vho-M. M. Mphaphuli

Government Agencies

AGRICULTURE

Venda Agricultural Corpn (Agriven): Private Bag 2346, Sibasa; tel (15581) 21141; fax (15581) 23200; f 1982; planning, promotion, co-ordination and devt of agriculture.

DEVELOPMENT

Venda Development Corpn: POB 9, Sibasa; tel (15581) 21131; telex 331718; fax (15581) 21298; Chair: Jack Botes; Chief Exec: J. S. Kruger; f 1975; planning, finance, co-ordination and promotion of industrial, commercial, mining, financial devt.

ENERGY

Venda Electricity Corpn: Private Bag X2539, Sibasa; tel (15581) 21062; telex 331953; fax (15581) 23131; Chief Exec: J. P. Rodger; Man, Finance and Admin: W. J. Botha; f 1987; maintenance of electricity supply.

MEDIA

Department of Information and Broadcasting: Private Bag X2309, Sibasa; tel (15581) 21340; telex 423317; fax (15581) 23172; Dir-Gen: L. S. Ramavhoya; Dep Dir-Gen: M. W. Madzihandila; Dir: U. M. Ramaite; f 1979; controls state publs and radio station.

Radio Thohoyandou: Private Bag X2309, Sibasa; tel (15581) 21121; Dir-Gen: N. D. Nethonanda.

SPAIN

Head of State

Spain is an hereditary monarchy, with the sovereign as Head of State. The monarch appoints the President of the Government (Prime Minister) and, on the latter's recommendation, other members of the Council of Ministers. The Government is responsible to the Cortes Generales. The Council of State, comprising 23 members is the supreme consultative organ.

Sovereign: HRH King Juan Carlos (succeeded to the throne, 22 November 1975).

Office of HM the King: Palacio de la Zarzuela, Madrid; tel (1) 2229075; telex 42003; Head of Royal Household: Gen Sabino Fernández Campo.

Council of State: Madrid; Pres: Tomás de la Cuadra Salcedo Fernández del Castillo.

Legislature

Legislative power is vested in the bicameral Cortes Generales. The Congress of Deputies comprises 350 members, elected by universal adult suffrage on the basis of proportional representation, and the Senate has 208 directly-elected members plus 49 regional representatives.All members serve four-year terms. The country consists of 50 provinces, each with its own Diputación Provincial (Council) and Civil Governor.

Senado (Senate): Plaza de la Marina Española 8, Madrid; tel (1) 9429614; telex 22318; fax (1) 5425862; Speaker: José Federico de Carvajal Pérez; Clerk: José Manuel Serrano.

Congreso de los Diputados (Congress of Deputies): Fernan Flor 1, Madrid 14; tel (1) 4295193; Pres: Félix Pons.

MINISTRIES AND GOVERNMENT DEPARTMENTS

PRIME MINISTER'S CHANCELLERY
Ministerio de Relaciones con las Cortes y de la Secretaría del Gobierno, Complejo de la Moncloa, Edif INIA, 28071 Madrid
Tel (1) 4491827; telex 22083; fax (1) 2442991
Prime Minister and President of the Council of Ministers: Felipe González Márquez

OFFICE OF THE DEPUTY PRIME MINISTER
Complejo de la Moncloa, Edif Semillas, Madrid
Tel (1) 2440200
Deputy Prime Minister: Alfonso Guerra González

MINISTRY OF AGRICULTURE, FISHERIES AND FOOD
Paseo Infanta Isabel 1, 28014 Madrid
Tel (1) 4687223; telex 47062
Minister: Carlos Romero Herrera

MINISTRY OF CULTURE
Madrid
Tel (1) 4552600; telex 27286
Minister: Jorge Semprún

MINISTRY OF DEFENCE
Paseo de la Castellana 109, Madrid 16
Tel (1) 4497000; telex 41523
Minister: Narcís Serra Serra

MINISTRY OF ECONOMY, FINANCE AND TRADE
Alcalá 9, Madrid 14
Tel (1) 2326124; telex 48387
Minister: Carlos Solchaga Catalán

MINISTRY OF EDUCATION AND SCIENCE
Alcalá 34, Madrid 14
Tel (1) 2321300; telex 23102
Minister: Javier Solana Madariaga

MINISTRY OF FOREIGN AFFAIRS
Plaza de la Provincia 1, Madrid 12
Tel (1) 2658605; telex 22645
Minister: Francisco Fernández Ordóñez

MINISTRY OF HEALTH AND CONSUMER AFFAIRS
Paseo del Prado 18-20, 28014 Madrid
Tel (1) 239700; telex 22608
Minister: Julián García Vargas

Secretaría General de Consumo (General Secretariat of Consumer Affairs): Madrid; Sec-Gen: César Braña; f 1990.

MINISTRY OF INDUSTRY AND ENERGY
Paseo de la Castellana 160, Madrid 16
Tel (1) 4588010; telex 42112
Minister: José Claudio Aranzadi Martínez

MINISTRY OF THE INTERIOR
Amador de los Rios 7 y Paseo de la Castellana 5, Madrid 4
Tel (1) 4192094; telex 46092
Minister: José Luis Corcuera

MINISTRY OF JUSTICE
San Bernando 45, Madrid 8
Tel (1) 2313070
Minister: Enrique Múgica Herzog

MINISTRY OF LABOUR AND SOCIAL SECURITY
Nuevos Ministerios, Paseo de la Castellana, 28071 Madrid
Tel (1) 2537600; telex 45843
Minister: Manuel Chaves

MINISTRY OF PUBLIC ADMINISTRATION
Paseo de la Castellana 3, 28046 Madrid
Tel (1) 4105190; telex 45567
Minister: Joaquín Almunia Amann

MINISTRY OF PUBLIC WORKS AND TOWN PLANNING
Sub Gral Relaciones Internacionales, Paseo de la
Castellana 67, 28071 Madrid
Tel (1) 2531600; telex 46388
Minister: Favier Sáenz de Cosculluela

MINISTRY OF RELATIONS WITH THE CORTES AND SECRETARIAT TO THE GOVERNMENT
Complejo de la Moncloa, Edif INIA, 28071 Madrid
Tel (1) 2440200; telex 22083; fax (1) 2442991
Minister and Secretary: Virgilio Zapatero
Chief Government Spokesperson: Rosa Conde de Espina

MINISTRY OF SOCIAL AFFAIRS
Calle de José Abascal, Madrid
Minister: Matilde Fernández

MINISTRY OF TRANSPORT, TOURISM AND COMMUNICATIONS
Nuevos Ministerios, Plaza San Juan de la Cruz 1, Madrid 3
Tel (1) 4561144
Minister of Transport and Communications:
José Barrionuevo Peña

GOVERNMENT AGENCIES AND ORGANIZATIONS

Advisory and Supervisory Bodies

Instituto Nacional de Administración Pública (INAP):
Santa Engracia 7, 28010 Madrid; tel (1) 4461700; telex 47399;
fax (1) 4450839; f 1940; selection and training of civil servants.

Organismo Nacional de Loteria y Apuestas del Estado:
Guzmán el Bueno 137, 28003 Madrid; tel (1) 2334100; lottery
and betting organization.

Registro de la Propiedad Industrial: Panamá 1, 28071
Madrid; tel (1) 4582200; registry of industrial property; under
the Ministry of Industry and Energy.

Tribunal de Cuentas: Fuencarral 81, 28027 Madrid; tel (1)
4478701; fax (1) 4467600; Pres: Pascual Sala Sánchez; supreme
financial accounting organization of the state and public sector.

Agriculture and the Environment

AGRICULTURE

**Fondo de Ordenación y Regulación de Producciones y
Precios Agrarios (FORPPA):** José Abascal 4, 7°, 28003
Madrid; tel (1) 4488000; under the Ministry of Agriculture,
Fisheries and Food; regulation of prices of agricultural products.

Instituto Andaluz de la Reforma Agraria (IARA): Avda
San Fco Javier s/n, Edif Sevilla 1, 1°, 41005 Sevilla; tel (54)
639000; Pres: Francisco Vásquez; empowered to expropriate
land under the agricultural reform programme.

THE ENVIRONMENT

**Instituto Nacional para la Conservación de la Naturaleza
(ICONA):** Gran Vía de San Francisco 35, 28005 Madrid; tel (1)
2668200; telex 48566; nature conservation.

FISHING

Secretaría General de Pesca Maritima: Ortega y Gasset 57,
28006 Madrid; tel (1) 4025000; tel 47457; fax (1) 4017940;
Sec-Gen: José Loira Rua; f 1980; national maritime fishing
secretariat.

Art and Culture

Biblioteca Nacional de España: Paseo de Recoletos 20-22,
28070 Madrid; tel (1) 2756800; fax (1) 5775634; Admin: María
Teresa Simarro; f 1712; national library.

Centro del Libro y de la Lectura: Santiago Rusiñol 8, 28040
Madrid; tel (1) 2330802.

Museo del Prado: Paseo del Prado s/n, 28014 Madrid; tel (1)
4687131.

Patrimonio Nacional: Palacio Real, Bailén s/n, 28013 Madrid;
tel (1) 2487404; fax (1) 2482691; Pres: Manuel Gómez de Pablos;
Man: Julio de la Guardia García; admin and conservation of
historical and cultural artefacts; under the Ministry of Relations
with the Cortes and Secretariat to the Government.

Business and Economy

BANKING

Banco de Crédito Agrícola (BCA): Gran Vía 19, 28013
Madrid; tel (1) 5317000; telex 47405; Pres: Luis Tarrafeta Puyal;
f 1962; wholly state-owned.

Banco de Crédito Industrial (BCI): Carrera de San Jerónimo
40, 28014 Madrid; tel (1) 4296068; telex 27586; fax (1) 4298424.

Banco de Crédito Local (BLC): Paseo del Prado 4, 28014
Madrid; tel (1) 5212840; Pres: Andrés García de la Riva; part
of Instituto de Crédito Oficial (see below).

Banco de España: Alcalá 50, 28014 Madrid; tel (1) 4469055;
telex 27783; Gov: Mariano Rubio Jiménez; f 1829; granted
exclusive right of issue in 1874; nationalized 1962; agents in
London and Paris; 52 brs.

Banco Exterior de España: Carrera de San Jerónimo 36,
28014 Madrid; tel (1) 4294477; telex 22033; Pres: Francisco
Luzón; f 1929; export finance bank; 477 brs.

Caja Postal de Ahorros: Paseo de Recoletos 5, 7, 9, 28070
Madrid; tel (1) 5327220; telex 48700; Man Dir: Baltasar
Aymerich Corominas; Sec-Gen: Manuel del Mazo Hernández; f
1909; retail banking.

Consejo Superior Bancario (Central Committee of Spanish
Banking): José Abascal 57, 28003 Madrid; tel (1) 4410611; telex
22937; Pres: Guillermo de la Dehesa; Vice-Pres: Juan Antonio
Ruiz de Alda; f 1946; banking supervisory body.

Corporación Bancaria: Alcalá 50, 28014 Madrid; tel (1)

4469055; f 1978; assumes temporary control of failed or failing banks.

FINANCIAL AGENCIES

Fondo de Garantía de Depósitos (FGD): José Ortega y Gasset 22, Madrid; tel (1) 4312902; Pres: Juan Antonio Ruiz de Alda; f 1977; deposit guarantee fund.

Instituto de Crédito Oficial—ICO (Official Institute of Credit): Paseo del Prado 4, 28014 Madrid.

INSURANCE

Comisión Liquidadora de Entidades Aseguradoras (CLEA): Serrano 51, Madrid; tel (1) 4312063; Pres: Alvaro Muñoz; empowered to dissolve and administer cos that find themselves in difficulties.

Compañía Española de Seguros de Crédito y Caución, SA: Raimundo Fernández Villaverde 61, Madrid 3; tel (1) 2536800; Pres: Jesús Serra Santamans.

Dirección General de Seguros: Paseo de la Castellana 44, 28046 Madrid; tel (1) 2768942; telex 47569; Dir-Gen: León Benelbas Tapiero; insurance supervisory body.

NATIONALIZED INDUSTRY

Instituto Nacional de Industria—INI (National Industrial Institute): Plaza Marqués de Salamanca 8, 28071 Madrid; tel (1) 4014004; telex 22213; fax (1) 2755641; Chair: Jorge Mercader Miró; Vice-Chair: Miguel Angel Feito; f 1941; public corpn; has direct or indirect control of around 700 cos in the following industrial sectors: electric power, steel manufacture, mining, defence, shipbuilding, capital equipment, aluminium, electronics, automotive industry, fertilizers, air and sea transport, engineering and construction, paper, handicrafts, foreign trade, financial services and industrial promotion; investment policy includes the modernization of industry, supply of energy, research and exchange of technology, promotion of exports and the expansion of regional industrialization.

TRADE

Consejo Asesor de Exportación (CAE): Secretaría de Estado de Comercio, Dirección General de Comercio Exterior, Paseo de la Castellana 162, 28046 Madrid; tel (1) 4566734; telex 27701; fax (1) 4581766; Pres: Minister of Economy, Finance and Trade, Carlos Solchaga Catalán; f 1987; export promotion; 18 mems.

Instituto Español de Comercio Exterior (ICEX): Paseo de la Castellana 14, 28046 Madrid; tel (1) 4311240; telex 44838; fax (1) 4316128; f 1982; fmrly INFE; state institute for export promotion.

Instituto Nacional del Consumo: Príncipe de Vergara 54, 28006 Madrid; tel (1) 4311836; fax (1) 2763927; Pres: César Braña Pino; Dir-Gen: Ana Corcés; f 1975; educates and informs consumers; quality control; devt of consumer associations.

Defence

Armed Forces: Vitruvio 1, Madrid 6; tel (1) 2612800; Commdr-in-Chief: King Juan Carlos; Chief of the Gen Staff: Gen Gonzalo Puigcerver Roma.

Air Force: Plaza de la Moncloa, Madrid 34; tel (1) 4490700; telex 27721; Chief of Staff: Air Chief Marshal Federico Michavila Pallarés.

Army: Prim 4, Madrid 4; tel (1) 2212961; telex 22069; Chief of Staff: Gen Miguel Iñiguez del Moral.

Navy: Montalván 2, Madrid 14; tel (1) 2226510; telex 27416; Chief of Staff: Adm Fernando María Nardiz Vial.

Dirección General de la Guardia Civil: Guzmán el Bueno 110, 28003 Madrid; tel (1) 2347766.

Dirección General de la Policía: Miguel Angel 5, 28010 Madrid; tel (1) 4103219.

Dirección General de Protección Civil: Evaristo San Miguel 8, 28008 Madrid; tel (1) 4468162.

Secretaría de Estado para la Seguridad—Dirección de la Seguridad de Estado: Amador de los Ríos 5, 28010 Madrid; tel (1) 4193900.

Development and Planning

PLANNING

Dirección General de Planificación: Paseo de la Castellana 162, CP 632, 28046 Madrid; tel (1) 5639690; telex 27701; fax (1) 5639630; planning office.

Instituto Nacional de Reforma y Desarrollo Agrario—IRYDA (National Institute for Agrarian Reform and Development): Paseo de la Castellana 112, 28046 Madrid; tel (1) 5816100; telex 48979; fax (1) 4113770; Structures Sec-Gen: Jesús Arango Fernández; IRYDA Sec-Gen: Conrado Herrero Gómez; f 1972; agricultural production technology and rural devt; implementation in Spain of the EEC's sociostructural policy; under the Ministry of Agriculture.

REGIONAL DEVELOPMENT

Instituto de Fomento de Andalucía (IFA): Avda San Francisco Javier 15, Edif Capitolio, 3a°, 41005 Sevilla; tel (54) 661711; telex 72706; incorporates Instituto para la Promoción Industrial en Andalucía (IPIA).

Instituto Madrileño de Desarrollo (IMADE): García de Paredes 92, 28010 Madrid; tel (1) 4102063; telex 44594; Dir-Gen: José Carlos López; f 1984; public devt institution for the Madrid region.

Sociedad para el Desarrollo Industrial de Andalucía (SODIAN): República Argentina 29 accessorio, Sevilla 11; tel (54) 278705.

Sociedad para el Desarrollo Industrial de Canarias (SODICAN): Lagasca 88, Madrid 1; tel (1) 2766386; telex 42121; Pres: Daniel Viera León.

Sociedad para el Desarrollo Industrial de Extremadura (SODIEX): Dr Marañon 2, Cáceres; tel (27) 227700; telex 28950; f 1977.

Sociedad para el Desarrollo Industrial de Galicia, SA (SODIGA): Orense 6, La Rosaleda, 15701 Santiago de Compostela; tel (81) 566100; telex 88454.

Education and Research

Secretaría de Estado de Universidades e Investigación (Secretariat of State for Universities and Research): Serrano 150, 28006 Madrid; tel (1) 4113159.

Health and Welfare

HEALTH

Instituto Nacional de la Salud (INSALUD): Alcalá 56, 28071 Madrid; tel (1) 5212518; Pres: José Luis Fernandez Noriega; Dir-Gen: Jesús Gutiérrez Morlote; national health institute.

WELFARE

Consejo de la Juventud de España (CJE): Monte Esquinza 42 Bajo Derecha, 28010 Madrid; tel (1) 3081605; fax (1) 3083484; Chair: José Felix García Calleja; f 1983; encourages young people to participate in youth associations; organizes seminars and activities for young people.

Instituto de la Mujer: Almagro 36, 28010 Madrid; tel (1) 4105112; telex 49156; fax (1) 3199178; Dir: Carmen Reyes; f 1983; under Ministry of Social Affairs; equal opportunities devt and advancement of women; runs advisory centres on women's rights.

Instituto Nacional de la Seguridad Social (INSS): Padre Damián 4, 28036 Madrid; tel (1) 4501900; national social security institute.

Instituto Nacional de Servicios Sociales (INSERSO): Agustín de Foxá 31, 28036 Madrid; tel (1) 7333600; social services institute.

Organización Nacional de Ciegos Españoles (ONCE): Prado 24, 28014 Madrid; tel (1) 4299642; Dir-Gen: Miguel Durán; national organization for the blind.

International Affairs

Instituto de Cooperación Iberoamericana: Avda de los Reyes Católicos 4, Ciudad Universitaria, 28040 Madrid; tel (1) 2445816; under the Ministry of Foreign Affairs.

Secretaría de Estado para las Comunidades Europeas (Secretariat of State for the European Community): Palacio de la Trinidad, Francisco Silvela 82, 28028 Madrid; tel (1) 2467001; under the Ministry of Foreign Affairs.

Legal and Judiciary

Audiencia Nacional (National High Court): García Gutiérrez 1, Madrid 4; tel (1) 4101941; Pres: Fernando de Mateo Lage; established in 1977 to supplement the functions of the Tribunal Supremo and Audiencias Territoriales; consists of a Tribunal for Criminal Matters, and one for Legal Administration, each with its president and respective judges; deals primarily with crimes associated with a modern industrial society; three Central Courts of Proceedings are attached.

Consejo General del Poder Judicial—CGPJ (General Council of Judicial Power): Paseo de la Habana 140, 28071 Madrid; tel (1) 4575000; telex 42087; fax (1) 4579571; Pres: Antonio Hernández Gil; Vice-Pres: Manuel Peris Gómez; Sec-Gen: Juan Solé Marí Tárrega; f 1980; comprises 20 mems elected (since 1985) by the Cortes for a five-year term (10 by the Congress of Deputies and 10 by the Senate); supervises the judicial system; independent of the Ministry of Justice.

Defensor del Pueblo (Office of the Attorney-General): Eduardo Dato 31, 28010 Madrid; tel (1) 4106666; telex 49194; fax (1) 4194171; Defensor del Pueblo (Attorney-Gen): Leopoldo Torres Boursault; First Asst: Margarita Retuerto Buades; Second Asst: Soledad Mestre García; Sec-Gen: Rafael García

Ormaechea; f 1982; control of public admin; defence of fundamental rights.

Tribunal Central de Trabajo: General Martínez Campos 27, 28010 Madrid; tel (1) 4193103; labour tribunal.

Tribunal Constitucional: Doménico Scarlatti 6, 28003 Madrid; tel (1) 4490400; constitutional tribunal.

Tribunal Supremo (Supreme Court): Palacio de Justicia, Plaza de la Villa de París s/n, Madrid 4; tel (1) 4194767; Pres: Antonio Hernández Gil; Fiscal-Gen: Leopoldo Torres Boursault; composed of six tribunals, each with its pres and its respective judges.

Media

BROADCASTING

Canal Sur: Sevilla; Dir: Francisco Cervantes; commenced transmissions in 1989; regional station for Andalucía; controlled by RTVE.

Catalunya Ràdio: Avda Diagonal 614-616, 08021 Barcelona; tel (3) 2019911; telex 97325; fax (3) 2006224; Dir: Lluís Oliva; run by Catalan autonomous Govt; 3 channels.

Compañía de Radio Televisión de Galicia (CRTVG): Apdo 707, San Marcos, 15780 Santiago de Compostela; tel (81) 564400; telex 86297; Dir-Gen: Abilio Bernaldo de Quirós; f 1985; Galician language station.

Corporación Catalana de Ràdio i Televisió (CCRTV): Avda Diagonal 477, 7°, 08036 Barcelona; tel (3) 4209696; telex 97012; fax (3) 410795; Dir-Gen: Joan Granados i Duran; f 1983; Catalan language station.

Euskadi Irratia: Andía 13, 7°, 20004 San Sebastián; tel (43) 423630; Dir: José María Otermín Urtizberea; run by Basque autonomous Govt.

Euskal Irrati Telebista—EITB (Radiotelevisión Vasca—RTV): Barrio Iurreta s/n, 48200 Durango; tel (4) 6816600; telex 34440; Dir-Gen: Josu Ortuondo Larrea; f 1983; Basque language station.

Euskal Telebista—ETB (TV Vasca): Barrio Iureta s/n, 48200 Durango; tel (4) 6816600; telex 34441; Dir: Josu Ortuondo Larrea; f 1983; broadcasts in northern Spain in Basque language on ETB-1 and in Spanish on ETB-2; controlled by RTVE.

Radio Exterior de España (REE): Casa de la Radio, Prado del Rey, 28032 Madrid; tel (1) 7112742; telex 27366; fax (1) 7112906; Dir: Homero Valencia; foreign service of RNE (see below); comprises a service in Spanish broadcasting to Europe, Australia and the Philippines, North and South America and the Atlantic, and the International Service which broadcasts in English, to Europe and America, in French to Europe, North Africa and the Middle East, and in Arabic and Spanish to North Africa and the Arab states.

Radio Nacional de España (RNE): Casa de la Radio, Prado del Rey, 28032 Madrid; tel (1) 7112742; telex 27366; fax (1) 7112906; Dir-Gen: Enric Sopena; Man Dir: Ramón García-Rubio; f 1937; production and broadcast of radio programmes; 22 regional stations.

Ràdio Televisió Valenciana (RTVV): Avda de Blasco Ibáñez 34, 46022 Valencia; tel (6) 3710055; Dir-Gen: Amadeu Fabregat; f 1984.

RTG—A Radio Galega: Pazo de San Caetano s/n, Santiago de Compostela; tel (81) 562323; telex 86225; fax (81) 561150; Dir: Ignacio Rodríguez Iglesias; f 1985; run by Galician autonomous Govt.

RTVE—Radiotelevisión Española: Casa de la Radio, Prado del Rey, 28023 Madrid; tel (1) 2186529; telex 27366; Dir-Gen: Jordi Garcí Candau; controls and co-ordinates radio and TV; legislation relating to the ending of TVE's monopoly and the regulation of private TV stations was approved in April 1988;

the establishment of three new national channels was envisaged; a new regulatory body, Red Técnica Española de Televisión (Retevisión) was to be established.

Televisió de Catalunya, SA: Jacint Verdaguer s/n, Sant Joan Despí, 08970 Barcelona; tel (3) 4730333; telex 53280; fax 4730671; Dir: Jaume Ferrús; Dir, Programming: Jaume Santacana; f 1984; runs two TV channels, broadcasting in Catalan over north-eastern Spain and Andorra.

Televisión Española (TVE): Prado del Rey, Apdo 26002, 28023 Madrid; tel (1) 7110400; telex 27694; Dir: Ramón Colom; broadcasts on TVE-1 and TVE-2; 15 regional centres.

Televisión de Galicia (TVG): Apdo 707, San Marcos, 15780 Santiago de Compostela; tel (81) 564400; telex 86243; Dir: Xerardo Rodríguez Rodríguez; f 1985; broadcasts in Galician; controlled by CRTVG.

GOVERNMENT PUBLISHERS

Boletín Oficial del Estado: Trafalgar 27, 28071 Madrid; tel (1) 4466000; fax (1) 5933916; Dir-Gen: Carmen Salanueva Urtiaga; Sec-Gen: Alfonso Marina Hernando; f 1661; publication of the official journal and legal and legislative publs; under the Ministry of Relations with the Cortes and Secretariat to the Government.

Servicio Central de Publicaciones: Ayala 5, 4°, 28001 Madrid; tel (1) 4487000; under the Ministry of Relations with the Cortes and Secretariat to the Government.

NEWS AND INFORMATION

Agencia EFE, SA: Espronceda 32, Apdo 1112, 28003 Madrid; tel (1) 4415599; Pres and Dir-Gen: Alfonso Sobrado Palamares; f 1939; national and international news agency; 59 offices and correspondents abroad; sports, features and photographic branches.

Instituto Nacional de Estadística: Paseo de la Castellana 183, 28046 Madrid; tel (1) 2799300; telex 22224.

Mining and Energy

ENERGY

Centro de Investigaciones Energéticas, Medioambientales y Tecnológicas (CIEMAT): Avda Complutense 22, 28040 Madrid; tel (1) 3466000; telex 23555; Pres: Fernando Maravall Herrero; Dir-Gen: José Angel Azuara Solís; f 1951; 2,087 mems; research and devt.

Consejo de Seguridad Nuclear (CSN): Sor Angela de la Cruz 3, Madrid; tel (1) 4561812; nuclear safety council.

Empresa Nacional de Electricidad, SA: Velázquez 132, Madrid; tel (1) 2614176; under the state holding co, INI (see above); partially privatized in 1988; the major producer of electricity in the north of Spain.

Empresa Nacional Hulleras del Norte, SA (HUNOSA): Avda de Galicia 44, 33005 Oviedo; Pres: J. Tesoro Oliver; Man: J. R. Madera Fernández; wholly owned by the state holding co, INI (see above); coal-mining in the Asturías region.

Empresa Nacional del Uranio, SA (ENUSA): Santiago Rusiñol 12, 28040 Madrid; tel (1) 2336207; telex 43042; fax (1) 2336953; Pres: José Manuel Jiménez Araña; f 1972; production of uranium concentrates; procurement of nuclear fuel, etc.

Instituto Nacional de Hidrocarburos: Paseo de la Castellana 89, 28046 Madrid; tel (1) 3488100; telex 48162; fax (1) 4557671; Chair: Oscar Fanjul; Vice-Chair: Guzman Solana; f 1981; holding co for oil, gas and petrochemical cos:

Empresa Nacional de Gas (Enagás): Avda América 38, 28028 Madrid; tel (1) 2457100; telex 4448; Chair: Juan Badosa; state gas co.

Repsol, SA: Paseo de la Castellana 89, 28046 Madrid; tel (1) 4565300; telex 48162; Chair: Oscar Fanjul; f 1987 following reorganization of oil interests; 26.58% of capital sold to private shareholders in May 1989; direct and indirect interests in more than 50 cos; four directly-owned subsidiaries:

Repsol Butano: Arcipreste de Hita 10, 28015 Madrid; tel (1) 3486622; telex 27358; fax (1) 4490881; Chair: Alejandro Cachán; f 1958, fmrly Butano; distribution of LPG and natural gas.

Repsol Exploración: Pez Volador 2, 28007 Madrid; tel (1) 2747200; telex 49544; Chair: Carlos Payá; fmrly Hispanoil.

Repsol Petróleo: José Abascal 4, 28003 Madrid; tel (1) 4465200; telex 27568; Chair: Juan Sancho; fmrly EMP; interests in Campsa, Repsol Distribución and Repsol Derivados.

Repsol Química, SA: Juan Bravo 3B, 28006 Madrid; tel (1) 3488500; telex 49840; fax (1) 2768028; Chair: Javier de la Peña; f 1987, fmrly Alcudia; manufacture and sale of chemical and petrochemical products.

MINING

Empresa Nacional Carbonífera de Sur, SA: Monte Esquinza 24, Madrid; tel (1) 4191494; state-owned mining co producing coal in central Spain.

Instituto Tecnológico Geominero de España (ITGE): Ríos Rosas 23, 28003 Madrid; tel (1) 4416500; telex 48054; fax (1) 4426216; Dir-Gen: Dr Emilio Llorente Gómez; f 1849; geology; underground water; mining; environment.

Science and Technology

Consejo Superior de Investigaciones Científicas: Serrano 113, 28006 Madrid; tel (1) 2615001; telex 42182.

Instituto Geográfico Nacional: General Ibáñez de Ibero 3, 28003 Madrid; tel (1) 2333121; telex 23465; fax (1) 2546743; Dir-Gen: Angel Arévalo Barroso; Sec-Gen: José Fernández Vega; f 1870; astronomy, geophysics, mapping and metrology.

Instituto Nacional de Meteorología: Paseo de las Moreras s/n, Ciudad Universitaria, 28040 Madrid; tel (1) 5819882; fax (1) 5819845; meteorological institute.

Telecommunications

Dirección General de Correos y Telegrafos: Palacio de Comunicaciones, Plaza de la Cibeles s/n, 28070 Madrid; tel (1) 2315039; under Ministry of Transport, Tourism and Communications.

Dirección General de Medios de Comunicación Social: Ayala 5, 28001 Madrid; tel (1) 4487000; telex 47092; under the Office of the Government Spokesperson.

Dirección General de Telecomunicaciones: CCP de Chamartín, 28070 Madrid; tel (1) 7335500; telex 44100; fax (1) 7333684; Dir: Javier Nadal Ariño; f 1985; admin of telecommunications; under Ministry of Transport, Tourism and Communications.

Secretaría General de Comunicaciones: Palacio de Comunicaciones, Plaza de Cibeles s/n, 28070 Madrid; tel (1) 5323368; telex 23334; Sec-Gen: Carmen Mestre Vergara; f 1985; telecommunications authority.

Telefónica de España, SA: Gran Via 28, Apdo 753, 28013 Madrid; tel (1) 004; telex 27320; Chair: Cándido Velázquez; f

1924; partly state-owned; provides telecommunications services.

maintenance and admin of civil airports and aerodromes.

Tourism

Secretaría General de Turismo: María de Molina 50, 28001 Madrid; tel (1) 4114014; telex 23100; Sec-Gen: Ignacio Fuejo Lago.

Turespaña: María de Molina 50, 28006 Madrid; tel (1) 4114014; telex 23100; Pres: Ignacio Fuejo; Dir-Gen: Julio Rodríguez Aramberri; fmrly Inprotur; autonomous organization.

Transport

CIVIL AVIATION

Aeropuertos Españoles: Arturo Soria 109, 28043 Madrid; tel (1) 4156912; under Ministry of Transport, Tourism and Communications.

Líneas Aéreas de España, SA—IBERIA (Airlines of Spain): Velásquez 130, 28006 Madrid; tel (1) 2619500; telex 27775; Pres: Narcís Andreu; f 1927; domestic and international passenger and freight services to Africa, Europe, North, Central and South America, the Middle East and Japan.

Aviación y Comercio, SA (AVIACO): Calle Maudes 51, 28003 Madrid; tel (1) 3543600; telex 27641; Pres: Narcís Andreu; Exec Vice-Pres: Manuel Esteve Ríos; f 1948; subsidiary of IBERIA; scheduled internal services and national and international charter flights.

Spanish Airports Authority: Arturo Soria 109, Madrid; tel (1) 4156862; telex 44533; fax (1) 4161647; Dir-Gen: Juan Rosas; f 1958; responsible for the management, co-ordination, devt,

RAILWAYS

Red Nacional de los Ferrocarriles Españoles—RENFE (National System of Spanish Railways): Avda Pío XII s/n, 28036 Madrid; tel (1) 7336200; telex 27632; Pres: Julián García Valverde.

ROADS

Dirección General de Carreteras—Servicio de Tele-Ruta: Paseo de la Castellana 67, 28071 Madrid; tel (1) 2531600; under Ministry of Public Works and Town Planning.

Dirección General de Trafico: Josefa Valcárcel 28, 28027 Madrid; tel (1) 7428492; telex 44510; fax (1) 7425380; Dir-Gen: Miguel Maria Muñoz Medina; f 1959; traffic and road safety; under Ministry of the Interior.

Empresa Nacional de Transportes por Carretera: Avda Aragón, 28022 Madrid; tel (1) 7501000; fax (1) 7479531; f 1985; road transport organization.

SHIPPING

Dirección General de la Marina Mercante: Ruíz de Alarcón 1, 28014 Madrid; tel (1) 5229932; telex 27298; merchant navy directorate.

Empresa Nacional Elcano de la Marina Mercante: General Martínez Campos 46, 28010 Madrid; tel (1) 4195222; telex 27708; Pres: Javier Targhetta Roza; runs bulk carriers and tankers; controlled by INI (see above).

SPANISH EXTERNAL TERRITORIES

CEUTA

The Government

DELEGACIÓN DEL GOBIERNO
Beatriz de Silva 4, Ceuta
Tel (56) 51-25-23
Mayor of Ceuta: Fructuoso Miaja Sánchez
Government Delegate in Ceuta: Pedro-Miguel
González Márquez
Commandant-General: Juan Pérez Crucells

Government Agency

TRADE

**Cámara Oficial de Comercio, Industria y Navegación de
Ceuta:** Muelle Dato s/n, 11701 Ceuta; tel (56) 511815; fax (56)
518208; Pres: José M. Campos Martínez; Sec-Gen: Francisco
Olivencia Ruiz; f 1906; chamber of commerce, industry and
navigation.

MELILLA

The Government

DELEGACIÓN DEL GOBIERNO
Plaza de España s/n, Melilla
Tel (52) 68-14-51
Mayor of Melilla: Gonzalo Hernández Martínez
Government Delegate in Melilla:
Manuel Céspedes Céspedes
Commandant-General: José Jiménez Pérez de Larraya

Government Agency

TRADE

Cámara Oficial de Comercio, Industria y Navegación:
Cervantes 7, 29801 Melilla; tel (52) 68-48-40; Pres: Francisco
Marqués Vivancos; Sec-Gen: Ramón Martínez Jurado; f 1906;
chamber of commerce, industry and navigation.

SRI LANKA

Head of State

Executive power is vested in the President, who is directly elected for a term of six years. The President is not accountable to Parliament and has the power to appoint and dismiss the Prime Minister and other Cabinet members, and to dismiss Parliament. Any portfolio may be assumed by the President.

President: Ranasinghe Premadasa (took office 2 Jan 1989).

President's Secretariat: Republic Sq, Colombo 1; tel (1) 24801.

Legislature

The unicameral Parliament is the supreme legislative body; representatives are directly elected by a system of modified proportional representation. The number of representatives is determined by a Delimitation Commission and stood at 225 in 1989.

House of Parliament: Parliamentary Complex, Sri Jayewardenepura Kotte, Battaramulla; tel (1) 564100; Speaker E. L. Senanayake.

MINISTRIES AND GOVERNMENT DEPARTMENTS

PRIME MINISTER'S OFFICE
58 Sir Ernest de Silva Mawatha, Colombo 7
Tel (1) 36281
Prime Minister: Dingiri Banda Wijetunga

MINISTRY OF AGRICULTURE
73/1 Galle Rd, Colombo 3
Tel (1) 26346; telex 21434
Minister: Lalith Athulathmudali

MINISTRY OF COCONUT INDUSTRIES
320 T. B. Jayah Mawatha, Colombo 10
Tel (1) 598289
Minister: (vacant)

MINISTRY OF CO-OPERATIVES
330 Union Place, Colombo 2
Tel (1) 21211; telex 1170
Minister: Lalith Athulathmudali

MINISTRY OF CULTURAL AFFAIRS
34 Malay St, Colombo 2
Tel (1) 545777
Minister: W. J. M. Lokubandara

MINISTRY OF DEFENCE
Republic Bldg, Colombo 1
Tel (1) 25371; telex 21139
Minister: President Ranasinghe Premadasa

MINISTRY OF EDUCATION
255 Bauddhaloka Mawatha, Colombo 7
Tel (1) 25371; telex 83417
Minister: W. J. M. Lokubandara

MINISTRY OF FINANCE AND PLANNING
Galle Face Secretariat, Colombo 1
Tel (1) 33937; telex 21409
Minister: Dingiri Banda Wijetunga

MINISTRY OF FISHERIES AND AQUATIC RESOURCES
New Secretariat, Maligawatte, Colombo 10
Tel (1) 546183; telex 21419
Minister: Joseph Michael Perera

MINISTRY OF FOREIGN AFFAIRS
Republic Bldg, Colombo 1
Tel (1) 25371; telex 21139
Minister: Ranjan Wijeratne

MINISTRY OF HEALTH
Inland Revenue Bldg, Sir Chittampalam A. Gardiner Mawatha, Colombo 2
Tel (1) 21121
Minister: Renuka Herath

MINISTRY OF HIGHER EDUCATION, SCIENCE AND TECHNOLOGY
18 Ward Place, Colombo 7
Tel (1) 93916
Minister: A. C. S. Hameed

MINISTRY OF HIGHWAYS
Sethsiripaya, Sri Jayewardenepura Kotte, Battaramulla
Tel (1) 562721
Minister: Wijepala Mendis

MINISTRY OF HOME AFFAIRS
Secretariat, Independence Sq, Colombo 7
Tel (1) 596211
Minister: U. B. Wijekoon

MINISTRY OF INDUSTRIES
48 Sri Jinaratana Rd, Colombo 2
Tel (1) 27551; telex 21248
Minister: Ranil Wickremasinghe

Janatha Estates Development Board: 55/57 Vauxhall Rd, Colombo 2; tel (1) 24083; telex 21276.

MINISTRY OF INTERNAL SECURITY
Republic Bldg, Colombo 1
Tel (1) 34081
Minister: (vacant)

MINISTRY OF JUSTICE
Hulftsdorp, Colombo 12
Tel (1) 23979
Minister: M. Vincent Perera

MINISTRY OF LABOUR
2nd Floor, Labour Secretariat, Narahenpita, Colombo 5
Tel (1) 81991; telex 22234
Minister: Dr Ranjith Atapattu

MINISTRY OF LANDS, IRRIGATION AND MAHAWELI DEVELOPMENT
500 T. B. Jayah Mawatha, Colombo 10
Tel (1) 545396; telex 21338; fax (1) 584984
Minister: P. Dayaratne
F 1977; responsible for Govt policies on the devt of land, irrigation and the Mahaweli river basin.

MINISTRY OF LOCAL GOVERNMENT, HOUSING AND CONSTRUCTION
Sethsiripaya, Sri Jayewardenepura Kotte, Battaramulla
Tel (1) 562721
Minister: B. Sirisena Cooray

MINISTRY OF PARLIAMENTARY AFFAIRS
33 Torrington Place, Colombo 7
Tel (1) 94213
Minister: M. Vincent Perera

MINISTRY OF PLANTATION INDUSTRIES
349 Galle Rd, Colombo 3
Tel (1) 573263
Minister: Gamini Dissanayake

MINISTRY OF POLICY PLANNING AND IMPLEMENTATION
7th and 8th Floors, North Tower, Central Bank Bldg, Colombo 1
Tel (1) 547358
Minister: Ranasinghe Premadasa

MINISTRY OF POSTS AND TELECOMMUNICATIONS
Old CTO Bldg, Lotus Rd, Colombo 1
Tel (1) 22951; telex 21490
Minister: Alick Aluvihare

MINISTRY OF POWER AND ENERGY
50 Sir Chittampalam A. Gardiner Mawatha, Colombo 2
Tel (1) 422051
Minister: Festus Perera
F 1980; responsible authority for Ceylon Electricity Board, Ceylon Petroleum Corpn, the Government Business Undertaking of Colombo Gas and Water Co, Atomic Energy Authority, Energy Conservation Fund and Lanka Electricity Co.

MINISTRY OF PUBLIC ADMINISTRATION
Secretariat, Independence Sq, Colombo 7
Tel 596211
Minister: U. B. Wijekoon

MINISTRY OF REGIONAL DEVELOPMENT
244 Galle Rd, Colombo 4
Tel (1) 580146
Minister: (vacant)

MINISTRY OF REHABILITATION
1 York St, Colombo 1
Tel (1) 34262
Minister: (vacant)

MINISTRY OF RURAL DEVELOPMENT
Independence Sq, Colombo 7
Tel (1) 596007
Minister: (vacant)

MINISTRY OF RURAL INDUSTRIAL DEVELOPMENT
45 St Michael's Rd, Colombo 3
Tel (1) 540221
Minister: S. Thondaman

MINISTRY OF SOCIAL SERVICES
307 T. B. Jayah Mawatha, Colombo 10
Tel (1) 94438
Minister: Dr Ranjith Atapattu

MINISTRY OF STATE PLANTATIONS
18 Gregory's Rd, Colombo 7
Tel (1) 31747
Minister: (vacant)

MINISTRY OF TEXTILE INDUSTRIES
Torrington Sq, Colombo 7
Tel (1) 596675
Minister: S. Thondaman

MINISTRY OF TRADE AND SHIPPING
21 Rakshana Mandlraya, Vauxhall St, Colombo 2
Tel (1) 35601; telex 21245
Minister: A. R. Mansoor

MINISTRY OF TRANSPORT
1 D. R. Wijewardene Mawatha, POB 588, Colombo 10
Tel (1) 33311
Minister: Wijepala Mendis

MINISTRY OF YOUTH AFFAIRS AND SPORTS
4th Floor, 111/1 Inland Revenue Bldg, Sir Chittampalam A. Gardiner Mawatha, Colombo 2
Tel (1) 22263
Minister: Nanda Mathew

OFFICE OF THE MINISTER OF STATE FOR INDIGENOUS MEDICINES
385 Deans Rd, POB 522, Colombo 10
Tel (1) 597344
Minister of State: H. B. Wanninayake
Aims to develop and strengthen the practice of indigenous medicines, and to encourage the cultivation of medicinal plants, trees and herbs; responsible for Dept of Ayurveda, Sri Lanka Ayurvedic Drugs Corpn, College of Indigenous Medicine, Bandaranaike Memorial Ayurveda Research Inst, Ayurveda Medical Council.

GOVERNMENT AGENCIES AND ORGANIZATIONS

Agriculture

Ceylon Fisheries Corpn: Rock House Lane, Mutwal, Colombo 15; tel (1) 523326; Chair: A. R. Weeraratne; f 1964; exports fish and fish products; principal harbours at Mutwal and Galle.

Coconut Development Authority: 11 Duke St, Colombo 1; tel (1) 21025; telex 21217; Chair: D. Wijesinghe; f 1972.

Sri Lanka Tea Board: 574 Galle Rd, POB 1750, Colombo 3;

tel (1) 582236; telex 21304; Chair: C. P. R. Perera; Dir-Gen: M. S. Jayasinghe; f 1976 for devt of the tea industry through research and promotion in Sri Lanka and in world markets.

Art and Culture

Arts Council of Sri Lanka: Dept of Cultural Affairs, 34 Malay St, Colombo 2; tel (1) 545985; Pres: Prof J. B. Dissanayake; Sec: D. M. Gunaratna; f 1952; planning and implementation of projects in all fields of the Arts in Sri Lanka, including exhibitions of paintings, drama, literature and music festivals, and dance competitions; five mems.

Business and Economy

BANKING

Agricultural and Industrial Credit Corpn of Ceylon: 292 Galle Rd, POB 20, Colombo 3; tel (1) 23783; Chair: V. P. Vittachi; Gen Man: H. S. F. Goonewardena; f 1943.

Bank of Ceylon: 75 Janadhipathi Mawatha, Colombo 1; tel (1) 546811; telex 21331; Chair: Dr Nimal E. H. Sanderatne; Gen Man: R. L. Nanayakkara; f 1939; 309 brs in Sri Lanka, 1 br in Maldives.

> **Merchant Bank of Sri Lanka:** 411 Galle Rd, Colombo 3; tel (1) 575198; telex 21331; Chair: A. S. Jayewardena; f 1982.

Central Bank of Sri Lanka: 34-36 Janadhipathi Mawatha, POB 590, Colombo 1; tel (1) 421191; telex 21176; Gov and Chair of the Monetary Bd: Dr H. N. S. Karunatilake; Sec: W. Jayasena; f 1950; central bank and sole bank of issue; acts as financial adviser to Govt and administers monetary policy.

Development Finance Corpn of Ceylon: 73/5 Galle Rd, POB 1397, Colombo 3; tel (1) 540366; telex 21681; Chair: C. A. Cooray; Gen Man and Chief Exec: M. R. Prelis; f. 1955; devt and merchant banking, and consultancy work.

National Development Bank of Sri Lanka: 40 Navam Mawatha, Colombo 2; tel (1) 437350; telex 21399; fax (1) 540262; Chair: B. Mahadeva; Gen Man: R. M. S. Fernando; f 1979; devt banking.

People's Bank: 75 Sir Chittampalam A. Gardiner Mawatha, POB 728, Colombo 2; tel (1) 27841; telex 21143; Chair: Lakshman R. Watawala; Gen Man: M. W. Panditha; f 1961; commercial bank; 313 brs.

Sampath Bank Ltd: 55 D. R. Wijewardene Mawatha, POB 997, Colombo 10; tel (1) 541332; telex 22760; Chair: N. U. Jayawardene; f 1987.

State Mortgage and Investment Bank: 269 Galle Rd, POB 20, Colombo 3; tel (1) 573563; Chair: Rudra Rajasingham; Gen Man: D. B. Rajapakse; f 1978; provides loans for construction, purchase, repair and extension of dwelling houses, and for purchase of building sites.

INSURANCE

Insurance Corpn of Sri Lanka: Rakshana Mandiraya, 21 Vauxhall St, POB 1337, Colombo 2; tel (1) 35301; telex 21772; Chair: R. Chanaka D. de Silva; f 1961; general insurance.

National Insurance Corpn: 47 Muttiah Rd, Colombo 2; tel (1) 545738; Chair: T. M. S. Nanayakkara; Sec: A. C. J. de Alwis; general insurance.

MARKETING

Ceylon Tea Promotion Bureau: 574/1 Galle Rd, POB 295, Colombo 3; tel (1) 582121; telex 21304; fax (1) 585701; Dir: Mervyn C. Wijeyaratne; f 1932; promotes demand for Sri Lankan tea in domestic and foreign markets.

NATIONALIZED INDUSTRY

Ceylon Ceramics Corpn: 696 Galle Rd, Colombo 3; tel (1) 587526; telex 21220; fax (1) 0662132; Chair: Tissa Jayaweera; Gen Man: N. C. W. Attanayake; Sec: F M A Ranaweera; f 1955; mining and sale of ball clay, feldspar, quartz, kaolin and lime; manufacture and sale of tableware, sanitary ware, electrical insulators, clay tiles, ornamental ware, and wire-cut bricks and tiles.

Ceylon Cold Stores Ltd: POB 220, Colombo; tel (1) 28221; telex 21180; manufacturers, wholesalers and retailers of food and beverages; exporters of sea foods, spices, essential oils, fruit juices and processed meats.

> **Lanka Porcelain Ltd:** Rattora.

> **Lanka Refractories Ltd:** Meepe.

> **Lanka Tiles Ltd:** Colombo.

> **Lanka Wall Tiles Ltd:** Balangoda.

Ceylon Galvanising Industries Ltd: Lady Catherine Estate Dr, POB 35, Ratmalana; tel (71) 6711; Man Dir: V. Balasubramaniam; f 1967; manufacture of galvanized steel sheets.

Ceylon Leather Products Corpn: 141 Church Rd, Colombo 15; tel (1) 522776; Chair: L. R. Watawala; manufacturers and exporters of leather, including footwear, sports and leather goods.

Ceylon Mineral Sands Corpn: 167 Sri Vipulasena Mawatha, POB 1212, Colombo 10; tel (1) 694632; telex 21174; fax (1) 699132; Chair: Prof B. L. Panditheratna; Gen Man: S. A. Nandadeva; f 1957; mining, processing and exporting of mineral sands.

Ceylon Oils & Fats Ltd: Seeduwa; tel (30) 3529; telex 21256; fax (30) 3537; Chair: Upul Jayasuriya; f 1958 as state corpn, became fully govt-owned limited liability company 1989; manufacturer of provender feeds, vegetable oils, fatty acids and glycerine.

Ceylon Plywoods Corpn: 420 Bauddhaloka Mawatha, Colombo 7; tel (1) 595846; Chair: N. G. Puvimanasinghe; factory at Gintota, woodwork complex at Kosgama, timber extraction project at Kanneliya.

Ceylon Silks Ltd: 50/22 Mayura Place, Colombo 6; tel (1) 586614; Gen Man: P. M. D. Gunesekere; f 1962; manufacturer of synthetic textiles.

Ceylon State Hardware Corpn: Kandy Rd, Yakkala; tel (33) 2154; telex 21248; Chair: H. C. O. Ebert; hardware factory at Yakkala, cast iron factory at Enderamulle.

Ceylon Steel Corpn: Oruwala, Arthurugiriya; tel (1) 561447; telex 21416; fax (1) 561440; Chair: C. M. Pereira; f 1957; steel melting; manufacturers of rolled steel, foundry castings and wire products.

Government of Sri Lanka (Ceylon) Successor to the Business Undertaking of British Ceylon Corpn Ltd: Huttsdorf Mills, POB 281, Colombo 12; tel (1) 22111; telex 21123; manufacturers and shippers of coconut oil, household and toilet soaps, etc.

National Paper Corpn: 356 Union Place, POB 1367, Colombo 2; tel (1) 546381; telex 21248; fax (1) 546381; Chair: A. B. Padmaperuma; Gen Man: H. M. Jayasinghe; f 1955; manufacturers of paper, paper boards and other paper products; import, sale and distribution of paper.

National Small Industries' Corpn: 181 Sir James Peries Mawatha, Colombo 2; tel (1) 22781.

National Textile Corpn: 16 Gregory's Rd, Colombo 7; tel (1) 595891; factories at Veyangoda, Thulhiriya, Mattegama and Pugoda.

Paranthan Chemicals Corpn: 292 Galle Rd, POB 1489, Colombo 3; tel (1) 575321; Chair (acting): K. D. L. Ratnasena; Working Dir: Upali de Silva; Gen Man: L. M. Deekiriwewa; f 1956; manufacture, sale and import of caustic soda and chlorine.

Sri Lanka Cement Corpn: 130 W. A. D. Ramanayake Mawatha, POB 1382, Colombo 2; tel (1) 540201; telex 21498; cement works at Puttalam, Kankesan and Ruhunu; produces cement for domestic requirements and for export.

Sri Lanka Fertilizer Corpn: 294 Galle Rd, POB 841, Colombo 3; tel (1) 575639; telex 21108.

Sri Lanka National Salt Corpn: 110 Sir James Peries Mawatha, Colombo 2; tel (1) 28128; salt urns at Hambantota, Palatupana, Palavi, Puttalam, Manmar, Elephant Pass, Kurinchativu, Nilaveli and Bundala.

Sri Lanka State Flour Milling Corpn: 7 Station Rd, Colombo 3; tel (1) 21300; mill at Mutwal, Colombo 15.

Sri Lanka Sugar Corpn: 651 Alvitigala Mawatha, POB 1486, Narahenpita, Colombo 5; tel (1) 586922; telex 21434; Chair and Man Dir: Lalith Hettiarachchi; Gen Man (acting): P. K. Jayatilake; f 1963; planting of sugar cane; production of sugar and of spirits from the by-product molasses.

Sri Lanka Tyre Corpn: POB 8, Kelaniya; tel (1) 521241; telex 21508; fax (1) 521585; Chair: Dr D. A. Kotelawele; Gen Man: R. S. R. Abeygunawardene; f 1962; manufacture and sale of tyres, tubes and flaps for domestic and export markets.

State Engineering Corpn: 130 W. A. D. Ramanayake Mawatha, POB 194, Colombo 2; tel (1) 21261.

State Fertilizer Manufacturing Corpn: POB 1344, Colombo; tel (1) 521820; Chair: A. N. Senanayaka; Works Dir: Premaratne Gunasekara; f 1966.

State Gem Corpn: 25 Galle Face Terrace, Colombo 3; tel (1) 29392; telex 1135; fax (1) 21639; f 1971; promotes devt of the gem industry through research, training and marketing.

State Timber Corpn: Rajamalwatte Rd, Battaramulla; tel (1) 566601; telex 21675; Chair: Brig Harsha Gunaratne; Gen Man: S. B. Manawatte; f 1968; responsible for all aspects of harvesting, import and export of timber; conducts reafforestation projects; manufacturer of furniture and timber by-products.

United Motors (Government Business Undertaking): 100 Hyde Park Corner, POB 697, Colombo 2; tel (1) 548112; telex 21600; Competent Authority: A. A. Justin Dias; Gen Man: S. D. Liyanage; f 1972; import and sale of motor vehicles and spare parts.

Wellawatee Spinning and Weaving Mills: 324 Havelock Rd, Colombo 6; tel (1) 582381; nationalized 1976; textiles.

TRADE

Ceylon Tea Export Corpn: Colombo; tel (1) 84844; f 1971; handles exports of tea to communist countries.

Department of Commerce: Rakshana Mandiraya, 4th Floor, 21 Vauxhall St, Colombo 2; tel (1) 22311; Dir: P. Kanagaratnam; responsible to Ministry of Trade and Shipping.

Sri Lanka Export Development Board: 310 Galle Rd, Colombo 3; tel (1) 573049; telex 21457; fax (1) 573083; Chair: K. Gunaratnam; Gen Man: K. H. Camillus Fernando; f 1979; formulates export policies and programmes on behalf of Govt; assists devt of products and services for export; provides incentives to exporters and seeks to remove obstacles to the export of goods.

Sri Lanka State Trading (Consolidated Exports) Corpn: 68-70 York St, POB 263, Colombo 1; tel (1) 26498; Chair: C. L. Wikramanayake; handles export of a wide range of agricultural and industrial goods.

Sri Lanka State Trading (General) Corpn: 119 Wekande Rd, Colombo 2; tel (1) 36234; telex 21175; fax (1) 547970; Chair: D. L. S. Wijesekera; Gen Man: P. Wijayatilake; f 1970; handles import and domestic trade.

Trade and Shipping Information Service: Galle Face Court 2, 2nd Floor, Flat 31, POB 1525, Colombo 3; tel (1) 35277; telex 21245; Dir (acting): L. J. Hewawasam; f 1981; collects and disseminates commercial information; advisory services.

Defence

Sri Lanka Air Force: Sir Chittampalam A. Gardiner Mawatha, POB 594, Colombo 2; tel (1) 433184; Commdr: Air Marshal A. W. Fernando; f 1951.

Sri Lanka Army: Baladaksha Mawatha, Colombo 3; tel (1) 32681; Commdr: Maj-Gen Nalin Seneviratne.

Sri Lanka Navy: Naval Headquarters, POB 593, Colombo; tel (1) 21151; telex 22443; fax (1) 545367; Commdr: Vice-Adm H. Asoka Silva; f 1950.

Development and Planning

Greater Colombo Economic Commission (GCEC): 14 Sir Baron Jayatillake Mawatha, POB 1768, Colombo 1; tel (1) 434403; telex 21332; fax (1) 547995; Dir-Gen: Nissanka Wijewardane; Dep Dir-Gen: F. R. S. Weeraratne; f 1978; promotes investment and administers the Export Processing Zones at Katunayake and Biyagama.

Industrial Development Board of Ceylon: 615 Galle Rd, Katubedde, Moratuwa; tel (1) 505326; Chair: Theobald Seneviratne; Gen Man: N. Senanayake; f 1969; responsible to the Ministry of Rural Industrial Development; promotes industrial devt.

Local Loans and Development Fund: Ministry of Finance and Planning, Old Secretariat Bldg, 2nd Floor, Colombo 1; responsible for the granting of loans to local authorities for economic devt purposes.

Education and Research

Tea Research Institute of Sri Lanka: St Coombs, Talawakele; tel (512) 601; Dir: Dr P. Sivapalan; f 1925; conducts research into all aspects of tea production and manufacture; provides and publishes information based on research; 5 brs.

Energy

Atomic Energy Authority: 696 1/1, Ceramics Corpn Bldg, Galle Rd, Colombo 3; tel (1) 501467; telex 21248; Chair: Dr K. G. Dharmawardena; Sec: G. M. R. Wimalaweera; f 1969; co-ordinates activities of organizations engaged in nuclear research, and conducts own research programmes; provides research grants and scholarships; information and educational services.

Ceylon Electricity Board: 50 Sir Chittampalam A. Gardiner Mawatha, Colombo 2.

Ceylon Petroleum Corpn: 113 Galle Rd, Colombo 3; tel (1) 25231; telex 21167; Chair: Daham Wimalasena; terminal at Kolonnawa, Colombo; refinery at Sapugaskanda.

Legal and Judiciary

Supreme Court: Hulftsdorp, Colombo 12; tel (1) 22142; Chief Justice: Kulatilaka Arthanayake Parinda Ranasinghe.

Media

BROADCASTING

Independent Television Network (ITN): POB 574, Colombo 7; tel (1) 564591; telex 22445; commenced operations in 1979; station at Wickramsinghapura; broadcasts 6 hours daily.

Sri Lanka Broadcasting Corpn: Torrington Sq, POB 574, Colombo 7; tel (1) 597491; telex 21408; Chair: Livy R. Wijemanne; Dir-Gen: Hudson Samarasinghe; f 1925; controls all broadcasting in Sri Lanka.

Sri Lanka Rupavahini Corpn (SLRC): Independence Sq, POB 2204, Colombo 7; tel (1) 501050; telex 22148; Chair: Kumar Abeysinghe; Dir-Gen: Shirley Perera; f 1982; five transmitting stations; broadcasts 6 hours daily.

GOVERNMENT PUBLISHER

Lake House Printers and Publishers Ltd: 41 W. A. D. Ramnayake Mawatha, POB 1458, Colombo 2; tel (1) 33271; telex 21266; Chair: R. S. Wijewardene; Sec: L. C. Gooneratne; f 1965.

NEWS AND INFORMATION

Associated Newspapers of Ceylon Ltd: Lake House, D. R. Wijewardene Mawatha, POB 248, Colombo 10; tel (1) 421181; telex 22262; Chair: Sunil K. Rodrigo; Sec: B. A. Jinadasa; f 1926, nationalized 1973; publishers of 5 daily newspapers (*Daily News, Dinamina, Janatha, Observer, Thinakaran*), 3 Sunday newspapers (*Silumina, Sunday Observer, Thinakaran Vaara Manjari*) and 11 periodicals.

Department of Census and Statistics: 6 Albert Crescent, POB 563, Colombo 7; tel (1) 565291.

Department of Information: 7 Sir Baron Jayatilaka Mawatha, Colombo 1; tel (1) 28376.

Lankapuvath: Transworks House, Lower Chatham St, Colombo 1; tel (1) 33173; telex 22582; Chair: Ranapala Bodinagoda; Chief Editor: Geoff Wijesinghe; f 1978; national news agency.

Tourism

Ceylon Hotels Corpn: 63 Janadhipathi Mawatha, POB 259, Colombo 1; tel (1) 20239; Chair: N. W. Dissanayake; Gen Man: A. K. Mallimaratchi.

Ceylon Tourist Board: 228 Havelock Rd, POB 1504, Colombo 5; tel (1) 581801; telex 21867; Chair: Asker S. Moosajee; Dir-Gen (acting): Pani Seneviratne; f 1966.

Transport

Air Lanka: Greater Colombo Economic Commission Bldg, 14 Sir Baron Jayatilleke Mawatha, POB 670, Colombo 1; tel (1) 21291; telex 21401; Chair and Man Dir: Lakshman de Mel; Chief Operating Officer: Roni Rajasinghe; f 1979; 60% state-owned; operates domestic and international airline services.

Ceylon Shipping Corpn: 6 Sir Baron Jayatilleke Mawatha, POB 1718, Colombo 1; tel (1) 28772; telex 21165; fax (1) 547547; Chair: D. G. W. Wijesinghe; f 1971; operates fully containerized services to Europe, Middle East, Far East, North America and Australia; fleet of 13 fully-containerized vessels (1989).

Ceylon Shipping Lines Ltd: 55 1/1 and 55 2/2 Iceland Bldg, Galle Rd, POB 891, Colombo 3; tel (1) 27052; telex 21113; Chair: D. F. D. Wijesingha; Gen Man: M. P. V. Ratnaike; shipping and travel agents; depot and freight station operators; coastal shippers.

Colombo Dockyard (Pvt) Ltd: Port of Colombo, POB 906, Colombo 15; tel (1) 522461; telex 22794; fax (1) 546441; Chair: T. D. Pieris; Man Dir: B. J. Subasinghe; f 1974; 75% owned by the Ceylon Shipping Corpn, 25% by Singapore-based interests; operates 4 dry-docks for dry-docking and repair of vessels up to 100,000 dwt; builds vessels up to 3,000 dwt.

Department of Motor Traffic: POB 533, Colombo 5; tel (1) 94331.

Sri Lanka Central Transport Board: 200 Kirula Rd, POB 1435, Colombo 5; tel (1) 581121; Chair: Amara Hewamadduma; Sec: Leo Sampson; f 1958; consists of a central board and 9 regional transport boards; responsible for road passenger transport services; fleet of 7,100 buses operating from 100 depots (1988).

Sri Lanka Ports Authority: 19 Church St, Colombo 1; tel (1) 21201; telex 21805; Chair: A. De Vass Gunawardena; Man Dir: K. S. C. Fonseka; Gen Man: S. K. W. Dias; f 1979; responsible for all cargo handling, warehousing operations, servicing vessels, and maintenance of port installations and facilities in all prescribed ports in Sri Lanka.

Sri Lanka Railways: POB 355, Colombo 10; tel (1) 21281; telex 21674; Gen Man: G. P. S. Weerasooriya; operates 9 railway lines with a total of 1,944 track-km, and 168 stations with 118 sub-stations.

SUDAN

Head of State and Legislature

Following the military coup of 30 June 1989 the transitional Constitution, approved in October 1985, was suspended. Executive and legislative authority are vested in the Revolutionary Command Council for National Salvation, headed by a Chairman and Vice-Chairman.

Chair of the Revolutionary Command Council for National Salvation: Lt-Gen Omar Hassan Ahmad al-Bashir (took power 30 June 1989).

Vice-Chair: Brig-Gen Zubair Muhammad Salih.

Revolutionary Command Council for National Salvation: Khartoum; tel (11) 75300.

MINISTRIES AND GOVERNMENT DEPARTMENTS

OFFICE OF THE PRIME MINISTER
Khartoum
Prime Minister: Lt-Gen Omar Hassan Ahmad al-Bashir
Deputy Prime Minister: Brig-Gen Zubair Muhammad Salih

MINISTRY OF AGRICULTURE AND NATURAL RESOURCES
Khartoum
Tel (11) 72300
Minister: Prof Ahmad Ali Junaid

MINISTRY OF BELIEFS AND REFUGEE AFFAIRS
Khartoum
Minister: Bashir Eduard

MINISTRY OF CULTURE AND INFORMATION
Khartoum
Tel (11) 79850; telex 22275
Minister: Ali Muhammad Shummo

MINISTRY OF DEFENCE
Khartoum
Tel (11) 74910; telex 22411
Minister: Lt-Gen Omar Hassan al-Bashir

MINISTRY OF EDUCATION AND TRAINING
Khartoum
Tel (11) 78900
Minister: Mahjoub al-Badawi Muhammad

MINISTRY OF ENERGY AND MINING
POB 2087, Khartoum
Tel (11) 75595; telex 22256
Minister: Abd al-Manaam Khoujli

MINISTRY OF FINANCE AND ECONOMIC PLANNING
POB 700, Khartoum
Tel (11) 77003; telex 22324
Minister: Dr Said Ali Zaki

MINISTRY OF FOREIGN AFFAIRS
Khartoum
Tel (11) 73101
Minister: Ali Sahloul

MINISTRY OF GUIDANCE
Khartoum
Minister: Abdullah Deng Lual

MINISTRY OF HEALTH AND SOCIAL WELFARE
Khartoum
Tel (11) 73000
Minister: Shakir as-Sarraj

MINISTRY OF HOUSING, WORKS AND PUBLIC UTILITIES
Khartoum
Tel (11) 78631
Minister: Maj-Gen Muhammad al-Hadi Maimun al-Mardi

MINISTRY OF INDUSTRY
Khartoum
Minister: Muhammad Omar Abdullah

MINISTRY OF THE INTERIOR
Khartoum
Tel (11) 79990; telex 22604
Minister: Brig-Gen Faisal Ali Abu Salih

MINISTRY OF IRRIGATION AND WATER RESOURCES
Khartoum
Tel (11) 77533
Minister: Dr Yaqub Abu Shura Musa

MINISTRY OF JUSTICE AND OFFICE OF THE ATTORNEY-GENERAL
Khartoum
Minister and Attorney-General: Hassan Ismail al-Bili

MINISTRY OF LABOUR AND SOCIAL INSURANCE
Khartoum
Minister: George Kinga

MINISTRY OF LOCAL GOVERNMENT AND REGIONAL CO-ORDINATION
Khartoum
Minister: Natali Yanko Ambu

MINISTRY OF PRESIDENTIAL AFFAIRS
Khartoum
Minister: Lt-Col Tayib Ibrahim Muhammad Khair

MINISTRY OF RELIGIOUS GUIDANCE
Khartoum
Minister: Abdullah Rijan

MINISTRY OF TRADE, CO-OPERATION AND FINANCE
POB 194, Khartoum
Tel (11) 730030; telex 22329
Minister: Faruq al-Bashri

Trade Information Centre (TIC): POB 194, Khartoum; tel (11) 72540; telex 22329; Dir: Mahamoud Quma; Dep Dir: Farouk Abd Elhatim; f 1978; provides information on trading opportunities.

MINISTRY OF TRANSPORT AND COMMUNICATIONS
POB 300, Khartoum
Tel (11) 79700
Minister: Ali Ahmad Ibrahim

GOVERNMENT AGENCIES AND ORGANIZATIONS

Agriculture

Agricultural Research Corpn: POB 126, Wadi Medani; Gen Man: Hamid Burhan.

Animal Production Public Corpn: POB 624, Khartoum; tel (11) 40503; Dir: Dr Fouad Ramadan Hamid; f 1975; devt and marketing of chicks and egg production, milk and milk products, fish production, animal feeding and meat production.

Kenana Sugar Co Ltd: POB 2632, Khartoum; tel (11) 44297; telex 24033; Man Dir: Osman Abdullah an-Nazir; f 1971; financed by Govt and other Arab nations.

Mechanized Farming Corpn: POB 2482, Khartoum; Man Dir: Awad al-Karim al-Yass.

Public Agricultural Production Corpn: POB 538, Khartoum; Chair and Man Dir: Abdallah Bayoumo; Sec: Saad ad-Din Muhammad Ali.

Public Corpn for Irrigation and Excavations: POB 619, Khartoum; tel (11) 80167; Sec-Gen: Osman an-Nur.

Rahad Corpn: POB 2523, Khartoum; tel (11) 81381; Man Dir: Osman Muhammad Beleil; financed by the World Bank, Kuwait and the USA to irrigate uncultivated land.

Sudan Gezira Board: HQ Barakat Wadi Medani, Gezira Province; tel 2412; telex 50001; Sales Office, POB 884, Khartoum; tel (11) 40145; Man Dir: Abdallah Muhammad az-Zubair; responsible for Sudan's main cotton-producing area; Govt provides the land and is responsible for irrigation, tenants pay a land and water charge and receive the work proceeds, while the Board provides agricultural services at cost, technical supervision and execution of Govt agricultural policies relating to the scheme. Tenants pay a percentage of their proceeds to the Social Development Fund. In addition to cotton, groundnuts, sorghum, wheat, rice, pulses and vegetables are grown for the benefit of tenant farmers.

Sugar Co-ordination Office: POB 511, Khartoum; tel (11) 75022; telex 22665; Gen Man: Badr el-Deen Habbani; Dep Gen Man: M. M. Taha; Financial Man: Amin Osman; f 1986; co-ordinates four sugar states, assists Ministry of Industry in policy-making with regard to sugar industry.

Business and Economy

BANKING

Agricultural Bank of Sudan: POB 1363, Khartoum; tel (11) 77432; telex 22610; Gen Man: Sayed Ahmad Osman; f 1957; provides finance for approved agricultural projects; 22 brs.

Al-Baraka Bank: Hashim Hago Bldg, POB 3583, Khartoum; tel (11) 73046; telex 22555; Chair: Fath ar-Rahman al-Bashir; f 1984; investment and export promotion; 5 brs.

An-Nilien Bank: Parliament Ave, POB 466, Khartoum; tel (11) 73939; telex 22243; Chair and Man Dir (acting): Awad Zein al-Abdin; f 1965; 24 brs.

Arab-African International Bank: POB 2721, Khartoum; tel (11) 75573; telex 22624; Rep: Sheikh Hassan Belail.

Bank of Khartoum: 8 Gamhouria Ave, POB 1008, Khartoum; tel (11) 72880; telex 22181; Chair and Gen Man: Sayed A. Gadir A. Moneim; f 1913; 42 brs.

Bank of Sudan: Gamaa Ave, POB 313, Khartoum; tel (11) 78064; telex 22352; Gov: (vacant); f 1960; central bank and bank of issue; 9 brs.

Industrial Bank of Sudan: United Nations Sq, POB 1722, Khartoum; tel (11) 80929; telex 22456; Chair: Sayed Hassan Ahmad Mekki; f 1961; technical and financial assistance for private sector industrial projects, and acquires shares in industrial enterprises.

Islamic Bank for Western Sudan: Gamhouria Ave, POB 3575, Khartoum; tel (11) 79583; telex 22382; Chair: Dr Adam Mahmoud Madibbo; Gen Man: Esh-Sharief el-Khatim; f 1984; 4 brs.

Islamic Co-operative Development Bank (ICDB): POB 62, Khartoum; tel (11) 80223; telex 22906; Chair: Prof Muhammad Hashim Awad; f 1983; 6 brs.

National Bank of Sudan: Al-Qasr Ave, POB 1183, Khartoum; tel (11) 78153; telex 22058; Chair: Dr Bashir el-Bakri; Gen Man: Isam Uzri; 3 brs.

National Development Bank: POB 655, Khartoum; tel (11) 79496; telex 22835; Gen Man: Kamal ash-Shaigi; f 1982; finances or co-finances economic and social devt projects.

National Export-Import Bank: El Niel Ave, POB 2732,

Khartoum; tel (11) 81606; telex 22928; Chair: Abd ar-Rahman Ahmad Osman; Gen Man: Sheikh Omar Abu al-Hassan; 2 brs.

People's Co-operative Bank: POB 922, Khartoum; tel (11) 73555; telex 22247; Gen Man: Abd ar-Razzaq Abd al-Hafiz Zamrawi.

Sudan Commercial Bank: Al-Qasr Ave, POB 1116, Khartoum; tel (11) 79836; telex 22434; Chair and Gen Man: Hussin Abd al-Gadir; f 1960; 17 brs.

Sudanese Estates Bank: Baladiya Ave, POB 309, Khartoum; tel (11) 78062; telex 22439; Man Dir: Dr Abdin Salam; f 1966; provides finance for housing devt; 6 brs.

Sudanese International Bank: Zubeir Pasha St, POB 2775, Khartoum; tel (11) 76542; telex 22204; Chair: Kamal Ibrahim Ahmad; f 1979; 6 brs.

Sudanese Savings Bank: POB 159, Wad Medani; tel (51) 2271; telex 50005; Asst Gen Man (Banking): A. G. Muhammad; Asst Gen Man, Finance and Admin: M. Gad Karim; f 1974; 6 brs.

Tadamun Islamic Bank of Sudan: Barlaman Ave, POB 3154, Khartoum; tel (11) 73640; telex 22158; Gen Man: Sayed Salah Ali Abu an-Naja; f 1983; 9 brs.

Unity Bank: Barlaman Ave, POB 408, Khartoum; tel (11) 74200; telex 22231; Chair and Gen Man: Ahmad Mohd Nur; f 1970; 29 brs.

MARKETING

Cotton Public Corpn: POB 1672, Khartoum; tel (11) 71567; telex 22245; Chair and Man Dir: Salih Muhammad Salih; f 1970; supervises all cotton marketing operations.

Alaktan Trading Co: POB 2067, Khartoum; tel (11) 81588; telex 22272; Gen Man: Abd ar-Rahman Abd al-Momeim.

National Cotton and Trade Co Ltd: POB 1552, Khartoum; telex 22267; Gen Man: Zubair Muhammad al-Bashir.

Port Sudan Cotton Trade Co Ltd: POB 261, Port Sudan; telex 22270; POB 590, Khartoum; Gen Man: Said Muhammad Adam.

Sudan Cotton Co Ltd: POB 1672, Khartoum; tel (11) 71567; telex 22245; Chair: Prof Ibrahim Hassan Abd al-Galil; Gen Man: Hasab ar-Rassoul Ahmad Orabi; f 1970; exports raw cotton.

NATIONALIZED INDUSTRY

Gum Arabic Co: POB 857, Khartoum; tel (11) 77288; telex 22314; Chair: Fuad Muhammad Abu al-Ela; Gen Man: Osman Muhammad al-Hassan; f 1969.

Industrial Production Corpn: POB 1034, Khartoum; tel (11) 71278; telex 22236; Dir-Gen: Osman Tammam; Dep Chair: Abd al-Latif Widatalla; incorporates:

Cement and Building Materials Sector Co-ordination Office: POB 2241, Khartoum; tel (11) 74269; telex 22079; Dir: T. M. Khogali.

Food Industries Corpn: POB 2341, Khartoum; tel (11) 75463; Dir: Muhammad al-Ghali Suliman.

Leather Trading and Manufacturing Co Ltd: POB 1639, Khartoum; tel (11) 78187; telex 22298; Man Dir: Ibrahim Salih Ali.

Oil Corpn: POB 64, Khartoum North; tel (11) 32044; telex 22198; Gen Man: Bukhari Mahmoud Bukhari.

Spinning and Weaving General Co Ltd: POB 765, Khartoum; tel (11) 74306; telex 22122; Dir: Muhammad Salih Muhammad Abdallah; f 1975.

Sudan Tea Co: POB 1219, Khartoum; tel (11) 81261; telex 22320.

Public Corpn for Building and Construction: POB 2110, Khartoum; tel (11) 74544; Dir: Naim ad-Din.

TRADE

The State Trading Corpn: POB 211, Khartoum; tel (11) 78555; telex 22355; Chair: E. R. M. Tom.

Automobile Corpn: POB 221, Khartoum; tel (11) 78555; telex 22230; Gen Man: Dafalla Ahmad Siddiq; importer of vehicles and spare parts.

Engineering Equipment Corpn: POB 97, Khartoum; tel (11) 73731; telex 22274; Gen Man: Izz ad-Din Hamid; importers and distributors of agricultural, engineering and electronic equipment.

Gezira Trade and Services Co Ltd: Gamaa Ave, POB 215, Khartoum; tel (11) 72687; telex 22302; Man Dir: Muhammad Ahmad Hamad; Dep Man Dir: Rahamtalla Ahmad Muhammad; f 1980; largest importer of general merchandise and services in storage, shipping and insurance; exporter of oilseeds and cereals.

Khartoum Commercial and Shipping Co: POB 221, Khartoum; tel (11) 78555; telex 22311; Gen Man: Idris M. Salih; import, export and shipping services, insurance and manufacturing.

Silos and Storage Corpn: POB 1183, Khartoum; Gen Man: Ahmad at-Taieb Harhoof; stores and handles agricultural products.

Sudan Exhibitions and Fairs Corpn (Sudanexpo): POB 2366, Khartoum; tel (11) 77702; telex 22407; Dir-Gen: Malik Amin Nabri; f 1976.

Sudan Oilseeds Co Ltd: Partlement Ave, POB 167, Khartoum; tel (11) 80120; telex 22312; Chair: Sadiq Karar at-Tayeb; Gen Man: Kamal Abd al-Halim; f 1974; 58% state-owned; exporter of oilseeds, importer of foodstuffs and other goods.

Defence

Armed Forces: Khartoum; tel (11) 72771; Commdr-in-Chief: Lt-Gen Omar Hassan Ahmad al-Bashir.

Air Force: Khartoum; tel (11) 79101; telex 22411.

Army: Khartoum; tel (11) 72771; telex 22441.

Navy: Port Sudan; tel (31) 3016.

Development and Planning

Sudan Development Corpn (SDC): 21 al-Marat, POB 710, Khartoum; tel (11) 42529; telex 24078; Chair and Man Dir: Sayed Mubarak Abd al-Azim; Dep Man Dir: Sayed Yousuf Adam Yousuf; f 1974 to promote and co-finance devt projects with special emphasis on projects in the agricultural, agri-business, and industrial sectors; affiliates:

Sudan Rural Development Co Ltd (SRDC): POB 2190, Khartoum; tel (11) 73855; telex 22813; Gen Man: Omran Muhammad Ali; f 1980.

Sudan Rural Development Finance Co (SRDFC): POB 2190, Khartoum; tel (11) 73855; telex 22813; Gen Man: Omran Muhammad Ali; f 1980.

Legal and Judiciary

Office of the Attorney-General: Khartoum; tel (11) 77513; Attorney-Gen: Hassan Ismail al-Bili (mem of cabinet); in 1987 a new legal code based on a 'Sudanese legal heritage' was introduced.

Media

BROADCASTING

National Radio and Television Corpn: Omdurman; Dir-Gen: Ahmad Hamdi Badr ad-Din.

Sudan Broadcasting Service: POB 572, Omdurman; tel (11) 53151; Dir-Gen: Salih al-Muhammad Salih; broadcasts daily in Amharic, Arabic, English, French, Somali and Tigrinya.

Sudan National Broadcasting Corpn: POB 6 Morada, Omdurman; tel (11) 55022; telex 28002; Dir-Gen: Muhammad Suleiman; Sec-Gen: Hasabu Ahmad; f 1981; directs the activities of both Sudan radio and TV authorities.

GOVERNMENT PUBLISHER

Government Printer: POB 38, Khartoum.

NEWS AND INFORMATION

Department of Statistics: c/o Ministry of Finance and Economic Planning, POB 700, Khartoum; tel (11) 77255; collection, analysis and publication of statistical information.

Sudan News Agency (SUNA): Sharia al-Gamhouria, POB 1506, Khartoum; tel (11) 75770; telex 22418; Dir-Gen: Tayyib Hai Atiyah.

Mining and Energy

ENERGY

General Petroleum Corpn: POB 2986, Khartoum; tel (11) 71809; telex 22638; Chair: Dr Adam Madibou; Gen Man: Abd al-Fatah Muhammad Salih; f 1976.

Public Corpn for Oil Products and Pipelines: POB 1704, Khartoum; tel (11) 78290; Gen Man: Abd ar-Rahman Suliman.

Public Electricity and Water Corpn: POB 1380, Khartoum; Gen Man: Muhammad al-Mahdi Mirghani.

MINING

Sudanese Mining Corpn: POB 1034, Khartoum; tel (11) 70840; telex 22298; Dir: Ibrahim Mudawi Babiker; affiliated to the Industrial Production Corpn (see above).

Tourism

Public Corpn of Tourism and Hotels: POB 7104, Khartoum; tel (11) 74053; telex 22203; Chair: Omer Babiker esh-Shafie; f 1977.

Transport

CIVIL AVIATION

Civil Aviation Department: Khartoum; tel (11) 72264; telex 22650; Dir-Gen: Sir Hassan Beshir.

Sudan Airways Co Ltd: SDC Bldg Complex, 19 Amarat St, POB 253, Khartoum; tel (11) 47597; telex 22257; Chair: Dr S. el-Khatim Mahgoub; f 1947; internal flights and international services to the Middle East, Africa and Europe.

RAILWAYS

Sudan Railways Corpn: POB 65, Atbara; tel (21) 2020; telex 4000; Gen Man: H. M. Ahmad.

ROADS

National Transport Corpn: POB 723, Khartoum; Gen Man: Mohi ad-Din Hassan Muhammad Nur.

Public Corpn for Roads and Bridges: POB 756, Khartoum; tel (11) 70794; Chair: Abd ar-Rahman Haboud; Dir-Gen: Abdou Muhammad Abdou; f 1976.

SHIPPING

River Navigation Corpn: Khartoum; f 1970; jointly owned by Govts of Egypt and Sudan; operates services between Aswan and Wadi Halfa.

River Transport Corpn (RTC): POB 284, Khartoum North; Chair: Ali Amir Taha; operates 2,500 route-km of steamers on the Nile.

Sea Ports Corpn: Port Sudan; tel (31) 2910; telex 70012; Gen Man: Ali Ahmad Abd ar-Rahim; f 1906.

SURINAME

Head of State

Under the 1987 Constitution, the President is Head of State. The National Assembly elects the President and Vice-President for a five-year term. The President appoints a Cabinet of Ministers, led by the Vice-President, who is also Prime Minister. A Council of State advises the President and the Cabinet of Ministers, and has power of veto over legislature approved by the National Assembly. There is also a Military Council.

President: Ramsewak Shankar (assumed office 25 January 1988).

Office of the President: Kleine Combeweg 1, Paramaribo; tel 72841.

Vice-President and Prime Minister: Henck Arron.

Legislature

Under the provisions of the 1987 Constitution, legislative power is vested in the National Assembly, comprising 51 members elected by universal adult suffrage for a five-year term. Suriname is divided into nine administrative districts.

National Assembly: Paramaribo; Chair: Jaggernath Lachmon.

MINISTRIES AND GOVERNMENT DEPARTMENTS

OFFICE OF THE VICE-PRESIDENT AND PRIME MINISTER
Gravenstraat 6, Paramaribo
Tel 74600
Vice-President and Prime Minister: Henck Arron

MINISTRY OF AGRICULTURE, LIVESTOCK, FISHERIES AND FORESTRY
Cultuurtuinlaan 10, POB 1807, Paramaribo
Tel 74177; telex 118
Minister: Saimin Redjosentono
Deputy Minister: Johan W. Esajas

MINISTRY OF THE ARMY
Gravenstraat 52-54, Paramaribo
Tel 74244
Minister: Maj Achmed Sheikkariem

MINISTRY OF ECONOMIC AFFAIRS
Kleine Waterstraat 6-8, Paramaribo
Tel 75080; telex 344
Minister: Wilfred Grep

MINISTRY OF EDUCATION, SCIENCE, CULTURE, SPORTS AND YOUTH AFFAIRS
Samuel Kaffiludistraat 117-123, Paramaribo
Tel 98850; telex 376
Minister: Ronald Venetiaan

MINISTRY OF FINANCE AND PLANNING
Tamarindelaan 3, Paramaribo
Tel 77775; telex 315; fax 76314
Minister: Subhas Chandra Mungra

MINISTRY OF FOREIGN AFFAIRS
Gravenstraat 6, Paramaribo
Tel 77030
Minister: Edwin Sedoc

MINISTRY OF HOME AFFAIRS
Onafhankelijkheidsplein, Paramaribo
Tel 76461
Minister: Evelyn Alexander Vanenburg
Deputy Minister: Soeratno Setroredjo

MINISTRY OF HOUSING AND SOCIAL AFFAIRS
Waterkant 30, Paramaribo
Tel 76941
Minister: Willy Soemita

MINISTRY OF JUSTICE AND POLICE
Gravenstraat 1, Paramaribo
Tel 73033
Minister: Jules R. Ajodhia

MINISTRY OF LABOUR
Wagenwegstraat 22, POB 922, Paramaribo
Tel 75241; telex 132
Minister: Romeo W. van Russel

MINISTRY OF NATURAL RESOURCES AND ENERGY
Mr Dr de Mirandastraat 13-15, Paramaribo
Tel 74666
Minister: Pretaap S. R. Radhakishun
Deputy Minister: Roy H. de Rooy

MINISTRY OF PUBLIC HEALTH
Gravenstraat 64 boven, Paramaribo
Tel 74941
Minister: Henk Alimohamed

MINISTRY OF PUBLIC WORKS
Coppenamestraat 167, POB 190, Paramaribo
Tel 62500; telex 390
Minister: Harnaraim Jankipersadsing
Deputy Minister: Paidi Todirijo

Hydraulic Research Division: Duisburglaan, POB 2110, Paramaribo; tel 60322; telex 390; Dir (acting): M. A. Amatali; f 1963; research into, investigation and monitoring of water resources at national level.

MINISTRY OF REGIONAL DEVELOPMENT
Sommelsdijckstraat 2, Paramaribo
Tel 71574
Minister: Werner Vreedzaam

GOVERNMENT AGENCIES AND ORGANIZATIONS

Banking

Centrale Bank van Suriname: Waterkant 20, POB 1801, Paramaribo; tel 73741; telex 152; Gov: Henk Goedschalk; Exec Dir: H. E. Rijsdijk; Man: G. F. Deerveld; f 1957; central bank.

De Surinaamsche Bank NV: Gravenstraat 26-28, POB 1806, Paramaribo; tel 71100; telex 134; fax 77835; Gen Man: Dr A. J. Brahim; Dep Gen Man: Dr R. E. C. Tjong A. Hung; f 1865.

Nationale Ontwikkelingsbank NV (National Development Bank): Coppenamestraat 160-162, POB 677, Paramaribo; tel 65000; telex 359; fax 97192; Man Dir: J. T. Tsai Meu Chong; f 1963; grants loans to branches of new enterprises and for the expansion of existing enterprises in the productive sector, especially small- and medium-sized businesses.

Defence

Armed Forces: Memre Boekoe Kazerne, Paramaribo; tel 71515.

Suriname Police Force: Duisburglaan 43-45, Paramaribo; tel 62136; Chief of Police: P. H. Monsels.

Development and Planning

Centre for Industrial Development and Export Promotion: Rust en Vredestraat 79-81, Paramaribo; tel 74830; telex 285; Dir: R. A. Leter; f 1981; industrial devt and export promotion.

Small-Scale Industries and Handicrafts Development Division: Kleine Waterstraat 6-8, POB 557, Paramaribo; tel 75339; telex 119; Head: Ruben Nahar; f 1985; promotes establishment and extending of small manufacturing enterprises; production of hand-made articles.

Stichting Planbureau Suriname: Dr Sophie Redmondstraat 118, POB 172, Paramaribo; tel 73146; telex 170; Dir: Dr I. E. Kortram; Dep Dir: H. L. Illes; f 1951; prepares Govt and regional devt programmes; evaluates the appropriateness of project implementation and the effectiveness of plans, projects and programmes already developed.

Energy

Staatsolie Maatschppij Suriname NV (State Oil Co of Suriname): Industrieterrein 21, POB 4069, Flora, Paramaribo; tel 99649; telex 217; fax 91105; Man Dir: Dr S. E. Jharap; Dep Man Dir: Dr R. M. Bergval; f 1980; produces, processes, transports, distributes and exports heavy crude oil.

Forestry and the Environment

Suriname Timber State Forest Industries Inc: Duisburglaan 18, POB 2980, Paramaribo; tel 10359; Dirs: J. E. Lenne, F. Essajas; f 1975; logging and saw-milling; production of hewn poles and electricity poles.

Stinasu—The Foundation for Nature Preservation in Suriname: Cornelis Jongbawstraat 14, POB 436, Paramaribo; tel 75845; Man: K. Mohadien; offers tours and accommodation in nature reserves.

Legal and Judiciary

Court of Justice: Onafhankelijkheidsplein 4, Paramaribo; tel 73841; Pres: R. J. H. Oosteeling; Attorney-Gen: R. M. Reeder; comprises six mems, nominated for life.

Media

BROADCASTING

ATV—Abonnee Televisie: Adrianusstraat, POB 2995, Paramaribo; tel 75811; telex 488; fax 79260; Co-ordinating Man: Ludwig T. Dirksz; f 1985; TV broadcasting in Dutch, English, Portuguese and Spanish; under Telesur (see below).

Radio Suriname International: Wicherstraat 40, POB 2979, Paramaribo; tel 10101; Dir (acting): Guno Cooman; broadcasts daily Monday-Friday; news service and political, economic and cultural programmes; overseas service in English, Dutch, Sranang Tongo.

Stichting Radio-omroep Suriname: J. van Eerstraat 20, POB 271, Paramaribo; tel 90000; Dir: L. Darthuizen; commercial; all local languages.

Surinaamse Televisie Stichting (STVS): Cultuurtuinlaan, POB 535, Paramaribo; tel 73100; telex 271; Dir: F. J. Pengel; f 1965; commercial; local languages, Dutch and English TV broadcasting.

NEWS AND INFORMATION

Algemeen Bureau voor de Statistiek: Regeringsgebouw, Dr Sophie Redmondstraat 118, POB 244, Paramaribo; tel 73927; statistical office.

Science and Technology

Meteorological Service: Duisburglaan, POB 2273, Paramaribo; tel 60029; telex 390; Dir: L. W. Fung; Dep Dir: C. R.

Becker; f 1963; weather information and advice; promotes the establishment and maintenance of systems for the national and international exchange of meteorological information; under the Ministry of Public Works.

Tourism

Suriname Tourism Department: Waterkant 8, POB 656, Paramaribo; tel 71163; telex 118; fax 10555; Head: Armand Bhagwandas; f 1977; under the Ministry of Economic Affairs; implements the Govt tourism policy.

Transport and Communications

TELECOMMUNICATIONS

Telesur NV: POB 1839, Paramaribo; tel 74242; telex 131; Dir: J. R. Neede; telecommunications corpn of Suriname.

TRANSPORT

Dienst voor de Scheepvaart: Cornelis Jongbawstraat 2, POB 888, Paramaribo; tel 72845; telex 163; Dir of Maritime Affairs: E. Fitz Jim; Govt authority supervising and controlling shipping in Surinamese waters.

Paramaribo Government Railway: Onverwacht, Paramaribo; Dir: M. Nahar; single-track narrow-gauge railway from Onverwacht, via Zanderij to Bronsweg (87km—54 miles).

Surinaamse Luchtvaart Maatschappij NV—SLM (Suriname Airways): Jodenbreestraat 65, POB 2029, Paramaribo; tel 73939; telex 292; Pres: Dr M. Mungra; f 1962; services to Amsterdam, Curaçao (Netherlands Antilles), the USA, Haiti, Guyana, French Guiana and Brazil; regular and charter domestic services based at Zorg-en-Hoop.

Suriname Bauxite Railway: POB 1893, Paramaribo; Pres: Henry R. Ferrier; 70km—44 miles from the Backhuis Mountains to Apoera on the Corantijn river; owing to the abandonment of plans to mine bauxite in the Backhuis mountains, the railway was, in mid-1987, inoperative.

SWAZILAND

Head of State

Executive authority is vested in the King and is exercised through a Cabinet presided over by a Prime Minister. All ministers are nominated by the King. Succession is governed by Swazi law and custom.

Sovereign: HM King Mswati III (succeeded to the throne 25 April 1986).

Office of HM the King: POB 1, Lobamba; tel 61080; telex 2134.

Legislature

Legislative authority is vested in the bicameral Parliament (Libandla). The House of Assembly comprises 50 deputies, 40 drawn from the members of an 80-member Electoral College and 10 appointed by the King. The Senate has 20 members, 10 elected by the House of Assembly and 10 appointed by the King. Parliament's functions are confined to debating Government proposals and advising the King.The country is divided into 40 chieftaincies (Tinkhundla), each of which elects two members to the Electoral College.

Senate: POB 37, Lobamba; tel 61286; Pres: Jacob Mavimbela.

House of Assembly: POB 37, Lobamba; tel 61286; Speaker: Seth Dlamini.

MINISTRIES AND GOVERNMENT DEPARTMENTS

OFFICE OF THE PRIME MINISTER
POB 395, Mbabane
Tel 42251
Prime Minister (acting): Obed Dlamini

MINISTRY OF AGRICULTURE AND CO-OPERATIVES
POB 162, Mbabane
Tel 42731; telex 2343
Minister: Sipho Hezekiel Mamba

MINISTRY OF COMMERCE, INDUSTRY AND TOURISM
POB 451, Mbabane
Tel 43101 (Commerce); 43201 (All sections); telex 2232
Minister: Douglas Ntiwane

MINISTRY OF EDUCATION
POB 39, Mbabane
Tel 42491; telex 2293
Minister: Chief Sipho Shongwe

MINISTRY OF FINANCE
POB 443, Mbabane
Tel 42141; telex 2109
Minister: Barnabas Sibusiso Dlamini

MINISTRY OF FOREIGN AFFAIRS
POB 518, Mbabane
Tel 42661; telex 2036
Minister: George M. Mamba

MINISTRY OF HEALTH
POB 5, Mbabane
Tel 42431
Minister: Dr Fanny Friedman

MINISTRY OF THE INTERIOR AND IMMIGRATION
Mbabane
Telex 2328
Minister: Senzenjani Tshabalala

MINISTRY OF JUSTICE
POB 924, Mbabane
Tel 43531
Minister: Reginald Dhladhla

MINISTRY OF LABOUR AND PUBLIC SERVICE
POB 170, Mbabane
Tel 43521
Minister: Ben Nsibandze

MINISTRY OF NATURAL RESOURCES, LAND UTILIZATION AND ENERGY
Mbabane
Telex 2301
Minister: Prince Nqaba

MINISTRY OF WORKS AND COMMUNICATIONS
POB 58, Mbabane
Tel 42321; telex 2104
Minister: Wilson Mkhonta

GOVERNMENT AGENCIES AND ORGANIZATIONS

Advisory and Supervisory Body

Tender Board: POB 38, Mbabane; invites and evaluates tenders for public works.

Agriculture

Swaziland Citrus Board: POB 343, Mbabane; tel 44263; telex 2018; fax 43548; Gen Man: R. E. Lockyer; f 1956 for devt of citrus industry.

Swaziland Cotton Board: POB 230, Manzini; tel 52775; Chair: S. Z. S. Dhlamini; Vice-Chair: E. B. Shiba; Chief Exec: T. P. M. Jele; f 1967; responsible for research on cotton varieties, agronomy and pest control; oversees cotton marketing.

Swaziland Meat Corpn Ltd: POB 446, Manzini; tel 84033; telex 2083; Man Dir: J. J. J. Fourie; f 1965; operates an abattoir and cannery at Matsapa to process meat for local and export markets.

Swaziland Sugar Association: POB 445, Mbabane; tel 42646; telex 2031; Gen Man: D. Johnson.

Business and Economy

BANKING

Central Bank of Swaziland: POB 546, Mbabane; tel 43221; telex 2029; Gov: H. B. B. Oliver; Asst Gen Man: M. B. Samketi; f 1974.

Swazi Bank (Swaziland Development and Savings Bank): Allister Miller St, POB 336, Mbabane; tel 42551; telex 2055; fax 23214; Gen Man: S. S. Kuhlase; Dep Gen Man: J. J. Dlamini; Advisor: Dr T. Deguefe; f 1965; 6 brs.

INSURANCE

Swaziland Insurance Brokers (Pty) Ltd: Allister Miller St, POB 222, Mbabane; tel 43227; telex 2101; Gen Man: M. Heaton; f 1970; partly state-owned; general and reinsurance.

Swaziland Royal Insurance Corpn: POB 917, Mbabane; tel 43231; telex 2043; Gen Man: M. W. Mkwanazi; 51% state-owned; sole authorized insurance co since 1974.

TRADE

Customs Department: POB 489, Manyiri.

Swaziland Commercial Board: POB 509, Mbabane; tel 42930; Man Dir: J. M. D. Fakudze.

Trade Promotion Unit: c/o Ministry of Commerce, Industry and Tourism, POB 451, Mbabane; tel 45180; telex 2232; fax 43833; Dirs: Abner Khumalo, Wellington Dlamini, Jane Maseko, Henry Zeeman; f 1987; trade promotion by organization of trade fairs, market research, trade missions and provision of trade information.

Defence

Royal Swaziland Police Force: POB 49, Mbabane; tel 42501; telex 2017; Commr: Sandile Mdziniso.

Swaziland Umbutfo Defence Force: POB 395, Mbabane; tel 42251; telex 2189; Commdr: Ndambi Dlamini.

Development and Planning

National Industrial Development Corpn of Swaziland (NIDCS): POB 886, Mbabane; tel 43391; telex 2052; Man Dir (acting): M. Matsebula; f 1971; holding co for Govt investments since 1987, when the majority of its assets were transferred to the Swaziland Industrial Development Co (see below).

Small Enterprises Development Co: Swazi Plaza, POB A186, Mbabane; tel 42811; telex 2130; f 1970; promotion of small businesses by provision of loans, market information, entrepreneurial training, etc.

Swaziland Industrial Development Co (SIDC): POB 866, Mbabane; tel 43391; telex 2052; Gen Man: S. Pottes; f 1986 to finance private-sector projects and to promote local and foreign investment.

> **Natex Swaziland:** f 1987 to take control of the National Textile Corpn of Swaziland (NTCS); partly-owned by Swaziland Industrial Development Co.

Tibiyo Taka Ngwane: POB 181, Kwaluseni; tel 84390; telex 2116; Gen Man: A. S. Dlamini; f 1968; national devt agency with investment interests in all sectors of the economy; participates in domestic and foreign joint investment ventures; also charged with responsibility of assisting in upholding the Swazi culture and heritage.

Energy

Swaziland Electricity Board: Mhlambanyati Rd, POB 258, Mbabane.

Legal and Judiciary

High Court: POB 19, Mbabane; tel 42901; Chief Justice: Nicholas Hannah; the High Court is a Superior Court of Record; the Court of Appeal also sits at Mbabane.

Media

BROADCASTING

Swaziland Broadcasting and Information Service: POB 338, Mbabane; tel 42761; telex 2035; Dir: A. T. Tembe; f 1966; radio broadcasts in English and siSwati.

Television Authority of Swaziland: Hospital Hill, Swazi Plaza, POB A146, Mbabane; tel 43036; telex 2138; fax 42093; Chair: Enos Mavuso; Man Dir: Dan Dlamini; f 1978; broadcasts in English for 40 hours each week.

NEWS AND INFORMATION

Central Statistical Office: POB 456, Mbabane; tel 42151; telex 2109; f 1967; data collection, analysis and dissemination.

Transport and Communications

TELECOMMUNICATIONS

Swaziland Posts and Telecommunications Corpn: Phutfumani Bldg, Warner St, POB 125, Mbabane; tel 43131; telex 2019; fax 45522; provision of telecommunications and postal services.

TRANSPORT

Air Cargo Swaziland: Matsapa Airport, Manzini; f 1980; cargo services throughout Southern Africa.

Royal Swazi National Airways Corpn: POB 939, Manzini; tel 84444; telex 2149; Exec Chair: Prince Gabheni; Chief Exec (acting): Godfrey Paris; f 1978; scheduled services throughout Africa; also charter services.

Royal Swazi National Shipping Corpn Ltd: POB 1915, Manzini; tel 53788; telex 2281; fax 53820; Man Dir: M. S. Dlamini; f 1978 to succeed Royal Swaziland Maritime Co; owns no ships, acting only as a freight agent.

Swaziland Railways Board: Swaziland Railway Bldg, Johnstone St, POB 475, Mbabane; tel 42486; telex 2053; Chair: R. P. Stephens; Chief Exec: G. S. Coates; f 1962.

Utilities

Water and Sewerage Board: Mbabane.

SWEDEN

Head of State

Sweden is a constitutional monarchy in which the Monarch has representative and ceremonial duties only. Government is by a Prime Minister, nominated by the Speaker in consultation with the Riksdag (Parliament), and a Regeringen (Cabinet), nominated by the Prime Minister. A Prime Minister can request to be dismissed by the Speaker; the Riksdag also has the power to dismiss the Prime Minister or any other Cabinet minister.

Sovereign: King Carl XVI Gustaf (succeeded to the throne 15 Sept 1973).

Royal Household of His Majesty the King of Sweden: Kungl Slottet, 111 30 Stockholm; tel (8) 789 85 00; Perm Sec: Sven-Olof Hedengren.

Legislature

The unicameral Riksdag (Parliament) is the prime representative of the Swedish people. Its 349 members are elected for a term of three years by a system of proportional representation, with all adults over 18 eligible to vote. The Riksdag enacts laws, determines fiscal policy and examines the Government's actions. Much parliamentary work is conducted through standing committees.

Riksdag (Parliament): 100 12 Stockholm; tel (8) 786 40 00; telex 10184; fax (8) 21 12 67; Speaker: Thage G. Peterson; Sec-Gen: Gunnar Grenfors; Admin Dir: Anders Forsberg.

MINISTRIES AND GOVERNMENT DEPARTMENTS

OFFICE OF THE PRIME MINISTER
103 33 Stockholm
Tel (8) 763 10 00; telex 17820
Prime Minister: Ingvar Carlsson
Deputy Prime Minister: Odd Engström

MINISTRY OF AGRICULTURE
Drottninggt 21, 103 33 Stockholm
Tel (8) 763 10 00; telex 15681
Minister: Mats Hellström

MINISTRY OF DEFENCE
Regeringsgt 1-3, 103 33 Stockholm
Tel (8) 763 10 00; telex 17946; fax (8) 723 11 89
Minister: Roine Carlsson

MINISTRY OF EDUCATION AND CULTURE
Mynttorget 1, 103 33 Stockholm
Tel (8) 763 10 00; telex 13284; fax (8) 723 11 92
Minister of Education and Cultural Affairs:
Bengt Göransson
Minster for Culture, Mass Media and Comprehensive Schools: Goran Persson

MINISTRY OF THE ENVIRONMENT
Fredsgt 8, 103 33 Stockholm
Tel (8) 763 10 00; telex 11741
Minister: Birgitta Dahl

MINISTRY OF FINANCE
Rödbodgt 6, 103 33 Stockholm
Tel (8) 763 10 00; telex 11741
Minister of Finance: Allan Larsson
Deputy Finance Minister: Erik Åsbrink

MINISTRY FOR FOREIGN AFFAIRS
Gustav Adolfstorg 1, POB 16121, 103 23 Stockholm
Tel (8) 786 60 00; telex 10590
Minister of Foreign Affairs: Sten Andersson
Minister for Development Co-operation:
Lena Hjelm-Wallén
Minister for Foreign Trade: Anita Gradin

MINISTRY OF HEALTH AND SOCIAL AFFAIRS
Jakobsgt 26, 103 33 Stockholm
Tel (8) 763 10 00; telex 11461; fax (8) 723 11 91
Minister of Health and Social Affairs: Ingela Thalén
Minister of Family Affairs and Matters Concerning the Disabled and the Elderly: Bengt Lindqvist

MINISTRY OF HOUSING AND PHYSICAL PLANNING
Jakobsgt 26, 103 33 Stockholm
Tel (8) 763 10 00; telex 11461
Minister: Ulf Lönnqvist

MINISTRY OF INDUSTRY AND ENERGY
Fredsgt 8, 103 33 Stockholm
Tel (8) 763 21 53; telex 14180; fax (8) 11 36 16
Minister: Rune Molin

MINISTRY OF JUSTICE
Rosenbad 4, 103 33 Stockholm
Tel (8) 763 10 00; telex 17820
Minister: Laila Freivalds

MINISTRY OF LABOUR
Drottninggt 21, 103 33 Stockholm
Tel (8) 763 10 00; telex 12533
Minister of Labour: Mona Sahlin
Minister for Immigrant Affairs: Majlis Lööw

MINISTRY OF PUBLIC ADMINISTRATION
Tegelbacken 2, 103 33 Stockholm
Tel (8) 763 10 00; telex 14368

Minister of Public Administration: Bengt K. Å. Johansson
Minister for Ecclesiastical, Equality and Youth Affairs: Margot Wallström

MINISTRY OF TRANSPORT AND COMMUNICATIONS
Vasagt 8-10, 103 33 Stockholm
Tel (8) 763 10 00; telex 17328
Minister: Georg Andersson

GOVERNMENT AGENCIES AND ORGANIZATIONS

Advisory and Supervisory Bodies

Riksdagens ombudsmän—JO (Parliamentary Ombudsmen): Västra Trädgårdsgt 4, POB 16327, 103 26 Stockholm; tel (8) 786 40 00; Justitieombudsmen: Claes Eklundh (Chief), Anders Wigelius, Gunnel Norell Söderblom, Hans Ragnemalm; f 1809; supervises the manner in which judges, Govt officials (but not Govt ministers) and other civil servants observe the laws, and prosecutes those who act illegally, misuse their position or neglect their duties.

Riksdagens revisorer—RR (Parliamentary Auditor): Stor-kyrkobrinken 13, 100 12 Stockholm; tel (8) 786 40 00; Chair: Allan Åkerlind; Man Dir: Göran Hagbergh; f 1809.

Art and Culture

Statens kulturråd (Swedish National Council for Cultural Affairs): POB 7843, 103 98 Stockholm; tel (8) 24 72 60; Chair: Lars Engqvist; Dir: Göran Löfdahl; f 1974; funding, advisory and investigatory body concerning state grants for cultural purposes; covers theatre, dance, music, literature, public libraries, art, popular education, museums and exhibitions.

Svenska Institutet (Swedish Institute): POB 7434, 103 91 Stockholm; tel (8) 789 20 00; telex 10025; fax (8) 21 35 55; Pres: Sven O. Andersson; Dir: Anders Clason; f 1945; aims to increase knowledge about Swedish culture abroad, and to encourage cultural and informational exchange with other countries; administers grants and scholarships for study in Sweden.

Business and Economy

BANKING

Bankinspektionen (Bank Inspection Board): POB 16096, 103 22 Stockholm; tel (8) 24 21 20; fax (8) 24 13 35; Dir-Gen: Hans Löwbeer; Dep Dir-Gen: Stig Danielsson; Man Dirs: Mats Josefsson, Lars Hedberg, Berit Lunning; f 1907; supervises commercial and savings banks, finance companies, mortgage institutions, stock dealers, stock exchanges and agricultural loan societies.

Post-och Kreditbanken (PKbanken): Hamngt 12, 105 71 Stockholm; tel (8) 781 80 00; telex 19130; Chair: Karl Erik Persson; Chief Exec: Christer Zetterberg; f 1974 by merger of Postbanken and Sveriges Kreditbank; 70% Govt controlled; 140 brs and access to 4,500 post offices and postal service units.

Riksbanken (Bank of Sweden): Brunkeborgs torg 11, POB 16283, 103 25 Stockholm; tel (8) 787 00 00; telex 19150; Chair: Erik Åsbrink; Gov: Bengt Dennis; f 1668; central bank and bank of issue; determines monetary policy in close co-operation with Govt; controlled by board of 8 delegates, 7 of which elected by the Riksdag (Parliament); delegates elect one of their number as Governor.

FINANCIAL AGENCIES

Riksgäldskonteret (National Debt Office): Jakobsgt 20, POB 16036, 103 26 Stockholm; tel (8) 22 12 20; Chair: Sven Heurgren; Man Dir: Staffan Crona; f 1789; under parliamentary control until June 1989; responsible for Govt borrowing; issues and sells Govt bonds and other financial securities.

Royal Mint: Smedjegatan 19, POB 401, 631 06 Eskilstuna; tel (16) 12 03 00; telex 46028; Gen Man: Bengt Ulvfot; responsible to the Ministry of Finance.

INSURANCE

Försäkringsinspektionen: Tegnérgt 23, 4th Floor, POB 3095, 103 61 Stockholm; tel (8) 14 07 20; Chief Exec: A. E. B. Gabrielsson; f 1904; Swedish private insurance supervisory service.

Riksförsäkringsverket (National Social Insurance Board): Adolf Fredriks Kyrkogt 8, 103 51 Stockholm; tel (8) 786 90 00; Dir-Gen: K. G. Scherman; Dir-in-Chief: G. Jönsson; f 1961; administers social insurance system.

NATIONALIZED INDUSTRY

Apoteksbolaget AB: Humlegardsgt 20, 105 14 Stockholm; tel (8) 783 95 00; telex 11553; fax (8) 783 95 16; Chair: Bertil Danielsson; Pres and Chief Exec: Åke Hallman; f 1971; national corpn of Swedish pharmacies; two-thirds state-owned; responsible for pharmaceutical distribution, owns all pharmacies in Sweden.

Procordia AB: Norra Bankogränd 2, POB 2278, 103 17 Stockholm; tel (8) 791 31 00; telex 11454; Man Dir: Sören Gyll; f 1970 as state holding co, Statsföretag; listed on Stockholm Stock Exchange 1987; health care, tobacco, beverages, restaurants, etc.

Svenskt Stål AB—SSAB (Swedish Steel Co): Birger Jarlsgt 58, POB 16344, 103 26 Stockholm; tel (8) 24 23 10; telex 50950; Pres and Chief Exec: L. Gustafsson; Govt controls 40% of share capital and 52% of voting shares.

Systembolaget AB: Kungsträdgådsgt 14, 103 84 Stockholm; tel (8) 789 35 00; telex 8105098; fax (8) 789 35 02; Chair: Bertil Göransson; Vice-Chair: Erik Åsbrink; Man Dir: Gabriel Romanus; f 1955; state monopoly enterprise for retail sale of wines, spirits and strong beers.

Tidningstjänst AB: Gamla Brogt 11, 111 20 Stockholm; telex 16970; Pres: Ove Rainer; Dir: Olof Jonsson; f 1969; distribution of newspapers and admin of state subsidies.

AB Tipstjänst: 106 10 Stockholm; tel (8) 757 77 00; telex 10789; Pres: Walter Slunge; Man Dir: Richard Frigren; f 1934; state monopoly for public betting on all sports except horse racing.

AB Trafikrestauranger: POB 746, 101 30 Stockholm; tel (8)

24 44 60; telex 11673; Chair: Bengt Furbäck; Man Dir: Per Jönsson; f 1938; train, station and ferry catering.

AB Vin- & Spritcentralen: Formansvägen 19, POB 43005, 100 72 Stockholm; Chair: Lars Lindmark; Man: Egon Jacobsson; f 1917; responsible for import, wholesale and export of wines and spirits, and for import of beer.

TRADE

Exportrådet (Trade Council): Storgt 19, POB 5513, 114 85 Stockholm; tel (8) 763 85 00; Pres: Hans Stahle; Man Dir: Bo Hampus Israelsson; f 1972; central organization for the promotion of the Swedish export industry; operates through about 30 offices abroad, and through the commercial depts of embassies and consulates; jointly controlled by Govt and private interests; 3,500 mems.

Handelsavdelningen (Department of Foreign Trade): Fredsgt 8, 103 33 Stockholm; tel (8) 786 60 00; telex 17920; responsible to Ministry of Foreign Affairs.

Kommerskollegium—KK (National Board of Trade): POB 1209, 111 82 Stockholm; tel (8) 791 05 00; telex 11835; Chair and Dir-Gen: Gunnar Söder; f 1651; central Govt agency concerned with trade; issues import and export licences; grants permits for foreigners and foreign cos to operate commercially in Sweden.

Patent- och Registreringsverket—PRV (Patent Office): POB 5055, 102 42 Stockholm; tel (8) 782 25 00; fax (8) 666 02 86; Dir-Gen: Sten Niklasson; Deputy Dir-Gen: Inga Martinsson; f 1892; examines and registers patents, names, trademarks, designs and cos.

Defence

Försvaret (Armed Forces): Lindingövägen 24, POB 80001; 104 50 Stockholm; tel (8) 788 75 00; telex 19633; Supreme Commdr: Bengt Gustafson; Chief of Defence Staff: Torsten Engberg.

> **Armen** (Army): POB 80002, 104 50 Stockholm; tel (8) 788 75 00; telex 19633; Commdr-in-Chief: Erik Bengtsson; Chief of Staff: Krister Larsson.

> **Flygvapet** (Air Force): POB 80004, 104 50 Stockholm; tel (8) 788 75 00; telex 19633; Commdr-in-Chief: Sven-Olof Olson; Chief of Staff: Bengt Lönnbom.

> **Marinen** (Navy): POB 80003, 104 50 Stockholm; tel (8) 788 75 00; telex 19633; Commdr-in-Chief: Bengt Schuback; Chief of Staff: Lars Persson.

Development and Planning

Economic Planning Council: Fack, 103 10 Stockholm; Chair: Allan Larsson; Govt body responsible for long-term planning and economic devt.

National Land Survey of Sweden: Lantmäterigt 2, 801 82 Gävle; tel (26) 15 30 00; telex 47359; fax (26) 68-75-94; Gen Dir: Jim Widmark; f 1628; responsible for national land surveying and mapping; supervises registration of land for fiscal purposes.

Statens Industriverk—SIND (National Industry Board): Liljeholmsvägen 30, 117 86 Stockholm; Dir-Gen: Eric Pettersson; f 1973; responsible for industrial devt, particularly in the public sector, and regional devt.

Education and Research

EDUCATION

Universitets- och Högskoleämbetet (National Swedish Board of Universities and Colleges): Drottninggt 95A, POB 45501, 104 30 Stockholm; tel (8) 728 36 00; telex 14132; fax (8) 34 27 25; Chancellor: Gunnar Brodin; Head of Information: Torsten Käalvemark; responsible for management of the higher education system.

RESEARCH

Konjunkturinstitutet: POB 1228, 111 82 Stockholm; tel (8) 24 07 40; fax (8) 723 15 69; Dir-in-Chief: Alf Carling; Dep Dir-in-Chief: Bengt Pettersson; f 1937; conducts investigations and analyses of the trade cycle; business tendency surveys and forecasting.

Swedish Board for Technical Development: POB 43200, 100 72 Stockholm; conducts research on behalf of the Ministry of Industry.

Forestry

Domänverket: 791 81 Falun; tel (23) 840 00; telex 74130; Dir-Gen: Bo S. Hedström; f 1859; forestry.

Health and Welfare

Bostadfformedling (Housing Office): St Eriksgarten 49, Stockholm.

Legal and Judiciary

Domstolsverket: Jönköping; Justitiekansler (Chancellor of Justice): H. Stark; responsible for admin of courts of justice; exercises no judicial authority.

Högsta Domstolen (Supreme Court): POB 2066, 103 12 Stockholm; tel (8) 23 67 20; Pres: O. Höglund; the Supreme Court has 25 mems.

Media

BROADCASTING

Sveriges Radio AB (Swedish Broadcasting Corporation): Oxenstiernsgt 20, 105 10 Stockholm; tel (8) 784 00 00; telex 1000; fax (8) 784 15 00; Dir-Gen: Örjan Wallqvist; f 1924; produces radio and TV programmes; broadcasts under licence from the Govt; non-commercial.

> **Sveriges Lokalradio AB** (Swedish Local Radio Co): POB 70490, 107 29 Stockholm; tel (8) 784 98 00; telex 11850; Man Dir: Jan Engdahl; administers 15 local radio stations.

> **Sveriges Riksradio AB** (Swedish National Radio Company): Oxenstiernsgt 20, 105 10 Stockholm; tel (8) 784 00 00; telex (10000); fax (8) 662 69 92; Man Dir: Ove Joanson; Dep Man Dir: Arvid Lagercrantz; f 1925; operates three nationwide networks; responsible for foreign service radio broadcasting.

> **Sveriges Utbildningsradio AB** (Swedish Educational

Broadcasting Company): 115 80 Stockholm; tel (8) 784 00 00; Man Dir: Lars Hansson.

Swedish Television Co: Oxenstiernsgt 20, 105 10 Stockholm; tel (8) 784 00 00; Man Dir: Sam Nilsson.

GOVERNMENT PUBLISHER

Liber AB: 162 89 Stockholm; tel (8) 739 90 00; Man Dir: Birgitta Johansson-Hedberg; general and educational publishing.

NEWS AND INFORMATION

Statistika Centralbyrån (Statistics Sweden): Karlavägen 100, 115 81 Stockholm; tel (8) 783 40 00; telex 15261; fax (8) 61 52 61; Gen Dir: Sten Johansson; f 1858; central authority for the production of Govt statistics in Sweden.

Örebro Office: 701 89 Örebro; tel (19) 17 60 00; telex 73170; fax (19) 12 97 84.

Mining and Energy

ENERGY

Statens Energiverk (National Energy Administration): 117 87 Stockholm; tel (8) 744 95 00; telex 12870; fax (8) 744 09 80; Dir-Gen: Hans Rode; Dep Dir-Gen: Jan Magnusson; f 1983; responsible for electricity safety regulations and energy emergency planning; grants concessions for electricity transmission and distribution, and for gas transmission; produces forecasts and analyses of international energy markets and of Swedish energy demand and supply; provides financial support for research and devt concerned with energy supply.

Statens kärnkraftinspektion (Nuclear Power Inspectorate): POB 27106, 102 52 Stockholm; tel (8) 663 55 60; telex 11961; Dir-Gen and Chair: Olof Hörmander; undertakes the control and inspection of atomic installations and atomic fuel.

Statens strålskyddsinstitut (National Institute of Radiation Protection): POB 60204, 104 01 Stockholm; tel (8) 729 71 00; telex 11771; Dir: Gunnar Bengtsson; f 1965; undertakes protection against ionizing and non-ionizing radiation.

Statens Vattenfallsverk—Vattenfall (Swedish State Power Board): Jämtlandsgt 99, 162 87 Vällingby; tel (8) 739 50 00; telex 19653; Dir-Gen: Carl-Erik Nyqvist; f 1909; production, distribution and sale of electricity; generally responsible for national electricity supply system; produces 50% of all electricity in Sweden; operates 7 light-water nuclear power reactors.

Studsvik AB (Atomic Energy Co): 611 82 Nyköping; tel (155) 210 00; telex 64013; Chair: Hans Stahle; Man Dir: Kjell Håkansson; f 1947; conducts applied research in nuclear and other energy fields.

MINING

Luossavaara–Kiirunavaara AB—LKAB: Varvsgt 45, POB 58, 951 21 Luleå; tel (920) 380 00; telex 80230; fax (920) 195 05; Pres: Wiking Sjöstrand; Exec Vice-Pres (Marketing): Carl Ameln; Exec Vice-Pres (Econ and Finance): Håkan Sundin; f 1897; iron ore mining; owns 22% of voting shares of Svenskt Stål AB (SSAB).

Science and Technology

Statens Provningsanstalt—SP (National Testing Institute): POB 857, 501 15 Borås; tel (33) 16 50 00; telex 36252; fax (33)

13 55 02; Dir-Gen: Claes Bankuall; f 1926; performs testing and technical evaluation of materials, products, constructions, systems and related activities; research and devt in these areas and in measurement technology and metrology; provides advisory services to Govt authorities, and to national and international standardization organizations.

Statskonsult AB: Anderstorpsvägen 12, POB 4040, 171 04 Solna 4; telex 12754; Pres: Stig Moback; f 1969; management and data processing consultation services.

Tourism

Sveriges Turistråd (Swedish Tourist Board): Kungsträdgården, POB 7473, 103 92 Stockholm; tel (8) 790 31 00; Chair: Gert Karlsson; Dir-Gen: Ulf Åberg.

Transport and Communications

TELECOMMUNICATIONS

Televerket (Swedish Telecommunications Administration): Mårbackagt 11, 123 86 Farsta; tel (8) 713 10 00; telex 14970; Dir-Gen: Tony Hagström; f 1853; supplies telecommunications facilities; owns Teleinvest Group and other cos; responsible for nation-wide distribution of radio and TV programmes produced by Sveriges Radio.

TRANSPORT

Board of Civil Aviation: Vikboplan 11, 601 79 Norrköping; tel (11) 19 20 00; telex 64250; Dir-Gen: Bengt A. W. Johansson; f 1923; central Govt authority for matters concerning civil aviation.

Scandinavian Airlines System—SAS: Frösundavik Allée 1, Bromma, 161 87 Stockholm; tel (8) 780 10 00; Pres and Chief Exec: Jan Carlzon; Chief Operating Officer: Lars Bergvall; national carrier of Denmark, Norway and Sweden; owned two-sevenths by Danish Airlines, two-sevenths by Norwegian Airlines and three-sevenths by AB Aerotransport (Swedish Airlines).

AB Aerotransport—ABA (Swedish Airlines): Bromma, 161 87 Stockholm; Chair: Krister Wickman; Pres: Olle Hedberg; Chair Exec Cttee: Curt Nicolin; Swedish partner of SAS; jointly owned by Govt and private interests.

Linjeflyg AB: Arlanda Flygplats, POB 550, 190 45 Stockholm; tel (8) 797 50 00; telex 19165; Chair: N. Hörjel; Man Dir: Christopher Nilsson; f 1957; operates domestic passenger, newspaper distribution and postal services; jointly owned by ABA and SAS.

Statens Järnvägar: 105 50 Stockholm; tel (8) 762 20 00; telex 19410; Dir-Gen: Stig Larsson; f 1856; railways; operates 11,157 km of track, of which 6,995 electrified; four ferry-boat lines; 21,000 km of bus routes (all 1987 figures).

GDG Biltrafik AB: Gullbergs Strandgt 34, 411 04 Göteborg; tel (31) 80 40 00; telex 27295; road transport by bus, and road haulage.

AB Svelast: Östermalmsgt 47, POB 26008, 100 41 Stockholm; telex 19604; Man Dir: Leif Axen; f 1937; transport and distribution of goods.

Traffic Safety Board: 781 86 Borlange.

SWITZERLAND

Head of State

The Head of State is the President of the Swiss Confederation, and is one of the Federal Councillors elected to the post by the Federal Assembly for one year at a time. Executive power is held by the Federal Council, which has seven members elected for four years by a joint session of the Federal Assembly.

President of the Swiss Confederation for 1990: Arnold Koller.

Office of the President of the Swiss Confederation: Bundeshaus-West, 3003 Berne; tel (31) 662111; telex 911191.

Vice-President: Flavio Cotti.

Legislature

Legislative power is held by the bicameral Federal Assembly, comprising a Council of States, with 46 members representing the cantons elected for three to four years, and the National Council, with 200 members directly-elected by universal adult suffrage for four years on the basis of proportional representation. The Swiss Confederation consists of 26 cantons and half-cantons, each with a constitution, government and legislative assembly. Communes operate at a local level.

Ständerat/Conseil des Etats (Council of States): Parlamentsgebäude, 3003 Berne; tel (31) 619701; fax (31) 617804; Pres: Luretn Mathias Cavelty.

Nationalrat/Conseil National (National Council): Parlamentsgebäude, 3003 Berne; tel (31) 619701; fax (31) 617804; Pres: Viktor Ruffy.

MINISTRIES AND GOVERNMENT DEPARTMENTS

FEDERAL CHANCELLERY
Bundeshaus-West, Bundesgasse, 3003 Berne
Tel (31) 613727; telex 911191
Chancellor: Walter Buser

FEDERAL DEPARTMENT OF FINANCE
Bundesgasse 3, 3003 Berne Bernerhof
Tel (31) 616111; telex 912868; fax (31) 616187
Head: Otto Stich

FEDERAL DEPARTMENT OF FOREIGN AFFAIRS
Bundeshaus-West, 3003 Berne
Tel (31) 612111; telex 911440; fax (31) 613237
Head: René Felber

FEDERAL DEPARTMENT OF HOME AFFAIRS
Bundeshaus, Inselgasse, 3003 Berne
Tel (31) 619111; telex 912890; fax (31) 618032
Head: Flavio Cotti

FEDERAL DEPARTMENT OF JUSTICE AND POLICE
Bundeshaus-West, Bundesgasse, 3003 Berne
Tel (31) 614111; telex 911199; fax (31) 617832
Head: Dr Arnold Koller

FEDERAL DEPARTMENT OF PUBLIC ECONOMY
Bundeshaus-Ost, 3003 Berne
Tel (31) 612111; telex 912889; fax (31) 612056
Head: Jean-Pascal Delamuraz

FEDERAL DEPARTMENT OF TRANSPORT, COMMUNICATIONS AND ENERGY
Bundeshaus-Nord, Kochergasse 10, 3003 Berne
Tel (31) 614111; telex 911282; fax (31) 229576
Head: Adolf Ogi

FEDERAL MILITARY (DEFENCE) DEPARTMENT
Bundeshaus-Ost, 3003 Berne
Tel (31) 671211; telex 912909
Head: Kaspar Villiger

GOVERNMENT AGENCIES AND ORGANIZATIONS

Advisory and Supervisory Bodies

Amt für Bundesbauten/Office des constructions fédérales (Federal Office of Construction): Effingerstr 20, 3003 Berne; tel (31) 618111; fax (31) 618184; Dir: Niki Piazzoli; Vice-Dirs: Daniel Baumann, Hans-Peter Jost; f 1888; under the Federal Dept of Home Affairs.

Bundesamt für Ausländerfragen/Office fédéral des étrangers: Taubenstr 16, 3003 Berne; tel (31) 614411; telex 912697; Dir: Alexander Hunziker; Dep Dir: Dr Walter Wüthrich; federal office for foreigners' affairs; under the Federal Dept of Justice and Police.

Bundesamt für Industrie, Gewerbe und Arbeit (BIGA)/ Office fédéral de l'industrie, des arts et métiers et du travail (OFIAMT)/Ufficio federale dell'industria, delle arti e mestieri e del lavoro (UFIAML) (Federal Office for Industry and Labour): Bundesgasse 8, 3003 Berne; tel (31) 612902; telex 913280; fax (31) 612749; Dir: Dr Klaus Hug; f 1930; under the Federal Dept of Public Economy; activity is focussed on the domestic economy, economic structure and employment; has divisions concerned with the Protection of Labour and Labour Legislation, Occupational Medicine, Manpower and Emigration, Unemployment Insurance, Vocational Training, the Swiss Vocational Teachers Training Institute, Industrial Promotion and Trade, Regional Policy and Economic Affairs and Statistics.

Bundesamt für Konjunkturfragen: Belpstr 53, 3003 Berne; tel (31) 612133; fax (31) 612057; Dir: Dr Hans Sieber; analyses the economic situation and outlook and estimates quarterly aggregates of national accounts; manages a scheme which aims at promotion applied research and devt.

Bundesamt für Organisation (BFO) (Federal Office for Organization): Feldeggweg 1, 3003 Berne; tel (31) 617011; fax (31) 617030; Dir: H. Garin; f 1954; staff office of the Swiss Federal Council; responsible for appropriate and economical organization of federal admin; advises on organization and use of information technology in Govt admin; promotion, co-ordination and supervision of information technology activities.

Eidg Alkoholverwaltung: Länggassstr 31, 3000 Berne 9; tel (31) 231233; telex 911288; fax (31) 235032; Dir: Dr Ernst Scheurer; Dep Dir: Dr Christoph Zurbrügg; f 1887; alcohol monopoly; taxation of spirits; public health.

Grundbuchamt/Office du registre foncier (Land Registry): Bundesgasse 32, 3003 Berne; tel (31) 614797; Section Head: Manuel Müller; under the Federal Dept of Justice and Police.

Agriculture and the Environment

AGRICULTURE

Bundesamt für Landwirtschaft (Federal Office of Agriculture): Mattenhofstr 5, 3003 Berne; tel (31) 612622; telex 913162; fax (31) 612634; Dir: Jean Claude Piot; f 1882; under the Federal Dept of Public Economy; maintenance and promotion of agriculture, especially in the hill and mountain regions; formation of agricultural policy; research.

Eidg Getreideverwaltung/Administration fédérale des blés (Federal Grain Administration): Hallwylstr 15, 3003 Berne; tel (31) 612688; fax (31) 612709; Dir: Josef Ackermann.

THE ENVIRONMENT

Bundesamt für Forstwesen und Landschaftsschutz/ Office fédéral des forêts et de la protection du paysage

(Federal Office for Forests and Countryside Protection): Postfach 1987, Laupenstr 20, 3001 Berne; tel (31) 618074; Dir: Dr Maurice de Coulon; Vice-Dirs: Heinz Wandeler, Bruno Wallimann.

Bundesamt für Umwelt, Wald und Landschaft (Federal Office for Environment, Forests and the Countryside): Hallwysltr 4, 3003 Berne; tel (31) 619311; telex 912304; fax (31) 619981; Dir: Dr Bruno Böhlen; f 1971; environment protection, nature and countryside preservation, forestry, inland fishery.

Bundesamt für Wasserwirtschaft/Office fédéral de l'économie des eaux (Federal Office of Water Economy): Effingerstr 77, 3001 Berne; tel (31) 615411; Dir: Dr Alexander Lässker; Vice-Dir: Michel Mayer; under the Dept of Transport, Communications and Energy.

Wasser- und Bodenschutz/Protection des eaux et du sol: Hallwylstr 4, 3003 Berne; tel (31) 619380; Head: Bruno Milani; water and soil protection; under the Federal Dept of Home Affairs.

Art and Culture

Archives Fédérales (Federal Archives): Archivstr 24, 3003 Berne; tel (31) 618989; fax (31) 617823; Dir: Dr Oscar Gauye; Vice-Dir: Dr Christoph Graf; f 1848.

Bundesamt für Kulturpflege/Office fédéral de la culture (Federal Office of Culture): Postfach, Thunstr 20, 3000 Berne 6; tel (31) 619266; Dir: Dr Alfred Defago; under the Federal Dept of Home Affairs.

Schweizerische Landesbibliothek/Bibliothèque nationale suisse (Swiss National Library): Hallwylstr 15, 3003 Berne; tel (31) 618911; Dir: Dr Franz Georg Maier; Vice-Dir: Dr Rätus Luck.

Schweizerisches Landesmuseum/Musée national suisse (Swiss National Museum): Museumstr 2, 8023 Zürich; tel (1) 2211010; fax (1) 2112949; Dir: Dr Andres Furger; Vice-Dir: Dr Maurus Birchler.

Business and Economy

BANKING

Eidg Bankenkommission/Commission fédérale des banques (Federal Banking Commission): Postfach 1211, Marktgasse 37, 3001 Berne; tel (31) 616911; Pres: Brig Dr Hermann Bodenmann; Dir: Dr Kurt Hauri.

Schweizerische Nationalbank/Banque nationale suisse (Swiss National Bank): Börsenstr 15, 8022 Zürich; tel (1) 2213750; telex 812400; fax (1) 2211875; Bundesplatz, 3003 Berne; tel (31) 210211; Chair of Board: Dr M. Lusser; Vice-Chair: Dr H. Meyer; f 1907; central bank; head offices in Zürich and Berne; regulates the circulation of money, facilitates payments transactions and pursues a credit and monetary policy serving the general interest; Dept I (Zürich) is responsible for economic studies, statistics, legal matters, personnel and internal auditing; Dept II (Berne) issues notes, manages metal reserves, runs the main accounting section and banking transactions for the Federal Govt; Dept III (Zürich) handles foreign exchange business and credits to the commercial banks in addition to giro and clearing functions; 8 brs.

FINANCIAL AGENCIES

Eidg Finanzkontrolle/Contrôle fédéral des finances (Federal Finance Control): Bundesgasse 3, 3003 Berne; tel (31) 616311; Dir: Dr Gottlieb Schläppi; Dep Dir: Werner Frei; under the Federal Dept of Finance.

Eidg Finanzverwaltung/Administration des finances (Federal Finance Administration): Bundesgasse 3, 3003 Berne Bernerhof; tel (31) 616011; Dir: Dr Waldemar Jucker; Dep Dir: Dr Peter Probst; under the Federal Dept of Finance.

Eidg Steuerverwaltung/Administration fédérale des contributions (Federal Tax Administration): Eigerstr 65, 3003 Berne; tel (31) 617106; fax (31) 617349; Dir: Dieter Metzger; Dep Dir: François Gendre.

INSURANCE

Bundesamt für Privatversicherungswesen/Office fédéral des assurances privées: Gutenbergstr 50, 3003 Berne; tel (31) 617911; fax (31) 617944; Dir: Peter Pfund; Dep Dir: Dr Otto Louis; f 1885; oversees private insurance institutions subject to state supervision.

Eidg Versicherungskasse/Caisse fédérale d'assurance: Bundesgasse 32, 3003 Berne; tel (31) 616420; fax (31) 617822; Dir: Dr Ellen H. Hülsen; Vice-Dir: David Gerber; under the Federal Dept of Finance.

Schweizerische Unfallversicherungsanstalt (SUVA)/ Caisse nationale suisse d'assurance en cas d'accidents: Fluhmattstr 1, 6002 Luzern; tel (41) 215111; Pres of Board: Luigi Generali; Vice-Pres: Fritz Leuthy, Heinz Allenspach.

TRADE

Büro für Konsumentenfragen/Bureau de la consommation (Office for Consumer Affairs): Belpstr 53, 3003 Berne; tel (31) 612021; Dir: Dr Hans Kelterborn; under the Federal Dept of Public Economy.

Comptoir Suisse (National Fair): ave des Bergières 10, CP 89, 1000 Lausanne 22; tel (21) 451111; telex 454044; fax (21) 453711; Gen Man: Antoine Hoefliger; f 1919; organization of exhibitions, fairs, congresses, assemblies, meetings, etc; trade fair every September.

Eidg Zollverwaltung/Administration fédérale des douanes (Federal Customs Administration) and **Oberzolldirektion/Direction générale des douanes** (General Directorate of Customs): Monbijoustr 40, 3003 Berne; tel (31) 616511; Dir of Customs: Dr Hans Lauri; Dep Dir: Samuel Moser; under the Federal Dept of Finance.

Kommission für die Exportrisikogarantie/Commission pour la garantie des risques à l'exportation: Kirchenweg 4, 8032 Zürich; tel (1) 476654; Pres: Dr Rolf Jeker; export risk guarantee commission.

Defence

Bundesamt für Polizeiwesen/Office fédéral de la police (Federal Police Office): Bundesrain 20, 3003 Berne; tel (31) 614224; telex 912240; fax (31) 615380; Dir: Dr Peter Hess; Vice-Dirs: Dr Lorenz Zünd, Pierre Schmid.

Bundesamt für Rüstungsbetriebe/Office fédéral de la production d'armements (Federal Office of Arms Production): Kasernenstr 27, 3000 Berne 25; tel (31) 675815; Dir: Dr Kurt Hübner.

Bundesamt für Zivilschutz (Federal Office for Civil Defence): Postfach, Monbijoustr 91, 3003 Berne; tel (31) 615011; telex 911479; fax (31) 615236; Exec Dir: Hans Mumenthaler; f 1963; aims at the protection, rescue and care of people and the protection of property through measures intended to prevent or mitigate the effects of armed conflicts; in peacetime and in times of active military duty, Civil Defence may be mobilized for assistance and aid in an emergency.

Defence Technology and Procurement Agency: Kasernenstr 19, 3000 Berne 25; tel (31) 675701; telex 912619; fax (31) 675763; procurement of defence equipment for the Swiss Armed Forces.

Direktion der Eidg Militärverwaltung/Direction de l'administration militaire fédérale: Bundeshaus-Ost, 3003 Berne; tel (31) 675037; Dir: Hans-Ulrich Ernst; Dep Dir: Dr Walter Tschanz.

Gruppe für Generalstabsdienste/Groupement de l'état-major général: Bundeshaus-Ost, 3003 Berne; tel (31) 671211; Chief of Gen Staff: Commdr Eugen Lüthy.

Oberkriegskommissariat/Commissariat central des guerres (Central War Commission): Wylerstr 52, 3000 Berne 25; tel (31) 674252; fax (31) 674389; War Commr: Brig Hans Schlup.

Polizeidienst/Service de police: Taubenstr 16, 3003 Bern; tel (31) 614511; Chief of Police: Dr Peter Huber.

Zentralpolizeibüro/Bureau central de police: Bundesrain 20, 3003 Berne; tel (31) 614689; Chief: Rudolf Wyss.

Development and Planning

Bundesamt für Raumplanung (BRP)/Office fédéral de l'aménagement du territoire (Federal Office for Spatial Planning): Eigerstr 65, 3003 Berne; tel (31) 614060; fax (31) 617869; Dir: Marius Baschung; f 1980; spatial planning.

Education and Research

EDUCATION

Bundesamt für Bildung und Wissenschaft/Office fédéral de l'éducation et de la science (Federal Office for Education and Science): Postfach 2732, Wildhainweg 9, 3001 Berne; tel (31) 619654; Dir: Dr Urs Hochstrasser; Vice-Dir: Gerhard M. Schuwey.

RESEARCH

Kommission zur Förderung der wissenschaftlichen Forschung/Commission pour l'encouragement des recherches scientifiques (Commission for the Promotion of Scientific Research): Wildhainweg 20, 3003 Berne; tel (31) 612146; Pres: Dr Hans Sieber; Sec: Dr Peter Kuentz.

Paul Scherrer Institut (PSI): Würenlingen and Villigen, 5232 Villigen; tel (56) 992111; telex 827414; fax (56) 982327; Dir: Dr J. P. Blaser; Dep Dir: Dr W. Hirt; f 1988; fmrly Swiss Federal Institute for Reactor Research; nuclear and particle physics; biology, medicine and health physics; solid state research and material science; nuclear and non-nuclear energy research and engineering services.

Schweizerische Physikalische Gesellschaft/Société suisse de physique (Swiss Physical Society): Institut de Physique Expérimentale, Université de Lausanne, 1015 Lausanne-Dorigny; tel (21) 6922322; Pres: Prof Samuel Steinmann; holds two official meetings per year.

Energy

Bundesamt für Energiewirtschaft: Kapellenstr 14, 3001 Berne; tel (31) 615611; telex 33065; Dir: Eduard Kiener; federal energy office; concerned with the general devt of energy supply in Switzerland.

Services Industriels de Genève: Pont de la Machine, CP 272, 1211 Geneva 11; tel (22) 20811; publicly-owned utility co supplying Geneva with electricity; also supplies gas and water; Geneva is supplied with natural gas under contract from the Netherlands and the Federal Republic of Germany.

Health and Welfare

HEALTH

Bundesamt für Gesundheitswesen/Office fédéral de la santé publique (Federal Office for Public Health): Postfach 2644, Bollwerk 27, 3001 Berne; tel (31) 619511; Dir: Dr Beat Roos.

WELFARE

Bundesamt für Sozialversicherung/Office fédéral des assurances sociales (Federal Office of National Insurance): Effingerstr 33, 3003 Bern; tel (31) 619011; Dir: Dr Sebastian Schnyder.

Bundesamt für Wohnungswesen/Office fédéral du logement (Federal Housing Office): Weltpoststr 4, 3000 Berne 15; tel (31) 612444; fax (31) 612466; Dir: T. C. Guggenheim; Vice-Dir: P. Gurtner; central Govt body responsible for housing policy in Switzerland; housing subsidies, tenant protection, promotion of housing construction and home ownership, etc.

> **Eidg Forschungskommission Wohnungswesen (FWW)/ Commission fédérale de recherche pour le logement (CRL)** (Federal Housing Research Commission): address as above; Pres: Prof Walter Hess; f 1975; housing research; co-ordination of research needs in housing and construction market; publication of research results.

Eidg Kommission für Frauenfragen/Commission fédérale pour les questions féminines (Federal Commission for Women's Affairs): Postfach, Thunstr 20, 3000 Berne 6; tel (31) 619276; Pres: Dr Lili Nabholz-Haidegger; under the Federal Dept of Home Affairs.

Eidg Kommission für Jugendfragen/Commission fédérale pour la jeunesse (Federal Commission for Youth Affairs): Postfach, Thunstr 20, 3000 Berne 6; tel (31) 619287; Pres: Guy-Olivier Segond; under the Federal Dept of Home Affairs.

International Affairs

Bundesamt für Außenwirtschaft/Office fédéral des affaires économiques extérieures (Federal Office for Foreign Economic Affairs): Bundeshaus-Ost, 3003 Berne; tel (31) 612211; fax (31) 612330; Dir: Dr Franz Blankart; under the Federal Dept of Public Economy.

Direktion für Entwicklungszusammenarbeit und humanitäre Hilfe (Directorate of Development Co-operation and Humanitarian Aid): 3003 Berne; tel (31) 613488; telex 33151; fax (31) 613505; Dir: Fritz Staehelin; f 1961.

Legal and Judiciary

Bundesamt für Justiz/Office fédéral de la justice (Federal Justice Office): Bundeshaus-West, 3003 Berne; tel (31) 614141; Dir: Dr Heinrich Koller; Dep Dir: Dr Paul Zweifel.

Bundesanwaltschaft/Ministère public de la Confédération: Taubenstr 16, 3003 Berne; tel (31) 614511; Bundesanwalt (Solicitor-Gen): Dr Rudolf Gerber.

Schweizerisches Bundesgericht/Tribunal Fédéral (Federal Supreme Court): Palais de Mon-Repos, 1000 Lausanne 14; tel (21) 218111; fax (21) 233700; comprises 30 judges elected for a six-year term by the Federal Assembly; the Pres of the Federal Supreme Court is elected by the Federal Assembly for a two-year term, with no possibility of re-election, from among the sen judges of the Court; consists of six permanent branches, and four non-permanent divisions.

Eidg Versicherungsgericht/Tribunal Fédéral des Assurances (Federal Insurance Tribunal): Adligenswilerstr 24, 6006 Luzern; tel (41) 509911; f 1918; consists of seven mems; since 1969 it has been considered as the Court of Social Insurance (Sozialversicherungsabteilung, Cour des assurances sociales, Corte delle assicurazioni sociali) of the Federal Supreme Court.

Media

GOVERNMENT PUBLISHER

Eidg Drucksachen- und Materialzentrale/Office central fédéral des imprimés et du matériel/Ufficio Federale degli Stampati e del Materiale: 3000 Berne; fax (31) 613975; central printing and supply office.

NEWS AND INFORMATION

Bundesamt für Statistik/Office fédéral de la statistique/ Ufficio federale de statistica (Federal Office of Statistics): Hallwylstr 15, 3003 Berne; tel (31) 618660; telex 912871; fax (31) 617856; collection and publication of statistics in the areas of population, employment, economy, prices, agriculture, construction and housing, tourism, transport and communications, health, education, political life.

Science and Technology

Bundesamt für Landestopographie/Office fédéral de la topographie (Federal Topography Office): Seftigenstr 264, 3084 Wabern; tel (31) 541331; fax (31) 549459; Dir: Francis Jeanrichard.

Eidg Amt für Messwesen/Office fédéral de métrologie (Federal Office of Metrology): Lindenweg 50, 3084 Wabern; tel (31) 596111; telex 912860; Dir: Dr Otto Piller; Dep Dir: Dr Pierre Koch; under the Federal Dept of Justice and Police.

Institut suisse de météorologie (ISM): Krähbühlstr 58, 8044 Zürich; tel (1) 2569111; telex 817373; fax (1) 2569339; Dir: Dr A. Junod; Dep Dir: Dr T. Gutermann; Sub-Dir: M. Haug; f 1880; meteorological institute.

Landeshydrologie und -geologie/Service hydrologique et géologique national (National Hydrological and Geological Service): Hallwylstr 4, 3003 Berne; tel (31) 619385; Head: Dr Charles Emmenegger; under the Federal Dept of Home Affairs.

Schweizerischer Nationalfonds zur Förderung der wissenschaftlichen Forschung (Swiss National Science Foundation): Wildhainweg 20, 3001 Berne; tel (31) 245424; telex 912423; fax (31) 233009; Pres of the Council: Prof Alfred

Schmid; Pres of National Research Council: Prof André Aeschli-mann; Sec-Gen: Dr Peter Fricker; f 1952.

Tourism

Swiss National Tourist Office: Bellariastr 38, 8027 Zürich; tel (1) 2881111; telex 815391; fax (1) 2881205; Chair: Jean-Jacques Cevey; Dir-Gen: Walter Leu; Dep Dir-Gen: Helmut Klee; Asst Dir-Gen: Hans Zimmermann; f 1941; promotion of tourism; offices in most major cities of the world.

Transport and Communications

TELECOMMUNICATIONS

PTT—Post-, Telefon- und Telegrafenbetriebe/Entreprise des postes, téléphones et télégraphes: Viktoriastr 21, 3030 Berne; tel (31) 621111; fax (31) 622549; Dir-Gen: Hans-Werner Binz; Dir, Telecommunications: Rudolf Trachsel; state-owned telecommunications authority.

Postdepartement/Département de la Poste: address as above; Dir-Gen: Jean Clivaz.

Fernmeldedepartement/Département des télécommunications: address as above; Dir-Gen: Rudolf Trachsel.

TRANSPORT

Bundesamt für Straßenbau (Federal Highways Office): Monbijoustr 40, 3003 Berne; tel (31) 619411; fax (31) 616296; Dir: K. Suter; Vice-Dirs: P. Hurni, H. Thalmann; supervision of design, construction and maintenance of federal highways.

Bundesamt für Verkehr/Office fédéral des transports (Federal Transport Office): Bundeshaus-Nord, Kochergasse 10, 3003 Berne; tel (31) 615711; Dir: Dr Fritz Bürki; Dep Dir: Dr Claude Mossu; under the Federal Dept of Transport, Communications and Energy.

Bundesamt für Zivilluftfahrt/Office fédéral de l'aviation civile: Inselgasse 1, 3003 Berne; tel (31) 615901; telex 912601; fax (31) 617885; Dir: Max Neuenschwander; Dep Dir: Andreas Deutsch; Sub-Dir: Ernst Aebi; f 1920; prepares and executes legislation concerning civil aviation; co-ordinates activities of offices, organizations and cos involved in civil aviation devt; responsible for civil aviation security measures.

Schweizerische Bundesbahnen (SBB)/Chemins de fer fédéraux suisses: Hochschulstr 6, 3030 Berne; tel (31) 601111; telex 991121; fax (31) 603273; Pres: C. Grosjean; Gen Man: W. Latscha; f 1901; railways.

Schweizerisches Seeschiffahrtsamt/Office suisse de la navigation maritime (Swiss Maritime Navigation Office): Elisabethenstr 31, 4002 Basel; tel (61) 235333; Dir: Jean Hulliger; under the Federal Dept of Foreign Affairs.

SYRIA

Head of State

Under the 1973 Constitution, executive power is vested in the President, who is elected by direct popular vote for a seven-year term. The President appoints the Vice-President, Prime Minister and other members of the Cabinet.

President: Lt-Gen Hafiz al-Assad (elected 12 March 1971; re-elected 8 February 1978 and 10 February 1985).

Office of the President: Presidential Palace, Muhajreen, Abu Rumanch, al-Rashid St, Damascus; tel (11) 331112.

Vice-Presidents: Abd al-Halim Khaddam (responsible for Political and Foreign Affairs), Zuheir Masharkah (responsible for Internal and Party Affairs).

Legislature

Legislative power is vested in the unicameral Majlis ash-Sha'ab (People's Assembly), with 195 members elected by universal adult suffrage. Syria has 14 administrative districts (mohafazat).

Majlis ash-Sha'ab (People's Assembly): Damascus; tel (11) 332000; Speaker: Abd al-Qadir Qaddurah.

MINISTRIES AND GOVERNMENT DEPARTMENTS

OFFICE OF THE PRIME MINISTER
Shahbandar St, Damascus
Tel (11) 226000
Prime Minister: Mahmoud az-Zoubi
Deputy Prime Minister: Gen Mustafa Tlass

OFFICE OF ECONOMIC AFFAIRS UNDER THE PRIME MINISTER
Shabandar St, Damascus
Deputy Prime Minister: Salim Yassin

OFFICE OF PUBLIC SERVICE AFFAIRS UNDER THE PRIME MINISTER
Shahbandar St, Damascus
Deputy Prime Minister: Mahmoud Qaddour

MINISTRY OF AGRICULTURE AND AGRARIAN REFORM
29 rue Ayar, Damascus
Tel (11) 113613
Minister: Muhammad Ghabbash

MINISTRY OF AWQAF (RELIGIOUS ENDOWMENTS)
Parliament/Sanaa St, Damascus
Tel (11) 115646
Minister: Abd al-Majid at-Tarabulsi

MINISTRY OF COMMUNICATIONS
nr Majlis ash-Sha'ab, Damascus
Tel (11) 226213; telex 411993
Minister: Mourad Kuwatli

MINISTRY OF CONSTRUCTION
Jabri/Furat St, Damascus
Tel (11) 223595
Minister: Dr Marwan Farrah

MINISTRY OF CULTURE AND NATIONAL GUIDANCE
Rawda St, Damascus
Tel (11) 331556
Minister: Dr Najah al-Attar

MINISTRY OF DEFENCE
Omayyad Sq, Damascus
Tel (11) 112101; telex 11371
Minister: Gen Mustafa Tlass

MINISTRY OF ECONOMY AND FOREIGN TRADE
Salhieh, Ma'mun Bitar St, Damascus
Tel (11) 113513; telex 411982
Minister: Dr Muhammad al-Imadi

MINISTRY OF EDUCATION
Shahbandar St, Damascus
Tel (11) 444800
Minister: Ghassan Halabi

MINISTRY OF ELECTRICITY
Sultan Salim St and Victoria St, Damascus
Tel (11) 227155; telex 411256
Minister: Kamal al-Baba

MINISTRY OF FINANCE
Jule Jamal St, Damascus
Tel (11) 116300; telex 411932
Minister: Khalid al-Mahayni

MINISTRY OF FOREIGN AFFAIRS
al-Rashid St, Damascus
Tel (11) 331200; telex 411922
Minister: Farouk ash-Shara'
Minister of State: Nasir Qaddour

MINISTRY OF HEALTH
Parliament St, Damascus
Tel (11) 333800
Minister: Dr Iyad ash-Shatti

MINISTRY OF HIGHER EDUCATION
Ziad bin Abi Sufian St, Damascus
Tel (11) 330700
Minister: Dr Kamal Sharaf

MINISTRY OF HOUSING AND UTILITIES
Azmeh Sq, Sanaa St, Damascus
Tel (11) 224194
Minister: Muhammad Nour Antabi

MINISTRY OF INDUSTRY
place Yousuf Ahmad, Damascus
Tel (11) 115647
Minister: Antoine Joubrane

MINISTRY OF INFORMATION
ave al-Mazzeh, Immeuble Dar al-Baath, Damascus
Tel (11) 660412
Minister: Muhammad Salman

MINISTRY OF THE INTERIOR
Merjeh Circle, Damascus
Tel (11) 220100
Minister: Dr Muhammad Harbah

MINISTRY OF IRRIGATION, PUBLIC WORKS AND WATER RESOURCES
rue Saadallah Jabri, Damascus
Minister: Abd ar-Rahman Madani

MINISTRY OF JUSTICE
Nasr St, Damascus
Tel (11) 114101
Minister: Khalid al-Ansari

MINISTRY OF LOCAL GOVERNMENT
Bahsa, Damascus
Tel (11) 117251
Minister: Ahmad Diyab

MINISTRY OF PETROLEUM AND MINERAL WEALTH
rue Moutanabbi, Damascus
Tel (11) 116783; telex 411006
Minister: Dr Mtanios Habib

MINISTRY OF SOCIAL AFFAIRS AND LABOUR
Azmeh Sq, rue Fardoss, Damascus
Tel (11) 113516
Minister: Haydar Buzu

MINISTRY OF SUPPLY AND INTERNAL TRADE
opposite Majlis ash-Sha'ab, Damascus
Tel (11) 445200
Minister: Hassan as-Saqqa

MINISTRY OF TOURISM
Victoria St, Damascus
Tel (11) 210122; telex 411672
Minister: Adnan Kuli
Deputy Minister: Issam Amiri

MINISTRY OF TRANSPORT
rue Abou Roumaneh, BP 134, Damascus
Tel (11) 336801; telex 411994
Minister: Yousuf al-Ahmad

OFFICE OF THE MINISTERS OF STATE
Damascus
Minister of State for Council of Ministers Affairs: Yassin Rajjouh
Minister of State for Environmental Affairs: Abd al-Hamid al Mounajjid
Minister of State for People's Assembly Affairs: Ghazi Mustafa
Minister of State for Planning Affairs: Dr Sabah Bakjaji
Minister of State for Presidential Affairs: Wahib Fadel
Ministers of State: Dr Muhammad Jumah, Ali Khalil

GOVERNMENT AGENCIES AND ORGANIZATIONS

Agriculture

Cotton Marketing Organization (CMO): Bab-el-Faraj St, POB 729, Aleppo; tel (21) 238486; telex 331227; Dir-Gen: Rateb Jaber; Mans: Abdul Sattar Osman, Nouri Dalati, Walid Shou-gouri, Ahmed Rajeb; f 1965; buying, ginning and selling cotton in local and external markets.

General Organization for Food Industries: POB 105, Damascus; tel (11) 225290; telex 419154; organization of food-processing and marketing.

General Organization for Sugar Industries: POB 266, Homs.

Business and Economy

BANKING

Agricultural Bank: rue Euphrates, BP 5325, Damascus; Dir-Gen: Maen Rislan; f 1924; 55 brs.

Central Bank of Syria: place at-Tajrida al-Moughrabia, BP 2254, Damascus; tel (11) 224800; telex 11007; Gov: Dr Hisham Mutewalli; f 1956; 9 brs.

Commercial Bank of Syria: place Yousuf al-Azmeh, BP 933, Damascus; tel (11) 218890; telex 411002; Chair and Gen Man: Muhammad Riyadh Hakim; f 1967; 36 brs.

Co-operative Agricultural Bank: Nanaa Garden, BP 4325, Damascus.

Industrial Bank: 29 rue May, BP 7578, Damascus; tel (11) 228200; Chair: Abd al-Qadir Obeido; f 1959; provides finance for industry; 13 brs.

Popular Credit Bank: rue Fardoss, Dar al-Mohandessin Blvd, 6th Floor, BP 2841, Damascus; tel (11) 114260; Chair and Gen Man: Muhammad Hassan al-Houjjeri; f 1967; provides loans to the services sector and is the sole authorized issuer of savings certificates; 43 brs.

Real Estate Bank: rue al-Furat, Damascus; tel (11) 218602; telex 419171; Chair and Gen Man: Muhammad A. Makhlouf; f 1966; provides loans and grants for housing, schools, hospitals and hotel construction; 13 brs.

INSURANCE

Syrian General Organization for Insurance: rue Tajheez, BP 2279, Damascus; tel (11) 218430; telex 411003; Chair and Gen Man: Salem Haddad; f 1953; operates throughout Syria.

NATIONALIZED INDUSTRY

General Establishment for Chemical Industries: Baramkeh, Abou Bakr el-Siddeeq St, BP 5447, Damascus.

General Organization for Cement and Building Materials: Mezzeh Autostrade, Damascus.

General Organization of Engineering Industries: Baramkeh, Abou Bakr el-Siddeeq, BP 3120, Damascus; tel (11) 214650; telex 411035; Dir-Gen: Mamdouh Mounajed; Dep Dir-Gen: Dr Daoud Bechara; f 1975; supervises, controls, inspects and promotes activities of industrial and commercial nature with regard to 13 state-owned engineering cos.

General Organization for Textile Industries: rue Fardoss, BP 620, Damascus; tel (11) 116200; telex 411011; control and planning of the textile industry and supervision of textile manufacture; 13 subsidiary cos.

TRADE

General Directory for Damascus International Fair: Barada St, Damascus.

General Organization for Free Zones: BP 2790, Damascus.

General Organization for Trading and Distribution (GOTA): al-Nasr Ave, BP 15, Damascus; tel (11) 210396; telex 411355; Chair and Gen Man: Muhammad Rateb Kweider; Dep Gen Man: Muhammad Younes; f 1897, nationalized 1965; import monopoly on arms and alcohol, responsible for duty free shops.

General Trade Organization for Machinery and Equipment (Sayarat): Sayarat Maysaloon St, BP 3130, Damascus; tel (11) 118156; telex 11036.

Geza: al-Jumhouriah St, BP 893, Damascus; tel (11) 226142; telex 11009; foreign trade organization for chemicals and foodstuffs.

Maaden (General Foreign Trade Organization for Metals and Building Materials): 94 al-Jumhouriah St, BP 3136, Damascus; tel 420495; telex 411459; Dir-Gen: Muhammad al-Mahamid; trade in metal, timber and cement products.

Nasige (Foreign Trade Organization for Textiles): al-Jumhouriah St, BP 814, Damascus; tel (11) 111571; telex 11008.

Pharmex (General Organization for the Trade of Pharmaceutical Products): Abi Firass al-Hamadani St, BP 3052, Damascus; tel (11) 110289; telex 11001.

Defence

Armed Forces: c/o Ministry of Defence, Omayyad Sq, Damascus; tel (11) 229100; telex 11371; Commdr-in-Chief: Lt-Gen Hafiz al-Assad; Dep Commdr-in-Chief and Minister of Defence: Maj-Gen Mustafa Tlass.

Syrian Arab Air Force: al-Mahdi Ben Barakeh St, BP 90, Damascus; tel (11) 339101; telex 11900; Commdr: Maj-Gen Subhi Haddad.

Syrian Arab Army: BP 3361, Damascus; tel (11) 233766; telex 11371; Chief of Staff: Maj-Gen Hikmat ash-Shehabi; Dep Chiefs of Staff: Maj-Gen Ali Aslan, Maj-Gen Hasan at-Turkmani.

Syrian Arab Navy: c/o Ministry of Defence, Omayyad Sq,

Damascus; tel (11) 229100; telex 11371; Commdr: Fadhaah Hossein.

Development and Planning

PLANNING

State Planning Commission: Parliament St, Damascus.

REGIONAL DEVELOPMENT

General Organization for the Exploitation and Development of the Euphrates Basin (GOEDEB): Raqqa; telex 31004; Dir-Gen: Abdo Kassem.

Legal and Judiciary

Supreme Constitutional Court: Justice Palace, Nasr St, Damascus; tel (11) 114101; Chief Justice: Nasrat Mounla-Haydar; highest court in Syria, composed of a Chief Justice and four Justices, who are appointed by decree of the President of the Republic for a renewable period of four years.

Media

BROADCASTING

Directorate-General of Broadcasting and Television: Omayyad Sq, Damascus; tel (11) 720700; telex 411138; Dir-Gen: Khudr Omran; f 1945.

NEWS AND INFORMATION

Agence Arabe Syrienne d'Information: Damascus; Dir-Gen: Dr Sabhir Falhut; f 1966; supplies bulletins on Syrian news to foreign news agencies.

Arab Advertising Organization: 28 rue Moutanabbi, BP 2842-3034, Damascus; tel (11) 225219; telex 411923; Dir-Gen: Mazen Sabbagh; f 1963; exclusive Govt establishment responsible for advertising.

Central Bureau of Statistics: rue Abd al-Malek bin Marwah, Malki Quarter, Damascus; tel (11) 335830; telex 411099; collection, analysis and dissemination of statistical data.

Mining and Energy

ENERGY

Al-Furat Petroleum Co: f 1985; 50% owned by SPC (see below); exploits the ath-Thayyem, al-Asharah and al-Ward oilfields.

Atomic Energy Commission: BP 6091, Damascus; tel (11) 668114; telex 411420; Dir-Gen: Dr I. Haddad; Dep Dir-Gen: Dr A. Lutfi; f 1979; research, fundamental and applied, into peaceful uses of atomic energy in various fields of science.

Homs Refinery Co: BP 252, Homs; tel (31) 22771; telex 41004; Dir-Gen: Kamal Karfoul.

Public Establishment of Electricity (EPE): al-Jumhouriah St, Damascus; tel (11) 223086; telex 11056.

Syrian Co for Oil Transport (SCOT): BP 13, Banias; tel

(421) 22300; telex 441012; Dir-Gen: Muhammad Douba; f 1972; responsible for admin of oil pipelines.

Syrian Co for the Storage and Distribution of Petroleum (SADCOP): Hijaz Sq, BP 40, Damascus; tel (11) 111355; telex 11260; Dir-Gen: M. Lujani.

Syrian Petroleum Co (SPC): rue al-Moutanabbi, BP 2849, Damascus; tel (11) 227007; telex 411031; Dir-Gen: Dr Ali Jebran; f 1958; holds the oil and gas concession for all Syria; also organizes exploration, production and marketing of oil and gas nationally.

MINING

General Establishment of Geology and Mineral Resources: Khatib St, BP 7645, Damascus; tel (11) 451671; telex 411528; Dir-Gen: Dr Muhammad Nagieb; f 1977; geological surveying, studies and research, prospecting and exploration of mineral resources.

General Organization for Phosphate and Mines (GECO-PHAM): BP 288, Homs; tel (31) 20405; telex 441000; production and export of phosphate rock.

Tourism

Middle East Tourism: rue Fardoss, BP 201, Damascus; tel (11) 211876; telex 411726; Pres: Muhammad Dadouche; f 1966; 7 brs.

Syrian Arab Co for Hotels and Tourism: Mezzeh, BP 5549, Damascus.

Transport

CIVIL AVIATION

Directorate-General of Civil Aviation: place Nejmeh, Damascus; tel (11) 331306; telex 411928.

Syrian Arab Airlines (Syrianair): Immeuble Red Crescent, place Yousuf al-Azmeh, BP 417, Damascus; tel (11) 455600; telex 411593; f 1946, refounded 1961 to succeed Syrian Airways, after revocation of merger with Misrair; domestic passenger and cargo services; international services throughout the Middle East and to Europe, North Africa and the Far East.

RAILWAYS

General Organization of the Hedjaz-Syrian Railway: place Hedjaz, BP 134, Damascus; tel (11) 215815; Gen Man: A. Ismail; 246 km of track.

Syrian Railways: BP 182, Aleppo; tel (21) 213009; telex 331009; Pres and Dir-Gen: Muhammad Ghassan al-Kaddour; f 1897; approx 2,000 km of track.

ROADS

General Co for Roads: BP 3143, Aleppo; tel (21) 555406; telex 331403; Gen Man: M. Walid al-Ajlani; f 1975.

SHIPPING

Syrian Crude Oil Transport Co: POB 331, Homs; telex 41003; Dir-Gen: Yousuf Hissamo.

Syrian General Authority for Maritime Transport: 2 Argentine St, BP 730, Damascus; tel (11) 225710; telex 412112; Dir-Gen: Akil Ismail; f 1959; shipping agent and broker for state sector.

Syrian Navigation Co: Baghdad St, Lattakia; tel (41) 33778; telex 451028; Dir-Gen: Muhammad Haroun; f 1975; ship owner.

Syro-Jordanian Shipping Co: rue Port Said, BP 148, Lattakia; tel (41) 316356; telex 451002; Chair: Osman Lebbady; operates two general cargo ships.

TANZANIA

Head of State

Executive power is vested in the President, who is elected by direct popular vote, based on universal adult suffrage, for five years. A single presidential candidate is nominated by the ruling party, Chama Cha Mapinduzi (CCM). The President's term is limited to a maximum of two five-year periods. The President appoints two Vice-Presidents, one of whom is the President of Zanzibar and the other the Prime Minister of Tanzania. The President selects the Cabinet in consultation with the Prime Minister.

President: Ali Hassan Mwinyi (took office 5 November 1985).

Office of the President: The State House, POB 9120, Dar es Salaam; tel (51) 23261; telex 41192.

First Vice-President: Joseph Warioba.

Office of the First Vice-President: POB 980, Dodoma; tel (61) 20511; telex 53159.

Second Vice-President and President of Zanzibar: Idirs Abdul Wakil.

Office of the Second Vice-President: POB 776, Zanzibar; tel (54) 20511.

Legislature

Tanzania is a one-party state. Legislative power is vested in the unicameral National Assembly, whose members serve for five years. The 244 members of the Assembly are all approved by the CCM. At the 1985 elections 169 members were elected by universal adult suffrage. The remaining seats were allocated to nominated members, including five nominated by the Zanzibar House of Representatives. Zanzibar has its own administration for internal affairs, including a separate Constitution and an elected President.

National Assembly: POB 9133, Dar es Salaam; tel (51) 26491; Speaker: Chief Adam Sapi Mkwawa.

MINISTRIES AND GOVERNMENT DEPARTMENTS

OFFICE OF THE PRIME MINISTER
POB 980, Dodoma
Tel (61) 20511; telex 53159
Prime Minister: Joseph Warioba
Deputy Prime Minister: Salim Ahmed Salim
Ministers without Portfolio: Rashidi Kawawa, Gertrude Mongella

MINISTRY OF AGRICULTURE AND LIVESTOCK DEVELOPMENT
POB 9192, Dar es Salaam
Tel (51) 27231
Minister: Stephen Wassira

MINISTRY OF COMMUNICATIONS AND WORKS
POB 9423, Dar es Salaam
Tel (51) 23235; telex 41392
Minister: Pius Ng'wandu

MINISTRY OF DEFENCE AND NATIONAL SERVICE
POB 9544, Dar es Salaam
Tel (51) 28291
Minister: Ali Hassan Mwinyi
Minister of State: Jackson Makweta

MINISTRY OF EDUCATION
POB 9121, Dar es Salaam
Tel (51) 27211
Minister: Amran Mayagila

MINISTRY OF ENERGY AND MINERALS
POB 9153, Dar es Salaam
Tel (51) 31433
Minister: Jakaya Kikwete

MINISTRY OF FINANCE
POB 9111, Dar es Salaam
Tel (51) 21271; telex 41329
Minister: Stephen Kibona
Minister of State: Amina Salum Ali

MINISTRY OF FOREIGN AFFAIRS
POB 9000, Dar es Salaam
Tel (51) 21234; telex 41086
Minister: Benjamin Mkapa

MINISTRY OF HEALTH
POB 9083, Dar es Salaam
Tel (51) 20261
Minister: Charles Kabeho

MINISTRY OF HOME AFFAIRS
POB 9223, Dar es Salaam
Tel (51) 27291; telex 41231
Minister: Nalaula Kiula

MINISTRY OF INDUSTRIES AND TRADE
POB 9503, Dar es Salaam
Tel (51) 27251
Minister: Cleopa Msuya

MINISTRY OF INFORMATION
Dar es Salaam
Minister: Hassan Diria

**MINISTRY OF JUSTICE AND OFFICE OF THE
ATTORNEY-GENERAL**
POB 9050, Dar es Salaam
Tel (51) 21234
Minister and Attorney-General: Damian Lubuva

**MINISTRY OF LABOUR, CULTURE AND SOCIAL
SERVICES**
POB 2483, Dar es Salaam
Tel (51) 20781
Minister: Joseph Rwegasira

**MINISTRY OF LANDS, NATURAL RESOURCES
AND TOURISM**
POB 9132, Dar es Salaam
Tel (51) 21241; telex 41725; fax (51) 23244
Minister: Marcel Komanya
Deputy Ministers: E. C. Mwanansao, H. C. Dyamwale

**MINISTRY OF LOCAL GOVERNMENT,
COMMUNITY DEVELOPMENT, CO-OPERATIVES
AND MARKETING**
Dar es Salaam
Minister: Anna Abdallah
Minister of State: Matoe Qaresi

MINISTRY OF WATER DEVELOPMENT
POB 9153, Dar es Salaam
Tel (51) 31433
Minister: Christian Kisanji

MINISTRY OF YOUTH AND SPORTS
POB 1422, Dar es Salaam
Tel (51) 25411; telex 41201
Minister: (vacant)

**MINISTRIES OF STATE IN THE OFFICE OF THE
PRESIDENT**
The State House, POB 9120, Dar es Salaam
Tel (51) 23161; telex 41192
Minister of State for the Civil Service: Fatma Said Ali
Minister of State for Planning: Prof Kighoma Malima

**MINISTRIES OF STATE IN THE OFFICE OF THE
FIRST VICE-PRESIDENT AND PRIME MINISTER**
POB 980, Dodoma
Tel (61) 20511; telex 53159
Minister of State for Capital Development:
Anna Abdullah
Ministers of State: Anna Makinda, Charles Kileo

**MINISTRY OF STATE IN THE OFFICE OF THE
SECOND VICE-PRESIDENT**
POB 776, Zanzibar
Tel (54) 20511
Minister of State: Mohammed Seif Khatibu

GOVERNMENT AGENCIES AND ORGANIZATIONS

Advisory and Supervisory Body

Tanzania Audit Corpn: Gailey and Roberts Bldg, Samora Ave, POB 580, Dar es Salaam; tel (51) 37721; telex 41762; fax (51) 25470; Dir-Gen: Simon F. Sayore; f 1968; provides audit and consultancy services to public and private organizations.

Agriculture

National Agricultural and Food Corpn (NAFCO): POB 903, Dar es Salaam; tel (51) 25961; telex 41295; Gen Man: V. Ngula; f 1969; largest single food producer in Tanzania; promotes agricultural devt with special emphasis on promotion of crops vital to the economy.

National Coconut Development Programme: POB 6226, Dar es Salaam; tel (51) 74832; telex 41456; Dirs: P. Kinyawa, Dr L. Diehl; f 1978; projects include training, disease and pest control, smallholder and plantation devt, breeding and agronomy trials.

National Milling Corpn (NMC): POB 9502, Dar es Salaam; tel (51) 64541; telex 41343; Chair: S. Kasusura; Gen Man: E. D. Z. Mollel; f 1968; stores and distributes basic foodstuffs, owns grain-milling establishments and imports cereals as required.

Sugar Development Corpn: Dar es Salaam; telex 41338; Gen Man: Reuben Naburi.

Tanganyika Coffee Curing Co Ltd: POB 3053, Moshi; tel (55) 4116; telex 43082; f 1947; processing raw coffee.

Tanganyika Coffee Growers' Association Ltd: POB 102, Moshi.

Tanganyika Pyrethrum Board: POB 149, Iringa; tel (64) 2107; telex 52226; Chief Exec: P. B. G. Hangaya; Man, Admin and Personnel: E. J. Materu; Man, Finance: M. S. Lupiana; Man, Marketing: D. L. Kyaruzi; f 1949; pyrethrum processors and marketers.

Tanzania Sisal Development Board: Dar es Salaam: Chair: Austin Shaba; Gen Man: Ibrahim Kaduma; f 1973; co-ordinates the marketing of sisal.

Tanzania Tea Authority: Tea-Tex Bldg, Pamba Rd, POB 2663, Dar es Salaam; tel (51) 30031; telex 41130; Chair: H. A. Karimjee; Gen Man: E. K. Sannda; f 1968; promotion, supervision and implementation of programmes for devt of tea industry.

Tea Association of Tanzania Co Ltd: POB 2177, Dar es Salaam; tel (51) 22033; Chair: E. K. Sannda; Vice-Chair: M. S. Keeley; Exec Dir: D. E. A. Mgwassa; f 1943; promotes the devt of the tea industry; provides statistical data on tea, encourages and supports manpower devt within the industry.

Tobacco Authority of Tanzania: POB 227, Morogoro; telex 55347; Chief Exec: J. N. Elinewinga.

Business and Economy

BANKING

Bank of Tanzania: 10 Mirambo St, POB 2939, Dar es Salaam;

tel (51) 21291; telex 41024; Gov: Gilman Rutihinda; Dep Gov: N. N. Kitomari; f 1966; central bank and bank of issue.

Co-operative and Rural Development Bank: Azikiwe St, POB 268, Dar es Salaam; tel (51) 26511; telex 41643; Chair and Man Dir: P. A. Magani; Gen Man: R. D. Swai; f 1971; provides medium- and long-term loans for rural devt, as well as technical assistance and advisory service; 20 regional and 25 district offices, and 8 commercial brs.

East Africa Development Bank: 4 Nile Ave, POB 7128, Kampala, Uganda; tel (41) 230021; telex 61074; Dir-Gen: Per Aasmundrud; f 1967; provides financial and technical assistance to promote industrial devt within Uganda, Kenya and Tanzania, whose Govts each hold 30.8% of the equity.

The National Bank of Commerce (NBC): POB 1863, Dar es Salaam; tel (51) 28671; telex 41518; Chair and Man Dir: Amon J. Nsekela; Gen Man: P. L. Kamuzora; f 1967 to acquire Tanzania Bank of Commerce and Tanzanian brs of foreign banks; 134 brs, 248 agencies.

People's Bank of Zanzibar (PBZ): Forodhani, POB 1173, Zanzibar; tel (54) 31118; telex 57365; Chair: I. P. Hassan; Gen Man: N. S. Nassor; f 1966; controlled by Zanzibar Govt.

Tanganyika Post Office Savings Bank (TPOSB): POB 9300, Dar es Salaam; tel (51) 31155; telex 41054; Dir-Gen: F. C. Kasambala; Man: A. Kihwele; f 1927; 360 brs.

Tanzania Housing Bank (THB): POB 1723, Dar es Salaam; tel (51) 31112; telex 41831; Chair: E. J. Mashasi; Gen Man: Z. Maginga; f 1972; 52% state-owned, 24% owned by National Insurance Corpn, 24% by National Provident Fund; provides loans for residential and commercial projects; 21 brs, 1 agency.

Tanzania Investment Bank (TIB): POB 9373, Dar es Salaam; tel (51) 28581; telex 41259; Chair: Amon J. Nsekela; Gen Man: J. C. Rubambe; f 1970; 60% state-owned, 30% by National Bank of Commerce, 10% by National Insurance Corpn; provides finance and technical assistance for economic devt.

INSURANCE

National Insurance Corpn of Tanzania Ltd (NIC): POB 9264, Dar es Salaam; tel (51) 26561; telex 41146; Chair and Man Dir: A. M. Maalim; Gen Man: G. Mwaikambo; f 1963, nationalized 1967; all classes of insurance; 21 brs.

MARKETING

Cashew Nut Marketing Board of Tanzania: POB 533, Mtwara; telex 56134; Chair: R. Ng'itu; Gen Man: E. M. Makota.

Coffee Marketing Board of Tanzania: POB 732, Moshi; telex 43088; Chair: W. Kapinga; Gen Man: A. M. Rulegura.

Tanzania Cotton Marketing Board: POB 9161, Dar es Salaam; tel (51) 22564; telex 41287; Dir: George Wasira; f 1973 as the Tanzania Cotton Authority; regulates the marketing and export of cotton lint.

NATIONALIZED INDUSTRY

National Pharmaceutical Co Ltd: POB 4798, Dar es Salaam; tel (51) 25561; telex 41491; Dirs: J. E. Makoye, F. Lutende, M. M. Ngabo, A. Kijugu; f 1973; import, wholesale and retail of human and veterinary pharmaceuticals; invests in related industries.

National Steel Corpn Ltd: POB 2818, Dar es Salaam; tel (51) 64743; telex 41002; f 1973; import and distribution of imported and locally made steel, aluminium, copper, brass and other related metals.

National Textile Corpn: POB 9531, Dar es Salaam; tel (51) 26681; telex 41247; Man Dir: S. H. Nkya; f 1974; holding corpn

with 14 subsidiaries; production and marketing of fabrics and textiles.

State Motor Corpn: POB 1307, Dar es Salaam; telex 41152; Gen Man: H. H. Iddi; f 1974 to control all activities of the motor trade; sole importer of cars, tractors and lorries.

Tanganyika Packers Ltd: POB 60138, Dar es Salaam; tel (51) 47511; telex 41333; Dirs: H. Senkoro, A. O. Lema; f 1950; manufacturers of corned beef and other food.

Tanzania Cigarette Co Ltd: 20 Pugu Rd, POB 40114, Dar es Salaam; tel (51) 63276; telex 41165; Chair: Walter Bgoya; Gen Man: Timon Msangi; f 1975; manufacture and distribution of cigarettes; generation of revenue for the Govt.

Tanzania Portland Cement Co Ltd: POB 1950, Dar es Salaam; tel (51) 37660; telex 41401; fax (51) 38564; Gen Man: B. P. Coleman; f 1960; cement production and sales.

Tanzania Wood Industry Corpn: POB 9160, Dar es Salaam; tel (51) 28271; telex 41577; Gen Man (acting): I. T. Kuringe; Dir, Finance: J. A. Nawita; Dir, Manpower, Devt and Admin: G. R. P. Kazimoto; f 1971; production and sale of timber and wood products.

TRADE

Board of External Trade: POB 5402, Dar es Salaam; tel (51) 35614; telex 41408; Dir-Gen: M. K. Mwandoro; Dir, Research and Planning: S. U. R. Mlay; Dir, Export Promotion: P. J. Mwenguo; f 1979; export promotion, marketing research, participation in trade fairs.

Board of Internal Trade: POB 883, Dar es Salaam; tel (51) 28305; telex 41082; Dir-Gen: H. Bakari Mwapachu; f 1973; provides management consultancy to state trading cos; co-ordinates and controls corporate activities of planning, financing, trading operations, marketing research, auditing, systems design/analysis, manpower devt and admin, etc; controls internal trade policy and ensures distribution of goods.

General Agricultural Products Export Corpn: Independence Ave, POB 9172, Dar es Salaam.

Tanzania Bureau of Standards: POB 9524, Dar es Salaam; tel (51) 25551; telex 41667; Dir: B. L. Mwobahe; Mans: D. Mwakyembe, B. Mutabazi, F. L. Dias, A. Napinda; f 1976; standardization, quality control and certification, calibration and testing.

Tanzania Textile Trading Co: POB 9211, Dar es Salaam.

Zanzibar State Trading Corpn: Kenyatta Rd, POB 26, Zanzibar; tel (54) 30271; telex 57208; f 1964; purchase of crops and export to overseas markets.

Defence

Armed Forces: POB 9000, Dar es Salaam; Commdr-in-Chief: President Ali Hassan Mwinyi.

Development and Planning

PLANNING

Economic Development Commission: Dar es Salaam; f 1962 to plan national economic devt.

National Development Corpn: POB 2669, Dar es Salaam; tel (51) 26271; telex 41068; Chair and Man Dir: A. B. S. Kilewo; f 1965; promotes progress and expansion in production and investment.

National Productivity Council: POB 7282, Dar es Salaam; tel (51) 26187; Chief Exec: Nikubuka N. P. Shimwela; Dir,

Production Analysis and Prices: Lewis W. Simonje; Dir, Production Targets and Incentives: Stephen S. Tonya; Dir, Incomes and Prices: Halonga M. N. Shitindi; f 1981; co-ordination of national policy on productivity, incomes and prices.

Small Industries Development Organization (SIDO): POB 2476, Dar es Salaam; tel (51) 27691; telex 41123; fax (51) 21011; Dir-Gen: E. B. Toroka; Dir, Admin: N. E. Foya; Dir, Extension Services: D. K. Rulagora; Dir, Research and Planning: A. Semkiwa; f 1973; promotes and assists the devt of small-scale industries (especially handicraft production) in public, co-operative and private sectors; aims to increase rural industrialization and the involvement of women in devt projects.

REGIONAL DEVELOPMENT

Capital Development Authority (CDA): POB 9453, Dar es Salaam; tel (51) 23311; f 1973; created to plan and organize the transfer of the Tanzanian capital from Dar es Salaam to Dodoma.

Employment

Permanent Labour Tribunal: POB 1619, Dar es Salaam; tel (51) 29718; Chair: D. S. Meela; Dep Chair: A. R. Manento; Registrar: B. E. Nyamubi; f 1967; hears and determines trade disputes, registers negotiated and voluntary agreements.

Legal and Judiciary

Court of Appeal: Dar es Salaam; Chief Justice: Francis Nyalali; f 1979.

High Court: POB 9004, Dar es Salaam; tel (51) 26011; Jaji Kiongozi: N. S. Mnzavas; consists of a Jaji Kiongozi and 29 Judges.

Permanent Commission of Enquiry (Office of the Tanzanian Ombudsman): POB 2643, Dar es Salaam; tel (51) 26181; Chair and Official Ombudsman: A. L. S. Mhina; Sec: F. P. S. Malika; f 1966; receives and analyses complaints from the public against administrative injustice and maladministration.

Media

BROADCASTING

Radio Tanzania: POB 9191, Dar es Salaam; tel (51) 38011; telex 41201; Dir: David Wakati; f 1951; domestic services in Swahili; schools service in English and Swahili; external services in English and Afrikaans, and in vernacular languages of South Africa.

Television Zanzibar: POB 314, Zanzibar; telex 57200; Dir: Abdullah Mwinyi Khamis; f 1973; colour service.

Voice of Tanzania Zanzibar: POB 1178, Zanzibar; tel (51) 31985; telex 57207; Dir: Hassani Mitani; f 1951; broadcasts in Swahili on three wavelengths.

GOVERNMENT PUBLISHER

Government Press: POB 9124, Dar es Salaam; tel (51) 20291; telex 41631; Dir: J. Oforo; printing and bookbinding.

NEWS AND INFORMATION

Bureau of Statistics: Dar es Salaam; collection, analysis and dissemination of statistical data.

Mining and Energy

ENERGY

Agip (Tanzania) Ltd: POB 9450, Dar es Salaam; tel (51) 22586; telex 41027; Man Dir: G. Carbone; f 1966; 50% state-owned; distribution and marketing of petroleum products.

National Petroleum Development Corpn: POB 2774, Dar es Salaam; tel (51) 20773; telex 41219; state oil co.

Tanzania Electric Supply Co (TANESCO): POB 9024, Dar es Salaam; Chair: Minister of Water Development, Christian Kisanji; Man Dir: S. L. Mosha.

MINING

State Mining Corpn: POB 4958, Dar es Salaam; tel (51) 28781; telex 41354; Gen Man: W. H. Manning; f 1973; mineral exploration and mining.

Williamson Diamonds Ltd: POB 9470, Dar es Salaam; tel (51) 41332; PO Mwadui, Shinyanga; telex 46165; Gen Man: S. Mipawa; f 1942; State Mining Corpn owns 50% of capital; diamond mining.

Tourism

Tanzania Tourist Corpn: IPS Bldg, Maktaba St, POB 2485, Dar es Salaam; tel (51) 27671; telex 41061; Gen Man: N. J. Kasella; f 1969; implementation of plans on tourism designed to improve infrastructure and boost tourism.

Tanzania Wildlife Corpn (TAWICO): POB 1144, Arusha; tel (57) 3501; telex 42080; fax (57) 2828; f 1974; deals with and conducts: big game safaris, game cropping, capture and sale of live animals and birds, manufacture of assorted goods.

Transport and Communications

TELECOMMUNICATIONS

Tanzania Posts and Telecommunications (TPTC): POB 9070, Dar es Salaam; telex 41054; fax (51) 34610; Dir-Gen: F. C. Kasambala; Dep Dir-Gen: A. B. Mapunda; f 1977; operates postal and telecommunications services.

TRANSPORT

Air Tanzania Corpn: Ohio St, POB 543, Dar es Salaam; tel (51) 38300; telex 41077; Chief Exec: E. M. Olekambainei; Technical Dir: D. Rwehumbiza; Commercial Dir: F. Makwaia; f 1977; domestic network and international services throughout Africa.

National Shipping Agencies Co Ltd: POB 9082, Dar es Salaam; tel (51) 27241; telex 41323; f 1975; shipping agency operations, warehousing, cargo canvassing and business information.

Tanzania Coastal Shipping Line Ltd: POB 9461, Dar es Salaam; tel (51) 26192; telex 41124; Gen Mans: M. S. Karani,

K. Flottum; f 1971; operation of shipping services in Tanzania and to other African countries.

Tanzania Harbours Authority: Bandari St, POB 9184, Dar es Salaam; tel (51) 21212; telex 41346; fax (51) 32066; Dir-Gen: Athumani Janguo; f 1977; port admin and cargo handling.

Tanzania Railways Corpn (TRC): POB 468, Dar es Salaam; tel (51) 26241; telex 41308; Chair: Prof S. A. Mawenya; Gen Man: P. C. Bakilana; f 1977 after dissolution of East African Railways; operates 2,600 km of track; also operates vessels on Lakes Victoria, Tanganyika and Malawi.

Tanzania-Zambia Railway Authority (TAZARA): POB 2834, Dar es Salaam; tel (51) 64191; telex 41059; Chair: Odira Ongara; Gen Man: S. I. C. Mapala; Regional Man (Tanzania): R. S. Seme; opened in 1975; 1,860 km railway link between Dar es Salaam and New Kapiri Mposhi, Zambia.

THAILAND

<table>
<tr><td>

Head of State

The King is Head of State, and appoints a Prime Minister on the advice of the National Assembly, and the Council of Ministers on the advice of the Prime Minister. The King may dismiss members of the Council of Ministers on the Prime Minister's advice. A Privy Council, appointed by the King, exists to advise the King on all matters pertaining to his functions.

Sovereign: HM King Bhumibol Adulyadej (King Rama IX) (succeeded to the throne June 1946).

Office of HM the King: The Grand Palace, Na Phra Lan Rd, Bangkok 10200; tel (2) 225-0136; telex 72222; fax (2) 224-3259.

Privy Council: Bangkok; Pres: Dr Sanya Dharmasakti.

</td><td>

Legislature

Legislative power is vested in the bicameral National Assembly, comprising a House of Representatives, with 357 members elected by universal adult suffrage for four years (subject to dissolution), and a Senate of 267 members appointed for a six-year term by the King on the recommendation of the incumbent Prime Minister. Martial law was declared in October 1976 and remained in force, although some martial law powers were subsequently relaxed.

Senate: U-Thong Nai Rd, Bangkok 10300; tel (2) 282-6181; Speaker: Wan Chansu.

House of Representatives: U-Thong Nai Rd, Bangkok 10300; tel (2) 282-6181.

</td></tr>
</table>

MINISTRIES AND GOVERNMENT DEPARTMENTS

OFFICE OF THE PRIME MINISTER
Govt House, Nakhon Pathom Rd, Bangkok 10300
Prime Minister:
Gen Chatichai Choonhavan
Deputy Prime Ministers: Pong Sarasin, Gen Tienchai Sirisumpan
Ministers to the Prime Minister's Office: Meechai Ruchupan, Boon-Eua Prasertsuwan, Korn Dabbaransi, Anuwat Wattanapongsiri, Chaisiri Ruangkanchanases, Supatra Masdit, Col Phol Rerngprasertvit, Chalerm Yubamrung

MINISTRY OF AGRICULTURE AND CO-OPERATIVES
Ratchadamnoen Nok Ave, Bangkok 10200
Tel (2) 281-5955
Minister: Maj-Gen Sanan Khachornprasart
Deputy Ministers: Charoen Kanthawong, Udomsak Tangthong, Udon Tantisunthorn

MINISTRY OF COMMERCE
Sanamchai Rd, Bangkok 10200
Tel (2) 220-0855; telex 82389
Minister: Subin Pinkhayan
Deputy Ministers: Shucheep Hansaward, Pinya Chuayplod

Insurance Department: 1053/1 Phahon Yothin Rd, Phaya Thai, Bangkok 10400; tel (2) 279-9870; telex 82389; fax (2) 271-4708; Dir-Gen: Chalaw Fuangaromya; f 1929; responsible for supervision of insurance cos; ensures cos are financially strong, that policy holders are fairly treated by cos and that co devt is in line with the economic and social policy of the country.

MINISTRY OF DEFENCE
Sanamchai Rd, Bangkok 10200
Tel (2) 222-1121
Minister: Gen Chatichai Choonhavan

MINISTRY OF EDUCATION
Chandrakasem Palace, Ratchadamnoen Nok Ave, Bangkok 10300
Tel (2) 281-7644
Minister: Gen Mana Ratanakoses
Deputy Minister: Sakul Sriprom, Mai Sirinawakul

MINISTRY OF FINANCE
Rama VI Rd, Bangkok 10400
Tel (2) 271-0207
Minister: Pramual Sabhavasu
Deputy Ministers: Suchon Champoonod, Niphon Phromphan

MINISTRY OF FOREIGN AFFAIRS
Saranrom Palace, Bangkok 10200
Tel (2) 221-9171; telex 82698
Minister: Air Chief Marshal Siddhi Savetsila
Deputy Minister: Sub-Lt Prapas Limpabandhu

MINISTRY OF INDUSTRY
Phra Ram Hok Rd, Bangkok 10400
Tel (2) 246-1137; telex 84375
Minister: Gen Praman Adireksarn
Deputy Ministers: Dusit Rangkhasiri, Paitoon Kaewthong

MINISTRY OF THE INTERIOR
Atsadang Rd, Bangkok 10200
Tel (2) 221-1141
Minister: Banharn Silpa-Archa
Deputy Ministers: Sanoh Thienthong, Santi Chaivirat, Trairong Suwannakhiri, Wattana Asswahem

MINISTRY OF JUSTICE
6 Rachinee Rd, Bangkok 10200
Tel (2) 221-3161
Minister: Chamras Mangkalarat

MINISTRY OF PUBLIC HEALTH
Devavesm Palace, Samsen Rd, Bangkok 10200
Tel (2) 282-2121
Minister: Chuan Leekpai
Deputy Ministers: Suthas Ngernmuen, Prasong Buranapong

MINISTRY OF SCIENCE, TECHNOLOGY AND ENERGY
Phra Ram Hok Rd, Phaya Thai, Bangkok 10400
Tel (2) 246-0064; telex 20838
Minister: Prachuab Chaiyasan

MINISTRY OF TRANSPORT AND COMMUNICATIONS
Ratchadamnoen Nok Ave, Bangkok 10100
Tel (2) 281-3422; telex 70000; fax (2) 280-1714
Minister: Montri Pongpanich
Deputy Ministers: Nikhom Saencharoen, Pratuan Romayanond, Anek Tabsuwan

MINISTRY OF UNIVERSITY AFFAIRS
328 Sri Ayudhya Rd, Bangkok 10400
Tel (2) 245-8268; telex 72610
Minister: Tavich Klinprathoom

GOVERNMENT AGENCIES AND ORGANIZATIONS

Advisory and Supervisory Bodies

Bureau of the Crown Property: Ratchasima Rd, Bangkok 10300; tel (2) 281-8532.

Fiscal Policy Office (FPO): Rama VI Rd, Bangkok 10400; tel (2) 271-0204; telex 82823; fax (2) 271-4685; Dir-Gen: Dr Aran Thammano; Dep Dirs-Gen: Dr Somchai Richupan, Bunnam Ourairat; f 1961; technical office of the Ministry of Finance; responsible for the study, monitoring, analysing, planning and policy formulations on fiscal and taxation, monetary and financial institutions, external borrowing and capital markets.

Office of the Auditor-General: Soi Areesampan, Rama VI Rd, Bangkok 10400; tel (2) 279-4470; f 1915; oversees the fair presentation of financial statements of Govt agencies and enterprises; has the power to conduct investigation into cases involving fraud and abuses of public funds; conclusions and recommendations are submitted to the National Assembly through the Prime Minister.

Office of the Commission of Counter Corruption: Petsanulek Rd, Bangkok 10300; tel (2) 282-3161; Sec-Gen: Amnouy Vengviehian; f 1975; investigates allegations of corruption by state officials.

Office of the Narcotics Control Board: Din Daeng Rd, Phaya Thai, Bangkok 10400; tel (2) 245-9350; telex 72050.

Agriculture and the Environment

AGRICULTURE

Agricultural Land Reform Office: Ministry of Agriculture and Co-operatives, Ratchadamnoen Nok Ave, Bangkok 10200; tel (2) 281-5955.

Dairy Farming Promotion Organization of Thailand: 160 Friendship Highway, Muak Lek Saraburi 18180; tel (36) 244973; Dir: Chalermchai Lekchom; f 1971; promotes the raising of dairy cattle and other dairy animals; provides training in dairy husbandry; buys, sells, exchange and donates dairy animals and products.

Department of Agriculture: Ministry of Agriculture and Co-operatives, Ratchadamnoen Nok Ave, Bangkok 10200; tel (2) 579-0151.

Department of Livestock Development: Ministry of Agriculture and Co-operatives, Ratchadamnoen Nok Ave, Bangkok 10200; tel (2) 251-5136.

Land Development Department: Ministry of Agriculture and Co-operatives, Ratchadamnoen Nok Ave, Bangkok 10200; tel (2) 579-0111.

Office of Agricultural Economics: Ministry of Agriculture and Co-operatives, Ratchadamnoen Nok Ave, Bangkok 10200; tel (2) 281-0685; Dir: Narong Chuprakob; f 1979; under the Ministry of Agriculture and Co-operatives.

Office of the Cane and Sugar Board: Rama VI Rd, Bangkok 10400; tel (2) 245-9918; telex 84375; Sec-Gen: Cherdpong Siriwit; f 1984; under the Ministry of Industry; promotes and disseminates information on production, use and sale of sugar-cane and granulated sugar and on marketing conditions of granulated sugar; co-ordinating work with foreign and international organizations.

Rubber Estate Organization: Nabon Station, Nakhon Si Thammarat Province 80220; tel (75) 411554; Man Dir: Thavorn Visesjinda.

THE ENVIRONMENT

Office of the National Environment Board: Ministry of Science, Technology and Energy, Phra Ram Hok Rd, Phaya Thai, Bangkok 10400; tel (2) 279-7180.

FISHING

Department of Fisheries: Ministry of Agriculture and Co-operatives, Ratchadamnoen Nok Ave, Bangkok 10200; tel (2) 281-5577; Dir-Gen: Vanich Varikul; f 1901; responsible for all activities in the areas of fishery promotion, devt, admin and control, conservation of aquatic natural resources, aquaculture, training of fishermen, etc.

FORESTRY

Forest Industry Organization: 76 Ratchadamnoen Nok Ave, Bangkok 10200; tel (2) 282-3243; Man Dir: Acom Saisa-at; f 1947; oversees all aspects of forestry and wood industries.

Royal Forest Department: 61 Phahon Yothin Rd, Bangkok 10900; tel (2) 579-1151; Dir-Gen (acting): Dr Yookti Sarikaphuti; Dep Dirs-Gen: Phairot Suvanakorn, Tiwa Sapakit, Preecha Obeye; f 1896; in charge of forestry services.

Business and Economy

BANKING

Bank for Agriculture and Agricultural Co-operatives (BAAC): 469 Nakorn Sawan Rd, Dusit, Bangkok 10300; tel (2) 280-0180; telex 72221; Chair: Pramuel Sabhavasu; Pres: Suwan Traipol; f 1966 to provide credit for agriculture.

Bank of Thailand: POB 154, 273 Samsen Rd, Bangkhunprom, Bangkok 10200; tel (2) 282-3322; telex 22527; Gov: Chavalit Thanachanan; f 1942; central bank and bank of issue.

Government Housing Bank: 212 Rama IX Rd, Huaykwang, Bangkok 10310; tel (2) 246-0303; telex 84474; fax (2) 246-1789; Chair: M. R. Chatumongkol Sonakul; Man Dir: Kitti Patpongpibul; Dep Man Dir: Sidhijai Tanphiphat; f 1953; housing bank.

Government Savings Bank of Thailand: 470 Phahonyothin Rd, Samsennai, Bangkok 10400; tel (2) 279-0060; Chair: Pandit Banyapana; Dirs-Gen: M. R. Chandram, S. Chandratat; f 1913; 445 brs.

Krung Thai Bank Ltd (State Commercial Bank of Thailand): 35 Sukhumvit Rd, Bangkok 10110; tel (2) 255-2222; telex 81179; fax (2) 253-2940; Chair: Panas Simasathien; Pres: Thienchai Sribichitr; Sen Exec Vice-Pres: Prayun Phuphatana, Panya Tantiyavarong; f 1966; merged with Siam Bank Ltd (fmrly Asia Trust Bank) in 1987; 296 brs.

FINANCIAL AGENCIES

Board of Investment (BOI): Thai Farmers Bank Bldg, 16th Floor, 400 Phaholyothin Rd, Bangkok 10400; tel (2) 270-1400; telex 72435; Chair: The Prime Minister, Gen Chatichai Choonavan; Sec-Gen: Chira Panupong; f 1958 to publicize investment potential and encourage economically and socially beneficial investments.

Treasury Department: Chakrapong Rd, Bangkok 10200; tel (2) 282-3183; telex 82823; fax (2) 271-4684; Dir-Gen: Manas Leeviraphan; f 1933; under the Ministry of Finance; production and issue of circulation and commemorative coins, medals, decorations and insignias; management of state-owned land, buildings and other real estate.

MARKETING

Central Sugar Marketing Centre: Bangkok; f 1981; responsible for domestic marketing and price stabilization.

TRADE

Board of Trade of Thailand: 150 Rajbopit Rd, Bangkok 10200; tel (2) 221-1827; telex 84309; Pres: Yukta Na Thalang; f 1955.

Customs Department: Sunthornkosa Rd, Klong Toey, Bangkok 10110; tel (2) 249-0431; telex 82355; fax (2) 249-2874; Dir-Gen: Viroj Lowhaphandu; collects revenue for the Govt; prevents and suppresses customs evasion; promotes export trade.

Department of Commercial Registration: Maharaj Rd, Bangkok 10200; tel (2) 222-2870; telex 82389; fax (2) 225-8439; Dir-Gen: Sukon Karnchanalai; f 1924; under the Ministry of Commerce; registers commercial activities such as limited cos, limited partnership, patents and trademarks; controls weights and measures.

Department of Foreign Trade: Ministry of Commerce, Sanamchai Rd, Bangkok 10200; tel (2) 222-1859.

Department of Internal Trade: Ministry of Commerce, Sanamchai Rd, Bangkok 10200; tel (2) 222-5139.

Thai Industrial Standards Institute (TISI): c/o Ministry of Industry, Rama VI St, Bangkok 10400; tel (2) 245-7802; telex 84375; Sec-Gen: Samnao Chulkarat; Dep Sec-Gen: Thien Mekanontchai; f 1969; prepares and publishes national standards; grants licences to use TISI Standards Mark; promotes the implementation of standards; national contact point of the joint FAO/WHO Food Standards Programme.

Culture

Office of the National Culture Commission: Chandrakasem Palace, Ratchadamnoen Nok Ave, Bangkok 10300; tel (2) 214-1407.

Defence

Armed Forces Supreme Command Headquarters: Ranchini Rd, Bangkok 10200; tel (2) 222-1121; Supreme Commdr: Gen Chaovalit Yongchaiyut.

Air Force: Phahonyothin Rd, Bangkhen, Bangkok 10210; tel (2) 523-6151; Commdr-in-Chief: Air Chief Marshal Kaset Rojananin.

Army: Sanamchai Rd, Bangkok 10200; tel (2) 281-8003; Commdr-in-Chief: Gen Chaovalit Yongchaiyut.

Navy: Arun-Amarin Rd, Bangkok 10600; tel (2) 466-1180; Commdr-in-Chief: Adm Niphon Sirithon.

Office of the National Security Council: Govt House, Pitsanuloke Rd, Bangkok 10300; tel (2) 281-2360; telex 10300; fax (2) 2801681; Sec-Gen: Suwit Suthanukul; f 1959; recommends options on national security policies; co-ordinates and monitors implementation of formulated security policies among various ministries.

National Intelligence Agency (NIA): Wang Parus (Civil), Dusit, Bangkok 10300; tel (2) 281-7035.

The National Police Department: Ministry of the Interior, Atsadang Rd, Bangkok 10200; tel (2) 251-4943.

Development and Planning

Department of Industrial Promotion: Rama VI Rd, Phaya Thai, Bangkok 10400; tel (2) 245-9433; telex 20562; fax (2) 24285; f 1936; under the Ministry of Industry; promotes the establishment of new manufacturing business, in particular new medium and small industries in regional areas, by providing technical assistance and other consultancy services to those interested in setting up businesses.

Industrial Estate Authority of Thailand: 618 Nikom Makkasan Rd, Phaya Thai, Bangkok 10400; tel (2) 253-0561; fax (2) 253-4086; Gov (acting): Prateeb Chuntaketta; f 1972; responsible for industrial estates; areas set aside for siting industrial plants, provided with infrastructure and utilities, ie roads, drainage and flood protection systems, a central waste water treatment plant, electricity, water supply, communications systems, etc.

National Economic and Social Development Board: 962 Krung Kasem Rd, Bangkok 10100; tel (2) 282-1151; Sec-Gen: Phisit Pakkasem; economic planning agency.

Education and Research

EDUCATION

Centre for Educational Technology: Sri Ayudhaya Rd, Bangkok 10400; tel (2) 246-0026; telex 20791; fax (2) 321-4946; Dir: K. Choochuay; f 1953; under the Ministry of Education; utilizes and applies mass media, audio-visual and modern technology for the improvement of formal and non-formal education; also carries out research and pilot projects on new technology for educational devt.

RESEARCH

The National Research Council: Ministry of Science, Technology and Energy, Phra Ram Hok Rd, Phaya Thai, Bangkok 10400; tel (2) 579-1121.

The Royal Institute: The Grand Palace, Na Phra Lan Rd, Bangkok 10200; tel (2) 222-0189; Pres: Lt-Gen Salwidhan Nidhes; Vice-Pres: Dr Boonbrugsa Chatamra; f 1933; independent public agency under the Ministry of Education; undertakes and encourages research in every branch of learning for the dissemination of information to the general public; advises and carries out academic work in accordance with the wishes of the Govt.

Health

Department of Health: Ministry of Public Health, Devavesm Palace, Samsen Rd, Bangkok 10200; tel (2) 281-7166.

International Affairs

Department of Technical and Economic Co-operation (DTEC): 962 Krung Kasem Rd, Bangkok 10100; tel (2) 280-0980; Dir-Gen: Wanchai Sirirattna; f 1963; co-ordinating agency; administers technical co-operation programmes between Thailand and her co-operating partners.

Legal and Judiciary

The Central Juvenile Court: 6 Rachinee Rd, Bangkok 10200; tel (2) 221-0813; Chief Justice: Chalerm Karnplemjit; Dep Chief Justices: Jira Boonpochanasoonthorn, Sanad Maisawat; Dir: Sakol Liurungraung; f 1952; original jurisdiction over juvenile delinquency and matters affecting children and young persons.

The Central Labour Court: 6 Rachinee Rd, Bangkok 10200; tel (2) 235-2473; jurisdiction in labour cases throughout the country.

The Civil Court: 6 Rachinee Rd, Bangkok 10200; tel (2) 222-8154; Chief Justice: Amphone Na Takuathung; court of first instance in civil and bankruptcy cases in Bangkok; two judges form a quorum.

The Court of Appeal: 6 Rachinee Rd, Bangkok 10200; tel (2) 222-7870; Chief Justice: (vacant); Dep Chief Justices: Damrong Saichua, Apin Pusparkhom, Somprasong Panichattra; appellate jurisdiction in all civil, bankruptcy, juvenile and criminal matters; appeals from all the Courts of First Instance throughout the country, except the Central Labour Court, come to this Court; two judges form a quorum.

The Criminal Court: 6 Rachinee Rd, Bangkok 10200; tel (2) 223-5651; Chief Justice: Surat Srianuphun; court of first instance in criminal cases in Bangkok; two judges form a quorum.

Department of Public Prosecutions: Atsadang Rd, Bangkok 10200; tel (2) 222-8121.

Supreme Court: Ratchadamnoen Nok Rd, Bangkok 10200; tel (2) 224-1601; Pres (Chief Justice): Amnak Klaisan; Vice-Pres: Somboon Bunphinon, Sophon Ratanakorn, Sakdi Snongchati; the final court of appeal in all civil, bankruptcy, labour, juvenile and criminal cases; its quorum consists of three judges; occasionally sits in plenary session to determine cases of exceptional importance or where there are reasons for reconsideration or overruling of its own precedents.

Media

BROADCASTING

Radio Thailand (RTH): National Broadcasting Services of Thailand, Govt Public Relations Dept, 236 Vibhavadi Rangsit Rd, Bangkok 10400; tel (2) 277-9125; telex 72167; Dir of Radio Thailand: Chan Poolsombat; f 1930; educational, entertainment, cultural and news programmes; operates 91 stations throughout Thailand.

Home Service: address as above; Dir: Chalermsri Hooncharoen; 10 stations in Bangkok and 85 affiliated stations in 49 provinces; operates three programmes.

External Services: address as above; Dir: Bubpha Laemluang; f 1928; in Thai, English, French, Vietnamese, Khmer, Japanese, Burmese, Lao, Malay and Chinese (Mandarin).

The Royal Thai Army Television HSA-TV (Channel 5): Phaholyothin St, Sanam Pao, Bangkok 10400; tel (2) 279-8854; telex 81080; Dir-Gen: Prateep Chaiyapani; f 1958; operates channels in Bangkok, Nakorn Sawan, Nakorn Rachasima and Chiang Mai.

Television of Thailand (TVT): National Broadcasting Services of Thailand, Public Relations Dept, Petchburi Rd, Bangkok 10200; tel (2) 314-4001; telex 72243; Dir-Gen: Vichit Vudhiamphol; operates 16 colour stations.

NEWS AND INFORMATION

National Statistical Office: Larn Luang Rd, Bangkok 10100; tel (2) 281-3022.

Public Relations Department: Ratchadamnoen Klang Rd, Bangkok 10200; tel (2) 281-8821; telex 72243; fax (2) 277-8028; Dir-Gen: Manit Varin; Dep Dirs-Gen: Tavach Meksawan, Arun Ngamdee; f 1933; under the Office of the Prime Minister; serves as a national public information service centre; owns and operates radio and TV stations.

Mining and Energy

ENERGY

Electricity Generating Authority of Thailand (EGAT): 53 Charan Sanit Wong Rd, Bang Kruai, Nonthaburi 11000; tel (2) 424-0101; telex 82711; fax (2) 433-6317; Gen Man: Paopat Javanalikikorn; f 1969; electricity generation and transmission throughout the country; lignite production and trade.

The National Energy Administration: Ministry of Science, Technology and Energy, Phra Ram Hok Rd, Phaya Thai, Bangkok 10400; tel (2) 223-0021.

Office of Atomic Energy for Peace: 16 Vibhavadi Rangsit Rd, Bangkhen, Bangkok 10900; tel (2) 579-0138; telex 87161; fax (2) 579-3552; Sec-Gen: Suchat Mongkolphantha; f 1961; under the Ministry of Science, Technology and Energy; initiates, promotes and co-ordinates studies and research into the uses of atomic energy; lays down rules and regulations to ensure safe use of atomic energy and radiation.

Petroleum Authority of Thailand (PTT): 14 Vibhavadi Rangsit Rd, Bangkok 10900; tel (2) 537-2000; telex 87940; Chair: Gen Ataya Paaopanchon; Gov: Dr Anat Arbhabhirama; f 1978; subsequently merged with National Gas Organization of Thailand (NGOT) and the Oil and Fuel Organization; supervises all activities relating to the devt, exploitation, production and distribution of petroleum and gas.

MINING

Department of Mineral Resources: Ministry of Industry, Phra Ram Hok Rd, Bangkok 10400; tel (2) 281-5970.

Mining Industry Council: Sinthorn Bldg, Room 111, Wireless Rd, Bangkok 10330; tel (2) 250-1808; fax (2) 255-2078; Pres: Darmp Tewthong; Sec-Gen: Punya Adulyapichit; f 1983; intermediary between Govt organizations and private mining enterprises.

Science and Technology

Meteorological Department: 612 Sukumvit Rd, Bangkok 10110; tel (2) 258-7054; telex 72004; f 1942; provides meteorological information services; co-operates with meteorological agencies and scientific institutions; carries out research in meteorology and related fields.

Telecommunications

The Communications Authority of Thailand (CAT): 12/46-48 Chaeng Wattana Rd, Bang Khen, Bangkok 10002; tel (2) 573-0099; telex 70022; fax (2) 573-0099; Pres: Sudhorn Limpisthien; Vice-Pres: Aswin Saovaros (Posts), Somlak Sachjapinan (Telecommunications), Tarworn Yaowakun (Economics and Finance), Prapass Yoothong (Admin); f 1977; provides postal, telecommunications and remittance services.

Telephone Organization of Thailand (TOT): 977 Ploenchit Rd, Pathumwan, Bangkok 10330; tel (2) 257-1170; Chair: Gen Dr Paiboon Limpaphayom.

Tourism

Tourism Authority of Thailand (TAT): Head Office: 4 Ratchadamnoen Nok Ave, Bangkok 10100; tel (2) 282-1143; telex 72059; Gov: Dharmnoon Prachuabmoh; Dep Govs: Seree Wangpaichitr, Pairote Thammapimuk, Virakiart Angkatavanich.

Tourist Association of Northern Thailand: Old Chiang Mai Cultural Centre, 185/3 Wualai Rd, Chiang Mai 50000; tel (53) 235097; Pres: Prof Phoon-Phon Asanachinta.

Transport

CIVIL AVIATION

Airports Authority of Thailand: Bangkok International Airport, Vibhavadi Rangsit Rd, Bangkok 10210; tel (2) 535-1111; telex 87424; Man Dir: Air Marshal Somboon Rahong; f 1979.

Department of Aviation: 71 Soi Ngarmuplee, Rama IV Rd, Bangkok 10120; tel (2) 286-2129; telex 72099; Dir-Gen: Dr

Srisook Chandrangsu; f 1963; promotes civil aviation; constructs and operates regional airports; provides air navigation aids, air traffic control services and domestic telecommunications; issues aircraft registration, operators' and personnel licences.

Thai Airways International Ltd (TAI): 89 Vibhavadi Rangsit Rd, Bangkok 10900; tel (2) 513-0121; telex 82359; Chair: Air Chief Marshal Kaset Rojananin; Pres: Air Chief Marshal Veera Kitchathorn; Exec Vice-Pres: Chatrachai Bunya-ananta; f 1959; merged with Thai Airways Co in 1988; international services from Bangkok to the Far and Middle East, Europe, North and South America and Africa.

RAILWAYS

Expressway and Rapid Transit Authority of Thailand: Phaholyothin Rd, Bangkok 10900; tel (2) 579-5380; telex 72346; fax (2) 579-5205; Gov: Charan Burapharat; f 1972; construction, maintenance and supervision of the rapid transit system in Bangkok.

State Railway of Thailand: Krung Kasem Rd, Pathumwan, Bangkok 10500; tel (2) 223-0341; telex 72242; fax (2) 225-3801; Chair: Maj Gen Chatchai Upapong; Gen Man: Chird Boonyaratavej; f 1897; provides freight and passenger transport services throughout the country.

ROADS

Bangkok Mass Transit Authority (BMTA): 888 Nai Lert Bldg, Phaya Thai, Bangkok 10400; tel (2) 251-6503; Chair: Lt-Gen Sak Boonthrakul; Dir: Anothai Utensute; controls Bangkok's urban transport system.

Department of Highways: Si Ayudhaya Rd, Bangkok 10400; tel (2) 281-7082; Dir-Gen: Sathien Vongvichien.

Department of Land Transport: Phaholyothin Rd, Bangkok 10900; tel (2) 271-0120; Dir-Gen: Banterng Vattanasiritham; f 1941; plans and regulates national road transport; promotes road transport safety; inspects and registers vehicles; licences transport operators and drivers.

Express Transportation Organization of Thailand (ETO): 485/1 Sri Ayudhaya Rd, Phaya Thai, Bangkok 10400; tel (2) 245-3231; telex 72053; fax (2) 246-4248; Pres: Pongpol Adireksarn; f 1953; Govt freight forwarder; international and domestic transportation service.

SHIPPING

Harbour Department: 1278 Yotha Rd, Bangkok 10100; tel (2) 233-5087; Dir-Gen: Sen Lt Chid Ongsuwan.

Office of the Mercantile Marine Promotion Commission: 19 Phra Atit Rd, Bangkok 10200; tel (2) 281-9367; Sec-Gen: Sachee Sirison; f 1979.

Port Authority of Thailand: Sunthornkosa Rd, Phrakanong, Klong Toey, Bangkok 10110; tel (2) 249-0399; telex 72331; fax (2) 249-0885; Dir-Gen: Sen Lt Pongsak Vongsmoot; f 1951; handles import and export cargo; carries out dredging; installs navigation aids, etc.

Utilities

Public Works Department: 2 Larn Luang Rd, Pan Fa Bridge, Bangkok 10100; tel (2) 281-0733; Dir-Gen: Niyom Niyamanusorn; Dep Dirs-Gen: Prajaya Sutabutr, Samroeng Komolsiri; f 1898.

TOGO

Head of State

Under the 1979 Constitution, executive power is vested in the President, who is elected for seven years by universal adult suffrage. The President appoints and leads a Council of Ministers, and can dissolve the National Assembly.

President: Gen Gnassingbe Eyadéma (assumed power 13 January 1967; proclaimed President 14 April 1967; elected 30 December 1979; re-elected 21 December 1986).

Office of the President: Palais Présidentiel, ave de la Marina, Lomé; tel 21-27-01; telex 5201.

Legislature

Legislative power is vested in the Assemblée Nationale (National Assembly), comprising 77 members directly elected for five years. The Rassemblement du peuple togolais, the sole authorized political party, mobilizes support for the Government. The country is divided into four regions, each administered by an appointed Inspector, who is assisted by an elected council.

Assemblée Nationale (National Assembly): BP 3227, Lomé; tel 21-20-61; Pres: M. Akuetey.

MINISTRIES AND GOVERNMENT DEPARTMENTS

MINISTRY OF DEFENCE
Lomé
Tel 21-28-91; telex 5321
Minister: Gen Gnassingbe Eyadéma

MINISTRY OF ECONOMY AND FINANCE
BP 387, Lomé
Tel 21-23-71; telex 5286
Minister: Komlan Alipui

MINISTRY OF EDUCATION
Immeuble des Quatre Ministères, rue Col de Roux, Lomé
Tel 21-38-01; telex 5322
Minister of National Education and Scientific Research: Tcha Koza Tchalim
Minister of Technical Education and Training: Koffi Edoh

MINISTRY OF THE ENVIRONMENT AND TOURISM
ave Sarawaka, BP 3114, Lomé
Tel 21-53-52; telex 5007; fax 21-62-66
Minister: Yao Komlavi

MINISTRY OF EQUIPMENT, POSTS AND TELECOMMUNICATIONS
Immeuble des Quatre Ministères, rue Col de Roux, Lomé
Tel 21-38-01
Minister: Nassirou Ayeva

MINISTRY OF FOREIGN AFFAIRS AND CO-OPERATION
place du Monument aux Morts, Lomé
Tel 21-29-10; telex 5239
Minister: Ayaovi Adodo

MINISTRY OF INDUSTRY AND STATE ENTERPRISES
BP 2748, Lomé
Tel 21-07-44; telex 5396
Minister: Koffi Djondo

MINISTRY OF INFORMATION
BP 40, Lomé
Tel 21-03-39; telex 5294
Minister Delegate to the Presidency in charge of Information: Gbegnon Amegboh

MINISTRY OF THE INTERIOR AND SECURITY
rue Albert Sarraut, Lomé
Tel 21-23-19
Minister: Gen Yao Mawulikplimi Amegi

MINISTRY OF JUSTICE
ave de la Marina, rue Col de Roux, Lomé
Tel 21-26-53
Minister: (vacant)

MINISTRY OF LABOUR AND THE CIVIL SERVICE
angle ave de la Marina et rue Kpalimé, Lomé
Tel 21-26-53
Minister: Yagninim Bitokotipou

MINISTRY OF PLANNING AND MINES
ave de la Marina, Lomé
Tel 21-27-01; telex 5380
Minister: Barry Moussa Barque

MINISTRY OF PUBLIC HEALTH, SOCIAL AND WOMEN'S AFFAIRS
rue Branly, Lomé
Tel 21-29-83
Minister: Aissah Agbetra

MINISTRY OF RURAL DEVELOPMENT
ave Sarawaka, Lomé
Tel 21-56-71
Minister: Yao Palli Tchalla

MINISTRY OF TRADE AND TRANSPORT
rue du Commerce, Lomé
Tel 21-09-09
Minister: Barry Moussa Barque

MINISTRY OF YOUTH, SPORTS AND CULTURE
Blvd du Mono, Lomé
Tel 21-23-52; telex 5103
Minister: Mensah Agbeyome Kodjo

GOVERNMENT AGENCIES AND ORGANIZATIONS

Advisory and Supervisory Body

Conseil Economique et Social: 20 rue du Commerce, Lomé; tel 21-53-01; telex 5237; Pres: Koffi Djondo; f 1967; advisory body of 25 mems, comprising five trade unionists, five reps of industry and commerce, five reps of agriculture, five economists and sociologists, and five technologists.

Agriculture and Forestry

AGRICULTURE

Office National des Produits Vivriers (TOGOGRAIN): 141 ave de la Libération, BP 3039, Lomé; tel 21-59-55; telex 5220; Man Dir: M. Walla; devt and marketing of staple food crops.

Office des Produits Agricoles du Togo (OPAT): angle rue Branly et ave no 3, BP 1334, Lomé; tel 21-44-71; telex 5220; Man Dir: Ogamo Bagnah; f 1964; controls prices and export sales of coffee, cocoa, cotton, groundnuts, tobacco, palm oil, copra, kapok, karite and castor oil, and is the sole exporter of these products; promotes devt in agriculture, finances research and grants loans.

Société Agricole Togolaise-Arabe-Libyenne (SATAL): 329 blvd du 13 janvier, BP 3554, Lomé; tel 21-69-18; telex 5051; Pres: Katanga Koffi Walla; Dir-Gen: Assaid Mohamed Raai; f 1978; 50% state-owned, 50% owned by Libya; production, processing and marketing of agricultural goods.

Société Nationale pour le Développement de la Palmeraie et des Huileries (SONAPH): BP 1755, Lomé; tel 21-22-32; telex 5268; Pres: Dr Foli Amaizo Bubuto; Man Dir: Anani Ernest Gassou; cultivation of palms and production of palm oil and palmettoes.

Société Togolaise du Coton (SOTOCO): BP 219, Lomé; tel 90-01-53; telex 5179; Man Dir: Tcha Katanga; f 1974; devt of cotton-growing.

FORESTRY

Office National de Développement et d'Exploitation des Ressources Forestières (ODEF): 15 rue des Conseillers Municipaux, BP 334, Lomé; tel 21-51-59; Man Dir: Yao Elee Pomevor; f 1971; promotes devt of forestry and related products.

Business and Economy

BANKING

Banque Arabe Libyenne-Togolaise du Commerce Extérieur (BALTEX): route d'Aného, BP 4874, Lomé; tel 21-28-30; telex 5301; Pres: Yaovi Adodo; Man Dir: Wanis M. Leogali; f 1975; 50% state-owned, 50% by Libyan Arab Foreign Bank.

Banque Centrale des Etats de l'Afrique de l'Ouest (BCEAO): ave Sarawaka, BP 120, Lomé; tel 21-25-12; telex 5216; Gov: Alassane Ouattara; Dir in Togo: Yao Messan Aho; f 1955; headquarters in Dakar, Senegal; bank of issue and central bank for the seven states of the Union monétaire ouest-africaine (UMOA), comprising Benin, Burkina Faso, Côte d'Ivoire, Mali, Niger, Senegal and Togo.

Banque Togolaise pour le Commerce et l'Industrie (BTCI): 169 blvd du 13 janvier, BP 363, Lomé; tel 21-46-41; telex 5386; Pres: Gbégnon Amegboh; Man Dir: Jean Claude Picolet; f 1974; 24% owned by Banque Nationale de Paris; 5 brs.

Banque Togolaise de Développement (BTD): angle ave de Nîmes et ave N. Grunitzky, BP 65, Lomé; tel 21-36-41; telex 5282; Pres: Kokuvi Dogbé; Man Dir: Napo Kakaye; 50% state-owned, 20% by BCEAO (see above); 5 brs.

Société Nationale d'Investissement et Fonds Annexes (SNI): 11 ave du 24 janvier, BP 2682, Lomé; tel 21-62-21; telex 5265; Pres: Ogamo Bagnah; Man Dir: Issa Affo; f 1971; devt bank.

INSURANCE

Groupement Togolais d'Assurances (GTA): 3 rue Brazza, BP 3298, Lomé; tel 21-60-75; telex 5069; Pres: Minister of Economy and Finance, Komlan Alipui; Man Dir: Kossi Nambea; Sec-Gen: Koffi Laban; f 1974; 62.9% state-owned; all aspects of insurance and reinsurance.

NATIONALIZED INDUSTRY

Société des Ciments du Togo (CIMTOGO): Zone Industrielle Portuaire PK 12, BP 1687, Lomé; tel 21-08-59; telex 5234; Pres: Paulin Eklou; Man Dir: V. Lerstad; f 1969; 50% state-owned, 50% by Norcem Cement (Norway); production and marketing of cement and clinker.

Société des Détergents du Togo (SODETO): 3 rue d'Amoutivé, BP 1669, Lomé; tel 21-45-12; Man Dir: A. Dengo; f 1971; 97% state-owned; manufacturers of detergents.

Société Togolaise de Galvanisation de Tôles (SOTO-TÔLES): BP 9103, Lomé; tel 21-06-91; Dir: Rolf Kohlgrüber; f 1979; 50% state-owned; manufacture of galvanized steel.

TRADE

Société Nationale de Commerce (SONACOM): 29 blvd Circulaire, BP 3009, Lomé; tel 21-31-18; telex 5281; Dir-Gen: Jean Ladoux; f 1972; has monopoly of imports of milk, rice and sugar.

Defence

Armed Forces: route d'Atakpamé, Agoényivé; tel 21-28-91; telex 5201; Commdr-in-Chief: President, Gen Gnassingbe Eyadéma.

Air Force: c/o Ministry of National Defence, Lomé; tel 21-29-79.

Navy: Base Navale, Lomé Port; tel 21-28-12.

Gendarmerie Nationale (National Police): Lomé; tel 21-26-01.

Legal and Judiciary

Cour Suprême du Togo: BP 906, Lomé; tel 21-22-58; Pres: Atsu-Koffi Amega; f 1961; highest judicial authority; consists of four chambers: constitutional, judicial, administrative and auditing.

Media

BROADCASTING

Radiodiffusion-Télévision de la Nouvelle Marche: BP 434, Lomé; tel 21-24-93; Dir: Pitang Tchalla; f 1953; radio programmes in French, English and vernacular languages.

Radiodiffusion Kara (Togo): BP 21, Lama-Kara; tel 60-60-60; Dir: M'Ba Kpenougou.

Télévision Togolaise: BP 3286, Lomé; tel 21-53-57; f 1973; three stations; programmes in French and vernacular languages.

GOVERNMENT PUBLISHER

Etablissement National des Editions du Togo (EDITOGO): BP 891, Lomé; tel 21-61-06; telex 5294; Dir-Gen: Kokou Amedegnato; Dep Dir-Gen: Toyitom Amelete; f 1961; general and educational printing.

NEWS AND INFORMATION

Agence Togolaise de Presse (ATOP): 35 rue des Média, BP 2327, Lomé; tel 21-25-07; telex 5320; Dir: Seshie Seyena Biava; f 1975.

Direction de la Statistique: BP 118, Lomé; tel 21-22-87; collection, analysis and dissemination of statistical data.

Mining and Energy

ENERGY

Communauté électrique du Bénin: BP 1368, Lomé; tel 21-61-32; Chair: Emile Nonan; Man Dir: Boukary Alidou; f 1968 as joint venture between Togo and Benin to harness and exploit the energy resources in the two countries. Ghana's Volta dam is currently supplying energy to both countries.

Compagnie Energie Electrique du Togo (CEET): 10 ave du Golfe, BP 42, Lomé; tel 21-27-43; telex 5230; Chair: Issa Affo; Man Dir: Kwame Agbebe; f 1963; production, transportation and distribution of electricity.

MINING

Office Togolais des Phosphates (OTP): BP 3200, Lomé; tel 21-22-28; telex 5287; Pres: Minister of Planning and Mines, Barry Moussa Barque; Man Dir: (vacant); production and commercialization of phosphates.

Tourism

Direction du Tourisme et d'Hôtellerie: BP 1289, Lomé; tel 21-56-62; Dir: Kokou Assiobo-Tipoh.

Transport

CIVIL AVIATION

Air Togo: rue du Commerce, BP 1090, Lomé; tel 21-33-10; Gen Man: Amadou Isaac Ade; f 1963; scheduled services between Lomé, Sokodé, Mango and Dapango.

RAILWAYS

Chemin de Fer Togolais: BP 340, Lomé; tel 21-43-01; telex 5178; Pres: N'Souwodji Kawo Ehe; Gen Man: T. Kpekpassi; f 1905; total length 525 km.

ROADS

Société Nationale des Transports Routiers (SNTR TOGOROUTE): km 9, route d'Atakpamé, BP 4730, Lomé; tel 21-35-26; telex 5312; Dir: Roger Bondoux; f 1976; 60% state-owned.

SHIPPING

Port Autonome de Lomé: BP 1225, Lomé; tel 21-47-42; telex 5243; Pres: Yao Pali Tchalla; Dir: Minister of Trade and Transport, Barry Moussa Barque; f 1967.

Société d'Affrètement Maritime du Togo (SAFT): BP 1085, Lomé; Man Dir: Koffi Francis Ames; f 1980.

Société Ouest-Africaine d'Enterprises Maritimes Togo (SOAEM-TOGO): BP 3285, Lomé; tel 21-07-20; telex 5207; Pres: Jean Fabry; Man Dir: John M. Aquereburu; f 1959.

Société Togolaise de Navigation Maritime (SOTONAM): 93 voie Express, BP 4086, Lomé; tel 21-51-73; telex 5285; Man Dir: M. S. Tchamdja.

TONGA

Head of State

Tonga is a hereditary monarchy, and the sovereign is Head of State and Head of Government. The sovereign appoints, and presides over, a Privy Council which acts as the national Cabinet. The Council includes the King, eight Ministers, appointed for life and led by the Prime Minister, and the Governors of Ha'apai and Vava'u.

Sovereign: HM King Taufa'ahau Tupou IV (succeeded to the throne 15 December 1965).

Office of HM the King: The Palace Office, POB 6, Nuku'alofa; tel 21-000.

Legislature

Legislative power is held by the unicameral Legislative Assembly, comprising the King and 28 members: the Privy Council, nine hereditary nobles (elected by their peers) and nine representatives elected by all adult Tongan citizens. Elected members hold office for three years.

Legislative Assembly: POB 62, Nuku'alofa; tel 21-599; Speaker and Chair: Malupo.

MINISTRIES AND GOVERNMENT DEPARTMENTS

OFFICE OF THE PRIME MINISTER, AND MINISTRY OF AGRICULTURE, FORESTRY AND FISHERIES, AND MARINE AFFAIRS
Nuku'alofa
Tel 21-300; telex 66269
Prime Minister and Minister: HRH Prince Fatafehi Tu'ipelehake
Minister without portfolio: Ma'afu

OFFICE OF THE DEPUTY PRIME MINISTER
Nuku'alofa
Tel 22-655; telex 66269
Deputy Prime Minister: Baron Vaea of Houma

MINISTRY OF CIVIL AVIATION
POB 845, Nuku'alofa
Tel 23-903; telex 66269; fax 24-145
Minister: Hu'akavameiliku

MINISTRY OF EDUCATION
Nuku'alofa
Tel 21-903
Minister: Hu'akavameiliku

MINISTRY OF FINANCE
Vuna Rd, POB 87, Nuku'alofa
Tel 23-066; telex 66277
Minister: J. Cecil Cocker

MINISTRY OF FOREIGN AFFAIRS AND DEFENCE
Nuku'alofa
Tel 23-600; telex 66235
Minister: HRH Crown Prince Tupouto'a

MINISTRY OF HEALTH
POB 59, Nuku'alofa
Tel 23-200; telex 66209; fax 23-938
Minister: Dr Sione Tapa

MINISTRY OF JUSTICE AND OFFICE OF THE ATTORNEY-GENERAL
POB 85, Nuku'alofa
Tel 21-055
Minister and Attorney-General: Tevita P. Tupou

MINISTRY OF LABOUR, COMMERCE AND INDUSTRIES
POB 110, Nuku'alofa
Tel 23-688; telex 66269; fax 23-887
Minister: Baron Vaea of Houma

MINISTRY OF POLICE, FIRE SERVICES AND PRISONS
Nuku'alofa
Tel 21-233
Minister: George 'Akau'ola

MINISTRY OF WORKS
Nuku'alofa
Tel 21-904
Minister (acting): Dr M. Toupou

OFFICE OF THE GOVERNOR OF HA'APAI
Nuku'alofa
Governor: Fakafanua

OFFICE OF THE GOVERNOR OF VAVA'U
Nuku'alofa
Governor (acting): Tu'i'afitu

GOVERNMENT AGENCIES AND ORGANIZATIONS

Business and Economy

BANKING

Bank of Tonga: POB 924, Nuku'alofa; tel 23-933; telex 66212; Chair: Frank J. Conroy; Gen Man: Brynmor D. Harris; f 1974; owned by Govt of Tonga, Bank of Hawaii International, Bank of New Zealand and Westpac Banking Corpn.

National Reserve Bank of Tonga: Nuku'alofa; f 1989 to assume central bank functions of Bank of Tonga; issues currency; manages exchange rates and international reserves.

Tonga Development Bank: Fatafehi Rd, POB 126, Nuku'-alofa; tel 23-333; telex 66206; Man Dir: Lisiate 'Aloveita 'Akolo; f 1977; 4 brs.

NATIONALIZED INDUSTRY

Construction Division: POB 28, Nuku'alofa; tel 21-388; telex 66233; Chair: HRH Prince Fatafegi Tu'ipelehake; Gen Man: Tevita T. Havili; f 1958 to undertake the construction programme of the Commodities Board (see below) as well as those of the Govt, local bodies and private concerns; commission agents for imports and exports.

TRADE

Commodities Board: POB 27, Nuku'alofa; tel 21-388; telex 66233; Chair: HRH Prince Fatafehi Tu'ipelehake; Dir (acting): T. Tapavalu; f 1974; statutory organization.

Copra Division: POB 27, Nuku'alofa; tel 21-388; telex 66233; Chair: HRH Prince Fatafehi Tu'ipelehake; Gen Man: S. 'Amanaki; f 1941; non-profit board controlling the export of coconut and all coconut products.

Primary Produce Division: POB 27, Nuku'alofa; tel 21-800; Chair: HRH Prince Fatafehi Tu'ipelehake; Gen Man: Nomani S. Vaka; non-profit board controlling the export of coconuts and all coconut products.

Defence

Army: c/o Ministry of Foreign Affairs and Defence, Nuku'alofa; tel 23-600; telex 66235.

Development and Planning

Central Planning Department: POB 827, Nuku'alofa; tel 21-366; advises Govt on economic devt; drafts plans for economic and social progress.

Industrial Promotion Unit (IPU): POB 110, Nuku'alofa; tel 21-888; under the Ministry of Labour, Commerce and Industries; information on financial incentives for foreign investors.

Legal and Judiciary

Supreme Court: Justice Dept, POB 11, Nuku'alofa; tel 21-598; Chief Justice: Geoffrey Martin; Puisne Judge: Robin Webster; appeals from the Magistrates' Courts are heard by the Supreme Court.

Media

BROADCASTING

Tonga Broadcasting Commission: POB 36, Nuku'alofa; tel 23-555; telex 66225; Man: S. Tavake Fusimalohi; f 1961; independent statutory body; commercially-operated; radio programmes in Tongan and English.

NEWS AND INFORMATION

Statistics Department: POB 149, Nuku'alofa; tel 23-913; telex 66277; Govt Statistician (acting): J. Mongi; f 1970; collects, compiles and disseminates statistical information about Tonga.

Tourism

Tonga Visitors' Bureau: Vuna Rd, POB 37, Nuku'alofa; tel 21-733; telex 66269; Dir: Semisi P. Taumoepeau; f 1978.

TRINIDAD AND TOBAGO

Head of State

The President is a constitutional Head of State, chosen by an electoral college of members of both the Senate and the House of Representatives. The Cabinet, presided over by the Prime Minister, is responsible for the general direction and control of the Government. It is collectively responsible to Parliament.

President: Noor Mohammed Hassanali (took office March 1987).

Office of the President: President's House, St Ann's; tel 624-1261.

Legislature

Legislative power is vested in the bicameral Parliament, consisting of the Senate, with 31 members, and the House of Representatives, with 36 members. Members of the Senate are nominated by the President in consultation with the Prime Minister and the Leader of the Opposition. Members of the House of Representatives are elected by universal adult suffrage. The duration of Parliament is five years. Tobago was granted its own House of Assembly in 1980 and given full internal self-government in 1987.

Senate: Red House, St Vincent St, Port of Spain; tel 623-2971; Pres: Michael Williams; Vice-Pres: Carlyle Walters.

House of Representatives: Red House, St Vincent St, Port of Spain; tel 623-2971; Speaker: Nizam Mohammed; Dep Speaker: Dr Anselm St George.

Tobago House of Assembly: Scarborough; Chair: Dr Jefferson Davidson.

MINISTRIES AND GOVERNMENT DEPARTMENTS

OFFICE OF THE PRIME MINISTER
Central Bank Tower, Eric Williams Plaza, Independence Sq, Port of Spain
Tel 623-3653
Prime Minister: Arthur N. R. Robinson
Minister without Portfolio: Dr Bhoe Tewarie

MINISTRY OF EDUCATION
Alexandra St, St Clair, Port of Spain
Tel 622-2181
Minister: Clive Pantin

MINISTRY OF ENERGY
Riverside Plaza, POB 96, Port of Spain
Tel 623-4241; telex 22715
Minister: Herbert Atwell

MINISTRY OF THE ENVIRONMENT AND NATIONAL SERVICE
Port of Spain
Minister: Lincoln Myers

MINISTRY OF EXTERNAL AFFAIRS AND INTERNATIONAL TRADE
Knowsley Bldg, Queen's Park West, Port of Spain
Tel 623-4116
Minister: Dr Sahadeo Basdeo

MINISTRY OF FINANCE AND ECONOMY
Eric Williams Finance Bldg, 8th Floor, Eric Williams Plaza, Independence Sq, Port of Spain
Tel 627-9700; telex 22450
Minister of Finance: Selby Wilson
Minister of Economy: Arthur N. R. Robinson

MINISTRY OF FOOD PRODUCTION AND MARINE EXPLOITATION
St Clair Circle, Port of Spain
Tel 622-1221
Minister: Dr Brinsley Samaroo

MINISTRY OF HEALTH
35-37 Sackville St, Port of Spain
Tel 625-4611
Minister: Dr Emmanuel Hosein

MINISTRY OF INDUSTRY, ENTERPRISE AND TOURISM
Riverside Plaza, cnr Piccadilly and Besson Sts, Port of Spain
Tel 627-8451; fax 627-8488
Minister: Kenneth Gordon

**MINISTRY OF JUSTICE AND NATIONAL
SECURITY**
Knox St, Port of Spain
Tel 623-2441
Minister: Selwyn Richardson

**MINISTRY OF LABOUR, EMPLOYMENT AND
MANPOWER RESOURCES**
Riverside Plaza, Port of Spain
Minister: Dr Albert Richards

MINISTRY OF PLANNING AND MOBILIZATION
Eric Williams Finance Bldg, Eric Williams Plaza,
Independence Sq, Port of Spain
Tel 627-9700
Minister: Winston Dookeran

**MINISTRY OF PUBLIC UTILITIES AND
SETTLEMENTS**
Port of Spain
Minister: Pamela Nicholson

**MINISTRY OF SOCIAL DEVELOPMENT AND
FAMILY SERVICES**
Port of Spain
Minister: Gloria Henry

**MINISTRY OF WORKS, INFRASTRUCTURE AND
DECENTRALIZATION**
Room 500, 5th Floor, Salvatori Bldg, Independence Sq,
Port of Spain
Tel 627-9197
Minister: Dr Carson Charles

**MINISTRY OF YOUTH, SPORT, CULTURE AND
CREATIVE ARTS**
69 Eastern Main Rd, Success Village, Laventille
Tel 625-5622
Minister: Jennifer Johnson

OFFICE OF THE ATTORNEY-GENERAL
Red House, St Vincent St, Port of Spain
Tel 623-2971
Attorney-General: Anthony Isidore Smart

GOVERNMENT AGENCIES AND ORGANIZATIONS

Advisory and Supervisory Bodies

Aliens Investment Committee: Port of Spain; monitors investment by non-Trinidadians in the economy; advises Govt on measures required to ensure national interests are not compromised by foreign investment.

Central Administrative Services for Tobago: Jerningham, Scarborough; tel 639-2696; administrative organization of Govt services in Tobago.

National Lotteries Control Board: Guardian Life Bldg, 80 Independence Sq, Port of Spain; tel 623-1831; Chair: Mark Chang; Dir: Trevor Hamilton; f 1968; promotes, organizes and conducts lotteries.

Agriculture and the Environment

AGRICULTURE

Caribbean Food Corpn (CFC): 30 Queen's Park West, POB 264, Port of Spain; tel 622-5211; telex 3000; fax 622-5232; Man Dir: Dr H. A. D. Chesney; Man, Admin and Finance: A. L. Phillips; f 1976; promotion of agricultural devt, mobilization of funds and technical skills for agricultural projects; established in co-operation with the member states of CARICOM (Caribbean Community and Common Market).

Caroni (1975) Ltd: Brechin Castle, Couva; tel 636-2311; telex 31361; fax 636-2622; Chair: Vishnu Ramlogan; Gen Man: J. R. Wotherspoon; sugar cane plantations and mills; producer of rum and other sugar by-products.

   Orange Grove National Co Ltd: c/o Caroni (1975) Ltd, Brechin Castle, Couva; tel 636-2371.

Cocoa and Coffee Industry Board: Room 301, Salvatori Bldg, Frederick St, Port of Spain; tel 625-0289; Man: Hubert C. Waldron; f 1962; marketing of coffee and cocoa beans and regulation of cocoa and coffee industry.

Fertilizers of Trinidad and Tobago Ltd (Fertrin): Goodrich Bay Rd, POB 201, Couva; tel 636-2205; Chair: Leonard Lewis.

Food and Agriculture Corpn of Trinidad and Tobago Ltd: Laughton Bldg, 37A Wrightson Rd, Port of Spain; tel 625-4384; Chair: Mobarack Ali Aziz.

National Fruit Processors Ltd: Orange Grove Estate, Trinalty; tel 662-5470; Chair: Liaquat Shah.

National Poultry Co Ltd: Central Farm Complex, Beeta Village Hall, Private Bag 326, Couva; tel 625-4384; Chair: Prof Laurie Wilson.

FISHING

National Fisheries Co Ltd: Sea Lots, Port of Spain; tel 623-7171; Chair: Michael Arneaud.

FORESTRY

Trinidad and Tobago Forest Products Ltd (TANTEAK): Connector Rd, Carlsen Field, Chaguanas; tel 665-0078; telex 3000; fax 665-0080; Chair: Ruskin Punch; Man Dir: Clarence Bacchus; f 1975; harvesting, processing and marketing of plantation-grown teak and pine from state-owned plantations.

Art and Culture

Public Library of Trinidad: 8 Knox St, POB 491, Port of Spain; tel 623-6124; Sec and Librarian: Monica Olivier-Rawlins; f 1851; provision of public lending and reference library.

Business and Economy

BANKING

Agricultural Development Bank of Trinidad and Tobago: 86 Duke St, POB 154, Port of Spain; tel 623-6251; Chair: Dr M. Sampath; f 1968; provides funding for devt of domestic food and agriculture sector.

Central Bank of Trinidad and Tobago: Financial Complex, Eric Williams Plaza, Independence Sq, POB 1250, Port of Spain; tel 625-4835; telex 3532; Pres: William Demas; f 1964.

Trinidad Co-operative Bank Ltd: 80-84 Charlotte St, Port of Spain; tel 623-5330; Chief Exec: Ganace Ramdial; f 1914; 3 brs.

FINANCIAL AGENCIES

Trinidad and Tobago Development Finance Co Ltd (DFC): 8-10 Cipriani Blvd, Port of Spain; tel 623-4665; fax 624-3563; Gen Man: Gerard Pemberton; Corp Man, Loan Operations: Brian Awang; f 1970; provides medium- and long-term finance for projects in manufacturing, agro-industries, fisheries, tourism and service enterprises.

Trinidad and Tobago Mortgage Finance Co Ltd: Albion Court, 61 Dundonald St, Port of Spain; tel 623-6112; Chair: Claude Mussibali; offers funding for the construction, improvement and purchase of housing.

INSURANCE

National Insurance Board: 2A Cipriani Blvd, POB 1195, Port of Spain; tel 625-2171; Chair: Errol Gregoire; Exec Dir: Kelvin Urquhart; f 1971.

Reinsurance Co of Trinidad and Tobago Ltd (TRINRE): Trinre House, 52 Jerningham Ave, POB 1087, Belmont, Port of Spain; tel 623-6194; telex 22811; fax 624-4021; Chair: Terrence W. Farrell; Gen Man: Bernard K. Aquing; Sec: Malcolm F. Williams; f 1978; 60% state-owned; reinsurance.

Trinidad and Tobago Export Credit Insurance Co Ltd: Mecalfab House, 92 Queen St, Port of Spain; tel 624-0028; Chair: N. Jones; Gen Man: L. Osbourne; f 1974; export credit insurance and financing.

MARKETING

Central Marketing Agency: Beetham Highway, POB 449, Port of Spain; tel 623-4348; Gen Man: Dr Lennox Sealy; f 1966; responsible for facilitating the devt of the domestic agricultural marketing system; provides market information as well as planning and research in food industry.

Trinidad and Tobago National Petroleum Marketing Co Ltd: NP House, National Drive, Sea Lots, Port of Spain; tel 625-1364; Chair: Noel Wyatt; Gen Man: Harold Cuffy.

NATIONALIZED INDUSTRY

Iron and Steel Co of Trinidad and Tobago Ltd (ISCOTT): POB 183, Couva, Point Lisas; tel 636-2381; telex 31254; fax 636-5696; Chair: Ian Dasent; producers of iron and steel wire and rods.

National Feed Mill Ltd: Lot 3A, Sea Lots, Port of Spain; tel 623-1904; fax 623-0956; Chair: Robert Clarke; Man Dir: E. C. Clyde Parris; f 1984; manufacture and sale of a wide range of livestock feeds.

National Flour Mills Ltd: Wrightson Rd, Port of Spain; tel 625-2416; Chair: Mervyn Assam.

Polymer (Caribbean) Ltd: 227 Western Main Rd, Cocorite; POB 1208, Port of Spain; tel 622-5266; fax 628-0927; Man Dir: Raymond Chin Choy; Dir, Manufacturing and Engineering: Lennox M. Aqui; Dir, Finance: Ronald V. Hogan; f 1969; manufacture of packaging products, both rigid and flexible.

Trinidad Cement Ltd: Southern Main Rd, Claxton Bay; tel 659-2381; telex 3004; fax 659-2540; Chair: Arlindo Nunes; Man Dir: Richard Jackman; f 1954; manufacture and sale of Portland, sulphate-resisting and oil-well cement.

Trinidad Nitrogen Co Ltd: POB 952, Port of Spain; tel 636-2782; fax 636-2073; Chair: Kerston M. Coombs; Pres: Calvin L. Conyette; f 1974; manufacture of anhydrous ammonia.

Trinidad and Tobago Meat Processors Ltd: POB 1166, Port of Spain; tel 667-3463; Chair: Dr Pooran Ramial.

Trinidad and Tobago Methanol Co Ltd: c/o National Energy Corpn of Trinidad and Tobago Ltd, 10-14 Phillip St, Port of Spain; tel 625-4358.

Trinidad and Tobago Printing and Packaging Co Ltd: O'Meara Rd, POB 112, Port of Spain; tel 642-3481; fax 642-1266; Chief Exec (acting): Neil Mollineau; Man, Finance: Osbert Holder; f 1971; manufacturer of stationery, folding cartons, etc.

Universal Metal Co Ltd: Macoya Rd and Churchill Roosevelt Highway, Arouca; tel 662-4464; Dir: Leroy Meyers.

TRADE

Trinidad and Tobago Export Development Corpn: Export House, 10-14 Philipps St, Port of Spain; tel 623-3591; telex 22732; fax 627-0050; Chief Exec: Oscar J. Alonzo; Dir, Marketing (acting): Albert Chow; f 1984; export promotion and devt, primarily in the non-oil and non-traditional products sectors.

Defence

Air Division: Heliport Chaguaramas, POB 3158, Carenage; tel 634-4267; telex 21271; Man: Nicholas Nothnagel; Dep Man: Elvin Weithers; f 1977; search and rescue services.

Trinidad and Tobago Coast Guard: Stauble's Bay, Chaguaramas; tel 625-4939; telex 21272; fax 637-2678; f 1962; naval arm of national security; surveillance, fishery protection, pollution monitoring, search and rescue.

Trinidad and Tobago Defence Force: Defence Force Headquarters, Chaguaramas; tel 625-1021.

Trinidad and Tobago Regiment: Teteron Barracks, Chaguaramas; tel 625-2211.

Development and Planning

Industrial Development Corpn: 10-12 Independence Sq, Port of Spain; tel 623-7291; f 1959; promotes the creation and devt of private-sector industrial cos by providing investment funds and advice.

National Economic Planning Commission: c/o Ministry of Finance, Eric Williams Finance Bldg, Eric Williams Plaza, Independence Sq, Port of Spain; consists of eight Govt ministers and ten reps from banking, commerce, industry, trade unions and other interests concerned with economic planning.

Trinidad and Tobago Management Development Centre: Room 212, 2nd Floor, Salvatori Bldg, POB 301, Port of Spain; tel 623-1961; Dir: Dr Neave Beckles; Dep Dir: Henry Makhan; f 1965; training, consultancy and advisory services, research and documentation, promotion of management awareness, information services.

Energy

National Energy Corpn of Trinidad and Tobago Ltd: Plipdeco House, Goodrich Bay Rd, Point Lisas Industrial Estate, Point Lisas; tel 636-3412; telex 31344; fax 636-2905; Chair: Doddridge Alleyne; Chief Exec: Basharat Ali; f 1979.

    Trinidad and Tobago Urea Co Ltd (TTUC): address as above; Chair: Mary K. King; f 1983; production of fertilizer and urea.

National Gas Co of Trinidad and Tobago Ltd: 134-138

Frederick St, POB 1127, Port of Spain; tel 623-1161; fax 624-0717; Chair: C. A. Beaubrun; Man Dir: M. A. Jones; f 1975; compression, transmission and distribution of natural gas.

Trinidad and Tobago Oil Co Ltd (TRINTOC): Albion Court, 61 Dundonald St, Port of Spain; tel 658-4220; telex 32367; fax 658-2513; Chair: Dodderidge Alleyne; Man Dir: Walton F. James; f 1974; exploration and production of oil and gas in onshore and offshore fields; operates two refineries and a manufacturing complex, producing a variety of petroleum and petrochemical products.

Trinidad and Tobago Petroleum Co Ltd (TRINTOPEC): Santa Flora; tel 649-5500; telex 36377; Chair: Dr Trevor Farrell; fmrly Trinidad-Tesoro Petroleum Co, nationalized 1985; petroleum and gas exploration and production.

Health and Welfare

HEALTH

National Hospital Management Co Ltd: 59-63 Edward St, Port of Spain; tel 625-4214; Chair: Dr Dipchan Rattan.

WELFARE

National Housing Authority: Eastern Foundry Bldg, 5-7 South Quay, POB 555, Port of Spain; tel 627-8752; Chair: Gwendoline Williams; Exec Dir: Dr Keith Bailey; Dep Exec Dir: Robert Drayton; f 1962; construction management, mortgage financing, land/settlements devt, property acquisition, etc.

Sugar Industry Labour Welfare Committee: Balisier Ave, Couva; tel 636-2771; Chair: Ronald Tagallie; Sec and Chief Exec: Claude W. Reid; Dep Chief Exec: Jean Carmino; f 1952; acquisition and devt of land and allocation of lots; maintenance of housing settlements and disbursement of loans to eligible sugar workers/cane farmers for the erection, completion, renovation and repair of houses, as well as purchasing and paying off debts on houses.

Legal and Judiciary

Supreme Court: Knox St, Port of Spain; tel 623-2416; Chief Justice: Clinton Bernard; Mems of Court of Appeal: Alcalde Warner, Gerard des Iles, Kester McMillan, George Edoo, James Davies; consists of High Court of Justice and Court of Appeal; has jurisdiction in civil and criminal cases.

Media

BROADCASTING

National Broadcasting Service (NBS): 17 Abercromby St, POB 610, Port of Spain; tel 623-2618; Chair: K. Ablack; Gen Man: F. Thompson; Dir of Programmes: Hamilton Clement; f 1957; AM and FM radio stations.

Trinidad and Tobago Television Co Ltd: Television House, 11A Maraval Rd, POB 665, Port of Spain; tel 622-4141; telex 22664; Dir: Ethel Bethelmy; f 1962; state-owned commercial station.

NEWS AND INFORMATION

Central Statistical Office: 23 Park St, POB 98, Port of Spain; tel 624-2436; f 1950; collection and publication of statistics on population, vital statistics, labour force, agriculture, national accounts, balance of payments and trade statistics.

Tourism

National Hotel Co of Trinidad and Tobago Ltd: c/o Ministry of Industry, Enterprise and Tourism, Level 14, Riverside Plaza, cnr Piccadilly and Besson Sts, Port of Spain.

Trinidad and Tobago Hotel and Tourism Association: Trinidad Hilton, POB 243, Port of Spain; tel 624-3065; fax 624-3065; Exec Dir: Jan Bocas-Ryan; f 1958 promotion and devt of tourist industry.

Trinidad and Tobago Tourism Development Authority: 122-124 Frederick St, POB 222, Port of Spain; tel 623-1933; telex 22318; fax 623-3848; Chair: Minister of Industry, Enterprise and Tourism, Kenneth Gordon; Exec Dir: Peter Hezekiah; f 1989; promotion of investment in tourist infrastructure, planning of policy devt in tourist industry.

Zoological Society of Trinidad and Tobago: Emperor Valley Zoo, Botanical Gdns, Port of Spain; tel 622-3530; f 1947.

Transport and Communications

TELECOMMUNICATIONS

Trinidad and Tobago External Telecommunications Co Ltd: 1 Edward St, Port of Spain; tel 625-4431; telex 9003; fax 627-0856; Gen Man: L. C. R. Worrell; Dep Gen Mans: N. Campbell, C. Lewis, C. Seecheran; f 1969; provision of international telecommunications services.

Trinidad and Tobago Telephone Co Ltd (TTT): 85 Abercromby St, Port of Spain; tel 625-4588; Chair: Audley Walker.

TRANSPORT

Airports Authority of Trinidad and Tobago: Airports Administration Centre, Piarco International Airport, Caroni North Bank Rd, Piarco; tel 669-1433; fax 669-2319; f 1979; operation and management of airports.

BWIA—Trinidad and Tobago (BWIA International) Airways Corpn: Piarco International Airport, Caroni North Bank Rd, POB 604, Piarco; tel 664-4871; telex 22231; Chair: Karl Hudson Phillips; Man Dir: Ian Bertrand; f 1980 as merger of BWIA International and Trinidad and Tobago Air Services; operates scheduled passenger and cargo services linking destinations in the Caribbean region, North America and Europe.

Port Authority of Trinidad and Tobago: 1D Wrightson Rd, POB 549, Port of Spain; Chair: Eustace Bernard.

Port Lisas Industrial Port Development Corpn Ltd: Goodrich Bay Rd, Port Lisas; tel 636-2201; fax 636-4061; Chief Exec: Ken Snaggs; Sec: A. F. Lazare; Port Man: Rawle Baddaloo; f 1966; port operations and estate devt.

Public Transport Service Corpn: Railway Bldg, South Quay, POB 391, Port of Spain; tel 623-2341; telex 22801; Chair: Dr Philbert Morris; Gen Man: Dr Trevor Townsend; f 1965; provision of public transport service.

Shipping Association of Trinidad and Tobago: Room 402, 4th Level, Mecalfab Bldg, 92 Queen St, Port of Spain; tel 623-8570; Pres: Arthur A. Lawlor; Exec Sec: Sheila Julumsingh; f 1938; advisory service, dialogue with port authorities etc on behalf of mems.

Shipping Corpn of Trinidad and Tobago: 12th and 13th Floors, Central Bank Tower, Eric Williams Plaza, Independence Sq, Port of Spain; tel 623-5295; telex 22590; fax 625-0844; Gen Man (acting): Kirk Ifill; Man, Admin: Dianne Joseph; Man, Liner: Paul Jardim; Man, Technical: Carlton Mends; f 1971;

shipowners and managers, liner services, chartering services, port agents.

Utilities

Trinidad and Tobago Solid Waste Management Co Ltd:
9A Stanmore St, Port of Spain; tel 625-6681; Man Dir (acting): Winston A. Thomas; Man, Technical (acting): Edison Garraway; Man, Public Relations and Education: Pat Bishop; f 1980; general waste disposal and collection; faecal waste disposal and collection; consultancy services on environmental management projects; devt and implementation of educational programmes on the environment.

TUNISIA

Head of State

The President, who is Head of State and Head of Government, serves a five-year term (renewable twice, consecutively) and is elected by popular vote at the same time as the National Assembly. The President appoints a Council of Ministers, headed by a Prime Minister.

President: Zine al-Abidine ben Ali (took office on 7 November 1987).

Office of the President: Palais Présidentiel, Tunis-Carthage; tel (1) 260-348; Minister, Dir of the Presidencial Office: Mohamed Jeri; Minister, Private Adviser to the Pres: Habib Boulares.

Legislature

Legislative power is held by the unicameral National Assembly, with 141 members elected by universal adult suffrage for five years. For the purpose of local administration, the country is divided into 18 governorates.

Assemblée Nationale (National Assembly): Le Bardo, Tunis; tel (1) 222-800; Pres: Slaheddine Bali.

MINISTRIES AND GOVERNMENT DEPARTMENTS

OFFICE OF THE PRIME MINISTER
place du Gouvernement, la Kasbah, Tunis
Tel (1) 260-322; telex 13566
Prime Minister: Hamid Karoui
Government Secretary-General: Taoufik Cheikhrouhou

MINISTRY OF AGRICULTURE
30 rue Alain Savery, Tunis
Tel (1) 660-088
Minister: Nouri Zorgati

MINISTRY OF CHILDREN AND YOUTH
89 ave Hédi Chaker, Tunis
Tel (1) 680-088; telex 13246
Minister: Hamouda ben Slama

MINISTRY OF COMMUNICATIONS
Tunis
Minister: Sadok Rabah

MINISTRY OF CULTURE AND INFORMATION
place du Gouvernement, la Kasbah, Tunis
Tel (1) 660-088; telex 12032
Minister: Ahmed Khaled

MINISTRY OF EQUIPMENT AND HOUSING
Cité Jardin, Tunis
Tel (1) 680-088; telex 13565
Minister: Ahmed Fria

MINISTRY OF FINANCE
place Alizouaui, Tunis
Tel (1) 650-621; telex 51922
Minister: Mohamed ben Hassouna Ghannouchi

MINISTRY OF FOREIGN AFFAIRS
place du Gouvernement, la Kasbah, Tunis
Tel (1) 660-088; telex 13470
Minister: Ismail Khelil

MINISTRY OF EDUCATION, HIGHER EDUCATION AND SCIENTIFIC RESEARCH
ave Ouled Haffouz, 1030 Tunis
Tel (1) 786-300; telex 13870
Minister: Mohamed Charfi

MINISTRY OF INDUSTRY AND TRADE
7 rue du Royaume d'Arabie Saoudite, 1035 Tunis
Tel (1) 285-134; telex 14341
Minister: (vacant)

MINISTRY OF THE INTERIOR
ave du 7 Novembre, Tunis
Tel (1) 243-000; telex 13994
Minister: Abdelhamid Escheikh

MINISTRY OF JUSTICE
ave Bab Benat, Tunis
Tel (1) 660-088
Minister: Chedli Neffati

MINISTRY OF NATIONAL DEFENCE
blvd Bab Menara, Tunis
Tel (1) 260-244; telex 12580
Minister: Abdallah Kallel

MINISTRY OF PLANNING
rue de Kairouan, Tunis
Tel (1) 660-088; telex 13488
Minister and Minister of Regional Development: Mustapha Nabli

MINISTRY OF PUBLIC HEALTH
Bab Saâdoun, 1030 Tunis
Tel (1) 660-088; telex 15235
Minister: Dali al-Jezi

MINISTRY OF SOCIAL AFFAIRS
blvd Bab Benat, 1006 Tunis
Tel (1) 262-201; telex 14268; fax (1) 262-348
Minister: Moncer Rouissi

MINISTRY OF STATE PROPERTIES
Tunis
Minister: Mustapha Bouaziz

MINISTRY OF TOURISM AND HANDICRAFTS
Tunis
Minister: Mohamed Jegham

MINISTRY OF TRANSPORT
3 rue d'Angleterre, Tunis
Tel (1) 660-088; telex 13040
Minister: Ahmad Smaoui

MINISTRY OF VOCATIONAL TRAINING AND EMPLOYMENT
Tunis
Minister: Tahar Azaiez

GOVERNMENT AGENCIES AND ORGANIZATIONS

Agriculture and Fishing

AGRICULTURE

Agence de la Réforme Agraire: 4 rue Claude Bernard, Tunis; agrarian reform.

Office des Céréales: 23 bis rue al-Djazira, Tunis; tel (1) 247-421; telex 13499; Chair and Dir-Gen: A. Eladeb; f 1962; responsible for the cereals industry.

Office de l'Elevage et des Pâturages (OEP): 30 rue Alain Savary, Tunis; tel (1) 681-021; telex 13630; Dir: Taïeb Belhadj; f 1966; assists farmers; pasture and cattle promotion and devt.

Office des Terres Domaniales (OTD): 43 rue d'Iran, Tunis; tel (1) 280-322; telex 13566; Dir: Bechir ben Smail; f 1961; responsible for agricultural production and the management of state-owned lands.

Société Tunisienne de l'Industrie Laitière (STIL): 25 rue Belhassen ben Chaâbane, El Omrane, 1005 Tunis; tel (1) 260-117; telex 15322; fax (1) 261-882; Pres and Dir-Gen: Ahmed Rafik ben Brahm; f 1962; milk production.

FISHING

Office National des Pêches (ONP): Le Port, La Goulette, Tunis; tel (1) 275-093; telex 12388; Pres: M. Zaouli; marine and fishing authority.

Business and Economy

BANKING

Banque Arabe Tuniso-Libyenne pour le Développement et le Commerce Extérieur: 25 ave Kheireddine Pacha, BP 102, 1002 Tunis-Belvédère; tel (1) 781-500; telex 14938; Pres and Dir-Gen: Ezzeddine Chelbi; f 1984; promotes trade and devt projects between Tunisia and Libya, and provides funds for investment in poorer areas.

Banque Centrale de Tunisie: rue de la Monnaie, BP 369, Tunis; tel (1) 340-588; telex 12375; Gov: Ismaïl Khelil (mem of the Cabinet); Man: Hamda Beji; f 1958; central bank.

Banque de Développement Economique de Tunisie (BDET): 68 ave du 7 Novembre, BP 280, 1000 Tunis; tel (1) 245-600; telex 14382; Chair and Man Dir: Habib Bourguiba, Jr; Man Dir: Chekib Nouira; f 1959; main source of long-term and equity finance for industrial and tourist enterprises.

Banque Internationale Arabe de Tunisie: 70-72 ave du 7 Novembre, BP 520, 1080 Tunis; tel (1) 340-733; telex 15396; Pres: Magr Mokhtar Fakhfakh; Gen Man: Hassen Zghal; f 1976 by consortium of banks and the Tunisian Govt; 44 brs.

Caisse Nationale d'Epargne Logement (Housing Bank): 4 rue Jean-Jacques Rousseau, 1002 Tunis-Belvédère; tel (1) 785-277; telex 14349; fax (1) 784-477; f 1973; loans to individuals; savings bank, etc.

INSURANCE

Compagnie Tunisienne pour l'Assurance du Commerce Extérieur: 5 rue du Brésil, 1002 Tunis-Belvédère; tel (1) 783-000; telex 14874; fax (1) 782-539; Man Dir: Mohamed Salah Bouaziz; f 1984; export credit insurance.

NATIONALIZED INDUSTRY

Office National de l'Artisanat Tunisien: ave de l'Indépendance, 2011 Den Den; tel (1) 512-400; telex 15238; Pres and Dir-Gen: Hédi Toumi; Dep Dir-Gen and Commercial Dir: Noureddine Gueddiche; f 1959; production and marketing of Tunisian handicraft goods, eg carpets, tapestries, ceramics, bird-cages, silver jewellery, embroidery, painted cloth, etc.

Société Générale des Industries Textiles (SOGITEX): Bir Kassaa, Ben Arous, Tunis; tel (1) 297-100; telex 12444; Chair: Bechir Saidane; responsible for the textile industry.

Société Tunisienne de Constructions et de Réparations Mécaniques et Navales (SOCOMENA): BP NB 10, 7050 Menzel Bourguiba; tel (2) 60-590; telex 21016; fax (2) 60-354; Chair: Moncef Driss; Vice-Chair: Cherif Jerbi; f 1963; ship-building and repairing; industrial activities.

TRADE

Centre de Promotion des Exportations (CEPEX): 8 rue de Médine, 1002 Tunis-Belvédère; tel (1) 890-003; telex 15358; f 1973; state export promotion organization.

Institut National de Normalisation et de la Propriété Industrielle: 10 bis rue Ibn el Jazzar, Tunis; standards and industrial property institute.

Office du Commerce de la Tunisie: ave Mohamed V, 1002 Tunis-Belvédère; tel (1) 682-905; telex 14159; f 1962; monopoly of importation of certain products, eg sugar, tea, coffee, cacao, pepper; controls exportation of Tunisian products and applies standardization laws.

Defence

Armed Forces: c/o Ministry of National Defence, blvd Bab Menara, Tunis; tel (1) 260-244; telex 12580.

Air Force: address as above; Chief of Staff: Gen Ridha Attar.

Army: address as above; Chief of Staff: Gen Mohamed Said al-Kateb.

Navy: address as above; Chief of Staff: Adm Habib Fedhila.

Development and Planning

Agence de Promotion de l'Industrie (API): 63 rue de Syrie, 1002 Tunis; tel (1) 287-600; telex 14166; fax (1) 782-482; Pres: Chahed; f 1973 by merger of Agence de Promotion des Investissements, Agence Foncière Industrielle and Centre National d'Etudes Industrielles; co-ordinates industrial policy, undertakes feasibility studies, organizes industrial training and establishes industrial zones; overseas offices in Belgium, France, the Federal Republic of Germany and Sweden.

Société Nationale de Mise en Valeur du Sud (SOMNIVAS): 23 ave des Etats-Unis d'Amérique, Tunis; implements and co-ordinates economic devt projects for the southern desert areas.

Education and Research

Centre National Universitaire de Documentation Scientifique et Technique: 1 ave de France, 1000 Tunis; tel (1) 258-603; telex 13415; Dir: Fatima Chamam; f 1980; provides postgraduates with primary documents; provides an on-line searching service and produces in-house databases; edits and publishes academic works.

Media

BROADCASTING

Radiodiffusion Télévision Tunisienne: 71 ave de la Liberté, Tunis; tel (1) 287-300; telex 12365; Dir-Gen: Slaheddine Maaouiya; Govt service; broadcasts in Arabic, French and Italian.

GOVERNMENT PUBLISHERS

Imprimerie Officielle de la République Tunisienne: ave Farhat Hached, 2040 Radès; tel (1) 299-914; telex 14939; Man Dir: Maher Kamoun; f 1860.

Maison Tunisienne de l'Edition: 36 rue Bab el Khadhra, Tunis; tel (1) 346-040; telex 14143; Pres and Dir-Gen: Mongi Bousnina; f 1966; publishes books on Tunisia, children's books, novels, etc.

NEWS AND INFORMATION

Institut National de Statistique: 27 rue de Liban, Tunis; tel (1) 282-500.

Mining and Energy

Compagnie des Phosphates de Gafsa: Bayache, 2100 Gafsa; tel (6) 283-522; telex 14475; fax (6) 288-453; Tunis Office: 9 rue du Royaume d'Arabie Saoudite, 1035 Tunis; Pres: Najib ben Debba; f 1897; production and marketing of phosphates.

Office National des Mines: 26 rue d'Angleterre, Tunis; tel (1) 253-122; telex 12004; Pres, Dir-Gen: Ali Attia; f 1962; mining of iron ores; research and study of mineral wealth.

Société Tunisienne de l'Electricité et du Gaz (STEG): BP 190, 1080 Tunis; tel (1) 341-345; telex 14020; fax (1) 349-981; Pres and Gen Man: Tahar Hadj Ali; Asst Gen Man: Mohamed Elloumi; f 1962; produces, transmits and sells electricity; monopoly of importing and exporting electricity; also distributes natural and manufactured gas.

Science and Technology

Institut National de la Météorologie: BP 156, 2035 Tunis-Carthage; tel (1) 782-400; telex 14195; fax (1) 784-608; Dir: Hamadi Trabelsi; f 1875; meteorology, climatology, hydrometeorology, seismology, etc.

Office de la Topographie et de la Cartographie: Cité Olympique Tunis, BP 156, 1080 Tunis; tel (1) 891-477; telex 14129; Pres and Dir-Gen: Ali Kallel; f 1886; mapping and map revision; cadastral surveys; national topographical, cartographical and aerial photographic archives.

Tourism

Office National du Tourisme Tunisien: 1 ave Mohamed V, Tunis; tel (1) 341-077; telex 14381; Dir-Gen: (vacant); Man: Mahjoub Gerfali; f 1958.

Transport

CIVIL AVIATION

Office des Ports Aériens: BP 60, Aérodrome de Tunis, Tunis-Carthage; tel (1) 289-000; telex 13809; Chair: Mohamed el Hedi Merchaoui; air traffic control and airport admin.

RAILWAYS

Société du Métro Léger de Tunis (SMLT): 6 rue Khartoum, 1002 Tunis; tel (1) 780-100; telex 14072; fax (1) 780-371; Pres and Dir-Gen: Lamine Riahi; f 1981; light railway system in and around Tunis.

Société Nationale des Chemins de Fer Tunisiens (SNCFT): 67 ave Farhat Hached, Tunis; tel (1) 249-999; telex 14019; Pres and Dir-Gen: Nouri Chaouch; f 1957; state organization controlling all Tunisian railways.

ROADS

Société Nationale du Transport Rural et Interurbain (SNTRI): ave Mohamed V, BP 40, 1012 Tunis; tel (1) 784-433; telex 13335; fax (1) 786-605; Dir-Gen: Houcine Chouk; f 1981; national and international passenger transportation by road; bus hire service.

Société Nationale des Transports (SNT): 1 ave Habib Bourguiba, 1001 Tunis; tel (1) 259-421; telex 12196; Chair and Man Dir: Mahmoud ben Fadhl; Gen Man: Hassine Massani; f 1963; operates 157 local bus routes with 713 buses.

SHIPPING

Compagnie Tunisienne de Navigation SA: 5 ave Dag Hammarskjoeld, BP 40, Tunis; tel (1) 242-999; telex 12475; fleet of general cargo vessels and tankers; brs at Bizerta, Gabès, La Skhirra, La Goulette Radès, Sfax and Sousse.

Office des Ports Nationaux: Bâtiments Administratifs, Port de Goulette, La Goulette, Tunis; tel (1) 730-000; telex 15386; Dir-Gen: S. Borgi; maritime port admin.

Utilities

Office National de l'Assainissement: 32 rue de la Monnaie, 1001 Tunis; tel (1) 343-819; telex 15080; fax (1) 350411; Dir: Mehdi Mlika; f 1974; urban sewerage and improvement of sanitation in urban areas; water pollution.

Société Nationale d'Exploitation et de Distribution des Eaux: 23 rue Nehru, Montfleury, Tunis; water exploitation and distribution.

Welfare

Agence de Réhabilitation et de Rénovation Urbaine: 17 rue Abderrahmane el Jaziri, 1002 Tunis; tel (1) 782-655; telex 14234; Pres and Dir-Gen: Khaled Limayem; Dep Dir-Gen: Rachid Bellalouna; f 1981; conducts Govt urban upgrading and renewal programmes; assists municipalities in locating over-crowded and deteriorating areas and designs and sets up special programmes for them.

Office National de la Famille et de la Population: 42 ave Madrid, Tunis; family and population office.

TURKEY

Head of State

Executive power is vested in the President, who is elected by the Turkish Grand National Assembly for a seven-year term, and who acts as Head of State with the assistance of a Presidential Council.

President: Turgut Özal (elected 31 October 1989; took office 9 November 1989).

Office of the President: Cumhurbaşkanlığı Köskü, Çankaya, Ankara; tel (4) 271338; telex 42303.

Presidential Council: Cumhurbaşkanlığı Konsey Üyesi, Ankara; tel (4) 271338; Sec-Gen: Sedat Güneral; Mems: Nurettin Ersin, Tahsin Şahinkaya, Nejat Tümer, Sedat Celasun.

Legislature

Legislative power is vested in the unicameral Turkish Grand National Assembly, which has 450 deputies (increased from 400 by a constitutional amendment in June 1987) who are elected by universal adult suffrage for a five-year term.

Turkish Grand National Assembly: Türkiye Buyuk Millet Meclisi (TBMM), Ankara; tel (4) 1183871; telex 43627; Speaker: (vacant).

MINISTRIES AND GOVERNMENT DEPARTMENTS

OFFICE OF THE PRIME MINISTER
Basbakanlık, Bakanlıklar, Ankara
Tel (4) 1186230; telex 43384
Prime Minister: Yildirim Akbulut
Ministers of State for Economic Affairs: Gunes Taner, Işin Çelebi

OFFICE OF THE DEPUTY PRIME MINISTER
Basbakan yard ve Devlet Bakani,
Bakanlıklar, Ankara
Tel (4) 2308919
Deputy Prime Minister and Minister of State:
Prof Ali Bozer

MINISTRY OF AGRICULTURE, FORESTRY AND RURAL AFFAIRS
Tarim, Orman ve Koyisleri Bakanlığı,
Bakanlıklar, Ankara
Tel (4) 1172235; telex 43298; fax (4) 1258967
Minister: Lutfullah Kayalar

MINISTRY OF CULTURE AND TOURISM
Kültür ve Turizm Bakanlığı,
Gazi Mustafa Kemal Bul 33,
Demirtepe, Ankara
Tel (4) 2317380; telex 42448; fax (4) 1254749
Minister, Culture: Namik Kemal Zeybek
Minister, Tourism: Ilham Akuzum

Directorate-General of Information and Promotion: 10 Kızılay, Ankara; telex 42448; fax (4) 1254749; Dir-Gen: Aydın Barlas.

MINISTRY OF ENERGY AND NATURAL RESOURCES
Enerji ve Tabii Kaynaklar Bakanlığı, Ankara
Tel (4) 1183180; telex 43287
Minister: Fahrettin Kurt

MINISTRY OF FINANCE AND CUSTOMS
Maliye ve gumruk Bakanlığı, Ankara
Tel (4) 1191200; telex 43445
Minister: Prof Ekrem Pakdermirli

MINISTRY OF FOREIGN AFFAIRS
Disisleri Bakanlığı,
Yeni Hizmet Binası Balgat, Ankara
Tel (4) 2872555; telex 42203
Minister: Ali Bozer

MINISTRY OF HEALTH AND SOCIAL WELFARE
Saglik ve Sosyal Yardim Bakanlığı,
Yenişehir, Ankara
Tel (4) 1258238; telex 43694
Minister: Halil Sivgin

MINISTRY OF INDUSTRY AND COMMERCE
Sanayi ve Ticaret Bakanlığı, Ankara
Telex 42598
Minister: Sukru Yurur

MINISTRY OF THE INTERIOR
Icisleri Bakanlığı,
Bakanlıklar, Ankara
Tel (4) 1285298; telex 46201
Minister: Abdulkadir Aksu

MINISTRY OF JUSTICE
Adalet Bakanlığı,
Bakanlıklar, Ankara
Tel (4) 1185260
Minister: Mahmut Oltan Sungurlu

MINISTRY OF LABOUR AND SOCIAL SECURITY
Calisma ve Sosyal Guvenlik Bakanlığı,
Mithat Pasa Cad, Ankara
Tel (4) 3113442; telex 42140
Minister: Imren Aykut

MINISTRY OF NATIONAL DEFENCE
Milli Savunma Bakanlığı, Ankara
Tel (4) 1176100
Minister: Safa Giray

MINISTRY OF NATIONAL EDUCATION, YOUTH AND SPORTS
Milli Egitim, Genclik ve Spor Bakanlığı,
Ankara
Tel (4) 2231160; telex 42903
Minister: Avni Aykol

MINISTRY OF PUBLIC WORKS AND HOUSING
Bayindirlik ve Iskan Bakanlığı, Ankara
Tel (4) 1339110; telex 42477
Minister: Cengiz Altinkaya

MINISTRY OF TRANSPORT AND COMMUNICATIONS
Ulaştirma Bakanlığı, Istasyon Cad, Ankara
Tel (4) 3113047; telex 42019
Minister: Cengiz Tuncer

GOVERNMENT AGENCIES AND ORGANIZATIONS

Advisory and Supervisory Body

Devlet Malzeme Ofisi (State Supply Office): Genel Müdürlüğü, Inönü Bul, 06041 Ankara; tel (4) 1175300; telex 42350; fax (4) 1187128; f 1926; supply of miscellaneous requirements to govt offices.

Directorate-General of State Economic Enterprises: Ulus, Ankara; supervises nationalized industries.

Higher Planning Council: Ankara; f 1988 to streamline econonic policymaking.

Agriculture

Soil Products Office (TMO): Ankara; Gen Man: Ahment Ozgunes; production and promotion of grains and pulses.

Art and Culture

State Archives: Istanbul; Dir: Prof Ismet Miroglu; maintenance of archives.

Business and Economy

BANKING

Denizçilik Bankası TAŞ (Turkish Maritime Bank): (see Transport section).

Devlet Yatırım Bankası (State Investment Bank): Milli Müdafaa Cad 29, Yenisehiri, Ankara; tel (4) 256310; telex 42606; Chair and Gen Man: Ertan Sakizli; f 1964; provides financial support and credit for state economic enterprises.

Etibank: Cihan Sok 2, Sıhhıye, Ankara; tel (4) 2317020; telex 42207; Gen Man: M. Fethi Ağalar; f 1935; 129 brs.

Türkiye Halk Bankası AŞ (Halkbank): İlkiz Sok 1, Sıhhıye, 06240 Ankara; tel (4) 2317500; telex 44201; Gen Man: Mümtaz Pehlivanli; f 1938; 659 brs.

İller Bankası (Municipalities Bank): Atatürk Bul 21, Opera, Ankara; tel (4) 3113044; telex 42723; Chair and Gen Man: Rafet Güney; f 1933; 1 br.

Sınai Yatırım ve Kredi Bankası AO (Industrial Investment

Bank of Turkey): Barbaros Bul Akdoğan Sok 41-43, 80690 Beşiktaş, Istanbul; tel (1) 1597414; telex 26263; Chair: Cahit Kocaömer; Gen Man: Dr Orhan Altan; f 1963; 1 br.

Sümerbank: Çankırı Cad 2, Ulus, Ankara; tel (4) 3103830; telex 44098; Gen Man: Ahmet Özerdim; f 1933; 46 brs.

Töbank (Türkiye Ögretmenler Bankası TAŞ): Taşocağı Cad 1, Naci Kasim Sok 7, 80493 Mecidiyeköy, Istanbul; tel (1) 1722250; telex 30072; Gen Man: Çetin Hacaloğlu; f 1959; 111 brs.

Türkiye Cumhuriyet Merkez Bankası AŞ (Central Bank of the Republic of Turkey): Istiklal Cad 10, 06100 Ulus, Ankara; tel (4) 3103646; telex 44031; Gov: Dr Rüşdü Saracoğlu; Dep Gov: Ercan Kumcu; Man: Perihan Üçer; f 1930; bank of issue; 25 brs.

Türkiye Cumhuriyeti Ziraat Bankası (Agricultural Bank of the Republic of Turkey): Atatürk Bul 42, Ulus, Ankara; tel (4) 2317560; telex 44217; Chair and Chief Exec: Kemal Akkaya; Gen Man: Dr Şerif Çoşkun Ulusoy; f 1863; 1,231 brs.

Türkiye Emlâk Bankası AŞ—Konutbank (Real Estate Bank of Turkey): Büyükdere Cad 43-45, 80670 Maslak, Istanbul; tel (1) 1761620; telex 26035; Gen Man: Engin Civan; Dep Gen Man: Z. Yalçin Sayin; f 1987 by merger of Anadolu Bankası AŞ and Türkiye Emlâk Kredi Bankası; commercial banking, trade finance, real estate and property devt; 438 brs.

Türkiye İhracat Kredi Bankası AŞ (Türk Eximbank) (Export Credit Bank of Turkey): Milli Müdafaa Cad 20, 06100 Bakanlıklar, Ankara; tel (4) 1171300; telex 46751; fax (4) 1257896; Chair: Yavuz Canevi; Pres: Dr Turgay Özkan; f 1987; supports exporters, manufacturers, contractors, etc, by means of finance, guarantee and insurance programmes.

Türkiye Kalkınma Bankası AŞ (Development Bank of Turkey): İzmir Cad 43, 06440 Kızılay, Ankara; tel (4) 1171220; telex 42457; Gen Man: Dr Halit Kara; f 1988 by merger of Devlet Sanayi ve İşçi Yatırım Bankası AŞ and Türkiye Cumhuriyeti Turizm Bankası AŞ; 2 brs.

Türkiye Sınai Kalkınma Bankası AŞ (Industrial Development Bank of Turkey): Meclisi Mebusan Cad 137, PK 17, Fındıklı, Istanbul; tel (1) 1512800; telex 24344; Chair: Burhan Karagöz; Gen Man: Özhan Eroğuz; f 1950; 5 brs.

Türkiye Vakıflar Bankası TAO (Foundation Bank of Turkey): Atatürk Bul 207, Kavaklıdere, Ankara; tel (4) 1261676; telex 44496; Chair: Şener Macun; Gen Man: Ismet Alver; f 1954; 289 brs.

INSURANCE

Güven Sigorta TAŞ: Bankalar Cad 122-124, 80000 Karaköy, Istanbul; tel (1) 1552790; telex 24336; fax (1) 1555888; Chair and Gen Man: Aytekin Tece; f 1924; state-owned insurance co, providing fire, accident, motor, engineering, marine and life cover.

NATIONALIZED INDUSTRY

Aselsan Askeri Elektronik Sanayii ve Tic AŞ (Aselsan): PK 101, Yenimahalle, Ankara; tel (4) 1541700; electronic goods.

Azot Sanayii TAŞ: Genel Müdürlüğü, Konya Devlet Yolu 70, Hipodrom, Ankara; nitrogen industry.

MKEK: Ankara; Chair: Adnan Ignebekçili; f 1827, passed to civilian management in 1950; production of munitions and small arms.

Northern Electric Telekomünikasyon AŞ (Netas): Ümranije, Alemanday Cad, Üsküdar, Istanbul; telecommunications apparatus.

Türkiye Cimento Sanayii TAŞ: Atatürk Bul 211, Kavaklidere; production of cement.

TRADE

Ihracatçı Geliştirme Etüd Merkezi (IGEME) (Export Promotion Research Centre): Mithatpasa Cad 60, Kızılay, Ankara; tel (4) 1172223; telex 42228; Dep Sec-Gen: Birkan Erdal; f 1960.

Türk Standartlar Enstitüsü (Turkish Standards Institute): Necatibey Cad 112, Bakanlıklar, Ankara; tel (4) 1341990; telex 42047.

Defence

Armed Forces: Genelkurmay Bakanlığı, Ankara; tel (4) 1335011; Chief of Gen Staff: Gen Necip Torumtay.

  Air Force: Haa Kuvvetleri, Komutanlığı, Ankara; tel (4) 1172150; telex 42688; Commdr: Gen Safter Necioğlu.

  Army: Kara Kuvvetleri, Komutanlığı, Ankara; tel (4) 1343610; Commdr: Gen Dogan Gures.

  Navy: Deniz Kuvvetleri, Komutanlığı, Ankara; tel (4) 1335011; Commdr: Adm Orhan Karabulut.

Defence Industry Development Administration (Dida): Ankara; Dir: Yahit Erdem; devt of arms industry through provision of financial incentives for foreign cos.

Gendarmerie General Command: Jandarma Genel Komutanlığı, Bakanlıklar 06100, Ankara; tel (4) 2306220; Commdr: Gen Burhanettin Bigali; f 1839.

Development and Planning

Devlet Planlama Tekilati Mustesarlığı (State Planning Organization): Necatibey Cad 108, Ankara; tel (4) 302497; Dir: Ali Tigrel; Dir, Foreign Investment: Ibrahim Cakir; prepares devt plans, monitors progress towards targets.

Forestry

Orman Genel Müdürlüğü (Directorate-General of Forestry): Tarim, Orman ve Köyileri Bakanlığı, Ankara; tel (4) 1187061; Dir-Gen: Mehmet Ali Karadeniz.

Legal and Judiciary

Anayasa Mahkemesi (Constitutional Court): Selanik Cad 37, Yenisehir, Ankara; tel (4) 1189286; Pres: Mahmut Cuhruk; f 1962; reviews constitutionality of laws, functions as high council empowered to try senior members of state.

Danistay (Council of State): Sihhiye, Ankara; tel (4) 1342980; administrative court of the first instance.

Uyusmazlik Mahkemesi (Court of Jurisdictional Dispute): Selanik Cad 37, Ankara; tel (4) 1173199; settles disputes among civil, administrative and military courts.

Yargitay (Supreme Court of Appeal): Kizilay, Ankara; tel (4) 1253099.

Media

BROADCASTING

Türkiye Radyo Televizyon Kurumu (TRT) (Turkish Radio-Television Corpn): Nevzat Tandoğan Cad 2, Kavaklıhidere, Ankara; tel (4) 1282230; telex 43164; Dir-Gen: Tunca Toskay; f 1964; controls Turkish radio and TV services.

NEWS AND INFORMATION

Devlet Istatistik Enstitusu (State Statistical Institute): Necatibey Cad 114, Ankara; tel (4) 1188719.

Mining and Energy

ENERGY

Turkish Atomic Energy Authority: Karanfil Sok 67, Bakanlıklar, Ankara; tel (4) 1188923; telex 42581; Pres (acting): Atilla Özmen; Sec: Gen Erol Barutçugil; f 1956; controls the devt of peaceful uses of atomic energy.

Turkish Electricity Authority: İnonü Bul 27, Bahçelievler, Ankara; tel (4) 2800875; telex 42245; Dir: Dr Ahmet Kütükçüoğlu; state enterprise to supervise building and operation of power stations.

Türkiye Petrolleri AO (Turkish Petroleum Corpn): PK 209, Bakanlıklar, Ankara; tel (4) 1179160; telex 42426; Turkey's largest state economic enterprise; drilling, exploration and production of crude petroleum.

MINING

Black Sea Copper Corpn: Ziva Gökaln Cad 17, Ankara.

Maden Tetkik ve Arama Enstitüsü (MTA) (Directorate-General of Mineral Research and Exploration): Eskişehir Yolu, Ankara; tel (4) 2234255; telex 42040; Dir-Gen: M. Sitki Sancar; f 1935.

Türkiye Demir ve Celik Isletmeleri Kurumu: Cankiri Cad 57, Diskapi, Ankara; tel (4) 1339985; telex 42506; state-owned mining and exploration co.

Türkiye Komur Isletmesi Kurumi: Genel Müdürlüğü, Zafer Meydani, Ankara; tel (4) 10126000; coal-mining organization.

Zinc and Lead Industries Inc: Cinkur PK 184, 38001 Kayseri; tel (351) 38460; telex 49517; fax (351) 33180; Gen Man: Aydin Keskin; f 1968; mining and metallurgy, production of zinc and cadmium.

Science and Technology

Türkiye Bilimsel ve Teknik Arastırma Kurumu (Scientific and Technical Research Council of Turkey): Atatürk Bul 221, Kavaklidere, Ankara; tel (4) 262770; telex 43186; f 1963; Govt body which promotes and co-ordinates research activities in pure and applied sciences.

Tourism

General Directorate of Information and Promotion: Şehit Adem Yavuz Sokak, 10 Kızılay, Ankara; telex 42448; fax (4) 1254749; Dir-Gen: Aydın Barlas; tourism authority.

Transport and Communications

TELECOMMUNICATIONS

Directorate-General of Posts, Telegraphs and Telephones (PTT): Milletlerarasi İlişkiler D. Bşk, 06101 Ulus, Ankara; tel (4) 3125252; telex 42291; Dir-Gen: Emin Başer; f 1840; provides all telephone, telegraph, telex and postal services.

TRANSPORT

Bayındırlık ve İskan Bakanlığı Karayolları (Directorate-General of Highways): Genel Müdürlüğü, Ankara; Dir-Gen: Atalay Coşkunoğlu.

Denizçilik Bankası TAŞ (Turkish Maritime Bank): Reşadiye Cad, Birlik Sok 3, Eminönü, Istanbul; tel (1) 5111042; telex 30066; Gen Man: Mete Kiliç; f 1952; operates ports, shipyards and drydocks, as well as providing passenger, cargo and ferry services; 52 brs.

Türk Hava Yolları AO (THY) (Turkish Airlines Inc): Cumhuriyet Cad 199-201, Harbiye, Istanbul; tel (1) 1462050; telex 22681; Chair and Gen Man: Yilmaz Oral; Sec-Gen: Atayar Aygün; 97.99% state-owned airline; extensive internal network and international services to the Middle East, North Africa, Far East and Europe.

Türkiye Cumhuriyeti Devlet Demiryolları İşletmesi (TCDD) (Turkish Republic State Railways): Genel Müdürlüğü, Ankara; tel (4) 3103500; telex 42571; Chair and Dir-Gen: Birkan Erdal; f 1924; operates all railways and connecting ports of the state railway admin.

TUVALU

<table>
<tr><td>

Head of State

Tuvalu is a constitutional monarchy. The British sovereign, as Head of State, is represented locally by a Governor-General, appointed on the recommendation of the Prime Minister, and who acts on the advice of the Cabinet. The Governor-General appoints the Cabinet, led by the Prime Minister, elected from and by the members of Parliament. The Cabinet is responsible to Parliament.

Sovereign: HM Queen Elizabeth II (succeeded to the throne 6 February 1952).

Governor-General: Sir Tupua Leupena (took office 1 March 1986).

Office of the Governor-General: Vaiaku, Funafuti.

</td><td>

Legislature

Legislative power is vested in the unicameral Parliament, with 12 members elected by universal adult suffrage for four years (subject to dissolution). Each of the inhabited atolls has an elected Island Council which is responsible for local government.

Parliament: Vaiaku, Funafuti; Speaker: Vasa Vave Founuku.

</td></tr>
</table>

MINISTRIES AND GOVERNMENT DEPARTMENTS

OFFICE OF THE PRIME MINISTER, AND MINISTRY OF CIVIL SERVICE ADMINISTRATION AND LOCAL GOVERNMENT, AND FOREIGN AFFAIRS
Vaiaku, Funafuti
Prime Minister and Minister: Bikenibeu Paeniu

OFFICE OF THE DEPUTY PRIME MINISTER AND MINISTRY OF FINANCE AND COMMERCE
Vaiaku, Funafuti
Deputy Prime Minister and Minister: Dr Alesana Seluka

MINISTRY OF HEALTH AND EDUCATION
Vaiaku, Funafuti
Minister: Naama Sapetalatasi

MINISTRY OF NATURAL RESOURCES AND HOME AFFAIRS
Vaiaku, Funafuti
Minister: Tomu Sione

MINISTRY OF WORKS AND COMMUNICATIONS
Vaiaku, Funafuti
Minister: Ionatona Ionatona

GOVERNMENT AGENCIES AND ORGANIZATIONS

Business and Economy

BANKING

National Bank of Tuvalu: POB 13, Vaiaku, Funafuti; tel 802; telex 4802; Gen Man: Mark Hitchenson; f 1980; commercial bank; managed by Westpac Banking Corpn of Australia.

TRADE

Tuvalu Coconut Traders' Co-operative Society Ltd (TCTC): POB 17, Funafuti; tel 724; telex 4800; Man (acting):

Pusinelli T. Lafai; f 1979; marketing of copra and other coconut products; management committee has mems representing each island of Tuvalu.

Defence

Police: Vaiaku, Funafuti; Chief: Saloa Tauia.

Development and Planning

Business Development Advisory Bureau: POB 9, Vaiaku, Funafuti; tel 850; telex 4800; Man: Simeona Iosia; f 1981;

established by the Govt to assist, promote and stimulate the devt of commercial activities in the country; provides financial assistance under its guarantee and subsidy scheme and provides advice to enterprises.

Legal and Judiciary

High Court: Vaiaku, Funafuti; superior court of record, presided over by the Chief Justice; has jurisdiction to consider appeals from judgements of the Magistrates' Courts and the Island Courts.

Office of the Attorney-General: Vaiaku, Funafuti; the principal legal adviser to the Govt.

Media

BROADCASTING

Radio Tuvalu: POB 92, Vaiaku, Funafuti; tel 732; telex 4801; Broadcasting and Information Officer: Lina Petaia; f 1975; daily broadcasts in Tuvaluan and English, 40 hours per week.

NEWS AND INFORMATION

Statistics Division: c/o Ministry of Finance and Commerce, Vaiaku, Funafuti.

UGANDA

Head of State

The 1967 Constitution was suspended following a coup in 1985. In January 1986 a further military coup established a broad-based interim Government, headed by an executive President, who is assisted by a Cabinet of ministers. In February 1989 a commission was appointed to review the Constitution, and to present, within 24 months, a new draft Constitution.

President: Lt-Gen Yoweri Kaguta Museveni (took office 29 January 1986).

Office of the President: Parliament Bldgs, POB 7006, Kampala; tel (41) 254881; telex 61389.

Legislature

Following the 1986 military coup a National Resistance Council (NRC) was established, to legislate by decree. The NRC comprises 278 members, of whom 68 are nominated by the President and 210 are elected. Resistance Committees (RCs) were formed at village, parish, county and district level, and these, in turn, elect representatives to the NRC. Political activity has been suspended, although political parties are not banned.

National Resistance Council (NRC): Kampala.

MINISTRIES AND GOVERNMENT DEPARTMENTS

OFFICE OF THE PRIME MINISTER
POB 341, Kampala
Tel (41) 259518; telex 62001
Prime Minister: Dr Samson Kisekka
First Deputy Prime Minister: Eriya Kategaya
Second Deputy Prime Minister: Paul Ssemogerere
Third Deputy Prime Minister: Abubakar Mayanja
Minister of State resident in North Central Uganda: Betty Bigombe

MINISTRY OF AGRICULTURE AND FORESTRY
POB 102, Entebbe
Tel (42) 20752; telex 61287
Minister: Victoria Ssekitoleko

MINISTRY OF ANIMAL INDUSTRY AND FISHERIES
POB 7003, Kampala
Tel (41) 533789; telex 62287
Minister: Prof George Kagonyera

MINISTRY OF COMMERCE
POB 7000, Kampala
Tel (41) 233561; telex 61403
Minister: Paul Etiang

MINISTRY OF CONSTITUTIONAL AFFAIRS
POB 7272, Kampala
Tel (41) 243401
Minister: Sam Njuba

MINISTRY OF CO-OPERATIVES AND MARKETING
POB 7103, Kampala
Tel (41) 258202; telex 61183
Minister: James Wapakabulo

MINISTRY OF DEFENCE
Republic House, POB 3798, Kampala
Tel (41) 270331; telex 61023
Minister: Lt-Gen Yoweri Kaguta Museveni
Minister of State: Maj-Gen Elly Tumwine

MINISTRY OF EDUCATION
POB 7063, Kampala
Tel (41) 234440; telex 61298
Minister: Maj Amanya Mushega
Minister of State: John Ntimba

MINISTRY OF ENERGY
POB 7270, Kampala
Tel (41) 234995; telex 61098
Minister: Richard Kaijuka

MINISTRY OF ENVIRONMENT PROTECTION
POB 4544, Kampala
Tel (41) 234733
Minister: Moses Kintu

MINISTRY OF FINANCE
POB 8147, Kampala
Tel (41) 234700; telex 61170
Minister: Crispus W. C. B. Kiyonga

MINISTRY OF FOREIGN AFFAIRS AND OF REGIONAL CO-OPERATION
POB 7048, Kampala
Tel (41) 258251; telex 61007
Minister: Paul Ssemgorerere
Minister of State: Omara Atubo

MINISTRY OF HEALTH
POB 8, Entebbe
Tel (42) 20201; telex 61372
Minister: Zak Kaberu
Minister of State: Dr Ronald Bata

MINISTRY OF HOUSING AND URBAN DEVELOPMENT
POB 7122, Kampala
Tel (41) 242931; telex 61274
Minister: Ssebaana-Kizito

MINISTRY OF INDUSTRY AND TECHNOLOGY
1 Parliament Ave, POB 7125, Kampala
Tel (41) 254092; telex 61296
Minister: Dr E. T. S. Adriko
Deputy Minister, Industry: Dr S. Wandira-Kazibwe
Deputy Minister, Research and Technology:
A. A. Kiiza-Kabango

MINISTRY OF INFORMATION AND BROADCASTING
POB 7142, Kampala
Tel (41) 256888; telex 61084
Minister: Kintu Musoke

MINISTRY OF INTERNAL AFFAIRS
POB 7191, Kampala
Tel (41) 231188; telex 61331
Minister: Ibrahim Mukiibi
Minister of State: Tom Butine

MINISTRY OF JUSTICE AND OFFICE OF THE ATTORNEY-GENERAL
POB 7183, Kampala
Tel (41) 233219
Minister: Prof George Kanyeihamba

MINISTRY OF LABOUR
POB 7009, Kampala
Tel (41) 242837; telex 62167
Minister: Stanislas Okurut

MINISTRY OF LANDS AND SURVEYS
POB 7096, Kampala
Tel (41) 254855; telex 61265
Minister: Ben Okello Luwum

MINISTRY OF LOCAL GOVERNMENT
POB 7037, Kampala
Tel (41) 241279; telex 61265
Minister: Jaberi Bidandi Ssali

MINISTRY OF MINERALS AND WATER DEVELOPMENT
POB 7096, Kampala
Tel (41) 254855
Minister: Henry Kajura

MINISTRY OF PLANNING AND ECONOMIC DEVELOPMENT
POB 7086, Kampala
Tel (41) 235051; telex 61117
Minister: Joshua Mayanja-Nkangi
Minister of State: M. Rukikaire

MINISTRY OF PUBLIC SERVICES AND CABINET AFFAIRS
POB 7168, Kampala
Tel (41) 254881
Minister: Tom Rubale

MINISTRY OF RELIEF AND SOCIAL REHABILITATION
POB 5261, Kampala
Tel (41) 233483
Minister: Adoko Nekyon

MINISTRY OF TOURISM AND WILDLIFE
Parliament Ave, POB 4241, Kampala
Tel (41) 232971; telex 62218
Minister: Samuel Sebagereka

MINISTRY OF TRANSPORT AND COMMUNICATIONS
POB 7087, Kampala
Tel (41) 230070; telex 62006
Minister: Dr Ruhakana Rugunda

MINISTRY OF WORKS
POB 10, Entebbe
Tel (42) 20103; telex 61313
Minister: Daniel Serwango Kigozi

MINISTRY OF YOUTH, CULTURE AND SPORTS
POB 7136, Kampala
Tel (41) 254253
Minister: Brig Moses Ali

MINISTRIES OF STATE IN THE OFFICE OF THE PRESIDENT
Parliament Bldgs, POB 7006, Kampala
Tel (41) 254881; telex 61389
Minister of State for Karamoja: Anthony Butele
Minister of State for Security: Balaki Kirya
Minister of State for Special Duties: Eteker Ejalu
Minister of State for Women's Development:
Joyce Mpanga
Minister of State without Portfolio: David Kibirango
National Political Commissar: Dr Kiiza Besigye

GOVERNMENT AGENCIES AND ORGANIZATIONS

Advisory and Supervisory Body

Office of the Auditor-General: Apolo Kapwa Rd, POB 7083, Kampala; tel (41) 244521; Auditor-Gen: L. Y. A. Outeke; Dir, Audit: G. Singh; Dir: F. Bugunya; audit of Govt, local authorities and parastatal organizations.

Agriculture

Blenders Uganda Ltd: POB 7054, Kampala; Gen Man: T. D. Muzito; tea- and coffee-blending, packaging and distribution.

Mitchell Cotts Uganda Ltd: 8 Burton St, POB 7032, Kampala; telex 61003; jointly owned by Govt and UK trading group

active in the tea sector; rehabilitation of the tea industry has been undertaken.

Business and Economy

BANKING

Bank of Uganda: 37-43 Kampala Rd, POB 7120, Kampala; tel (41) 258441; telex 61059; Gov: Suleimann Kigundu; Dep Gov: P. Bukumune; Gen Man: E. Rukyarekere; f 1966; bank of issue.

The Co-operative Bank: 7/9 Burton St, POB 6863, Kampala; tel (41) 258323; telex 61263; Gen Man: A. B. K. Ntate; f 1970.

East African Development Bank: 4 Nile Ave, POB 7128, Kampala; tel (41) 230021; telex 61074; Dir-Gen: G. F. Mbowe;

Dir, Operations: M. B. Ngatunga; Dir, Services: D. Mulira; Dir, Finance: E. Mukasa; Dir, Planning and Devt: Dr K. Gatere; f 1967; provides financial and technical assistance to promote industrial devt within Uganda, Kenya and Tanzania, whose Govts each own 30.8% of the equity; regional offices in Nairobi and Dar es Salaam.

Uganda Commercial Bank: 12 Kampala Rd, POB 973, Kampala; tel (41) 234710; telex 61073; Chair and Man Dir: Frank Mwine; f 1965; 58 brs.

Uganda Development Bank: IPS Bldg, 14 Parliament St, POB 7210, Kampala; tel (41) 230740; telex 61143; Gen Man: John Kiggundu; f 1972; finances devt projects in agriculture and industry.

FINANCIAL AGENCY

Agriculture and Livestock Development Fund: Kampala; f 1976; provides loans to farmers.

INSURANCE

National Insurance Co of Uganda: POB 7134, Kampala; tel (41) 233974; telex 61222; Man Dir: Dr I. Kabumba; Dep Man Dir: F. F. Magezi; Gen Man: P. E. Okwi; Sec: L. E. Oweka-Laboke; f 1964; all classes of insurance.

MARKETING

Coffee Marketing Board: POB 7154, Kampala; telex 61157; Chair and Man Dir: Alfred Mubanda; Gen Man: Ernest B. Kakwano; sells all processed coffee produced in Uganda.

Lint Marketing Board: POB 7018, Kampala; tel (41) 232660; telex 61008; Gen Man: J. W. Obbo; Sec: M. A. Dramotu; sole exporter of cotton lint and cottonseed cake; manufacturer of edible oil, soap and candles.

NATIONALIZED INDUSTRY

African Textile Mill: POB 242, Mbale; telex 66274; f 1970; manufacture of textiles.

British-American Tobacco (BAT) Uganda 1984 Ltd: POB 7100, Kampala; tel (41) 243231; telex 61075; f 1928; jointly owned by the Govt and BAT (UK); manufacture of tobacco.

East African Distilleries Ltd: POB 3221, Kampala; tel (41) 221111; Gen Man: Eva Adengo; Chief Accountant: David Sserunjogi; f 1963; manufacture of spirits.

Nile Breweries Ltd: POB 762, Jinja; tel (43) 20177; telex 64067; Man Dir: A. B. Abaliwano; Production Man: S. K. Ndaula; f 1951; brewing.

Nyanza Textile Industries Ltd: POB 408, Jinja; tel (43) 202059; telex 64133; Man Dir: Oneg Obel; f 1949; textile manufacturers.

Pamba Textiles Ltd: POB 472, Jinja; f 1963; manufacture of cotton textiles.

Steel Corpn of East Africa: POB 1023, Jinja.

Tororo Industrial Chemicals and Fertilizers Ltd: POB 254, Tororo; f 1962; manufacture of single super-phosphate fertilizer, sulphuric acid and insecticide.

Uganda Breweries Ltd: POB 7130, Kampala; tel (41) 220224; telex 61218.

Uganda Metal Products and Enamelling Co Ltd: POB 3151, Kampala; f 1956; manufacture of enamelware, furniture, beds, etc.

TRADE

Customs and Excise Department: POB 444, Kampala.

Uganda Advisory Board on Trade: POB 6877, Kampala; tel (41) 33311; telex 61085; f 1974; issues trade licences and is also an import agency; advisory service for exporters.

Uganda Export Promotion Council: POB 5045, Kampala; tel (41) 259779; telex 62033; Exec Sec: Frank Nabwiso; f 1983; undertakes market intelligence work and research, engages in export promotion activities, provides advisory services, formulates and recommends to the Govt export plans and policies.

Uganda Tea Authority: POB 4161, Kampala; tel (41) 231003; telex 61120; Sec: M. M. Mugabi; f 1974; monopoly tea exporter.

Defence

Armed Forces: Kampala; Commdr: Col Mugisha Muntu.

Development and Planning

Departmnet of Physical Planning: Post Office Bldg, Kitante Rd, POB 1911, Kampala; tel (41) 243543; Chief Planner: Deo K. Kajugir; f 1953; preparation and supervision of physical devt plans for urban and rural regions.

Uganda Development Corpn Ltd (UDC): 9-11 Parliament Ave, POB 7042, Kampala; telex 61069; Chair: J. M. S. Kanakulya; Sec: S. B. Okidi; f 1952.

Legal and Judiciary

Court of Appeal: Kampala; Pres: Samson William Wambuzi; hears appeals from the High Court.

High Court: POB 7085, Kampala; tel (41) 233420; Chief Justice: Samson William Wambuzi; has full criminal and civil jurisdiction over all persons and matters in the country; consists of the Chief Justice and 11 Puisne Judges.

Media

BROADCASTING

Radio Uganda: c/o Ministry of Information and Broadcasting, POB 7142, Kampala; tel (41) 254461; telex 61084; Dir: John C. Sserwadda; f 1954; broadcasts in 22 languages, including English, French, Arabic and vernacular languages.

Uganda Television Service: c/o Ministry of Information and Broadcasting, POB 4260, Kampala; tel (41) 254461; telex 61084; Controller: Faustin Misanvu; f 1962; state-controlled commercial service; programmes mainly in English, also in Swahili and Luganda.

GOVERNMENT PUBLISHER

Government Printer: POB 33, Entebbe; telex 61336.

NEWS AND INFORMATION

Statistics Department: c/o Ministry of Planning and Economic Development, POB 13, Entebbe; tel (42) 20741; f 1948; statistical work.

Uganda News Agency (UNA): POB 7142, Kampala; tel (41) 32734; telex 61188; Dir: (vacant); Editor-in-Chief: F. A. Otai.

Mining

Geological Survey and Mines Department: Entebbe Pier, POB 9, Entebbe; reconstruction of copper and cobalt mining industries, as well as other mining and exploration projects.

Science

Meteorological Department: POB 7025, Kampala; tel (41) 255875; telex 61061; Dir: P. C. Okot; Dep Dir: Bwangu-Apuuli; f 1938; weather and climate surveillance, analysis and weather forecasting.

Telecommunications

Telecommunications Corpn: Kampala.

Transport

Directorate of Civil Aviation: Crested Towers Bldg, Nile Ave, POB 5536, Kampala; tel (41) 245514; telex 62006; Dir-Gen (acting): John Ojambo; f 1977; responsible for civil aviation activities in the country.

Uganda Airlines Corpn: 6 Colville St, POB 5740, Kampala; tel (41) 322990; telex 61239; fax (41) 257279; Chief Exec: C. S. K. Mboijana; f 1976; scheduled cargo and passenger services within Africa and to the Middle East and Europe.

Uganda Railways Corpn: Nasser Rd, POB 7150, Kampala; tel (41) 254961; telex 61111; fax (41) 244405; Man Dir: Charles Karamagi; f 1977; 1,286 km of track in 1986.

Welfare

National Housing and Construction Corpn: POB 659, Kampala; tel (41) 257461; telex 61156; Gen Man: G. J. Semwogerere; Technical Man: Martin Kasekende; f 1964; construction, devt and management of housing estates.

THE UNION OF SOVIET SOCIALIST REPUBLICS

Head of State

Following constitutional changes, which were approved by the Congress of People's Deputies in March 1990, the functions of Head of State were vested in the President, who was elected by a majority vote of the Congress. A provision has been made that the President be elected by universal adult suffrage in future elections. The President, who is elected for five years, appoints a Council of Ministers, which is responsible to the Congress, to assist in government.

President: Mikhail Sergeyevich Gorbachev (elected 14 March 1990).

Office of the President: Moscow, Kremlin; tel (095) 295-90-51.

Legislature

Following constitutional changes approved in March 1990 legislative power is vested in the Congress of the People's Deputies of the USSR, comprising 2,250 members, and the Supreme Soviet, comprising the Soviet of the Union and the Soviet of Nationalities. The leading role of the Communist Party of the Soviet Union (CPSU) was abolished in March 1990, and a framework for the development of a multi-party system was established. Each of the 15 Union Republics has a constitution and state structure on the same pattern as the central Government.

Supreme Soviet: Moscow, Kremlin; Chair: Anatoly Lukyanov.

Soviet of the Union: Moscow, Kremlin; Chair: Yevgeni Primakov.

Soviet of Nationalities: Moscow, Kremlin; Chair: Rafik N. Nishanov.

MINISTRIES AND GOVERNMENT DEPARTMENTS

OFFICE OF THE CHAIRMAN OF THE PRESIDIUM OF THE COUNCIL OF MINISTERS
Moscow, Kremlin
Tel (095) 295-90-51
Chair (Prime Minister): Nikolai I. Ryzhkov
First Vice-Chairs: Yuri Maslyukov, Lev Voronin (General Questions)
Vice-Chairs: Leonid Abalkin (Economic Reform), Igor Belousov (Military and Industrial Complexes), Alexandra Biryukova (Social Questions), Vitali Doguzhiev (Emergencies), Vladimir Gusev (Chemical and Forestry Resources), Nikolai Laverov (Science and Technology), Pavel Mostovoi, Lev Ryabev (Fuel and Energy Resources), Ivan Silayev (Machine Building)

MINISTRY OF AGRICULTURE AND TRACTOR MACHINE BUILDING
Moscow, Kuznetsky most 21/5
Tel (095) 925-11-32
Minister: Nikolai A. Pugin

MINISTRY OF THE AIRCRAFT INDUSTRY (Minaviaprom)
Moscow, Ulansky per 16
Tel (095) 207-02-73
Minister: Apollon S. Systsov

MINISTRY OF ATOMIC ENERGY
Moscow, Staromonetny per 26
Minister: Nikolai F. Lukonin

MINISTRY OF THE AUTOMOBILE INDUSTRY (Minavtoprom)
Moscow
Tel (095) 925-11-32; telex 41109
Minister: Nikolai A. Pugin

MINISTRY OF THE BUILDING MATERIALS INDUSTRY
Moscow 103713, pl Nogina 2/5
Tel (095) 928-44-82; telex 411887
Minister: Sergei F. Voyenushkin
Deputy Minister, Foreign Relations: V. I. Kushidi

MINISTRY OF THE CHEMICAL INDUSTRY (Minkhimprom)
Moscow, ul Kirova 20
Tel (095) 927-73-63
Minister: Yuri A. Bespalov

MINISTRY OF CHEMICAL AND OIL ENGINEERING (Minkhimmash)
Moscow, Bezbozhny per 25
Tel (095) 288-40-10
Minister: Vladimir M. Lukyanenko

MINISTRY OF CIVIL AVIATION (MGA)
Moscow 125167, Leningradsky prospekt 37
Tel (095) 155-54-94; telex 411182
Minister: Aleksandr N. Volkov

MINISTRY OF THE COAL INDUSTRY
(Minugleprom)
Moscow, prospekt Kalinina 23
Tel (095) 202-63-96
Minister: Mikhail Shchadov
Deputy Minister: Alexander Fisun

MINISTRY OF COMPUTER ENGINEERING AND INFORMATION SCIENCE
Moscow
Minister: Boris Tolstykh

MINISTRY OF CONSTRUCTION IN EASTERN REGIONS OF THE USSR (Minvostokstroi)
Moscow, prospekt Vernadskovo 41
Tel (095) 202-80-81
Minister: (vacant)

MINISTRY OF CONSTRUCTION IN NORTHERN AND WESTERN REGIONS OF THE USSR
Moscow
Minister: Vladimir I. Reshetilov

MINISTRY FOR THE CONSTRUCTION OF OIL AND GAS INDUSTRY ENTERPRISES (Minneftegazstroi)
Moscow, Zhitnaya ul 14
Tel (095) 238-50-00
Minister: Vladimir G. Chirskov

MINISTRY OF CONSTRUCTION IN THE REGIONS OF THE URALS AND WESTERN SIBERIA, USSR
Moscow
Tel (095) 930-17-49
Minister: (vacant)

MINISTRY OF CONSTRUCTION IN SOUTHERN REGIONS OF THE USSR
Moscow
Minister: Arkady N. Shchepetilnikov

MINISTRY OF CULTURE (Minkultury SSSR)
Moscow, ul Arbat 35
Tel (095) 241-07-09
Minister: Nikolai Gubenko

MINISTRY OF DEFENCE (Minoborony)
103160 Moscow, ul Kirova 37
Tel (095) 296-89-00
Minister: Gen Dmitri T. Yazov
Deputy Minister: Adm Vladimir Chernavin

MINISTRY OF THE DEFENCE INDUSTRY
(Minoboronprom)
Moscow
Tel (095) 209-85-97
Minister: Boris Belousov

MINISTRY OF DOMESTIC TRADE (Mintorg SSSR)
Moscow, ul Razina 14
Tel (095) 298-48-64
Minister: Kondrat Z. Terekh

MINISTRY OF ELECTRIC POWER DEVELOPMENT AND ELECTRIFICATION (Minenergo SSSR)
Moscow, Kitaisky proyezd 7
Tel (095) 228-00-72
Minister: Yuri Semyonov

MINISTRY OF THE ELECTRICAL ENGINEERING AND INSTRUMENTATION INDUSTRIES
(Minelectrotekhpribor)
103918 Moscow, ul Ogariov 5
Tel (095) 229-75-73; telex 411390; fax (095) 291-42-81
Minister: Oleg G. Anfimov

MINISTRY OF THE ELECTRONIC INDUSTRY
(Minelektronprom)
Moscow, Kitaisky proyezd 7
Tel (095) 220-66-00
Minister: Vladislav G. Kolesnikov

MINISTRY OF FERROUS METALLURGY
(Minchernmet)
Moscow, Nogin pl
Tel (095) 220-81-80
Minister: Serafim V. Kolpakov

MINISTRY OF FINANCE (Minfin SSSR)
Moscow, ul Kuybysheva 9
Tel (095) 298-91-01
Minister: Valentin Pavlov

MINISTRY OF FISHERIES (Minrybkhoz SSSR)
Moscow, Rozhdestvensky bul 12
Tel (095) 923-76-34; telex 411208
Minister: Nikolai I. Kotlyar

MINISTRY OF FOREIGN AFFAIRS (MID SSSR)
Moscow, Smolenskaya-Sennaya pl 32/34
Tel (095) 244-16-06
Minister: Eduard A. Shevardnadze
Deputy Ministers: Ivan Oboimov, Vladimir Petrovsky, Anatoly Kovalyev, Igor Rogachev, Gennady Tarasov (Special Representative for the Middle East)

MINISTRY OF FOREIGN ECONOMIC RELATIONS
Moscow, Smolenskaya-Sennaya pl 32/34
Tel (095) 244-19-47
Minister: Konstantin F. Katushev
Deputy Minister: Vladimir Mordvinov

MINISTRY OF THE FORESTRY INDUSTRY
Moscow, Telegrapny per 1
Tel (095) 208-00-56
Minister: Mikhail I. Busygin

MINISTRY OF THE GAS INDUSTRY (Mingazprom)
Moscow, ul Stroitelei 8, kor 1
Tel (095) 133-13-00
Minister: Leonid Filimonov

MINISTRY OF GENERAL MACHINE BUILDING
(Minodshchemash)
Moscow
Tel (095) 251-94-83
Minister: Oleg Shishkin

MINISTRY OF GEOLOGY (Mingeo)
123242 Moscow, Bolshaya Gruzinskaya ul 4/6
Tel (095) 254-11-33
Minister: Yevgeni A. Kovlovsky

MINISTRY OF GRAIN PRODUCTS (Minkhleb SSSR)
101859 Moscow, K-451, 12a Chistoprudny bul
Tel (095) 227-92-05
Minister: Aleksandr D. Budyka

MINISTRY OF HEALTH (Minzdrav SSSR)
Moscow, Rakhmanovsky per 3
Tel (095) 925-11-40; telex 411407
Minister: Yevgeni I. Chazov

MINISTRY OF HEAVY, POWER AND TRANSPORT MACHINE BUILDING
Moscow, Nizhny Kislovsky per 5
Tel (095) 291-07-62; telex 411337
Minister: Vladimir M. Velichko

MINISTRY FOR INDUSTRIAL ERECTION AND SPECIAL CONSTRUCTION WORK
103379 Moscow, ul Bolshaya Sadovaya 8
Tel (095) 299-01-59
Minister: Aleksandr Mikhalchenko

MINISTRY OF THE INTERIOR (MVD SSSR)
Moscow, ul Ogariov 6
Tel (095) 924-65-72
Minister: Vadim V. Bakatin
Deputy Minister: Ivan Shilov

MINISTRY OF JUSTICE (Minyust SSSR)
Moscow, ul Obukha 4
Tel (095) 206-05-54
Minister: Veniamin Yakovlev

MINISTRY OF LAND RECLAMATION AND WATER RESOURCES (Minvodkhoz SSSR)
Moscow, Novobasmannaya ul 10
Tel (095) 265-91-09
Minister: (vacant)

MINISTRY OF MACHINE BUILDING (Minmash)
Moscow
Tel (095) 924-77-22
Minister: Boris M. Belousov

MINISTRY OF MACHINE BUILDING FOR CONSTRUCTION, ROAD BUILDING AND MUNICIPAL SERVICES (Minstroidormash)
Moscow, prospekt Kalinina 23
Tel (095) 202-96-32
Minister: Yevgeni A. Varnachev

MINISTRY OF THE MACHINE TOOL INDUSTRY
Moscow, ul Gorkovo 20
Tel (095) 209-55-20; telex 411053
Minister: Nikolai A. Panichev

MINISTRY OF THE MANUFACTURE OF THE MEANS OF COMMUNICATION (Minpromsvyazi)
Moscow, Vtoroy Spasonalivkovsky per 6
Tel (095) 238-72-42
Minister: Erlen K. Pervyshin

MINISTRY OF THE MEDICAL EQUIPMENT INDUSTRY (Minmedprom)
Moscow, proyezd Khudozhestvennovo teatra 2
Tel (095) 292-60-75
Minister: Valeri A. Bykov

MINISTRY OF MEDIUM MACHINE BUILDING (Minsredmash)
Moscow
Minister: Lev D. Ryabev

MINISTRY OF THE MERCHANT MARINE (Minmorflot)
103759 Moscow, ul Zhdanova 1/4
Tel (095) 926-10-00; telex 411197
Minister: Yuri M. Volmer

MINISTRY OF NON-FERROUS METALLURGY (Mintsvetmet)
Moscow, prospekt Kalinina 27
Tel (095) 202-65-92
Minister: Vladimir A. Durasov

MINISTRY OF THE NUCLEAR POWER INDUSTRY
Moscow
Minister: Vitaly Konavalov

MINISTRY OF THE OIL INDUSTRY (Minnefteprom)
Moscow, nab Morisa Toreza 26/1
Tel (095) 239-88-00
Minister: Leonid Filimonov

MINISTRY OF OIL-REFINING AND PETROCHEMICAL INDUSTRY (Minneftekhimprom)
Moscow, ul Gilyarovskovo 31
Tel (095) 281-94-79
Minister: Nikolai V. Lemayev

MINISTRY OF POST AND TELECOMMUNICATIONS (Minpostsvyazi SSSR)
103375 Moscow, ul Gorkovo 7
Tel (095) 925-51-08; telex 412961
Minister: Vasili A. Shamshin

MINISTRY OF PRODUCT QUALITY CONTROL AND STANDARDS
Moscow
Minister: Valery Sychev

MINISTRY FOR THE PRODUCTION OF MINERAL FERTILIZERS (Minudobrenii)
Moscow, ul Gritsebets 2/16
Tel (095) 203-23-52; telex 412622
Minister: Nikolai M. Olshansky

MINISTRY OF RADIO ENGINEERING (Minradioprom)
Moscow, Kitaisky proyezd 7
Tel (095) 207-96-27; telex 411376
Minister: Vladimir Shimko

MINISTRY OF RAILWAYS (MPS)
Moscow, Novobasmannaya ul 2
Tel (095) 262-16-28; telex 411832
Minister: (vacant)

MINISTRY OF SHIPBUILDING (Minsudprom)
Moscow, Sadovaya-Kudrinskaya ul 11
Tel (095) 255-09-41; telex 411272
Minister: Igor K. Koksanov

MINISTRY OF TRANSPORT CONSTRUCTION (Mintransstroi)
Moscow, Sadovaya-Spasskaya ul 21
Tel (095) 262-99-01
Minister: Vladimir A. Brezhnev

MINISTRY OF THE WOOD INDUSTRY
Moscow
Minister: Vladimir Melnikov

PEOPLE'S CONTROL COMMITTEE (KNK SSSR)
Moscow, ul Kuybysheva 21
Tel (095) 206-19-47
Chair: Sergei I. Manyakin

STATE BANK OF THE USSR (Gosbank)
103016 Moscow, Neglinnaya ul 12
Tel (095) 923-18-70; telex 411283; fax (095) 921-64-65
Chair: Viktor V. Gerashchenko
F 1921; co-ordinates and controls the activities of specialized, commercial and co-operative banks; formulates and implements Govt's credit, monetary and foreign exchange policies; bank of issue.

STATE COMMISSION FOR FOOD AND PROCUREMENT
Moscow, Orlikovsky per 1/11
Tel (095) 207-80-00
Chair: Vsevolod S. Murakhovsky

STATE COMMISSION FOR FOREIGN TOURISM (Goskominturist SSSR)
103009 Moscow, prospekt Marksa 16
Tel (095) 292-24-50; telex 411211
Chair: Vladimir Y. Pavlov

STATE COMMITTEE FOR CINEMATOGRAPHY (Goskino USSR)
Moscow, Maly Gnezdnikovsky per 7
Tel (095) 229-13-30; telex 411417
Chair: Aleksandr I. Kamshalov

STATE COMMITTEE FOR COMPUTER TECHNOLOGY AND INFORMATION SCIENCE
Moscow
Chair: Nikolai V. Gorshkov

STATE COMMITTEE FOR CONSTRUCTION (Gosstroi)
Moscow, Pushkinskaya ul 26
Tel (095) 292-76-23
Chair: Valery Serov
Deputy Chair (with rank of Minister): Leonid A. Bibin

STATE COMMITTEE FOR FORESTS
117418 Moscow, Novocheremushkinskaya 69
Tel (095) 332-21-13; telex 411667
Chair: Aleksandr Isaev

STATE COMMITTEE FOR HYDROMETEOROLOGY AND ENVIRONMENTAL CONTROL (Goskomgidromet)
Moscow, per Pavlika Morozova 12
Tel (095) 255-00-03
Chair: Yuri A. Izrael

STATE COMMITTEE FOR INDUSTRIAL SAFETY AND THE SUPERVISION OF MINES (Gosgortekhnadzor SSSR)
Moscow, ul Kuybysheva 4
Tel (095) 221-93-86
Chair: Ivan M. Vladychenko

STATE COMMITTEE FOR INVENTIONS AND DISCOVERIES
Moscow, M. Cherkassy per 2/6
Tel (095) 206-88-06; telex 411248
Chair: Dr Y. A. Bespalov
Vice-Chairs: Dr L. E. Komarov, V. M. Torbenko

STATE COMMITTEE FOR LABOUR AND SOCIAL AFFAIRS (Goskomtrud SSSR)
103706 Moscow, pl Kuybysheva 1
Tel (095) 298-39-24
Chair: Vladimir Shcherbakov

STATE COMMITTEE FOR LIGHT INDUSTRY
Moscow, prospekt Kalinina 29
Tel (095) 291-47-10
Chair: Ludmila Dovletova

STATE COMMITTEE FOR MATERIAL RESERVES (Goskomrezerv)
Moscow, Bolshoy Cherkassky per 6
Chair: Fyodor I. Loshchenkov

STATE COMMITTEE FOR MATERIAL AND TECHNICAL SUPPLY (Gossnab SSSR)
Moscow, Orlikovsky per 5
Tel (095) 204-01-11
Chair: Pavel Mostovoi
Deputy Chair: Sergei Vinogradov

STATE COMMITTEE FOR PHYSICAL CULTURE AND SPORT
119871 Moscow, Luzhnetskaya nab 8
Tel (095) 201-00-94; telex 411287
Chair: Nikolai Rusak

STATE COMMITTEE ON PRICES (Goskomtsen SSSR)
Moscow, Bersenevskaya nab 20
Tel (095) 230-07-64
Chair: (vacant)

STATE COMMITTEE FOR THE PROTECTION OF NATURE (Goskompriroda)
Moscow
Chair: Nikolai Vorontsov

STATE COMMITTEE FOR PUBLIC EDUCATION
Moscow
Chair: Gennadi A. Yagodin
First Deputy Chairs (with rank of Minister): Feliks I. Peregudov, Vladimir D. Shadrikov

STATE COMMITTEE FOR PUBLISHING, PRINTING AND THE BOOK TRADE (Goskomizdat)
101409 Moscow, Strastnoi bul 5
Tel (095) 229-93-59; telex 411871
Chair: Nikolai Yefimov

STATE COMMITTEE FOR SCIENCE AND TECHNOLOGY (GKNT)
Moscow, ul Gorkovo 11
Tel (095) 229-11-92
Chair: Boris L. Tolstykh

STATE COMMITTEE FOR STANDARDS (Gosstandart)
Moscow, Leninsky prospekt 9
Tel (095) 236-03-00
Chair: Georgi D. Kolmogorov

STATE COMMITTEE FOR STATISTICS (Goskomstat)
103450 Moscow, ul Kirova 39
Tel (095) 228-16-33
Chair: Vadim Kirichenko
Deputy Chair: Nikolai Belov

STATE COMMITTEE FOR THE SUPERVISION OF INDUSTRIAL AND NUCLEAR SAFETY (Gospromatomnadzor)
109143 Moscow, ul Taganskaya 34
Tel (095) 272-47-10; telex 411743
Chair: Vadim M. Malyshev
First Deputy Chairs: Prof Viktor A. Sidorenko (Nuclear Safety), Dr Marat P. Vasilchuk (Industrial Safety)

STATE COMMITTEE FOR TELEVISION AND RADIO (Gosteleradio SSSR)
12700 Moscow, ul Korolyov 12
Tel (095) 217-78-98; telex 411140; fax (095) 288-9508
Chair: Mikhail Nenashev

STATE PLANNING COMMITTEE (Gosplan SSSR)
Moscow, prospekt Marksa 12
Tel (095) 292-80-00
Chair: Yuri D. Maslyukov
First Deputy Chair: Vladimir Durasov

STATE SECURITY COMMITTEE (KGB SSSR)
Moscow, ul Dzerzhinskovo 2
Tel (095) 221-07-62
Chair: Vladimir A. Kryuchkov

GOVERNMENT AGENCIES AND ORGANIZATIONS

Advisory and Supervisory Body

USSR Chamber of Commerce and Industry: 103684 Moscow, ul Kuybysheva 6; tel (095) 221-08-11; telex 411126; Pres: Vladislav L. Malkevich; Sec-Gen: Ivan I. Gaidayenko; f 1932; promotes trade, economic, scientific and technical relations between the USSR and other countries; assists Soviet enterprises to secure contacts with foreign partners; establishes associations for business co-operation with foreign countries; organizes Soviet trade and industrial exhibitions abroad and international exhibitions in the USSR; handles patenting and registration of trade marks.

Art and Culture

Committee for Lenin Prizes and State Prizes in Literature, Art and Architecture: 103051 Moscow, ul Nealinnaya 15; tel (095) 223-44-67.

Melodia: Moscow; record production and distribution.

Sovinterfest: 109028 Moscow, Hohlovsky per 10; tel (095) 227-54-17; telex 411263; Exec Dir: Yuri Khodjaev; Dep Dir: Stanislav Voitelev; f 1975; management of international film festivals and exhibitions.

Business and Economy

BANKING

The State Bank of the USSR (Gosbank USSR): see entry under Govt Depts and Ministries above.

Agroprombank (Agro-Industrial Bank): Moscow; Chair: A. A. Obozintsev; f 1988; assumed responsibility from Gosbank for credits and settlements in the agro-industrial sector of the economy; 148 regional and town offices, and 3,306 brs throughout the USSR.

Promstroibank (Industry and Construction Bank): Moscow; Chair: M. S. Zotov; f 1988; assumed responsibility from Gosbank to grant credits and effect settlements in industrial and transport sectors of the economy; 155 regional and town offices, and 1,237 brs throughout the USSR.

Sberbank (Savings and Credit Bank): Moscow; Chair: A. S. Burkov; First Dep Chair: Vladimir Belokon; f 1988; assumed responsibility from Sberkassa for deposits of public and consumer credits; 155 regional and town offices, and 4,100 brs throughout the USSR.

Vneshekonombank (Bank of Foreign Economic Affairs): Moscow 107078, 15 Kirovsky Prospekt; Chair: Y. S. Moskovsky; Gen Man: Yevgeny Ulyanov; telex 411174; f 1988; assumed responsibility for all the functions of Vneshtorgbank in 1987; 6 regional and town offices, 7 brs throughout the USSR, brs in Zurich and New York and offices in Bombay and Cairo.

Zhilsotsbank (Bank of Housing, Communal Services and Social Development): Moscow; Chair: V. I. Bukato; f 1988; assumed responsibility from Gosbank for credits and settlements in the housing construction industry, and the spheres of communal services and social devt; 154 regional and town offices, and 477 brs throughout the USSR.

INSURANCE

Gosstrakh (State Insurance Society): Moscow; Chair: Vyacheslav Shakov; undertakes domestic insurance; insurance is a state monopoly.

Ingosstrakh (Joint Stock Insurance Society): Moscow, Pyatnitskaya ul 12; telex 411144; Chair: L. L. Bogdanov; undertakes all kinds of international insurance and reinsurance.

TRADE

Almazyuvelireksport: 119021 Moscow, bul Zubovsky 25, d 1; tel (095) 245-34-10; telex 411115; Dir-Gen: I. V. Gorbunov; Dep Dirs-Gen: B. N. Ossipov, B. V. Sergeev; f 1970; exports jewellery, gems, articles of precious metals; imports equipment for diamond cutting and polishing industry.

Atomenergoexport: 113324 Moscow, Ovchinnikovskaya nab 18/1; tel (095) 220-14-36; telex 411397; Chair: V. Gulko; Dep Chairs: M. Katkov, V. Kulikov; f 1973; trade in nuclear power engineering and scientific research equipment, materials and plants; construction of nuclear power stations and research centres in the USSR and in the Third World.

Aviyaeksport: 121817 Moscow, Trubnikovsky per 19; tel (095) 290-01-71; telex 411257; Chair: V. S. Studenikin; trade in aircraft, air navigation aids and other civil aviation equipment.

Avtoeksport: 119902 Moscow, ul Volkhonka 14; tel (095) 202-85-35; telex 411936; Chair: N. M. Dmitriyev; trade in motor vehicles including motorcycles, bicycles, tools and spare parts.

Avtopromimport: 109017 Moscow, Pyatnitskaya ul 50/2; tel (095) 231-81-26; telex 411961; Chair: A. A. Butko; imports equipment for engineering industries: car, power generating, tractor, agricultural machinery, etc.

Centrosoyus (Central Union of Consumer Societies): 103626 Moscow, Cherkassky bul 15; tel (095) 430-71-18; telex 411127; Chair: Pavel S. Fedirko; Dir: Alexander I. Krasheninnikov; f 1898; organization of trade with foreign co-operatives, organizes trade services and public catering, procurement of farm produce and its processing, provision of wholesale supplies to local co-operatives.

Dalintorg: 692900 Nadhodka, Nakhodkinsky per 16A; tel 4-48-77; telex 213814; Dir: F. D. Zhitnikov; f 1964; trade of Eastern Siberia and Soviet Far East with Australia, Japan and the Democratic Peopla's Republic of Korea.

Eksportkhleb: 121200 Moscow, Smolenskaya-Sennaya pl 32/34; tel (095) 244-47-01; telex 411145; Chair: V. I. Pershin; trade in cereals, rice, pulses, flour, oil seeds and other grain and fodder products, seeds and seedlings.

Eksportlen: 117393 Moscow, ul Arkhitektora Vlasova 33; tel (095) 128-07-86; telex 411203; Chair: V. A. Sobolev; trade in cotton, flax, hemp, wool, raw silk, cotton and silk fabrics and other textile products.

Eksportles: 121803 Moscow, Trubnikovsky per 19; tel (095)

291-61-16; telex 411229; Dir-Gen: Yuri V. Vardashkin; f 1926; trade in timber and woodpulp/paper products.

Elektronorgtekhnika: Moscow, ul Chaikovskovo 11A, tel (095) 205-35-21; telex 411386; Chair: Y. D. Shcherbina; trade in computers and electronic equipment.

Energomachexport: 121019 Moscow, Kalinina per 19; tel (095) 203-15-71; telex 411965; Dir-Gen: Vladimir I. Filimonov; Dep Dir-Gen: Mikhail V. Nosanov; f 1966; export of heavy, power and transport machinery.

Lenfintorg: 196084 Leningrad, Moskovsky prospekt 98; tel (812) 292-56-33; telex 518; Dir: O. Y. Rumyantsev; trade in consumer, timber and semi-finished goods of the timber industry; also trades in general goods with Finland and Norway.

Litsenzintorg: 121108 Moscow, Minskaya ul 11; tel (095) 145-11-11; telex 411415; Chair: V. V. Ignatov; provision, acquisition and exchange of patents, licences and other industrial property rights; provision of technical services including engineering, raw materials testing, drawing up of technical designs.

Mashinoeksport: 117330 Moscow, Mosfilmovskaya ul 35; tel (095) 143-89-27; telex 411207; Chair: V. I. Vorontsov; exports equipment and tools for oil and gas drilling, geological and geophysical prospecting; equipment for the steel and non-ferrous metals industries, pipeline construction, and mine construction and mining.

Mashinoimport: 121200 Moscow, Smolenskaya-Sennaya pl 32/34; tel (095) 244-33-09; telex 411231; Chair: S. F. Volchkov; imports power and electrical engineering equipment, railway rolling stock, oil extracting and refining equipment, industrial fittings.

Mashpriborintorg: 121200 Moscow, Smolenskaya-Sennaya pl 32/34; tel (095) 244-27-75; telex 411235; Chair: V. F. Klimov; trade in wire and wireless communication equipment, control and automation instruments, material testing equipment, complete laboratories, physical and hydro-meteorological instruments; import of geophysical equipment.

Medeksport: 113461 Moscow, Kakhovka ul 31, kor 2; tel (095) 121-01-54; telex 411247; Chair: I. N. Filimonov; trade in medicines, pharmaceuticals and raw materials, medical equipment and instruments.

Metallurgimport: 117393 Moscow, ul Arkhitektora Vlasova 33; tel (095) 128-09-32; telex 411388; Dir-Gen: N. P. Maksimov; imports mining and ore-dressing equipment, metallurgical and foundry equipment, iron and steel works machinery and equipment, rotor excavators.

Mezhdunarodnaya Kniga: 121200 Moscow, Smolenskaya-Sennaya pl 32/34; tel (095) 244-10-22; telex 411160; Chair: Y. B. Leonov; trade in books, periodicals, newspapers, pictures, maps, gramophone records, postage stamps, slides and filmstrips; recording of Soviet performers abroad.

Neftekhimpromexport: 113324 Moscow, Ovchinnikovskaya nab 18/1; tel (095) 220-11-09; telex 411113; Chair: V. I. Grib; exports petroleum and chemical products.

Novoeksport: Moscow, ul Chekhova 12; tel (095) 299-00-06; telex 411254; Dir-Gen: V. K. Slovtsov; exports peat, secondary raw materials and production waste, carpets, handicrafts, antiques, ceramics, leisure and sports equipment, semi-precious and decorative stones, gardening equipment, etc.

Prodintorg: 121200 Moscow, Smolenskaya-Sennaya pl 32/34; tel (095) 244-26-29; telex 411201; Chair: V. Y. Golanov; trade in food and animal by-products; horses, pedigree cattle and animals for zoos.

Prommasheksport: 113324 Moscow, Ovchinnikovskaya nab 18/1; tel (095) 220-15-05; telex 411932; Chair: I. E. Vodopianov; assists in establishment of engineering, machine-tool building, casting, metal working, tool-making, electrical and radio engineering enterprises, radio and TV stations, fish processing enterprises, sugar refineries, printing works, airfields and airports; complete equipment for film studios, instrument-making plants and watch factories.

Prommashimport: 121200 Moscow, Smolenskaya-Sennaya pl 32/34; tel (095) 244-43-57; telex 411261; Chair: G. F. Rakhimbayev; imports equipment for the pulp and paper, woodworking and timber and electrical industries; hothouses and equipment, complete retail shops, prefabricated dwellings, railcar houses, industrial construction.

Promsyrioimport: 121834 Moscow, ul Chaikovsky 13; tel (095) 203-55-77; telex 411151; Pres: O. M. Smirnov; Vice-Pres: A. I. Gourco, V. G. Carpov, L. N. Sadovsky, E. D. Pozdnjakov, E. F. Chichoulin; f 1936; trade in iron and steel products through its subsidiaries: Promstallist, Promlistimpex, Promstalprofil, Promtrubimpex, Promstalsyrio, Promspetsstal, Prommetiz, Promtrubimport.

Raznoexport: 107896 Moscow, Verkhnaya Krasnoselskaya 15; tel (095) 264-01-83; telex 411408; fax (095) 288-95-39; Dir-Gen: Yuri T. Kostrov; f 1930; trade in consumer goods.

Raznoimport: 121200 Moscow, Smolenskaya-Sennaya pl 32/34; tel (095) 244-37-61; telex 411153; Chair: I. A. Russov; trade in non-ferrous metal and alloys, metal foil and powders, electrical cables, natural and synthetic rubber, tyres and tubes, rubber products, linoleum.

Selkhozpromeksport: 113324 Moscow, Ovchinnikovskaya nab 18/1; tel (095) 220-16-92; telex 411933; Chair: Y. A. Borisov; assists in construction of hydrotechnical and irrigation facilities, pump stations, water wells and establishment of agricultural projects.

Soveksportfilm: 103009 Moscow, Kalashny per 14; tel (095) 290-50-09; telex 411143; Chair: V. Y. Mayatsky; trade in films.

Sovfrakht: 103759 Moscow, Zhdanova ul 1/4; tel (095) 926-11-18; telex 411219; Chair: G. A. Maslov; tanker and cargo ship chartering and broking.

Sovinfilm: 121069 Moscow, Skatertny per 20; tel (095) 290-10-00; telex 411114; Chair: A. K. Surikov; establishes and co-ordinates commercial ties between Soviet film studios and foreign firms.

Sovincentr: 123610 Moscow, Krasnopresnenskaya nab 12; tel (095) 256-63-03; telex 411486; Dir-Gen: Gen F. K. Krioutchko; assists foreign cos in making contact with Soviet cos, and in representing their interests in the Soviet market.

Soyuzagrochimeksport: 119900 Moscow, Gritsevetskaya ul 2; tel (095) 202-49-04; telex 411678; fax (095) 230-23-04; Dir-Gen: Yuri A. Orlov; Dep Dir-Gen: V. M. Smirnov; f 1988; trade in mineral fertilizers and chemical products, and technical assistance in these fields.

Soyuzgazeksport: 117071 Moscow, Leninsky prospekt 20, tel (095) 244-22-84; telex 411987; Chair: Y. V. Baranovsky; trade in natural gas, liquefied petroleum gas, inert and other gases.

Soyuzkhimeksport: 121200 Moscow, Smolenskaya-Sennaya pl 32/34; tel (095) 244-22-84; telex 411295; Chair: V. G. Molodtsov; trade in chemical products: synthetic resins and plastics, chemicals for agriculture, varnishes, paints, chemical reagents and pure preparations, cine-photo materials, essential oils, including perfumes and scents, etc.

Soyuzkoopvneshtorg: 103626 Moscow, Bolshoy Cherkassy per 15; tel (095) 924-81-71; telex 411127; fax (095) 230-28-19; Dir-Gen: Alexander N. Starykh; Dep Dir-Gen: Alexander S. Astakhov; f 1962; trade in consumer goods; foreign trade organization of the Central Council of Union of Consumers' Co-operative Societies.

Soyuznefteeksport: 121200 Moscow, Smolemskaya-Sennaya pl 32/34; tel (095) 244-40-48; telex 411148; Chair: Vladimir A. Arutunyan; exports crude oil, naphtha, automobile and aviation fuel, paraffin, diesel oil and fuels, lubricants, petroleum coke, etc; imports petroleum products.

Soyuzplodoimport: 121200 Moscow, Smolenskaya-Sennaya pl 32/34; tel (095) 244-22-58; telex 411262; Chair: Y. B. Zhizhin; trade in fruit, vegetables, spirits, confectionery, spices, etc.

Soyuzpromeksport: 121200 Moscow, Smolenskaya-Sennaya

pl 32/34; tel (095) 244-19-79; telex 411268; Chair: B. K. Kosolapov; exports coal and coal by-products, manganese, chrome and iron ore, asbestos and other mineral and semi-finished products.

Soyuzpushnina: 102012 Moscow, ul Kuybysheva 6; tel (095) 923-09-23; telex 411150; Chair: V. M. Ivanov; trade in animal skins, hides, furs, oils etc; organization of fur auctions in Leningrad.

Soyuztransit: 121200 Moscow, Smolenskaya-Sennaya pl 32/34; tel (095) 244-39-51; telex 411266; Man Dir: S. G. Melnik; Dep Dirs: V. A. Aksyutenko, V. V. Shvanev, Y. E. Puchkov; f 1980; handles transit of goods through the USSR.

Soyuzvneshstroyimport: 103009 Moscow, Tverskoy bul 6; tel (095) 290-06-84; telex 411434; Chair: G. T. Grigoryan; f 1974; with the participation of foreign firms, carries out construction of industrial and civil installations in the USSR.

Soyuzvneshtrans: 121019 Moscow, Gogolevsky bul 17/16; tel (095) 203-11-79; telex 411441; Pres: V. I. Alisseychik; f 1962; handles transport and forwarding of imports and exports.

Stankoimport: 117342 Moscow, Obrucheva ul 34/63; tel (095) 333-51-01; telex 411991; Chair: G. G. Lebyazhiyev; exports and imports metal-cutting machines, flexible manufacturing systems, forging and pressing equipment, measuring machines, instruments and tools, spare parts, components and accessories, equipment and instruments, hard-alloy articles, abrasives, diamond tools, spares and components.

Stroymaterialintorg: 107113 Moscow, Sokolnichesky val 50, kor 2; tel (095) 269-05-54; telex 411889; Chair: V. V. Devyatov; trade in cement, glass, asbestos and other building materials.

Sudoimport: 103006 Moscow, Kalayevskaya ul 5; tel (095) 251-05-05; telex 411272; Chair: O. S. Kropotov; exports sea vessels, floating docks and cranes, shipboard equipment; imports sea and river vessels and shipboard equipment; trade in rigs, equipment for off-shore oil exploration and production; ship-repairing abroad.

Tekhmasheksport: 101850 Moscow, Mosfilmovskaya ul 35; tel (095) 206-91-14; telex 411068; Dir-Gen: V. F. Fadeyev; exports machinery and equipment for the textile, printing, oil refining and other industries, including refrigeration equipment, air separation units, compressors.

Tekhmashimport: 121069 Moscow, Trubnikovsky per 19; tel (095) 202-48-00; telex 411194; Chair: V. I. Grib; f 1958; imports equipment and machinery for industries producing chemicals, rubber goods, fertilizers, refrigeration equipment, plastics, synthetic fibres.

Tekhnoeksport: 113324 Moscow, Ovchinnikovskaya nab 18/1; tel (095) 220-17-82; telex 411338; Chair: Y. V. Chugunov; assists in organization of oil production and construction of light industry factories, pharmaceutical plants, hospitals, secondary and technical schools.

Tekhnointorg: 121200 Moscow, Smolenskaya-Sennaya pl 32/34; tel (095) 244-17-03; telex 411235; Chair: M. S. Kozin; trade in TV, radio, cine and photographic equipment, time measuring instruments and electrical household appliances.

Tekhnopromexport: 113324 Moscow, Ovchinnikovskaya nab 18/1; tel (095) 220-15-23; telex 411158; Chair: A. S. Postovalov; assists in construction of thermal and diesel power stations.

Tekhnopromimport: 117330 Moscow, Mosfilmovskaya ul 35; tel (095) 147-21-77; telex 411233; Chair: G. A. Konoplev; import of equipment for the light, food, electro-technical and electronics industries; also involved in polygraphic enterprises, cable- and glass-producing plants, plants for the production of building materials.

Tekhnostroieksport: 113324 Moscow, Ovchinnikovskaya nab 18/1; tel (095) 220-14-48; telex 411474; Chair: D. M. Shipilev; assists in construction of plants producing building materials.

Tekhsnabeksport: 109180 Moscow, Staromonetny per 26; tel (095) 233-48-46; telex 411328; Dir-Gen: B. K. Pushkin; trade in isotopes, ionising radiation sources, fuel elements, rare metals and their concentrates, rare-earth metals and their compounds, nuclear physics equipment; exports of components for nuclear power stations, technical assistance to other eastern European countries.

Tekhveshntrans: 113324 Moscow, Ovchinnikovskaya nab 18/1; tel (095) 220-19-53; telex 411110; Chair: A. P. Sobolev; organizes transportation of foreign trade freight turnover connected with the construction of industrial projects overseas and in the USSR.

Tjazhpromeksport: 113324 Moscow, Ovchinnikovskaya nab 18/1; tel (095) 220-16-10; telex 411931; Chair: Y. N. Kalashnikov; assists in construction and extension of integrated iron and steel mining complexes and hardware plants.

Traktoroeksport: 103055 Moscow, Lesnaya 43; tel (095) 258-59-34; telex 411273; fax (095) 288-99-99; Dir-Gen: D. N. Monaencov; f 1961; trade in agricultural machines and equipment, crawler industrial tractors and repairing equipment.

Tsvetmetpromeksport: 113324 Moscow, Ovchinnikovskaya nab 18/1; tel (095) 220-18-61; telex 411983; Chair: R. I. Kuprevich; assists in construction of non-ferrous metallurgy projects, mines, quarries, metallurgical works.

Vneshposyltorg: 109147 Moscow, Masrksistskaya ul 5; tel (095) 271-90-12; telex 411250; Dir-Gen: Yu. G. Bulakh; trade in foodstuffs, industrial and consumer goods including sanitary goods and equipment; wholesale of goods to diplomatic missions, cos and individuals with payment in freely convertible currencies.

Vneshtorgreklama: 113461 Moscow, ul Kakhovka 31, kor 2; tel (095) 331-83-11; telex 411265; fax (095) 310-70-05; Dir-Gen: Y. M. Deomidov; f 1964; trade in advertising services.

Vostokintorg: 121200 Moscow, Smolenskaya-Sennaya pl 32/34; tel (095) 244-20-34; telex 411123; Chair: A. A. Alekperov; trade in a wide variety of goods with Mongolia, Afghanistan, Iran, Turkey, Yemen Arab Republic, and the People's Democratic Republic of Yemen.

Zapchasteksport: 109029 Moscow, Skotoprogonnaya ul 35, kor 2; tel (095) 278-63-05; telex 411243; Chair: F. F. Yarotsky; trade in spare parts for tractors, cars, lorries, agricultural, road-building and special machines, motor cycles and bicycles.

Zaroubejneftegasstroi: 113184 Moscow, Novokuznetskaya ul 23b; tel (095) 231-12-19; telex 411482; Pres: V. V. Kopyshevski; Commercial Man: A. V. Koudriavtsev; f 1970; construction of pipelines, compressor stations, gas pumping and distribution stations, provision of technical assistance in these fields; trade in construction materials and equipment.

Defence

Armed Forces: c/o Ministry of Defence, 103160 Moscow, ul Kirova 37; tel (095) 223-61-08; Chief of Gen Staff: Gen Mikhail Moiseyev.

Air Forces: address as above; Commdr-in-Chief: Aleksandr Nikolayevich Yefimov.

Ground Forces: address as above; Commdr-in-Chief: Gen Valentin Varennikov; Dep Commdr-in-Chief: Gen Nikolai Ter-Grigoriants.

Joint Supreme Command for Warsaw Pact Forces: address as above; Commdr-in-Chief: Viktor Georgiyevich Kulikov.

Navy: address as above; Commdr-in-Chief: Vladimir Nikolayevich Chernavin.

Strategic Rocket Forces: address as above; Commdr-in-Chief: Yuri Pavlovich Maksimov.

Defence and State Security Committee: Moscow; f 1989; supervisory body of the KGB and defence forces.

Legal and Judiciary

Office of the Procurator-General: 103009 Moscow, Pushkinskaya ul 15A; Procurator-Gen: Aleksandr Y. Sukharev; supervises the strict observance of the law by all ministerial and executive bodies, economic institutions, co-operative and public organizations, officials and individuals, etc. The Procurator-Gen is elected by the Supreme Soviet for a five year term, and is responsible to that body and to the Congress of People's Deputies of the USSR. The Procurators of the Republics are appointed by the Procurator-Gen.

Supreme Court: 103009 Moscow, ul Vorovskogo 15; Chair: (vacant); Vice-Chairs: Sergei I. Gusev, Aleksandr M. Filatov; Chair of the Collegium for Civil Cases: V. I. Zamyatin; Chair of the Collegium for Criminal Cases: Robert G. Tikhomirnov; Chair of the Military Collegium: Georgi I. Bushuyev; highest judicial organ, exercising supervision of the activities of all the USSR's judicial organs. The members of the Supreme Court are elected by the Supreme Soviet for a ten-year term. The Supreme Court consists of the Plenum and three Collegia (civil cases, criminal cases and military). Supreme Courts are formed in Union and Autonomous Republics.

Media

BROADCASTING

National Television: Moscow, ul Akademika Koroleva 12; tel (095) 217-78-98; telex 411140; broadcasts in all of the union republics, territories and regions through 117 TV centres.

Radio Moscow: 113326 Moscow, Pyatnitskaya ul 25; tel (095) 233-60-60; telex 411136; programmes are broadcast daily from Moscow on four channels via long, medium, short and VHF wavebands to all parts of the country. All the union and autonomous republics, territories and regions have their own local stations.

NEWS AND INFORMATION

Agenstvo Pechati Novosti—APN (Novosti Press Agency): Moscow, Zubovsky bul 4; tel (095) 201-24-24; telex 411101; Chair: Albert I. Vlasov; f 1961 to provide information and general features on Soviet life; collaborates by arrangement with foreign press and publishing organizations in 110 countries.

Telegrafnoye Agenstvo Sovetskovo Soyuza—TASS (Telegraphic Agency of the Soviet Union): 103009 Moscow, Tverskoy bul 10; tel (095) 229-80-53; telex 411186; Dir-Gen: Leonid P. Kravchenko; f 1925; serves 4,000 Soviet newspapers and more than 550 foreign news agencies.

Science and Technology

Intercosmos (Council on International Co-operation in Research and Uses of Outer Space): 117901 Moscow, Leninsky prospekt 14; tel (095) 234-38-28; telex 411964; Chair: V. A. Kotelnikov; Vice-Chair: G. I. Kharitonov; f 1967; promotion of international co-operation in space exploration for peaceful purposes.

Tourism

USSR Co for Foreign Travel—Intourist: 103009 Moscow, prospekt Marksa 16; tel (095) 292-22-60; telex 411211; Chair: Igor Konovalov; f 1929; organizes tours in numerous Soviet cities, and has contracts with more than 700 foreign cos.

Transport

Azov Shipping Co: 341010 Zhdanov, prospekt Admirala Lunina 89; Pres: L. N. Shunin.

Baltic Shipping Co: 198035 Leningrad, Mezhevoy kanal 5; Pres: V. I. Kharchenko.

Black Sea Shipping Co: 270026 Odessa, ul Lastochkina 1; Pres: V. V. Pilipenko.

Caspian Shipping Co: 370005 Baku, ul Dzhaparidze 3; Pres: T. K. Akhmedov.

Estonian Shipping Co: 200101 Tallinn, bul Estonia 3/5; tel (0142) 44-38-02; telex 173272; Pres: T. A. Ninnas.

Far Eastern Shipping Co: 690019 Vladivostok, ul 25 Oktyabrya 15; Pres: V. M. Miskov.

Georgian Shipping Co: 384517 Batumi, ul Gogebashvili 60; Pres: D. K. Chigvariya.

Kamchatka Shipping Co: 683000 Petropavlovsk-Kamchatsky, ul Radiosvyazi 26; telex 113; Pres: Yu. P. Tereshin; f 1949.

Latvian Shipping Co: 226807 Riga, bul Padomju 2; Pres: Y. L. Paderov.

Lithuanian Shipping Co: 235813 Klaipeda, ul Yuliusa Yanonisa 24; Pres: A. V. Ramanauskas.

Middle-Asia Shipping Co: 746100 Tchardzhou, Flotilskaya ul 8; Pres: N. B. Bazarov.

Murmansk Shipping Co: 183636 Murmansk, ul Kominterna 15; Pres: V. V. Beletsky.

Northern Shipping Co: 163061 Arkhangelsk, nab Lenina 36; Pres: A. N. Gagarin.

Novorossiysk Shipping Co: 353900 Novorossiysk, ul Svobody 1; tel (3832) 5-12-76; telex 279113; Pres: Leonid I. Loza.

Primorsk Shipping Co: 692900 Nakhodka, Pogranichnaya 6; tel 5-53-09; telex 213812; Pres: P. K. Chernysh; f 1972.

Sakhalin Shipping Co: 694620 Sakhalin, Kholmsk, Pobedy 16; tel 2-28-38; Pres: M. A. Romanovsky.

Soviet Danube Shipping Co: 272630 Izmail, prospekt Suvorova 2; Pres: A. F. Tekhov.

USSR Register of Shipping: 191065 Leningrad, Dvortsovaya nab 8; tel (812) 312-88-78; telex 121525; fax (812) 314-10-87; Dir: R. A. Belik; Technical Dir: Y. I. Bykov; f 1914; control and approval of design, specifications, classification, safety requirements, etc, of Soviet shipping.

Welfare

Committee of Youth Organizations of the USSR: 101000 Moscow, ul Bogdana Khmel'Nitskogo 7/8; tel (095) 206-89-09.

Soviet Committee of War Veterans: 121019 Moscow, Gogolevski bul 4; tel (095) 202-59-52.

THE UNITED ARAB EMIRATES

Head of State

Under the 1971 Constitution, the highest federal authority is the Supreme Council of Rulers, comprising the hereditary rulers of the seven emirates. From its seven members, the Council elects a President and a Vice-President. The President appoints a Prime Minister and a Federal Council of Ministers, responsible to the Supreme Council, to hold executive authority.

President: Sheikh Zayed bin Sultan an-Nahayan, Ruler of Abu Dhabi (took office as President on 2 December 1971; re-elected 1976 and 1981).

Office of the President: Manhal Palace, POB 280, Abu Dhabi; tel (2) 341010; telex 22220.

Vice-President: Sheikh Rashid bin Said al-Maktoum, Ruler of Dubai.

Office of the Vice-President: Za'beel Palace, Dubai; tel (4) 431001; telex 45688.

Legislature

Legislative authority is vested in the Federal National Council, a consultative assembly, comprising 40 members appointed for two years by the emirates, which considers laws proposed by the Council of Ministers. There are no political parties. In local affairs, each ruler has considerable authority.

Federal National Council: POB 836, Abu Dhabi; tel (2) 324000; Speaker: Hilal bin Ahmad Lootah.

MINISTRIES AND GOVERNMENT DEPARTMENTS

OFFICE OF THE PRIME MINISTER
POB 899, Abu Dhabi
Tel (2) 361555; telex 23245
Prime Minister: Sheikh Rashid bin Said al-Maktoum
Minister of State without Portfolio: Sheikh Ahmad bin Sultan al-Qasimi

OFFICE OF THE DEPUTY PRIME MINISTERS
POB 831, Abu Dhabi
Tel (2) 451900; telex 45427
Deputy Prime Minsters: Sheikh Maktoum bin Rashid al-Maktoum, Sheikh Hamdan bin Muhammad an-Nahayan

MINISTRY OF AGRICULTURE AND FISHERIES
POB 1509, Abu Dhabi
Tel (2) 228161; telex 42590
Minister: Said Muhammad ar-Raghbani

MINISTRY OF COMMUNICATIONS
POB 900, Abu Dhabi
Tel (2) 362900; telex 22668
Minister: Muhammad Said al-Mu'alla

MINISTRY OF DEFENCE
POB 2838, Dubai
Tel (4) 532330; telex 45554
Minister: Sheikh Muhammad bin Rashid al-Maktoum

MINISTRY OF ECONOMY AND COMMERCE
POB 901, Abu Dhabi
Tel (2) 215455; telex 22897
Minister: Saif Ali al-Jarwan

MINISTRY OF EDUCATION
POB 295, Abu Dhabi
Tel (2) 334141; telex 22581
Minister: Faraj Fadhil al-Mazroui

MINISTRY OF ELECTRICITY AND WATER
POB 1672, Dubai
Tel (4) 660575; telex 46453
Minister: Humaid Nasser al-Owais

MINISTRY OF FINANCE AND INDUSTRY
POB 433, Abu Dhabi
Tel (2) 726000; telex 22937
Minister: Sheikh Hamdan bin Rashid al-Maktoum
Minister of State: Ahmad Humaid at-Tayer

MINISTRY OF FOREIGN AFFAIRS
POB 1, Abu Dhabi
Tel (2) 362000; telex 22217
Minister of State: Rashid Abdullah an-Nuaimi

MINISTRY OF HEALTH
POB 848, Abu Dhabi
Tel (2) 334000; telex 22678
Minister: Hamad Abd ar-Rahman al-Midfa

MINISTRY OF INFORMATION AND CULTURE
POB 17, Abu Dhabi
Tel (2) 326000; telex 22283
Minister: Sheikh Ahmad bin Hamid

MINISTRY OF THE INTERIOR
POB 398, Abu Dhabi
Tel (2) 377666; telex 22398
Minister: Sheikh Mubarak bin Muhammad an-Nahayan
Minister of State: Hamouda bin Ali Dhairi

MINISTRY OF JUSTICE AND ISLAMIC AFFAIRS AND AWQAF (RELIGIOUS ENDOWWMENTS)
POB 2272, Abu Dhabi
Tel (2) 323200
Minister: Sheikh Muhammad bin Hassan al-Khazraji

MINISTRY OF LABOUR AND SOCIAL AFFAIRS
POB 809, Abu Dhabi
Tel (2) 362890
Minister: Khalfan Muhammad ar-Roumi

MINISTRY OF PETROLEUM AND MINERAL RESOURCES
POB 59, Abu Dhabi

Tel (2) 651810; telex 22544
Minister: Dr Mana bin Said al-Oteiba

MINISTRY OF PLANNING
POB 904, Abu Dhabi
Tel (2) 362270; telex 22920
Minister: Sheikh Humaid bin Ahmad al Mu'alla

MINISTRY OF PUBLIC WORKS AND HOUSING
POB 1828, Dubai
Tel (4) 693900; telex 23833; fax (4) 692931
Minister: Muhammad Khalifa al-Kindi
Deputy Minister: Ahmad Jassim al-Abdouli

MINISTRY OF STATE FOR AFFAIRS OF THE COUNCIL OF MINISTERS
POB 899, Abu Dhabi
Tel (2) 361555; telex 23245
Minister of State: Said al-Ghaith

MINISTRY OF STATE FOR AFFAIRS OF THE SUPREME COUNCIL
POB 545, Abu Dhabi
Tel (2) 343921
Minister of State: Sheikh Abd al-Aziz bin Humaid al-Qasimi

GOVERNMENT AGENCIES AND ORGANIZATIONS

Advisory and Supervisory Bodies

General Secretariat of UAE Municipalities: POB 5665, Dubai; tel (4) 237785; fax (4) 236136; Undersec: Jassem Muhammad Darwish; f 1980; unifies the laws between all municipalities, organising seminars for local govt, and co-ordination between municipalities and ministries.

Office of Naturalization and Immigration Administration: Mussafah Rd, POB 228, Abu Dhabi; tel (2) 377355; Dir-Gen: Hilal Said al-Dhahiri.

Supreme Petroleum Council (SPC): POB 26555, Abu Dhabi; tel (2) 666000; telex 26555; Exec Dir: Sheikh Khalifa bin Zayed an-Nahayan; Sec-Gen: Sohail Fares al-Mazrui; f 1988; assumed authority and responsibility of the former Dept of Petroleum for the admin and supervision of all petroleum affairs in the UAE.

UAE State Audit Institution: Soroor bin Shahwan Aldhahir Bldg, Sheikh Zayid First St, POB 3320, Abu Dhabi.

Business and Economy

BANKING

Abu Dhabi Commercial Bank (ADCB): POB 939, Abu Dhabi; tel (2) 721122; telex 22244; fax (2) 776499; Chair: Sheikh Suroor bin Sultan adh-Dhaheri; Chief Exec and Man Dir: Sultan Nasser as-Suweidi; f 1985 by merger of Khalij, Emirates and Federal Commercial Banks; 60% state-owned; 24 brs in UAE, 1 abroad.

Central Bank of the United Arab Emirates: POB 854, Abu Dhabi; tel (2) 368200; telex 22330; Chair: Sheikh Suroor bin Muhammad an-Nahayan; Gov: Abd al-Malik Yousuf al-Hamar; f 1973; bank of issue.

Emirates Bank International: POB 2923, Dubai; tel (4) 281181; telex 46425; Chair: Ahmad Humaid at-Tayer; Gen Man: John R. M. Lewis; f 1977 by amalgamation of Emirates National Bank, Dubai Bank and Union Bank of the Middle East Ltd; the Central Bank and Govt of Dubai hold an 80% share; 7 brs in Dubai, 8 brs overseas.

Emirates Industrial Bank: POB 2722, Abu Dhabi; tel (2) 339700; telex 23324; Chair: Ahmad at-Tayer; Gen Man: Muhammad Abd al-Baki; f 1982; 51% state-owned; offers low-cost loans to industries with at least 70% local ownership.

National Bank of Abu Dhabi (NBAD): Sheikh Khalifa St, POB 4, Abu Dhabi; tel (2) 335262; telex 22266; Chair: Sheikh Muhammad Habroush as-Suwaidi; Chief Exec: John S. W. Coombs; f 1968; owned jointly by Abu Dhabi Investment Authority and UAE citizens; 33 brs in UAE, 14 brs overseas.

National Bank of Dubai Ltd: POB 777, Dubai; tel (4) 222241; telex 45421; Chair Sultan Ali al-Owais; Gen Man: D. F. McKenzie; f 1963; 16 brs.

National Bank of Fujairah: POB 887, Fujairah; tel (70) 24518; telex 89050; Chair: Sheikh Saleh bin Muhammad ash-Sharqi; Gen Man: Michael J. Connor; f 1982; owned jointly by Govt of Fujairah (43%), Govt of Dubai (19.56%) and UAE citizens (37.44%); brs in Abu Dhabi, Fujairah, Dubai and Dibba.

United Arab Emirates Development Bank: POB 2449, Abu Dhabi; tel (2) 344986; telex 22427; f 1974; finances devt projects in agricultural, fisheries and construction sectors.

FINANCIAL AGENCY

Abu Dhabi Development Finance Corpn: POB 30, Abu Dhabi; tel (2) 22656; telex 820431; Dep Man Dir: Said Muhammad; provides finance to the private sector.

NATIONALIZED INDUSTRY

Abu Dhabi Pipeline Construction Co (ADPIC): POB 3840, Abu Dhabi; tel (2) 827400; telex 23624; Gen Man: Amin Khawaja; 60% state-owned.

TRADE

Customs Department: POB 246, Abu Dhabi.

Defence

Armed Forces: POB 309, Abu Dhabi; tel (2) 343492; telex 22368; Supreme Commdr: Sheikh Zayed bin Sultan an-Nahayan; Dep Commdr-in-Chief: Khalifa bin Zayed an-Nahayan; Chief of Staff: Brig-Gen: Muhammad Sa'id al-Badi.

Air Force: POB 906, Abu Dhabi; tel (2) 377300; Commdr: Muhammad Rashid.

Army: POB 3755, Abu Dhabi; tel (2) 334334; telex 22368.

Navy: POB 309, Abu Dhabi: tel (2) 341980; Commdr: Muhammad Nabel Radha Mudawwar.

Directorate-General of Police: POB 253, Abu Dhabi; Commdr: Ahmad bin Mubarak an-Nahayan.

Development and Planning

INVESTMENT

Abu Dhabi Investment Authority (ADIA): POB 3600, Abu Dhabi; tel (2) 213100; telex 22674; Chair: Sheikh Khalifa bin Zayed an-Nahayan; Gen Man: Sheikh Muhammad Habroush as-Suwaidi; f 1976; responsible for co-ordination of investment policy.

Abu Dhabi Investment Co (ADIC): POB 6309, Abu Dhabi; tel (2) 328200; telex 23824; Chair: Hareb ad-Darmaki; Gen Man: Yasus Mujazaki; f 1977; 90% owned by ADIA, 10% by National Bank of Abu Dhabi; investment and merchant banking activities in UAE and abroad.

International Petroleum Investment Co (IPIC): POB 7528, Abu Dhabi; tel (2) 336200; telex 22510; fax (2) 216045; Man Dir: Khalifa Muhammad al-Shamsi; Man, Admin: Adil as-Sheikhly; Man, Investment: M. D. Cunningham; f 1984; investment in petroleum activities, particularly in refining and distribution networks.

PLANNING

General Industry Corpn (GIC): POB 4499, Abu Dhabi; tel (2) 214900; telex 22938; f 1979; responsible for the promotion of non-oil-related industry.

Town Planning Department: Municipality Bldg, Sheikh Hamdan St, POB 862, Abu Dhabi.

REGIONAL DEVELOPMENT

Abu Dhabi Planning Department: POB 12, Abu Dhabi; tel (2) 329300; telex 23194; Chair: Sheikh Saif bin Muhammad an-Nahayan; Undersec: Hassan Mousa al-Qamzi; supervises Abu Dhabi's Devt Programme.

Sharjah Economic Development Corpn (SHEDCO): POB 3458, Sharjah; tel (6) 371212; telex 68789; Gen Man: J. T. Pickles; promotes economic devt and investment; joint venture between Sharjah Govt and private sector.

Umm al-Dalkh Development Co (UDECO): POB 6866, Abu Dhabi; tel (2) 333300; telex 23686; 50% state-owned.

Zakum Development Co (ZADCO): POB 6808, Abu Dhabi; tel (2) 321700; telex 22948; 50% state-owned.

Employment

Civil Service Commission: Salem Samaw Bldg, Hamdan St, POB 2350, Abu Dhabi; control of employment procedures within the civil service.

Energy

Abu Dhabi National Oil Co (ADNOC): POB 898, Abu Dhabi; tel (2) 666000; telex 22215; Chair: Sheikh Tahnoun bin Muhammad an-Nahayan; Gen Man: Dr Mahmoud Hamra Krouha; f 1971; deals in all phases of oil industry.

Abu Dhabi Co for Onshore Oil Operations (ADCO): Corniche Rd, POB 270, Abu Dhabi; tel (2) 666100; telex 22222; fax (2) 669785; Gen Man: T. D. Adams; Dep Gen Man, Operations: Z. R. Fakhouri; f 1979; 60% owned by ADNOC; exploration, drilling, production and export of crude oil from onshore areas of Abu Dhabi.

Abu Dhabi Drilling Chemicals and Products Ltd (ADDCAP): POB 6121, Abu Dhabi; tel (2) 772400; telex 23267; 75% owned by ADNOC; manufacture and marketing of drilling chemicals and operation of an offshore supply marine base.

Abu Dhabi Gas Industries Co (GASCO): POB 665, Abu Dhabi; tel (2) 651100; telex 22365; Chair: Sheikh Tahnoun bin Muhammad an-Nahayan; Gen Man: Aziz Ait-Said; started production in 1981; recovers condensate and LPG from Asab, Bab and Bu Hasa fields for delivery to Ruwais natural gas liquids fractionation plant; ADNOC holds 68% of capital.

Abu Dhabi Gas Liquefaction Co (ADGAS): POB 3500, Abu Dhabi; tel (2) 333888; telex 22698; Chair: Minister of Petroleum and Mineral Resources, Dr Mana bin Said al-Oteiba; Gen Man: Ronald I. Wiseman; f 1973; 51% owned by ADNOC.

Abu Dhabi Marine Operating Co (ADMA-OPCO): POB 303, Abu Dhabi; tel (2) 776600; telex 22284; Gen Man: André Durand de Boursingen; operates a concession 60% owned by ADNOC and 40% by Abu Dhabi Marine Areas Ltd (UK).

Abu Dhabi National Oil Co for Distribution (ADNOC-FOD): POB 4188, Abu Dhabi; tel (2) 720200; telex 22358; Dir-Gen: Abdullah Said al-Badi; distributes petroleum products in Abu Dhabi.

Abu Dhabi National Plastic Pipe Fabrication Co (NPP): POB 2915, Abu Dhabi; tel (2) 724400; telex 22627; ADNOC holds a 51% share.

Abu Dhabi Petroleum Ports Operating Co (ADPPOC): POB 61, Abu Dhabi; tel (2) 336700; telex 22209; Chair: Sohail F. Mazrui; Gen Man: Gerald E. Maynard; f 1979; ADNOC holds a 60% share.

The Liquefied Gas Shipping Co Ltd (LGSC): POB 3500, Abu Dhabi; tel (2) 333888; telex 22698; Gen Man: R. I. Wiseman; ADNOC holds 51% share.

National Drilling Co (NDC): POB 4017, Abu Dhabi; tel (2) 820330; telex 22553; Gen Man: Ahmad Juma adh-Dharif.

National Petroleum Construction Co Ltd (NPCC): POB 2058, Abu Dhabi; tel (2) 774100; telex 22638; Chair: Muhammad Khalifa al-Kindi; Gen Man: Najjad A. Zeenni; f 1973; manufacture and maintenance of on- and offshore facilities for the petroleum industry.

Ruwais Fertilizer Industries (Fertil): POB 6159, Abu Dhabi; tel (2) 727100; telex 24205; fax (2) 728084; Gen Man: Yousef al-Noweis; Marketing Man: Muhammad A. Daoudi; f 1980; 66.66% owned by ADNOC, 33.34% by Total-Compagnie (France); production and marketing of ammonia and urea.

Ajman National Oil Co (AJNOC): POB 410, Ajman; tel (6) 421218; f 1983; 50% state-owned.

Department of Ruler's Affairs and Petroleum Affairs: POB 207, Dubai; Dir: Mahdi at-Tajir; state supervisory body for the petroleum industry.

Dubai National Gas Co Ltd (DUGAS): POB 4311, Dubai; tel (84) 56234; telex 45741; Dep Chair and Dir: Mirza H. as-Sayegh; wholly owned by Dubai Govt.

Dubai Petroleum Co (DPC): POB 2222, Dubai; tel (4) 442990; telex 45423; Pres: John I. Horning; holds offshore concession which began production in 1969; wholly owned by Dubai Govt.

Emirates General Petroleum Corpn (EGPC): POB 9400, Dubai; tel (4) 373300; telex 47980; f 1981; wholly owned by Ministry of Finance and Industry; distribution of petroleum.

Emirates Petroleum Products Co (EPPCO): Dubai; f 1980; joint venture between Dept of the Ruler's Affairs and Petroleum Affairs and Caltex; sales of bunkering fuel and bitumen.

Petroleum and Mineral Affairs Department: POB 188, Sharjah; tel (6) 541888; telex 68708; Dir: Ismail A. Wahid.

Petroleum and Mineral Affairs Department: POB 9, Umm al-Qaiwain; tel (6) 666034; Chair: Sheikh Sultan bin Ahmad al-Mualla.

Sharjah Liquefied Petroleum Gas Co (SHALCO): POB 787, Sharjah; tel (6) 68799; f 1984; 60% owned by Govt of Sharjah.

International Affairs

Abu Dhabi Fund for Arab Economic Development (ADFAED): POB 814, Abu Dhabi; tel (2) 822865; telex 22287; Chair: Sheikh Khalifa bin Zayed an-Nahayan; Gen Man: Nasser M. an-Nowais; f 1971; offers economic aid to other Arab states and other developing countries in support of their devt.

Legal and Judiciary

United Supreme Court: Abu Dhabi; tel (2) 343764; telex 22220; Chief Shari'a Justice: Ahmad Abd al-Aziz al-Mubarak; f 1971.

Media

BROADCASTING

Abu Dhabi Radio: POB 63, Abu Dhabi; tel (2) 461800; telex 22557; Dir-Gen: Abd al-Wahab Radwan; f 1968; stations in Abu Dhabi, Dubai, Umm al-Qaiwain and Ras al-Khaimah all broadcasting in Arabic over a wide area; some broadcasts in English, French, Bengali and Urdu.

Abu Dhabi Television: POB 637, Abu Dhabi; tel (2) 461400; telex 22557; Dir-Gen: Ahmad Mousa al-Hamili.

Capital Radio: POB 63, Abu Dhabi; tel (2) 464555; telex 23321; fax (2) 335129; Station Dir: Archibald Quadros; f 1977; commercial station.

NEWS AND INFORMATION

Central Statistics Department: c/o Ministry of Planning, POB 1134, Sharjah; tel (6) 22704; collection, analysis and dissemination of statistical data.

Emirates News Agency (WAM): POB 3790, Abu Dhabi; tel (2) 464600; telex 22979; fax (2) 464695; Dir-Gen: Ibrahim al-Abed; f 1977; news gathering and distribution.

Science and Technology

National Computer Centre: POB 3870, Abu Dhabi.

Telecommunications

Emirates Telecommunications Corpn Ltd (Etisalat): POB 3838, Abu Dhabi; tel (2) 283333; telex 22135; fax (2) 727842; Gen Man: Ali Salim al-Owais; f 1976; provides telecommunications service for UAE.

General Postal Administration: POB 8888, Dubai.

Tourism

Dubai Information Department: POB 1420, Dubai; Dir: Omar Deesi.

Ras as-Khaimah Information and Tourism Department: POB 141, Ras al-Khaimah; tel (77) 51151; Chair: Sheikh Abd al-Aziz bin Humaid al-Qassimi.

Sharjah Department of Tourism: POB 5119, Sharjah; tel (6) 581111; telex 68185; Dir: Muhammad Saif al-Hajri; f 1980.

Transport

CIVIL AVIATION

Civil Aviation Department: POB 20, Abu Dhabi; tel (2) 757500; telex 24406; Chair: Ali bin Khalfan adh-Dhahri; responsible for all aspects of civil aviation.

Emirates (EK) Dubai: POB 686, Dubai; tel (4) 223698; telex 48085; Chair: Sheikh Ahmad bin Said al-Maktoum; Man Dir: Maurice Flanagan; owned by the Dubai Govt; services throughout the Middle East, and to the Far East and Europe.

Gulf Air Co GSC (Gulf Air): POB 5015, Sharjah; tel (6) 354024; f 1950; jointly owned by the Govts of Bahrain, Oman, Qatar and Abu Dhabi.

Gulf Air Dubai: Sheikh as-Sabah Bldg, al-Maktoum St, POB 4410, Deira; tel (4) 283599; internal services and flights to the Far East, Paris and London.

SHIPPING

Abu Dhabi National Tanker Co (ADNATCO): POB 2977, Abu Dhabi; tel (2) 331800; telex 22747; Chair: Khalaf Rashid al-Otaibah; Gen Man: Bader M. as-Sowaidi; subsidiary co of ADNOC (see above), operating owned and chartered tankships, and transporting crude petroleum and refined products.

Abu Dhabi Petroleum Ports Operating Co (ADPPOC): POB 61, Dubai.

Ahmad bin Rashid Port and Free Trade Zone: POB 279, Umm al-Qaiwain; tel (6) 665882; telex 69717; Man: D. F. Munro; f 1987; free port operations and warehousing.

Dubai Drydock Co: POB 8988, Dubai; tel (4) 450626; telex 48838; Chief Exec: E. S. Ware; state-owned dry docks with cleaning facilities, galvanizing plant, transport systems and facilities for maintenance and repair of ships of any size.

Jebel Ali Free Zone Authority (JAFZA): POB 3258, Dubai; tel (84) 56578; telex 46580; Chair: Sultan Ahmad bin Sulayem; administers Jebel Ali port and industrial area; facilities for handling container, bulk, general and liquid traffic.

Jebel Dhanna Port: c/o ADCO, POB 270, Dubai; tel (2) 71008;

telex 22222; Man: J. B. Sheehan; facilities include four tanker berths.

National Marine Services Co (NMS): POB 7202, Abu Dhabi; tel (2) 339800; telex 22965; Chair: S. F. al-Mazrui; Gen Man: Capt Hassan A. Shareef; ADNOC holds a 60% share; operation, charter and lease of specialized offshore support vessels.

Port of Fujairah: POB 787, Fujairah; tel (70) 24231; telex 89085; fax (70) 24240; Gen Man: Capt Roger Saunders; Marketing Man: Tony P. Restall; f 1982; container port and free trade zone.

Port Rashid Authority (PRA): POB 2149, Dubai; tel (4) 451545; telex 47530; Gen Man: John Arundell; offers duty-free storage areas and facilities for loading and discharge of vessels.

Port Zayed Authority: POB 422, Abu Dhabi; tel (2) 823360; telex 22731; Chair: Dr Adnan al-Bajahji; Gen Man: Said Bakeet al-Mansouri; facilities include 19 general berths, two container berths and a bulk grain terminal.

Ras al-Khaimah Port Services: POB 5130, Ras al-Khaimah; tel (77) 66444; telex 99280; Chair: Sheikh Muhammad bin Saqr al-Qasimi; Govt holds majority share; operates Mina Saqr port.

Ruwais Petroleum Port: c/o ADNOC, POB 898, Abu Dhabi; tel (2) 366029; telex 52207.

Sharjah Port Authority: POB 510, Sharjah; tel (6) 541666; telex 68138; Chair, Ports and Customs: Sheikh Saud bin Khalid al-Qasemi; Dir-Gen: Abd al-Aziz Suleiman as-Sarkal; administers Port Khalid and Port Khor Fakkan and offers specialized facilities for container and roll-on, roll-off traffic, reefer cargo and project and general cargo.

Umm al-Qaiwain Port: POB 225, Umm al-Qaiwain; tel (6) 666126; telex 69611.

THE UNITED KINGDOM

Great Britain

Head of State

The United Kingdom (UK) is a constitutional monarchy, with the sovereign as Head of State. Executive power is held by the Cabinet, headed by the Prime Minister, which is responsible to the House of Commons. A Privy Council, presided over by the monarch, is empowered to make Orders in Council and plays an advisory role.

Sovereign: HM Queen Elizabeth II (succeeded to the throne 6 February 1952).

The Queen's Household: Buckingham Palace, London, SW1; tel (71) 930-4832; Lord Chamberlain: The Earl of Airlie.

Privy Council Office: 68 Whitehall, London, SW1A 2AT; tel (71) 270-0472; Lord Pres of the Council and Leader of the Commons: Sir Geoffrey Howe; Lord Privy Seal and Leader of the House of Lords: Lord Belstead; Minister of State and Minister for the Civil Service: Richard Luce.

Legislature

Supreme legislative authority is vested in the bicameral Parliament, comprising the House of Lords (composed of hereditary Peers of the Realm and Life Peers and Peeresses created by the sovereign), and the House of Commons (composed of 650 members elected for a maximum of five years by direct adult suffrage, using single-member constituencies). The House of Lords may delay, but cannot prevent, any bill becoming law once it has been passed by the Commons.

House of Lords: Westminster, London SW1A 0PW; tel (71) 219-5242; telex 916318; fax (71) 219-6396; Chair of Committees: Lord Aberdare; Principal Dep Chair of Committees: The Baroness Serota.

House of Commons: Westminster, London, SW1A 0AA; tel (71) 219-3000; Speaker: Bernard Weatherill.

MINISTRIES AND GOVERNMENT DEPARTMENTS

PRIME MINISTER'S OFFICE
10 Downing St, London, SW1A 2AA
Tel (71) 270-3000
Prime Minister: Margaret Thatcher

CABINET OFFICE (OFFICE OF THE MINISTER FOR THE CIVIL SERVICE)
Horse Guards Rd, London, SW1P 3AL
Tel (71) 270-3000; fax (71) 270 5828
Minister for the Civil Service: Margaret Thatcher
Maintains standards of integrity and competence for the Civil Service; acts as an agent for the selection, devt and training of staff; acts as a source of policy advice on the management of civil servants and on the structure and practice of Govt; promotes equal opportunity and merit throughout the Civil Service.

DEPARTMENT OF EDUCATION AND SCIENCE
Elizabeth House, York Rd, London, SE1 7PH
Tel (71) 934-9000; telex 23171; fax (71) 934-9082
Secretary of State: John MacGregor
Minister of State: Angela Rumbold
Under Secretaries of State: Robert Jackson, Alan Howarth

DEPARTMENT OF EMPLOYMENT
Caxton House, Tothill St, London, SW1 9NF
Tel (71) 273-3000; telex 915564; fax (71) 273-5124
Secretary of State: Michael Howard
Minister of State: Tim Eggar
Under Secretaries of State: Patrick Nicholls, Lord Strathclyde

DEPARTMENT OF ENERGY
Thames House South, Millbank, London, SW1P 4QJ
Tel (71) 211-3000; telex 918777
Secretary of State: John Wakeham
Minister of State: Peter Morrison
Under Secretary of State: Tony Baldry

DEPARTMENT OF THE ENVIRONMENT
2 Marsham St, London, SW1P 3EB
Tel (71) 276-3000; telex 22221
Secretary of State: Christopher Patten
Minister for Housing and Planning: Michael Spicer
Minister for Local Government and Inner Cities:
David Hunt

Minister for Environment and Countryside:
David Trippier
Under Secretaries of State: Christopher Chope,
Lord Hesketh, David Heathcoat-Amory
Minister for Sport: Colin Moynihan

DEPARTMENT OF HEALTH
Richmond House, 79 Whitehall, London, SW1A 2NS
Tel (71) 210-3000
Secretary of State: Kenneth Clarke
Minister of State: Virginia Bottomley
Under Secretaries of State: Roger Freeman, Lady Hooper

DEPARTMENT OF SOCIAL SECURITY
Richmond House, 79 Whitehall, London, SW1A 2NS
Tel (71) 210-3000
Secretary of State: Tony Newton
Minister for Social Security: Nicholas Scott
Under Secretaries of State: Lord Henley, Gillian Shephard
It was announced in May 1989 that social security was to be
hived off from Whitehall into two or three agencies.

DEPARTMENT OF TRADE AND INDUSTRY
1 Victoria St, London, SW1H 0ET
Tel (71) 215-5000; telex 8811074; fax (71) 222-2629
Secretary of State: Nicholas Ridley
Minister for Industry: Douglas Hogg
Minister for Trade: Lord Trefgarne
**Under Secretary of State for Industry and Consumer
Affairs:** Eric Forth
Under Secretary of State for Corporate Affairs:
John Redwood

DEPARTMENT OF TRANSPORT
2 Marsham St, London, SW1P 3EB
Tel (71) 276-3000; telex 22221; fax (71) 276-0818
Secretary of State: Cecil Parkinson
Minister for Public Transport: Michael Portillo
Under Secretaries of State: Robert Atkins,
Patrick McLoughlin

FOREIGN AND COMMONWEALTH OFFICE
Downing St, London, SW1A 2AL
Tel (71) 270-3000; telex 297711
Secretary of State: Douglas Hurd
Ministers of State: William Waldegrave, Francis Maude,
Lord Brabazon of Tara
Under Secretary of State: Tim Sainsbury

HER MAJESTY'S TREASURY
Parliament St, London, SW1P 3AG
Tel (71) 270-3000; telex 9413704
First Lord of the Treasury: Margaret Thatcher
Chancellor of the Exchequer: John Major
Chief Secretary: Norman Lamont
Paymaster-General: The Earl of Caithness
Financial Secretary: Peter Lilley
Economic Secretary: Richard Ryder

HOME OFFICE
50 Queen Anne's Gate, London, SW1H 9AT
Tel (71) 273-3000; telex 24986; fax (71) 273-2190
Secretary of State: David Waddington
Ministers of State: Earl Ferrers, John Patten, David Mellor
Under Secretary of State: Peter Lloyd

LORD CHANCELLOR'S DEPARTMENT
Lord Chancellor's Office, House of Lords,
London, SW1A 0PW
Tel (71) 210-8500; fax (71) 210-8549
Lord Chancellor: Lord Mackay of Clashfern
Responsible for general reforms in the civil law, for the pro-
cedure of the civil courts and for various tribunals and the Legal
Aid scheme; administers the Supreme Court and County Courts
in England and Wales; advises the Crown on the appointment
of judges and other officers; appoints certain judicial officers.

MINISTRY OF AGRICULTURE, FISHERIES AND FOOD
Whitehall Place, London, SW1A 2HH
Tel (71) 233-5550; telex 889351
Minister: John Gummer
Minister of State: Lady Trumpington
Parliamentary Secretary in charge of Food Safety:
David Maclean
**Parliamentary Secretary in charge of the Food and
Farming Industries:** David Curry

MINISTRY OF DEFENCE
Main Bldg, Whitehall, London SW1A 2HB
Tel (71) 218-9000; telex 825911
Secretary of State: Tom King
Minister of State for Defence Procurement: Alan Clark
Minister of State for the Armed Forces: Archie Hamilton
Under Secretary of State for the Armed Forces:
The Earl of Arran
Under Secretary of State for Defence Procurement:
Michael Neubert

NORTHERN IRELAND OFFICE
Whitehall, London, SW1A 2AZ
Tel (71) 210-3000; telex 918889
Stormont Castle, Belfast, BT4 3ST
Tel (232) 63011; telex 74272
Secretary of State: Peter Brooke
Minister of State: John Cope
Under Secretaries of State: Richard Needham, Dr Brian
Mawhinney, Peter Bottomley, Lord Skelmersdale

OFFICE OF ARTS AND LIBRARIES
Horse Guards Rd, London, SW1P 3AL
Tel (71) 270-3000
Minister for the Arts: Richard Luce

OFFICE OF THE CHANCELLOR OF THE DUCHY OF LANCASTER
1-19 Victoria St, London, SW1H 0ET
Tel (71) 215-5147
Chancellor of the Duchy of Lancaster: Kenneth Baker

OVERSEAS DEVELOPMENT ADMINISTRATION (ODA)
Eland House, Stag Place, London, SW1E 5DH
Tel (71) 273-3000; telex 263907; fax (71) 273-0019
Minister for Overseas Development: Lynda Chalker
Manages Britain's aid programme to developing countries.

SCOTTISH OFFICE
Dover House, Whitehall, London, SW1A 2AU
Tel (71) 270-3000; telex 22890
St Andrew's House, Edinburgh, EH1 3DE
Tel (31) 556-8400; telex 727301
Secretary of State: Malcolm Rifkind
Ministers of State: Ian Lang, Lord Sanderson of Bowden
Under Secretaries of State: Lord James
Douglas-Hamilton, Michael Forsyth

WELSH OFFICE
Gwydyr House, Whitehall, London, SW1A 2ER
Tel (71) 270-3000
Cathays Park, Cardiff, CF1 3NQ
Tel (222) 825-111; telex 498228
Secretary of State: Peter Walker
(to be succeeded by David Hunt in June 1990)
Minister of State: Wyn Roberts
Under Secretary of State: Ian Grist

GOVERNMENT AGENCIES AND ORGANIZATIONS

Advisory and Supervisory Bodies

Advisory, Conciliation and Arbitration Service (ACAS): 27 Wilton St, London, SW1X 7AZ; tel (71) 210-3000; fax (71) 210-3708; Chair: Douglas B. Smith; f 1974; independent service, under the management of a Council appointed by the Sec of State for Employment; offers advice and practical assistance on industrial relations issues to everyone concerned with employment; provides conciliation services in collective and individual disputes, mediation and arbitration; promotes improvements in collective bargaining; advises in respect of alleged infringement of individual rights under industrial relations legislation, with particular responsibility for dealing with complaints of alleged unfair dismissal.

The Audit Commission: 1 Vincent Sq, London SW1P 2PN; tel (71) 828-1212; fax (71) 828-1212; Controller: Howard Davies; Dep Controller: Cliff Nicolson; f 1983; appoints auditors to local authorities and helps authorities bring about improvements in economy, efficiency and effectiveness; undertakes studies into the effects of central Govt's actions on the economy, efficiency and effectiveness of local govt; responsible to the Dept of the Environment.

British Council of Productivity Associations: POB 378, Reading, Berks, RG4 0BD; tel (734) 471702; Gen Man: K. Robbins; f 1952; supported by the Dept of Trade and Industry, CBI, National Economic Devt Office and TUC; promotes higher productivity by spreading knowledge of better methods; publishes and makes films on all productivity matters.

Central Arbitration Committee: 39 Grosvenor Place, London SW1X 7BD; tel (71) 210-3737; fax (71) 210-3708; Chair: Sir John Wood; Sec: S. Gouldstone; f 1975; independent standing arbitration body working nationally in the field of industrial relations; provides boards of arbitration for the settlement of trade disputes referred to it with the consent of the parties concerned or unilaterally under the Employment Protection Act 1975.

Charity Commission: St Alban's House, 57-60 Haymarket, London, SW1Y 4QX; tel (71) 210-3000; fax (71) 930-9173; Chief Commr: R. I. L. Guthrie; Sec: D. Forrest; Commrs are appointed under the Charities Act 1960 principally to further the work of charities; maintains a register of charities; holds investments for charities.

Commission for Racial Equality: Elliot House, 10-12 Allington St, London, SW1E 5EH; tel (71) 828-7022; fax (71) 630-7605; f 1977; set up by the Race Relations Act 1976 with the duties of working towards the elimination of discrimination on racial grounds and promoting equality and good relations between persons of different racial groups.

Companies House: Crown Way, Cardiff, CF4 3UZ; tel (222) 388588; telex 497768; fax (222) 374092; 102 George St, Edinburgh, EH2 3DJ; tel (31) 225-5774; Chief Exec and Registrar of Cos (England and Wales): Stephen R. Curtis; Registrar (Scotland): J. Leighead; f 1844; registration of cos; became a Govt Executive Agency in Oct 1988, headed by a Chief Exec, who is also Registrar of Cos.

The Crown Estate: 16 Carlton House Terrace, London, SW1Y 5AH; tel (71) 210-4377; fax (71) 930-8259; First Commr and Chair of the Board: The Earl of Mansfield; Second Commr and Chief Exec: Christopher Howes; f 1760; responsible for the management of Crown Estate interests in the UK, including agriculture and forestry, commercial and housing properties, etc; the Estate, which is vested in the sovereign in right of the Crown, is managed by the Crown Estate Commrs under the provisions of the Crown Estate Act 1961.

Government Actuary's Department: 22 Kingsway, London, WC2R 6LE; tel (71) 242-6828; fax (71) 831-6653; Govt Actuary: C. D. Daykin; f 1919; provides a consultancy service to depts, nationalized industries and Commonwealth Govt; gives advice on social security and superannuation schemes, population and other studies, the supervision of insurance cos and friendly societies and any other actuarial matter.

HM Land Registry: Lincolns Inn Fields, London, WC2A 3PH; tel (71) 405-3488; telex 929779; fax (71) 242-0825; Chief Land Registrar: E. J. Pryer; Chief Exec: J. Manthorpe; f 1862; registration of title to land in England and Wales.

Monopolies and Mergers Commission: New Court, 48 Carey St, London, WC2A 2JT; tel (71) 324-0467; fax (71) 324-1400; Chair: M. S. Lipworth; Sec: S. N. Burbridge; f 1948; inquires into and reports on matters relating to monopolies, mergers or other commercial or industrial matters affecting the public interest, referred to it by the Sec of State for Trade and by the Dir-Gen of Fair Trading.

National Audit Office: 157-197 Buckingham Palace Rd, Victoria, London, SW1W 9SP; tel (71) 798-7000; fax (71) 828-3774; Comptroller and Auditor-Gen: John Bourn; Dep Comptroller and Auditor-Gen: H. D. Myland; fmrly Exchequer and Audit Dept; responsible for controlling receipts into and issues from the Consolidated and National Loans Funds; examines the accounts of Govt depts, certain public bodies and international organizations; reports to Parliament on public spending.

Offshore Supplies Office (OSO): c/o Department of Energy, Alhambra House, 45 Waterloo St, Glasgow, G2 6AS; tel (41) 221-8777; telex 779379; fax (41) 221-1718; Dir-Gen: J. E. d'Ancona; f 1973; promotion of supply of goods and services by British firms for the exploitation of off-shore oil and gas.

Agriculture and the Environment

AGRICULTURE

Crofters Commission: 4-6 Castle Wynd, Inverness, EV2 3EQ; tel (463) 237231; Chair: A. Macleod; Sec: I. A. Macpherson; advises the Sec of State for Scotland on all matters relating to crofting; controls the letting, subletting, and in some cases, the assignation or enlargement of crofts, the removal of land from crofting tenure and the regulation of common grazing; administers schemes of agricultural assistance to crofters.

Department of Agriculture and Fisheries for Scotland: Pentland House, Robb's Loan, Edinburgh, EH14 1TY; tel (31) 556-8400; telex 22890; promotion of agriculture and the fishing industry in Scotland.

Intervention Board for Agricultural Produce: Fountain House, 2 Queen's Walk, Reading, Berks, RG1 7QW; tel (734) 583626; telex 848302; Chair: A. J. Ellis; Chief Exec: G. Stapleton; responsible to the Agricultural Ministers for the implementation of the market support measures of the Common Agricultural Policy of the European Community.

THE ENVIRONMENT

Countryside Commission: John Dower House, Crescent Place, Cheltenham, Glos, GL50 3RA; tel (242) 521381; fax (242) 584270; Chair: Sir Derek Barber; Dir-Gen: A. A. C. Phillips; established 1968 to succeed the National Parks Commission, became an independent Govt agency in 1982; funded by the Dept of the Environment; advisory and promotional body concerned with landscape conservation and informal recreation in the countryside in England and Wales.

Countryside Commission for Scotland: Battleby, Redgorton, Perth, PH1 3EW; tel (738) 27921; Chair: J. Roger Carr; Dir: D. Campbell; conservation of the Scottish countryside; provision of facilities for the public's enjoyment of the countryside.

HM's Inspectorate of Pollution: Romney House, 43 Marsham St, London, SW1P 3PY; tel (71) 276-8642; telex 22221; fax (71) 276-8605; f 1987; plant assessment and enforcement of pollution control legislation in England and Wales.

The National Rivers Authority: 30-34 Albert Embankment, London, SE1 7TL; Chair: Lord Crickhowell; Chief Exec: Dr John Bowman; f 1989 under the Water Act; independent watchdog aiming to improve the standards of rivers, lakes and coastal waters by controlling pollution from the water industry as well as other industries and agriculture; takes over the responsibilities of the water authorities for water resource management, flood defence, fisheries and navigation.

Nature Conservancy Council (NCC): Northminster House, Peterborough, Cambs, PE1 1UA; tel (733) 40345; fax (733) 68834; Chair: Sir William Wilkinson; Dir-Gen: T. R. Hornsby; f 1973; advises Govt on nature conservation in Great Britain; selects, establishes and manages National Nature Reserves and Marine Nature Reserves; identifies and notifies Sites of Special Scientific Interest; disseminates information about nature conservation; conducts and supports research relevant to these functions; in January 1990 it was confirmed the Council would be broken up, and from April 1991 Prof Fred Holliday was to be the first Chair of a UK joint committee to maintain the NCC's scientific work, Lord Cranbrook was to be the first Chair of the Nature Conservancy Council for England, and Magnus Magnusson was to be the head of the new Nature Conservancy Council for Scotland, which it was planned to merge with the Countryside Commission for Scotland in 1992.

FISHING

Sea Fish Industry Authority: 10 Young St, Edinburgh, EH2 4JQ; tel (31) 225-2515; telex 727225; fax (31) 220-0445; Chair: Ben Davies; Chief Exec: Christopher Davies; f 1981 from the White Fish Authority and the Herring Industry Board; statutory body concerned with all sectors of the fishing industry.

FORESTRY

Forestry Commission: 231 Corstorphine Rd, Edinburgh, EH12 7AT; tel (31) 334-0303; telex 727879; fax (31) 334-3047; Chair: Sir David Montgomery; Dir-Gen: G. J. Francis; f 1919; national forestry authority charged with promoting the interests of forestry and the devt of afforestation and production and supply of timber and other forest products in Great Britain; seeks a reasonable balance between forestry and conservation; involved in research and a range of regulatory functions, including the admin of grant-aid schemes for planting by private owners, the licensing of tree-felling and the combatting of tree pests and diseases.

Art and Culture

Arts Council of Great Britain: 105 Piccadilly, London, W1V 0AU; tel (71) 629-9495; Chair: Peter Palumbo; Sec-Gen: L. Rittner; promotes knowledge, understanding and practice of the arts and aims to increase their accessibility to the public; plans to devolve funding of the arts to Regional Arts Boards within three years were announced in March 1990.

British Library: British Library Board Headquarters: 2 Sheraton St, London, W1V 4BH; tel (71) 323-7111; Chair: Lord Quinton; Dep Chair and Chief Exec: K. R. Cooper; provides reference, lending, bibliographic and other services; holds collections of books, manuscripts, maps, music, periodicals, sound recordings, etc.

British Museum: Great Russell St, London, WC1B 3KG; contains the national collection of antiquities, ethnography, prints, drawings, coins, medals and banknotes; British Museum

(Natural History) conducts research and contains natural history exhibits, and the Geological Museum displays gems and earth science.

Historic Buildings and Monuments Commission for England (English Heritage): Fortress House, 23 Savile Row, London, W1X 2HE; tel (71) 734-6010; Chair: Lord Montagu of Beaulieu; Chief Exec: P. W. Rumble; f 1983; conservation and presentation of England's heritage of ancient monuments and historic bldgs; statutory adviser to the Sec of State for the Environment on heritage preservation and protection; designates areas of archaeological importance; gives grants.

National Library of Scotland: George IV Bridge, Edinburgh, EH1 1EW; tel (31) 226-4531; telex 72638; fax (31) 226-4531; Chair of the Board of Trustees: M. F. Strachan; Librarian and Sec to the Board of Trustees: Prof E. F. D. Roberts; reference and research library.

National Library of Wales: Aberystwyth, Dyfed, SY23 3BU; tel (970) 623816; Librarian: Dr Brynley F. Roberts; founded by Royal Charter in 1907; specializes in manuscripts and books relating to Wales and the Celtic people; repository for pre-1858 Welsh probate records, manorial records, tithe documents, maps, prints and drawings.

National Museum of Wales: Cathays Park, Cardiff, CF1 3NP; tel (222) 397951; Dir: Dr D. W. Dykes; Sec: Gerwyn Morgan; geology, botany and zoology of Wales, archeology, industry and art of the people.

National Museums of Scotland: Chambers St, Edinburgh, EH1 1JF; tel (31) 225-7534; Chair of the Board of Trustees: The Marquess of Bute; Dir: Dr R. G. W. Anderson; collections comprise material made or used in Scotland from earliest times to the present day, and exhibits from all over the world.

Public Record Office: Ruskin Ave, Kew, Richmond, Surrey, TW9 4DU; Chancery Lane, London, WC2A 1LR; tel (71) 876-3444; fax (71) 878-7231; Keeper of Public Records: Michael Roper; f 1838; preserves the archives of the central Govt.

Scottish Record Office: HM General Register House, Edinburgh, EH1 3YY; tel (31) 556-6585; Keeper of the Records: Dr Athol L. Murray; preserves Govt archives in Scotland, public registers of Scotland and private archives deposited in or gifted to the office.

Business and Economy

BANKING

Bank of England: Threadneedle St, London, EC2R 8AH; tel (71) 601-4444; telex 885001; fax (71) 601-4771; Gov: Rt Hon Robert Leigh-Pemberton; Chief Cashier: G. M. Gill; Sec: G. A. Croughton; inc by Royal Charter in 1694, nationalized by Act of Parliament on 1 March 1946; is the Govt's banker and on its behalf manages the note issue and the National Debt; also the bankers' bank.

FINANCIAL AGENCIES

Board of Inland Revenue: Somerset House, London, WC2R 1LB; tel (71) 438-6622; Chair: Sir Anthony Battishill; Dep Chairs: A. J. G. Isaac, T. J. Painter; administers and collects direct taxes, mainly income tax, corpn tax, capital gains tax, stamp duty and petroleum revenue tax; advises the Chancellor of the Exchequer on policy questions involving these taxes; the dept's Valuation Office values property for tax purposes, etc.

Department for National Savings: Headquarters: Charles House, 375 Kensington High St, London, W14 8SD; tel (71) 605-9300; National Savings Bank, Boydstone Rd, Cowglen, Glasgow, G58 1SB; Savings Certificate and SAYE Office, Millburngate House, Durham, DH99 1NS; Bonds and Stock Office (Govt Stock and Bonds), Marton, Blackpool, Lancs,

FY3 9YP; Bonds and Stock Office (Premium Savings Bonds), Lytham St Annes, Lancs, FY0 1YN; Dir of Savings: John Patterson; f 1861.

National Debt Office: National Investment and Loans Office, Royex House, Aldermanbury Sq, London, EC2V 7LR; tel (71) 606-7321; Comptroller-Gen: I. H. Peattie; Asst Comptroller and Establishment Officer: A. G. Ladd; management of the investment portfolios of certain public funds, including the funds of the National Insurance scheme and the National Savings Bank; responsibilities for the reduction of the National Debt.

The Royal Mint: Llantrisant, Pontyclun, Mid Glamorgan, CF7 8YT; tel (443) 222111; telex 498353; fax (443) 228799; Dep Master and Controller (Chief Exec): A. D. Garrett; manufacture of coins, blanks and medals.

TRADE

Export Credits Guarantee Department (ECGD): POB 272, Export House, 50 Ludgate Hill, London, EC4M 7AY; tel (71) 382-7000; telex 883601; fax (71) 382-7469; Chief Exec: Malcolm G. Stephens; f 1919; UK's official export credit insurer; responsible to the Sec of State for Trade and Industry; encourages exports by protecting British exporters against the main risks of non-payment by overseas buyers or their Govts.

HM Customs and Excise: New King's Beam House, 22 Upper Ground, London, SE1 9PJ; tel (71) 620-1313; telex 886231; fax (71) 620-1313; Chair: J. B. Unwin; Dep Chairs: V. P. M. Strachan, P. Jefferson Smith; collects and administers customs and excise duties and Value Added Tax, advising the Chancellor of the Exchequer on any matters connected with them; responsible for preventing and detecting the evasion of revenue laws and for enforcing a range of prohibitions and restrictions on the importation of certain classes of goods; compiles UK overseas trade statistics.

National Consumer Council: 20 Grosvenor Gdns, London, SW1; tel (71) 730-3469; fax (71) 730-0191; Chair: Lady Wilcox; Dir: Maurice Healy; consumer affairs in England.

Office of Fair Trading: Field House, 15-25 Bream's Bldgs, London, EC4A 1PR; tel (71) 242-2858; telex 269009; fax (71) 831-2195; Dir-Gen: Sir Gordon Borrie; f 1973; monitors consumer affairs, consumer credit, estate agencies; maintains registers relating to restrictive trade practices, etc.

Patent Office and Industrial Property and Copyright Department: State House, 66-71 High Holborn, London, WC1R 4TP; tel (71) 831-2525; Comptroller-Gen: P. J. Cooper; under the Dept of Trade and Industry; has branches concerned with patents and designs, trade marks, and industrial property and copyright.

Scottish Consumer Council: 314 St Vincent St, Glasgow, G3 8XW; tel (41) 226-5261; fax (41) 221-0731; Chair: Barbara Kelly; Dir: Peter Gibson; f 1975; speaks up for consumers; monitors public services and issues related to goods and private services; identifies specific Scottish consumer issues.

Welsh Consumer Council (Cyngor Defnyddwyr Cymru): Castle Bldgs, Womanby St, Cardiff, CF1 2BN; tel (222) 396056; fax (222) 238360; Chair: Rhiannon Bevan; Dir: Katherine Hughes; f 1975; self-governing branch of the National Consumer Council; funded by a grant-in-aid from the Dept of Trade and Industry; speaks out on behalf of consumers and presses for changes in policies and practices.

Defence

Air Force Department: Main Bldg, Whitehall, London, SW1A 2HB; tel (71) 218-6813; Chief of the Air Staff: Air Chief Marshal Sir David Craig; Asst Chief of Air Staff: Air Vice-Marshal M. G. Simmons.

Army Department: Main Bldg, Whitehall, London, SW1A 2HB; tel (71) 218-7114; Chief of the Defence Staff: Air Chief Marshal Sir David Craig (until March 1991), Gen Sir Richard Vincent (after March 1991); Chief of the Gen Staff: Gen Sir John Chapple; Asst Chief of the Gen Staff: Maj-Gen C. R. L. Guthrie.

Navy Department: Main Bldg, Whitehall, London, SW1A 2HB; tel (71) 218-2214; Chief of Naval Staff and First Sea Lord: Adm Sir William Staveley; Asst Chief of the Naval Staff: Rear-Adm M. H. Livesay.

Procurement Executive: Main Bldg, Whitehall, London, SW1A 2HB; tel (71) 218-9000; telex 825911; Chief of Defence Procurement: Permanent Under Sec of State, Sir Peter Levene; part of the Ministry of Defence; research, devt, production and purchase of weapons and equipment for the armed forces; promotes export of defence equipment and research and devt projects.

Development and Planning

DEVELOPMENT

British Technology Group: 101 Newington Causeway, London, SE1 6BU; tel (71) 403-6666; telex 894397; fax (71) 403-7586; Chair: Colin Barker; Chief Exec: Ian Harvey; f 1948 by merger of National Enterprise Board and National Research Development Corpn; technology transfer organization; licenses new scientific and engineering products to industry world-wide and provides finance for the devt of new technology.

Commonwealth Development Corpn (CDC): 1 Bessborough Gdns, London, SW1V 2JQ; tel (71) 828-4488; telex 21431; fax (71) 828-6505; Gen Man: John Eccles; f 1948; public corpn established to assist overseas countries to develop their economies through direct investment.

Co-operative Development Agency: Broadmead House, 21 Panton St, London, SW1Y 4DR; tel (71) 839-2985; fax (71) 839-1215; Chief Exec: George Jones; f 1978; promotes the concept of co-operatives as an alternative to the public and private sectors; advises potential new business co-operatives.

Industrial Development Advisory Board: Kingsgate House, 68-74 Victoria St, London, SW1E 6SW; Chair: Sir Ronald Halstead; Sec: A. Berry; f 1972; under Dept of Trade and Industry.

National Economic Development Council (NEDC): Millbank Tower, Millbank London, SW1P 4QX; tel (71) 211-3100; telex 945059; Dir-Gen: Walter Eltis; f 1962; independent forum for discussions between Govt, management and unions; the Sector Groups, working parties and the Committee on Industry and Finance (f 1988) set up by the NEDC, examine the prospects and performance of key individual industrial industries in the private sector; the National Economic Development Office (NEDO) provides the professional staff for the NEDC and other organizations; mems: six Govt ministers, six from the CBI, six from the TUC, two from nationalized industries, three independents.

Rural Development Commission: 11 Cowley St, London, SW1P 3NA; tel (71) 276-6969; fax (71) 276-6940; 141 Castle St, Salisbury, Wilts, SP1 3TP; tel (722) 336255; fax (722) 332769; Chair: Lord Vinson; Chief Exec: Richard Butt; f 1988 following the merger of the Development Commission and the Council for Small Industries in Rural Areas (COSIRA); promotes economic and social well-being of rural communities; stimulates job creation and the provision of essential services in the countryside; provides advice, training and finance to small firms in rural England; advises Govt on all matters concerning rural England; responsible to the Dept of the Environment.

REGIONAL DEVELOPMENT

Development Board for Rural Wales: Ladywell House, Newtown, Powys, SY16 1JB; tel (686) 626965; f 1977; promotes economic and social devt of mid-Wales; develops industrial and business premises; gives financial assistance to business and industry.

Devon and Cornwall Development Bureau: 5 Derriford Park, Derriford, Plymouth, Devon, PL6 5QZ; tel (752) 793379; fax (752) 788660; Exec Dir: Ivor Simpson; f 1985; promotes investment in Devon and Cornwall; overseas offices in Massachusetts, USA and Tokyo, Japan.

English Estates: St George's House, Kingsway, Team Valley, Gateshead, Tyne and Wear, NE11 0NA; tel (91) 487-8941; fax (91) 487-5690; Chief Exec: A. R. Pender; provides and manages industrial and commercial sites in rural and devt areas; gives advice on the availability of business premises.

Greater Manchester Economic Development Ltd: Bernard House, Piccadilly Gdns, Manchester, M1 4DD; tel (61) 236-4412; telex 665770; fax (61) 228-6462; Man Dir: Alan McGarvey; f 1979; promotes and develops businesses throughout the county of Greater Manchester; provides information on industrial sites and premises; puts together loan and investment packages; stages trade missions and seminars and other activities to market Greater Manchester.

Highlands and Islands Development Board: Bridge House, 20 Bridge St, Inverness, IV1 1QR; tel (463) 234171; telex 75267; fax (463) 244469; Chair: Sir Robert Cowan; Sec: Iain MacAskill; f 1965; Govt devt agency, established to promote the economic and social devt of the Highlands and Islands of Scotland; incentives available for a wide range of devts, including manufacturing, tourism and crafts businesses; plans were unveiled in July 1989 to rename it Highland Enterprise, responsible for 8 local enterprise cos.

Land Authority for Wales: Custom House, Custom House St, Cardiff, CF1 5AP; tel (222) 223444; telex 498024; fax (222) 223330; Chair: G. D. Inkin; Chief Exec: Bernard Ryan; f 1976; acquires land for devt and disposes of it to others to develop; provides land for residential, commercial and industrial purposes.

London Docklands Development Corpn: Unit A, Great Eastern Enterprise, Millharbour, London, E14 9TJ; tel (71) 515-3000; telex 894041; fax (71) 987-7070; Chair: David Hardy; Chief Exec: Michael Honey; f 1981; set up by the Govt to regenerate 8 sq miles of derelict and underused land in East London by encouraging private sector investment in new homes, work-places, leisure and recreation.

Merseyside Development Corpn: Royal Liver Bldg, Pierhead, Liverpool, L31 JH; tel (51) 236-6090; fax (51) 227-3174; Chair: Philip Carter; Chief Exec: Dr John Ritchie; f 1981; regeneration of derelict docklands; supports skill and enterprise training schemes.

North East Scotland Development Authority (NESDA): 8 Albyn Place, Aberdeen, AB1 1YH; tel (224) 643322; fax (224) 631187; f 1969; promotes industrial devt of the Grampian region; advises on business premises and assistance available for local industry.

Scottish Development Agency: 120 Bothwell St, Glasgow, G1 7JP; tel (41) 248-2700; telex 777600; Chair: Dir David Nickson; Chief Exec: I. S. Robertson; promotes economic devt of Scotland and improvement of the environment; advises on industrial premises and enterprise in Scotland; assists in the provision of loan and equity finance to cos; plans were unveiled in July 1989 to merge it with the Training Agency to create Scottish Enterprise, an umbrella organization for 12 local enterprise cos.

Welsh Development Agency: Pearl Assurance House, Greyfriars Rd, Cardiff, CF1 3XX; tel (222) 222666; telex 497513; Chair: Dr M. G. Jones; Chief Exec: D. Waterstone; f 1976; furthers the regeneration of the Welsh economy and the improvement of the environment; provides venture capital for new and expanding businesses; acts as an agent for the European Coal and Steel Community; provides business advice.

Employment

Civil Service Commission: Alencon Link, Basingstoke, Hants, RG21 1JB; tel (256) 29222; First Commr: D. J. Trevelyan; recruitment and selection of civil servants.

Equal Opportunities Commission: Overseas House, Quay St, Manchester, M3 3HN; tel (61) 833-9244; fax (61) 833-9244; Chair: Joanna Foster; Chief Exec: Alan Hart; f 1975; statutory body set up to fight discrimination due to sex or marital status; promotes equality of opportunity between men and women.

The Training Agency: Moorfoot, Sheffield, S1 4PQ; tel (742) 753275; telex 547885; fax (742) 758316; Dir-Gen: Roger Dawe; Dep Dir-Gen and Dir, Policy and Programmes Division: I. Johnston; f 1973 as the Manpower Services Commission; Govt dept providing adult and youth training to combat unemployment; provides help for people setting up small businesses.

Health

Health Education Authority: Hamilton House, Mabledon Place, London, WC1H 9TX; tel (71) 631-0930; fax (71) 387-0550; Chair: Sir Donald Maitland; Chief Exec: Dr Spencer Hagard; f 1987; health education in England and education on AIDS throughout the UK.

Health and Safety Commission: Baynards House, 1 Chepstow Place, Westbourne Grove, London W2 4TF; tel (71) 243-6000; Chair: Dr E. J. Cullen; Sec: A. J. Lord; responsible to appropriate Ministers for the admin of the Health and Safety at Work Act 1974; reviews health and safety legislation and submits proposals for new or revised regulations.

Health and Safety Executive: Broad Lane, Sheffield, S3 7HQ; tel (742) 768141; telex 54556; fax (742) 755792; Dir-Gen: John D. Rimington; f 1974; statutory body under the Dept of Employment; responsible for implementing the provisions of the Health and Safety at Work Act 1974 and reports to the Commission.

National Health Service Management Board: Richmond House, 79 Whitehall, London, SW1A 2NS; Chair: the Sec of State for Health, Kenneth Clarke; Dep Chair: Sir Roy Griffiths; Chief Exec of the National Health Service: Duncan Nichol; Chief Medical Officer: Sir Donald Acheson.

Legal and Judiciary

Court of Appeal: Royal Courts of Justice, Strand, London, WC2A 2LL; tel (71) 936-6000; fax (71) 936-9000 (Criminal Division), (71) 936-6810 (Civil Division); Master of the Rolls: Sir John Francis Donaldson; Pres of the Family Division: Sir John Lewis Arnold; Vice-Chancellor: Sir Nicolas C. H. Browne-Wilkinson; hears appeals in civil cases from County Courts and the High Court of Justice, and in criminal cases from the Crown Courts; the Master of the Rolls is the effective head of the court; the House of Lords is the final court of appeal in civil and criminal cases.

Court of Session: Parliament House, 11 Parliament Sq, Edinburgh, EH1 1RQ; tel (31) 225-2595; Pres: Lord Emslie; supreme civil court in Scotland; comprises an Inner House, which is mainly an appeal court, whence further appeal may be made to the House of Lords, and an Outer House, dealing with the major civil cases and divorce actions; the judges are those of the High Court of Justiciary.

Crown Office: 5-7 Regent Rd, Edinburgh, EH7 5BL; tel (31) 557-3800; public prosecution of crime in Scotland.

Crown Prosecution Service: 4-12 Queen Anne's Gate, London, SW1H 9AZ; tel (71) 273-8030; fax (71) 222-0392; Dir of Public Prosecutions: Allan Green; Dep Dir of Public Prosecutions: David Gandy; f 1986; prosecution of all police-initiated prosecutions in England and Wales.

High Court of Justice: Royal Courts of Justice, Strand, London, WC2A 2LL; tel (71) 936-6000; Pres, Chancery Division: Lord Mackay of Clashfern (Lord High Chancellor); Lord Chief Justice of England and Pres, Queen's Bench Division: Lord Lane; Pres, Family Division: Sir Stephen Brown; certain civil cases are heard in the three divisions—Chancery, dealing with litigation about property, patents, family trusts, cos, dissolution of partnerships and disputed estates, Queen's Bench, hearing cases involving damage to property, personal injuries, etc, and also includes the Commercial and Admiralty Courts, and Family, hearing contested or complex divorce and separation cases and matters relating to children such as adoption, wardship or guardianship of minors.

High Court of Justiciary: Parliament House, 11 Parliament Sq, Edinburgh, EH1 1RQ; tel (31) 225-2595; Lord Justice Gen: Lord Emslie; Lord Justice Clerk: Lord Ross; supreme criminal court in Scotland; appeal may be made to it from the Sheriff Court and from the District courts; the 24 judges are known as Lords Commrs of Justiciary, headed by the Lord Justice Gen.

The Law Commission: Conquest House, 37-38 John St, Theobalds Rd, London, WC1N 2BQ; tel (71) 242-0861; fax (71) 242-1885; Chair: Justice Beldam; Commrs: Trevor M. Aldridge, Richard Buxton, Prof Brenda Hoggett; Sec: Michael Collon; f 1965; promotes the reform of the law.

Law Officers' Department/Attorney-General's Chambers: Royal Courts of Justice, Strand, London WC2A 2LL; tel (71) 936-6602; Attorney-Gen: Sir Patrick Mayhew; Solicitor-Gen: Sir Nicholas Lyell; the Attorney-Gen, also the Attorney-Gen for Northern Ireland, is the chief legal adviser to the Govt, and is assisted by the Solicitor-Gen.

Lord Advocate's Department: Fielden House, 10 Great College St, Westminster, London, SW1P 3SL; tel (71) 276-3000; Lord Advocate: Lord Fraser of Carmyllie; Solicitor-Gen for Scotland: Alan Rodger; the Lord Advocate and the Solicitor-Gen for Scotland are the Law Officers of the Crown for Scotland and the chief legal advisers to the Govt on Scottish questions.

Scottish Law Commission: 140 Causewayside, Edinburgh, EH9 1PR; tel (31) 668-2131; Chair: Lord Davidson; f 1965; systematic devt and reform of the law of Scotland.

Media

BROADCASTING

British Broadcasting Corpn (BBC): Broadcasting House, London, W1A 1AA; tel (71) 580-4468; telex 265781; Chair: Marmaduke Hussey; Dir-Gen: Michael Checkland; Man Dir, Network TV: Paul Fox; Man Dir, World Service: John Tusa; Man Dir, Regional Broadcasting: Ron Neil; Man Dir, Network Radio: David Hatch; f 1922; operates under Royal Charter and a licence from the Home Department; financed by TV licence fees, less Post Office expenses.

BBC External Services: Bush House, Strand, London, WC2B 4PH; tel (71) 240-3456; telex 265781; the World Service (in English) is broadcast for 24 hours daily and directed to all areas of the world; there are special services to: the Far East (in Mandarin, Cantonese, Indonesian, Japanese, Malay, Thai and Vietnamese); the sub-continent (in Bengali, Burmese, Hindi, Nepali, Pashto, Persian, Urdu and Tamil); the Middle East and North Africa (in Arabic and French); Central, East, West and South Africa (in English, French, Hausa, Portuguese, Somali and Swahili); and the Western Hemisphere (in Portuguese for Brazil and Spanish for Latin America); services for listeners in Europe in Bulgarian, Czech and Slovak, Finnish, French, German, Greek, Hungarian,

Polish, Portuguese, Romanian, Russian, Serbo-Croat, Slovene and Turkish.

BBC Television: Television Centre, Wood Lane, London, W12; tel (81) 743-8000; Controller, BBC-1: Jonathan Powell; Controller, BBC-2: Alan Yentob; operates two television services, BBC-1 and BBC-2.

GOVERNMENT PUBLISHER

Her Majesty's Stationery Office (HMSO): St Crispins, Duke St, Norwich, NR3 1PD; tel (603) 622211; telex 97301; fax (603) 695582; f 1786; Executive Agency; purchases gen office supplies and print; publishes on behalf of Parliament and Govt depts.

NEWS AND INFORMATION

Central Office of Information: Hercules Rd, London, SE1 7DU; tel (71) 927-2345; telex 915444; Dir-Gen: Mike Devereau; f 1946; supplies publicity material, services and advice to Govt depts on a repayment basis.

Central Statistical Office: Great George St, London SW1P 3AQ; tel (71) 270-3000; telex 27582; Dir and Head of the Govt Statistical Service: Jack Hibbert; executive agency; co-ordinates the statistics collected by depts and produces statistics needed for central economic and social policies and management; responsible for a number of statistical publs; responsible to the Treasury.

General Register Office for Scotland: New Register House, Edinburgh, EH1 3YT; tel (31) 556-3952; Registrar-Gen: Dr C. M. Glennie; Dep Registrar-Gen: J. M. Randall; f 1855; registration of births, deaths and marriages; provides a facility for record searching; holds the old parochial registers, statutory registers and census records.

Office of Population Censuses and Surveys: Head Office, St Catherines House, 10 Kingsway, London, WC2B 6JP; tel (71) 242-0262; Dir and Registrar-Gen for England and Wales: G. T. Banks; incorporates the Gen Register Office; regulation of civil marriages, the registration of births, marriages and deaths in England and Wales, and control of the registration services; carries out censuses of the population and analyses statistics.

Mining and Energy

AEA Technology: 11 Charles II St, London, SW1Y 4QP; tel (71) 930-5454; telex 22565; Chair: J. G. Collier; Sec: Mark Baker; fmrly United Kingdom Atomic Energy Authority (UKAEA); f 1954 to take responsibility for UK research and devt into the generation of electricity from nuclear energy, reactor systems for installation as part of the UK nuclear power programme, research into safety and environmental aspects of nuclear power, the devt of the fast reactor and its fuel cycle and fusion; most work is now carried out for the Dept of Energy and the electricity supply industry.

The British Coal Corpn: Hobart House, Grosvenor Place, London, SW1X 7AE; tel (71) 235-2020; telex 882161; Chair: Sir Robert Haslam; established 1947 under the Coal Industry Nationalisation Act of 1946; charged with the duties of working and getting the coal in Great Britain to the exclusion of any other person, securing the efficient devt of the coal-mining industry, and making supplies of coal available of such qualities and sizes, in such quantities and at such prices as may seem best calculated to further the public interest in all respects.

British Nuclear Fuels PLC: Risley, Warrington, Cheshire, WA3 6AS; tel (925) 832000; telex 627581; fax (925) 817625; Chair: Christopher Harding; Chief Exec: Neville Chamberlain; f 1971; provision of nuclear fuel cycle services, including reprocessing of irradiated nuclear fuels, manufacture of plutonium and plutonium oxide fuels, uranium ore treatment, fuel element manufacture and hexafluoride production; operation of centrifuge plants producing enriched uranium.

Electricity Council: 30 Millbank, London, W1P 4RD; tel (71) 834-2333; telex 23385; Chair: Sir Philip Jones; Sec: R. Savinson; advises the Sec of State for Energy on all matters affecting the electricity supply industry; promotes maintenance and devt of an efficient, co-ordinated and economical system of electricity supply; after privatization of electricity cos, was to be replaced by the Electricity Association, provisional Pres: John Wilson; provisional Vice-Pres: John Baker.

National Grid (GridCo): Bankside House, Sumner St, London; tel (71) 620-8000; f 1990 as successor to the Central Electricity Generating Board (CEGB); Chair: David Jeffries; the Govt plans to privatize the co within the life of the current Parliament; to be owned collectively by the distribution cos which will succeed the 12 Area Electricity Boards.

National Nuclear Corpn Ltd: Booths Hall, Chelford Rd, Knutsford, Cheshire, WA16 8QZ; tel (565) 3800; telex 666000; Chair: R. J. Davidson; Man Dir: D. Taylor; f 1973 as the supplier and contractor for nuclear stations in the UK, aiming to promote and develop the nuclear power industry.

National Power: Sudbury House, 15 Newgate St, London, EC1A 7AU; tel (71) 634-5111; telex 883141; Chair: Lord Marshall of Goring; Finance Dir: Brian Birkenhead; Commercial Dir: Colin Webster; f 1990 as electricity generating successor to the Central Electricity Generating Board (CEGB); the Govt plans to privatize the co within the life of the current Parliament; an Office of Electricity Regulation (Offer), headed by the Dir-Gen of the Electricity Supplies, Prof Stephen Littlechild, is to oversee terms on which individual power stations feed into the National Grid, the special position of nuclear power stations, etc.

North of Scotland Hydro-Electric Board: 16 Rothesay Terrace, Edinburgh, EH3 7SE; tel (31) 225-1361; telex 72480; Chair: Michael Joughin; Dep Chair and Chief Exec: Kenneth R. Vernon; responsible for electricity supply in North Scotland; in March 1988 the Govt announced the privatization of both Scottish electricity boards as two separated cos within two or three years.

Nuclear Electric: Bedminster Down, Bridgewater Rd, Bristol, BS13 8AN; tel (272) 648111; Chair: John Collier; f 1990 as public successor to the Central Electricity Generating Board (CEGB) responsible for nuclear power installations; was to remain in public ownership after privatization of other electric power cos.

Office of Gas Supply (Ofgas): 2nd Floor, Southside, 105 Victoria St, London, SW1E 6QT; tel (71) 828-0898; telex 928591; fax (71) 630-8164; Dir-Gen: James McKinnon; Dep Dir-Gen: Malcolm Keay; f 1986; monitors the activities of British Gas as a public gas supplier; enforces the price formula governing the maximum average price that British Gas is allowed to charge tariff customers; protects the interests of gas consumers.

Power Generation (PowerGen): 53 New Broad St, London EC2M 1JJ; tel (71) 638-5742; Chair: Robert Malpas; Dir, Finance: John Rennocks; f 1990 from the Central Electricity Generating Board (CEGB); electricity generation; the Govt plans to privatize the co within the life of the current Parliament.

South of Scotland Electricity Board: Cathcart House, Spean St, Glasgow, G44 4BE; tel (41) 637-7177; telex 777703; fax (41) 637-3470; Chair: D. J. Miller; Dep Chair: I. M. H. Preston; Sec: D. A. S. MacLaren; f 1955; generation, transmission and distribution of electricity in south Scotland; in March 1988 the Govt announced the privatization of both Scottish electricity boards as two separated cos within two or three years.

United Kingdom Nirex Ltd: Curie Ave, Harwell, Didcot, Oxon, OX11 0RH; tel (235) 835153; telex 837567; fax (235) 831239; Man Dir: P. T. McInerney; Sec: G. R. Evans; f 1985; devt of a national disposal centre for low and intermediate level radioactive waste.

Research

Agricultural Food and Research Council: Wiltshire Court, Farnsey Streed, Swindon, Wilts, SN1 5AT; tel (793) 514242; fax (793) 514788; Chair: The Earl of Selborne; Dep Chair and Sec: Prof W. D. P. Stewart; Dep Sec: Prof J. P. Hearn; f 1931; operates research institutes; supports research in universities and polytechnics throughout the UK.

Building Research Establishment: Bucknall Lane, Garston, Watford, Herts, WD2 7JR; tel (923) 894040; telex 923220; fax (923) 664010; Dir: R. G. Courtney; f 1921; part of the Dept of the Environment; carries out work on the design, performance and planning of bldgs, fire prevention and mechanical equipment; technical consultancy and an advisory service available.

Economic and Social Research Council: Cherry Orchard East, Kembrey Park, Swindon, Wilts, SN2 6UQ; tel (793) 513838; fax (793) 487916; Chair: Prof Howard Newby; Sec: David Stafford; f 1965; fmrly Social Science Research Council; supports research and training in UK universities, polytechnics and research institutes in the social sciences.

Medical Research Council: 20 Park Cres, London, W1N 4AL; tel (71) 636-5422; Chair: Earl Jellicoe; Sec: Dr D. A. Rees; Second Sec: Dr D. C. Evered; promotes devt of medical and related biological research to advance knowledge that will lead to better health care; has over 55 research establishments; provides grants for individual scientists to undertake research.

Natural Environment Research Council: Polaris House, North Star Ave, Swindon, Wilts, SN2 1EU; tel (793) 411500; telex 444293; fax (793) 411501; Chair: Prof John Knill; f 1965; carries out research in the physical and biological sciences which explain the processes of the natural environment, taking account of man's impact, so that industry and Govt can form sensible management policies; also supports research in universities and polytechnics.

Science and Engineering Research Council: Polaris House, North Star Ave, Swindon, Wilts, SN2 1ET; tel (793) 26222; 160 Great Portland St, London, W1N 6DT; tel (71) 636-8955; Chair: Sir Mark Richmond; Private Sec and Sen Scientific Officer: Dr J. Wand; supports and encourages scientific research and education in tertiary institutions, in its own establishments and in collaboration with international organizations.

Science and Technology

British National Space Centre: Millbank Tower, Millbank, London, SW1P 4QU; tel (71) 217-4290; telex 8811074; fax (71) 821-5387; Dir: A. Pryor; f 1985; Britain's official space agency; directs UK civil space activities and develops future policy.

Meteorological Office: London Rd, Bracknell, Berks, RG12 2SZ; tel (344) 420242; telex 849801; fax (344) 422907; Chief Exec: Dr John T. Houghton; f 1855; management of the state weather service; activities include implementing the objectives of the World Meteorological Organization, research into the atmospheric sciences and provision of meteorological forecast and consultative services.

Ordnance Survey: Romsey Rd, Maybush, Southampton, SO9 4DH; tel (703) 7922763; telex 477843; fax (703) 792404; Dir-Gen: Peter McMaster; f 1791; national mapping agency responsible for the official surveying and mapping of Great Britain; digital mapping, devt of a topographic database, surveying and mapping in the Third World.

Tourism

British Tourist Authority: Thames Tower, Black's Rd, London, W6 9EL; tel (81) 846-9000; telex 21231; fax (81) 563-0302; Chair: Duncan Bluck; Chief Exec: Michael Medlicott; f

1969; responsible for the promotion of tourism to Great Britain from overseas; advises central Govt on tourism matters.

English Tourist Board: Thames Tower, Black's Rd, London, W6 9EL; tel (81) 846-9000; telex 260975; fax (81) 563-0302; Chair: Duncan Bluck; Chief Exec: John East; f 1969; responsible for the devt, improvement and promotion of facilities and amenities for tourism and leisure in England; encourages British people to holiday in England and influences and services the movements of overseas visitors within the country.

Scottish Tourist Board: 23 Ravelston Terrace, Edinburgh, EH4 3EU; tel (31) 332-2433; telex 72272; fax (31) 343-1513; Chief Exec: Tom Band; promotion of Scotland as a holiday destination.

Wales Tourist Board: Brunel House, Cardiff, CF2 1UY; tel (222) 499909; telex 497269; fax (222) 498151; Chief Exec: Paul E. Loveluck; f 1969; promotion of tourism in Wales; administers grants and loans to tourism businesses in Wales.

Transport and Communications

TELECOMMUNICATIONS

Office of Telecommunications (Oftel): Atlantic House, Holborn Viaduct, London, EC1N 2HQ; tel (71) 353-4020; telex 883484; fax (71) 822-1643; Dir-Gen: Sir Bryan Carsberg; f 1984; independent regulatory body set up under the Telecommunications Act 1984; responsible for the monitoring and enforcement of licences; acts to promote the interests of telecommunication users.

The Post Office: 33 Grosvenor Place, London, SW1X 1PX; tel (71) 235-8000; Chair: Sir Bryan Nicholson; Sec: M. MacDonald; f 1969 as a public corpn; established in 1981 as a separate corpn from telecommunications; provides Royal Mail postal and National Girobank services.

TRANSPORT

British Railways Board: Euston House, 24 Eversholt St, London, NW1 1DZ; tel (71) 928-5151; telex 299431; fax (71) 922-6994; Chair: Bob Reid; Vice-Chairs: David Kirby, Derek Fowler; Chief Exec, Railways: J. K. Welsby; Head, Channel Tunnel Division: John Palmer; f 1963; provision of rail services in Great Britain; responsible for policies to meet objectives set by the Sec of State for Transport.

British Rail, Anglia Region: Hamilton House, Appold St, London, EC2 2AT; tel (71) 928-5151; Gen Man: J. C. P. Edmonds.

British Rail, Eastern Region: York, Y01 1HT; tel (904) 653022; telex 299431; Gen Man: John G. Nelson.

British Rail, London Midland Region: Stanier House, Holliday St, Birmingham, B1 1TG; tel (21) 643-4444; telex 299431; Gen Man: Cyril Bleasdale.

British Rail, Southern Region: Waterloo Station, London, SE1 8SE; tel (71) 928-5151; telex 299431; Gen Man: G. C. Pettitt.

British Rail, Western Region: 125 House, 1 Gloucester St, Swindon, Wilts, SN1 1DL; tel (793) 26100; telex 299431; Gen Man: B. D. Scott.

ScotRail: ScotRail House, 58 Port Dundas Rd, Glasgow, G4 0HG; tel (41) 332-9811; telex 299431; Gen Man: J. R. Ellis.

British Waterways Board: Melbury House, Melbury Terrace, London, NW1 6JX; tel (71) 262-6711; telex 263605; fax (71) 402-0168; Chair: D. Ingman; Vice-Chair: Sir Peter Craft Hutchison; Chief Exec: B. C. Dice; Sec and Parliamentary Adviser: T. T. Luckcuck; f 1963 established by the Transport Act 1962; owns or manages 2,000 miles of canals and river navigations; waterways are divides into three categories: Commercial (359 miles), Cruising (1071 miles), and the Remainder (570 miles).

Civil Aviation Authority (CAA): CAA House, 45-59 Kingsway, London, WC2B 6TE; tel (71) 379-7311; telex 883092; Chair: Christopher Tugendhat; Man Dir: Thomas Murphy; f 1972; responsible for economic and safety regulation of civil aviation; provides National Air Traffic Services (jointly with the Ministry of Defence).

Driver and Vehicle Licensing Agency: Longview Rd, Swansea, W. Glam, SA6 7JL; tel (792) 782341; telex 48102; fax (792) 782793; f 1969; fmrly Driver and Vehicle Licensing Directorate; registers and licences drivers and vehicles in Great Britain and collects and enforces vehicle excise duty; provides a wide range of services for the Dept of Transport, other Govt depts and various external organizations; is supported by a network of 53 Vehicle Registration Offices across Great Britain.

London Regional Transport (LRT): 55 Broadway, London, SW1H 0BD; tel (71) 222-5600; telex 893633; fax (71) 222-5719; Chair and Chief Exec and Chair, London Underground: Wilfrid Newton; Dep Chief Exec and Chair, London Buses: John Telford Beasley; Man Dir: London Underground: Denis Tunnicliffe; Man Dir, London Buses: Clive Hodson; Man Dir, Docklands Light Railway: Kenneth J. Fergusson; f 1933 as London Passenger Transport Board, present name since 1984; operates by far the largest urban passenger transport undertaking in the world, through subsidiaries London Buses, London Underground and Docklands Light Railway.

Utilities

Office of Water Services (Ofwat): Floors 13-15, Centre City Tower, 7 Hill St, Birmingham, B5 4UA; tel (21) 6251300; Dir-Gen of Water Services: Ian Byatt; f 1989 under the Water Act; non-ministerial Govt dept; water regulatory authority; monitors the performance of water and sewage cos; ensures customer interests are protected by limiting increases in standard charges and comparing the performance of the different cos to encourage greater efficiency; up to 10 Customer Service Committees are to advise the Dir-Gen on customer issues.

Northern Ireland

Legislature

The Secretary of State for Northern Ireland and the Secretary's ministers are answerable to Parliament at Westminster under a Parliamentary order which is renewable annually. Northern Ireland returns 17 members to the UK Parliament. The Northern Ireland Assembly, elected in 1982, was dissolved in 1986 following a boycott of meetings by some members. The 1985 Anglo-Irish Agreement gave the Republic of Ireland a consultative role in Northern Irish affairs.

MINISTRIES AND GOVERNMENT DEPARTMENTS

NORTHERN IRELAND OFFICE
Whitehall, London, SW1A 2AZ
Tel (71) 210-3000; telex 918889
Stormont Castle, Belfast, BT4 3ST
Tel (232) 63011; telex 74272
Secretary of State: Peter Brooke
Minister of State: John Cope
Under Secretaries of State: Richard Needham, Dr Brian Mawhinney, Peter Bottomley, Lord Skelmersdale

Department of Agriculture for Northern Ireland: Dundonald House, Upper Newtownards Rd, Belfast, BT4 3SB; tel (232) 650111; telex 74578; agent of the Ministry of Agriculture, Fisheries and Food; devt of agricultural, forestry and fishing industries; advisory service for farmers; agricultural research and education; application in Northern Ireland of the agricultural policy of the EEC.

Department of Education for Northern Ireland: Rathgael House, Balloo Rd, Bangor, Co Down, BT19 2PR; tel (247) 270077; devt of education; responsible for teacher training, examinations, arts and libraries, youth services, sport and recreation, community services and facilities, improvement of community relations, etc.

Department of Finance and Personnel: Parliament Bldgs, Stormont, Belfast, BT4 3SW; tel (232) 63210; fax (232) 63716; controls expenditure of Northern Ireland depts.

Policy Planning and Research Unit: Economics Division, Dept of Finance and Personnel, Parliament Bldgs, Stormont, Belfast, BT4 3SW; Head, Economics Division: Dr D. Slattery; Head, Statistics and Social Division: E. Jardine; provision of professional services in economics, statistics and social research to assist Northern Ireland depts in carrying out their responsibilities over the broad range of public policy.

Department of Health and Social Services Northern Ireland: Dundonald House, Upper Newtownards Rd, Belfast, BT4 3SB; tel (232) 650111; health and social services; administers social security schemes.

GOVERNMENT AGENCIES AND ORGANIZATIONS

Advisory and Supervisory Bodies

Northern Ireland Audit Office: Rosepark House, Upper Newtownards Rd, Belfast, BT4 3NS; tel (2318) 4567; Comptroller and Auditor-Gen: L. V. D. Calvert; Sec: J. G. W. McComish; examines the accounts of Govt depts and certain public bodies; reports to the UK Parliament.

Northern Ireland Civil Service: Stormont Castle, Belfast, BT4 3TT; tel (232) 63011; Head: Sir Kenneth Bloomfield; Private Sec: J. Cairns.

Northern Ireland Economic Council: 2 Linenhall St, Belfast, BT2 8BA; tel (232) 232125; Chair: Prof C. M. Campbell; Dir: V. N. Hewitt; f 1977; provides independent advice to Govt on matters of economic policy and the devt of the economy in Northern Ireland in the medium term; 15 mems representing trade union, employer, and independent interests.

Broadcasting

British Broadcasting Corpn (BBC): Broadcasting House, 22-27 Ormeau Ave, Belfast, BT2 8HQ; tel (232) 244400; telex 265781; National Gov for Northern Ireland: Dr James Kincade; Controller BBC, Northern Ireland: Dr Colin Morris; radio and TV broadcasting.

Defence

Police Authority for Northern Ireland: River House, 48 High St, Belfast, BT1 2DR; tel (232) 230111; Sec: C. Radcliffe.

Development and Planning

Department of Economic Development Northern Ireland: Netherleigh, Massey Ave, Belfast, BT4 2JP; tel (232) 63244; responsible for vocational training, employment services, youth and adult employment schemes, industrial relations, promotion of industrial devt and investment through the Industrial Devt Board.

Industrial Development Board for Northern Ireland: IDB House, Chichester St, Belfast; tel (232) 233233; telex 747025; fax (232) 231328; Chief Exec: A. S. Hopkins; f 1982; supports industry and investment through a variety of schemes including capital, employment, rent, interest relief and marketing grants, loans, etc.

LEDU (Northern Ireland Small Business Agency): Ledu House, Upper Galwally, Belfast, BT8 4TB; tel (232) 491031; Chair: M. Hadden; Chief Exec: George Mackey; f 1971 as the Local Enterprise Devt Unit; encourages the formation, growth and survival of small businesses in Northern Ireland.

Legal and Judiciary

Crown Solicitor's Office for Northern Ireland: Royal Courts of Justice, Chichester St, Belfast, BT1 3JY; tel (232) 235111; Crown Solicitor: H. A. Nelson.

Department of the Director of Public Prosecutions for Northern Ireland: Royal Courts of Justice, Chichester St, Belfast, BT1 3NX; tel (232) 235111; Dir of Public Prosecutions: Alasdair M. Fraser; conducts certain criminal proceedings in Northern Ireland on behalf of the Crown.

Supreme Court of Judicature of Northern Ireland: Royal Courts of Justice, Chichester St, Belfast, BT1 3JF; tel (232) 235111; Lord Chief Justice and Pres of the Court of Appeal and High Court: Sir Brian Hutton.

Tourism

Northern Ireland Tourist Board: River House, 48 High St Belfast, BT1 2OS; tel (232) 231221; telex 748087; fax (232) 240960; Chief Exec: R. J. O'Hare; f 1948; tourist promotion and devt in Northern Ireland.

Transport

Northern Ireland Transport Holding Co: Chamber of Commerce House, 22 Great Victoria St, Belfast, BT2 7LX; tel (232) 243456; telex 747538; fax (232) 333845; Chair: Sir Myles Humphreys; Chief Exec: J. M. Irvine; f 1968; monitors subsidiary transport operating cos.

Citybus Ltd: Milewater Rd, Belfast, BT3 9BG; tel (232) 351201; fax (232) 351474; Man Dir: E. Hesketh; Sec: B. Lyle; f 1973; public transport in Belfast; bus and coach hire; city tours.

Northern Ireland Airports Ltd: Belfast International Airport, Belfast, BT29 4AB; tel (8494) 22888; telex 747980; Chief Exec: Jack McConnell; f 1961; subsidiary of Northern Ireland Transport Holding Co.

Northern Ireland Railways Co Ltd: Central Station, East Bridge St, Belfast, BT1 3PB; tel (232) 235282; telex 747623; fax (232) 230630; Chief Exec: R. P. Beattie; Dep Chief Exec: S. G. Shaw; f 1967; subsidiary of Northern Ireland Transport Holding Co; operates rail services for passengers and freight over 357 km (221 miles) of railway track.

Ulsterbus Ltd: Milewater Rd, Belfast, BT3 9BG; tel (232) 351201; fax (232) 351474; Man Dir: E. Hesketh; Sec: B. Lyle; f 1967; local and express bus services throughout Northern Ireland; bus and coach hire; bus parcels service; coach touring holidays.

UNITED KINGDOM CROWN DEPENDENCIES

THE ISLE OF MAN

The Government

ISLE OF MAN GOVERNMENT
Govt Offices, Bucks Rd, Douglas
Tel (624) 26262; fax (624) 26288
Lord of Mann: HM Queen Elizabeth II
Chief Minister: M. R. Walker

TYNWALD—LEGISLATIVE COUNCIL
Douglas
Lieutenant-Governor: Maj-Gen Laurence New
Lord Bishop of Sodor and Man: Rt Rev Noel Debroy Jones
President of the Council: J. A. Nivison
Attorney-General: T. W. Cain
Clerk: T. A. Bawden
Upper House, comprising a President, the Lord Bishop of Sodor and Man, the Attorney-General and seven mems elected by the House of Keys.

TYNWALD—HOUSE OF KEYS
Douglas
Speaker: Sir Charles Kerruish
Secretary: Prof T. S. N. Bates
Lower House, comprising 24 mems, elected by adult suffrage—eight for Douglas, two for Ramsey, one each for Peel and Castletown and 12 for rural districts.

Department of Agriculture, Fisheries and Forestry: Govt Offices, Bucks Rd, Douglas.

Department of Education: Govt Offices, Bucks Rd, Douglas.

Department of Health and Social Security: Markwell House, Market St, Douglas.

Department of Home Affairs: Homefield, 88 Woodbourne Rd, Douglas; tel (624) 23355; fax (624) 21298; Minister: E. G. Lowey; Sec: W. P. Creer; f 1986; dept of the Isle of Man Govt; responsible for police, fire service, civil defence, broadcasting, radio communications, prison and probation services.

Department of Industry: Govt Offices, Bucks Rd, Douglas; tel (624) 26262; telex 6288612; fax (624) 26288; Chief Exec: K. Bawden; promotion of industrial devt, particularly manufacturing, through direct financial support and training measures.

Department of Local Government and the Environment: Govt Offices, Bucks Rd, Douglas.

Government Agencies

BANKING

Isle of Man Bank Ltd: POB 13, 2 Athol St, Douglas; tel (624) 26232; telex 627071; Chair: J. C. Dean; Gen Man: J. C. Allen; bankers to Isle of Man Govt; mem of the National Westminster Group; 16 brs.

BROADCASTING

Department of Home Affairs (Broadcasting Division): Homefield, 88 Woodbourne Rd, Douglas; tel (624) 23355; fax (624) 21298; Chair of Radio Manx Ltd: W. A. Wilcocks; represents the Island's interests in all matters of radio and TV.

FINANCIAL AGENCIES

Isle of Man Government Financial Supervision Commission: POB 58, 1-4 Goldie Terrace, Upper Church St, Douglas; tel (624) 24487; telex 628612; Dir: M. W. Solly.

Isle of Man Treasury: Govt Offices, Bucks Rd, Douglas; tel (624) 26262; telex 628612; fax (624) 26288; Minister: J. D. Q. Cannan; Chief Financial Officer: W. Dawson; Banking Supervisor: Jim Noakes; control of Govt finances; collection of taxes.

  Economic Affairs Division: 14 Hill St, Douglas; tel (624) 26262; telex 628612; fax (624) 26288; Economic Adviser: S. Carse; f 1975; provides economic and statistical advice to Govt and the private sector.

TOURISM

Department of Tourism and Transport: 13 Victoria St, Douglas; tel (624) 74323; telex 627793; Chief Exec: T. P. Toohey; f 1896.

TRADE

Board of Consumer Affairs: 21A Athol St, Douglas.

TRANSPORT

Department of Highways, Ports and Properties: Sea Terminal Bldg, Douglas; tel (624) 23813; telex 629335; fax (624) 27238; Chief Exec: N. R. Cooil; Surveyor-Gen: W. S. Basnett; admin of the Island's roads, harbours and airports.

  Airports Division: Ronaldsway Airport, Ballasalla.

Isle of Man Transport: Strathallan Cres, Douglas; tel (624) 74549; Chief Exec: R. H. Smith.

THE CHANNEL ISLANDS

GUERNSEY

The Government

OFFICE OF THE LIEUTENANT-GOVERNOR AND COMMANDER-IN-CHIEF OF THE BAILIWICK OF GUERNSEY
St Peter Port
Lieutenant-Governor and Commander-in-Chief:
Lt-Gen Sir Alexander Boswell
Secretary to the Lieutenant-Governor and ADC:
Capt D. P. L. Hodgetts
The Lieutenant-Governor and Commander-in-Chief of Guernsey is the personal representative of the sovereign and the channel of communication between the Crown and the Insular Government, and is appointed by the Crown.

ASSEMBLY OF THE STATES
St Peter Port
Bailiff of Guernsey, President of the Assembly of the States and the Royal Court of Guernsey:
Sir Charles Frossard
Deputy Bailiff: G. M. Dorey
HM Procureur (Attorney-General): de Vic G. Carey
HM Comptroller (Solicitor-General): A. C. K. Day
States Supervisor: F. N. Le Cheminant
The insular legislature; government of the island is conducted by Committees appointed by the States; the States consist of 12 Conseillers, 33 People's Deputies, 10 Douzaine Representatives, two Alderney Representatives and the Bailiff who has a casting vote; HM Procureur and HM Comptroller, appointed by the Crown, are entitled to sit in the States and to speak, but not to vote.

Government Agencies

BROADCASTING

BBC Radio Guernsey: Commerce House, St Peter Port; tel (481) 28977; telex 4191456; Man (acting): Reg Brookes; f 1982; broadcasts 42 hours a week.

TOURISM

Guernsey Tourist Board: POB 23, St Peter Port; tel (481) 26611; telex 4191612; Dir of Tourism: M. J. Walden.

JERSEY

The Government

OFFICE OF THE LIEUTENANT-GOVERNOR AND COMMANDER-IN-CHIEF OF JERSEY
St Helier
Lieutenant-Governor and Commander-in-Chief:
Adm Sir William Pillar
Secretary to the Lieutenant-Governor and ADC:
Commdr D. M. L. Baybrooke
The Lieutenant-Governor and Commander-in-Chief of Jersey is the personal representative of the sovereign, and the channel of communication between the Crown and the Insular Government, and is appointed by the Crown.

ASSEMBLY OF THE STATES
St Helier
Bailiff, President of the Assembly of the States and the Royal Court of Jersey: Sir P. J. Crill
Deputy Bailiff: Vernon A. Tomes
Dean of Jersey: Very Rev Basil O'Ferrall
Attorney-General: Philip M. Bailhache
Solicitor-General: Terence Sowden
Greffier of the States: E. J. M. Potter
The insular legislature; government of the island is conducted by Committees appointed by the States; the States consist of 12 Senators, 12 Constables and 29 Deputies elected by universal suffrage; the Lieutenant-Governor, the Dean of Jersey, the Attorney-General and Solicitor-General are entitled to sit and speak in the States, but not to vote.

Government Agencies

BROADCASTING

BBC Radio Jersey: Broadcasting House, Rouge Bouillon, St Helier; tel (534) 70000; Station Man: Mike Warr; f 1982; broadcasts 40-45 hours per week.

BRITISH DEPENDENT TERRITORIES

ANGUILLA

The Government

OFFICE OF THE GOVERNOR
Govt House, The Valley
Tel 2622; telex 9351
Governor: G. O. Whittaker
Appointed by the British sovereign, and holds executive power; responsible for external affairs, defence and internal security; in most other matters the Governor acts on the advice of the Executive Council, led by the Chief Minister.

HOUSE OF ASSEMBLY
The Valley
Clerk: Eualie Bradley
Holds legislative power; comprises 11 mems, two ex-officio, two nominated by the Governor, and seven elected for five years by universal adult suffrage.

OFFICE OF THE CHIEF MINISTER
The Secretariat, The Valley
Tel 2518; telex 9313
Chief Minister and Minister of Home Affairs, Tourism and Economic Development: Emile R. Gumbs

GOVERNMENT OF ANGUILLA
The Secretariat, The Valley
Tel 2518; telex 9313
Minister of Communications, Public Utilities and Works: Kenneth Harrigan
Minister of Finance, Education and Community Development: Osborne Fleming
Minister of Lands, Agriculture, Fisheries and Health: Eric Reid
Attorney-General: Richard Whitehead
Permanent Secretary for Finance: Franklin Connor
Secretary to the Executive Council: Edison Hughes
The Executive Council, headed by the Chief Minister, is responsible to the House of Assembly.

Government Agencies

BANKING

Eastern Caribbean Central Bank (ECCB): POB 89, Basseterre, St Christopher and Nevis; tel 465-2537; telex 6828; Gov: Cecil A. Jacobs; f 1965 as East Caribbean Currency Authority, expanded responsibilities and changed name in 1983; responsible for issue of currency in Anguilla, Antigua and Barbuda, Dominica, Grenada, Montserrat, Saint Christopher and Nevis, Saint Lucia and Saint Vincent and the Grenadines.

BROADCASTING

Radio Anguilla: The Valley; tel 2218; Dir of Information and Broadcasting: Vanier Menes Hodge; Information Officer and News Editor: Alfred Nathaniel Hodge; f 1969; owned and operated by the Govt of Anguilla since 1976; 250,000 listeners throughout the North Eastern Caribbean; broadcasts 14 hours daily.

LEGAL AND JUDICIARY

Eastern Caribbean Supreme Court: POB 1093, Castries, St Lucia; tel 22573; Chief Justice: Sir Lascelles Robotham; f 1967; jurisdiction extends to Anguilla, Antigua and Barbuda, the British Virgin Islands, Dominica, Montserrat, Saint Christopher and Nevis, Saint Lucia and Saint Vincent and the Grenadines; comprises a High Court of Justice and a Court of Appeal; High Court is composed of the Chief Justice and seven Puisne Judges; the Court of Appeal is presided over by the Chief Justice and includes two other Justices of Appeal.

NEWS AND INFORMATION

Government Information Service Bulletin: The Valley; monthly; contains feature articles on Anguilla and items of local news.

Official Gazette: The Valley; monthly; Govt news-sheet.

TOURISM

National Tourist Agency: The Valley; tel 2759; telex 9313.

TRANSPORT

Air Anguilla: POB 110, The Valley; tel 2643; Pres: Restormel Franklin; scheduled services to St Thomas, St Maarten/St Martin, St Christopher and Beef Island (British Virgin Islands).

BERMUDA

The Government

OFFICE OF THE GOVERNOR
Govt House, 11 Langton Hill, Pembroke HM 13
Tel 292-3600; telex 3202
Governor and Commander-in-Chief:
Sir Desmond Langley
Deputy Governor: Brian Canty
Represents the British sovereign, and is responsible for external affairs, defence and internal security.

SENATE
Hamilton
President: Albert S. Jackson
Has 11 nominated mems.

HOUSE OF ASSEMBLY
Hamilton
Speaker: F. John Barritt
Has 40 mems elected for five years by universal adult suffrage; the Governor appoints the majority leader in the House as Premier, and the latter nominates other Ministers; the Cabinet is responsible to the legislature.

OFFICE OF THE PREMIER
Cabinet Bldg, 105 Front St, Hamilton HM 12
Tel 292-5501; telex 3775
Premier: John W. Swan
Deputy Premier: Ann Cartwright DeCouto
Minister without Portfolio: Ralph Marshall
Secretary to the Cabinet: Kenneth Richardson

DEPARTMENT OF TOURISM
Global House, 43 Church St, Hamilton HM 12
Tel 292-0023; telex 3243
Minister: Jim Woolridge
Dir of Tourism: Gary L. Phillips

MINISTRY OF COMMUNITY AND CULTURAL AFFAIRS
Old Fire Station Bldg, 81 Court St, Hamilton HM 12
Tel 292-1681
Minister of Community Affairs: Sid Stallard
Minister of Cultural Affairs: Gerald Simons

MINISTRY OF EDUCATION
POB HM 1185, Hamilton HM EX
Tel 236-6904
Minister: Gerald Simons

MINISTRY OF THE ENVIRONMENT
Govt Admin Bldg, 30 Parliament St, Hamilton HM 12
Tel 295-5151
Minister: Ann Cartwright DeCouto

MINISTRY OF EXTERNAL AND LEGISLATIVE AFFAIRS
Hamilton
Minister: Sir John H. Sharpe

MINISTRY OF FINANCE
Govt Admin Bldg, 30 Parliament St, Hamilton HM 12
Tel 295-5151; telex 3609; fax 292-8152
Minister: David Saul

MINISTRY OF HEALTH, SOCIAL SERVICES AND HOUSING
Old Hospital Bldg, 7 Point Finger Rd, Paget DV 04
Tel 236-0224
Minister: Quinton L. Edness

MINISTRY OF LABOUR AND HOME AFFAIRS
Govt Admin Bldg, 30 Parliament St, Hamilton HM 12
Tel 295-5151; telex 3775
Minister: J. Irving Pearman

MINISTRY OF TELECOMMUNICATIONS
Hamilton
Minister: Charles Collis

MINISTRY OF TRANSPORT
Global House, 43 Church St, Hamilton HM 12
Tel 292-2463; telex 3243
Minister of Transport and Sport: Harry Soares

MINISTRY OF WORKS AND ENGINEERING
POB HM 525, Hamilton HM CX
Tel 295-5151; fax 295-0170
Minister: Clarence Terceira

Government Agencies

BANKING

Bank of Bermuda Ltd: Front St, Hamilton HM 11; tel 295-4000; telex 3212; Chief Gen Man: D. P. Lines; f 1889; 8 domestic brs, 5 overseas brs.

DEVELOPMENT

Bermuda Small Business Development Corpn: POB HM 637, Hamilton HM CX; tel 292-5570; Dir: Thomas R. Wall III; f 1980; funded jointly by the Govt and private banks; guarantees loans to small businesses.

BROADCASTING

Bermuda Broadcasting Co Ltd: POB HM 452, Hamilton HM BX; 6 Fort Hill Rd, Prospect, Devonshire DV 04; tel 295-2828; telex 3702; fax 295-4282; Gen Man: Malcolm R. Fletcher; f 1943; radio and TV commercial broadcasting.

LEGAL AND JUDICIARY

Supreme Court and Court of Appeal: Hamilton; Chief Justice: Sir James R. Astwood; Puisne Judges: Gerald Collett, Vincent Melville; Sen Magistrate: Granville O'Neal Cox; Registrar of Supreme Court and Court of Appeal: Norma Wade; Attorney-Gen: Saul Froomkin; Supreme Court has jurisdiction over all serious criminal matters and has unlimited civil jurisdiction; the Court of Appeal was established in 1964, with powers and jurisdiction of equivalent courts in other parts of the Commonwealth.

NEWS AND INFORMATION

The Bermuda Sun: King St, POB HM 1241, Hamilton HM FX; tel 295-3902; Editor: Keith Blackmore; f 1964; weekly; official Govt gazette.

Department of Information Services: 113 Front St, Hamilton.

TRANSPORT

Department of Civil Aviation: Civil Air Terminal, 2 Kindley Field Rd, St George's GE CX; tel 293-1640; telex 3248; fax 293-2417; Dir of Civil Aviation: James Pitman; f 1949; regulation of

international and domestic aviation activities; participates in the operation of the Bermuda Airport jointly with the United States authorities; responsible to the Minister of Transport.

THE BRITISH VIRGIN ISLANDS

The Government

OFFICE OF THE GOVERNOR
Govt House, Tortola
Tel 494-2345; telex 7984
Governor: John Mark Ambrose Herdman
Appointed by the British monarch and is responsible for external affairs, defence and internal security; the Governor is Chair of the Executive Council, which comprises five other mems.

LEGISLATIVE COUNCIL
Tortola
Speaker: Keith Flax
Comprises 11 mems: a Speaker, one ex-officio mem, and nine mems elected by universal adult suffrage.

OFFICE OF THE CHIEF MINISTER
Tortola
Tel 494-3701
Chief Minister: H. Lavity Stoutt
Deputy Chief Minister: Ralph O'Neal

MINISTRY OF COMMUNICATIONS, WORKS AND PUBLIC UTILITIES
Road Town, Tortola
Tel 494-3701; telex 7959; fax 494-4435
Minister: Oliver Cills

MINISTRY OF FINANCE
Road Town, Tortola
Tel 494-3701
Minister: H. Lavity Stoutt

MINISTRY OF HEALTH, EDUCATION AND WELFARE
Road Town, Tortola
Tel 494-3701
Minister: Louis Walters

MINISTRY OF NATURAL RESOURCES AND LABOUR
Road Town, Tortola
Tel 494-3701
Minister: Ralph O'Neal

OFFICE OF THE ATTORNEY-GENERAL
Tortola
Attorney-General: Karl Sinclair Atterbury

Government Agencies

BANKING

Development Bank of the British Virgin Islands: POB 275, Wickhams Cay 1, Road Town, Tortola; tel 494-3737; devt bank.

BROADCASTING

Virgin Islands Broadcasting Ltd—Radio ZBVI: POB 78, Road Town, Tortola; tel 494-2250; Gen Man: Merrit Nerbert; f 1965; commercial radio broadcasting.

DEVELOPMENT

Development Control Authority: POB 142, Road Town, Tortola; tel 494-3444; telex 7959; fax 494-4435; Chair: James Morris; Sec: Vicotreen Romnay-Varlack; Chief Physical Planning Officer: Louis Potter; f 1969; reviews subdivision, devt and advertisement signs by private individuals or cos; ensures land use.

LEGAL AND JUDICIARY

Eastern Caribbean Supreme Court: POB 1093, Castries, St Lucia; tel 22573; Chief Justice: Sir Lascelles Robotham; f 1967; jurisdiction extends to Anguilla, Antigua and Barbuda, the British Virgin Islands, Dominica, Montserrat, Saint Christopher and Nevis, Saint Lucia and Saint Vincent and the Grenadines; comprises a High Court of Justice and a Court of Appeal; High Court is composed of the Chief Justice and seven Puisne Judges; the Court of Appeal is presided over by the Chief Justice and includes two other Justices of Appeal.

TOURISM

British Virgin Islands Tourist Board: POB 134, Road Town, Tortola; tel 494-3134; telex 7968; Chair: Elihu Rhymer; Dir: (vacant).

TRANSPORT

Air BVI: POB 85, Road Town, Tortola; tel 495-2346; telex 7950; Pres: Elihu Rhymer; Dir: Capt T. C. Branson; f 1971; national airline; internal flights and external services to US Virgin Islands and other destinations in the Eastern Caribbean.

CAYMAN ISLANDS

The Government

OFFICE OF THE GOVERNOR
Govt House, Grand Cayman
Tel 92290; telex 4260
Governor: Alan Scott
Responsible for defence and internal security, external affairs, and the public services; the Governor chairs the Executive Council.

LEGISLATIVE ASSEMBLY
Grand Cayman
Mems are the Financial Secretary, the Attorney-General, the Administrative Secretary and 12 elected mems; the Governor is President of the Assembly.

EXECUTIVE COUNCIL
Grand Cayman
Attorney-General: Richard W. Ground
Administrative Secretary: Lemuel Hurlson
Financial Secretary: Thomas C. Jefferson
Elected Members: Benson O. Ebanks (Education, Recreation and Culture), W. Norman Bodden (Tourism, Aviation and Trade), Ezzard Miller (Health and Social Services), Linford Pierson (Communication, Works and Natural Resources)
The Council comprises the Financial Secretary, the Attorney-General and the Administrative Secretary, and four other mems elected by the Legislative Assembly from their own number.

Government Agencies

BROADCASTING

Radio Cayman: POB 1110, George Town, Grand Cayman; tel 97799; telex 4260; Dir: Loxley E. M. Banks; Dep Dir: Doren Miller; started full-time broadcasting 1976; Govt-run commercial radio station.

FINANCIAL AGENCY

Agricultural and Industrial Development Board (AIDB): POB 1271, Tower Bldg, George Town, Grand Cayman; tel 95277; telex 94260; fax 98487; Chair: Financial Sec, Thomas C. Jefferson; Man: Angela J. Miller; Dep Man: Herman L. Simpson; f 1978; devt finance institution; promotes agricultural, industrial and tourism devt in the Islands by providing medium- to long-term financing to Caymanian enterprises; also provides loans for higher education.

LEGAL AND JUDICIARY

Grand Court: Grand Cayman; Chief Justice: Gerald D. M. Collett; has Supreme Court status; sits six times a year and has jurisdiction in civil matters, bankruptcy, equity, probate and admin, and in felonies and indictable misdemeanours.

NEWS AND INFORMATION

Government Information Services: 3rd Floor, Tower Bldg, George Town, Grand Cayman; tel 98092; telex 4260; fax 98487; Sen Information Officer: Jim Graves; Information Officer: Pat Ebanks; f 1971; main channel of public information about all depts and agencies of the Govt except tourism; issues news releases and liaises with the media.

TOURISM

Cayman Islands Department of Tourism: Tower Bldg, POB 67, George Town, Grand Cayman; tel 97999; Dir: Edward Remington; f 1965.

TRANSPORT

Cayman Airways Ltd: POB 1101, George Town, Grand Cayman; tel 92672; telex 4272; Chair: Arthur Hunter; Man Dir: Florentino Gonzalez; f 1968; operates local services and scheduled flights to Jamaica and the USA.

Port Authority of the Cayman Islands: POB 1358, Harbour Drive, George Town, Grand Cayman; tel 92055; fax 95820; Dir of Ports: Errol L. Bush; Dep Dir, Operations: A. Brent Bush; Dep Dir, Marine: Ned Miller; f 1976; maritime affairs and cargo handling and shipping.

FALKLAND ISLANDS

The Government

OFFICE OF THE GOVERNOR
Govt House, Stanley
Tel 48; telex 2414
Governor: William H. Fullerton
Attorney-General: D. G. Lang
Military Commander: Maj-Gen P. T. Stevenson
The Governor is the personal representative of the British monarch and is advised by an Executive Council.

LEGISLATIVE COUNCIL
Stanley
The Legislative Council is composed of the Governor, eight elected mems and two non-voting ex-officio mems (the Chief Executive and the Financial Secretary of the Falkland Islands Govt).

EXECUTIVE COUNCIL
Falkland Islands Govt, Stanley
Chief Executive of the Falkland Islands Government:
David Taylor
Financial Secretary: J. H. Buckland-James
Government Secretary: C. F. Redston
Consists of six mems: the Governor, three mems elected by the Legislative Council and two ex-officio mems, the Chief Executive and the Financial Secretary of the Falkland Islands Govt, who are non-voting.

Government Agencies

BROADCASTING

Falkland Islands Broadcasting Station: John St, Stanley;

tel 90; Broadcasting Officer: Patrick J. Watts; Sec: Sarah Lurcock; sponsored by local Govt in association with SSVC of London, England; provides local and BBC World Service news programmes, in conjunction with the British Forces Broadcasting Service (BFBS) over a 24-hour period.

DEVELOPMENT

Falkland Islands Development Corpn (FIDC): Old Transmitting Station, Stanley; tel 2211; telex 2428; fax 2606; Gen Man: M. V. Summers; f 1983; promotion of devt in agriculture, industry and services, fisheries and tourism.

LEGAL AND JUDICIARY

Supreme Court: Stanley; Judge: Sir D. Renn-Davies; Sen Magistrate: R. McIlroy; Registrar: S. Halford; presided over by a non-resident Chief Justice; a Court of Appeal, Pres: Sir Alistair Forbes; Registrar: Michael J. Elks, sits in England and appeals therefrom may be heard by the Judicial Committee of the Privy Council.

TOURISM

Falkland Islands Tourism Ltd (FIT): Old Transmitting Station, Stanley; tel 2211; telex 2428; fax 2606; Man Dir: Graham L. Bound; f 1983; tourism bureau.

TRANSPORT

Falkland Islands Government Air Service (FIGAS): c/o Falkland Islands Govt, Stanley; tel 219; telex 2423; Dir of Civil Aviation: G. W. Cheek; f 1948 to maintain services between the settlements and Stanley.

GIBRALTAR

The Government

OFFICE OF THE GOVERNOR AND COMMANDER-IN-CHIEF
The Convent, Gibraltar
Tel 75908; telex 2223
Governor and Commander-in-Chief: Air Chief Marshal Sir Peter Terry
Deputy Governor: W. E. Quantrill
Representative of the British sovereign, responsible for external affairs, defence and internal security; the Governor is also head of the executive and administers Gibraltar, acting generally on the advice of the Gibraltar Council.

GIBRALTAR COUNCIL
Gibraltar
Ex-oficio Members: W. E. Quantrill (Deputy Governor), J. M. Jones (Deputy Fortress Commander), E. Thistlethwaite (Attorney-General), B. Traynor (Financial and Devt Secretary)
The Governor is President of the Council; comprises the ex-oficio mems, the Chief Minister and four other Ministers designated by the Governor after consultation with the Chief Minister; the Council advises the Governor.

HOUSE OF ASSEMBLY
Gibraltar
Speaker: Maj Robert J. Peliza
Comprises a Speaker, 15 elected mems and two ex-officio mems (the Attorney-General and the Financial and Development Secretary); mems serve four-year terms, and elect the Mayor from amongst themselves to carry out ceremonial and representational functions.

OFFICE OF THE CHIEF MINISTER
Gibraltar
Chief Minister with responsibility for Information: Joe Bossano
Deputy Chief Minister: Joe Pilcher

DEPARTMENT OF EDUCATION
40 Town Range, Gibraltar
Tel 75987; telex 2223; fax 76396
Minister of Education, Culture and Youth Affairs: Joseph Moss
Director of Education: J. J. Alcantara

MINISTRY OF HOUSING
Gibraltar
Minister: Joseph Baldachino

MINISTRY OF LABOUR AND SOCIAL SECURITY
Gibraltar
Minister: Robert Mor

MINISTRY OF MEDICAL SERVICES AND SPORT
Gibraltar
Minister: Mary Montegriffo

MINISTRY OF PUBLIC WORKS, ELECTRICITY AND TELECOMMUNICATIONS
Gibraltar
Minister: Juan Carlos Perez

MINISTRY OF TRADE AND INDUSTRY
Gibraltar
Minister: Michael Feetham

Government Agencies

BANKING

Gibraltar Government Savings Bank: Gibraltar Post Office Savings Bank, 104 Main St, Gibraltar; tel 75624; telex 2223; fax 76396; Minister for Govt Services: J. C. Perez; Dir, Postal Services: E. R. Howes; offers facilities for savings and investments; deposits guaranteed by the Govt.

BROADCASTING

Gibraltar Broadcasting Corpn (GBC): Broadcasting House, 18 South Barrack Rd, Gibraltar; tel 79760; telex 2229; fax 78673; Chair: E. C. Ellul; Gen Man: G. J. Valarino; f 1963; public service radio and TV broadcasting; statutory corpn governed by an independent Chair and Board, appointed by the Gov of Gibraltar.

HEALTH

Environmental and Health Department: Casemates, Gibraltar; tel 71648; telex 2223; fax 76396; Chief Environmental

Health Officer: Alexis Almeda; Dep Chief Environmental Health Officer: P. Delgado; responsibility for sanitation and food control, living conditions, building conditions, etc.

Gibraltar Health Authority: Flat 3, St Bernard's Hospital, Gibraltar; tel 76881; telex 2223; fax 76396; Gen Man: Ralph Murray; f 1988; medical services.

LEGAL AND JUDICIARY

Court of Appeal: Gibraltar; Pres: Sir John Farley Spry; Justices of Appeal: John Fieldsend, Sir Geoffrey Briggs, Sir Alan Huggins.

Supreme Court: Gibraltar; Chief Justice: Alister Kneller; Additional Justice: John Alcantara; Registrar: Mario Balban.

TOURISM

Gibraltar Tourism Agency Ltd: Cathedral Sq, Gibraltar; tel 76400; fax 79980; Minister of Tourism: Joe Pilcher (mem of the Council of Ministers); Man: Dr C. Finlayson; Business Man: J. Viale; f 1989; tourism.

TRANSPORT

Public Works Department: Gibraltar; responsible for the maintenance of all public highways.

HONG KONG

The Government

OFFICE OF THE GOVERNOR
Govt House, Upper Albert Rd, Hong Kong
Tel 5-232031; telex 73380
Governor: Sir David Clive Wilson
(assumed office 9 April 1987)
Representative of the British monarch.

LEGISLATIVE COUNCIL
Legislative Council Bldg, 8 Jackson Rd, Central, Hong Kong
Tel 5-8440868; telex 73380; fax 5-8101691
President: Sir David Clive Wilson
F 1843; consists of three ex-officio mems, (the Chief Secretary, the Attorney-General and the Financial Secretary), seven official mems, 22 appointed unofficial mems and 26 elected mems; advises on and approves the enactment of the territory's laws and approves all expenditure from public funds.

EXECUTIVE COUNCIL
Central Govt Offices, Lower Albert Rd, Hong Kong
Tel 5-8102717; telex 73380
President: Sir David Clive Wilson
Chief Secretary: Sir David Ford
Commander, British Forces: Maj-Gen Garry Johnson
Financial Secretary: Piers Jacobs
Attorney-General: Jeremy Mathews
Nominated Official Member: Donald Liao (Secretary of District Admin)
In addition to four ex-officio mems (the Chief Secretary, Commander of British Forces, Financial Secretary and Attorney-General), there are 10 appointed mems, including one official mem; the Council is consulted by the Governor on all important administrative questions.

Government Agencies

ADVISORY AND SUPERVISORY BODIES

Audit Department: 13th Floor, West Wing, Central Govt Offices, 11 Ice House, St, Central, Hong Kong; tel 5-8102739; telex 60770; fax 5-8684193; Dir of Audit: R. J. Hutt; f 1844; provides Legislative Council with an overall assurance that the Govt's financial and accounting transactions are accurate and conform with accepted accounting standards; sees that public funds are prudently managed.

Hong Kong Productivity Council: 12th Floor, World Commerce Centre, 11 Canton Rd, Tsimshatsui, Kowloon; tel 3-7351656; telex 32842; fax 3-7357229; Chair of Council and Exec Cttee: James Tien; Exec Dir: A. K. Chan; Dep Exec Dir: Dr D.

F. Taylor; f 1967; promotes increased industrial productivity and encourages optimum utilization of resources; 21-mem council appointed by the Gov of Hong Kong, representing management, labour, academic and professional interests, and Govt depts associated with productivity matters.

Inland Revenue Department: 26th Floor, Windsor House, 311 Gloucester Rd, Causeway Bay, Hong Kong.

Public Records Office: Mezzanine Floor, 2 Murray Rd, Murray Rd Multi-Storey Car Park Bldg, Central, Hong Kong; tel 5-260031; Archivist: Dr Thomas Lau; f 1972; management of public records; provides services for public and official research.

Urban Council of Hong Kong: 3 Edinburgh Place, Central, Hong Kong; tel 5-244891; telex 60645; fax 5-8452697; Chair: H. M. G. Forsgate; Sec: Roy Spencer; f 1883; environmental hygiene; public health; culture and cultural activities; recreational activities; control of markets and street traders.

AGRICULTURE

Agriculture and Fisheries Department: Canton Rd Govt Offices, 393 Canton Rd, Kowloon; tel 3-7332211; fax 3-3113731; Dir and Registrar of Co-operatives: L. H. Y. Lee; responsible for the registration, audit of accounts and general supervision of co-operative socs, research and devt of the agriculture and fishing industries, control of wholesale marketing of primary produce, protection of endangered species, management of country parks.

BANKING

Office of the Commissioner of Banking: 9th Floor, Queensway Govt Offices, 66 Queensway, Hong Kong; tel 5-8622671; telex 64282; Commr: A. W. Nicolle; Dep Commr: C. W. Lau; f 1964; supervises banks and deposit-taking cos in Hong Kong as well as their overseas brs and representative offices.

Overseas Trust Bank: OTB Bldg, 160 Gloucester Rd, Hong Kong; tel 5-756657; telex 74545; fax 5-727535; Chair: D. A. C. Nendick; Dep Chair and Man Dir: D. F. L. Turner; f 1955; wholly owned by the Hong Kong Govt.

BROADCASTING

British Forces Broadcasting Service: BFPO 1, Hong Kong; tel 0-986083; telex 34513; Gen Man: Bryan Hamilton; Nepali Network Editor: Kishorkumar Gurung; English Programme Dir: Jon Shilling; f 1971; broadcasts in English and Nepali.

Hong Kong Television Broadcasts Ltd: 77 Broadcast Drive,

Kowloon; tel 3-360111; telex 43596; Gen Man: Robert H. C. Chan; f 1967; operates Chinese and English language services.

Radio Television Hong Kong: POB 70200, Broadcasting House, 30 Broadcast Drive, Kowloon; tel 3-370211; telex 45568; fax 3-380279; Dir: Man-yee Cheung; f 1929; provides radio and TV programmes; also acts as a production house for the Education Department in producing school TV programmes.

DEFENCE

Royal Hong Kong Police Force: Arsenal St, Wan Chai, Hong Kong.

DEVELOPMENT

Industry Department: 14th Floor, Ocean Centre, 5 Canton Rd, Kowloon; tel 3-7222573; telex 50151; fax 3-7304633; Dir: T. H. Barma; provides infrastructural and developmental support for industries and promotes inward investment.

EDUCATION

University and Polytechnic Grants Committee: Suite 202, Hutchison House, 10 Harcourt Rd, Hong Kong; tel 5-243987; fax 5-8451596; Chair: Andrew Li; Sec: L. F. Spark; f 1962; advises the Govt on the provision and devt of tertiary education in Hong Kong; provides funding.

FINANCIAL AGENCIES

J. E. Joseph Trust Fund: c/o Director of Agriculture and Fisheries, 12th-14th Floors, Canton Rd Govt Offices, 393 Canton Rd, Kowloon; tel 3-7332211; grants credit facilities to farmers.

Kadoorie Agricultural Aid Association: Lam Kam Rd, Lam Tsuen Valley, Tai Po, New Territories; tel 0-4881317; Dirs: Lord Kadoorie, Horace Kadoorie; Man: Y. H. Chung; f 1951; assists farmers in capital construction by technical direction and by donations of livestock, trees, plants, seeds, fertilizers, cement, road and building materials, farming equipment, etc.

> **Kadoorie Agricultural Aid Loan Fund:** address as above; f 1954; in conjunction with the Hong Kong Govt, provides low-interest loans to assist farmers in the devt of projects.

Securities and Futures Commission (SFC): Hong Kong; Chair: Robert Owen; f 1989; encourages self regulation; has the right to issue directives to stock and futures exchanges, and the power to intervene in the affairs of securities dealers.

The Treasury: 8th Floor, West Wing, Central Govt Offices, 11 Ice House St, Hong Kong; tel 5-8102263; telex 60770; fax 5-8684193; Dir of Accounting Services: C. F. M. O'Kelly; Dep Dir: Sze-hung Chiu; f 1937; management of the Govt's accounting and financial operations and of various statutory funds; collection of Govt revenue; acts as the Govt's paymaster-gen.

INSURANCE

Hong Kong Export Credit Insurance Corpn: 2nd Floor, South Seas Centre, Tower I, 75 Mody Rd, Tsim Sha Tsui East, Kowloon.

LEGAL AND JUDICIARY

Supreme Court: Hong Kong; Chief Justice: Sir Ti-Liang Yang; consists of a Court of Appeal and a High Court.

MARKETING

Fish Marketing Organization: Hong Kong; f 1945; statutory organization controlling wholesale fish marketing.

Vegetable Marketing Organization: Hong Kong; f 1946; Govt agency for collection, transport and sale of vegetables; loan fund to farmers.

NEWS AND INFORMATION

Information Services Department: Beaconsfield House, 1 Queen's Rd, Central, Hong Kong; tel 5-8428777; telex 61190; fax 5-8459078; Dir: Irene Yau; Dep Dir: Anthony Woo; Asst Dir, Publicity: Peter Moss; Asst Dir, News: Chris Wong; Asst Dir, Public Relations: Harold Yau; f 1959; dissemination of information on the Hong Kong admin; issues press releases, arranges press conferences, promotes and distributes all Govt publications, etc.

TOURISM

Hong Kong Tourist Association: 35th Floor, Jardine House, 1 Connaught Place, Central, Hong Kong; tel 5-244191; telex 74720; fax 5-8104877; Chair: Martin G. Barrow; Exec Dir: Eugene C. Sullivan; f 1957; promotes and develops tourism to Hong Kong; co-ordinates the activities of the travel trade; advises the Govt on matters relating to the tourism industry.

TRADE

Consumer Council: 3rd Floor, Asian House, 1 Hennessy Rd, Wan Chai, Hong Kong.

Customs and Excise Department: 14th Floor, Hong Kong Trade Centre, 161-167 Des Voeux Rd, Central, Hong Kong.

Trade Department: 14th Floor, Ocean Centre, 5 Canton Rd, Kowloon; tel 3-7372333; telex 45126; fax 3-7356135; Chair: C. C. Michael; Dir: H. C. C. Sze; f 1982; overseas commercial relations; issues certificates of origin, import and export licences, etc.

Trade Development Council: 31st Floor, Great Eagle Centre, 23 Harbour Rd, Wan Chai, Hong Kong; tel 5-8334333; telex 73595; fax 5-730249; Chair: Dame Lydia Dunn; Exec Dir: Jack So; f 1966; promotion of Hong Kong's trade overseas; has 28 offices around the world.

TRANSPORT

Civil Aviation Department: 46th Floor, Queensway Govt Offices, 66 Queensway, Hong Kong; tel 5-8674332; telex 61361; fax 5-8690093; Dir of Civil Aviation: P. K. N. Lok; Airport Gen Man: R. A. Siegel; Air Traffic Gen Man: M. P. K. Pang; f 1947; responsible for all aspects of civil aviation, including air traffic control, aviation safety, technical and planning matters, air services and airport management.

Highways Department: 10th Floor, Empire Centre, 68 Mody Rd, Tsim Sha Tsui, Kowloon; tel 3-682734; fax 3-3113648; Technical Sec: F. K. C. Lee; f 1986; planning, design, construction and maintenance of the public road system; co-ordination of major highway projects.

Kowloon-Canton Railway Corpn: KCR House, Sha Tin, New Territories; tel 0-6069333; telex 51666; fax 0-6951168; Man Dir: Peter V. Quick; Heavy Rail Dir: Ian McPherson; Light Rail Dir: Jonathan Yu; f 1983; 100% owned by the Hong Kong Govt; operation of an electrified railway linking the territory in the north-east to the border with China; also operation of a light rail transit system in the north-west.

Land Transport Agency: 25th Floor, Wan Chai Tower I, 12 Harbour Rd, Hong Kong; tel 5-8235281; Controller: P. B. Walker; f 1979; transport management.

Marine Department: Harbour Bldg, 38 Pier Rd, Central, Hong Kong; tel 5-8523001; telex 64553; fax 5-449241; Dir of Marine: D. A. Hall; Dep Dir: I. R. Strachan; port admin; ship surveying and registration; recruiting and certification of seamen; maritime search and rescue; provision of port facilities and aids to navigation; maintenance of the Govt fleet, etc.

Mass Transit Railway Corpn: MTRC Headquarters, 33 Wai Yip St, Kowloon Bay, Kowloon; tel 3-7512111; telex 56257; fax 3-7988822; Chair and Chief Exec: H. T. Mathers; f 1975; underground railway system.

Transport Department: 28th Floor, Queensway Govt Offices, 66 Queensway; tel 5-8623194; Transport Commr: Gordon Kwing Chue Siu.

WELFARE

Hong Kong Housing Authority: 101 Princess Margaret Rd, Kowloon; tel 3-7602119; telex 31861; Chair: Sir David Akers-Jones; Chief Exec and Dir of Housing: Fred Y. L. Pang; f 1973; plans, builds and manages public housing.

MONTSERRAT

The Government

OFFICE OF THE GOVERNOR
Govt House, Peebles St, Plymouth
Tel 2409; telex 5727
Governor: Christopher J. Turner
Attorney-General: Odel Adams
Financial Secretary: John E. Ryan
The Governor represents the British sovereign and retains responsibility for defence, external affairs and internal security.

LEGISLATIVE COUNCIL
Plymouth
Speaker: Dr Howard A. Fergus
Comprises a Speaker chosen outside the Council, seven elected, two official and two nominated mems.

OFFICE OF THE CHIEF MINISTER
Govt Headquarters, Church Rd, Plymouth
Tel 2444; telex 5727; fax 2367
Chief Minister: John A. Osborne
Deputy Chief Minister: J. Benjamin Chalmers

MINISTRY OF AGRICULTURE, TRADE, LANDS AND HOUSING
POB 272, The Groves, Plymouth
Tel 2075; telex 5720
Minister: Nowell Tuitt

MINISTRY OF COMMUNICATIONS AND WORKS
General Turning Rd, Plymouth
Tel 2521
Minister: J. Benjamin Chalmers

MINISTRY OF EDUCATION, HEALTH AND COMMUNITY SERVICES
Plymouth
Tel 3321
Minister: Vernon Jeffers

MINISTRY OF FINANCE AND ECONOMIC DEVELOPMENT
Govt Headquarters, Church Rd, Plymouth
Tel 2444; telex 5727; fax 2367
Minister: John A. Osborne

Government Agencies

AGRICULTURE

Office of the Director of Agriculture: Plymouth; Dir of Agriculture: Franklyn Michaels

ADVISORY AND SUPERVISORY BODIES

Audit Office: Plymouth; Dir of Audit: Lorenzo Cassell.

Office of the Accountant-Gen: Plymouth; Accountant-General: Betty Browne.

Office of the Chief Surveyor/Registrar of Lands: Plymouth; Chief Surveyor/Registrar of Lands: B. Burke

Office of the Comptroller of Inland Revenue: Plymouth; Comptroller: L. Dyett.

ART AND CULTURE

Office of the Principal Librarian: Plymouth; Principal Librarian: J. Grell.

BANKING

Eastern Caribbean Central Bank (ECCB): POB 89, Basseterre, St Christopher and Nevis; tel 465-2537; telex 6828; Gov: Cecil A. Jacobs; f 1965 as East Caribbean Currency Authority, expanded responsibilities and changed name in 1983; responsible for issue of currency in Anguilla, Antigua and Barbuda, Dominica, Grenada, Montserrat, Saint Christopher and Nevis, Saint Lucia and Saint Vincent and the Grenadines.

Government Savings Bank: Plymouth; 675 depositors (1984).

BROADCASTING

Radio Montserrat—ZJB: POB 51, Plymouth; tel 2451; Station Man: Michael Jarvis; f 1952; Govt station.

DEFENCE

Police: Plymouth; Commr: Thomas Richard; Dep Commr: Sydney Charles.

DEVELOPMENT

Office of the Principal Community Devt Officer: Plymouth; Principal Community Devt Officer: M. Bass

HEALTH AND WELFARE

Office of the Chief Medical Officer: Plymouth; Chief Medical Officer: L. Lewis

LEGAL AND JUDICIARY

Eastern Caribbean Supreme Court: POB 1093, Castries, St Lucia; tel 22573; Chief Justice: Sir Lascelles Robotham; f 1967; jurisdiction extends to Anguilla, Antigua and Barbuda, the British Virgin Islands, Dominica, Montserrat, Saint Christopher and Nevis, Saint Lucia and Saint Vincent and the Grenadines; comprises a High Court of Justice and a Court of Appeal; High Court is composed of the Chief Justice and seven Puisne Judges; the Court of Appeal is presided over by the Chief Justice and includes two other Justices of Appeal.

TOURISM

Department of Tourism: POB 7, Plymouth; tel 2230; telex 5720; fax 2367; f 1984; clearing house for consumer mail enquiries; promotion of and upkeep of tourist attractions.

TRADE

Office of the Comptroller of Customs: Plymouth; Comptroller: R. A. Jemmotte.

TRANSPORT

Office of the Airport Manager: Plymouth; Airport Man: John O'Garro

UTILITIES

Office of the Director of Public Works: Plymouth; Dir of Public Works: Ken Sparkes

PITCAIRN ISLANDS

The Government

ISLAND COUNCIL
Pitcairn Islands
Island Magistrate: Brian Young
Island Secretary (ex-officio): Olive Christian
Chair of the Internal Committee: Jay Warren
The British High Commissioner in New Zealand acts as Governor; the Island Council is presided over by the island magistrate (who is elected triennially) and comprises one ex-officio mem (the island secretary), four elected and five nominated mems.

Government Agency

NEWS AND INFORMATION

Pitcairn Miscellany: Pitcairn Islands; f 1959; monthly four-page mimeographed news sheet edited by the Education Officer.

ST HELENA AND DEPENDENCIES

ASCENSION

The Government

OFFICE OF THE ADMINISTRATOR
The Residency, Ascension
Tel 6311; telex 214
Administrator: J. J. Beale
Representative of the Govt of St Helena.

ST HELENA

The Government

OFFICE OF THE GOVERNOR
Plantation House, Jamestown
Telex 202
Governor: Robert Frederick Stimson

LEGISLATIVE COUNCIL
Jamestown
Comprises the Governor, two ex-officio mems (the Government Secretary and the Treasurer) and 12 elected mems.

EXECUTIVE COUNCIL
Jamestown
Chief Secretary: (vacant)
Financial Secretary: M. Rosling
Government Secretary: A. A. Green
Chair, Agriculture and Natural Resources Committee: T. S. George
Chair, Education Committee: E. W. Benjamin
Chair, Finance Committee: P. C. Knights
Chair, Public Works and Services Committee: H. B. Legg
Chair, Public Health Committee: I. D. Hudson
Chair, Social Welfare Committee: R. Pridham
Consists of the Government Secretary and the Treasurer as ex-officio mems and the Chairs of the Council Committees (all of whom must be mems of the Legislative Council); the Governor presides at meetings of the Executive Council.

Government Agencies

BANKING

Government Savings Bank: Jamestown; tel 291; telex 202.

BROADCASTING

Government Broadcasting Service: Radio St Helena, Broadway House, Main St, Jamestown; tel 669; telex 202; Information Officer: John Cranfield; Station Man: Anthony D. Leo; f 1967; broadcasts 30 hours weekly.

LEGAL AND JUDICIARY

Supreme Court: Jamestown; Chief Justice: Sir John Farley Spry (non-resident); Attorney-Gen: (vacant); Sheriff: B. Dillon; Sen Magistrate: J. R. H. Beadon; there are four Courts: the Supreme Court; the Magistrate's Court, the Small Debts Court and the Juvenile Court; provision exists for a St Helena Court of Appeal which can sit in Jamestown or London.

NEWS AND INFORMATION

St Helena News: Broadway House, Jamestown; tel 612; telex 202; Editor: John Cranfield; f 1986; Govt-sponsored weekly.

TRISTAN DA CUNHA

The Government

OFFICE OF THE ADMINISTRATOR
The Residency, Tristan da Cunha
Administrator: Bernard E. Pauncefort
Chief Islander: Anne Green
Represents the British Govt and is aided by a Council of eight elected and three appointed mems, including at least one woman, which has advisory powers in legislative and executive functions; small committees of the Council deal with the separate branches of administration.

TURKS AND CAICOS ISLANDS

The Government

OFFICE OF THE GOVERNOR
Waterloo, Govt House, Grand Turk
Tel 2309; telex 8212
Governor: Michael J. Bradley
Appointed representative of the British sovereign, who also holds responsibility for external affairs, internal security, defence, the appointment of any person to any public office and the suspension and termination of appointment of any public officer.

LEGISLATIVE COUNCIL
Grand Turk
Speaker: L. Coalbrooke
Consists of a Speaker, the three ex-officio mems of the Executive Council, 13 mems elected by residents aged 18 and over, and three nominated mems.

EXECUTIVE COUNCIL
Chief Secretary's Office, Grand Turk
Tel 2702; fax 2886
Chief Secretary: M. Cox
Attorney-General: Ian Lamb
Financial Secretary: Austin Robinson
Chief Minister and Minister of Tourism and Home Affairs: Oswald O. Skippings
Minister of Development and Commerce: Derek Taylor
Minister of Natural Resources: Llewellyn Handfield
Minister of Social Services: Wendal Swann
Minister of Works: Samuel Harvey
Comprises three ex-officio mems (the Financial Secretary, the Chief Secretary and the Attorney-General, a Chief Minister (appointed by the Governor), and four other ministers appointed by the Governor on the advice of the Chief Minister; the Executive Council is presided over by the Governor.

Government Agencies

BROADCASTING

Radio Turks and Caicos (RTC): POB 69, Grand Turk; tel 2041; telex 8212; Man (acting): Richard Williams.

DEVELOPMENT

Development Board of the Turks and Caicos Islands: POB 105, Hibiscus Sq, Pond St, Grand Turk; tel 2058; f 1974; promotion and direction of agricultural, industrial, tourism, housing and student devt.

LEGAL AND JUDICIARY

Supreme Court: Grand Turk; Chief Justice: Sir Frederic Gladstone Smith (resident in Barbados); Magistrate: M. Jackson; the Magistrate acts a Judge of the Supreme Court during the absence from the island of the non-resident Judge.

TOURISM

Turks and Caicos Tourist Board: Govt Headquarters, Grand Turk; tel 2321; telex 8227; fax 2777; Chair: Leon Wilson; Chief Tourism Officer: N. Outten; f 1970; promotion of tourism.

THE UNITED STATES OF AMERICA

Head of State

The President is Head of the State and of the executive, and is elected to serve a four-year term by a college of representatives elected directly from each state. The President appoints the other members of the executive, subject to the consent of the Senate.

President: George Herbert Walker Bush (took office 20 January 1989).

Executive Office Of The President: The White House, 1600 Pennsylvania Ave, NW, Washington, DC 20500; tel (202) 456-1414; telex 440074.

Vice-President: James Danforth Quayle.

Office of the Vice-President: 1600 Pennsylvania Ave, NW, Washington, DC 20500; tel (202) 456-2326; telex 440402; Chief of Staff: Robert M. Guttman.

Legislature

The bicameral Congress holds legislative power and comprises the Senate (100 members, two elected directly in each state for a six-year term, one-third of the membership being renewable every two years) and the House of Representatives (435 members elected by direct universal suffrage for two years). Each of the 50 constituent states and the District of Columbia exercises a measure of internal self-government.

Senate: Capitol Bldg, Washington, DC 20510; tel (202) 224-3121; Pres: Vice-Pres, James Danforth Quayle; Pres Pro Tempore: Robert C. Byrd.

House of Representatives: Capitol Bldg, Washington, DC 20515; tel (202) 225-8040; Speaker: Thomas S. Foley.

MINISTRIES AND GOVERNMENT DEPARTMENTS

COUNCIL OF ECONOMIC ADVISERS
Old Executive Office Bldg, Washington, DC 20500
Tel (202) 395-5042
Chair (with Cabinet rank): Michael Jay Boskin

DEPARTMENT OF AGRICULTURE
14th St and Independence Ave, SW, Washington, DC 20250
Tel (202) 655-4000
Secretary: Dr Clayton Keith Yeutter

DEPARTMENT OF COMMERCE
14th St between Constitution Ave and E St, NW, Washington, DC 20230
Tel (202) 377-2000
Secretary: Robert Adam Mosbacher

DEPARTMENT OF DEFENSE
The Pentagon, Washington, DC 10301
Tel (202) 697-5737
Secretary: Richard Bruce Cheney

DEPARTMENT OF EDUCATION
400 Maryland Ave, SW, Washington, DC 20202
Tel (202) 245-3192
Secretary: Lauro Fred Cavazos

DEPARTMENT OF ENERGY
James Forrestal Bldg, 1000 Independence Ave, SW, Washington, DC 20585
Tel (202) 586-5000; fax (202) 586-8134
Secretary: James David Watkins

DEPARTMENT OF HEALTH AND HUMAN SERVICES
200 Independence Ave, SW, Washington, DC 20201
Tel (202) 245-7000
Secretary: Dr Louis Wade Sullivan

DEPARTMENT OF HOUSING AND URBAN DEVELOPMENT
451 Seventh St, SW, Washington, DC 20410
Tel (202) 755-5111
Secretary: Jack F. Kemp

DEPARTMENT OF THE INTERIOR
C St between 18th and 19th Sts, NW, Washington, DC 20240
Tel (202) 343-7351
Secretary: Manuel Lujan, Jr

DEPARTMENT OF JUSTICE
Office of the Attorney-General, 10th St and Constitution Ave, NW, Washington, DC 20530
Tel (202) 633-2007
Attorney-General: Richard Lewis Thornburgh

DEPARTMENT OF LABOR
200 Constitution Ave, NW, Washington, DC 20210
Tel (202) 523-666; fax (202) 523-6354
Secretary: Elizabeth Hanford Dole

DEPARTMENT OF STATE
2210 C St, NW, Washington, DC 20520
Tel (202) 647-4000
Secretary: James Addison Baker, III

DEPARTMENT OF TRANSPORTATION
400 Seventh St, SW, Wahington, DC 20590
Tel (202) 426-4000
Secretary: Samuel K. Skinner

DEPARTMENT OF THE TREASURY
15th St and Pennsylvania Ave, NW, Washington, DC 20220
Tel (202) 566-2041
Secretary: Nicholas Frederick Brady

DEPARTMENT OF VETERAN AFFAIRS
810 Vermont Ave, NW, Washington, DC 20420
Tel (202) 389-3775
Secretary: Edward Joseph Derwinski

OFFICE OF MANAGEMENT AND BUDGET
Old Executive Office Bldg, Washington, DC 20500
Tel (202) 395-4840
Director (with Cabinet rank): Richard Gordon Darman

OFFICE OF THE UNITED STATES TRADE REPRESENTATIVE
600 17th St, NW, Washington, DC 20506
Tel (202) 395-3204
Trade Representative (with Cabinet rank):
Carla Anderson Hills

GOVERNMENT AGENCIES AND ORGANIZATIONS

Advisory and Supervisory Bodies

Administrative Conference of the United States: 2120 L St, NW, Washington, DC 20037; tel (202) 254-7020; Chair: Marshall J. Breger; f 1964.

Bureau of Alcohol, Tobacco and Firearms: 1200 Pennsylvania Ave, NW, Washington, DC 20226; tel (202) 566-7511; Dir: Stephen E. Higgins; under the Dept of the Treasury.

Bureau of Economic Analysis (BEA): US Dept of Commerce, 14th St between Constitution Ave and E St, NW, Washington, DC 20230; tel (202) 523-0777; Dir: Allan H. Young; Dep Dir: Carol S. Carson; f 1953; measures and analyses the economy of the US at national, regional, state and local levels; products include national income and product accounts, gross national product estimates, personal income estimates, international transactions accounts, etc.

Bureau of Engraving and Printing: 14th and C Sts, SW, Washington, DC 20223; tel (202) 447-1364; Dir: Peter H. Daly; under the Dept of the Treasury.

Federal Election Commission: 999 E St, NW, Washington, DC 20463; tel (202) 376-5140; Chair: D. McDonald; f 1971.

Federal Emergency Management Agency: 500 C St, SW, Washington, DC 20472; tel (202) 646-4600; Dir: Calvin G. Franklin; f 1979.

Federal Mediation and Conciliation Service: 2100 K St, NW, Washington, DC 20427; tel (202) 653-5290; Dir (acting): Robert P. Baker; f 1947; assists labour and management settle disputes through mediation.

Food and Drug Administration: 5600 Fishers Lane, Rockville, MD 20857; Commr: Frank Young; protection of the nation's health against impure and unsafe foods, drugs, cosmetics and other potential hazards; in charge of the Bureau of Biologics, Bureau of Drugs, Bureau of Foods, Bureau of Radiological Health, Bureau of Veterinary Medicine, Bureau of Medical Devices, and the National Center for Toxicological Research.

General Accounting Office: 441 G St, NW, Washington, DC 20548; tel (202) 275-5481; Comptroller-Gen of the USA: Charles A. Bowsher; f 1921.

General Services Administration: 18th and F Sts, NW, Washington, DC 20405; tel (202) 535-0800; Admin: Richard Astin; f 1949; provides Govt with an economical and efficient system for the management of its property and records, eg the construction and operation of bldgs, procurement and distribution of supplies, transportation and communications management, management of the automatic data processing resources programme, etc.

Immigration and Naturalization Service: 425 Eye St, NW, Washington, DC 20536; tel (202) 633-1900; Commr: Alan C. Nelson; under the Dept of Justice.

Intelligence Oversight Board: Old Executive Office Bldg, Washington, DC 20500; tel (202) 456-2530; Chair: W. Glenn Campbell; under the Executive Office of the Pres.

Office of Administration: Executive Office Bldg, Washington, DC 20500; tel (202) 395-4980; Dir: Gordon Riggle; under the Executive Office of the Pres; provides information, personnel, financial management, library services, etc, to units within the Executive Office of the Pres.

Office of Federal Procurement Policy: Executive Office Bldg, Washington, DC 20503; tel (202) 395-5802; under the Executive Office of the Pres; direction of procurement policies, regulations, procedures and forms.

Office of Policy Development: Old Executive Office Bldg, Washington, DC 20500; tel (202) 456-6515; Dep Asst to the Pres for Policy Devt: Franmarie Kennedy-Keel; under the Executive Office of the Pres.

National Mediation Board: 1425 K St, NW, Washington, DC 20572; tel (202) 523-5920; Chair: Walter C. Wallace; f 1934; provides railways and airline industries with specific mechanisms for the settlement of labour-management disputes.

Office of Personnel Management: 1900 E St, NW, Washington, DC 20415; tel (202) 632-6106; telex 4931447; Dir: Constance Newman; f 1978.

Peace Corps: 1990 K St, NW, Washington, DC 20024; tel (202) 254-5010; fax (202) 254-4010; Dir: Paul D. Coverdell; Dep Dir: Barbara Zartman; f 1961; promotes world peace and friendship; volunteers work and live in 68 countries around the world.

Regulatory Information Service Center: Executive Office Bldg, Washington, DC 20503; tel (202) 395-6693; Exec Dir: Mark G. Schoenberg; under the Executive Office of the Pres.

Small Business Administration: 1441 L St, NW, Washington, DC 20435; tel (202) 653-6565; Admin: Susan Engeleiter; f 1953; aids, assists and protects the interests of small businesses; provides loans; licenses and regulates small business investment cos; guarantees surety bonds for small contractors.

The White House Office: 1600 Pennsylvania Ave, NW, Washington, DC 20500; tel (202) 456-1414; telex 440074; White House Chief of Staff: John H. Sununu; aids the Pres; maintains communication with the Congress, heads of depts and agencies, the media and the public.

World Agricultural Outlook Board: 14th St and Independence Ave, SW, Rm 5143-S, Washington, DC 20250; tel (202) 447-5447; fax (202) 472-5805; Chair: James R. Donald; f 1977; issues monthly world agricultural supply and demand estimates reports; monitors impact of global weather on crops; co-ordinates weather and remote sensing activities of the Dept of Agriculture.

Art and Culture

American Battle Monuments Commission: 5127 Pulaski Bldg, Washington, DC 20314; tel (202) 272-0532; Chair: Gen (retd) Andrew J. Goodpaster; f 1923.

Commission of Fine Arts: 708 Jackson Pl, NW, Washington, DC 20006; tel (202) 566-1066; Chair: J. Carter Brown; f 1910.

Library of Congress: 101 Independence Ave, SE, Washington, DC 20540; tel (202) 707-5000; telex 8220185; fax (202) 707-9199; Librarian of Congress: James H. Billington; f 1800; the Nation's library; the Copyright Office in the library administers the operation of the US copyright law; provides services for Congress, the executive and judicial branches of Govt, libraries and researchers.

National Archives and Records Administration (NARA): Seventh and Pennsylvania Ave, NW, Washington, DC 20408; tel (202) 523-3000; fax (202) 523-4357; Archivist of the USA: Dr Don W. Wilson; Dep Archivist: Claudine Weiher; f 1934; independent executive branch agency of the Govt; preserves and makes available for use the official records and archives of all parts of the US Govt.

National Endowment for the Humanities: 1100 Pennsylvania Ave, NW, Washington, DC 20506; tel (202) 786-0438; Chair: Lynne Cheney; Dep Chair: Celeste Colgan; f 1965; advances and disseminates knowledge in all disciplines of the humanities, eg history, philosophy, languages, linguistics, literature, archaeology, jurisprudence, theory, history and criticism of the arts, ethics, comparative religion, etc.

National Foundation for the Arts and Humanities: 1100 Pennsylvania Ave, NW, Washington, DC 20506; tel (202) 682-5414; Chair (acting): Hugh Southern; f 1965.

Smithsonian Institution: 1000 Jefferson Drive, Washington, DC 20560; tel (202) 357-2700; telex 264729; fax (202) 786-2515; Sec: Robert McCormick Adams; Under Sec: Dean W. Anderson; f 1846; independent trust; holds artefacts and specimens to increase and diffuse knowledge; research centre dedicated to public education, national service and scholarship in the arts, science and history.

Business and Economy

BANKING

Comptroller of the Currency: 490 L'Enfant Plaza East, SW, Washington, DC 20219; tel (202) 447-1810; Comptroller: Robert L. Clarke; has supervisory control over all federally-chartered banks (the national banks).

Export-Import Bank of the United States (Eximbank): 811 Vermont Ave, Washington, DC 20571; tel (202) 566-8144; telex 248460; Chair: John Macombe; f 1934, independent agency since 1945; finances and facilitates US trade with other countries, guarantees payment to US foreign traders and banks, extends credit to foreign governmental and private concerns.

Federal Home Loan Bank Board: 1700 G St, NW, Washington, DC 20552; tel (202) 377-6677; Chair: (vacant); f 1932; supervises and regulates savings and loan associations specializing in lending money on homes and which provide funds to pay for building and buying housing; operates the Federal Savings and Loan Insurance Corpn; directs the Federal Home Loan Bank System, providing reserve credit and assuring that mem savings and loan associations will continue to finance housing.

Federal Reserve System: Board of Governors: 20th St and Constitution Ave, NW, Washington, DC 20551; tel (202) 452-3204; telex 197668; Chair: Alan Greenspan; Vice-Chair: Manuel H. Johnson; f 1913; comprises the Board of Govs, the Federal Open Market Committee and the 12 Federal Reserve Banks with 25 brs; the seven mems of the Federal Reserve Board of

Govs are appointed by the Pres of the USA, with the advice and consent of the Senate, to serve a 14-year term; the Chair and Vice-Chair serve renewable four-year terms; the Board of Govs supervises the budgets and operations of the Federal Reserve Banks; the Reserve Banks are empowered to issue Federal Reserve notes, they hold the cash reserves of depository institutions and make loans to them, move currency and coin into and out of circulation, and collect and process cheques; they provide banking services for the Treasury, issue and redeem Govt securities and act in other ways as fiscal agent for the US Govt; they also take part in the primary responsibility of the Federal Reserve System, the setting of monetary policy, through participation on the Federal Open Market Committee.

FINANCIAL AGENCIES

Bureau of Public Debt: 999 E St, NW, Washington, DC 20226; tel (202) 376-4300; Commr: Richard L. Gregg; under the Dept of the Treasury.

Commodity Futures Trading Commission: 2033 K St, NW, Washington, DC 20581; tel (202) 254-8630; Chair: Wendy Lee Gramm; f 1974 to strengthen the regulations of futures trading and bring under regulation all agricultural and other commodities which are traded on commodity exchanges; aims to prevent price manipulation, the dissemination of false and misleading information affecting prices, etc; protects market users against fraud and establishes minimum financial requirements for futures commission traders.

Farm Credit Administration: 1501 Farm Credit Drive, McLean, VA 22102-5090; tel (703) 883-4000; Chair (acting): Marvin Duncan; co-ordinates and supervises the borrower-owned banks and associations comprising the co-operative Farm Credit System, whose institutions provide loans to farmers, ranchers, rural homeowners, etc.

National Credit Union Administration: 1776 G St, NW, Washington, DC 20576; tel (202) 357-1100; Chair: Roger W. Jepsen; f 1970; charters, insures, supervises and examines federal credit unions, and administers the National Credit Union Share Insurance Fund.

Overseas Private Investment Corpn: 1615 M St, NW, Washington, DC 20527; tel (202) 457-7010; Pres and Chief Exec: Fred M. Zeder, III; f 1970; assists investors in making profitable investments in about 80 developing countries, and encourages projects beneficial to these countries; provides loans, insurance and loan guarantees.

Securities and Exchange Commission: 450 Fifth St, NW, Washington, DC 20549; tel (202) 272-3101; telex 89513; fax (202) 272-7050; Chair: Richard C. Breeden; f 1934; regulation of US securities markets; enforcement of securities laws.

United States Mint: 633 Third St, NW, Washington, DC 20020; tel (202) 376-0560; Dir: Donna Pope; under the Dept of the Treasury.

INSURANCE

Federal Deposit Insurance Corpn: 550 17th St, NW, Washington, DC 20429; tel (202) 389-4221; Chair: L. William Seidman; f 1933; protects the money supply through providing insurance cover for bank deposits.

TRADE

Bureau of Trade Regulation: 14th St between E St and Constitution Ave, NW, Washington, DC 20230; manages export admin and related activities; assists in regulating exports of US goods and technology.

Consumer Product Safety Commission: 5401 Westbard Ave, Bethesda, MD 20207; Chair (acting): Anne Graham; f 1972;

protection of consumers through devt of uniform product safety standards and promotion of research into the causes and prevention of product-related injuries and deaths.

Federal Trade Commission: Sixth St and Pennsylvania Ave, NW, Washington, DC 20580; tel (202) 326-2100; Chair: Daniel Oliver; f 1914; responsible for the maintenance of the free enterprise system by maintaining free and fair competition.

National Institute of Standards and Technology: Bldg 101, Route 270, Gaithersburg, MD 20899; tel (301) 975-2411; Dir (acting): Raymond Kammer.

Patent and Trademark Office: 2021 Jefferson Davis Highway, Arlington, VA.

United States Customs Service: 1301 Constitution Ave, NW, Washington, DC 20229; collects revenue from imports and enforces customs and related laws.

Defence

Central Intelligence Agency: Washington, DC 20505; tel (703) 351-7676; Dir: William H. Webster; f 1947; under the Pres and the National Security Council (see below); carries out intelligence activities in foreign countries; has no internal security or law enforcement powers.

Defense Advanced Research Projects Agency: 1400 Wilson Bldg, Arlington, VA 22209; tel (703) 694-3007; Dir: Craig Fields; under the Dept of Defense.

Defense Communications Agency: Eighth St and Court House Rd, Arlington, VA 22204; tel (703) 692-0018; Dir: John T. Myers; Vice-Dir: T. R. M. Emery; under the Dept of Defense.

Defense Intelligence Agency: The Pentagon, Washington, DC 20301; tel (202) 695-7353; Dir: Harry E. Soyster; under the Dept of Defense.

Defense Nuclear Agency: 6801 Telegraph Rd, Alexandria, VA 22310; tel (703) 325-7004; Dir: John T. Parker, Jr; under the Dept of Defense.

Federal Bureau of Investigation (FBI): Ninth St and Pennsylvania Ave, NW, Washington, DC 20535; tel (202) 324-3444; Dir: William S. Sessions; under the Dept of Justice.

National Security Council: Executive Office Bldg, Washington, DC 20506; tel (202) 395-3440; Asst to the Pres for National Security Affairs: Gen Brent Scowcroft; under the Executive Office of the Pres; advises the Pres on matters relating to national security.

United States Air Force: The Pentagon, Washington, DC 10330; tel (202) 697-7376; Sec: Donald B. Rice; Gen Counsel: Anne Foreman; Comptroller: Claudius E. Watts.

United States Arms Control and Disarmament Agency: 320 21st St, NW, Washington, DC 20451; tel (202) 632-0392; Dir: Ronald F. Lehman, II; f 1961.

United States Army: The Pentagon, Washington, DC 20310-0101; tel (202) 695-3211; telex 89459; Chair, Joint Chiefs of Staff: Gen Colin Powell; Chief of Staff: Carl Vunono; Sec: John O. Marsh, Jr; Under-Sec: Michael P. W. Stone; Gen Counsel: Susan J. Crawford; Inspector-Gen: Henry Doctor, Jr.

United States Coast Guard: 2100 Second St, SW, Washington, DC 20590; tel (202) 267-2390; Commdt: Paul A. Yost, Jr.

United States Navy: The Pentagon, Washington, DC 20350-1000; tel (202) 695-3131; Sec: H. Lawrence Garrett, III; Gen Counsel: Larry L. Lamade.

United States Secret Service: 1800 G St, NW, Washington, DC 20223; tel (202) 535-5700; Dir: John R. Simpson; under the Dept of the Treasury.

Development and Planning

Appalachian Regional Commission: 1666 Connecticut Ave, NW, Washington, DC 20235; tel (202) 673-7968; Fed Co-Chair: Winifred A. Pizzano; States' Co-Chair: Gov Carroll A. Campbell, Jr (South Carolina); f 1965; federal and state Govt agency concerned with the economic, physical and social devt of the 13-state Appalachian region; involved in community devt and housing, education, the environment, health, industrial devt, tourism and transport.

Pennsylvania Avenue Development Corpn: 1331 Pennsylvania Ave, NW, Suite 1220 North, Washington, DC 20004-1703; tel (202) 724-9091; Chair: Henry A. Berliner; f 1972; devt of Pennsylvania Ave and the adjacent blocks between the Capitol and the White House.

Tennessee Valley Authority: 400 West Summit Hill Drive, Knoxville, TN 37902; tel (615) 632-8000; Chair of Board of Dirs: Marvin T. Runyon; f 1933; Govt-owned corpn; programme of resource devt for the advancement of economic growth in the region of the Tennessee Valley, including flood control, devt of navigation, production of electric power, fertilizer devt, forestry and wildlife devt, etc.

Employment

Equal Employment Opportunity Commission: 2401 E St, NW, Washington, DC 20507; tel (202) 634-6922; fax (202) 634-7332; Chair: Clarence Thomas; Vice-Chair: R. Gaull Silberman; Commrs: Tony Gallegos, Evan Kemp, Dr Joy Cherian; f 1965; enforces Title VII of the Civil Rights Act of 1964, which prohibits employment discrimination based on race, colour, sex, religion or national origin, the Age Discrimination in Employment Act and the Equal Pay Act.

Federal Labor Relations Authority: 500 C St, SW, Washington, DC 20424; tel (202) 382-0700; Chair (acting): Jean McKee; f 1978.

National Labor Relations Board: 1717 Pennsylvania Ave, NE, Washington, DC 20570; tel (202) 254-9430; Chair: James M. Stephens; f 1935; admin of laws relating to labour relations; safeguards employees' rights to unions and prevents unfair labour practices.

Occupational Safety and Health Review Commission: 1825 K St, NW, Washington, DC 20006-1246; tel (202) 634-7943; Chair: E. Ross Buckley; f 1970; concerned with the provision of safe and healthy working conditions.

Pension Benefit Guaranty Corpn: 2020 K St, NW, Washington, DC 20006; tel (202) 254-4817; Exec Dir: Kathleen P. Utgoff; f 1974; guarantees basic pension benefits in covered private plans if they terminate with insufficient assets.

Energy

Energy Information Administration: US Dept of Energy, James Forrestal Bldg, 1000 Independence Ave, SW, Washington, DC 20585; tel (202) 586-8800; Admin: Dr H. A. Merklein; f 1977; collects, assembles, evaluates, analyses and disseminates energy statistics and forecasts.

Federal Energy Regulatory Commission (FERC): 825 North Capitol St, NE, Washington, DC 20426; tel (202) 357-8200; Chair: Martha O. Hesse; under the Dept of Energy.

Nuclear Energy Research: US Dept of Energy, Nuclear Energy, Rm 5A-115, Washington, DC 20585; tel (202) 586-6456; provides information on research into nuclear energy, including fuel technology, nuclear-waste management and the admin of nuclear power installations.

Nuclear Regulatory Commission: 1717 H St, NW, Washington, DC 20555; tel (202) 492-7715; Chair: Lando W. Zech, Jr; f 1975; licensing and regulation of the uses of nuclear energy in order to protect public health and safety and the environment; inspects licensed cos to ensure safety regulations are not violated.

Nuclear Safety Information Center (NSIC): Oak Ridge National Laboratory, POB Y, Oak Ridge, TN 37830; tel (615) 574-0391; collects and disseminates information on the safety aspects of nuclear technology.

Nuclear Task Force: US Dept of Energy, Nuclear Energy, 1000 Independence Ave, SW, Washington, DC 20585; tel (202) 252-4710; co-ordinates programme strategies for the planning and devt of nuclear power plant construction.

Office of the Associate Deputy Assistant Secretary for Reactor Systems Development and Technology: US Dept of Energy, NE-40, Washington, DC 20545; tel (301) 353-3950; develops and co-ordinates programmes exploiting the inherent characteristics of liquid metal-cooled reactors as attractive concepts for application in the 1990s and beyond; develops and recommends goals, policies and associated strategies for devt of High-Temperature Gas-Cooled Reactors (HTGR) for a broad range of applications in support of commercial-user interests in these plants.

Office of Technology Support Programs: US Dept of Energy, Office of Nuclear Energy, NE-46, Washington, DC; tel (301) 353-3424; telex 8280475; fax (301) 353-3870; Dir: Bernard J. Rock; f 1985; research and devt programmes on the Liquid Metal Reactor Program.

The Environment

ACTION (American Council to Improve Our Neighbourhood): 806 Connecticut Ave, NW, Washington, DC 20525; tel (202) 634-9282; Dir: Donna M. Alvarado; f 1971.

Council on Environmental Quality: 722 Jackson Pl, NW, Washington, DC 20503; tel (202) 395-5080; Chair: A. Alan Hill; under the Executive Office of the Pres; recommends to the Pres national policies to promote environmental quality; assesses energy research and devt from an environmental stand-point.

Environmental Protection Agency: 401 M St, SW, Washington, DC 20460; tel (202) 382-4700; telex 892757; fax (202) 382-7886; Admin: William Reilly; f 1970; protection of the environment; aims to control and abate pollution in air, water, solid waste, etc; concerned also with noise, radiation and toxic substances; co-operates with state and local govts.

Health and Welfare

HEALTH

National Center for Health Services Research: 5600 Fishers Lane, Rockville, MD 20857; tel (301) 443-5650; Dir: J. Michael Fitzmaurice; under the Dept of Housing and Urban Development.

WELFARE

Commission on Civil Rights: 1121 Vermont Ave, NW, Washington, DC 20425; tel (202) 523-5571; Chair: William Allen; f 1957; promotion of equal opportunity.

Office of National Drug Control Policy: Old Executive Office Bldg, Washington, DC 20506; Dir: William John Bennett; under the Executive Office of the Pres.

International Affairs

Panama Canal Commission: APO Miami, Fl 34011-5000; Chair of Board of Dirs: William R. Gianelli; Admin: D. P. McAuliffe; Dep Admin: Fernando Manfredo; f 1979; provides inter-oceanic canal transit service to world shipping.

United States Mission to the United Nations: 799 United Nations Plaza, New York, NY 10017; tel (212) 415-4000; US Rep to the United Nations: Thomas R. Pickering; under the Executive Office of the Pres.

United States International Trade Commission: 701 E St, NW, Washington, DC 20436; tel (202) 523-0161; Chair: Anne E. Brunsdale; f 1916; reports and makes recommendations to the Pres, the Congress and other Govt agencies on international trade and tariffs; conducts investigations, public hearings and research projects relating to the international policies of the USA.

Legal and Judiciary

Bureau of Prisons: 320 First St, NW, Washington, DC 20534; tel (202) 724-6300; Dir: J. Michael Quinlan; under the Dept of Justice.

Supreme Court of the United States: Supreme Court Bldg, 1 First St, NE, Washington, DC 20543; tel (202) 479-3000; Chief Justice: William Hubbs Rehnquist; the only federal court established by the constitution; it is the highest court in the nation, comprising a Chief Justice and eight associate justices; appointments, which are for life or until retirement, are made by the Pres, subject to confirmation by the US Senate; the Supreme Court has the power to disallow legislation and to overthrow executive actions which it deems unconstitutional.

United States Claims Court: 717 Madison Pl, NW, Washington, DC 20005; tel (202) 633-7257.

United States Parole Commission: 5550 Friendship Blvd, Chevy Case, MD 20815; tel (301) 492-5990; Chair: Benjamin F. Baer.

United States Tax Court: 400 Second St, NW, Washington, DC 20217; tel (202) 376-2754.

US Courts of Appeals: c/o Administrative Office of the US Courts, Washington, DC 20544; tel (202) 633-6097; the country is divided into 12 judicial circuits including one in the District of Columbia, in each of which there is one Court of Appeals; there is also a Court of Appeals for the federal circuit, having nation-wide specialized jurisdiction; federal courts hear cases involving federal law, cases involving participants from more than one state, crimes committed in more than one state and civil or corporate cases that cross state lines.

US Court of International Trade: 1 Federal Plaza, New York, NY 10007; tel (212) 264-2814.

Media

BROADCASTING

Board for International Broadcasting: 1201 Connecticut Ave, Suite 400, NW, Washington, DC 20036; tel (202) 254-8040; Chair: Malcolm S. Forbes, Jr; f 1973.

Department of Defense, American Forces Radio and Television Service (AFRTS): 1088 La Tuna Canyon Rd, Los Angeles, CA 91352-2098; tel (818) 504-1200; telex 6831327; Commdr: Capt John A. Martin; Govt-operated; provides US radio and TV programming in English by satellite and mail for use by AFRTS networks and stations where US military personnel are stationed; c 800 radio and TV outlets in more than 20 countries.

Office of Education: US Dept of Education, 400 Maryland Ave, SW, Washington, DC 20202; 100 broadcasting stations; makes grants for educational programming and broadcasting facilities.

Public Broadcasting Service (PBS): 1320 Braddock Pl, Alexandria, VA 22314; tel (703) 739-5000; fax (703) 739-0775; Pres and Chief Exec: Bruce L. Christensen; f 1969; non-profit making; financed by private subscriptions and federal Govt funds; provides programming to 314 affiliated, non-commercial TV stations.

Radio Free Europe/Radio Liberty: 1201 Connecticut Ave, NW, Washington, DC 20036; tel (202) 457-6900; Pres: E. Eugene Pell; Dirs: A. Ross Johnson (RFE Div), S. Enders Wimbush (Radio Liberty Div); f 1950; financed by the federal Govt; broadcasts from Munich, Federal Republic of Germany to Eastern Europe and the USSR; c 1,000 hours weekly in 23 languages.

Voice of America: US Information Agency, 400 C St, SW, Washington, DC 20547; tel (202) 485-7860; Dir: Richard W. Carlson; f 1942; broadcasts in 42 languages to all areas of the world; under the US Information Agency (see below).

GOVERNMENT PUBLISHER

Government Printing Office: 710 North Capitol St, NW, Washington, DC 20401; tel (202) 783-3238; telex 8229413; fax (202) 275-0019; Public Printer (acting): Joseph E. Jenifer.

NEWS AND INFORMATION

Bureau of the Census: Dept of Commerce, Public Information Office, Rm 2705, FB3, Washington, DC 20233; tel (301) 763-4040; fax (301) 763-4644; Dir: (vacant); Dep Dir: C. Louis Kincannon; f 1902; carries out censuses of population and housing, economics, governments and agriculture.

Bureau of Labor Statistics: 441 G St, NW, Washington, DC 20212; tel (202) 523-1221; Commr: Janet L. Norwood; f 1884; data-gathering agency of the federal Govt in the field of labour economics; conducts surveys of businesses or households and collects data in co-operation with the Bureau of the Census (see above) and state and federal agencies; programme areas include employment and unemployment statistics, economic growth and employment projections, prices and living conditions, productivity and technology, and compensation and working conditions.

United States Information Agency: 301 Fourth St, SW, Washington, DC 20547; tel (202) 485-7700; Dir: Bruce S. Gelb; f 1978; the Dir reports to the Pres of the US and receives policy guidance from the Sec of State; maintains 204 posts in 127 countries; purposes are to strengthen foreign understanding and support for US policies and actions, advise key officials on the implications of foreign opinion for US policies, promote and administer educational and cultural exchange programmes, assist in the devt of a comprehensive policy on the free flow of information and international communication, etc.

Science and Technology

National Aeronautics and Space Administration (NASA): 400 Maryland Ave, SW, Washington, DC 20546; tel (202) 453-1000; telex 4979843; fax (202) 755-9234; Admin: Dr James C. Fletcher; Dep Admin: Dale D. Myers; f 1958; research, devt, construction and operation of aeronautical and space vehicles, both manned and unmanned.

National Science Foundation: 1800 G St, NW, Washington, DC 20550; tel (202) 357-7748; Chair: Erich Bloch; f 1950.

Office of Science and Technology Policy: Old Executive Office Bldg, Washington, DC 20506; tel (202) 456-7116; Dir: Dr

William R. Graham, Jr; under the Executive Office of the Pres; advises the Pres on scientific and technological issues concerned with the economy, national security, health, foreign relations and the environment.

US National Hurricane Centre: Coral Gables, FL; Dir: Bob Sheets.

Tourism

United States Travel and Tourism Administration: US Dept of Commerce, Rm 1865, 14th St between Constitution Ave and E St, NW, Washington, DC 20230; tel (202) 377-0136; Under-Sec for Travel and Tourism: Charles E. Cobb, Jr; f 1961; promotes US tourist industry and collects and analyses data on tourism.

Transport and Communications

TELECOMMUNICATIONS

Federal Communications Commission: 1919 M St, NW, Washington, DC 20554; tel (202) 632-7000; Chair: Dennis R. Patrick; f 1934; regulation of inter-state and foreign communications by radio, TV wire and cable; responsible for the orderly devt and operation of broadcasting.

National Telecommunications and Information Administration: 1800 G St, NW, Washington, DC 20504; provides telecommunications planners and users with techniques for evaluating performance of systems, models for estimating transmission characteristics, research in the application of telecommunications technology, etc.

Postal Rate Commission: 1333 H St, NW, Washington, DC 20268-0001; tel (202) 789-6800; Chair: Janet D. Steiger; f 1970.

United States Postal Service: 475 L'Enfant Plaza West, SW, Washington, DC 20260-0001; tel (202) 268-2000; Postmaster-Gen: Anthony M. Frank; f 1970; mail processing and delivery services.

TRANSPORT

Alaska Railroad Corpn: POB 7-211, Anchorage, AK 99510-7069; tel (907) 265-2403; telex 26658; Pres and Chief Exec: F. G. Turpin; f 1912; operated by the Federal Railroad Administration; 526 track-miles.

AMTRAK (National Railroad Passenger Corpn): 400 North Capitol St, NW, Washington, DC 20001; tel (202) 383-3000; Chair: W. Graham Claytor, Jr; f 1970; public corpn operating the passenger services in 43 states of 20 fmrly investor-owned railways; 23,600 track-miles.

Federal Aviation Administration: US Dept of Transportation, 800 Independence Ave, SW, Washington, DC 20591; tel (202) 426-8058; Admin: James B. Busey; f 1958; promotes safety in the air, regulates air commerce and assists in the devt of an effective national airport system.

Federal Highway Administration: 400 Seventh St, SW, Washington, DC 20590; tel (202) 366-0650; telex 8229426; fax (202) 366-1078; Admin: Dr Thomas Larson; Dep Admin: Eugene McCormick; Exec Dir (acting): Dean Carlson; f 1967; oversees the expenditure of federal funds on highway projects; technology transfer activities throughout the US; operates the Federal Highway Research Center; directly oversees the design and construction of roads on federal lands; acts as liaison between the US Govt and other national govts and international organizations for highway-related issues.

Federal Maritime Commission: 1100 L St, NW, Washington, DC 20573; tel (202) 523-5707; telex 204796; fax (202) 523-3782;

Chair (acting): James J. Carey; f 1961; regulates foreign and domestic ocean shipping; reviews agreements on rates, schedules, etc and grants anti-trust immunity; reviews activities for compliance with shipping laws and regulations of the Commission.

Federal Railroad Administration: US Dept of Transportation, 400 Seventh St, SW, Washington, DC 20590; tel (202) 426-0881; Admin: John Riley; formulates federal railway policies and administers and enforces safety regulations.

Interstate Commerce Commission: 12th St and Constitution Ave, NW, Washington, DC 20423; tel (202) 275-7524; Chair: Heather J. Gradison; f 1887; regulation of interstate surface transportation, including trains, buses, trucks, shipping, etc; certification of carriers, assuring rates and services are reasonable.

Maritime Administration: US Dept of Transportation, Nasif Bldg, 400 Seventh St, SW, Washington, DC 20590; tel (202) 366-5807; Admin: John Gaughan; concerned with promoting the US Merchant Marine; also administers subsidy programme to ship operators.

National Transportation Safety Board (NTSB): 800 Independence Ave, SW, Washington, DC 20594; tel (202) 382-6830; fax (202) 382-6819; Chair (acting): James L. Kolstad; f 1974; aviation accident investigation.

St Lawrence Seaway Corpn: US Dept of Transportation, POB 44090, Washington, DC 20026-4090; tel (202) 366-0091; responsible for sections of the St Lawrence Seaway within the territorial limits of the USA.

United States Railway Association: 955 L'Enfant Plaza North, SW, Washington, DC 20595; tel (202) 488-8877; f 1973; creation and maintenance of a financially self-sustaining, competitive and efficient rail service system in the Midwest and Northeast regions.

UNITED STATES EXTERNAL TERRITORIES

AMERICAN SAMOA

The Government

GOVERNMENT OF AMERICAN SAMOA
Pago Pago, AS 96799
Tel 633-4116; telex 782501; fax 633-2269
Governor: Peter Tali Coleman
Lieutenant-Governor: Galia'i Poumele
The Governor holds executive power, is elected by popular vote and has authority which extends to all operations within the territory of American Samoa. The Governor has veto power with respect to bills passed by the Fono, and has the authority to appoint heads of Govt depts with the approval of the Fono.

FONO (LEGISLATURE)
Pago Pago, AS 96799
Tel 633-4116; telex 782501; fax 633-2269
Pres of the Senate: Letuli Toloa
Speaker of the House of Representatives:
Tuanaitau F. Tuia
The Senate is composed of 18 mems elected from local chiefs or *matai*, for a term of four years; the House of Representatives comprises 20 mems elected by popular vote for two years, and a non-voting delegate from Swain's Island.

Government Agencies

BANKING

Development Bank of American Samoa: POB 9, Pago Pago, AS 96799; tel 633-4031; Chair and Pres: Auina To'oto'o; f 1969; Govt-owned and non-profit-making.

BROADCASTING

KVZK: Office of Public Information, Pago Pago, AS 96799; tel 633-4191; telex 770519; Dir: Leo'o V. Ma'o; f 1964; Govt-owned; non-commercial; English and Samoan; broadcasts 18 hours daily on three channels.

DEVELOPMENT

Office of Economic Development and Planning: Govt of American Samoa, Pago Pago, AS 96799; tel 633-5155; Dir: Alfonso P. Galea'i.

Territorial Planning Office: Devt Planning Office, Govt of American Samoa, Pago Pago, AS 96799; tel 633-5155; telex 541; Chair: Soli Aolaolagi; Exec Dir: Alfonso P. Galea'i; f 1964.

LEGAL AND JUDICIARY

District Court: Pago Pago, AS 96799; Judge: Malaetasi Togafau; hears preliminary felony proceedings, misdemeanours, infractions, civil and small claims, etc.

High Court: Pago Pago, AS 96799; Chief Justice: Michael Kruse; Associate Justice: Grover Joseph Rees, III; consists of three Divisions: Appellate, which has limited original jurisdiction and hears appeals from the Trial Division, the Land and Titles Division and from the District Court when it has operated as a court of record, Trial, which has general jurisdiction over all cases, and Land and Titles, which hears cases involving land or *matai* titles.

NEWS AND INFORMATION

News Bulletin: Office of Public Information, American Samoa Govt, Utulei; tel 633-5490; Editor: Philip Swett; daily Monday to Friday; English non-commercial.

TRANSPORT

Samoa Air: Pago Pago, AS 96799; Pres and Chair: Ron Pritchard; f 1985; operates service between Pago Pago and Western Samoa, Niue and Honolulu (Hawaii).

GUAM

The Government

OFFICE OF THE GOVERNOR
Guam
Governor: Joseph F. Ada
Lieutenant-Governor: Frank F. Blas
The Governor holds executive power and is elected by popular vote every four years; the Govt has 48 executive depts, whose heads are appointed by the Governor with the consent of the Guam Legislature.

LEGISLATURE
Guam
Speaker: Joe T. San Agustin
Comprises 21 mems elected by popular vote every two years; it

is empowered to pass laws on local matters, including taxation and fiscal appropriations.

Government Agencies

DEVELOPMENT

Guam Economic Development Authority (GEDA): Guam International Trade Center Bldg, Suite 911, 590 South Marine Drive, Tamuning, 96911; tel 649-4141; telex 6132; fax 649-4146; Chair of Board: Anthony A. Leon Guerrero; Vice-Chair: Dr Shinkyung Kim; Sec: Cecilia C. A. Perez; Admin: Charles P. Crisostomo; f 1965; controls and supervises an integrated programme for the economic devt of Guam in the areas of commerce, agriculture, industry and tourism; conducts research in the areas of Guam's natural resources and market potential; promotes investment, operates industries and maintains facilities for sale or lease; makes loans, sells bonds, recommends to the Gov of Guam those firms or individuals deemed worthy of receiving qualifying certificates for tax relief.

LEGAL AND JUDICIARY

District Court of Guam: Guam; Presiding Judge: Cristobal C. Duenas; the Judge is appointed by the Pres of the USA; has the jurisdiction of the federal district court and of a bankruptcy court of the USA in all cases arising under the laws of the USA.

Superior Court of Guam: Guam; Presiding Judge: Alberto C. Lamorena, III; Judges are appointed by the Governor of Guam for an initial eight-year term and are thereafter elected by popular vote; the Superior Court has jurisdiction over cases arising in Guam other than those heard in the District Court.

TOURISM

Guam Visitors Bureau: 1220 Pale San Vitores Rd, Tumon, 96911; POB 3520, Agaña, 96910; tel 646-5278; telex 6432; fax 646-8861; Chair of the Board: Gerhard H. Zimmer; Vice-Chair: Carl T. C. Gutierrez; Gen Man: Joey B. Cepeda; Sec: Joyce Bamba; f 1962; promotion of tourism.

TRADE

Guam Department of Commerce: Guam International Trade Center Bldg, Suite 601, 590 South Marine Drive, Tamuning, 96911; tel 646-5841; telex 7431520; fax 646-7242; Dir: Peter R. Barcinas; f 1950; facilitates trade and investment between domestic and foreign investors; gives information on trade and commerce; collects and disseminates business and economic statistics; economic planning and devt; customs and quarantine; population dynamics and research.

MARSHALL ISLANDS

The Government

THE NITIJELA (LEGISLATURE)
Majuro, 96960
Speaker: Atlan Anien
Comprises 33 mems, who elect a Pres of the Marshall Islands from amongst their mems.

OFFICE OF THE PRESIDENT AND MINISTRY OF RESOURCES AND DEVELOPMENT
Majuro, 96960
President and Minister: Amata Kabua

MINISTRY OF EDUCATION
Majuro, 96960
Minister: Phillip Miller

MINISTRY OF FINANCE
Majuro, 96960
Minister: Tom Kijiner

MINISTRY OF FOREIGN AFFAIRS
Majuro, 96960
Minister: Charles Dominick

MINISTRY OF HEALTH SERVICES
POB 16, Majuro, 96960
Tel 3355; telex 7300908; fax 3432
Minister: Rubin Zackhras

MINISTRY OF INTERNAL AFFAIRS
Majuro, 96960
Minister: Rubin Zackhras

MINISTRY OF JUSTICE
Majuro, 96960
Minister: Lanari Kunio

MINISTRY OF PUBLIC WORKS
Majuro, 96960
Minister: Kunar Abnes

MINISTRY OF SOCIAL SERVICES, RESOURCES AND DEVELOPMENT
Majuro, 96960
Minister: Brenson Wase

MINISTRY OF TRANSPORTATION AND COMMUNICATIONS
Majuro, 96960
Minister: Kunio Lemari

OFFICE OF THE ATTORNEY-GENERAL
Majuro, 96960
Attorney-General: (vacant)

OFFICE OF THE AUDITOR-GENERAL
Majuro, 96960
Auditor-General: Greg Bonz

Government Agencies

ADVISORY AND SUPERVISORY BODY

Public Service Commission: POB 90, Majuro, 96960; tel 3298; fax 3382; Chair: Tibrikrik Samuel; f 1978; the employing authority for the public service, and controls its organization and management; responsible for reviewing the efficiency and economy of all depts and offices of the Govt.

LEGAL AND JUDICIARY

High Court of the Republic of the Marshall Islands: Majuro, 96960; tel 3652; Chief Justice: A. D. Tennekone.

Supreme Court of the Republic of the Marshall Islands: Majuro, 96960; tel 3652; Chief Justice: Harold W. Burnett.

Traditional Rights Court of the Marshall Islands: Majuro, 96960; Chief Judge: Berson Joseph.

NEWS AND INFORMATION

Marshall Islands Gazette: Office of the Chief Sec, Marshall Islands Govt, Majuro, 96960; tel 3143; Editor: Giff Johnson; f 1982.

TRANSPORT

Airline of the Marshall Islands: POB 959, Majuro, 96960; tel 3373; telex 0929; fax 3216; Pres: the Pres, Amata Kabua; Gen Man and Chief Exec: Neville Hill; f 1980; internal services and international flights to Fiji, Kiribati and Tuvalu.

THE FEDERATED STATES OF MICRONESIA

The Government

LEGISLATURE
Kolonia, Pohnpei, Eastern Caroline Islands, 96941
Speaker, Senate of the Federated States of Micronesia: Jack Fritz
Speaker, House of Representatives of the Congress of the Federated States of Micronesia: Bethwel Henry
Each of the four districts has its own legislature: the Kosrae State Legislature, Gov: Yosiwo George, is a unicameral body of 14 mems serving for four years; the Pohnpei State Legislature, Gov: Resio Moses, has 27 representatives elected for four years (terms staggered); the Truk State Legislature, Gov: Erhart Aten, has 28 mems elected for four years (terms staggered); and the Yap State Legislature, Gov: John de Avilla Mangefel, has 10 mems, six elected from the Yap Islands and four elected from the Outer Islands of Ulithi and Woleai, for a four-year term.

OFFICE OF THE PRESIDENT
Kolonia, Pohnpei, Eastern Caroline Islands, 96941
President: Yapese John R. Haglelgam
Vice-President: Bailey Olter

DEPARTMENT OF EXTERNAL AFFAIRS
Kolonia, Pohnpei, Eastern Caroline Islands, 96941
Secretary: Andon L. Amaraich

DEPARTMENT OF FINANCE
Kolonia, Pohnpei, Eastern Caroline Islands, 96941
Secretary: Aloysius Tuuth

DEPARTMENT OF RESOURCES AND DEVELOPMENT
Kolonia, Pohnpei, Eastern Caroline Islands, 96941
Secretary: Bernard Helgenberger

DEPARTMENT OF SOCIAL SERVICES
Kolonia, Pohnpei, Eastern Caroline Islands, 96941
Secretary: Dr Eliuel Pretrick

OFFICE OF THE ATTORNEY-GENERAL
Kolonia, Pohnpei, Eastern Caroline Islands, 96941
Attorney-General: Bill Mann

Government Agencies

BROADCASTING

Federated States of Micronesia Information Office: POB 490, Kolonia, Pohnpei, Eastern Caroline Islands, 96941; Information Officer: Ketson Johnson; Broadcasting Officer: E. Lippwe; four regional stations, each broadcasting 18 hours daily.

Station WSZA: POB 117, Colonia, Yap, Western Caroline Islands, 96943; Man: A. Yug; programmes in English, Yapese, Ulithian and Woleaian.

Station WSZC: Moen, Truk, Eastern Caroline Islands, 96942; Man: P. J. Maipi; programmes in Trukese and English.

Station WSZD: POB 1086, Kolonia, Pohnpei, Eastern Caroline Islands, 96941; Man: Dusty Frederick; programmes in English and Ponapean.

Station WTFL: POB 147, Leln, Kosrae, Eastern Caroline Islands, 96944; tel 3040; telex 6874; Man: H. Nena; programmes in English and Kosraean.

TV Station Yap—WAAB: Colonia, Yap, Western Caroline Islands, 96943.

DEVELOPMENT

Federated Development Authority: Kolonia, Pohnpei, Eastern Caroline Islands, 96941; Chair: the Pres, Yapese John R. Haglelgam.

LEGAL AND JUDICIARY

Supreme Court of the Federated States of Micronesia: Kolonia, Pohnpei, Eastern Caroline Islands, 96941; Chief Justice: Edward C. King.

THE NORTHERN MARIANA ISLANDS

The Government

OFFICE OF THE GOVERNOR
Capitol Hill, Saipan, CM 96950
Governor: Pedro P. Tenorio
Lieutenant-Governor: Pedro A. Tenorio

Executive authority is vested in the Governor, who is elected by popular vote.

NORTHERN MARIANAS COMMONWEALTH LEGISLATURE
Capitol Hill, Saipan, CM 96950
Tel 322-3670
Pres of the Senate: Benjamin T. Manglona
Speaker of the House of Representatives:
Pedro R. Guerrero
Legislative body comprising a Senate of nine mems elected for two-year terms, and a House of Representatives of 15 mems also elected for two-year terms.

Government Agencies

DEVELOPMENT

Commonwealth Development Authority: Wakins Bldg, Gualo Rai, Saipan, CM 96950; tel 234-7145; foreign sales corpn and Govt lending institution; invests Federal funds available under the Covenant.

LEGAL AND JUDICIARY

High Court of the Trust Territory of the Pacific Islands: Saipan, Northern Mariana Islands, CM 96950; tel 322-9739; Chief Justice: Alex R. Munson; Appellate and Trial Divisions.

TOURISM

Marianas Visitors Bureau: POB 861, Saipan, CM 96950; tel 234-8325; telex 676; fax 234-3596; Chair of Board: Peter J. L. Igitol; Vice-Chair: P. Thomas Picarro; f 1976; devt and coordination of tourist industry.

TRANSPORT

Commonwealth Ports Authority: Saipan International Airport, POB 1055, Saipan, CM 96950; tel 234-8315.

Saipan Shipping Co (Saiship): POB 8, Saipan, CM 96950; weekly service from Guam to Saipan and Tinian, and services to Micronesia and the Far East.

UTILITIES

Commonwealth Utilities Corpn: POB 1220, Saipan, CM 96950; tel 322-9450.

Marianas Public Land Corpn: POB 380, Saipan, CM 96950; tel 322-6914; management of public land, which constitutes 73% of total land area in the Commonwealth (38% on Saipan).

PALAU

The Government

OFFICE OF THE PRESIDENT
POB 100, Koror, Palau, Western Caroline Islands, 96960
High Commissioner of the Trust Territory: Janet McCoy
Attorney-General of the Trust Territory: Kent Harvey
President and Minister of Justice: Ngiratkel Etpison
Vice-President: Kuniwo Nakamura
Minister of Administration: Franz Reksid
Minister of National Resources: Wilhelm Renjill
Minister of Social Services: Nobuo Swei
Minister of State: John O. Ngiraked
Attorney-General: (vacant)
The Trust Territory of the Pacific Islands is a United Nations Trusteeship administered by the USA; executive and administrative authority is exercised by a High Commissioner, appointed by the Pres of the USA with the consent and approval of the US Senate; the High Commissioner acts under the direction of the US Secretary of the Interior; executive authority is vested in the directly-elected President and Vice-President, serving four-year terms.

OLBIIL ERA KELULAU (PALAU NATIONAL CONGRESS)
Koror, Palau, Western Caroline Islands, 96960

President of the Senate: Joshua Koshiba
Speaker of the House of Delegates: (vacant)
The Republic is divided into 16 states, each with an elected governor and legislature.

Government Agencies

BANKING

National Development Bank of Palau: Palau, Western Caroline Islands, 96960; tel 578; Chair: Polycarp Basilius.

LEGAL AND JUDICIARY

High Court of the Trust Territory of the Pacific Islands: Saipan, Northern Mariana Islands, CM 96950; tel 322-9739; Chief Justice: Alex R. Munson; Appellate and Trial Divisions.

Supreme Court of the Republic of Palau: Koror, Palau, Western Caroline Islands, 96960; tel 461; Chief Justice: Mamoru Nakamura.

PUERTO RICO

The Government

OFFICE OF THE GOVERNOR
La Fortaleza, San Juan
Governor: Rafael Hernández Colón
(inaugurated 2 January 1989)
Elected by universal adult suffrage for a four-year term; the Governor is Commdr-in-Chief of the militia and has the power to proclaim martial law, and chooses Secretaries of Depts as assistants, led by the Secretary of State, subject to the approval of the Legislative Assembly.

SENATE
San Juan
Pres: Miguel Hernández Agosto
27 mems elected by direct vote for four-year terms.

HOUSE OF REPRESENTATIVES
San Juan
Speaker: José R. Jarabo
Resident Commissioner in Washington: Jaime B. Fuster
51 mems elected by direct vote for four-year terms; a Resident Commissioner, also elected for a four-year term, represents Puerto Rico in the US House of Representatives, but is permitted to vote only in committees of the House.

DEPARTMENT OF STATE
San Juan
Secretary: Sila M. Calderón

DEPARTMENT OF AGRICULTURE
Fernández Juncos Ave, Stop 19.5, POB 10163,
Santurce, PR 00908
Tel 722-0871; fax 723-9747
Secretary: Juan Bauzá Salas
Under-Secretary: Felipe N. Rodríguez

DEPARTMENT OF COMMERCE
San Juan
Secretary: Jorge R. Santiago

DEPARTMENT OF CONSUMER AFFAIRS
Minillas Governmental Center, North Bldg, POB 41059,
Minillas Station, Santurce, PR 00940
Tel 721-3280
Secretary: Jorge Ocasio Rodríguez

DEPARTMENT OF DRUG ADDICTION SERVICES
San Juan
Secretary: Isabel S. de Martínez

DEPARTMENT OF EDUCATION
San Juan
Secretary: Rafael Cartagena

DEPARTMENT OF HEALTH
San Juan
Secretary: Enrique Méndez Grau

DEPARTMENT OF HOUSING
San Juan
Secretary: Vydia García Gómez

DEPARTMENT OF JUSTICE
San Juan
Secretary: Héctor Rivera Cruz

DEPARTMENT OF LABOUR AND HUMAN RESOURCES
San Juan
Secretary: Ruy N. Delgado Zayas

DEPARTMENT OF NATURAL RESOURCES
San Juan
Secretary: José Laborde Rivera

DEPARTMENT OF RECREATION AND SPORTS
San Juan
Secretary: Leonardo González Rivera

DEPARTMENT OF TRANSPORTATION AND PUBLIC WORKS
San Juan
Secretary: Hermengildo Ortiz Quinones

DEPARTMENT OF THE TREASURY
San Juan
Secretary: Juan Agosto Alicea

Government Agencies

BANKING

Government Development Bank for Puerto Rico: POB 42001, Minillas Station, San Juan, PR 00940; tel 722-2525; telex 3857265; fax 726-1440; Pres: José Ramón González; f 1942; independent Govt agency; acts as fiscal (borrowing) agent to the Commonwealth Govt and its public corpns and provides long- and medium-term loans to private businesses; also acts as cheque clearing agency for Puerto Rico's commercial banks.

DEVELOPMENT

Commonwealth of Puerto Rico Economic Development Administration—EDA: POB 2350, San Juan, PR 00936; 355 Roosevelt Ave, Hato Rey, San Juan, PR 00918; tel 758-4747; telex 2345; Admin: Antonio J. Colorado; f 1950, fmrly Puerto Rico Industrial Devt Co; public agency responsible, with its subsidiary the Puerto Rico Industrial Development Co (PRIDCO), for the Govt-sponsored industrial devt programme.

Puerto Rico Planning Board: San Juan, PR 00940-9985.

ENERGY

Center for Energy and Environment Research: POB 3682, San Juan, PR 00936; tel 767-0350; Dir: Dr Juan A. Bonnet, Jr; f 1957; operated by the University of Puerto Rico for the US Dept of Energy; research in renewable energy technologies, tropical marine and terrestrial ecology.

LEGAL AND JUDICIARY

Supreme Court of Puerto Rico: POB 2392, San Juan, PR 00903; tel 723-0297; Chief Judge: Victor Pons Nuñez.

US District Court for Puerto Rico: San Juan; Chief Judge: Juan Pérez Giménez; District Attorney for Puerto Rico: Daniel López Romo.

NEWS AND INFORMATION

División Editorial Departamento de Instrucción Pública: Avda Teniente César González, esq Calaf, Urb Tres Monjitas, Hato Rey, San Juan, PR 00917; Dir: Adrian Santos Tirado; Govt publishing house.

TOURISM

Commonwealth of Puerto Rico Tourism Co: POB 4435, Old San Juan Station, San Juan, PR 00905; tel 721-2400; telex 3450158; Dir: Miguel A. Domenech.

Tourism Development Corpn: POB 3072, San Juan, PR 00903; Exec Dir: Miguel Domenech; f 1970.

TRANSPORT

Puerto Rico Maritime Shipping Authority (Navieras): POB 71105, Hato Rey, San Juan, PR 00936; tel 754-6565; telex 3859777; weekly cargo services to US Atlantic and Gulf ports, US Virgin Islands, Haiti, Dominican Republic, Trinidad and Tobago.

Puerto Rico Ports Authority: POB 2829, San Juan, PR 00936; tel 723-2260; telex 9464; Exec Dir: Guillermo F. Valls; manages and administers all ports and port facilities.

UNITED STATES VIRGIN ISLANDS

The Government

OFFICE OF THE GOVERNOR
Govt House, 21-22 Kongens Gade, St Thomas, 00802
Tel 774-0001; telex 3470060; fax 774-1361
Governor: Alexander A. Farrelly
Lieutenant-Governor: Derek M. Hodge
Administrator for St Croix: Richard Roebuck, Jr
Administrator for St John: William Lomax
Administrator for St Thomas: Harold Robinson
Regional Audit Manager (acting): Roger E. Michaud
The Governor holds executive power and is elected, with the Lieutenant-Governor, by popular election; the Governor appoints the heads of the executive depts and may appoint administrative assistants as his representatives on St John and St Croix.

SENATE
St Thomas
President of the Senate: Bent Lawaetz
Secretary of the Senate: St Clair Williams
The Legislature is a unicameral body composed of 15 Senators, elected by popular vote; legislation is subject to the approval of the Governor.

Government Agencies

BROADCASTING

WTJX—TV (Public Television Service): Barbel Plaza, POB 7879, St Thomas, 00801; Gen Man: Calvin Bastian; one channel.

DEVELOPMENT

Department of Economic Development and Agriculture: POB 6400, St Thomas, 00801; tel 744-8784; responsible for promotion and devt of tourism.

LEGAL AND JUDICIARY

Territorial Court of the Virgin Islands: Barbel Plaza, POB 70, St Thomas, 00801; tel 774-6680; Chief Judge: Verne A. Hodge; jurisdiction in violations of police and executive regulations, in criminal cases and civil actions involving not more than $50,000, in domestic and juvenile matters concurrently with the US District Court; judges are appointed by the Gov.

US District Court of the Virgin Islands: Federal Bldg, POB 720, St Thomas, 00801; tel 774-0640; Chief Judge: Almeric L. Christian; jurisdiction in civil, criminal and federal actions; the judges are appointed by the Pres of the USA with the advice and consent of the Senate.

TRANSPORT

Aero Virgin Islands: Cyril E. King Airport, POB 546, St Thomas, 00801; tel 774-5000; daily flights to San Juan (Puerto Rico) from St Thomas and St Croix.

Virgin Islands Port Authority: Cyril E. King Airport, St Thomas, 00801; tel 774-1629; Alexander Hamilton Airport, St Croix, 00840; tel 778-1012; Dir: John E. Harding; f 1968; semi-autonomous Govt agency; maintains, operates and develops marine and aviation facilities.

URUGUAY

Head of State

Under the 1966 Constitution, executive power is held by the President, who is directly elected by universal adult suffrage for a five-year term. The President is assisted by a Vice-President and an appointed Council of Ministers.

President: Luis Alberto Lacalle (elected 26 November 1989; took office 15 February 1990).

Office of the President: Casa de Gobierno, Edif Libertad, Avda Luis Alberto de Herrera 3050 esq Avda José Pedro Varela, Montevideo; tel (2) 80-81-10; Sec-Gen: Augusto Durán Martínez

Vice-President: (vacant).

Office of the Vice-President: Palacio Legislativo, Montevideo.

Legislature

Legislative authority is vested in a bicameral Congreso (Congress), comprising the Senado (Senate) with 30 members, and the Cámara de Diputados (Chamber of Deputies) with 99 members. Members of both houses are elected for five years by universal adult suffrage based on a system of proportional representation.

Senado (Senate): Palacio Legislativo, Montevideo; tel (2) 20-13-34; Pres: (vacant).

Cámara de Diputados (Chamber of Deputies): Palacio Legislativo, Montevideo; Pres: (vacant).

MINISTRIES AND GOVERNMENT DEPARTMENTS

MINISTRY OF ECONOMY AND FINANCE
Colonia 1089, 3°, Montevideo
Tel (2) 91-91-02; telex 6269
Minister: Enrique Braga Silva

MINISTRY OF EDUCATION AND CULTURE
Reconquista 535, Montevideo
Tel (2) 95-01-03; telex 23133
Minister: Guillermo Francisco García Costa

MINISTRY OF ELECTORAL AFFAIRS
Montevideo
Minister: (vacant)

MINISTRY OF FOREIGN AFFAIRS
Avda 18 de Julio 1205, Montevideo
Tel (2) 92-10-07; telex 22074; fax (2) 92-13-27
Minister: Héctor Gross Espiell

MINISTRY OF HOUSING AND ENVIRONMENT
Montevideo
Minister: Raúl Lago Finsterwald

MINISTRY OF INDUSTRY AND ENERGY
Rincón 747, Montevideo
Tel (2) 90-26-00; telex 22072
Minister: Augusto Montesdeoca Galagorri

MINISTRY OF THE INTERIOR
Mercedes 993, Montevideo
Tel (2) 98-93-10; telex 22045
Minister: Juan Andrés Ramírez

MINISTRY OF LABOUR AND SOCIAL SECURITY
Juncal 1511, 4°, Montevideo
Tel (2) 91-54-11
Minister: Carlos Alfredo Cat Vidal

MINISTRY OF LIVESTOCK, AGRICULTURE AND FISHING
Avda Constituyentes 1476, Montevideo
Tel (2) 40-41-55; telex 937
Minister: Alvaro Ramos Trigo

MINISTRY OF NATIONAL DEFENCE
8 de Octubre 2628, Montevideo
Tel (2) 80-71-09; telex 23317
Minister: Mariano Romeo Brito Cecchi

MINISTRY OF PUBLIC HEALTH
18 de Julio 1892, Montevideo
Tel (2) 40-01-01
Minister: Alfredo Solari Damonte

MINISTRY OF PUBLIC WORKS AND TRANSPORT
Rincón 561, Montevideo
Tel (2) 90-65-71; telex 22071
Minister: Wilson Santiago Elso Goñi

MINISTRY OF TOURISM
Avda Libertador Brig Gral Lavelleja 1409, Montevideo
Tel (2) 91-32-43
Minister: José Villar Gómez

OFFICE OF THE SECRETARY OF PLANNING AND BUDGET
Edif Libertad, 2/3/4°, Montevideo
Tel (2) 81-95-25
Secretary: (vacant)

GOVERNMENT AGENCIES AND ORGANIZATIONS

Advisory and Supervisory Bodies

Contaduría General de la Nación (National Audit Office): Montevideo; responsible for audit of state accounts and supervision of expenditure by Govt agencies.

Dirección Nacional de Costos, Precios e Ingresos (Dinacoprín): Montevideo; tel (2) 98-10-25; determines rates for minimum wages and maximum retail prices.

Agriculture

Comisión Honoraria del Plan Agropecuario: Bulevar Artigas 3802 esq Burgues, Montevideo; tel (2) 23-68-66; Pres: Rodolfo Raffo; f 1957; devt of livestock farms.

Business and Economy

BANKING

Banco La Caja Obrera: 25 de Mayo 500, Montevideo; tel (2) 95-05-01; telex 26613; Pres: Yamandú D'Elía; Gen Man: Enrique Ferreiro Camejo; f 1905; taken over by the Banco de la República Oriental in 1987; 42 brs.

Banco Central del Uruguay: Avda Juan P. Fabini esq Florida, Montevideo; tel (2) 91-71-17; telex 6659; Pres: Juan Carlos Protasi; Gen Man: Jorge Sambarino; f 1967; bank of issue; also supervisory authority for all banks.

Banco Hipotecario del Uruguay: Avda Fernández Crespo 1508, Montevideo; Pres: Dr Julio Kneit; f 1892; state mortgage bank; in 1977 assumed responsibility for housing projects in Uruguay.

Banco Pan de Azúcar: Rincón 518/528, Casilla 1891, Montevideo; tel (2) 95-80-13; telex 803; Pres: Federico Slinger; Gen Man: Fructuoso Novo; f 1945; under control of Banco de la República Oriental del Uruguay; 18 brs.

Banco de la República Oriental del Uruguay: Calles Cerrito y Zabala, Montevideo; tel (2) 95-01-57; telex 6634; Pres: Federico Slinger; Mans: José Pedro Laffite, Juan Young; f 1896; 135 brs.

FINANCIAL AGENCIES

Tesorería General (National Treasury): Montevideo; responsible for control and allocation of Govt funds.

INSURANCE

Banco de Seguros del Estado: Avda Libertador Brig Gral Lavalleja 1465, Montevideo; telex 26938; Pres: Nelson Costanzo; Vice-Pres: Jorge Luis Franzini; f 1912; state insurance organization; has monopoly of all types of insurance.

TRADE

Dirección General de Comercio Exterior: Cuareim 1384, Montevideo; tel (2) 92-03-19; telex 22330; fax (2) 92-17-26; Dir-Gen: Isidoro Hodara; Librarian: María Teresa Castilla; f 1989; foreign trade directorate.

Defence

Air Force: Comando General de la Fuerza Aérea, Avda Don Pedro de Mendoza 5553, Montevideo; tel (2) 22-44-01.

Army: Comando General del Ejército, Avda General Garibaldi 2313, Montevideo; tel (2) 28-15-42; telex 931.

Navy: Comando General de la Armada, Edif Aduana, 4°, Montevideo; tel (2) 95-55-00.

Development and Planning

INVESTMENT

Fondo Nacional de Inversiones: Montevideo; investment fund controlled by Ministry of Public Works and Transport for infrastructure devt schemes.

PLANNING

Corporación Nacional para el Desarrollo: Rincón 528, 7°, 11000 Montevideo; tel (2) 95-57-64; telex 6652; fax (2) 96-14-93; Pres: Enrique Vispo; Dirs: Pablo Cristina, Mauricio Geppert, Agustín Barbato, Roberto Horta; f 1985; national devt corpn; helps in the creation of new enterprises, strengthens existing ones and promotes devt of exports.

Secretaría de Planificación, Coordinación y Difusión (Seplacodi): Coronel Lorenzo Latorre 1366, Montevideo; tel (2) 90-03-09; supervises and implements devt plans.

Energy

Administración Nacional de Combustibles, Alcohol y Portland (ANCAP): Paysandú y Avda Libertador Brig Gral Lavalleja, Casilla 1090, Montevideo; tel (2) 92-11-36; telex 23168; fax (2) 92-11-36; Pres: José Luis Batlle; Gen Man: Andrés Tierno Abreu; f 1931; deals with the transport, refining and sale of petroleum products, and the manufacture of alcohol, spirit and cement.

Administración Nacional de las Usinas y Transmisiones Eléctricas del Estado (UTE): Paraguay 2431, Montevideo; tel (2) 215; telex 326627; Pres: Roberto d'Amado Campos; f 1912; sole purveyor of electricity.

Comisión Nacional de Energía Atómica: Soriano 1014, Casilla 970, Montevideo; telex 22072; Pres: José L. Bozzo; f 1955; atomic energy commission.

Fishing

Instituto Nacional de Pesca (INAPE): Calle Constituyente 1497, Montevideo; tel (2) 4-31-80; Man: Pedro C. Márquez Straga; f 1975; promotion and devt of the fishing industry in all its aspects.

Legal and Judiciary

Suprema Corte Administrativa (Supreme Administrative Tribunal): Mercedes 961, Montevideo; tel (2) 90-80-47; five mems appointed by the executive to hear cases involving the functioning of the State admin.

Suprema Corte de Justicia (Supreme Court): Gutiérrez Ruiz 1310, 11100 Montevideo; tel (2) 90-10-41; Pres: Dr Nelson Nicoliello; Mems: Dra Jacinta Balbela del Delgue, Dr Armando Tommasino, Dr Nelson García Otero, Dr Rafale Addiego; f 1907; supreme judicial organ; declares on constitutionality of laws, resolution of international conflicts and on conflict between state institutions; five mems appointed for five years by the executive.

Media

BROADCASTING

SODRE—Servicio Oficial de Difusión Radiotelevisión y Espectáculos: Blvd Artigas 2552, Montevideo; tel (2) 80-64-48; telex 26602; Dir: Dr Daniel Álvarez Ferretjans; national TV service.

NEWS AND INFORMATION

CENCI-Uruguay: Misiones 1361, Casilla 1510, Montevideo; tel (2) 95-45-78; collection, analysis and dissemination of statistical data.

Dirección General de Estadística y Censos: Cuareim 2052, Montevideo; tel (2) 20-11-05; telex 22280; Dir-Gen: Rosa Grosskoff; f 1912; collection and dissemination of national statistics.

Telecommunications

Administración Nacional de Telecomunicaciones— ANTEL: Avda Daniel Fernández Crespo 1534, Montevideo; tel (2) 41-27-03; telex 850; Pres: Prof Manuel Buela; Vice-Pres: Miguel Vieites; f 1974; national telecommunications admin.

Dirección Nacional de Correos: Mesa Central, Misiones 451, Montevideo; national postal co.

Tourism

Dirección Nacional de Turismo: Agraciada 1409, 4/5/6°, Montevideo; tel (2) 90-41-48; supervises and executes national tourism policy.

Transport

CIVIL AVIATION

Primeras Líneas Uruguayas de Navegación Aérea (PLUNA): Colonia 1021, Casilla 1360, Montevideo; tel (2) 98-35-16; telex 753; Pres: Emilio A. Conforte; Sec-Gen: Col Fernando R. Blanco; f 1936, nationalized 1951; operates international services to Argentina, Brazil, Chile, Paraguay and Spain under management of the Govt.

Transporte Aéreo Militar Uruguayo (TAMU): Colonia 959, Montevideo; tel (2) 92-09-45; telex 22457; fax (2) 22-43-02; Dir: Col Roque A. Aita; Dep Dir: Lt-Gen Rafael J. Becerra; f 1970; branch of the Air Force; operates domestic flights only.

RAILWAYS

Administración de los Ferrocarriles del Estado—AFE: La Paz 1095, Casilla 419, Montevideo; tel (2) 28-95-51; Pres: Juan F. Berchesi; Vice-Pres: Víctor Antonio Delgado; f 1952; 2,991 km of track.

SHIPPING

Administración Nacional de Puertos (ANP): Rambla 25 de Agosto de 1825 160, Montevideo; tel (2) 95-03-58; f 1916; national ports admin.

Prefectura Nacional Naval: Edif Comando General de la Armada, 5°, Rambla 25 de Agosto de 1825 s/n, Montevideo; tel (2) 96-09-86; telex 23929; Dir: Adm Ramon Robatto; f 1829; maritime supervisory body, responsible for rescue services, protection of sea against pollution, etc.

Utilities

Administración de las Obras Sanitarias (OSE): Carlos Roxlo 1275, Montevideo; tel (2) 40-11-51; telex 22054; f 1952; provision of drinking water and maintenance of sewerage system.

VANUATU

Head of State

The Head of State is the President, who is elected for a five-year term by an electoral college consisting of Parliament and the Presidents of the Regional Councils. Executive power is vested in the Council of Ministers, appointed by the Prime Minister and responsible to Parliament. The Prime Minister is elected by and from members of Parliament.

President: Fred Timakata (took office 30 January 1989).

Office of the President: Port Vila; tel 3055; telex 1040.

Legislature

Legislative power is vested in the unicameral Parliament, comprising 46 members elected by universal adult suffrage for four years. The National Council of Chiefs, composed of custom chiefs elected by their peers, may make recommendations to Parliament concerning the preservation and promotion of Vanuatu's cultural heritage.

Parliament: Port Vila; Speaker: Onneyn Tahi.

MINISTRIES AND GOVERNMENT DEPARTMENTS

OFFICE OF THE PRIME MINISTER
Private Mail Bag, Port Vila
Tel 2413; telex 1040; fax 3142
Prime Minister: Fr Walter Hadye Lini
First Secretary: Joe Natuman

MINISTRY OF AGRICULTURE, FORESTRY AND FISHERIES
POB 129, Port Vila
Tel 3406; telex 1040
Minister: Jack T. Hopa

MINISTRY OF CIVIL AVIATION AND TOURISM
Port Vila
Minister: Edward Natapei

MINISTRY OF EDUCATION AND SPORT
POB 153, Port Vila
Tel 2309; telex 1040
Minister: Sethy Regenvanu

MINISTRY OF FINANCE AND HOUSING
POB 31, Port Vila
Tel 2951; telex 1040
Minister: Sela Molisa

MINISTRY OF FOREIGN AFFAIRS AND JUDICIAL SERVICES
Private Mail Bag, Port Vila

Tel 2913; telex 1040; fax 3142
Minister: Donald Kalpokas
Secretary: Nikenike Vurobaravu

MINISTRY OF HEALTH
Port Vila
Minister: Jimmy Meto Chilia

MINISTRY OF HOME AFFAIRS AND LABOUR
POB 157, Port Vila
Tel 2252; telex 1040
Minister: Iolu Abil

MINISTRY OF LANDS, MINERALS AND RURAL WATER SUPPLY
POB 151, Port Vila
Tel 3105; telex 1040
Minister: William Mahit

MINISTRY OF TRADE, CO-OPERATIVES, ENERGY AND INDUSTRY
Private Mail Bag 011, Port Vila
Tel 3979; telex 1040; fax 3499
Minister: Harold Qualao

MINISTRY OF TRANSPORT, COMMUNICATIONS AND PUBLIC WORKS
POB 381, Port Vila
Tel 2790; telex 1040
Minister: Edward Natapei

GOVERNMENT AGENCIES AND ORGANIZATIONS

Business and Economy

BANKING

Central Bank of Vanuatu: POB 271, Port Vila; tel 3333; telex 1049; Gen Man: Franklyn Kere.

Development Bank of Vanuatu: rue de Paris, POB 241, Port Vila; tel 2181; telex 1049; Man Dir: Augustine Garae; f 1979.

MARKETING

Vanuatu Commodities Marketing Board: POB 81, Port Vila; tel 3123; telex 1036; Gen Man: Meto Nganga; f 1982; sole exporter of major commodities, including copra, kava and cocoa.

TRADE

Vanuatu Chamber of Commerce: POB 189, Port Vila; tel 3255; telex 1107; Gen Man: Joel George Toa; f 1982; devt of new enterprises and trading opportunities.

Development and Planning

National Planning Office: Port Vila; responsible for national devt and planning.

Legal and Judiciary

Supreme Court of Vanuatu: rue Querios, Port Vila; tel 2420; Chief Justice: Frederick Cooke; Chief Prosecutor: John Baxter-Wright; Attorney-Gen: Silas Hakwa; highest judicial authority; unlimited jurisdiction to hear and determine any civil or criminal proceedings; consists of five mems appointed by the President, after consultation with the Prime Minister and the Leader of the Opposition.

Media

BROADCASTING

Radio Vanuatu: Private Bag, Port Vila; tel 2999; telex 1046; Dir: Bob Makin; f 1966; broadcasts in English, French and Bislama.

NEWS AND INFORMATION

Statistics Office: Private Mail Bag, Port Vila; tel 2111; telex 1040; fax 3142; responsible for the collection and dissemination of Govt statistics, and the co-ordination of all statistical data in Vanuatu.

Tourism

National Tourism Office of Vanuatu: Kumul Highway, POB 209, Port Vila; tel 2685; telex 1102; Gen Man: Peter K. Taurakoto.

Transport and Communications

TELECOMMUNICATIONS

Posts and Telecommunications: c/o Post Office, Port Vila.

TRANSPORT

Air Vanuatu: POB 148, Port Vila; tel 3838; telex 1117; fax 3250; Chief Exec: Peter W. Roberts; Gen Man: Keith J. Molloy; f 1987; services to Melbourne, Sydney and Auckland.

THE VATICAN CITY

Head of State and Legislature

The Vatican City State is under the temporal jurisdiction of the Pope, the Supreme Pontiff elected for life by a conclave comprising members of the Sacred College of Cardinals. He appoints a Pontifical Commission, headed by a President, to conduct the administrative affairs of the Vatican City State.

The Supreme Pontiff: His Holiness Pope John Paul II (elected 16 October 1978).

Office of the Supreme Pontiff: Palazzo Apostolico del Vaticano, 00120 Vatican City.

Pontifical Commission: Palazzo Apostolico del Vaticano, Vatican City; tel (6) 6983306; telex 2019; Mems: Cardinal Sebastiano Baggio (Pres), Archbishop Paul Marcinkus (Pro-Pres), Cardinal Luigi Dadaglio, Cardinal Antonio Innocenti, Cardinal Jozef Tomko, Cardinal Andrzej Maria Deskur, Cardinal Rosalio José Castillo Lara, Marchese Giulio Sacchetti (Special Delegate).

THE ROMAN CURIA

SECRETARIAT OF STATE
Palazzina della Zecca, 00120 Vatican City
Tel (6) 6985098
Secretary of State: Cardinal Agostino Casaroli
The Secretariat of State is divided into two sections:

First Section—General Affairs: Palazzo Apostolico Vaticano, 00120 Vatican City; tel (6) 6983438; telex 2015; Asst Sec of State: Most Rev Edward Cassidy, Titular Archbishop of Amantia.

Second Section—Relations with States: Palazzo Apostolico Vaticano, 00120 Vatican City; tel (6) 6983014; telex 2029; Sec: Most Rev Angelo Sodano, Titular Archbishop of Nova Caesaris.

ADMINISTRATION OF THE PATRIMONY OF THE HOLY SEE
Palazzo Apostolico, 00120 Vatican City
Tel (6) 6984306
President: Cardinal Agnelo Rossi
Secretary: Mgr Giovanni Lajolo, Titular Archbishop of Caesariana

APOSTOLIC CHAMBER
Palazzo Apostolico, 00120 Vatican City
Tel (6) 6983554
Chamberlain of Holy Roman Church:
Cardinal Sebastiano Baggio
Vice-Chamberlain: Mgr Ettore Cunial

PREFECTURE OF THE ECONOMIC AFFAIRS OF THE HOLY SEE
Palazzo delle Congregazioni, Largo del Colonnato 3, 00193 Rome
Tel (6) 6984263
Prefect: Cardinal Giuseppe Caprio
Secretary: Mgr Luigi Sposito

PREFECTURE OF THE PAPAL HOUSEHOLD
00120 Vatican City
Prefect: Mgr Dino Monduzzi, Titular Bishop of Capri
Responsible for domestic admin and organization.

GOVERNMENT AGENCIES AND ORGANIZATIONS

Financial Agency

Istituto per le Opere di Religione (IOR): 00120 Vatican City; telex 2012; Chair: Giovanni Bodio; Man Dir: Luigi Mennini; f 1887 and re-named in 1942; oversees the distribution of capital designated for religious works; takes deposits from Vatican residents, including the Pope; from 1989 a commission of five cardinals, assisted by a committee of financial experts will be responsible for the institution.

Media

BROADCASTING

Centro Televisivo Vaticano (Vatican Television Centre):
Palazzo Belvedere, 00120 Vatican City; tel (6) 6985497; telex 2011; Pres: Mgr John Foley, Titular Archbishop of Neapolis in Proconsulari; Sec-Gen: (vacant); f 1983; produces and distributes religious programmes.

Radio Vaticana: Palazzo Pio, Palazza Pia 3, 00193 Rome; tel (6) 6983551; telex 2023; Pres: Rev Roberto P. Tucci; Dir-Gen: Rev Pasquale Borgomeo; f 1931; broadcasts papal teaching and events affecting the Catholic religion in 35 languages.

NEWS AND INFORMATION

Agenzia Internazionale Fides (AIF): Palazzo di Propaganda Fide, Via di Propaganda 1c, 00187 Rome; tel (6) 6792414; Dir: Mgr Jesús Urtasun Irigoyen; f 1926; handles news of missions throughout the world.

VENEZUELA

Head of State

Executive authority is vested in the President, who is elected for five years by universal adult suffrage. The President may not serve two consecutive terms. The President appoints a Council of Ministers to assist in government, and nominates the Governors of the Federal District, Federal Territories and the States.

President: Carlos Andrés Pérez (elected 4 December 1988; took office 2 February 1989).

Office of the President: Palacio de Miraflores, Avda Urdaneta, Caracas 1010; tel (2) 810-811; telex 21162.

Legislature

Legislative authority is vested in the bicameral Congreso Nacional (National Congress). The Senado (Senate) comprises 49 elected members as well as former Presidents. The Cámara de Diputados (Chamber of Deputies) comprises 201 members. Members of both houses are elected for five years by universal adult suffrage. Venezuela is made up of 20 States, two Federal Territories and a Federal District, each with an executive Governor and an elected legislature.

Senado (Senate): Congreso Nacional, Caracas 1010; tel (2) 483-3568; Pres: Octavio Lepage.

Cámara de Diputados (Chamber of Deputies): Congreso Nacional, Caracas 1010; tel (2) 483-3347; Pres: José Rodríguez Iturbe.

MINISTRIES AND GOVERNMENT DEPARTMENTS

MINISTRY OF AGRICULTURE AND LIVESTOCK
Torre Este, 1°, Parque Central, Caracas 1010
Tel (2) 509-01-11; telex 21483
Minister: Fanny Bello

MINISTRY OF CO-ORDINATION AND PLANNING
Caracas
Minister: Miguel Antonio Rodríguez Fandeo

MINISTRY OF CULTURE, SCIENCE AND TECHNOLOGY
Palacio de Miraflores, Avda Urdaneta, Caracas 1010
Minister, Culture: José Antonio Abreu
Minister, Science and Technology: Dulce Arnao de Uzcategui

MINISTRY OF DEVELOPMENT
Edif Sur, Centro Simón Bolívar, Caracas 1010
Tel (2) 419-341; telex 22753
Minister: Moíses Naime

MINISTRY OF EDUCATION
Edif Educación, esq El Conde, Caracas
Minister: Gustavo Roosen

MINISTRY OF ENERGY AND MINES
Torre Oeste, Avda Lecuna, Parque Central, Caracas 1010
Tel (2) 507-50-80; telex 29550
Minister: Celestino Armas

MINISTRY OF THE ENVIRONMENT AND RENEWABLE NATURAL RESOURCES
Torre Norte, Centro Simón Bolívar, Caracas 1010
Tel (2) 408-11-11; telex 22661
Minister: Dr Enrique Colmenares Finol

MINISTRY OF THE FAMILY
Torre Oeste, 41°, Avda Lecuna, Parque Central, Caracas 1010
Tel (2) 574-71-11; telex 24402
Minister: Teresa Albáñez

MINISTRY OF FINANCE
Torre Norte, Centro Simón Bolívar, Caracas 1010
Tel (2) 419-341; telex 22763
Minister: Eglée Iturbe de Blanco

MINISTRY OF FOREIGN AFFAIRS
Casa Amarilla, esq de Principal, Caracas
Tel (2) 818-521; telex 22721
Minister: Alejandro Tejera Parise

MINISTRY OF HEALTH AND SOCIAL ASSISTANCE
Edif Sur, Centro Simón Bolívar, Caracas 1010
Minister: Felipe Bello González

MINISTRY OF THE INTERIOR
Carmelitas a Santa Capilla, Caracas
Tel (2) 813-851; telex 29679
Minister: Alejandro Izaguirre Angelie

MINISTRY OF JUSTICE
Edif Lincoln, Calle Real de Sabana Grande, Caracas
Tel (2) 725-831; telex 21320
Minister: Luis Beltrán Guerra

MINISTRY OF LABOUR AND SOCIAL DEVELOPMENT
Edif Sur, Centro Simón Bolívar, Caracas 1010
Minister: Marisela Padrón Quero

MINISTRY OF NATIONAL DEFENCE
La Planicie, Caracas
Tel (2) 662-12-53; telex 22598
Minister: Gen Italo del Valle Allegroe

**MINISTRY OF THE SECRETARIAT OF THE
PRESIDENCY**
Palacio de Miraflores, Avda Urdaneta, Caracas 1010
Tel (2) 810-811; telex 28115; fax (2) 571-31-34
Minister: Dr Reinaldo Figueredo Planchart
Deputy Minister: Beatrice Rangel Mantilla

**MINISTRY OF TRANPORT AND
COMMUNICATIONS**
Torre Este, Parque Central, Caracas 1010
Tel (2) 509-10-00; telex 21785
Minister: Gustavo José Rada Aristiguieta

MINISTRY OF URBAN DEVELOPMENT
Edif Banco de Venezuela, Reducto a Miranda, Caracas
Tel (2) 419-711; telex 24135
Minister: Luis Penzini Fleury

MINISTRY OF WOMEN'S AFFAIRS
Edif Administrativo de Miraflores, 3°, Avda Urdaneta,
Caracas 1010
Tel (2) 810-811
Minister: Aura Loret de Range

OFFICE OF THE COMPTROLLER-GENERAL
Avda Andrés Bello, frente al Mercado Guaicaipuro, Caracas
Tel (2) 571-64-11
Comptroller-General: Jesús Ramón Carmona Borjas

**OFFICE OF THE GOVERNOR OF THE FEDERAL
DISTRICT**
Esq de Principal, Caracas 1010
Tel (2) 811-111; telex 28256
Governor: Virgilio Avila Vivas

**OFFICE OF THE PRESIDENT OF THE
VENEZUELAN OFFICE FOR GUAYANAN
DEVELOPMENT**
Avda La Estancia 10, 13°, Apdo 7000, Caracas
President: Leopoldo Sucre Figarella

GOVERNMENT AGENCIES AND ORGANIZATIONS

Advisory and Supervisory Body

Consejo Supremo Electoral: Centro Simón Bolívar, esq de Pajaritos, Caracas 1010; tel (2) 419-881; electoral council and supervisory body.

Agriculture

Corporación de Mercadeo Agrícola (Corpomercadeo): Edif Torre Industrial, C. Vargas-Boleíta, Caracas; tel (2) 358-044; Pres: Dr Alberto Silva Guillén; responsible for the marketing and promotion of agricultural products.

Instituto Agrario Nacional (IAN): Quinta Barrancas, La Quebradita, Caracas; Pres: Antonio Alvarez Fernández; f 1945 under Agrarian Law to assure ownership of the land to those who worked on it; now authorized to expropriate and redistribute idle or unproductive lands.

Instituto de Crédito Agrícola y Pecuario: 40-44 Salvador de León a Socarras, Caracas; Dir-Gen: Dr Antonio José Alvarez Fernández; fmrly the Banco Agrícola y Pecuario; administers Govt crop credit scheme for small farmers.

Art and Culture

Consejo Nacional de la Cultura (CONAC): Edif Los Roques, 7°, Avda Principal de Chuao, Caracas; tel (2) 911-180; national council for culture.

Business and Economy

BANKING

Banco Central de Venezuela: Avda Urdaneta esq de las Carmelitas, Caracas 1010; tel (2) 829-811; telex 28250; Pres: Pedro Tinoco, Jr; Vice-Pres: José Benjamín Escobar; f 1940; bank of issue and clearing house for commercial banks.

Banco de Comercio, SACA: Edif Banco de Comercio, 1°, esq

San Jacinto, Apdo 2330, Caracas; tel (2) 545-59-54; telex 21594; Pres: Ramón Carrasco; f 1953; came under state control in 1985; 28 brs.

Banco de Desarrollo Agropecuario, CA: Carrera 19 con Calle 25, Barquisimeto, Lara; tel (51) 20940; telex 51293; Pres: Antonio Alvarez Fernández; Vice-Pres: Italo Masobrio; f 1967.

Banco de Fomento Comercial de Venezuela, CA: Avda 20, entre Calles 31 y 32, Apdo 128, Barquisimeto, Lara; tel (51) 26020; telex 51149; Pres: Félix Pineda Galaviz; Exec Vice-Pres: Dr Jesús Rafael Flores; f 1949.

Banco de Fomento Regional Coro, CA: Avda Manaure, entre Calles Falcón y Zamora, Coro, Falcón; tel (68) 514-421; telex 56168; Pres: Abraham Naín Senior Urbina; Gen Man: Dimas Bueno Arenas; f 1950.

Banco de Fomento Regional Los Andes, CA: Carrera 6, esq Calle 5, San Cristóbal, Táchira; tel (76) 431-269; telex 76113; Pres: Edgar Moreno Méndez; Exec Vice-Pres: Pedro Roa Sánchez; f 1951.

Banco Guayana, CA: Edif Banguayana, Prologación Paseo Orinoco, Apdo 156, Ciudad Bolívar, Bolívar; tel (85) 25511; telex 85175; Pres: Andrés E. Bello Bilancieri; Gen Man: Omaira Uncein de Natera; f 1955.

Banco Industrial de Venezuela, CA: Avda Universidad, esq Traposos, Caracas 1010; tel (2) 545-92-22; telex 21354; Pres: Bernardo Martínez; Exec Vice-Pres: Carlos L. Mendiri; f 1937; 58 brs.

Banco Italo-Venezolano, CA: Edif Banco Italo-Venezolano, Avda Urdaneta, esq Pelota a esq Punceres 23, Caracas; tel (2) 561-65-66; telex 26316; Pres: Dr Antonio Morales S.; Gen Man: Amilcar Guevara; f 1952.

Banco Nacional de Ahorro y Préstamo (BANAP): Edif Torre BANAP, 8°, Avda Venezuela, Caracas; tel (2) 323-835.

Banco Occidental de Descuento, CA: Avda 5 de Julio, esq Avda 17, Apdo 695, Maracaibo, Zulia; tel (61) 523-044; telex 64348; Pres: Dr Alfredo Belloso; Exec Vice-Pres: Giorgio Vignali Erli; f 1957; 12 brs.

Banco Popular, CA: Edif Comercial de Maracaibo, Avda 5 de Julio, Apdo 46, Maracaibo, Zulia; tel (61) 70622; telex 62558; Pres: Antonio Quintero Parra; Gen Man: Carlos Rodríguez Rojas; f 1916.

Banco República, CA: Edif EDSAM, Madrices a San Jacinto, Apdo 6688, Caracas 1010-A; tel (2) 563-38-89; telex 21333; Pres:

Eglée Iturbe de Blanco; Vice-Pres: Antonio Golding Hernández; f 1958.

Banco de los Trabajadores de Venezuela (BTV), CA: Avda Universidad, esq Colón a esq Dr Díaz, Apdo 888, Caracas; tel (2) 541-73-22; telex 22604; Pres: Juan José Delpino; Man: Silverio Antonio Narváez; f 1968 to channel workers' savings for the financing of artisans and small industrial firms; came under state control in 1982; 11 agencies.

INSURANCE

Superintendencia de Seguros: Torre Metálica, 1°-4°, Avda Francisco de Miranda, cruce con Avda Loyola, Chacao, Caracas 1061; tel (2) 263-13-44; telex 24684; Supt: Dr Juan F. Ramírez Giraud; insurance supervisory board.

NATIONALIZED INDUSTRY

Siderúrgica del Orinoco, CA (Sidor): Edif La Estancia, Chuao, Caracas; Pres: César Mendoza; steel producer.

Venezolana de Aluminio, CA (Venalum): Caracas; production of aluminium; Pres: (vacant).

TRADE

Instituto de Comercio Exterior (ICE): Centro Comercial Los Cedros, Apdo 51852, Caracas 1050; tel (2) 729-960; Pres: Gabriela Febres Cordero; responsible for promotion of exports, linked to Ministry of Foreign Affairs.

Defence

Armed Forces: Fuerte Tiuna, El Valle, Caracas; tel (2) 692-685.

> **Air Force:** Base Generalísimo, Avda Francisco de Miranda, La Carlota, Caracas 1070; tel (2) 239-2311.

> **Army:** Fuerte Tiuna, La Valle, Caracas; tel (2) 692-685; telex 21491.

> **Navy:** Avda Vollmer, 2°, San Bernardino, Caracas 1010; tel (2) 521-404; telex 21168.

Development and Planning

INVESTMENT

Fondo de Inversiones de Venezuela (FIV): Edif Banco Central, esq de Carmelitas con esq Santa Capilla, Caracas; tel (2) 838-338; Pres: Eduardo Quinteros; f 1974 as a fund using surplus oil revenue for internal investment; in 1977 it was made into a holding co with responsibility for co-ordinating, supervising and controlling the activities of all public financial and credit cos.

Superintendencia de Inversiones Extranjeras (SIEX): Torre Europa, Avda Francisco de Miranda, Apdo 64582, Caracas 1064; tel (2) 926-511; telex 24534; Supt: Jesús María Ponce Torrealba; f 1974; supervises foreign investment in Venezuela.

PLANNING

Consejo de Economía Nacional: Caracas; economic planning advisory board.

Cordiplán: Palacio Blanco, Avda Urdaneta, Miraflores, Caracas; tel (2) 818-011; telex 21202; Dir: Minister of Co-ordination and Planning, Miguel Antonio Rodríguez Fandeo; co-ordination and planning office.

Corporación de Desarrollo de la Pequeña y Mediana Industria (Corpoindustria): Avda Páez, esq Avda Las Delicias, Maracay, Aragua; tel (43) 23459; telex 43472; Pres: Dr Carlos González López; promotes the devt of small- and medium-sized industries.

Corporación Venezolana de Fomento: Prolongación Edif Norte, Centro Simón Bolívar, Caracas 1010; tel (2) 419-441; telex 21314; José Vincente Sánchez Piña; devt corpn.

REGIONAL DEVELOPMENT

Corporación Venezolana de Guayana (CVG): Avda La Estancia 10, 13°, Apdo 7000, Caracas; Pres: Leopoldo Sucre Figarella; f 1960 to organize the devt of the Guayana region, paticularly its iron ore and hydroelectric resources.

Legal and Judiciary

Fiscalía General de la República: Edif Banco Exterior, 8°, Avda Urdaneta esq Urapal, Caracas; tel (2) 572-95-11; office of the State Prosecutor.

Supreme Court: Avda Universidad, esq La Bolsa, Caracas 1010; tel (2) 483-11-52; Pres: Dr René de Solas; Attorney-Gen: Pedro J. Mantellini González; comprises 15 judges appointed by the Congress in joint session for nine years, five to be appointed every three years; highest judicial authority divided into three courts, each with five judges: political-administrative; civil, mercantile and labour cassation; penal cassation.

Media

BROADCASTING

Radio Nacional: Apdo 3979, Caracas 1010; Dir: Silvia Rodríguez; f 1946; eight stations.

Televisora Nacional: Apdo 3979, Caracas; Dir-Gen: Ricardo Tirado.

Venezolana de Televisión—Canal 5: Apdo 3979, Caracas; tel (2) 239-98-11; Dir-Gen: Osorio Canales; f 1964; 14 relay stations; there are plans to convert the network to satellite transmission.

Venezolana de Televisión—Canal 8: Avda Montecristo, Los Ruices, Apdo 2739, Caracas; tel (2) 349-571; telex 25401; Dir-Gen: Osorio Canales; 12 relay stations.

NEWS AND INFORMATION

Oficina Central de Estadística e Informática (OCEI): Edif Fundación La Salle, Avda Boyacá, Cota Mil, Maripérez, Caracas; Apdo 4593, San Martín, Caracas 1010; tel (2) 782-11-33; telex 21241; fax (2) 781-72-77; Dir-Gen: Dr Leonardo Seijas Zerpa; Dir, Information: Dr Francisco Ortega; Dir, Statistics: Dr Myrna Cisneros; f 1978; collection, analysis and publication of demographic, commercial, social and administrative statistics; also responsible for population, economic, housing, farming and other censuses.

Mining and Energy

ENERGY

Dirección General Sectorial de Hidrocarburos: Torre Oeste, 12°, Avda Lecuna, Parque Central, Caracas 1010; tel (2) 507-62-01; Dir-Gen: Manuel Alayeto E.; division of Ministry of Energy and Mines responsible for determining national policy for the exploration and exploitation of petroleum reserves and for the marketing of petroleum and its products.

Petróleos de Venezuela, SA (Petrovén/PDVSA): Edif Petróleos de Venezuela, Avda Libertador, La Campiña, Apdo 169, Caracas 1010-A; tel (2) 708-41-11; telex 21890; Pres: Juan Chaci Guzmán; First Vice-Pres: Pablo Reimpell; f 1975; holding co for national petroleum industry; responsible for petrochemical sector since 1978 and for devt of coal resources in Western Venezuela since 1985; the following are subsidiaries of PDVSA:

Barivén, SA: Edif Centro Empresarial Parque del Este, Avda Francisco de Miranda, La Carlota, Apdo 893, Caracas 1010-A; tel (2) 203-11-11; telex 29542; handles the petroleum, petrochemical and hydrocarbons industries' overseas purchases of equipment and materials.

Carbozulia, SA: c/o Edif Petróleos de Venezuela, Avda Libertador, La Campiña, Apdo 169, Caracas 1010-A; tel (2) 708-41-11; telex 21890; Pres: Luis Urdaneta Vásquez; f 1978 to administer coal mining operations at Zulia.

Corpovén, SA: Avda Libertador, La Campiña, Apdo 61373, Caracas 1060-A; telex 21363; Pres: Roberto Mandini; Vice-Pres: Dr Eduardo López Quevedo; petroleum drilling, production, refining and marketing and gas distribution; merged with Menevén in 1986.

Intervén, SA: Edif Centro Empresarial Parque del Este, Avda Francisco de Miranda, La Carlota, Apdo 60564, Caracas 1060-A; tel (2) 203-13-00; telex 21854; Pres: Remigio Fernández; Vice-Pres: Arnoldo Volkenborn; f 1986 to manage PDVSA's joint ventures overseas.

INTEVEP, SA: Urb Santa Rosa, Los Teques, Apdo 76343, Caracas 1070-A; tel (2) 908-61-11; telex 21672; Pres: Gustavo Inciarte; Vice-Pres: Néstor Barroeta; research and devt branch of Petróleos de Venezuela; undertakes applied research and devt in new products and processes and provides specialized technical services for the petroleum and petrochemical industries.

Lagovén, SA: Edif Lagovén, Avda Leonardo da Vinci, Los Chaguaramos, Apdo 889, Caracas; tel (2) 661-10-11; telex 227726; Pres: Renato Urdaneta.

Maravén, SA: Edif Maravén, Avda La Estancia 10, Chuao, Apdo 829, Caracas 1010-A; tel (2) 908-21-11; telex 23227; Pres: Dr A. Quiros Corradi; f 1976; petroleum exploration, production, transport, refining and both domestic and international marketing.

Petroquímica de Venezuela, SA (Pequivén): Edif Pequivén, Calle Cali, Las Mercedes, Caracas; tel (2) 208-31-11; telex 23206; Pres: Hugo Finol; f 1956 as Instituto Venezolano de Petroquímica, became Pequivén in 1977; affiliate of PDVSA since 1978; involved in many joint ventures with foreign and private Venezuelan interests for expanding the petrochemical industry; active in regional economic integration.

Refinería Isla (Curazao), SA: c/o Edif Petróleos de Venezuela, Avda Libertador, La Campiña, Apdo 169, Caracas 1010-A; tel (2) 708-41-11; telex 21890; f 1985; operates a refinery and deep-water terminal on Curaçao (Netherlands Antilles), fmrly owned the Royal Dutch-Shell group.

MINING

CVG Bauxita Venezolana (Bauxivén): Caracas; Pres: José Tomás Milano; f 1978 to develop the bauxite deposits at Los Pijiguaos; financed by the Fondo de Inversiones de Venezuela (FIV) (see above) and Corporación Venezolana de Guayana (CVG) (see above), which has a majority shareholding.

Dirección General Sectorial de Minas y Geología: Torre Oeste, 8°, Avda Lecuna, Parque Central, Caracas 1010; tel (2) 507-58-34; Dir-Gen: José G. Mendez; division of the Ministry of Energy and Mines responsible for formulating and implementing national policy on non-petroleum mineral reserves.

Ferrominera Orinoco, CA: Apdo 76500, Caracas 1070; Pres: Leopoldo Sucre Figarella; Gen Man: Antonio Giliberti; responsible for production and processing of iron ore.

Science and Technology

Instituto Venezolano de Investigaciones Científicas (IVIC): Altos de Pipe, Apdo 21827, Caracas 1020-A; tel (2) 572-11-20; telex 21338; Dir: Prof Horacio Vanegas; Dep Dir: Dr Roberto Sánchez-Delgado; f 1959; research in biology, medicine, chemistry, physics, mathematics, anthropology and technology; also atomic energy research facilities.

Tourism

Corporación de Turismo de Venezuela: Torre Oeste, 36°, Avda Lecuna, Parque Central, Caracas; tel (2) 507-87-26; telex 27328; fax (2) 574-22-20; Dir: Dr Armando Durán; f 1974; tourist information centre.

Departamento de Turismo: c/o Central Office of Information, Palacio de Miraflores, Avda Urdaneta, Caracas 1010; Dir: Dr Jesús Federico Ravel; dept of tourism.

Sociedad Financiera para el Fomento del Turismo y de Recreo Público (FOMTUR): Caracas; f 1962; tourist devt agency.

Transport and Communications

TELECOMMUNICATIONS

CA Nacional Teléfonos de Venezuela (CANTV): Apdo 6353, Caracas; tel (2) 782-30-89; national telephone co.

TRANSPORT

Aerovías Venezolanas, SA (AVENSA): Edif Banco de la Construcción y de Oriente, 1/11/15/16°, esq de Platanal, Avda Urdaneta, Caracas 1010; Chair: Andrés Boulton; Pres: Henry Lord Boulton; f 1943; provides extensive domestic services from Caracas and an international service to Panama and Mexico.

CA Metro de Caracas: Multicentro Empresarial del Este, Conjunto Miranda, Torre B, 1-7°, Avda Francisco Miranda, Chacao, Caracas; tel (2) 208-21-11; telex 24936; fax (2) 261-68-80; Pres: José González Lander; Vice-Pres: Manuel Antonio Díaz Díaz; f 1977; underground railway system serving Caracas.

Instituto Autónomo de Ferrocarriles del Estado (FERROCAR): Torre Este, 37/45°, Parque Central, Caracas 1010; tel (2) 509-35-01; telex 28522; fax (2) 574-70-21; Pres: Eduardo Santos Castillo; Vice-Pres: Pedro José Briceño Q.; f 1946; 336 km of track.

Instituto Nacional de Canalizaciones: Edif INC, Calle

Caracas, Chuao, Caracas; tel (2) 915-033; telex 23170; fax (2) 910-506; Pres: Rear-Adm Aguedo Felipe Hernández; Vice-Pres: Fernando Martí O.; f 1952; semi-autonomous institution dealing with inland waterways; linked to Ministry of Transport and Communications.

Instituto Nacional de Puertos: Calle Veracruz con Calle Cali, Urb Las Mercedes, Caracas; tel (2) 922-811; telex 23138; fax (2) 928-085; Pres: Vice-Adm Freddy J. Mota Carpio; f 1975; operation, admin, construction and devt of port facilities.

Venezolana Internacional de Aviación, SA (VIASA): Torre Viasa, Avda Sur 25, Plaza Morelos, Apdo 6857, Caracas 1050; telex 21125; Pres: José Luís Ignacio Mendoza; international flights to Europe, North, Central and South America and the Caribbean.

Utilities

Instituto Nacional de Obras Sanitarias (INOS): Edif La Paz, Caracas; Pres: Dr Alexis Carstens Ramos; administers water supply and sewerage projects.

Welfare

Instituto Nacional de la Vivienda (INAVI): Torre INAVI, Edif Anexo, 2°, Avda Francisco de Miranda, Caracas; tel (2) 261-08-71; telex 21407; Pres: Pedro Sosa Franco; f 1975; provision of low-cost housing.

VIETNAM

Head of State

Vietnam has a collective Presidency, the Council of State, which is elected for five years by the National Assembly. Executive power is exercised by a Council of Ministers, appointed by, and responsible to, the Assembly.

President of the Council of State: Vo Chi Cong.

Office of the President of the Council of State: Hanoi.

Vice-Presidents: Le Quang Dao, Nguyen Quyet, Dam Quang Trung, Nguyen Thi Dinh, Nguyen Huu Tho; Sec-Gen: Nguyen Viet Dung.

Legislature

Legislative power is vested in the 496-member National Assembly, elected for five years by universal adult suffrage. Locally elected People's Councils operate at district, town and village level. Government is effectively in the hands of the Communist Party of Vietnam.

Quoc Hoi (National Assembly): Hanoi; Chair: Le Quang Dao; Vice-Chairs: Tran Do, Hong Truoong Minh, Phung Van Tuu, Nguyen Thi Ngoc Phuong, Huynh Cuong.

MINISTRIES AND GOVERNMENT DEPARTMENTS

COUNCIL OF MINISTERS
Hanoi
Chair (Prime Minister): Do Muoi
Vice-Chairs: Vo Van Kiet, Gen Vo Nguyen Giap, Nguyen Khanh, Gen Dong Si Nguyen, Nguyen Co Thach, Tran Duc Luong
Minister, General Secretary and Director, Council of Ministers' Office: Nguyen Khanh

GOVERNMENT COMMISSION FOR ECONOMIC RELATIONS WITH FOREIGN COUNTRIES
Hanoi

MINISTRY OF AGRICULTURE AND FOOD INDUSTRY
Bach Thao, Hanoi
Tel 54013
Minister: Nguyen Cong Tan

MINISTRY OF BUILDING
37 Le Dai Hanh, Hanoi
Tel 54191
Minister: Ngo Xuan Loc

MINISTRY OF COMMUNICATIONS AND TRANSPORT
80 Tran Hung Dao, Hanoi
Tel 52362
Minister: Bui Danh Luu

MINISTRY OF CULTURE
53 Ngo Quyen, Hanoi
Tel 52915
Minister: Tran Van Phac

MINISTRY OF EDUCATION
21 Le Thanh Tong, Hanoi
Tel 53352
Minister: Pham Minh Hac

MINISTRY OF ENERGY, MINES AND COAL
54 Hai Ba Trung, Hanoi
Tel 55659
Minister: Vu Ngoc Hai

MINISTRY OF FINANCE
8 Phan Huy Chu, Hanoi
Tel 58111
Minister: Hoang Quy

MINISTRY OF FOREIGN AFFAIRS
Dien Bien Phu, Hanoi
Tel 58201
Minister: Nguyen Co Thach
Deputy Minister: Tran Quang Co

MINISTRY OF FOREIGN ECONOMIC RELATIONS
21 Ngo Quyen, Hanoi
Tel 62521; telex 4251
Minister: Doan Duy Thanh

MINISTRY OF FORESTRY
123 Lo Duc, Hanoi
Tel 53236
Minister: Phan Xuan Dot

MINISTRY OF HIGHER VOCATIONAL EDUCATION AND JOB TRAINING
9 Hai Ba Trung, Hanoi
Tel 53230
Minister: Tran Hong Quan

MINISTRY OF INFORMATION
Hanoi
Minister: (vacant)

MINISTRY OF THE INTERIOR
Tran Binh Trong, Hanoi
Tel 58300
Minister: Maj-Gen Mai Chi Tho

MINISTRY OF INTERNAL TRADE
91 Dinh Tien Hoang, Hanoi
Tel 55713
Minister: Hoang Minh Thang

MINISTRY OF JUSTICE
5 Ong Ich Khiem, Hanoi
Tel 55375
Minister: Phan Hien

MINISTRY OF LABOUR, DISABLED SOLDIERS AND SOCIAL WELFARE
12 Ngo Quyen, Hanoi
Tel 52236
Minister: Tran Dinh Hoan

MINISTRY OF LIGHT INDUSTRY
7 Trang Thi, Hanoi
Tel 53831
Minister: Vu Tuan

MINISTRY OF MARINE PRODUCTS
Bach Thao, Hanoi
Tel 52696
Minister: Nguyen Tan Trinh

MINISTRY OF MECHANICAL ENGINEERING AND METALLURGY
54 Hai Ba Trung, Hanoi
Tel 58311
Minister: Phan Thang Liem

MINISTRY OF NATIONAL DEFENCE
42 Tran Phu, Hanoi
Tel 58101
Minister: Gen Le Duc Anh

MINISTRY OF PUBLIC HEALTH
138A Giang Vo, Hanoi
Tel 52035
Minister: Pham Song

MINISTRY OF SUPPLY
37 Nguyen Binh Khiem, Hanoi
Tel 54731
Minister: Hoang Duc Nghi

MINISTRY OF WATER RESOURCES
164 Tran Quang Khai, Hanoi
Tel 58141
Minister: Nguyen Canh Dinh

STATE COMMISSION FOR CO-OPERATION AND INVESTMENT
Ho Chi Minh City
Minister and Chair: Dau Ngoc Xuan

STATE COMMISSION FOR PLANNING
6B Hoang Dieu, Hanoi
Tel 53169
Chair: Phan Van Kahi

STATE COMMISSION FOR PRICES
3 Mai Xuan Thuong, Hanoi
Tel 54453
Chair: Phan Van Tiem

STATE COMMISSION FOR SCIENCE AND TECHNOLOGY
39 Tran Hung Dao, Hanoi
Tel 52733
Chair: Dang Huu

STATE INSPECTORATE
28 Tang Bat Ho, Hanoi
Tel 54497
Chair: Nguyen Ky Cam

GOVERNMENT AGENCIES AND ORGANIZATIONS

Business and Economy

BANKING

Bank for Investment and Reconstruction: 10 Phan Huy Chu, Hanoi; Dir: Pham Ngoc Lam.

Ho Chi Minh Bank for Industry and Trade (BIT): Ho Chi Minh City; tel 53824; Dir: Lu' Sanh Thoa; f 1987; first bank operating without direct Govt control; authorized to receive personal savings, extend loans, issue stocks and invest in export-orientated cos and joint ventures with foreigners.

Indovina Bank: Ho Chi Minh City: f 1989; joint venture established by Summa Handelsbank AG (an Indonesian bank based in the Federal Republic of Germany) and the Ho Chi Minh Industrial and Commercial Bank.

Savings Fund for Socialism: 7 Le Lai, Hanoi; Dir (acting): Ngo Quat; Dep Dir: Cao Van Dang.

Vietbank (State Bank of Vietnam): 49 Ly Thai To, Hanoi; tel 52833; telex 244; Dir-Gen: Cao Si Khiem; f 1951; bank of issue; provides a national network of banking services and supervises the operation of the state banking system; 532 brs and sub-brs.

Vietcombank (Bank for Foreign Trade of Vietnam): 47-49 Ly Thai To, Hanoi; tel 52831; telex 4244; Chair: Nguyen Manh Thuy; f 1963; authorized to deal with foreign currencies and international payments; 8 brs.

Vietnam Export-Import Bank: Ho Ci Minh City; f 1989; authorized to undertake banking transactions for the production and processing of export-import products and export-import operations.

INSURANCE

Baoviet (the Vietnam Insurance Co): 7 Ly Thuong Kiet St, Hanoi; tel 62642; telex 4283; Dir-Gen: Pham Van Trong; Dep Dirs-Gen: Trinh Doanh, Nguyen Dang Diem; f 1965; marine, aviation, liability, offshore oil, motor vehicles, property, personal accidents and agriculture insurance; reinsurance.

TRADE

Agrexport (Vietnam National Agricultural Produce Export-Import Corpn): 6 Trang Tien, Hanoi; tel 54234; telex 4510; Dir-Gen: Tong Tran Dao; f 1957; imports and exports agricultural produce and coffee, natural silk, insecticides and agrochemicals.

Animex (Vietnam National Animal and Poultry Products

Import-Export Corpn): 33 Batrieu St, Hanoi; tel 55539; telex 4553; Dir-Gen: Nguyen Van Khac; f 1969; export and import of animal and poultry products.

Artexport (Vietnam National Handicrafts and Art Articles Export-Import Corpn): 31-33 Ngo Quyen, Hanoi; tel 56456; telex 4519; Dir-Gen: Ngo Dai Hanh; f 1964; deals in craft products and art articles.

Barotex (Vietnam National Bamboo and Rattan Export-Import Corpn): 37 Ly Thuong Kiet, Hanoi; tel 56428; telex 4508; Dir-Gen: Nghiem Minh Le; f 1971; specializes in export of cane, rattan and bamboo products.

Centrimex (National General Export-Import Corpn): 48 Tran Phu Rd, Nhatrang City; tel 21239; telex 8303; Dir-Gen: Hoang Tich Phuc; Dep Dir-Gen: Tran Ve; f 1987; export of commodities, especially sea products; import of commodities, especially cement and fertilizer.

Coalimex (Vietnam National Coal Export-Import and Material Supply Corpn): 47 Quang Trung, Hanoi; tel 55684; telex 4517; Dir-Gen: Dinh Tien Dat; f 1982; exports anthracite coal, imports mining machinery and equipment.

Confectimex (The Vietnam Foreign Trade Co for Garments): 25 Ba Trieu St, Hanoi; tel 57700; telex 4549; Dir-Gen: Nguyen Truong Sinh; Dep Dirs-Gen: Hoang Hien, Nguyen Thi Minh; f 1986; exports ready-made garments; imports fabrics and accessories, equipment and spare parts for the garment industry.

Constrexim (Vietnam National Construction Materials and Technique Export-Import Corpn): 37 Le Dai Hanh, Hanoi; tel 54171; Dir-Gen: Doan Mong Hung; exports and imports building materials and technical services.

Generalexim Hanoi (Vietnam National General Export-Import Corpn): 46 Ngo Quyen St, Hanoi; tel 64009; telex 4527; Dir-Gen: Maivan Dau; f 1982; exports and imports all kinds of commodities from and to Northern Vietnam, covering 19 provinces.

Intimex (Vietnam National Foreign Trade Enterprise): 96 Trân Hung Dao St, Hanoi; tel 56161; telex 4240; Dir-Gen: Vu Kim Ngân; f 1979; imports and exports agricultural, forestry and fishing products, manufactured and consumer goods.

Machinoimport (Vietnam National Machinery Export-Import Corpn): 8 Trang Thi, Hanoi; tel 52265; telex 4275; Dir-Gen: Nguyen Sinh; f 1957; imports and exports machinery and tools.

Marine Supply (Vietnam Marine Technical Materials Export-Import Co): 276A Danang St, Haiphong; tel 46539; telex 45243; Dir-Gen: Le Quoc Hung; f 1973; involved in ship demolition and export of steel scrap; imports and exports equipment for merchant shipping and the maritime industry; acts as forwarding agent and consignment agent for inland and foreign importers and exporters.

Mecanimex (Vietnam National Mechanical Products Export-Import Co): 54 Hai Ba Trung, Hanoi; Dir-Gen: Tran Bao Gioc; exports and imports mechanical products and hand tools.

Minexport (Vietnam National Minerals Export-Import Corpn): 35 Hai Ba Trung, Hanoi; tel 55264; telex 4515; Dir-Gen: Vo Trong Cuong; f 1956; exports minerals and metals, quarry products, chemical products; imports metals, chemical products, industrial materials, fuels and oils, fertilizers.

Naforimex (Vietnam National Forest and Native Produce Export-Import Corpn): 19 Ba Trieu, Hanoi; tel 54034; telex 4503; Dir-Gen: Lam Quang Thanh; f 1960; imports chemicals, machinery and spare parts for the forestry industry, linseed oil and essences; exports oils, forest products, gum benzoin and resin.

Petechim (National Petroleum Export-Import Corpn): 72 Xo Viet Nghe Tinh Q3, Ho Chi Minh City; tel 99299; telex 8241; Pres: Tran Huu Lac; f 1981; imports oil-field equipment and machinery; exports crude oil; general trading in all kinds of products.

Petrovietnam (Vietnam Oil and Gas Corpn): 80 Nguyen Du, Hanoi; tel 52526; telex 263; Dir-Gen: Truong Thien; f 1977;

arranges contracts with foreign countries concerning oil and gas exploration and exploitation and supplies services.

Rubexim (Vietnam National Rubber Export-Import Corpn): 64 Truong Dinh, Ho Chi Minh City; tel 91593; telex 8358; Dir-Gen: Ngo Chi Trong; exports natural rubber; imports machinery, spare parts and chemicals for rubber plantation and processing.

Seaprodex (Vietnam National Sea Products Export-Import Corpn): 2-6 Dong Khoi, Ho Chi Minh City; tel 91333; Dir-Gen: Nguyen Hong Can; f 1980; exports frozen and processed sea products; imports machinery and materials for fishing and processing.

Sobexim (The Union of Song Be Export-Import Corpn): Phu Loi, Thu Dau Mot Town, Song Be Province; tel 98186; telex 8112; Dir-Gen: Ngo Quang Ngoc; f 1976; farm and forest products.

Technimex (Vietnam Technical Export-Import Corpn): 70 Tran Mung Dao St, Hanoi; tel 55655; telex 4287; Dir: Nguyen Tram; Dep Dir: Nguyen Huy Binh; f 1982; technology transfer; import of equipment, spare parts and other products; sets up agencies for foreign organizations and individuals wanting to introduce equipment, scientific products, new technology to the Vietnamese market; organizes conferences and professional courses.

Technoimport (Vietnam National Complete Equipment Import and Technical Exchange Corpn): 16-18 Trang Thi, Hanoi; tel 53776; telex 4243; Dir-Gen: Tran Chi Kinh; f 1959; imports industrial plant and secures technical service of foreign specialists.

Textimex (Vietnam National Textiles Export-Import Corpn): 25 Ba Trieu, Hanoi; tel 57700; telex 4507; Dir-Gen: Pham Van Mot; f 1978; imports textile machinery and materials, spare parts; exports textile products, garments, jute fibres, woollen carpets.

Vegetexco (Vietnam National Vegetables and Fruit Export-Import Corpn): 46 Ngo Quyen, Hanoi; tel 53307; telex 4512; Dir-Gen: Le Ngoc Sau; f 1971; exports fresh and processed vegetables and fruit, spices and flowers; imports vegetable seeds and processing materials.

Vieco (Vungtau-Condau Import-Export Co): 36A National Rd No 51, Vungtau; tel 97129; telex 8310; Dir: Bui Chi Thanh; Dep Gen Man: Vo Van Cao; Man: Nguyen Thanh Binh; f 1981; import-export and general trading.

Vietcochamber (Chamber of Commerce and Industry of the Socialist Republic of Vietnam): 33 Ba Trieu, Hanoi; tel 52961; telex 4264; Pres: Hoang Trong Dai; f 1963; br office in Ho Chi Minh City; promotes business between foreign and Vietnamese cos; organizes exhibitions and fairs in Vietnam and abroad; provides information about Vietnam's trade and industry; represents foreign applicants for patents and documentation; associated organizations are:

   Foreign Trade Arbitration Committee: 33 Ba Trieu, Hanoi; tel 52961; telex 4524; Pres: Luu Van Dat; adjudicates in trade disputes between Vietnamese and foreign economic organizations.

   Marine Arbitration Committee: 33 Ba Trieu, Hanoi; tel 52961; telex 4524; Pres: Luu Van Dat; adjudicates in disputes arising from sea transportation.

   Vinacontrol (The Vietnam Superintendence and Inspection Co): 54 Tran Nhan Tong St, Hanoi; tel 52105; Dir-Gen: Bui Huy Huong; Dir, Foreign Relations Dept: Tran Van Chuong; f 1959; brs in all main Vietnamese ports; controls quality and volume of exports and imports and transit of goods; conducts inspections of deliveries and production processes.

   Vinexad (Vietnam National Exhibition and Advertising Agency): 33 Ba Trieu, Hanoi; tel 52961; Exec Dir: Nguyen Trong Nhuan; f 1975; organizes commercial exhibitions in Vietnam and abroad.

Vietrans (Vietnam National Forwarding and Warehousing Corpn): 13 Ly Nam De, Hanoi; tel 54913; telex 4505; Dir-Gen:

VIETNAM

Nguyen Van Hung; f 1970; freight forwarding, warehousing, booking and chartering, customs clearance, insurance, and other services relating to international forwarding.

Viettronimex (Vietnam Electronics Export-Import Corpn): 74-76 Nguyen Hue, Ho Chi Minh City; tel 98200; telex 8252; Dir-Gen: Nguyen Ngoc Ngoan; imports and exports electronic goods.

Vimedimex (Vietnam Medical Products Export-Import Co): 34 Nguyen Hue St and 246 Cong Quynh St, Hanoi; tel 98441; telex 8287; Dir: Nguyen Van En; Vice-Dir: Bui Quang Duc; f 1984; import and export of pharmaceutical products, medicinal plants and essential oils, and medical equipment.

Vinafim (Vietnam Film Import, Export and Film Service Corpn): 73 Nguyen Trai, Hanoi; tel 44566; Gen Man: Ngô Manh Lan; f 1953; export and import of films; film distribution; organization of film shows and participation of Vietnamese films in international film festivals.

Vinafood (Vietnam National Food Export-Import Corpn): 24 Vo Van Tan, Ho Chi Minh City; tel 97676; telex 8228; Dir-Gen: Nguyen Nhat Tan; exports and imports rice, maize, tapioca, wheat and wheat flour.

Vinalimex (Vietnam National Foodstuffs Export-Import Corpn): 63 Ly Thai To, Hanoi; tel 55768; telex 4533; Dir-Gen: Nguyen Van Thach; Dep Dir-Gen: Do Thanh Che; f 1984; exports tea, sugar, peanuts, confectionery, coconut oil, salt and other foodstuffs, spirit, liqueurs and cigarettes; imports sugar, hops, malt, sweets, brandy.

Xunhasaba (Vietnam State Enterprise for Export and Import of Books, Periodicals and other Cultural Commodities): 32 Hai Ba Trung, Hanoi; tel 52313; Mans: Nguyen Anh Tuan, Tran Phu Son; exports and imports books, periodicals, postage stamps and paintings.

Defence

Armed Forces: Hanoi; Commdr-in-Chief: Sen Gen Van Tien Dung; Chief of Gen Staff (Army): Gen Doan Khue.

National Defence Council: Hanoi; Chair: Vo Chi Cong; Vice-Chair: Do Muoi; Mems: Gen Le Duc Anh, Nguyen Co Thach, Maj-Gen Mai Chi Tho.

Legal and Judiciary

Supreme People's Court: Hanoi; Pres: Pham Hung; highest court and exercises civil and criminal jurisdiction over all lower courts; may also conduct trials of the first instance in certain cases.

Supreme People's Organ of Control: Hanoi; Pres: Tran Guyet; concerned with the observance of the law by ministries, Govt offices and all citizens.

Media

BROADCASTING

Central Television: Giang Vo, Hanoi; tel 55933; telex 279; Dir-Gen: Nguyen Van Han; broadcasts from Hanoi, Vinh, Hué, Qui Nhon, Da Nang, Nha Trang, Ho Chi Minh City and Can Tho; Vietnamese, Russian.

Voice of Vietnam: 58 Quan Su, Hanoi; tel 54134; Editor-in-Chief: Tran Lam; separate programme network operating from Ho Chi Minh City; home service in Vietnamese; foreign service in English, Japanese, French, Khmer, Laotian, Spanish, Thai, Cantonese and Standard Chinese, Indonesian and Russian.

NEWS AND INFORMATION

General Statistical Office of the Socialist Republic of Vietnam: Hanoi.

Vietnam News Agency (VNA): 5 Ly Thuong Kiet, Hanoi; Dir-Gen: Dào Tùng; mem of Organization of Asian and Pacific News Agencies.

Tourism

Du Lich Viet-Nam—Vietnamtourist (Vietnam National Administration of Tourism): 54 Nguyen Du, Hanoi; tel 55963; telex 4269; Dir-Gen: Nguyen Quyen Sinh; f 1979; controlled by the Vietnam Gen Dept of Tourism.

Hanoi Tourism Association: Hanoi; Chair: Pham Huy Thong; f 1988 to encourage the devt of tourism in the capital.

Transport

CIVIL AVIATION

Haong Khong Viet-Nam (Vietnam Airline): Gia Lam Airport, Hanoi; Chief of Directorate of Civil Aviation: Khoang Igok Zieu; fmrly the Gen Civil Aviation Admin of Vietnam; operates domestic passenger services from Hanoi to nine cities and from Ho Chi Minh City to six cities, and international services from Hanoi to Moscow, Berlin, Vientiane, Phnom-Penh, Prague, Manila and Bangkok, and from Ho Chi Minh City to Moscow, Sofia, Vancouver and Paris.

RAILWAYS

Duong Sat Viet-Nam—DSVN (Vietnam Railway Central Department): 180 Nam Bo, Hanoi; tel 54998; Dir-Gen: Tuu; controlled by the Vietnam Gen Dept of Railways.

ROADS

National Automobile Transport Undertaking: Hanoi; f 1951; operates municipal and long-distance bus services.

SHIPPING

Cong Ty Van Tai Duong Bien Viet Nam—VOSCO (Vietnam Ocean Shipping Co): 15 Cu Chinh Lan, Haiphong; tel 212; telex 45251; Dir-Gen: Tran Xuan Nhon; controlled by the Vietnam Gen Dept of Marine Transport; tankers, roll-on/roll-off vessels and bulk carriers.

Dai Ly Tau Bien Viet Nam—VOSA (Vietnam Ocean Shipping Agency): 25 Dien Bien Phu St, Haiphong; tel 46301; telex 45245; Dir-Gen: Pham Thiet Quat; Dep Dir-Gen: Nguyen Kim Long; f 1957; controlled by the Vietnam Gen Dept of Marine Transport; carries out all formalities for in-coming and out-going merchant shipping, ie arranges port working, cargo handling, settlement of claims for damaged or lost cargo, forwarding, booking space, tallying, etc; ship broking, ship repairing and surveys; arranges embarkation and disembarkation formalities for passengers.

Nam-Hai: 20 Nguyen Cong Tru, Ho Chi Minh City.

Vietnam Chartering and Shipbroking Corpn: 74 Nguyen Du, Hanoi; tel 56342; telex 4264; Dir-Gen: Truong Thi Nhan; f 1963; ship broking, chartering; ship management; provides regular services to and from South East Asian ports and arranges shipments from Vietnam to all ports.

Vietnam Coastal Shipping Co: 4 Cu Chinh Lan, Haiphong; tel 629; eight vessels; South East Asian Trade.

Transchart (Vietnam Sea Transport and Chartering Co): 428-432 Nguyen Tat Thanh St, Ho Chi Minh City; tel 91977; telex 8261; 10 vessels.

Vietnam Tanker Co: 83 Nguyen Cong Tru, Ho Chi Minh City; one tanker.

WESTERN SAMOA

<table>
<tr><td>

Head of State

The Head of State is HH Malietoa Tanumafili II, who will hold this post for life. Subsequently the Head of State will be elected by the Fono (Legislative Assembly) for a term of five years. Executive power is vested in the Cabinet, headed by the Prime Minister. Cabinet decisions are subject to review by the Executive Council, which is made up of the Head of State and the Cabinet.

O le Ao le Malo: HH Malietoa Tanumafili II (took office as joint Head of State 1 January 1962; became sole Head of State 5 April 1963).

Office of the Head of State: Government House, Vailima, Apia; tel 20840; telex 221.

</td><td>

Legislature

Legislative authority is vested in the unicameral Fono (Legislative Assembly), comprising 47 members, each serving a three-year term. Two members of the Assembly are elected from the individual voters' roll by universal adult suffrage, while the remaining 45 members are chosen by Matai (elected clan leaders) in 41 traditional electoral constituencies.

Fono (Legislative Assembly): Apia; tel 21811; telex 221; Speaker: Aeau Peniamina; Dep Speaker: Tuilagi Vavae.

</td></tr>
</table>

MINISTRIES AND GOVERNMENT DEPARTMENTS

PRIME MINISTER'S DEPARTMENT
POB 193, Apia
Tel 21500; telex 221
Prime Minister: Tofilau Eti Alesana

AGRICULTURE DEPARTMENT
POB 206, Apia
Tel 22561
Minister: Pule G. Lameko

BROADCASTING DEPARTMENT
POB 200, Apia
Tel 21420
Minister: (vacant)

CUSTOMS DEPARTMENT
POB 44, Apia
Tel 21561
Minister: (vacant)

ECONOMIC AFFAIRS DEPARTMENT
POB 862, Apia
Tel 20471
Minister: Tanuvasa Livi

EDUCATION DEPARTMENT
POB 201, Apia
Tel 21911
Minister: Patu Afaese

FINANCE DEPARTMENT
Private Bag, Apia
Tel 22822; telex 233
Minister: Tuilaepa Sailele Malielegaoi

HEALTH DEPARTMENT
Private Bag, Apia
Tel 21212; telex 277
Minister: Polataivao Fosi

INLAND REVENUE DEPARTMENT
POB 209, Apia
Tel 20411
Minister: (vacant)

JUSTICE DEPARTMENT
POB 48, Apia
Tel 22671
Minister: (vacant)

LANDS AND SURVEY DEPARTMENT
Private Bag, Apia
Tel 22481
Minister: Sifuiva Sione

MINISTRY OF FOREIGN AFFAIRS
POB 193, Apia
Tel 21500; telex 221
Minister: (vacant)

MINISTRY OF TRANSPORT AND CIVIL AVIATION
POB 1607, Apia
Tel 23700; telex 221
Minister: Jack Netzler

MINISTRY OF YOUTH, SPORTS AND CULTURE
Apia
Tel 23315
Minister: (vacant)

**POSTAL AND TELECOMMUNICATIONS
DEPARTMENT**
Private Bag, Apia
Tel 23456; telex 220; fax 24000
Minister: Jack Netzler

PUBLIC WORKS DEPARTMENT
Private Bag, Apia
Tel 21611; telex 256
Minister: Leia'Taua Vaiao Alailima

GOVERNMENT AGENCIES AND ORGANIZATIONS

Agriculture

Cocoa Board of Western Samoa: POB 589, Apia; tel 21041; telex 236; Minister of Agriculture and Dir: Pule G. Lameko; Sec: Ueligitone Sasagi; f 1972; marketing, devt and promotion of cocoa industry.

Western Samoa Trust Estates Corpn (WSTEC): Apia; f 1957 to hold and administer land confiscated from German planters after the First World War; holdings include copra and cocoa plantations.

Business and Economy

BANKING

Bank of Western Samoa: Beach Rd, POB 187, Apia; tel 22422; telex 258; Chair: Sir Ronald Brierley; Gen Man: Keith Jenvey; f 1959.

Central Bank of Samoa: Private Bag, Apia; tel 24100; telex 200; fax 20293; Chair: Terrence Betham; Gen Man: Papali'i T. Scanlan; f 1984; bank of issue; advises Govt on banking and monetary matters and acts as supervisory body for banking system.

Development Bank of Western Samoa: POB 1232, Apia; tel 22861; telex 212; Gen Man: Tuatagaloa A. Schwalger; f 1974 to foster economic and social devt.

INSURANCE

Western Samoa Life Assurance Corpn: POB 494, Apia; tel 23360; Gen. Man: Aniseto S. Chan-Ting; f 1977; life assurance and superannuation.

Defence

Department of Police and Prisons: POB 193, Apia; tel 21500; telex 221.

Legal and Judiciary

Office of the Attorney-General: POB 27, Apia; tel 20295; telex 221; Attorney-Gen: Tiava'asue Falefatu Maka Sapolu.

Supreme Court: c/o Justice Department, POB 48, Apia; tel 22671; Chief Justice: (vacant); Sec: Asi Falanaipupu Vaimasanu'u Niko Apa; full jurisdiction for both civil and criminal cases.

Media

BROADCASTING

Western Samoa Broadcasting Service: c/o Broadcasting Department, POB 200, Apia; tel 21420; Dir: J. K. Brown; f 1948; state-controlled with commercial sponsorship; broadcasts on two channels in Samoan and English.

NEWS AND INFORMATION

Western Samoa Department of Statistics: POB 1151, Apia; tel 21371; collection, analysis and dissemination of statistical data.

Tourism

Western Samoa Visitors' Bureau: POB 862, Apia; tel 20471; promotion and devt of tourist industry.

Transport

Polynesian Airlines Ltd: Beach Rd, POB 599, Apia; tel 21261; telex 249; Chair: T. S. Toalepasalii; Gen Man: James K. Moynihan; f 1959; international services to American Samoa, Fiji, Cook Islands, Tonga, Australia and New Zealand; domestic services between islands of Upolu and Savai'i.

YEMEN ARAB REPUBLIC

Head of State

Executive power is vested in the President, elected for a five-year term by the Majlis ash-Shura (Consultative Council). The President governs with the assistance of an appointed Council of Ministers, led by a Prime Minister.

President: Col Ali Abdullah Saleh (took office 18 July 1978; re-elected for third five-year term by the new Consultative Council on 17 July 1988).

Office of the President: Zubairi St, San'a; tel (2) 71392; telex 2422; Special Sec (with Ministerial rank): Maj Ali Muhammad al-Anisi).

Vice-President: Qadi Abd al-Karim al-Arashi.

Office of the Vice-President: 26 September St, San'a.

Legislature

Legislative power is vested in the Majlis ash-Shura (Consultative Council), comprising 159 members, including 128 elected at the general election held on 5 July 1988. The remaining 31 members were appointed by presidential decree. The General People's Congress, comprising 1,000 members, meets every two years and acts as an advisory body.

Majlis ash-Shura: San'a; Speaker: Qadi Abd al-Karim al-Arashi.

MINISTRIES AND GOVERNMENT DEPARTMENTS

OFFICE OF THE PRIME MINISTER
26th September St, San'a
Tel (2) 73092
Prime Minister: Maj Abd al-Aziz Abd al-Ghani
Deputy Prime Ministers: Dr Hassan Muhammad Makki, Lt-Col Mujahid Yahya Abu Shuwarib, Dr Abd al-Karim al-Irryani, Dr Muhammad Said al-Attar

MINISTRY OF AGRICULTURE AND FISHERIES
Alziraa St, San'a
Tel (2) 70348
Minister: Dr Nasir Abdullah al-Awlaqi

MINISTRY OF AWQAF (RELIGIOUS ENDOWMENTS) AND RELIGIOUS GUIDANCE
San'a
Tel (2) 72381
Minister: Qadi Ali bin Ali as-Samman

MINISTRY OF CIVIL SERVICE AND ADMINISTRATIVE REFORM
San'a
Minister: Muhammad Abdullah al-Jayfi

MINISTRY OF COMMUNICATIONS AND TELECOMMUNICATIONS
Altahrir Sq, San'a
Tel (2) 72991; telex 2340
Minister: Muhammad al-Khadim al-Wajih

MINISTRY OF DEVELOPMENT AND THE CENTRAL PLANNING ORGANIZATION
Abaunia St, San'a
Tel (2) 73506
Minister and Head of the Central Planning Organization: Dr Muhammad Said al-Attar

MINSTRY OF ECONOMY, TRADE AND SUPPLY
Alquiadah St, San'a
Tel (2) 75009; telex 2360
Minister: Dr Abd al-Wahhab Mahmoud Abd al-Hamid

MINISTRY OF EDUCATION
Gamal Abdul Nasser St, San'a
Tel (2) 75881
Minister: Ahmad Muhammad al-Ansi

MINISTRY OF ELECTRICITY AND WATER
San'a
Minister: Jamal Muhammad Abduh

MINISTRY OF FINANCE
Ring Rd, San'a
Tel (2) 89502; telex 2254
Minister: Alawi Salih as-Salami

MINISTRY OF FOREIGN AFFAIRS
Alolofi Sq, San'a
Tel (2) 73534; telex 2216
Minister: Dr Abd al-Karim al-Iryani

MINISTRY OF HEALTH
Altahrir Sq, San'a
Tel (2) 73286; telex 3281
Minister: Dr Muhammad Ali Muqbil

MINISTRY OF INFORMATION AND CULTURE
San'a
Tel (2) 74761; telex 2464
Minister: Hassan Ahmad al-Lawzi

MINISTRY OF THE INTERIOR
Almatar Rd, San'a
Tel (2) 72677; telex 2274
Ministers: Lt-Col Abdullah Hussain Barakat, Lt-Col
Mujahid Yahya Abu Shuwarib

MINISTRY OF JUSTICE
Wadi Dhahr St, San'a
Tel (2) 78607
Minister: Lt-Col Muhsin Muhammad al-Ulufi

**MINISTRY OF LEGAL AND CONSULTATIVE
COUNCIL AFFAIRS**
San'a
Minister: Ismail Ahmad al-Wazir

MINISTRY OF MUNICIPALITIES AND HOUSING
San'a
Minister: Muhsin Ali al-Hamdani

**MINISTRY OF PETROLEUM AND MINERAL
RESOURCES**
San'a
Minister: Ahmad Ali al-Mahanni

MINISTRY OF SOCIAL AFFAIRS AND LABOUR
Zubairi St, San'a
Tel (2) 72097
Minister: Ahmad Muhammad Luqman

MINISTRY OF TRANSPORT AND PUBLIC WORKS
Zubairi St, POB 1180, San'a
Tel (2) 276291; telex 2208; fax (2) 274145
Minister: Abdullah Hussain al-Kurshumi

MINISTRY OF YOUTH AND SPORTS
San'a
Minister: Dr Muhammad Ahmad al-Kabab

**MINISTRY OF STATE FOR AFFAIRS OF THE
COUNCIL OF MINISTERS**
San'a
Minister of State: Ahmad Saleh ar-Roueini

**MINISTRY OF STATE FOR YEMEN UNITY
AFFAIRS**
San'a
Minister of State: Yahya Hussain al-Arashi
A draft Constitution which would unify the Yemen Arab Republic and the People's Democratic Republic of Yemen was approved in December 1989. The Constitution was to be referred to the legislatures of both countries for ratification within six months. This was to be followed by a plebiscite on the draft Constitution and the election of a single legislative body for the new Yemen Republic.

GOVERNMENT AGENCIES AND ORGANIZATIONS

Advisory and Supervisory Bodies

Government Consumption Assembly for Public and Semi-Public Sector Employees: POB 833, San'a.

Military and Police Economical Corpn (Public Sector): POB 1207, San'a; tel (2) 79340; telex 2244; Commercial Man: A. Karim Sayaghi.

Agriculture

General Corpn for Foreign Trade and Grain: POB 710, San'a; tel (2) 207571; telex 2349; Chair: Abdullah al-Barakani; Gen Man: Kassim M. as-Sabri; fmrly Yemen General Grain Corpn, present name adopted in 1987.

General Cotton Co: POB 2603, Hodeida; tel (3) 238390; telex 5562.

Yemen Agricultural Evolution Office: Taiz; telex 8837.

Business and Economy

BANKING

Central Bank of Yemen: Ali Abd al-Mughni St, POB 59, San'a; tel (2) 279351; telex 2280; Gov: Abdullah as-Sanabani; Gen Man: Ali Ali an-Nuseif; f 1971; 10 brs.

Housing Credit Bank: Az-Zubairi Bldg, POB 638, San'a; tel (2) 77126; Chair: Ali Abd ar-Rahman al-Bahr; f 1977.

Industrial Bank of Yemen: Banks Complex, Az-Zubairi St, POB 323, San'a; tel (2) 207381; telex 2580; Chair and Man Dir: Abbas Abdu Muhammad al-Kirshy; Gen Man: Abd al-Karim Ismail al-Arhabi; f 1976; industrial investment.

The Yemen Bank for Reconstruction and Development (YBRD): 26 September St, POB 541, San'a; tel (2) 271621;

telex 2291; Chair: Ahmad As-Samawi; Gen Man: Ahmad Muhammad Ali; Man, Foreign Dept: Muhammad Khushafa; f 1962; consolidated bank; 38 brs.

MARKETING

Yemen Agricultural Marketing Corpn: POB 10159, San'a; tel (2) 202467; telex 2767.

NATIONALIZED INDUSTRY

National Co for Industrial and Construction Materials (YEMROC): POB 2564, San'a; tel (2) 70058; telex 2257; Gen Man: Abdulwase Kaid Ahmad; Dir, Projects Dept: Hilal A. Faraj; Dir, Finance: Abdullah Y. Nufaish; f 1978; extraction and devt of marble, granite and other construction materials.

Yemen Cement Industry Corpn: POB 3393, Hodeida; tel (3) 72952; telex 5594; Chair: Amin Abd al-Wahid Ahmad.

Yemen Co for Industry and Commerce Ltd: POB 5302, Taiz; tel (4) 215171; telex 8804; Chair: Ali Muhammad Said.

Yemen Construction Co: San'a; f 1984.

Yemen Drug Co for Industry and Commerce: POB 40, San'a; tel (2) 234250; telex 2289; fax (2) 251595; Chair: Hazem A. R. Baker; Gen Man: Dr Ali S. al-Hamdani; Commercial Man: A. Rehman Ghaleb; f 1974; import, distribution, manufacture and marketing of pharmaceuticals.

Yemen Textile and Weaving Corpn: POB 214, San'a; tel (2) 202460; telex 2249.

Defence

Armed Forces: Zubairi St, San'a; tel (2) 71392; Commdr-in-Chief: Col Ali Abdullah Saleh; Chief of Staff: Lt-Col Abd al-Wallah Hussain al-Busheiry.

Air Force: International Airport, San'a; tel (2) 74411.

Army: Alquiadah St, San'a; tel (2) 75772.

Navy: Hodeida.

Development and Planning

INVESTMENT

Yemen Co for Investment and Finance: POB 2789, San'a; tel (2) 72089; telex 2564; Chair: Abdullah Ishaq; Gen Man: Omar al-Kumaim.

PLANNING

Industrial Estate Development Authority: POB 195, San'a.

Central Planning Organization: POB 175, San'a; tel 3506; telex 2266; Chair: Minister of Development, Dr Muhammad Said al-Attar; responsible for formulation and implementation of devt programmes.

Legal and Judiciary

State Security Court: San'a; Pres: Ghaleb Mutahir al-Qanish; Public Prosecutor: Abd ar-Rizaq ar-Roqaihi; Attorney-Gen: Muhammad al-Badri.

Media

BROADCASTING

Radio Hodeida: POB 3263, Hodeida; f 1967; broadcasts in Arabic, four hours daily.

Radio San'a: c/o Ministry of Information and Culture, San'a; Dir-Gen: A. Sarham; broadcasts in Arabic, 15 hours daily.

Radio Taiz: Taiz; broadcasts in Arabic, 4 hours daily.

NEWS AND INFORMATION

Data Processing Centre: c/o Central Planning Organization, POB 175, San'a; tel (2) 3506; telex 2266; collection, analysis and dissemination of statistical data.

Saba News Agency: POB 1475, San'a; tel (2) 233228; telex 2568; Dir: Dr Hassan al-Ulufi; f 1970.

Mining and Energy

ENERGY

Yemen General Electricity Corpn (YGEC): POB 178, San'a; telex 2275; Gen Man: Ahmad al-Aini.

Yemen Petroleum Co: POB 81, San'a; tel (2) 70432; telex 2257; Chair: Hussain Abdullah al-Makdani.

MINING

Yemen Oil and Mineral Industrial Co (YEMINCO): San'a; Chair: Ali Abd ar-Rahman al-Bahr; f 1970.

Tourism

General Corpn for Tourism: San'a; telex 2592.

Yemen Tourist Co: POB 1526, San'a; Chair: Abd al-Hadi al-Hamdani.

Transport and Communications

TELECOMMUNICATIONS

Public Telecommunications Corpn: POB 17045, San'a; tel (2) 251140; telex 2617.

TRANSPORT

General Corpn for Transport: POB 1827, San'a; tel (2) 77711; telex 2400.

General Ports and Marine Affairs Corpn: POB 3183, Hodeida; tel (3) 79034; telex 5565.

Yemen Airways (Yemenia): Airport Rd, POB 1183, San'a; tel (2) 232389; telex 2204; Chair: Muhammad Ahmad al-Haimi; Man Dir: Rida T. Hakim; supervised by a ministerial committee headed by the Minister of Communications and Telecommunications; f 1963, present name adopted 1978 following establishment of new airline, owned 51% by Govt of YAR and 49% by Govt of Saudi Arabia; internal services and international flights throughout the Middle East and to Europe and the Far East.

Yemen Land Transport Corpn: Taiz St, POB 279, San'a; tel (2) 262108; telex 2400; Chair: Col Ali Ahmad al-Wasi; Gen Man: Hamid Mukrid; f 1961.

Yemen Sea Transport Corpn: San'a.

PEOPLE'S DEMOCRATIC REPUBLIC OF YEMEN

Head of State

Executive power is vested in the Chairman of the Presidium, which is appointed by the Supreme People's Council (SPC). The Chairman is Head of State, and also appoints a Council of Ministers to assist in government.

Chairman of the Presidium: Haidar Abu Bakr al-Attas (took office 24 January 1986).

Office of the Chairman of the Presidium: Aden.

Vice-Chairman of the Presidium: Dr Muhammad Awad as-Sa'adi.

Legislature

Under the 1970 Constitution, legislative power is vested in the unicameral Supreme People's Council (SPC), comprising 111 directly-elected members. Effective political control lies with the Yemen Socialist Party (YSP), the only legal political party. The country is divided into six administrative governorates comprising 28 provinces.

Supreme People's Council (SPC): Aden.

MINISTRIES AND GOVERNMENT DEPARTMENTS

OFFICE OF THE PRIME MINISTER
Aden
Prime Minister: Dr Yasin Said Numan
Deputy Prime Ministers: Brig-Gen Salih Muntassar as-Siyaili

MINISTRY OF AGRICULTURE AND AGRARIAN REFORM
Aden
Minister: Dr Ahmad Ali Muqbil

MINISTRY OF CULTURE AND INFORMATION
POB 1187, Tawahi 102, Aden
Tel 24874; telex 2286
Minister: Dr Muhammad Ahmad Jirghum

MINISTRY OF DEFENCE
Aden
Minister: Salih Obaid Ahmad

MINISTRY OF EDUCATION
Aden
Minister: Dr Salim Abu Bakr ba Salim

MINISTRY OF ENERGY AND MINERALS
POB 5176, Maalla, Aden
Tel 24542; telex 2215
Minister: Saleh Abu Bakr bin Husseinoun

MINISTRY OF FINANCE
Aden
Minister: Dr Ahmad Nasir ad-Danami

MINISTRY OF FISH WEALTH
Aden
Minister: Salim Muhammad Joubran

MINISTRY OF FOREIGN AFFAIRS
Madinet al-Shaab, Aden
Telex 222
Minister: Dr Abd al-Aziz ad-Dali

MINISTRY OF HEALTH
Aden
Minister: Dr Said Sharaf

MINISTRY OF HOUSING AND CONSTRUCTION
Aden
Minister: Abd al-Qawi Muthanna Hadi

MINISTRY OF INDUSTRY AND OF TRADE AND SUPPLY
Aidroos Rd, Aden
Telex 273
Minister: Abdullah Muhammad Othman

MINISTRY OF THE INTERIOR
Aden
Minister: Brig-Gen Salih Muntassar as-Siyaili

MINISTRY OF JUSTICE AND AWQAF (RELIGIOUS ENDOWMENTS)
Aden
Minister: Abd al-Wasi Ahmad Salam

MINISTRY OF LABOUR AND THE CIVIL SERVICE
Aden
Minister: Uthman Abd al-Jabbar Rashid

MINISTRY OF PLANNING
POB 1193, Tawahi, Aden
Tel 22235; telex 2289
Minister: Dr Faraj bin Ghanim

MINISTRY OF STATE SECURITY
Aden
Minister: Said Salih Salim

MINISTRY OF TRANSPORT AND COMMUNICATIONS
Aden
Minister: Salih Abdullah Muthannah

MINISTRY OF STATE FOR YEMEN UNITY AFFAIRS
Aden
Minister of State: Rashid Muhammad Thabit
A draft Constitution which would unify the Yemen Arab Republic and the People's Democratic Republic of Yemen was approved in December 1989. The Constitution was to be referred to the legislatures of both countries for ratification within six months. This was to be followed by a plebiscite on the draft Constitution and the election of a single legislative body for the new Yemen Republic.

GOVERNMENT AGENCIES AND ORGANIZATIONS

Advisory and Supervisory Body

National Chamber of Commerce and Industry: 14th October St, Crater 101, POB 473, Aden; tel 51104; telex 2233; Pres: Ali Abd al-Karim Muhammad; Gen Man: Abdullah Salem al-Khader; f 1886.

Agriculture and Fishing

AGRICULTURE

Public Corpn for Poultry Development: POB 4145, al-Mansoura, Aden; tel 82201; f 1984 to replace General Corpn for Poultry Development.

Public Organization for Dairy Products: POB 1416, Crater, Aden; tel 31257; telex 2273.

Public Organization for Salt: POB 1169, Tawahi, Aden; tel 22048; telex 2250; f 1970.

FISHING

National Corpn for Marketing Fish: POB 1139, Tawahi, Aden; tel 24275; telex 2244; Gen Man: Abd al-Majeed Murshed; operates 18 deep-sea fishing vessels.

Public Corpn for Fish Wealth: Pier Rd, POB 2242, Tawahi, Aden; telex 2244; operates 1 fishing vessel.

Business and Economy

BANKING

Bank of Yemen: POB 452, Crater, Aden; tel 51814; telex 2279; Gov: Ahmad Obaid al-Fadhli; f 1972, replaced Yemeni Currency Authority.

National Bank of Yemen: Arwa Rd, POB 5, Crater, Aden; tel 52481; telex 2224; Chair: Salem al-Ashwali; Gen Man: Muhammad Ali Omaya; f 1970 as National Bank of Southern Yemen by nationalizing and amalgamating the local brs of the seven foreign banks in Aden; adopted current name in 1971; 27 brs.

INSURANCE

National Insurance and Re-insurance Co: POB 456, Aden; tel 51464; telex 2245; Chair and Gen Man: Farouq Nasser Ali; f 1970; Lloyd's agent.

NATIONALIZED INDUSTRY

Cottonseed Oil Factory: Main Pass Roundabout, Maalla, Aden; manufacture and export of cottonseed oil.

National Corpn for Bottling Soft Drinks: POB 352, Crater, Aden; tel 82237; telex 2500; Gen Man: Abd al-Hafez Muqbil; f 1972; manufacturer and distributor of soft drinks, distilled water, ice and carbon dioxide.

National Tanning Factory: POB 4073, Sheikh Othman, Aden; tel 81449; Gen Man: Mansour A. Mansoor; f 1972.

Public Corpn for Construction and Industrial Installation: POB 7022, Almansura, Aden; tel 82124; telex 2260; Dirs: Sultan bin Brek, Salih A. Assani, A. A. Bakathir; f 1974; construction of Govt devts, especially housing and hospital projects.

Public Corpn for Manufacturing Textiles: POB 2063, Sheikh Othman, Aden; tel 82364; telex 2273; Gen Man: Saeed Sharaf.

Public Organization for Carpentry: POB 5034, Maalla, Aden; tel 23619; telex 2273.

Yemen Co for Perfumes and Cosmetics Ltd: POB 5042, Maalla, Aden; tel 23830; telex 2273.

TRADE

National Co for Foreign Trade: POB 90, Crater, Aden; tel 42793; telex 2211; Gen Man (acting): Ahmad Muhammad Saleh; f 1969; incorporates main foreign trading businesses (nationalized in 1970) and arranges their supply to the National Co for Home Trade.

National Co for Home Trade: POB 90, Crater, Aden; tel 41483; telex 2266; Man Dir: Abd ar-Rahman as-Sailani; marketing of general consumer goods, building materials, electrical goods, motor cars and spare parts, agricultural machinery, etc.

National Drug Co: POB 192, Crater, Aden; tel 24912; telex 2293; Chair and Gen Man: Dr Awadh Salam Issa Bamatraf; f 1972; import of pharmaceutical products, chemicals, medical supplies, baby foods and scientific instruments.

Public Trading Corpn for Textile and Electrical Goods: 1st Floor, Ministry of Industry, Trade and Supplies Bldg, POB 4490, Maalla, Aden; tel 42242; telex 2223; Gen Man: Salem Abd as-Salem; f 1982; import of textiles and clothing and electrical goods.

Defence

Air Force: Aden; Commdr: Col Ali Muthannah Hadi.

Army: Aden; Chief of Gen Staff: Col Haitham Saleh Qasim

Tahir; Commdr of the Popular Militia National Command: Maj Said Ahmad Sulum.

Navy: Aden; Commdr: Maj Ali Qasim Talib.

Energy

Aden Refinery Co: POB 3003, Little Aden 110, Aden; tel 76234; telex 2213; fax 76600; Exec Dir: Muhammad Hussein al-Haj; f 1952; refining of crude petroleum.

Public Corpn for Electric Power: POB 5245, Hedjuff, Aden; tel 24821; telex 2263.

Yemen National Oil Co: POB 5050, Maalla, Aden; Gen Man: Muhammad Abd Hussein; sole petroleum concessionaire, importer and distributor of petroleum products.

Legal and Judiciary

Supreme Court: Aden; Pres: Dr Mustafa Abd al-Kahliq; Islamic law (Shari'a) and local common law (Urfi) are applied.

Media

BROADCASTING

State Committee for Information: POB 1222, Aden; tel 22809; telex 2317; Chair: Muhammad Abd al-Qawi; Dep Chair: Awadh Alhamza; controls radio, TV, news agency and press.

Democratic Yemen Broadcasting Service: POB 1222, Aden; tel 22809; Dir-Gen: Gamal ud-Din al-Khatib; radio broadcasts in Arabic.

Democratic Yemen Broadcasting Service: POB 1264, Aden; tel 22809; Dir-Gen: Umar Abd al-Aziz Muhammad; programmes for four hours daily, mainly in Arabic; other series in English and French.

GOVERNMENT PUBLISHER

14 October Corpn for Printing, Publishing, Distribution and Advertising: POB 4227, Crater, Aden; Chair and Gen Man: Salih Ahmad Salih; under control of Ministry of Culture and Information.

NEWS AND INFORMATION

Aden News Agency (ANA): c/o Ministry of Culture and Information, POB 1187, Tawahi 102, Aden; tel 24874; telex 2286; Dir-Gen: Ahmad Muhammad Ibrahim; f 1970.

Transport

Alyemda (Democratic Yemen Airlines): POB 6006, Khormaksar, Aden; tel 33811; telex 2269; Chair and Gen Man: Abdullah Ali Abdullah; Dep Gen Man: Said Nagi Sinan; f 1971; domestic services and international flights throughout the Middle East, and to Europe and the Far East.

National Dockyards Co: POB 1244, Maalla, Aden; tel 22504; telex 268; Gen Man: Dr S. al-Muntasser; Dep Gen Man: M. Modhesh; f 1969; ship repairs and shipbuilding facilities.

National Shipping Co: POB 1228, Steamer Point, Aden; tel 24861; telex 2216; Gen Man: Muhammad bin Muhammad Shaker; f 1970, following nationalization and amalgamation of foreign shipping cos; freight and passenger services to Red Sea ports, East Africa and Bombay.

Yemen Land Transport Co: Aden; telex 2307; Chair: Abd al-Jalil Tahir Badr; Gen Man: Salih Awad al-Amudi; f 1980; incorporates former Yemen Bus Co and all other local public transport.

Yemen Navigation Line: POB 4190, Aden; tel 24861; telex 295; fleet of three general cargo ships.

Yemen Ports Authority: POB 1316, Tawahi, Aden; tel 22666; telex 2278; Chair and Dir-Gen: Ahmad Said al-Dahi; f 1888; pilotage, lighterage and stevedoring in ports of Aden, Mukalla and Nishtun.

YUGOSLAVIA

Head of State

The rights and duties of the Head of State are exercised by a nine-member collective state Presidency, consisting of one representative of each republic and autonomous province and the President of the Presidium of the League of Communists of Yugoslavia's (LCY) Central Committee. The Members of the Presidency are elected for five years by both chambers of the Socialist Federal Republic of Yugoslavia (SFRY) Assembly, with the posts of President and Vice-President rotating annually. The administrative branch of government is the Federal Executive Council, led by a President and two Vice-Presidents, which is elected by the SFRY Assembly for four years.

President of the Collective Presidency: Janez Drnovsek (May 1989-May 1990).

Vice-President of the Collective Presidency: Borisav Jović.

Office of the Presidency: 11000 Belgrade, Bul Lenjina 2; tel (11) 636-466; 11448.

Legislature

The SFRY Assembly is composed of two chambers. The Federal Chamber has 220 members (30 from each of the six republics and 20 from each of the two provinces). The Chamber of Republics and Provinces has 88 members (12 from each Republican Assembly and eight from each Provincial Assembly). The delegates are chosen by each basic self-managing organization or community to serve a four-year term. In January 1990 the LCY voted to abolish its leading role in society and to set up a multi-party system.

Savezna Skupština (Federal Assembly): 11000 Belgrade, trg Marksa i Engelsa 13; tel (11) 339-484; telex 12388; Pres: Dr Slobodan Gligorijević; Pres, Federal Chamber: Bogdana Glumac-Levakov; Pres, Chamber of Republics and Provinces: Dr Miran Mejak.

MINISTRIES AND GOVERNMENT DEPARTMENTS

OFFICE OF THE PRESIDENT OF THE FEDERAL EXECUTIVE COUNCIL
11070 Belgrade, Bul Lenjina 2
Tel (11) 334-281
President: Ante Marković
Vice-Presidents: Aleksandar Mitrović, Zivko Pregl
Federal Secretaries without Portfolio: Dzevad Mujezinović, Branimir Pajković, Nikola Gasovski

FEDERAL SECRETARIAT FOR AGRICULTURE
11070 Belgrade, Omladinskih brigada 1
Tel (11) 338-281; telex 11448
Federal Secretary: Dr Stevo Mirjanić

FEDERAL SECRETARIAT FOR DEVELOPMENT
Belgrade
Federal Secretary: Dr Bozidar Marendić

FEDERAL SECRETARIAT FOR ENERGY AND INDUSTRY
11070 Belgrade, Omladinskih brigada 1
Tel (11) 338-281; telex 11448
Federal Secretary: Stevan Santo

FEDERAL SECRETARIAT FOR FINANCE
11070 Belgrade, Omladinskih brigada 1
Tel (11) 338-281; telex 11448
Federal Secretary: Branko Zekan

FEDERAL SECRETARIAT FOR FOREIGN AFFAIRS
11000 Belgrade, Kneza Miloša 24
Tel (11) 682-555; telex 11173
Federal Secretary: Budimir Lončar

FEDERAL SECRETARIAT FOR FOREIGN ECONOMIC RELATIONS
11070 Belgrade, Omladinskih brigada 1
Tel (11) 195-444; telex 12110
Federal Secretary: Franc Horvat

FEDERAL SECRETARIAT FOR INTERNAL AFFAIRS
11000 Belgrade, Kneza Miloša 100
Tel (11) 685-765; telex 11448
Federal Secretary: Petar Gračanin

FEDERAL SECRETARIAT FOR JUSTICE AND ADMINISTRATION
11070 Belgrade, bul Lenjina 2
Tel (11) 334-281; telex 11448
Federal Secretary: Dr Vlado Kambovski

FEDERAL SECRETARIAT FOR LABOUR, HEALTH, VETERANS' AFFAIRS AND SOCIAL POLICY
11070 Belgrade, bul AVNOJ-a 104
Tel (11) 602-555; telex 11062; fax (11) 195-244
Federal Secretary: Radiasa Gačić

FEDERAL SECRETARIAT FOR NATIONAL DEFENCE
11000 Belgrade, Kneza Miloša 29
Tel (11) 656-122
Federal Secretary: Col-Gen Veljko Kadijević

FEDERAL SECRETARIAT FOR TRADE
Belgrade
Federal Secretary: Nazmi Mustafa

FEDERAL SECRETARIAT FOR TRANSPORT AND COMMUNICATIONS
11070 Belgrade, bul AVNOJ-a 104
Tel (11) 338-281; telex 12062
Federal Secretary: Jože Slokar

GOVERNMENT AGENCIES AND ORGANIZATIONS

Advisory and Supervisory Body

Savezni zavod za medjunarodnu naucnu prosvetnokul-turnu i technicku saradnju (Federal Administration for International Scientific, Educational, Cultural and Technical Co-operation): 11000 Belgrade, Kosančićev venac 29, POB 384; tel (11) 625-955; telex 11661; Dir-Gen: Dr Marijan Strbašić; f 1971; responsible for bilateral and multilateral co-operation in fields of science, education, culture and technology.

Business and Economy

BANKING

Beobanka—Beogradska Osnovna Banka (Belgrade Basic Bank): 11000 Belgrade, Zeleni venac 16; tel (11) 629-455; telex 11802; Pres: Vladan Ikonić; f 1978; associated with Udružena Beogradska Banka.

Investiciona Banka Titograd—Udružena Banka (Titograd Investment Associated Bank): 81000 Titograd, bul Revolucije 1; tel (81) 42-922; telex 61118; Pres: Veselin Babić; f 1966.

Jugobanka—Osnovna Banka, Beograd (Jugobanka—Basic Bank, Belgrade): 11000 Belgrade, Maršala Tita 11; tel (11) 334-931; telex 11280; Pres: Stevan Vrapčević; f 1956.

Jugobanka—Osnovna Komercijalna Banka, Beograd (Jugobanka—Basic Commercial Bank, Belgrade): 11000 Belgrade, Radivoja Koraća 6; tel (11) 455-666; telex 12133; Chair: Ljubomir Potkonjak; f 1970 as br of Sremska banka, joined Jugobanka 1977.

Jugobanka—Udružena Banka, Beograd (United Bank—Belgrade): 11000 Belgrade, 7 Jula 19-21, POB 400; tel (11) 630-022; telex 11145; Chair: Branislav Penević; Dep Chair: Luka Reljić; f 1955 as Yugoslav Bank for Foreign Trade, name changed 1971.

Jugoslovenska Banka Za Medjunarodnu Ekonomsku Saradnju (Yugoslav Bank for International Economic Co-operation): 11070 Belgrade, Bul AVNOJ-a 121, POB 219; tel (11) 143-004; telex 11710; Pres: Ivan Stambolić; Dep Man: Ilija Marjanović; f 1979; replaced the Export Credit and Insurance Fund and assumed the assets and liabilities of the Fund; established by a special law; grants export credits; underwrites insurance of exports against non-commercial risks, etc.

Ljubljanska Banka—Kreditna Banka, Maribor (Ljubljana Bank—Credit Bank, Maribor): 62000 Maribor, Vita Kraigherja 4; tel (61) 27-441; telex 33167; Pres: Franc Hvalec.

Ljubljanska Banka—Združena Banka (Ljubljana Bank—Associated Bank): 61001 Ljubljana, trg revolucije 2, POB 534; tel (61) 215-511; telex 31256; fax (61) 222-422; Pres: Metod Rotar; Exec Vice-Pres, International: Ciril Krpač; f 1955; 421 brs.

Narodna Banka Jugoslavije (National Bank of Yugoslavia):

11001 Belgrade, Bul Revolucije 15, POB 1010; tel (11) 332-001; telex 72000; Gov: Dušan Vlatković; Dep Gov: Mitja Gaspari; f 1883, received its present name in 1963; sole right of issue, performs the usual functions of a central bank; there are also National Banks in the capitals of the Yugoslav Republics and Autonomous Provinces.

Osnovna Privredno—Investiciona Banka u Beograda—Investbanka (Basic Economic Investment Bank of Belgrade): 11000 Belgrade, Terazije 7-9; tel (11) 335-201; telex 11147; Pres: Budimir Kostić; f 1862; associated with Udružena Beogradska Banka.

Privredna Banka Sarajevo—Udružena Banka (Sarajevo Economic Bank—Associated Bank): 71000 Belgrade, Vojvode Stepe Obala 19, POB 160; tel (71) 213-144; telex 41280; Pres: Božidar Martinović; f 1971.

Stopanska Banka—Osnovna Banka, Bitola (Economic Bank—Basic Bank, Bitola): 97000 Bitola, G. Radosavljević bb; tel (97) 31-720; telex 53123; Gen Man: Jakim Ivanovski; associated with Stopanska Banka—Združena Banka, Skopje.

Stopanska Banka—Osnovna Banka, Ohrid (Economic Bank—Basic Bank, Ohrid): 96000 Ohrid, B. Kidrić 19; tel (96) 31-400; telex 53871; Gen Man: Najdenko Popovski; associated with Stopanska Banka—Združena Banka, Skopje.

Stopanska Banka—Osnovna Banka, Skopje (Economic Bank—Basic Bank, Skopje): 91000 Skopje, Kej Dimitar Vlahov 4; tel (91) 236-111; telex 51162; Gen Man: Aleksandar Manevski; associated with Stopanska Banka—Združena Banka.

Stopanska Banka—Združena Banka, Skopje (Associated Bank, Skopje): 91000 Skopje, Str 11 Oktomvri 7; tel (91) 235-111; telex 51140; fax (91) 226-276; Pres: Ljubomir Popovski; f 1944; associated with Stopanska Banka—Združena Banka.

Udružena Banka Hrvatske (Associated Bank of Croatia): 41000 Zagreb, Ksaver 208; tel (41) 431-222; telex 22560; Pres: Dr Tomislav Badovinac; f 1983; 80 brs.

Udružena Banka Hrvatske—Dubrovačka Banka Dubrovnik (Bank of Dubrovnik): 50000 Dubrovnik, put Republike 5; tel (50) 32-366; telex 27540; Gen Man: Nikola Sambrailo; f 1956.

Udružena Banka Hrvatske—Istarska Banka Pula (Bank of Istria): 52000 Pula, Premanturska 2; tel (52) 33-966; telex 25241; Gen Man: Anton Racan; f 1956.

Udružena Banka Hravatske—Komercijalna Banka Zadar: 57000 Zadar, trg 27 marta 3; tel (57) 437-111; telex 27224; Gen Man: Neven Dobrović; f 1957.

Udružena Banka Hrvatske—Riječka Banka Rijeka (Bank of Rijeka): 51000 Rijeka, trg P. Togliattia 3a; tel (51) 31-211; telex 24143; Gen Man: Nikola Pavletić; f 1954.

Udružena Banka Hrvatske—Slavonska Banka Osijek (Bank of Slavonia): 54000 Osijek, Bul JNA 29; tel (54) 125-022; telex 28090; Gen Man: Josip Harangozo; f 1977.

Udružena Banka Hrvatske—Splitska Banka Split (Bank of Split): 58000 Split, R. Boškovića 16; tel (58) 521-777; telex 26161; Gen Man: Ante Krstulović; f 1966.

Udružena Banka Hrvatske—Privredna Banka Zagreb
(Zagreb Economic Bank): 41000 Zagreb, Račkoga 6; tel (41)
410-822; telex 21120; Pres: Andjelko Radovinović; f 1966.

**Udružena Banka Hrvatske—Vukovarska Banka
Vukovar:** 56230 Vukovar, Maršala Tita 1; tel (56) 44-690; telex
28296; Gen Man: Milan Maksimović; f 1965.

Udružena Banka Hrvatske—Zagrebačka Banka Zagreb
(Bank of Zagreb): 41000 Zagreb, Paromlinska 2; tel (41) 530-
444; telex 21463; Gen Man: Josip Pribanić; f 1978.

Udružena Beogradska Banka (Associated Belgrade Bank):
11001 Belgrade, Knez Mihajlova 2, POB 955; tel (11) 624-455;
telex 11712; Pres: Borka Vučič; f 1978.

Udružena Kosovska Banka (Kosovo Associated Bank):
38000 Priština, Maršala Tita 4; tel (38) 34-111; Pres: Muharem
Ismailji.

Udruženje banaka Jugoslavije (Association of Yugoslav
Banks): 11001 Belgrade, Masarikova 5/IX; tel (11) 684-797; telex
11767; Pres: Muharem Ismailji; Sec-Gen: Milovan Milutinović; f
1955; works on improving inter-bank co-operation, organizes
agreements of mutual interest, gives assistance, organizes co-
operation with foreign banks, other financial institutions and
their associations, represents banks in their relations with the
Govt and National Bank of Yugoslavia.

Vojvodjanska Banka—Udružena Banka (Bank of Vojvo-
dina—Associated Bank): 21001 Novi Sad, bul Maršala Tita 14,
POB 272; tel (21) 57-222; telex 14129; Pres: Dr Andraš Mora; f
1978.

INSURANCE

'DUNAV' Zajednica Osiguranja Imovine i Lica (Dunav
Insurance Community): 11000 Belgrade, Makedonska 4, POB
624; tel (11) 324-001; telex 11359; f 1974; all classes of insurance.

NATIONALIZED INDUSTRIES

Brodosplit: 58000 Split, Put Udarnika 19, POB 107; tel (58)
521-222; telex 26125; shipbuilding and ship design.

Energoprojekt: 11000 Belgrade, 12 Lenjinov Bul; tel (11) 131-
516; telex 11181; fax (11) 146-466; design and contracting of
engineering projects.

Iskra: 61000 Ljubljana, Trg Revolucije 3; tel (61) 213-213;
telex 31356; manufacture of electrical and telecommunications
equipment.

SCT: 61000 Ljubljana, Titova 38; tel (61) 319-273; telex 31469;
fax (61) 319-389; civil engineering and building projects both if
Yugoslavia and abroad.

TRADE

Belgrade Fair: 11000 Belgrade, Bul Vojvode Mišića 14, POB
408; tel (11) 655-555; telex 11306; Pres: Djurdje Miković; promotes and holds several trade fairs throughout the year,
including Motor Show, Chemical Fair, International Technical
Fair, Clothing Fair and Book Fair.

Generalexport: 11070 Belgrade, Narodnih Heroja 43, POB
636; tel (11) 691-512; telex 11228; international trading co
dealing in trade of products from all sectors of the economy.

Institut za Spoljnu Trgovinu: 11000 Belgrade, Moše Pijade
8; tel (11) 339-041; foreign trade institute.

Jugometal: 11000 Belgrade, Deligradska 28, POB 311; tel (11)
687-999; telex 885932; fax (11) 643-925; trade in ores and metals,
chemicals, jewellery and industrial equipment.

Novosadski Sajam (Novi Sad Fair): 21000 Novi Sad, Hajduk
Veljkova 11; tel (21) 51-648; telex 14180; fax (21) 20-649; Gen

Man: Jovan Nešin; f 1923; organization of trade fairs and
exhibitions.

Privredna Komora Jugoslavije (Federal Chamber of
Economy): 11000 Belgrade, Terazije 23, POB 1003; tel (11) 339-
461; telex 11638; affiliates all economic organizations; promotes
economic and commercial relations with foreign cos and countries.

Rade Končar: 41000 Zagreb, Fallerovo šetalište 22; tel (41)
561-022; telex 21204; export of electrical equipment.

Zagreb Fair: Zagrebački Velesajam, 41020 Zagreb, av Borisa
Kidriča 2, POB 41020-16; tel (41) 511-666; telex 21385; Dir-
Gen: Bohumil Bernašek; f 1909.

Defence

Armed Forces: c/o Federal Secretariat for National Defence,
11000 Belgrade, Kneza Miloša 29; tel (11) 454-061; Chief of
Staff: Zorko Canadi.

Air Force: address as above; tel (11) 656-122; Commdr:
Anton Tus.

Army: address as above; tel (11) 454-061; Commdr: Slavko
Djurdjević.

Navy: address as above; tel (11) 656-122; Commdr: Sveto
Letica.

Energy

JUGEL (Union of Yugoslav Electric Power Industry): 11000
Belgrade, Balkanska 13; tel (11) 686-337; telex 11876; Head of
Nuclear Power Dept: Milan Gavrilović.

JUMEL (Business Association of Yugoslav Machine Industry):
11070 Belgrade, Bul Lenjina 143; tel (11) 130-195; telex 11076;
Sec: Dušan Radojković.

Komisija Saveznog izršnog veća nuklearnu energiju
(Nuclear Energy Commission of the Federal Executive Council):
11070 Belgrade, Palata Federacije; tel (11) 636-797; telex 11448;
Sec: Milan Pavićević.

INA Group: 41000 Zagreb, Ulica Proleterskih 78; tel (41) 517-
230; telex 21223; exploration, devt and production of oil and
gas.

NUKLIN (Associated Nuclear Research Institutes of Yugoslavia): 11001 Belgrade, POB 522; tel (11) 455-663; telex 11563;
fax (11) 458-676; Dir: Naim Afgan; Dep Dir: Zoran Drače; f
1983; co-ordination of research and devt projects in field of
nuclear sciences.

Legal and Judiciary

Constitutional Court: 11070 Belgrade, Ustavni sud Jugoslavije, Bul Lenjina 2; tel (11) 339-590; telex 11448; Pres: Dušan
Strbac; consists of 14 mems (two from each republic and one
from each autonomous province) elected for eight years; judicial
review of constitutionality of laws; settles disputes between
republic Govts, between courts and other state bodies and
between the constitutional courts of the republics.

Federal Court: 11000 Belgrade, Svetozara Markovića 21; tel
(11) 333-911; Pres: Rajko Nisavić; highest organ of justice
comprising 13 mems elected by the Federal Chamber of the
SFRY Assembly.

Media

BROADCASTING

Federal Radiocommunication Administration: 11000 Belgrade, Terazije 41; tel (11) 344-414; telex 12405; Dir: Dr Drasko Marin; f 1957; frequency management.

Jugoslovenska Radio-Televizija—JRT (Association of Yugoslav Radio and Television Organizations): 11000 Belgrade, Generala Ždanova 28; tel (11) 330-194; telex 11469; Pres: Živojin Radojlović; Chair: Hrvoje Ištuk; Exec Sec: Aleksandar Todorović; f 1952.

Radio Jugoslavija: 11000 Belgrade, Hilendarska 2; tel (11) 344-455; telex 12432; fax (11) 332-014; Dir: Dr Dragan Marković; f 1945; foreign service broadcasting in Albanian, Arabic, Bulgarian, English, French, German, Greek, Italian, Russian and Spanish.

Radio-Televizija Beograd: 11000 Belgrade, Hilendarska 2; tel (11) 346-801; telex 11727 (Radio); Takovska 10; tel (11) 342001; telex 11884 (TV); Dir-Gen: Dušan Mitević; Dir, Radio: Dragan Nitiković; Dir, TV: Nenad Ristić; five radio and two TV channels.

Radio-Televizija Ljubljana: 61000 Ljubljana, Tavčarjeva 17; tel (61) 311-922; telex 31118 (Radio); tel (61) 312-447; telex 32283 (TV); Dir-Gen: Vlado Janžić; Dir, Radio: Boris Dolničar; Dir, TV: Stane Grah; f 1928; four radio and three TV channels broadcasting in Slovene and Italian/Koper-Capodistria languages.

Radio-Televizija Novi Sad: 21000 Novi Sad, Žarka Zrenjanina 3; tel (21) 611-588; telex 14127 (Radio); Kamenički put 45; tel (21) 56-855; telex 14303 (TV); Dir-Gen: (vacant); Dir, Radio: (vacant); Dir, TV: (vacant); five radio and one TV channel broadcasting in Serbo-Croat, Slovak, Romanian, Hungarian and Ruthenian.

Radio-Televizija Priština: 38000 Priština, Zejnel Ajdina bb; tel (38) 26-171; telex 18134 (Radio); tel (38) 31-211; telex 18186 (TV); Dir-Gen: Ćemajl Hasani; Dir, Radio: (vacant); Dir,TV: Baškim Hisari; two radio and one TV channel broadcasting in Albanian, Serbo-Croat and Turkish.

Radio-Televizija Sarajevo: 71000 Sarajevo, VI Proleterske brigada 4; tel (71) 652-333; telex 41122; Dir-Gen: Hrvoje Ištuk; Dir, Radio: Nedeljko Miljanović; Dir, TV: Radivoje Budalić; four radio and two TV channels.

Radio-Televizija Skopje: 91001 Skopje, Bul Goce Delčev bb; tel (91) 227-711; telex 51157; Dir-Gen: Ljubomir Jakimovski; Dir, Radio: Vjekoslav Prokopenko; Dir, TV: Ivan Andreevski; three radio and two TV channels.

Radio-Televizija Titograd: 81000 Titograd, Cetinjski put bb; tel (81) 52-622; telex 61133; Dir-Gen: Milutin Vukašinović; Dir, Radio: Čedomir Lješević; Dir, TV: Pero Radović; f 1944; one radio and two TV channels.

Radio-Televizija Zagreb: 41000 Zagreb, Jurišićeva 4; tel (41) 426-333; telex 21154 (Radio); Dežmanova 10; tel (41) 276-611; telex 21477 (TV); Dir-Gen: Veljko Knezević; Dir, Radio: Josip Grubišić-Cabo; Dir, TV: Goran Radman; f 1926; four radio and two TV channels.

NEWS AND INFORMATION

Federal Statistical Office: 11000 Belgrade, Kneza Miloša 20; tel (11) 681-999; telex 11317; fax (11) 681-995; f 1944; collection, processing and dissemination of data.

Novinska Agengija Tanjug: 11001 Belgrade, Obilićev venac 2, POB 439; tel (11) 332-230; telex 11220; Dir: Mihailo Šaranović; Editor-in-Chief: Mladen Arnautović; f 1943; state news agency providing news to domestic and foreign sources.

Science and Technology

Energoinvest-RO ITEN (Institute for Thermal and Nuclear Technologies): 71000 Sarajevo, Stup, Tvornička 3; tel (71) 542-969; telex 41826; fax (71) 629-681; Dir: Dr Alija Lekić; f 1961; research organization.

GEOINSTITUT: 11000 Belgrade, Rovinjska st 12; tel (11) 4889-966; telex 11903; Dirs: Dimitrije Cvetković, Milan Obrenović; f 1948; research organization for geological, geophysical and mining exploration of nuclear and other raw materials, exploratory drilling, engineering geology and hydrogeology.

Geološki zavod (Geological Survey): 61000 Ljubljana, Parmova 37; tel (61) 344-261; telex 31448; research in geology, geophysics and geo-engineering; operates uranium mine.

Institut 'Jozef Stefan': 61000 Ljubljana, Jamova 39; tel (61) 214-399; telex 31296; fax (61) 219-385; Dir: Prof Tomaž Kalin; f 1949; basic and applied research work in some fields of physics, chemistry, electronics, reactor engineering, applied mathematics, environmental protection.

Institut za nuklearne nauke Boris Kidrič (Boris Kidrič Institute of Nuclear Sciences): 11001 Belgrade, POB 522; tel (11) 438-906; telex 11563; Dir-Gen: Dr Miodrag Stojić; f 1948; basic and applied research in the fields of natural, mathematical, techno-technological and nuclear sciences.

Institut Rudjer Bošković (Rudjer Bošković Institute): 41000 Zagreb, Bijenička 54; tel (41) 435-111; telex 21383; fax (41) 425-497; Dir-Gen: Dr K. Pisk; f 1950; fundamental and applied research in natural sciences.

Tourism

Atlas: 50000 Dubrovnik, Pile 1; tel (50) 27-333; telex 27515; f 1923; travel agency with 41 brs, one overseas office.

Autotehna: 11000 Belgrade, Bul Revolucije 94; tel (11) 433-323; telex 11713; car hire service with 17 brs.

Dalmacijaturist: 58000 Split, Titova Obala 5; tel (58) 44-666; telex 26145; f 1923; tourist agency with 21 brs, one office abroad.

Emona Glogtour: 61000 Ljubljana, Šmartinska 130/X; tel (61) 444-177; telex 31146; tourist agency with 32 brs, two foreign offices.

Generalturist: 41000 Zagreb, Praška 5; tel (41) 420-888; telex 21467; f 1923; 34 brs, four reps overseas.

Inex: 11000 Belgrade, trg Republike 5/VII; tel (11) 622-360; telex 12990; 17 brs.

Jugoslavenska tankerska plovidba (Turisthotel): 57000 Zadar, I. L. Ribara bb; tel (57) 24-255; telex 27136; Dir-Gen: Ivan Aralica; Vice-Pres: Andjelo Lordanić; f 1964; tourism, hotel management.

Kompas: 61000 Ljubljana, Pražakova 4; tel (61) 327-661; telex 31209; Pres: Egon Conradi; f 1923; 100 brs, 11 offices overseas.

Kvarner Express: 51410 Opatija, Maršala Tita 186-192; tel (51) 711-111; telex 24174; f 1952; arranges accomodation, tours, conventions, etc; 40 brs, one foreign office.

Putnik: 11000 Belgrade, Dragoslava Jovanovića 1; tel (11) 332-591; telex 11324; 60 brs.

Srbijaturist: 18000 Niš, Voždova 12; tel (18) 22-077; telex 16256; f 1951; hotels and tourism enterprise.

Turistički savez Jugoslavije (Tourist Association of Yugoslavia): 11001 Belgrade, Moše Pijade 8/IV, Poštanski fah 595; tel (11) 339-041; telex 11863; Pres: Nikola Ban; Sec-Gen: Pero Djoković; f 1953; promotion and devt of tourism.

Vojvodinatours: 21000 Novi Sad, Bul Maršala Tita 19; tel (21) 616-322; telex 14472; 11 brs.

Yugotours: 11000 Belgrade, Djure Djakovića 31; tel (11) 764-622; telex 11000; f 1957; organizes travel and accomodation arrangements for foreign and domestic tourists; nine brs, 24 offices overseas.

Transport

CIVIL AVIATION

Adria Airways: 61001 Ljubljana, Kuzmičeva 7; tel (61) 313-366; telex 31268; fax (61) 323-356; Pres: Janez Kocijančič; f 1961; domestic passenger and cargo services between all the major cities; international flights to Larnaca, Munich, London, Bari and Tel-Aviv.

Air Jugoslavia: 11000 Belgrade, Moše Pijade 1/III; tel (11) 338-812; telex 12125; Man Dir: Zvonimir Sokčić; f 1969; wholly-owned subsidiary of JAT (see below); overseas passenger and cargo charter flights.

Aviogenex: 11070 Belgrade, Milentija Popovića 9; tel (11) 603-198; telex 11711; fax (11) 541-664; Gen Man: Miroslav Spasić; Dep Gen Mans: Dragoslav Andjelković, Miroslav Vrbaški; f 1968; passenger and cargo flights within Europe, the Mediterranean and the Middle East.

Jugoslovenski Aerotransport—JAT (Yugoslav Airlines): 11070 Belgrade, Centar Sava, Milentija Popovića 9; tel (11) 145-789; telex 12035; Chair: Miljenko Zrelec; f 1947; internal services and international flights to Europe, Africa, Asia, Australia and North America.

RAILWAYS

Zajednica Jugoslovenskih Železnica (Community of Yugoslav Railways): 11000 Belgrade, Nemanjina 6, POB 553; tel (11) 685-822; telex 12495; Pres: Zoran Nastić; 9,270 km of track in 1987.

SHIPPING

Jadrolinija (Adriatic Lines): 51000 Rijeka, Obala Jugoslavenske mornarice 16, POB 123; tel (51) 30-899; telex 24225; fax (51) 213-116; Dirs: Capt Anton Lenac, Aleksej Antonini; f 1947; ferry and cruise services.

Jugolinija (Yugoslav Shipping Line): 51001 Rijeka, Obala Jugoslavenske mornarice 16, POB 379; tel (51) 33-111; telex 24218; fax (51) 32-914; f 1947; cargo and passenger services throughout the world.

Jugoslovenska Oceanska Plovidba (Yugoslav Ocean Lines): 85330 Kotor; tel (85) 25-011; telex 61116; Pres: Anton Moškov; regular services to North America.

Jugoslovenska Pomorska Agencija (Yugoslav Shipping Agency): 11070 Belgrade, Lenjinov Bul 165A; tel (11) 130-004; telex 11140; fax (11) 138-882; Dir: Stevan Obradović; f 1947; chartering, liner/container transport, port agency, passenger service and air cargo routes.

ZAIRE

Head of State

Executive power is vested in the President, who is directly-elected for seven years. The President appoints and leads the National Executive Council, a cabinet of State Commissioners with departmental responsibilities. A National Security Council advises the President on questions of security.

President: Marshal Mobutu Sese Seko Kuku Ngbendu Wa Za Banga (assumed power 24 November 1965; elected by popular vote 31 October-1 November 1970; re-elected 28-29 July 1984).

Office of the President: Mont Ngaliema, Kinshasa; tel (12) 31312; telex 21368.

Legislature

Legislative power is held by the unicameral National Legislative Council, which has 210 members elected for five years by universal adult suffrage. Since 1970 the only authorized political party has been the ruling Mouvement populaire de la révolution (MPR). Zaire comprises 10 regions, each headed by an appointed Commissioner, and the city of Kinshasa, headed by a Governor.

Conseil National Législatif (National Legislative Council): Palais de la Nation, Kinshasa-Gombe; tel (12) 30918; Speaker: (vacant).

MINISTRIES AND GOVERNMENT DEPARTMENTS

OFFICE OF THE FIRST STATE COMMISSIONER
Hôtel du Conseil Exécutif, ave des 3Z, Kinshasa-Gombe
Tel (12) 30892
First State Commissioner: Kengo Wa Dondo
Deputy First State Commissioner in charge of Political, Administrative and Social Affairs:
Nimy Mayidika Ngimbi
Deputy First State Commissioner in charge of Economic, Financial and Monetary Affairs:
Mwando Nsimba
Deputy First State Commissioner in charge of Territorial Administration and Decentralization:
Mozagba Ngbuka
State Commissioner without Portfolio: Kinzonzi Mvutudiki Ngindu Kogbia

DEPARTMENT OF AGRICULTURE AND RURAL DEVELOPMENT
BP 8722, Kinshasa-Gombe
Tel (12) 31821
State Commissioner for Agriculture: Takizala Luyuna Musi Mbingini
State Commissioner for Rural Development:
Mwando Nsimba

DEPARTMENT OF CITIZENS' RIGHTS AND LIBERTIES
Kinshasa-Gombe
State Commissioner for Citizens' Rights and Liberties:
Nimy Mayidika Ngimbi

DEPARTMENT OF THE CIVIL SERVICE
Kinshasa-Gombe
State Commissioner: Ntawiniga Balezi

DEPARTMENT OF CULTURE, ARTS AND TOURISM
Immeuble CCIZ, Kinshasa-Gombe
Tel (12) 32071
State Commissioner: Ngogo Kamanda

DEPARTMENT OF ENERGY AND MINES
77 ave de la Justice, Kinshasa-Gombe
Tel (12) 30120; telex 21362
State Commissioner: Beyeye Djema

DEPARTMENT OF THE ENVIRONMENT AND CONSERVATION
15 ave de la Clinique, BP 1248, Kinshasa
Tel (12) 31252
State Commissioner: Pendje Demodetdo Yako

DEPARTMENT OF FINANCE AND BUDGET
blvd du 30 juin, BP 12997, Kinshasa-Gombe
Tel (12) 31197; telex 21161
State Commissioner for Finance: Katanga Mukumadi Wa Mutumba
State Commissioner for the Budget: Kaseraka Kasai

DEPARTMENT OF FOREIGN AFFAIRS AND INTERNATIONAL CO-OPERATION
BP 7100, Kinshasa-Gombe
Tel (12) 32450; telex 21364
State Commissioner for Foreign Affairs:
Nguza Karl-I-Bond
State Commissioner for International Co-operation:
Nyiwa Mobutu

DEPARTMENT OF FOREIGN TRADE
BP 3095, Kinshasa-Gombe
Tel (12) 32071; telex 21232
State Commissioner: Nzanda Buana Kalemba

DEPARTMENT OF HIGHER EDUCATION
ave Col Tshatshi, Kinshasa-Gombe
Tel (12) 32074; telex 21394
**State Commissioner for Higher and University
Education and Scientific Research:** Lombeye Bosongo

DEPARTMENT OF INFORMATION AND PRESS
BP 3171, Kinshasa
Tel (12) 23171
State Commissioner: Sakombi Inongo

DEPARTMENT OF JUSTICE
BP 3137, Kinshasa-Gombe
Tel (12) 32432
State Commissioner: Nsinga Udjuu Ongwakebi Untube

DEPARTMENT OF LABOUR AND SOCIAL SECURITY
blvd du 30 juin, Kinshasa-Gombe
Tel (12) 26727
State Commissioner: Muduka Inyanza

DEPARTMENT OF LAND AFFAIRS
ave du Fleuve, BP 7367, Kinshasa-Gombe
Tel (12) 30236
State Commissioner: Pendje Demodetdo Yako

DEPARTMENT OF NATIONAL DEFENCE
Mont Ngaliema, Kinshasa
Tel (12) 31312; telex 21368
State Commissioner: Marshal Mobutu Sese Seko Kuku
Ngbendu Wa Za Banga

DEPARTMENT OF NATIONAL ECONOMY AND INDUSTRY
Immeuble ONATRA, BP 8500, Kinshasa-Gombe
Tel (12) 22945; telex 21232
State Commissioner: Ndele Bamu

DEPARTMENT OF PLANNING
4155 rue des Coteaux, BP 9378, Kinshasa-Gombe
Tel (12) 32874; telex 21195
State Commissioner: Bieme Ngalisame

DEPARTMENT OF POSTS, TELEPHONES AND TELECOMMUNICATIONS
BP 800, Kinshasa-Gombe
Tel (12) 24854; telex 21403
State Commissioner: Okuka Wa Katako

DEPARTMENT OF PRIMARY AND SECONDARY EDUCATION
ave des Ambassadeurs, BP 32, Kinshasa-Gombe
Tel (12) 30098; telex 21460
State Commissioner: Nzege Aliaziambina

DEPARTMENT OF PUBLIC HEALTH
BP 3088, Kinshasa-Gombe
Tel (12) 31750
State Commissioner: Dr Ngandu Kabeya

DEPARTMENT OF PUBLIC WORKS AND TERRITORIAL DEVELOPMENT
BP 26, Kinshasa-Gombe
Tel (12) 30578
State Commissioner: Kabangula Kia Makonga

DEPARTMENT OF SPORTS AND LEISURE
BP 8541, Kinshasa 1
Tel (12) 31005
State Commissioner: Kibassa Maliba

DEPARTMENT OF TERRITORIAL ADMINISTRATION
blvd Col Tshatshi, BP 3468, Kinshasa-Gombe
Tel (12) 31147; telex 21358
State Commissioner: Mozagba Ngbuka

DEPARTMENT OF TRANSPORT AND COMMUNICATIONS
Immeuble ONATRA, BP 3304, Kinshasa-Gombe
Tel (12) 23660; telex 21404
State Commissioner: Mokolo Wa Mpombo

DEPARTMENT OF URBAN DEVELOPMENT
Kinshasa
State Commissioner: Ileo Itambala

DEPARTMENT OF VETERANS' AFFAIRS AND TERRITORIAL SECURITY
Kinshasa
State Commissioner: Gen Nsinga Boyenge Mosambay

GOVERNMENT AGENCIES AND ORGANIZATIONS

Advisory and Supervisory Body

Direction des Titres Fonciers et Cadastre: cnr ave Haut-Zaïre and ave Plateau, BP 7367, Kinshasa-Gombe; land registry.

Agriculture and the Environment

Institut National pour l'Etude et la Recherche Agronomiques: BP 1513, Kisangani, Haut-Zaïre; Dir-Gen: Dr Botula Manyala; f 1933; agricultural research.

Industries Zaïroises des Bois (IZB): 23 ave de l'Ouganda, BP 10399, Kinshasa; state forestry and saw-milling enterprise.

Institut Zaïrois pour la Conservation de la Nature: 5 ave de la Clinique, BP 4019, Kinshasa-Gombe; tel (12) 31401; nature conservation institute.

Office Zaïrois du Café (OZACAF): ave Général Bobozo, BP 8931, Kinshasa; tel (12) 77144; telex 20062; Exec Pres: Nendaka Bika; Man Dir: Unen Can; state agency for coffee.

Pêcherie Maritime Zaïroise (PEMARZA): Kinshasa; the sole sea-fishing enterprise.

Business and Economy

BANKING

Banque de Crédit Agricole (BCA): cnr aves Kasavubu and M'Polo, BP 8837, Kinshasa-Gombe; tel (12) 22801; telex 21383; Pres: Bofossa W'Ambea Nkoso; f 1982; devt bank; provides short-, medium- and long-term credit to the agricultural sector.

Banque du Zaïre: blvd Col Tshatshi au nord, BP 2697, Kinshasa; tel (12) 30681; telex 21227; Gov: Pay Pay Wa Syakasighe; Dir: Mamadou Touré; central bank; 6 brs, 16 agencies.

Banque Zaïroise du Commerce Extérieur (BZCE): blvd du 30 juin, BP 400, Kinshasa; tel (12) 25161; telex 21108; Chair and Gen Man: N'Sele·Ekofo Anyenga; f 1947; 32 brs.

Caisse Générale d'Epargne du Zaïre (CADEZA): 38 ave de la Caisse d'Epargne, BP 8147, Kinshasa-Gombe; tel (12) 31464; telex 21384; Chair and Man Dir: Nyembo Ya Lumbu; f 1950; 45 brs.

Caisse Nationale d'Epargne et de Crédit Immobilier: BP 11196, Kinshasa; Dir-Gen: Biangala Elonga Mbaü; f 1971.

Nouvelle Banque de Kinshasa: 1 place du Marché, BP 8033, Kinshasa 1 ; tel (12) 26361; telex 21304; Man Dir: N'Sele Ekofo Anyenga; f 1969 as Banque de Kinshasa; nationalized 1986; control transferred to National Union of Zairean Workers (UNTZA) in 1988; 6 brs.

Union Zaïroise de Banques SARL: angle ave de la Nation et ave des Aviateurs, BP 197, Kinshasa; tel (12) 25801; telex 21206; Chair and Gen Man: Tshilombo Wa Nshimba; Man Dir: Jacques Waerseggers; Gen Man: Gérard Godefroid; f 1949; partly state-owned; 12 brs.

FINANCIAL AGENCY

Société Financière de Développement (SOFIDE): Immeuble UZB Centre, 7ème étage, ave des Aviateurs, BP 1148, Kinshasa-Gombe; tel (12) 25619; telex 21476; Pres and Dir-Gen: Kazadi Membu; Man Dir: A. Delforge; f 1970; partly state-owned; provides technical and financial aid, primarily for agricultural devt; 4 brs.

INSURANCE

Société Nationale d'Assurances (SONAS): Immeuble SAN-KURU, blvd du 30 juin 3473, BP 3443, Kinshasa-Gombe; tel (12) 23051; telex 21653; Pres and Dir-Gen: Baza Luemba; f 1966; insurance and reinsurance.

NATIONALIZED INDUSTRY

Caisse de Stabilisation Cotonnière (CSCo): BP 3058, Kinshasa-Gombe; tel (12) 31206; telex 21174; Exec Chair: A. Kibangula; f 1978 to replace Office National des Fibres Textiles; acts as an intermediary between the Govt, cotton ginners and textile factories, and co-ordinates international financing of cotton sector.

Société Générale d'Alimentation (SGA): BP 15898, Kinshasa; state enterprise for the importation, processing and distribution of foodstuffs; largest chain of distributors in Zaire.

TRADE

Douane (Customs): Aéroport de Ndjili, BP 10007, Kinkasha 24; tel (12) 23760.

FIKIN—Foire Internationale de Kinshasa (Kinshasa International Trade Fair): BP 1397 Kinshasa; tel (12) 77506; telex 20145; Pres and Del-Gen: Togba Mata Boboy; f 1968; state-sponsored; held annually in July.

Defence

Armed Forces: c/o Dept of National Defence, Mont Ngaliema, Kinshasa; tel (12) 31312; telex 21368; Commdr-in-Chief: Marshal Mobutu Sese Seko Kuku Ngbendu Wa Za Banga; Chief of the Defence Staff: Vice-Adm Lomponda Wa Botende; Chief of Staff of the Naval Forces: Commdr Mambu Nsenga.

Gendarmerie Nationale (Constabulary): c/o Dept of National Defence, Mont Ngaliema, Kinshasa; tel (12) 31312; telex 21368.

Education

Presses Universitaires du Zaïre (PUZ): BP 1682, Kinshasa 1; tel (12) 30652; telex 21394; Dir: Prof Mumbanza Mwa Bawele; f 1972; publication of scientific research theses and university courses.

Legal and Judiciary

Cour Suprême de Justice (Supreme Court): cnr ave de la Justice and ave des 3Z, BP 3382, Kinshasa-Gombe; tel (12) 25104; First Pres: Balanda Mikuin Leliel; Pres: Okitakula Djambakote; Procurator-Gen of the Republic: Mongulu T'Apangane.

Justice Department: cnr ave de la Justice and ave des 3Z, BP 3382, Kinshasa-Gombe; tel (12) 25104; f 1980; under the control of the State Commr for Justice; responsible for the organization and definition of competence of the judiciary; civil, penal and commercial law and civil and penal procedures; the status of persons and property; the system of obligations and questions pertaining to Zairean nationality; international private law; status of magistrates; organization of the lawyers' profession, counsels for the defence, notaries and judicial auxiliaries; supervision of cemeteries, non-profit-making organizations, cults and institutions working in the public interest; the operation of penitentiaries; confiscated property.

Media

BROADCASTING

Radio Candip: Centre d'Animation et de Diffusion Pédagogique, BP 373, Bunia; educational broadcasts in French, Lingala, Swahili and six local dialects.

La Voix du Zaïre: Station Nationale, BP 3171, Kinshasa-Gombe; tel (12) 23175; telex 21583; Pres: Dongo Badjanga; home service broadcasts in French, Swahili, Lingala, Tshiluba, Kikongo; operates regional stations.

Zaïre Television: BP 3171, Kinshasa-Gombe; tel (12) 23171; telex 21583; Dir-Gen: Dongo Badjanga; Govt commercial station; broadcasts for 5 hours daily on weekdays and 10 hours daily at weekends.

NEWS AND INFORMATION

Agence Zaïroise de Presse (AZAP): 44-48 ave Tombalbaye, BP 1595, Kinshasa 1; tel (12) 22035; telex 21096; Del-Gen: Landu Lusala Khasa; f 1957.

Institut National de la Statistique: BP 20, Kinshasa-Gombe; tel (12) 30693; Pres and Del-Gen: Charles Durand; Dep Del-Gen: Manya Ndjadi; f 1978; collection of statistics.

Mining and Energy

La Générale des Carrières et des Mines (GÉCAMINES—Holding): blvd du 30 juin, BP 8714, Kinshasa; tel (12) 22270; Pres: Isungu ky-Maka; f 1984; state holding co; operates the following enterprises:

GÉCAMINES—Commercial: Chair: Djamboleka Loma Okitongono; marketing of mineral products.

GÉCAMINES—Développement: Chair: Kanobana Kigesa; operates agricultural and stock-farming ventures in Shaba region.

GÉCAMINES—Exploitation: Chair: Mulenda Mbo; mining operations.

Office des Mines d'Or de Kilo-Moto: BP 219-220 Bunia; Pres: Issiaka Tabu; Sec-Gen: Kaite Mutijima; operates gold mines.

PetroZaïre: 1513 blvd du 30 juin, BP 7617, Kinshasa 1; tel (12) 25356; telex 21066; f 1974; petroleum refining, processing, stocking and transporting.

Société de Développement Industriel et Minier de Zaïre (SODIMIZA): 4219 ave d l'Ouganda, BP 7064, Kinshasa; tel (12) 32511; telex 21370; copper-mining consortium exploiting mines of Musoshi and Kinsenda in Shaba.

Société Minière de Bakwanga (MIBA): place de la Coopération 4, BP 377-378, Mbujimayi; tel 285; blvd du 30 juin 116, BP 8633, Kinshasa; tel (12) 32109; telex 21063; Pres: Mukamba Kadiata Nzemba; Vice-Pres: Bele Mongungu, Bruno Morelli; f 1961; diamond mining.

Société Nationale d'Electricité (SNEL): 49 blvd du 30 juin, BP 500, Kinshasa 1; tel (12) 26893; telex 21570; Gen Man: M. Mutondo; f 1970; operates mainly hydroelectric power stations, but in 1979 assumed control of thermal power stations in the interior.

Tourism

Office National du Tourisme: 2A/2B ave des Orangers, BP 9502, Kinshasa 1; tel (12) 30070; Man Dir: Botolo Magoza; f 1959.

Transport

Air Zaïre (SARL): 4 ave du Port, BP 8552, Kinshasa; tel (12) 24986; telex 21313; Dir-Gen: Hubert Andrade; f 1961 as Air Congo; name changed 1971; 80% state-owned; domestic and international services to Angola, Burundi, Cameroon, Côte d'Ivoire, Gabon, Guinea, Kenya, Nigeria, Senegal, Togo, Belgium, France and Italy.

Compagnie Maritime Zaïroise (CMZ): Immeuble CMZ-AMIZA, place de la Poste, BP 9496, Kinshasa 1; tel (12) 25816; telex 21626; Pres and Del-Gen: Bombutsi Entombo; Dep Del-Gen: Mayilukila Lusiasia; f 1974; maritime transport; 100% state-owned; mem of UK/West Africa Lines (UKWAL); services to Antwerp, North Continental Range to East Africa, USA, Mediterranean ports to West Africa, Japan, Hong Kong and Singapore.

Office National des Transports au Zaïre (ONATRA): BP 98, Kinshasa 1; tel (12) 24761; Dir-Gen: Umba Kyamitala; operates waterways, railways and road transport; administers ports of Kinshasa, Matadi, Boma and Banana.

Office des Routes: Direction Générale, ave Ex-Descamp, BP 10899, Kinshasa-Gombe; tel (12) 32036; telex 21327; construction and maintenance of roads.

Régie des Voies Aériennes: BP 6574, Kinshasa 1; tel (12) 24812; telex 926; airways admin.

Régie des Voies Fluviales: 109 ave Lumpungu, Kinshasa-Gombe; BP 11697, Kinshasa 1; Gen Man: Mondombo Sisa Ebambe; administers river navigation.

Société Nationale des Chemins de Fer Zaïrois (SNCZ): place de la Gare, BP 297, Lubumbashi, Shaba; tel (2) 223430; telex 41056; Pres and Del-Gen: Mbatshi Batshia; Dir, Admin: Yandi Kaniki; Dir, Finance: Ruboz Difand; f 1974; administers all internal railway sections as well as river transport and transport on lakes Tanganyika and Kivu.

Utilities

Régie de Distribution d'Eau et d'Electricité (REGIDESCO): 65 blvd du 30 juin, BP 12599, Kinshasa; tel (12) 22792; telex 21077; electricity and water supply admin.

ZAMBIA

Head of State

Zambia's 1973 Constitution declared the country to be a one-party state. The President of the United National Independence Party (UNIP) is thus also the state President, although general elections are held every five years to elect the President. The President appoints a Cabinet of 20 ministers (from the 68-member UNIP Central Committee), led by a Prime Minister, chooses Supreme Court judges, and is Commander-in-Chief of the Armed Forces. The UNIP Central Committee, to which the Cabinet is subordinate, is the highest policy-making body in the country.

President: Dr Kenneth David Kaunda (took office 24 October 1964, re-elected for sixth five-year term 26 October 1988).

Office of the President: State House, POB 30208, Lusaka; tel (1) 211833; telex 41460.

United National Independence Party (UNIP): Freedom House, POB 30302, Lusaka; tel (1) 211411; telex 43640; Pres: Dr Kenneth David Kaunda; Sec-Gen: Alexander Grey Zulu; f 1958.

Legislature

Legislative power is held by the unicameral National Assembly, which has 135 members: 125 are elected for a five-year term by universal adult suffrage, with up to three candidates per constituency, and 10 are nominated by the President. All members of the Assembly must be members of UNIP. Laws passed in the Assembly require presidential assent. There is also a House of Chiefs, with 27 members, which represents traditional tribal authorities and may submit resolutions to be debated by the National Assembly.

National Assembly: POB 31299, Lusaka; tel (1) 218991; Speaker: Dr Robinson Nabulyato.

MINISTRIES AND GOVERNMENT DEPARTMENTS

OFFICE OF THE SECRETARY-GENERAL OF THE PARTY
United National Independence Party (UNIP), Freedom House, POB 30302, Lusaka
Tel (1) 211411; telex 43640
Secretary-General: Alexander Grey Zulu

OFFICE OF THE PRIME MINISTER
POB 30208, Lusaka
Tel (1) 218282; telex 42240
Prime Minister: Gen Malimbe Masheke
Secretary to the Cabinet: Charles Manyema

Personnel Division: New Secretariat, Independence Ave, POB 30587, Lusaka; tel (1) 218282; telex 42240; Minister of State for the Civil Service: Kennedy Shepande.

OFFICE OF THE SECRETARY OF STATE FOR DEFENCE AND SECURITY
POB 30208, Lusaka
Tel (1) 211411; telex 43640
Secretary of State: Alex K. Shapi.

MINISTRY OF AGRICULTURE
Mulungushi House, Independence Ave, Nationalist Rd, POB RW50291, Lusaka
Tel (1) 213551; telex 43950
Minister: Justin Mukando

MINISTRY OF COMMERCE AND INDUSTRY
Kwacha Annex, Cairo Rd, POB 31968, Lusaka
Tel (1) 213767; telex 45630
Minister: Rabson Chonga

MINISTRY OF CO-OPERATIVES
Mulungushi House, Independence Ave, Nationalist Rd, POB RW50291, Lusaka
Tel (1) 213551; telex 43950
Minister: Malimba Masheke

Department of Marketing and Co-operatives: POB 50595, Lusaka; tel (1) 214933; Dir: S. B. Chiwala.

MINISTRY OF DEFENCE
POB 31931, Lusaka
Tel (1) 252366
Minister: Frederick Hapunda

MINISTRY OF FINANCE AND TECHNICAL CO-OPERATION
Finance Bldg, POB RW50062, Lusaka
Tel (1) 213822; telex 42221
Minister of Finance and of the National Commission for Development Planning: Gibson Chigaga.

MINISTRY OF FOREIGN AFFAIRS
POB RW50069, Lusaka
Tel (1) 217171; telex 41290
Minister: Luke Mwananshiku

MINISTRY OF GENERAL EDUCATION, YOUTH AND SPORT
POB RW50093, Lusaka
Tel (1) 211100; telex 42621
Minister: Eli Mwanang'onze

MINISTRY OF HEALTH
1st and 2nd Floors, Woodgate House, Cairo Rd, POB 30205, Lusaka
Tel (1) 211528
Minister: Mavis Muyanda

MINISTRY OF HIGHER EDUCATION, SCIENCE AND TECHNOLOGY
Haile Selassie Ave, POB 50464, Lusaka
Tel (1) 219744
Minister: Prof Lameck Goma
F 1982; responsible for university education, teacher education, technical education and scientific research.

MINISTRY OF HOME AFFAIRS
POB 32862, Lusaka
Tel (1) 213505
Minister: Gen Kingsley Chinkuli

Department of Passport and National Registration: Kundalila House, POB 32311, Lusaka; tel (1) 213288; Registrar-Gen: L. K. Nyirongo; Dep Registrar-Gen: W. S. Meja; Chief Passport and Citizenship Officer: H. A. Munkombwe; f 1965; responsible for registration of births, marriages and deaths, for issue of national registration cards and passports, and for the granting of citizenship.

MINISTRY OF INFORMATION AND BROADCASTING SERVICES
Independence Ave, POB 32245, Lusaka
Tel (1) 214034; telex 41240
Minister: Arnold Simuchimba

MINISTRY OF LABOUR, SOCIAL DEVELOPMENT AND CULTURE
Lechwe House, Freedom Way, POB 32186, Lusaka
Tel (1) 212020
Minister: Lavu Malimba

MINISTRY OF LEGAL AFFAIRS
Fairley Rd, POB RW50106, Lusaka
Tel (1) 214771
Minister and Attorney-General: Frederick Chomba

MINISTRY OF MINES
Chilufya Mulenga Rd, POB 31969, Lusaka
Tel (1) 211220
Minister: Bernard Fumbelo

MINISTRY OF NATIONAL GUIDANCE
Old Bank of Zambia Bldg, Cairo Rd, POB 34011, Lusaka
Tel (1) 218066
Minister: (vacant)

MINISTRY OF POWER, TRANSPORT AND COMMUNICATIONS
Fairley Rd, POB RW50065, Lusaka
Tel (1) 213211; telex 41680
Minister: Enos Haimbe

MINISTRY OF TOURISM
Electra House, Cairo Rd, POB 30575, Lusaka
Tel (1) 211110; telex 45510
Minister: Pickson S. Chitambala

MINISTRY OF WATER, LANDS AND NATURAL RESOURCES
Mulungushi House, Independence Ave, Nationalist Rd, POB 30055, Lusaka
Tel (1) 214988
Minister: Paul Malukutila

MINISTRY OF WORKS AND SUPPLY
Block 28, Independence Ave, POB RW50236, Lusaka
Tel (1) 215580; telex 43980
Minister: Haswell Mwale

GOVERNMENT AGENCIES AND ORGANIZATIONS

Advisory and Supervisory Bodies

Anti-Corruption Commission: Block 25, Independence Ave, POB 50486, Lusaka; tel (1) 251392.

Commission for Investigations: Old Bank of Zambia Bldg, POB 50494, Lusaka; tel (1) 214016; f 1973; investigates administrative abuse.

House of Chiefs: POB RW50027, Lusaka; tel (1) 216310; advisory body representing traditional tribal authorities; may submit resolutions to the National Assembly; mems are 27 Chiefs, four each from the Northern, Western, Southern and Eastern Provinces, three each from the North-Western, Luapula and Central Provinces, and two from the Copperbelt Province.

Office of the Auditor-General: POB 50071, Lusaka; tel (1) 217377; f 1964; responsible for conducting audits of Govt and parastatal organizations.

Agriculture and Forestry

AGRICULTURE

Central Veterinary Research Station: POB 50, Mazabuka; Asst Dir, Veterinary Research: Dr M. A. Q. Awan; f 1926.

Dairy Produce and Marketing Corpn Ltd: Kwacha House, Cairo Rd, POB 30124, Lusaka; tel (1) 214770; telex 41520; f 1975; purchasing, processing, distribution and sale of milk and milk products.

National Agricultural Marketing Board of Zambia (NAMBOARD): Kwacha House, Cairo Rd, POB 30122, Lusaka; tel (1) 214833; telex 42310; Chair: U. Mwila; Gen Man: Maj-Gen C. Nyirenda; imports fertilizers, pesticides and agricultural implements.

Tobacco Board of Zambia: POB 31963, Lusaka; tel (1) 218373; telex 40370; Sec: V. S. Mwaba.

Veterinary and Tsetse Control Department: Mulungushi House, Independence Ave, Nationalist Rd, POB RW50060, Lusaka; tel (1) 213551; dept of Ministry of Water, Lands and Natural Resources.

FORESTRY

Division of Forest Research: POB 22099, Kitwe; tel (2) 210288; telex 52051; Chief Forest Research Officer: A. C. Mubita; f 1956.

Forestry Department: Lusaka North Plantation, POB 80864, Lusaka; tel (1) 216280.

Art and Culture

Department of Cultural Services: POB RW50177, Lusaka; tel (1) 252388.

National Archives of Zambia: Government Rd, POB RW50010, Lusaka; tel (1) 214844; Dir: P. M. Mukula; Archivist: M. F. Mbewe; Librarian: H. K. Nyendwa; f 1947; responsible to Ministry of Home Affairs; covers national literature from earliest times to the present day; holds the National Archives Library, a reference and legal deposit library for all printed publs published in Zambia.

National Monuments Commission: POB 60124, Livingstone; tel (3) 320481; Dir: N. M. Katanekwa; f 1948; administers antiquities legislation; records and investigates archaeological sites; controls the export of relics; protects, develops and manages national monuments.

Business and Economy

BANKING

Bank of Zambia: POB 30080, Lusaka; tel (1) 216529; telex 41560; Gov: Jacques Bussières; Gen Man: James Ng'oma; f 1964; central bank and bank of issue; br in Ndola.

Development Bank of Zambia: Katondo Rd, POB 33955, Lusaka; tel (1) 214884; telex 45040; Chair: C. M. Fundanga; Man Dir: L. M. Nyambe; f 1972; 72% state-owned, subsidiary of Zambia Industrial and Mining Corpn (ZIMCO); provides medium- and long-term loans and offers business consultancy and research services.

Zambia Agricultural Development Bank: Society House, Cairo Rd, POB 30847, Lusaka; tel (1) 219251; telex 40126; Chair: K. Makasa; Man Dir: Amon Chibiya; f 1982; loan finance for devt of agriculture and fishing; authorized cap 75m Kwacha.

Zambia National Commercial Bank Ltd: POB 33611, Lusaka; tel (1) 215100; telex 42360; Chair: E. Willima; Man Dir: F. C. Ndhlovu; f 1969; subsidiary of State Finance and Development Corpn (FINDECO); 31 brs.

FINANCIAL AGENCY

State Finance and Development Corpn (FINDECO): POB 31930, Lusaka; tel (1) 212226; telex 41821; Chair: Gibson Chigaga; f 1971; subsidiary of Zambia Industrial and Mining Corpn (ZIMCO) with overall responsibility for the Govt financial sector and investment agencies.

INSURANCE

Zambia State Insurance Corpn Ltd: Premium House, Independence Ave, POB 30894, Lusaka; tel (1) 218888; telex 42521;

Chair: E. Willima; Man Dir: Mwene Mwinga; f 1968, became national insurance monopoly in 1971.

MARKETING

Department of Marketing and Co-operatives: Mulungushi House, Independence Ave, Nationalist Rd, POB 50595, Lusaka; tel (1) 214933.

Metal Marketing Corpn (Zambia) Ltd (MEMACO): Memaco House, Sapele Rd, POB 35570, Lusaka; tel (1) 213299; telex 40070; Chair: E. Willima; Man Dir: L. C. Mutakasha; f 1973; sole agents for sales of all metals and minerals production.

NATIONALIZED INDUSTRY

Dunlop Zambia Ltd: Cnr Kabwe Rd and Mushili Rd, POB 71650, Ndola; tel (2) 650789; telex 34110; fax (2) 650138; Man Dir: R. M. May; f 1969; manufacturers of rubber tyres and other rubber products.

Nitrogen Chemicals of Zambia Ltd: POB 32483, Lusaka; tel (1) 311531; telex 70030; Chair: D. Mhango; Man Dir: B. J. Walker; Gen Man: A. Pizzirani; f 1965; manufacturers of ammonia, ammonium nitrate, ammonium sulphate, NPK fertilizers, sulphuric acid, nitric acid, carbon dioxide and methanol.

ROP (1975) Ltd: Nakambala Rd, POB 71570, Ndola; tel (2) 650549; telex 33120; Gen Man: D. Mhango; f 1975 by merger of Refined Oil Products Ltd and Lever Brothers, Zambia; manufacturers of soaps, detergents, toilet preparations and edible oils.

Zambia Breweries Ltd: POB 70091, Ndola; tel (2) 3601; telex 42330; Gen Man: Zacks Musonda; f 1951; brewing, bottling and distribution of lager beers.

Zambia Breweries Ltd (Lusaka): 74 Independence Ave, Lusaka; f 1966.

Zambia Industrial and Mining Corpn (ZIMCO) Ltd: Zimco House, Cairo Rd, POB 30090, Lusaka; tel (1) 212487; telex 40790; Chair: Dr Kenneth David Kaunda; Dir-Gen: E. Willima; f 1970; holding co for Govt interests in mining, industry, finance, agriculture, commercial transport, energy, communications, hotels and land; about 135 subsidiaries and associate cos.

Industrial Development Corpn of Zambia (INDECO) Ltd: Indeco House, Buteko Place, POB 31935, Lusaka; tel (1) 214555; telex 41821; Chair: E. Willima; Man Dir: A. D. Zulu; f 1956; parastatal holding co with 42 subsidiaries in food, engineering, building materials, transport, and consumer goods sectors.

Kafue Textiles of Zambia Ltd: POB 131, Kafue; tel (1) 311501; telex 70050; Gen Man: Rolf Klein; f 1969; 55% of shares owned by INDECO; manufacturers of drills, denims, twills and polions; dress prints and African prints; industrial and household textiles.

National Breweries Ltd: POB 22699, Kitwe; tel (2) 211333; telex 51740; Chair: D. H. Luzongo; Gen Man: H. G. Muzabazi; inc 1968; operates 14 breweries.

Zambesi Sawmills (1968) Ltd: Chishimba Falls Rd, POB 60041, Livingstone; tel (3) 20329; telex 24003; Commercial Man: H. M. Chombe; sawmillers and manufacturers of railway sleepers, mining timbers, sawn timber, etc.

TRADE

Customs and Excise Department: Customs House, Dedan Kimathi Rd, POB 30085, Lusaka; tel (1) 211932; dept of the Ministry of Finance.

National Import and Export Corpn (NIEC): National Housing Authority Bldg, POB 30283, Lusaka; tel (1) 212810;

telex 44490; Chair: E. C. Kaunga; Man Dir: C. C. F. Mabwe; f 1974.

Development and Planning

PLANNING

Buildings Branch: Government Rd, POB 50800, Lusaka; tel (1) 212621; dept of the Ministry of Works and Supply.

Lands Department: Mulungushi House, Independence Ave, Nationalist Rd, POB 30069, Lusaka; tel (1) 214988; dept of the Ministry of Water, Lands and Natural Resources.

National Commission for Development Planning: Lusaka, Zambia; Chair: Gibson Chigaga.

Survey Department: Mulungushi House, Independence Ave, Nationalist Rd, POB 30250, Lusaka; tel (1) 214988; dept of the Ministry of Water, Lands and Natural Resources.

REGIONAL DEVELOPMENT

Office of the Provincial Commissioner of Works: Church Rd, POB 30098, Lusaka; tel (1) 214211; dept of the Ministry of Works and Supply.

Rural Development Corpn of Zambia (RDC): POB 31957, Lusaka; tel (1) 213111; telex 43280; f 1968; promotes economic and social devt in rural areas.

Small Industries Development Organisation (SIDO): Sido House, Cairo Rd, POB 35373, Lusaka; tel (1) 219801; telex 40169; Chair: Kapasa Makasa; Dir: Dr C. O. Ngandwe; f 1981; promotes the planning, co-ordination and implementation of national policies and programmes for the devt of the small industrial sector, particularly in villages.

   Northern Regional Office: POB 21318, Kitwe; tel (2) 215795.

Education and Research

EDUCATION

Department of Technical Education and Vocational Training (DTEVT): POB RW16, Lusaka; tel (1) 212716; Dir S. K. Simutoine; Dep Dir: E. L. Phiri; f 1967; main training agency for all technical and vocational education programmes at craft, technician and diploma levels; subjects covered include commercial and enginnering studies for the public, parastatal and private sectors.

Education Services Centre: Haile Selassie Rd, POB RW50097, Lusaka; tel (1) 215975; dept of the Ministry of General Education, Youth and Sport.

   Zambia Library Service: POB 30802, Lusaka; tel (1) 254993; Librarian: M. Walubita; f 1962; maintains 900 library centres, six regional libraries, 6 branch libraries and a central library of 500,000 volumes.

Teaching Service Commission: Office of the Prime Minister, 5th Floor, Kulima Tower, Katunjila Rd, POB 33644; tel (1) 216729; Chair: L. M. A. Simukonda.

RESEARCH

National Council for Scientific Research: POB CH158, Lusaka; tel (1) 281081; Chair: Gen Malimba Masheke; Sec-Gen: Dr S. M. Silangwa; f 1967; statutory body set up to advise the Govt on scientific research policy, to promote and co-ordinate research and to collect and disseminate scientific information.

Employment

Community Development Department: Fidelity House, Cnr Cha Cha Cha Rd and Katondo Rd, POB 31958, Lusaka; tel (1) 213852; dept of the Ministry of Labour, Social Development and Culture.

Educational and Occupational Assessment Service: Lechwe House, Freedom Way, POB 32186, Lusaka; tel (1) 217717; Dir: N. M. J. Ngulbe; Asst Dir: C. G. Zeko; Chief Assessment Officer: E. C. Nsofwa; f 1965; dept of the Ministry of Labour, Social Development and Culture; conducts psychological testing in the educational and occupational fields; consultancy work.

Health

National Food and Nutrition Commission: POB 32669, Lusaka; tel (1) 211724; Chair: Anthony Ndalama; Exec Dir: Alexander B. Vermoer; f 1967; statutory body which aims to improve the nutritional status of the people of Zambia.

Legal and Judiciary

Administrator-General's and Official Receiver's Office: Kundalila House, POB 37778, Lusaka; tel (1) 217631; f 1925; dept of the Ministry of Legal Affairs; responsible for the admin of the estates of the bankrupt and deceased.

Department of Legal Aid: Kundalila House, Dedan Kimathi Rd, POB 32761, Lusaka; tel (1) 214871; dept of the Ministry of Legal Affairs.

Law Development Commission: 11th Floor, Profound House, Kabwe Roundabout, POB 34670, Lusaka; tel (1) 253436; f 1976; reviews law reform matters.

Supreme Court of Zambia: Independence Ave, POB RW50067, Lusaka; tel (1) 214040; Chief Justice: Annel M. Silungwe; Dep Chief Justice: M. M. S. W. Ngulube; final Court of Appeal; Chief Justice and other judges are appointed by the President.

   High Court of Zambia (Kitwe): Nsansa Lane, POB 20135, Kitwe; tel (2) 213482; Judges: A. R. Lawrence, Commr V. H. Chileshe.

   High Court of Zambia (Lusaka): Independence Ave, POB RW50067, Lusaka; tel (1) 214040; Judges: B. K. Bweupe, M. S. Chaila, W. M. Muzyamba, L. Chibesakinda, Commr T. A. Kabalata, Commr J. M. Phiri, Commr J. C. M. Mambilima.

   High Court of Zambia (Ndola): POB 70004, Ndola; tel (2) 2648; Judges: D. K. Chirwa, D. M. Lewanika, Commr C. N. Musumali, Commr Chishala.

Media

BROADCASTING

Educational Broadcasting Services: Headquarters, POB 50231, Lusaka; tel (1) 251724; Controller of Educational Broadcasting and Television: Michael P. Mulombe; radio broadcasts.

   Educational Broadcasting Services (Television): POB 21106, Kitwe; TV broadcasting for schools.

   Educational Broadcasting Services (Audio-Visual Aids): POB 50295, Lusaka; audio-visual aids service.

Zambia National Broadcasting Corpn: Mass Media Complex, POB 50015, Lusaka; tel (1) 219673; telex 41221; Dir-Gen: Dr Steven P. C. Moyo; Controller, Sound: Festus Siliya;

Controller, Television (acting): Frank Mutubila; f 1966 as Zambia Broadcasting Services, name changed 1987; radio services in English and seven Zambian languages; TV services in English.

GOVERNMENT PUBLISHER

Government Printing Department: Off Kabelenga Rd, POB 30136, Lusaka; tel (1) 215401; telex 40437; Govt Printer: T. K. Mwanza; f 1901; responsible for the printing of Govt stationery, law books and other related publs.

NEWS AND INFORMATION

Central Statistical Office: POB 31908, Lusaka; tel (1) 211231; telex 40430; dept of the National Commission for Development Planning.

Zambia Information Services: Mass Media Complex, POB 50020, Lusaka; tel (1) 219673; telex 41350; Dir: Daniel P. Kapaya; Dep Dir (acting): Bernard Mukuwa; co-ordinates press relations for all Govt depts and ministries; publishes booklets on Govt policy.

Zambia Institute of Mass Communication: Broadcasting House, Independence Ave, POB 50386, Lusaka; tel (1) 219070; telex 43710; fax (1) 253368; Dir: Mann V. Sichalwe; f 1980; provides further training facilities for African media practitioners and other communicators.

Zambia News Agency (ZANA): Mass Media Complex, POB 30007, Lusaka; tel (1) 219673; telex 42120; Editor-in-Chief: David Kashweka.

Mining and Energy

ENERGY

Zambezi River Authority: POB 30233, Lusaka; tel (1) 214436; telex 42421; Chief Exec: A. S. Mpala; Corporate Sec: S. Mweene; f 1987; operates, monitors and maintains the Kariba Dam Complex and any other dams on the Zambezi River; collects, accumulates and processes hydrological and environmental data on the Zambezi River.

Zambia Electricity Supply Corpn (ZESCO) Ltd: POB 33304, Lusaka; tel (1) 213177; telex 40150; Gen Man: John Kaluzi; f 1969 by merger of various electricity undertakings; acquired all assets in Zambia of the Central African Power Corpn in 1986.

Zambia National Energy Corpn: POB 34585, Lusaka; tel (1) 21922; telex 40640; Man Dir: Dancewell Bowa; controls electricity supplies and the refining and distribution of petroleum products.

MINING

Geological Survey Department: POB RW50135, Lusaka; tel (1) 212553; telex 40107; Dir (acting): N. J. Money; f 1951; dept of the Ministry of Mines; statutory depository for all mining and prospecting records and reports; geological mapping; economic mineral investigation.

Zambia Consolidated Copper Mines Ltd: 5309 Dedan Kimathi Rd, Independence Ave, POB 30048, Lusaka; tel (1) 218033; telex 44540; Chair and Chief Exec: Francis Kaunda; Dir

of Operations (acting): Alex Malama; f 1982 by merger of Nchanga Consolidated Copper Mines and Roan Consolidated Mines; Govt holds 60.3% of shares through Zambia Industrial and Mining Corpn (ZIMCO).

Tourism

Hotel Board: Electra House, Cairo Rd, Lusaka; tel (1) 211110; dept of the Ministry of Tourism.

National Hotels Development Corpn: POB 33200, Lusaka; tel (1) 211023; telex 44130; Dir: Patrick D. Chisanga; subsidiary of Zambia Industrial and Mining Corpn (ZIMCO); responsible for 11 hotels, three casinos and five lodges in the national parks.

Zambia National Tourist Board: Century House, Cairo Rd, POB 30017, Lusaka; tel (1) 217761; telex 41780; Chair: Solomon Kalulu; dept of the Ministry of Tourism.

Transport and Communications

TELECOMMUNICATIONS

Posts and Telecommunicatons Corpn: POB 76120, Ndola; tel (2) 2281; telex 33430.

TRANSPORT

Department of Civil Aviation: POB 50137, Lusaka; tel (1) 251861; telex 42280; f 1964; responsible for admin of the Zambian Aviation Act; inspects aircraft airworthiness; licenses air crews; airport planning and construction; telecommunications and navigational aids.

Department of Roads: POB 50003, Lusaka; tel (1) 253088; Dir of Roads: T. Ngoma; dept of the Ministry of Works and Supply.

National Air Charters (Z) Ltd (NAC): POB 33650, Lusaka; tel (1) 216779; telex 43850; Gen Man: Brian B. Nanchengwa; f 1973; operates air cargo services.

Tanzania–Zambia Railway: POB 98, Mpika; Chair: O. Ongara; Gen Man: S. I. C. Mapala; f 1975; jointly owned and controlled by Tanzanian and Zambian Govts; operates passenger and freight services linking Kapiri Mposhi, north of Lusaka, with Dar es Salaam (Tanzania).

Zambia Airways Corpn (ZAC): Ndeke House, Haile Selassie Ave, POB 30272, Lusaka; tel (1) 213674; telex 43850; Chair: R. M. Chomba; Man Dir: Capt M. Geoffrey Mulundika; f 1967; operates internal services and scheduled passenger and cargo services to African, European and North American cities.

Zambia National Shipping Line: Lusaka; Gen Man: Martin Phiri; operates cargo and passenger services from Dar es Salaam (Tanzania) to northern Europe.

Zambia Railways: POB 80935, Kabwe; tel (5) 222201; telex 8100; Chair: Oliver Chama; Man Dir: E. Hachipuka; f 1967; controlled by Zambia Industrial and Mining Corpn (ZIMCO).

Utilities

Water Affairs Department: Mulungushi House, Independence Ave, Nationalist Rd, POB RW50288, Lusaka; tel (1) 215281.

ZIMBABWE

Head of State

The President is Head of State and holds executive power, and is elected by Parliament for six years, though in the 1990 elections the President is to be elected by universal suffrage. The President, who heads the Cabinet, appoints a Vice-President and other members of the Cabinet. The Cabinet must have the confidence of Parliament, to which it is responsible.

President: Robert Gabriel Mugabe (took office 31 December 1987).

Office of the President: Munhumutapa Bldg, Samora Machel Ave, Private Bag 7700, Causeway, Harare; tel (4) 707091; telex 24478; Sen Minister in the President's Office without portfolio: Joshua Mqabuko Nkomo; Sen Minister in the President's Office for Political Affairs (acting): Simon Vengayi Muzenda.

Vice-President: Simon Vengayi Muzenda.

Office of the Vice-President: Munhumutapa Bldg, Samora Machel Ave, Private Bag 7700, Causeway, Harare; tel (4) 707091; telex 24478.

Legislature

Legislative power is vested in the bicameral Parliament, which comprises a House of Assembly with 100 members, and a Senate, which has delaying powers only and consists of 40 members. The life of Parliament is ordinarily five years; it was announced in September 1989 that the Senate was to be abolished in 1990 to give way to a unicameral Parliament of 150 members: 120 elected on a single constituency basis, eight provincial governors, 10 chiefs and 12 members appointed by the President.

Senate: Baker Ave, POB 8055, Causeway, Harare; tel (4) 700181; telex 24064; Pres: Nolan Makombe.

House of Assembly: Baker Ave, POB 8055, Causeway, Harare; tel (4) 700181; telex 24064; Speaker: Didymus Noel Edwin Mutasa; Dep Speaker and Chair of Committees: Abraham Kabasa; Sec: Dr J. W. Z. Kurewa; Dep Secs: A. N. Nyarota, A. M. Zvoma.

MINISTRIES AND GOVERNMENT DEPARTMENTS

MINISTRY OF DEFENCE
Munhumutapa Bldg, Samora Machel Ave, Private Bag 7713, Causeway, Harare
Tel (4) 700155; telex 22141
Minister (acting): Dr Sydney Tigere Sekeramayi

MINISTRY OF ENERGY AND WATER RESOURCES AND DEVELOPMENT
Rhodes Ave Complex, Block 3, Private Bag 7712, Causeway, Harare
Tel (4) 707861; telex 22141
Minister: Kumbirai Kangai

MINISTRY OF FINANCE, ECONOMIC PLANNING AND DEVELOPMENT
Ground Floor, Munhumutapa Bldg, Samora Machel Ave, Private Bag 7705, Causeway, Harare
Tel (4) 794571; telex 22141
Senior Minister in the President's Office: Dr Bernard Thomas Chidzero

MINISTRY OF FOREIGN AFFAIRS
Munhumutapa Bldg, Samora Machel Ave, POB 4240, Causeway, Harare
Tel (4) 794681; telex 22141
Minister: Dr Nathan Marwirakuwa Shamuyarira

MINISTRY OF HEALTH
Kaguvi Bldg, Fourth St, POB 8204, Causeway, Harare
Tel (4) 730011; telex 22141
Minister: Dr Felix Muchemwa

MINISTRY OF HOME AFFAIRS
Mukwati Bldg, Samora Machel Ave, Private Bag 505D, Causeway, Harare
Tel (4) 703641; telex 22141
Minister: Moven Enock Mahachi

MINISTRY OF INDUSTRY AND TECHNOLOGY
18th Floor, Kaguvi Bldg, POB 8434, Causeway, Harare
Tel (4) 791823; telex 22141
Minister (acting): Bernard Chidzero

MINISTRY OF INFORMATION, POSTS AND TELECOMMUNICATIONS
Linquenda House, Baker Ave, POB 8150, Causeway, Harare
Tel (4) 703894; telex 24142
Minister: Dr Witness Mangwende
Deputy Minister: K. V. Manyonda

MINISTRY OF JUSTICE, LEGAL AND PARLIAMENTARY AFFAIRS
Mapondera Bldg, Samora Machel Ave, Private Bag 7751, Causeway, Harare
Tel (4) 790901
Minister: Emmerson Dambudzo Mnangagwa

MINISTRY OF LABOUR, MANPOWER PLANNING AND SOCIAL WELFARE
Compensation House, Central Ave, Fourth St, Private Bag 7707, Causeway, Harare
Tel (4) 790871; telex 22079
Minister: John Landa Nkomo
Deputy Minister: H. S. Mahlaba

MINISTRY OF LANDS, AGRICULTURE AND RURAL RESETTLEMENT
Robert Fletcher Bldg, Private Bag 7701, Causeway, Harare
Tel (4) 706081; telex 22455
Minister: David Ishemunyoro Karimanzira

MINISTRY OF LOCAL GOVERNMENT, RURAL AND URBAN DEVELOPMENT
Mukwati Bldg, Private Bag 7706, Causeway, Harare
Tel (4) 790601; telex 22179
Minister: Enos Chamunorwa Chikowore

MINISTRY OF MINES
Private Bag 7709, Causeway, Harare
Tel (4) 703781; telex 22416
Minister: Richard Chemist Hove

MINISTRY OF NATIONAL SUPPLIES
Atlas Bldg, 62 Manica Rd, Private Bag 7742, Harare
Tel (4) 706446; telex 22141
Minister: Simbi Veke Mubako

MINISTRY OF NATURAL RESOURCES AND TOURISM
Karigamombe Centre, Private Bag 7753, Causeway, Harare
Tel (4) 794455
Minister: Victoria Fikile Chitepo

MINISTRY OF PRIMARY AND SECONDARY EDUCATION
Ambassador House, Union Ave, POB 8022, Causeway, Harare
Tel (4) 734051; telex 2141
Minister of Primary and Secondary Education and Acting Minister of Higher Education: Fay Chung

MINISTRY OF PUBLIC CONSTRUCTION AND NATIONAL HOUSING
POB 8081, Causeway, Harare
Tel (4) 704561; telex 22589
Minister: Joseph Msika

MINISTRY OF THE PUBLIC SERVICE
Pax House, Union Ave, POB 8080, Causeway, Harare
Tel (4) 700811; telex 22141
Minister of State in the President's Office:
Jonas Christian Andersen

MINISTRY OF SECURITY
Chaminuka Bldg, POB 2278, Causeway, Harare
Tel (4) 700501
Minister of State in the President's Office for National Security: Dr Sydney Tigere Sekeremayi

MINISTRY OF TRADE AND COMMERCE
Mukwati Bldg, Fourth St, Private Bag 7708, Causeway, Harare
Tel (4) 702731; telex 24472
Minister: Dr Oliver Munyaradzi

MINISTRY OF TRANSPORT
Kaguvi Bldg, POB 8109, Causeway, Harare
Tel (4) 700991; telex 22141
Minister: Simbarashe Simbanenduku Mumbengegwe

MINISTRY OF WOMEN'S AFFAIRS, CO-OPERATIVES AND COMMUNITY DEVELOPMENT
Chaminuka Bldg, Private Bag 7735, Causeway, Harare
Tel (4) 792351
Minister: Joyce Teurai Ropa Mujuru

MINISTRY OF YOUTH, SPORT AND CULTURE
Makombe Bldg, Rhodes Ave, Private Bag 7749, Causeway, Harare
Tel (4) 794531; telex 22141
Minister: David Kwidini

OFFICE OF THE MINISTER OF STATE FOR NATIONAL SCHOLARSHIPS
Harare
Minister of State in the President's Office:
Joseph Culverwell

OFFICE OF THE MINISTERS OF STATE FOR POLITICAL AFFAIRS
Harare
Ministers of State: Ernest Rusununguko Kadungure, Eddison Jonas Mudadirwa Zvobgo, Herbert Sylvester Masiyiwa Ushewokunze

GOVERNMENT AGENCIES AND ORGANIZATIONS

Advisory and Supervisory Bodies

Census of Population: Trafalgar Court, Julius, Harare; tel (4) 703727; under the Ministry of Finance, Economic Planning and Devt.

Deeds and Companies Registry: Electra House, Samora Machel Ave, Central Box 8033, Causeway, Harare; tel (4) 791871; comprises the Registrar of Deeds and Farmers and the Registrar of Cos, Patents and Trademarks.

Department of Immigration Control: 2nd Floor, Linquenda House, Baker Ave, Private Bag 7717, Causeway, Harare; tel (4) 791913; under the Ministry of Home Affairs.

Central Registry for Births, Marriages, Deaths, Citizenship, Voters and Cattle Brands: Makombe Bldg, Moffat St, Private Bag 7734, Causeway, Harare; tel (4) 702295; under the Ministry of Home Affairs.

Office of the Ombudsman: 2nd Floor, Burroughs House, 48 Gordon Ave, Private Bag 7759, Causeway, Harare; tel (4) 700907; appointed by the Pres, acting on the advice of the Judicial Service Commission, to investigate complaints against actions taken by employees of the Govt or of a local authority,

State Lotteries: 27 Speke Ave, Julius Nyerere Way, POB 1188, Harare; tel (4) 705477; telex 22426; Dir: G. H. Mafico; f 1935; sells lottery tickets for the purpose of raising funds for social service, public welfare and for the relief of distress.

Taxes: Kaguvi Bldg, Central Ave between Fourth and Fifth Sts, Harare; tel (4) 795711; income and sales taxes, stamp duties, etc; under the Ministry of Finance, Economic Planning and Devt.

Agriculture and the Environment

Department of Co-operative Development: Makombe Bldg, Block 2, Rhodes Ave and Salisbury St, POB 8158, Causeway, Harare; tel (4) 707311; under the Ministry of Lands, Agriculture and Rural Resettlement.

Department of National Parks and Wildlife Management: North Ave and Colquhoun St, POB 8365, Causeway, Harare; tel (4) 707624; under the Ministry of Natural Resources and Tourism.

Art and Culture

National Archives: Borrowdale Rd, Gun Hill, Private Bag 7729, Causeway, Harare; tel (4) 792741.

National Museums and Monuments: 107 Rotten Row, POB 8540, Causeway, Harare; tel (4) 790044.

Business and Economy

BANKING

Bank of Credit and Commerce: Union House, 60 Union Ave, POB 3313, Harare; tel (4) 794624; telex 4245.

Reserve Bank of Zimbabwe: 76 Samora Machel Ave, POB 1283, Causeway, Harare; tel (4) 790731; telex 26033; Gov: Dr Kombo J. Moyana; Dep Gov: Richard V. Wilde; Gen Man: J. B. Cooke; f 1964; central bank and bank of issue.

Zimbabwe Banking Corpn Ltd: Zimbank House, 46 Speke Ave, POB 3198, Harare; tel (4) 735011; telex 24163; fax (4) 735600; Chair: C. G. Tracey; Man Dir: D. H. D. Johnston; f 1951; Govt-controlled; 34 brs, sub-brs and agencies.

Zimbabwe Development Bank (ZDB): POB 1720, Harare; tel (4) 705471; telex 22602; Chair: Dr Liberty Mhlanga; Man Dir: Xavier Khadhani; f 1985; devt bank.

FINANCIAL AGENCY

Agricultural Finance Corpn (AFC): Harare; provides credit to farmers.

MARKETING

Agricultural Marketing Authority: POB 8094, Causeway, Harare; tel (4) 730944; telex 22586; Chair: Cephas Msipa; f 1967.

Cotton Marketing Board: POB 2697, Harare; tel (4) 739061; telex 24216; fax (4) 66429; Gen Man: Peter Dove; Asst Gen Man, Admin: Timothy M. Shoko; f 1969; purchasing of cotton from farmers; ginning and marketing of lint and seed.

Dairy Marketing Board: POB 587, Harare; tel (4) 705701; telex 24420; f 1952; milk procurement and processing, and milk product marketing.

Grain Marketing Board: Kurima House, 89 Baker Ave, POB 8014, Causeway, Harare; tel (4) 732011; telex 22336; Gen Man: R. M. Gasela; Dep Gen Mans: L. Zana, A. R. Hawke; grain trading.

Minerals Marketing Corpn of Zimbabwe: 5th Floor, Globe House, 51 Stanley Ave, POB 2628, Causeway, Harare; tel (4) 705682; telex 24579; fax (4) 722441; Chair: C. Ushewokunze; Gen Man: (vacant); f 1982; central authority for marketing of mineral production.

Tobacco Marketing Board: POB UA2214, Harare; tel (4) 66311; telex 24656.

NATIONALIZED INDUSTRY

Zimbabwe Iron and Steel Corpn Ltd (ZISCO): 5th Floor, Pearl Assurance House, Samora Machel Ave, POB 3491, Causeway, Harare; tel (4) 708961; telex 4697.

TRADE

Department of Customs and Excise: Custom House, 3 South Ave, POB 8015, Causeway, Harare; tel (4) 790801.

Zimbabwe State Trading Corpn: Globe House, 51 Stanley Ave, POB 7765, Causeway, Harare; tel (4) 729353; telex 26117; import and export co.

Defence

Air Force of Zimbabwe Headquarters: Private Bag 7721, Causeway, Harare; tel (4) 705050; Commdr: J. Tungamirai.

Zimbabwe National Army Headquarters: Private Bag, 7720, Causeway, Harare; tel (4) 707451; Commdr-in-Chief of the Armed Forces: The President, Robert Gabriel Mugabe; Commdr, Zimbabwe National Army: Lt-Gen Mujuru.

Zimbabwe Republic Police (ZRP): Montagu Ave, POB 8007, Causeway, Harare; tel (4) 700171; telex 24328; f 1980.

Development and Planning

Department of the Rural Development: Makombe Bldg, Block 2, Rhodes Ave and Salisbury St, Private Bag 7743, Causeway, Harare; tel (4) 700596; under the Ministry of Lands, Agriculture and Rural Devt.

Industrial Development Corpn of Zimbabwe Ltd: 93 Park Lane, POB 8531, Causeway, Harare; tel (4) 706971; telex 24409; fax (4) 796028; Gen Man: C. M. D. Sanyanga; Dep Gen Man, Finance and Admin: S. S. Neube; f 1963; invests in industry; plans, co-ordinates and implements industrial devt projects on behalf of the state.

Zimbabwe Investment Centre: Private Bag 7705, Causeway, Harare; tel (4) 794571; telex 2141.

Employment

Employment Council for the Motor Industry: 167 Sinoia St, POB 2943, Harare; tel (4) 723925; Chair: E. G. G. Marsh; Chief Exec: B. R. Charlesworth; f 1964; established under the terms of the Labour Relations Act 1985 to administer the industrial agreement; fosters and promotes the interests and well-being of the motor industry.

National Employment Council for the Construction Industry of Zimbabwe: St Barbara House, Moffat St, POB 2995, Harare; tel (4) 726740; Sec-Gen: D. G. Semmons.

National Employment Council for the Engineering and Iron and Steel Industry: 5th Floor, Chancellor House, Samora Machel Ave, POB 1922, Causeway, Harare; tel (4) 705607; Chair: G. D. Cox; f 1943.

Legal and Judiciary

High Court: Mapondera Bldg, Samora Machel Ave, POB 8050, Causeway, Harare; tel (4) 726113; Chief Justice: Enoch Dumbutshena; consists of the Chief Justice, the Judge President and 11 other judges.

Office of the Attorney-General: Mapondera Bldg, Samora Machel Ave, Private Bag 7714, Causeway, Harare; tel (4) 703353; Attorney-Gen: P. Chinamasa.

Public Prosecutor: Mother Patrick Rd, off Belvedere Rd and Rotten Row, POB 8065, Causeway, Harare; tel (4) 703081.

The Supreme Court of Zimbabwe: cnr Third St and Union Ave, POB 8159, Causeway, Harare; tel (4) 736951; Chief Justice: Enoch Dumbutshena; Judges of Appeal: A. R. Gubbay, N. J. McNally, J. A. Manyarara, R. K. Korsah; f 1981 as successor to the appellate division of the High Court; consists of the Chief Justice and four Judges of Appeal; final court of appeal and constitutional court of Zimbabwe; hears appeals from the High Court, the Administrative Court, numerous Magistrates Courts and other tribunals.

Media

BROADCASTING

Zimbabwe Broadcasting Corpn: Broadcasting Centre, POB HG444, Highlands, Harare; tel (4) 707222; telex 24175; Dir-Gen: T. J. Kangai; Dep Dir-Gen: O. O. Chekeche; f 1933 (Radio), 1965 (TV); radio broadcasting on four channels, and TV on two channels.

GOVERNMENT PUBLISHER

The Literature Bureau: POB 8137, Causeway, Harare; tel (4) 726929; Chief Publications Officer: B. C. Chitsike; f 1953; controlled by the Ministry of Education.

NEWS AND INFORMATION

Central Statistical Office: Kaguvi Bldg, Fourth St, POB 8063, Causeway, Harare; tel (4) 706681; under the Ministry of Finance, Economic Planning and Devt.

Zimbabwe Inter-Africa News Agency (ZIANA): POB 8166, Causeway, Harare; tel (4) 725101; telex 22290; fax (4) 794336; Editor-in-Chief: Farayi Munyuki; f 1981; collects and distributes local and international news.

Mining and Energy

Department of Mining Engineering: 148 Victoria St, POB 8009, Causeway, Harare; tel (4) 706591.

Zambezi River Authority: POB 30233 Lusaka, Zambia; POB 630, Harare; tel (4) 704031; telex 42421; Chief Exec: A. S. Mpala; Corporate Sec/Chief Accountant: S. Mweene; f 1987; operation, monitoring and maintenance of the Kariba hydro-electric power complex; construction, operation and maintenance of other dams on the Zambezi river; collection and processing of hydro-logical and environmental data on the Zambezi river.

Zimbabwe Electricity Supply Authority (ZESA): Electricity Centre, 25 Samora Machel Ave, POB 377, Causeway, Harare; telex 24323; Gen Man: Dr Z. Sydney Gata.

Science and Technology

Department of Geological Survey: Maufe Bldg, Selous Ave and Fifth St, POB 8039, Causeway, Harare; tel (4) 790701; under the Ministry of Mines.

Department of the Surveyor-General: Electra House, Samora Machel Ave, POB 8099, Causeway, Harare; tel (4) 794545; under the Ministry of Lands, Agriculture and Rural Devt.

Meteorological Services: Gaul Ave, Belvedere, POB BE150, Belvedere, Harare; tel (4) 704955; under the Ministry of Transport.

Tourism

Zimbabwe Tourist Development Corpn: Tourism House, cnr Stanley ave and Fourth St, POB 8052, Causeway, Harare; tel (4) 793666; telex 4435; Dir-Gen: M. W. Chihuri; f 1984; promotes, fosters and develops tourism in Zimbabwe; co-ordinates the activities of people engaged in the provision of services for tourists within the country; invests in the tourism industry.

Transport and Communications

TELECOMMUNICATIONS

Posts and Telecommunications Corpn Zimbabwe (PTC): POB 8061, Harare; tel (4) 791711; telex 24753; fax (4) 731989; posts and telecommunications; runs savings bank.

TRANSPORT

Air Zimbabwe Corpn (AirZim): POB AP1, Harare Airport, Harare; tel (4) 737011; telex 24548; Chair: Xavier Khadhani; Gen Man: F. S. Musara; f 1967; scheduled domestic and international passenger and cargo services to destinations in Africa and Europe.

Affretair: POB 655, Harare; tel (4) 731781; telex 24493; f 1965 as Air Trans Africa; wholly-owned subsidiary of Air Zimbabwe; national freight carrier; regular services to West Africa and Europe, and charter services world-wide.

Civil Aviation Department: c/o Ministry of Transport, Sarum House, Manica Rd, Private Bag 7716, Causeway, Harare; tel (4) 792631; telex 4738.

National Railways of Zimbabwe (NRZ): cnr Fife St and 10th Ave, POB 596, Bulawayo; tel (9) 363111; telex 33173; Chair: Rex Chiwara; Gen Man: N. N. Singh; runs national railway system and is the prime mover of goods import and export traffic through Mozambique and South African ports; also runs a local road transport service, the Road Motor Service (RMS).